SAVEUR

THE NEW
CLASSICS
COOKBOOK

THE EDITORS OF SAVEUR

Contents

"Classic recipes are maps, biographies, history lessons on a plate."

I N 2014, THEN-EDITOR-IN-CHIEF JAMES OSLAND defined the dishes and techniques collected in the ambitious SAVEUR *The New Classics Cookbook*. "A classic epitomizes—and helps us understand—provenance," he explained, "but it also goes beyond that: It's a direct link to a culture, a location, an aesthetic, a moment."

The updated edition to this book grew out of a moment of global pandemic. Huddled in our home kitchens, we at SAVEUR sought comfort and connection in soup dumplings (page 375) and stroganoff (page 194), crispy roast chicken (page 153), and the perfect martini (page 540). Again and again, we found ourselves returning to the recipes in this book, and it quickly became clear that it was time for a refresh.

When SAVEUR launched in 1994, the magazine's founding editors set out to bring readers face to face with the food, people, and cultures of the world through unprecedented in-depth storytelling. *The New Classics* is not just a compendium of global recipes and techniques; it's a culinary record of that legacy. Technology has since dramatically changed how we interact with food and recipe content, but despite this digital sea change, a deeply felt need for trustworthy and transportive cookbooks persists.

As Osland wrote in his original introduction, *New Classics* was never intended to be the "final word." How could its editors rest on the laurels of a thousand recipes when, "out there in the big, beautiful, delicious world, there are thousands more to discover"?

However aspirational, SAVEUR's recipe content has always been presented with usability in mind—after all, we really do want you to cook and eat these dishes at home. Nowadays, many international ingredients are far easier to source than when the recipes were originally published, so where it made sense to do so, we have made updates to the text to provide information about traditional spices, chiles, and assorted pantry sundries which are now mere clicks away.

We've also expanded the already sweeping and comprehensive text to include 70 *new* new classics. We added subsections containing some of our favorite dishes, including seafood stews and chowders; calzone; tacos; and even a living larder of fermented foods. Since this new edition is a celebratory occasion—and since all great accomplishments call for a toast—we included a few great new cocktails and a subsection on cordials, infusions, and liqueurs. And finally, as a capstone to this revised edition, we've added a festive new chapter of 20 recipes perfect for holiday entertaining.

We hope you find cooking through this updated and expanded edition as informative and inspiring as we do. Check back in with us on SAVEUR.com daily for even more new classics.

– SAVEUR EDITORS

INTRODUCTION

I WAS TWELVE YEARS OLD when I first tried duck à l'orange. My father had taken me to one of Chicago's great old continental restaurants, and as soon as I saw it on the menu, I knew it was what I wanted. It was glorious to behold: the lacquered leg pointed elegantly upward, the breast meat fanned over a sweep of colorful sauce. It was that exquisite first bite, though, that I'll always remember: gamy and rich, sweet and savory, subtle and exuberant all at once. Instantly I was transported to a time and place far from that Midwestern dining room.

That plate of duck marked my first encounter with a truly classic dish. Over my years on this earth as a cook, an eater, and a traveler, I've come across countless more classics in tiny home kitchens and grand dining rooms, at Heartland county fairs and Southeast Asian hawker centers. Whether a lobster soufflé or a grilled cheese sandwich, a plate of pad thai or a Lebanese kibbeh, these recipes always carry a deeper importance (and, frequently, a deeper deliciousness) than others. A classic epitomizes—and helps us understand—provenance, but it also goes beyond that: It's a direct link to a culture, a location, an aesthetic, a moment. Classic recipes are maps, biographies, history lessons on a plate.

Our notion of what constitutes a classic recipe is ever evolving, ever growing. A century ago, the pinnacle of American culinary sophistication was a cream-sauced blanquette de veau right out of Escoffier, and in the 1970s, nothing was more iconic than fondue. Today, we eat—and learn from, and love—an entire world of classic foods, from California-style kale salads to aromatic Moroccan tagines.

This quest for the truly classic is at the heart of what we do at SAVEUR. Our mission—and our passion—is to learn and share those ways of cooking that exemplify people and places. We've been on this journey for 20 years, and this book is the result of those two decades of obsessive eating, cooking, and exploring. (Recipes from our very first cover story, on the moles of Oaxaca, are here on page 170.) This volume is not, however, the final word. There are a thousand classic recipes between these covers (including my beloved duck à l'orange, on page 181), but out there in the big, beautiful, delicious world, there are thousands more to discover.

JAMES OSELAND
SAVEUR EDITOR-IN-CHIEF

HOW TO USE THIS BOOK

THE SAVEUR TEST KITCHEN HAS SEEN thousands upon thousands of recipes pass through its ovens and over its stovetops over the years. We rigorously test each recipe multiple times, using consistent methods. As you cook through this book, here are a few things worth keeping in mind.

RECIPES

Always read a recipe start to finish before beginning to cook, to familiarize yourself with the ingredients and techniques, and to get a sense of how long the recipe will take. Some recipes have Cook's Notes at the end; these are there to help you with a particular technique, help you source an ingredient or tool, or give you options for modifying the recipe.

COOKING EQUIPMENT

If a recipe specifies a pot or pan of a certain size (like a 6-qt. saucepan or 10" skillet), use a comparable vessel in order to maintain the integrity of the recipe. Too small a pan, and you may end up steaming chicken rather than searing it; too big a pot, and you may over-reduce a sauce because there's too much surface area.

WATER

We specify water in an ingredient list only if it needs to be heated or chilled to a specific temperature, or if a recipe demands filtered or distilled water that needs to be acquired ahead of time. Otherwise, you'll find water listed in the instructions.

SALT

With a few exceptions, our recipes are tested using kosher salt, which tastes better and dissolves faster than table salt.

PEPPER

Pre-ground black pepper rarely stands up to the bite or fragrance of its fresh counterpart. Invest in a pepper grinder and whole peppercorns, and grind your pepper as you need it.

BUTTER

We believe butter should add fat and flavor, but not a briny bite—that's salt's job. So unless specified, we use only unsalted butter in our recipes.

OIL

For frying and sautéing, our preferred neutral oil is canola. Some recipes benefit from olive oil; when its grassy flavor shines, we use extra-virgin, but if the ingredients don't specify, the standard variety is sufficient. Some recipes call for sesame oil, also sold as "toasted sesame oil." Be sure not to use light sesame oil; the flavor is very different.

PARSLEY

Unless otherwise noted, we prefer flat-leaf (also known as Italian) parsley, rather than the curly variety, because flat-leaf has a cleaner flavor and texture.

TAMARIND

In recipes that call for tamarind, we generally specify tamarind extract. To make tamarind extract, soak ¼ lb. tamarind paste, broken into small pieces, in 1 cup boiling water, occasionally mashing the pulp with your fingers. The strained liquid will keep in the refrigerator for up to 2 weeks.

TOMATOES

To maintain quality and consistency when it comes to canned tomatoes, we use only whole, peeled tomatoes. We then crush, dice, or purée them as needed, with or without their juices. (Note that if a recipe calls for "canned whole tomatoes, crushed" and you substitute canned crushed tomatoes, the recipe may not turn out exactly.)

FLOUR

When a recipe refers to "flour," we mean all-purpose flour. If a recipe calls for a certain variety—like cake flour, rice flour, or whole wheat flour—the ingredient list will specify. We measure flour by volume, using a consistent method: Use a spoon to stir the flour in its container. Transfer flour into a measuring cup one spoonful at a time until the cup overflows, then sweep a knife across the rim to make an even surface.

ALCOHOL

We test our cocktails using widely available national brands that are in the middle of the price spectrum. Avoid bargain-priced spirits; they're often harsh and poorly balanced. When you're cooking with liquor, always use something you'd be more than happy to drink on its own. The alcohol itself may cook off, but the flavor of the drink will remain in the finished dish.

TO MARKET, TO MARKET

While most of the recipes in this book call for ingredients readily found at your favorite local supermarket—where you can increasingly find ingredients ranging from Thai rice noodles to dried Mexican chiles—in a few cases, you'll need to look a bit further.

For hard-to-find packaged goods, the internet is your grocery store. There are countless specialty retailers with robust mail-order services online: Just plug your desired product into your favorite search engine and up will pop dozens of specialty retailers that ship quickly and affordably. (More often than not, what you're looking for is right there on amazon.com.) For spices, extracts, and dried fruits and nuts we especially recommend Kalustyan's (kalustyans.com); for hard-to-find produce, we usually order from Melissa's (melissas.com); and for specialty meats, we turn to Marx Foods (marxfoods.com).

We also encourage you to seek out specialty grocery stores in your area. In most parts of the US, you can find stores specializing in Mexican, Asian, Indian and Caribbean foods, which can be an excellent source for hard-to-find ingredients—and usually at a lower price than what you will find online.

Appetizers

APPETIZERS

O F ALL THE PLEASURES associated with eating, anticipation is one of the best. The moment when a heavenly aroma sneaks around the kitchen door, heralding the repast to come, is wonderful. But it can also be tough: Our stomachs grumble; our mouths water. How can we bear the wait until dinner is served? Enter appetizers, those much-loved nibbles that precede the meal, calming the appetite in advance of the dishes to come.

For cooks the world over, these savory tidbits buy time and set the mood, curbing hunger and putting an edible welcome on the table.

The first known use of the English word *appetizer* was in 1820, but, of course, preprandial treats have been around a lot longer. Ancient Greeks snacked on raw and cured olives, bits of fish and nuts. According to Apicius, early Romans were likely to start with what may be one of the original versions of deviled eggs. French aristocrats of the 17th century sated themselves with small plates of oysters, pâtés, and, yes, stuffed eggs. They called these bites *hors d'oeuvres,* meaning "out of the ordinary course of things." In other words, such foods were not the meal, but rather the meal's extraordinary accompaniments. It's a definition we heartily endorse: Spanish-style *pan con tomate,* the juice of the ripe tomato soaking into the garlicky bread; *pissaladière,* a French tart pungent with onion and anchovy; Malaysian chicken satay fragrant with ginger and lemongrass—all are indeed extraordinary.

Modest in size and extravagant in flavor, appetizers like these prime everyone at the table for enjoyment. We can think of nothing better to offer the people with whom we choose to dine than a delectable morsel made with care. Whether oysters Rockefeller from the broiler, topped with bread crumbs laced with butter and tarragon, pita slathered with baba ghannouj, a smoky mashed eggplant spread, or a quickly made batch of Mexican spiced nuts, an appetizer gives our dining companions the license to dig in with gusto. By any name—antipasto, tapa, mezze, *entrada*—it's an edible greeting of immediate impact delivering the simple message, "We're glad you're here."

Hors d'Oeuvres

BAKED FETA

SERVES 4

Crumbly, salty feta takes on a whole new dimension when it's baked in the oven.

- ½ lb. firm feta
- 3 tsp. extra-virgin olive oil
- Crushed red chile flakes
- Crusty bread, for serving

1 Heat oven to 400°. Cut feta into 4 slices about 3″×4″ and ½″ thick. Place each slice on a large piece of aluminum foil, drizzle with 1 tsp. oil, and sprinkle with chile flakes. Wrap foil around cheese, closing it and folding it over to seal.

2 Place foil packets on a baking sheet and bake until cheese is slightly soft, about 10 minutes. Transfer to 4 plates, remove foil, and drizzle with remaining 2 tsp. oil. Serve with bread.

COOK'S NOTE Use tinned feta rather than the barrel-aged variety, which can be too soft and creamy for this dish.

THE FACTS ON FETA

Feta, the definitive Greek cheese, salty and sourish and earthy, is descended from the soft, tart goat's-milk cheeses that have been made in the Balkans, and especially in Greece and Bulgaria, for centuries. The Greek word *feta* means "slice"– the form in which the cheese is customarily served. (It is not an old name; it was probably coined by a market-savvy cheese-monger or producer around the turn of the 20th century.) Greek law decrees that feta must be made from at least 70 percent ewe's milk and up to 30 percent goat's milk. Each animal produces one to three kilos of milk per day; it takes at least four kilos to make a kilo of cheese. The more goat's milk in the mix, the firmer the cheese will be.

ELLA FITZGERALD'S FAVORITE CHEDDAR CHEESE LOG

MAKES ONE 8″ LOG

No less than jazz legend Ella Fitzgerald flagged this recipe in her copy of *James Beard's American Cookery*. This vintage hors d'oeuvre has won over cocktail partygoers for decades with its smooth cheddar cheese texture sharpened with the heat of Tabasco and Dijon mustard.

- 2 lb. cheddar cheese (mild, medium or sharp), grated
- 1 tbsp. Dijon mustard
- ½ tsp. Tabasco sauce
- ½ cup finely chopped fresh flat-leaf parsley
- ¼ cup finely chopped pimiento
- ¼ cup coarsely chopped pecans

1 Put room-temperature cheddar cheese in a large bowl. Add mustard, Tabasco, parsley, and pimientos. Mix until ingredients are evenly distributed.

2 Place a piece of plastic wrap about 9″ long on a clean surface. Mound cheese mixture along edge nearest you, then roll in plastic, pressing and molding to form a log about 1½″ wide and 8″ long.

3 Carefully remove plastic wrap and roll log in chopped pecans, pressing nuts into log as you roll. Rewrap log with fresh plastic wrap and chill for at least 1 hour. Serve with crackers.

CHICKEN LIVER PÂTÉ

MAKES ABOUT 1⅓ CUPS

A smart cook never tosses the jewels found inside a whole chicken, especially the liver. Sautéed and blended, liver transforms into a velvety pâté, spiked with cognac and mellowed with sweet sautéed onions.

- ½ lb. chicken livers, cleaned
- 4 cups chicken stock
- 2 tbsp. rendered chicken fat or unsalted butter
- ½ medium yellow onion, minced
- 1½ tbsp. cognac or brandy

2   hard-cooked eggs
    Kosher salt and freshly ground black pepper,
    to taste
    Toast points, for serving

Bring livers and stock to a boil in a 4-qt. saucepan over medium-high heat. Reduce heat to medium-low and cook until just cooked through, about 8 minutes. Drain, reserving ¼ cup cooking liquid, then transfer to a food processor. Heat fat in a 10″ skillet over high heat, add onion, and cook until browned, about 4 minutes. Transfer to food processor. Add reserved cooking liquid, cognac, egg, salt, and pepper and purée. Serve with toast points.

GOUGÈRES
MAKES ABOUT 2½ DOZEN

These feather light, tender pastry puffs are flavored with Gruyère cheese and baked until golden brown. They're best eaten right out of the oven, when the warm cheese is at its most aromatic.

½   cup milk
8   tbsp. unsalted butter, cubed
½   tsp. kosher salt
1   cup flour
4   eggs, at room temperature
6   oz. Gruyère cheese, grated

1 Heat oven to 425°. Bring milk, butter, salt, and ½ cup water to a boil in a 4-qt. saucepan over high heat. Add flour and stir until dough forms. Reduce heat to medium and cook, stirring dough constantly with a wooden spoon, until slightly dried, about 2 minutes. Transfer to a bowl. Using a hand mixer, beat in one egg until smooth. Repeat with remaining eggs, beating them in one at a time, until dough is smooth. Stir in cheese.

2 Using a large tablespoon, drop balls of dough onto parchment paper–lined baking sheets. Reduce oven temperature to 375° and bake until golden brown, about 30 minutes.

PIMENTO CHEESE
SERVES 4–6

Chefs John Bates and Brandon Martinez of Austin, Texas' now-shuttered Noble Sandwich Co. added Sriracha to their beloved chunky pimento cheese, upping the spice factor and helping to offset the creaminess of the rich cheddar spread. We still like to slather it on everything, from romaine spears to sandwiches.

PUFF PERFECT

Gougères, the irresistible French cheese puffs traditionally served with apéritifs in Burgundy, might well be the perfect hors d'oeuvre: With their delicate crisp walls and soft, cheese-laced, eggy interior, they are light enough to whet your appetite but rich enough to satisfy premeal cravings. The secret of the puff? According to chef Jean-Pierre Silva of Le Vieux Moulin in Bouilland, it's all in how you construct the dough: Adding the flour all at once, and the eggs one at a time. This produces a perfectly airy, lofty dough.

---

6   oz. grated sharp cheddar cheese
¼   cup plus 2 tbsp. garlic aïoli
2   tsp. Sriracha chile sauce
1   tsp. apple cider vinegar
¾   tsp. paprika
¾   tsp. Worcestershire sauce
2   medium scallions, finely chopped
1   roasted red bell pepper, peeled, seeded, and finely
    chopped
    Kosher salt and freshly ground black pepper
    Romaine lettuce (optional)

Combine cheddar cheese, aïoli, Sriracha, cider vinegar, paprika, Worcestershire, scallions, and roasted bell pepper in a medium bowl. Season to taste with salt and pepper, and stir to combine. Spread on sandwiches, or simply transfer to a wide bowl and serve with romaine spears for dipping.

CHINESE-AMERICAN MINCED CHICKEN LETTUCE WRAPS
San Choy Bow
SERVES 4

These crisp wraps are a lesson in textural contrast—and they're packed with flavor. The chicken marinates in a powerful combination of soy sauce, oyster sauce, and rice wine.

1   lb. ground chicken
20 cashews, roughly chopped
3   dried shiitake mushrooms, softened in hot water,
    stemmed, and finely chopped
3   scallions, 2 finely chopped, the green part
    of 1 julienned
4   tsp. soy sauce

1 tbsp. oyster sauce
1 tbsp. Shaoxing wine
1 tsp. cornstarch
½ tsp. sugar
Kosher salt and freshly ground white pepper, to taste
2 tbsp. peanut oil
3 cloves garlic, finely chopped
16 leaves iceberg lettuce
Sweet chile sauce, for serving

1 Put chicken, cashews, mushrooms, and chopped scallions into a bowl. Mix soy sauce, oyster sauce, wine, cornstarch, sugar, salt, and pepper in a bowl. Pour over chicken and toss well. Let marinate for 15 minutes.

2 Heat oil in a 12″ skillet over high heat. Add garlic and cook for 10 seconds. Add chicken mixture and cook, stirring, until browned, about 3 minutes. Transfer chicken to a bowl. To serve, spoon some chicken onto each lettuce leaf. Garnish with julienned scallion and chile sauce.

NEGIMA YAKITORI

Chicken & Scallion Skewers with Yakitori Sauce

SERVES 6–8

Japanese chicken skewers are marvels of simplicity. A basting of homemade yakitori sauce, salty and deep thanks to roasted chicken bones, combines with the smoke of the grill and the sweetness of scallions to bring out remarkable flavor in the chicken.

4 whole, bone-in chicken legs
2 cups mirin
2 cups soy sauce
1 cup dry sake
2 tbsp. packed dark brown sugar
2 tsp. freshly ground black pepper
16 large scallions, cut into 1″ pieces
5 cloves garlic, crushed
1 2″ piece fresh ginger, peeled and thinly sliced
16 bamboo skewers, soaked in water for 30 minutes

1 Make the yakitori sauce: Arrange an oven rack 4″ from broiler and heat broiler. Remove bones from chicken legs and cut bones into small pieces. Cut chicken meat into ¼″-thick slices; refrigerate until ready to use. Transfer bones to a foil-lined baking sheet and broil, turning, until browned all over, about 10 minutes. Transfer bones to a 4-qt. saucepan and add mirin, soy sauce, sake, sugar, pepper, green parts of scallions, garlic, ginger, and 1 cup

water. Bring to a boil, reduce heat to medium-low, and cook until liquid is reduced by half, about 1½ hours. Pour through a fine-mesh sieve into a bowl and let sauce cool.

2 Working with 1 skewer at a time, alternately thread 4 slices chicken with 3 pieces of white parts of scallions, piercing chicken slices through their ends to form folded slices and piercing scallion pieces perpendicular to skewer.

3 Build a medium fire in a charcoal grill or heat a gas grill to medium. (Alternatively, heat a cast-iron grill pan over medium-high heat.) Add skewers and cook, turning, until beginning to brown, about 6 minutes. Brush with yakitori sauce and continue cooking, turning and basting with sauce every 30 seconds, until cooked through and sauce forms a glaze on chicken, about 2 minutes more. Transfer to a serving plate and drizzle with more yakitori sauce; serve immediately.

MALAYSIAN CHICKEN SATAY

Satay Ayam

MAKES 30 SKEWERS

Malaysia's version of chicken satay, called *satay ayam*, comes from the northeast coast and is marinated in a spice market's worth of seasonings, from ginger to fennel to coriander. It's served with a rich, piquant peanut sauce—in Malaysia, the street hawkers who sell satay each have their own variation, some spicier, some sweeter, some more sour.

6 tbsp. peanut oil
¼ cup packed dark brown sugar
1 tbsp. ground coriander
2½ tsp. ground turmeric
1½ tsp. ground fennel
1½ tsp. kosher salt
3 cloves garlic, chopped
6 stalks lemongrass, trimmed and chopped, plus 1 stalk, whole
3 large shallots, chopped
1 5″ piece fresh ginger, peeled and chopped
3¼ lb. skinless, boneless chicken thighs, cut into 1″-wide, ¼″-thick slices
30 bamboo skewers, soaked in water for 30 minutes
Peanut Sauce (page 595), for serving

1 Process 2 tbsp. oil with sugar, coriander, turmeric, fennel, salt, garlic, chopped lemongrass, shallots, and ginger in a food processor until smooth. Mix paste and chicken in a bowl; chill for 4 hours. Using a meat mallet, strike thick end of lemongrass stalk until it splits into threads resembling a brush. Place shattered end in a bowl and pour in remaining 4 tbsp. oil.

2 Build a hot fire in a charcoal grill or heat a gas grill to high. Thread 2 pieces of chicken on each skewer. Grill, turning once and brushing with oil from lemongrass brush, until charred, 5–6 minutes. Serve at once with peanut sauce.

THE WORLD OF SATAY

> **"**Satay is the quintessence of fast food in Southeast Asia. You'll find it sizzling over hot coals practically 24 hours a day—at night markets, in busy hawker stalls, or offered by mobile vendors who prepare it to order. These cooks carry bamboo rods across their shoulders, balancing a basketful of the marinated meat and condiments on one side and a small grill filled with hot coals on the other. When a vendor is waved down by a customer, he sets up his mobile kitchen on the ground and starts cooking. Within minutes, the skewers are charred and ready to eat. **"**
>
> JAMES OSELAND

TOFU WANZI

Fried Tofu & Bacon Fritters

MAKES ABOUT 3½ DOZEN

China meets the American South in these exquisite tofu, bacon, and scallion fritters, an invention of author Mei Chin's grandmother, who emigrated from China to Richmond, Virginia.

- 2 12½-oz. boxes soft or silken tofu
- 1 12½-oz. box firm tofu
- ⅔ cup panko bread crumbs
- ⅓ cup flour
- ¼ cup sesame oil
- 5 scallions, finely chopped
- 4 slices bacon, cooked and finely chopped
- 2 eggs, lightly beaten
   Kosher salt and freshly ground white pepper, to taste
   Canola oil, for frying

1 Place all the tofu on a bed of paper towels on a baking sheet and cover with more paper towels and another baking sheet. Place a cast-iron skillet on sheet to weight it down; refrigerate until tofu is drained of most of its liquid, at least 6 hours or up to overnight. Transfer pressed tofu to a large bowl and mash coarsely with a fork. Stir in panko, flour, sesame oil, scallions, bacon, eggs, and salt and pepper until evenly combined.

2 Pour oil to a depth of 2″ into a 6-qt. Dutch oven and heat over medium-high heat until a deep-fry thermometer reads 350°. Portion 2 tbsp. of the tofu mixture and form into a quenelle using 2 spoons; repeat with remaining tofu mixture. Fry until golden brown and crisp, about 2 minutes. Season with salt and serve immediately.

TUNA MELT CANAPÉS

SERVES 2

This bite-size riff on a tuna melt gets a face-lift from curry powder, raisins, and chutney—unexpected partners, but they work together beautifully.

- 2–3 tbsp. mayonnaise
- 1½ tbsp. raisins
- 1 tbsp. mango chutney, chopped
- ½ tsp. curry powder
- 1 5-oz. can oil- or water-packed tuna, drained
   Kosher salt and freshly ground black pepper, to taste
- 2 slices white bread, crusts removed
- 2 thin, square slices cheddar cheese
- 8 1″ pieces fresh chives, for garnish

1 Arrange an oven rack 10″ from broiler and heat broiler. Combine mayonnaise, raisins, chutney, curry, and tuna in a bowl and season with salt and pepper; set aside.

2 Cut each slice of bread and cheese into 4 triangles. Spoon tuna salad on top of bread pieces and top with cheese. Broil triangles until cheese is melted, 3–4 minutes. Serve garnished with chives.

FRIED WHITEBAIT

SERVES 4

A standard menu item in the ouzo bars of Athens, these tiny, deep-fried fish—about 3″ long and eaten whole, heads and all—are as addictive as French fries.

BETTER WITH BACON

From artichokes to zucchini, almost everything is improved when it's wrapped in smoky, salty bacon.

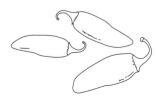

JALAPEÑOS

You don't need breading to make perfect poppers. Grill seeded jalapeños and stuff them with cream cheese; wrap the peppers in bacon and grill until golden and crispy, about 10 minutes. Serve them with fresh tomato salsa to tame the heat.

SCALLIONS

Butcher shops all across Sicily sell bacon-wrapped scallions called *cipollate con pancetta*. Bunch 3 scallions together and tie with bacon. Sauté in a skillet until bacon is browned and crispy on all sides, 6–8 minutes. Serve immediately, or snack on them at room temperature.

CHICKEN LIVERS

To make *rumaki,* the tiki bar appetizer that took the 1960s by storm, place a water chestnut in the middle of a raw slice of bacon, then top with ½ a chicken liver. Place a drop of soy sauce, a pinch of minced fresh ginger, and a sprinkle of brown sugar on top, then wrap in bacon and secure with a skewer. Bake, turning once, in a 400° oven until crisp and golden all over.

ARTICHOKES

Place a drained, jarred artichoke heart on the end of a piece of raw bacon, sprinkle it with Parmigiano and black pepper, roll it up, and secure with a toothpick. Heat canola oil poured to a depth of 2″ into a Dutch oven to 350° and fry the artichokes until golden brown, about 3 minutes. Sprinkle with more cheese.

DATES

At The Red Cat, a New York City restaurant, almost every table orders these dates. Insert an almond into the cavity of a pitted Medjool date, and pipe in soft goat cheese to fill any empty space. Wrap each date in a ½ slice bacon and place seam side down on a baking sheet. Cook at 500° until bacon is crisp, 6–8 minutes.

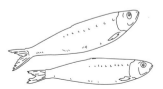

SARDINES

Wrap oil-packed sardines from a tin in 1 slice of bacon per sardine and secure with a toothpick. Heat canola oil poured to a depth of 2″ into a Dutch oven to 350° and fry until bacon is crisp, about 2 minutes. Serve over toasted white bread, sprinkled with chopped fresh herbs like parsley or chervil.

1 lb. whitebait or smelts
1 cup flour
1 tsp. kosher salt
   Freshly ground black pepper, to taste
4 cups vegetable oil, for frying
   Coarse salt (optional) and lemon wedges,
   for serving

1 Wash and drain fish (since they're so small, it is not necessary to clean or bone them). On a large plate, combine flour with salt and several grinds of pepper. Dredge fish in flour, shaking off any excess.

2 Pour oil to a depth of 2″ into a 6-qt. Dutch oven and heat over medium-high until a deep-fry thermometer reads 350°. (Test the oil by dropping in a fish; it should sizzle vigorously and, after sinking to the bottom, quickly rise to the top.) Gently place half the fish in the oil and fry until crisp and golden, about 3 minutes. Remove with a slotted spoon and drain on paper towels. Repeat with remaining fish.

3 Mound hot fried fish on a plate and sprinkle with coarse salt, if desired. Serve immediately with lemon wedges.

COOK'S NOTE Don't crowd the fry pot with too many fish. The temperature will drop and the fish won't be crisp.

SHRIMP & HERB CANAPÉS
SERVES 14–16

Time-Life's *Good Cook* series of cookbooks from the 1970s and 1980s is filled with timeless classics. Among our favorite recipes is this one for a duo of canapés made with herb and shrimp butters, which we've adapted.

2 cups packed watercress leaves
1 cup packed fresh flat-leaf parsley leaves
1 cup packed fresh tarragon leaves
1 lb. (4 sticks) unsalted butter, softened
4 tbsp. fresh lemon juice
   Kosher salt and freshly ground black pepper,
   to taste
½ lb. medium shrimp, unpeeled
1 loaf Pullman bread, cut lengthwise into six
   ¼″-thick slices, crusts removed
1 tbsp. capers, rinsed, for garnish
4 radishes, thinly sliced, for garnish
3 fresh chives, cut into 2″ lengths, for garnish

1 To make the herb butter: Combine watercress, parsley, tarragon, and ½ cup water in a food processor and purée

into a smooth paste. Transfer to a 2-qt. saucepan, place over medium heat, and cook, without stirring, until mixture barely begins to simmer. Remove from heat and let sit for 10 minutes. Using a slotted spoon, scoop the herb solids from the liquid and transfer to paper towels to drain. Squeeze paper towels around herbs to remove any excess liquid, and then transfer herb solids to a food processor along with 2 sticks butter and 2 tbsp. lemon juice; process until smooth. Transfer to a bowl, season with salt and pepper, and set herb butter aside.

2 To make the shrimp butter: Bring a 2-qt. saucepan of water to a boil. Add shrimp and cook until just cooked through, about 4 minutes. Drain, peel, and devein. Set aside 4 shrimp to slice thinly lengthwise for garnish. Finely chop remaining shrimp; transfer to a food processor along with remaining butter and lemon juice and process until smooth. Transfer to a bowl, season with salt and pepper, and set aside.

3 Thinly spread some of the herb butter over half the bread slices; thinly spread some of the shrimp butter over the remaining bread slices. Transfer each butter to a separate piping bag fitted with a ⅜″ star tip, and pipe rows of butter along the long edges of the corresponding herb- and shrimp-buttered bread slices; chill to firm butters. Cut each bread slice crosswise into 5 rectangles. Garnish rectangles with capers, cooked shrimp slices, radishes, and chives.

LOWCOUNTRY SHRIMP PASTE
MAKES 2½ CUPS

A specialty of Charleston and the Carolina Lowcountry, this shrimp paste—similar to what the English call potted shrimp—is delicious spread on buttered toast.

½ lb. (2 sticks) unsalted butter
1 lb. shrimp, peeled and deveined
½ tsp. kosher salt
½ tsp. freshly ground black pepper
¼ cup sherry
2 tbsp. fresh lemon juice
¼ tsp. cayenne pepper

1 Heat 6 tbsp. butter in a large skillet until it is hot and foaming. Add the shrimp, salt, and black pepper and cook over high heat, stirring often, until the shrimp are pink and cooked through, 4–7 minutes.

> **"One of the very nicest things about life is the way we must regularly stop whatever it is we are doing and devote our attention to eating."**
>
> LUCIANO PAVAROTTI

2 Remove the skillet from the stove and use a slotted spoon to transfer the cooked shrimp to a food processor. Return the skillet to the stove and add sherry, lemon juice, and cayenne. Cook over high heat until the liquid in the skillet is reduced to about 3 tbsp. and is quite syrupy. Immediately add this to the shrimp in the food processor and process until the shrimp are thoroughly puréed. Cut remaining 10 tbsp. butter into pieces. With the motor running, add the butter, a few pieces at a time, and process until thoroughly blended. Turn the food processor off and taste the shrimp paste for seasoning, adding more salt, black pepper, sherry, lemon juice, or cayenne as needed. Transfer the shrimp paste to a crock or bowl and allow to cool completely. If not using right away, cover the shrimp paste and refrigerate for up to 1 week.

DEVILS ON HORSEBACK
SERVES 4–6

In this version of the classic hors d'oeuvre, oysters are cooked with garlic and wine, then set "astride" toasted garlic bread slices and sprinkled with bacon.

- 6 tbsp. unsalted butter
- 2 tbsp. finely chopped garlic
- ½ small baguette (about ¼ lb.), cut into eight 1"-thick slices
- 10 slices bacon, cut into 2" pieces
- 3 scallions, finely chopped
- ¼ cup white wine
- 2 tsp. fresh lemon juice, plus wedges for serving
- 8 oysters, such as bluepoint, shucked, juices reserved
  Kosher salt and freshly ground black pepper, to taste
- 2 tbsp. roughly chopped fresh flat-leaf parsley, for garnish

1 Heat oven to 400°. Melt 4 tbsp. butter in a small pan; mix with 1 tsp. garlic. Brush baguette slices with the garlic butter and arrange on a baking sheet. Bake until lightly toasted, about 10 minutes. Set aside.

2 Meanwhile, cook bacon in a 12" skillet over medium-high heat until crispy, about 10 minutes. Using a slotted spoon, transfer bacon to paper towels to drain, reserving bacon fat for another use; set aside. Heat remaining 2 tbsp. butter in the skillet. Add remaining 5 tsp. garlic and the scallions and cook, stirring, until soft, about 3 minutes. Add wine, lemon juice, oysters with their juices, and salt and pepper. Cook, stirring, until oysters begin to curl at the edges, about 3 minutes. Using a slotted spoon, transfer oysters to a bowl; cover to keep warm. Continue to cook sauce until thickened and reduced by half, about 10 minutes. Divide oysters and sauce among baguette slices; top with reserved bacon and garnish with parsley.

FRIED ARTICHOKE HEARTS WITH TAHINI SAUCE
Ardî Shawkî Maqli bil-Taratur
SERVES 4 (SEE PHOTO, PAGE 212)

We found this recipe—a flavorful preparation, in which tender artichoke bottoms are fried and served with an intense, tahini-based sauce—at al-Az, a casual but well-known restaurant in Damascus.

FOR THE TAHINI SAUCE
- 6 cloves garlic, peeled
- 2 tsp. kosher salt
- ½ cup tahini
- ½ cup fresh lemon juice
- 3 tsp. chopped fresh flat-leaf parsley

FOR THE ARTICHOKES
- 4 cups olive oil
- 8 hearts of steamed medium artichokes, halved if large
- ½ cup flour
  Kosher salt, to taste

1 Make the sauce: Combine garlic and salt in a mortar and grind to a paste with pestle. (Garlic can also be very finely chopped.) Transfer garlic paste to a bowl and add tahini. While stirring, drizzle in lemon juice. Thin to the consistency of a thick dip with up to 3 tbsp. water. Stir in 2 tsp. parsley.

2 Heat oil in a medium saucepan over medium-high heat until a deep-fry thermometer reads 375°. Dredge artichokes in flour and shake off excess. Fry artichokes, a few at a time, turning occasionally, until golden, about 2 minutes. Remove with a slotted spoon, drain on paper towels, and sprinkle with salt. Serve with sauce, garnished with remaining 1 tsp. parsley.

COOK'S NOTE To test if the oil is hot enough, drop in a toothpick. If it quickly turns dark brown, the oil is ready.

LEMON & CORIANDER MARINATED OLIVES

Elies Tsakkistes me Koliandro

SERVES 8–10

Chunks of lemon and cracked coriander seeds lend a bright flavor to these classic Greek-style olives.

3	cups cracked (but not pitted) green olives
⅓	cup extra-virgin olive oil
¼	cup fresh lemon juice
2	tbsp. cracked whole coriander seeds
4	cloves garlic, smashed
3	fresh or dried bay leaves
1	lemon

1 In a large bowl, mix olives with oil, lemon juice, coriander, garlic, and bay leaves.

2 Cut lemon into wedges lengthwise; cut each wedge crosswise into ½"-thick pieces. Add lemon pieces to olives; stir well to combine. Cover olives with plastic wrap and refrigerate for at least 8 hours or up to 1 month. Bring olives to room temperature before serving.

COOK'S NOTE When making this dish, we prefer to use the nutty, cracked Cypriot olives called *kipriakes elies,* but you can use Italian Cerignola or Spanish Gordal olives and get equally good results.

FRIED OLIVES

SERVES 2

Briny olives take on a whole new dimension when fried in a crisp bread crumb crust. They're a perfect cocktail party snack.

	Olive oil, for frying
1	egg, beaten
½	cup fine dry bread crumbs
1	cup pitted green olives, drained

1 Pour oil to a depth of 2" into a 2-qt. saucepan and heat over medium-high heat until a deep-fry thermometer reads 350°.

2 Meanwhile, place the beaten egg and the bread crumbs in separate bowls. Coat olives in egg, then roll in bread crumbs until fully coated. Fry one-quarter of the olives until golden, about 45 seconds. Drain on paper towels and repeat with remaining olives. Serve warm.

EGGPLANT CAPONATA

SERVES 6–8

This classic Sicilian dish of fried eggplant sops up the flavors of onions, celery, tomatoes, olives, raisins, capers, basil, pine nuts, and chocolate—yes, chocolate. It's the perfect example of sweet and salty marrying well together.

3	cups olive oil
2	lb. eggplant, cut into 1" cubes
1	large yellow onion, chopped
1	rib celery, roughly chopped
	Kosher salt and freshly ground black pepper, to taste
3	tbsp. tomato paste, thinned with ¼ cup water
1	cup canned whole, peeled tomatoes, crushed by hand
1¼	cups green olives, pitted and roughly chopped
½	cup white wine vinegar
½	cup golden raisins
¼	cup salt-packed capers, rinsed and drained
3	tbsp. sugar
2	tbsp. finely grated unsweetened chocolate
½	cup finely chopped fresh basil
2	tbsp. pine nuts

1 Heat oil in a 12″ skillet over medium-high heat. Working in batches, add eggplant and fry, tossing occasionally, until browned, 3–4 minutes. Using a slotted spoon, transfer eggplant to a large bowl; set aside.

2 Pour off all but ¼ cup oil and reserve for another use. Return skillet to heat, add onions and celery, and season with salt and pepper. Cook, stirring often, until beginning to brown, 10 minutes. Reduce heat to medium, add tomato paste, and cook, stirring, until caramelized and almost evaporated, 1–2 minutes. Add crushed tomatoes and continue cooking for 10 minutes. Stir in olives, vinegar, raisins, capers, sugar, and chocolate and cook, stirring occasionally, until thickened, about 15 minutes. Transfer to bowl with eggplant, along with basil and pine nuts, and mix together. Season with salt and pepper and let cool to room temperature before serving.

POTATO SKORDALIA

MAKES 2 CUPS

This garlicky purée of olive oil, almonds, and potatoes is a staple in a Greek mezze spread. It's traditionally served with bread and raw vegetables.

- 1 medium russet potato, peeled and cut into 1″ cubes
  Kosher salt, to taste
- ⅓ cup ground blanched almonds
- 8 cloves garlic, smashed and minced into a paste
- 1 cup extra-virgin olive oil
- 1 tbsp. red wine vinegar

1 Put potatoes into a 2-qt. saucepan and add enough salted water to cover by 1″. Bring to a boil and cook until tender, about 15 minutes. Drain and transfer to a bowl.

2 Mash potatoes until smooth; stir in almonds and garlic. Add oil, then vinegar, in a thin stream while whisking vigorously, and season with salt. Skordalia will keep, refrigerated and covered, for up to 4 days.

HERBED TOMATO TART

SERVES 12–16

Made with ripe cherry tomatoes and fragrant herbs, this sweet-savory tart makes a regular appearance during the annual midsummer communal feast held in the hilltop town of Buggiano, in northern Tuscany.

- 2 9″×11″ sheets frozen puff pastry, thawed and chilled
- ½ cup grated Parmigiano-Reggiano
- 4 tbsp. extra-virgin olive oil
- 12 oil-packed anchovy filets, drained and finely chopped
- 3 lb. cherry or grape tomatoes
  Kosher salt and freshly ground black pepper, to taste
- ¼ cup finely chopped fresh flat-leaf parsley
- 2 tbsp. finely chopped fresh chives
- 2 tbsp. finely chopped fresh oregano
  Freshly grated nutmeg, to taste

1 Heat oven to 375°. Fit pastry sheets side by side in a parchment paper–lined 13″×18″ rimmed baking pan, pressing pastry against bottom and sides. Trim inner edges of pastry sheets so that they form a seam in center; trim pastry hanging over sides of pan. Prick bottom of pastry with a fork. Line bottom and sides of pastry with parchment paper and fill with pie weights or dried beans. Bake until edges of tart are golden, about 25 minutes. Remove weights and parchment, sprinkle Parmigiano over tart shell, and bake until cheese is melted and tart shell is golden all over, 15–20 minutes. Transfer to a rack and let cool.

2 Arrange an oven rack 4″ from broiler and heat broiler. In a large bowl, mix together oil and anchovies; add tomatoes and season with salt and pepper. Toss to coat. Transfer tomato mixture to a baking sheet and broil, shaking pan once or twice, until tomatoes blister, 12–14 minutes. Let cool slightly. Use a slotted spoon to transfer tomato mixture to the prepared tart shell; distribute tomatoes evenly.

3 Heat oven to 425°. In a medium bowl, mix parsley, chives, oregano, and nutmeg; sprinkle herb mixture evenly over tomatoes. Return tart to oven and bake until hot, about 15 minutes. Let tart cool slightly before serving.

PISSALADIÈRE

Caramelized Onion Tart

SERVES 12

This southern French tart takes its name from *pissala,* a pungent anchovy paste that gives the flatbread its distinctive flavor. Serve this savory bread as an appetizer or as a snack, served with a glass of rosé.

1 ¼-oz. package active dry yeast
1 cup water, heated to 115°
3 cups flour
¾ cup extra-virgin olive oil, plus more for greasing
1 tbsp. kosher salt, plus more to taste
20 oil-packed anchovy filets, drained and finely chopped
12 medium yellow onions, thinly sliced lengthwise
4 sprigs fresh thyme
2 sprigs fresh rosemary
2 bay leaves
   Freshly ground black pepper, to taste
½ cup pitted, halved black olives

1 Make the dough: Whisk together yeast and water in a large bowl; let sit until foamy, about 10 minutes. Add flour, ¼ cup oil, and salt and stir until dough forms; transfer to a floured work surface and knead until smooth, about 6 minutes. Transfer to a greased bowl, cover with plastic wrap, and let sit in a warm spot until doubled in size, about 1 hour.

2 Meanwhile, make the topping: Heat remaining ½ cup oil in a 6-qt. saucepan over medium-low heat. Add anchovies and cook, stirring, until dissolved in the oil, about 7 minutes. Add onions, thyme, rosemary, bay leaves, and salt and pepper and cook, covered and stirring occasionally, until reduced and softened, about 1 hour. Uncover and cook, stirring occasionally, until liquid evaporates and onions are golden brown, about 30 minutes. Remove from heat and discard herb sprigs and bay leaves; let cool.

3 Heat oven to 425°. Uncover dough and transfer to a work surface; using a rolling pin, roll dough into a 12″×18″ rectangle. Transfer dough rectangle to a greased 13″×18″ rimmed baking sheet and then cover evenly with onion mixture; place olive halves decoratively over onion mixture.

Cover tart loosely with plastic wrap and let sit until dough is puffed, about 1 hour. Bake until golden brown at the edges, about 20 minutes. Let cool for 10 minutes before cutting into squares to serve.

TREVISO & GORGONZOLA TART
SERVES 4–6

Treviso, the long-leaved cousin of round Verona radicchio, is wilted and tossed with blue cheese as a topping for this light and crispy tart.

1 7½″×14½″ sheet frozen puff pastry, thawed
3 tbsp. extra-virgin olive oil
1 clove garlic, crushed
2 heads Treviso radicchio, cored and coarsely chopped
   Kosher salt and freshly ground black pepper, to taste
3 oz. Gorgonzola cheese, crumbled

1 Put a pizza stone on oven rack set in middle of oven. Heat oven to 400°.

2 Heat 3 tbsp. oil in a large skillet over medium heat, add garlic, and cook until golden, 3–4 minutes. Add radicchio, raise heat to medium-high, and cook until wilted, 2–3 minutes. Season with salt and pepper. Set aside.

3 Place a pastry sheet on a floured inverted baking sheet, prick all over with a fork, then scatter radicchio and Gorgonzola on top.

4 Put into freezer for 15 minutes, then loosen pastry from baking sheet with a metal spatula and slide onto pizza stone. Bake until pastry is golden, 18–20 minutes. Let cool for 5–10 minutes before cutting into squares to serve.

Dips & Spreads

LEMON PARMESAN DIP

MAKES 2 CUPS

Cheesy and bright-tasting, this crudité dip also makes a great salad dressing.

- 1½ cups mayonnaise
- ¾ cup grated Parmigiano-Reggiano
- 2 tbsp. fresh lemon juice
- 1 tsp. Dijon mustard
- 1 tsp. Worcestershire sauce
- 1 clove garlic, mashed to a paste
  Grated zest of 1 lemon
  Kosher salt and freshly ground black pepper

Stir all ingredients together in a bowl until smooth.

FETA CHEESE SPREAD

MAKES 1 CUP

In this Greek recipe, feta is blended with olive oil and red chiles into a savory spread. It's delicious right away, but it's even better when left to marinate for several hours so the flavors can blend.

- ½ lb. feta, crumbled
- 3 tbsp. extra-virgin olive oil, plus more as needed
- 2 small dried red chiles
  Freshly ground black pepper, to taste
  Juice of ½ lemon
  Kalamata olives, for serving
  Pita bread, for serving

1 Combine feta, oil, chiles, a few grinds of pepper, and lemon juice in a food processor and blend until very smooth. Transfer to a bowl. Cover and refrigerate for several hours so that the flavors develop and the cheese spread sets up.

2 Bring to room temperature. Drizzle a little oil over the top. Serve with olives and pita. Spread will keep, refrigerated, for up to 1 week.

MAYTAG BLUE CHEESE DIP

MAKES ABOUT 2 CUPS

The most celebrated American blue cheese, Maytag Blue—made on a dairy farm in Newton, Iowa, and cave-aged for six months for a full, rich flavor—is available in quality cheese shops. Other blue cheeses may be substituted, but Maytag is worth looking for. Celery sticks make an ideal vehicle for this rich dip.

- 8 oz. cream cheese, softened
- ¼ cup sour cream
- ¼ cup heavy cream
- ¼ lb. Maytag Blue cheese
- 3 scallions, chopped
  Freshly ground black pepper, to taste

Mix cream cheese, sour cream, and heavy cream together in a medium bowl. Crumble in blue cheese, add two-thirds of the scallions, and stir until well mixed but still slightly chunky. Season to taste with pepper and garnish with remaining scallions.

ARTICHOKE DIP

MAKES 3 CUPS

Artichokes mixed with salty parmesan cheese and creamy mayo are baked together until bubbling hot. This quintessential appetizer is served all across the South, from New Orleans, Louisiana, to Norfolk, Virginia.

- 3–4 cups cooked artichoke hearts, or one 15-oz. can artichoke hearts, drained and chopped
- 1 cup grated Parmigiano-Reggiano
- 1 cup mayonnaise
  Minced onions, to taste
  Assorted crackers, for serving

Heat oven to 350°. Combine artichokes, cheese, and mayonnaise, mixing well. Stir in onions to taste. Spoon into an 8″ square baking dish. Bake until bubbly and lightly browned. Serve with crackers.

RAW DEAL

There's nothing new about eating raw vegetables, but in the States it wasn't until the first half of the 20th century that an austere serving of celery sticks was recast as crudités—an opulent appetizer. The distinction is partly semantic: Fashionable French restaurants in America offered first-course relish plates of raw vegetables, referring to them in their native tongue (the word *crudité* itself is French for "rawness," though the presentation may include cooked or cured ingredients), and the term caught on. The definition is also an aesthetic one: Crudités live or die by their composition, by their balance of colors, and the allure of the arrangement. Whether it's a single sliced carrot or a polychromatic cornucopia, it's a dish that's meant to attract, to be admired. (James Beard called crudités "the most appetizing dish imaginable.") Compose your crudités using whatever looks best at the market: Broccoli, cauliflower, carrots, and cucumbers are just starting points; try wedges of raw fennel, elegant breakfast radishes, pickled caperberries, or blanched green beans, and always several dips, like Lemon Parmesan Dip (page 25), Muhammara (page 28), and Bagna Cauda (this page).

TAPÉNADE

MAKES ½ CUP

Tapénade speaks to salt lovers. Briny olives, salty capers, and anchovy filets are mixed into a piquant spread that's brightened by the addition of lemon juice, parsley, and olive oil.

- 1 clove garlic
- 1 oil-packed anchovy filet
- 1 tsp. chopped, rinsed salt-packed capers
- ½ cup chopped, pitted niçoise olives
- 1 tbsp. chopped fresh flat-leaf parsley
- ¼ cup extra-virgin olive oil
- ½ tbsp. fresh lemon juice

Crush garlic and anchovy filet with a mortar and pestle, then mix in capers, olives, and parsley. Stir in oil, add lemon juice, and combine well with a fork.

FRENCH ONION DIP

MAKES ABOUT 3½ CUPS (SEE PHOTO, PAGE 221)

Our favorite recipe for this classic dip showcases onions three ways: fried, roasted, and fresh.

- 4 medium yellow onions, 2 quartered lengthwise, 2 finely chopped
- 1 cup olive oil
   Kosher salt and freshly ground black pepper, to taste
- 1 cup mayonnaise
- 4 oz. cream cheese, softened
- ½ cup sour cream
- 1 tbsp. fresh lemon juice
- 1 tsp. Worcestershire sauce
   Tabasco sauce, to taste
- 4 scallions, minced
   Cut raw vegetables, such as cucumber, carrot, and cauliflower, for serving

1 Heat oven to 425°. Toss quartered onions with 2 tbsp. oil on a foil-lined baking sheet, and season with salt and pepper. Roast, turning occasionally, until soft and slightly caramelized, about 45 minutes. Set roasted onions aside to cool.

2 Purée roasted onions in a food processor until smooth. Add mayonnaise, cream cheese, sour cream, lemon juice, Worcestershire, hot sauce, salt, and pepper, and purée until smooth. Transfer to a bowl, cover with plastic wrap, and refrigerate until set, at least 4 hours or up to overnight.

3 Heat remaining oil in a 10″ skillet over medium-high heat. Add finely chopped onions and cook, stirring, until beginning to brown, about 10 minutes. Reduce heat to medium-low and cook, stirring occasionally, until deep golden brown, about 16 minutes more. Transfer onions to a sieve set over a bowl to drain; discard oil or reserve for another use. Transfer fried onions to paper towels to drain.

4 To serve, stir two-thirds of the fried onions and the scallions into dip, and transfer to a serving bowl. Top with remaining fried onions and serve with raw vegetables.

BAGNA CAUDA

Anchovy & Garlic Dip

SERVES 4–6

This lusty hot dip, whose Italian name means "warm bath," provides the perfect counterpoint to raw vegetables.

½ cup extra-virgin olive oil

3 tbsp. unsalted butter

2 cloves garlic, finely chopped

10 salt-cured anchovy filets, rinsed and finely chopped
   Kosher salt, to taste
   Cut raw cauliflower, carrots, celery, radicchio, and radishes, for serving

1 Heat oil and butter in a pot over medium-high heat until butter begins to foam. Add garlic and cook for 10 seconds.

2 Reduce heat to medium-low and add anchovies. Cook, stirring and mashing anchovies with a wooden spoon, until anchovies are broken into very small pieces and dip is cloudy, 3–4 minutes.

3 Season with salt and serve immediately with raw vegetables.

GALILEAN-STYLE HUMMUS

Mashaushe

MAKES 3 CUPS

Generous spice, a good dose of olive oil, and whole chickpeas piled high are the hallmarks of this Galilean-style hummus.

1½ cups dried chickpeas, soaked overnight and drained

½ cup tahini

¾ cup extra-virgin olive oil, plus more

¼ cup fresh lemon juice

2 tsp. ground cumin

2 cloves garlic, peeled

1 small hot red chile, stemmed and seeded
   Kosher salt, to taste
   Pita Bread (page 458, or store-bought), for serving

Bring chickpeas and 4 cups water to a boil in a 4-qt. saucepan. Reduce heat to medium-low and cook, covered, until chickpeas are very tender, 1–1½ hours. Drain, reserving ½ cup cooking liquid; cool to room temperature. Transfer all but ¾ cup chickpeas to a food processor with the tahini, oil, juice, cumin, garlic, chile, and salt; purée until smooth. Add reserved cooking liquid and continue to purée until airy in consistency, about 5 minutes. Transfer hummus to a serving dish. Top with remaining whole chickpeas, drizzle with more oil, and sprinkle with salt. Serve with pita bread.

BABA GHANNOUJ

Mashed Eggplant Spread

SERVES 4

The classic Middle Eastern eggplant spread, redolent of garlic and smoky charred eggplant, is made even creamier with the addition of a small quantity of mayonnaise.

8 cloves garlic, unpeeled

2 medium eggplants

⅓ cup fresh lemon juice

¼ cup plus 2 tbsp. tahini

2 tbsp. mayonnaise

3 tsp. finely chopped fresh flat-leaf parsley

1 tsp. ground cumin

1 tsp. paprika
   Kosher salt and freshly ground black pepper, to taste

Heat broiler. Place garlic and eggplants on a foil-lined baking sheet and broil until tender and charred all over, about 10 minutes for garlic and 40 minutes for eggplant. Peel garlic and peel and seed eggplants. Mash eggplant flesh, garlic, lemon juice, tahini, mayonnaise, 2 tsp. parsley, the cumin, paprika, salt, and pepper in a bowl. Sprinkle with remaining 1 tsp. parsley.

LABNEH

SERVES 4

Thick, tart, and luscious, this yogurt-like cheese, when eaten together with olive oil, pita bread, and the sumac-based spice blend *za'atar,* makes a typical breakfast throughout the Middle East.

8 cups whole milk

1 cup plain yogurt
   Kosher salt, to taste
   Extra-virgin olive oil, for serving

1 Bring milk just to a boil in a 4-qt. nonreactive saucepan fitted with a deep-fry thermometer. Remove from heat and let cool until thermometer reads 118°. Transfer 1 cup milk to a bowl and whisk in yogurt until combined. Add yogurt mixture to saucepan and whisk until smooth; cover tightly with plastic wrap and let sit at room temperature (70°–75°) until thickened, 6–8 hours.

2 Line a fine-mesh sieve with 3 layers of cheesecloth and set over a bowl. Transfer mixture to sieve and let drain for at least 8 hours or up to overnight. Transfer to a serving dish. Season with salt and drizzle with oil.

MUHAMMARA

MAKES 2 CUPS

Diana Abu-Jaber, author of the book *The Language of Baklava*, grew up with a Jordanian father who would lure his children back home by making their favorite foods. According to Abu-Jaber, "This dip or spread is good for when you want everyone to quit running around and come to the table." Serve with warm pita bread, or use as a spread on your favorite sandwich.

- 2 roasted red bell peppers, peeled, seeded, and chopped
- 1½ cups walnuts, toasted
- ½ cup dried bread crumbs
- ¼ cup extra-virgin olive oil, plus more for serving
- ¼ cup tomato purée
- 2 tbsp. unsweetened pomegranate juice
- 1 tbsp. crushed red chile flakes
- 1 tsp. ground cumin
- ½ tsp. ground allspice
- ½ tsp. sugar
- ¼ tsp. kosher salt
- ¼ cup chopped fresh flat-leaf parsley

1 Combine all ingredients except parsley in a food processor or blender. Purée until smooth.

2 Spoon dip into small bowls and garnish with parsley. Cover and chill until ready to serve. Before serving, top with drizzle of oil.

SALSA DE PIÑA

Fresh Pineapple Salsa

MAKES ABOUT 5 CUPS

Pineapple's bright flavor shines in this fragrant, spicy Mexican salsa. It's a terrific foil for rich meats, stewed chicken, and roasted fish—or, on its own, as a brilliantly tart-sweet counterpoint to salty tortilla chips.

- 2 cups finely chopped pineapple
- ½ cup finely chopped fresh cilantro
- ½ cup fresh lime juice
- 1 tbsp. sugar
- 2 tsp. kosher salt
- 4 serrano chiles, stemmed and minced
- 1 small red onion, minced
  Tortilla chips, for serving

Combine all ingredients in a large bowl and toss until evenly combined. Let sit at room temperature to meld flavors, at least 30 minutes. Serve with tortilla chips.

SALSA VERDE

Green Tomatillo Salsa

MAKES ABOUT 4 CUPS

Bright and fruity, this Mexican salsa is a perfect partner to rich cheesy dishes and grilled meats.

- ¼ lb. tomatillos, husked and rinsed
- 4 cloves garlic, peeled
- 2 medium white onions, quartered
- 2 jalapeños, stemmed
- 1 tsp. sugar
- 1 bunch cilantro, stemmed
  Kosher salt and freshly ground black pepper, to taste

1 Combine tomatillos, garlic, onions, and jalapeños in a 4-qt. saucepan; add water to cover by 1″. Bring to a boil and cook until slightly soft, about 5 minutes. Drain, reserving 1 cup cooking liquid.

2 Transfer to a blender along with reserved liquid, sugar, cilantro, and salt and pepper, and pulse until chunky. Transfer to a bowl and serve at room temperature.

OAXACAN SHRIMP PICO DE GALLO

Salsa con Camarón Seco

MAKES ABOUT 3 CUPS

In coastal Oaxaca, Mexico, dried shrimp appear in all kinds of preparations. Here, they bring texture and intense flavor to a classic *pico de gallo*–style salsa.

- 1 lb. plum tomatoes, cored and roughly chopped
- ¼ lb. Mexican dried shrimp, soaked overnight, drained, and roughly chopped
- ¼ cup roughly chopped pickled jalapeños, plus 2 tbsp. brine from jar
- ¼ cup roughly chopped fresh cilantro
- ½ small white onion, roughly chopped
  Juice of 2 limes
  Kosher salt, to taste

In a large bowl, mix tomatoes, shrimp, jalapeños plus brine, cilantro, onion, lime juice, and salt. Let sit at room temperature to meld flavors, at least 1 hour.

TEX-MEX CHILE CON QUESO

SERVES 4

You'll find this creamy, cheesy dip on the menu at virtually every Tex-Mex restaurant in San Antonio, Texas, generally with a basket of tortilla chips.

- 1 cup grated extra-sharp cheddar cheese
- ½ cup Velveeta, cut into pieces
- ½ cup heavy cream
- 2 tbsp. chopped peeled yellow onion
- 2 tbsp. diced tomato
- 1 jalapeño, stemmed, seeded, and diced
  Tortilla chips, for serving

1 Put cheddar and Velveeta in a medium pot. Set it over a pot of simmering water over medium heat and heat until cheese mixture is nearly melted. Add cream and stir constantly with a wooden spoon until cheese mixture is hot and smooth, 3–5 minutes.

2 Transfer cheese mixture to a serving dish and sprinkle onions, tomatoes, and jalapeños on top. Serve immediately with tortilla chips.

CASA DRAGONES GUACAMOLE

MAKES ABOUT 4 CUPS

This guacamole, sourced from the Casa Dragones tequila-making operation in San Miguel de Allende, Mexico, offers a hit of flavor thanks to a rough paste made from white onion, cilantro, serrano chiles, and garlic, into which chunks of ripe avocado are gently incorporated.

- ¼ cup finely chopped white onion
- 2 tbsp. minced fresh cilantro
- 4 serrano chiles, stemmed, seeded, and finely chopped
- 2 cloves garlic, minced
  Kosher salt, to taste
- 3 avocados, pitted, peeled, and cut into 1″ chunks
- 1 plum tomato, seeded and finely chopped
  Juice of 1 lime
  Tortilla chips, for serving

1 In a large bowl or molcajete, combine onion, cilantro, chiles, and garlic; sprinkle heavily with salt and mash with a fork or pestle into a chunky paste.

2 Add avocados, tomato, and lime juice and stir to combine, mashing some of the avocado slightly as you stir. Season with salt and serve with tortilla chips.

AVOCADO SALAD

MAKES 3½ CUPS

This dish, originally created by the late chef Floyd Cardoz is spiked with cayenne and cumin and served with naan chips.

FOR THE SALAD

- 4 avocados, pitted, peeled, and cut into ½″ pieces
- 1 small red onion, finely chopped
- 1 plum tomato, chopped
- 3 tbsp. finely sliced fresh cilantro leaves, plus more for garnish
- 3 tbsp. fresh lime juice
- 2 tbsp. extra-virgin olive oil
- 1–2 tsp. ground cumin
- ½ tsp. sugar
- ⅛ tsp. cayenne pepper
  Fine sea salt and freshly ground black pepper, to taste

FOR THE CHIPS

- 2 8″–9″ naan breads (page 459, or store-bought)
- 2 tbsp. extra-virgin olive oil
  Fine sea salt and freshly ground black pepper, to taste

1 To make the salad: Put all the ingredients, except the garnish, in a medium bowl and stir well. Press plastic wrap directly onto surface of salad and refrigerate for 2–3 hours.

2 To make the chips: Heat oven to 350°. Using a rolling pin, roll each naan ⅛″ thick. Cut each bread into 12 triangles. Put triangles into large bowl, drizzle with oil, add salt and pepper, and toss well. Arrange triangles in a single layer on a baking sheet. Bake until crisp, about 20 minutes, turning chips over and rotating baking sheet front to back after 10 minutes. Set aside to cool.

3 Garnish salad with cilantro and serve with naan chips.

Snacks

SCOTCH EGGS

MAKES 6

A hard-cooked egg encased in sausage and bread crumbs and then deep-fried may seem like a product of modern pub culture, but the Scotch egg debuted at London department store Fortnum & Mason in 1738.

- 6 eggs in their shells, plus 1 egg lightly beaten
- 1 lb. pork sausage, casings removed
- 1 tbsp. Worcestershire sauce
- 1 tbsp. English mustard
- 2 tsp. cornstarch
- ¼ tsp. ground mace
- 2 leaves fresh sage, finely chopped
- 2 sprigs fresh thyme, finely chopped
  Kosher salt and freshly ground black pepper
  Canola oil, for frying
- ¼ cup milk
- ½ cup flour
- 2 cups panko bread crumbs

1 Place 6 eggs in a 2-qt. saucepan and cover by 1″ with cold water. Place over medium-high heat and bring to boil; cover, remove from heat, and let sit for 6 minutes. Drain eggs and transfer to a bowl of ice water; let sit for 5 minutes. Drain eggs and peel and discard shells; set aside.

2 Combine sausage, Worcestershire, mustard, cornstarch, mace, and herbs in a bowl; season with salt and pepper and mix until evenly combined. Divide into 6 equal portions, and press a portion around each cooked egg to cover completely. Place on a plate and refrigerate for 30 minutes.

3 Pour oil to a depth of 2″ into a 6-qt. Dutch oven and heat over medium-high until a deep-fry thermometer reads 350°. Combine beaten egg and milk in a bowl, and place flour and bread crumbs in separate bowls. Working in batches, coat each meat-covered egg in flour, shaking off excess, and then dip in milk mixture to coat. Dredge in bread crumbs, and then fry until crumbs are golden brown and meat is cooked through, about 7 minutes. Transfer to paper towels to drain briefly, and let cool for 10 minutes before serving.

CHINESE TEA EGGS

Cha Ye Dan

MAKES 8

Cooked in a flavorful marinade of soy sauce, star anise, and cinnamon, these tea-stained eggs are a Lunar New Year staple and a favorite everyday snack in China.

- ½ cup soy sauce
- ½ cup sugar
- ½ tsp. black peppercorns
- ½ tsp. fennel seeds
- 8 whole cloves
- 2 star anise pods
- 2 sticks cinnamon
- 1 tbsp. loose-leaf smoked tea, such as Lapsang souchong
- 8 eggs

1 Combine soy sauce, sugar, peppercorns, fennel, cloves, star anise, cinnamon, and 2 cups water in a 2-qt. saucepan and bring to a boil; remove from heat and add tea. Let steep for 10 minutes, then pour marinade through a fine-mesh sieve into a bowl. Keep warm.

2 Place eggs in a 4-qt. saucepan and cover by ½″ with cold water. Place saucepan over medium-high heat and bring to a boil; cover, remove from heat, and let sit until eggs are soft-boiled, about 5 minutes.

3 Drain eggs. Crack shells all over but do not peel eggs; return to saucepan along with marinade. Bring to a boil and cook, stirring, for 5 minutes. Remove from heat and add 2 cups ice. Let eggs cool in marinade before serving.

CLASSIC DEVILED EGGS

MAKES 24

Deviled eggs come in a seeming infinity of variations, but originally, deviled foods got their name from the addition of an assertive ingredient, such as horseradish, chiles, or, in the case of this recipe, mustard and vinegar.

12   hard-cooked eggs (see Eggs, Perfected, this page)
4½   tbsp. mayonnaise
1½   tbsp. cider vinegar
1½   tbsp. melted butter
1   tbsp. yellow mustard
1   tbsp. sugar
Kosher salt, freshly ground black pepper,
and paprika, to taste

1 Gently peel eggs and halve each lengthwise. Remove yolk from each egg half and transfer to a large bowl. Arrange whites on a large platter.

2 Mash yolks well with a fork, then add mayonnaise, vinegar, butter, mustard, sugar, and salt and pepper. Stir the egg yolk mixture until smooth. Using a small spoon, fill each egg white half with a rounded dollop of the egg yolk mixture. Loosely cover deviled eggs with plastic wrap and refrigerate until chilled. When ready to serve, sprinkle the eggs with paprika.

DEVILED EGGS WITH SMOKED TROUT
MAKES 24

Deviled-egg enthusiast Carolynn Spence, chef at the Chateau Marmont in Los Angeles, shared her version of this classic hors d'oeuvre with us, which pairs the egg with smoked fish.

12   hard-cooked eggs (see Eggs, Perfected, this page)
½   cup mayonnaise
2   tbsp. extra-virgin olive oil
2   tsp. fresh lemon juice
½   tsp. dry mustard
½   tsp. whole-grain mustard
¼   tsp. cayenne pepper
Kosher salt and freshly ground black pepper,
to taste
¼   cup shredded smoked trout
Smoked paprika, minced fresh chives, and thinly
shaved red onion, for garnish

1 Gently peel eggs and halve each lengthwise. Remove yolk from each egg half and transfer to a fine sieve set over a bowl. Arrange whites on a large platter.

2 Using a rubber spatula, press yolks through sieve. Add mayonnaise, oil, lemon juice, mustards, and cayenne. Season with salt and pepper and stir vigorously with spatula until smooth.

EGGS, PERFECTED

The best way to make perfect hard-boiled eggs is not to actually boil them. Arrange eggs in a single layer in a medium pot and cover with cold water by 1″. Bring to a boil over medium-high heat, then immediately remove pot from heat. Cover and let rest for 8–10 minutes undisturbed. Drain eggs, leaving them in the pot; tap the eggs with a spoon to crack their shells. This will allow water to seep under the shells, which helps with peeling. Cover eggs with cold water, swish around, then drain. Cover again, this time with icy-cold water (add a few ice cubes if necessary). As soon as the eggs are cool, peel them, starting at the broad end and holding the egg under running water to loosen any bits of stubborn shell clinging to the sides. The longer eggs sit without peeling, the more difficult they will be to peel.

3 Transfer mixture to a piping bag fitted with a plain tip and pipe into egg whites. Top each egg with a bit of trout; garnish with smoked paprika, chives, and red onion. Serve cold or at room temperature.

SOUTHERN-STYLE DEVILED EGGS
MAKES 24

The secret to these traditional Southern deviled eggs, from a recipe shared by home cook Sandra Livesay of Tarboro, North Carolina, is the addition of Durkee Famous Sauce (a tangy, vinegary sandwich spread) and sweet pickle relish.

12   hard-cooked eggs (see Eggs, Perfected, this page)
4   tbsp. Durkee Famous Sauce, or 1 tbsp. each
mayonnaise and Dijon mustard
2   tbsp. sweet pickle relish
½   tsp. paprika, plus more for garnish (optional)
Kosher salt, freshly ground black pepper, and
Tabasco sauce, to taste

1 Gently peel eggs and halve each lengthwise. Remove yolk from each egg half and transfer to a medium bowl. Arrange whites on a large platter.

2 Using a fork, mash yolks. Add Durkee sauce, relish, and paprika and season with salt, pepper, and Tabasco. Stir vigorously with rubber spatula until smooth.

3 Transfer mixture to a piping bag fitted with a plain tip and pipe into egg whites. Garnish eggs with more paprika, if you like. Serve cold or at room temperature.

AJI

Persian Trail Mix

MAKES ABOUT 5 CUPS

This traditional Iranian mixture of nuts, seeds, and dried fruits—often set out for snacking before or between meals—is an inspired mix of sweet and salty.

- 1 cup roasted, salted pumpkin seeds
- 1 cup salted whole pistachios
- 1 cup sugar-coated slivered almonds
- ⅔ cup dried mulberries
- ½ cup roasted, unsalted almonds
- ½ cup dried, salted chickpeas
- ½ cup golden raisins
- ½ cup dried currants
- 8 dried Mission figs
- 8 dried Turkish figs

Stir together all ingredients in a bowl until evenly combined; store in an airtight container for up to 2 weeks.

SPICY FRIED PEANUTS

SERVES 8

In this Mexican bar snack, peanuts get a boost from the addition of ground dried Oaxacan *chile de onza,* hot and sweet, as well as tiny, whole dried *chiles pequíns.* Serve them alongside your best mezcal cocktail.

- 1 dried chile de onza or chile de árbol
- 1 tsp. kosher salt
  Juice of 1 lemon
- ½ lb. skinned raw peanuts
- 8 small cloves garlic, peeled
- 1 tbsp. dried whole chiles pequíns, or 1 dried chile de árbol, chopped

1 Toast chile de onza in a nonstick skillet over low heat. Discard stem, then grind chile with salt in a mortar and pestle. Add lemon juice, mix well, and set aside.

2 Toast peanuts and garlic in a skillet over low heat for about 5 minutes (shake pan to prevent burning). Add chiles pequíns and toast for 1 minute more. Transfer to a dish and drizzle chile-lemon mixture over peanuts.

SPICED PECANS

MAKES 2 CUPS

Fragrant, skillet-roasted pecans are a staple in the South during the holidays. These get their earthy, spicy savor from rosemary, smoked paprika, and chili powder.

- 4 tbsp. unsalted butter
- 2 cups pecan halves
- 2 tbsp. light brown sugar
- 2 tbsp. roughly chopped fresh rosemary leaves
- 2 tsp. Worcestershire sauce
- 2 tsp. smoked paprika
- 1 tsp. chile powder
- 1 tsp. kosher salt
- ½ tsp. Tabasco sauce
- ¼ tsp. freshly ground black pepper
- ¼ tsp. ground cinnamon

1 Melt butter in a 12″ skillet over medium heat. Add pecans and cook, swirling skillet constantly, until nuts are toasted, about 5 minutes.

2 Add brown sugar, rosemary, Worcestershire, paprika, chile powder, salt, Tabasco, black pepper, and cinnamon and stir until pecans are evenly coated. Continue cooking pecans, stirring constantly, until fragrant, 1–2 minutes.

3 Transfer pecans to a parchment paper–lined baking sheet, spread into a single layer, and let cool, stirring pecans and breaking up sugar and spices occasionally.

KHANDVI

Spiced Chickpea-Flour Snacks

SERVES 4–6

In this popular street snack from the Indian state of Gujarat, yogurt, ginger, chiles, and chickpea flour are whisked together to make a thick batter that's rolled up into paper-thin coils and garnished with a riot of spices, seeds, and chiles.

FOR THE KHANDVI

- 4 serrano chiles, stemmed
- 1 1″ piece ginger, peeled and minced
- 1 cup plain yogurt
- 1 cup chickpea flour
- 2 tsp. kosher salt
- ½ tsp. ground turmeric

FOR THE GARNISH

- ¼ cup peanut oil
- 2 tsp. black mustard seeds
- 2 tsp. sesame seeds
- ¾ tsp. asafoetida
- 10 fresh or frozen curry leaves
- 6 serrano chiles, stemmed and julienned
- 5 chiles de árbol
- 2 tbsp. roughly chopped fresh cilantro
- 2 tbsp. freshly grated coconut

1 Make the khandvi: Purée serranos, ginger, and ¼ cup water in a food processor until smooth; set paste aside. In a bowl, whisk together yogurt, flour, salt, turmeric, and 1 cup water. Whisk reserved paste into batter; transfer batter to a 4-qt. saucepan over medium-high heat. Whisking constantly, bring to a boil, then reduce heat to medium-low and cook until very thick, about 15 minutes. Spread the batter onto inverted baking sheets. Let cool, then slice into strips and roll into coils. (See Forming Khandvi, below, for illustrated step-by-step instructions.)

2 Make the garnish: Heat oil in a 10″ skillet over high heat. Add mustard seeds, sesame seeds, asafoetida, curry leaves, serranos, and chiles de árbol and cook, stirring, until fragrant, about 2 minutes. To serve, pour garnish over roll-ups; sprinkle with cilantro and coconut.

COOK'S NOTE When you spread it out for rolling, the batter for this snack has to be of the right consistency—not too wet, not too dry—so test a spoonful of it on a plate first.

SOUR CREAM NACHOS
Nachos Agrios
SERVES 4

We found these indulgent nachos at the San Antonio, Texas, eatery Los Barrios, where, with no false modesty, the menu called them "the most outstanding appetizer there is."

- 2½ cups refried beans
- 5–6 oz. tortilla chips
- 1 cup grated Swiss cheese
- 1 cup grated provolone
- 1 jalapeño, stemmed, seeded, and diced
- ½ cup sour cream
- 1 tbsp. chopped, drained jarred pimientos

1 Heat oven to 300°. Heat refried beans in a pan over medium heat until hot.

2 Spread chips out evenly on a large oval ovenproof dish. Spread beans on top of chips, sprinkle cheeses evenly over beans, and scatter jalapeños over cheese. Bake until cheese is completely melted, about 5 minutes. Garnish with dollops of sour cream, then scatter pimientos over nachos. Serve immediately.

FORMING KHANDVI

1 Arrange 2 baking sheets upside down. Spoon half the batter onto the side of one of the sheets. Using a spatula, spread batter toward far edge of sheet, creating an even layer.

2 Let batter cool for 5 minutes. Using a paring knife, trim uneven edges of dried batter. Cut each sheet of batter into eight 5″×2″ strips.

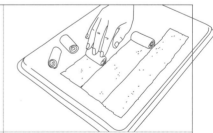

3 Roll up each strip of dried batter into a neat cylinder shape that's about the size of a quarter in diameter. Transfer roll-ups to a platter.

GABHOR UTOMO

APPLE & STILTON WELSH RAREBIT BITES

MAKES 24 BITES

To our minds, the classic "rabbit," that creamy amalgam of cheddar and beer bearing a misleading name (the origins of which remain murky), is the pinnacle of cheese cookery. Pungent Stilton replaces the more traditional cheddar in this bite-size twist on the classic British dish.

½   thin baguette, cut into ½″-thick slices

3   tbsp. unsalted butter, melted

1   small tart apple, such as Granny Smith, peeled, halved, cored, and thinly sliced

½   lb. crumbled Stilton or blue cheese, at room temperature

3   tbsp. crème fraîche

1   tsp. Worcestershire sauce

1   tsp. Dijon mustard

1   tsp. honey

     Kosher salt and freshly ground black pepper, to taste

1 Heat a grill pan over medium-high heat. Brush baguette slices with melted butter; working in batches, grill, flipping once, until golden on both sides, about 2 minutes. Transfer to a parchment paper–lined baking sheet. Layer 2 apple slices on each toast; set aside.

2 Arrange an oven rack 4″ from broiler and heat broiler. Mix cheese, crème fraîche, Worcestershire, mustard, honey, salt, and pepper in a small bowl. Spread about 1 tbsp. of the cheese mixture over each toast. Broil until topping is melted and golden brown, about 4 minutes.

OVEN-DRIED PINEAPPLE SNACKS

MAKES ABOUT 3 CUPS

Dressed in a flavor-bomb combination of sugar, salt, nutmeg, and hot chiles, chewy dried pineapple pieces make for an addictive cocktail snack. (We particularly love them alongside a gin and tonic.)

2   ripe pineapples, peeled, cored, and cut into ¾″–1″ chunks

¼   cup demerara sugar

2   tsp. flaky sea salt

1   tsp. freshly grated nutmeg

2   red bird's eye chiles, stemmed, seeded, and finely chopped

     Grated zest of 2 limes

1 Heat oven to 225°. Divide pineapple chunks between 2 large baking sheets and spread out in a single layer. Bake, rotating pans front to back and flipping pineapple chunks halfway through, until chunks are light golden brown and dried around the edges but still juicy in the center, about 4½ hours. Transfer pans to a cooling rack; let pineapple cool to room temperature.

2 Put sugar, salt, nutmeg, chiles, and zest into a medium bowl and stir to combine. Add pineapple and toss to coat. Transfer to a serving bowl and serve immediately.

COOK'S NOTE You may also leave the pineapple overnight in a gas oven, turned off; the heat from the pilot light will dry the fruit.

Small Dishes

PEPPERS STUFFED WITH FETA

Piperies Gemistes me Feta

SERVES 4-6 (SEE PHOTO, PAGE 426)

You might find peppers stuffed with cheese in a taverna in Athens or in other parts of Greece, but this classic mezze is associated above all with the region of Macedonia, in the north. Peppers—mild and hot, fresh and dried—are one of the agricultural glories of the region, and the queen of them all is the sweet, firm-fleshed, long red pepper grown around the town of Florina, in the mountains of Macedonia's far northwest. Florina peppers can be hard to find in the States; Fresno or (if you like a bit of spice) Anaheim chiles are acceptable substitutes.

- 10 3"–4" Fresno chiles or six 4"–5" Anaheim chiles
- 9 oz. feta, crumbled
- 2 tbsp. extra-virgin olive oil
- 2 tbsp. Greek yogurt
- 1 tbsp. minced fresh flat-leaf parsley
- ½ tsp. grated lemon zest
- ¼ tsp. dried oregano
- 2 egg yolks
  Kosher salt and freshly ground black pepper, to taste
- ¼ cup grated Parmigiano-Reggiano cheese

1 Arrange an oven rack 6" from broiler and heat broiler. Put peppers on a baking sheet and broil, turning once, until just soft, about 5 minutes. Transfer to a rack; let cool.

2 In a large bowl, use a hand mixer to whip feta, oil, yogurt, parsley, lemon zest, oregano, and egg yolks; season with salt and pepper. Make a lengthwise cut from the stem to the tip of each pepper; scoop out seeds and ribs. Stuff each pepper with some of the feta filling and transfer to a foil-lined baking sheet; chill for 30 minutes.

3 Sprinkle peppers with grated cheese. Broil peppers until cheese is golden brown and bubbly, about 6 minutes. Transfer peppers to a platter and serve hot.

CHAWANMUSHI

Japanese Egg Custard

SERVES 4

This tender egg custard reveals treasures upon digging in: succulent morsels of chicken and shrimp. The name translates to "steamed in a teacup," but ramekins will do.

- 2 iriko (Japanese-style dried anchovies), heads removed
- ½ 2"×15" piece kombu (dried kelp)
- 2 tbsp. dried bonito flakes
- 1 boneless, skinless chicken breast, cut crosswise into slices ½" thick and 1½" long
- 4 medium shrimp, peeled, deveined, and halved lengthwise
- 1½ tsp. soy sauce
- 1½ tsp. mirin
- 3 eggs
- 2 shiitake mushrooms, stemmed and cut into 2 triangles each
- 4 fresh flat-leaf parsley leaves
  Grated zest of ½ lemon

1 Bring anchovies, kombu, and 1½ cups water to a boil in a 4-qt. saucepan; remove and discard anchovies and kombu with a slotted spoon. Add bonito. Remove from heat, and let steep for 5 minutes. Pour through a sieve and set dashi aside.

2 Heat oven to 325°. Bring a large pot of salted water to a boil over high heat. Add chicken and cook until opaque, about 3 minutes. Using a slotted spoon, transfer to a bowl; set aside. Add shrimp and cook until opaque, about 30 seconds. Drain and add to bowl with chicken. Divide mixture among four 6-oz. ramekins and place in a 9"×13" baking dish.

3 Whisk dashi, soy sauce, mirin, and eggs in a bowl and pour through a fine-mesh sieve into a liquid measuring cup. Pour over shrimp and chicken in ramekins and top with mushroom triangle. Pour boiling water into baking dish to come halfway up sides of ramekins. Bake until custard is just set, about 30 minutes.

THE CULTURE OF TAPAS

Arguing about the evolution of tapas is a favorite Spanish pastime. But this much is beyond dispute: Spain's iconic little plates have a long history. One story is that the 13th-century Castilian king Alfonso X was instructed by his doctor to eat several mini-meals a day with wine; hence, tapas. Cervantes, in his 17th-century classic *Don Quijote*, refers to *llamativos*, or "lures"—tidbits designed to arouse hunger or thirst. However, the most commonly accepted theory is that tapas as we know them originated in Andalusia in the 19th century as small saucers set over wineglasses in taverns to keep the aroma in. Today, there are more than a thousand varieties of tapas, and every region, city, and bar in Spain has its own specialties, from baked scallops in Galicia to stuffed peppers in San Sebastián to Casa Bigote's cod. But on almost every tapas menu you'll find a variation of four essential recipes: Pan con Tomate (this page), Albóndigas en Salsa (this page), Patatas Bravas (page 37), and Tortilla Española con Fritas (page 37), the pillars—and, as Spanish tapas have become a global phenomenon, the ambassadors—of the genre.

4 Divide parsley among custard tops and continue cooking until parsley is slightly wilted, about 2 minutes. Remove from oven and transfer ramekins to serving plates; sprinkle with lemon zest before serving.

COOK'S NOTE Keep the water bath simmering, never boiling, to ensure a smooth, crater-free surface on the custards.

PAN CON TOMATE

Spanish-Style Toast with Tomato

SERVES 2

This utterly essential Spanish dish, emblematic of Barcelona's tapas tradition but found throughout the country, is simplicity at its best. The pulp from a ripe tomato is spooned over garlic-rubbed bread and seasoned with sea salt.

- 1 **6″ piece baguette, halved lengthwise**
- 1 **clove garlic**
- 2 **tbsp. extra-virgin olive oil**
- 1 **very ripe large tomato**
   Coarse sea salt, to taste

1 Heat oven to 500°. Put bread, cut side up, on a baking sheet and toast until golden brown, about 8 minutes. Rub garlic over cut surface and drizzle with oil.

2 Put a box grater into a large bowl and grate tomato over largest holes, discarding skin. Spoon grated tomato onto warm toast and sprinkle with sea salt. Serve immediately.

ALBÓNDIGAS EN SALSA

Spanish-Style Meatballs

SERVES 4

These saucy meatballs figure in a wide range of dishes that make up the constellation of little snacks served in tapas bars all over Spain. Pick them up and pop them into your mouth with toothpicks—at some tapas bars, the discarded picks are tallied up so that the bar owner can compile the bill at the end of meal.

FOR THE MEATBALLS
- 1½ **lb. coarsely ground beef**
- 1½ **lb. coarsely ground pork**
- ½ **cup fresh white bread crumbs**
- ¼ **cup finely chopped fresh flat-leaf parsley**
- 4 **eggs, lightly beaten**
- 4 **cloves garlic, finely chopped**
   Kosher salt and freshly ground black pepper, to taste
- 1 **cup flour**
- 1 **cup Spanish olive oil**

FOR THE SAUCE
- 4 **cloves garlic, finely chopped**
- 1 **large yellow onion, chopped**
- 1 **large leek, white part only, chopped**
- 1 **bay leaf**
- 2 **tbsp. flour**
- 2½ **cups beef stock**
- 1½ **cups dry white wine**

1 Make the meatballs: Mix together the beef, pork, bread crumbs, parsley, eggs, garlic, and salt and pepper in a large bowl. Chill for 1 hour.

2 Put flour into a bowl. Using wet hands, form meat mixture into 20 even-size meatballs. Roll each in flour, shaking off excess; transfer to a baking sheet.

3 Heat half the oil in a large skillet over medium-high heat. Brown half the meatballs in the skillet, 10–12 minutes. Transfer meatballs to a plate. Wipe out skillet and repeat with remaining oil and meatballs, leaving oil and caramelized bits in skillet.

4 Make the sauce: Heat skillet (with reserved oil) over medium-low heat. Add garlic, onion, leeks, and bay leaf and cook until softened, 12–15 minutes. Add flour and cook for 2 minutes. Whisk in stock and wine, raise heat to medium-high, and bring to a boil while whisking constantly. Reduce heat to medium-low and simmer until thickened, 12–14 minutes. Let cool.

5 Discard bay leaf and purée sauce in blender in batches. Return sauce to skillet along with meatballs; bring to a boil over medium-high heat. Reduce heat to medium-low and simmer until thickened and meatballs are cooked, 16–18 minutes. Season with salt and pepper.

PATATAS BRAVAS

Fried Potatoes with Spicy Sauce

SERVES 2

Invented at the Madrid restaurant Vinícola Aurora in the 1950s, these "fierce potatoes"—crisp on the outside and melting on the inside, served with a fiery tomato sauce and a rich, garlicky *allioli*—are now a staple on tapas menus throughout Spain and beyond. The key to this particular version is poaching and then frying the potatoes in olive oil.

FOR THE SALSA BRAVA
- ½ cup crushed canned tomatoes
- 1 tbsp. extra-virgin olive oil
- 1½ tsp. red wine
- 1 tsp. hot smoked paprika
- ¼ tsp. sugar
- 1 serrano chile, stemmed and minced
  Kosher salt, to taste

FOR THE ALLIOLI
- 1 egg yolk
- 1 clove garlic, minced
- 8 tbsp. olive oil
- 1 tsp. fresh lemon juice
- 1 tsp. milk

FOR THE POTATOES
- Olive oil, for frying
- 4 russet potatoes, peeled and quartered

1 Make the salsa brava: Purée tomatoes, oil, wine, paprika, sugar, and chile in a blender. Season with salt, transfer to a bowl, and set aside.

2 Make the allioli: Vigorously whisk egg yolk and garlic. While whisking, add 1 tbsp. oil in a thin stream until mixture thickens. Continue whisking, adding remaining 7 tbsp. oil in a thin stream. Add lemon juice and milk and season with salt; chill.

3 Make the potatoes: Pour oil to a depth of 1½″ into a 5-qt. pot and heat over medium heat until a deep-fry thermometer reads 220°. Transfer potatoes to oil and cook, turning occasionally, until tender and pale golden, 15–20 minutes. Using a slotted spoon, transfer potatoes to paper towels; chill. Remove pot from heat; reserve.

4 Heat reserved oil over medium-high heat until a deep-fry thermometer reads 350°. Add potatoes and cook until golden brown, 3–5 minutes. Transfer to paper towels and season with salt. Serve potatoes with the reserved brava salsa and allioli.

TORTILLA ESPAÑOLA CON FRITAS

Spanish Potato-Chip Omelette

SERVES 6–8

Tortilla española is everything we love about Spanish cooking—lusty, elemental, assuredly straightforward. Traditionally this Iberian omelette gets its heft from thin-sliced potatoes, but the version from inventive chef Ferran Adrià proposes an audacious update. Eschewing the dirty work of peeling, slicing, and frying the potato, Adrià substitutes a generous handful of store-bought thick-cut potato chips, which soften to just the right tenderness thanks to a soak in the beaten egg before the omelette is cooked.

- 4 oz. thick-cut potato chips, gently crushed
- 2 oz. serrano ham or prosciutto, finely chopped
- ¼ cup finely chopped canned piquillo peppers or pimientos
- 1 tbsp. fresh thyme leaves
- 8 eggs, lightly beaten
  Kosher salt and freshly ground black pepper, to taste
- 2 tbsp. olive oil

Heat broiler. Combine potato chips, ham, peppers, thyme, eggs, and salt and black pepper in a bowl and let sit to allow chips to soften in eggs, about 5 minutes. Heat oil in a 10″ nonstick skillet over medium-high heat; add egg mixture and cook, without stirring, until bottom begins to brown, about 3 minutes. Transfer to broiler and broil until set and golden on top, about 3 minutes. Cut into wedges to serve.

RAZOR CLAMS WITH CHILES & GARLIC

Navajas al Ajillo

SERVES 2–4 (SEE PHOTO, PAGE 224)

With their long, narrow shells, razor clams are undeniably dramatic on the plate. Their sweet meat takes well to quick-cooked preparations like this fiery sauté of wine, garlic, and chiles. It's a popular order at Bar Pinotxo, a revered tapas counter in La Boqueria, Barcelona's covered market.

- 5 tbsp. extra-virgin olive oil
- 4 cloves garlic, minced
- 3–4 dried chiles de árbol, crumbled, or 2 tsp. red chile flakes
- 1½ lb. razor clams, rinsed thoroughly
- ¼ cup white wine
- 1½ cups loosely packed fresh flat-leaf parsley leaves, minced
  Kosher salt, to taste

Heat oil, garlic, and chiles in a 12″ skillet over medium heat. Cook, swirling pan occasionally, until garlic is pale golden brown, about 6 minutes. Increase heat to high, add razor clams and wine, and cook, covered, until clams are just cooked through, about 3 minutes. Add parsley and season with salt; toss razor clams to coat with sauce. Transfer clams to a serving platter and drizzle with remaining sauce. Discard any clams that do not open.

RICOTTA & ROASTED PEPPER FRITTATA

Frittata con Ricotta & Peperoni

SERVES 4–6

Calabrians in Italy sometimes add sliced cured sausage to this popular frittata on Easter, to celebrate the end of Lent. It makes a welcome addition to a meal of small plates or as a main course for brunch.

- ½ cup grated pecorino romano
- 2 tbsp. roughly chopped fresh flat-leaf parsley leaves
- 1½ tsp. kosher salt
- 1 tsp. chopped fresh oregano
- 8 eggs, beaten
  Freshly ground black pepper, to taste
- 3 tbsp. extra-virgin olive oil
- 1 large onion, halved and thinly sliced
- 1 small Yukon gold potato, peeled and sliced into ⅛″ rounds
- 1 red bell pepper, roasted, peeled, seeded, and cut into ¼″-wide strips
- ¾ cup ricotta

1 Heat oven to 425°. In a large bowl, whisk together ¼ cup pecorino, parsley, ½ tsp. salt, oregano, and eggs and season with pepper. Set egg mixture aside.

2 Heat oil in a 10″ nonstick ovenproof skillet over medium-high heat. Add remaining 1 tsp. salt, onions, and potatoes and cook, stirring occasionally, until lightly browned and soft, about 20 minutes.

3 Remove skillet from heat. Add egg mixture to skillet and stir to distribute onion and potatoes evenly. Scatter peppers over top, spoon ricotta over mixture in 6 dollops, and sprinkle with remaining ¼ cup pecorino. Bake until lightly browned and set in center, about 15 minutes. Run a rubber spatula around edges of frittata to loosen it. Slide frittata onto a serving plate. Season with more pepper, if you like.

NIÇOISE SALAD QUICHE

SERVES 6–8

A nod to the composed salad of southern France (page 55), this elegant quiche combines green beans, olives, potatoes, tuna, and just-wilted butter lettuce.

- 1 medium Yukon gold potato, peeled and sliced ¼″ thick
  Kosher salt
- 7 green beans, trimmed and cut into 1″ pieces
- 1 head butter lettuce, trimmed and torn into 1″ pieces
- 1 3-oz. can water-packed tuna; drained
- ½ cup heavy cream
- ½ cup milk
- 3 tbsp. olive oil
- 1 tbsp. Dijon mustard
- 3 eggs
- 1 oil-packed anchovy filet
- 1 clove garlic, peeled
- 1 small shallot, peeled
  Freshly ground black pepper, to taste
- 1 recipe Perfect Quiche Crust (page 476)
- 1 plum tomato, thinly sliced

½ cup pitted niçoise olives
Finely chopped fresh flat-leaf parsley, for garnish

1 Boil potatoes in a 2-qt. pot of salted water until tender, 6–8 minutes. Add green beans and cook for 1 minute more. Using a slotted spoon, transfer vegetables to a bowl of ice water until cold; drain and place in a bowl. Add lettuce and tuna; set salad aside.

2 Purée cream, milk, oil, mustard, eggs, anchovy, garlic, and shallot. Season with salt and pepper, pour over salad, and gently stir to combine. Refrigerate filling until ready to use.

3 Preheat oven to 325°. Spread filling evenly into crust, arrange tomatoes and olives over top, and bake until filling is set, about 20 minutes. Let quiche cool briefly, garnish with parsley, and serve.

BEEF & BULGUR WHEAT MEATBALLS
Kibbeh
MAKES 16

Middle Eastern *kibbeh* is a finely ground paste of bulgur, onions, and lamb or beef, which is formed into patties or balls, filled with coarsely ground, sweetly spiced meat, onions, and pine nuts, and deep-fried.

FOR THE FILLING

1	tbsp. extra-virgin olive oil, plus more for garnish
1	medium onion, roughly chopped
½	lb. ground beef sirloin
1	tsp. kosher salt
¼	tsp. ground allspice
¼	tsp. ground cinnamon
¼	cup pine nuts, toasted
1	tbsp. ground sumac, plus more for garnish

FOR THE SHELL

1½	cups fine bulgur
1	tbsp. kosher salt
½	tsp. ground allspice
½	tsp. ground cinnamon
¼	tsp. ground black pepper
1	small onion, finely chopped
1½	lb. lamb shoulder, trimmed

Canola oil, for frying
Plain yogurt, for serving
Fresh mint leaves, for garnish

1 Make the filling: Heat oil in a 12″ skillet over medium heat. Add onion and cook, stirring, until soft, about

10 minutes. Add beef and cook, breaking it up with a wooden spoon, until no longer pink, about 7 minutes. Add salt, allspice, and cinnamon and cook, stirring, until meat begins to brown, about 4 minutes more. Transfer to a bowl, stir in nuts and sumac, and let cool.

2 Make the shell: Rinse bulgur, squeeze out excess water, and place in a large bowl. Add salt, allspice, cinnamon, pepper, and onion, and set aside. Grind lamb twice in a meat grinder and add to bulgur mixture; knead mixture in bowl into a pliable paste, about 5 minutes. Cover bowl with a clean towel.

3 Shape about ¼ cup of the bulgur-meat paste into a ball, moistening your hands with water as you work. Hold ball in one hand and insert index finger of other hand into center to form a hole. Shape ball into a thin-walled (about ¼″ thick) oval with an opening at one end by molding ball around finger, gradually tapering closed end. Mend any cracks in shell with a moistened finger. Fill hole with 1½ tbsp. of the filling. Moisten edges of opening, then gather edges together to seal. Gently form kibbeh into the shape of an egg, and keep moist under a clean dish towel. Repeat shaping with remaining filling and bulgur-meat paste to make 16 egg-shaped balls in all.

4 Pour oil to a depth of 2″ into a 6-qt. Dutch oven and heat over medium heat until a deep-fry thermometer reads 375°. Working in batches, fry kibbeh until browned all over, about 4 minutes. Drain on paper towels. Transfer to a serving platter and spoon some yogurt alongside the kibbeh. Drizzle oil over yogurt, and sprinkle with more sumac. Serve with mint leaves on the side.

STEAK TARTARE
Tartare de Filet de Bœuf
SERVES 4

This steak tartare recipe, inspired by the tableside preparation at Brasserie Georges in Lyon, France, gets a zip of acidity from cornichons, capers, and Dijon mustard.

14	oz. center-cut beef tenderloin, trimmed
1½	tbsp. Dijon mustard
2	egg yolks
¼	cup canola oil
6	tbsp. salt-packed capers, rinsed, drained, and minced
2	tbsp. minced green niçoise olives
2	tbsp. minced fresh flat-leaf parsley

1½ tsp. Worcestershire sauce
¼   tsp. Tabasco sauce
4   cornichons, minced
1   small onion, minced
    Kosher salt and freshly ground black pepper,
    to taste
    Bistro French Fries (page 407), for serving
    (optional)
    Mixed salad greens, for serving (optional)

1 Put beef in the freezer to firm, about 30 minutes; this will make it easier to chop finely. Meanwhile, whisk mustard and egg yolks in a large bowl; while whisking constantly, slowly pour in oil to create a mayonnaise. Add capers, olives, parsley, Worcestershire, hot sauce, cornichons, and onion and season with salt and pepper; refrigerate flavorings until ready to use.

2 Remove beef from freezer and cut into ¼″ cubes. Transfer beef to bowl of flavorings and stir to combine. Keep beef mixture chilled until ready to serve.

3 To serve, divide beef mixture into 4 equal portions, and shape each into an oval disk on a serving plate. Serve immediately with fries and mixed greens, if you like.

BEEF CARPACCIO

SERVES 6

Today, almost anything thinly sliced gets called "carpaccio," but the name of this 1950 Harry's Bar creation originally referred to its color: It was named for the great Venetian painter Vittorio Carpaccio, noted for his vivid use of reds and whites. The dish was inspired by the Contessa Amalia Nani Mocenigo, a steady customer whose doctor had forbidden her to eat cooked meat.

1   egg yolk
1   tsp. white wine vinegar or red wine vinegar
2   pinches of dry mustard
     Kosher salt and freshly ground white pepper,
     to taste
¾   cup olive oil
     Juice of ½ lemon
1–2 dashes Worcestershire sauce, or to taste
1½   tsp. milk
1½   lb. top sirloin or other best-quality beef,
     trimmed of all fat, sinew, and gristle

1 Make a mayonnaise by combining egg yolk, vinegar, mustard, and a little salt and pepper in a medium mixing bowl and whisking until foamy and thoroughly blended. Add ¼ cup oil drop by drop, whisking constantly. Gradually add the rest of the oil in a thin, steady stream, continuing to whisk as the mayonnaise thickens. Add 1 tbsp. lemon juice, or to taste, and adjust seasonings, whisking in a little water to thin the mayonnaise, if you like.

2 Put ½ cup mayonnaise (reserve the rest for another use) in a small bowl; whisk in Worcestershire and ¼ tsp. lemon juice, then enough milk to make a thin sauce that just coats the back of a wooden spoon. Season with salt and pepper.

3 To assemble, make sure the beef is very cold, then slice into the thinnest possible slices, using a razor-sharp, long-bladed slicing knife (see Slicing Carpaccio, below). Divide slices among 6 small chilled plates, arranging them in one thin layer, covering the surface completely. Drizzle some of the sauce over the meat on each plate and serve immediately.

COUNTRY-STYLE PÂTÉ

SERVES 10–20

There are as many variations on this rustic French terrine as there are picturesque French farmhouses; this recipe brings together our favorite elements of the many dozens we've tried.

2   lb. whole chicken legs
⅓   cup white wine
2   tbsp. extra-virgin olive oil
3   tsp. fresh thyme leaves

SLICING CARPACCIO

The secret to slicing carpaccio is a very cold—nearly frozen—piece of meat trimmed of all fat and gristle, and a long, sharp slicing knife. Cut at an angle across the grain, shaving off thin pieces until you've got a wide, even surface. The goal: sheets about ⅛″ thick.

2	tsp. chopped fresh rosemary
8–10	bay leaves
4	sprigs fresh flat-leaf parsley
1	small yellow onion, peeled and chopped
¼	lb. rind from pork fat
	Kosher salt and freshly ground black pepper
2	slices stale bread, crusts removed
1	clove garlic, minced
¾	lb. veal, finely chopped
¾	lb. pork, finely chopped
¾	lb. ground pork
½	lb. chicken livers, trimmed and halved
7	oz. prosciutto, diced
6	oz. cold fresh fatback, diced
⅓	cup cognac
	Pinch *each* of ground allspice and mace
½	tsp. saltpeter (potassium nitrate)
3	large sheets caul fat, or thinly sliced fatback

1 Cut chicken legs into drumsticks and thighs, then remove thigh meat from the bone, remove skin, and cut meat into thick strips. Reserve skin, bones, and drumsticks for stock. Mix together wine, oil, 1 tsp. thyme, 1 tsp. rosemary, and 2 bay leaves in a small bowl, then add thigh meat, cover, and refrigerate for 4 hours or up to overnight.

2 Pour 6 cups water in a heavy pot; add reserved chicken drumsticks, bones, and skin, 1 bay leaf, 3 sprigs parsley, onions, pork rind, and salt and pepper; bring to a boil over medium heat. Reduce heat to low and gently simmer for about 2½ hours. Strain stock, discard solids, return stock to pot, and increase heat to high. Boil until stock has reduced to about ½ cup. Remove from heat and let cool.

3 Heat oven to 325°. Pulse bread, garlic, and remaining 1 sprig parsley in a food processor to make fine crumbs. Put stock, bread crumbs, veal, chopped and ground pork, livers, prosciutto, fatback, cognac, allspice, mace, saltpeter, and remaining 2 tsp. thyme and 1 tsp. rosemary in a large bowl and season liberally with salt and pepper. Mix thoroughly.

4 Line a 6-cup terrine with caul fat, draping it over sides, then pack one-third of meat mixture evenly into terrine. Lay half the marinated chicken pieces on top of meat. Repeat layers, ending with meat. Fold caul fat over meat to wrap completely, arrange remaining 5–7 bay leaves on top, and cover with a double layer of aluminum foil. Set terrine in a baking pan, add enough boiling water to come two-thirds of the way up sides of terrine, and bake

until a thermometer inserted in center reads 160°, about 2¾ hours. Remove from oven, pour off water, then return terrine to baking pan. Remove foil, cover terrine with plastic wrap, then place a piece of heavy cardboard, cut to fit, inside the terrine. Weight with a couple of heavy cans. Refrigerate, still weighted, for 1–3 days, then serve in ½"-thick slices.

SEARED FOIE GRAS WITH CARAMELIZED PINEAPPLE
SERVES 4

Buttery foie gras is seared and placed atop caramelized pineapple and drizzled with a syrupy port sauce. This appetizer is a famous and now classic dish that's served at Wolfgang Puck's Chinois on Main in Santa Monica.

PÂTÉ 101

THE MOLD Hinged rectangular metal molds are often used for pâtés; the sides unhook, so the pastry isn't damaged when unmolding. Terrines are baked in rectangular, oval, or round molds with straight, high sides. Traditionally made of earthenware, they also come in porcelain and enameled cast iron. Game pâtés are sometimes baked in oval molds whose sculpted lids depict a duck, rabbit, or the like, to indicate the contents.

THE FAT To keep terrines from drying out during baking, molds are lined with caul fat (the white lacy membrane that lines the pig's stomach) or thin sheets of fatback (the pure-white fat found under the skin on the pig's back; ask your butcher to thinly slice the fatback for you). Diced fatback is often added to meat pâtés and terrines to provide moisture and to make them more tender.

THE SALTPETER Also known as potassium nitrate, this natural substance is used (in tiny amounts) to inhibit spoilage and preserve the rosy color of meats.

TO STORE Wrapped tightly in plastic and refrigerated, a meat terrine will keep for about 7 days; those made of fish or liver, about 2 days.

FOR THE SAUCE

- 1⅓ cups port
- 1⅓ cups red wine
- ⅔ cup plum wine
- 2 shallots, minced
- 2 cups veal stock
- 1 cinnamon stick
- 2 tbsp. cold unsalted butter, cubed

FOR THE GARNISH

- ½ cup port
- ½ cup plum wine
- ½ tsp. light brown sugar
- 1 4″ piece fresh ginger, peeled and julienned

FOR THE FOIE GRAS & PINEAPPLE

- 1½ tsp. sugar
- 4 ¼″-thick rings fresh ripe pineapple
- 2 tbsp. peanut oil
- 4 2-oz. slices cold foie gras
  Kosher salt and freshly ground black pepper
- ½ cup flour

1 Make the sauce: Combine port, red wine, plum wine, and shallots into a medium saucepan and bring to a boil over medium-high heat. Reduce heat to medium and cook, stirring occasionally, until reduced by half, about 30 minutes. Add stock and cinnamon and cook until liquid has reduced to about 1 cup, about 30–35 minutes. Strain through a fine-mesh sieve and return sauce to pan. Set aside.

2 Make the garnish: Put port, plum wine, sugar, and ginger in a small pot and bring to a boil over medium heat. Reduce heat to medium-low and cook until syrupy, about 35 minutes. Remove from heat and set aside.

3 Make the foie gras and pineapple: Sprinkle sugar evenly over tops of pineapple slices and caramelize with a kitchen torch. Set aside in a single layer. Heat oil in a large skillet over medium-high heat. Season each piece of foie gras, then dredge lightly in flour, shaking off any excess. Sear foie gras on both sides until crisp and golden brown, 1–1½ minutes per side. Transfer to a paper towel–lined plate.

4 To assemble, bring sauce to a simmer over medium heat. Reduce heat to low and whisk in butter, a little at a time, until smooth and glossy. Place 1 piece of pineapple on each of 4 warm plates and top each with a slice of foie gras. Spoon sauce over foie gras, then top with a dollop of the ginger garnish and some of its syrup. Serve immediately.

HOR MOK

Steamed Thai Fish Custard

SERVES 8

Typically steamed in intricately folded banana leaves, in our simplified version these Thai-style fish custards are baked in banana leaf–lined ramekins set in a water bath.

- 1½ lb. boneless, skinless halibut, grouper, or snapper filets, finely chopped
- 2 cups canned coconut milk
- ⅓ cup Thai red curry paste
- 1 tbsp. nam pla (Thai fish sauce)
- 2½ tsp. finely chopped palm sugar or packed dark brown sugar
- 2 eggs
- 13 makrut lime leaves, very thinly shredded
  Kosher salt, to taste
- 4 large fresh or frozen banana leaves, wiped with a damp towel
- ¼ cup packed finely torn fresh Thai basil leaves
- 1½ tsp. cornstarch
- 1 red bird's eye chile, stemmed, very thinly sliced crosswise

1 Heat oven to 350°. Process fish, 1 cup coconut milk, curry paste, fish sauce, 2 tsp. sugar, and eggs in a food processor until very smooth, 1–2 minutes. Stir in 12 shredded lime leaves, season with salt, and set fish custard aside.

2 Lay the banana leaves out on a surface and use scissors to cut out 8 circles, each 6″ in diameter. Place a banana leaf circle, shiny side down, over each of eight 8-oz. ramekins. Press circles into bottom and up the sides of ramekins so that they are nestled snugly inside. Divide half the fish custard among ramekins, top each with basil leaves, and cover with remaining custard. Place ramekins in a 9″×13″ baking pan; pour boiling water into pan so that it comes halfway up sides of ramekins. Bake until custards set and begin to pull away from banana leaves or sides of ramekins, about 16 minutes. Meanwhile, heat remaining 1 cup coconut milk and ½ tsp. sugar with cornstarch in a 1-qt. saucepan over medium-high heat; cook, stirring, until thickened, about 2 minutes.

3 Remove pan from oven and remove ramekins from water. Top each with some of the thickened coconut milk, and sprinkle with remaining shredded lime leaf and chiles.

GRAVLAX

Cured Salmon

SERVES 8–10

Silky, luxurious Scandinavian-cured salmon requires little more than salt, sugar, and time. Dill is the traditional flavoring, but the seasonings can be adjusted to suit your taste—we like adding fennel and caraway seeds, to bring out the flavor of the aquavit.

- 2 tbsp. white peppercorns
- 1 tbsp. fennel seeds
- 1 tbsp. caraway seeds
- ⅔ cup kosher salt
- ⅓ cup sugar
- 1 2-lb. center-cut, skin-on salmon filet
- 1 cup fresh dill sprigs, plus ⅓ cup chopped dill
- ¼ cup aquavit
  Mustard-Dill Sauce (page 593), for serving

1 In a small food processor, pulse peppercorns, fennel seeds, and caraway seeds until coarsely ground; combine with salt and sugar. Stretch plastic wrap over a plate; sprinkle with half the salt mixture. Place salmon filet on top, flesh side up. Cover with remaining salt mixture, dill sprigs, and aquavit.

2 Fold plastic wrap ends around salmon; wrap tightly with more plastic wrap. Refrigerate the fish on the plate for 48–72 hours, turning the package every 12 hours and using your fingers to redistribute the herb-and-spice-infused brine that accumulates as the salt pulls moisture from the salmon. The gravlax should be firm to the touch at the thickest part when fully cured.

3 Unwrap salmon, discarding the spices, dill, and brine. Rinse the filet under cold running water and pat dry with paper towels. Cover a large plate with the chopped dill. Firmly press the flesh side of the gravlax into the dill to coat it evenly.

4 Place gravlax skin side down on a board. With a long, narrow-bladed knife, slice gravlax against grain, on the diagonal, into thin pieces. Serve with mustard-dill sauce. Refrigerate any remaining gravlax, wrapped in plastic wrap, for up to 2 weeks.

COOK'S NOTE The longer the gravlax cures, the drier the flesh will become, the more intense its flavor, and the easier it will be to slice.

HAWAIIAN POKE

SERVES 4

Poke, a popular Hawaiian dish, is a mixture of cubed raw fish combined with inamona (roasted candlenuts and sea salt), seaweed, and chiles. Be sure to use only the freshest fish.

- 1 lb. fresh ahi tuna or other tuna
- 1 medium tomato, chopped
- 1 cup limu seaweed (or any rehydrated or sashimi-grade seaweed), chopped
- ½ cup finely chopped sweet onion
- 1 tsp. candlenut or sesame oil
- ½ tsp. crushed red chile flakes
- 2 tbsp. soy sauce

Chop tuna into ½" cubes. Place in a large bowl and gently toss with tomatoes, seaweed, onions, oil, and chile flakes. Add soy sauce.

COOK'S NOTE For fried poke, a less common but nevertheless traditional variation, prepare the poke as instructed. Heat 1 tbsp. vegetable oil in a wok or skillet over high heat. Fry the poke over high heat for 2–3 minutes. Serve hot.

VUELVE A LA VIDA

Veracruzan Shellfish Cocktail

SERVES 4–6

This dish from the Mexican state of Veracruz is reputed to be a hangover remedy—its name literally means "return to life." Use whatever shellfish is freshest.

- 1 cup ketchup
- ¼ cup finely chopped white onion
- 2 tbsp. extra-virgin olive oil
- 2 tbsp. orange juice
  Juice of 2 limes
- ½ cup clam juice
- 2 lb. cooked shelled seafood (for instance, 1½ lb. lobster, ¼ lb. shrimp, and ¼ lb. crab)
  Kosher salt and freshly ground white pepper, to taste
  Diced avocado, chopped fresh cilantro, and chopped white onion, for serving
  Lime wedges, for garnish

1 In a large bowl, stir together ketchup, onions, oil, orange juice, lime juice, clam juice, and 1½ cups water.

2 Roughly chop seafood and stir into sauce. Season with salt and pepper. Top with avocado, cilantro, and onions. Garnish with lime wedges.

FRITTO MISTO DI MARE

Mixed Seafood Fry

SERVES 4–6

Simply fried assorted seafood is a popular appetizer all over coastal Italy—and especially along the shores of the Adriatic.

- 2 cups flour
  Kosher salt and freshly ground black pepper
- 1 cup milk
  Vegetable oil for frying
- ½ lb. whitebait or smelts
- ¾ lb. cleaned squid or cuttlefish bodies, cut into 1″ rings
- ¼ lb. small shrimp, peeled and deveined
  Arugula, for serving
- 2 lemons, cut into wedges, for serving

1 Put flour in a medium bowl, season with salt and pepper, and mix thoroughly. Pour milk into a separate bowl. Pour oil to a depth of about 3″ into a deep skillet and heat over medium-high heat until a deep-fry thermometer reads 350°. Meanwhile, dip fish in milk, a few pieces at a time, then dredge in flour. Repeat process, dipping squid and shrimp first in milk, then in flour.

2 Shake excess flour from fish and seafood, then fry in batches, turning occasionally, until crisp and golden, about 3 minutes per batch. Drain on paper towels, sprinkle with salt, and then transfer to a large platter. Serve on a bed of arugula, with lemon wedges on the side.

SHRIMP COCKTAIL

SERVES 4

No dish showcases shrimp quite so elegantly as a shrimp cocktail. Poaching the shrimp in advance in an aromatic, wine-enriched broth brings out their sweetness, the better to pair with a piquant cocktail sauce. The classic steak-house presentation has the cocktail sauce divided among martini glasses with the shrimp perched along the rim of each glass. But for a less formal presentation, a communal platter will do.

HOT TIP

Monitoring oil temperature is crucial when you're frying foods (like *fritto misto*, this page): too hot, your food will burn; not hot enough, it'll come out greasy. A deep-fry thermometer works, but another method appeals to the minimalist in us: Asian cooks simply stick an unvarnished wooden or bamboo chopstick into the oil to test the heat. If the oil is hot enough, a steady stream of bubbles will issue from the submerged end, as moisture trapped inside the wood or bamboo boils and escapes as steam when exposed to the hot oil. The hotter the oil, the more bubbles there will be. Give the chopstick a dip at 350°, there will be a swirl of bubbles all over; by 375°, the swirl will reach Jacuzzi-esque force. It takes a few fry-ups to master the reading of bubble intensity as clearly as one would the needles of a thermometer, but once one has, there's something wonderfully Zen about dispensing with cooking by the numbers.

FOR THE COCKTAIL SAUCE

- ¾ cup ketchup
- 3 tbsp. drained prepared horseradish
- 2 tbsp. fresh lemon juice
- 2 tsp. Worcestershire sauce
- ¼ tsp. Tabasco sauce
  Pinch of kosher salt

FOR THE SHRIMP

- 2 cups dry white wine
- 1 tbsp. black peppercorns
- 6 sprigs fresh thyme
- 1 small bunch fresh flat-leaf parsley
- 1 yellow onion, sliced
- 1 rib celery, chopped
- 1 bay leaf
  Kosher salt
- 16 jumbo shrimp (about 1 lb.), unpeeled

1 Make the cocktail sauce: Put ketchup, horseradish, lemon juice, Worcestershire, Tabasco, and salt into a medium bowl and stir well. Cover and refrigerate.

2 Make the shrimp: Put wine, peppercorns, thyme, parsley, onions, celery, bay leaf, and 8 cups water into a large pot. Season the liquid generously with salt and bring to a boil. Reduce heat to medium-low and simmer for 30 minutes.

3 Add shrimp and cook, stirring occasionally, until just cooked through, 2–3 minutes. Drain shrimp, transfer to a baking sheet, and spread into a single layer; let cool to room temperature. Refrigerate shrimp until completely chilled, then peel them and serve with the cocktail sauce.

NEW ORLEANS BARBECUED SHRIMP

SERVES 4

There's no barbecue involved in this classic New Orleans dish, just a lip-smacking combination of Worcestershire and hot sauces, butter, and tangy spices—a recipe that was perfected, in our opinion, at Mr. B's Bistro in New Orleans. The sweet peel-and-eat jumbo shrimp may look like the main attraction, but sopping up the sauce juices with a hunk of bread is, by all accounts, truly the best part.

- 3 tbsp. unsalted butter, plus 12 tbsp., cut into ½″ cubes and chilled
- 2 cloves garlic, finely chopped
- ½ cup hot sauce, such as Crystal
- ¼ cup Worcestershire sauce
- 2 tbsp. fresh lemon juice
- 1 tbsp. Creole seasoning
- 4 tsp. freshly ground black pepper
- 1½ lb. large shrimp, heads on, unpeeled
  Kosher salt, to taste
  French bread, for serving

Heat 3 tbsp. butter in a 12″ skillet over medium-high heat. Add garlic and cook until soft, 1–2 minutes. Add hot sauce, Worcestershire, juice, Creole seasoning, and pepper and bring to a simmer. Cook until sauce is reduced by half, 5–7 minutes. Add shrimp and cook, flipping once, until cooked through, 3–4 minutes. Reduce heat to medium-low and stir in chilled butter to make a smooth sauce. Season with salt. Serve with French bread.

OYSTERS ROCKEFELLER

SERVES 4–6

Oysters Rockefeller were created in New Orleans, at the legendary restaurant Antoine's. The precise recipe is kept a secret, but we do know that neither bacon nor spinach is involved—common inclusions at other restaurants. Instead, the oysters are topped with a roux full of herbs and aromatics, then combined with bread crumbs and broiled until a delicate crust forms.

- Rock salt, as needed
- 12 oysters, such as bluepoint, chilled
- 4 tbsp. unsalted butter
- 4 tbsp. flour
- ¼ tsp. cayenne pepper
- 6 scallions, minced
- 2 ribs celery, minced
  Leaves from 2 sprigs fresh tarragon, minced
  Leaves from 1 bunch fresh parsley, minced, plus sprigs for garnish
  Kosher salt and freshly ground white pepper
- 3 tbsp. fresh bread crumbs

1 Fill 2 ovenproof baking dishes halfway with rock salt. Shuck oysters over a bowl to catch their liquor (you should have about ½ cup), discarding flat top shells. Loosen oysters from bottom shells with a knife. Nestle 6 shucked oysters in their shells into each bed of rock salt; chill.

2 Melt butter in a 2-qt. saucepan over medium heat. Add flour and cook, stirring, until smooth, about 2 minutes. Add oyster liquor; cook until thickened to a paste, about 2 minutes. Stir in cayenne, scallions, celery, tarragon, parsley, and salt and pepper. Reduce heat to medium-low and cook until soft, about 1 hour. Transfer to a food processor, add bread crumbs, and process into a smooth paste, about 2 minutes.

3 Heat broiler. Place paste in a pastry bag fitted with a ½″ fluted tip. Pipe paste completely over oysters. Broil until paste begins to brown and oysters are just cooked through, 5–7 minutes. Garnish with parsley sprigs.

FRIED OYSTERS WITH SPICY RÉMOULADE

SERVES 4

Chef Frank Stitt of Highlands Bar and Grill in Birmingham, Alabama, uses the bottom oyster shells as serving platters for these crispy fried oysters with a piquant rémoulade sauce.

FOR THE RÉMOULADE

- 1 cup mayonnaise
- 2 tbsp. minced cornichons
- 2 tbsp. minced fresh flat-leaf parsley
- 2 tbsp. minced capers
- 1 tbsp. whole-grain mustard
- 1 tbsp. minced fresh tarragon
- 1 tbsp. minced shallots
- 2 tsp. sherry vinegar
- 1 tsp. minced oil-packed anchovies
- ½ tsp. paprika
- 2 dashes Tabasco sauce
- Grated zest of 1 lemon
- Kosher salt and freshly ground black pepper, to taste

FOR THE OYSTERS

- Canola or peanut oil, for frying
- 2 cups cornmeal
- ¾ cup flour
- 2 cups buttermilk
- 24 medium oysters, such as bluepoint or Apalachicola, shucked, bottom shells reserved

1 Make the rémoulade: In a medium bowl, combine all the ingredients. Stir to combine; season with salt and pepper. Cover and set aside.

2 Make the oysters: Pour oil to a depth of 2″ into a 4-qt. pot and heat over medium heat until a deep-fry thermometer reads 350°. Meanwhile, whisk together cornmeal and flour in a shallow dish and season with salt and pepper. Pour buttermilk into another shallow dish. Working in small batches, dip oysters in buttermilk and then in cornmeal mixture, tossing to coat. Transfer oysters to a rack set inside a baking sheet. Working in batches, add oysters to oil and fry, turning occasionally, until golden brown and crisp, about 2 minutes. Using a slotted spoon, transfer oysters to paper towels. Spoon some of the reserved rémoulade into the reserved oyster shells and top with fried oysters. Serve warm.

NEW ORLEANS, OYSTER CITY

New Orleans is an oyster lover's town: They're emblematic, hungrily sought after, and seemingly everywhere. At the raw bar at Pascal's Manale, shucker Thomas Stewart opens them by the thousands to be eaten the Gulf way: raw on a saltine with hot sauce and horseradish. The white-tiled oyster sanctuary Casamento's charbroils them, each shell a vessel for gurgling butter, garlic, and parmesan cheese. At Upperline, they're deep-fried and served atop a zesty, garlicky sauce. At Antoine's, there's a kingly platter known as the 2-2-2: oysters Bienville, baked in a white wine–cream sauce; Rockefeller, smothered in puréed herbs (page 45); and Thermidor, with bacon and tomato sauce. New Orleans' oyster cookery is so evolved largely due to abundance: Louisiana is a prolific oyster-producing state. The type in the Gulf of Mexico, *Crassostrea virginica*, are large, plump, mild specimens that lend themselves well to both raw and cooked preparations. Early on, the plentiful mollusks were swapped in for escargots in Creole versions of classic French dishes, and cooks kept going from there. Sal Sunseri, a coproprietor of P&J's Oyster Company with his brother Al, told us what he looks for in one: "Louisiana oystermen say they're looking for a 'cock' oyster, because it has the colors, like purple and copper, you'd see on a cockleshell. Those show that the oyster's feeding well, and everything's salty and good—all you have to do is suck it up."

BRIGTSEN'S OYSTERS LERUTH

SERVES 4–6

Sweet crabmeat and shrimp enrich the stuffing of these broiled mollusks, famously served at Brigtsen's restaurant in New Orleans.

- 2½ tbsp. unsalted butter
- 2 cloves garlic, finely chopped
- 2 scallions, finely chopped
- 1 rib celery, finely chopped
- ½ small yellow onion, finely chopped
- 1 tbsp. finely chopped fresh flat-leaf parsley

> "As I ate the oysters with their strong taste of the sea and their faint metallic taste that the cold white wine washed away, leaving only the sea taste and the succulent texture, and as I drank their cold liquid from each shell and washed it down with the crisp taste of the wine, I lost the empty feeling and began to be happy and to make plans."
>
> ERNEST HEMINGWAY

½ tsp. finely chopped fresh thyme
½ tsp. cayenne pepper
¼ tsp. celery seeds
1 bay leaf
  Kosher salt and freshly ground white pepper, to taste
¼ lb. medium shrimp (about 5), peeled, deveined, and finely chopped
1 tbsp. flour
1 cup heavy cream
2 oz. crabmeat, picked of shells
1 cup fresh bread crumbs
¼ cup grated Parmigiano-Reggiano
  Coarse rock salt, for pan
12 large bluepoint oysters, on the half shell
½ tsp. paprika

1 Melt butter in a 2-qt. saucepan over medium-high heat. Add garlic, scallions, celery, and onion and cook, stirring occasionally, until golden, 4–6 minutes. Add parsley, thyme, cayenne, celery seeds, bay, salt, and pepper and cook until fragrant, 1 minute. Add shrimp and cook until just pink, 1–2 minutes. Add flour and cook for 1 minute. Add cream and bring to a boil; remove from heat and stir in crab, bread crumbs, and cheese. Transfer to a pastry bag fitted with a ½" fluted tip; refrigerate until cold, at least 1 hour.

2 Heat broiler. Line a baking sheet with rock salt about ¼" deep. Nestle oysters into bed of rock salt. Pipe filling over oysters and sprinkle with paprika; broil until tops are browned, about 4 minutes.

CLAMS CASINO
SERVES 6–8

Butter, shallots, paprika, and salt slathered over littleneck clams is an inspired combination that you'll find in restaurants across the country. The dish, however, is thought to have been invented in 1917 by restaurateur Julius Keller, proprietor of the Little Casino in Narragansett, Rhode Island—a true clam town.

  Rock salt
24 littleneck or cherrystone clams, scrubbed
8 tbsp. unsalted butter, softened
2 shallots, finely chopped
¼ tsp. paprika
  Kosher salt and freshly ground black pepper
4 slices bacon, cut crosswise into 1" pieces

1 Move oven rack to top third of oven and heat oven to 500°. Fill a large baking dish halfway with rock salt and set aside. Using a clam or paring knife, shuck clams, loosening clam meat from top shell, and discard top shell, then loosen clam meat from bottom shell. Nestle shucked clams in their shell into rock salt and set aside.

2 Put butter, shallots, paprika, and salt and pepper to taste into a small bowl and mix well. Spoon about 1 tsp. of the seasoned butter onto each clam and top each with a piece of bacon.

3 Bake clams until edges of bacon are crisp and butter is golden brown and bubbling, about 5 minutes. Serve hot.

COOK'S NOTE Can't find rock salt at the supermarket? Look for it in a hardware store.

STAMP & GO
Jamaican Salt Cod Fritters
SERVES 6–8

The Jamaican journalist Novia McDonald-Whyte suggests that these popular local road snacks were named for a term used by 18th-century British sailors living on the island. If an officer wanted something to be done in a hurry, she writes, the order was to "Stamp and Go!"

FOR THE CULANTRO SAUCE

- 2 cups mayonnaise
- ½ cup finely chopped fresh culantro or cilantro
- ¼ cup finely chopped fresh flat-leaf parsley
- 1 tbsp. white wine vinegar
- 1 tbsp. fresh lime juice
- 2 tsp. grated lime zest
- 1 tsp. finely chopped fresh basil
- 1 tsp. finely chopped fresh thyme
- 2 cloves garlic, finely chopped
- ½ Scotch bonnet or habanero chile, stemmed, seeded, and minced
  Kosher salt and freshly ground black pepper, to taste

FOR THE FRITTERS

- 1 lb. dried salt cod
- 1 tbsp. canola oil, plus more for frying
- 6 cloves garlic, minced
- 2 small yellow onions, minced
- 2 scallions, finely chopped
- ½ Scotch bonnet or habanero chile, stemmed, seeded, and finely chopped
- 2 cups flour
- 3 tbsp. baking powder
- 2 tsp. kosher salt
- 1 tsp. ground black pepper
- 6 eggs, lightly beaten

1 Make the culantro sauce: Whisk together all ingredients in a bowl and season with salt and pepper; chill.

2 Make the fritters: Place cod in a 2-qt. saucepan, and cover by 2″ with cold water; bring to a boil over high heat, and cook for 20 minutes. Drain cod, return to saucepan, and repeat process twice more. Transfer cod to a bowl, and flake with a fork into large chunks; set aside.

3 Heat 1 tbsp. oil in a 12″ skillet over medium-high heat. Add garlic, onions, scallions, and chile and cook, stirring, until soft, about 10 minutes. Remove from heat and let cool; set aside. In a large bowl, whisk together flour, baking powder, salt, and pepper; add eggs and stir until a dough forms. Add reserved cod and cooked vegetables and stir gently until combined.

4 Pour oil to a depth of 2″ into a 6-qt. Dutch oven, and heat over medium-high heat until a deep-fry thermometer reads 350°. Using a tablespoon, drop rounds of dough into oil and fry until golden brown, about 3 minutes; repeat

with remaining dough. Using a slotted spoon, transfer fritters to paper towels to drain briefly. Serve immediately with culantro sauce.

STUFFED ROMAINE LEAVES WITH AVGOLÉMONO SAUCE

SERVES 4

Avgolémono sauce is a traditional Greek lemon sauce, often drizzled over dolmades. This recipe, in which lettuce leaves are filled with an herbaceous meat mixture, was inspired by the new breed of Athenian ouzo bar owner-chefs, who mix traditional foods and flavors with new ingredients to enhance their eclectic menus.

FOR THE FILLING

- ⅓ lb. ground lamb
- ⅓ lb, ground beef
- ⅓ lb. ground pork
- ½ cup toasted pine nuts
- ½ cup dried currants
- 1 tbsp. finely chopped fresh dill
- 1 tbsp. finely chopped fresh mint
- 1 tbsp. finely chopped fresh flat-leaf parsley
- ½ tsp. ground cloves
- 1 tsp. ground cinnamon
- 1 cup cooked white rice
  Kosher salt and freshly ground black pepper, to taste

FOR THE AVGOLÉMONO SAUCE

- 1 cup chicken stock
- 2 eggs
- 3 tbsp. lemon juice
- ½ tsp. cornstarch

- 2 heads romaine lettuce

1 Make the filling: In a large heavy skillet, sauté lamb, beef, and pork until cooked, about 10 minutes. Remove from heat and drain fat. Stir in pine nuts, currants, dill, mint, parsley, cloves, cinnamon, rice, and salt and pepper, then remove from heat and set aside.

2 Make the sauce: Heat stock. In a separate bowl, beat together eggs and lemon juice mixed with cornstarch. Whisk hot stock into egg-lemon mixture, ¼ cup at a time, and place in the top of a double boiler over low heat. Cook until sauce thickens to the consistency of yogurt, about 10 minutes.

3 Bring a large pot of salted water to a boil. Remove outer dark leaves of heads of lettuce, cutting off and reserving top half of each leaf (reserve inner leaves and cores for another use). Blanch leaf halves in boiling water for 5 seconds to soften. Place 2 heaping tbsp. filling at the base of a leaf. Fold over sides and carefully roll up. Repeat with remaining leaves. Place seam side down on a platter. Spoon extra filling around the stuffed leaves. Top with warm avgolémono sauce.

SCALLION PANCAKES

Cong You Bing

SERVES 6

These light and flaky scallion pancakes, an iconic, hugely popular dish throughout China and now a staple of Chinese restaurants in America, get a hit of heat from crushed red chile flakes.

4	cups flour
1	tbsp. baking powder
1	tbsp. kosher salt
⅓	cup canola oil
2	tbsp. sesame oil
1½	cup thinly sliced scallions
1	tsp. crushed red chile flakes
½	tsp. ground white pepper

1 Process 2 cups flour and baking powder in a food processor. With motor running, add ⅔ cup cold water and process until dough forms, about 40 seconds. Transfer to a plate; set aside. Add remaining 2 cups flour and the salt to food processor. With motor running, add ⅔ cup boiling water and process until dough forms, about 30 seconds. Return reserved dough to food processor; pulse until both doughs come together, about 35 seconds. Transfer to a lightly floured work surface and knead until smooth, about 4 minutes. Transfer to a greased bowl, cover, and let sit at room temperature for 2 hours.

2 Halve dough; using a rolling pin, roll 1 dough half into a 10"×20" rectangle. Brush with 1 tbsp. canola oil and half the sesame oil. Sprinkle with half the scallions, half the chile flakes, and half the white pepper. Beginning with one long side, tightly roll dough like a jelly roll. Cut roll crosswise into 3 pieces, slightly stretch each piece, and starting from one edge, coil piece horizontally, tucking the end

underneath. Using your hand, gently flatten coil into a disk; using a rolling pin, flatten into a 5" circle. Repeat with remaining pieces and second dough half, 1 tbsp. canola oil, remaining sesame oil, scallions, chile flakes, and white pepper. Let pancakes sit for about 10 minutes.

3 Heat oven to 200°. Heat 2 tsp. canola oil in a 10" nonstick skillet over medium heat. Add 1 pancake to skillet and cook, swirling skillet and turning once, until golden and crisp, about 10 minutes. Transfer to a baking sheet; place in oven to keep warm. Repeat with remaining oil and pancakes. Cut into wedges to serve.

KOREAN MUNG BEAN PANCAKES

Bindae-tteok

MAKES ABOUT 30 PANCAKES

These savory Korean pancakes are made from a batter of ground mung beans flecked with pork, scallions, and pungent kimchi.

2	cups peeled, dried mung beans, soaked overnight and drained
¼	lb. boneless pork loin, trimmed and finely chopped
¼	lb. Cabbage Kimchi (page 584, or store-bought), rinsed, drained, and finely chopped (about ½ cup), plus ½ cup kimchi pickling liquid
1½	cups mung bean sprouts, roughly chopped
1	tbsp. kosher salt
6	scallions, halved lengthwise and cut crosswise into 1" pieces
5	cloves garlic, finely chopped
½	cup canola oil
¼	cup soy sauce
1	tbsp. white vinegar

1 Purée mung beans and 1¾ cups water in a food processor until smooth; transfer to a bowl. Add pork, kimchi and pickling liquid, sprouts, salt, scallions, and garlic; stir until combined.

2 Heat 2 tbsp. oil in a 12" nonstick skillet over medium heat. Working in batches and adding more oil as needed, place ¼ cup of mixture in pan for each pancake. Cook, flipping once, until golden, 8–10 minutes. Transfer to paper towels to drain briefly, then place on a serving platter. Stir soy sauce and vinegar in a bowl; serve on the side for dipping.

Salads

SALADS

THERE'S NOTHING quite as bright and satisfying as a simple green salad. In America, lettuce piques the appetite at the start of a meal; in Europe, it's a palate-cleansing intermezzo or a final crunchy counterpoint to a hearty main course. But you don't need lettuce to have a salad.

The world of salads is vast, ranging far beyond the typical assembly of garden-harvested lettuces tossed with a dressing. The word *salad* itself comes from the Latin for salt, a reference to the seasoning used by ancient Romans for their wild greens. But the term has come to encompass a seemingly endless array of preparations. Salads can be cooked or raw, warm or chilled, spritzed with lemon or bound with mayonnaise, built with vegetables or bolstered with meats, made up of just a few components or elaborately composed from an ingredients list longer than the platter they are served on.

With all that variation, what, then, is a salad? Why do we consider a plate of thin-sliced raw baby artichokes drizzled with lemon and olive oil and crowned with a few curls of cheese to be in the same category as Guatemala's riotous *fiambre,* in which as many as 50 different ingredients—every imaginable in-season vegetable, half a dozen cured meats, pickles and cheeses, head-on shrimp—constitute a wild-hearted culinary adventure?

What makes a salad is not just its role as costar to the main course. It's also the careful selection and arrangement of ingredients. Whether you're serving a finely minced Lebanese tabbouleh, a knife-and-fork California-style Chinese chicken salad, or a juicy, garlicky summertime *panzanella,* no component is an afterthought. Above all, a successful salad embodies balance: the sour with the sweet, the crisp with the creamy, the rich with the piquant. From the lemon-scented mezze found around the Mediterranean to the spicy-sweet grilled-meat salads of Southeast Asia to the slaws and lettuce wedges of the American Midwest, a salad's miscellany of ingredients—its beauty on the plate, its flavors and aromas—resolves in a satisfying harmony.

It's a harmony that tells a unique story. Japan's quick-pickled daikon and sunflower sprouts nibbled between helpings of grilled fish and rice; Eastern Europe's *selyodka pod shuboy,* a composed masterpiece of pickled herring striated with sour cream, boiled potatoes, fresh dill, and chopped eggs; Senegal's mix of avocado, mango, and coconut that complements the country's rich stews—whatever the ingredients, oils, and spices, each salad tells something of who we are and where we come from.

Composed & Entrée Salads

COBB SALAD

SERVES 4–6

The Brown Derby on Wilshire Boulevard in Los Angeles closed its doors long ago, but this classic salad—defined by its artful arrangement of blue cheese, bacon, hard-cooked egg, tomato, chicken, and avocado—which was invented there in 1937 by the restaurant's owner Robert H. Cobb, lives on.

FOR THE DRESSING

- ¾ cup canola oil
- ¼ cup extra-virgin olive oil
- ¼ cup red wine vinegar
- 1 tbsp. fresh lemon juice
- ¾ tsp. dry mustard
- ½ tsp. Worcestershire sauce
- ¼ tsp. sugar
- 1 clove garlic, minced
  Kosher salt and freshly ground black pepper, to taste

FOR THE SALAD

- ½ head iceberg lettuce, cored and shredded
- ½ head romaine lettuce, chopped
- ½ bunch watercress, some of the stems trimmed, chopped
- 2 oz. blue cheese, preferably Roquefort, crumbled
- 6 slices bacon, cooked and roughly chopped
- 3 hard-cooked eggs, peeled and cut into ½″ cubes
- 2 medium tomatoes, peeled, seeded, and cut into ½″ cubes
- 1 boneless skinless chicken breast, cooked and cut into ½″ cubes
- 1 avocado, pitted, peeled, and cut into ½″ cubes
  Kosher salt and freshly ground black pepper, to taste
- 2 tbsp. minced fresh chives

1 Make the dressing: Combine the canola oil, olive oil, vinegar, lemon juice, mustard, Worcestershire, sugar, and garlic in a blender. Purée the ingredients to make a smooth dressing and season with salt and pepper. Set the dressing aside (or refrigerate, covered, for up to 1 week).

2 Make the salad: On a large platter, combine the iceberg and romaine lettuces along with the watercress. Arrange the blue cheese, bacon, eggs, tomatoes, chicken, and avocado on top of the greens in neat rows. To serve, drizzle salad with dressing, season with salt and pepper, and top with chives. Alternatively, toss everything together in a bowl.

A SALAD CELEBRITY

The first Brown Derby Restaurant opened on Wilshire Boulevard in Los Angeles in 1926 and quickly became known as much for the glittering Hollywood movie crowd it attracted as for the food it served. But the food was hardly negligible—and without question, the restaurant's most famous creation was the Cobb salad, improvised one day early in the restaurant's history by Robert H. Cobb, a protégé of the restaurant's founder. According to the Derby's chef at the time, Cobb got hungry one day and "he chopped up whatever was around—some lettuce, an avocado from the icebox, some bacon left over from the breakfast service—and stirred it all up in a bowl. He liked what he came up with and, by adding a few new ingredients, developed a recipe." He remembers the eventual salad, which became an instant hit, as "a bowl filled with lettuce . . . topped with stripes of ingredients—red tomatoes, blue cheese, white chicken, and the rest—so that it resembled a flag. The waitress would arrive with it at the table, dribble the dressing over it, and toss it there."

CHINESE CHICKEN SALAD

SERVES 4–6

This Chinese-American salad probably originated in Los Angeles, and has been attributed to restaurateur Sylvia Cheng Wu. Variations have been served everywhere from the Fox Studios commissary to Wolfgang Puck's longstanding Santa Monica spot Chinois on Main—the origin of this particular version.

FOR THE DRESSING

- ½ cup canola oil
- ¼ cup rice vinegar
- 3 tbsp. soy sauce
- 3 tbsp. smooth peanut butter
- 1½ tbsp. sesame oil
- 1 tbsp. fresh lime juice
- 1 tbsp. dry mustard
- ½ tbsp. honey
- ½ tbsp. white sesame seeds, toasted
- ½ tsp. minced fresh ginger
- 1 clove garlic, minced
  Kosher salt and freshly ground black pepper, to taste

FOR THE FRIED WONTON STRIPS

- Canola oil, for frying
- 5 wonton wrappers, cut into ¼″ strips

FOR THE SALAD

- ½ head napa cabbage, cored and shredded
- ½ head romaine lettuce, shredded
- 2 cups shredded cooked chicken
- ½ cup loosely packed fresh cilantro leaves
- 1 cup mung bean sprouts
- 10 snow peas, julienned
- 4 scallions, thinly sliced
- 1 red bell pepper, stemmed, seeded, and julienned
- 1 carrot, peeled and julienned
- 1 cucumber, peeled, seeded, and thinly sliced
- 1 Thai or serrano chile, thinly sliced, for garnish
  Black sesame seeds, for garnish
  Roasted crushed peanuts, for garnish

1 Make the dressing: Whisk together oil, vinegar, soy sauce, peanut butter, sesame oil, lime juice, mustard, honey, sesame seeds, ginger, and garlic in a bowl. Season with salt and pepper; set dressing aside.

2 Make the fried wonton strips: Pour oil to a depth of 2″ into a 1-qt. saucepan and heat over medium-high heat until a deep-fry thermometer reads 350°. Add wonton strips and cook until crisp, 20–30 seconds. Using tongs, transfer strips to paper towels; set aside.

3 Make the salad: Combine cabbage, lettuce, chicken, and cilantro in a bowl; divide among plates. Arrange sprouts, peas, scallions, peppers, carrots, and cucumbers over each salad; drizzle with dressing. Garnish with chiles, sesame seeds, peanuts, and wonton strips. Alternatively, toss everything together in a bowl.

VIETNAMESE SHREDDED CHICKEN SALAD

Gỏi gà bắp cả

SERVES 4

Leftover chicken takes on new life when it's brought together with pungent fish sauce, spicy chiles, and fresh mint in a bright and simple salad you'll find all over Vietnam.

- 2 fresh green bird's eye chiles, stemmed, seeded, and rinsed
- 3 cloves garlic, minced
- 2 tbsp. sugar
- 1 tbsp. rice vinegar
- 3 tbsp. fresh lime juice
- 3 tbsp. nuoc mam (Vietnamese fish sauce)
- 3 tbsp. vegetable oil
- 1 small onion, thinly sliced
- 2 cups shredded cooked chicken
- 4 cups shredded napa cabbage
- 2 medium carrots, julienned
- ½ cup roughly chopped fresh mint
  Freshly ground black pepper, to taste
  Fresh cilantro, for garnish

1 Put chiles in a large bowl. Add garlic, sugar, vinegar, lime juice, fish sauce, vegetable oil, and onion. Mix until sugar dissolves.

2 Add chicken, cabbage, carrots, and mint. Season with pepper, mix, and garnish with cilantro.

COOK'S NOTE It is always best to wear rubber gloves when working with hot chiles and to wash hands thoroughly afterward.

COMPOSE YOURSELF

A composed salad is almost by definition a thing of beauty. Unlike its tossed or dressing-bound cousins, it's a thoughtful arrangement of ingredients, a showpiece for regional abundance. These three bear the global standard.

FIAMBRE (page 56) Guatemala's exuberant *fiambre* can contain up to 50 ingredients, from hearts of palm to chorizo to sardines, and can take days to prepare; consequently it's eaten only once a year, on All Saint's Day. The salad's origins are murky, but it's likely that over time the dozens of little dishes families would carry to the cemetery got mixed together, resulting in something simpler to carry—if not necessarily to put together.

NIÇOISE (this page) This rustic salad is a platform for the bounty of southeastern France. While the ingredients vary by season, it's always anchored by delicacies such as oil-cured olives, anchovies, and tuna. While traditional versions eschew cooked vegetables, French chef Auguste Escoffier is credited with the now-standard addition of potato and green beans, while Julia Child is responsible for the popularity (in America, at least) of serving the dish on a bed of lettuce.

GADO-GADO (page 60) Indonesia's iconic *gado-gado*—the name means "mix mix"—can be made up of as many different types of cooked and raw vegetables as you can get your hands on. Cabbage, spinach, bean sprouts, chayote, bitter melon, and cucumber are all good places to start, along with tofu, eggs, and potatoes. All are artfully arranged on a platter with a bowl of peanut dressing on the side, bright with lime and fiery with chile heat.

CHEF'S SALAD

SERVES 1

This recipe for chef's salad—the classic luncheon dish of greens topped with an assortment of chilled meats—is based on one developed by Louis Diat, onetime chef at New York's Ritz-Carlton Hotel and the purported inventor of the dish.

- 3 cups loosely packed chopped mixed escarole, green leaf lettuce, and iceberg lettuce
- ¼ cup julienned smoked ham
- ¼ cup julienned cooked beef tongue
- ¼ cup thinly sliced boiled chicken breast
- ¼ hard-cooked egg
- 1 cup loosely packed trimmed watercress
- ¼ cup American French Dressing (page 77)

Spread lettuce mix on a salad plate. Arrange ham, beef tongue, chicken, and egg on top of greens. Tuck watercress into center. Drizzle with dressing.

SALADE NIÇOISE

SERVES 4–6 (SEE PHOTO, PAGE 209)

Traditionally made with ingredients local to the Provençal town of Nice, such as olives, oil-cured tuna, and anchovies, this hearty salad—which according to custom ought not to be served over lettuce—has become a staple of brasseries all over France.

FOR THE DRESSING

- 1 clove garlic
  Kosher salt and freshly ground black pepper, to taste
- ⅓ cup extra-virgin olive oil
- 2 tbsp. fresh lemon juice
- 1 tbsp. Dijon mustard
- 1 shallot, minced

FOR THE SALAD

- 1 lb. small new potatoes, boiled until tender
- 6 oz. yellow baby beets, boiled until tender, peeled
- 6 oz. red baby beets, boiled until tender, peeled
- 8 oz. haricot verts or green beans, blanched
- 12 oz. cherry tomatoes, halved
- ½ cup black niçoise olives
- 8 small radishes, trimmed and thinly sliced
- 8 salt-packed anchovies, rinsed and drained
- 4 hard-cooked eggs, halved lengthwise
- 3 4-oz. cans tuna packed in olive oil, drained
- 1 small cucumber, thinly sliced
- ½ cup loosely packed fresh basil leaves, for garnish
- ¼ cup thinly sliced scallions, for garnish

1 Make the dressing: Mince garlic on a cutting board and sprinkle heavily with salt. Using a knife, scrape garlic and salt together to form a smooth paste. Transfer paste to a bowl and whisk in oil, lemon juice, mustard, shallot, salt, and pepper; set aside.

2 Make the salad: Arrange all ingredients in separate rows on a large serving platter; drizzle dressing over all ingredients, season with salt and pepper, and garnish with basil and scallions just before serving.

LATVIAN LAYERED HERRING SALAD

Selyodka Pod Shuboy

SERVES 6–8

Salt-cured herring becomes a lavish centerpiece when layered with apples and a sour cream–mayonnaise dressing in this beautiful Eastern European composed salad.

- 1 cup mayonnaise
- 1 cup sour cream
  Kosher salt and freshly ground black pepper, to taste
- 3 filets salted herring, rinsed and roughly chopped
- ½ small yellow onion, minced
- 2 Yukon gold potatoes, boiled, peeled, and grated
- 3 medium carrots, peeled, boiled, and grated
- 6 hard-cooked eggs, whites and yolks separated, each passed through a fine sieve
- ½ Granny Smith apple, cored, peeled, and grated
- 2 medium beets, boiled, peeled, and grated
- ¼ cup chopped fresh dill

1 Whisk together mayonnaise and sour cream in a small bowl and season with salt and pepper; set dressing aside.

2 Place herring in the bottom of a shallow 1½-qt. oval dish, and top with one-third of the dressing. Sprinkle onions on top, then cover with potatoes. Top potatoes with carrots and half the remaining dressing. Combine half the sieved egg yolks and half the sieved whites in a small bowl, then spread over dressing. Top with apples, then beets. Spread remaining dressing over beets to cover. Create 3 even rows across top of salad with remaining egg yolks and 3 rows with remaining whites. Fill in gaps with rows of dill.

FIAMBRE

Guatemalan Composed Salad

SERVES 12–16

Fiambre, whose name has come to mean "cold cuts," is a salad eaten in Guatemala only on All Saint's Day. Though its origins are murky, it seems likely that as families took dozens of little dishes to the cemetery for the traditional picnic to honor the dead, over time they got mixed together, resulting in this easier-to-carry creation.

FOR THE DRESSING

- ¾ cup chopped fresh flat-leaf parsley
- ½ cup white wine vinegar
- 2 tbsp. capers, drained
- 1 tbsp. Dijon mustard
- 6 scallions, roughly chopped
- 1 7-oz. jar pimientos, drained
- 1 clove garlic, thinly sliced
- 1 1″ piece fresh ginger, peeled and thinly sliced
- 1 cup extra-virgin olive oil
  Kosher salt and freshly ground black pepper

FOR THE SALAD

- 1 lb. boneless, skinless chicken breasts, poached and cut into 1″ cubes
- 1 lb. cooked medium shrimp, heads on, unpeeled
- 1 lb. Yukon gold potatoes, peeled, boiled, and halved
- ½ lb. uncured chorizo sausage, cooked and cut into ¼″ slices
- ½ lb. linguiça sausage, cooked and cut into ¼″ slices
- ¼ lb. green beans, trimmed and blanched
- 3 oz. salami, cut into ½″ strips
- 3 oz. smoked ham, cut into ½″ strips
- 1 cup frozen peas, thawed
- 4 medium carrots, cut into ½″ rounds, boiled until tender
- 4 ribs celery, cut into ½″ slices, boiled until tender
- 1 head cauliflower, cut into florets, boiled until tender
- 4 medium beets, roasted, peeled, and quartered
- 1 small head green leaf lettuce, leaves separated
- 1 small head red leaf lettuce, leaves separated
- ½ lb. farmer's or feta cheese
- 3 oz. mini gherkins, drained
- 3 oz. Spanish olives, pitted
- 5 radishes, quartered
- 4 hard-cooked eggs, quartered

1 Make the dressing: Purée ½ cup parsley, vinegar, capers, mustard, scallions, pimientos, garlic, and ginger in a blender. Drizzle in oil until emulsified; season with salt and pepper and set vinaigrette aside.

2 Make the salad: Toss chicken, shrimp, potatoes, chorizo, linguiça, green beans, salami, ham, peas, carrots, celery, and cauliflower with ¾ cup vinaigrette in a bowl. Toss beets with ¼ cup vinaigrette in another bowl. Cover both bowls; chill 30 minutes to blend flavors.

3 Arrange lettuce on bottom of a large platter; top with marinated meats and vegetables. Garnish with beets, cheese, gherkins, olives, radishes, and eggs. Sprinkle with remaining parsley.

Side Salads

RAW ARTICHOKE SALAD WITH PARMESAN & MINT

SERVES 4

In this classic Italian salad, thinly sliced, pleasantly bitter baby artichoke hearts are lightened with fresh mint, lemon juice, and Parmigiano.

- 2 lb. (about 20) baby artichokes
- 2 lemons, halved
- 4 tbsp. extra-virgin olive oil
- ½ cup baby arugula
- ¼ cup torn fresh mint leaves
  Kosher salt and freshly ground black pepper
- 2 oz. Parmigiano-Reggiano, thinly shaved with a vegetable peeler

1 Trim away tough outer leaves of artichokes to expose their tender pale green interior. Using a serrated-blade knife, cut off the spiky top third of the artichokes. Use a vegetable peeler to remove tough outer layers around the base and stem. Squeeze 1 lemon into a bowl filled with cold water and submerge artichokes in water.

2 Drain artichokes and pat dry with paper towels. Using a mandoline or a chef's knife, cut artichokes into thin slices and transfer to medium bowl. Squeeze remaining lemon over artichokes, add oil, and toss to coat. Add arugula and mint and season with salt and pepper; toss gently. Garnish with Parmigiano shavings.

BEET & SUMAC SALAD

SERVES 6

This Middle Eastern salad has a creamy, nutty taste and a bracing bite of onions, sumac, and lemon.

- 3 large beets
  Red wine vinegar
- 2 tsp. ground sumac
- 2 handfuls arugula leaves
- 1 large red onion, thinly sliced
- 1 cup whole-milk yogurt
- 2 tbsp. fresh lemon juice
- 2 tsp. tahini
- 2 cloves garlic, smashed
  Kosher salt and freshly ground black pepper, to taste

1 Cook beets in a large pan of gently boiling water until tender, 30–40 minutes, with a few drops of vinegar added (this helps set the beets' color). Drain beets and let cool. Peel beets, then cut them into quarters and thinly slice. Put sliced beets, sumac, arugula, and red onion into a serving bowl.

2 Mix yogurt, lemon juice, tahini, garlic, salt, and pepper to taste in a bowl. Pour dressing over the salad and toss gently.

FENNEL, SUNCHOKE & APPLE SALAD

SERVES 6–8

Crisp, sweet, earthy sunchokes are rarely served raw, but in this preparation they are sliced paper-thin and tossed with fennel, radishes, and apples and marinated in a delicate vinaigrette. The result is a surprising and delicious cold-weather salad.

- ½ cup extra-virgin olive oil
- 2 tbsp. rice vinegar
- 2 tbsp. fresh lemon juice
- 2 tbsp. chopped fresh chives
- 2 fennel bulbs, trimmed and very thinly sliced, 2 tbsp. fronds reserved and finely chopped
  Kosher salt and freshly ground black pepper, to taste
- 8 radishes, very thinly sliced
- 6 sunchokes, peeled and very thinly sliced
- 2 Gala or Fuji apples, cored and very thinly sliced

1 In a bowl, whisk together oil, vinegar, lemon juice, chives, and fennel fronds to make a smooth vinaigrette. Season with salt and pepper to taste.

2 Add radishes, sunchokes, apples, and fennel. Toss well, cover, and refrigerate for at least 30 minutes or up to 1 day, to allow the flavors to come together. Season with salt and pepper before serving.

CHICORY IN ANCHOVY SAUCE

Puntarelle in Salsa di Alici

SERVES 4

In the winter, you'll find puntarelle on restaurant menus throughout Rome: The bitter green, from the chicory family, inspires passion in cooks during its short growing season. Its biting flavor is the perfect counterpoint to this garlicky anchovy dressing.

½ lb. young puntarelle or dandelion greens, trimmed and thinly sliced

4 oil-packed anchovy filets

1 clove garlic, minced

6 tbsp. extra-virgin olive oil

3 tbsp. red or white wine vinegar
   Kosher salt and freshly ground black pepper, to taste

Put puntarelle into a bowl of ice water; let sit for 1 hour. Meanwhile, finely chop and smash anchovies and garlic to make a paste; whisk in oil and vinegar to make a smooth dressing. Season with salt and pepper. Drain puntarelle and pat dry, then toss with dressing.

THE BITTER END

Among all winter greens, perhaps the most underappreciated is *puntarelle* (literally "little points"), a type of chicory that comes into season in November and stays until February. Each head is about a foot long, with a healthy fringe of feathery green leaves—but most are too bitter for many palates. The real prize is the cluster of hollow white stalks from which the leaves grow. These are bitter, too, but their bitterness may be tempered with a good long soak in ice water. In Rome, where *puntarelle* is much appreciated—it's been known to incite a bit of a frenzy in the markets—it's served as a simple salad with an anchovy dressing (above), but the stalks and leaves can also be sautéed with garlic, wilted in soups, or braised with beans.

SOM TUM

Thai Green Papaya Salad

SERVES 6

At Seattle's now-shuttered Little Uncle, chefs Poncharee Kounpungchart and Wiley Frank dehydrated and ground Oregon bay shrimp for their take on this Southeast Asian salad.

10 small home-dehydrated (see below) or store-bought dried shrimp

2 small red bird's eye chiles, stemmed

1 clove garlic, peeled

¼ cup tamarind juice

1 tbsp. grated palm sugar

1 tbsp. nam pla (Thai fish sauce)

1 lime, cut into 1″ pieces

4 cherry tomatoes, halved

3 long beans or 6 green beans, trimmed and cut into 1″ pieces

1 carrot, coarsely shredded

½ English cucumber, seeded and coarsely shredded

⅛ small green cabbage, cored and thinly sliced

1 lb. unripe green papaya, peeled, quartered, seeded, and finely shredded using a mandoline (about 2 cups)

3 tbsp. unsalted roasted peanuts

1 For home-dehydrated shrimp: dry bay shrimp in a dehydrator at 155° for 9 hours.

2 Using a mortar and pestle, crush shrimp, chiles, and garlic. Add tamarind juice, palm sugar, and fish sauce. Squeeze three-quarters of the lime pieces over the top and drop into mortar; grind to make a rough dressing. Add remaining ingredients, except peanuts, adding papaya last. Use pestle and a spoon to grind and mix salad until vegetables and fruit are bruised and coated in dressing. Transfer to a serving dish; garnish with remaining lime pieces and peanuts.

HAWAIIAN PICKLED SEAWEED SALAD

SERVES 6

Seaweed takes a dip in a sweet and nutty toasted sesame oil marinade in this briny-sweet salad. We got this recipe from Manago Hotel, in the town of Captain Cook on the Island of Hawaii.

1 2-oz. package dried seaweed, such as mehijiki

¼ cup white vinegar

3 tbsp. sugar

3 tbsp. soy sauce
1 tbsp. sesame seeds
2 tsp. sesame oil
1 tsp. kosher salt
½ small onion, halved and thinly sliced, for garnish
1 plum tomato, coarsely chopped, for garnish

1 Put seaweed into a sieve; rinse under cold water. Transfer seaweed to a bowl and cover with 6 cups cold water. Let soak until plump and soft, about 30 minutes. Drain seaweed and pat dry with paper towels. Transfer seaweed to a large bowl.

2 Meanwhile, whisk together vinegar, sugar, soy sauce, sesame seeds, sesame oil, and salt in a bowl.

3 Add soy mixture to seaweed; toss to combine. Cover with plastic wrap and chill for at least 3 hours or overnight to allow the flavors to meld. Divide salad among 6 small plates and garnish with onions and tomato.

SUMMER PANZANELLA
SERVES 4

The juiciness of vine-ripened tomatoes is sopped up by crusty bread that's been infused with garlic butter in this indulgent rendition of the classic Italian bread salad.

½ cup extra-virgin olive oil
4 tbsp. unsalted butter
3 cloves garlic, sliced
½ baguette, cut into ½″ cubes
3–4 lb. tomatoes
2 tbsp. balsamic vinegar
Kosher salt and freshly ground black pepper, to taste
1 handful fresh basil leaves, thinly sliced, plus sprigs for garnish (optional)

1 Heat oven to 350°. Heat ¼ cup oil and the butter together in a large ovenproof skillet over medium heat. When butter has melted, remove skillet from heat and add garlic and bread cubes and mix well. Place skillet in oven and bake until bread cubes are golden and crisp, 10–15 minutes. Remove skillet from oven and set aside to cool.

2 Meanwhile, prepare the tomatoes: If using cherry tomatoes, remove stems and slice in half. For larger tomatoes, core and slice into medium cubes. Put tomatoes in a large bowl, add vinegar and remaining ¼ cup oil, then season with salt and pepper. Mix well.

3 Shortly before serving, toss bread and basil with the tomatoes. Adjust seasonings. Spoon panzanella into each of 4 shallow soup bowls and garnish with sprigs of basil, if you like.

MOROCCAN TOMATO SALAD
SERVES 4–6

Tomatoes don't need much embellishment, and this Moroccan staple is a good example of that. A simple dressing of cumin and white vinegar beautifully offsets sweet tomatoes and fresh parsley.

3 medium tomatoes
Kosher salt and freshly ground black pepper, to taste
½ cup coarsely chopped fresh flat-leaf parsley
1 green chile, stemmed, seeded, and minced
1 tsp. ground cumin
1 tbsp. white vinegar
1 tbsp. extra-virgin olive oil

1 Dice tomatoes and place in a colander. Sprinkle with salt, toss gently, and allow to drain for 30 minutes.

2 Combine parsley, chile, cumin, vinegar, and oil in a medium bowl. Season with salt and pepper. Add tomatoes, mix thoroughly, and serve at room temperature.

ISRAELI CHOPPED SALAD
SERVES 4

This staple salad is found on virtually every table in Israel. The simplicity of the recipe demands that you use only the freshest and most flavorful vegetables you can find, along with a high-quality olive oil.

2 large tomatoes, diced
2 cucumbers, diced
1 large onion, diced
Juice of ½ lemon
½ cup finely chopped fresh flat-leaf parsley
Kosher salt and freshly ground black pepper, to taste
Chopped fresh mint

Combine tomatoes, cucumbers, and onion in a bowl. Pour lemon juice over the vegetables. Add parsley, salt, pepper, and mint and toss well before serving.

TOMATO SALAD WITH HERBS & POMEGRANATE

SERVES 6

Chock-full of parsley, mint, thyme, onions, and tomatoes, this bright Middle Eastern salad gets a bit of heat from ground Aleppo pepper. It's a great garnish for Fava Falafel (page 388) and also delicious on its own.

- ¾ cup chopped fresh flat-leaf parsley
- ½ cup chopped fresh mint leaves
- ¼ cup finely chopped red onion
- 3 tbsp. pomegranate molasses
- 3 tbsp. fresh lemon juice
- 2 tbsp. chopped fresh thyme
- ½ tsp. ground Aleppo pepper or paprika
- 8 scallions, finely chopped
- 6 medium tomatoes, cored and finely chopped
- 2 large banana peppers or cubanelle peppers, stemmed, seeded, and finely chopped
- 1 clove garlic, finely chopped
  Kosher salt and freshly ground black pepper, to taste
- 1 tsp. ground sumac, for garnish

Stir all ingredients except sumac together in a large bowl. Garnish with sumac and serve.

WATERMELON & TOMATO SALAD

SERVES 4–6

Chef Bill Smith of Crook's Corner, a restaurant in Chapel Hill, North Carolina, serves a version of this refreshing dish during the late summer. Smith says he developed his recipe after paying a visit to a few of his former cooks in Mexico, where he discovered a range of dishes that melded sweet, spicy, and sour flavors. Serve this cool, crisp salad as a side for grilled fish or meat.

- ¼ cup champagne vinegar or white wine vinegar
- 1 tbsp. sugar
- 1 tsp. kosher salt
- ¼ tsp. cayenne pepper
- ½ small red onion
- 1 4-lb. piece seedless watermelon, peeled and cut into 1″ chunks
- 4 beefsteak tomatoes, cored and cut into 1″ chunks
- ¼ cup extra-virgin olive oil
- 1 cup loosely packed roughly torn fresh basil leaves
- 1 cup loosely packed roughly torn fresh mint leaves
  Kosher salt and freshly ground black pepper, to taste

1 Whisk together sugar, salt, and cayenne in a small bowl. Quarter and thinly slice onion and toss it in the vinegar mixture. Set aside to let rest until the onion softens and mellows, about 30 minutes.

2 Combine tomatoes and watermelon chunks in a large bowl. Pour in onion-vinegar mixture along with oil and toss gently with your hands. Add basil and mint and toss gently. Season with salt and pepper and serve at room temperature.

MARINATED ZUCCHINI & GREEN BEAN SALAD

SERVES 4

The *ouzerí*—ouzo bar—is to Greece what the tapas bar is to Spain: a place to gather and eat (and drink) with friends. This summer salad is a favorite found in many *ouzerís* around Athens.

- 1 large zucchini, trimmed
- ½ lb. green beans, trimmed
- 1 tbsp. finely chopped fresh dill
- ¼ cup finely chopped scallions
- 1 cup sliced white mushrooms
- ⅓ cup white wine vinegar
- ⅓ cup extra-virgin olive oil
  Kosher salt and freshly ground black pepper, to taste

1 Using a mandoline or a knife, julienne zucchini. Halve green beans lengthwise and again crosswise. (Zucchini and beans should be about the same size.) Bring a medium pot of water to a boil. Blanch vegetables for 60 seconds, drain, pat dry, and transfer to a bowl.

2 Add dill, scallions, and mushrooms to bowl. Toss with vinegar and oil and season with salt and pepper. Refrigerate salad for at least 1 hour before serving.

GADO-GADO

Indonesian Vegetable Salad with Peanut Dressing
SERVES 6

An array of vegetables and starches are brought together in beautiful harmony by a sweet-spicy peanut dressing in this iconic Indonesian salad. Use the best produce available at the market—this ingredient list is just a starting point.

FOR THE PEANUT DRESSING

- 1½ cups unsalted roasted peanuts
- 1½ tsp. terasi shrimp paste
- ¼ cup grated palm or dark brown sugar
- 2 cloves garlic, peeled
- 1 red Holland or Fresno chile, stemmed and chopped
- ¾ cup coconut milk, preferably UHT from a carton
- 1 tbsp. palm or rice vinegar
  Kosher salt, to taste

FOR THE SALAD

- Peanut oil, for frying
- 1 lb. medium Yukon gold potatoes, peeled and sliced ⅓" thick
- 7 oz. firm tofu, drained, pressed, and cut into ½"-thick triangles
- 5 oz. kangkung water spinach or regular spinach, tough stems trimmed, leaves cut into 2" pieces
- ¼ lb. long beans or regular green beans, trimmed and cut into 2" pieces
- 2 cups mung bean sprouts
- 2 medium carrots, peeled and sliced ¼" thick on the diagonal
- ¼ head green cabbage, cored and cut into 1½" pieces
- 1 Kirby cucumber, sliced ½" thick on the diagonal
- 3 hard-cooked eggs, peeled and halved (optional)
  Shrimp chips or prawn crackers, fried (optional)

1 Make the peanut dressing: Heat a 12" nonstick skillet over medium heat. Cook peanuts until golden, 8–10 minutes; let cool. Transfer to a food processor and pulse until ground. Return skillet to medium-high heat. Enclose shrimp paste in aluminum foil in a flat packet, add to skillet, and cook, flipping once, until toasted and fragrant, 2–4 minutes. Let cool, unwrap, and transfer to food processor. Add sugar, garlic, and chile and purée to a paste. Transfer paste to skillet, add coconut milk, and cook over medium heat, stirring constantly, until mixture begins to separate, 5–7 minutes. Stir in vinegar, salt, and ½ cup water and simmer until dressing is thickened, 2–3 minutes.

2 Make the salad: Heat 2" oil in a 6-qt. saucepan until a deep-fry thermometer reads 350°. Working in batches, fry potatoes until golden and cooked through, 3–4 minutes. Using a slotted spoon, transfer to paper towels to drain. Fry tofu until puffed and golden, about 2 minutes; drain on paper towels. Bring a large pot of salted water to a boil. Working in batches, cook spinach, beans, sprouts, carrots, and cabbage until just tender, 30 seconds to 1 minute for

spinach, beans, and sprouts and 2–3 minutes for carrots and cabbage. Using a slotted spoon, transfer vegetables to a bowl of ice water until chilled; drain, spread on paper towels to dry, and transfer to a large platter. Add potatoes, tofu, and cucumber. Top with dressing, eggs, and shrimp chips, if using.

SENEGALESE AVOCADO-MANGO SALAD
SERVES 4–6

The creamy avocado, sweet mango, and bright citrus in this Senegalese salad come together to create a fresh counterpoint to the country's rich and savory stews.

- ½ cup finely chopped fresh flat-leaf parsley
- ¼ cup peanut or canola oil
- ¼ cup fresh lime juice
- 2 tbsp. fresh orange juice
- 1 jalapeño, stemmed, seeded, and minced
  Kosher salt and freshly ground black pepper, to taste
- 2 ripe mangoes, peeled, pitted, and cut into ¼" cubes
- 2 ripe avocados, peeled, pitted, and cut into 1" chunks
- 1 small navel orange, peeled and cut into segments
- 2 tsp. unsweetened shredded dried coconut

1 Whisk together 6 tbsp. parsley, peanut oil, lime and orange juices, jalapeño, salt, and pepper in a large bowl. Add mangoes and avocados and toss gently to combine. Cover with plastic wrap and refrigerate to meld flavors, about 1 hour.

2 To serve, transfer avocado salad to a serving bowl; halve orange segments crosswise and lay over salad. Sprinkle with remaining parsley and with coconut. Serve chilled.

CHERRY & HERB SALAD
SERVES 4–6

This sweet-tart cherry, cilantro, and walnut salad came to us as an Israeli riff on a classic Turkish recipe. It's delicious on its own, or as a relish for grilled meats or fish.

- 2 red Holland or Fresno chiles
- 1 lb. dark cherries, pitted
- 1 cup fresh cilantro leaves
- ½ cup walnut halves, toasted and roughly chopped
- 3 tbsp. extra-virgin olive oil

1½   tbsp. pomegranate molasses
1   tbsp. fresh lemon juice
    Kosher salt and freshly ground black pepper,
    to taste

1 Heat broiler. Place chiles on a baking sheet and broil, turning as needed, until charred and tender, 4–5 minutes.

2 Transfer to a bowl, cover with plastic wrap, and let sit for 5 minutes. Discard stems, skin, and seeds from chiles; finely chop and transfer to a bowl. Add cherries, cilantro, walnuts, oil, molasses, lemon juice, salt, and pepper; toss to combine. Serve chilled or at room temperature.

GREEN BEAN & PEACH SALAD

SERVES 6–8

Summer peaches pair remarkably well with sweet caramelized onions and crisp green beans in this summer salad, shared with us by Deb Miller, a home cook in Lawrence, Kansas. She serves it at an annual potluck held at the former home of writer William S. Burroughs.

½   cup olive oil
1   medium onion, thinly sliced
1   lb. firm-ripe yellow peaches, pitted and sliced
1   tbsp. finely chopped fresh oregano
2   tbsp. white balsamic vinegar
    Kosher salt and freshly ground black pepper
2   lb. green beans, trimmed

1 Heat 3 tbsp. oil in a 12″ skillet over medium-high heat. Add onion and cook until slightly caramelized, 7–10 minutes. Stir in peaches and oregano and cook until peaches are soft, 5–7 minutes. Whisk remaining oil with vinegar, salt, and pepper in a large bowl; add onion and peaches.

2 Bring a 6-qt. saucepan of salted water to a boil. Add beans and cook until crisp-tender, 1–2 minutes. Transfer to a bowl of ice water until chilled. Drain, add to peach mixture, and toss to combine.

ROJAK

Pineapple & Jicama Salad

SERVES 4

Rojak is a colloquial expression that means "eclectic mix" in Malay, the national language of Malaysia, where this dish originated.

½   tbsp. belacan (Malaysian dried shrimp paste)
6   tbsp. gula jawa (Indonesian palm sugar)
5   tbsp. kecap manis (Indonesian sweet soy sauce)
2   tbsp. fresh lime juice
3–6   red bird's eye chiles, stemmed and coarsely
    chopped
    Kosher salt, to taste
2   Kirby cucumbers, cut into 2″ chunks
1   medium green (unripe) mango, peeled, cored,
    and cut into 2″ chunks
1   small jicama (about ¾ lb.), peeled and cut
    into 2″ chunks
½   large, ripe pineapple, peeled, cored, and cut
    into 2″ chunks
⅓   cup unsalted roasted peanuts, finely chopped

1 Wrap shrimp paste in a 5″-square piece of aluminum foil to form a package; press down with the heel of your hand to flatten paste into a ¼″-thick disk. Heat a gas burner to medium-low or an electric burner to medium-high, place package directly on burner, and toast until paste begins to smoke, about 1 minute. Turn with tongs and cook for 1 minute more. Unwrap disk and let cool.

2 Put shrimp paste, sugar, soy sauce, lime juice, chiles, and salt into a blender; pulse to form a smooth paste. Transfer dressing to a large nonreactive bowl, add cucumbers, mango, jicama, and pineapple and toss to combine. Season with salt. (Alternatively, arrange on a plate and drizzle with dressing.) Transfer salad to a platter, sprinkle with peanuts, and serve immediately.

BURMESE GINGER SALAD

SERVES 4

Freshly pickled ginger adds a subtle heat and a welcome brightness to this salad, which combines crispy shallots, fried chickpeas, and crunchy peanuts.

1   3″ piece young fresh ginger, peeled and thinly
    sliced lengthwise
    Kosher salt, to taste
    Juice of 2 limes
2   tbsp. dried small chickpeas
½   cup peanut oil
10   shallots, thinly sliced
6   cloves garlic, thinly sliced
½   tsp. fish sauce
¼   cup unsalted roasted peanuts
2   tsp. sesame seeds, toasted
4   green bird's eye chiles, stemmed

1 Toss ginger and 1 tsp. salt together in a medium glass or ceramic bowl, cover with plastic wrap, and refrigerate for 24 hours, stirring every 8 hours. Rinse ginger, drain well, and put into a clean glass or ceramic bowl. Add lime juice and mix with your fingers until ginger is well coated. Cover with plastic wrap and refrigerate for 24 hours, stirring every 8 hours. Soak chickpeas in a small bowl of water for 8 hours.

2 Drain ginger, then slice into long, thin strips. Put ginger into a clean glass or ceramic bowl and set aside. Drain chickpeas, thoroughly dry with paper towels, and set aside.

3 Heat oil in a wok or a large heavy-bottomed skillet over medium heat. Add shallots and fry, stirring constantly with a slotted spoon, until lightly golden and crisp, 6–8 minutes. Transfer shallots with slotted spoon to paper towels to drain. Fry garlic in the hot oil, stirring constantly, until it just begins to to turn golden around the edges, 1–2 minutes, then transfer to paper towels to drain. Fry chickpeas in the hot oil, stirring constantly, until golden, 4–5 minutes, then transfer to paper towels to drain, setting wok with oil aside. Set shallots, ginger, and chickpeas aside separately to cool completely.

4 Add fish sauce, peanuts, sesame seeds, and chiles to bowl with ginger. Add fried shallots, garlic, and chickpeas and 2 tsp. of the frying oil, season to taste with salt, and toss well. Adjust seasonings. Serve at room temperature.

COOK'S NOTE We recommend using young ginger, which has very thin, delicate, pinkish skin and is more succulent than mature ginger. Young ginger is easiest to find in markets during the spring; if it's not available, use the smaller knobs of only very fresh mature ginger.

LEMONGRASS SALAD
Yum Takrai
SERVES 4

Cooks in southern Thailand adore the crunchy texture and intensely citrusy flavor of fresh lemongrass. This salad displays lemongrass at its best.

15	stalks lemongrass, trimmed and sliced into rings
¼	cup finely chopped fresh ginger
2	tbsp. cashews, toasted
2	tbsp. whole dried shrimp
1½	tbsp. nam pla (Thai fish sauce)
1½	tbsp. fresh lime juice
1½	tbsp. sugar
1	tbsp. whole dried shrimp, finely ground
4–6	red bird's eye chiles, stemmed and thinly sliced
2	shallots, very thinly sliced lengthwise
3	long beans or green beans, trimmed and cut into 4″ pieces, for garnish

Place lemongrass in a medium bowl; separate rings with your fingers. Add ginger, cashews, whole shrimp, fish sauce, lime juice, sugar, ground shrimp, chiles, and shallots and toss well. Garnish with long beans.

CELERY ROOT RÉMOULADE
SERVES 6–8

This Parisian bistro salad of crisp, raw celery root tossed in a briny mustard aïoli makes for a quick and elegant side dish.

3	tbsp. Dijon mustard
3	egg yolks
1½	cups canola oil
¼	tsp. cayenne pepper
	Juice of 2 lemons
3	lb. celery root, peeled and cut into ⅛″-thick matchsticks
1	tbsp. minced Kalamata olives
	Kosher salt and freshly ground black pepper, to taste
¼	cup thinly sliced fresh flat-leaf parsley

Whisk together mustard and yolks in a bowl; while whisking constantly, slowly drizzle in oil, a few drops at a time, to emulsify. Continue slowly streaming oil into bowl and whisking until a smooth mayonnaise forms. Stir in cayenne and juice. Add celery root, olives, and salt and pepper and toss to coat. Cover with plastic wrap and chill until celery root wilts slightly, about 40 minutes. Stir in parsley before serving.

ICEBERG SLAW
SERVES 4–6

This crunchy slaw isn't weighed down by a mayonnaise-based dressing. Instead, earthy coriander seeds are toasted and whisked into a mustard vinaigrette subtly sweetened by honey and tossed with iceberg lettuce, onions, and carrots. Make this slaw just before serving, so that the lettuce is as crisp as possible.

2 tsp. coriander seeds

6 tbsp. extra-virgin olive oil

2 tbsp. cider vinegar

2 tsp. honey

1 tsp. Dijon mustard
   Kosher salt and freshly ground black pepper,
   to taste

2 medium carrots, peeled and julienned

½ head iceberg lettuce, cored, halved,
   and thinly sliced

¼ red onion, thinly sliced

Put coriander into a skillet over medium heat. Toast, swirling, for 2 minutes. Transfer coriander to a medium bowl and whisk in oil, vinegar, honey, and mustard until smooth. Season with salt and pepper. Add carrots, lettuce, and onions and toss. Serve immediately.

CLASSIC COLESLAW

SERVES 12

This platonic ideal of a dinner-style coleslaw recipe—meeting the necessary requirements of shredded green cabbage, julienned carrots, and a mayonnaise dressing—demands to be served next to a perfectly grilled burger.

1 medium head green cabbage, cored
   and finely shredded

2 small carrots, peeled and shredded

2 ribs celery, minced

½ red onion, minced

½ tsp. kosher salt

½ tsp. sugar

½ cup mayonnaise

Put cabbage, carrots, celery, red onion, salt, sugar, and mayonnaise into a large bowl and toss until well combined. Adjust seasonings. Cover and refrigerate until well chilled.

COOK'S NOTE You can use a food processor to shred cabbage, but hand shredding, though time-consuming and old-fashioned, produces crunchier slaw.

GERMAN COLESLAW

SERVES 6–8

In Milwaukee, coleslaw is an essential component of the traditional Friday-night fish fry. We enjoyed this crisp German-style slaw, dressed with a sweet vinaigrette, at the Historic Turner Restaurant, a former German-American meeting place and gymnasium.

FOR THE DRESSING

⅓ cup white vinegar

1 tsp. dry mustard

½ tsp. celery seeds

⅓ cup sugar

½ cup vegetable oil
   Kosher salt, to taste

FOR THE COLESLAW

½ medium head green cabbage, cored
   and thinly sliced

1 small head red cabbage, cored
   and thinly sliced

1 small carrot, peeled and coarsely grated

1 Make the dressing: Put the vinegar, mustard, and celery seeds into a medium bowl and whisk to combine. Add the sugar and whisk vigorously until dissolved. Pour in oil in a thin stream while whisking constantly, until it is well combined with other ingredients and a smooth dressing has formed. Season with salt and set aside.

2 Make the coleslaw: Put the green and red cabbages and carrots into a large bowl. Add the dressing and toss well to combine. Store the coleslaw in the refrigerator until ready to use, up to 1 day. Serve chilled.

HAWAIIAN-STYLE RAMEN CABBAGE SALAD

SERVES 4–6

Cabbage salads featuring crushed instant ramen noodles are a staple of Hawaiian home cooking. The noodles add crunch, texture, and sweetness to this terrifically versatile slaw. As the salad sits and the noodles soak up the sesame dressing, they soften slightly, so be sure to serve this salad straightaway.

1 large head green cabbage, shredded
   into ¼" ribbons

6–8 scallions, thinly sliced

¼ cup mirin

¼ cup rice vinegar

2 tbsp. sugar

½ tbsp. kosher salt

½ tsp. white pepper

¼ cup sesame oil

¼ cup vegetable oil

¼ cup white sesame seeds, toasted

¼ cup black sesame seeds

1 package instant ramen noodles, crushed
   lightly (save seasoning packet for another use)

In a large bowl, combine cabbage and scallions. In a medium bowl, whisk together mirin, vinegar, sugar, salt, and white pepper. Combine sesame and vegetable oils in a separate vessel and slowly add to mirin mixture, whisking steadily, until all oil is added and dressing has emulsified. Add vinaigrette to the bowl of cabbage and scallions, then add both types of sesame seeds and crushed ramen noodles. Toss to combine and serve immediately.

CLASSIC POTATO SALAD

SERVES 4–6

This cool, creamy potato salad is our take on the backyard barbecue staple, spiked with pickle relish and red onion.

- 2 lb. small Yukon gold potatoes, peeled and quartered
- 2 ribs celery, minced
- ½ medium red onion, minced
- ½ cup mayonnaise
- 2 tbsp. dill pickle relish
- 2 tbsp. finely chopped fresh flat-leaf parsley
- 1 tbsp. yellow mustard
- 1 tsp. kosher salt
  Freshly ground black pepper, to taste
- 2 hard-cooked eggs, chopped

Put potatoes in a 6-qt. pot and cover with salted water by 2″. Bring to a boil over medium-high heat, reduce to medium, and gently boil until just tender, about 12 minutes. Drain and transfer to a large bowl along with celery and onions. In a small bowl, whisk together mayonnaise, relish, parsley, mustard, salt, and pepper; add to potatoes along with eggs and toss. Chill before serving.

GERMAN POTATO SALAD

Kartoffelsalat

SERVES 4–6

The potatoes in this salad are tossed in a rich and piquant vinaigrette made from rendered bacon fat. With sweet onions and crisp bacon, it's an irresistible side dish.

- 6–8 medium waxy potatoes, peeled and quartered
  Kosher salt and freshly ground black pepper
- 12 thick slices bacon
- 1 large yellow onion, thinly sliced

- 6 tbsp. white wine vinegar
- ¼ cup chopped fresh flat-leaf parsley

1 Put potatoes in a 6-qt. pot and cover with salted water by 2″. Bring to a boil over medium-high heat, reduce to medium, and gently boil until just tender, about 12 minutes.

2 Meanwhile, cook bacon in a large skillet over medium heat until crisp, 10–15 minutes. Drain on paper towels, setting skillet with rendered fat aside. Crumble bacon into large pieces.

3 Drain potatoes and transfer to a large warm serving bowl and add bacon and onions. Return skillet with bacon fat to medium-high heat until hot. Carefully add vinegar and salt and pepper to taste. Pour hot dressing over potato mixture and toss well. Garnish with parsley. Serve warm.

NORTH AFRICAN POTATO SALAD

SERVES 4–6

Bright and aromatic with plenty of fresh parsley, this potato salad is a terrific accompaniment to grilled chicken or lamb.

- 1 lb. new potatoes, scrubbed
- ¾ cup minced fresh flat-leaf parsley
- 1 small red onion, minced
- 1 clove garlic, minced
- 1 tbsp. extra-virgin olive oil
  Kosher salt and freshly ground black pepper, to taste

1 Put potatoes in a 4-qt. pot and cover with salted water by 2″. Bring to a boil over medium-high heat, reduce to medium, and gently boil until tender, about 18 minutes. Drain potatoes and let cool.

2 Combine parsley, red onion, garlic, and oil in a medium bowl. Season with salt and pepper. Peel potatoes, then coarsely chop; add to dressing and mix. Serve at room temperature.

Starter Salads

BABY BEETS WITH HERB SALAD & WARM CHÈVRE TOASTS

SERVES 6

Beets and goat cheese make a classic pair; the combination began showing up in force on restaurant menus in the 1990s, often in elegant first-course preparations such as this one.

30	baby beets, preferably of assorted colors, trimmed, rinsed, and patted dry
8–9	tbsp. fruity extra-virgin olive oil
	Sea salt and freshly ground black pepper, to taste
6	thin slices walnut bread (not sweet)
2–3	tbsp. champagne vinegar
1	medium shallot, minced
3	¼-lb. logs soft goat cheese, halved
6	oz. (about 7 cups) mixed baby salad greens
5	fresh chives, coarsely chopped
	Leaves from 5 sprigs fresh chervil
	Leaves from 3 sprigs fresh tarragon
	Small sprigs from 2 stems fresh dill
	Leaves from 2 sprigs fresh flat-leaf parsley
	Pinch sugar

1 Heat oven to 400°. Toss beets with 1 tbsp. oil and salt, transfer to a large sheet of foil, and fold foil edges together, tightly sealing packet. Roast beets until soft, 30–60 minutes, depending on size of beets. Meanwhile, spread bread slices on a baking sheet, drizzle with 1 tbsp. oil, and lightly toast in the oven. Set toast aside.

2 Unwrap beets, peel, and cut in half. Toss beets with vinegar, shallots, salt, and pepper in a bowl and marinate for 1 hour. Put cheese on a plate, drizzle with 4 tbsp. oil, season with pepper, and marinate for 1 hour.

3 Put 1 piece cheese on each piece of toast, setting plate of oil aside, and heat in 400° oven until warm, 6–8 minutes.

4 Put salad greens, chives, chervil, tarragon, dill, parsley, remaining 2–3 tbsp. oil, sugar, salt, and pepper into a bowl and toss well. Add beets and toss again. Adjust seasonings. Divide salad among 6 plates. Drizzle reserved marinating oil over cheese toasts, then divide toasts among the plates.

SICILIAN FENNEL SALAD WITH ORANGES, ARUGULA & BLACK OLIVES

SERVES 4

In Sicily, this salad is traditionally prepared with wild chicory, a slightly peppery, tender-leaved green. Substitute arugula or dandelion leaves if you can't find wild chicory.

3	navel oranges
¼	cup extra-virgin olive oil
1	tbsp. red wine vinegar
	Kosher salt and freshly ground black pepper, to taste
2	bunches wild chicory, arugula, or dandelion leaves, trimmed
2	medium fennel bulbs, trimmed and halved
¼	cup oil-cured black olives

Trim off and discard peel and all of the white pith from oranges, then slice crosswise into thin rounds and set aside. Mix together oil and vinegar in a large salad bowl, then season with salt and pepper. Tear arugula into large pieces, slice fennel into long, narrow strips, and arrange them in the bowl. Just before serving, toss salad, adjust seasonings, and arrange orange slices and olives on top.

CAVOLO NERO SALAD WITH PECORINO

SERVES 4

Freshly toasted bread crumbs add depth to this lemony, garlicky salad of *cavolo nero,* a dark, slightly bitter variety of kale.

1	cup coarse fresh bread crumbs
2	tbsp. unsalted butter, melted
	Kosher salt and freshly ground black pepper, to taste
1	clove garlic, chopped
3	tbsp. extra-virgin olive oil, plus more for drizzling
2	tbsp. fresh lemon juice
⅛	tsp. crushed red chile flakes
¼	cup grated pecorino romano
1	lb. cavolo nero or flat-leafed kale, trimmed and thinly sliced

1 Heat oven to 400°. Toss bread crumbs with butter, salt, and pepper. Spread on a baking sheet and toast until golden, 5–7 minutes. Let cool.

2 Sprinkle a little salt over garlic, mash with the side of a knife to make a paste, and transfer to a bowl. Whisk in oil, lemon juice, chile flakes, and salt and pepper. Stir in cheese to make a dressing.

3 Add cavolo nero to dressing and toss. Sprinkle with bread crumbs and more pecorino and finish with a drizzle of oil.

KALE & AVOCADO SALAD

SERVES 4–6

Creamy avocado is enlivened with a citrus dressing and tossed with hearty kale and hemp seeds in this dish from now-shuttered Elf restaurant in Echo Park, Los Angeles.

- ½ cup fresh orange juice
- 3 tbsp. fresh lemon juice
- 2 tsp. soy sauce
- 1 clove garlic, smashed and chopped into a paste
- 4 tbsp. extra-virgin olive oil
- 3 avocados, pitted and peeled
- 2 tbsp. raw hemp seeds (optional)
- 1 bunch kale, stemmed and finely chopped
  Kosher salt and freshly ground black pepper

1 Whisk together orange and lemon juices, soy sauce, and garlic in a bowl. Slowly whisk in oil; set dressing aside.

2 Cut 2 avocados into ½″ cubes and thinly slice the remaining avocado. Put cubed avocados, half of the hemp seeds (if using), and kale into a serving bowl. Toss kale mixture with dressing and season generously with salt and pepper. Divide salad among plates and garnish with sliced avocado and remaining hemp seeds.

CAESAR SALAD

SERVES 2 (SEE PHOTO, PAGE 210)

The origins of the Caesar salad are a matter of much dispute. But the most widely accepted version traces it back to Caesar Cardini, an Italian restaurateur who was working in Tijuana, Mexico, when he came up with the recipe in the 1920s. The salad, a mixture of lettuce, croutons, cheese, a garlicky egg-based vinaigrette, and

A LIFELONG LOVE

❝At nine years old, the closest I'd come to cooking was upending a box of Cap'n Crunch into a bowl. One Sunday, I found myself glued to *The French Chef;* Julia Child was making Caesar salad. It seemed like the best thing I could possibly eat. I asked my dad for permission to make it. As luck would have it, we had the ingredients. With my chicken-scratched notes, I assembled it. By God, it was good: the tang of the parmesan and lemon, the sweet flash of the Worcestershire, the mellow egg, all draped upon an interplay of romaine and crouton crunches. It's been 40 years, and I could still eat it every day. Caesar salad is that perfect.❞

JAMES OSELAND

other ingredients, is quite simple, so the quality of the ingredients is paramount.

- 1½ cups olive oil
- 3 cloves garlic, smashed
- ½ lb. day-old crusty Italian or French white bread, cut into 1″ cubes
- 1 tbsp. fresh lemon juice
- 1½ tsp. Worcestershire sauce
- ½ tsp. Tabasco sauce
- 4 oil-packed anchovy filets, drained and roughly chopped
  Kosher salt and freshly ground black pepper, to taste
- ¾ lb. whole romaine lettuce leaves, inner leaves only
- 1 egg, lightly beaten
- 1 cup finely grated Parmigiano-Reggiano

1 Heat 1 cup oil and 1 garlic clove in a 12″ skillet over medium heat. Add bread and cook, tossing often, until golden brown and crisp, about 5 minutes. Transfer to paper towels to drain and set aside.

2 Rub remaining garlic over inside of a large wooden serving bowl and leave in bowl. Add lemon juice, Worcestershire, hot sauce, anchovies, salt, and pepper and whisk until anchovies break down. Add remaining oil and whisk just until blended. Add lettuce leaves and toss to coat in dressing. Drizzle egg over leaves and toss again until evenly coated. Add reserved croutons, Parmigiano, salt, and pepper, and toss until evenly combined. Serve immediately.

CANLIS SALAD

SERVES 4

This rich salad, reminiscent of a Caesar, is full of bright flavors from fresh herbs and savory depth from bacon and pecorino. It comes from—and is still served at—the eponymous Seattle restaurant, where it's been on the menu since 1950.

FOR THE CROUTONS

- 2 tbsp. unsalted butter, melted
- 1 tsp. dried oregano
- 1 tsp. dried thyme
- 4 slices country white bread, cut into ½″ cubes
- 1 clove garlic, finely chopped
  Kosher salt and freshly ground black pepper, to taste

FOR THE DRESSING

- 1 egg, at room temperature
- ¼ cup fresh lemon juice
- ¼ cup extra-virgin olive oil
  Kosher salt and freshly ground black pepper, to taste

FOR THE SALAD

- ½ lb. slab bacon, cut into ½″ cubes
- 1 cup grated pecorino cheese
- 1 cup mixed red and yellow grape tomatoes, halved
- ½ cup torn fresh mint leaves
- 3 tbsp. fresh oregano leaves
- 5 scallions, chopped
- 2 heads romaine ettuce, cored and cut crosswise into
  1″ strips

1 Make the croutons: Heat oven to 325°. Toss butter, oregano, thyme, bread, and garlic together in a large bowl and season with salt and pepper. Spread on a baking sheet and toast, stirring frequently, until croutons are golden, about 15 minutes. Let croutons cool.

2 Make the dressing: Whisk together egg and lemon juice in a medium bowl. Slowly drizzle in oil, whisking constantly to make a smooth vinaigrette. Season with salt and pepper; set aside.

3 In a 10″ skillet, bring 1 cup water to a boil. Add bacon and cook, stirring occasionally, until water evaporates, about 10 minutes. Reduce heat to medium and cook until bacon crisps, about 5 minutes; let cool. Toss bacon, croutons, cheese, tomatoes, mint, scallions, and romaine lettuce with vinaigrette in a salad bowl and season with salt and pepper.

FATTOUSH

Green Salad with Toasted Pita Bread

SERVES 6

This bread salad, packed with cucumbers, fresh mint, and parsley, is a favorite throughout the Levant.

- 2 small rounds pita bread
- ½ cup plus 2 tbsp. extra-virgin olive oil
- 1 clove garlic, peeled
- 2 tsp. fresh lemon juice
  Kosher salt and freshly ground black pepper, to taste
- 2 medium cucumbers, peeled, seeded, and coarsely chopped
- ½ heart romaine lettuce, coarsely chopped
- 3 tbsp. coarsely chopped fresh mint
- 3 tbsp. coarsely chopped fresh flat-leaf parsley

1 Heat oven to 400°. Split open pita rounds. Cut each into wedges. Toss pita with 2 tbsp. oil, then place in a single layer on a baking sheet and toast until crisp, about 5 minutes. Let cool.

2 Rub a large salad bowl with garlic clove, then discard. Combine lemon juice and remaining ½ cup oil in a bowl. Season dressing with salt and pepper. Place cucumber, lettuce, mint, and parsley in a salad bowl. Add pita crisps and dressing and toss gently. Serve immediately.

BLUE CHEESE WEDGE SALAD

SERVES 4

While most iceberg wedge salads wear a blue cheese dressing, the one at Anthony's Steakhouse in Omaha, Nebraska—one of the best we've tried—is decadently adorned with both blue cheese *and* Italian dressings.

- 1 head iceberg lettuce, cored and quartered
- 20 grape or cherry tomatoes
- ½ cucumber, thinly sliced crosswise
- 1 small red onion, thinly sliced into rings

Italian Dressing (page 74)
Blue Cheese Dressing (page 76)
⅓ cup crumbled blue cheese
Fresh flat-leaf parsley, for garnish

Divide iceberg quarters, tomatoes, and cucumber among 4 plates. Top with onion rings and drizzle with Italian dressing. Sprinkle blue cheese over top and spoon over blue cheese dressing. Garnish with parsley.

GRILLED ROMAINE SALAD WITH BLUE CHEESE & BACON

SERVES 4–6

Fresh heads of romaine lettuce are exquisite when split down the middle, grilled until charred and smoky, and then topped with blue cheese and bacon in this salad served to us at a summer feast on a ranch in California's Central Valley.

6 slices bacon
2 tbsp. extra-virgin olive oil

THE ORIGINS OF ICEBERG

Like any field, the science of plant breeding has its own pantheon of superstars. Foremost among them is Edward J. Ryder, the inventor of the most popular variety of the most popular lettuce in the world. If you've got a head of crisp iceberg lettuce in your fridge, chances are it's a kind called Salinas, and it's better than the iceberg your grandparents ate: it's more compact, it lasts longer, it has more flavor, and it comes in a greater range of colors and textures, from its dark green and supple outer leaves to its crunchy, pale yellow ones. Ryder, who was a Bronx-born plant geneticist with the U.S. Department of Agriculture, came up with this hardy hybrid in 1975, building on a legacy of crossbreeding that can be traced back to the very first iceberg variety, developed by Burpee in 1894. Today Salinas is grown all over the world, both conventionally and organically. "I try to be as humble as I can, but Salinas was sensational," Ryder says. "Few breeds take off like Salinas has. It made my reputation."

---

2 tbsp. balsamic vinegar
2 tbsp. Worcestershire sauce
5 heads romaine lettuce, halved lengthwise
1 cup red grape tomatoes, halved
Kosher salt and freshly ground black pepper, to taste
¼ lb. blue cheese, crumbled

1 Heat bacon in a 12″ skillet over medium heat and cook, turning once, until crisp and fat is rendered, about 10 minutes. Transfer bacon to a plate, reserving 2 tbsp. drippings, and let cool; crumble and set aside. Transfer reserved drippings to a bowl and add oil, vinegar, and Worcestershire; whisk until smooth and set dressing aside.

2 Build a medium-hot fire in a charcoal grill, or heat a gas grill to medium-high. (Alternatively, heat a cast-iron grill pan over medium-high heat.) Working in batches, if necessary, place romaine halves, cut side down, on grill and cook, turning once, until charred and slightly wilted, about 4 minutes.

3 Transfer lettuce, cut side up, to a serving platter, and scatter with tomatoes. Season with salt and pepper, drizzle with dressing, and sprinkle with reserved bacon and with blue cheese.

MIXED GREEN SALAD WITH SICHUAN PEPPERCORNS

SERVES 4

This salad, a staple on the menu at the restaurant Chase's Daily in Belfast, Maine, uses the heat of pink-hued Sichuan peppercorns to its best advantage by offsetting it with fresh herbs, fresh orange juice, and sesame oil.

1½ tbsp. finely chopped fresh ginger
1 tbsp. tamari
1 tbsp. rice vinegar
2 tbsp. sesame oil
2 tbsp. extra-virgin olive oil
2 tbsp. fresh orange juice
1 tsp. chile oil
1 tsp. Sichuan peppercorns
6 cups loosely packed mixed Asian salad greens, like mizuna and tatsoi
3 cups thinly sliced napa cabbage
4 small red radishes, thinly sliced crosswise
3 radishes, quartered lengthwise

½ medium carrot, peeled and julienned
1 kohlrabi, cut into matchsticks
 Fresh Thai basil leaves, for garnish
 Fresh cilantro leaves, for garnish
 Fresh mint leaves, for garnish

1 Combine the ginger, tamari, vinegar, sesame oil, olive oil, orange juice, and chile oil in a small bowl.

2 Heat an 8″ skillet over medium heat. Add the peppercorns and cook, swirling the pan constantly, until the peppercorns are toasted and fragrant, about 1 minute. Transfer peppercorns to a spice grinder and grind into a fine powder. Whisk ground peppercorns into dressing.

3 In a large bowl, combine greens, cabbage, and vegetables and toss with the dressing. Serve the salad garnished with basil, cilantro, and mint.

SPINACH SALAD WITH
HOT BACON DRESSING
SERVES 4–6

A descendant of the sauce used in classic German potato salad (page 65), a rich and flavorful bacon dressing was used by German-Americans to coat dandelion greens during the 19th century (and perhaps before). The bitter greens were eventually supplanted by spinach, creating this hearty—and classic—salad, which is best served immediately after tossing, so the spinach is just wilted.

6 slices bacon, roughly chopped
2 shallots, finely chopped
⅓ cup malt vinegar
1 tbsp. Dijon mustard
2 tsp. sugar
 Kosher salt and freshly ground black pepper, to taste
1 lb. spinach, washed and trimmed
½ cup chopped fresh chives
2 tbsp. chopped fresh savory

1 Cook bacon in a small pot over medium-high heat, stirring often, until crisp, 8–10 minutes. Using a slotted spoon, transfer bacon to a paper towel–lined plate to drain.

2 Add shallots to pot with bacon fat and cook until just softened, 1–2 minutes. Whisk in vinegar, mustard, sugar, salt, and pepper. Continue whisking until heated, about 30 seconds. Pour immediately over spinach and toss. Sprinkle with bacon, chives, and savory and serve.

WARM CHANTERELLE
& PANCETTA SALAD
SERVES 4

Earthy chanterelle mushrooms are slightly caramelized with pine nuts and tossed with mixed greens in this warm Italian salad.

¼ lb. pancetta, diced
2 shallots, minced
½ lb. chanterelles, trimmed and quartered
¼ cup pine nuts
7 tbsp. extra-virgin olive oil
1 tbsp. fresh lemon juice
2 tbsp. red wine vinegar
6 cups mixed frisée, arugula, and Bibb lettuce
 Freshly ground black pepper, to taste

1 Cook pancetta in a medium sauté pan over low heat until crisp, about 20 minutes. Drain on paper towels and transfer to a large bowl. Pour off fat from pan (a thin film should remain). Increase heat to medium, add shallots to pan, and cook until tender, about 5 minutes.

2 Increase the heat to high, add chanterelles and pine nuts, and sauté until lightly browned, about 5 minutes. Transfer mixture to bowl with pancetta.

3 In the same pan, warm oil over medium heat, then whisk in lemon juice and vinegar and heat through, scraping up the flavorful browned bits from the bottom of the pan.

4 Add mixed greens to bowl with pancetta, chanterelles, and shallots. Add the warm vinaigrette and toss well. Divide among 4 plates and season with pepper.

NOPALES SALAD WITH
JALAPEÑO DRESSING
SERVES 4

Beneath the prickly exterior of *nopales*—prickly pear cactus pads—lies pure, delicious flavor that's fresh, crisp, and slightly acidic. They're an integral part of traditional Mexican cuisine—to the point where it's a prickly pear cactus that the eagle in the center of the Mexican flag is perched upon.

2 jalapeños, stemmed, seeded, and chopped
½ cup sour cream
⅓ cup fresh cilantro leaves, coarsely chopped
1 tbsp. fresh lime juice
 Pinch ground cumin

Kosher salt, to taste
4 medium nopales (prickly pear cactus pads)
1 tomatillo, husked and cored
1 small red onion, diced
½ red bell pepper, seeded and diced
1 ripe avocado

1 Purée jalapeños, sour cream, ¼ cup cilantro, lime juice, and cumin in a food processor until smooth. Transfer to a bowl, season with salt, cover, and refrigerate for 3 hours.

2 Place each cactus pad on a work surface, hold base with a kitchen towel, and shave off thorny bumps on each side with a sharp knife. Blanch cactus and tomatillo in a large pot of boiling salted water over high heat. Remove tomatillo when tender, after about 5 minutes, rinse in cold water, and transfer to a plate. Cook cactus until tender, about 5 minutes more, rinse in cold water, and transfer to plate. Cut cactus crosswise into ½"-wide strips and return to pot to cook for 2–3 minutes to remove excess slime. Drain cactus, rinse in cold water, and dry with paper towels. Transfer cactus to a bowl. Dice tomatillo and add to bowl. Add onions and peppers, season with salt, cover, and refrigerate for 3 hours.

3 To serve, halve avocado, discard pit and peel, and thinly slice lengthwise. Toss together avocado, cactus mixture, dressing, and salt in a serving bowl. Garnish with remaining cilantro.

PARSLEY & ONION SALAD
SERVES 4 (SEE PHOTO, PAGE 211)

Chef Jeremiah Tower rose to fame in the 1980s thanks to his San Francisco restaurant Stars, a pulpit from which he evangelized for the bright, lucid flavors of Californian produce. This salad—a mélange of mint, red onions, parsley, capers, and lemon juice, served atop grilled bread—epitomizes his culinary philosophy.

2 tbsp. finely chopped mint
1 large red onion, halved and thinly sliced lengthwise
Kosher salt and freshly ground black pepper, to taste
2 cups loosely packed fresh flat-leaf parsley leaves
¼ cup salt-packed capers, rinsed and drained
¼ cup extra-virgin olive oil
2 tbsp. fresh lemon juice
1 tbsp. lemon zest
4 slices grilled country white bread, cut into quarters, to serve

In a medium bowl, toss together mint, onion, salt, and pepper; let sit until onion softens, about 10 minutes. Add parsley, capers, oil, lemon juice, and lime zest and toss until evenly combined. Serve immediately piled on top of grilled bread.

RADISH & ORANGE SALAD
SERVES 4

Fragrant orange flower water, called *ilma zhar* in Morocco, is made from the blossoms of bergamot orange trees. It perfumes this delicate salad in which sweet citrus is offset by peppery radish.

1–2 bunches red radishes, trimmed
1½ tbsp. sugar
1 tsp. orange flower water
1½ tbsp. fresh lemon juice
2 tbsp. fresh orange juice
Kosher salt, to taste
1 navel orange
Leaves from 2 sprigs fresh mint, for garnish

1 Shred radishes using a mandoline or food processor, or slice thinly and julienne. Place in a small bowl and sprinkle with sugar. Stir and set aside to macerate for 15 minutes. Drain off excess liquid. Cover and refrigerate until well chilled, about 20 minutes.

2 Just before serving, whisk together orange flower water, lemon juice, and orange juice in a small bowl and season with salt. Pour dressing over radishes and lightly toss.

3 Peel and section orange, removing any pith. (For a more elegant plating, slice orange into thin wheels or supremes.) Arrange orange sections over radishes and serve garnished with mint.

GREEK SALAD
Horiatiki
SERVES 2

This refreshing salad takes on various guises in Greece depending on what vegetables are in season, but it almost always features feta and a dusting of dried oregano. Classically, it's served without lettuce, though in the United States—particularly in Greek diners—you'll often find this preparation tossed with romaine.

2 tbsp. roughly chopped fresh flat-leaf parsley,
 plus more for garnish
2 medium tomatoes, cut into 1½″ pieces
1 small cucumber, peeled, halved lengthwise,
 and sliced crosswise into ¼″ pieces
½ medium onion, thinly sliced
3 tbsp. extra-virgin olive oil
1 tbsp. red wine vinegar
⅛ tsp. dried oregano, plus more for garnish
 Kosher salt and freshly ground black pepper,
 to taste
6 oz. feta, cut into thick slabs
8 Kalamata olives

Combine parsley, tomatoes, cucumbers, and onion in
a bowl. In a small bowl, whisk together oil, vinegar, and
oregano and season with salt and pepper. Pour over
cucumber mixture and toss. Transfer salad to a serving
bowl and top with feta and olives. Garnish with more
oregano and season with pepper.

ARUGULA SALAD WITH FRIED DOUGH
SERVES 2–4

Fried strips of tender pizza dough are tossed in a colorful
salad of marinated cherry tomatoes and arugula—a much
beloved menu item at Starita, a century-old pizza shop
in Naples, Italy.

⅓ cup extra-virgin olive oil
½ tsp. dried oregano
4 cloves garlic, thinly sliced
1 pint cherry or grape tomatoes, halved
 (see Cutting Grape Tomatoes, above)
 Kosher salt and freshly ground black pepper,
 to taste
 Canola oil, for frying
1 12-oz. ball Naples-Style Pizza Dough
 (page 136)
 Fine semolina flour, for dusting
4½ cups baby arugula

1 Mix olive oil, oregano, garlic, tomatoes, salt, and pepper
in a bowl and set aside.

2 Pour enough canola oil into a 6-qt. saucepan to reach a
depth of 2″. Heat until a deep-fry thermometer reads 350°.
Dust dough with semolina, then roll dough into a 4″×9″
rectangle about ⅓″ thick. Cut dough into ½″×2″ strips.
Fry strips until puffed and golden, 3–4 minutes. Drain.

3 Toss fried dough with tomatoes and their juices, arugula,
salt, and pepper. Divide among bowls and serve.

CUTTING GRAPE TOMATOES

Halved grape tomatoes bring sweetness and
color to many dishes, including Arugula Salad with
Fried Dough (this page) and the bacon-studded
Canlis Salad (page 68). Slicing the tiny orbs,
however, can be time-consuming. So, instead
of halving them individually, we use an ingenious
restaurant trick to slice a dozen in the time
it would normally take to slice one.

In the shallow plastic lid of a take-out container,
arrange grape tomatoes on their sides so that
they're arrayed snugly. Place another, identical
lid, upside down over the tomatoes; hold the top
lid down firmly. Using smooth, strong horizontal
motions, pass a sharp chef's knife between the
lids, slicing through the tomatoes as you go.
Remove the top lid and, *voilà*, your work is done.

COOKED & RAW WINTER SALAD
SERVES 6–8

Frozen peas and lima beans can have nearly as much
sweetness and flavor as their fresh counterparts, lending a
bit of summer to this cold-weather salad. It can be adapted
for just about any assortment of vegetables, fresh or frozen,
but we particularly like the balance in this version, which
creates an enticing contrast of flavors and textures.

6 slices bacon, roughly chopped
½ cup olive oil
½ cup pine nuts
2 shallots, finely chopped
 Kosher salt and freshly ground black pepper
1 16-oz. package frozen lima beans
1 16-oz. package frozen peas
1 cup roughly chopped fresh mint
1 cup roughly chopped fresh flat-leaf parsley
⅓ cup grated Parmigiano-Reggiano
7 scallions, finely chopped
1 bunch watercress, roughly chopped
1 head Bibb lettuce, cored and torn into small pieces
1 medium bulb fennel, trimmed and finely chopped,
 plus ⅓ cup roughly chopped fronds, for garnish
⅓ cup fresh lemon juice

1 Heat bacon in a 12″ skillet over medium-high heat and
cook until crisp, about 6 minutes. Using a slotted spoon,
transfer bacon to paper towels to drain; set aside. Add

> **"Lettuce is like conversation; it must be fresh and crisp, so sparkling that you scarcely notice the bitter in it."**
>
> CHARLES DUDLEY WARNER

2 tbsp. oil to pan and return to medium-high heat. Add pine nuts, shallots, salt, and pepper and cook until shallots are soft, 2–4 minutes. Transfer mixture to a bowl; set aside.

2 Bring a large pot of salted water to a boil. Cook lima beans and peas until bright green, about 1 minute. Drain and transfer to a bowl of ice water. Drain and spread on paper towels to dry; transfer to bowl with pine nuts and shallots. Add reserved bacon, remaining 6 tbsp. oil, mint, parsley, half the Parmigiano, the scallions, watercress, lettuce, fennel and half the fronds, lemon juice, salt, and pepper; toss. Garnish with remaining Parmigiano and fennel fronds.

SALADE LYONNAISE

Frisée Salad with Poached Eggs & Bacon

SERVES 4

Slivers of bacon create a pleasing taste and textural contrast in this iconic French bistro salad. After serving, break the egg yolks and quickly toss the warm egg with the salad to add body and richness to the dressing.

- 5 ½"-thick slices bacon, sliced crosswise into ½"-wide strips
- 1 tbsp. white wine vinegar
- 4 eggs
- 1 tbsp. finely chopped shallots
- 1 tbsp. fresh lemon juice
- 2 tsp. Dijon mustard
- 2 tbsp. extra-virgin olive oil
   Kosher salt and freshly ground black pepper
- ½ lb. frisée lettuce, torn

1 Combine bacon and 1 cup water in a 12" skillet over medium-high heat. Cook, stirring, until water evaporates and bacon crisps, 10–15 minutes. Using a slotted spoon, transfer bacon to a plate. Reserve fat in skillet.

2 Prepare eggs for poaching: Bring a 4-qt. saucepan of water to a boil. Add vinegar and reduce heat to medium-low. Crack each egg into its own ramekin and set aside. (Don't cook the eggs yet.)

3 In a medium bowl, whisk together shallots, lemon juice, mustard, and 3 tbsp. reserved bacon fat. While whisking, slowly drizzle in oil to make a smooth vinaigrette. Season with salt and pepper. In a large bowl, toss frisée with vinaigrette. Divide frisée and bacon among 4 plates.

4 In the saucepan, swirl simmering water with a spoon to create a whirlpool effect. Slide 2 eggs into water; cook until just firm, about 2 minutes. Using a slotted spoon, top first 2 salads with 1 egg apiece; repeat with remaining eggs. Season salads with salt and pepper. Serve immediately.

THE SECRET TO CRISPY BACON

Water? Really! It may sound counterintuitive to plunge raw bacon in water and expect a crisp strip to emerge, but it does. Adding water in the beginning helps to keep the cooking temperature low and keeps the bacon moist. Once the water evaporates, the bacon fat has already been rendered (read: no splattering hot oil), and at this point you're less likely to turn your bacon into dry, crumbly strips. Here's how to do it: In a 12" skillet, bring 1 cup water to a boil. Add bacon and cook, stirring occasionally, until water evaporates, about 10 minutes. Reduce heat to medium and cook until bacon crisps, about 5 minutes; let cool.

Dressings

ITALIAN DRESSING

MAKES ABOUT 2 CUPS

You have no excuse for buying the bottled version of this popular salad dressing. Italian dressing is simply (and deliciously) a heavy helping of garlic, parsley, and oregano whisked into the delicate flavor of white wine vinegar and olive oil.

- ⅓ cup white wine vinegar
- 3 tbsp. finely chopped fresh flat-leaf parsley
- 1 tbsp. dried oregano
- 3 cloves garlic, finely chopped
  Kosher salt and freshly ground black pepper, to taste
- 1⅓ cups extra-virgin olive oil

Whisk vinegar, parsley, oregano, garlic, salt, and pepper in a bowl. While whisking, slowly drizzle in oil until emulsified. Dressing will keep refrigerated for up to 1 week.

LA VRAIE VINAIGRETTE

We got a favorite vinaigrette from a veteran French home cook, who told us the recipe in her own words: "Place a small clove of chopped garlic into a wooden salad bowl, add a pinch of coarse salt and some freshly ground black pepper, and use the back of a wooden salad spoon to mash them into a coarse paste. To this add Dijon mustard (about 1 tsp.) and some red wine vinegar (about 1 tbsp.), mix that around a bit, then pour in some good olive oil (about 4 tbsp.) and stir it all together. Let the vinaigrette sit there, in the bottom of the bowl, until just before dinner, then add the salad greens—some Bibb or leaf lettuce or curly endive and maybe a few fresh tarragon leaves. Bring the bowl to the table and toss the salad toward the end of the meal (so un-American!)."

BACON VINAIGRETTE

MAKES 2 CUPS

This salty and savory take on a vinaigrette incorporates bacon directly into the dressing and is fantastic drizzled over a simple caprese salad, as it's served at the Everyday People Cafe in Douglas, Michigan.

- ¾ lb. bacon, diced
- ½ cup chopped celery
- ½ cup honey
- ½ cup rice vinegar
- ½ cup sliced shallots
- ¼ cup roasted garlic
- 4 tbsp. fresh lemon juice
- ½ tbsp. Dijon mustard
- ¼ cup canola oil
  Kosher salt and freshly ground black pepper, to taste

1 Cook bacon in a 12″ skillet over medium heat until extremely crisp, about 8 minutes. Remove bacon pieces with a slotted spoon, reserving rendered fat.

2 In a food processor, process the crisp bacon, celery, honey, vinegar, shallots, garlic, lemon juice, and mustard until smooth. With the processor running, slowly add oil and the reserved bacon fat; season with salt and pepper. Dressing will keep refrigerated for up to 3 days.

OREGANO VINAIGRETTE

MAKES ½ CUP

This pungent vinaigrette gets body from anchovy, lemon, and plenty of garlic, all of which enhance oregano's dusty, herbal flavor. We like it served with greens like spinach or kale.

- ⅛ tsp. crushed red chile flakes
- 2 cloves garlic, peeled
- 1 oil-packed anchovy filet, drained
  Kosher salt and freshly ground black pepper, to taste
  Rind of ½ preserved lemon, roughly chopped
- ¼ cup loosely packed fresh oregano leaves

1½   tbsp. red wine vinegar

6   tbsp. extra-virgin olive oil

1 Combine the chile flakes, garlic, anchovy, and a pinch of salt in a mortar and smash with the pestle until ingredients are finely ground. Add the lemon and oregano and continue smashing until the oregano has broken down into tiny pieces. (Alternatively, put the garlic, anchovy, salt, lemon, and oregano on a cutting board, finely chop with a large knife, and transfer to a bowl; stir in chile flakes.)

2 Add vinegar, whisk in oil, and season with salt and pepper. Cover with plastic wrap and let vinaigrette sit for at least 30 minutes. Dressing will keep refrigerated for up to 3 days.

COOK'S NOTE To make this recipe vegetarian or vegan, omit the anchovy and replace with 1 tbsp. black olive tapenade.

CURRANDOOLEY DRESSING

MAKES 1 CUP

Tangy and bright, this simple Australian citronette can be used to dress any combination of mixed greens.

3   cloves garlic, peeled

1   tbsp. kosher salt

½   cup mild extra-virgin olive oil

     Freshly ground black pepper, to taste

½   cup Meyer lemon juice

1 Using a fork, crush garlic and coarse salt together in a small bowl until mixture is soft and moist, interspersed with large chunks of garlic. Gradually drizzle in oil while mixing vigorously with the fork. Add a generous sprinkling of pepper and continue to mix.

2 Whisk in lemon juice to make a smooth dressing. Strain dressing through a fine sieve, discard solids, and adjust the seasonings. Dressing will keep refrigerated for up to 1 week.

COOK'S NOTE We've made this dressing with juice from regular lemons, and the results were just as delicious, if a bit more tart.

CARROT-GINGER DRESSING

MAKES ABOUT 3 CUPS

This vibrantly orange dressing was made famous by Japanese-American steak houses. It gets its incomparably clean flavor from puréed carrot and fresh ginger. Serve it simply tossed with iceberg lettuce.

1   cup vegetable oil

½   cup rice vinegar

¼   cup soy sauce

1   tbsp. sugar

1½   tsp. finely grated fresh ginger

2   medium carrots (about ½ lb.), peeled and roughly chopped

½   medium yellow onion (about 6 oz.), roughly chopped

     Kosher salt and freshly ground black pepper, to taste

Combine all ingredients in a food processor and blend until smooth. Dressing will keep refrigerated for up to 2 weeks.

PONZU DRESSING

MAKES ABOUT 2 CUPS

This richly savory Japanese dressing takes two weeks to make, but the flavor is well worth the wait.

1   cup bottled ponzu sauce

1   cup soy sauce

½   cup mirin

½   cup rice vinegar

1   5″ piece kombu (dried kelp)

1   tbsp. katsuobushi (dried, smoked bonito flakes)

     Juice of ½ orange

1   tsp. chile oil, for serving

1   tsp. chile sauce, for serving

1 Combine ponzu sauce, soy sauce, mirin, vinegar, kombu, bonito flakes, and orange juice in a medium bowl. Cover with plastic wrap and transfer to the refrigerator to let mature for 2 weeks.

2 Strain ponzu mixture through a fine sieve into a clean 24-oz. glass jar with a tight-fitting lid and discard solids. (Dressing will keep, tightly sealed, for up to 3 months in the refrigerator.)

3 When ready to serve, whisk together chile oil, chile sauce, and ⅓ cup ponzu dressing. Toss with your favorite greens. Dressing will keep refrigerated for up to 1 week.

POPPY SEED DRESSING

MAKES ABOUT 2 CUPS

Popularized by Texas-based cookbook author Helen Corbitt in the 1950s, this sweet-tart dressing, enriched with poppy seeds, is perfect for a delicate lettuce such as butter or Bibb.

2 tbsp. poppy seeds
½ cup sugar
⅓ cup white wine vinegar
2 tsp. dry mustard
2 tsp. kosher salt
1 tsp. freshly ground black pepper
1 small onion, finely grated, juice reserved
¾ cup canola oil
¼ cup olive oil

Heat a 2-qt. saucepan over medium-high heat. Add poppy seeds and cook, swirling pan constantly, until lightly toasted and fragrant, about 3 minutes. Add sugar, vinegar, mustard, salt, pepper, and onion with juice and cook, stirring constantly, until sugar dissolves and mixture begins to simmer. Remove from heat and transfer to a blender. Add both oils and blend until smooth. Let cool. Dressing will keep refrigerated for up to 2 weeks.

GREEN GODDESS DRESSING

MAKES 2 CUPS

According to food authority Marion Cunningham, this exquisitely herbaceous dressing was created circa 1925 at San Francisco's Palace Hotel.

1 2-oz. can oil-packed anchovy filets
3 tbsp. chopped fresh chives
3 tbsp. tarragon vinegar
1 tbsp. fresh lemon juice
1 cup sour cream
1 cup mayonnaise
½ cup chopped fresh flat-leaf parsley
½ tsp. kosher salt
  Freshly ground black pepper, to taste

Combine all ingredients in a blender and blend until smooth. Cover and refrigerate until needed, up to 1 week.

LEMON OLIVE OIL

MAKES ABOUT 2 CUPS

Chef and writer Carla Hall shared this great trick with us: Throw a lemon—rind, pith, seeds, and all—into a blender with olive oil, blitz the heck out of it, and what do you get? A bright and bracing emulsion that's terrific in virtually everything: tossed with roasted potatoes, added to marinades, even mixed into pancake batter for some zip.

1 lemon, quartered
2 cups extra-virgin olive oil
  Kosher salt and freshly ground black pepper, to taste

Blend lemon and oil until emulsified; season with salt and pepper. Refrigerate in an airtight container for up to 3 weeks.

BLUE CHEESE DRESSING

MAKES ABOUT 1½ CUPS

This steak-house classic is extra creamy thanks to the addition of half-and-half, in addition to mayonnaise and sour cream.

⅓ cup crumbled blue cheese
¼ cup half-and-half
¼ cup mayonnaise
3 tbsp. sour cream
1 tbsp. fresh lemon juice
1 tsp. granulated garlic
½ tsp. onion powder
¼ tsp. celery seeds
  Kosher salt and freshly ground black pepper, to taste

Using a fork, stir together blue cheese, half-and-half, mayonnaise, sour cream, lemon juice, granulated garlic, onion powder, and celery seeds in a bowl. Season with salt and pepper. Dressing will keep refrigerated for up to 1 week.

THOUSAND ISLAND DRESSING

MAKES ABOUT 1 CUP

The invention of thousand island dressing is often attributed to Theo Rooms, a chef at the Blackstone Hotel in Chicago when it opened in 1910. Other accounts hold that the thick, satisfying condiment was devised on one of the Thousand Islands, in the St. Lawrence River in Canada. Wherever it originated, we like it best spooned over wedges of crisp iceberg lettuce.

1 cup mayonnaise
2 tbsp. bottled chile sauce
1 tbsp. finely chopped white onion
1 tbsp. finely chopped dill pickle
1 tbsp. finely chopped cooked beet
1 tbsp. finely chopped hard-cooked egg
1 tbsp. finely chopped fresh chives
1 tbsp. finely chopped pimientos
1 tbsp. finely chopped fresh flat-leaf parsley

½ tsp. Worcestershire sauce
   Kosher salt and freshly ground black pepper,
   to taste

Fold together mayonnaise, chile sauce, onion, pickle, beet, egg, chives, pimiento, parsley, and Worcestershire in a bowl with a rubber spatula. Season with salt and pepper. Dressing will keep refrigerated for up to 1 week.

RANCH DRESSING
MAKES ABOUT 1½ CUPS

Ranch dressing was originally sold by its inventor, Steve Henson, as a seasoning packet that contained, among other ingredients, dehydrated garlic, dehydrated onion, black pepper, and dried parsley; all cooks had to do was add mayonnaise and buttermilk. Our version uses fresh herbs, but fresh garlic and onion won't do—only the dried powders produce this dressing's characteristic flavor.

½ cup buttermilk
½ cup sour cream
½ cup mayonnaise
1 tbsp. finely chopped fresh chives
1 tbsp. finely chopped fresh flat-leaf parsley
1 tsp. garlic powder
½ tsp. onion powder
   Kosher salt and freshly ground black pepper,
   to taste

Combine buttermilk, sour cream, mayonnaise, chives, parsley, garlic powder, and onion powder in a bowl and stir well. Season with salt and pepper. Dressing will keep refrigerated for up to 1 week.

AMERICAN FRENCH DRESSING
MAKES ABOUT 1 CUP

This classic dressing, which gets its orange hue from a mélange of ketchup and paprika, is mellowed by homemade mayonnaise.

3 tbsp. ketchup
3 tbsp. red wine vinegar
1 tbsp. sugar
1 tsp. dry mustard
½ tsp. paprika
   Pinch white pepper
1 egg yolk
¾ cup extra-virgin olive oil
   Kosher salt, to taste

Combine ketchup, vinegar, sugar, dry mustard, paprika, white pepper, and egg yolk in a bowl and whisk well. Slowly drizzle in oil while whisking constantly until smooth. Season with salt. Dressing will keep refrigerated for up to 1 week.

THE ALL-STAR AMERICAN DRESSING

Ranch dressing, a creamy, vaguely tart, vaguely garlicky emulsion of mayonnaise and buttermilk, is more than a mere condiment for salads. It's a dip (for raw vegetables, potato chips, fried onion rings), a marinade, and a flavoring (for Doritos and CornNuts, among other snack foods). It is so well liked in West Texas that Houston restaurant critic and food writer Robb Walsh once noted that "some restaurant patrons seem to regard it as a beverage."

Of course, it was a dressing to begin with, and one first concocted—it is perhaps surprising to learn, in this day of made-up brand legends—at an actual ranch. Well, a sort of dude ranch rather than, say, a cattle spread, but a ranch nonetheless: Hidden Valley Ranch, in the hills of Santa Barbara, California, opened in 1954 by a former Alaska plumbing contractor named Steve Henson and his family.

In Alaska, Henson, who was also a cook, had created a buttermilk-based salad dressing for his crew. He later improved on the recipe for the Hidden Valley dining room. Guests loved it, and he developed a dry-mix version to sell. It was such a hit that in 1964 Henson closed the ranch and went into the dressing business full-time. In 1972 he sold the Hidden Valley name and formula to the Clorox Company. Clorox began marketing the dry mix in 1974 and the bottled dressing—which now comes in countless variations—a decade later. Today, there are a number of ranch dressing brands on the shelves, and Steve Henson's modest creation has become the most popular salad dressing in America.

Soups & Stews

SOUPS & STEWS

WHEN A COOK SETS OUT TO MAKE SOUP, the possibilities are endless. Some soups are thin and clear, like a crystalline oxtail consommé served as a first course to awaken the appetite; others, like a roux-thickened gumbo chock-full of andouille sausage and chicken, are ample meals in themselves. The elements that elevate the world's soups speak to the universal ingenuity of soup makers everywhere.

Broth can be bolstered with a bonanza of tiny *galuska* dumplings; swimming with tiny meatballs, pasta, and greens; bobbing with ethereal matzo balls; or fortified simply with stale bread and a topping of just-set eggs, as in Portugal's rustic, garlicky *açorda* from the region of Alentejo.

As comforting as they are in cool weather, soups and stews are a warm-weather delight, too: Syrian cooks welcome the spring with *yakhnit al-ardî shawkî,* a stew of artichoke, mint, and lamb lavishly spiced with allspice, cinnamon, and nutmeg, and around the world, home cooks make refreshing, restorative soups in the height of summer, such as Mexico's chilled avocado soup or Spain's bright gazpacho of cucumbers, ripe-to-bursting tomatoes, fruity olive oil, and nip of red wine vinegar, all gently thickened with country-style bread.

In the West, "Soup's on!" usually means it's time for lunch or dinner, but elsewhere in the world, many people start the day with soups and stews. In Japan, a warming bowl of miso soup rounds out a morning meal of rice, pickles, and broiled fish, and Peruvians breakfast on a hearty chicken soup thick with potatoes and noodles and garnished with hard-cooked eggs, sliced scallions, cilantro, chiles, and lime wedges.

Soups and stews have historically been among the most economical of foods, the means by which clever home cooks transformed leftover meats, vegetables, stocks, and more into satisfying meals. But the recipes featured in the following pages go beyond that venerable tradition to showcase scores of classic recipes—both modest and elegant—from around the globe.

Hot Soups

SOPA DE TORTILLA

Tortilla Soup

SERVES 4

This take on classic tortilla soup comes from celebrated Mexican chef Martha Ortiz. It's garnished with silky goat cheese and crisp pork rinds, as well as the more traditional diced avocado and crunchy tortilla strips.

- 3 dried guajillo chiles
- ¾ cup canola oil
- 6 cloves garlic, finely chopped
- 1 medium onion, finely chopped
- 3 plum tomatoes, cored and chopped
- 2 6″ corn tortillas, torn into small pieces
- 2 sprigs fresh cilantro
- 2 tbsp. dried oregano
- 1 tbsp. ground cumin
  Kosher salt and freshly ground black pepper, to taste
- 3 small dried pasilla chiles, stemmed, seeded, and thinly sliced
- 4 cups chicken stock
- 2 oz. fresh goat cheese, softened, for serving
- 3 fried pork rinds, crumbled, for serving
- 1 small avocado, pitted, peeled, and finely chopped, for serving
  Fried tortilla strips, for serving

1 Toast the guajillo chiles in a 6-qt. saucepan over medium-high heat. Transfer chiles to a bowl with 1 cup boiling water; let soften for 30 minutes. Drain, reserving ½ cup soaking liquid. Remove and discard stems and seeds from chiles. Transfer chiles and reserved liquid to a blender.

2 Return pan to medium-high heat and add ¼ cup canola oil to pot. Add garlic and onion and cook until soft, 6–8 minutes. Add tomatoes, tortillas, cilantro, oregano, cumin, salt, and pepper and cook until tomatoes are soft, about 6 minutes. Add guajillo to chiles in blender, purée until smooth, and set aside.

3 Return pan to medium-high heat with ¼ cup oil. Add pasilla chiles and fry until crisp, about 2 minutes. Using a slotted spoon, transfer to paper towels to drain. Discard oil and wipe pan clean.

4 Add remaining ¼ cup oil to pan and heat over medium-high heat. Add purée and cook until slightly reduced, 3–5 minutes. Add stock and simmer until thick, 40–45 minutes more. Strain soup through a fine-mesh sieve and divide among 4 bowls. Top with fried pasillas, goat cheese, pork rinds, avocado, and tortilla strips.

PORTUGUESE BREAD & GARLIC SOUP WITH CILANTRO

Açorda à Alentejana

SERVES 6–8 (SEE PHOTO, PAGE 213)

The recipe for this hearty, garlicky bread soup comes from Rosa Filipe of O Barro restaurant in Redondo, Portugal. According to Filipe, the soup is often nicknamed "beggar's soup" because it contains no meat or fish.

- 4 cups roughly chopped fresh cilantro leaves and stems
- 7 cloves garlic, peeled
- 1 large green bell pepper, seeded and roughly chopped
- 1 serrano chile, stemmed, seeded, and roughly chopped
  Kosher salt and freshly ground black pepper, to taste
- ½ cup olive oil
- ½ lb. Portuguese pão bread or 2 kaiser rolls, cut into 1″ cubes and toasted
- 8 cups chicken stock
- 4 eggs, lightly beaten

1 Pulse cilantro, garlic, bell pepper, chile, salt, and pepper in a food processor until roughly chopped. Add oil and purée to a smooth paste. Put ½ cup of paste in a bowl. Add bread, toss to coat, and set aside.

2 Heat remaining paste in a 6-qt. saucepan over medium heat. Cook until fragrant, 2–3 minutes. Add stock and bring to a boil. While stirring constantly, slowly drizzle in eggs and cook until eggs are just set, about 1 minute. Remove from heat, stir in bread mixture, and serve hot.

TORTELLINI IN BRODO

Tortellini in Broth

SERVES 6–8

A deceptively simple soup, this Italian classic hangs its hat on a meaty, intensely flavored, perfectly clear broth that takes many hours to come together. It's worth it, though: complex and satisfying, with heft from the cheese-filled tortellini.

4 lb. turkey wings, cut into 3″ pieces
2 lb. beef shank bones, trimmed
2 ribs celery, roughly chopped
2 large carrots, roughly chopped
2 large onions, roughly chopped
2 sprigs fresh flat-leaf parsley
1 bay leaf
1 clove garlic, crushed
1 lb. fresh cheese-filled tortellini pasta
   Kosher salt and freshly ground
   black pepper, to taste
   Grated Parmigiano-Reggiano,
   for serving

1 Put turkey wings and beef bones in a 12-qt. saucepan and cover with cold water by 4″. Place over medium heat and let mixture come to a very slow simmer, skimming off any foam that rises to the surface in the meantime. Add celery, carrots, onions, parsley, bay leaf, and garlic and return to a slow simmer. Cook, occasionally skimming fat from the surface, for 6 hours. Add 5 cups boiling water, and continue cooking, adding more boiling water as necessary to keep solids submerged, for 6 hours more.

2 Remove from heat, pour through a fine sieve into a large container, and discard solids. Let broth cool to room temperature, then refrigerate until chilled. Remove hardened layer of fat from surface of broth and discard.

3 To serve, reheat broth in a 4-qt. saucepan over medium-high heat. Bring broth to a boil and then add pasta. Cook, stirring, until al dente, about 7 minutes. Taste and season with salt and pepper. Ladle pasta and broth into serving bowls and top with Parmigiano.

GILLIE'S MATZO BALL SOUP

SERVES 12

This spectacular take on the iconic Jewish soup, from home cook Gillie Feuer of Long Island, New York, was a tightly held secret, until we pried it loose. The key? Lots of veggies in the stock, and her light and floaty matzo balls: "They're very well behaved," she told us. "They plump up just like little dolls."

FOR THE BROTH

1 3-lb. chicken
3 carrots, halved
2 onions, halved
5 ribs celery, with leaves, halved
3 parsnips, halved
1 head garlic, split
1 bunch fresh flat-leaf parsley

FOR THE MATZO BALLS

1 onion
8 eggs
½ cup margarine or butter, melted
   and slightly cooled
2½ cups matzo meal
   Kosher salt and freshly ground
   black pepper, to taste

   Small fresh dill sprigs, for garnish

1 Make the broth: Combine chicken, carrots, onions, celery, parsnips, and garlic in a large stockpot with water to cover. Finely chop enough parsley leaves to yield about 2 tbsp. and set aside; add remainder to pot. Bring mixture just to a boil over medium-high heat, skimming off any foam that rises to the surface. Reduce heat and simmer for 2½ hours. Strain, let cool, and refrigerate for at least 3 hours. Remove hardened layer of fat from surface of broth and discard.

2 Make the matzo balls: Grate enough onion to yield about 2 tbsp. and set aside the rest. In a large bowl, combine grated onions, eggs, margarine, matzo meal, reserved chopped parsley, and ¼ cup water or stock. Season with salt and pepper and let sit for at least 30 minutes.

3 Wet hands and roll dough into twenty-four 2″ balls (they will expand as they cook). Meanwhile, bring a large pot of water to a boil. Add 2 tbsp. salt and remaining onion. Drop matzo balls into water one at a time. (They won't stick together if the pot is large enough.) Reduce heat, cover, and simmer for 30–40 minutes. Drain. Store, covered, on a plate until ready to use. Matzo balls will keep up to 3 days in the refrigerator.

4 To serve, heat broth over medium heat and season with salt and pepper. Add matzo balls and heat through. Garnish with dill.

A WARM TRADITION

In Hungary, the soup course is a point of national pride, and Hungarian cooks have developed a whole battery of soup-making techniques unknown in other European cooking traditions. One secret behind *karfiolleves* (below), a warming, brick-red cauliflower soup, is the handling of the paprika, a spice introduced by occupying Turks in the 16th century and thereafter embraced by Hungarians as their own. Paprika is fat-soluble, so it makes sense to begin by cooking it in butter, but it also releases its flavor quickly and scorches easily, so broth is added to the pot soon after. Whereas cooks elsewhere rely on rich meat or vegetable broths as building blocks of flavor, Hungarians tend to use very light broths or even water. In a soup like this one, the idea is to let the pure flavor of the vegetables shine through.

PAPRIKA-SPICED CAULIFLOWER SOUP

Karfiolleves

SERVES 4 (SEE PHOTO, PAGE 215)

This recipe for paprika-spiced cauliflower soup comes from chef Andrea Németh at the restaurant Bagolyvár in Budapest, Hungary. To form the tiny dumplings, called *galuska*, she simply drops bits of dough into the simmering broth.

- ⅓ cup flour
- ½ tsp. kosher salt
- 6 tbsp. cold unsalted butter, cubed
- 1 egg
- 1½ tbsp. Hungarian hot paprika
- 1 large yellow onion, finely chopped
- 6 cups vegetable stock
- 1 small head cauliflower, cored and cut into florets
- 1 medium carrot, peeled and finely chopped
  Kosher salt and freshly ground black pepper, to taste
- 1 small bunch fresh flat-leaf parsley, stemmed and finely chopped, for garnish

1 Make the dumplings: In a bowl, stir together flour and salt. Add 2 tbsp. butter and, using your fingers, rub into flour until pea-size crumbles form. Add egg and stir until dough forms. Refrigerate until ready to use.

2 Heat remaining 4 tbsp. butter in a 6-qt. saucepan over medium-high heat. Add paprika and onion and cook, stirring, until soft, about 5 minutes. Add stock, cauliflower, and carrot, season with salt and pepper, and bring to a boil. Reduce heat to medium and cook, stirring occasionally, until vegetables are tender, about 15 minutes. Using a ½-tsp. measuring spoon, portion out and drop all dumpling dough into simmering soup. Cook, stirring occasionally, until dumplings are cooked through, about 3 minutes. Season with salt and pepper.

3 To serve, ladle soup and dumplings into 4 serving bowls and garnish with parsley.

STRACCIATELLA

Roman Egg-Drop Soup

SERVES 8

The Italian name for this simple, hearty soup of eggs stirred into hot broth with lemon and cheese is derived from the fact that the eggs take on the appearance of *straccetti*, or "little rags."

- 8 cups chicken stock
- 2 eggs
- ½ cup grated Parmigiano-Reggiano
- 2 tbsp. chopped fresh flat-leaf parsley (optional)
  Fresh lemon juice, to taste
  Kosher salt and freshly ground black pepper, to taste

1 Bring stock to a boil over medium-high heat, then reduce heat to medium-low and simmer.

2 Beat eggs in a bowl and add Parmigiano and the parsley, if desired.

3 Slowly pour egg mixture into stock, stirring with a whisk. (The faster you stir, the finer the pieces of egg.) Season to taste with lemon juice, salt, and pepper before serving.

AVGOLÉMONO
Greek Lemon Chicken Soup
SERVES 8

Straightforward and slightly tangy, this riff on chicken soup is an essential home cure in Greece when someone is feeling ill. It's thick and rich but contains no cream: All that body is thanks to well-whisked eggs, tempered with a bit of stock so they don't curdle.

- 8 cups chicken stock
- 1 cup long-grain white rice
- 4 eggs
  Juice of 3 lemons
  Kosher salt and freshly ground black pepper, to taste
  Fresh flat-leaf parsley leaves, for garnish

1 Bring stock to a boil in a 4-qt. saucepan over high heat. Reduce heat to medium and stir in rice. Cook, partially covered and stirring occasionally, until rice is tender, about 20 minutes.

2 Whisk eggs and lemon juice in a bowl until frothy. Whisking constantly, add 1 cup of the simmering stock, then return to the pot. Cook, stirring, about 2 minutes. Season with salt and pepper and garnish with parsley.

COCK-A-LEEKIE SOUP
SERVES 6–8

This traditional Scottish soup is thought to have originated as a way to use chickens that had been killed in a cockfight. The traditional inclusion of prunes enriches the stock, and their sweetness highlights the flavor of the chicken and leeks.

- 1 3–4-lb. chicken
- ½ cup long-grain white rice
- 6 leeks, trimmed and cut into 1″ slices
  Kosher salt and freshly ground black pepper, to taste
- 1 lb. pitted prunes
- ¼ cup finely chopped fresh flat-leaf parsley

1 Place chicken in an 8-qt. pot and cover with water. Bring to a boil over medium-high heat. Add rice, leeks, salt, and pepper. Reduce heat to medium and simmer gently, partially covered, until chicken is tender, about 2 hours.

2 Add prunes and simmer for 30 minutes longer. Remove chicken and let cool slightly. Remove meat, discarding

bones and cartilage, and thinly slice. Return meat to pot and season with salt and pepper. Sprinkle with parsley before serving.

PERUVIAN CHICKEN SOUP
Aguadito de Pollo
SERVES 6

This bright, aromatic soup is a popular Peruvian morning dish, though it's a welcome treat on the table any time of day. There are all sorts of ways it can be garnished; residents of Lima, Peru's capital, often choose halved hard-cooked eggs.

- 1 5–6-lb. chicken
- 2 leeks, trimmed and roughly chopped
- 2 ribs celery, roughly chopped
- 2 carrots, peeled and roughly chopped
- 1 1″ piece fresh ginger, peeled and smashed
- 1 head garlic, halved crosswise
- 6 medium Yukon gold potatoes, peeled and left whole
- 6 oz. dried egg noodles
  Kosher salt, to taste
- 6 hard-cooked eggs, halved, for garnish
- 2 tbsp. chopped fresh cilantro, for garnish
- 4 scallions, thinly sliced, for garnish
- 2 limes, quartered, for garnish
- 1 fresh red chile, such as Fresno, stemmed, seeded, and finely chopped, for garnish

1 Put chicken, leeks, celery, carrots, ginger, garlic, and 5 qt. cold water into an 8-qt. stockpot. Bring to a boil over high heat, then reduce heat to medium-low and simmer, skimming occasionally, until the broth becomes rich and golden, 3½ hours.

2 Transfer chicken to a large plate and set aside. Set a fine sieve over a clean pot and strain broth into pot. Discard vegetables and ginger. Add potatoes to broth, bring to a boil over medium-high heat, and cook until potatoes are very tender, about 25 minutes.

3 Meanwhile, remove and discard skin from chicken. Pull the chicken meat from the carcass and discard carcass. Tear chicken meat into at least 6 large chunks.

4 Bring the broth to a boil over high heat. Add the egg noodles and cook until al dente, about 10 minutes. Add the reserved chicken pieces and allow them to warm through. Season soup with salt. Divide soup among 6 deep serving bowls. Garnish each portion with eggs and some of the cilantro, scallions, limes, and chiles. Serve immediately.

CHINESE HOT & SOUR SOUP

Suan La Tang

SERVES 4–6

Hot and sour soup is a culinary contradiction. In it, the mildest ingredients—pork, mushrooms, tofu—are nestled in a fiery, vinegar-laced broth. This soup doesn't just warm you; it burns through you and brings you back to life.

FOR THE PORK

- 1 tbsp. soy sauce
- 1 tbsp. brandy
- 1 tsp. cornstarch
- ¼ lb. pork tenderloin, cut into ¼″ cubes

FOR THE SOUP

- 8 cups chicken stock
- 3 tbsp. soy sauce
- 3 tbsp. white wine vinegar
- 3 tbsp. cornstarch
- 1 tsp. ground white pepper
- 1 tsp. kosher salt
- ½ tsp. cayenne pepper, or more to taste
- ¾ lb. firm tofu, drained and cut into ¼″ cubes
- 6 shiitake or wood ear mushrooms, stems discarded and cut into ¼″ pieces
- 1 egg, lightly beaten
- 1 tsp. sesame oil
- 2 tbsp. finely chopped fresh cilantro, for garnish

1 Make the pork: Combine the soy sauce, brandy, and cornstarch in a medium bowl. Add pork and toss until combined. Let sit at room temperature for 15 minutes.

2 Make the soup: Whisk together stock, soy sauce, vinegar, cornstarch, pepper, salt, cayenne, and ¼ cup water in a 4-qt. saucepan and bring to a boil over medium-high heat. Add pork, reduce heat to medium-low, and cook, stirring occasionally, until soup thickens, about 30 minutes. Add tofu, and mushrooms and cook until potatoes are tender, about 15 minutes.

3 Without stirring, slowly drizzle egg into simmering soup in a thin, steady stream. When egg strands float to surface, stir in oil. Ladle soup into serving bowls and garnish with cilantro.

WONTON SOUP

SERVES 4–6

Filled dumplings floating in savory broth is a staple of Chinese cuisine. To form dainty, single-bite wontons, be sure to restrict the filling amount to 1 teaspoon per wonton.

- 8 cups chicken stock, plus 2 tbsp.
- 3 whole scallions, plus 1 tbsp. minced
- 1 3″ piece fresh ginger, peeled (2″ sliced into thin disks, 1″ finely chopped)
  Kosher salt, to taste
- 2¼ tsp. cornstarch
- ¼ lb. ground pork
- 1 tbsp. soy sauce
- 2¼ tsp. dry Shaoxing wine
- 1 tsp. sesame oil
  Pinch of sugar
- 20 3½″ square wonton wrappers
- 1 packed cup gai lan or spinach leaves, torn into large pieces

1 Put 8 cups stock, whole scallions, sliced ginger, and salt into a large pot. Bring to a boil over medium-high heat, then reduce heat to medium-low, cover, and simmer until flavors have come together, about 10 minutes. Remove from heat and set aside.

2 Put remaining 2 tbsp. stock and cornstarch into a large bowl and stir to combine. Add minced scallions, chopped ginger, pork, soy sauce, sherry, sesame oil, and sugar and stir well to make a filling for the wontons.

3 Fill a cup with water and set aside. Arrange a wrapper in front of you so that it looks like a diamond; dip your finger in the water and moisten the 4 edges of the wrapper. Place about 1 tsp. filling in center of wrapper and fold in half over filling to make a triangle. Press firmly along sides to seal and remove all excess trapped air. Moisten the left and right corners, then draw them together and pinch to seal. Place stuffed wonton on a wax paper–lined sheet pan and cover with a towel to prevent drying. Repeat with remaining filling and wrappers.

4 Bring reserved broth to a boil, covered, over medium-high heat. Uncover and reduce heat to medium-low. Add wontons and cook, stirring occasionally, until wonton filling is firm and cooked through, about 5 minutes. Stir in gai lan and cook for 30 seconds more. Ladle into bowls and serve hot.

GERMAN BARLEY SOUP

Graupensuppe

SERVES 8

Klaus Weiler, the chef at Weinhaus Weiler in Oberwesel, Germany, gave us the recipe for this classic barley soup. Fortified with sausage, bacon, and plenty of vegetables, it's substantial enough to make a meal in itself.

- 4 tbsp. unsalted butter
- 1 medium onion, finely chopped
- 1 cup pearl barley
- 8 cups chicken or vegetable stock
- ½ cup finely chopped, peeled russet potato
- ½ cup finely chopped carrot
- ½ cup finely chopped celery root
- ½ cup finely chopped leek
- 1 tsp. dried marjoram
- 2 German sausages, like bockwurst or bratwurst
- 1 2-oz. piece bacon
  Freshly grated nutmeg, to taste
  Kosher salt and freshly ground black pepper, to taste
- ⅓ cup thinly sliced fresh flat-leaf parsley leaves, for garnish

1 Melt butter in a 6-qt. saucepan over medium-high heat. Add onion and cook, stirring, until soft, about 5 minutes. Add barley and cook, stirring, until lightly toasted, about 5 minutes. Add stock, potato, carrot, celery root, leek, marjoram, sausages, and bacon and cook, stirring occasionally, until sausages are tender, about 35 minutes. Remove sausages and bacon from saucepan, thinly slice sausages, and discard bacon.

2 Season soup with nutmeg, salt, and pepper. To serve, ladle soup into 8 bowls and garnish with parsley and sausage.

RED BEET BORSCHT

SERVES 10–12

Eaten hot or cold, enriched with a dollop of sour cream and wisps of dill, this beet-based soup is the quintessence of good Eastern European cooking. It's hearty yet fine-tuned, dramatic in color yet humble in its ingredients.

- 2¾ lb. trimmed boneless pork shoulder
- 2¼ lb. trimmed boneless beef chuck
- 10 cups beef stock
- 4 ham hocks
- 1 bouquet garni (below)
- 1½ lb. beets, roasted and cut into ¼"-thick half-moons
- 4 leeks, white part only, finely chopped
- 1 large onion, finely chopped
- 1 small head Savoy cabbage, cored and shredded
- 1 cup white wine vinegar
  Kosher salt and freshly ground black pepper, to taste
  Sour cream and fresh dill fronds, for garnish

1 Bring pork, beef, stock, ham hocks, and bouquet garni to a boil in an 8-qt. Dutch oven over medium-high heat. Reduce heat to medium-low and cook, stirring occasionally, until meat is tender, about 3 hours.

2 Using tongs, remove meats from broth, transfer to a cutting board, and let cool. Discard bouquet garni. Cut pork and beef into ½" chunks. Shred meat from ham hocks, and cut into ½" chunks. Discard bone, skin, and excess fat from hocks. Return chopped meats to broth, add beets, leeks, onion, and cabbage and bring to a boil. Reduce heat to medium-low and cook, stirring, until soft, about 25 minutes. Stir in vinegar and season with salt and pepper. Divide among bowls and garnish with sour cream and dill.

Bouquet Garni

MAKES 1

A bouquet garni (translated literally from the French, the phrase means "garnished bouquet") is a bundle of herbs and aromatics that lend their flavor and delicious scent to a soup or stew but is removed before serving. Depending on the recipe, they can range from the beautifully simple (perhaps just a leek and a sprig of parsley) to the extravagant. We've found that this combination serves well in everything from chicken stock to beet borscht.

- 3 sprigs fresh thyme
- 3 sprigs fresh flat-leaf parsley
- 3 sprigs fresh marjoram
- 1 small leek, trimmed
- 1 rib celery, trimmed
- 1 dried bay leaf, or 2 fresh bay leaves

Tie all ingredients together securely with kitchen twine. Alternatively, bundle all ingredients together in a loose cheesecloth pouch and secure with kitchen twine.

POLISH WHITE BORSCHT

Bialy Barszcz

SERVES 4–6

This pale cousin to red borscht uses potatoes in place of beets. In Poland, it's traditionally served at Easter.

- 2 lb. smoked kielbasa
- 2 tbsp. unsalted butter
- 4 cloves garlic, finely chopped
- 2 leeks, trimmed, sliced, and rinsed
- 1 small onion, sliced
- 2 medium russet potatoes, peeled and cut into 1″ cubes
- 2 sprigs fresh marjoram
- 1 bay leaf
- 1½ cups sour cream
- ¼ cup flour
- ¼ cup freshly grated horseradish
  Kosher salt and freshly ground black pepper, to taste
- ¼ cup roughly chopped fresh dill, for garnish
- 2 tbsp. chopped fresh flat-leaf parsley, for garnish
- 4 hard-cooked eggs, cut into wedges, for garnish

1 Bring kielbasa and 8 cups water to a boil in a 6-qt. saucepan. Reduce heat to medium-low and cook to flavor broth, about 25 minutes longer. Pour liquid and kielbasa into a bowl and reserve. Return saucepan to medium heat. Add butter, garlic, leeks, and onion and cook until soft, about 10 minutes. Add reserved liquid, potatoes, marjoram, and bay leaf and bring to a boil. Reduce heat to medium-low and cook until potatoes are tender, about 30 minutes. Discard marjoram and bay leaf. Transfer soup to a blender and purée.

2 Return soup to pan and bring to a simmer. Meanwhile, whisk sour cream and flour in a bowl, add ½ cup soup, and whisk until smooth. Pour mixture into soup and cook, stirring, until thickened, about 5 minutes. Cut kielbasa into ½″ slices and add to soup along with horseradish, salt, and pepper. Divide among individual bowls and garnish with dill, parsley, and eggs.

PHO BÒ

Vietnamese Beef & Noodle Soup

SERVES 6–8

Vietnamese noodle soup, known as *pho* (pronounced "fuh," with a rising intonation), is a fragrant study in textural contrasts—silky broth, soft noodles, toothsome beef, crisp sprouts, leafy herbs.

- 6 lb. oxtails or meaty beef bones
- 2 onions, quartered
- 4 turnips, quartered
- 4 star anise pods
- 8 whole cloves
- 1 3″ piece fresh ginger, crushed
- 1 cinnamon stick
- 4 fresh or frozen makrut lime leaves (optional)
  Nuoc mam (Vietnamese fish sauce)
- 1 lb. dried flat rice noodles
  Vegetable oil, for frying
- 5 shallots, thinly sliced
- 2 cups bean sprouts
- 2 scallions, thinly sliced
- 7 fresh hot red chiles (Thai or serrano), thinly sliced
- 1 cup fresh cilantro leaves
- 1 cup fresh Thai or sweet basil leaves
- 2 limes, cut into wedges
- ½ lb. top sirloin, thinly sliced
  Hoisin sauce, for dipping

1 Combine oxtails, onions, turnips, star anise, cloves, ginger, cinnamon stick, lime leaves, and 16 cups water in a large pot. Bring to a boil over high heat, then reduce to medium, skim foam, and stir in 1 tbsp. fish sauce. Simmer, adding water as needed to cover bones, for 5 hours. Strain and set aside. (Broth improves if refrigerated overnight; skim before heating.)

2 Soak noodles in a bowl of hot water until soft, about 30 minutes. Drain. Meanwhile, heat 1″ oil in a saucepan over medium heat. Add shallots and fry until golden, 4–7 minutes. Drain on paper towels.

3 Bring broth to a simmer over medium heat. Arrange shallots, bean sprouts, scallions, chiles, cilantro, basil, and lime wedges on a platter. Divide noodles and sirloin among soup bowls, cover with hot broth, then add vegetables and herbs as desired and season to taste with lime and fish sauce. Serve with small individual bowls of hoisin sauce for dipping.

TOM YUM GOONG
Sweet-and-Sour Prawn Soup
SERVES 4

Fragrant with lime juice and lemongrass, this hot, sweet, sour, and savory soup is a true Thai classic.

- 8 fresh or frozen makrut lime leaves
- 2 cloves garlic, crushed
- 1 stalk lemongrass, trimmed and halved lengthwise
- 1 3″ piece peeled fresh or frozen galangal, cut crosswise into ¼″-thick disks
- 5 head-on, shell-on jumbo prawns, halved lengthwise
- ¾ cup fresh lime juice
- ¼ cup nam pla (Thai fish sauce)
- 3–4 tbsp. semi-moist Thai palm sugar
- 5 red or green bird's eye chiles, stemmed and halved lengthwise
- 2 plum tomatoes, cored and quartered
  Kosher salt, to taste
- ½ cup roughly chopped fresh cilantro, for serving

Bring 4 cups water to a boil in a large pot. Add makrut lime leaves, garlic, lemongrass, and galangal. Reduce heat to medium and cook until fragrant, 3–4 minutes. Add prawns and boil gently until just cooked through, about 30 seconds. Add lime juice, fish sauce, palm sugar, chiles, tomatoes, and salt. Reduce heat to medium-low and simmer until tomatoes are softened, 4–5 minutes. Transfer to a serving bowl and top with cilantro.

FRENCH ONION SOUP
Soupe à l'Oignon
SERVES 6

Oven-braised onions, bread, and melted cheese are the main components of this timeless dish, which epitomizes the robust cuisine of Parisian brasseries. To make it, you'll need six sturdy ceramic bowls that can withstand the heat of a broiler.

- 1 cup white wine
- ½ cup plus 3 tbsp. sherry
- 10 tbsp. unsalted butter
- 1 tsp. sugar
- 3 large onions, thinly sliced
  Kosher salt and freshly ground black pepper
- 6 sprigs fresh flat-leaf parsley
- 6 sprigs fresh thyme
- 2 fresh bay leaves
- 8 cups beef stock
- 12 ½″-thick baguette slices
- 2 cloves garlic, smashed
- 6 cups grated Gruyère cheese
- 2 cups grated Parmigiano-Reggiano

1 Heat oven to 425°. Combine wine, ½ cup sherry, 8 tbsp. butter, sugar, onions, salt, and pepper in a 9″×13″ baking dish. Braise, uncovered, stirring occasionally, until the onions just begin to brown, 40–45 minutes. Remove from oven, cover with foil, and then continue braising in oven, stirring occasionally, until caramelized, about 1 hour more. Keep onions warm.

2 Meanwhile, tie parsley, thyme, and bay leaves together with kitchen twine to make a bouquet garni (page 86). Put bouquet garni and stock into a pot and bring to a boil. Reduce heat to medium-low and simmer, partially covered, for 30 minutes. Remove and discard bouquet garni. Stir in remaining 3 tbsp. sherry and cook for 5 minutes more.

3 Meanwhile, spread baguette slices with remaining 2 tbsp. butter. Toast in a skillet over medium heat, turning once, until golden, 5–7 minutes. Rub the slices generously with garlic and set aside.

4 Arrange an oven rack 6″ from broiler and heat broiler. Arrange 6 heatproof bowls on a foil-lined baking sheet, divide onions and broth among bowls, and stir together. Place 2 baguette slices in each bowl and top each with about 1 cup Gruyère and about ⅓ cup Parmigiano. Broil until cheeses are browned and bubbly, 3–5 minutes. Serve immediately.

PROVENÇAL VEGETABLE SOUP WITH PESTO
Soupe au Pistou
SERVES 8–10

Pistou, the Provençal cousin of pesto, is stirred into this summer soup just before serving, its herbaceous freshness an elegant balance to the delicate broth.

FOR THE PISTOU
- 4 cups packed fresh basil leaves
- 1 cup grated Parmigiano-Reggiano
- ¼ cup extra-virgin olive oil
- 1 tsp. kosher salt
- 2 cloves garlic, chopped
- 1 plum tomato, cored

> ## "An Italian vegetable soup is an excellent illustration of the principle of *insaporire*, the extraction and building up of flavor."
>
> MARCELLA HAZAN

FOR THE SOUP

- ¼ cup extra-virgin olive oil
- 1 oz. pancetta, minced
- 5 cloves garlic, finely chopped
- 3 medium carrots, peeled and finely chopped
- 2 ribs celery, finely chopped
- 1 yellow onion, finely chopped
- ½ medium zucchini, chopped
- ¼ head Savoy cabbage, cored and thinly shredded
- 8 cups chicken stock
- 7 canned whole, peeled tomatoes, chopped
- ⅓ cup broken dried spaghetti
- 1 15-oz. can cannellini beans, drained and rinsed
  Kosher salt and freshly ground
  black pepper, to taste

1 Make the pistou: Process basil, Parmigiano, oil, salt, garlic, and tomato in a food processor until finely ground. Season with salt and pepper and set aside.

2 Make the soup: Heat oil in a 6-qt. saucepan over medium-high heat. Add pancetta and cook, stirring often, until fat has rendered, about 2 minutes. Add garlic, carrots, celery, and onions, reduce heat to medium, cover, and cook, stirring occasionally, until crisp-tender, 12–15 minutes. Add zucchini and cabbage and cook, covered, until wilted, 3–5 minutes. Add stock and tomatoes and bring to a boil. Add pasta and cook until al dente, about 8 minutes. Mash half the beans with a fork and add to soup along with whole beans and cook until warmed through. Season with salt and pepper. Ladle soup into bowls and serve with pistou dolloped on top.

ITALIAN WEDDING SOUP

Minestra Maritata

SERVES 8

In fact, this soup has nothing to do with weddings. In Italian, it is called "married soup" for its harmonious mingling of ingredients, and somewhere along the line the name was charmingly mistranslated.

- 1 3½–4-lb. chicken
- 2 carrots, peeled

- 2 ribs celery
- 2 cups canned whole, peeled tomatoes
- ½ tsp. kosher salt, plus more to taste
- ½ cup acini de pepe or other tiny round pasta
- 1 head escarole, coarsely chopped
- ½ lb. ground beef
- 1 egg yolk
- 2 tbsp. dried bread crumbs
- 1 tbsp. grated Parmigiano-Reggiano
- 1 tbsp. grated pecorino romano
  Leaves from 2 sprigs fresh flat-leaf parsley, chopped, plus more for garnish
- 1 clove garlic, finely chopped
- ¼ tsp. chopped fresh oregano
- ¼ tsp. freshly ground black pepper, plus more to taste

1 Put chicken, carrots, celery, tomatoes, 14 cups water, and salt in a large pot. Bring to a boil over high heat, skimming any foam that rises to the surface, then reduce heat to medium-low. Simmer until chicken is just cooked through, about 40 minutes.

2 Meanwhile, cook pasta in a small pot of boiling salted water until just tender, 5–7 minutes. Drain, rinse, and set aside. Put escarole and 2 tbsp. water into a large skillet, cover, and cook over medium heat until wilted, 4–5 minutes; set aside. Gently mix beef, egg yolk, bread crumbs, cheeses, parsley, garlic, oregano, ½ tsp. salt, and ¼ tsp. pepper together in a large bowl. Form into ½″ meatballs and set aside.

3 Using a slotted spoon, transfer chicken to a large bowl and set aside to cool. Strain broth through a cheesecloth-lined colander into a clean medium pot, discarding solids. Shred chicken meat and set aside, discarding skin and bones.

4 Bring broth to a boil over high heat. Add meatballs, reduce heat to medium, and simmer until cooked through, 10–15 minutes. Add shredded chicken, escarole, and pasta and season to taste with salt and pepper. Simmer for 15 minutes more. Serve garnished with parsley leaves.

POLITICS ASIDE

"No claim to fame, political or otherwise, goes unquestioned in Washington. So it seems fitting that not even the Historical Office of the Senate can say for sure who ordained that bean soup should appear every day, until the end of time, on the menus of the Senate's restaurants—both the starchy place reserved for senators and their guests and the casual ones open to hoi polloi. We do know that the custom arose early in the last century. According to one account, Senator Fred Thomas Dubois of Idaho, a politically supple Yale man who served one term as a Republican and another as a Democrat, originated it; Senator Knute Nelson, a Norwegian-born Republican from Minnesota, is the rival claimant. Both grew up in the Midwest.

This is a nonpartisan dish. For decades, Bob Dole, the Republican conservative from Kansas, ate bean soup and cherry pie for lunch almost every day. For many of the same years, Daniel Patrick Moynihan, the New York liberal Democrat, ate bean soup and a tuna fish sandwich on thin whole wheat.

The soup is made simply with navy beans, water, ham hocks, and onions (apparently, an earlier recipe also included mashed potatoes, celery, garlic, and parsley). In 1943, the soup cost ten cents a cup, 15 cents a bowl. One day in the summer of 2000, when Senator John McCain of Arizona invited me into the inner sanctum, the prices were $3.10 and $4.35, respectively. I ordered a bowl, and when my taste of tradition arrived, it was beige and creamy, studded with shreds of mildly smoky ham. The soup, which cried out for salt and pepper, is unlikely to offend (or arouse) any palate, but this is more about politics than about flavor."

R. W. APPLE JR.

SENATE BEAN SOUP

SERVES 4–6

In the early 20th century, this humble bean soup first appeared on the menus at the restaurants of the U.S. Senate. It's still served there today.

1 lb. dried navy beans, soaked overnight
1 smoked ham hock
1 tbsp. unsalted butter
1 small onion, finely chopped
    Kosher salt and freshly ground black pepper, to taste

1 Bring beans, ham hock, and 8 cups water to a boil in a 6-qt. Dutch oven over medium-high heat. Reduce heat to medium-low and cook until beans are tender, about 1 hour.

2 Meanwhile, melt butter in a 10″ skillet over medium heat. Add onion and cook, stirring, until soft, about 5 minutes. Transfer to pot with beans and reduce heat to low to keep warm. Remove ham hock, let cool slightly, and then remove meat, discarding bone, skin, and excess fat. Finely chop meat and add back to soup. Lightly mash some of the beans in the pot to create a thick, creamy texture. Season with salt and pepper and serve.

LENTIL SOUP

SERVES 6–8

Soup is one of the most common ways for Americans to eat lentils—perhaps because the most common domestic variety of the legume, U.S.A. Regular, lends itself well to such treatment. While many lentil soups are enriched with bacon, sausages, or ham hocks, this recipe is lighter, unadulterated, and full of pure lentil flavor.

1 whole clove
1 medium onion, peeled
8 cups chicken stock
1 bay leaf
1 lb. American brown lentils, picked over and rinsed
    Kosher salt and freshly ground black pepper, to taste
2 cloves garlic, minced
1 tsp. finely chopped fresh thyme
2 tbsp. unsalted butter
2 tsp. chopped fresh mint, for garnish

1 Press clove into onion and place onion in a large saucepan. Add stock, bay leaf, lentils, and a pinch each of salt and pepper. Bring to a boil over high heat, then reduce heat to medium and simmer, skimming occasionally, until lentils are tender, 30–35 minutes.

2 Discard cloves, onion, and bay leaf and stir in garlic, thyme, and butter. Reduce heat to medium-low and cook, just below a simmer, for 10 minutes, allowing flavors to blend. Season with salt and pepper, then ladle into bowls. Garnish with mint and serve. (If desired, soup can also be puréed before serving.)

VARIATION For a richer, more traditional lentil soup, dice 2 slices of bacon, place them in a large saucepan, and cook over medium heat until crisp, about 10 minutes. Using a slotted spoon, remove bacon and drain on paper towels. To the rendered fat, add 1 thinly sliced medium yellow onion and 2 minced garlic cloves and cook until soft, about 20 minutes. Add 1 lb. lentils, 8 cups chicken stock, and 1 tsp. finely chopped fresh thyme and cook as above until tender. Garnish with bacon.

PASTA & FAGIOLI

Pasta & Bean Soup

SERVES 4–6

The Italians love beans—both the legumes of the Old World, like chickpeas, favas, and lentils, and New World–derived varieties such as borlotti and cannellini. In an aromatic broth alongside pieces of pasta, the beans' texture and flavor shine.

- ¾ lb. dried borlotti or cranberry beans, soaked overnight
- 2 oz. pancetta, minced
- 1½ cups extra-virgin olive oil
- 1 yellow onion, minced
- ½ rib celery, minced
- 3 sprigs fresh flat-leaf parsley, minced
- 2 tbsp. tomato paste
- 3 cloves garlic, crushed
- 2 small sprigs fresh rosemary
- 3 fresh sage leaves
  Kosher salt and freshly ground black pepper, to taste
- 6 oz. dried fettuccine, broken into small pieces

1 Put beans in a large heavy pot. Add pancetta, 1 cup oil, onions, celery, parsley, tomato paste, and 6½ cups water. Mince 1 clove garlic and 1 sprig of rosemary and add to pot. Bring to a boil over high heat, then reduce heat to medium-low and simmer, stirring occasionally, until beans are very tender, about 2½ hours.

2 Meanwhile, heat remaining ½ cup oil in a medium skillet over medium heat. Add sage and remaining 2 cloves garlic, and 1 sprig rosemary and cook until garlic is golden, about 3 minutes. Remove sage, garlic, and rosemary from oil and discard, reserving flavored oil.

3 Transfer half the soup to a food processor and purée until smooth. Stir back into pot, then stir in flavored oil and season with salt and pepper.

4 Add pasta to soup and cook, stirring often, until tender, about 15 minutes. Garnish with parsley and a drizzle of oil, if you like.

BLACK BEAN SOUP

Sopa de Frijol

SERVES 8

This long-simmered Mexican soup matches spiced black beans with a roasted tomato purée, producing exuberantly savory results.

- ½ cup canola oil
- ½ lb. dried black beans, soaked overnight
- ½ tsp. dried oregano
- ½ tsp. ground cumin
- 4 cloves garlic, peeled
- 2 medium onions, cut in half
  Kosher salt and freshly ground black pepper, to taste
- 2 plum tomatoes, cored
- 4 cups chicken stock
- ¼ cup crema or sour cream
- ½ lb. queso fresco or Monterey Jack, cut into ¼" cubes
  Fried tortilla strips, for garnish

1 Heat ¼ cup oil in a 4-qt. saucepan over medium-high heat. Add beans, oregano, cumin, 3 cloves garlic, 2 onion halves, and 5 cups water. Bring to a boil, then reduce heat to medium-low. Cover and cook, stirring occasionally, until beans are tender, about 2 hours. Remove from heat and purée in a blender until smooth, at least 2 minutes. Season with salt and pepper and set beans aside.

2 Arrange an oven rack 4" from broiler and heat broiler. Place remaining garlic clove and 1 onion half along with tomatoes on a foil-lined baking sheet. Broil, turning as needed, until blackened all over, about 8 minutes for garlic and tomatoes, about 16 minutes for onion. Transfer to a food processor and purée until smooth, at least 2 minutes. Pour through a fine-mesh sieve into a bowl and set aside.

3 Heat remaining ¼ cup oil in a 6-qt. saucepan over medium-high heat. Finely chop remaining onion half, add to pan, and cook, stirring, until soft, about 8 minutes. Add tomato purée and cook, stirring constantly, until slightly reduced, about 3 minutes. Add beans and stock and bring to a boil. Reduce heat to medium-low and cook, stirring occasionally, until slightly reduced, about 45 minutes. Working in batches, purée soup in blender until very smooth, at least 2 minutes. Stir in crema and season with salt and pepper. To serve, divide soup among bowls and sprinkle with cheese and tortilla strips.

MULLIGATAWNY
SERVES 4–6

The Indian antecedent to mulligatawny was likely a thin, spicy lentil broth, but the colonizing British thickened it. Thankfully, this cultural hybrid kept the Indian spices.

- 9 tbsp. unsalted butter
- 1 tsp. ground dried Aleppo pepper (optional)
- ½ tsp. cumin seeds
- ½ tsp. coriander seeds
- ½ tsp. black mustard seeds
- 2 dried chiles de árbol
- 1 plum tomato, minced
- 3 tbsp. minced fresh ginger
- 6 cloves garlic, minced
- 1 large onion, minced
- ½ jalapeño, minced
- ¼ cup flour
- 1 tbsp. ground coriander
- 2 tsp. ground cumin
- 1½ tsp. ground turmeric
- 9 cups chicken stock or vegetable stock
- 1¾ cups red lentils
- 3 tbsp. minced fresh cilantro
- 1 cup canned coconut milk
- ¼ cup fresh lemon juice
  Kosher salt and freshly ground black pepper, to taste
  Plain yogurt, for garnish

Cook 5 tbsp. butter, Aleppo (if using), cumin, coriander, mustard, chiles, and tomato in an 8″ skillet over high heat until fragrant. Set sauce aside. Heat remaining 4 tbsp. butter in a 6-qt. saucepan over medium-high heat. Add ginger, garlic, onion, and jalapeño and cook until browned, about 15 minutes. Add flour, coriander, cumin, and turmeric and cook until smooth, about 2 minutes. Add stock and lentils and bring to a boil. Reduce heat to medium-low, cover, and cook until tender, about 45 minutes. Add cilantro and purée. Add coconut milk, lemon juice, salt, and pepper. Divide among bowls, garnish with sauce and yogurt, and serve.

CALIFORNIA CLASSIC

"After my parents' divorce in the 1970s, Mom and I did the best we could to cobble a new family unit together. Part of that was creating new traditions. We found one in our regular pilgrimages to Duarte's Tavern in Pescadero, California. After a two-hour drive from our Bay Area home and a brisk walk along the craggy coast, we would head to Duarte's and warm up over steamy bowls of cream of artichoke soup. Opened in 1894, Duarte's was everything you wanted a California diner to be, and still is. Unlike other such establishments, which have been what I like to call "arugulaized," Duarte's still serves classics like BLTs and burgers, along with local specialties, including Pacific-caught fish and plenty of artichoke dishes. Then there are the desserts, my favorite being the olallieberry pie, made with the tangy West Coast hybrid berries. It's quite possibly the best pie on Earth. My mother is gone now. But when I go back to Duarte's for a bowl of that artichoke soup, I can't help thinking I'm keeping our relationship alive."

JAMES OSELAND

DUARTE'S CREAM OF ARTICHOKE SOUP
SERVES 6

Diners at the 118-year-old Duarte's Tavern in Pescadero, California, have been dipping hunks of sourdough bread into this soup for as long as anyone can remember.

- 2 tbsp. unsalted butter
- 2 cloves garlic, finely chopped
- 1 small onion, finely chopped
- 2 lb. frozen artichoke hearts, thawed and roughly chopped
- 3 cups chicken stock
- 2 cups heavy cream
  Kosher salt and freshly ground black pepper, to taste
  Lemon wedges, for serving

Melt butter in 4-qt. saucepan over medium heat. Add garlic and onion and cook, stirring occasionally, until soft, about 8 minutes. Add artichokes and cook, stirring, until soft, about 3 minutes. Add stock and bring to a boil. Reduce heat to medium-low and cook until artichokes are very tender, about 20 minutes. Working in batches, transfer stock and vegetables to a blender and purée until smooth. Return to saucepan, add cream, and bring to a simmer over medium heat. Cook, stirring occasionally, until reduced by one-third, about 45 minutes. Season with salt and pepper and serve with lemon wedges on the side.

CREAMY CHESTNUT SOUP

Velouté de Châtaignes

SERVES 6

Earthy roasted chestnuts are simmered in an aromatic stock until tender, then puréed to make a lush cream-thickened soup, a winter staple in the southwest of France.

4	slices bacon, roughly chopped
2	tbsp. unsalted butter
1	large shallot, roughly chopped
1	medium carrot, peeled and roughly chopped
1	small leek, roughly chopped
1	rib celery, roughly chopped
4½	cups chicken stock
2½	lb. fresh chestnuts, roasted and peeled, or two 15-oz. jars whole roasted chestnuts, drained
1	bay leaf
1	sprig fresh thyme
½	cup heavy cream
½	tsp. freshly grated nutmeg
	Kosher salt and freshly ground black pepper, to taste

1 Heat bacon in a 6-qt. saucepan over medium-high heat and cook, stirring occasionally, until fat is rendered and bacon is almost crisp, 3–4 minutes. Add butter, shallot, carrot, leek, and celery and cook, stirring occasionally, until vegetables are soft, 5–7 minutes. Add stock, chestnuts, bay leaf, and thyme and bring to a boil. Reduce heat to medium and cook, partially covered, until chestnuts are very tender, about 25 minutes. Remove from heat and let cool slightly. Discard bay leaf and thyme.

2 Working in batches, purée soup in a blender until smooth. Return soup to saucepan and place over medium heat. Stir in cream, nutmeg, salt, and pepper and cook until soup is slightly thick, about 5 minutes more.

CREAM OF GREEN PEA SOUP

SERVES 4

Rich, bright, and sweet, this verdant recipe has little in common with the thick forest-green purée that is most associated with the phrase "pea soup." Made with frozen peas, it is remarkable and easy; made with fresh peas in the early summer, it's a revelation.

3	cups milk, at room temperature
2	cups fresh or frozen peas
	Leaves from 3 sprigs fresh marjoram
1	sprig fresh thyme
1	fresh mint leaf
1½	tsp. onion salt
½	tsp. garlic salt
1½	tsp. sugar
	Kosher salt and freshly ground black pepper, to taste

1 Combine milk, peas, marjoram, thyme, mint, onion salt, garlic salt, and sugar in a blender and purée until smooth, 1–2 minutes. Place a fine-mesh sieve over a medium saucepan and strain the pea mixture into the saucepan. Press as much liquid as possible through the sieve with a spatula, discarding the pulp.

2 Place saucepan over medium-low heat and bring to just below boiling, about 5 minutes. Season with salt and pepper before serving.

GERMAN SPLIT PEA SOUP

Erbsensuppe

SERVES 6–8

Smoked ham hocks are a traditional ingredient in Germany's famous split pea soup; the addition of silky rendered bacon fat deepens the flavor. A little flour gives this soup a smooth texture, while celery root adds an earthy note.

2	tbsp. extra-virgin olive oil
2	slices bacon, finely chopped
1	large onion, finely chopped
1	rib celery, finely chopped
1	large carrot, peeled and finely chopped
1	small celery root, peeled and finely chopped
	Kosher salt, to taste
2	tbsp. flour
10	sprigs fresh flat-leaf parsley

> "There is nothing like soup. It is by nature eccentric: No two are ever alike, unless of course you get your soup in a can."
>
> LAURIE COLWIN

8   sprigs fresh thyme
2   bay leaves
1   lb. green split peas, rinsed and drained
2   large smoked ham hocks (about 2 lb. total)
    Freshly ground black pepper, to taste

1 Place oil and bacon in a 6-qt. pot and cook over medium-high heat until crisp, about 6 minutes. Using a slotted spoon, transfer bacon to a paper towel to drain and set aside. Add onions, celery, carrots, and celery root, season with salt, and cook, stirring occasionally, until soft, about 10 minutes. Stir in flour and cook for 3 minutes.

2 Tie parsley, thyme, and bay leaves together with kitchen twine and add to pot with peas, ham hocks, and 7 cups water. Bring to a boil over high heat. Reduce heat and simmer, covered, until peas are very tender, about 1 hour. Remove from heat. Discard herbs. Transfer hocks to a plate to cool. Pull off and chop the meat, discarding fat, skin, and bones. Stir meat into soup, season with salt and pepper, and ladle soup into bowls. Sprinkle with reserved bacon.

CREAM OF TOMATO SOUP

SERVES 4–6

To those of us who grew up loving the ready-made stuff, a first taste of homemade cream of tomato soup is nothing short of revelatory. Crushed tomatoes bring brightness and body; bacon, a smoky backbone; and a generous finish of crème fraîche infuses that signature luxuriousness. It's nuanced and vibrant in ways that the canned variety just can't be, and it remains the ideal partner for the Ultimate Grilled Cheese Sandwich (page 121).

4   slices thick-cut bacon, finely chopped
2   tbsp. unsalted butter
4   cloves garlic, finely chopped
1   medium onion, finely chopped
1   medium carrot, peeled and finely chopped
3   tbsp. tomato paste
1   tbsp. flour
4   cups chicken stock

2   sprigs fresh thyme
1   bay leaf
1   15-oz. can whole, peeled tomatoes in juice, crushed by hand
¼   cup heavy cream
    Kosher salt and freshly ground black pepper, to taste
    Crème fraîche and finely chopped fresh chives, for garnish (optional)

1 Heat bacon in a 4-qt. saucepan over medium heat and cook until its fat renders and bacon is crisp, about 10 minutes. Add butter and increase temperature to medium-high. Add garlic, onion, and carrot and cook, stirring, until soft, about 10 minutes. Add tomato paste and cook, stirring, until lightly caramelized, about 3 minutes. Add flour and cook, stirring, until smooth, about 2 minutes more. Add stock, thyme, bay leaf, and tomatoes and bring to a boil. Reduce heat to medium-low and cook, stirring occasionally, until slightly reduced, about 30 minutes.

2 Working in batches, transfer to a blender and purée. Return to saucepan and stir in cream. Season with salt and pepper. Divide among bowls, dollop with crème fraîche and sprinkle with chives (if using), and serve.

LOBSTER BISQUE

SERVES 4

A silky lobster bisque is one of the great luxuries to be found with the soup course, and there's no better version than this, as once served by the great chef Raymond Oliver, of Paris' celebrated midcentury restaurant Le Grand Véfour. The bisque is particularly wonderful paired with champagne, as the wine's tang offers such a pleasing contrast to the soup's creamy texture.

12   sprigs fresh flat-leaf parsley
6   sprigs fresh thyme
1   fresh bay leaf
1   4-lb. lobster, cooked
6   tbsp. unsalted butter

2   tbsp. extra-virgin olive oil
¼   cup brandy
3   large shallots, finely chopped
2   carrots, peeled and finely chopped
2   ribs celery, finely chopped
1   clove garlic, finely chopped
1   large onion, finely chopped
     Kosher salt, to taste
2   tbsp. tomato paste
2   cups white wine
5   cups fish stock (page 569)
     Pinch of cayenne pepper
1   cup heavy cream
1   tbsp. cornstarch
4   egg yolks
2   tbsp. chopped fresh chives

1 Tie 6 sprigs parsley, thyme, and bay leaf together with kitchen twine to make a bouquet garni and set aside. Working over a sieve set over a bowl to collect the lobster's juices, separate claws and tail from body and crack claws. Remove meat from shells. Cut tail into quarters crosswise and halve body lengthwise. Discard intestinal tract and sac behind head. Reserve lobster parts and juices separately.

2 Heat butter and oil in a deep skillet over high heat. Add lobster parts and cook, covered and turning once, until bright red, 6–7 minutes. Remove skillet from heat. Pour the lobster-infused butter into a bowl and set aside. Pour brandy over lobster and ignite with a match. When the flames subside, transfer lobster to a plate.

3 Heat reserved lobster-infused butter in the skillet over medium-high heat. Add remaining 6 parsley sprigs, shallots, carrots, celery, garlic, onions, and salt. Cook until caramelized, 18–20 minutes. Add tomato paste and cook until browned, 3–4 minutes. Add wine and cook, scraping up browned bits, 2–3 minutes. Transfer mixture to a large pot. Add reserved bouquet garni, stock, cayenne, salt, and cream and bring to a boil. Reduce heat to medium-low, cover, and simmer, 15–20 minutes. Remove soup from heat and strain, then return to pot.

4 Meanwhile, put cornstarch and egg yolks into a medium bowl and whisk until smooth. Gradually whisk about ¼ cup of the bisque into yolks, then stir egg mixture back into pot of bisque. Place bisque back over medium heat and stir until thickened, about 10 minutes. Add reserved lobster and juices and season with salt and pepper. Divide among bowls and serve garnished with chives.

SCALLOP BISQUE

SERVES 4

This unusual Irish soup uses fish bones and trimmings to get its flavor. Creamy and delicate, it makes a lovely simple supper on a cold evening.

5   lb. bones and trimmings from a non-oily fish, such as red snapper or flounder
2   carrots, peeled and halved
2   onions, halved
3   ribs celery, halved
2   cups dry white wine
2   bay leaves
1   stalk lemongrass, trimmed and coarsely chopped
     Kosher salt, to taste
2   tbsp. extra-virgin olive oil
1   lb. large sea scallops
1   cup heavy cream
1   tbsp. chopped chives

1 Make a stock by combining fish parts, carrots, onions, celery, wine, bay leaves, lemongrass, and salt to taste with 8 cups water in a large stockpot. Bring to a simmer, skim foam, and cook for 40 minutes. Strain. Return stock to pot and simmer until reduced by half.

2 Heat oil in a large skillet until very hot but not smoking. Sear scallops for about 1 minute on each side. Set aside.

3 Strain stock into a heavy saucepan. Add cream. Simmer until slightly thickened, about 15 minutes. Add scallops. Adjust seasoning. Garnish with chives.

COLLARD GREENS CHOWDER

SERVES 8

During greens season, chef Matt Register of Garland, North Carolina's Southern Smoke BBQ stews nearly 30 pounds of collards a week for his hearty, fish-free riff on creamy clam chowder.

2½   lb. collard greens, coarsely chopped
1   tbsp. kosher salt
8   oz. dry-cured country ham such as Benton's, coarsely chopped (about 1½ cups)
1   large sweet onion, finely chopped (about 2 cups)
2   tbsp. salted butter
1   tsp. ground turmeric
2   medium russet potatoes, peeled and diced (about 2½ cups)
1   cup heavy cream
1   tsp. freshly ground black pepper

> "But when that smoking chowder came in, the mystery was delightfully explained. Oh! sweet friends, hearken to me. It was made of small juicy clams, scarcely bigger than hazel nuts, mixed with pounded ship biscuits and salted pork cut up into little flakes! the whole enriched with butter, and plentifully seasoned with pepper and salt . . . we dispatched it with great expedition."
>
> HERMAN MELVILLE, *MOBY-DICK*

1 Combine collard greens, salt, and 6 cups cold water in a large stockpot over medium-high heat. Bring to a boil, then lower heat and simmer, stirring occasionally, until greens are tender but not mushy, 50–60 minutes. Drain, reserving potlikker, and set greens and potlikker aside.

2 Rinse out pot and return it to medium heat. Add ham and cook, stirring occasionally, until its fat begins to render and edges begin to brown, 3–5 minutes. Add onion and butter and cook, stirring frequently, until onion is translucent, 4–6 minutes. Stir in turmeric, then add 3 cups of reserved potlikker and the potatoes. Bring to a simmer and cook until potatoes are tender, 4–6 minutes more. Stir in 3 cups of reserved greens, heavy cream, and black pepper, then bring to a simmer and cook until greens are very tender and heated through, 6–8 minutes. Serve hot.

COOK'S NOTE Dry-cured country ham can be found in specialty markets or online. But if you can't track some down locally, substitute thickly sliced prosciutto.

ELOTE-STYLE CORN CHOWDER

SERVES 6 (SEE PHOTO, PAGE 214)

Inspired by elote, a popular street food in Mexico, this creamy chowder is an excellent way to use up leftover grilled corn. Even the cobs are added to the soup for an extra boost of sweetness and depth of flavor.

- 8 medium ears corn, shucked
- 4 tbsp. unsalted butter
- 1 medium yellow onion, finely chopped (1½ cups)
- 1 rib celery, finely chopped (½ cup)
- 1 medium poblano pepper, seeded, stemmed, and finely chopped (½ cup)
- 4 cloves garlic, finely chopped (1 tbsp. plus 1 tsp.)
- 1 tsp. dried Mexican oregano
- 1 fresh bay leaf
- 3½ cups whole milk
- 3 medium yellow potatoes (about 1½ lb.), peeled and cut into ½" pieces
- 1 cup heavy cream
  Kosher salt, to taste
- 1 tbsp. ancho chile powder, plus more for topping
- ¼ cup thinly sliced cilantro
- ½ cup Mexican crema or sour cream
- ½ cup crumbled Cotija cheese
  Lime wedges, for serving

1 On a medium-hot grill or hot grill pan, char corn all over, 15–20 minutes. Transfer to a platter and set aside until cool enough to handle.

2 Working over a large bowl, slice corn kernels off each cob, scraping the cob with the knife to extract the flavorful juices. Halve 5 bare corn cobs crosswise, discarding the rest. Set kernels and cobs aside.

3 Melt butter in a medium pot over medium heat. When foam begins to subside, add onion, celery, poblano, garlic, oregano, and bay leaf. Cover and cook, stirring occasionally, until onion softens, 7–8 minutes. Add reserved corn kernels and cobs, milk, potatoes, and cream. Bring to a boil, cover, and lower heat to maintain a simmer. Cook, stirring occasionally, until potatoes are tender, about 25 minutes. Remove and discard cobs and bay leaf. Transfer 1½ cups of the soup to a blender and purée until smooth. Stir puréed soup back into pot of remaining soup to thicken. Season with salt and the ancho chile powder, then ladle into wide soup bowls and garnish with cilantro, crema, Cotija, and additional ancho chile powder. Serve with lime wedges.

Chilled Soups

CHILLED CARROT SOUP WITH FINES HERBES MOUSSE

SERVES 4

This intensely carroty soup from chef Thomas Keller of the French Laundry in Yountville, California, captures the very essence of fresh carrots.

FOR THE SOUP

3	medium carrots, peeled and cut into 1″ rounds
2½	cups fresh carrot juice
1	tsp. unsalted butter
1	tsp. honey
	Pinch of curry powder
½	cup heavy cream
	Kosher salt and freshly ground white pepper, to taste

FOR THE MOUSSE

¼	cup crème fraîche
1	fresh chive, finely chopped
1	small sprig fresh parsley, minced
1	small sprig fresh chervil, minced
1	small sprig fresh tarragon, minced

1 Make the soup: Put carrots, 1¼ cups carrot juice, butter, honey, and curry powder into a medium pot and bring to a simmer over medium heat. Reduce heat to medium-low and simmer until liquid has evaporated and carrots are very soft, about 1 hour. Add cream, increase heat to medium, and simmer for 3 minutes.

2 Purée carrot mixture and remaining 1¼ cups carrot juice in a blender. Pass soup through a fine sieve into a medium bowl and season to taste with salt and pepper. Cover and refrigerate until chilled.

3 Make the mousse: Whisk crème fraîche in a medium bowl until stiff peaks form. Fold in chives, parsley, chervil, and tarragon.

4 Divide soup among 4 chilled soup bowls and place a spoonful of mousse in center of each bowl.

GAZPACHO ANDALUZ

SERVES 4

Most likely invented in Seville, gazpacho was originally served at the end of a meal. Although there are many versions of this soup, the traditional, tomato-based, bread-thickened Andalusian variety is the one we want on a hot afternoon or warm evening. It's salad in a blender, summer in a bowl.

1	slice country-style bread, about 1″ thick, crust removed
2	small cucumbers, peeled, seeded, and chopped
2	lb. very ripe tomatoes, seeded and coarsely chopped
1	clove garlic, chopped
2	tbsp. sherry vinegar
½	cup extra-virgin olive oil
	Kosher salt, to taste

OPTIONAL GARNISHES

½	green pepper, seeded and finely diced
½	cucumber, peeled, seeded, and finely diced
1	cup ½″ croutons
½	small white onion, finely diced
1	small tomato, seeded and finely diced

1 Soak bread in a small bowl in water to cover for 30 minutes. Squeeze out moisture with your hands.

2 Purée bread, cucumbers, tomatoes, garlic, vinegar, oil, and 1 cup water in a blender or food processor until very smooth.

3 Push purée through a coarse sieve with the back of a wooden spoon. Gazpacho should be fairly thin. Season to taste with salt.

4 Chill gazpacho in refrigerator for at least 2 hours. Adjust seasoning. Serve in glasses or soup bowls, with garnishes on the side.

SALMOREJO
Spanish Tomato-Bread Soup

SERVES 8

Salmorejo is gazpacho's deeper, richer cousin, its tomato base intensified by garnishes of chopped hard-cooked egg and strips of salty, fatty *jamón ibérico*.

3	tbsp. kosher salt, plus more to taste
8	plum tomatoes, cored, halved, and seeded
1	clove garlic, crushed
1	baguette, cut into large pieces
½	small onion
1	cup extra-virgin olive oil, plus more for drizzling
2	tbsp. sherry vinegar
	Freshly ground black pepper, to taste
3	hard-cooked eggs, chopped
1½	cups finely chopped Iberian ham or prosciutto

1 Combine salt, tomatoes, garlic, bread, and onion in a bowl, cover with boiling water, and let sit for 1 hour.

2 Drain vegetables, reserving 1 cup soaking liquid, and place in blender. Squeeze water from bread, then add to blender with reserved soaking liquid, oil, and vinegar. Purée until smooth. Season with salt and pepper and chill for at least 1 hour.

3 Pour soup into serving bowls and top with eggs, ham, and a drizzle of oil.

VICHYSSOISE
Creamy Chilled Potato & Leek Soup

SERVES 8

Legend has it that chef Louis Diat of New York City's original Ritz-Carlton Hotel once prepared eight portions of his famous soup to be delivered to the Manhattan town house of Sara Delano Roosevelt, Franklin's mother, at her request—and enclosed this recipe, so she could have her cook prepare it without his further assistance.

4	tbsp. unsalted butter
4	leeks, white and light green parts only, thinly sliced
1	medium onion, thinly sliced
5	medium white boiling potatoes (about 2¼ pounds), peeled and thinly sliced
	Kosher salt
2	cups milk
2	cups cream
1	cup heavy cream
2	tbsp. finely chopped fresh chives

1 Melt butter in a large pot over medium-low heat. Add leeks and onion and cook, stirring occasionally, until soft but not browned, about 20 minutes. Add potatoes, salt to taste, and 4 cups water and increase heat to high. Bring to a boil, reduce heat to medium-low, and simmer, stirring occasionally, until potatoes are soft, 50–60 minutes.

2 Strain soup through a fine-mesh sieve into a bowl, pressing and scraping the solids with a spoon. Wipe out pot and return soup to it. Whisk in milk and light cream, bring to a boil over high heat, then remove from heat and let cool. Strain soup through a fine-mesh sieve (finer than the first), pressing and scraping it into a bowl with the spoon, leaving behind a thick paste of solids. Discard solids. Stir heavy cream into soup, cover with plastic wrap, and refrigerate until chilled. Season soup with salt to taste. Divide soup among 8 soup bowls and garnish with chives.

CHILLED AVOCADO SOUP
Sopa Fría de Aguacate

SERVES 6–8

Brightened with chiles and lime juice, this silky, cold Mexican avocado soup gets an added dose of richness from heavy cream.

4	serrano chiles, stemmed, seeded, and finely chopped
2	large ripe avocados, pitted, peeled, and roughly chopped
1	medium onion, finely chopped
6	cups chicken stock
1	cup heavy cream
⅓	cup fresh lime juice
	Kosher salt and freshly ground black pepper, to taste
2	plum tomatoes, cored, seeded, and finely chopped

1 Combine half the serrano chiles, the avocados, and half the onion in a food processor and process until a smooth paste forms. Add stock, cream, and lime juice and purée until very smooth. Pour through a fine-mesh sieve into a bowl or pitcher and season with salt and pepper; cover and refrigerate until chilled, at least 2 hours.

2 To serve, divide soup among bowls and top with a spoonful each of remaining chiles and onion, along with the tomatoes.

Stews

CHICKEN & SAUSAGE GUMBO

SERVES 6–8

Gumbos are a staple of Acadian cuisine, evolving over many years as new ingredients and techniques enlivened generations-old recipes. During cooking, okra exudes a thick liquid that gives this stew a sumptuous, silky texture; a little filé powder, made from dried sassafras leaves, further thickens and enriches it. The backbone of this gumbo, however, and the source of its smoky flavor, is the roux made by toasting flour in hot oil until it is a deep red-brown.

½	cup canola oil
2	lb. bone-in, skin-on chicken thighs
	Kosher salt and freshly ground black pepper, to taste
½	lb. andouille sausage, cut into ½″ pieces
4	slices bacon, cut into ½″ pieces
1	cup flour
2	ribs celery, finely chopped
1	small onion, finely chopped
1	small green bell pepper, seeded and finely chopped
2	tsp. dried thyme
1	tsp. cayenne pepper
6	canned whole, peeled tomatoes, crushed by hand
6	cloves garlic, finely chopped
1	bay leaf
10	oz. okra, trimmed and cut into ½″ slices
4	cups chicken stock
	Cooked white rice, for serving
	Hot sauce and filé powder, for serving

1 Heat ¼ cup oil in an 8-qt. Dutch oven over medium-high heat. Working in batches, season chicken with salt and pepper, and add chicken to pot. Cook, turning once, until lightly browned, about 12 minutes. Transfer to a plate. Add sausage and bacon and cook, stirring, until fat renders and bacon is browned, about 5 minutes. Transfer to plate with chicken.

2 Add remaining oil and reduce heat to medium-low. Stir in flour and cook, stirring constantly, until this mixture (called a roux) is the color of dark, reddish caramel, about 8 minutes. Add celery, onion, and pepper and cook until

soft, about 6 minutes. Add thyme, cayenne, tomatoes, garlic, and bay leaf and cook for 3 minutes. Return chicken, sausage, and bacon to pot along with okra and stock and bring to a boil over high heat. Reduce to medium and cook, stirring occasionally, until chicken is cooked through, okra is tender, and gumbo is thickened, about 30 minutes. Remove chicken from pot and let cool for 5 minutes. Remove and shred meat, discarding bones and skin, then stir meat back into gumbo. Season with salt and pepper. Serve with white rice, hot sauce, and filé powder.

GUMBO Z'HERBES

SERVES 10–12

This meatless gumbo, made with various greens, is a traditional Lenten dish in Louisiana's Catholic communities.

4	tbsp. canola oil
4	tbsp. flour
3	large onions, chopped
3	ribs celery, chopped
1	green bell pepper, seeded and chopped
5–6	cloves garlic, chopped
2	tsp. Tabasco sauce
1	tsp. cayenne pepper
3	lb. greens, such as mustard, beet, turnip, collards, kale, spinach, swiss chard, carrot tops, or parsley, or any combination, chopped
2	bay leaves
	Kosher salt and freshly ground black pepper, to taste
2	tbsp. filé powder
	Cooked white rice, for serving

1 Heat oil in a large, heavy pot over medium heat. Add flour and cook, stirring constantly with a wooden spoon, until deep golden brown, 12–15 minutes. Add onions, celery, bell pepper, and garlic and cook, stirring often, until soft, 8–10 minutes.

2 Stir 8 cups water into pot, then add Tabasco sauce and cayenne pepper. Increase heat to high and bring to a boil. Add greens and bay leaves and season to taste with salt and pepper. Reduce heat to medium-low and simmer, stirring occasionally, until greens are very soft, about 1 hour. Stir in filé powder, taste, and adjust seasonings. Remove bay leaves before serving. Serve gumbo over rice.

CHILI VERDE
SERVES 4–6

You can find a bowl of green chili with alarming frequency in the American Southwest, but New Mexicans are particularly proud of their chili verde, with its hunks of juicy pork shoulder and tart tomatillo-based sauce. The dish gets its oomph from green chiles, ideally the gorgeous ones grown around the town of Hatch, of which New Mexicans are also quite proud.

- ¼ cup canola oil
- 2 lb. boneless pork shoulder, cut into ½" cubes
  Kosher salt and freshly ground black pepper, to taste
- ½ cup flour
- ½ lb. ground breakfast sausage
- 2 tbsp. ground cumin
- 1 tbsp. green chile powder
- 1 dried pasilla chile, stemmed, seeded, and chopped
- ½ cup chopped scallions
- 12 tomatillos, husked, rinsed, and finely chopped
- 2 medium onions, finely chopped
- 2 serrano chiles, stemmed and finely chopped
- 2 Anaheim chiles, stemmed, seeded, and finely chopped
- 1 green bell pepper, seeded and finely chopped
- 2 cups chicken stock
- 1 15-oz. can green enchilada sauce, such as Hatch
  Roughly torn fresh cilantro leaves, for garnish
  Hot sauce, for serving

1 Heat oil in an 8-qt. saucepan over medium-high heat. Season pork with salt and pepper and toss with flour. Working in batches, add pork to pan and cook until browned, about 6 minutes. Transfer to a bowl and set aside.

2 Add sausage to pan and cook, breaking up with a spoon, until browned, about 4 minutes. Transfer to bowl with pork.

3 Add cumin, chile powder, and pasilla chile to pan and cook until fragrant, about 1 minute. Add scallions, tomatillos, onions, serranos, Anaheim chiles, and bell pepper and cook until soft, about 15 minutes. Add reserved pork and sausage, stock, and enchilada sauce and cook until pork is tender, about 30 minutes. Garnish with cilantro and serve with hot sauce.

TEXAS-STYLE CHILI CON CARNE
SERVES 4

You won't find beans or tomatoes in a true Texan chili con carne—just tender cubes of beef and pork, fiery chiles, and plenty of garlic, onion, oregano, and cumin for flavor. A little bacon fat gives this one a rich and smoky undertone.

- 6 large dried guajillo chiles
- 6 dried chiles de árbol
- 2 tbsp. rendered bacon fat
- 1 lb. boneless beef shoulder, cut into ¼" cubes
- 1 lb. boneless pork shoulder, cut into ¼" cubes
- 5 cloves garlic, finely chopped
- 1 small onion, finely chopped
- 1 tbsp. dried oregano
- 1 tbsp. ground cumin
- 1 tbsp. flour
- 1½ cups beef stock
  Kosher salt and freshly ground black pepper, to taste

1 Place both chiles in a bowl, cover with 4 cups boiling water, and let sit until softened, about 30 minutes. Remove chiles from water and discard stems and seeds. Transfer chiles to a blender along with soaking liquid and purée until smooth, at least 30 seconds. Set purée aside.

2 Heat bacon fat in a 6-qt. saucepan over medium-high heat. Add beef and pork and cook, stirring occasionally, until lightly browned all over, about 12 minutes. Using a wooden spoon, push meat to the perimeter of the pan, and add garlic and onion to the center of the pan. Cook, stirring, until soft, about 2 minutes. Add oregano, cumin, and flour, stir ingredients together, and cook until fragrant, about 2 minutes. Add reserved chile purée and stock and bring to a boil. Reduce heat to medium-low and cook, covered partially and stirring occasionally, until meat is very tender and sauce is reduced slightly, about 1 hour. Season with salt and pepper and serve ladled into bowls.

JIM CLARK'S CHILI

SERVES 6

The Southwest doesn't get all the chili glory! Home cook Jim Clark won the 1980 Great Chili Cookoff in Galena, Illinois, with this recipe, and Benjamin's, a local eatery, served it for years. Clark believes that freezing improves this chili's flavor, so consider making it in advance.

- 3 tbsp. vegetable oil
- 2 lb. boneless beef chuck, cut into ¼″ cubes
- 1 lb. boneless pork shoulder, cut into ¼″ cubes
- 2 onions, diced
- 8 cloves garlic, diced
- 4 shallots, diced
- 1 large green bell pepper, seeded and diced
- 3 tbsp. chili powder
- 2 28-oz. cans whole, peeled tomatoes with juice
  Kosher salt
- 2 tbsp. ground cumin
- 1 tbsp. dried oregano
- 1 tbsp. dried rosemary
- 2 cups cooked kidney beans

1 Heat oil in a large pot over medium-high heat. Add beef and pork and brown, turning, for 5 minutes. Add onions, garlic, shallots, and peppers, mix well, then add chili powder. Cover pot, reduce heat to medium-low, and simmer, stirring occasionally, for 20 minutes.

2 Add tomatoes, crushing them with your hand, along with salt, cumin, and herbs, then return to a simmer. Lower heat, cover, and barely simmer until meat is tender, about 2 hours. Add beans, cook for an additional 30 minutes, and serve.

TAMING THE CHILE

Much of a pepper's capsaicin (the chemical responsible for spiciness) resides in the interior tissue that holds the seeds. When cooking for spice-averse diners, dial back a chile's heat by simply slitting it up the side before adding it—whole—to the pot. Make a lengthwise incision from the shoulder of each pepper's stem to the tip—it'll coax out just enough of the pepper's floral sweetness and burn. (Be sure to remove it before serving!)

CINCINNATI CHILI

SERVES 4

Redolent of warm spices and rounded out with a touch of cocoa powder, Cincinnati-style chili, whether prepared two-way (chili over spaghetti), three-way (with cheese), four-way (with onions), or five-way (with a finishing flourish of kidney beans), is an enduring American classic.

- 2 tbsp. olive oil
- 5 cloves garlic, finely chopped
- 2 medium onions, finely chopped
- 1½ lb. ground beef
- 2 tbsp. chili powder
- 1½ tsp. ground cinnamon
- ½ tsp. ground allspice
- ½ tsp. ground cloves
- ½ tsp. ground cumin
- 1 tsp. dried oregano
- ½ tsp. ground nutmeg
- ½ tsp. celery seeds
- 1 bay leaf
  Kosher salt and freshly ground black pepper, to taste
- 2 cups tomato sauce
- 1 tbsp. unsweetened cocoa powder
- ¾ lb. dried spaghetti
- 1 15-oz. can red kidney beans, drained and rinsed
- 2 cups finely grated cheddar cheese
  Oyster crackers, for serving

1 Heat oil in a large skillet over medium-high heat. Add garlic and half of onions and cook, stirring occasionally, until lightly browned, 5–6 minutes. Add beef, chili powder, cinnamon, allspice, cloves, cumin, oregano, nutmeg, celery seeds, bay leaf, and salt and pepper and cook, stirring occasionally, until well browned, 6–8 minutes. Tilt skillet and spoon out and discard any accumulated fat. Add tomato sauce, cocoa powder, and 1 cup water and bring to a boil. Reduce heat to medium-low and cook, partially covered, until somewhat thick, about 25 minutes.

2 Meanwhile, bring a large pot of salted water to a boil over medium-high heat. Add spaghetti and cook, stirring occasionally, until tender, 8–10 minutes; drain. Put beans into a small pot, cover, and cook over medium heat, stirring occasionally, until heated through. Divide spaghetti among 4 large bowls. Top with chili, cheese, remaining onions, and beans. Serve hot, with oyster crackers on the side.

VEGETARIAN CHILI

SERVES 6–8

Writer Suketu Mehta gave us the recipe for this vegetable-laden, vibrantly spicy chili. Making a lengthwise slit down the side of each of the fresh chiles releases more of their intense floral heat.

- ¾ lb. dried dark kidney beans, soaked overnight
- ¾ lb. dried pinto beans, soaked overnight
-      Kosher salt, to taste
- ¼ cup extra-virgin olive oil
- 12 cloves garlic, minced
- 3 dried chipotle chiles
- 2 bay leaves
- 2 large white onions, chopped
- 1 dried ancho chile
- ½ lb. button mushrooms, quartered
- 6 medium tomatoes, chopped
- 1½ cups canned hominy, drained and rinsed
- ½ cup tomato paste
- 2 tbsp. red wine vinegar
- 2 tsp. fresh thyme leaves
- 1 tsp. dried oregano
- 1 tsp. ground cumin
- 8 sun-dried tomatoes, chopped
- 3–6 habanero chiles, slit lengthwise down one side
-      Freshly ground black pepper, to taste
-      Sour cream, for serving
-      Minced fresh cilantro, for serving
-      Minced red onion, for serving

1 Put kidney beans and pinto beans into a large pot and cover with 3″ water. Bring to a boil, reduce heat to medium-low, and simmer, stirring occasionally, until beans are tender, about 1 hour. Season with salt and set aside.

2 Heat oil in a 6-qt. pot over medium-high heat. Add garlic, chipotle chiles, bay leaves, onions, and ancho chile and cook, stirring often, until onions are golden, 12–15 minutes. Add mushrooms and cook, stirring often, until tender, about 8 minutes. Add tomatoes and cook, stirring, until they release their juices, about 5 minutes. Stir in reserved beans and their cooking liquid, hominy, tomato paste, vinegar, thyme, oregano, cumin, sun-dried tomatoes, and habaneros and season with salt and pepper. Reduce heat to medium-low and simmer, stirring occasionally, until chili thickens and flavors meld, about 1 hour. Serve chili topped with sour cream, cilantro, and red onions.

PEPPER POT SOUP

SERVES 6–8

This vegetarian soup, a Jamaican classic, is made with callaloo, a spinach-like green that can be found canned or fresh in Caribbean groceries. Serve with minced fresh Scotch bonnet chiles sprinkled on top for extra heat.

- 2 tbsp. vegetable oil
- 6 scallions, roughly chopped
- 3 sprigs thyme, stems removed
- 2 cloves garlic, minced
- 1 small white onion, roughly chopped
- 8 oz. fresh or canned callaloo or spinach, roughly chopped
- 4 cups vegetable stock
- 3 Scotch bonnet chiles (1 halved; 2 stemmed, seeded, and minced)
- 1 yellow yam or russet potato, peeled and cut into 1″ cubes
-      Kosher salt and freshly ground black pepper, to taste

1 Heat oil in a large saucepan over medium heat. Add scallions, thyme, garlic, and onion and cook, stirring, until soft, about 7 minutes. Stir in callaloo, stock, and halved chile. Bring to a simmer over medium heat and cook, stirring, until callaloo is tender, about 10 minutes.

2 Transfer soup to a blender, discard chile, and purée until smooth. Return soup to pan over medium heat, stir in yam, and cook, stirring, until yam is tender, about 15 minutes. Season with salt and pepper, then serve soup with minced chiles on the side.

SENEGALESE PEANUT STEW

Maafe Ginaa

SERVES 4–6

Peanut, or groundnut, stews are found across West Africa and its disapora. The list of ingredients often extends to okra, tomatoes, chiles, and other bright foils for the stew's intense richness, but it's the indispensable peanut that gives this version from Senegal its essential earthy character.

- ⅓ cup canola oil
- 2 lb. bone-in chicken thighs, skinned
-      Kosher salt, to taste
- ¼ cup finely chopped fresh ginger
- 1 large onion, finely chopped
- 4 dried chiles de árbol

1 tsp. ground coriander
1 tsp. turmeric
½ tsp. ground cumin
½ tsp. ground black pepper
¼ tsp. ground cinnamon
⅓ tsp. fenugreek seeds
3 whole cloves
2 tbsp. tomato paste
¾ cup smooth peanut butter
1 cup diced plum tomatoes
1 lb. eggplant, peeled and cut into 1″ cubes
¼ lb. okra, cut into 1″ pieces
1 fresh red chile, sliced, for garnish
  Chopped roasted peanuts, for garnish
  Cooked white rice or fonio, for serving

1 Heat 3 tbsp. oil in a 6-qt. Dutch oven over medium-high heat. Season chicken with salt and add to pot. Cook, turning once, until lightly browned on both sides, about 10 minutes. Transfer to a plate and set aside.

2 Add remaining oil to pot. Add ginger, onion, and chiles de árbol and cook, stirring, until fragrant, about 6 minutes. Add spices and cook, stirring, until fragrant, about 1 minute. Add tomato paste and cook, stirring, until lightly caramelized, about 3 minutes. Stir in peanut butter and then return chicken to pot with 6 cups water and tomatoes. Bring to a boil, reduce heat to medium-low, and cook, partially covered, until chicken is half-cooked, about 25 minutes. Add eggplant and okra and cook, stirring occasionally, until chicken is cooked through and eggplant and okra are tender, about 30 minutes. Season with salt and sprinkle with red chile and peanuts. Serve with rice or fonio.

SIMPLE CHICKEN STEW

SERVES 6–8

This chicken stew isn't fussy, but its deep flavor and remarkable cold-weather-overpowering properties make it a very special meal. Plus, it comes together quickly with a short list of ingredients.

4 tbsp. unsalted butter
4 lb. boneless, skinless chicken thighs
4 ribs celery, sliced
4 carrots, peeled and sliced
1 small onion, sliced
2 tbsp. tarragon vinegar or champagne vinegar
1 tsp. fines herbes (a blend of parsley, chervil, tarragon, and chives)
1 bay leaf
  Kosher salt and freshly ground black pepper

1 Melt butter in a large cast-iron pot or other heavy-bottomed pot over medium-high heat. Working in batches to avoid crowding pot, add chicken and cook until well browned, 5–6 minutes per side. Transfer chicken to a plate and set aside.

2 Meanwhile, bring 4 cups water to a boil in a small pot over high heat. Reduce heat to low to keep water hot.

3 Add celery, carrots, onions, vinegar, fines herbes, and bay leaf to the large pot containing the butter and rendered chicken fat, scraping any browned bits stuck to bottom of pot. Season with salt and pepper and cook until vegetables begin to soften, about 3 minutes.

4 Return chicken and any accumulated juices to pot, add enough hot water just to cover chicken (about 3 cups), and bring to a boil. Reduce heat to low, cover, and simmer until chicken is tender, about 40 minutes. Discard bay leaf before serving.

IRANIAN CHICKEN & WALNUT STEW

Khoresht-e Fesenjān

SERVES 6–8

Pomegranate molasses and walnuts bring intense sweet, sour, and bitter notes to this essential Iranian dish.

¼ cup canola oil
2 lb. boneless, skinless chicken thighs, cut into 2½″ pieces
  Kosher salt and freshly ground black pepper, to taste
1½ tbsp. ground turmeric
1 large onion, thinly sliced
2 cups finely chopped spinach
1½ lb. walnuts
2 cups pomegranate molasses
¼ cup sugar
  Sliced red onion, for garnish

1 Heat oil in a 12″ skillet over medium-high heat. Working in batches, season chicken with salt and pepper, add to skillet, and cook, turning, until browned, about 8 minutes. Transfer to a plate and set aside. Add turmeric and onion and cook until soft, about 10 minutes. Add spinach and cook until wilted, about 1 minute. Remove from heat and set aside.

2 Meanwhile, process walnuts in a food processor into a very fine paste, about 2 minutes. Transfer to a 6-qt. Dutch

oven and heat over medium-low heat. Cook until fragrant, about 15 minutes. Stir in 8 cups water and bring to a simmer over medium heat. Cook, skimming any oil that floats to the surface, until light brown and thickened, about 2 hours. Add molasses and sugar and cook until thickened once more, about 25 minutes. Add reserved chicken and onion-spinach mixture and cook until chicken is cooked through, about 30 minutes. Garnish with onions.

VEAL STEW WITH POTATO DUMPLINGS

SERVES 6

This hearty recipe, a staple of writer Geraldine Campbell's childhood, is warming and homey. Its fall-apart tender pieces of veal and rich potato dumplings make it a perfect one-pot meal for a cold-weather weekend.

FOR THE STEW

- ½ cup flour
- 2 tsp. kosher salt
- 1 tsp. freshly ground black pepper
- 3 lb. boneless veal shoulder, cut into 1″ pieces
- 4 tbsp. unsalted butter
- 4 carrots, peeled and cut into 1″ pieces
- 1 large onion, chopped
- ¾ lb. cremini mushrooms, halved
- 4 cups chicken stock

FOR THE DUMPLINGS

- 1½ lb. Yukon gold potatoes (about 5 medium)
- ¾ cup dried bread crumbs or panko
- 4 egg yolks
- 2 tbsp. milk
- 1½ tbsp. finely chopped fresh dill
- 1 tsp. kosher salt
- ½ tsp. freshly ground black pepper
- ½ cup flour

1 Make the stew: Combine flour, salt, and pepper in a large resealable plastic bag. Add veal pieces to flour mixture and toss to coat evenly. Heat 1 tbsp. butter in a large, heavy pot over medium heat. Brown veal in 3 batches, adding an additional tbsp. butter to the pot with each new batch, turning meat occasionally, until golden on all sides but not cooked through, about 6 minutes per batch. Reserve browned veal.

2 Add remaining 1 tbsp. butter to pot, allow to heat just short of browning. Stir in carrots, onion, and mushrooms, scraping up any browned bits from bottom of pot. Increase

heat to medium-high and cook vegetables, stirring occasionally, until golden, 8–10 minutes.

3 Add stock and reserved veal, along with any accumulated juices, and bring to a boil. Reduce heat to a simmer and cook until veal is very tender and broth is thickened, about 2 hours.

4 Make the dumplings: While the stew simmers, in a separate pot, cover potatoes with salted water and bring to a boil. Cook until potatoes are easily pierced with a knife, 20–30 minutes. Drain potatoes and let cool until they are easily handled. Peel potatoes, then force through a ricer into a large bowl. Add bread crumbs, egg yolks, milk, dill, salt, and pepper to the riced potatoes; knead together using your hands until mixture is just combined (do not overwork the dumpling mixture). Form dough into golf ball–size dumplings. Pour flour out onto a flat surface, then evenly coat dumplings with a thin layer of flour, using a rolling motion. Boil dumplings in salted water until cooked through, about 15 minutes. To serve, place 3–4 dumplings in each bowl and top generously with stew.

ARGENTINE HOMINY STEW

Locro

SERVES 12

This autumnal Argentine stew of squash, meat, and hominy is creamy and slightly sweet. Its garnishing sauce, made with paprika, provides a festive burst of spice and color.

- 2 cups dried, broken hominy
- 1 cup dried lima beans
- 1 cup dried chickpeas
- ¾ cup olive oil
- 1½ tsp. sweet paprika
- ½ tsp. crushed red chile flakes
- 8 cloves garlic, minced
- 1 lb. boneless veal shoulder, cut into 1″ pieces
- 1 lb. boneless pork shoulder, cut into 1″ pieces
  Kosher salt and freshly ground black pepper, to taste
- 10 oz. cured chorizo, cut into ½″ slices
- 1 large onion, minced
- 1 tbsp. tomato paste
- 1 tsp. dried oregano
- ½ tsp. ground cumin
- 1 bay leaf
- 1 small acorn squash, peeled, seeded, and finely chopped

Juice of 1 lemon
1   cup finely chopped scallions

1 Rinse hominy under running water until water runs clear. Combine in a bowl with limas and chickpeas. Cover with water and soak for at least 8 hours or overnight before draining.

2 Whisk ½ cup oil, paprika, chile flakes, and one-quarter of the garlic in a bowl and set sauce aside. Heat remaining ¼ cup oil in an 8-qt. saucepan over medium-high heat. Season veal and pork with salt and pepper. Working in batches, add to pan and cook, turning, until browned all over, about 5 minutes. Transfer to a plate.

3 Add chorizo and cook until fat renders, about 2 minutes. Add remaining garlic and onion and cook until soft, about 3 minutes. Add tomato paste, oregano, cumin, and bay leaf and cook for 2 minutes. Return meat to pan with hominy, beans, chickpeas, squash, and 10 cups water. Bring to a boil, then reduce heat to medium-low and cook until hominy and beans are tender, about 2 hours.

4 Stir lemon juice into stew and season with salt and pepper. Divide among bowls, drizzle with sauce, and sprinkle with scallions.

BIGOS

Polish Pork & Sauerkraut Stew

SERVES 8

Bigos—a rib-sticking stew of pork shoulder, bacon, kielbasa, and sauerkraut—is a centerpiece of Polish celebrations.

¼   oz. dried porcini mushrooms
¼   lb. bacon, cut into ½″ pieces
1   lb. boneless pork shoulder, cut into 1″ cubes
Kosher salt and freshly ground black pepper, to taste
½   lb. smoked kielbasa, cut into 1″ rounds
1   tsp. caraway seeds
8   whole allspice berries
2   large onions, chopped
2   bay leaves
½   cup tomato paste
3   tbsp. flour
4   lb. sauerkraut, drained
⅓   cup pitted prunes, chopped
6   cups beef stock
½   cup madeira wine

2   medium tart apples, peeled, cored, and cut into ½″ cubes
Minced fresh chives, for garnish

1 Put mushrooms in a bowl and cover with 1½ cups boiling water. Let sit until mushrooms rehydrate, about 1 hour. Using a slotted spoon, transfer mushrooms to a cutting board, roughly chop, and set aside. Slowly pour soaking liquid into another bowl, leaving any sediment in the bottom of the first bowl, and set aside.

2 Heat bacon in an 8-qt. Dutch oven over medium heat and cook until fat renders, about 12 minutes. Transfer bacon to a plate. Increase heat to medium-high. Working in batches, season pork with salt and pepper, add to pot, and cook, turning, until browned all over, about 8 minutes. Transfer to plate with bacon. Add kielbasa and cook until browned, about 6 minutes. Transfer to plate.

3 Add caraway, allspice, onions, and bay leaves and cook, scraping bottom of pot, until onions are soft, about 10 minutes. Add tomato paste and cook until caramelized, about 8 minutes. Add flour and cook, stirring, until smooth, about 2 minutes. Add sauerkraut and cook, stirring, until slightly wilted, about 3 minutes. Return meat to pot along with reserved mushrooms and their soaking liquid, and then add prunes, stock, and wine and bring to a boil. Season with salt and pepper and reduce heat to medium-low. Cover and cook, stirring occasionally, for 30 minutes. Add apples and cook, covered, until pork is tender, about 30 minutes more. To serve, divide among bowls and garnish with chives.

SYRIAN ARTICHOKE & LAMB STEW

Yakhnet al-Ardî Shawkî

SERVES 4

The flavors of spring leap out in this bright stew, lifted with a dose of *baharat*—an Arabic term for spices in general, which also refers to a specific spice mixture that, in Syria, might include black pepper, allspice, cinnamon, and nutmeg.

6   tbsp. extra-virgin olive oil
8   raw artichoke hearts, halved
1   2-lb. piece boneless leg of lamb, cut into 1″ pieces
Kosher salt and freshly ground black pepper
1   large onion, grated
1   tsp. Baharat (page 586)
2   tbsp. chopped fresh mint, for garnish

1 Heat oil in a large Dutch oven over medium heat. Add artichokes and cook, turning once, until lightly browned, 3–5 minutes. Remove and set aside.

2 Season lamb with salt and pepper. In the same pot, brown lamb on all sides, in batches if necessary, turning the meat occasionally, for 4–6 minutes. Remove and set aside.

3 Add onion and spice mix to pot and cook, stirring frequently, until onion and spices are fragrant, about 5 minutes. Add lamb and 3 cups water. Season to taste with salt, then reduce heat to medium-low. Cover and simmer until meat is tender, 1½–2 hours. Increase heat to medium, add artichokes, and cook uncovered until stew thickens, about 45 minutes. Serve garnished with mint.

THARID

Emirati Lamb Stew

SERVES 4–6

A satisfying lamb and vegetable stew, tharid is often cited as the Prophet Muhammad's favorite dish, and many versions of the recipe are still enjoyed throughout the Arab world today. This one from the United Arab Emirates includes chiles, tomatoes, and potatoes—New World cultivars that were introduced to the region a thousand years after Muhammad's birth.

- ¼ cup canola oil
- 3 lb. bone-in lamb shoulder, trimmed and cut into 3″ pieces
- 2 tbsp. Bzar (page 587)
- 5 whole cloves
- 2 chiles de árbol, stemmed
- 1 large onion, thinly sliced lengthwise
- 6 cloves garlic, minced
- 1 4″ piece fresh ginger, peeled and minced
- 1 tbsp. ground cumin
- 1 tsp. freshly ground black pepper, plus more to taste
- ¼ tsp. ground cardamom
- 4 plum tomatoes, quartered lengthwise
- 2 bay leaves
- 15 baby Yukon gold potatoes
- 2 medium carrots, peeled and halved crosswise
- 2 small zucchini, halved crosswise
- 2 large cubanelle peppers, quartered lengthwise and seeded
  Kosher salt, to taste
- 4 12″ pieces pita bread, toasted

1 Heat oil in an 8-qt. Dutch oven over medium-high heat. Season lamb all over with spice mix. Working in batches, add lamb to pot and cook, turning as needed, until browned on all sides, about 6 minutes. Transfer lamb to a plate and set aside. Add cloves, chiles, and onion to pot and cook, stirring occasionally, until onion is soft and begins to caramelize, about 10 minutes. Add garlic and ginger and cook, stirring, until fragrant, about 2 minutes. Add cumin, pepper, cardamom, tomatoes, and bay leaves and cook, stirring, until tomatoes are soft, about 2 minutes. Return lamb to pot, and any drippings that accumulated on the plate. Add the potatoes, carrots, zucchini, peppers, and 12 cups water. Bring to a boil, reduce heat to medium-low, and simmer, partially covered, until lamb is tender, about 1½ hours. Season with salt and pepper.

2 Line a large, deep serving dish with pita. Using a slotted spoon, arrange meat and vegetables over bread. Pour liquid into a large bowl and serve on the side.

LAMB NAVARIN

Navarin d'Agneau

SERVES 4

We based our version of this French lamb stew on the recipe used in courses at the International Culinary Center in New York City. Over the years it's been made by thousands of students, and as far as we can tell, it's come out deliciously every time.

- 2 tbsp. canola oil
- 1½ lb. trimmed boneless lamb shoulder, cut into 1″ cubes
  Kosher salt and freshly ground black pepper, to taste
- 5 carrots (1 chopped, 4 peeled and cut into 2″ pieces)
- 1 medium yellow onion, chopped
- 2 cloves garlic, crushed
- 2 tbsp. flour
- 1 tbsp. tomato paste
- 4 medium turnips, peeled and cut into 2″ pieces
- 4 medium new potatoes, peeled and cut into 2″ pieces
- 3 tbsp. unsalted butter
- 2 tsp. sugar
- 12 pearl onions, peeled
- ⅓ cup fresh or frozen peas
  Finely chopped fresh flat-leaf parsley, for garnish

1 Heat oven to 350°. Heat oil in a 6-qt. Dutch oven over medium-high heat. Season lamb with salt and pepper. Working in batches, add lamb and cook, turning once, until browned, 8–10 minutes. Transfer lamb to a plate and set aside. Add chopped carrot and yellow onion and cook, stirring occasionally, until vegetables are soft and brown, about 10 minutes. Add garlic, flour, and tomato paste and cook, stirring often, until tomato paste begins to brown, about 2 minutes. Stir in 6 cups water and reserved lamb. Cover, bring to a boil, transfer to oven, and cook until lamb is tender, about 50 minutes.

2 Using a slotted spoon, transfer lamb to a plate and cover with foil to keep warm. Set a sieve over a 4-qt. saucepan and strain cooking liquid. Discard solids. Bring liquid to a boil over medium-high heat, skimming surface occasionally. Cook until reduced to 2½ cups, about 25 minutes. Set liquid aside.

3 Meanwhile, using a paring knife, trim each piece of remaining carrots, as well as the turnips and potatoes, into elegantly tapered football shapes (alternatively, cut them into large dice). Set potatoes aside in a bowl of water. Heat a 12″ skillet over medium-high heat and add carrots, butter, sugar, salt, and 1 cup water. Partially cover and cook for 10 minutes. Add turnips and pearl onions, partially cover, and continue cooking until liquid has evaporated and vegetables are tender, about 10 more minutes. Uncover and continue to cook, swirling skillet, until vegetables are golden brown, about 3 minutes. Add 2 tbsp. water, swirl skillet to glaze vegetables, and remove from heat. Set aside and keep warm.

4 Bring a 4-qt. saucepan of salted water to a boil. Drain potatoes, add to boiling water, reduce heat to medium-low, and simmer until tender, about 15 minutes. Using a slotted spoon, transfer potatoes to a bowl; set aside.

5 To serve, put the lamb, carrots, turnips, pearl onions, potatoes, and peas into the sauce and cook until hot, about 2 minutes. Divide the stew among bowls and garnish with parsley.

CARBONNADE
Flemish Beef & Beer Stew
SERVES 4

More properly known by its full name, *carbonnade de bœuf à la flamande,* this Flemish beef and onion stew relies on the dark, complex flavor of Belgian abbey-style beer. But what really gives carbonnade its distinctive character is the addition of brown sugar and a fillip of cider vinegar, a sweet-sour combination that plays beautifully against the caramelized onions and rich brew.

2   lb. beef chuck, cut into 2″ × ½″-thick slices
    Kosher salt and freshly ground black pepper, to taste
¼   cup flour
4   tbsp. unsalted butter
4   slices bacon, finely chopped
6   cloves garlic, finely chopped
3   medium onions, thinly sliced lengthwise
2   cups Belgian-style ale
1   cup beef stock
2   tbsp. dark brown sugar
2   tbsp. cider vinegar
3   sprigs fresh thyme
3   sprigs fresh flat-leaf parsley
2   sprigs fresh tarragon
1   bay leaf

1 Season beef with salt and pepper in a bowl, then add flour and toss to coat. Heat 2 tbsp. butter in a 6-qt. Dutch oven over medium-high heat. Working in batches, add beef and cook, turning, until browned, about 8 minutes. Transfer to a plate and set aside.

2 Add bacon to pan and cook until fat renders, about 8 minutes. Add remaining 2 tbsp. butter, garlic, and onions and cook until caramelized, about 30 minutes. Add half the beer and cook, scraping bottom of pot, until slightly reduced, about 4 minutes. Return beef to pot with remaining beer, stock, sugar, vinegar, thyme, parsley, tarragon, bay leaf, and salt and pepper and bring to a boil. Reduce heat to medium-low; cook, covered, until beef is tender, about 1½ hours.

BŒUF À LA BOURGUIGNONNE
Burgundy-Style Beef Stew
SERVES 4–6

What is there to say about *bœuf à la bourguignonne* that hasn't been said before? This is a classic French stew, made rich with a good bottle of burgundy wine. Variations abound, ranging from the quick and minimalist to hours-long, baroquely complex preparations, but we think this classic, straightforward recipe—inspired by Julia Child's unimpeachable version—is the best one out there.

1   bay leaf
4   cloves garlic, peeled
5   black peppercorns
1   sprig fresh flat-leaf parsley
1   sprig fresh thyme
3   lb. boneless beef chuck, cut into large pieces
1   large onion, finely chopped
2   carrots, peeled and finely chopped
1   750-ml bottle good red burgundy
6   oz. lean salt pork, diced
    Kosher salt and freshly ground black pepper
⅓   cup flour
1   lb. small white button mushrooms,
    stems trimmed

1 Make a bouquet garni by wrapping bay leaf, 2 cloves garlic, peppercorns, parsley, and thyme in a square piece of cheesecloth, then tying into a pouch with kitchen twine. Put beef, onion, carrots, remaining 2 cloves garlic, and bouquet garni in a large bowl and add wine. Using your hands, mix all the ingredients together, then cover bowl with plastic wrap and refrigerate for 24 hours.

2 Remove beef from marinade, reserving marinade, and dry well on paper towels. Fry salt pork in a large pot over medium heat until crisp, about 7 minutes. Season beef with salt and pepper to taste. Add to pot and brown on all sides, about 7 minutes. Sprinkle in flour and cook, stirring constantly, for 3 minutes. Add marinade and 2 cups water and bring to a boil over high heat, scraping up brown bits.

3 Reduce heat to low, cover, and cook until meat is tender, about 3 hours. Add mushrooms and cook for 30 minutes more. Remove bouquet garni before serving.

TIBETAN BEEF & POTATO STEW
SERVES 4

In Tibet, this recipe is traditionally made with yak meat; we've found that beef is a serviceable substitute.

3   lb. Yukon gold potatoes
1   lb. carrots, peeled
    Kosher salt, to taste
3   tbsp. peanut oil
1   tbsp. minced garlic
1   tbsp. coarsely ground celery seeds
3   scallions, cut into 1″ pieces
1   lb. boneless beef chuck, cut into 1½″ pieces
    Freshly ground black pepper, to taste
4   tbsp. unsalted butter

2   tsp. finely chopped fresh ginger
½   tbsp. ground coriander
½   tbsp. ground cumin
    Cooked white rice, for serving

1 Place potatoes and carrots in a large pot with 5 cups water; season with salt. Bring to a boil, reduce heat to medium, and simmer, covered, until potatoes and carrots are cooked, 35–40 minutes. Strain, reserving cooking liquid, and let ingredients cool. Once cool, remove and discard skins from potatoes and cut into 1½″ chunks. Cut carrots into 1″ lengths. Set aside.

2 Return the pot to medium-high heat and add oil. When hot, add garlic and cook, stirring, until fragrant, about 30 seconds. Stir in celery seeds and scallions. Carefully pour in ½ cup water and cook until scallions are crisp-tender, about 1 minute. Add beef, season with salt and pepper, reduce heat to medium, and cook, stirring occasionally, for 5 minutes. Add the reserved cooking liquid, potatoes, and carrots along with the butter, ginger, coriander, and cumin. Bring to a boil, reduce heat to medium-low, and simmer, partially covered and stirring occasionally, until beef is tender and sauce has thickened, 30–35 minutes. Season with salt and pepper and serve with rice.

IRISH STEW
SERVES 6–8

This Emerald Isle favorite is traditionally made with mutton or fatty, chewy cuts of lamb. We recommend using at least some neck or shoulder meat for better texture and flavor. There's an Irish saying that a stew boiled is a stew spoiled, so watch the pot closely as you bring the liquid to a simmer.

3   lb. trimmed boneless lamb stew meat (preferably from the neck and shoulder), cut into 1″ chunks
2   lb. russet potatoes, peeled and cut crosswise into thirds
7   carrots, peeled and halved crosswise
2   medium onions, peeled and thinly sliced
2   tbsp. chopped fresh flat-leaf parsley
     Kosher salt and freshly ground black pepper
1½   cups shelled fresh or frozen peas

1 Heat oven to 250°. Put the lamb, potatoes, carrots, onions, parsley, and 2 cups water into a large ovenproof pot with a tight-fitting lid. Season to taste with salt and pepper and gently stir to combine. Bring to a simmer over medium-high heat.

2 Once the stew comes to a simmer, cover the pot and transfer to the oven to cook until the lamb is just tender, about 2 hours. Remove the pot from the oven and gently stir in the peas. Cover and return the pot to the oven. Continue cooking until lamb is fork tender, about 30 minutes more.

3 Allow the stew to sit, covered, for 20 minutes, then spoon into bowls and serve hot.

HUNGARIAN GOULASH

Gulyásleves

SERVES 4–6

The recipe for this satisfying, savory beef stew comes from Katalin Bánfalvi, a home cook in the village of Bõny, in northwestern Hungary.

- 4 tbsp. sunflower or canola oil
- 2 onions, chopped
- 1½ lb. beef chuck, trimmed and cut into ½″ cubes
  Kosher salt and freshly ground black pepper, to taste
- ¼ cup Hungarian sweet paprika
- 2 tsp. dried marjoram
- 2 tsp. caraway seeds
- 2 cloves garlic, finely chopped
- 2 medium carrots, peeled and cut into ½″ cubes
- 2 medium parsnips, peeled and cut into ½″ cubes
- 1½ lb. new potatoes, peeled and cut into ½″ cubes
- 1 tomato, chopped
- 1 cubanelle pepper, seeded and chopped
  Rye bread, for serving

1 Heat oil in a 5-qt. Dutch oven over medium heat. Add onions, cover, and cook, stirring occasionally, until soft and translucent, about 10 minutes. Increase heat to high. Add beef and season with salt and pepper. Cook, uncovered, stirring only once or twice, until meat is lightly browned, about 6 minutes. Stir in paprika, marjoram, caraway, and garlic and cook until fragrant, about 2 minutes. Add carrots, parsnips, and 5 cups water. Bring to a boil, reduce heat to medium, and simmer, covered, until the beef is nearly tender, about 40 minutes.

2 Add potatoes and cook, uncovered, until tender, about 25 minutes. Stir in tomatoes and peppers and cook for 2 minutes. Season with salt and pepper to taste and serve with rye bread.

CARIBBEAN OXTAIL STEW

SERVES 6

You know it's a traditional meal in the English-speaking Caribbean when you are presented with a dish of fragrant oxtail stew. Historian and cookbook author Jessica B. Harris explains that the slow-cooked dish likely originated during the region's plantation era, when tails were leftovers after slaughter and given to the enslaved. Today though, for anyone from the Caribbean, oxtail stew means family, friends, and home.

- 3 tbsp. canola oil
- 2 lb. oxtails, cut into 2″ pieces
  Kosher salt and freshly ground black pepper, to taste
- 3 tbsp. tomato paste
- 1 tbsp. minced fresh ginger
- 6 cloves garlic, minced
- 2 large yellow onions, chopped
- 1 small carrot, peeled and chopped
- 1 rib celery, chopped
- 2 tbsp. flour
- 4 cups beef stock
- 1 tbsp. allspice berries
- 4 sprigs fresh thyme
- 2 habanero chiles
- 2 tbsp. light brown sugar
- 1 tbsp. Worcestershire sauce
- 4 scallions, roughly chopped
  Cooked white rice, for serving

1 Heat oil in an 8-qt. Dutch oven over medium-high heat. Season oxtails with salt and pepper. Add to pot and cook, turning once, until golden brown, about 5 minutes. Transfer to a plate and set aside. Add tomato paste, ginger, garlic, onions, carrot, and celery and cook until soft, about 4 minutes. Add flour and cook until smooth, about 2 minutes. Return oxtails to pot with stock, allspice, thyme, and chiles and bring to a boil. Reduce heat to medium-low and cook, covered, until oxtails are tender, about 1½ hours.

2 Add sugar and Worcestershire to pot and cook for 5 minutes more. Garnish with scallions and serve with rice.

BRUNSWICK STEW

SERVES 8–10

This North Carolina specialty was historically made with whatever meat was on hand, including squirrel. This version, featuring chicken and pork, is a more approachable variation.

¼	cup canola oil
1	lb. boneless, skinless chicken thighs
1	lb. boneless pork shoulder, cut into 2″ chunks
	Kosher salt and freshly ground black pepper, to taste
8	cloves garlic, minced
1	large yellow onion, minced
3	tbsp. tomato paste
1	tsp. crushed red chile flakes
1	tsp. dried thyme
1	bay leaf
1	lb. Yukon gold potatoes, peeled and cut into 1″ cubes
1	lb. fresh or frozen corn kernels
4	cups chicken stock
1	28-oz. can whole, peeled tomatoes in juice, crushed by hand
1	15-oz. can butter beans, drained and rinsed

1 Heat oil in an 8-qt. Dutch oven over medium-high heat. Season chicken and pork with salt and pepper. Working in batches, add to pot and cook, turning once, until golden brown, about 12 minutes. Transfer to a bowl.

2 Add garlic and onion to pot and cook, stirring, until soft, about 3 minutes. Add tomato paste, chile flakes, thyme, and bay leaf; cook for 2 minutes. Add meat back to pot along with potatoes, corn, stock, tomatoes, and beans. Bring to a boil and then reduce heat to medium-low. Cook, stirring, until meat is tender and potatoes begin to fall apart, about 1 hour.

3 Remove meat from pot, shred with 2 forks, and return to pot. Season to taste and serve.

GREEK RABBIT & ONION STEW

Kouneli Stifado

SERVES 4

Sweetened with prunes and studded with pearl onions, this country-style rabbit stew is a home-cooked specialty on the Greek island of Crete.

2	lb. pearl onions, root ends trimmed
1	rabbit (about 3 lb.), cut into 8 pieces
	Kosher salt and freshly ground black pepper, to taste
½	cup olive oil
1	lb. medium tomatoes, roughly chopped
½	cup chicken stock
1	tbsp. tomato paste
12	prunes
6	whole cloves
5	cloves garlic, peeled smashed
3	bay leaves
2	small sprigs fresh rosemary
1	2″ stick cinnamon
	Fresh flat-leaf parsley, for garnish

1 Bring a 4-qt. pot of water to a boil. Add onions and cook for 1 minute. Using a slotted spoon, transfer onions to a large bowl of ice water and let sit for 5 minutes. Drain onions and, using a small knife, remove skins. Set aside.

2 Season rabbit with salt and pepper. Heat oil in a 5-qt. Dutch oven over medium-high heat. Working in 3 batches, add rabbit and cook, turning once, until browned, about 8 minutes. Transfer rabbit to a plate and set aside. Add onions and cook, stirring occasionally, until golden brown, about 5 minutes. Add tomatoes, stock, tomato paste, prunes, cloves, garlic, bay leaves, rosemary, and cinnamon. Nestle the rabbit in the pot, cover, and bring to a boil. Reduce heat to low and cook until rabbit is very tender, about 45 minutes.

3 Transfer rabbit to a large platter. Set a medium sieve over a 1-qt. saucepan. Strain the cooking liquid, discarding bay leaves, rosemary, and cinnamon stick. Transfer the onions and prunes to the platter. Simmer the strained sauce over medium-high heat until slightly thickened, about 8 minutes. Skim excess fat from surface, season sauce with salt and pepper, and spoon over rabbit. Serve stew garnished with parsley.

Seafood Stews & Chowders

BOUILLABAISSE

SERVES 8

This saffron-infused Marseille classic is traditionally served as two courses: A first of the broth, topped with toasted bread spread with a garlicky *rouille;* a second of a platter of the simmered fish, shellfish, and potatoes. This recipe came from Provençal fisherman Lucien Vitiello, who told us that it's not *what* fish you use that matters, but how many kinds you can get in at once.

- 1   24″ baguette, cut into ½″-thick slices
- 7   cloves garlic, peeled; 2 left whole, 5 crushed
- ½   cup extra-virgin olive oil
- 2   medium onions, sliced
- 3   sprigs fresh parsley
- 3   sprigs fresh thyme
- 1   bay leaf
- ¼   cup fennel tops or coarsely chopped fennel bulbs
- 2   lb. new potatoes, peeled and sliced
- 1½   lb. tomatoes, peeled, seeded, and chopped (or left whole if small)
- 5–6 lb. cleaned assorted seafood (such as red snapper, sea bass, tilefish, grouper, striped bass, monkfish, halibut, cuttlefish, squid)
- 16   favouilles (small Mediterranean crabs), optional
- 16   mussels, scrubbed and debearded
- 10   cups fish stock, hot
- 1   tsp. crushed saffron threads
- ½   cup Pernod
-      Kosher salt and freshly ground black pepper, to taste
-      Rouille (this page)

1 Heat oven to 350°. Place bread on a baking sheet and toast until golden, about 10 minutes. Rub with whole garlic cloves while warm. Set aside.

2 Pour ¼ cup oil into a 10–12-qt. pot. Add onions, crushed garlic, parsley, thyme, bay leaf, and fennel. Add potatoes, then tomatoes. Add large, whole, and firm fish, then smaller, more delicate fish. Finally, add favouilles, if using, and mussels.

3 Pour in stock and remaining ¼ cup oil. Add saffron and Pernod, season with salt and pepper, and place over high heat. Depending on the types of seafood you use, the ingredients will cook at varying rates as the soup comes to a boil. Start checking for doneness after about 5 minutes

and as each type of seafood cooks, transfer it to a platter, discarding any mussels that do not open. Once all seafood is removed, continue boiling until potatoes are cooked through, up to 25 minutes. Remove potatoes to platter with the seafood, keep at room temperature. Strain broth, discarding any remaining solids.

4 To serve as two courses, prepare the first course: Spread rouille on toast, divide toast between 8 warmed soup bowls, and fill with strained broth, reserving 1 cup (or more). For the second course, ladle the 1 cup broth (or more) over the platter of fish and potatoes, top with a dollop of rouille, and serve at room temperature.

COOK'S NOTE Bouillabaisse can also be served in a single course. Divide seafood among 8 deep soup bowls, ladle broth over seafood, and top with rouille-topped toasts.

Rouille

MAKES ABOUT 1 CUP

Rouille—a saffron-scented aïoli—is best served the day it's made.

-      Pinch of saffron threads
- 2   tbsp. fish stock
- 4   cloves garlic, minced
- 1   cup mayonnaise
- ½   tsp. sweet paprika
-      Pinch of cayenne pepper
-      Kosher salt, to taste

Crush saffron threads into stock in a mini food processor or mortar. Add garlic and purée, or grind with a pestle, until smooth. Transfer to a bowl and stir in mayonnaise, paprika, and cayenne. Season with salt.

CIOPPINO

SERVES 8

This wine-enriched seafood stew was developed in San Francisco by the Genovese immigrants who settled there. Derived from the traditional *ciuppin*—which means "little soup" in Genovese dialect—the dish was originally a purée of cooked vegetables and leftover fish scraps.

Our crab-filled version comes from the city's beloved Hayes Street Grill.

- ½ cup extra-virgin olive oil
- 1 large onion, chopped
- 6 cloves garlic, chopped
- 2 medium carrots, diced
- 1 28-oz. can whole, peeled tomatoes, drained and chopped
- 2 cups light red wine
- 4 cups fish stock
- 4 bay leaves
- 1 bunch fresh flat-leaf parsley, trimmed and chopped
- 1 tbsp. lemon zest
- 1 tbsp. finely chopped fresh oregano
- 1 tbsp. fresh thyme leaves
- 2 tbsp. chopped fresh basil
- 1 tsp. cayenne pepper
  Kosher salt and freshly ground black pepper, to taste
- 12 Dungeness crab legs, cracked
- 8 mussels, well-scrubbed
- 16 manila clams, well-scrubbed
- 16 medium shrimp
- 4 black sea bass or rockfish filets (about 2 lb. total)

1 Heat oil in a large pot over medium heat. Add onion, garlic, and carrots and cook, stirring occasionally, until vegetables are tender, about 8 minutes. Add tomatoes, wine, stock, bay leaves, parsley (reserve about ¼ cup for garnish), lemon zest, oregano, thyme, basil, and cayenne. Bring to a boil, then reduce heat to low and simmer, partially covered, for about 40 minutes. Strain, discarding vegetables and herbs, and return broth to pot. Season with salt and pepper.

2 Add crab legs, mussels, clams, and shrimp to broth, stir gently, and cook over medium heat until mussels and clams open. (Discard any that don't open.) Add bass filets and simmer for another 7 minutes or until fish turns opaque. Ladle soup into large bowls and garnish with reserved parsley.

CACCIUCCO
Tuscan Seafood Stew
SERVES 6–8

This Tuscan soup traditionally uses fish considered "bottom of the boat": those left behind after more valuable fish have sold. The base is octopus and squid, along with tomatoes, wine, garlic, sage, and dried red chiles; other fish are added at the end of cooking, before the soup is served over garlic-rubbed bread.

- ¼ cup extra-virgin olive oil
- 1 tbsp. minced fresh flat-leaf parsley
- 1 tbsp. minced fresh sage leaves
- ½ tsp. crushed red chile flakes
- 5 cloves garlic, peeled; 4 minced, 1 left whole
- 12 oz. calamari, cleaned and cut into 1″ pieces
- 12 oz. baby octopus, cleaned and cut into 1″ pieces
- 1 tbsp. tomato paste
- 1 cup dry white wine
- 1 14-oz. can diced tomatoes with juice
  Kosher salt and freshly ground black pepper
- 1 cup fish stock
- 1 1-lb. monkfish filet, cut into 2″ pieces
- 1 1-lb. red snapper filet, cut into 2″ pieces
- 12 oz. large shell-on shrimp
- 12 oz. mussels, scrubbed and debearded
- 8 1″-thick slices country-style white bread

1 Heat oil in a 6-qt. saucepan over medium heat. Add parsley, sage, chile flakes, and minced garlic and cook until fragrant, about 1 minute. Add calamari and octopus and cook, stirring occasionally, until opaque, about 4 minutes. Add tomato paste, stir well, and cook until paste has darkened slightly, about 1 minute. Add wine and cook, stirring often, until the liquid has evaporated, about 20 minutes.

2 Add tomatoes and their juice, season with salt and pepper, and cook, stirring occasionally, until seafood is tender, about 10 minutes. Stir in stock, cover, and simmer for 10 minutes. Add monkfish and cook, covered, until just firm, about 5 minutes. Add snapper and shrimp to the pot and scatter mussels over top. Cover and cook, without stirring (so as not to break up the seafood), until the snapper is just cooked through and the mussels have just opened, about 10 minutes. (Discard any that don't open.)

3 Toast bread and rub liberally with remaining whole garlic clove. Place 1 piece of garlic-rubbed bread in each bowl, ladle stew over bread, or serve bread on the side.

VATAPÁ
Brazilian Shrimp Stew
SERVES 6–8

This versatile stew is from the Brazilian state of Bahia, where Iberian, indigenous, and African foodways intermingle in one of the country's most dynamic cuisines. Onions, tomatoes, ginger, okra, and chiles might go into the pot, along with chicken, salt cod, or shrimp. There's always coconut milk and palm oil, though, which provide silky texture and signature floral notes.

6   oz. dried salt cod filet
½   cup small dried shrimp
¼   cup cashews
¼   cup unsalted raw peanuts
3   scallions, thinly sliced
2   dried chiles de árbol, stemmed
2   cloves garlic
1   1″ piece fresh ginger, peeled and thinly sliced
5   oz. country-style white bread, thinly sliced
1   14-oz. can coconut milk
½   cup dendê (palm oil)
1   small onion, finely chopped
3   canned whole, peeled tomatoes, crushed by hand
3   cups fish stock
½   lb. raw medium shrimp, peeled and deveined
    Kosher salt and freshly ground black pepper, to taste
    Cooked white rice, for serving

1 Place cod in a 2-qt. saucepan and cover with cold water by 2″. Boil for 20 minutes, then drain. Repeat process twice more, then finely shred cod, discarding any errant bones, and set aside. Purée dried shrimp, cashews, peanuts, scallions, chiles, garlic, and ginger in the food processor and set shrimp paste aside. Combine bread and coconut milk in a food processor. Let sit for 20 minutes, then purée. Set bread paste aside.

2 Heat oil in a 4-qt. saucepan over medium-high heat. Add onion and cook until soft, about 10 minutes. Add shrimp paste and cook for 2 minutes. Add tomatoes and cook until broken down, about 6 minutes. Add cod, bread paste, and stock and bring to a boil. Reduce heat to medium and cook until reduced by one-quarter, about 30 minutes. Add shrimp and cook until shrimp are pink and cooked through, about 3 minutes. Season with salt and pepper and serve with rice.

JFK'S LOBSTER STEW

SERVES 6

At Locke-Ober, the storied but now-closed Boston restaurant, this exquisitely rich lobster stew was a signature of the menu. It was so beloved by President John F. Kennedy that the restaurant officially renamed it in his honor. It takes two days to prepare, but the opulent, richly flavored result is worth every minute.

6   1-lb. live lobsters, rinsed
    Kosher salt and freshly ground black pepper, to taste
14 tbsp. unsalted butter, softened

1   cup medium-dry or cream sherry
6   cups milk
2   cups heavy cream
    Pinch cayenne
1–2 pinches of paprika
½   tsp. fresh lemon juice
1   tsp. finely julienned fresh flat-leaf parsley

1 Plunge lobsters into a large pot of boiling salted water over high heat and boil until just cooked through, about 4 minutes. Transfer lobsters to a large bowl of ice water to prevent them from cooking any longer, and keep them submerged until completely cool. Drain lobsters, separate tails and claws from bodies, setting bodies aside. Crack shells and remove meat from tails and claws, reserving tail shells. Discard claw shells. Cut lobster meat into large pieces and set aside in the refrigerator.

2 Melt 8 tbsp. of the butter in a large, wide, heavy-bottomed pot over medium-high heat. Add lobster bodies and tail shells and cook, turning often, until shells turn a deep red, 5–8 minutes. Add sherry and boil for 2 minutes, then add milk and cream and return to a boil. Reduce heat to medium-low and simmer, stirring often, until milk and cream reduce by one-quarter and thicken slightly, 20–25 minutes. Add cayenne and paprika and season to taste with salt and pepper. Remove pot from heat, set milk infusion aside to cool, cover, and refrigerate overnight.

3 The following day, strain milk infusion into another medium pot, discarding solids, and bring just to a simmer over medium heat.

4 Meanwhile, melt 4 tbsp. butter in a large skillet over medium heat. Add lobster meat and heat until warmed through, 3–5 minutes, then add to milk infusion in pot. Add lemon juice and adjust seasonings. Divide stew among 6 warm bowls, adding some of the remaining 2 tbsp. butter to each bowl. Garnish with parsley.

MARYLAND CRAB SOUP

SERVES 4–8

This ideal version of vegetable-laden, richly spiced crab soup is served at Eddie's Market in Baltimore, Maryland; it's a great way to use up any steamed crab left over from a crab feast (page 290).

3   carrots, peeled and chopped
1   medium boiling potato, peeled and cubed
1   medium onion, chopped
1   rib celery, chopped

½ lb. green beans, cut into 1″ pieces
1 cup fresh corn kernels (about 2 ears)
1 cup fresh or frozen lima beans
½ cup fresh or frozen peas
4 tbsp. Worcestershire sauce
2 tbsp. Old Bay seasoning
1½ tbsp. dry mustard
   Pinch of crushed red chile flakes
1 28-oz. can whole, peeled tomatoes in juice
1 lb. jumbo lump crabmeat, picked of shells
   Kosher salt and freshly ground black pepper, to taste

1 Combine carrots, potatoes, onion, celery, green beans, corn, lima beans, peas, Worcestershire, Old Bay, mustard, chile flakes, and 6 cups water in a large pot. Add tomatoes, crushing them in your hand, and juice from can. Bring to a boil over medium-high heat, then reduce heat to medium-low and simmer for 30 minutes.

2 Add crabmeat to soup and simmer for 45 minutes more, stirring often. Season with salt and pepper.

COCONUT CRAB
Caranguejo e Coco
SERVES 2

Mozambique was colonized by Portugal for almost five centuries. At Lisbon's Cantinho do Aziz, Khalid Aziz draws crowds with Mozambican dishes that honor his family's heritage, like this take on a traditional crab curry. The first step for this dish calls for making coconut milk from unsweetened coconut, which has a cleaner flavor and lighter texture than the canned variety.

8 cups (1½ lb.) unsweetened dried coconut
¼ cup plus 1 tbsp. olive oil
2 medium white onions, minced
1 cup canned crushed tomatoes
2 cloves garlic, chopped
1 lb. cooked Mozambican or Alaskan king crab legs, broken apart at the joints
1 tbsp. kosher salt
   Cilantro leaves, for garnish
   Cooked white rice, for serving

1 Bring 8 cups water to a boil in a large pot over high heat. Add coconut and let cook for 1 minute. Remove pot from heat and let rest until coconut is cool enough to handle. Using your hands, squeeze the coconut flesh in batches to extract the coconut milk (you should have about 4½ cups milk).

2 Heat oil in a large skillet over medium-high heat. Add onions and cook, stirring occasionally, until softened and caramelized, about 25 minutes. Add tomatoes, garlic, and crab, and cook, stirring occasionally, 3 minutes. Add coconut milk and bring to a gentle boil. Reduce heat to a simmer and cook, stirring occasionally, for 30 minutes. Season with salt to taste. Garnish with cilantro and serve with rice.

NORWEGIAN COD & ROOT VEGETABLE CHOWDER
Fiskesuppe
SERVES 6–8

When making this creamy fish stew, you should feel free to substitute mahimahi, salmon, scallops, or shrimp for the cod. Local cooks on the Lofoten Islands of northern Norway like to add accents like red pepper, chunks of bacon, or chive oil.

6 tbsp. unsalted butter
4 cloves garlic, chopped
2 ribs celery, chopped
1 small onion, chopped
1 green bell pepper, seeded and chopped
1 small leek, sliced ¼″ thick
   Kosher salt and freshly ground black pepper, to taste
2 medium carrots, sliced ¼″ thick
1 large parsnip, peeled and chopped
1 small celery root, peeled and chopped
4 medium new potatoes, peeled and cut into 1″ pieces
3 cups fish stock
2 cups milk
1 cup heavy cream
1½ tbsp. Worcestershire sauce
2 lb. boneless, skinless cod filet, cut into 2″ pieces
⅓ cup dill, chopped, plus more for garnish
¼ cup fresh flat-leaf parsley leaves, chopped
   Juice of 1 lemon
   Crusty bread, for serving

1 Heat butter in a medium pot over medium-high heat. Add garlic, celery, onion, pepper, and leek, and season with salt and pepper. Cook, stirring, until soft, 8–10 minutes.

2 Add carrots, parsnip, celery root, potatoes, fish stock, milk, cream, and Worcestershire; bring to a boil. Reduce heat to medium and cook, stirring occasionally, until vegetables are tender, about 25 minutes.

3 Add cod and continue to cook, stirring gently, until fish is cooked through, 6–8 minutes. Stir in dill, parsley, lemon juice, and salt and pepper. Serve with bread.

NICARAGUAN RUNDOWN SEAFOOD SOUP

SERVES 8 (SEE PHOTO, PAGE 225)

"Rundown" is a dish found throughout the Caribbean and on the eastern coast of Central America, but recipes differ. In Jamaica, it manifests as a slow-cooked custardy stew. On the Corn Islands of Nicaragua, a lighter, heady broth of spices and fresh-pressed coconut milk is simmered with tubers and whatever fresh seafood local cooks find when they "run down" to the harbor market.

- 6   cups unsweetened coconut milk
- 1   lb. conch meat, cut into ½″ cubes
- 6   cloves garlic, finely chopped
- 2   large Cuban oregano leaves (available at garden nurseries) or 1 sprig Italian oregano
- 2   green bananas, peeled and each cut crosswise into 4 pieces
- 1   green plantain, peeled and cut crosswise into 8 pieces
- 1   yellow plantain, peeled and cut crosswise into 8 pieces
- 1   medium cassava root, peeled and cut into 2″ pieces
- 1   medium malanga or taro root, peeled and cut into 2″ pieces
- 1   small yellow onion, coarsely chopped
     Kosher salt and freshly ground black pepper, to taste
- 2   skinless king mackerel filets, about 8 oz. each, cut into 8 pieces
- 4   rock lobster tails, halved lengthwise
     Lime wedges, for serving

1 Combine coconut milk with 4 cups water in a large Dutch oven. Add conch, garlic, oregano, bananas, both plantains, cassava, malanga, and onion. Season with salt and pepper and bring to a boil. Reduce heat to a steady simmer and cook, stirring occasionally, until liquid reduces and vegetables are just tender, about 1 hour.

2 Add mackerel and lobster and cook until seafood is tender, about 10 minutes. Remove pot from heat, season with salt and pepper, and serve with lime wedges.

CONCH SOUP

SERVES 6–8

Sweet conch meat meets fiery chiles in this aromatic stew; the classic recipe came to us from Delvin Powell of Jamaica's St. Elizabeth parish.

- ¼   cup canola oil
- 10   cloves garlic, finely chopped
- 1   large yellow onion, finely chopped
- 1   tbsp. sugar
- 1   tsp. ground turmeric
- 1   tsp. paprika
- ¼   cup flour
- 1½   lb. conch meat, cut into ½″ cubes
- 1   tbsp. fresh thyme leaves
- 1   large yellow yam or sweet potato, peeled and cut into ½″ cubes
- 1   medium carrot, peeled and cut into ½″ cubes
- 1   chayote squash, cut into ½″ cubes
- 1   green banana, peeled and cut into ½″ cubes
- 1   Scotch bonnet or habanero chile, slit in half lengthwise
     Kosher salt and freshly ground black pepper, to taste
- 2   tbsp. finely chopped fresh flat-leaf parsley
- 4   scallions, roughly chopped

1 Heat oil in a medium Dutch oven over medium-high heat. Add garlic and onion and cook, stirring often, until soft, about 6 minutes. Add sugar, turmeric, and paprika and cook, stirring, until fragrant, about 1 minute. Sprinkle in flour and cook, stirring, until smooth, about 1 minute. Add conch meat and 6 cups water, and bring to a boil. Reduce heat to medium-low, and simmer until conch meat is tender, about 2 hours.

2 Add thyme, yam, carrot, chayote, banana, and chile and cook, stirring occasionally, until vegetables are tender, about 10 minutes. Remove from heat and season with salt and pepper. Sprinkle with parsley and scallions to serve.

GARIFUNA-STYLE SEAFOOD SOUP

SERVES 8

Fresh herbs and five types of seafood lend their heady fragrance to this rich coconut soup, adapted from a version served at the restaurant Chef Guity in Honduras.

- ¼   cup canola oil
- 4   cloves garlic, minced
- 1   small yellow onion, minced
- 1   small green bell pepper, minced
- 4   cups coconut milk
- 2   cups fish stock
- ¼   cup packed basil leaves, thinly sliced
- 2   tbsp. finely chopped oregano
- 1   tbsp. finely chopped sage
- 1½   tsp. ground cumin
- 1   tsp. sugar

1   lb. conch meat, pounded thin and cut into 1″ pieces
8   oz. calamari, sliced crosswise into ¼″ rings
1   lb. large shrimp, peeled and deveined
8   oz. cooked lobster meat, cut into 1″ pieces
8   oz. mussels, scrubbed and debearded
    Kosher salt and freshly ground black pepper, to taste
    Lime wedges, for serving

1 Heat oil in an 8-qt. saucepan over medium-high heat. Add garlic, onion, and bell pepper and cook until golden brown, about 6 minutes. Add coconut milk, stock, basil, oregano, sage, cumin, and sugar and bring to a boil. Reduce heat to medium, add conch and calamari, and cook, covered, until tender, about 8 minutes.

2 Add shrimp, lobster, and mussels and cook, covered, until mussel shells open, about 7 minutes more. Season with salt and pepper to taste. Serve with lime wedges on the side.

NEW ENGLAND CLAM CHOWDER
SERVES 8

This comforting, cream-based wonder is briny with clam liquor, smoky with bacon, and contains a high ratio of fresh clams to potato chunks.

10   lb. clams in the shell, preferably cherrystone, scrubbed
¼   lb. thick-cut bacon, finely chopped
2   tbsp. unsalted butter
1   tbsp. finely chopped fresh thyme
2   medium yellow onions, roughly chopped
2   bay leaves
2½   lb. new potatoes, cut into ¼″ cubes
2   cups heavy cream
     Kosher salt and freshly ground black pepper, to taste
     Oyster crackers and hot sauce, for serving

1 Bring 2 cups water to a boil in a 6-qt. saucepan over high heat. Add clams, cover, and cook until clams are steamed open, about 10 minutes (discard any that do not open). Remove from heat and let cool. Remove clam meat from shells, roughly chop, and set aside. Pour cooking liquid from pan through a fine-mesh sieve into another bowl (you should have about 6 cups; if not, add enough water to make 6 cups) and set aside.

2 Heat bacon in a 6-qt. saucepan over medium heat and cook, stirring, until its fat renders and bacon is crisp, about

10 minutes. Add butter, thyme, onions, and bay leaves and cook, stirring, until soft, about 8 minutes. Add reserved cooking liquid and potatoes and bring to a boil. Reduce heat to medium-low and cook, stirring, until potatoes are cooked through, about 20 minutes. Add chopped clam meat and cream and cook until warmed through, about 5 minutes. Season with salt and pepper and serve with crackers and hot sauce.

MANHATTAN CLAM CHOWDER
SERVES 6

When it comes to clam chowder, Imogene Wolcott got right to the point. Writing in the 1939 classic *The New England Yankee Cook Book,* she said: "Rhode Island and Connecticut housewives uphold the tomato. The rest of New England scorns it." The red version is named for Manhattan, but this version is based on one served at Champlin's restaurant in Narragansett, Rhode Island.

2   tbsp. unsalted butter
1   medium onion, chopped
½   tsp. Lawry's seasoned salt or kosher salt
2   cups chopped clams, fresh or canned
4   cups clam juice
4   large white potatoes (about 1¾ lb.), peeled and cut into ½″ cubes
1   10¾-oz. can condensed tomato soup
½   cup canned tomato purée
¼   tsp. cayenne pepper
     Kosher salt and freshly ground black pepper, to taste
     Oyster crackers, for serving

1 Melt butter in a large pot over medium heat. Add onion and seasoned salt and cook until softened, 8–10 minutes. Add clams, clam juice, and 1 qt. water, raise heat to medium-high, and bring to a boil. Reduce heat to medium-low, cover, and simmer for 30 minutes.

2 Add potatoes, increase heat to medium-high, and bring to a boil. Reduce heat to medium-low and simmer until potatoes are almost cooked through, 6–8 minutes. Stir in tomato soup, tomato purée, cayenne, and salt and pepper and continue simmering until potatoes are tender, 8–10 minutes more.

3 Ladle into soup bowls. (The chowder tastes even better when chilled overnight and reheated.) Serve with oyster crackers.

RHODE ISLAND CLAM CHOWDER

SERVES 4 (SEE PHOTO, PAGE 428)

A true taste of the sea, Rhode Island–style clam chowder is made with a clear, light broth that lets the flavor of fresh clams shine through. For the best value and yield, look for very fresh, medium to large hard-shell clams (known as quahogs in New England). The hefty bellies enrich the soup, and when cooked gently and chopped, the tougher, muscly bits lend the dish a pleasant chew.

4	lb. cherrystone clams (about 20 large)
	Kosher salt and freshly ground black pepper, to taste
4	cloves garlic, thinly sliced
2	tbsp. extra-virgin olive oil
2	medium russet potatoes, cut into ⅓″ dice
1	large yellow onion, finely chopped
2	large ribs celery, finely chopped
1	bay leaf
2	tbsp. finely chopped fresh flat-leaf parsley
1	tbsp. finely chopped fresh dill

1 Purge clams to remove any excess sand: place clams in a large bowl of generously salted cold water and set aside at room temperature for 15 minutes.

2 Transfer clams to a large pot, leaving sand behind in bowl. Add garlic and 2 cups fresh cold water to pot, cover, and cook over highest heat possible until steam escapes from the edges of the lid and clams begin to open, 3–6 minutes (start checking after 3 minutes). Use tongs to transfer clams to a large bowl as they open, allowing up to 15 minutes; discard any that don't open. Strain cooking liquid through a fine-mesh strainer set over a heat-resistant liquid-measuring cup, discarding any solids. Add enough water to bring amount to 8 cups; set aside.

3 Rinse out pot and return to medium heat. When pot is dry and hot, add oil. When oil shimmers, add potatoes, onion, celery, and bay leaf; cook, stirring frequently, until onion is translucent and softened, 10–11 minutes. Add parsley and dill; continue cooking for 2 minutes more. Add reserved cooking liquid, then bring to a strong simmer and cook until vegetables are tender and broth has reduced slightly, 20–22 minutes.

4 Meanwhile, remove clams from their shells, and add any accumulated juices to pot. Chop clams into ½″ pieces. Immediately before serving, stir clams into chowder and turn off heat. Season to taste with pepper and additional salt. Serve hot.

OYSTER CHOWDER WITH BACON, CORN & FENNEL

SERVES 4

One of the easiest ways to cook oysters is to slip them out of their shells and into quick-cooking soups, stews, and chowders. This one—a creamy, flourless chowder with fresh corn, crispy bacon, and some of the oysters' natural juices—is the type of iconic summer recipe that should get tacked to the refrigerator door.

1	trimmed medium fennel bulb, outermost layer peeled and discarded
3	thick slices bacon
½	large yellow onion, finely chopped
1	medium carrot, finely chopped
1	medium russet potato, peeled and diced into ⅓″ dice
2	medium cloves garlic, finely chopped
¾	cup dry white wine
½	cup fresh oyster brine or bottled clam juice
1½	cups heavy cream
½	cup whole milk
½	tsp. kosher salt
	Freshly ground black pepper, to taste
	Corn kernels from 1 fresh cob (about ⅔ cup)
18	medium, briny oysters, shucked
	Dill or fennel fronds, for garnish
	Oyster crackers or crusty bread

1 Slice the fennel bulb in half lengthwise, then very thinly slice each half. Set aside.

2 Arrange bacon slices a large, heavy pot over medium-low heat. Cook, turning as needed, until well-browned and crispy, 10–12 minutes. Remove slices, but leave fat in pan.

3 Add fennel, onion, carrot, potato, and garlic to pan and cook, stirring frequently, until onion is translucent, about 4 minutes. Pour in wine and oyster brine and boil for 1 minute.

4 Reduce heat to a light simmer and stir in cream, followed by whole milk, kosher salt, and a generous pinch of black pepper; let simmer gently until potatoes are tender, about 5 minutes (do not boil, or dairy might curdle). Add corn and chop oysters into bite-size pieces. Add oysters and let cook until firmed slightly, about 3 minutes.

5 Break bacon up into small pieces and stir half of it into chowder. Ladle into bowls and top with dill and remaining bacon. Serve with crackers or bread.

Sandwiches, Pizzas & Burgers

SANDWICHES, PIZZAS & BURGERS

A VERITABLE FEAST OF MARINATED TUNA, anchovies, hard-cooked eggs, and vegetables devoured on a rustic loaf just outside a Provençal bakery; a red-sauce-smothered pizza marinara savored while watching life go by on a bustling Neapolitan street; a favorite cheeseburger consumed at a classic American diner—all are quick to get, easy to eat, and utterly satisfying.

Sure, sandwiches, pizzas, and burgers are convenience foods. They all involve bread in one form or another, since most are made for grabbing and eating out of hand. But the best qualities shared by these culinary icons are much greater than that. Unfussy, intimate, and often gloriously messy, these are the foods we reach for when we are looking not only for sustenance but also for comfort.

Because comfort is personal, there's a sandwich to please everyone. Diverse fillings and a big world of breads are mixed and matched across countless variations to create a wild array of classics from every corner of the globe. The grilled cheese that Mom served for lunch; an Italian beef sandwich loaded with hot, thinly sliced sirloin that you discovered on Chicago's South Side; a pork-laden *bánh mì* on a crusty baguette made to order by a Vietnamese street vendor—each is the product of a delectable alchemy of flavors that invariably soothes the appetite.

The same is true of pizza, with its limitless toppings and styles, from thin crust to deep dish to a plump calzone. Although recently the wood-fired Neapolitan with its perfectly blistered crust has become the go-to choice for pizza lovers everywhere, it's a revelation how creative some Naples' *pizzaioli* can get with their hallowed classic. Whether it's that iconic trio of tomato, basil, and mozzarella or a pairing of pistachio cream and mortadella, there's a pizza guaranteed to appeal to every eater.

When it comes to burgers, we love them every which way, from a saucy Sloppy Joe at a diner to a duck fat–enriched hunk of herb-laced beef at a high-end restaurant. But for comfort, a homemade burger, seared on a charcoal grill, is nearly an American birthright, whether made with the traditional beef or fashioned from lamb or even a meaty portobello.

As much a part of our daily lives as these foods are, the origins of many them remain shrouded in mystery: Was the sandwich actually "invented" by the Earl of Sandwich? Was a Connecticut lunch wagon the originator of the burger? And is Naples where pizza was first dreamed up? We don't know the answers for sure, so for now we'll simply turn to eating these much beloved classics.

Sandwiches

THE ULTIMATE GRILLED CHEESE SANDWICH

SERVES 2

The secret to making a perfect grilled cheese sandwich is cooking it over low heat, which brings out the subtle flavors of the cheese, and slathering the bread with butter, which crisps it in the pan.

- 4 tbsp. unsalted butter, softened
- 4 ½″-thick slices sourdough bread
- ½ lb Comté cheese, grated

1 Spread butter evenly on both sides of each slice of bread. Put half the cheese on one slice and half on another. Top each with remaining bread slices. Heat a 12″ cast-iron skillet over medium-low heat.

2 Add sandwiches to skillet and cook, turning once, until golden brown and crusty on both sides, 18–20 minutes. Transfer sandwiches to a cutting board and cut in half. Serve warm.

CUBAN TURKEY TEA SANDWICH

Elena Ruz

SERVES 1

Commonly served during *merienda* (afternoon tea) in Cuba, this pressed sandwich of turkey, jam, and cream cheese on a roll is sweet and savory all in one. It's named for a 1930s-era Cuban socialite who ordered it regularly from her favorite Havana restaurant.

- 2 tbsp. cream cheese, softened
- 1 Cuban roll or brioche bun, split
- 3 oz. sliced cooked turkey breast
- 2 tbsp. strawberry jam
- 1 tbsp. unsalted butter

Spread cream cheese on bottom half of roll and top with turkey. Spread jam on top half of roll and close sandwich. Melt butter in a 10″ skillet over medium heat; cook sandwich, weighting down with a cast-iron skillet and turning once, until golden brown and heated through, 3–4 minutes. Cut in half and serve hot.

VENETIAN TEA SANDWICHES

Tramezzini

SERVES 4

A Venetian tradition, *cicchetti* are small bites enjoyed as snacks and appetizers in wine bars, or *bacari*, all over the city. Venetian tea sandwiches are staples there; diners especially favor these three varieties: asparagus and eggs, tuna and olives, and arugula with cured beef.

- 12 slices white sandwich bread, crusts removed
- ¾ cup mayonnaise
  Kosher salt and freshly ground black pepper
- 1 5-oz. can olive oil–packed tuna, drained and flaked
- ⅓ cup pitted black olives, halved
- 2 tsp. capers, drained and rinsed
- 6 asparagus spears, blanched and halved lengthwise
- 2 hard-cooked eggs, sliced
- 1 medium tomato, cored and sliced
- 6 oz. thinly sliced bresaola
- 2 oz. thinly shaved Parmigiano-Reggiano
- 1 cup baby arugula leaves

Remove crusts from bread and spread 1 tbsp. mayonnaise over each slice; season with salt and pepper. Layer tuna, olives, and capers over 2 slices; layer asparagus, eggs, and tomato over 2 slices; and layer bresaola, Parmigiano, and arugula over 2 slices. Top each with a slice of bread and halve sandwiches on diagonal.

SHIT ON A SHINGLE

Creamed Chipped Beef on Toast

SERVES 10

This recipe for the American military classic, more delicately known as creamed chipped beef on toast, is based on one in the *Manual for Navy Cooks*, published in 1945.

- 10 oz. dried sliced beef, chopped into ½″ pieces
- 7½ cups milk
- 1 cup flour
- ⅓ cup bacon grease, melted
  Kosher salt and freshly ground black pepper
- 20 slices white sandwich bread, toasted

1 Put beef into a large bowl, cover with cold water, and soak for 3–5 minutes (depending on how salty you'd like the finished product to be). Drain beef and set aside.

2 Put milk into a large pot and bring to a boil over medium-high heat. Meanwhile, put flour and bacon grease into a medium bowl and stir well to form a smooth paste. Reduce heat to medium-low, whisk flour paste into milk, and cook, stirring constantly, until thickened, 2–3 minutes. Add beef, season with salt and pepper to taste, and simmer until sauce thickens, about 5 minutes more. Ladle the creamed chipped beef over toast and serve immediately. No griping!

SOUTH AMERICAN STEAK SANDWICH
Lomito Completo

SERVES 1

The lomito completo, popular in Uruguay and Argentina, lavishes sirloin steak with sauerkraut, mayonnaise, ketchup, mustard, and a runny fried egg.

- ¼ lb cooked sirloin steak, sliced
- 1 crusty round bun, split
- 1 tbsp. mayonnaise
- 1 tbsp. yellow mustard
- 1 tbsp. ketchup
- ¼ cup drained sauerkraut
- 1 fried egg
- 2 slices tomato
- 2 leaves iceberg lettuce

Place steak on bottom half of bun; top with mayonnaise, mustard, ketchup, sauerkraut, egg, tomato, and lettuce. Cover with bun top.

CHICAGO-STYLE ITALIAN BEEF

SERVES 6

This Windy City icon is no insipid deli sandwich. Beef is roasted under a coating of basil, oregano, and garlic, thinly sliced, then drenched in a garlicky gravy that permeates the crusty roll.

- 1½ tbsp. crushed red chile flakes
- 1 tsp. red wine vinegar
- 3 pickled jalapeños, stemmed and thinly sliced
- 3 ribs celery, thinly sliced
  Kosher salt and freshly ground black pepper
- 1 tbsp. dried basil
- 1 tbsp. dried oregano
- 4 cloves garlic, finely chopped
- 1 2½-lb. beef sirloin tip roast, trimmed
- 6 6″ crusty Italian rolls, split
- 3 green bell peppers, seeded, thickly sliced, and boiled until soft

1 Stir together half the chile flakes, the vinegar, jalapeños, celery, and salt and pepper to taste in a small bowl. Cover pepper relish and refrigerate for 8 hours or up to overnight.

2 Heat oven to 425°. Combine remaining chile flakes with basil, oregano, garlic, salt, and pepper in a small bowl. Place beef in a roasting pan, rub with half the spice mixture, and roast for 20 minutes. Reduce heat to 350° and roast for another 20 minutes. Combine remaining spice mixture with 4 cups water and add to roasting pan; continue roasting until an instant-read thermometer inserted into the thickest part of the meat reads 135°, 20–30 minutes. Transfer roast to a cutting board and let rest for 15 minutes. Skim fat from broth and keep broth warm.

3 Thinly slice beef with a deli slicer or an electric knife and return to broth until hot. Stuff each roll with some of the beef, broth, and green peppers and top with pepper relish.

COOK'S NOTE Unless you have access to a deli slicer, the best way to achieve the ultrathin slices of beef needed for this sandwich is to freeze the beef after cooking it, then thaw slightly before slicing with an electric knife.

HOW TO ORDER AN ITALIAN BEEF

An Italian beef shop, of which Chicago has scores, is not the sort of place where waiters patiently explain the menu. It is crucial to know the lingo. Order "a beef," not "a beef sandwich." The latter is redundant, because all Italian beef is served as a sandwich. "Double-dipped" says you want the whole sandwich submerged in gravy after it's been assembled. "Dry" is the opposite: a request for the server to pluck a heap of sliced, oven-roasted meat from the pan with tongs and shake off the excess juice before packing it into the roll. Say "hot" and your beef will be topped with spicy pickled-vegetable relish *giardiniera*; "sweet" refers to a garnish of roasted peppers. "Combo" means the sandwich is freighted with a length of charcoal-grilled Italian sausage. Cheese or other condiments are anathema—don't even ask about them.

CUBANO

SERVES 1

This sumptuous grilled sandwich—a crusty roll filled with roast pork, ham, Swiss cheese, and pickles—most likely originated in Tampa, Florida's Cuban cafés.

- 2 tbsp. mayonnaise
- 1 Cuban roll, split
- ½ cup cooked roast pork shoulder, shredded
- 3 slices deli ham
- 3 slices Swiss cheese
- 10 dill pickle chips
- 1 tbsp. yellow mustard
- 1 tbsp. canola oil

Spread mayonnaise on the bottom half of the roll and top with pork, ham, cheese, and pickle chips. Spread mustard on top half of roll; cover the sandwich. Heat oil in a 10″ skillet over medium-high heat and cook sandwich, weighting it down with a cast-iron skillet and turning once, until golden brown and cheese is melted, 8–10 minutes. Cut in half and serve hot.

HAM, CHEESE, EGG & LEMON SANDWICH

SERVES 1 (SEE PHOTO, PAGE 436)

The unusual combination of lemon curd and goat cheese adds a bright and tangy lightness to this omelette sandwich, a favorite menu item at the Big Egg in Portland, Oregon.

- 2 1″-thick slices brioche
  Unsalted butter, melted, for brushing
- ½ oz. goat cheese, softened
- 2½ tbsp. lemon curd
- 1 egg
- ¼ tsp. finely chopped fresh thyme
  Kosher salt and freshly ground black pepper, to taste
- 4 slices Black Forest ham
- ¼ cup mâche or other salad greens

1 Heat a 10″ nonstick skillet over medium-high heat. Brush one side of each slice of brioche with butter, place in skillet, buttered side down, and toast, about 1 minute. Transfer slices, toasted side down, to a plate and spread goat cheese over 1 slice and lemon curd over the other slice.

2 Meanwhile, whisk egg in a bowl and add to skillet. Sprinkle with thyme, salt, and pepper and cook, flipping once, until just set, about 2 minutes. Fold up omelette and place on top of goat cheese. Place ham in skillet and cook, flipping once, until heated through, about 35 seconds; place on top of omelette. Place mâche on top of ham, then top with the bread slice slathered with lemon curd.

CROQUE-MONSIEUR

SERVES 6

The *croque-monsieur*—on the menu in any bistro worth its salt—is a classic French ham and cheese sandwich covered in béchamel.

- 3 tbsp. unsalted butter
- 3 tbsp. flour
- 2 cups milk
- 1 cup grated Gruyère cheese
- ½ cup finely grated Parmigiano-Reggiano
  Freshly grated nutmeg, to taste
  Kosher salt and freshly ground black pepper, to taste
- 12 ¾″-thick slices pain de mie or Pullman bread, toasted
- 6 tbsp. Dijon mustard
- 12 thin slices baked ham

1 Melt butter in a 2-qt. saucepan over medium-high heat. Add flour and cook, whisking, until smooth, about 1 minute. Whisk in milk and bring to a boil. Reduce heat to medium-low and let simmer until slightly reduced and thickened, 6–8 minutes. Add ½ cup grated Gruyère and the Parmigiano and whisk until smooth. Season with nutmeg, salt, and pepper.

2 Heat broiler. Place 6 slices bread on a parchment paper–lined baking sheet and spread 1 tbsp. mustard over each. Top each with 2 slices ham and divide remaining Gruyère. Broil until cheese begins to melt, 1–2 minutes. Top with remaining bread slices, then pour a generous amount of béchamel on top of each sandwich. Broil until cheese sauce is bubbling and evenly browned, 3–4 minutes.

COOK'S NOTE Top a *croque-monsieur* with a fried egg and it becomes a *croque-madame*. Heat 1 tbsp. canola oil in a nonstick skillet over medium heat. Crack in an egg, season with salt and pepper, and cook until white is opaque but yolk is still runny, about 3 minutes. Place an egg on top of each sandwich and serve hot.

IN SEARCH OF MONTE CRISTO

It's safe to say that the Monte Cristo sandwich has nothing to do with the tiny Italian island of Montecristo, nor with the Bolivian town of Monte Cristo. Neither is there any apparent link with Alexandre Dumas' *The Count of Monte Cristo*—though that novel, published in 1845, did inspire a crop of movies, the most famous being the Robert Donat version, which appeared in 1934, somewhat before the sandwich came into vogue. One theory holds that the Monte Cristo is a Californian elaboration on the *croque-monsieur* (page 123); another possibility is that it derived from the Neapolitan battered and fried cheese sandwich called *mozzarella in carrozza* (page 131)—which might sound a bit like "Monte Cristo" to a foreign ear.

Wherever it came from, by the 1950s it could be found in diners and hotel dining rooms across America. Writer Helen Evans Brown, in her *West Coast Cook Book* (1952), suggests that the Monte Cristo originated in San Francisco; she includes not only the basic sandwich but also the Monte Carlo (made with tongue) and a cocktail variant called the Monte Benito.

MONTE CRISTO

SERVES 2

People tend to have strong opinions about the Monte Cristo sandwich, a double-decker of Swiss cheese, ham, and chicken or turkey, battered, fried, and dusted with confectioners' sugar, served with jelly on the side. Some consider it a marvel; others, an absurdity. Whatever it may be, the Monte Cristo is a stunning creation, requiring careful assembly and, at the table, a knife and fork.

- ¼ cup milk
- 2 eggs
  Kosher salt and freshly ground black pepper, to taste
- 5 tbsp. unsalted butter, softened
- 6 thin slices white sandwich bread
- 4 thin slices deli-style ham
- 4 thin slices deli-style turkey
- 4 thin slices Swiss cheese
  Confectioners' sugar, for garnish
  Red currant jelly, for serving

1 Lightly beat milk and eggs in a shallow bowl. Season with salt and pepper and set aside. For each sandwich, lightly butter 3 slices of bread on both sides (using about ½ tbsp. butter for each sandwich). Place 2 slices each of ham and turkey between 2 slices of bread. Top each with 2 slices of cheese, and then top with third slice of buttered bread. Trim crusts, secure with toothpicks, and cut in half on the diagonal.

2 Melt 2 tbsp. butter in a 12″ nonstick skillet over medium heat. Dip sandwich halves in milk mixture to coat. When butter foams, place sandwiches in skillet and fry until golden brown on bottom, about 2 minutes. Add remaining 2 tbsp. butter to skillet, turn sandwiches, and fry until browned on other side, about 2 minutes more. Transfer to plates, sprinkle with confectioners' sugar, and serve with jelly.

SCHNITZEL SANDWICH

SERVES 4

Schnitzi Schnitzel Bar, in Brooklyn, New York, makes nine different types of schnitzel—a breaded chicken sandwich popular in Israel and in Orthodox Jewish enclaves in the U.S.—and serves them with 13 varieties of homemade sauce. This recipe is an adaptation of the restaurant's chile-flecked "Spanish" schnitzel, one of its most popular variations.

FOR THE PESTO SAUCE

- 6½ cups packed fresh basil leaves
- ¾ cup plus 2 tbsp. extra-virgin olive oil
- 3 tbsp. pine nuts, toasted
- 3 cloves garlic, peeled
  Kosher salt and freshly ground black pepper, to taste

FOR THE RED CHIMICHURRI SAUCE

- ½ cup extra-virgin olive oil
- ¾ cup roughly chopped roasted red bell peppers
- ¼ cup white vinegar
- 1½ tbsp. kosher salt
- 1 tbsp. red wine vinegar
- 1 tbsp. sweet paprika

1 tbsp. finely chopped oregano

1½ tsp. crushed red chile flakes

½ tsp. freshly ground black pepper

¼ tsp. ground cumin

3 cloves garlic

1 bunch fresh flat-leaf parsley

FOR THE SCHNITZEL

4 cups flour

8 eggs, beaten

4 cups dried bread crumbs

½ cup crushed red chile flakes

12 ¼"-thick chicken cutlets
Kosher salt and freshly ground black pepper, to taste

¼ cup canola oil

2 medium onions, thinly sliced lengthwise

4 12" French baguettes, split
Sweet chile sauce, to taste

4 cups loosely packed shredded romaine lettuce

3 ripe tomatoes, thinly sliced

½ cup sliced dill pickles

1 Make the pesto: Combine basil, oil, nuts, garlic, salt, and pepper in a food processor and process until smooth; transfer to a small bowl and set aside.

2 Make the chimichurri: Clean the food processor, then add oil, peppers, white vinegar, salt, wine vinegar, paprika, oregano, chile flakes, pepper, cumin, garlic, parsley, and ¼ cup water. Process until smooth; transfer to a small bowl and set aside.

3 Place flour, eggs, and bread crumbs mixed with the chile flakes in three separate shallow dishes. Season flour and chicken with salt and pepper. Working in batches, coat cutlets with flour, shaking off excess. Dip in eggs, then dredge in bread crumb mixture. Set aside.

4 Heat oil in a 12" skillet over medium-high heat. Working in batches, add cutlets and cook, turning once, until golden brown, 4–6 minutes. Transfer to paper towels to drain. Once all cutlets are cooked, add half the onions to skillet and cook, stirring often, until soft and caramelized, about 8 minutes.

5 Place 3 cutlets on bottom half of each baguette and cover with sauces, to taste. Top each with lettuce, tomatoes, remaining raw onions, cooked onions, and pickles. Cover with top half of baguette.

THE SCHNITZEL LEGACY

For a country known for Middle Eastern food, Israel's national obsession with schnitzel represents one of the lone culinary holdovers of Zionism's Austro-Hungarian roots. It's been a staple since the early days of the country's existence, found everywhere from the frozen-food aisles of supermarkets to kibbutz dining halls to take-out windows in bustling nightlife areas, where it comes in sandwich form. Turkey or chicken breasts are pounded; marinated in olive oil, garlic, and lemon juice; dipped in flour, then egg; dredged in bread crumbs—sometimes with sesame seeds or za'atar spice—and fried in oil. Fresh-from-the-fryer schnitzels are stuffed into baguettes or pitas and layered with toppings that bridge the gap between Ashkenazic (Eastern European) and Mizrahic (Middle Eastern) tastes: mayonnaise and mustard, but also hummus, tahini, tomato and cucumber salad, and harissa. The sandwiches are so popular, you can find them outside the Holy Land wherever Israelis congregate. On Brooklyn's Coney Island Avenue, a thriving artery of Orthodox Jewish culture, a slew of outlets vie for the appetites of students with flavors that go far beyond the sandwich's origins—like the "Spanish" version (in a spicy breading with red chile sauce, page 124) served at Schnitzi's, a popular joint.

MUFFULETTA
SERVES 4

Salvatore Lupo, who opened Central Grocery in New Orleans in 1906, created the muffuletta for the Sicilian farmers selling their goods at the French Quarter market. (The name derives from *muffuliette*, a Sicilian colloquialism for soft rolls.) At Central Grocery, they use their famous olive salad—brimming with green niçoise olives, black Kalamata olives, roasted peppers, and banana peppers, all marinated in red wine vinegar—to dress deli meats and cheeses in this irresistible sandwich.

FOR THE OLIVE SALAD

1¼ cups coarsely chopped cauliflower florets

½ cup extra-virgin olive oil

½ tsp. dried oregano

½ tsp. dried thyme

2 small carrots, peeled and roughly chopped

2 small ribs celery, thinly sliced

¾ cup chopped pitted green niçoise olives

½ cup chopped pitted Kalamata olives

½ cup chopped roasted red peppers

¼ cup jarred sliced banana peppers, drained

2 tbsp. red wine vinegar

Kosher salt and freshly ground black pepper, to taste

FOR THE SANDWICH

1 8″–10″ round loaf Italian bread with sesame seeds, halved

6 oz. thinly sliced deli-style ham

6 oz. thinly sliced Genoa salami

6 oz. thinly sliced mortadella

6 oz. thinly sliced provolone

1 Make the olive salad: Bring cauliflower, oil, oregano, thyme, carrots, celery, and 3 tbsp. water to a simmer in a 2-qt. saucepan over medium-high heat. Reduce heat to medium-low; cook until vegetables are just tender, 10–12 minutes. Transfer to a medium bowl and stir in olives, peppers, vinegar, salt, and pepper; let cool.

2 Make the sandwich: Using your hands, hollow out both loaf halves; spread olive salad over bottom half. Layer ham, salami, mortadella, and provolone over salad, then top with remaining salad and top half of loaf. Wrap entire sandwich in plastic wrap and refrigerate for 8 hours or up to overnight, allowing the sandwich to marinate and the flavors to intermingle. Cut into quarters and serve.

BÁNH MÌ

SERVES 4

Originating on the streets of Saigon (now Ho Chi Minh City), the *bánh mì* sandwich is a French-Vietnamese hybrid consisting of an airy baguette, sour pickled daikon and carrot, fresh cilantro, spicy chiles, and cool slices of cucumber surrounding any number of protein options, from sweet minced pork to fatty pâté to sardines. This is the classic version: hoisin-marinated pork, julienned daikon radishes, carrots, cilantro, and chile oil.

FOR THE SLAW

¼ cup white vinegar

¼ cup sugar

½ cup julienned carrots

½ cup julienned daikon radish

Kosher salt, to taste

FOR THE SEASONED PORK

1 tsp. canola oil

1 tbsp. finely chopped yellow onion

¾ lb ground pork

2 tbsp. hoisin sauce

2 tsp. soy sauce

1 tsp. sesame oil

½ tsp. hot sauce

½ tsp. five-spice powder

¼ tsp. onion powder

¼ tsp. garlic powder

¼ tsp. freshly ground black pepper

FOR THE SANDWICH

4 baguette lengths, each 10″ long and split

½ cup mayonnaise

8 ⅛″-thick slices giò lụa (Vietnamese-style pork sausage)

8 ⅛″-thick slices headcheese

4 tsp. soy sauce

½ cup cilantro sprigs

½ medium English cucumber, cut lengthwise into 4 slices

Chile oil, to taste

Freshly ground black pepper, to taste

1 Make the slaw: Bring vinegar, sugar, and ½ cup water to a boil in a 2-qt. saucepan over high heat; transfer to a medium bowl. Stir in carrots, radish, and salt and set the slaw aside for 30 minutes. Drain.

2 Make the seasoned pork: Heat oil in a 10″ nonstick skillet over medium heat. Add onion and cook, stirring often, until soft, 2–3 minutes. Add pork, hoisin, soy sauce, sesame oil, hot sauce, five-spice powder, onion and garlic powders, and pepper. Cook, stirring often, until browned, 5–6 minutes. Remove from heat and set aside.

3 Make the sandwich: Heat oven to 400°. Place baguettes, cut side up, on a baking sheet and spread 1 tbsp. mayonnaise on all cut sides. Bake until hot and slightly crisped, about 5 minutes. Remove from oven and divide seasoned pork evenly among half the baguettes. Top each with 2 slices pork roll, 2 slices salami, 1 tsp. soy sauce, ¼ of the cilantro, and 1 cucumber slice. Season with chile oil and pepper and top with the slaw. Close sandwiches, slice each in half, and serve.

STREET HERO

> **"**When I'm exploring Vietnam, a thousand street snacks beckon, but I inevitably seek out *bánh mì*, the ubiquitous Franco-Viet sandwich. I order the *đặc biệt,* "the special." The vendor slashes open a crisp baguette, moistens it with mayonnaise and soy sauce, adds garlicky pork liver pâté and Vietnamese cold cuts—silky *giò lụa* sausage, marbled headcheese, rich pork shank—and finishes it with daikon and carrot pickles, chile slices, cucumber, and cilantro. My expectations are met at first bite: crisp, earthy, bright. The bread, condiments, and meats are the legacy of French and Chinese colonialism, but *bánh mì đặc biệt* is 100 percent Viet.**"**
>
> ANDREA NGUYEN

TUNISIAN TUNA SANDWICH

Casse-Croûte Tunisien

SERVES 4

You'll need both hands to eat this overstuffed tuna sandwich. Lavished with fiery condiments and stacks of fixings, it's a North African take on the famous French *pan bagnat* (page 128).

- 3 tbsp. olive oil
- 2 cloves garlic, minced
- ½ small yellow onion, minced
- ½ small green bell pepper, seeded and minced
- 1 15-oz. can whole, peeled tomatoes, drained and crushed by hand
- 1 bay leaf
  Kosher salt and freshly ground black pepper, to taste
- 2 baguettes, cut into four 8″ lengths
- 2 medium Yukon gold potatoes, boiled until tender, peeled, and thinly sliced
- 1 small English cucumber, thinly sliced
- 1 medium ripe tomato, thinly sliced
- 2 5-oz. cans olive oil–packed tuna, drained
- ½ cup pitted black olives
- ¼ cup capers, rinsed and drained
- 4 peperoncini peppers, drained, stemmed, and halved lengthwise
- ½ cup Harissa (page 592, or store-bought)

1 Heat oil in a 10″ skillet over medium-high heat. Add garlic, onion, and pepper and cook, stirring, until soft, about 6 minutes. Add tomatoes and bay leaf and cook, stirring, until sauce is thick, about 3 minutes. Remove and discard bay leaf, season with salt and pepper, and set aside.

2 Split baguettes horizontally, leaving them intact on one side. Divide tomato sauce among baguettes, top with potatoes, cucumber, and tomato and then tuna; top with olives, capers, and peperoncini. Drizzle the top of each with harissa; halve sandwiches crosswise to serve.

OYSTER PO'BOY

SERVES 4

This New Orleans sandwich is classically dressed with shredded iceberg lettuce, thin-sliced tomato, pickles, and a generous smear of mayonnaise. At Crabby Jack's restaurant in Jefferson, Louisiana, the source of this recipe, the oysters are fried in a spicy cornmeal breading.

- Canola oil, for frying
- 2 tbsp. kosher salt, plus more to taste
- 1 tbsp. freshly ground black pepper
- 1 tbsp. paprika
- 1 tbsp. garlic powder
- 1½ tsp. onion powder
- ¾ tsp. cayenne pepper
- ¾ tsp. chipotle chile powder
- ¾ tsp. dried oregano, crumbled
- ¾ tsp. dried rosemary, crumbled
- ¾ tsp. dried thyme, crumbled
- 40 large oysters, shucked
- 2 cups yellow cornmeal
- 4 8″ New Orleans–style French bread rolls
  Mayonnaise, shredded iceberg lettuce, tomato slices, and dill pickle chips, for serving

Pour oil to a depth of 2″ into a 6-qt. Dutch oven and heat over medium-high heat until a deep-fry thermometer reads 350°. Whisk together salt, pepper, paprika, garlic and onion powders, cayenne, chile powder, oregano, rosemary, and thyme in a bowl; add oysters and toss to coat with seasoning. Add cornmeal and toss until oysters are evenly coated; dust off excess cornmeal. Working in batches, add oysters to oil and fry until golden brown, about 3 minutes. Transfer to paper towels to drain and sprinkle with salt. Spread insides of rolls with mayonnaise and divide oysters among rolls; top with lettuce, tomato, and pickles.

SANDWICH TO GO

> "When my husband and I acquired our farmhouse in Provence in 1984, our visits were generally limited to weekend getaways from Paris. For the train ride back to the city, a snack was essential, and *pan bagnat*, or "bathed bread," the Provençal sandwich found at every bakery and market in the region, became our standby. It's inexpensive, travels well, and includes many of our favorite Provençal ingredients: tomatoes, local bell peppers, black niçoise olives, anchovies and tuna, salt, and pepper—a salade niçoise, effectively, between slices of crusty bread. I'd prepare the sandwiches on Saturday, scooping out some of the crumb of the bread, then letting the *pan bagnat* marinate, tightly wrapped and weighted down in the refrigerator, until departure time the next day, which always made for moist and satisfying sandwiches."
>
> PATRICIA WELLS

PAN BAGNAT

Provençal Tuna Sandwich

SERVES 4 (SEE PHOTO, PAGE 217)

This stuffed sandwich captures the heart and flavors of Provence with fresh tomatoes, niçoise olives, fennel, cucumber, red bell peppers, and oil-packed tuna.

- 2   plum tomatoes, cored and thinly sliced crosswise
     Kosher salt, to taste
- 1   5-oz. can olive oil–packed tuna, drained
- 4   scallions, thinly sliced
- ½   small red bell pepper, seeded and thinly sliced into 2″ lengths
- ⅓   cup extra-virgin olive oil
- 1   tbsp. Dijon mustard
- 1   7″ round rustic bread loaf, split
- 1   small bulb fennel, cored and thinly sliced crosswise
- 1   small cucumber, thinly sliced crosswise
- 2   hard-cooked eggs, thinly sliced crosswise
- 8   oil-cured anchovies, drained
- 10   salt-cured black olives, pitted and halved
     Freshly ground black pepper, to taste

1 Sprinkle tomato slices liberally with salt and transfer to a colander; set aside to drain for 30 minutes. In a small bowl, break up tuna with a fork and stir in scallions and bell pepper; set aside. In another small bowl, whisk together oil and mustard; set dressing aside. Scoop the insides from the bread loaf and discard or reserve for another use. Place tomatoes evenly over bottom of bread and then top with fennel and cucumbers; spread tuna mixture over top and then add egg slices, anchovies, and olives. Pour dressing evenly over ingredients and season with salt and pepper. Cover with top of bread, pressing lightly to compact.

2 Wrap sandwich tightly in plastic wrap and place on a baking sheet; top with another baking sheet and weight with a cast-iron skillet. Refrigerate for at least 4 hours or up to overnight. Slice into quarters to serve.

SOFT-SHELL CRAB SANDWICHES

SERVES 2

Crunchy soft-shell crabs used to be a seasonal delicacy, available only in warm months when blue crabs molted their hard exoskeletons. Now, thanks to flash-freezing, they're available year-round, but this sandwich—in which the crabs are lightly fried until golden brown and then wedged between two slices of soft white bread—is a summer classic.

- ½   cup flour
     Kosher salt and freshly ground black pepper, to taste
- 2   tbsp. unsalted butter
- 1   tbsp. canola oil
- 2   cleaned soft-shell crabs
- 4   slices soft white sandwich bread
     Tartar Sauce (page 591)
     Bibb lettuce, for serving

1 Season flour with salt and pepper in a shallow bowl or plate.

2 Heat butter and oil in a medium skillet over medium-high heat. Dredge crabs in flour, shake off excess, then fry until brown and crisp, about 2 minutes on each side. Drain on paper towels.

3 Make up 2 sandwiches, using 1 crab per sandwich, 2 slices of bread, a little tartar sauce, and 1 or 2 lettuce leaves. Serve with additional tartar sauce.

MAINE-STYLE LOBSTER ROLL

SERVES 2

The combination of lobster and mayonnaise is unbeatable in a split, buttered roll. It instantly transports us to the Maine coast on a sunny summer's day.

- 1 lb. cooked lobster meat, cut into ½" chunks
- ½ cup mayonnaise
- 3 scallions, thinly sliced
  Kosher salt and freshly ground black pepper, to taste
- 2 split-top hot dog rolls

In a large bowl, gently stir together lobster, mayonnaise, scallions, salt, and pepper. Split lobster salad between rolls.

JACQUES PÉPIN'S CONNECTICUT-STYLE LOBSTER ROLL

SERVES 2

Outside of Maine, and particularly along the Connecticut beachline, lobster rolls come not with mayonnaise, but bathed in warm butter. We're enamored of Jacques Pépin's version, with the very French addition of fresh tarragon.

- ½ cup unsalted butter
- 2 split-top hot dog rolls
- 1 tbsp. fresh minced tarragon
- 1 tbsp. fresh lemon juice
  Kosher salt and freshly ground black pepper, to taste
- 1 lb. cooked lobster meat, cut into ½" chunks
  Lettuce leaves, for serving

1 Melt butter in a small saucepan over low heat. Brush insides and outsides of hot dog rolls with some of the butter and brown on both sides in a skillet over medium heat.

2 Add tarragon and lemon juice to the saucepan, season with salt and pepper, and add lobster meat. Heat until just warmed through.

3 Tuck 2 lettuce leaves into each roll, fill with lobster, and spoon butter on top.

CURRIED HERRING OPEN-FACE SANDWICHES

Smørrebrød med Karrysild

SERVES 6

You'll find *smørrebrød*—open-face sandwiches—throughout Scandinavia, topped with almost anything you can imagine. Curried herring *(karry sild)* is a popular option; this version, served at the restaurant Gammel Strand in Copenhagen, is one of our favorites.

- 4 pickled herring filets
- 2 tbsp. sugar
- ½ tbsp. hot curry powder
- ½ cup crème fraîche
- 6 thin slices pumpernickel bread, buttered
- 6 Leaves lettuce
  Red onion slices
  Finely chopped hard-cooked egg
- 6 sprigs fresh dill

1 Cut herring filets into thirds crosswise, then place in a medium bowl and set aside.

2 Combine sugar and 1 tbsp. water in a small saucepan and bring to a boil over medium-high heat. Let cool completely. Whisk in hot curry powder and crème fraîche. Pour curry mixture over herring, cover with plastic wrap, and refrigerate for 24 hours.

3 Cover each pumpernickel slice with lettuce and 2 pieces of herring. Top each with red onion, egg, and a sprig of fresh dill.

WARM OPEN-FACE AVOCADO & GOAT CHEESE SANDWICHES

SERVES 6

Creamy avocado is lightly mashed together with goat cheese, making this open-face sandwich especially tangy. This sandwich was a staple at the Los Angeles restaurant City Café in the 1980s.

- 3 tbsp. fresh lemon juice
- 1 tbsp. freshly cracked black pepper
  Kosher salt, to taste
- ¼ cup extra-virgin olive oil
- ¼ lb soft goat cheese
- ⅛ tsp. finely ground black pepper
- 4 ripe avocados, pitted and peeled
  Tabasco sauce

6   small baguettes, split and lightly toasted
    Tomato slices, for serving
    Cucumber slices, for serving

1 Put 1 tbsp. lemon juice, the cracked black pepper, and salt to taste into a bowl; stir well. While whisking constantly, drizzle in olive oil to make a dressing; set aside.

2 Put goat cheese, remaining 2 tbsp. lemon juice, finely ground black pepper, the flesh from the avocados, and a few dashes of Tabasco into a bowl. Lightly mash with a fork, then season with salt.

3 Heat broiler to high. Divide avocado mixture among the 12 baguette halves and spread to cover each. Transfer baguettes to baking sheet and broil until just warmed through, 1–2 minutes. Top baguette halves with tomato and cucumber slices, in any arrangement you wish. Drizzle some dressing onto each sandwich.

BLT BASICS

There are operatic sandwiches—the big, lavish muffuletta and *bánh mì*—but the all-American BLT is more like finely wrought chamber music. Each of its five elements—bread, bacon, lettuce, tomato, and mayonnaise—plays in counterpoint to the others in a subtle and satisfying harmony. Ostentatious embellishments are to be avoided. Substitute unsmoked pork belly for smoky rashers or split ciabatta for sliced white bread and you'll upset the delicate balance.

For a BLT, the bread should be white and toasted; Pullman loaf works best. This kind of bread has a soft, tight crumb that will soak up some of the tomato's juices, and toasting it helps prevent it from becoming overly sodden. The bacon must be smoked, to adequately offset a tomato's sweetness. We like a medium-thick cut; take care as you cook to avoid a result that's too leathery, as that impedes biting through the sandwich's layers with ease and tasting all the ingredients in each mouthful. Crisp iceberg lettuce lends the right note of freshness, and the tomato should be absolutely ripe and sweet. Mayonnaise is not optional; its creaminess tempers the tomato's acidity. The matter of whether to slice your BLT into triangles or rectangles, however, is up to you.

EGGPLANT & CUCUMBER SALAD SANDWICH

Sabich

SERVES 4

This earthy vegetarian sandwich is a traditional breakfast for Iraqi Jews. It's filled to bursting with fried eggplant, tea-steeped hard-cooked eggs, tahini, parsley, *amba* (a jarred mango relish), and cucumber salad.

4   Black tea bags
    Peel of 1 large yellow onion
4   hard-cooked eggs, peeled
7   tbsp. canola oil
1   1½-lb. eggplant, cut crosswise into ¼″-thick slices
    Kosher salt, to taste
2   Kirby cucumbers, finely chopped
1   plum tomato, cored and finely chopped
1   small red onion, finely chopped
3   tbsp. fresh lemon juice
2   tbsp. extra-virgin olive oil
    Freshly ground black pepper, to taste
5   tbsp. tahini
1   clove garlic, finely chopped
4   Pita pockets, warmed
    Amba or mango chutney, for serving
¼   cup packed fresh flat-leaf parsley leaves

1 Place tea bags and onion peel in a 4-qt. saucepan with 8 cups water; bring to a boil. Reduce heat to lowest setting, add eggs, and cover; let eggs steep until they've darkened in color, about 1 hour. Drain, and slice each egg into ¼″ rounds.

2 Meanwhile, heat oil in a 12″ cast-iron skillet over medium-high heat until oil is shimmering. Season eggplant with salt. Working in batches, add eggplant and cook, flipping once, until golden and very soft, 3–4 minutes. Transfer eggplant to paper towels and set aside.

3 In a small bowl, combine cucumbers, tomatoes, onion, 1 tbsp. lemon juice, and olive oil; season cucumber salad with salt and pepper and set aside. In a small bowl, combine remaining 2 tbsp. lemon juice, tahini, garlic, and 5 tbsp. ice water. Whisk ingredients until creamy and season with salt; set tahini mixture aside.

4 To serve, slice off one-fourth of each pita round and spread some of the tahini mixture on the inside of each pita pocket. Put one-fourth of the eggplant into each pita and 1 egg. Add some of the cucumber salad, top with amba, and stuff with some parsley. Drizzle the top of each sandwich with remaining tahini sauce.

"Too few people understand a really good sandwich."

JAMES BEARD

MEXICAN BEAN & CHEESE SANDWICHES
Molletes
SERVES 8

For this popular Mexican sandwich, warm, freshly made refried beans are spooned into hollowed-out rolls, topped with *queso Oaxaca,* and then broiled until the cheese is bubbling.

FOR THE SALSA

- 2 lb. plum tomatoes, cored and cut into ½″ cubes
- ⅔ cup roughly chopped cilantro
- 6 serrano chiles, stemmed, seeded, and finely chopped
- 1 large white onion, finely chopped
  Kosher salt, to taste

FOR THE REFRIED BEANS & SANDWICHES

- ½ cup lard or canola oil
- 4 cloves garlic, minced
- 1 small white onion, finely chopped
- 2 cups chicken stock
- 3 15-oz. cans pinto beans, drained and rinsed
  Kosher salt and freshly ground black pepper, to taste
- 4 bolillos or kaiser rolls, split
- ¾ lb. queso Oaxaca, grated

1 Make the salsa: Combine tomatoes, cilantro, chiles, and onion in a bowl and season liberally with salt; fold gently to combine. Cover and refrigerate for about 1 hour.

2 Make the refried beans: Heat lard in a 12″ skillet over medium-high heat. Add garlic and onion and cook, stirring, until soft, about 8 minutes. Add stock and beans and cook, stirring and mashing, until almost all beans are smooth and mixture is slightly soupy, about 5 minutes. Season with salt and pepper and keep warm.

3 Heat broiler to high. Using your fingers, scoop out and discard insides of rolls, leaving a ½″-thick shell. Place roll halves on a foil-lined baking sheet, cut side up, and broil until lightly toasted, about 2 minutes. Pour about ½ cup refried beans over each roll half so that the beans are spilling over the edges, and then sprinkle with cheese.

Return to broiler and heat until beans are heated through and cheese is just melted but not browned, about 2 minutes. Transfer 1 roll half to each serving plate and top each with a couple of large spoonfuls of salsa. Serve immediately.

COOK'S NOTE The *bolillo,* a French-style crusty white bread roll from Mexico, is the traditional foundation of this comforting dish, but a kaiser or most any other sandwich roll will work well.

FRIED MOZZARELLA SANDWICHES
Mozzarella in Carrozza
SERVES 4

These crisp mini-sandwiches from Campania are deep-fried and filled with molten cheese.

- Canola oil, for frying
- 6 oz. sliced mozzarella
- 8 slices white sandwich bread
  Kosher salt and freshly ground black pepper, to taste
- ½ cup flour
- 2 eggs, lightly beaten
- 1 cup plain bread crumbs

1 Pour oil to a depth of 2″ in a medium Dutch oven and heat over medium-high heat until a deep-fry thermometer reads 350°. Divide mozzarella slices among 4 slices of bread, season with salt and pepper, and cover with remaining bread slices to make 4 sandwiches. Trim crusts and halve sandwiches diagonally.

2 Place flour, eggs, and bread crumbs in 3 separate bowls. Dredge sandwiches in flour, coat in eggs, and coat in bread crumbs; fry, turning once, until golden brown, about 2 minutes.

BURRATA & MARINATED CHERRY TOMATO SANDWICHES

SERVES 4

Crusty bread sops up creamy burrata cheese and juicy marinated tomatoes in this pleasantly messy sandwich from Casa del Vino in Florence.

2	cups halved cherry tomatoes
¼	cup plus 2 tbsp. extra-virgin olive oil
¼	cup balsamic vinegar
1	tbsp. capers
10	oil-packed anchovy filets, minced
	Crushed red chile flakes
	Kosher salt and freshly ground black pepper, to taste
4	small crusty sandwich rolls
1	8-oz. ball burrata or fresh mozzarella

1 Combine tomatoes, oil, vinegar, capers, anchovies, a pinch of crushed red chile, and a generous pinch each of salt and black pepper in a large bowl. Stir well to combine. Cover with plastic wrap and let rest on the countertop or in the fridge for at least 8 hours or up to overnight.

2 When ready to serve, let tomato mixture come to room temperature. Stir briefly, then put a generous dollop of tomato mixture on each roll and top with burrata, dividing evenly. Season with salt, pepper, and more crushed red chile to taste, and serve.

ITALIAN PECORINO, PARSLEY & ANCHOVY SANDWICHES

SERVES 4

This crusty sandwich from Florence's Casa del Vino calls for only a handful of ingredients, but goes big on bold Italian flavors.

2	cups fresh flat-leaf parsley leaves, finely chopped
6	cloves garlic, finely chopped
	Kosher salt and freshly ground black pepper
16	oil-packed anchovies
¼–½	cup extra-virgin olive oil
4	oz. pecorino cheese, thinly sliced (about 8 slices)
4	small crusty sandwich rolls, halved crosswise

1 Combine the parsley, garlic, and a pinch each of salt and pepper in a medium bowl; stir well. Gently stir in the anchovies and olive oil, starting with ¼ cup oil and adding more as needed to saturate the parsley (it should be shiny and moist but not runny). Let rest for 30 minutes.

2 When ready to serve, distribute sliced pecorino atop the bottom halves of rolls, followed by the parsley mixture and anchovies. Top with other halves of rolls.

WAFFLE SANDWICHES WITH CECINA, AVOCADO & ARUGULA

SERVES 4

This all-day-appropriate sandwich was born out of Parisian restaurant Mokonuts' staff meals as a way to use up leftover waffles from breakfast service. Whipped egg whites folded into the batter help create airy, crisp waffles. Cecina is a smoky cured beef from Spain, but any dry Spanish ham will do.

FOR THE WAFFLES

1⅓	cups sour cream
½	cup whole milk
4	large egg yolks
¼	cup sugar
¼	tsp. kosher salt
1½	cups flour, sifted
8	tbsp. unsalted butter, melted and cooled
4	large egg whites

FOR THE SANDWICHES

½	cup mayonnaise, or to taste
2	firm-ripe avocados, sliced
12	oz. (16–20 thin slices) cecina or Spanish ham
8	oz. smoked scamorza or provolone cheese, thinly sliced
½	cup arugula

1 Make the waffles: Whisk together sour cream, milk, egg yolks, 2 tbsp. sugar, and salt in a large bowl. Whisk in flour, followed by melted butter, and set aside.

2 Preheat a standard waffle iron according to manufacturer's directions. Preheat oven to 400°.

3 In a separate bowl, whisk or use an electric mixer to beat egg whites with remaining sugar until mixture holds soft peaks. Gently fold meringue into prepared batter just before cooking.

4 Ladle ⅓ cup batter onto waffle iron and cook until waffle is lightly browned around the edges, 8–10 minutes. Remove to a rack to cool while you continue until batter is all used and you have 8 waffles.

5 Make the sandwiches: Spread mayonnaise evenly over 4 waffles. Top each with sliced avocado, cecina, cheese, and arugula. Cover with remaining waffles, then transfer sandwiches to a large baking sheet. Place an ovenproof weight on top (such as a large skillet) and bake until warm, 10–12 minutes.

PORCHETTA SANDWICHES WITH MARINATED ONIONS & SALSA VERDE

SERVES 10 (SEE PHOTO, PAGE 226)

Florence's Casa del Vino serves its fatty homemade porchetta on soft ciabatta rolls with plenty of pickley condiments.

FOR THE PORCHETTA

- 1   **6-lb. porchetta (boneless pork loin encased in a piece of skin-on pork belly)**
      Salt and freshly ground black pepper
- 3   **tbsp. fennel seeds**
- 1   **tbsp. fennel pollen**
- ⅓   **cup finely chopped fennel fronds**
- ⅓   **cup finely chopped fresh flat-leaf parsley**
- ⅓   **cup finely chopped fresh sage**
- ¼   **cup finely chopped fresh rosemary**
- ½   **cup white wine (optional)**

FOR THE MARINATED ONIONS

- 2   **medium red onions, halved and thinly sliced (3 cups)**
- ½   **cup red wine vinegar**
- ¼   **cup extra-virgin olive oil**

FOR THE SALSA VERDE

- 1   **cup coarse dried bread crumbs**
- 2   **tbsp. red wine vinegar**
- 1   **cup flat-leaf parsley, minced**
- ¾   **cup extra-virgin olive oil**
- 1   **tbsp. capers, minced**
- 12   **anchovy filets in oil, minced**
- 2   **hard-boiled eggs (page 31; optional), finely chopped**
- 1   **small head garlic, finely chopped (about ⅓ cup)**

    Hearty sandwich rolls, for serving

1 Prepare the porchetta: On a rimmed baking sheet, lay pork belly skin side up and rub skin side generously with salt. Refrigerate uncovered for at least 12 hours or ideally 24 hours.

2 Meanwhile, put fennel seeds in a small skillet over medium heat. Cook, stirring or shaking the pan occasionally, until lightly toasted and fragrant, 4–5 minutes. Remove and coarsely grind.

3 Set a rack in the center of the oven and preheat to 300°. Retrieve pork belly and place skin side down on a clean work surface. Rub inside of pork belly all over with salt and pepper, then with ground fennel seeds, fennel pollen, fennel fronds, parsley, sage, and rosemary. Baste or rub loin with white wine, if using. Wrap seasoned pork belly tightly around loin to cover completely, then tie porchetta tightly every 2–3 inches with kitchen twine. Transfer to a roasting rack set in a high-sided roasting pan (if pork belly does not fit around entire loin, be sure the largest piece of the belly is facing the top of the oven, to keep loin from drying out).

4 Roast until skin looks firm and ends of pork look cooked, about 2 hours 15 minutes. Raise heat to 425° and cook, basting skin once with drippings halfway through, until skin is well browned and a thermometer inserted into the center of the loin registers 145–150°, about 1 hour longer.

5 Meanwhile, make the marinated onions: Combine onions and vinegar in a large bowl. Let rest, stirring occasionally, until onions soften, 1 hour or up to overnight. When ready to serve, stir in olive oil.

6 Make the salsa verde: Stir together bread crumbs and red wine vinegar in a large bowl. Add parsley, olive oil, capers, anchovies, eggs (if using), and garlic, and stir to combine.

7 Remove porchetta from oven and let rest for 15 minutes before slicing into thin ½″ slices.

8 Spread some of the salsa verde onto the bottom half of each sandwich roll. Top with porchetta slices and marinated onions to taste.

Sandwich Salads

KNIFE-AND-FORK EGG SALAD

SERVES 4

This piquant egg salad is traditionally served on slices of buttered brown bread with watercress—to be eaten with a knife and fork, a dainty presentation fit for a refined occasion. It's also delicious atop any bread, or even eaten on its own.

6   hard-cooked eggs, peeled and coarsely chopped
½   cup finely chopped fresh chives
2   tbsp. finely chopped celery leaves
    Kosher salt and freshly ground black pepper, to taste
⅓   cup mayonnaise
2   tsp. white wine vinegar
2   tsp. Dijon mustard

Combine eggs, half the chives, celery leaves, and salt and pepper in a medium bowl and fold together gently to combine. Add mayonnaise, vinegar, and mustard and fold again, being careful not to mash up the eggs.

HELEN CORBITT'S CHICKEN SALAD

MAKES ABOUT 6 CUPS

Famed Texas cook Helen Corbitt created this rich chicken salad—studded with almonds, red grapes, celery, parsley, and a touch of whipped cream—for the café menu at Neiman Marcus department stores in the 1950s.

1   lb. boneless, skinless chicken breasts, cooked and cut into ½" cubes
1   cup mayonnaise
1   cup thinly sliced celery
1   cup halved red grapes
½   cup sliced almonds, toasted
1   tbsp. finely chopped fresh parsley
1   tsp. kosher salt
½   cup heavy cream, whipped
    Freshly ground black pepper, to taste

ALL HAIL HELEN CORBITT

Helen Corbitt—chef, writer, and champion of Texas cuisine—created many of our most-loved recipes, including Poppy Seed Dressing (page 75) and grape-studded chicken salad (this page). She oversaw the restaurants at Neiman Marcus from 1955 onward, where Stanley Marcus, owner of the fashion-forward department store, dubbed her "the Balenciaga of Food."

Combine chicken, mayonnaise, celery, grapes, almonds, parsley, and salt in a bowl. Add whipped cream and pepper and fold to combine.

SOUTHERN-STYLE CHICKEN SALAD

SERVES 4

In the South, chicken salad often gets a sweet kick from a generous dose of pickle relish. This version comes from the kitchen of Charlottesville, Virginia, home cook Sharon Sant. It's perfect on soft rolls or white toast, and we particularly like it with saltines.

4   cups shredded cooked chicken breast
¾   cup finely chopped celery
¾   cup finely chopped onion
¾   cup sweet pickle relish
2   hard-cooked eggs, peeled and finely chopped
¾   cup mayonnaise
    Kosher salt and freshly ground black pepper, to taste

Combine chicken, celery, onion, relish, and eggs in a large bowl. Add the mayonnaise in increments, until the chicken salad reaches the desired consistency: rich but not too creamy. Season with salt and pepper.

> "A man's social rank is determined by the amount
> of bread he eats in a sandwich."
>
> F. SCOTT FITZGERALD

HAM SALAD

MAKES ABOUT 4 CUPS

This spicy salad—brightened with jalapeño, parsley, and red onions—is ideal for that day-after holiday ham taking up too much space in your refrigerator.

- 1   lb. baked ham, cut into 1" chunks
- 8   gherkins
- 1   pickled jalapeño
- ½   cup mayonnaise
- 2   tbsp. Dijon mustard
- 2   tbsp. finely chopped fresh flat-leaf parsley
- 3   scallions, thinly sliced
- 2   ribs celery, thinly sliced
- ½   small red onion, finely chopped
      Kosher salt and freshly ground black pepper, to taste

Place ham, gherkins, and jalapeño in a food processor and pulse until roughly chopped. Transfer to a large bowl and add mayonnaise, mustard, parsley, scallions, celery, onion, salt, and pepper; stir until combined. Chill before serving.

CLASSIC TUNA SALAD

SERVES 4

Preserved tuna has taken on something of a prestigious image now that pricey brands of the ubiquitous fish—often imported from Spain and packed in olive oil—are selling quickly at specialty stores. This best-quality tuna is terrific on its own, but it's also a surefire way to elevate the old lunchbox staple, tuna salad. If you prefer to use water-packed tuna, increase the amount of mayonnaise called for below to ½ cup.

- 2   6-oz. cans olive oil–packed tuna, undrained
- ⅓   cup mayonnaise, or as needed
- 1   tsp. fresh lemon juice
- ½   rib celery, finely chopped
- ½   bunch fresh chives, minced

Leaves from 3–4 fresh flat-leaf parsley sprigs, finely chopped
Kosher salt and freshly ground black pepper, to taste

Put tuna and its oil in a medium bowl and break it up with a fork. Add mayonnaise and lemon juice and mash into tuna until mixture has the consistency of a coarse purée (not a paste), adding a bit more mayonnaise if necessary. Stir in celery, chives, and parsley and season with salt and pepper before serving.

RASCAL HOUSE WHITEFISH SALAD

MAKES ABOUT 2 CUPS

We love this creamy salad on a toasted bagel half, topped with tomato and onion slices. It was a staple at the now-closed Miami Beach delicatessen Wolfie Cohen's Rascal House, which anchored the city's Jewish-style restaurant culture from its opening in 1954 until it shuttered in 2008.

- ½   small red onion, finely chopped
- 1   lb. smoked whitefish or trout, skinned and bones removed
- ⅓   cup mayonnaise
- ¼   cup sour cream
- 1   tbsp. chopped fresh dill
- 1   tbsp. fresh lemon juice
- 1   hard-cooked egg, peeled and finely chopped
- 1   rib celery, finely chopped
      Freshly ground black pepper, to taste

1 Place the onion in a bowl and cover with cold water. Let soak (to mellow its bite), about 15 minutes. Drain and set aside.

2 Use a fork to flake the fish into a bowl. Add onion, mayonnaise, sour cream, dill, lemon juice, egg, and celery. Stir to combine, then season with pepper. Serve immediately, or cover and refrigerate for up to 4 days.

Pizzas

NAPLES-STYLE PIZZA DOUGH

Pasta da Pizza

MAKES FOUR ¾-LB BALLS

The key to this pizza dough is to let it slowly rise in the refrigerator for 48 hours—that's what gives it its deep flavor and tender structure.

- 2 tbsp. sugar
- 1 tbsp. olive oil, plus more for greasing and brushing
- ½ tsp. active dry yeast
- 5½ cups farina "00" (Italian-style flour), preferably Caputo Pizzeria Flour
- 2 tbsp. kosher salt

1 Combine sugar, oil, yeast, and 2 cups cold water in bowl of a stand mixer fitted with a dough hook; let sit until foamy, 8–10 minutes. Mix flour and salt in a bowl. With motor running, slowly add flour mixture, then mix until a smooth dough forms, 8–10 minutes. Transfer dough to a greased baking sheet and cover with plastic wrap. Let sit at room temperature for 1 hour.

2 Divide dough into 4 equal balls. Transfer to a greased 9″×13″ dish and brush tops with oil. Cover with plastic wrap and refrigerate for 48 hours.

GLUTEN-FREE PIZZA DOUGH

MAKES TWO 12″ PIZZAS

For people who are gluten intolerant, pizza is often one of the most-missed indulgences. This gluten-free pizza crust holds its own against the authentic Neapolitan version.

- 1 ¼-oz. package active dry yeast
- 1 tbsp. olive oil, plus more to taste
- 1 tsp. sugar
- 1 egg
- 1 18-oz. package Cup4Cup brand gluten-free pizza crust mix or other all-purpose gluten-free pizza flour blend

- 1 tsp. kosher salt, plus more to taste
  White rice flour or fine cornmeal, for dusting

1 Combine yeast, oil, sugar, egg, and 1 cup cold water in bowl of a stand mixer fitted with a dough hook; let sit until yeast begins to foam and float on surface of water, about 10 minutes. Mix flour and 1 tsp. salt in a bowl. With motor running, slowly add flour mixture, then mix until a smooth dough forms, about 10 minutes. Transfer dough to a greased baking sheet and cover with plastic wrap. Let sit at room temperature for 1 hour.

2 Divide dough into 2 equal balls. Dust 1 ball with rice flour and roll out into a 12″ round about ¼″ thick. Transfer to a rice flour-dusted pizza peel and top as desired. Repeat with second ball.

NAPLES-STYLE PIZZA SAUCE

Salsa di Pomodoro Fresco

MAKES ABOUT 4 CUPS

Neapolitan *pizzaioli* use a simple uncooked tomato sauce based on whole, peeled tomatoes straight from the can, which preserves the bright taste and color.

- 2 28-oz. cans whole, peeled tomatoes packed in purée
  Kosher salt, to taste

1 Remove tomatoes from each can and reserve 3 cups purée. Cut tomatoes in half and, using your fingers, remove and discard the seeds (don't rinse).

2 Place tomatoes in a food processor and pulse until just crushed but not puréed. (Alternatively, crush the tomatoes by hand or pass them through a food mill.)

3 Transfer the crushed tomatoes to a bowl and stir in the reserved 3 cups purée and the salt.

A PERFECT PIE

A perfect Neapolitan crust requires a very gentle approach. First, dust the dough in fine semolina flour so it doesn't stick to your fingers or the work surface. Then, using your fingertips, press the dough outward from the center, working in a clockwise motion, spiraling gradually outward until you get within one to two inches of the edge; this edge will become the crust (Italians call it the *cornicione*). To stretch the dough while ensuring the crust remains airy and crisp, follow the steps below.

STEP 1 Using both hands, pick up the dough by the crust as if holding the top of a steering wheel; rotate the dough, passing it from one hand to the next, as though you were turning the wheel.

STEP 2 Taking care not to compress the dough, continue to pass it from one hand to the next; gravity will help it fall and stretch naturally.

STEP 3 Stop when the center of the dough is stretched to about ⅛″ thick and the diameter is about 12″ across.

PIZZA MARGHERITA

MAKES FOUR 10″ PIZZAS (SEE PHOTO, PAGE 216)

This most iconic of pizzas is topped with tomato sauce, fresh mozzarella, and basil leaves, the colors of the Italian flag.

  1   recipe Naples-Style Pizza Dough (page 136)
      Fine semolina flour, for dusting
  2   cups Naples-Style Pizza Sauce (page 136)
  1   lb. fresh mozzarella, thinly sliced
 16   fresh basil leaves
      Olive oil, to taste

Place a pizza stone under the broiler; heat for 30 minutes. Working in 4 batches, dust 1 ball dough with semolina. Using your fingertips, press dough into a 10″ circle about ¼″ thick, leaving a 1″ crust around the edges. Hold dough straight up and, with fingertips circling crust, slide fingers around crust in a circular motion as you would turn a steering wheel, until dough in the center is stretched to about ⅛″ thick; transfer to a semolina-dusted pizza peel.

Spread ½ cup sauce over dough and top with one-fourth each of the cheese and basil leaves; drizzle with oil. Slide pizza onto stone and broil until cheese melts and crust is puffed and charred in spots, 3–4 minutes. Serve hot.

30-Minute Mozzarella

MAKES ¾–1 LB.

Making mozzarella at home rewards you with fresher, softer, and creamier cheese than you'll buy at the store.

      2   tsp. citric acid
      1   gal. pasteurized whole milk
 ⅛–¼   tsp. lipase powder, dissolved in ¼ cup cool water and allowed to sit for 20 minutes, for a stronger flavor (optional)
      ¼   tsp. liquid rennet (or ¼ rennet tablet)
           Kosher salt for sprinkling (optional)

1 Add the citric acid to the milk and mix thoroughly. If using lipase, add it as well.

2 Heat the milk to 88°. (The milk will begin to curdle.)

3 Gently stir in the diluted rennet with an up-and-down motion and continue heating until the temperature reaches 105°. Turn off the heat and let the curd set for a few minutes.

4 The curds should look like thick yogurt. If the whey is still milky white, wait a few more minutes.

5 Scoop out the curds with a slotted spoon and put into a 2-qt. microwave-safe bowl. Press the curds gently with your hands, pouring off as much whey as possible. Reserve the whey.

6 You may want to put on heavy rubber gloves at this point; the cheese has to be almost too hot to touch before it will stretch. Microwave the curds on high for 1 minute. More whey will precipitate from the curd. Again, drain off all excess whey. Quickly work the cheese with a spoon or your hands, forming it into a ball until it is cool enough to touch.

7 Microwave 2 more times for 35 seconds each. After each heating, work the cheese into a ball until it is cool enough to touch. Drain all excess whey each time.

8 Knead quickly like bread dough until smooth. Sprinkle on the salt, if desired, while kneading and stretching. When the cheese stretches like taffy, it is done. If it comes apart, the curds need to be reheated.

9 When the cheese is smooth and shiny, it is ready to eat. Although this mozzarella is best eaten right away, if you must wait, cover it and store in the refrigerator.

PISTACHIO & MORTADELLA PIZZA
MAKES FOUR 10″ PIZZAS

A buttery pistachio purée is the ideal backdrop for salty mortadella and mozzarella on this Neapolitan-style pizza.

- 1½ cups shelled pistachios
- ½ tbsp. grated Parmigiano-Reggiano
- ½ cup extra-virgin olive oil, plus more to taste
- 3 tbsp. fresh lemon juice
  Kosher salt, to taste
- 1 recipe Naples-Style Pizza Dough (page 136)
  Fine semolina flour, for dusting
- ¼ lb. mortadella, thinly sliced and cut into quarters
- 1 lb. fresh mozzarella, thinly sliced
- ¼ cup grated pecorino romano
- 16 fresh basil leaves

Place a pizza stone under the broiler; heat for 30 minutes. Purée pistachios, Parmigiano, oil, lemon juice, salt, and ¼ cup water in a food processor until smooth. Working in 4 batches, dust 1 ball dough with semolina. Using your fingertips, press dough into a 10″ circle about ¼″ thick, leaving a 1″ crust around the edges. Hold dough straight up and, with fingertips circling crust, slide fingers around crust in a circular motion as you would turn a steering wheel, until dough in the center is stretched to about ⅛″ thick; transfer to a semolina-dusted pizza peel. Spread ½ cup pistachio purée over dough and distribute one-fourth each of the mortadella, cheeses, and basil over the top; drizzle with oil. Slide pizza onto stone and broil until cheese melts and crust is puffed and charred in spots, 3–4 minutes. Serve hot.

SIX-ONION PIZZA
MAKES FOUR 12″ PIZZAS

This sweet and savory pizza, adapted from a recipe by Michael Leviton, chef and co-owner of Area Four in Cambridge, Massachusetts, showcases the multifarious flavors of a half-dozen members of the onion family: conventional white and red onions, plus leeks, shallots, scallions, and chives.

- 5 tbsp. extra-virgin olive oil
- 12 sprigs fresh thyme
- 2 large onions, very thinly sliced lengthwise
- 1 bay leaf
  Kosher salt and freshly ground black pepper, to taste
- 8 oz. leeks, white part only, halved lengthwise, cut into ¼″-thick slices
- 8 oz. shallots, very thinly sliced lengthwise
- 8 oz. red onions, very thinly sliced lengthwise
- 1 recipe Naples-Style Pizza Dough (page 136)
- 8 oz. finely grated pecorino
- 5 scallions, very thinly sliced
- 1 bunch fresh chives, thinly sliced

1 Heat 2 tbsp. oil, thyme, onions, bay leaf, salt, and pepper in a 12″ skillet over medium-low heat and cook, stirring occasionally, until onions are very soft but not browned, about 30 minutes. Remove and discard thyme stems and bay leaf. Transfer onion to a food processor or blender and purée until smooth; set aside.

2 Make an onion compote: Heat 1 tbsp. oil in a 12″ skillet over medium heat. Add leeks, season with salt and pepper, and cook, stirring occasionally, until very soft but not browned, about 15 minutes. Transfer to a bowl and set aside. Heat remaining oil in skillet, add shallots and red onions, and season with salt and pepper. Cook, stirring occasionally, until very tender and lightly browned, about 18 minutes. Transfer to bowl with leeks and stir to combine; set aside.

3 Heat oven to 500°. Place 1 piece dough on a lightly floured work surface and flatten with your fingertips. Pick up dough circle and gently feed edges of dough between your thumbs and forefingers, letting the weight of the dough stretch edges until the circle of dough is 12″ in diameter. Place dough circle on a parchment paper–lined baking sheet, and working quickly, spread about 2 tbsp. onion purée over dough, leaving a ¾″ border around edge; sprinkle evenly with about ¼ cup onion compote. Sprinkle one-fourth of the pecorino over onions, then transfer to oven. Bake until browned and crisp at the edges, about 12 minutes. Repeat with remaining dough balls, purée, compote, and pecorino. Sprinkle each pizza with one-fourth each of the scallions and chives before serving.

HOT, HOT, HEAT

The biggest difference between making pizza in a pizza shop and making one at home is the oven. The wood-burning types you'll find at most Neapolitan pizzerias burn steadily at temperatures of 750° to 1,000°F—temperatures at which the pizza cooks in a minute, resulting in crusts that crackle but stay pliant, mozzarella that remains milky, toppings that stay fresh, and tomato sauce that retains its raw brightness. Below are two methods we devised to reliably hit these volcanic temperatures at home.

THE BROILER Most home ovens won't go higher than 500°, so we concentrated on the broiler, where the heat is most intense. We placed a pizza stone on a shelf three inches from the broiler, set the dial to high, and waited. After 30 minutes, a temperature gun registered the stone's surface at 770°. At this temperature, our pizzas cooked in two minutes, and came out with an airy crust, just-melted cheese, and fresh, pulpy tomato sauce.

THE GRILL A grilling kit and a pizza stone atop a grill create an ad hoc wood-fired oven. We banked our coals and wood chips to one side, let the temperature reach 775°, and put in the pizza. In two minutes it emerged, its crust beautifully blistered and imbued with a kiss of smoke that's pure Naples.

SQUASH BLOSSOM PIZZA
MAKES FOUR 10″ PIZZAS

A blistered, pillowy crust is an ideal vessel for the combination of delicate squash blossoms and creamy, rich *burrata* cheese. This recipe was inspired by a pie served at Pizzeria Mozza in Hollywood, California.

- 9 tbsp. extra-virgin olive oil, plus more for drizzling
- 1 tbsp. active dry yeast
- 1 tbsp. sugar
- 1 tsp. kosher salt, plus more to taste
- 6 cups flour
- 2 cups Naples-Style Pizza Sauce (page 136)
- 60 squash blossoms, stemmed
- 1 lb. burrata cheese

1 In a bowl, combine 1 tbsp. oil, yeast, sugar, salt, and 2 cups 115° water; let sit until foamy, 10–12 minutes. Stir in flour to make a dough. Transfer dough to a floured surface and knead until smooth, 8–10 minutes. Divide dough into 4 equal balls. Put balls on a floured baking sheet. Cover with plastic wrap and let sit in a warm place until soft and tripled in size, 2–3 hours.

2 Place a pizza stone on a rack in lower third of oven. Heat oven to 500° for 1 hour. Transfer 1 dough ball to a floured 16½″×12¼″ piece parchment paper. Working from center, gently flatten dough with fingertips, leaving edges thicker than middle. Stretch dough to a 10″ diameter. Cover dough with a tea towel and let rest for 15 minutes. Brush edges with 2 tbsp. oil. Season dough with salt. Spread ½ cup pizza sauce over dough, leaving a 1″ border. Arrange 15 squash blossoms over sauce in concentric circles. Transfer pizza (on paper) to stone and bake until golden brown, 10–14 minutes. Remove pizza with a spatula. Top with spoonfuls of burrata and drizzle with oil. Repeat with remaining dough balls.

Calzone & Beyond

CALZONE NAPOLETANO

MAKES 4

The original calzone is a specialty of Naples—San Marzano tomato territory.

FOR THE DOUGH
- 1 ¼-oz. packet active dry yeast
- 1½ cups all-purpose flour
- 1½ cups cake flour
- 1 tsp. kosher salt
-   Extra-virgin olive oil
- ½ cup cornmeal

FOR THE FILLING
- ½ lb. fresh mozzarella, sliced into 8 pieces
- 16 oil-packed anchovy filets
- 1 14-oz. can peeled whole San Marzano tomatoes, drained and chopped
- 2 tsp. fresh oregano leaves

1 Make the dough: Dissolve yeast in ¼ cup lukewarm water in a large bowl and set aside until foamy, about 10 minutes. Combine flours and salt in a bowl. Add 1 cup flour mixture to yeast. Stir with a wooden spoon. Add ½ cup water, then another 1 cup flour. Mix well, then work in remaining 1 cup flour. Gradually add another ¼ cup water to make a soft, moist dough.

2 Turn out dough onto a lightly floured surface and knead until smooth, 10–12 minutes. Divide dough into 4 balls. Lightly coat insides of 4 small bowls with olive oil. Place 1 ball of dough in each bowl. Cover with damp cloths and set aside to rise until dough nearly doubles in size, 2½–3 hours.

3 Place pizza stone in oven and preheat oven to 450°. On a floured work surface, stretch 1 ball of dough into a thin 9″ round. Place 2 slices mozzarella, 4 anchovy filets, and 2–3 tbsp. chopped tomatoes on one side of a dough round. Sprinkle with oregano, fold dough over, and pinch to seal. Repeat process to make a total of 4 calzones.

4 Sprinkle cornmeal on pizza stone, place calzones on top, and brush tops with a little oil. Bake until golden, about 15 minutes.

CHICKEN & BROCCOLI RABE STROMBOLI

SERVES 8

The recipe for this crispy rolled pizzeria classic is adapted from one served at Romano's Pizzeria in Philadelphia.

FOR THE DOUGH
- 1½ cups lukewarm water (115°)
- 2 tsp. sugar
- 1 ¼-oz. package active dry yeast
- 1 tbsp. vegetable shortening
- 2½ cups bread flour, plus more for dusting
- 2 tsp. kosher salt

FOR THE FILLING
-   Kosher salt and freshly ground pepper, to taste
- 12 oz. boneless, skinless chicken breasts
- ⅓ cup olive oil, plus more as needed
- 2 tsp. dried oregano
- 4 cloves garlic, minced
- 1 bunch broccoli rabe (about 12 oz.), tough stems trimmed
- ½ tsp. crushed red chile flakes
- 2 cups shredded mozzarella
- 16 jarred sweet cherry peppers, stemmed, seeded, and cut into ½″ strips
- 3 oz. thinly sliced provolone
-   Marinara sauce (page 356; optional), heated, for serving

1 Make the dough: Combine lukewarm water, sugar, and yeast in the bowl of a stand mixer fitted with a hook and let sit until foamy, about 10 minutes. Add shortening, then flour and salt. Mix on low speed until dough forms, then increase speed to medium-high and knead dough until smooth, 8–10 minutes. Cover with plastic wrap and let sit in a warm place until nearly doubled in size, 1½–2 hours.

2 Make the filling: Heat oven to 350° and grease a large baking sheet. Bring a medium saucepan of salted water to a boil. Rub chicken with 3 tbsp. oil, the oregano, half the garlic, and salt and pepper to taste; place in a 9″ × 13″ baking dish. Bake until nearly cooked, or an instant-read thermometer inserted into the thickest part of the chicken reads 140°, 16–18 minutes. Let cool, then cut into 1″ pieces.

3 Add broccoli rabe to boiling water and cook until just tender, 1–2 minutes. Transfer rabe to an ice bath, then drain, roughly chop, and spread onto paper towels to dry. Heat remaining olive oil and garlic in a large skillet over medium-high heat. Add broccoli rabe and chile flakes and cook until golden, 3–4 minutes. Remove from heat.

4 Assemble the stromboli: Increase oven temperature to 425°. Place dough on prepared baking sheet and, using greased fingers, press into a rectangle about ¼″ thick. Sprinkle mozzarella lengthwise down the center. Top with chicken, broccoli rabe, peppers, and provolone. Tuck short sides of dough over the filling, then fold long sides, overlapping, over the filling. Pinch to seal and roll stromboli over so its seam is on the bottom. Bake until puffed and golden, about 1 hour. Let cool slightly, then slice and serve with marinara, if you like.

LASAGNA BREAD

Scaccia

SERVES 4–6

A street food popular in its native Ragusa, scaccia is an exercise in rustic simplicity: A pizza-style dough is rolled super-thin, smeared with tomato sauce, showered with D.O.P. Caciocavallo cheese (similar to a spicy provolone), and folded into a lasagna-like loaf. In some versions, yeast is left out, which results in a more pasta-like dough that gets layered into a thinner, free-form rectangular pie, which is served cut into squares. Whatever the shape, the scaccia is best served warm from the oven while the cheese is still gooey.

- 1¼ tsp. sugar
- ¼ tsp. active dry yeast
- ½ cup plus 2 tbsp. lukewarm water (115°)
- 2 cups durum wheat semolina flour
- 2 tbsp. extra-virgin olive oil
- ½ tsp. kosher salt, plus more to taste
  All-purpose flour, for dusting
- 2 cups whole peeled canned tomatoes in juice
- 1 clove garlic, finely chopped
- ½ cup loosely packed basil leaves, roughly chopped
  Freshly ground black pepper
- 8 oz. Caciocavallo or aged provolone cheese, thinly sliced

1 Whisk together ¼ tsp. sugar and the yeast in a large bowl. Add lukewarm water and let stand until foamy, about 10 minutes. Stir in semolina flour, 1 tbsp. olive oil, and ½ tsp. salt until dough comes together. Scrape dough onto a lightly floured work surface and knead until smooth, about 8 minutes. Transfer dough to a clean bowl, cover with plastic wrap, and let stand at room temperature until doubled in size, about 2 hours.

2 Meanwhile, pour tomatoes and their juice into a blender and purée until smooth. Heat remaining 1 tbsp. olive oil in a small pot over medium heat. Add garlic and cook, stirring, until fragrant and beginning to brown, about 2 minutes. Pour tomatoes into saucepan along with remaining 1 tsp. sugar, bring to a simmer, and cook, stirring occasionally, until sauce thickens slightly, about 10 minutes. Remove sauce from heat, stir in basil, and season liberally with salt and pepper.

3 Heat oven to 450°. Line a 9″× 5″ loaf pan with parchment paper. Scrape dough onto a lightly floured work surface. Using a rolling pin, flatten dough into a ⅟₁₆″ thick, 26″×18″ rectangle, and position rectangle so that a long side is nearest to you. Spread half the tomato sauce over the middle three-fifths of the rectangle, then sprinkle sauce with half the cheese slices. Fold two uncovered sides of dough over so their edges overlap in the middle of the rectangle by 2″.

4 Spread remaining sauce over left two-thirds of the dough, and sprinkle sauce with remaining cheese slices. Fold the right-hand third of the dough over the sauce, then fold the left-hand side of dough over, like completing the tri-fold of a letter. Fold dough crosswise to create a 9″ long rectangular pie. Transfer pie to prepared loaf pan, pierce top with the tines of a fork, and bake until loaf is dark brown on top and lightly charred at the edges, about 1 hour.

5 Immediately invert the scaccia onto a rack, remove loaf pan and parchment paper, and let cool in this position for 10 minutes. Flip loaf right-side up before serving.

Hamburgers & Hot Dogs

'21' CLUB HAMBURGER
SERVES 4

The chef at New York City's now-shuttered '21' Club ground beef chuck and round with duck fat to make this tasty burger, so full of spices it hardly needs condiments.

- 2 lb. ground beef
- ¼ cup minced yellow onion
- 2 tsp. minced fresh thyme
- 1 tsp. ground black pepper
- 1 tsp. minced fresh rosemary
- ¼ tsp. ground coriander
- ¼ tsp. ground fennel seeds
- ⅛ tsp. cayenne pepper
- 1 egg, lightly beaten
- 2–3 tbsp. rendered duck fat, melted, at room temperature (optional)
  Kosher salt, to taste
  Canola oil (optional)
- 4 brioche buns, toasted

1 In a large bowl, gently mix together beef, onions, thyme, pepper, rosemary, coriander, fennel, cayenne, egg, and fat (if using). Season with salt. Divide the meat into 4 portions and shape them into 1″-thick patties. Wrap patties in plastic wrap; refrigerate until cold.

2 Build a medium-hot fire in a charcoal grill or heat a gas grill to medium-high. (Alternatively, heat a tablespoon of canola oil in a large cast-iron skillet over medium-high heat.) Cook burgers, flipping once, until cooked to desired doneness, about 12 minutes total for medium rare. Serve on buns.

PATTY MELT
SERVES 6

Some say that the patty melt—the classic diner griddled sandwich of ground beef, caramelized onions, and cheese—isn't technically a burger because it's served on sliced rye bread instead of a bun. We love it just the same.

- 1½ lb. ground beef
  Kosher salt and freshly ground black pepper

- 5 tbsp. canola oil
- 2 yellow onions, halved and thinly sliced
- 12 slices rye bread
- 12 thin slices cheddar, Swiss, or American cheese
- ½ cup unsalted butter, softened

1 Season beef with salt and pepper. Divide meat into six ¼″-thick patties that are slightly wider and longer than the bread.

2 Heat 2 tbsp. oil in a 12″ cast-iron skillet over medium-high heat. Add onions, season with salt and pepper, and cook, stirring occasionally, until softened and browned, about 12 minutes. Transfer the onions to a bowl; wipe out skillet. Working in 3 batches, heat 1 tbsp. oil in skillet over high heat. Add 2 burger patties and cook, flipping once, until well browned, about 4 minutes total. Transfer patties to a plate.

3 Top 6 bread slices each with some of the onions, a cheese slice, and a burger patty. Top each burger with a cheese slice and a slice of bread. Using a table knife, spread butter over the top and bottom of each sandwich.

4 Heat a 12″ nonstick skillet over medium heat. Working in 3 batches, cook sandwiches, flipping once, until golden brown and hot, about 6 minutes.

SID'S ONION BURGER
SERVES 6

For these burgers, ground beef is pressed onto the griddle with paper-thin slices of onion and seared until crisp around the edges. The recipe comes from Sid's Diner, in El Reno, Oklahoma.

- 4 tbsp. canola oil
- 1 lb. ground beef, gently formed into 6 balls
- 2 medium yellow onions, very thinly sliced with a mandoline or a sharp knife and divided into 6 equal portions
  Kosher salt, to taste
- 6 slices American cheese
- 6 hamburger buns, toasted

1 Working in 2 batches, heat 2 tbsp. oil in a 12″ cast-iron skillet over medium-high heat. Add 3 beef balls and, using the back of a spatula, press down on them until they're thin; cook for 1 minute. Top each patty with a portion of the onions; season with salt. Press onions into the meat and cook for 1 minute more.

2 Flip burgers and flatten with the spatula. Place a cheese slice on each patty and let melt while onions and meat brown. Serve on buns.

SWEDISH BEEF BURGER
Biff a la Lindström
SERVES 4

Loaded with capers, pickles, and beets, this piquant burger captures the flavors of Sweden in one juicy bite. Its Swedish name is a reference to 19th-century industrialist Henrik Lindström, who famously taught the head cook at his favorite hotel how to make the dish.

- 1 lb. ground beef
- ½ cup dried bread crumbs
- 5 tbsp. finely chopped pickled red beets, plus 2 tbsp. juice
- 3 tbsp. finely chopped dill pickles
- 2 tbsp. capers, drained and chopped
- 2 tbsp. dark beer
- 1 tsp. kosher salt
- ½ tsp. freshly ground black pepper
- 2 eggs, beaten
- 1 clove garlic, finely chopped
- ½ medium yellow onion, finely chopped
- 6 tbsp. unsalted butter, with 2 tbsp. diced
- 2 tbsp. finely chopped fresh flat-leaf parsley

1 In a bowl, combine beef, bread crumbs, beets with their juice, pickles, capers, beer, salt, pepper, eggs, garlic, onions, and diced butter; mix to combine. Divide the mixture into 8 portions and form into 1″-thick patties.

2 Heat 2 tbsp. butter in a nonstick skillet over medium heat. Add half the patties and cook, flipping once, until browned and cooked through, about 5 minutes per side. Wipe out skillet and repeat with remaining butter and patties. Sprinkle burgers with the parsley.

BLUE CHEESE–STUFFED BURGERS
SERVES 4

A "juicy lucy" is a hamburger that has the cheese baked inside the patty, rather than just melted on top. In this variation, quick-pickled mushrooms and onions pair well with a burger filled with sharp blue cheese.

- 6 oz. cremini mushrooms, thinly sliced
- 1 red onion, thinly sliced into rings
- 1 cup red wine vinegar
- ½ cup olive oil
- 1 tsp. dried basil
- 1 tsp. dried oregano
  Kosher salt, to taste
  Freshly ground black pepper, to taste, plus 1 tbsp.
- 2 lb. ground beef
- ¼ lb. blue cheese
- 2 tbsp. dehydrated garlic flakes
- 1 tbsp. coriander seeds
- ½ tbsp. dill seeds
- ½ tbsp. crushed red chile flakes
- ½ tbsp. dried onion flakes
- 4 hamburger buns, toasted
  Dijon mustard, for serving

1 Place mushrooms and onions in a bowl. Bring vinegar, oil, basil, oregano, salt, and pepper to a boil in a 1-qt. saucepan; pour over mushrooms and onions. Let cool, then cover with plastic wrap and refrigerate for 1 hour.

2 Season beef with salt; divide into 4 flat patties about ⅛″ thick. Put one-fourth of cheese into center of each patty; fold sides of meat up and over cheese. In a spice grinder, grind 1 tbsp. black pepper, garlic flakes, coriander, dill, chile flakes, and onion flakes to a coarse powder. Rub spice mixture over each burger, coating evenly.

3 Build a hot fire in a charcoal grill or set a gas grill to high; bank coals or turn burner off on one side for indirect grilling (page 191). Grill burgers, flipping them once, until cooked to desired doneness, about 12 minutes for medium rare. If outside starts to burn before burgers are cooked, move to cooler section of grill until done. Serve on buns with pickled mushrooms, red onions, and mustard.

> ### "Anybody who doesn't think that the best hamburger place in the world is in his hometown is a sissy."
>
> CALVIN TRILLIN

HEMINGWAY'S HAMBURGER
SERVES 4

In 2013, Ernest Hemingway's hamburger recipe resurfaced among the writer's papers at the John F. Kennedy Presidential Library and Museum in Boston. The maximalist patty (identified in Hemingway's papers as "Papa's Favorite Wild West Hamburger") calls for minced carrot and tomato, cheddar cheese, grated apple, capers, India relish, and a brace of spices, all mixed directly into the beef. The result is juicy and vibrant, its many constituent parts melding into a single, intensely savory whole.

- 1   lb. lean ground beef
- 2   oz. sliced ham, minced
- ⅓   cup dry red or white wine
- ¼   cup grated cheddar cheese
- 2   tbsp. capers, drained
- 2   tbsp. grated tart apple
- 1   tbsp. minced fresh flat-leaf parsley
- 1   tbsp. soy sauce
- 1½ tsp. ground sage
- 1½ tsp. India relish or pickle relish
- ½   tsp. Beau Monde seasoning
- 2   cloves garlic, minced
- 2   small scallions, minced
- 1   egg, beaten
- 1   plum tomato, cored, peeled, and grated
- ½   small carrot, peeled and grated
- ½   small yellow onion, grated
      Kosher salt and freshly ground black pepper, to taste
- 1   tbsp. canola oil
      Hamburger buns, lettuce, sliced tomato and onion, ketchup, mustard, and mayonnaise, for serving

Mix ingredients, except for oil, buns, and condiments, in a bowl. Form meat mixture into 4 patties. Heat oil in a 12″ skillet over medium-high heat. Cook patties, flipping once, until cooked to desired doneness, 8–10 minutes for medium rare. Serve on buns with lettuce, tomato, onion, ketchup, mustard, and mayonnaise.

SLOPPY JOES
SERVES 6

A version of this recipe was published in *My Best Meat Recipes* (National Live Stock and Meat Board, 1945) under the title "Barbecued Ground Beef." Scanning the ingredients list we immediately recognized it as an early recipe for sloppy joes.

- 2   tbsp. unsalted butter
- 1   small yellow onion, finely chopped
- 1   small green bell pepper, seeded and finely chopped
- 1   lb. ground beef
- 1   cup ketchup
- 2   tbsp. prepared mustard
- 1   tbsp. white vinegar
- 1   tbsp. sugar
- ½   tsp. ground cloves
      Kosher salt and freshly ground black pepper, to taste
- 6   hamburger buns, split, buttered, and toasted

1 Melt butter in a large skillet over medium heat. Add onion and pepper and cook until softened, about 15 minutes. Add ground beef and cook until browned, 6–8 minutes. Add ketchup, mustard, vinegar, sugar, and ground cloves.

2 Reduce heat to medium-low, cover, and cook, stirring occasionally, until thick and dark, 25–30 minutes. Season with salt and pepper. Divide among buns and serve.

GRILLED LAMB BURGER WITH RED ONION AÏOLI
SERVES 4

Grilled red onion aïoli, smashed avocado, and a sunny-side-up egg top this rich cumin-spiced lamb burger, a favorite of Los Angeles–based, Australia-born chef Curtis Stone.

- 1½ lb. ground lamb
- 1½ tsp. ground cumin

Kosher salt and freshly ground black pepper,
to taste

5 cloves garlic, peeled and wrapped in aluminum foil

1 large red onion, sliced crosswise into ¼"-thick rings

1 cup olive oil

2 egg yolks

Zest and juice of 1 lemon

½ cup canola oil

2 ripe avocados

Juice of 1 lime

4 hamburger buns, split

Thinly sliced romaine lettuce and tomatoes,
for serving

4 fried eggs, for serving

1 Gently mix lamb, 1 tsp. cumin, salt, and pepper in a bowl; divide mixture into 4 patties about 1" thick. Transfer patties to a plate and cover with plastic wrap; refrigerate until ready to grill.

2 Build a hot fire in a charcoal grill or set a gas grill to high; bank coals or turn off burner on one side for indirect grilling (page 191). Grill garlic until tender, 8–10 minutes; remove from foil and transfer to a food processor. Mix onions and ¼ cup olive oil in a bowl; grill onions, flipping once, until charred in spots and tender, 8–10 minutes. Transfer onions to food processor along with yolks, lemon zest and juice, salt, and pepper; purée until smooth. With the motor running, drizzle in ½ cup olive oil plus canola oil until emulsified. Transfer aïoli to a bowl, cover, and refrigerate. Cut avocados in half lengthwise; discard pits. Scoop out flesh and mash with remaining cumin, plus lime juice, salt, and pepper in a bowl; cover and refrigerate.

3 Return grill to high heat. Brush buns with remaining ¼ cup olive oil; grill until lightly toasted, 1–2 minutes, and transfer to a serving platter. Grill burgers on hottest part of grill, flipping once, until cooked to desired doneness, about 10 minutes for medium rare. If outside starts to burn before burgers are fully cooked, move to cooler section until done. Serve on buns with aïoli, avocado, lettuce, and tomatoes and top with fried eggs.

BLACK BEAN BURGER WITH SALSA FRESCA & AVOCADO CREMA

SERVES 6

Cumin, paprika, coriander, and poblano and chipotle chiles lend their robust flavor to this vegetarian black bean burger. Dredged in cornmeal, it's a hearty base for a garlicky *salsa fresca* and smooth avocado *crema*.

FOR THE BLACK BEAN BURGERS

5 tbsp. olive oil

1 medium yellow onion, finely chopped

6 cloves garlic, finely chopped

2 poblano chiles, stemmed, seeded, and finely chopped

2 tsp. ground cumin

2 tsp. paprika

1 tsp. ground coriander

1 tsp. dried oregano

1 chipotle chile in adobo sauce, finely chopped

½ cup dried bread crumbs

2 15-oz. cans black beans, rinsed, drained, and mashed

2 eggs

Kosher salt and freshly ground black pepper, to taste

½ cup finely ground cornmeal

FOR THE SALSA FRESCA

¼ cup red wine vinegar

2 tbsp. finely chopped fresh cilantro

3 medium tomatoes, cored, seeded, and finely chopped

2 cloves garlic, minced

FOR THE AVOCADO CREMA

½ cup sour cream

2 tbsp. fresh lime juice

2 avocados, pitted and peeled

6 hamburger buns, split

1 Make the black bean burgers: Heat 3 tbsp. oil in a 12" skillet over medium-high heat. Add onion and cook, stirring, until soft, about 4 minutes. Add garlic and poblanos and cook, stirring, until soft and slightly caramelized, about 5 minutes. Add cumin, paprika, coriander, oregano, and chipotle chiles and cook, stirring, until fragrant, about 1 minute more. Transfer to a bowl and let cool slightly. Add bread crumbs, beans, and eggs, season with salt and pepper, and mix well to combine. Divide mixture into 6 patties about 3" wide by 1" thick. Place on a plate and refrigerate for 20 minutes or until ready to use.

2 Make the salsa: Mix vinegar, cilantro, tomatoes, garlic, and salt and pepper to taste in a bowl. Cover with plastic wrap and let sit for 20 minutes to allow flavors to marry.

3 Make the crema: Combine sour cream, lime juice, avocado, and salt and pepper to taste in a blender and purée until smooth. Transfer to a bowl and cover with plastic wrap; store in the refrigerator until ready to use.

4 Heat remaining 2 tbsp. oil in skillet over medium-high heat. Dredge 3 burgers in cornmeal and cook, flipping once, until toasted on each side and cooked through, about 4 minutes. Repeat with remaining burgers and cornmeal.

5 Spread bottom half of each bun with avocado crema, top with a burger, some salsa, and the top of the bun, and serve.

PORTOBELLO BURGER WITH CARAMELIZED RED ONIONS
SERVES 4

A far cry from the standard grilled-mushroom-cap-as-burger, these portobello patties get a further umami boost from garlic and steak sauce—a winning match for a flavorful topping of melted blue cheese and caramelized red onions.

FOR THE PORTOBELLO BURGERS
- 8 large portobello mushroom caps
- 4 cloves garlic, minced
- 3 tbsp. steak sauce, such as A1
- ¾ cup dried bread crumbs
- 1 egg
- ½ tsp. freshly ground black pepper

FOR THE CARAMELIZED ONIONS
- 3 tbsp. unsalted butter
- 1 large red onion, thinly sliced
- 2 tbsp. balsamic vinegar
- 2 tsp. dried thyme
  Kosher salt and freshly ground black pepper, to taste
- 2 tbsp. olive oil
- ¼ lb. blue cheese, crumbled
- 4 hamburger buns, split and toasted

1 Make the portobello burgers: Place mushroom caps in a bamboo steamer over simmering water, or over a steamer inserted in a 6 qt. saucepan. Cover and steam until mushrooms are tender, about 7 minutes. Place cooked mushrooms in a food processor with garlic, steak sauce, bread crumbs, and egg and season with black pepper. Pulse just until mixture comes together, about 20 pulses or 30 seconds. Divide mixture into 4 patties about 4″ wide by ⅓″ thick. Place on a plate and refrigerate for 20 minutes or until ready to use.

2 Make the caramelized onions: Melt butter in a 12″ skillet over medium-high heat. Sauté onions until soft, about 8 minutes. Add vinegar, thyme, salt, and pepper and cook until onions are slightly caramelized, about 7 minutes more. Remove from the pan and reserve.

3 Wipe out skillet and heat olive oil over medium-high. Cook portobello burgers until toasted on each side and cooked through, about 6 minutes per side. Top each burger with blue cheese and continue to cook until just melted, about 2 minutes. Divide burgers among buns, top with onions, and serve.

COOK'S NOTE Individual portobello burgers can be formed and then frozen, tightly wrapped, for up to 1 month. Thaw in the refrigerator and cook as needed.

CORN DOGS
SERVES 8

Deep-fried, cornmeal-covered hot dogs on a stick are a county-fair essential. Spiked with cayenne and flavored with tangy buttermilk, this batter stands up to the robust wieners within.

- 1 cup flour
- ⅔ cup yellow cornmeal
- 2 tbsp. sugar
- 1 tsp. baking powder
- ¼ tsp. baking soda
- ¼ tsp. dry mustard
- ¼ tsp. cayenne pepper
- 1 tsp. kosher salt
- ¾ cup milk
- ¼ cup buttermilk
- 1 egg, lightly beaten
  Canola oil, for frying
- 8 6″ hot dogs
- 8 wooden skewers

1 In a large bowl, whisk together flour, cornmeal, sugar, baking powder and soda, mustard, cayenne, and salt. Add milk, buttermilk, and egg and whisk until smooth; set batter aside. Pour batter into a pint glass or other tall, narrow container, leaving a 1″ space between the top of the batter and the rim of the glass.

HOT DOG NATION

American cities may have their sports teams, their skylines, and their landmarks, but nothing gives rise to hometown pride quite like the local take on the hot dog. You can pinpoint your location in America with startling accuracy based on what's found atop your frankfurter.

Sonoran hot dogs (originally from Hermosillo, in Sonora, Mexico), which flourish in border states like **Arizona** and **New Mexico**, feature all-beef franks wrapped in bacon, grilled, and festooned with tomatoes, pinto beans, onions, mustard, hot sauce, and mayonnaise.

In **New York City**, street vendors sell hot dogs topped with sauerkraut, onions cooked in a thin tomato sauce, and a squirt of mustard.

Rhode Island's "New York–System" wieners are served in a steamed bun, under a blanket of chili, a dash of celery salt, and mustard.

In **North Carolina**, hot dogs are heaped with coleslaw and smothered with hot sauce.

Chicago-style dogs, served on a poppy seed bun, are piled high with sweet pickle relish, pickled sport peppers, wedges of tomato, dill pickle spears, celery salt, and mustard—never, ever ketchup.

California is home to a variety of hot dog styles, but in Los Angeles, the Tijuana dog, wrapped in bacon, deep-fried, then topped with mayonnaise, reigns supreme.

Michigan is ground zero for the Coney, a frankfurter covered in a tomato and beef chili, scattered with onions, and topped with cheese.

Reuben-like **Kansas City** hot dogs are dressed with sauerkraut, caraway seeds, Thousand Island dressing, and melted Swiss cheese.

Seattle's hot dogs are garnished with grilled onions, cabbage, and jalapeños and served on a toasted bun slathered with cream cheese.

In the area around **Newark, New Jersey**, hot dogs are deep-fried and smothered with fried potatoes, onions, bell peppers, and mustard.

2 Pour oil to a depth of 2″ into an 8-qt. Dutch oven and heat over medium-high heat until a deep-fry thermometer reads 350°.

3 Skewer 1 hot dog with a wooden skewer and dip into batter. Fry until golden brown, about 3 minutes. Using tongs, transfer corn dog to paper towels to drain; repeat with remaining hot dogs and batter.

SAUSAGES WITH PEPPERS & ONIONS
SERVES 4

We love Italian sausage piled high with peppers and onions on a hard roll. It's an unbeatable combination, popular at Italian-American restaurants throughout the country.

> 6–8 small onions, peeled
> 2 cloves garlic, peeled
> 4 bell peppers
> 4 tbsp. extra-virgin olive oil
> Kosher salt and freshly ground black pepper, to taste
> 4 sweet Italian sausages, cooked and kept hot
> 4 hard rolls, split

1 Cut onions in half crosswise and set aside. Thinly slice garlic and set aside. Cut peppers in half lengthwise, discard stem and seeds, slice lengthwise into medium-wide strips, and set aside.

2 Heat oil in a large skillet over medium-high heat. Add onions, cut side down, and cook until browned, about 5 minutes, then turn and brown other side, about 3 minutes longer. Add garlic, sauté until just beginning to color, then add peppers and season with salt and pepper. Sauté, stirring occasionally, until peppers begin to brown, 5–10 minutes. Reduce heat to medium and continue to cook until onions and peppers are soft, about 5 minutes longer.

3 Divide sausages evenly among rolls, top with peppers and onions, and serve.

Tacos

SAN ANTONIO PUFFY CHICKEN TACOS

SERVES 12

Corn or flour tortillas that are deep-fried until they puff are a specialty of San Antonio's Tex-Mex cuisine. This recipe for puffy tacos filled with shredded chicken and guacamole comes from Rolando's Super Tacos.

- ¼ cup olive oil
- 2½ lb. bone-in, skin-on chicken thighs
  Kosher salt and freshly ground black pepper, to taste
- 6 cloves garlic, finely chopped, plus 2 cloves minced
- 1 medium yellow onion, finely chopped
- 1 rib celery, finely chopped
- 1 small carrot, finely chopped
- 1 small red bell pepper, finely chopped
- 3 cups chicken stock
- 1 14-oz. can whole peeled tomatoes in juice, crushed by hand
- 2 avocados, pitted, peeled, and mashed
  Juice of 1 lime
  Canola oil, for frying
- 3 cups masa harina
- 1½ tbsp. unsalted butter, softened
  Shredded iceberg lettuce, diced tomato, and shredded cheddar cheese, to garnish

1 Heat olive oil in a large pot over medium-high heat. Season chicken with salt and pepper and add to pan, skin side down; cook, turning once, until browned on both sides, about 8 minutes. Transfer chicken to a plate and set aside. Add chopped garlic, onion, celery, carrot, and bell pepper; cook, stirring, until soft, about 20 minutes. Add stock and tomatoes, and return chicken to pan. Bring to a boil. Turn heat to medium-low; and cook until chicken is very tender, about 1½ hours. Remove chicken from sauce, and set aside until cool enough to handle; reserve sauce for another use. Discard skin and bones, shred chicken, and set aside. Meanwhile, combine avocados, minced garlic, lime juice, and salt and pepper to taste in a bowl; chill guacamole until ready to use, covering to avoid browning.

2 Pour canola oil to a depth of 2" in a medium Dutch oven and heat over medium-high heat until a deep-fry thermometer reads 375°. Stir together masa, butter, and

2¼ cups warm water in a bowl until dough forms; divide dough into 12 pieces and shape each piece into a ball. Using a tortilla press or rolling pin, flatten each ball into a 6½" disk. Place 1 disk in the oil. When tortilla begins to puff, press the end of a metal spatula into the center so that it bends into a taco shape; hold the spatula within the fold of the tortilla until it is golden and crisp, about 1½ minutes. Transfer to paper towels to drain; repeat with the remaining tortillas. Divide chicken and guacamole among tacos; top with lettuce, tomato, and cheese.

CARNITAS TACOS

Michoacán-Style Braised Pork Tacos

SERVES 8–10 (SEE PHOTO, PAGE 229)

At the Viva Taco bus in Turlock, California, Silvestre Valencia adds jalapeño pickling liquid to the pork braise, which tenderizes the meat and keeps it from drying out.

FOR THE CARNITAS

- 3 tbsp. lard or canola oil
- 3 lb. skinless, bone-in pork shoulder, cut into 3" pieces (have your butcher do this)
  Kosher salt, to taste
- ¾ cup whole milk
- 8 cloves garlic, peeled and smashed
- 6 canned or jarred whole pickled jalapeños, plus ⅓ cup pickling liquid
- 1 large white onion, roughly chopped
- 2 limes, juiced
- 2 oranges, juiced

FOR SERVING

  Warm corn tortillas, for serving
  Salsa Verde (page 28), for serving
  Roughly chopped cilantro and thinly sliced radishes, for garnish
  Orange wedges, for serving

1 Make the carnitas: Melt lard in a large pot over medium-high. Season pork with salt; cook, turning as needed, until browned, 10–12 minutes. Add milk, garlic, jalapeños and pickling liquid, onion, and lime and orange juices; boil. Reduce heat to medium-low; cook, covered, until pork is tender, about 2 hours. Let pork cool and transfer to a cutting board; chop into bite-size pieces. Strain cooking liquid and return to pan; stir in pork and keep warm.

2 Serve carnitas on tortillas, dolloped with salsa and garnished with cilantro and radishes. Serve with more pickled jalapeños and the orange wedges on the side.

TACOS DE PAPA HWY 99

Potato Tacos

SERVES 6

Inspired by the potato tacos at Loncheria Otro Rollo in Bakersfield, California, this version from Bay Area restaurateur Sara Deseran is stuffed with fluffy mashed potatoes and pan-fried until crisp. The accompanying smoky ranchero sauce is also great spooned over meat, fish, or eggs.

5	tbsp. olive oil
6	cloves garlic, roughly chopped
1	small white onion, roughly chopped
4	canned chipotle chiles en adobo
1	15-oz. can whole, peeled tomatoes
	Kosher salt, to taste
1½	lb. russet potatoes, peeled and quartered
2	tsp. ground cumin
12	6″ corn tortillas
½	cup canola oil
	Thinly sliced green and red cabbage, for garnish
	Thinly sliced red radishes, for garnish
	Crumbled queso fresco, for garnish

1 Heat 3 tbsp. olive oil in a small pot over medium heat. Cook garlic and onion until soft, about 5 minutes; transfer to a blender. Add chiles, tomatoes, and salt; purée until smooth and set sauce aside.

2 Cook potatoes in a medium pot of salted boiling water until cooked through, about 15 minutes; drain and return to pan over medium heat. Add the remaining olive oil and the cumin and mash the potatoes. Season with salt.

3 Working in batches, place about ¼ cup mashed potatoes in the center of a tortilla; fold tortilla in half and secure with a toothpick. Heat canola oil in a large skillet over medium. Fry tacos, flipping once, until golden and crisp, 2–3 minutes. Discard toothpicks and transfer tacos to a platter; top with reserved sauce, the cabbage, radishes, and queso fresco, and serve hot.

SHRIMP TACOS

SERVES 6

Every element of this taco—inspired by those at Don Pepe Taqueria in Fresno, California—is amped up, from the red rice simmered in a blend of chicken stock and puréed tomatoes to the quick-marinated shrimp to the jumbo tortillas. If the oversized taco proves unwieldy, just wrap the whole thing up like a burrito and dig in. For a homemade salsa and guacamole, try Salsa Verde on page 28 and Casa Dragones Guacamole on page 29.

FOR THE RICE

1½	cups chicken stock
2	plum tomatoes, cored and roughly chopped
2	tbsp. canola oil
2	cloves garlic, minced
1	small white onion, minced
1	cup long-grain white rice
	Kosher salt and freshly ground black pepper, to taste

FOR THE SHRIMP & SERVING

1½	lb. medium shrimp, peeled and deveined, tails removed
1	tsp. Worcestershire sauce
2	cloves garlic, minced
1	lime, juiced
2	tbsp. canola oil
	Large flour tortillas, warmed, for serving
	Salsa, for serving
	Guacamole, for serving
	Shredded jack cheese, for serving
	Roughly chopped cilantro and white onion, for garnish
	Lime wedges, for serving

1 Make the rice: Purée stock and tomatoes in a blender until smooth; set aside. Heat oil in a medium pot over medium-high. Cook garlic and onion until soft, about 5 minutes. Add rice; cook until golden, about 6 minutes. Stir in reserved tomato mixture, and salt and pepper; boil. Reduce heat to low; cook, covered, until rice is tender, 25–30 minutes. Remove from heat and set aside, covered, for 10 minutes.

2 Make the shrimp: Stir shrimp, Worcestershire, garlic, lime juice, and salt and pepper to taste in a bowl; set aside for 10 minutes. To a large skillet over medium-high heat, add oil. When oil is hot, working in batches, cook shrimp until pink and cooked through, 2–3 minutes. To serve, divide rice and shrimp between tortillas; top with salsa and guacamole, cheese, cilantro, and onion. Serve with lime wedges.

Poultry

POETRY

THESE ARE PRETTY GOOD TIMES for the domesticated bird—at least from the cook's point of view. Chickens, turkeys, ducks, and geese find their way into kitchens around the world with delicious results, which are then showcased on dinner tables from India and Jamaica to France and Thailand.

Chicken has become a bit of a punch line for good reason: Tastes like chicken? That means you're going to like it. It's also a safe bet that pretty much every night of the week a large number of Americans are sitting down to chicken for dinner. It's popular because of its flavor, of course, but also because of its seemingly infinite versatility. A blank slate just waiting for spices and sauces to write on it, chicken blends seamlessly with whatever comes its way, whether a savory garlic purée, a deep, sweet kick of chocolate, or handfuls of chiles and peanuts. A dip in spicy-sweet Korean barbecue sauce—why not? Decadently enveloped in truffles and cream—*mais oui!* Even an old bird has its place, nestled in a big Dutch oven where it keeps company with mushrooms, onions, a bottle of wine, and a parsley sprig or two in a classic coq au vin.

Of course, there's also the glory of a crisp-skinned, tender-fleshed roast chicken, astonishing in its ease, its simplicity, and its deliciousness. But for a smart home cook, the whole chicken is just the beginning. Sunday's roast becomes Monday's sandwiches; Tuesday's hash; and Wednesday's stock: the bones (and, though unlikely, any meat that remains) simmer away in a pot with water and aromatics, resulting in a rich brew that will lends its depth and body to a slew of pleasing soups, stews, and other dishes.

But there's so much more to the glory of poultry. The gloriously fatty, flavorful duck deserves just as much love as its cousin the chicken. From a tender confited leg to a firm slice of Cantonese-style roast duck—its skin paper-crisp thanks to a day or more of drying—the duck's firm, dark flesh appeals to a carnivore's appetite more than chicken ever could.

For a celebratory meal, the center of the table demands something larger and something richer. Sitting in splendor on a porcelain platter, a stately Thanksgiving turkey—dressed to the nines with chestnut-studded stuffing and a bowl of smooth, dark gravy—is more than just a main course. It's a symbol, a reminder of the bounty of autumn and an expression of gratitude for all that we have. And a classic Christmas goose fills hearts with Dickensian good cheer: it's a centerpiece around which we come together to share the joy of a holiday spent in the warm company of family and friends.

Chicken

PERFECT ROAST CHICKEN

SERVES 2–4

Christian Delouvrier, chef of Manhattan's La Mangeoire restaurant, serves perhaps our favorite roast chicken, a spectacularly moist bird with bronze, crisp skin. The key to perfecting the dish at home is basting the chicken throughout the cooking process with an umami-rich mixture of soy sauce and butter. Delouvrier serves his roast chicken atop a bed of French fries (page 407) to absorb all the pan juices.

- ½ cup unsalted butter
- ½ cup soy sauce
- 1 3–4-lb. chicken
  Kosher salt and freshly ground black pepper, to taste
- 4 cloves garlic, crushed
- 1 bunch fresh thyme

1 Heat oven to 475°. Melt butter in a 2-qt. saucepan over medium heat and stir in soy sauce; set aside. Season chicken with salt and pepper and stuff cavity with garlic and thyme; tie legs together with kitchen twine. Transfer to 9"×13" baking dish.

2 Brush the chicken generously with some of the soy-butter mixture and cook, basting twice more during cooking, until an instant-read thermometer inserted into the thickest part of a thigh reads 165°, about 1 hour. Let rest for 10 minutes before carving.

ROAST CHICKEN WITH SAFFRON & LEMON

SERVES 4

In Spain, the bitter-briny flavor of saffron and the tart bite of citrus are paired in dishes throughout the country; this elegant roast chicken brings the two together in beautiful harmony.

- Large pinch of saffron threads
- 2 tsp. kosher salt
- ¼ tsp. black peppercorns
- 1 3-lb. chicken
- 1 lemon, thinly sliced
  Sprigs fresh rosemary

1 Heat oven to 400°. Grind saffron threads, salt, and peppercorns with a mortar and pestle. Use your fingers to gently separate the skin from the flesh of the chicken. Rub spices over and under the skin and inside the cavity. Place lemon slices and rosemary under the skin and inside the cavity.

2 Tuck the wings under the back and tie the bird with a kitchen twine to hold the legs together for even cooking. Place in a roasting pan and roast for 1 hour. Let rest for 10 minutes before carving.

TUTU-MAN'S TERIYAKI CHICKEN

SERVES 4

Hawaiian cookbook author Kaui Philpotts gave us this family recipe. Her father, known as Tutu-Man, considered fresh ginger an essential ingredient in his teriyaki sauce. This sauce can also be used as a marinade for pork chops, short ribs, or thinly sliced flank steak, so make more than you need—it will keep in the refrigerator for up to a week.

FOR THE SAUCE
- ½ cup soy sauce
- ½ cup sugar
- 1 1½" piece fresh ginger, peeled and sliced
- 2 cloves garlic, crushed
- 1 tbsp. bourbon

- 1 3½-lb. chicken
  Scallion greens or fresh garlic chives, for garnish

1 Make the sauce: Cook soy sauce and sugar in a small saucepan over medium-low heat until sugar dissolves, about 2 minutes. Stir in ginger, garlic, and bourbon and cook for 30 minutes. Remove ginger and garlic. Pour sauce into a small bowl.

2 Heat oven to 375°. Pat chicken dry. Truss the chicken by tucking wings under the back and tying legs together with kitchen string. Using a pastry brush, coat chicken with sauce both inside the cavity and on the outside.

3 Place chicken in a roasting pan and roast for about 1 hour, basting every 15 minutes. Chicken is done when an instant-read thermometer inserted into the thickest part of a thigh reads 165°. Let chicken rest for 15 minutes before carving. Garnish with lengths of scallion greens and serve.

LEMON & ROSEMARY CHICKEN

Pollo Arrosto

SERVES 4

Evan Kleiman of the now-closed Angeli Caffè in Los Angeles gave us the recipe for her simple, aromatic roast chicken. We like to serve it with crusty bread for sopping up the tart, savory sauce.

- 1 3½-lb. chicken, cut into 8 pieces
- ½ cup extra-virgin olive oil
- ½ cup fresh rosemary leaves
- ¼ cup fresh lemon juice
- 10 cloves garlic, thinly sliced
- 1 lemon, peel removed, pith and pulp chopped
  Kosher salt and freshly ground black pepper, to taste

1 Toss chicken with oil, rosemary, lemon juice, garlic, lemon, salt, and pepper in bowl. Marinate for 1 hour.

2 Heat oven to 475°. Arrange chicken in a 9″×13″ baking dish; add remaining marinade. Roast, flipping once, until cooked through, 30–40 minutes. Serve hot.

CHICKEN WITH 40 CLOVES OF GARLIC

SERVES 6–8

This rustic French dish is gorgeously rich in flavor. Don't be intimidated by the quantity of garlic: After braising in the oven, the cloves lose their bite and retain nothing but mellow sweetness.

- 3 tbsp. olive oil
- 1 3½-lb. chicken, cut into 8 pieces
  Kosher salt and freshly ground black pepper
- 40 cloves garlic, peeled (or up to 100 cloves)
- ½ cup dry vermouth
- ¾ cup chicken stock
- 1 tbsp. chopped fresh tarragon

Heat oven to 350°. Heat oil in a 6-qt. Dutch oven over medium-high heat. Season chicken with salt and pepper; add to pot and cook, turning once, until browned, about 15 minutes. Transfer to an 8″×8″ baking dish; set aside. Add garlic to pot and cook until browned in spots, about 6 minutes. Add vermouth and cook, scraping bottom of pot, until slightly reduced, about 2 minutes. Add stock and bring to a boil. Transfer half of the garlic to baking dish; mash remaining into stock and pour over chicken. Bake until glazed and tender, 20–25 minutes. Garnish with tarragon and serve.

HOW TO PEEL A HEAD OF GARLIC IN UNDER A MINUTE

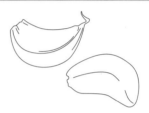

We're of the mind that there's no such thing as too much garlic. When it comes to a dish like Chicken with 40 Cloves of Garlic (this page), which showcases the allium's sweet qualities, we've been known to up the title quantity as high as a hundred. Peeling that many cloves can appear to be daunting task, but there's a devastatingly simple trick that cuts it down to the work of seconds.

Smash a dry head of garlic with the heel of your hand to separate the cloves. Sweep it all into a large metal or Pyrex bowl (the trick won't work with plastic bowls; it needs to be a very hard material), and invert a second bowl of the same size and material over the first, making a hollow globe filled with unpeeled garlic. Hold the bowls together where the rims meet and just shake the heck out of it for 10–20 seconds (it'll make a riotously cacophonous noise). When you lift off the top bowl, you'll find that the garlic cloves slip right out of their skins.

GABHOR UTOMO

TANDOORI CHICKEN

SERVES 4–6

This version of India's tandoori chicken—intricately spiced, juicy, and tender—tastes even better if you allow the chicken to rest in the second, yogurt-based marinade overnight.

- 4 skinless, bone-in whole chicken legs
- 3 skinless, bone-in chicken breast halves, halved crosswise
- 6 cloves garlic, roughly chopped
- 1 3″ piece fresh ginger, peeled and coarsely chopped
  Kosher salt
- 3 tbsp. canola oil
- 1 tbsp. distilled white vinegar
- 1 tbsp. Kashmiri red chile powder or paprika
- 1½ tsp. cardamom seeds
- 1½ tsp. garlic powder
- 1½ tsp. ground bay leaf
- 1½ tsp. ground cinnamon
- 1½ tsp. ground clove
- 1½ tsp. ground ginger
- 1 cup plain yogurt
- ½ tsp. ground black salt (optional)
- 6 green bird's eye chiles, stemmed and finely chopped

1 Make 2″-wide slashes about ½″ deep all over chicken pieces. Cut knee joints on legs halfway. Transfer all the chicken to a large bowl.

2 Purée garlic, ginger, and ¼ cup water in a blender; add to chicken along with 2 tsp. salt, half the oil, vinegar, 1 tsp. chile powder, and half each of the following: cardamom, garlic powder, bay leaf, cinnamon, cloves, and ground ginger. Toss to coat; refrigerate overnight.

3 Put yogurt, black salt, chiles, and all remaining oil, chile powder, cardamom, garlic powder, bay leaf, cinnamon, cloves, ground ginger, and salt to taste into a bowl. Mix well. Pour yogurt mixture over chicken; massage into flesh for 2–3 minutes. Cover with plastic wrap and let marinate at room temperature for at least 1 hour or up to overnight.

4 Place a baking stone on the middle oven rack; heat oven to highest setting (500°, or 550° if possible). Line a baking sheet with foil; place a baking rack directly on top of the foil. Arrange chicken pieces with any marinade that clings to them on the rack in a single layer. Bake, rotating baking sheet once back to front, until crisp, lightly charred, and cooked through, about 25 minutes for breasts and 35 minutes for legs. Serve hot.

COOK'S NOTE To re-create the heat of a clay tandoor oven, we placed a baking stone in our conventional oven and cranked up the oven as high as it would go.

POLLO ALLA DIAVOLA

Chicken Devil Style

SERVES 4–8

Roman "devil style" chicken is liberally seasoned with crushed red pepper flakes; their heat is tamed by tangy lemon juice and—for serving—plenty of good bread.

- 2 3½-lb. chickens, spatchcocked (see Backing Out, page 156)
- 3 lemons
- ¾ cup extra-virgin olive oil
  Crushed red pepper flakes, to taste
  Kosher salt and freshly ground black pepper
  Crusty bread, for serving

1 Place each spatchcocked chicken, skin side up, on a cutting board, and roll a rolling pin on it, leaning heavily on the pin to flatten the birds.

2 Place chicken in a wide, deep dish. Squeeze the juice from 2 of the lemons over bird, add ½ cup of the oil, and season with lots of red pepper and with salt and black pepper. Set aside to marinate for 30–60 minutes.

3 Build a medium fire in a charcoal grill or set a gas grill to medium; bank coals or turn burner off on one side for indirect grilling (page 191). Squeeze juice from the remaining lemon into a small bowl, whisk in the remaining ¼ cup oil, and season to taste with salt and lots of pepper, then set aside. Remove chickens from marinade, discarding marinade. Grill birds on hottest part of grill, basting occasionally with the reserved lemon and oil, until skin is well browned on both sides and an instant-read thermometer inserted into the thickest part of a thigh reads 165°, about 50 minutes. If outside starts to burn before chicken is cooked, move to cooler side of grill until done. Set chickens aside to rest for 10 minutes, then cut into quarters and serve with bread.

ALABAMA-STYLE BBQ CHICKEN WITH WHITE SAUCE

SERVES 8

What distinguishes this pulled chicken from other Southern versions is the creamy spiced sauce that both bastes and dresses the chicken. Eat it on its own with a side of greens, or slap it on a potato roll with some pickle chips and let it soak up the sauce.

2 cups mayonnaise

½ cup prepared horseradish

¼ cup cider vinegar

2 tbsp. sugar

4 tsp. kosher salt, plus more to taste

2 tbsp. freshly ground black pepper, plus more to taste

½ tsp. cayenne pepper

2¼ tsp. paprika

1½ tsp. garlic powder

¾ tsp. celery seeds

¼ tsp. ground cumin

¼ tsp. ground coriander

1 4-lb. chicken, spatchcocked or quartered (see Backing Out, this page)

1 In a bowl, whisk together mayonnaise, horseradish, vinegar, sugar, 3 tsp. salt, 1½ tsp. pepper, and cayenne. Place half of the sauce in another bowl; one bowl will be for basting and one for serving. In a third bowl, mix remaining 1 tsp. salt and pepper with paprika, garlic powder, celery seeds, cumin, and coriander; set rub aside.

2 Prepare for barbecuing using the kettle grill (facing page), bullet smoker, or gas grill method using apple wood chunks or chips. Season chicken with the rub mixture and place it, skin side up, on grill grate. Maintaining a temperature of 225°–250° (replenish fire with unlit coals as needed to maintain temperature), cook, turning once and basting chicken with sauce every 20 minutes, until an instant-read thermometer inserted into the thickest part of a thigh reads 165°, about 1½ hours. Remove chicken from grill; let rest, covered loosely with foil, for 10 minutes.

3 Shred the chicken meat with forks and discard bones and skin. Serve with reserved sauce for dressing.

BACKING OUT

Spatchcocking is a technique that removes the backbone and sternum from a chicken so that it can lie flat while cooking. To do it, place the chicken thigh side up and, using kitchen shears, cut along each side of the backbone so the bird can open like a book. Flip chicken over and press down on breast to flatten.

CORNELL CHICKEN

SERVES 4

We have Cornell University poultry science professor Robert C. Baker to thank for this juicy, flavorful marinade. The dish is served at the New York State Fair in Syracuse each autumn, but we find ourselves making it year-round.

2 2½–3-lb. chickens, halved

2 cups cider vinegar

1 cup vegetable oil

1 tbsp. Homemade Fresh Poultry Seasoning (page 588, or store-bought)

1 egg

Kosher salt and freshly ground black pepper, to taste

1 Place chicken in a bowl. Purée vinegar, oil, seasoning, and egg in a blender until smooth. Pour half the marinade over chicken and toss to coat. Cover with plastic wrap and chill for 2 hours. Reserve remaining marinade.

2 Build a hot fire in a charcoal grill or set a gas grill to high; bank coals or turn burner off on one side for indirect grilling (page 191). Remove chicken from marinade and, using paper towels, wipe excess marinade from chicken and pat dry. Grill chicken on hottest part of grill, turning as needed and, using a brush, basting often with reserved marinade, until slightly charred and cooked through, about 30 minutes or until an instant-read thermometer inserted into the thickest part of a thigh reads 165°. If outside starts to burn before chicken is cooked, move to cooler side of grill until done. Let rest before serving.

IRAQI YELLOW SPICE–RUBBED CHICKEN
Djaj Bil-Bahar il-Asfar

SERVES 2–4 (SEE PHOTO, PAGE 230)

This fragrant spice-rubbed grilled chicken was a favorite of author Felicia Campbell when she was deployed as a soldier in Iraq.

2 tsp. coriander seeds

2 tsp. cumin seeds

2 tsp. black peppercorns

6 cardamom pods

4 dried chiles de árbol, stemmed

4 whole allspice

4 whole cloves

4 dried rose hips

1 tbsp. curry powder

1 tbsp. ground cinnamon

1 tbsp. ground sumac

2 tsp. ground ginger

1½ tsp. freshly grated nutmeg

1 tsp. ground fenugreek

8 cloves garlic, mashed into a paste
Kosher salt and freshly ground
black pepper, to taste

1 3-lb. chicken, halved
Flatbread, such as Naan (page 459,
or store-bought), for serving

1 Heat coriander, cumin, peppercorns, cardamom, chiles, allspice, and cloves in a 10″ skillet over medium heat until seeds pop, 1–2 minutes; let cool. Transfer to a spice grinder with rose hips; grind and transfer to a bowl. Stir in curry, cinnamon, sumac, ginger, nutmeg, fenugreek, garlic, salt, and pepper; add chicken and toss to coat. Cover and refrigerate overnight.

2 Build a hot fire in a charcoal grill or set a gas grill to high; bank coals or turn burner off on one side for indirect grilling (page 191). Grill chicken on hottest part of grill, flipping once, until slightly charred and cooked through, about 45 minutes or until an instant-read thermometer inserted into the thickest part of a thigh reads 165°. If outside starts to burn before chicken is cooked, move to cooler side of grill until done. Let rest for 10 minutes. Serve with flatbread.

JAMAICAN JERK CHICKEN

SERVES 8

Full of fiery chiles and warm spices, the all-purpose Jamaican seasoning for this dish can be used as a rub on pork, goat, fish, and vegetables, as well as on its most popular vehicle, chicken.

¾ cup packed light brown sugar

¾ cup ground allspice

¾ cup minced scallions

½ cup peanut or canola oil

⅓ cup ground black pepper

¼ cup kosher salt

¼ cup minced fresh ginger

¼ cup fresh lime juice

2 tbsp. soy sauce

1 tbsp. dried thyme

1 tsp. ground cinnamon

1 tsp. freshly grated nutmeg

½ tsp. ground cloves

8 cloves garlic, minced

3 Scotch bonnet or habanero chiles,
stemmed and minced

2 3–4-lb. chickens, each quartered

1 Combine sugar, allspice, scallions, oil, pepper, salt, ginger, juice, soy sauce, thyme, cinnamon, nutmeg, cloves, garlic, and chiles in a bowl. Add chicken and toss to coat

BARBECUING IN A KETTLE GRILL

Barbecuing calls for low-and-slow cooking over indirect heat. Here's how to do it in a kettle grill.

1 Heat 50 coals in chimney starter until ashy; pour over half the bottom grate. Place a foil pan filled with water over other half.

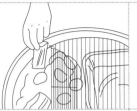

2 Place top grill grate into grill and open grate door over coals. Insert 3 or 4 soaked wood chunks onto coals; close grate.

3 Cover grill with lid and heat for 10 minutes. Scrape grate with grill brush, then place meat over water-filled foil pan.

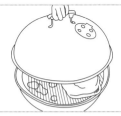

4 Cover grill and open vents; position top vents over meat. Replenish with coals as needed to maintain desired temperature.

VALERIYA FATEYCHEVA

in jerk marinade. Cover with plastic wrap and chill for at least 6 hours or up to overnight.

2 Build a hot fire in a charcoal grill or set a gas grill to high; bank coals or turn burner off on one side for indirect grilling (page 191). (Alternatively, heat a cast-iron grill pan over medium-high heat.) Place chicken, skin side down, over hottest part of grill. Grill, turning once, until marinade forms a crust on the outside, about 8 minutes. Move chicken to cooler side of grill. Cover grill and continue cooking until cooked through, about 35 minutes or until an instant-read thermometer inserted into the thickest part of a thigh reads 165°. (Alternatively, transfer chicken to a foil-lined baking sheet and bake in a 350° oven until done.) If outside starts to burn before chicken is cooked, move to cooler side of grill until done.

WHAT A JERK

The key to the tremendous appeal of Jerk Chicken (page 157) lies in the unique way it's prepared. At Jamaica's most celebrated "jerk centres," the meat is cooked atop wood set over charcoal in long, troughlike grills. The white smoke from the branches is captured beneath sheets of galvanized zinc that are laid on top of the grill, so the jerk steams as it smokes, resulting in moist, tender meat. Allspice, ginger, cinnamon, and thyme lend fragrance to the complex paste in which the meat marinates before it's cooked; scallions and citrus give it sharpness and tang; and plenty of black pepper and Scotch bonnet chile add heat.

Today, the jerk meat of choice is chicken, though the dish originated in the 18th century with Jamaica's enslaved Africans, who hunted feral pigs, rubbed the carcasses in foraged herbs and spices, and cooked the meat in covered pits. The salt and smoke preserved the meat so it lasted longer and, as later visitors attested, it had the excellent side effect of tasting wonderful. On a visit to Jamaica in the late 1930s, the writer and anthropologist Zora Neale Hurston raved that jerk was "more delicious than our American barbecue."

PESTO-RUBBED CHICKEN

SERVES 4 (SEE PHOTO, PAGE 228)

Pesto—vibrant with fresh basil and garlic—adds herbal brightness to this grilled chicken. We like it served with a toasted bread salad, like Summer Panzanella (page 59). Any flavor pesto will work for the chicken.

- 1 3– to 4-lb. chicken, cut into 6 pieces
- ¾ cup Pesto Genovese (page 356)
  Kosher salt and freshly ground black pepper, to taste

1 Using your fingers, gently loosen skin from flesh on chicken and spread ½ cup pesto between them. Transfer chicken to a baking sheet and season generously with salt and pepper; set aside.

2 Build a hot fire in a charcoal grill or heat a gas grill to high. Place chicken, skin side down, on grill and cook, covered and turning once, until an instant-read thermometer inserted into the thickest part of a thigh reads 165°, about 25 minutes. Rub with remaining pesto and cook until a thermometer inserted into the thickest part of a thigh reads 165°, about 5 minutes more. (Alternatively, heat an oven to 475° and cook chicken, skin side up, for 25 minutes; rub with remaining pesto and cook until chicken reaches an internal temperature of 165°.) Transfer chicken to a plate and tent with foil; rest for 20 minutes before serving.

THAI GRILLED CHICKEN WITH SWEET CHILE SAUCE

Kai Yang

SERVES 4

Kai yang is a specialty of Isan, a region in northeast Thailand. The chicken is succulent and crisp-skinned, thanks to an overnight marinating in cilantro, garlic, and other ingredients. Street vendors sell the chicken split, splayed, and grilled whole, then served with a sticky-spicy chile sauce. If you have small chickens (under 2 pounds), you can spatchcock (see Backing Out, page 156) and grill them whole; if not, we've found that grilling pieces achieves the best balance of flavors.

FOR THE CHICKEN
- 1 3–4-lb. chicken, cut into 8 pieces
- 1 cup roughly chopped fresh cilantro leaves and stems
- ⅓ cup soy sauce

2 tbsp. canola oil
2½ tsp. ground white pepper
10 cloves garlic, peeled

FOR THE SWEET CHILE SAUCE

5 cloves garlic, finely chopped
1 cup sugar
½ cup white vinegar
Kosher salt, to taste
1 tbsp. crushed red chile flakes

1 Make the chicken: Place chicken in a 9″×13″ baking dish. Pulse cilantro, soy sauce, oil, white pepper, and 10 whole garlic cloves in a food processor until smooth; rub three-quarters of marinade over chicken, reserving remaining marinade. Cover and refrigerate overnight.

2 Make the sweet chile sauce: Bring garlic, sugar, vinegar, salt, and 1 cup water to a boil in a 2-qt. saucepan. Cook, stirring, until sauce is reduced by half, 12–15 minutes. Stir in chile flakes; let sauce cool.

3 Build a hot fire in a charcoal grill or heat a gas grill to high; bank coals or turn burner off on one side for indirect grilling (page 191). Grill chicken on hottest part of grill, turning as needed and, using a brush, basting with reserved marinade, until slightly charred and cooked through, 25–30 minutes or until an instant-read thermometer inserted into the thickest part of a thigh reads 165°. If the outside starts to burn before the chicken is fully cooked, move to the cooler side of the grill until done. Serve with chile sauce on the side.

YASSA POULET

Senegalese Grilled Chicken in Caramelized Onion Sauce
SERVES 4–6

Here, the rich, savory marinade is cooked down into a sweet-tart sauce for the grilled chicken.

⅓ cup cider vinegar
⅓ cup fresh lime juice
1 tbsp. lime zest
2 tbsp. minced fresh ginger
2 tsp. coarsely cracked black peppercorns, plus more to taste
1 tsp. cayenne pepper
6 cloves garlic, minced
2 large yellow onions, thinly sliced
1 medium carrot, thinly sliced
1 habanero or Scotch bonnet chile, stemmed, seeded, and minced

1 bay leaf
Kosher salt, to taste
2 lb. bone-in, skin-on chicken thighs and drumsticks
2 tbsp. peanut or canola oil, plus more for brushing
1 tsp. whole allspice
Cooked white rice, for serving

1 Combine vinegar, lime juice and zest, ginger, pepper, cayenne, garlic, onion, carrot, chile, bay leaf, and salt in a large resealable plastic bag; add chicken and seal bag. Refrigerate, tossing chicken with marinade occasionally, for 4 hours.

2 Heat oil in a 6-qt. Dutch oven over medium-high heat. Remove chicken from marinade. Working in batches, add to pot and cook, turning once, until golden brown on both sides, about 8 minutes; transfer to a plate. Add allspice to pot and cook until fragrant, about 2 minutes. Pour marinade through a fine sieve, reserving liquid, and transfer solids to pot. Cook, stirring, until softened, about 5 minutes. Add reserved liquid and chicken and cook, covered and stirring occasionally, until chicken is cooked through, about 30 minutes.

3 Transfer chicken to a serving platter. Continue cooking onions until liquid evaporates and onions are lightly caramelized, about 20 minutes. Season with salt and pepper and pour onions over chicken. Serve with rice.

RAO'S FAMOUS LEMON CHICKEN

SERVES 6

Platters of lemon chicken seem to go out to almost every table at Rao's, a century-old Italian restaurant in Manhattan's East Harlem that's known, in relatively equal measure, for this dish and for the Herculean difficulty of landing a reservation.

2 cups fresh lemon juice
1 cup extra-virgin olive oil
1 tbsp. red wine vinegar
1 clove garlic, minced
½ tsp. dried oregano
Salt and freshly ground black pepper
2 2½-lb. chickens with legs, thighs, and wings separated and breasts quartered on the bone
¼ cup chopped fresh parsley

1 Place an oven rack in the upper third of the oven and heat broiler. Whisk together lemon juice, oil, vinegar, garlic, and oregano in a large bowl. Season to taste with salt and pepper. Set aside.

2 Place chicken, skin side down, on a baking sheet and broil for 15 minutes. Turn chicken skin side up and broil until skin is crisp and golden and juices run clear, about 15 minutes more.

3 Remove chicken from broiler and toss in lemon mixture. Return chicken, skin side up, to broiler and broil for 3 minutes. Transfer chicken to a platter.

4 Pour pan drippings into a saucepan, add lemon sauce, bring to a boil over high heat until thickened, and cook until thickened, about 5 minutes. Stir in parsley, drizzle a little sauce on chicken, and serve remaining sauce on the side.

CHICKEN TIKKA MASALA
SERVES 6

The chicken in this Anglo-Indian dish (which, despite its complement of Indian spices, likely originated in Great Britain) is kept separate from its creamy, complex tomato-laced sauce until the very end, to preserve its succulence.

- 1 tbsp. ground turmeric
- 4 tsp. garam masala
- 6 cloves garlic, crushed
- 1 2½" piece fresh ginger, peeled and chopped, plus julienned strips for garnish
- 1 jalapeño, stemmed and chopped
- 1 28-oz. can whole, peeled tomatoes, undrained
- 2 lb. boneless, skinless chicken breasts, cut into 1½" cubes
- ¼ cup plain Greek yogurt
  Kosher salt, to taste
- 6 tbsp. unsalted butter
- 1 tsp. coriander seeds
- ½ tsp. cumin seeds
- 1 tbsp. paprika
- 2 small yellow onions, finely chopped
- 1 cup heavy cream
  Fresh cilantro leaves, for garnish
  Cooked basmati rice, for serving

1 In a blender, purée turmeric, 2 tsp. garam masala, garlic, ginger, jalapeños, and ½ cup water. Put paste into a bowl. In the same blender, purée tomatoes and strain through a sieve. In a bowl, mix 2 tbsp. paste, chicken, yogurt, and salt; marinate for 30 minutes. Arrange an oven rack 4" from broiler and heat broiler. Transfer chicken to a foil-lined baking sheet and broil until cooked through, 5–6 minutes; set aside.

2 Melt butter in 6-qt. saucepan over medium-high heat. Add coriander and cumin and toast for 4–6 minutes. Add paprika and onions and cook until soft, 6–8 minutes. Add remaining paste and brown for 5–6 minutes. Add tomatoes and cook for 2 minutes. Stir in cream and 1 cup water and bring to a boil. Reduce heat and simmer until thickened, 6–8 minutes. Stir in remaining garam masala and chicken, then season with salt. Garnish with cilantro and serve with rice.

BRICK CHICKEN
SERVES 4–6

Using a weight (such as a brick or a few soup cans) to press down on a partially deboned chicken as it cooks in a skillet reduces cooking time and yields an especially juicy, crisp bird. This recipe is adapted from the excellent version served at Brooklyn's Marlow & Sons restaurant.

- 1 4-lb. chicken, halved; backbone, ribcage, and thighbones removed
  Kosher salt and freshly ground black pepper, to taste
- 2 tbsp. canola oil
- ⅓ cup chicken stock
- 1 tbsp. fresh lemon juice

1 Season chicken generously with salt and pepper. Heat oil in a 10" skillet over high heat. When oil begins to smoke, add the 2 chicken halves, skin side down, to skillet. Place another 10" skillet, right side up, on top of chicken and gently place a heavy brick or several soup cans in it (weight should be at least 20 pounds).

2 Reduce heat to medium-high and cook chicken until the skin is golden brown and crisp, about 18 minutes. Remove the top skillet and weight, flip the chicken halves with tongs, and pour off excess fat.

3 Add stock and lemon juice and cook until an instant-read thermometer inserted into the thickest part of a thigh reads 165°, about 3 more minutes. Serve with pan drippings.

CHICKEN GALLIANO
SERVES 4–6

Galliano, an Italian liqueur flavored with 30 herbs and spices, including anise and vanilla, gives a complex sweetness to the sauce for these stuffed chicken breasts. The recipe, a staple in the dinner repertoire of SAVEUR senior editor Keith Pandolfi's father, Ron, was printed on Galliano bottles in the 1960s.

6 boneless, skinless chicken breast halves, pounded ⅛″ thick
Kosher salt and freshly ground black pepper, to taste
12 tbsp. herbed goat cheese, softened
6 thin slices prosciutto
8 tbsp. unsalted butter, chilled
10 oz. cremini mushrooms, sliced
Flour, for dredging
2 tbsp. canola oil
1½ cups chicken stock
¼ cup Galliano liqueur
1 tbsp. finely chopped fresh flat-leaf parsley
Cooked white rice, for serving

1 Season chicken with salt and pepper. Working with one breast half at a time, spread one side with 2 tbsp. goat cheese and top with 1 slice prosciutto; roll into a tight cylinder. Using kitchen twine, tie chicken roll 1″ in from each end. Snip off excess twine.

2 Heat 3 tbsp. butter in a 12″ skillet over medium-high heat. Add mushrooms and cook, without stirring, until browned, 4–5 minutes. Stir mushrooms and continue cooking until softened, about 8 minutes. Transfer to a plate; wipe out skillet. Put flour on a plate and dredge each chicken roll in flour. Heat 2 tbsp. butter and the oil in skillet over medium-high heat. Add chicken and cook, turning, until browned and cooked through, 12–14 minutes. Transfer chicken rolls to a plate. Add stock and Galliano to skillet and boil, stirring, until sauce has reduced by one-third, 4–5 minutes. Return mushrooms and chicken to skillet and cook, turning to coat in sauce, until warmed through, about 5 minutes.

3 Transfer chicken to a platter. Remove skillet from heat and swirl in remaining 3 tbsp. butter to make a smooth sauce. Spoon sauce over chicken and sprinkle with parsley. Serve with rice.

CHICKEN MARSALA
SERVES 6–8

Pounding the chicken cutlets renders them terrifically tender. Deglazing the pan with Marsala and stock creates a quick, silky sauce, proving it's a stalwart of Italian-American restaurant menus for a reason.

8 boneless, skinless chicken breast halves, pounded ¼″ thick
Kosher salt and freshly ground black pepper, to taste

5 tbsp. flour
5 tbsp. olive oil
5 tbsp. unsalted butter
½ lb. white button mushrooms
2 tbsp. minced shallots
1 clove garlic, minced
⅓ cup dry marsala wine
⅓ cup chicken stock

1 Season chicken with salt and pepper and dredge in 2 tbsp. flour. Heat 2 tbsp. oil and 1 tbsp. butter in a 12″ skillet over medium-high heat. Working in batches, add chicken and cook, turning once, until golden brown, about 3 minutes. Transfer to a plate, and set aside. Add 2 tbsp. oil and 1 tbsp. butter and then add mushrooms and cook until golden brown, about 8 minutes. Transfer to plate with chicken and set aside.

2 Heat remaining 1 tbsp. oil in skillet, add shallots and garlic and cook, stirring, until soft, about 1 minute. Add remaining 3 tbsp. flour and cook for 2 minutes. Add marsala and stock and cook, scraping bottom of pan to loosen any brown bits, until slightly reduced, about 2 minutes. Return chicken and mushrooms to skillet and cook until heated through, about 2 minutes. Remove from heat and stir in remaining butter. Season with salt and pepper before serving.

GENERAL TSO'S CHICKEN
SERVES 4

Apricot jam lends a touch of sweetness, acidity, and sheen to this riff on the classic Hunanese dish. The pectin in the preserves also gives it a glossy, alluring sheen.

1½ lb. boneless, skinless chicken thighs, cut into 2″ pieces
⅓ cup plus 1 tbsp. cornstarch
1 large egg, lightly beaten
¼ cup soy sauce
½ cup low-sodium chicken stock
1 tbsp. rice vinegar
1 tbsp. Shaoxing wine or dry sherry
2 tbsp. apricot jam
1 tbsp. tomato paste
2 tbsp. canola or peanut oil, plus more for frying
1 tbsp. grated ginger
1 tsp. grated garlic
¼ cup dried Tianjin or cayenne chiles
Toasted sesame oil, for serving (optional)
Thinly sliced scallions, for serving
Steamed jasmine rice, for serving

1 Combine chicken, ⅓ cup cornstarch, egg, and 2 tbsp. soy sauce in a medium bowl. Toss well to coat, then set aside to marinate at room temperature for 15 minutes.

2 Combine chicken stock, remaining 1 tbsp. cornstarch, vinegar, wine, apricot jam, tomato paste, remaining 2 tbsp. soy sauce, and ½ cup cold water in a small bowl. Whisk to combine.

3 Line a large plate or baking sheet with paper towels and set by the stove. In a wok or large, deep skillet fitted with a deep-fry thermometer, add enough canola oil to reach 3″ up the sides of the wok. Preheat oil to 375° over medium-high heat. Working in batches, use your hands or a slotted spoon to lift prepared chicken from marinade, shake off any excess, and add to oil. Cook, stirring occasionally, until crispy and cooked through, about 4 minutes per batch. Using tongs or a heat-resistant slotted spoon, transfer chicken to prepared plate. Repeat this process with remaining chicken.

4 Discard frying oil. Return wok to high heat and add 2 tbsp. canola oil. When oil is hot, swirl to coat the wok, then add ginger and garlic. Stir-fry until aromatics are fragrant but not yet browned, about 20 seconds, then stir in chiles and cook until they begin to soften, plump, and turn a deep tobacco-brown color, 15–20 seconds more. Keeping your head away from the area above the stove, add chicken stock mixture (it will sizzle and steam up violently). Bring to a boil, then adjust heat to maintain a strong simmer. Cook, stirring occasionally, until sauce is thickened and glossy, 7–10 minutes. Return chicken to wok, stirring well to coat. Continue cooking until chicken is heated through, about 2 minutes more. Remove wok from heat, then transfer chicken to a serving platter. Drizzle with sesame oil (if using), top with scallions, and serve with rice.

DICED CHICKEN & PEANUTS SAUTEED WITH DRIED CHILES

Kong Bao Ji Ding

SERVES 4

This Sichuan dish—often better known by its Americanized name, "kung pao chicken"—is only moderately spicy.

- 1 tbsp. cornstarch
- 4 tbsp. light soy sauce
- 1 lb. boneless, skinless chicken breasts, cubed
- 3 tbsp. Shaoxing wine

- 2 tbsp. sugar
- 3 tbsp. chicken stock
- 4 tsp. black vinegar or balsamic vinegar
- 1 tbsp. sesame oil
- 2 tsp. dark soy sauce
- 3 tbsp. peanut oil
- 12 dried hot red chiles, stemmed, halved crosswise, and seeded
- 5 scallions, white part only, thickly sliced crosswise
- 1 large clove garlic, ends trimmed off and thinly sliced
- 1 ½″ piece fresh ginger, peeled and minced
- ½ cup shelled raw skinless peanuts
  Cooked white rice, for serving

1 Mix together cornstarch and 1 tbsp. light soy sauce in a medium bowl, add chicken, toss well, and set aside to marinate for 30 minutes. Meanwhile, mix together the remaining 3 tbsp. light soy sauce, wine, sugar, stock, vinegar, sesame oil, and dark soy sauce. Set aside.

2 Heat peanut oil in a wok or large nonstick skillet over high heat until just beginning to smoke. Add chiles, half the scallions, garlic, ginger, and chicken and stir-fry until chicken is golden, 3–5 minutes. Add soy sauce mixture and stir-fry until sauce thickens, about 2 minutes. Stir in peanuts. Garnish with remaining scallions and serve with rice.

STIR-FRIED CHICKEN WITH CELERY

Jirou Chao Qincai

SERVES 2–4

In this dish from Beijing, a mix of egg white and cornstarch coats the chicken and a quick blanching in a little oil in the wok preserves its succulence—a technique called velveting. The payoff comes when the chicken is reintroduced to the wok: the cornstarch–egg white coating soaks up the flavors of the aromatics, and the bright, crunchy celery contrasts beautifully with the silky texture and delicate taste of the chicken.

- 2 tsp. cornstarch
- 2 boneless, skinless chicken breasts, frozen for 20 minutes, halved lengthwise, and cut crosswise into ⅛″-thick strips
- 1 egg white
  Kosher salt, to taste
- 3 tbsp. canola oil
- 1½″ piece fresh ginger, peeled and julienned
- 1 leek, halved crosswise and julienned
- 5 ribs nan ling celery, cut on diagonal into ¼″-thick slices

1½ tbsp. light soy sauce
Cooked white rice, for serving

1 Combine cornstarch, chicken, egg white, and a pinch of salt in a medium bowl and toss vigorously to combine; set aside for 10 minutes.

2 Heat a 14″ wok (or stainless-steel skillet) over high heat until wok starts smoking. Add 2 tbsp. oil around edge of wok and swirl to coat the bottom and sides. Add chicken and cook, tossing constantly, until chicken is opaque, about 1–2 minutes. Transfer chicken to a plate and set aside.

3 Return wok to high heat and add remaining 1 tbsp. oil around edge of wok. Add ginger and leeks and cook, tossing constantly, until fragrant, about 30 seconds. Add celery and cook, tossing often, until crisp-tender, about 1 minute.

4 Return chicken and any juices from the plate to wok, along with soy sauce. Cook, tossing, until chicken is cooked, 1–2 minutes. Serve with rice.

HOLLYHOCK FRIED CHICKEN
SERVES 2–4

When preparing a chicken for frying, cook Tom Sheron of the Hollyhock Hill restaurant in Indianapolis halves the breast crosswise instead of lengthwise, leaving the wishbone intact. "It's the way fried chicken used to be cut," he says. In the same spirit, his recipe keeps things as simple and pure as possible.

1 3–4-lb. chicken, cut into 8 pieces
Kosher salt
Lard or vegetable shortening
2 cups flour

1 Season chicken generously with salt; transfer to a bowl and refrigerate, covered, for at least 1 hour or overnight.

2 Melt lard or shortening to a depth of ¾″ in a deep 12″ cast-iron skillet and heat over high heat until a deep-fry thermometer reads 350°.

3 Place flour on a plate. Dredge chicken in flour and fry, turning occasionally, until light brown, about 10 minutes. Reduce heat to medium; fry, turning occasionally, until golden brown and cooked through, about 10 minutes more. Transfer to a paper towel–lined plate. Serve immediately.

IZOLA'S FRIED CHICKEN
SERVES 4–6

Southern transplants to Chicago once considered Izola's restaurant a home base for real Southern cooking. Izola White, originally from Alabama, opened the restaurant in 1940, serving a no-nonsense fried chicken that always came out of the kitchen crispy and juicy. Although the restaurant closed in 2011, Izola's legend, and this unforgettable recipe, live on.

2 cups milk
2 eggs
3 cups flour
1 tbsp. garlic powder
Kosher salt and freshly ground black pepper, to taste
Canola oil
2 3½-lb. chickens, each cut into 8 pieces

1 Whisk together milk and eggs in a wide, deep dish; set aside. Whisk together flour, garlic powder, and salt and pepper in a second dish; set aside.

2 Pour oil into a large cast-iron skillet to a depth of 1″ and heat over medium to medium-high heat until a deep-fry thermometer reads 350°.

3 Working in batches of 3 or 4 pieces, season chicken with salt and pepper to taste, then coat in milk-egg mixture. Coat chicken well in flour mixture, shake off any excess, and fry, turning once at the halfway point, until deep golden brown and cooked through, 10–15 minutes a batch. Transfer to a paper towel–lined plate. Serve immediately.

NASHVILLE HOT CHICKEN
SERVES 2–4

For Nashville's iconic take on fried chicken, the bird is tenderized in spiced buttermilk a day ahead of time, twice-fried, and then slathered in a fiery paste. Adjust the heat by adding as much—or as little—cayenne as you like.

3 cups buttermilk
¾ cup cayenne pepper
9 tbsp. granulated garlic
9 tbsp. paprika
6 tbsp. onion powder
3 tbsp. sugar
1 2½–3-lb. chicken, cut into 8 pieces, or 3 lb. chicken wings

"The best comfort food will always be greens, corn bread, and fried chicken."

MAYA ANGELOU

Kosher salt and freshly ground black pepper
Canola oil, for frying

2 cups self-rising flour

6 tbsp. unsalted butter, melted
Sliced white sandwich bread and dill pickle chips, for serving

1 Combine buttermilk, ¼ cup cayenne, 3 tbsp. each granulated garlic and paprika, 2 tbsp. onion powder, and 1 tbsp. sugar in a bowl; whisk until smooth. Add chicken and toss to coat; cover and refrigerate for at least 4 hours or up to overnight.

2 The next day, drain chicken, rinse, and pat dry; season with salt and pepper. Heat 2″ oil in a 6-qt. saucepan until a deep-fry thermometer reads 300°. Stir together remaining cayenne, granulated garlic, paprika, onion powder, and sugar in a bowl; transfer half to another bowl and whisk in flour. Working in batches, dredge chicken in flour mixture, then fry, flipping once, until golden and almost cooked through, 6–7 minutes or until a deep-fry thermometer inserted into the thickest part of a thigh reads 150°. Transfer chicken to paper towels.

3 Increase oil temperature to 350°. Stir together remaining cayenne mixture and melted butter in a bowl; set paste aside. Dredge chicken once more in flour mixture and fry until cooked through, 2–3 minutes more; drain briefly on paper towels and brush with reserved paste. Serve with bread and pickles.

BUFFALO WINGS

SERVES 4 (SEE PHOTO, PAGE 218)

For residents of Buffalo, New York, true Buffalo wings come only from Frank and Teressa's Anchor Bar, where owner Teressa Bellissimo invented the dish in 1964. There, wings are fried, then tossed in a combination of melted margarine and hot sauce. Today, the Anchor Bar serves two thousand pounds of wings each day.

Peanut oil, for frying

4 lb. chicken wings, separated into 2 pieces, wing tips removed

¾ cup margarine

1 cup hot sauce, preferably Frank's Red Hot Original Cayenne Pepper Sauce

1⅓ cups Blue Cheese Dressing (page 76)

4 ribs celery, halved lengthwise, then cut crosswise into 3″ sticks

1 Heat oven to 200°. Pour oil to a depth of 2″ into a 6-qt. Dutch oven and heat over medium heat until a deep-fry thermometer reads 350°. Dry wings thoroughly with paper towels. Working in batches, fry wings until golden brown and cooked through, about 12 minutes. Transfer wings to a wire rack set over a baking sheet, and place in oven to keep warm until all wings are fried.

2 Heat margarine in a 12″ deep-sided skillet over medium heat; stir in hot sauce until smooth. Add wings and toss until completely coated. Serve wings in a large bowl with dressing and celery on the side.

KOREAN FRIED CHICKEN WINGS

Yangnyeom Dak

SERVES 2–4

The secret to achieving the delicate crackly crust that is the hallmark of this popular Korean specialty is double-frying the wings. Doing so creates a crisp-fried exterior that holds up well to the sweet-spicy sauce—Korea's answer to American-style barbecue sauce—in which the chicken is tossed before it's served.

FOR THE SAUCE

5 cloves garlic

1 1½″ piece fresh ginger, peeled

3 tbsp. soy sauce

3 tbsp. gochujang (Korean chile paste)

1½ tbsp. rice vinegar

1 tbsp. sesame oil

1 tbsp. honey

FOR THE CHICKEN

Canola oil, for frying

⅔ cup flour

1 tbsp. cornstarch

1¾ lb. chicken wings

THE OTHER KFC

Twice-fried sweet-spicy chicken has long been a favorite in Korean homes and eateries. Today, fast food versions of the dish have a global following. The key to its perfection lies in precision frying.

When an order comes in at the popular restaurant chain Kyochon, a cook takes a batch of unseasoned wings and drumsticks—pared from small, fresh chickens and chilled overnight to decrease their moisture before frying—and dunks them in a thin batter of wheat flour, water, and cornstarch.

Then he gives the wings and drumsticks a nine-minute sizzle in a deep-fryer containing 356-degree canola oil, which cooks the meat and forms a light crust.

Next, he tosses the chicken in a wire sieve to shake off loose bits of fried batter before plunging it into a second fryer, which contains oil left over from the previous day; the darker oil gives the skin a deeper flavor and hue.

Three minutes later, the chicken emerges with a delicate texture and crackly crust. Finally, he brushes on the sauce. What emerges is a habit-forming finger food, with a flavor that's nothing short of explosive.

1 Make the sauce: Chop garlic and ginger in a food processor. Add soy, gochujang, vinegar, sesame oil, and honey and purée until smooth. Transfer to a large bowl.

2 Make the chicken: Pour oil to a depth of 2″ into a 6-qt. pot. Heat over medium-high heat until a deep-fry thermometer reads 350°. Whisk flour, cornstarch, and ⅔ cup water in another bowl. Add chicken and toss well. Working in 3 batches, fry chicken until golden, 6–8 minutes. Drain on paper towels. Return oil to 350°. Fry chicken until crisp, 6–8 minutes more. Drain again. Toss hot chicken wings in sauce before serving.

BEIJING-STYLE CHICKEN WINGS
Mi Zhi Ji Chi Chuan
SERVES 4

These crisp-skinned, deeply savory wings get their tingly, mouth-numbing heat from Sichuan peppercorns.

- 5 tbsp. soy sauce
- 4 tbsp. peanut oil
- 4 tbsp. Sichuan peppercorns, lightly crushed
- 2 tsp. coarsely ground black pepper, plus more to taste
- 2 tsp. honey
- 2 tsp. sesame oil
- 8 cloves garlic, finely chopped
- 2 scallions, finely chopped
- 1 2″ piece fresh ginger, peeled and finely chopped
   Kosher salt, to taste
- 2 lb. chicken wings, tips removed
- 6 12″ bamboo skewers, soaked in water for 30 minutes
- ¼ cup brown rice vinegar
- 2 tbsp. sesame-chile oil

1 Stir together 4 tbsp. soy, 1 tbsp. peanut oil, half the Sichuan peppercorns, 2 tsp. black pepper, honey, toasted sesame oil, two-thirds of the garlic, scallions, ginger, and salt in a bowl. Add chicken wings and toss to coat. Cover and refrigerate for at least 4 hours or up to overnight.

2 Build a hot fire in a charcoal grill or set a gas grill to high; bank coals or turn off burner on one side for indirect grilling (page 191). Remove chicken from marinade and, working in batches, thread 2 wings lengthwise onto each skewer; set aside. Strain marinade into a 1-qt. saucepan, discarding solids; bring to a boil and remove from heat. Brush chicken with remaining 3 tbsp. peanut oil and season with salt and pepper. Grill wings on hottest part of grill, brushing often with marinade and turning as needed, until charred in spots and cooked through, 12–15 minutes. If outside starts to burn before wings are cooked, move to cooler section of grill until done. Whisk remaining 1 tbsp. soy and garlic, pepper to taste, vinegar, and sesame-chile oil in a bowl; drizzle over wings.

SUTTON'S CHICKEN
SERVES 4

This hearty preparation of fried chicken breasts with country ham and redeye gravy over grits was inspired by Charleston restaurateur Ruth Fales' memories of meals served on her family's working farm in rural Hartsville, South Carolina. Serve with fried okra (page 322).

2 eggs
4 boneless, skinless chicken breast halves
1 cup flour
1 cup cornmeal
2 tbsp. vegetable oil
4 thin slices country ham
1 cup chicken stock
1 cup strong black coffee
2 tbsp. butter
¼ cup heavy cream
¼ cup chopped scallions
Kosher salt and freshly ground black pepper
Prepared grits (page 401), for serving

1 Whisk together eggs with an equal amount of water in a wide, deep dish; set aside. Dust chicken with flour, then coat in egg wash. Dredge chicken in cornmeal until well coated.

2 Heat oil in a large skillet over medium-high heat. Fry chicken until golden-brown, 5–7 minutes on each side. Place a ham slice on top of each chicken breast, then turn carefully so ham is on the bottom. Lower heat to medium-low and cook until ham has crisped around the edges and chicken is cooked through, about 5 minutes more. Remove chicken and ham from skillet and place on a large plate; cover chicken with foil to keep warm.

3 Add stock and coffee to the skillet with the drippings, increase heat to medium-high, and reduce by half, about 10 minutes. Lower heat to medium-low, stir in butter and cream, and cook, stirring, until gravy is thickened, about 3 minutes. Stir in scallions and season with salt and pepper. To serve, divide grits among 4 plates. Top grits with chicken, ham side up, and douse with gravy.

MITZI'S CHICKEN FINGERS

SERVES 6

At the restaurant Mitzi's in Winnipeg, Canada, these chicken fingers are served with crinkle-cut fries, coleslaw, and a honey-dill dipping sauce. They're so good that even grown-ups line up for them.

FOR THE DIPPING SAUCE
1½ cups mayonnaise
¼ cup honey
2 tbsp. roughly chopped fresh dill
2 tbsp. fresh lemon juice
1 tbsp. dry mustard powder
Kosher salt and freshly ground black pepper, to taste

FOR THE CHICKEN FINGERS
2 lb. boneless, skinless chicken breasts, cut into 3" × 1" strips
1 tbsp. sugar
1 tbsp. kosher salt
1 tbsp. freshly ground black pepper
1½ tsp. garlic powder
1 tsp. paprika
1 tsp. dry mustard
1 cup flour
4 eggs, lightly beaten
3 cups finely ground dried bread crumbs or panko
Canola oil, for frying

1 Make the dipping sauce: In a medium bowl, whisk together the mayonnaise, honey, dill, lemon juice, and mustard. Season with salt and pepper and stir together until smooth; set aside.

2 Make the chicken fingers: In a medium bowl, toss together chicken, sugar, salt, pepper, garlic powder, paprika, and mustard; set aside. Place flour, eggs, and bread crumbs in 3 separate shallow dishes; set aside. Pour oil to a depth of 2" into a 6-qt. Dutch oven and heat over medium-high heat until a deep-fry thermometer reads 325°. Working in batches, coat chicken in flour, shaking off excess; dip in eggs, then coat in bread crumbs. Fry chicken until golden brown and crisp, about 3 minutes. Transfer to paper towels to drain. Repeat with remaining chicken. Serve with dipping sauce.

COUNTRY CAPTAIN

SERVES 4

This curried chicken dish is a Southern Lowcountry classic whose name harks back to the days when ships' captains in port cities like Charleston, South Carolina, and Savannah, Georgia, traded in spices acquired during their travels abroad.

1 3–4-lb. chicken, cut into 8 pieces
1 tsp. dried thyme
Kosher salt and freshly ground black pepper, to taste
¼ cup canola oil
6 slices bacon, chopped
4 cloves garlic, finely chopped
3 ribs celery, chopped
2 green bell peppers, seeded and chopped
1 large yellow onion, chopped
1 28-oz. can whole, peeled tomatoes, chopped; ¾ cup juice reserved

3 tbsp. curry powder
2 tbsp. unsalted butter
⅓ cup currants, plus more for garnish
2 bay leaves
  Crushed roasted peanuts, for garnish
  Cooked white rice, for serving

1 Rub chicken with thyme, salt, and pepper. Heat oil in a 5-qt. Dutch oven over high heat. Add chicken, skin side down, and cook, turning once, until golden brown, about 12 minutes. Using tongs, transfer chicken to a plate and set aside.

2 Discard oil and return Dutch oven to medium heat. Add bacon and cook, stirring occasionally, until crisp, about 7 minutes. Using a slotted spoon, transfer bacon to a paper towel–lined plate; set aside. Add garlic, celery, peppers, and onions to the pot and cook, stirring occasionally, until soft, about 10 minutes. Add tomatoes and their juice and cook, stirring frequently, until the juice thickens, about 10 minutes. Stir in the curry powder, butter, currants, and bay leaves and season with salt and pepper. Reduce heat to medium-low, cover, and simmer, stirring occasionally, until mixture thickens into a chunky sauce, about 30 minutes.

3 Heat oven to 325°. Add the reserved chicken to the pot, nestling it into the curry sauce; spoon some of the sauce over chicken. Cover and cook until chicken is very tender, about 1¼ hours. Discard bay leaves. Garnish with reserved bacon, more currants, and peanuts and serve with rice.

DOLORES' BROKENHEARTED CHICKEN
SERVES 4

Caramelized garlic and dry sherry make a luscious sauce for this simple but delectable braised chicken dish. The name refers to Dolores, a fruit vendor in the Spanish city of Cádiz, who proclaimed that the recipe was good enough to make you hungry even if you have a broken heart. We're inclined to agree.

½ cup flour
1 3-lb. chicken, cut into 8 pieces
  Kosher salt and freshly ground
  black pepper, to taste
2 slices bacon, roughly chopped

3 tbsp. olive oil
5 cloves garlic, thinly sliced
1 cup chicken stock
½ cup dry sherry
2 tbsp. roughly chopped fresh flat-leaf parsley
2 tbsp. unsalted butter, cut into ¼" cubes
  Country bread, for serving

1 Heat oven to 350°. Place flour in a bowl. Season chicken with salt and pepper and dredge in flour; set aside. Heat bacon in a 12″ ovenproof skillet over medium-high heat and cook, stirring, until its fat renders, about 4 minutes. Using a slotted spoon, transfer bacon to a bowl; set aside. Add oil to skillet, add half of the chicken, and cook, turning once, until browned on both sides, about 12 minutes. Transfer to a plate and repeat with remaining chicken.

2 Add garlic to the skillet and cook, stirring, until golden brown, about 2 minutes. Add stock and sherry and return chicken, skin side up, to the skillet; sprinkle with reserved bacon along with parsley and then dot with butter. Transfer skillet to oven and cook, basting twice during cooking, until chicken is cooked through and tender, about 40 minutes. Serve with country bread.

MUSTARD & WHITE WINE BRAISED CHICKEN
SERVES 4

An adaptation of a regional French classic, this version swaps out the traditional Dijon in favor of a grainy, seeded mustard, for a milder flavor and a more enticing texture.

2 tbsp. olive oil
2 lb. chicken thighs and drumsticks
  Kosher salt and freshly ground black pepper
4 shallots, halved lengthwise and thinly sliced
3 cloves garlic, thinly sliced
½ cup dry white wine
1 cup chicken stock
¼ cup whole-grain mustard
1 tbsp. finely chopped fresh thyme
2 tbsp. roughly chopped fresh tarragon, for garnish

1 Heat oven to 375°. Heat oil in a 6-qt. saucepan over medium-high heat. Season chicken with salt and pepper. Working in batches, cook chicken, flipping once, until browned, about 10 minutes. Transfer chicken to a plate; set aside. Add shallots and garlic to pan and cook, stirring occasionally, until golden, 3–5 minutes. Add wine, stock, mustard, and thyme and bring to a boil. Return chicken to the pan with any juices, cover with a lid, and transfer to the oven. Bake until chicken is cooked through, about 45 minutes or until an instant-read thermometer inserted into the thickest part of a thigh reads 165°.

2 Transfer chicken to a serving platter and keep warm. Return pan to stove top and bring to a boil. Cook, stirring occasionally, until reduced by half, 8–10 minutes. Spoon sauce over chicken and garnish with tarragon.

COQ AU VIN

SERVES 4–6

This winey chicken braise dotted with pearl onions and button mushrooms is often one of the first French dishes American cooks make, and no wonder: It's as simple to prepare as it is delicious.

- 4 cups red wine
- 1 3–4-lb. chicken, cut into 8 pieces
- 1 large onion, halved and thinly sliced lengthwise
- 1 Bouquet Garni (page 86)
- 2 tbsp. olive oil
- 10 oz. pearl onions, peeled
- ¾ lb. white button mushrooms, quartered
- 10 oz. bacon, cut into ½" pieces
- 3 tbsp. unsalted butter
  Kosher salt and freshly ground black pepper, to taste
- 2 tbsp. flour
- 1 cup chicken stock
  Finely chopped fresh flat-leaf parsley, for garnish

1 Combine wine, chicken, yellow onion, and bouquet garni in a bowl; cover with plastic wrap and marinate in the refrigerator for at least 4 hours or up to overnight. Drain chicken, onions, and bouquet garni, reserving wine, and set aside. Dry chicken thoroughly with paper towels.

2 Heat oil in a 6-qt. Dutch oven over medium-high heat. Add pearl onions and cook, stirring often, until lightly browned and tender, about 8 minutes. Using a slotted spoon, transfer to a bowl and set aside. Add mushrooms to pot and cook, stirring, until they release all their moisture

and brown lightly, about 8 minutes. Transfer to bowl with pearl onions; set aside. Add bacon to pot and cook, stirring, until it renders its fat and is crisp, about 10 minutes. Using a slotted spoon, transfer to paper towels to drain; set aside. Add 1 tbsp. butter to pot, season chicken with salt and pepper, and then add to pot. Cook, turning once, until browned on both sides, about 10 minutes. Transfer to a plate and set aside. Add drained yellow onions to pot and cook, stirring, until soft, about 10 minutes. Add flour and cook, stirring, until smooth, about 2 minutes. Stir in reserved wine and stock and then return chicken to pot along with bouquet garni; bring to a boil. Reduce heat to medium-low and cook, covered and stirring occasionally, until chicken is tender, about 15 minutes.

3 Remove from heat, and stir in pearl onions and mushrooms. Divide between serving bowls, and garnish with reserved bacon and parsley.

ROOSTER & GOOD RED WINE

The main reason Burgundians traditionally don't make *coq au vin* with chicken is probably that they'd consider it a waste. They know their birds, be they the renowned *poulets de Bresse* or any other local fowl, and they know that the best way to cook full-grown chickens is to roast them; that smaller birds are usually best cut up and sautéed or grilled; and that poussins, or baby chickens, are delicious roasted or braised whole. The tough old rooster, on the other hand, is all but inedible unless cooked for three or four hours in an acidic liquid (like wine). Beyond the wine, though, recipes vary. Traditionally, the dish's rich sauce is thickened with the bird's own blood—a practice frowned upon in this country, for reasons of health and squeamishness—and sometimes also with mashed-up rooster (or chicken) livers. Some chefs perfume the dish with cloves, or add sugar. To color the sauce, they might even stir in some unsweetened cocoa powder.

HAINANESE CHICKEN RICE

SERVES 4

Despite its name, a reference to the Chinese island of Hainan, this dish is remarkably common in Singapore, where it can be found at restaurants and food stalls all over the city. The combination of chicken, broth, and rice makes for a hearty meal.

FOR THE CHICKEN & STOCK

- 1 3-lb. chicken
  Kosher salt
- 1 small piece fresh ginger, peeled and crushed
- 2 cloves garlic, crushed
- 1 scallion, tied in a knot

FOR THE RICE

- 1½ cups jasmine or other long-grain white rice
- 2 tbsp. vegetable oil
- 3 shallots, finely chopped
- 5 cloves garlic, finely chopped
  Kosher salt, to taste
- 1 cucumber, sliced, for garnish
- 1 tomato, sliced, for garnish
- 1 carrot, sliced, for garnish
  Fresh cilantro leaves, for garnish

1 Make the chicken and stock: Sprinkle chicken with salt inside and out. Tuck ginger, garlic, and scallion into cavity of chicken, then tie legs together with kitchen string.

2 Bring 5 qt. water to a boil in a large pot over high heat. Completely submerge chicken, breast side down. Bring to a boil again, cover pot, and turn heat down to very low. Simmer for 30 minutes, turning chicken once and skimming any foam from stock. Remove chicken and set aside to cool; reserve stock, keeping it warm. Remove chicken skin; pull meat from bones and cut into thick slices.

3 Make the rice: Wash rice in a large bowl of cold water and drain. Repeat process until water is almost clear. Drain in colander and shake to remove as much remaining water as you can.

4 Heat oil in a wok or medium skillet over high heat. Add shallots and garlic and stir-fry for 30 seconds. Add rice and stir-fry for 1–2 minutes more. Pour in 3 cups chicken stock and season with salt. Bring to a boil over high heat, cover, reduce heat to very low, and cook for 20 minutes. Stir, cover, and let rest for 5 minutes. Serve the chicken accompanied with the rice and broth in separate small bowls with garnishes on the side.

ARROZ CON POLLO

Chicken with Rice

SERVES 8

This simple one-pot Latin American classic is bursting with flavor, thanks to a robust array of spices like cumin, allspice, and thyme, with briny olives and capers for good measure.

- ½ cup olive oil
- 1½ lb. boneless, skinless chicken thighs
  Kosher salt and freshly ground black pepper, to taste
- 8 cloves garlic, minced
- 1 medium white onion, finely chopped
- 1 red bell pepper, seeded and minced
- 1 habanero chile, stemmed, seeded, and minced (optional)
- 3 tbsp. tomato paste
- 2 tsp. ground cumin
- 1 tsp. ground annatto
- 1 tsp. ground allspice
- 3 tbsp. finely chopped fresh thyme leaves
- 1 bay leaf
- 1 12-oz. bottle lager beer
- 1 15-oz. can whole, peeled tomatoes, crushed by hand
- 2¾ cups chicken stock
- 1½ cups long-grain white rice, rinsed, drained, and soaked in cold water for 1 hour
- ⅓ cup pimiento-stuffed Spanish olives, thinly sliced
- ¼ cup large Spanish capers, rinsed and drained
- ¼ cup minced fresh cilantro
- 3 tbsp. fresh lime juice

1 Heat oven to 350°. Heat oil in an 8-qt. Dutch oven over medium-high heat. Season chicken with salt and pepper, then cook, flipping once, until browned and almost cooked through, 8–10 minutes. Transfer to a plate; let cool, then shred and set aside.

2 Add garlic, onions, bell pepper, and chile (if using) to the pot and cook until soft, 6–8 minutes. Add tomato paste, cumin, annatto, allspice, thyme, and bay and cook until slightly caramelized, about 2 minutes. Add beer and cook, stirring, until reduced by half, about 6 minutes. Add tomatoes and stock and bring to a boil. Add reserved chicken along with rice, then cover and bake until rice is tender, about 30 minutes.

3 Uncover pot and stir in olives, capers, cilantro, and lime juice and season with salt and pepper.

MOLE NEGRO

Black Mole Sauce with Chicken

MAKES 3 CUPS

Nuts, chocolate, herbs, and spices all impart color to this mole, but it's the charring of the stems and seeds of the chiles that really gives it the dark hue. One of the seven classic moles of Oaxaca, Mexico, this sauce is typically served over chicken.

FOR THE CHICKEN

1	3–4-lb. whole chicken, cut into 8 pieces
½	cup chopped fresh cilantro stems
2	tbsp. kosher salt
1	tsp. black peppercorns
2	cloves garlic, chopped
1	large onion, chopped
1	bay leaf

FOR THE MOLE

10	dried guajillo chiles, washed
7	dried mulato negro chiles, washed
7	dried pasilla chiles, washed
4	tbsp. corn oil
1	6″ square dry bread
8	cloves garlic, peeled
1	small white onion, quartered
2	whole cloves
1	tsp. ground canela (Mexican cinnamon) or cinnamon
1	tsp. ground anise
3	black peppercorns
4	whole allspice
1	large plantain, peeled and cut into chunks
2	prunes, pitted
1	oz. bittersweet chocolate, melted
1	oz. almonds
1	oz. sesame seeds, toasted until golden
⅓	cup raisins

1 Make the chicken: Place chicken, cilantro, salt, peppercorns, garlic, onion, bay leaf, and 12 cups water in a 6-qt. saucepan and bring to a boil; reduce heat to medium-low and cook, covered and stirring occasionally, until chicken is tender, about 30 minutes.

2 Remove chicken from saucepan and strain liquid through a fine sieve; reserve 4 cups and save remaining liquid for another use. Set chicken and liquid aside.

3 Make the mole: Stem, seed, and devein chiles, reserving everything. Sear stems, seeds, and ribs in a cast-iron skillet over high heat until charred black. (Don't worry, this is a secret of real mole, but avoid breathing smoke or getting it in your eyes.) Cool, then rinse in a fine sieve to wash out white ashes, which are bitter. Set aside.

4 In the same pan, heat 2 tbsp. of the oil and brown bread on both sides. Remove from pan. Add 1 tbsp. oil, add garlic and onions and cook until tender and golden, 3–5 minutes. Set aside.

5 Soak chiles in 3 cups very hot water until soft. Meanwhile, mix cloves, canela, anise, peppercorns, and allspice. Using a spice mill or mortar and pestle, grind spices finely. Combine charred stems, seeds, ribs, chiles (reserve soaking water), garlic and onions, ground spices, plantain, prunes, chocolate, almonds, sesame seeds, raisins, and bread. Using the food grinder attachment on an electric mixer or a blender, grind in small batches until very smooth. Use soaking water as needed to process the mole into a thick paste.

6 Put paste in a nonstick pan brushed with remaining 1 tbsp. oil. Fry paste until thick, fragrant, and slightly golden on all surfaces, about 20 minutes. It should be a dense, dry, toasty-looking smooth paste. Cool, then refrigerate or freeze until needed. Thin with chicken cooking liquid to a sauce consistency. Serve over reserved chicken.

MOLE VERDE ZACATECANO

Zacatecas-Style Green Mole with Chicken

SERVES 6

This Zacatecan version of mole, unlike the better-known nut- and chocolate-enriched variants from Puebla and Oaxaca (like Mole Negro, page 170), is bright and simple, thanks to fresh tomatillos, cilantro, jalapeños, and garlic. Serve with Mexican rice and tortillas.

FOR THE CHICKEN

1	3–4-lb. whole chicken, cut into 8 pieces
½	cup chopped fresh cilantro stems
2	tbsp. kosher salt
1	tsp. whole black peppercorns
2	cloves garlic, chopped
1	large onion, chopped
1	bay leaf

FOR THE MOLE

½	lb. tomatillos, husked, rinsed, and chopped
2	jalapeños, stemmed and chopped

½ cup fresh cilantro leaves
2 tbsp. kosher salt, plus more to taste
2 cloves garlic, chopped
2 8″ flour tortillas, toasted
3 tbsp. canola oil

1 Make the chicken: Place chicken, cilantro, salt, peppercorns, garlic, onion, bay leaf, and 12 cups water in a 6-qt. saucepan and bring to a boil; reduce heat to medium-low and cook, covered and stirring occasionally, until chicken is tender, about 30 minutes.

2 Remove chicken from saucepan and strain liquid through a fine sieve; reserve 4 cups and save remaining liquid for another use. Set chicken and liquid aside.

3 Make the mole: Heat tomatillos and jalapeños in a 4-qt. saucepan over medium heat and cook, stirring occasionally, until darkened and thick, about 10 minutes. Transfer to a blender with cilantro, salt, garlic, tortillas, and 1 cup reserved cooking liquid; purée.

4 Heat oil in a 6-qt. saucepan over medium-high heat. Add tomatillo sauce and fry, stirring constantly, until it thickens into a paste, about 5 minutes. Whisk in remaining cooking liquid and bring to a boil. Reduce heat to medium-low and cook, stirring, until reduced and thickened, about 30 minutes. Add chicken pieces and cook until heated through, about 10 minutes.

CHICKEN IN TRUFFLE CREAM SAUCE

Poulet aux Truffes à la Crème

SERVES 6

While researching black truffles in Provence, food writer Peggy Knickerbocker was served this hearty dish by private chef Henri Sanègre. No truffles on hand? No matter. The recipe is delicious even without them.

1 4–5-lb. chicken, cut into 8 pieces
4 onions, quartered
2 750-ml bottles dry white wine
 Kosher salt, to taste
1 Bouquet Garni (page 86)
3 medium Yukon gold potatoes, peeled and quartered
3 medium carrots, trimmed and halved lengthwise
3 medium leeks, white part only, trimmed, halved lengthwise
12 pearl onions, peeled

2 tbsp. butter
2 tbsp. flour
½ cup heavy cream
½ cup fresh flat-leaf parsley leaves, finely chopped
1 medium fresh black truffle, cleaned
 Pinch of freshly grated nutmeg
6 sprigs fresh rosemary

1 Put chicken, onions, wine, and 2 large pinches salt into a large pot. Add enough cold water to cover and bring to a boil over high heat, skimming any foam as it appears. Reduce heat to medium-low, add bouquet garni, and poach, partially covered, until chicken is cooked through, 40–50 minutes. Transfer chicken to a platter, cover with foil, and keep warm in oven set at lowest setting. Remove onions and bouquet garni from stock with a slotted spoon and discard.

2 Add potatoes, carrots, leeks, and pearl onions to pot with stock. Increase heat to medium and simmer until vegetables are soft, 20–30 minutes. Transfer vegetables to platter with chicken, cover, and return to oven to keep warm. Keep stock warm over low heat.

3 Melt butter in a saucepan over medium heat. Add flour and cook, stirring, for 2 minutes. Whisk in 1½ cups of the stock (save the rest for another use). Add cream and parsley and simmer, stirring, until sauce thickens, 3–5 minutes. Grate truffles on large holes of a box grater, then add to sauce. Add nutmeg and season to taste with salt. Divide chicken and vegetables among 6 plates, spoon sauce over chicken, and garnish each with a rosemary sprig.

CHICKEN & ONION CURRY

Murgh Dopiaza

SERVES 6

The word *dopiaza,* which means "two onions" in the South Asian language Urdu, refers to the large quantity of onions that's typically used in this style of curry.

4 large sweet onions, such as Walla Walla
6 cloves garlic
1 1½″ piece fresh ginger, peeled
7 tbsp. canola oil
5 tbsp. tomato paste
1 tbsp. ground coriander
1 tbsp. ground cumin
½ tsp. ground turmeric
½ tsp. cayenne pepper

¼ cup plain yogurt

6 whole, peeled canned tomatoes, drained and crushed by hand

1 3–4-lb. chicken, cut into 8 pieces, skin removed
Kosher salt, to taste

½ tsp. garam masala

1 tbsp. chopped fresh cilantro

3 serrano chiles, stemmed and quartered
Cooked basmati rice, for serving

1 Roughly chop 2 onions; put into a food processor with garlic and ginger. Process to a paste; set aside. Thinly slice remaining 2 onions; set aside.

2 Heat oil in an 8-qt. pot over medium-high heat. Add sliced onions and cook, stirring often, until well browned, 18–20 minutes. Using a slotted spoon, transfer onions to a bowl. Add reserved onion-garlic paste to pot and cook, stirring, until golden brown, 8–10 minutes. Add tomato paste, coriander, cumin, turmeric, and cayenne and cook until paste is browned, 1–2 minutes. Add yogurt, tomatoes, and chicken, season with salt, and cook, stirring, until browned, 3–4 minutes. Cover, turn heat to low, and simmer, stirring occasionally, until chicken is fully cooked, about 20 minutes.

3 Increase heat to medium-high, uncover, add sautéed onions and garam masala, and cook, stirring, until sauce thickens slightly, about 8 minutes. Stir in cilantro and chiles and serve with rice.

KENYAN COCONUT CHICKEN STEW

Kuku Wa Nazi

SERVES 4

Coconut milk–based chicken stews are found in equatorial regions around the world, including Kenya, from where this dish hails. This recipe was given to us by Lela Abdulaziz, a home cook in Mombasa.

¼ cup canola oil

1½ tsp. ground turmeric

4 cloves garlic, minced

4 pili pili or red bird's eye chiles, stemmed, seeded, and minced

4 plum tomatoes, cored and minced

1 medium red onion, minced

4 bone-in chicken thighs, skin removed

4 bone-in chicken drumsticks, skin removed

¼ cup fresh lime juice

2 14-oz. cans coconut milk

Kosher salt and freshly ground black pepper
Cooked basmati rice, for serving

1 Heat oil in a 6-qt. pot over medium-high heat. Add turmeric, garlic, chiles, tomatoes, and onions and cook, stirring often, until the onions are caramelized, 20–25 minutes. Add chicken to pot along with lime juice and coconut milk. Bring mixture to a boil and reduce heat to medium-low; simmer, stirring occasionally, until chicken is tender, about 30 minutes. Season with salt and pepper.

2 To serve, divide rice into serving bowls and spoon chicken and sauce over rice. Season with more black pepper before serving.

CHICKEN PAPRIKASH

Paprikás Csirke

SERVES 4–6

Chicken is braised in a brick red, paprika-laced sauce in this elemental Hungarian dish, perhaps the Eastern European nation's best-known culinary export.

¼ cup lard or canola oil

1 3–4-lb. chicken, cut into 8 pieces
Kosher salt and freshly ground black pepper, to taste

1 large yellow onion, minced

3 tbsp. Hungarian sweet paprika, plus more for garnish

2 cups chicken stock

2 plum tomatoes, seeded and cut into 1″ pieces

1 cubanelle pepper, seeded and cut into 1″ pieces

½ cup sour cream, for serving

1 Melt lard or heat oil in a 6-qt. saucepan over medium-high heat. Season chicken with salt and pepper. Working in batches, cook, flipping once, until browned, 8–10 minutes. Transfer chicken to a plate; set aside.

2 Add onion to pan and cook, stirring occasionally, until soft, about 8 minutes. Add paprika and cook, stirring, for 2 minutes.

3 Return chicken and its juices to pan. Add stock, tomatoes, and cubanelle pepper and bring to a boil. Reduce heat to medium-low and simmer, partially covered, until chicken is fully cooked, about 30 minutes. Transfer chicken and sauce to a serving platter. Spoon sour cream over top and garnish with more paprika.

CHICKEN, OLIVE & LEMON TAGINE

Djaj Mqualli

SERVES 6

Tagine, the Moroccan stew, shares its name with the terra-cotta pot it's traditionally cooked in, whose neat conical lid promotes convection and even cooking. There are many versions of the stew; maybe the most classic is this combination of braised chicken, green olives, and lemons in a sauce fragrant with ginger and coriander.

- 3 tbsp. olive oil
- 6 whole chicken legs
  Kosher salt and freshly ground black pepper, to taste
- 2 large yellow onions, sliced
- 2 tbsp. ground coriander
- 2 tsp. ground white pepper
- 2 tsp. ground ginger
- 1 tsp. ground turmeric
- ½ tsp. crushed saffron threads
- 1½ cups chicken stock
- 1¼ cups green olives, cracked
- 2 tbsp. unsalted butter
- 1 tbsp. finely chopped fresh flat-leaf parsley
- 2 tsp. finely chopped fresh cilantro
- 2 Preserved Lemons (page 580, or store-bought), cut into slices
  Cooked rice or flatbread, for serving

1 Heat oven to 350°. Heat oil in a large tagine or an 8-qt. Dutch oven over medium-high heat. Season chicken with salt and pepper, add to pot, and cook, turning, until browned, 12–15 minutes. Transfer chicken to a plate.

2 Add onions to pot and cook until golden, 10–12 minutes. Add spices; cook for 2 minutes. Return chicken to pot with stock and bring to a boil.

3 Bake chicken, covered, until tender, 35–40 minutes. Stir olives, butter, parsley, cilantro, and lemons into pot and cook for 6 minutes. Serve with rice or flatbread.

ETHIOPIAN CHICKEN STEW

Doro Wot

SERVES 6

This long-cooking braised chicken dish is emblematic of Ethiopian cuisine. The spiced butter and *berbere* spice mix are essential to the dish's earthy, layered flavors. It's best served with *injera,* the spongy Ethiopian flatbread, though it's also good with rice.

- 4 tbsp. Nit'r qibe (page 595), Ghee (page 595), or melted butter
- 2½ tbsp. peeled and minced fresh ginger
- 5 small red onions, finely chopped
- 5 cloves garlic, minced
- 3 tbsp. Berbere (page 586)
- 1 plum tomato, chopped
- ¾ tsp. ground cardamom
- 8 chicken drumsticks
  Kosher salt and freshly ground black pepper, to taste
- 4 hard-cooked eggs
  Injera (page 460) or cooked white rice, for serving

1 Heat spiced butter in a 6-qt. saucepan over low heat. Add ginger, onions, and garlic and cook, stirring, until soft, about 30 minutes. Add spice mixture and tomato and cook, stirring, until reduced and darkened, about 15 minutes.

2 Add 4 cups water, cardamom, and chicken, seasoning with salt and pepper. Bring to a boil, then reduce heat to medium-low and cook, covered, until chicken is tender, about 1 hour.

3 Transfer chicken to a plate. Cook sauce until reduced, about 15 minutes. Add eggs and warm. Pour reduced sauce over chicken. Serve with flatbread or rice.

CREAMY CHICKEN CURRY

Murgh Korma

SERVES 6–8

Chicken korma is a beloved Indian recipe that came by way of the Moghuls (the Muslim rulers of much of India from the 16th to 19th centuries). The meat is lightly browned, then simmered in yogurt with puréed almonds and cashew nuts, which give the dish its characteristic creaminess. But what makes it really special are the fragrant spices.

- 2 lb. boneless, skinless chicken thighs and breasts, cut into 2″ chunks
- 1 tbsp. plus 1 tsp. minced fresh ginger, plus one 2″ piece, peeled and sliced
- 1 tbsp. minced garlic, plus 3 cloves, thinly sliced
- 1 tbsp. fresh lemon juice
  Kosher salt, to taste
- ¼ cup blanched almonds
- ¼ cup raw cashews
- 1 tbsp. poppy seeds
- ¾ cup canola oil

1 tbsp. black peppercorns
2 tsp. fennel seeds
12 dried rose petals (optional)
3 green cardamom pods
2 whole cloves
1 bay leaf
½ stick cinnamon
3 large yellow onions, thinly sliced
3 green serrano chiles, stemmed
and minced
1 tsp. ground turmeric
½ tsp. paprika
1 cup plain yogurt
6 tbsp. heavy cream
Cooked white rice, for serving

1 Toss chicken, 1 tbsp. minced ginger, minced garlic, lemon juice, and salt in a bowl; chill for 1 hour.

2 Purée almonds, cashews, poppy seeds, and ⅓ cup water in a blender to make a nut paste. Set aside.

3 Heat ½ cup oil in a 6-qt. saucepan over medium-high heat. Add peppercorns, fennel, rose petals, cardamom, cloves, bay leaf, and cinnamon and cook until toasted, about 2 minutes. Add sliced ginger, remaining garlic, and onions and cook until deeply caramelized, about 45 minutes. Purée mixture with ⅓ cup water to make an onion paste. Set aside.

4 Add remaining ¼ cup oil to pot over high heat. Add onion paste, remaining minced ginger, and chiles and cook until oil separates, about 6 minutes. Add turmeric, paprika, and salt and cook for 1 minute. Add chicken and cook until lightly browned, about 8 minutes. Add 1 cup water and bring to a boil, then reduce heat to medium-low and cook, covered, for 15 minutes.

5 Add nut paste and yogurt and cook until emulsified, about 3 minutes. Stir in 4 tbsp. cream and drizzle with remaining cream to garnish. Serve with rice.

GEORGIAN CHICKEN WITH WALNUT SAUCE

Katmis Satsivi

SERVES 6–8

A thick, aromatic sauce of puréed walnuts adds luscious body and earthy flavor to this spiced chicken dish from the Republic of Georgia.

3 cups toasted walnuts, plus ½ cup roughly chopped
5 cups chicken stock
1½ cups roughly chopped fresh cilantro
10 cloves garlic, finely chopped
1 large yellow onion, finely chopped
1 red Holland chile, stemmed, seeded, and finely chopped (optional)
Kosher salt and freshly ground black pepper, to taste
¼ cup olive oil
2 lb. boneless, skinless chicken thighs, cut into 1½″ pieces
3 tsp. sweet paprika
1 tsp. hot paprika
1 tsp. ground coriander
1 tsp. ground fenugreek
½ tsp. ground cinnamon
2 egg yolks
2 tbsp. red wine vinegar

1 Place 3 cups walnuts and ½ cup stock in a food processor; purée until very smooth. Add half each of the cilantro, garlic, and onion, plus chiles, salt, and pepper; purée until very smooth and set sauce aside.

2 Heat oil in a 6-qt. saucepan over medium-high heat. Season chicken with salt and pepper and add to pan; cook, turning as needed, until browned, about 8 minutes. Add remaining garlic and onion and cook, stirring occasionally, until golden, about 4 minutes. Add paprikas, coriander, fenugreek, and cinnamon and cook until fragrant, about 1 minute. Add reserved walnut sauce and remaining 4½ cups stock and bring to a boil. Reduce heat to medium; cook, stirring occasionally, until chicken is tender and sauce is reduced by one-third, 30–35 minutes.

3 Place yolks in a bowl; whisk in 1 ladle of sauce from stew. Return sauce to the stew and cook for 5 minutes more. Stir in vinegar, salt, and pepper. Ladle into bowls and garnish with chopped walnuts and remaining cilantro.

JAPANESE-STYLE CURRY

Wafuu Curry

SERVES 4

Wafuu curry has a cult following in Japan, where many fondly remember eating it at home and at school functions. The recipes vary from cook to cook—some might add chocolate, milk, miso, or dashi—but all have followed the same wandering path, from colonial India to Britain, and from there to Japan, where the dish was popularized in the late-19th century by British sailors. Unlike most curries in other Asian countries, this one is thickened with flour, which creates a silky texture.

3 cups chicken stock
1 tbsp. canola or peanut oil
1 lb. boneless, skinless chicken thighs, cut into 1″ chunks
Salt and freshly ground black pepper
3 tbsp. butter
1 tsp. finely chopped fresh ginger
1 medium onion, ½ finely chopped, ½ cut into 1″ pieces
1 clove garlic, finely chopped
3 tbsp. flour
2 tbsp. curry powder
2 tbsp. crushed tomatoes
1 bay leaf
1 medium carrot, cut crosswise into ½″-thick rounds
1 medium russet potato, peeled and cut into 1″ chunks
1 small apple, peeled, cored, and coarsely grated
1 tsp. honey
1 tbsp. soy sauce
Cooked white rice, for serving

1 Bring stock to a simmer in a medium pot over medium-high heat; reduce heat to medium-low to maintain a simmer. Meanwhile, heat oil in a large skillet over high heat. Season chicken thighs with salt and pepper, add to the skillet, and cook, turning frequently, until deep golden brown on all sides, about 4 minutes. Remove skillet from heat, transfer chicken to a plate, and set chicken aside.

2 Return skillet with chicken drippings to medium-high heat and melt butter. Add ginger, chopped onions, and garlic and cook, stirring often to scrape up any browned bits, until the onions are translucent, about 3 minutes. Sprinkle in flour and cook, stirring constantly, until mixture is evenly browned, about 2 minutes. Add curry powder and tomatoes, stir well to combine, and remove the skillet from the heat. Add ½ cup of hot stock and whisk vigorously to combine, scraping up any browned bits from bottom of skillet. (The browned bits will contribute greatly to the taste and color of the curry.) Whisk the curry mixture into the pot of simmering stock, then add reserved browned chicken thighs, onion pieces, bay leaf, carrots, and potatoes. Bring curry to a boil, reduce the heat to medium-low, and simmer, stirring occasionally, until thickened and vegetables are tender, about 30 minutes.

3 Add apple, honey, soy sauce, and salt to taste and stir well to combine. Cook curry over medium-low heat, stirring occasionally, until flavors meld, about 5 minutes more. Serve curry with steamed rice.

CHICKEN & DUMPLINGS
SERVES 8

There's not much that can make chicken and dumplings—one of America's great comfort-food dishes—even better than it already is. This hearty version, from chef Andrea Reusing of the restaurant Lantern, in Chapel Hill, North Carolina, is an exceptional take on the classic.

1 4-lb. chicken, legs removed
Kosher salt and freshly ground black pepper, to taste
¼ lb. slab bacon, cut into slivers
2 tbsp. canola oil
2 tsp. dried thyme
4 cloves garlic, chopped
4 medium carrots, peeled and thickly sliced
4 ribs celery, thickly sliced
2 large onions, cut into 1″ chunks
1 fresh or dried bay leaf
2⅔ cups flour
1 cup white wine
1 tbsp. baking powder
½ tsp. baking soda
5½ tbsp. butter, melted and cooled slightly
¾ cup buttermilk
2 tbsp. finely chopped fresh parsley

1 Halve chicken legs, separating thigh from drumstick; season with salt and pepper and set aside. Put remaining chicken into a pot, cover with salted water, and bring to a boil. Reduce heat and simmer, until breast is just cooked, 12–15 minutes. Remove chicken. Cut breast and wings from carcass. Discard any skin and bones from breast and wing meat and cut meat into 1″ chunks; chill. Return carcass to pot and simmer for 1 hour. Strain; reserve 4 cups broth (save remainder for another use).

2 Meanwhile, cook bacon in a large, wide pot over medium heat until crisp, 8–10 minutes. Transfer bacon to a plate, leaving rendered fat in pot. Add oil and heat over medium-high heat; add drumsticks and thighs and brown, 8–10 minutes. Transfer chicken to a plate. Add thyme, garlic, carrots, celery, onions, and bay leaf and cook until light brown, 18–20 minutes. Add ⅔ cup flour and cook for 1 minute. Add wine and cook for 1 minute.

> **"There is nothing better on a cold wintry day than a properly made potpie."**
> CRAIG CLAIBORNE

Whisk in reserved broth and salt and pepper to taste. Nestle in drumsticks, thighs, and reserved bacon. Reduce heat to medium-low and simmer, covered, for 15 minutes.

3 Whisk together remaining 2 cups flour, baking powder, baking soda, 1½ tsp. salt, and ¼ tsp. pepper in a bowl. Combine butter, buttermilk, and parsley in a second bowl; pour into flour mixture and stir to make a thick batter. Uncover pot and add breast and wing meat. Drop batter in 8 large spoonfuls over the top. Simmer, covered, until dumplings are cooked, 20–25 minutes.

VERMONT CHICKEN POTPIE
SERVES 12

This savory church-supper staple has epitomized the Green Mountain State's simple, frugal cooking for generations. Over the years, Molly Turner, a writer based in Amherst, Massachusetts, who married into an old Vermont family, has experimented with different versions of this traditional dish. Here's her favorite one.

FOR THE FILLING
- 1 7–10-lb. stewing chicken, cut into 4 pieces
- 3 medium onions, sliced
- 2 carrots, peeled and sliced
- 1 rib celery, sliced
- ½ cup celery leaves, chopped
- 3 sprigs fresh parsley
- 2 sprigs fresh sage
- ½ tsp. freshly ground white pepper
- ½ cup flour
- Kosher salt, to taste

FOR THE BISCUITS
- 3⅓ cups flour
- 2 tbsp. baking powder
- 1 tsp. salt
- 9 tbsp. cold unsalted butter, cut into pieces
- 1 cup plus 2 tbsp. milk

1 Make the filling: Put chicken, onions, carrots, celery, celery leaves, parsley, sage, pepper, and 12 cups cold water into a large pot. Bring to a boil over high heat, skimming off any foam as it appears. Reduce heat to low and simmer until chicken is very tender, 1½–2 hours, depending on weight and age of bird. Transfer chicken with a slotted spoon to a bowl and set aside to let cool briefly. Remove meat from bones and transfer to a bowl; discard skin and return bones to stock. Cover meat with plastic wrap and refrigerate overnight. Increase heat to medium and continue simmering stock until rich and golden, about 3 hours more. Strain stock, discarding solids. Set aside to let cool, then cover and refrigerate overnight.

2 The next day, remove and discard solid layer of fat from stock, then transfer stock to a medium pot and boil over medium heat until reduced by half, to about 5 cups, 1–1½ hours.

3 Heat oven to 475°. Cut chicken meat into large pieces and put into a large baking dish in an even layer. Whisk flour and 1 cup water together in a bowl until smooth, then whisk into hot stock in pot over medium heat, whisking constantly, until thickened, 4–6 minutes. Season to taste with salt, then ladle gravy over chicken. Bake until hot and bubbling, 10 minutes.

4 Make the biscuits: Sift flour, baking powder, and salt together into a large bowl. Use 2 table knives to work butter into flour until it resembles coarse meal. Stir in milk with a fork until dough holds together. Transfer to a floured surface and roll dough out to about ½″ thickness. Use a 3″ round cookie cutter to cut out 12 disks, rolling dough out again, if necessary.

5 Remove baking dish from oven and arrange biscuits on top of chicken and gravy in a single layer. Return dish to oven and bake until biscuits are fluffy and golden brown, about 20 minutes. Set pie aside on a rack to let cool for 10 minutes before serving.

Turkey

LEAH CHASE'S ROASTED TURKEY

SERVES 8–12

Leah Chase, the late chef at New Orleans restaurant Dooky Chase, prepares a roasted turkey with astonishingly tender, juicy breast meat. The secret, we learned, is to seal the bird in an oversize packet of aluminum foil, which locks in the moisture. To brown the skin, she unwraps it and roasts it at a high temperature for the last 30 minutes.

- 1   12-lb. turkey, giblets removed
     Kosher salt and freshly ground black pepper, to taste
- 1   onion, roughly chopped
- 3   ribs celery, roughly chopped
- ½   cup unsalted butter
- 1   tsp. dried thyme
- 1   tsp. rubbed sage
- 4   crumbled dried bay leaves

1 Heat oven to 350°. Season cavity and skin of turkey generously with salt and pepper. Stuff cavity with onion and celery.

2 Tie legs together with kitchen twine, tuck wings under body, and place turkey on top of an 18″×26″ sheet of heavy-duty aluminum foil. Top with another sheet of foil of equal size. Crimp and seal edges tightly to form a packet. Transfer sealed turkey to a large roasting pan fitted with a rack and roast for 2½ hours.

3 Melt butter in a 1-qt. saucepan, then add thyme, sage, and bay leaves. Remove top sheet of foil from turkey and raise oven temperature to 500°; cook, basting with herb butter every 5 minutes, until turkey is browned and an instant-read thermometer inserted into the thickest part of a thigh reads 165°, about 30 minutes more. Let turkey rest for at least 20 minutes before carving.

CHILE-RUBBED TURKEY WITH BEET STUFFING & GRAVY

SERVES 10–12

This recipe is the centerpiece of Mexican-American writer Javier Cabral's family Thanksgiving. New Mexico chiles and *chiles de árbol* create a dark sauce similar to a mole that coats the turkey while adding spice and depth. It's a dramatic presentation, too, with the skin of the bird burnished to a deep red.

- 12   tbsp. unsalted butter
- 2   lb. ground beef
- 16   cloves garlic
- 8   ribs celery
- 5   medium carrots
- 3   bunches scallions, minced
- 2   lb. beets, roasted, peeled, and roughly chopped
- 1¼   cups pitted Kalamata olives
- 2   cups fresh or frozen corn
- 1   cup fresh cilantro leaves, chopped
     Kosher salt and freshly ground black pepper, to taste
- 20   dried New Mexico chiles, stemmed and seeded
- 8   dried chiles de árbol, stemmed
- 1   tbsp. ground cumin
- 1   tsp. ground cloves
- 8   saltine crackers
- 1   16-lb. turkey, neck and giblets reserved
- 1   medium yellow onion, roughly chopped
- 1   cup flour
- 8   cups chicken or turkey stock

1 Make the stuffing: Heat 4 tbsp. butter in a 12″ skillet over medium-high heat. Add beef and cook, stirring, until well-browned, about 10 minutes. Finely chop half the garlic, 5 ribs celery, and 3 carrots, and add to skillet along with scallions; cook, stirring, until vegetables are soft, about 25 minutes. Transfer to a bowl and add beets, olives, corn, and cilantro. Season with salt and pepper; transfer to a 9″×13″ baking dish. Refrigerate until ready to use.

2 Make the chile sauce: Place both chiles in a bowl; cover with boiling water and let sit until softened, about

10 minutes. Drain, reserving 2 cups soaking liquid, and transfer chiles to a blender with remaining garlic, cumin, cloves, crackers, and 2 cups soaking liquid. Purée until smooth; set aside.

3 Heat oven to 450°. Arrange neck and giblets on the bottom of a large roasting pan; place turkey, breast side up, in pan. Season with salt and pepper and rub with remaining butter. Roast until skin is golden brown, about 1 hour. Reduce oven temperature to 350°, pour chile sauce over turkey, and cook, basting every 30 minutes, until an instant-read thermometer inserted into the thickest part of a thigh reads 165°, about 2 hours. Transfer turkey to a cutting board; set aside. Pour pan drippings through a fine sieve into a bowl; discard solids. Meanwhile, place stuffing in oven and cook until golden brown on top, about 30 minutes; set aside.

4 Meanwhile, make the gravy: Return 1 cup fat from the drippings to pan and place over two burners of the stove; heat over medium-high heat. Roughly chop remaining celery and carrots and add to skillet along with onion. Cook, stirring, until soft, about 15 minutes. Add flour and cook, stirring, until smooth, about 3 minutes. Add stock and bring to a boil. Reduce heat to medium and cook, stirring, until gravy thickens, about 15 minutes. Pour through a fine sieve into a serving bowl and season with salt and pepper. Serve turkey with stuffing and gravy on the side.

TAMARIND & HONEY–GLAZED ROAST TURKEY

SERVES 6–8

Sweet and sour tamarind pulp is a prized ingredient in Senegal, where it's formed into candies, mixed into a cooling drink, or slathered over grilled fish. Chef Pierre Thiam transforms the iconic Thanksgiving bird with his own glaze made with tamarind, Scotch bonnet chiles, and fish sauce, which lends the turkey skin a pleasantly sticky texture and the meat an umami-rich flavor. Be sure to use fresh, or "wet," tamarind pulp, which is packed in blocks with the seeds mixed throughout, and not tamarind concentrate or syrup; they are too sweet.

- 6 oz. "wet" tamarind pulp, roughly chopped
- ¾ cup honey
- ¼ cup Vietnamese or Thai fish sauce
- 2 cloves garlic, minced
- 1 Scotch bonnet or habanero chile, stemmed seeded, and finely chopped

- 1 12-lb. whole turkey, rinsed and dried thoroughly Kosher salt and freshly ground black pepper, to taste
- 2 cups chicken stock
- 2 tbsp. cornstarch

1 In a small bowl, cover tamarind pulp with ½ cup boiling water and let stand for 10 minutes to soften. Using your fingers, break tamarind apart and then let stand for another 5 minutes. Pour tamarind through a fine sieve set over a medium bowl and, using a rubber spatula or spoon, press tamarind through sieve, discarding solids. Add honey, fish sauce, garlic, and chile to tamarind liquid and stir into a smooth glaze; you should have 1½ cups.

2 Heat oven to 450°. Place turkey on a rack set in a large roasting pan and season cavity and outside liberally with salt and pepper. Pour stock into pan and roast turkey until golden brown, about 1 hour. Reduce oven temperature to 350°, cover turkey with foil, and roast until almost cooked through, 1 hour more. Uncover turkey and roast, basting with ½ cup of the tamarind glaze every 10 minutes, until an instant-read thermometer inserted into the thigh of the turkey reads 160°, 30 minutes more.

3 Transfer turkey on its rack to a cutting board, tent with foil, and let rest for 20 minutes. Meanwhile, pour pan juices into a small saucepan. In a small bowl, stir cornstarch with 2 tbsp. cold water, and then stir cornstarch slurry into pan juices. Place pan over medium-high heat, bring to a boil, and cook, stirring, until thickened into a gravy, about 5 minutes. Pour gravy through a fine sieve into a bowl and serve alongside turkey.

TURKEY BREAST ROULADE WITH CHESTNUT STUFFING

SERVES 6

This rolled turkey breast cooks in about an hour, making it perfect for last-minute Thanksgiving get-togethers. The delicately flavored chestnut stuffing keeps the white meat moist, while reduced chicken stock adds rich flavor to the quick gravy.

- 4 cups chicken stock
- 4 tbsp. butter
- ½ cup finely chopped celery
- ¾ cup finely chopped onion
- ½ cup finely chopped carrot
- 1 clove garlic, finely chopped

ALL TRUSSED UP

Trussing a turkey brings all the parts in close together so that the bird cooks evenly. It results in moist, beautifully cooked meat—and the four-step French technique is easy to master. (For a chicken, which also benefits from being trussed, simply use a smaller needle and shorter lengths of twine.)

1. THREADING Thread an 8″ trussing needle with a 24″ piece of cotton kitchen twine and use it to sew up the cavity of the stuffed turkey, tucking the tail up and under and then sewing it closed.

2. TRUSSING Rethread the needle with a 48″ piece of twine, and push it through the soft part of the lower thigh and out the other side in the middle of the leg. Leave enough twine to tie off at the end.

3. TURNING Turn the bird over, breast side down. Push the needle through the wing and neck skin and out through the opposite wing. Then truss through the center of leg to lowest part of opposite thigh.

4. TYING Push the needle under the legs through the thigh and the soft flesh under the breast and out to where you started. Pull the two ends taut and tie them in a double bow. As you tie the two ends of twine, the bird will pull together into a solid "package."

⅓ cup grated Parmigiano-Reggiano
⅓ cup flour
1 tsp. chopped fresh rosemary
1 tsp. chopped fresh thyme
1 tbsp. chopped fresh parsley
1 15-oz. can chestnut purée (or 1 lb. jarred peeled chestnuts, puréed)
   Kosher salt and freshly ground black pepper, to taste
1 3–4 lb. boneless turkey breast with skin
2 tbsp. olive oil
¼ cup white wine
1 tbsp. potato or corn starch

1 Heat oven to 425° with the rack in the center position. Bring stock to a simmer in a small saucepan and reduce to 2 cups, 25–30 minutes.

2 In a medium skillet, melt butter over medium heat until foamy. Add celery, onion, carrot, and garlic and sauté until vegetables are slightly soft and onions are translucent, 10–12 minutes. Remove from heat and transfer mixture to a large bowl. Mix in Parmigiano, flour, and herbs until thoroughly combined. Crumble in chestnut purée and mix well to incorporate. Season with salt and pepper.

3 Pat turkey breast dry with paper towels. Lay skin side down on clean work surface and, if needed, slice butterfly-style to create a larger surface area. Season interior liberally with salt and pepper. Spread filling mixture evenly over surface, leaving 1″ border at edges. Starting at shortest edge, gently roll breast up and over stuffing. Place seam side down and tie securely with kitchen twine. Season outside of breast liberally with salt and pepper.

4 Wipe out skillet and heat oil over medium-high heat. Brown turkey breast on all sides until golden brown, 10–12 minutes. Transfer breast to a foil-lined baking sheet or small roasting pan and roast 12–15 minutes per pound until interior temperature in thickest part of breast reads 155°. Remove from oven, tent loosely with foil, and let rest for 15 minutes.

5 While turkey roasts, add wine to hot skillet and reduce by half, scraping up any brown bits in the pan. Add reduced stock and bring to a simmer. Mix potato starch with 2 tbsp. cool water to form a slurry and whisk into simmering stock. Simmer, stirring constantly, until mixture has thickened, 2–3 minutes. Remove from heat, strain gravy through a fine-mesh sieve, and season to taste. Untie turkey breast and slice crosswise into 1½″–2″ slices. Serve with gravy.

Duck & Goose

AMAZING FIVE-HOUR DUCK

SERVES 4

Long cooking yields a tender roast duck with perfectly crisped skin—with amazingly little hands-on effort.

- 1 **5–6-lb. Long Island duck**
  Kosher salt and freshly ground black pepper, to taste
- 3 **cloves garlic, chopped**
- 1 **bunch fresh thyme**

1 Heat oven to 300°. Pat duck dry with paper towels. Discard any large pieces of fat from cavity, then trim off wing tips (reserve along with giblets for stock, if you like). Season cavity with salt and pepper to taste, then rub with garlic. Stuff cavity with a few sprigs of thyme.

2 Pierce duck skin and fat with a sharp paring knife—being careful not to cut into flesh—by inserting tip of knife on the diagonal (not straight in) and making dozens of slits all over duck. Place duck, breast side up, on a rack set on a shallow roasting pan. Roast duck for 4 hours, removing bird from oven every hour and piercing skin and fat again, as described above, and pouring off fat (reserve fat for another use, like Duck Confit, page 182) and turn bird over, allowing it to roast for 2 hours total on each side.

3 After 4 hours of roasting time, increase oven temperature to 350°. Season duck skin with salt and pepper and cook until skin is crisp and browned, 1 hour more. Let duck rest for 20 minutes, then garnish cavity with remaining fresh thyme, if you like. Using a sharp cleaver, hack duck into small pieces, bones and all, and serve.

CANTONESE ROAST DUCK

SERVES 4

Chinese restaurants and butcher shops often specialize in serving Cantonese-style roast duck, with its shatteringly crisp skin and succulently spiced meat. It's the result of a meticulous, multi-day process of marinating, scalding, air-drying, and slow-cooking, and as such, most cooks find it's best left to the professionals. But we can't resist a

challenge: The techniques for making this duck at home may verge on the absurd (yes, you'll need to figure out a way to jury-rig an electric fan inside your refrigerator, or else set the bird to dry in an unheated room in winter), but if your ambition matches your appetite, this exquisite bird is absolutely worth it.

FOR THE DUCK

- 1 **5–6-lb. Long Island duck, with or without head and feet**
- 1 **tbsp. dry sherry**
- 1 **tbsp. soy sauce**
- ½ **tsp. kosher salt**
- 2 **pinches of ground white pepper**
- ¼ **tsp. Chinese five-spice powder**
- 3 **thick slices peeled ginger, crushed**
- 1 **clove garlic, crushed**
- 1 **scallion, cut into 2″ pieces and crushed**
- 1 **tbsp. honey**
- 2 **tsp. rice vinegar**

FOR THE SAUCE

- 2 **tbsp. soy sauce**
- 1 **tbsp. dry sherry**
- 1 **tbsp. Chinese ground bean or black bean sauce**
- 1½ **tsp. sugar**
- ¼ **tsp. salt**
- ¼ **tsp. freshly ground white pepper**
- ½ **bunch fresh cilantro, trimmed**
  Zest of ½ orange
- 1 **tbsp. peanut oil**
- 3 **thick slices peeled ginger, crushed**
- 2 **cloves garlic, crushed and peeled**
- 2 **scallions, crushed**

1 Make the duck: Remove any quills with tweezers, then pat duck dry. Remove fat from inside of cavity and discard. Cut off wing tips and (if attached) feet and set aside. (If duck comes without neck attached, leave long piece of neck skin intact and tuck skinned neck inside cavity.) Combine sherry, soy sauce, salt, pepper, five-spice powder, ginger, garlic, and scallion in a medium bowl, then rub mixture inside cavity. Truss closed with a thin metal skewer.

2 Bring 8 cups water to a boil in a large pot over high heat. Meanwhile, combine honey, rice vinegar, and ¼ cup water in a small saucepan, bring to a boil over high heat, then set aside. Tie a long piece of strong kitchen twine securely around the duck's neck (or neck skin). Place duck in sink, then pour half the boiling water over duck, making sure that it runs over every part of the skin. Turn duck over and repeat with remaining water. Brush duck with reserved honey mixture. Suspend duck in a cool place (33°-39°). Aim an electric fan at duck, set fan on high, and air-dry duck for 24 hours.

3 Heat oven to 350°. Cut duck down and remove and discard kitchen twine. Cut off head and neck from duck if necessary and discard head (or trim and discard neck skin). Cut neck (or reserved skinned neck) into 4–5 pieces and set aside. Place duck, breast side up, on a rack in a shallow roasting pan. Pour ¼″ water into pan and roast duck for 2½–3 hours, adding more water as necessary. Halfway through roasting, baste with honey mixture blended with ¼ cup of sauce.

4 Make the sauce: Combine soy sauce, sherry, bean sauce, sugar, salt, pepper, a few sprigs of cilantro, orange zest, and 2 cups water in a small bowl. Mix well, then set aside. Heat peanut oil in a medium saucepan over medium-high heat. Add ginger, garlic, reserved wing tips, feet (if any), and neck pieces and stir-fry until duck pieces are browned, about 3 minutes. Add scallions and stir-fry for 1 minute. Add reserved soy sauce mixture and bring to a boil, stirring constantly. Reduce heat to medium-low and simmer, covered, for 45 minutes. Strain sauce, then return to saucepan and bring to a boil over medium-high heat. Boil until reduced by half, about 15 minutes. Remove from heat and set aside.

5 Remove duck from oven and let rest for 15 minutes. Remove skewer, discard stuffing, chop duck into 2″ pieces, and arrange on platter. Garnish with remaining cilantro. Serve with warm sauce on side.

DUCK À L'ORANGE
Roast Duck with Orange Sauce

SERVES 4

Duck *à l'orange* is only as French as Catherine de' Medici, who popularized what was originally a Florentine dish in France. It was first made with bitter oranges, to offset the richness of the duck, but the recipe has evolved to accommodate conventional oranges.

1	orange
4	1½-lb. mallard ducks
	Kosher salt and freshly ground black pepper
4	cloves garlic, peeled
1	yellow onion, quartered
4	sprigs fresh rosemary
½	cup butter, melted
½	cup madeira wine
1	cup duck stock or Brown Chicken Stock (page 568)
1	tbsp. sugar
2	tbsp. red wine vinegar

1 Heat oven to 500°. Using a vegetable peeler, zest orange. Julienne half the zest, set aside, and cut orange into quarters. Pat ducks dry and season inside and out with salt and pepper. Tuck wings under back, and stuff each duck with 1 orange quarter, 1 garlic clove, 1 onion quarter, and 1 sprig rosemary. Tie legs with kitchen twine. Place ducks in large roasting pan and brush with butter. Roast until skin is crisp, 25–30 minutes. Remove ducks from pan.

2 Place pan over medium-high heat and cook just until juices are caramelized, about 5 minutes. Skim fat, then deglaze with madeira and stock, scraping up any brown bits from bottom of pan. Add orange zest and cook over medium heat until reduced by about one-third, 3–5 minutes.

3 Combine sugar and 1 tbsp. water in a small saucepan. Cook over medium heat until golden, 2–3 minutes. Remove from heat, stir in vinegar, then reduced pan juices. Return to heat and cook for 5–8 minutes. Top ducks with sauce and serve.

CHRISTMAS GOOSE WITH STUFFING
SERVES 8

This recipe for roast goose, perhaps the most iconic (and extravagant) of all Christmas centerpieces, comes from executive chef Brian Alberg of the Red Lion Inn in Stockbridge, Massachusetts.

FOR THE STUFFING

½	lb. bacon, cut into ¼″ cubes
½	lb. Brussels sprouts, quartered
2	cups minced celery
1	large yellow onion, minced
1	lb. cooked chestnuts, roughly chopped
4½	oz. country white bread, cut into ½″ cubes (about 4 cups)

4   cups cooked wild rice

1   cup chicken stock

1   cup unsalted butter, melted, plus more
    for buttering casserole dish

½   cup finely chopped fresh flat-leaf parsley

2   tbsp. finely chopped fresh thyme

2   tbsp. finely chopped fresh sage

2   tart apples, cored and chopped
    Kosher salt and freshly ground black pepper,
    to taste

FOR THE GOOSE & GRAVY

1   12-lb. goose, wing tips, neck, and giblets reserved
    Kosher salt and freshly ground black pepper,
    to taste

1   lemon, halved

8   sprigs fresh thyme

4   sprigs fresh sage

8   cups chicken stock

2   ribs celery, roughly chopped

2   small yellow onions, chopped

1   large carrot, peeled and roughly chopped

4   tbsp. unsalted butter

¼   cup extra-virgin olive oil

¼   lb. baby carrots, peeled

1   lb. baby beets, peeled

1   lb. small potatoes, halved

6   cipolline or pearl onions, peeled

2   large parsnips, peeled and cut on diagonal
    into 1″-thick slices

1   celery root, peeled, halved, and cut into
    1″-thick slices

1   head garlic, cloves peeled

1   sprig fresh rosemary

¼   cup flour

1 Make the stuffing: Render bacon in a 12″ skillet over medium-high heat for 10 minutes. Add sprouts, celery, and onion and cook until lightly browned, about 10 minutes. Remove from heat and stir in chestnuts, bread, rice, stock, butter, parsley, thyme, sage, and apples, then season with salt and pepper. Set aside.

2 Roast the goose: Prick skin all over with a fork; season with salt and pepper and squeeze lemon juice over skin. Place spent lemon halves in cavity along with 3 sprigs each thyme and sage. Place goose on a rack in a roasting pan and heat pan on stove top over high heat. Add stock and bring to a boil. Reduce heat to medium-low, cover with foil, and steam (to render goose fat) for 1 hour. Discard lemon and

herbs. Heat oven to 325°. Uncover goose; remove it with rack. Pour pan liquid into a measuring cup; let sit until fat rises to top. Skim off fat and reserve for another use. Add 2 cups pan liquid to roasting pan along with celery, onion, and large carrot; reserve remaining pan liquid. Return goose and rack to pan. Stuff goose with some of the stuffing (place remaining stuffing in a buttered casserole; heat alongside goose the last 15 minutes of cooking); tie legs together with kitchen twine. Place goose breast side down, cover with foil, and roast for 1 hour.

3 Begin the gravy: Melt butter in a 6-qt. saucepan over medium-high heat. Add wing tips, neck, giblets, and 2 sprigs thyme and cook until browned, about 15 minutes. Add reserved pan liquid and bring to a boil. Reduce heat to medium-low and cook until reduced by half, about 1 hour. Strain goose stock; set aside.

4 Increase oven temperature to 475°. Uncover goose; turn breast side up. Roast until golden and temperature of stuffing is 180°, about 70 minutes.

5 Meanwhile, roast the vegetables: Toss remaining thyme and sage, oil, baby carrots, beets, potatoes, onions, parsnips, celery root, garlic, rosemary, salt, and pepper on 2 baking sheets. Roast, stirring, until golden brown, about 45 minutes. Keep warm.

6 Transfer goose to a cutting board; let rest for 15 minutes. Strain pan liquid into a measuring cup; let sit until fat rises to top. Skim off fat and return liquid to pan with the celery, onion, and carrot. Heat over medium-high heat and brown vegetables for 8 minutes. Add flour and cook for 4 minutes. Add strained pan juices and goose stock and bring to a boil. Cook until slightly thickened, about 3 minutes. Strain gravy; season with salt and pepper. Remove stuffing from goose before carving. Serve with gravy and roasted vegetables on the side.

DUCK CONFIT
SERVES 6–8

You'll need two days and plenty of duck fat on hand to make confit, an indulgent preparation in which meaty duck legs are cooked at a relatively cool temperature, and then stored in a blanket of their braising fat. Confited duck legs are an essential part of many French dishes, including Cassoulet (page 235), but they're also delicious browned in a hot oven until the skin crisps.

4   duck legs
2   tbsp. finely chopped fresh thyme
3   bay leaves
¼   cup kosher salt
1½   tbsp. sugar
1   tbsp. freshly ground black pepper
1   tbsp. garlic powder
1   tbsp. ground ginger
6   cups rendered duck fat

1 Trim skin on drumsticks about 1" below the tip of the bone and scrape down toward the meat, exposing the bone; place legs on a baking sheet and set aside. Grind thyme and bay leaves in a spice grinder; transfer to a bowl. Stir in salt, sugar, pepper, garlic powder, and ginger. Rub mixture all over duck, pressing it into the skin and coating completely. Cover with plastic wrap; chill overnight or up to 2 days.

2 The next day, rinse duck and pat completely dry with paper towels. Melt duck fat in an 8-qt. saucepan until a deep-fry thermometer reads 200°. Add duck legs and cook until tender, about 2 hours. Let cool to room temperature, then cover and chill. The confit can be used right away or will keep for up to 1 month.

3 To serve: Heat oven to 400°. Remove duck from fat and place skin side up on a baking sheet with a wire rack. Bake until skin is browned and crisp, about 40 minutes.

THE PLEASURES OF DUCK

Given duck's universal appeal, it's surprising that it's not more popular in American home kitchens. Perhaps it's because, short of shooting the fowl ourselves, the only ducks most of us could get until the 1980s (when specialty purveyors like D'Artagnan began selling pasture-raised birds) were frozen and factory-farmed. These days, thankfully, Americans can find fresh ducks at many farmers' markets, even heritage breeds such as the Rouen, introduced by the French. We can also increasingly find better-quality fresh or frozen Pekin or Long Island ducks packaged whole, or as breasts and legs. Other varieties, such as the ultra-plump French Moulard often used to produce foie gras and the gamier Muscovy, can be ordered online.

THAI RED CURRY WITH ROASTED DUCK
SERVES 4

Known as *gaed phed ped yang*, this sweet and savory recipe, studded with pineapple and cherry tomatoes, is one of those interpretive Westernized dishes that often appears on Thai restaurant menus. Ask the counterperson at your local Chinese market (where freshly roasted, crisp-skinned ducks ought to be available in the butcher department) to cut the roasted duck into pieces.

2½   cups canned coconut milk
¼   cup Thai red curry paste
½   Chinese roasted duck, cut into 2" pieces
10   fresh or frozen makrut lime leaves
1   cup cut-up fresh pineapple, in 1" chunks
1½   tbsp. nam pla (Thai fish sauce)
1   tbsp. Thai palm sugar
6   bird's eye chiles, stemmed
20   cherry tomatoes
    Leaves from 10 stems Thai basil
    Cooked white rice, for serving

1 Heat 1 cup of the coconut milk in a large pot over medium heat until it just begins to boil. Reduce heat to medium-low and simmer, stirring often, until liquid is slightly reduced, about 5 minutes. Whisk in the curry paste and continue to simmer the mixture, stirring occasionally, until the liquid is very aromatic, about 5 minutes more.

2 Add the cut-up duck to the curry mixture and increase the heat to medium. Cook, stirring occasionally, until the duck is heated through, about 7 minutes. Add the remaining coconut milk, lime leaves, and ¾ cup water. Increase the heat to medium-high, bring to a boil, then reduce the heat to medium-low. Simmer, stirring, until the flavors have melded, about 2 minutes. Add the pineapple, fish sauce, sugar, and chiles and continue to simmer on medium-low heat, stirring occasionally, until the pineapple is fork tender, about 5 minutes more.

3 If you like, skim off and discard oil from the top of the curry. Stir in tomatoes and basil and simmer the curry for 1 minute more; the tomatoes and basil should retain their shape and bright color. Serve curry with rice.

Meat & Game

MEAT & GAME

THE ORANGE LEAP OF THE FIRE, its flames hissing and sputtering, the heat and smoke and aromas, the hefty hunk of meat charring and dripping fat and juices—nothing excites many of us quite as much as cooking meat. And as the paintings on cave walls from Western Europe to eastern Australia tell us, it's one of our oldest and most primal pleasures.

In mountainous Greece, the meat might be earthy lamb culled from herds that roam the hillsides and munch on wild herbs, the meat slowly roasted with plenty of garlic and oregano. In Italy, it is tender veal, sauced with red gravy and slathered in melted cheese, or wrapped in prosciutto and pan-fried with a buttery marsala sauce. Asia favors pork, which features in everything from lemongrass-marinated Vietnamese chops to China's red-braised pork belly. And then there are good, old Texas ribs, the pride of the state's cattle ranchers.

But no matter the cut or the animal it came from, one thing that unites all of this meat-based cooking is its essential role in celebrations. Sure, we like a warming stew on any cold night. But there's something about a big, gorgeous roast rich with pan juices or a prime rib fresh from the fire that makes us want to gather a group and throw a party. In North Africa, for the Muslim feast of Eid Al-Adha, a lamb *tagine* might be served, the cubed meat spooned over couscous. At Christmastime, what could be more festive than a crown roast of pork with dried-fruit stuffing, or a rack of venison with a rich cherry-port sauce? And for Ashkenazi Jews, a Shabbat dinner wouldn't be the same without a long-braised brisket. Even casual get-togethers feel more festive with a meat dish on the table: pork kebabs from the grill, Korean short ribs, game-season venison sausage.

The aim of all meat cookery, regardless of the type of meat or where you are in the world, is to coax out the most delicious flavors and textures through tenderizing, seasoning, and applying heat. Broiling, grilling, or searing marinated meat caramelizes its exterior and locks in moisture. Oven-braising chunks of beef, lamb, and pork for hours in a flavorful liquid, as we do in our vegetable-loaded Alsatian Bacheofe, breaks down the proteins in the meats and makes each bite melt-in-your-mouth tender. All of these cooking methods are aimed toward one goal: to create the type of indulgence that humans have shared with one another since the days of the first cooking fires some 250,000 years ago.

Beef & Veal

ROAST PRIME RIB

SERVES 10

A glorious piece of meat needs little more than a dusting of seasonings—and this classic American recipe proves just that.

- 1 prime rib, trimmed (see Cook's Note)
- 3 tbsp. flour
- 1 tbsp. dry mustard
- 2 tsp. salt
- 2 tsp. freshly ground black pepper
- 1 cup dry red wine

1 Before cooking, let prime rib come to room temperature. Heat oven to 450°. Combine flour, mustard, salt, and pepper in a bowl and mix well. Rub mixture all over prime rib.

2 Tie short ribs with kitchen twine and place in a large roasting pan. Place prime rib, fat side up, on top of ribs. Roast meat for 20 minutes on lowest rack. Reduce heat to 325° and continue roasting, basting frequently with pan juices, for about 15 minutes per pound.

3 After 1¾ hours, pour wine over meat. Continue roasting and basting until an instant-read meat thermometer reads 120° for medium rare. Remove meat from oven, allow to rest for 30 minutes, then carve and serve.

COOK'S NOTE Have your butcher trim the fat and remove the chine bone and short ribs from a prime rib roast. Ask your butcher to tie and weigh the roast after trimming, as cooking time is calculated by trimmed weight.

Keens Steakhouse Prime Rib Hash

SERVES 2–3

Chef Bill Rodgers makes this holy mash-up of leftover prime rib and russet potatoes at Manhattan's legendary Keens Steakhouse. A robust main dish, it's lightened with fresh and fragrant rosemary and parsley.

- 1 large russet potato, peeled and cut into ½″ pieces
- 2 tbsp. unsalted butter
- ½ small white onion, finely chopped
- 1 rib celery, finely chopped
- 10 oz. cooked prime rib, cut into ½″ pieces
- 1 tbsp. finely chopped fresh flat-leaf parsley
- 1 tsp. finely chopped fresh rosemary
- 2–3 tbsp. ketchup
- ½ tsp. Tabasco or other hot sauce
  Kosher salt and freshly ground black pepper
- 1 sunny-side-up egg, for serving
  Chopped fresh chives, for garnish

1 Heat oven to 450°. Boil potatoes in a 2-qt. saucepan of salted water until tender, 5–10 minutes. Drain, transfer to a bowl, and mash slightly, leaving some diced pieces intact.

2 Melt butter in an 8″ oven-safe nonstick skillet over medium-high heat. Add onion and celery and cook for 2 minutes. Transfer to bowl with potatoes. Add beef, parsley, rosemary, ketchup, hot sauce, and salt and pepper; stir to combine. Return pan to medium-high heat; add potato mixture and, using spatula, form into a compact cake. Cook, without stirring, until bottom is browned, 2–3 minutes. Transfer to oven and cook until top is browned, 15–20 minutes. Invert onto a plate. Garnish with egg and chives.

LEFTOVER LESSONS

What to do with pieces of leftover roasted meat? Reheating them in the oven or the microwave generally renders the meat dry, overcooked, and tough. Sandwiches are a good—but predictable—option. Here are some other ideas we like: Cube cold pieces of meat and toss with capers, onions, parsley, and a sharp Dijon mustard vinaigrette. Panfry thick slices until browned and crisp on both sides; shred meat, make a hash (this page), and top with poached eggs. Serve cold slices with garlicky homemade mayonnaise or a good chutney.

ETHIOPIAN SIZZLING SPICED BEEF

Siga Tibs

SERVES 4

This dish is popular and prepared year-round in Ethiopia, though it has a special place on the table for the fast-breaking feasts of Easter and Christmas. For a slightly saucier version, stir in a splash of *tej* (Ethiopian mead), red wine, or water with the chiles, and cook for an additional 2 minutes. This recipe is adapted from *Ethiopia: Recipes and Traditions from the Horn of Africa* by Yohanis Gebreyesus and Jeff Koehler.

2   lb. boneless, lean beef, such as top round or sirloin, thinly sliced against the grain, then cut into 1″ × 2″-wide strips
    Kosher salt and freshly ground black pepper, to taste
3   tbsp. vegetable oil
2   large yellow onions, thinly sliced
1   tbsp. plus 1½ tsp. clarified butter
¼   tsp. Berbere (page 286), plus more for serving
1   sprig fresh rosemary
1   medium jalapeño, seeded and thinly sliced
    Injera (page 460) or another flatbread, for serving

1 Put beef strips in a medium bowl. Season lightly with salt and pepper, and set aside.

2 Heat oil in a large skillet over medium heat. Once hot, add onions and cook, stirring occasionally, lowering heat or adding a tablespoon of water as needed, until deep golden brown, 25–30 minutes. Move onions to the edges of the pan, raise heat to medium-high, and add about 1 cup of the meat in the center. Let cook, turning once, until seared on both sides, about 2 minutes total. Move cooked meat to the pan's edges, and repeat with another cup of meat. When all of the meat has been browned in this manner, stir in clarified butter, ¼ tsp. berbere, and the rosemary. Taste and adjust the seasoning with more berbere, salt, or pepper as desired. Scatter jalapeño slices over the top.

3 Remove from heat and serve dish hot with injera or another flatbread for scooping, and a bowl of extra berbere on the side for dipping, if desired.

ROSEMARY-RUBBED BEEF TENDERLOIN

SERVES 4 (SEE PHOTO, PAGE 231)

Fresh rosemary and garlic form a flavorful crust for this elegant cut of beef, which emerges from the oven rosy-pink on the inside and shot through with a delicate herbal flavor. Served with a sharp green salad and roasted potatoes, it's perfect dinner-party fare.

1   2-lb. beef tenderloin, trimmed of sinew and excess fat, and tied with kitchen twine
¼   cup canola oil
3   tbsp. finely chopped fresh rosemary
3   large cloves garlic, finely chopped
    Kosher salt and freshly ground black pepper, to taste
2   tbsp. unsalted butter

1 Place beef tenderloin on a sheet of aluminum foil and rub all over with 2 tbsp. oil, rosemary, and garlic. Season tenderloin generously with salt and pepper, then let beef sit at room temperature for 1 hour, allowing seasonings to penetrate meat.

2 Heat oven to 425°. Heat remaining oil and butter in a 12″ ovenproof skillet over medium-high heat. Carefully place tenderloin in skillet and cook, turning as needed, until beef is browned on all sides, about 7 minutes.

3 Transfer skillet to oven and cook tenderloin until an instant-read thermometer inserted into center of beef reads 125° for medium rare, about 20 minutes.

4 Remove tenderloin from oven and let rest for an additional 20 minutes. (During this resting period, tenderloin will continue to rise in temperature to produce a perfect medium-rare interior.) To serve, remove twine and use a carving knife to cut beef into ½″-thick slices. Transfer slices to a large serving platter, and pour any accumulated juices from cutting board over meat to moisten it. Serve immediately or at room temperature.

STEAK SAUCES

CHIMICHURRI Put 10 minced cloves garlic, ½ cup minced fresh flat-leaf parsley, 2 tbsp. dried oregano, and 1 tbsp. crushed red chile flakes (or more, if you like) in a bowl and mix well. Whisk in 1 cup olive oil and ¼ cup red wine vinegar. Season with salt and freshly ground black pepper. Set mixture aside for 2–3 hours to develop flavor. Keep in a jar in refrigerator for up to 1 week. Makes about 2 cups.

SALSA DELLE ERBE Combine 1 cup chopped basil, 1 cup chopped fresh flat-leaf parsley, 2 tbsp. chopped fresh oregano, 1 tbsp. chopped fresh rosemary, 1 tbsp. chopped fresh thyme, 1 tbsp. chopped fresh tarragon, 2 minced cloves garlic, and ¾ cup extra-virgin olive oil. Season with salt and freshly ground black pepper, cover with plastic wrap, and set aside for at least 1 hour to let the flavors meld. Makes about 1½ cups.

PEPPERCORN SAUCE Using the same pan from searing steaks, add 2 finely chopped shallots and stir until fragrant, about 30 seconds. Add 1½ cups ruby port and bring to a boil over medium-high heat. Cook until mixture is reduced to about ¼ cup, 5–6 minutes. Add 2 cups beef stock and boil until syrupy, 10–12 minutes. Remove from heat and whisk in 1 cup heavy cream. Return skillet to medium heat and boil gently until thickened, 6–8 minutes. Stir in ¼ cup rinsed and coarsely chopped brine-cured green peppercorns, 2 tsp. vinegar, and salt to taste. Makes about 2 cups.

CHIVE BUTTER Beat 1 cup softened butter in a bowl with a wooden spoon until smooth. Put 2 large coarsely chopped bunches chives (about 2 cups) and ½ tsp. salt into a small food processor and purée until smooth. Add chive purée, 1 tsp. Dijon mustard, ½ tsp. fresh lemon juice, and salt and freshly ground white pepper to taste to butter; stir well. Transfer chive butter to a large sheet of parchment paper, roll tightly into a log, and twist the paper ends; chill until firm. Slice off what you need to adorn steak (or poultry). Store in the freezer for up to 6 months. Makes about 1 cup.

HORSERADISH SAUCE Using an electric mixer, whip 1⅓ cups heavy cream with 1 tbsp. sugar until stiff. Fold in 5 tbsp. peeled and grated fresh horseradish root. Makes 1 cup.

SEARED SIRLOIN STEAKS
SERVES 4

A true test of a cook's culinary aptitude lies in searing a steak to the correct temperature. You'll need only four ingredients to make a steak truly perfect every time. Serve with the sauce of your choice (this page).

- 4 1½″ thick sirloin steaks
  Kosher salt and freshly ground black pepper, to taste
- 2 tbsp. canola oil

Pat steaks dry with paper towels and season generously with salt and pepper. Heat a cast-iron grill pan or skillet over medium-high heat until very hot, then lightly grease with oil. Add steaks. For medium rare, sear 2 minutes per side, then reduce heat to medium and cook for 3 minutes per side. Allow steaks to rest for 5 minutes before serving.

ROLLED STUFFED FLANK STEAK
Matambre
SERVES 6–8

We fell in love with this hearty Argentine dish of flank steak stuffed with eggs and vegetables after Rosa Angelita Castro de Flores made it for us at the estancia El Bordo de las Lanzas in Salta, Argentina.

- 2 2½-lb. flank steaks, butterflied and pounded thin
  Kosher salt, to taste
- 6 cloves garlic, minced
- 2 tbsp. red wine vinegar
- 1 tbsp. ground cumin
- 1 tsp. crushed red chile flakes
  Freshly ground white pepper, to taste
- 4 large carrots, peeled and quartered lengthwise
- 1 large green bell pepper, seeded and cut into strips
- 1 cup fresh or frozen peas
- 6 hard-cooked eggs, peeled

1 Generously season both sides of meat with salt, then rub into meat. Lay 1 steak on a baking sheet and scatter half the garlic over meat. Sprinkle half the vinegar on top and cover with the other steak. Scatter the remaining garlic and vinegar over the meat and cover pan with plastic wrap. Marinate overnight in the refrigerator.

2 Heat oven to 350°. Lay 1 steak on a clean surface with the grain running horizontally toward you. Lay the other steak, also with the grain running horizontally, in front of the first, overlapping the ends by 2″. (That way you'll slice the cooked *matambre* across the grain for more tender meat.) Sprinkle with cumin and chile flakes and season with white pepper. Lay one-third of carrot and pepper strips horizontally (with grain of meat), beginning about 2″ in from end nearest to you. Sprinkle one-third of peas over vegetables. Then arrange a row of 3 eggs on top of vegetables. Carefully roll meat over filling in a tight jelly-roll style, tucking the near end of the meat under the filling. Repeat with another one-third of carrots, peppers, and peas and remaining 3 eggs and roll again, then lay remaining carrots, peppers, and peas on meat and finish rolling. Pin edges of roll together with trussing skewers, then tie kitchen twine around roll to keep ingredients packed.

3 Put meat in a large, heavy pot and add water to come halfway up meat. Cover, place in oven, and cook until meat is fork-tender, about 3 hours, turning meat once halfway through. Remove from oven and uncover. Place a sturdy plate on top of meat, weight it down with heavy unopened cans, and set aside until meat cools to room temperature. Transfer meat to a pan and cover loosely with plastic wrap, then reweight with plate and cans. Refrigerate overnight. To serve, bring meat to room temperature, remove string and skewers, then carve into 1″-thick slices.

COFFEE- & SOY-MARINATED FLANK STEAK

SERVES 6–8

In this recipe from one-time SAVEUR managing editor Greg Ferro, strong coffee pairs with soy sauce and lightly caramelized garlic and onions in a powerful marinade that results in extra-juicy steak.

- 4 tbsp. unsalted butter
- 8 cloves garlic, roughly chopped
- 1 large yellow onion, roughly chopped
- 1 cup strong coffee
- 1 cup soy sauce
- ¼ cup Worcestershire sauce
- 3 tbsp. white vinegar
- 1 tbsp. crushed red chile flakes
- ½ tbsp. dried oregano
  Kosher salt, to taste
- 1 2-lb. flank steak

1 Melt butter in a 12″ skillet over medium-high heat. Add garlic and onion and cook until slightly caramelized, 12–15 minutes. Transfer to a bowl. Whisk in coffee, soy, Worcestershire, vinegar, chile flakes, oregano, and salt. Reserve 1 cup marinade. Add steak to bowl; cover with plastic wrap and refrigerate overnight.

2 Build a hot fire in a charcoal grill or set a gas grill to high; bank coals or turn burner off on one side (facing page). Remove steak from marinade and grill, flipping once, until browned, about 10 minutes. Using a brush, baste with reserved marinade and cook, turning as needed, until cooked to desired doneness, 10–15 minutes for medium. If outside starts to burn before steak is cooked, move to cooler section of grill until done. Rest steak for 10 minutes; slice thinly on the diagonal, against the grain.

KOREAN GRILLED BEEF SHORT RIBS
Kalbi

SERVES 4

Pineapple juice sweetens and tenderizes beef short ribs in this classic Korean grilled dish. It's served with pungent kimchi and crisp lettuce leaves for wrapping.

- 1 lb. bone-in beef short ribs, cut crosswise about 3″ thick by butcher
- ½ cup fresh pineapple juice
- ¼ cup soy sauce
- ¼ cup sugar
- 2 tbsp. rice vinegar
- 2 tbsp. sesame oil
- 2 tbsp. sesame seeds, lightly toasted, plus more for garnish
- 2 tsp. freshly ground black pepper
- 5 cloves garlic, mashed into a paste
- 1 small white onion, grated
- 2 scallions, thinly sliced
  Gochujang (Korean chile paste), for serving
  Kimchi (page 584, or store-bought), for serving
  Green leaf lettuce, for wrapping

1 Place short ribs in a bowl. Whisk juice, soy, sugar, vinegar, oil, sesame seeds, pepper, garlic, and grated onion in a bowl; rub mixture over ribs. Cover and refrigerate for 45 minutes.

2 Build a hot fire in a charcoal grill or set a gas grill to high; bank coals or turn off burner on one side (facing page). Remove ribs from marinade and cook on hottest part of grill, flipping once, until charred in spots and cooked to desired doneness, 2–4 minutes for medium rare. If outside starts to burn before beef is fully cooked, move to cooler section of grill until done. Garnish with sesame seeds and scallions; serve with gochujang, kimchi, and lettuce leaves for wrapping.

COOK'S NOTE Many markets sell "flanken cut" beef short ribs perfectly sliced for kalbi.

TEXAS-STYLE BEEF RIBS

SERVES 6-8

These beef ribs are rubbed with an array of potent spices, which transform into a flavorful crust once grilled. Our Texas-style mopping sauce partners perfectly.

1 rack beef spareribs (about 3 lb.)
Texas-Style Barbecue Rub (page 587)
Texas Mopping Sauce (page 192), for serving

INDIRECT VS. DIRECT GRILLING

Indirect grilling makes use of the ambient heat a short distance away from the coals and is great for foods such as bone-in chicken and thick-cut steaks that take longer to cook all the way through; placing these foods to one side of the coals exposes them to a gentler heat, where they cook more slowly without burning on the outside.

Since most of us tend to grill different kinds of meats and vegetables all at once, it's best to organize your grill so that it has both direct and indirect grilling zones. Such a setup lets you move foods back and forth between zones, alternating between high-heat direct grilling and lower-heat indirect grilling. Creating dual zones for a gas grill is easy: just turn burners on one side on and keep them off on the other side. Here's how to do it for a charcoal grill:

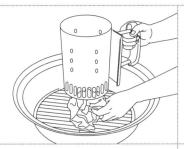

1 Remove top grill grate; set a chimney starter over bottom grate. Place crumpled newspaper under chimney starter.

2 Fill starter to the top with charcoal and light newspaper with a match. Let coals burn until white-hot and covered with gray ash.

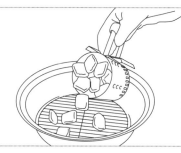

3 Using a heatproof glove or mitt, pour coals from chimney starter onto bottom grill grate. Replace top grate and cover grill.

4 Using a heatproof glove or mitt, remove top grill grate. Then, using tongs, spread coals in an even layer for direct grilling (pictured). For indirect grilling, using the tongs or a shovel, push all coals to one side of grill. Replace top grate.

5 Allow grill to heat for 30 minutes before starting to cook. To tell if the temperature is high enough for cooking, hold your hand about 3" over the grill grate. If you have to pull away after 4 seconds, it's time to start grilling.

6 Use the hottest area on the grill—directly over the coals—for your direct grilling zone. The area without coals will become gradually cooler; use this part of the grill for indirect grilling.

GABHOR UTOMO

1 Rub ribs all over with barbecue rub. Let sit at room temperature for 1 hour or refrigerate for up to overnight.

2 Prepare for barbecuing using a kettle grill, bullet smoker, or gas grill (see Barbecue Fuel, this page, and Barbecue Flavor, facing page), using applewood chunks or chips. Place ribs, meat side up, on grill grate. Maintaining a grill temperature of 225°–250° (if using a kettle grill or bullet smoker, replenish fire with unlit coals, as needed, to maintain temperature), cook, turning once, until the tip of a small knife slips easily in and out of meat, 3–4 hours. Serve with mopping sauce.

BARBECUE FUEL

Successful barbecue relies largely on controlling two variables: heat and smoke. Choosing a fuel that can burn for hours at a low, steady temperature, as well as the right wood to impart that signature smoky flavor, is essential.

Maintaining a low, even temperature is key for transforming tough cuts into tender barbecue, and for that, charcoal is the ideal fuel. It burns steadily and cleanly, which is imperative for barbecue's long smoke times. Charcoal comes in two forms: lump charcoal and briquettes.

Lump charcoal—wood that's been burned in the absence of oxygen, which reduces it to almost pure carbon—has the advantage of being free of chemical additives and binders. But because it's made from wood only, it has wood's irregularities. It comes
in different sizes and densities, which can make keeping a steady temperature challenging in vessels where airflow cannot be controlled, such as a kettle grill, as some pieces will burn faster than others.

Charcoal briquettes, made from charcoal combined with binding elements and ignition aids and formed into bricks, are the most widely available barbecue fuel. Their uniform shape, size, and density make them great for cooking in kettle grills. You can also get natural briquettes, which contain only charcoal and a natural binder. These combine the best qualities of lump charcoal and briquettes: clean-burning, even heat. (Avoid briquettes that have been impregnated with lighter fluid, as they'll impart a chemical flavor to meat.)

Texas Mopping Sauce
MAKES 3 CUPS

This spicy sauce is "mopped" onto ribs as they smoke to moisten and flavor them.

- 1 cup cider vinegar
- 2 tbsp. light brown sugar
- 1 tbsp. Worcestershire sauce
- 1 tbsp. crushed red chile flakes
- 1 tbsp. finely chopped fresh cilantro
- 1 tsp. kosher salt
- ½ tsp. aniseeds
- ½ tsp. cumin seeds
- 2 cloves garlic, chopped
- 2 cups ketchup

Purée vinegar, sugar, Worcestershire, chile, cilantro, salt, aniseeds, cumin, and garlic in a blender. Pour into a 4-qt. saucepan and add ketchup. Cook over medium heat, stirring, until thickened, about 30 minutes.

KANSAS CITY BARBECUED BRISKET
SERVES 6–8

Danny Edwards, son of legendary Kansas City pit master Jake Edwards, makes his alluringly tender brisket by simmering it in water with onions atop glowing coals for six to seven hours.

- 1 8-lb. beef brisket, untrimmed
- ½ cup Paul Kirk's Dry Rub (facing page)
  Freshly ground black pepper, to taste
- 2 large yellow onions, quartered (optional)

1 Prepare for barbecuing using a kettle grill, bullet smoker, or gas grill (see Barbecue Fuel, this page, and Barbecue Flavor, facing page), using hickory wood chunks or chips. Grill is ready when the temperature reaches 265°.

2 Blot brisket with paper towels, then sprinkle rub on both sides. Place brisket, fat side up, in a disposable aluminum pan. Arrange onions around meat, then add water to come just to top of brisket.

3 Place pan on grill rack, close lid, and cook for 6–7 hours, adding coals and wood as needed. Because grills have hot spots, rotate pan occasionally. If water boils, your fire is too hot; close a vent to lower heat. Midway through cooking, turn brisket over and add more water. Do not let water boil away.

4 Brisket, which will shrink by almost half in cooking, is done when fork-tender. Remove pan from grill, transfer meat to a cutting board, and let rest for 15 minutes. Trim fat and discard. Slice and serve.

Paul Kirk's Dry Rub

MAKES 3 CUPS

Kansas City chef and "Baron of Barbecue" Paul Kirk, who gave us this recipe, told us that the anatomy of the dry rub consists of a balance of sugar and salt, with paprika added for color, chili powder for flavor, and a touch of mustard "just because." Despite its name, this spice blend is best when sprinkled onto, not rubbed into, the meat.

- 1 cup sugar
- ¼ cup seasoned salt, such as Lawry's
- ¼ cup garlic salt
- ¼ cup celery salt
- ¼ cup onion salt
- ½ cup paprika
- 3 tbsp. chili powder
- 2 tbsp. freshly ground black pepper
- 1 tbsp. lemon pepper
- 2 tsp. ground sage
- 1 tsp. dry mustard
- ½ tsp. ground thyme
- ½ tsp. cayenne pepper

Stir together sugar, seasoned salt, garlic salt, celery salt, onion salt, paprika, chili powder, black pepper, lemon pepper, sage, mustard, thyme, and cayenne into a bowl. Store in a jar away from direct sunlight for up to 6 months.

STEAK DIANE

SERVES 4

A tender, lean cut like filet mignon takes well to sautéing, as in this classic preparation with a pan sauce laced with brandy and set aflame—the brief, exuberant fire cooks off the alcohol and contributes deep, smoky flavors.

- 2 tbsp. canola oil
- 4 ¼-lb. filet mignon steaks
  Kosher salt and freshly ground black pepper
- 1½ cups beef stock
- 2 tbsp. unsalted butter
- 2 cloves garlic, minced
- 1 shallot, minced

- 4 oz. oyster or hen-of-the-woods mushrooms, torn into small pieces
- ¼ cup cognac or brandy
- ¼ cup heavy cream
- 1 tbsp. Dijon mustard
- 1 tbsp. Worcestershire sauce

BARBECUE FLAVOR

While charcoal provides the low heat required for slow-cooking meat, wood, added in chunks or chips to a bed of coals, accounts for the smoky flavor. The best ones for barbecuing are hardwoods: close-grained, low-resin woods that burn slowly and give off aromatic smoke.

Different varieties bring distinct flavors to meat. The two most widely used woods in the United States, hickory and oak, emit medium to strong smoke and are a good match for a wide range of meats. The smoke of milder woods, like alder (used to smoke salmon) and maple (ideal for pork), provides a soft, sweet flavor. Fruitwoods like cherry and apple are more assertive, with a fruity fragrance that enhances poultry and pork. Post oak is found almost exclusively in Texas, where its subtle smoke is a hallmark of Hill Country barbecue. Mesquite, common throughout the Southwest, is a highly resinous wood, and its smoke has a sweet perfume.

All of these woods come in forms suited to different kinds of cookers. Wood shavings are great for a smoker, as they burn quickly. Wood chips, roughly two inches in size, work well in gas grills, where you want a wood that smolders longer than shavings but doesn't take long to ignite. Larger and denser wood chunks (about fist size) are the best choice for the widest range of applications; they're slower burning, won't require replenishing over the course of long cooking, and allow you to control the level of smoke by removing or adding chunks. Use wood that's been dried for at least three months after cutting; if the wood is fresh-cut, the smoke will be sooty and impart a bitter taste to the meat. To ensure a slow burn, soak wood overnight in water before using so that it smolders when it hits the coals (if you add it dry, the wood will catch fire and burn out of control).

¼ tsp. Tabasco or other hot sauce
1 tbsp. minced fresh flat-leaf parsley
1 tbsp. fresh minced chives

1 Heat oil in a 12″ skillet over medium-high heat. Season steaks and add to skillet; cook, turning once, until browned on both sides and cooked to desired doneness, about 4–5 minutes for medium rare. Transfer steaks to a plate.

2 Return skillet to high heat, add stock, and cook until reduced to ½ cup, about 10 minutes. Pour into a bowl and set aside. Return skillet to medium-high heat and add butter; add garlic and shallot and cook, stirring, until soft, about 2 minutes. Add mushrooms and cook, stirring, until they release any liquid and it evaporates and mushrooms begin to brown, about 2 minutes.

3 Add cognac and light with a match to flambé. When flame dies down, stir in reserved stock, the cream, mustard, Worcestershire, and hot sauce, then return steaks to skillet. Cook, turning, until steaks are warmed through and sauce is thickened, about 4 minutes. Transfer steak to serving plates and stir parsley and chives into sauce; pour sauce over steaks to serve.

BEEF STROGANOFF
SERVES 4

This stick-to-your-ribs Russian classic is an exercise in textures: rich, creamy sauce, succulent pieces of beef tenderloin, and crisp-fried matchstick potatoes come together to create an exquisite final product.

4 tbsp. unsalted butter
2 tbsp. flour
1 tsp. dry mustard
1 cup beef stock
¼ cup sour cream
1 small onion, thinly sliced
1½ lb. beef tenderloin, cut into 3″ × 1″ × ⅛″ slices
 Kosher salt and freshly ground black pepper, to taste
 Canola oil, for frying
4 russet potatoes, peeled and sliced into ⅛″ matchsticks
2 tbsp. finely chopped fresh flat-leaf parsley

1 Heat 2 tbsp. butter in a 2-qt. saucepan over medium heat. Add the flour and dry mustard and cook, stirring, for about 2 minutes. Gradually add stock, whisking constantly, and

bring to a boil; cook until thick, about 2 minutes. Stir in the sour cream, remove pan from heat, and set aside.

2 Heat remaining butter in a 12″ skillet over medium heat. Add onion and cook until soft and lightly golden, about 5 minutes. Increase heat to high, add meat, and cook until just cooked through, about 3 minutes. Reduce heat to low, add reserved sauce, and season to taste with salt and pepper. Cover to keep warm.

3 Meanwhile, pour oil to a depth of 1½″ into a 4-qt. saucepan, and heat over medium heat until a deep-fry thermometer reads 365°. Working in batches, fry potatoes until golden and crisp, about 3 minutes. Drain on paper towels; season to taste with salt.

4 Spoon stroganoff onto a serving platter and top with fried potatoes. Garnish with parsley.

VIETNAMESE SHAKING BEEF WITH LIME DIPPING SAUCE
Bò Lúc Lắc
SERVES 4

The key to making this dish—a Vietnamese classic vibrant with garlic, red onion, and scallions, as interpreted by chef Charles Phan of San Francisco's Slanted Door—is to sear the meat in small batches in a very hot wok or skillet so that it browns quickly.

1 lb. beef tenderloin, trimmed and cut into 1″ cubes
6 tbsp. canola oil
7 tsp. sugar
4 tsp. freshly ground black pepper
 Kosher salt, to taste
1 bunch watercress, for garnish
¼ cup rice vinegar
¼ cup soy sauce
1 tbsp. nuoc mam (Vietnamese fish sauce)
 Juice of 2 limes
3 scallions, sliced into 1″ pieces
2 cloves garlic, finely chopped
1 medium red onion, thinly sliced
1 tbsp. unsalted butter

1 Toss the beef with 2 tbsp. oil, 1 tsp. sugar, and 2 tsp. pepper in a bowl and season with salt. Cover bowl and set aside to marinate at room temperature for 1 hour, or refrigerate overnight.

2 Dress a platter with watercress and set aside. In a medium bowl, whisk together vinegar, soy sauce, 2 tsp. sugar, and fish sauce to make a vinaigrette; set aside. In a small bowl, make a dipping sauce by whisking together remaining 4 tsp. sugar and 2 tsp. pepper with the lime juice; season dipping sauce with salt and set aside.

3 Drain beef, pat dry with paper towels, and discard marinade. Working in 2 batches, heat 2 tbsp. oil in a flat-bottomed wok or a 12″ nonstick skillet over high heat. When oil begins to smoke, add half of beef. Cook, stirring, until well browned and medium rare, 3–4 minutes. Add half of scallions, garlic, and red onion and cook, stirring constantly, until wilted, about 30 seconds. Add half of vinaigrette and butter and toss to combine. Spoon beef and vegetables over platter of watercress. Repeat with remaining beef, vegetables, vinaigrette, and butter. Serve with dipping sauce.

HOME-STYLE TOMATO BEEF STIR-FRY

SERVES 2

This traditional Shanghainese stir-fry shines with fresh plum tomatoes, basil, and ginger.

- 8 oz. flank steak, trimmed and sliced very thinly across the grain
- 2 tbsp. soy sauce
- 2 tsp. minced garlic
- 1 tsp. minced fresh ginger
- 1 tsp. cornstarch
- 1 tsp. Shaoxing wine
- 2 tsp. canola oil
- ½ lb. plum tomatoes, cored and cut into 1″ pieces
- 2 tsp. sugar
- ¼ cup fresh basil leaves, for garnish
  Cooked white rice, for serving

1 In a bowl, combine beef, soy sauce, garlic, ginger, cornstarch, and wine. Mix well and let sit for about 20 minutes.

2 Heat a 14″ flat-bottomed wok or high-sided skillet over high heat. Add oil and tomatoes and cook until tomatoes begin to break down and release their juice, about 3 minutes. Add marinated beef and sugar and cook, tossing often, until meat is just cooked through but still tender, about 2 minutes. Garnish with basil leaves and serve with rice.

CHICKEN FRIED STEAK WITH SAWMILL GRAVY

SERVES 4

The thick, crunchy crust is one of our favorite things about Southern-style chicken fried steak. The sawmill gravy—a creamy gravy, likely named for its 19th-century popularity as a meal served to lumberjacks working at, yes, sawmills in Appalachia—isn't so bad, either.

- 2 cups flour
- 2 tsp. paprika
  Kosher salt and freshly ground black pepper, to taste
- 1 cup buttermilk
- 1 tsp. Tabasco or other hot sauce
- 1 egg
- 4 4–6-oz. cube steaks, pounded to ¼″ thickness
  Canola oil, for frying
  Sawmill Gravy (page 196)

1 Heat oven to 200°; put a baking sheet fitted with a rack inside. In a shallow dish, whisk together flour, paprika, salt, and pepper. In another dish, whisk together buttermilk, Tabasco, and egg. Season steaks with salt and pepper. Working with 1 steak at a time, dredge in flour mixture, then egg mixture, and again in flour; shake off excess. Transfer to plate.

2 Pour oil to a depth of ½″ into a 12″ cast-iron skillet and heat over medium-high heat until a deep-fry thermometer reads 320°. Working in 2 batches, fry steaks, flipping once, until golden brown, 6–8 minutes. Place steaks on rack in oven to keep warm.

3 Make gravy as directed, then serve steaks with gravy.

COUNTRY FRIED

It ain't steak and it ain't chicken. So what is it? Chicken fried steak (some Texans shorten the name and just call it CFS) is a slice of tenderized beef round that is dipped in egg and flour, then fried and served smothered in a creamy, peppery pan gravy. This quintessential Texan dish got its name simply because it's cooked the same way fried chicken is.

Sawmill Gravy

SERVES 6

A hint of cayenne cuts through the richness of this sausage-studded white gravy. It is great over chicken fried steaks and also over split biscuits.

- 2 slices bacon, finely chopped
- ½ lb. pork breakfast sausage (page 477, or store-bought), casings removed
- ½ cup flour
- 3 cups milk
- ½ cup heavy cream
- 1 tbsp. cider vinegar
- ¼ tsp. cayenne pepper
  Kosher salt and freshly ground black pepper, to taste

1 Place bacon in a 4-qt. saucepan over medium-high heat and cook, stirring occasionally, until its fat renders, about 3 minutes.

2 Add sausage and cook, breaking it into small pieces with a wooden spoon, until browned, about 5 minutes. Add flour and cook, stirring, for 2 minutes. Add milk and cream and bring to a boil; reduce heat to medium and cook, stirring occasionally, until gravy is thickened, about 5 minutes.

3 Add vinegar, cayenne, and salt and pepper and stir until combined. Serve immediately.

RUSSIAN BRAISED BEEF BRISKET WITH PICKLED WALNUTS

SERVES 4

This piquant Russian classic gets its unique flavor from pickled walnuts—plus a healthy dose of their liquor—as well as small but powerful amounts of anchovy paste and mushroom ketchup.

- 1 2-lb. beef brisket, trimmed
  Kosher salt and freshly ground black pepper, to taste
  Flour, for dredging
- 3 tbsp. lard
- 8 small onions, quartered
- 1 medium leek, trimmed and thickly sliced on the diagonal
- 3 ribs celery, thickly sliced
- 4 small turnips, peeled and quartered
- 1 tbsp. mushroom ketchup or Worcestershire sauce
- 1 tbsp. anchovy paste
- 6 pickled walnuts, quartered lengthwise, plus 3 tbsp. pickling liquor
- 2 bay leaves
- 4 cups beef stock

1 Heat oven to 325°. Generously season beef with salt and pepper, then dredge in flour. Melt lard in a deep cast-iron pot over medium-high heat. Add beef to pot and cook until well browned on both sides, about 10 minutes. Transfer beef to a plate and set aside.

2 Reduce heat to medium. Add onions, leeks, celery, and turnips and cook, stirring often, until lightly browned, about 10 minutes. Add mushroom ketchup, anchovy paste, pickled walnuts, walnut liquor, bay leaves, and stock. Return beef and any accumulated juices to pot.

3 Bring liquid to a gentle simmer for 10 minutes, skimming off any froth that surfaces. Cover pot and put in oven. Cook until beef is very tender when poked with a skewer, about 3 hours, removing cover for final half hour. Remove bay leaves. Use 2 forks to separate beef into 4 pieces. Transfer to a platter and ladle vegetables and broth over meat.

BEEF RENDANG

Rendang Daging Sapi

SERVES 6

Former SAVEUR editor-in-chief James Oseland, who lived in West Sumatra for a year in the late '90s, learned to make the dish from a home cook there named Ibu Rohati.

- 5 medium shallots, chopped (about 1¼ cups)
- 4 medium garlic cloves, minced
- 1 2″ piece fresh galangal, peeled and finely chopped
- 1 2″ piece fresh ginger, peeled and finely chopped
- 1 ½″ piece fresh turmeric, peeled and finely chopped
- 3 candlenuts, toasted and ground
- 2 tsp. freshly grated nutmeg
  Kosher salt
- 2 lb. well-marbled boneless beef chuck, cut into 1½″ pieces
- 2 stalks fresh lemongrass
- 2½ cups unsweetened coconut milk
- 6 makrut lime leaves
- 5 fresh curry leaves
  Banana leaves, for serving (optional)
- 4–6 cups steamed, long-grain white rice, for serving (optional)

1 Using a large mortar and pestle, grind together aromatics and spices (the first 7 ingredients), plus a pinch of salt, to yield a mostly smooth paste. In a large bowl, toss paste with beef, and set aside to marinate for 1 hour.

2 Meanwhile, using dull side of a cleaver or a large chef's knife, bruise lemongrass to soften; tie each stalk into a knot.

3 Bring coconut milk to a simmer in a wok or large pot over medium heat. Add meat and marinade, lemongrass knots, and lime and curry leaves. Bring to a boil, then lower heat to medium-low and cook, stirring occasionally, until liquid reduces to a thick sauce and beef begins to sizzle and fry, about 1½ hours. Continue cooking, stirring frequently, until meat browns, about 30 minutes more. Remove lime and curry leaves and lemongrass just before serving at room temperature, atop banana leaves with rice on the side, if desired.

CORNED BEEF & CABBAGE

SERVES 10

This Irish dish shouldn't be relegated to St. Patrick's Day only: The marriage between briny meat and buttery cabbage is a winning match that deserves to be served far more often than once a year.

- ¾ tbsp. allspice
- ¾ tbsp. cloves
- ¾ tbsp. coriander
- ¾ tbsp. crushed red chile flakes
- ¾ tbsp. mustard seeds
- ¾ tbsp. black peppercorns
- 5 bay leaves, crumbled
- 1¼ cups kosher salt, plus more to taste
- ¾ cup sugar
- 1 tbsp. saltpeter (optional)
- 1 5-lb. first-cut beef brisket
- 4 cloves garlic, peeled
- 1 medium onion, peeled
- 3 lb. small new potatoes, peeled
- 1 head green or Savoy cabbage, cored and shredded
- 1 tbsp. fresh lemon juice

1 Combine spices and 3 bay leaves in a 12″ skillet over medium heat. Cook, swirling pan constantly, until spices are toasted and fragrant, about 3 minutes. Transfer half the spice mixture to a 5-qt. pot and add 8 cups water, kosher salt, sugar, and saltpeter, if using. Bring to a simmer,

remove pot from heat, and let cool to room temperature. Refrigerate brine until chilled. Add brisket and weight it down with a plate so brisket is submerged. Refrigerate for 5 days.

2 Drain corned beef and rinse. Transfer beef to a 5-qt. pot along with the remaining spice mixture, the garlic, and onion. Cover corned beef with cold water. Bring to a simmer over medium heat and simmer until corned beef is tender, about 1 hour. Remove pot from heat and set aside.

3 Meanwhile, put potatoes into a 4-qt. pot of salted water and bring to a boil. Reduce heat to medium-low and simmer until potatoes are tender; drain. Put cabbage into a 3-qt. pot over medium-low heat, season with salt, add lemon juice and ½ cup water, cover, and bring to a boil. Reduce heat to low and cook, stirring occasionally, until cabbage is tender, about 30 minutes. To serve, transfer potatoes and cabbage to a large serving platter. Transfer corned beef to a cutting board, thinly slice beef against the grain, and transfer to the platter. Spoon some of the cooking liquid over the beef and serve warm.

COOK'S NOTE If your butcher sells whole corned beef briskets, omit step 1, buy 5 lb. of corned beef from your butcher, and proceed to step 2.

SAUERBRATEN

SERVES 8–10

This sweet-sauced, sour-marinated German pot roast calls for five days in a wine-and-vinegar marinade. As it bakes, your house will fill not only with warmth from the oven but also with rich, transportive aromas.

- 1 5-lb. beef eye of round
  Kosher salt, to taste
- 2 cups red wine
- 1½ cups red wine vinegar
- 3 large onions, thinly sliced
- 1 large carrot, peeled and thinly sliced
- 1 Bouquet Garni (page 86)
- 4 tbsp. unsalted butter
- 4 slices bacon, finely chopped
- 3 tbsp. flour
- 2 tbsp. sugar
- ½ cup golden raisins
- 6 gingersnaps, crumbled
- 2 tbsp. fresh lemon juice
- 2 tbsp. chopped fresh flat-leaf parsley

1 Season beef liberally with salt in a large bowl. Bring wine, vinegar, 1 onion, the carrot, bouquet garni, and 4 cups water to a boil in a 4-qt. saucepan, then pour this marinade over beef. Cover and refrigerate, turning once or twice a day, for 5 days. Remove beef from marinade; pour marinade through a fine sieve into a bowl and dry beef thoroughly. Reserve 5 cups of the marinade and the bouquet garni.

2 Heat 2 tbsp. butter and bacon in an 8-qt. Dutch oven over medium-high heat and cook until bacon renders its fat, about 10 minutes. Transfer bacon to a plate. Add beef and cook, turning, until browned all over, about 25 minutes. Transfer to a plate.

3 Heat oven to 325°. Add remaining 2 onions to pot and cook, stirring, until caramelized, about 18 minutes. Return beef to pot with reserved marinade and bouquet garni and bring to a boil. Cover and bake until beef is very tender, about 2½ hours. Transfer beef to a platter and pour sauce through a fine sieve into a bowl.

4 Return pot to medium-high heat and add remaining butter. Add flour and sugar and cook, whisking constantly, until lightly browned, about 5 minutes. Add sauce, raisins, gingersnaps, and lemon juice; return beef to sauce. Bring to a simmer, cover, and cook until slightly reduced, about 10 minutes. Thinly slice beef and arrange on a platter. Spoon sauce over top and sprinkle with bacon and parsley.

THE SECRET TO SAUERBRATEN

"It was in Cologne in 1963 that I finally solved the riddle of preparing sauerbraten. What I could not achieve until then was the golden glow that shimmers over the deep brown gravy; browning flour in the conventional *Einbrenne* (roux) never yielded that result. But a generous chef demonstrated the secret: the addition of sugar to the *Einbrenne*. It gilds the gravy even as its sweetness balances the sour lemon note and the zing of pickling spices."

MIMI SHERATON

BRACIOLA

Italian Steak Rolls

SERVES 6

For Italians, there's nothing more comforting than meat slowly braising in a thick and fragrant tomato sauce. Here, a lean cut of beef is pounded thin, then spread with a mixture of cheese, herbs, prosciutto, raisins, and pine nuts. It's then rolled, tied, seared, and simmered for hours.

⅓	cup raisins
5	tbsp. chopped fresh flat-leaf parsley
¼	cup pine nuts
¼	cup grated Parmigiano-Reggiano
3	cloves garlic, finely chopped
12	6″ × 4″ slices boneless beef chuck, pounded to ¹⁄₁₆″ thickness
	Kosher salt and freshly ground black pepper, to taste
¼	cup olive oil
1	medium yellow onion, finely chopped
½	cup red wine
½	tsp. crushed red chile flakes
2	28-oz. cans whole, peeled tomatoes in juice, crushed by hand
1	bay leaf

1 Make the filling: Mix together raisins, 4 tbsp. parsley, pine nuts, Parmigiano, and garlic in a bowl; set aside. Place a slice of beef on a work surface perpendicular to you, season with salt and pepper, and place about 1 tbsp. filling on the bottom half. Starting with the filled half, roll beef up around the filling into a tight cylinder. Secure roll with toothpicks, then repeat with remaining beef and filling.

2 Heat oil in a 6-qt. Dutch oven over medium-high heat. Working in batches, add beef rolls and cook, turning as needed, until browned on all sides, about 6 minutes. Transfer to a plate and set aside. Add onion to pot and cook, stirring, until soft, about 5 minutes. Add wine, and cook, stirring to scrape bottom of pot, until almost evaporated, about 5 minutes. Stir in chile flakes, tomatoes, and bay leaf and then return beef rolls to pot. Bring to a boil and then reduce heat to medium-low; cook, covered partially and gently stirring occasionally, until meat is cooked through and tender, about 2 hours.

3 Remove meat rolls from sauce, remove toothpicks, and transfer to a serving platter; continue cooking sauce until reduced and thickened, about 20 minutes. Pour sauce over meat rolls and sprinkle with remaining parsley.

GRILLADES & GRITS

SERVES 4

Your French-English dictionary definition notwith-standing, *grillades* are never grilled; instead, they're simmered until tender in a Creole-inflected version of Italian tomato gravy. Resting atop creamy grits, they're an essential New Orleans dish.

- 3 cups chicken stock
- 1 cup stone-ground grits
- 4 tbsp. unsalted butter, cubed, plus more for serving
- 1 tsp. minced fresh thyme
  Kosher salt and freshly ground black pepper, to taste
- 1 tbsp. canola oil
- 1 lb. beef tenderloin, cut into ¼"-thick slices
- 1 cup flour, for dredging
- 3 cloves garlic, finely chopped
- ½ small yellow onion, finely chopped

- ¼ medium red onion, finely chopped
- ¼ green bell pepper, seeded and finely chopped
- ¼ red bell pepper, seeded and finely chopped
- 1 plum tomato, seeded and finely chopped
- ¼ cup red wine
- 1 cup beef stock
- 2 tbsp. roughly chopped fresh parsley
  Warm biscuits, for serving (page 451)

1 Bring stock and 2 cups water to a boil in a 4-qt. saucepan over high heat. Whisking constantly, add grits; reduce heat to medium. Cook, stirring often, until grits are tender, about 25 minutes. Stir in 3 tbsp. butter and the thyme, season with salt and pepper, and keep grits warm.

2 Heat oil in a 12″ skillet over medium-high heat. Season beef with salt and pepper; dredge in flour. Working in batches, add to skillet and cook, turning once, until lightly browned, about 4 minutes. Transfer to a plate; set aside. Return skillet to heat and add remaining butter. Add garlic, both onions, and both peppers and cook until soft, about 4 minutes. Add tomato and cook for 5 minutes. Add wine and cook until evaporated, about 3 minutes. Return beef to skillet and add stock; cook until reduced, about 5 minutes. Spoon grits onto plates, top with beef, and pour pan juices over the top. Sprinkle with parsley and serve with biscuits.

THAI YELLOW CURRY WITH BEEF & POTATOES

Kaeng Kari

SERVES 8–10

Chef and author Andy Ricker gave us good advice for making this recipe: Make it exactly as written the first time, then adjust the seasonings and the quantity of coconut milk on your later attempts. "Put your stamp on it," says Ricker. "After all, that's what the Thai do."

FOR THE PASTE

- 6 small Asian shallots or 2 medium regular shallots, unpeeled
- 2 small heads garlic, unpeeled
- 1 3″-piece galangal, peeled and thinly sliced
- 1 2″-piece fresh ginger, peeled and thinly sliced
- 1 tsp. coriander seeds
- 20 dried red bird's eye chiles, stemmed and roughly chopped

---

A SUNDAY DINNER CLASSIC

"Many of my favorite memories are of the epic Sunday dinners at my grandparents' house in Philadelphia. My grandmother, Nancy DiRenzo, would be up at dawn cooking. By 2:00 p.m., family would start piling in for what would inevitably become a six-hour meal; guests spilled from the dining room to the kitchen to the living room, eating off folding TV trays. The centerpiece was the rich tomato gravy. What gave it its heft were the meats that Grandmom cooked in it: pork sausages, meatballs, and, my favorite, *braciola*. I've had similar dishes with names like *involtini* or *rollatini*; what these recipes share is the art of stretching a little protein to feed as many mouths as possible. These days, I find myself putting up a pot of "red gravy" on Sundays, just like Grandmom's, studded with meatballs, good sausage, and, of course, *braciola*. For some reason, maybe it's just a trick of memory, but hers was better than mine."

MICHAEL COLAMECO

2 tbsp. ground turmeric

2 tbsp. mild curry powder

2 tbsp. roughly chopped cilantro root or stems

2 tbsp. shrimp paste

1½ tbsp. kosher salt

6 stalks lemongrass, trimmed and thinly sliced

FOR THE CURRY

1½ lb. beef chuck, trimmed and cut into 2″ strips about ½″ thick

3 cups canned coconut milk

1 cup canned coconut cream

10 small Asian shallots, halved, or 3 medium regular shallots, quartered

3 large Yukon gold potatoes, peeled and cut into 1½″ pieces

2 tbsp. grated palm sugar

1 tbsp. nam pla (Thai fish sauce)

Cooked jasmine rice, for serving

1 Make the paste: Heat a 12″ cast-iron skillet over medium-high heat. Place shallots and garlic on a piece of foil and fold into a tight package; add to pan. Cook, flipping once, until soft, about 25 minutes. Let cool, then peel and roughly chop; set aside. Place galangal and ginger in a single layer on a piece of foil and fold into a flat package; add to pan. Cook, flipping once, until soft, about 7 minutes; set aside. Heat coriander seeds in pan until seeds begin to pop, 1–2 minutes; let cool slightly. Place in a spice grinder and pulse until finely ground; set aside.

2 Place chiles in a bowl and cover with 2 cups boiling water; let sit until soft, about 15 minutes. Drain, reserving 2 tbsp. liquid. Place chiles in a small food processor with shallots, garlic, galangal, ginger, coriander, turmeric, curry powder, cilantro root, shrimp paste, salt, and lemongrass; pulse until roughly chopped. Add reserved liquid and purée until smooth. Set 1 cup of the curry paste aside; refrigerate remaining paste for future use up to 2 weeks.

3 Make the curry: Bring beef and coconut milk to a simmer in a 4-qt. saucepan over medium heat. Cook, stirring occasionally, until beef is very tender, about 1 hour. Using a slotted spoon, transfer beef to a bowl and reserve 1½ cups coconut milk; set beef and coconut milk aside.

4 Heat coconut cream in a 6-qt. saucepan or 13″–14″ wok over medium heat. Cook, stirring occasionally, until oil is

separated, about 30 minutes. Add the 1 cup reserved curry paste and cook, stirring, until slightly browned, about 7 minutes. Add reserved coconut milk along with 3 cups water; bring to a boil. Add reserved beef, plus shallots and potatoes. Reduce heat to medium-low and cook, stirring occasionally, until potatoes are very tender, about 40 minutes. Stir in palm sugar and fish sauce. Serve with jasmine rice.

BACHEOFE
Alsatian Meat & Vegetable Stew
SERVES 6

This wine-simmered dish of meat and vegetables cooked in a dough-sealed pot is Alsatian through and through. It's an improvised meal of odds and ends that cooks for hours at low heat, while you go about your business, and emerges from the oven with enormous flavor. According to the French culinary bible *Larousse Gastronomique,* on Monday washdays in Alsace, women would take a filled terrine to the baker, who would cook the *Bacheofe* in the residual heat of the oven—the dish's name literally means "baker's oven"—to be retrieved post-laundry.

1 lb. boneless beef chuck, trimmed and cut into 1½″ pieces

1 lb. boneless pork shoulder, trimmed and cut into 1½″ pieces

1 lb. boneless lamb shoulder, trimmed and cut into 1½″ pieces

Kosher salt and freshly ground black pepper, to taste

3 cups dry white wine

¼ cup fresh flat-leaf parsley leaves, finely chopped

2 tsp. juniper berries

5 cloves garlic, chopped

2 bay leaves

2 medium carrots, peeled and thinly sliced

2 medium yellow onions, thinly sliced

2 small leeks, trimmed and thinly sliced

2 sprigs fresh thyme

¼ cup rendered duck or goose fat or butter

3 lb. Yukon gold potatoes, peeled and sliced

1 lb. thick-cut bacon

1 cup flour, plus more for dusting

1 Place beef, pork, and lamb in a bowl; season with salt and pepper. Add wine, parsley, juniper berries, garlic, bay, carrots, onions, leeks, and thyme; mix together, cover with plastic wrap, and refrigerate overnight or up to 2 days.

2 Heat oven to 350°. Rub a 10-qt. Dutch oven with fat. Layer potatoes, marinated meat, and vegetables in the pot, seasoning between each layer with salt and pepper and ending with a layer of potatoes. Pour in remaining marinade and arrange the bacon, overlapping the slices slightly, over the top.

3 Mix flour and 5 tbsp. water in a bowl; transfer to a floured surface and knead briefly. Roll dough into a rope and transfer to rim of pot; press to adhere and cover with lid. Bake for 3½ hours. Using a paring knife, carefully break the seal and discard pastry rope; remove lid to serve.

JOE'S SPECIAL

SERVES 4

Joe's Special is one of the most odd and divine scrambles known to man. Consisting of egg, garlic, spinach, and ground beef, the dish originated in San Francisco in the 1920s, at a long-gone Italian-American restaurant, New Joe's. Later, it was the signature dish of a Bay Area chain called Original Joe's—and a standby for countless home cooks in Northern California.

- 2 tbsp. olive oil
- 5 cloves garlic, minced
- 1 medium yellow onion, finely chopped
- ½ lb. ground beef chuck
- 1 10-oz. package frozen chopped spinach, thawed and squeezed dry
- 8 eggs, lightly beaten
  Kosher salt and freshly ground black pepper, to taste
- ¼ cup grated Parmigiano-Reggiano
  Crusty Italian bread, for serving

Heat oil in a 12″ skillet over medium-high heat. Add garlic and onion and cook until soft, about 5 minutes. Add chuck and cook, stirring, until browned and all moisture evaporates, about 10 minutes. Add spinach and cook until heated through, about 2 minutes. Add eggs and cook until eggs are cooked and mixture is slightly dry, about 4 minutes. Season with salt and pepper and sprinkle with Parmigiano. Serve with bread.

STUFFED CABBAGE ROLLS

Holishkes

SERVES 6–8

These beef-stuffed cabbage rolls are a Jewish holiday mainstay. They stay tender and moist while baking, thanks to a layer of lightly sweetened tomato sauce.

- Kosher salt, to taste
- 1 large head cabbage, cored
- 2 tbsp. canola oil
- 3 medium onions, 2 thinly sliced, 1 finely grated (about ½ cup)
- 2 ribs celery, finely chopped
  Freshly ground black pepper, to taste
- ¼ cup tomato paste
- ⅓ cup raisins
- ¼ cup honey
- ¼ cup fresh lemon juice
- 1 32-oz. can whole, peeled tomatoes in juice, puréed
- 1 lb. ground beef chuck
- ¼ cup uncooked long-grain white rice, soaked in hot water for 10 minutes, then drained
- 3 tbsp. beef stock
- 1 tsp. paprika
- ¼ tsp. cayenne pepper
- 1 egg, lightly beaten

1 Bring a large pot of salted water to a boil over high heat. Add cabbage and cook, pulling off each outer leaf with tongs as it becomes tender, about 2 minutes per leaf. Transfer leaves to a baking sheet and continue until you have 20 leaves.

2 Heat oil in a 6-qt. saucepan over medium-high heat. Add sliced onions and celery, season with salt and pepper, and cook, stirring, until lightly caramelized, about 15 minutes. Add tomato paste and cook, stirring, until lightly caramelized, about 2 minutes. Add raisins, honey, lemon juice, and tomatoes and bring to a boil. Reduce heat to medium-low and cook, partially covered, until reduced, about 30 minutes.

3 Heat oven to 350°. Combine remaining grated onion, beef, rice, stock, paprika, cayenne, egg, salt, and pepper in a bowl. Place 2 tbsp. beef mixture in center of each cabbage leaf, fold sides over filling, and then roll up. Transfer rolls, seam side down, to a 9″×13″ baking dish. Pour tomato sauce over rolls and bake until filling is cooked through, about 45 minutes.

> "There are many miracles in the world to be celebrated and, for me, garlic is the most deserving."
>
> LEO BUSCAGLIA

PICADILLO

SERVES 4

A traditional ground meat dish throughout Latin America and the Philippines, picadillo may be served on its own, with rice or tortillas, as a stuffing for empanadas (this page), or any of a thousand other ways. This version combines the meat with a sweet-savory blend of garlic, bell peppers, scallions, green olives, raisins, capers, and tomato sauce.

3	lb. ground beef
10	cloves garlic, minced
1	green bell pepper, seeded and chopped
2	scallions, finely chopped
25	pitted green olives, chopped
½	cup raisins
3	tbsp. capers, drained
2	bay leaves
1½	tsp. ground cumin
1	tsp. dried oregano
1	cup tomato sauce
½	cup dry sherry
3	tbsp. olive oil
	Kosher salt, to taste

1 Mix together beef, garlic, peppers, scallions, olives, raisins, capers, bay leaves, cumin, oregano, tomato sauce, and sherry in a bowl. Cover and set aside for 30 minutes.

2 Heat oil in a large pot over medium heat. Add beef mixture and cook, breaking up meat with the back of a spoon, for 30–40 minutes. Season with salt. Remove bay leaves.

PICADILLO-STUFFED EMPANADAS

MAKES ABOUT 2 DOZEN

Picadillo makes a fragrant filling for these sugar-dusted, savory-sweet empanadas.

4	cups flour
6	tbsp. unsalted butter, cubed
1½	tsp. kosher salt, plus more to taste
½	recipe Picadillo (this page)
	Freshly ground black pepper, to taste
	Canola oil, for frying
	Confectioners' sugar, for dusting

1 Combine flour, butter, and salt in a large bowl and, using your fingers, rub butter into flour until pea-size crumbles form. Add 1½ cups warm water and stir until dough forms. Knead in the bowl until smooth, about 4 minutes. Wrap in plastic wrap and refrigerate for 1 hour.

2 Divide dough into 24 balls and place on a work surface. Using a small rolling pin or the heel of your hand, flatten each ball into a 5″ disk, brush edges with water and place 2 tbsp. filling in the center. Fold disks in half to form half-moons and seal edges together using the tines of a fork. Refrigerate empanadas for at least 1 hour or up to overnight.

3 Pour oil to a depth of 2″ into a 6-qt. saucepan and heat over medium-high heat until a deep-fry thermometer reads 350°. Working in batches, fry empanadas until browned and crisp, about 6 minutes. Transfer to paper towels to drain. Dust lightly with confectioners' sugar before serving.

MEATBALLS IN TOMATO SAUCE

Keftedes me Saltsa Domata

SERVES 4–6

Redolent of oregano and mint, these meatballs—which are sometimes flattened circles, sometimes elongated ovals, and sometimes perfect spheres, depending on the cook—are served in northern Greece with fried potatoes or steamed rice.

- 1 tbsp. dried mint
- 5 tbsp. extra-virgin olive oil, plus more for frying
- 2 tbsp. dried oregano
- ¼ tsp. ground cinnamon
- ¼ tsp. freshly grated nutmeg
- ⅛ tsp. cayenne pepper
- 1 medium red onion, grated
- 1 large egg and 1 yolk, beaten
  Kosher salt and freshly ground black pepper, to taste
- 1 cup milk
- 3 ½"-thick slices stale country bread, crusts removed
- 1 lb. ground beef, pork, or lamb
- ½ cup flour, for dredging
- 4 cloves garlic, minced
- 1½ tbsp. tomato paste
- 2 bay leaves
- 1 28-oz. can whole, peeled tomatoes in juice, drained and puréed
- 1 cup beef stock
- 1 tbsp. fresh lemon juice
- 2 tbsp. chopped fresh flat-leaf parsley, for garnish

1 In a medium bowl, combine mint, 2 tbsp. oil, 1 tbsp. oregano, ⅛ tsp. cinnamon, ⅛ tsp. nutmeg, cayenne, onion, and eggs; season with salt and pepper. Put milk and bread in a bowl and let soak 5 minutes. Drain bread and squeeze out milk. Mix bread, onion mixture, and meat. Divide mixture into 20 balls; flatten slightly into patties or roll into ovals. Dredge each meatball in flour. Pour enough oil into a 12" skillet to reach a depth of ½"; heat over medium-high heat. Working in 3 batches, cook meatballs until browned, 6–8 minutes. Transfer meatballs to paper towels. Discard oil; wipe out skillet.

2 Heat remaining oil in skillet over medium heat. Add garlic and cook 1 minute. Stir in tomato paste and bay leaves; cook for 2 minutes. Add remaining oregano, cinnamon, and nutmeg, along with the tomatoes and stock. Cook, stirring, until thickened, 15–20 minutes.

Season with salt, pepper, and lemon juice. Nestle meatballs in sauce and cook until sauce coats meatballs, about 5 minutes. Garnish with parsley.

SWEDISH MEATBALLS WITH MASHED POTATOES

Köttbullar med Potatismos

SERVES 6

In Sweden, meatballs are served every which way: plain, as a snack, on a sandwich with beet salad, or, as they are here, with mashed potatoes, creamy gravy, and tart lingonberry preserves.

- 4 lb. (about 5 large) russet potatoes, peeled and cut into 1" chunks
- 2¼ cups heavy cream
- 14 tbsp. unsalted butter, cubed
  Kosher salt and freshly ground black or white pepper, to taste
- 2 slices crustless white bread, torn into small pieces
- ¾ lb. ground pork
- ¾ lb. ground beef
- ¼ tsp. ground allspice
- 1 egg, lightly beaten
- ½ small onion, minced
- 3 tbsp. flour
- 3 cups beef stock
  Lingonberry preserves, for serving

1 Make the mashed potatoes: Place potatoes in a 4-qt. saucepan and cover with water by 1"; bring to a boil over high heat and cook until potatoes are tender, about 15 minutes. Drain potatoes and pass through a ricer or food mill set over a bowl; set aside. Meanwhile bring 1½ cups cream and 12 tbsp. butter to a boil in a 1-qt. saucepan; pour over potatoes and whisk until smooth. Season with salt and pepper and keep warm until ready to serve.

2 Make the meatballs: Place ½ cup cream and bread in a small bowl; let sit until soft, about 5 minutes. Transfer to a large bowl along with pork, beef, allspice, egg, and onion, season with salt and pepper, and mix until evenly combined. Shape mixture into about thirty 1-oz. balls, about 1" in diameter. Heat remaining 2 tbsp. butter in a 12" skillet over medium heat. Working in batches, add meatballs and cook, turning as needed, until browned all over and cooked through, about 12 minutes. Using a slotted spoon, transfer meatballs to a plate and set aside.

3 Return skillet to medium-high heat. Add flour and cook, stirring, until smooth and light brown, about 4 minutes. Whisk in stock until smooth and then bring to a boil; stir in remaining ¼ cup cream and return meatballs to gravy. Reduce heat to medium and cook, stirring gently, until meatballs are warmed through, about 3 minutes; season with salt and pepper. Serve meatballs and gravy over mashed potatoes and garnish with a generous dollop of lingonberry preserves.

HERB MEATBALLS IN TOMATO-PLUM SAUCE

Kufteh

SERVES 4–6

These tender Iranian meatballs perfumed with dill, tarragon, parsley, and chives have a hidden secret: Bite into one and you'll find a dried, sour plum in the middle that's been rehydrated thanks to the moist meat and sweet-tart tomato sauce in which they've been simmering.

- ½ cup yellow split peas
- 1 lb. ground beef
- 1 cup cooked basmati rice
- ½ cup finely chopped fresh dill
- ½ cup finely chopped fresh tarragon
- ¼ cup finely chopped fresh parsley
- ¼ cup finely chopped fresh chives
- 1 tbsp. ground turmeric
- ½ tsp. crushed saffron threads
- 1 egg, lightly beaten
  Kosher salt and freshly ground black pepper, to taste
- 1 cup dried sour plums
- ¼ cup olive oil
- 2 medium onions, sliced
- ¼ cup tomato paste
- 2 plum tomatoes, seeded and roughly chopped

1 Bring peas and 2 cups water to a boil in a 2-qt. saucepan over high heat; cook until tender, about 40 minutes. Drain; transfer to a bowl. Add beef, rice, dill, tarragon, parsley, chives, turmeric, saffron, egg, salt and pepper and mix well. Place ⅓ cup meat mixture in your hand and place a dried plum in the center; form around plum into a 2″ ball. Repeat with remaining meat; chill. Reserve unused plums.

2 Heat oil in a 6-qt. saucepan over medium-high heat. Add onions and cook until softened, about 15 minutes.

Add tomato paste and cook until lightly caramelized, about 2 minutes. Add tomatoes and cook until soft, about 5 minutes. Add remaining dried plums and 3 cups water and bring to a boil. Add meatballs to sauce, reduce heat to medium-low and cook, covered, until cooked through, about 45 minutes. Season with salt and pepper.

VEAL CHOP AU JUS

SERVES 2

A rich, concentrated sauce made from veal stock, like the traditional one accompanying this dish from Las Vegas' Joël Robuchon, takes time—but it's a great way to add a richer flavor to a simply seared veal chop.

FOR THE JUS

- 4 tbsp. canola oil
- 4 lb. boneless veal breast, trimmed of fat, cut into 1″ cubes
- 1 yellow onion, roughly chopped
- 1 carrot, roughly chopped
- 1 head garlic, halved crosswise
- 4 sprigs fresh thyme

FOR THE VEAL CHOP

- 1 1½-lb. bone-in veal chop, about 2½″ thick
- 4 tbsp. extra-virgin olive oil
  Kosher salt and freshly ground black pepper
- 2 tbsp. unsalted butter
- 2 sprigs fresh rosemary
- 4 sprigs fresh thyme
- 2 cloves garlic
- ¼ lb. shiitake mushrooms, stemmed and quartered

1 Make the jus: Heat 2 tbsp. oil in 6-qt. wide-bottomed pot. Working in 2 batches, add veal and cook, stirring occasionally, until well browned, about 6 minutes. Using a slotted spoon, transfer veal to a plate.

2 Add onion, carrot, garlic, and thyme and cook, stirring occasionally, until browned. Add 1 cup water and stir vigorously to loosen browned bits from bottom of pot. Add veal and 16 cups water and bring to a boil. Reduce heat to medium-low and simmer, without stirring, until the broth has reduced by roughly half, about 3 hours.

3 Strain liquid through a fine-mesh sieve into a 4-qt. saucepan set over high heat; reserve solids for stew or soup. Bring liquid to a boil over medium-high heat and cook until it reduces to about ½ cup, about 1 hour; cover and set sauce aside.

4 Heat oven to 350°. Rub veal chop with 1 tbsp. oil and massage in salt and pepper. Heat 1 tbsp. oil in an ovenproof 10″ skillet over high heat. Add veal and cook, turning occasionally, until browned on all sides, about 12 minutes. Add butter, rosemary, thyme, and garlic to the skillet and transfer to the oven. Roast, basting frequently with the juices, until veal is medium rare and an instant-read thermometer inserted into center of the chop reads 140°, about 30 minutes. Transfer veal to a plate and let rest for 10 minutes. Discard herbs and garlic from skillet.

5 Heat remaining 2 tbsp. oil in the skillet over medium-high heat, add mushrooms, and cook, stirring occasionally, until golden brown, 5 minutes. Carve veal into ½″-thick slices and serve with sauce and mushrooms.

VEAL CUTLETS WITH HERB-TOMATO SAUCE

Chuletas de Ternera al Sartén con Salsa de Tomate & Hierbas

SERVES 4

Veal cutlets are topped with a pan sauce of onion, tomato, olive, and pickled peppers in our rendition of a dish served at the restaurant El Renaciente in Buenos Aires.

- ½ cup olive oil
- 1½ lb. veal cutlets
  Kosher salt and freshly ground black pepper
- ½ tsp. crushed red chile flakes
- 8 cloves garlic, thinly sliced
- 1 small onion, thinly sliced
- ⅓ cup dry white wine
- 1 15-oz. can whole, peeled tomatoes, drained and crushed by hand
- 1 bay leaf
- 3 tbsp. roughly chopped fresh flat-leaf parsley
- 2½ tbsp. roughly chopped oregano
- 2 tbsp. fresh lemon juice
- 10 Spanish green olives, pitted and smashed
- 6 pickled cherry peppers, stemmed, seeded, and halved

1 Heat 2 tbsp. oil in a 12″ skillet over medium-high heat. Season veal with salt and pepper. Working in batches and adding more oil as needed, cook veal, flipping once, until browned and cooked to desired doneness, 4–6 minutes for medium. Transfer veal to a serving platter; keep warm.

2 Add remaining 6 tbsp. oil to pan. Add chile flakes, garlic, and onion and cook, stirring occasionally, until golden,

6–8 minutes. Add wine and bring to a boil. Cook, stirring and scraping the bottom of the pan, until reduced by half, about 3 minutes. Add tomatoes, bay leaf, and salt. Cook until tomatoes begin to break down, 3–5 minutes. Stir in parsley, oregano, lemon juice, olives, and peppers, then spoon sauce over veal.

VEAL PICCATA

SERVES 6 (SEE PHOTO, PAGE 232)

In this Italian-American classic, tender veal cutlets are pounded into thin scaloppine and then dredged in flour and sautéed in butter, getting a boost from a simple pan sauce made with white wine and a generous squeeze of lemon.

- 12 2–3-oz. veal cutlets, pounded until ¼″ thick (see How to Pound Scaloppine, this page)
  Kosher salt and freshly ground black pepper, to taste
- ½ cup flour
- 4 tbsp. unsalted butter
- 2 tbsp. olive oil
- ½ cup dry white wine
- 1¼ cups chicken stock
- 1 lemon, thinly sliced
- 1 tbsp. fresh lemon juice
- ¼ cup capers, drained
- 2 tbsp. chopped fresh flat-leaf parsley

HOW TO POUND SCALOPPINE

Very thin cutlets, called scaloppine, are essential to dishes such as veal piccata (this page), saltimbocca (page 206), and parmesan (page 206). Pounding them until they're thin tenderizes the meat and allows it to cook quickly. The key is to achieve maximal thinness without tearing or damaging the meat.

STEP 1 Place a 2–3-oz. veal top round cutlet between 2 sheets of plastic wrap.

STEP 2 With a meat mallet held waffled side down, begin pounding the veal cutlet using medium force, taking care not to work one part of the cutlet more than any other. When the cutlet is about ¼″ thick or less, tap it all over with the flat side of the mallet to smooth out the surface of the meat.

1 Season veal with salt and pepper and dredge in flour, shaking off excess. Heat 2 tbsp. butter and oil in a 12″ skillet over medium-high heat. Working in batches, add veal and cook, turning once, until golden brown, about 3 minutes. Transfer to a serving platter, and set aside.

2 Add wine to skillet and cook, scraping bottom of pan, until reduced by half, about 3 minutes. Add stock and lemon slices and bring to a boil; cook until reduced by half, about 8 minutes. Add remaining 2 tbsp. butter, lemon juice, capers, and parsley and season with salt and pepper. Pour sauce over veal and serve immediately.

VEAL SALTIMBOCCA ALLA ROMANA
SERVES 2–4

In this Roman preparation, pounded veal cutlets are pressed with prosciutto and then seared, giving them a crispy exterior. This flavorful dish is slightly salty, slightly woodsy—thanks to the fresh sage leaves—and entirely sumptuous.

8	3-oz. veal cutlets, pounded until ¼″ thick (see How to Pound Scaloppine, page 205) Kosher salt and freshly ground black pepper, to taste
16–24	thin slices prosciutto
16	fresh sage leaves
½	cup flour
4	tbsp. olive oil
8	tbsp. unsalted butter
¼	cup marsala wine
1	cup chicken stock

1 Lightly season veal with salt and pepper.

2 Lay 2–3 thin slices of prosciutto atop each piece of veal, gently pressing prosciutto against veal to adhere. Place 2 sage leaves on top of the prosciutto and attach them into the veal with a toothpick. Place flour on a large plate. Dredge each piece of veal in flour, shake off any excess, and set aside.

3 Heat 2 tbsp. oil and 2 tbsp. butter in a 12″ skillet over medium-high heat. Add half the meat and cook, turning once, until prosciutto side is crisp and the veal side is lightly browned, about 1 minute per side. Transfer the meat to a paper towel–lined plate. Repeat with remaining 1 tbsp. oil, 2 tbsp. butter, and remaining meat. Remove and discard the toothpicks.

4 Discard oil and butter from skillet and place over high heat. Add marsala and cook, scraping up browned bits, until reduced by half, 1–2 minutes. Add stock and reduce by half, about 3 minutes. Stir in remaining 4 tbsp. of butter and reduce heat to medium. Return meat to pan and cook, turning occasionally, until sauce thickens slightly, 1–2 minutes. Serve immediately.

WIENER SCHNITZEL
SERVES 2

Breaded, sautéed schnitzel in Vienna is often made with pork—but that's just an inexpensive alternative to veal, the meat original to the dish. This recipe comes from Weibel's Wirtshaus, a cozy little restaurant near the city center.

4	¼-lb. pieces veal top round, pounded until ¼″ thick Kosher salt, to taste
1	cup flour
2	eggs
2	cups fresh bread crumbs
½	cup Clarified Butter (page 595)
½	cup vegetable oil
1	lemon, halved crosswise

1 Season veal with salt and set aside. Put flour into a wide, shallow dish and set aside. Lightly beat eggs in a second wide, shallow dish and set aside. Put bread crumbs into a third wide, shallow dish and set aside. Dredge 1 piece of veal at a time in flour, shaking off excess, then dip into egg, evenly coating each side, then dredge in bread crumbs.

2 Heat ¼ cup clarified butter and ¼ cup oil together in each of 2 large heavy-bottomed skillets over medium-high heat until hot but not smoking. Cook 2 pieces of veal at a time in each skillet, turning once and gently shaking skillet over heat, until golden brown and puffed slightly, 1–1½ minutes per side. Drain on paper towels.

3 Divide veal between 2 large warmed plates and serve each with half a lemon for squeezing over.

VEAL PARMESAN
SERVES 4

This rich and cheesy Italian-American favorite—breaded, fried veal cutlets topped with tomato sauce and a blanket of broiled cheese—is great over pasta, or pile the cutlets on an Italian roll for a seriously satisfying sandwich.

½ cup flour
4 eggs, beaten
1½ cups dried bread crumbs
8 3-oz. veal cutlets, pounded until ¼″ thick
(see How to Pound Scaloppine, page 205)
Kosher salt and freshly ground black pepper,
to taste
8 tbsp. olive oil
3 cups tomato sauce (page 357, or store-bought)
8 slices provolone cheese
¾ cup grated Parmigiano-Reggiano
2 tbsp. roughly chopped fresh flat-leaf parsley

1 Arrange a rack 10″ from broiler and heat broiler. Place flour, eggs, and bread crumbs into separate shallow dishes. Season veal with salt and pepper. Working with 1 piece of veal at a time, dredge in flour, dip in eggs, coat in bread crumbs, and transfer to a plate.

2 Heat 2 tbsp. oil in a 12″ skillet over medium-high heat. Working in batches, and adding more oil as needed, cook veal, flipping once, until golden, 3–4 minutes. Transfer veal cutlets to a foil-lined baking sheet in a single layer. Spoon about ⅓ cup tomato sauce over each cutlet, then top with 1 slice provolone and sprinkle with 1½ tbsp. Parmigiano. Broil until cheese is golden and bubbly, 4–5 minutes. Garnish with parsley.

OSSO BUCO

SERVES 6

Rick Moonen, chef of RM Seafood in Las Vegas, gave us his mother's recipe for these falling-off-the-bone veal shanks. We like to serve them with mashed potatoes (page 409) to soak up the rich gravy from the pan.

6 1½″-thick crosscut veal shanks, tied with
kitchen twine
Kosher salt and freshly ground black pepper,
to taste
1 cup flour
2 tbsp. canola oil
3 tbsp. unsalted butter
2 large onions, minced
2 medium carrots, peeled and minced
2 ribs celery, minced
2 tbsp. tomato paste
1 bunch fresh flat-leaf parsley
5 sprigs fresh thyme
2 bay leaves
1 750-ml bottle dry white wine

1 cup veal stock (optional)
8 cloves garlic, minced
Grated zest of 3 lemons

1 Heat oven to 325°. Season veal shanks with salt and pepper. Put flour on a large plate and dredge each shank veal in flour, shaking off excess; transfer to a plate.

2 Heat oil in a 6-qt. Dutch oven over medium-high heat. Working in 2 batches, add veal shanks and cook, flipping once, until browned, about 10 minutes. Transfer veal shanks to a plate; cover.

3 Add butter to pot, then stir in onions, carrots, and celery and cook, stirring and scraping any browned bits from bottom of pot with a wooden spoon, until soft, about 10 minutes. Stir in tomato paste and cook for 2 minutes. Tie 3 parsley sprigs and thyme with kitchen twine and add to pot along with bay leaves, veal shanks, wine, and veal stock (if using) or 1 cup water. Bring to a simmer, season lightly with salt and pepper, and cover.

4 Transfer pot to oven and cook until veal is nearly falling off the bone, about 1½ hours.

5 Transfer veal shanks to a plate and cover with aluminum foil. Discard herb bundle and bay leaves. Heat pot over medium heat and reduce liquid by half. Return veal shanks to pot, spoon over liquid, and cover to keep warm. Meanwhile, finely chop remaining parsley leaves and toss in a bowl with garlic and lemon zest. Sprinkle some of parsley mixture over veal shanks and serve family-style from the pot along with the remaining parsley mixture.

VITELLO TONNATO

Veal with Tuna Sauce

SERVES 6–8

A briny purée of canned tuna, mayonnaise, anchovy filets, lemon juice, and capers are layered with tender slices of veal in this classic Piedmontese dish, which is served at room temperature.

FOR THE VEAL
2½ lb. boneless lean veal roast, preferably
top round, firmly trussed
1 medium carrot, peeled and chopped
1 rib celery, without leaves, chopped
1 medium onion, chopped
4 sprigs fresh flat-leaf parsley
1 bay leaf

> ## "The only time to eat diet food is while you're waiting for the steak to cook."
> JULIA CHILD

FOR THE TUNA SAUCE

1	7-oz. can olive oil–packed tuna, drained
5	oil-packed anchovy filets
1	cup extra-virgin olive oil
1	tbsp. fresh lemon juice
3	tbsp. capers, soaked and rinsed
1¼	cups mayonnaise

FOR GARNISH

Thin lemon slices
Pitted black olives, slivered
Capers
Fresh flat-leaf parsley leaves
Oil-packed anchovy filets

1 Make the veal: Place veal in a deep, heavy pan. Add carrot, celery, onion, parsley, bay leaf, and enough water to cover. Remove meat from pan and set it aside. Cover pan, bring water to a boil, then add veal. Return to a boil, cover, reduce heat, and gently simmer for 2 hours. Add more water if necessary. Remove from heat, set aside, and allow meat to cool in stock.

2 Make the tuna sauce: Put tuna into a food processor with anchovies, oil, lemon juice, and capers. Process until it becomes a creamy, beige sauce. Fold sauce gently but thoroughly into mayonnaise. If made ahead of time, cover and refrigerate.

3 When meat is cool, transfer to a cutting board. Remove trussing strings, and carefully cut into ¼" slices.

4 Spread some tuna sauce on bottom of a platter. Arrange a single layer of veal slices over sauce, edge to edge and without overlapping; cover with sauce. Repeat layering, ending with sauce.

5 Cover veal with plastic wrap and refrigerate for at least 24 hours. (It will keep for at least 1 week.) Bring to room temperature before serving. Use a spatula to smooth the sauce on top, and garnish with a mix of garnishes.

BLANQUETTE DE VEAU
SERVES 6–8

This delicate, rich preparation of veal, butter, cream, and carrots consistently ranks in the top ten when the French are surveyed about their favorite dishes.

3	lb. boneless veal shoulder, cut into 1″ chunks
1	Bouquet Garni (page 86)
10	oz. pearl onions, peeled
16	baby carrots, peeled
2	small bulbs fennel, each cut into 8 wedges
10	oz. button mushrooms, quartered
5	ribs celery, cut into 1″ pieces
3	tbsp. unsalted butter
2½	tbsp. flour
2	cups heavy cream
1	tbsp. fresh lemon juice
	Kosher salt and freshly ground white pepper, to taste
	Cayenne pepper, to taste
	Cooked white rice, for serving
⅓	cup crème fraîche, for serving
	Fresh flat-leaf parsley leaves, for garnish

1 Bring veal, bouquet garni, and 10 cups water to a boil in a 6-qt. saucepan over high heat; reduce heat to medium-low and cook, occasionally skimming any impurities that rise to the surface, for 30 minutes. Add onions, carrots, and fennel and cook for 30 minutes. Add mushrooms and celery and cook until veal is very tender and vegetables are tender, about 20 minutes. Using a slotted spoon, transfer veal and vegetables to a bowl; cover and keep warm. Pour cooking liquid through a fine sieve into a bowl; place 4 cups in a 2-qt. saucepan. Bring to a boil and reduce to 2 cups, about 30 minutes.

2 Wipe 6-qt. saucepan clean and return to medium heat; add butter. Add flour and cook, stirring, until smooth, about 2 minutes. Add reduced stock and cream and bring to a boil; cook until thickened and slightly reduced, about 15 minutes. Return veal and vegetables to sauce and cook until warmed through, about 5 minutes. Stir in lemon juice, salt, pepper, and cayenne; divide among bowls with rice. Drizzle with crème fraîche and garnish with parsley leaves.

Preceding page: Salade Niçoise (page 55); this page: Caesar Salad (page 67); facing page: Parsley & Onion Salad (page 71).

Facing page: Fried Artichoke Hearts with Tahini Sauce (page 21); this page: Portuguese Bread & Garlic Soup with Cilantro (page 81); following page: Elote-Style Corn Chowder (page 96).

Preceding page: Paprika-Spiced Cauliflower Soup (page 83); facing page: Pizza Margherita (page 137); this page: Pan Bagnat (page 128).

This page: Buffalo Wings (page 164); facing page: Beer-Battered Onion Rings (page 324)

Facing page: Bibimbap (page 400); this page: French Onion Dip (page 26); following spread: Salt-Roasted Sea Bass with Celery Salsa Verde (page 259).

Clockwise from top left: Shrimp with Tomatoes & Feta (page 277); Bourbon-Roasted Lobster (page 284); Razor Clams with Chiles & Garlic (page 38); Red Snapper with Cherry Tomatoes (page 266); facing page: Nicaraguan Rundown Seafood Soup (page 115).

Facing page: Porchetta Sandwiches with Marinated Onions & Salsa Verde (page 133); this page: Spiedies (page 237).

This page: Pesto-Rubbed Chicken (page 158); facing page: Carnitas Tacos (page 148).

Facing page: Iraqi Yellow Spice–Rubbed Chicken (page 156); this page: Rosemary-Rubbed Beef Tenderloin (page 188); following page: Veal Piccata (page 205).

Pork

ROAST CROWN OF PORK WITH DRIED-FRUIT STUFFING

SERVES 8–10

This regal roast consists of two center-cut pork rib sections tied together by the butcher in the shape of a crown. It's a dramatic holiday presentation that's easy to carve: Just slice between the ribs and serve.

FOR THE ROAST

- ¼ cup fresh lemon juice
- 2 cloves garlic, minced
- 1 tbsp. finely chopped fresh sage
- 1 tbsp. finely chopped fresh rosemary
- 1 tsp. grated fresh ginger
- 12 juniper berries, crushed
  Kosher salt and freshly ground black pepper
- 1 10-lb. crown roast of pork

FOR THE STUFFING

- 1 cup coarsely chopped dried pears
- 1 cup coarsely chopped dried pitted prunes
- 2 cups fresh orange juice
- ½ cup brandy
- 6 tbsp. butter
- 1 large yellow onion, chopped
- 4 cloves garlic, minced
- ½ lb. sweet Italian sausage, casings removed
- 1 loaf country bread, torn into coarse crumbs (about 8 cups)
  Kosher salt and freshly ground black pepper

1 Make the roast: Heat oven to 350°. Mix lemon juice, garlic, sage, rosemary, ginger, juniper berries, and salt and pepper in a small bowl. Rub meat with spice mixture, then put roast, bone side down (to give a good crust), into a roasting pan. Roast meat until an instant-read thermometer inserted into center (not touching bone) reads 160°, 2½–3 hours.

2 Make the stuffing: Put pears, prunes, orange juice, and brandy into a large bowl and set aside to soak for 1 hour. Melt butter in a large skillet over low heat, add onions and garlic, and cook until soft, 10–15 minutes. Increase heat to medium, add sausage, and cook, breaking up meat with

a spoon, until lightly browned, 8–10 minutes. Add sausage mixture, bread crumbs, and salt and pepper to soaked fruit and mix well. Transfer to a 9″×11″ baking dish and bake alongside roast for last 40 minutes.

3 To serve, invert roast onto a warm serving platter and fill with stuffing. Serve remaining stuffing on the side.

PERNIL ASADO

Roast Pork Shoulder

SERVES 8

We adapted the recipe for Puerto Rican *lechón,* a roasted whole pig traditionally served at Christmastime, using pork shoulder.

- 1 cup fresh orange juice
- ½ cup red wine vinegar
- ⅓ cup packed dark brown sugar
- ¼ cup kosher salt
- ¼ cup ground black pepper
- 2 tbsp. olive oil
- 2 tbsp. dried oregano
- 2 tbsp. ground cumin
- 40 cloves garlic, minced (about 7 tbsp.)
- 1 8-lb. bone-in, skin-on pork picnic shoulder

1 Mix orange juice, vinegar, sugar, salt, pepper, oil, oregano, cumin, and garlic in a bowl to make a marinade. Using a paring knife, cut 1½″-wide, 1″-deep slits all over pork in a roasting pan; pour marinade over pork. Chill, turning pork every few hours, for at least 6 hours.

2 Heat oven to 325°. Roast pork, basting with marinade every 30 minutes, until an instant-read thermometer inserted into center (not touching bone) reads 190°, about 5 hours. Let pork rest for 20 minutes before serving.

BRAISED PORK ROAST WITH ROOT VEGETABLES

Schweineschmorbraten mit Rübengemüse

SERVES 6–8

The juniper berries and caraway seeds in this Bavarian roast give it a floral, woodsy flavor, while the bacon that wraps it helps keep the meat moist. Ask your butcher to butterfly the pork shoulder.

1	5-lb. boneless pork shoulder, butterflied Kosher salt and freshly ground black pepper, to taste
2	tbsp. juniper berries
4½	tsp. caraway seeds
8	cloves garlic, roughly chopped
8	slices bacon
¼	cup olive oil
3	medium parsnips, peeled and cut into 1″ chunks
3	medium carrots, peeled and cut into 1″ chunks
1	large russet potato, peeled and cut into 1″ chunks
1	small celery root, peeled and cut into 1″ chunks
1	medium yellow onion, cut into 1″ chunks
½	cup dry red wine
1½	cups chicken stock
6	sprigs fresh thyme
3	bay leaves
2	tbsp. cornstarch
2	tbsp. red wine vinegar

1 Heat oven to 350°. Season pork with salt and pepper, rub with juniper, caraway, and garlic, and lay 4 slices bacon across pork, parallel to short sides and spaced about 2″ apart. Starting at one of the short edges, roll pork into a tight bundle and place seam side down; lay remaining bacon lengthwise across the top of the roast, and tie securely with kitchen twine at 1″ intervals. Season the outside of the pork with salt and pepper and set aside.

2 Set a large roasting pan over two burners and heat oil over medium-high heat. Place roast, bacon side down, in pan and cook, turning as needed, until browned all over, about 25 minutes. Push roast to one side of the pan, add parsnips, carrots, potato, celery root, and onion, and cook, stirring occasionally, until soft, about 15 minutes. Add wine and cook, stirring to scrape the bottom of the pan, until liquid is reduced by half, about 2 minutes. Add stock, thyme, and bay leaves and, using tongs, arrange roast, bacon-side up, on top of vegetables. Cover with foil and roast until an instant-read thermometer inserted into the thickest part of the roast reads 165°, about 2 hours.

3 Transfer pork to a cutting board and let rest for 20 minutes. Discard bay leaves and thyme, and arrange vegetables on a large serving platter. Slice pork and arrange over vegetables.

4 Bring roasting pan with pan juices to a boil over high heat. Mix cornstarch and 2 tbsp. water in a bowl. When juices boil, whisk in cornstarch mixture and cook until gravy is thick, about 2 minutes more. Strain gravy through a fine-mesh strainer, stir in vinegar, and season with salt and pepper. Serve alongside roast.

CRISPY CHINESE ROAST PORK
Siew Yoke
SERVES 8

With a luscious interior and perfectly crisp crackling, this elemental Chinese pork belly is everything roast meat should be.

1	4-lb. slab pork belly (1¾″ thick)
1½	tbsp. baking soda
5	tbsp. Shaoxing wine
3	tbsp. sugar
1	tbsp. fine sea salt
1¼	tsp. five-spice powder

1 Place pork, skin side up, on a work surface. Using a pork-skin pricking tool, an ice pick, or a carving fork, prick skin all over, making hundreds of small, shallow holes that just puncture the surface. Set pork aside.

2 Dissolve baking soda in 5 cups boiling water. Transfer water to a measuring cup with a spout. Grasp one corner of pork belly with tongs. Holding pork belly over a bowl or the sink, slowly pour the baking soda mixture in a thin stream over pork skin to scald it.

3 Transfer pork to a work surface, skin side down. Using a knife, score the meat, making 1″-deep parallel slits spaced 1½″ apart.

4 Combine 3 tbsp. rice wine, sugar, salt, and five-spice powder in a small bowl and pour marinade over the meat.

5 Rub marinade all over meat, pushing it into the slits. Transfer pork, skin side up, to a baking dish. Wipe any moisture from skin with a paper towel. Refrigerate pork belly, uncovered, overnight to marinate as the skin air-dries.

6 Heat oven to 375°. Thread 3 metal skewers horizontally through the meat layer of the pork belly to prevent the pork from curling as it cooks. Transfer pork, skin side up, to a rack set over a foil-lined roasting pan or rimmed baking sheet. Wipe skin again with a paper towel.

7 Pour remaining 2 tbsp. rice wine over skin and brush to distribute. Pour hot water into pan to a depth of ¼". Cook pork on center of oven rack until an instant-read thermometer inserted into the thickest part reads 160°, about 1 hour. Raise heat to broil and cook until skin is blistered and browned, 5–10 minutes. Before serving, let pork rest for 15 minutes. To serve, cut into 1" slices.

CHOUCROUTE GARNIE À L'ALSACIENNE

Alsatian Garnished Sauerkraut

SERVES 6–8

No other dish shows off the richly varied charcuterie of the northeastern French region of Alsace quite like *choucroute garnie,* which was traditionally served at home on Sundays after families returned from church.

1½	lb. fresh ham hocks
¼	cup rendered duck or goose fat or butter
3	small yellow onions, finely chopped
4½	lb. sauerkraut, drained and rinsed
3¼	cups Alsatian riesling or other dry but fruity white wine
1½	lb. boneless pork loin
1	lb. smoked ham
½	lb. slab bacon
1	Bouquet Garni (page 86)
	Kosher salt and freshly ground black pepper, to taste
12	medium red bliss potatoes, peeled
6	fresh pork sausages, such as saucisse de Strasbourg
3	blood sausages
1	tbsp. canola oil
6	smoked pork sausages, such as saucisse de Montbéliard or de Strasbourg

1 Place ham hocks in a large pot. Cover with water and simmer over medium heat for 1½ hours. Drain and set aside.

2 Heat oven to 350°. Melt fat in a Dutch oven over medium heat. Add onions and cook until soft, 10–15 minutes. Add sauerkraut, wine, ham hocks, pork loin, ham, bacon, and bouquet garni. Season with salt and pepper, cover, and cook in oven until meats are tender, about 1½ hours.

3 About 35 minutes before serving, place potatoes in a pot of salted water over medium-high heat and cook until tender, 20–25 minutes. Drain and keep warm.

4 Prick fresh and blood sausages with a fork, then place in a skillet, cover with water, and simmer over medium heat for 10 minutes. Drain. Dry skillet, add oil, and heat over medium heat. Brown fresh and blood sausages, turning occasionally, then remove. In the same oil, adding more if necessary, brown smoked sausages, turning occasionally, then remove. To serve, spoon sauerkraut onto a large platter, discarding bouquet garni. Slice pork loin, ham, and bacon and arrange on platter with ham hocks, potatoes, and all sausages.

"ELEGANT" IOWA PORK CHOPS

SERVES 4

This recipe came to us from Virginia Miller, a home cook from Iowa who bakes thick-cut pork chops in a sweet, tomatoey sauce that caramelizes as it cooks.

4	double-cut, bone-in pork chops
	Kosher salt and freshly ground black pepper, to taste
2	cups packed brown sugar
2	cups soy sauce
1	tbsp. molasses
1¾	cups ketchup
1½	cups bottled chile sauce
2	tbsp. American French Dressing (page 77, or store-bought)
1	tbsp. dry mustard

1 Put pork chops into a baking dish and season with salt and pepper. In a small bowl, whisk together ½ cup brown sugar, soy sauce, molasses, and 1 cup water and pour over meat. Cover with plastic wrap and marinate chops in the refrigerator for at least 4 hours.

2 Heat oven to 375°. Drain pork chops and transfer to a 9"×13" baking dish. Whisk together remaining 1½ cups brown sugar, ketchup, chile sauce, French dressing, mustard, and ⅓ cup water in a small bowl. Pour sauce over pork chops and bake, turning pork chops and basting with sauce occasionally, until pork chops are tender and sauce has thickened, about 45 minutes. Let pork chops rest for 10 minutes before serving.

CASSOULET

SERVES 6–8

A slow-simmered mix of beans, pork sausages, pork shoulder, pancetta, and duck, cassoulet, a classic of southwestern France, takes its name from the earthenware *cassole* in which it was traditionally made.

1   lb. dried great northern beans
10 tbsp. rendered duck fat or olive oil
16 cloves garlic, smashed
2   onions, chopped
2   carrots, peeled and chopped
2   large fresh ham hocks
1   lb. pork shoulder, cut into 1"cubes
½   lb. pancetta, cubed
4   sprigs fresh oregano
4   sprigs fresh thyme
3   bay leaves
1   cup canned whole, peeled tomatoes
1   cup white wine
2   cups chicken stock
4   legs Duck Confit (page 182, or store-bought)
1   lb. pork sausages
2   cups dried bread crumbs

1 Soak beans in a 4-qt. bowl in 7½ cups water overnight. Heat 2 tbsp. duck fat in a 6-qt. pot over medium-high heat. Add half the garlic, onions, and carrots and cook until lightly browned, about 10 minutes. Add ham hocks along with beans and their water and boil. Reduce heat and simmer beans until tender, about 1½ hours.

2 Transfer hocks to a plate; let cool. Pull off meat; discard skin, bone, and gristle. Chop meat; add to beans. Set aside.

3 Heat 2 tbsp. duck fat in a 5-qt. Dutch oven over medium-high heat. Add pork and brown for 8 minutes. Add pancetta and cook for 5 minutes. Add remaining garlic, onions, and carrots; cook until lightly browned, about 10 minutes. Tie together oregano, thyme, and bay leaves with twine; add to pan with tomatoes and cook until liquid thickens, 8–10 minutes. Add wine; reduce by half. Add stock and bring to a boil. Reduce heat to medium-low and cook, uncovered, until liquid has thickened, about 1 hour. Discard herbs; set Dutch oven aside.

4 Meanwhile, sear duck legs in 2 tbsp. duck fat in a 12" skillet over medium-high heat for 8 minutes; transfer to a plate. Brown sausages in the fat, about 8 minutes. Cut sausages into ½" slices. Pull duck meat off bones. Discard fat and bones. Stir duck and sausages into pork stew.

5 Heat oven to 300°. Mix beans and pork stew in a 4-qt. casserole. Cover with bread crumbs and drizzle with remaining 4 tbsp. duck fat. Bake, uncovered, for 3 hours. Raise temperature to 500°; cook until crust is golden, about 5 minutes.

THE CASSOLE ITSELF

Among the many mysteries surrounding cassoulet is the question of its exact origins. It is believed to have been born in Castelnaudary, France, but this has been disputed. More certain is the provenance of the dish's name, which derives from *cassole*—originally *cassolo* in the Occitan language—a brick-colored earthenware bowl that was, it seems, first fabricated in Issel, a village north of Castelnaudary once famous for its pottery. Today, a single enterprise continues to craft cassoles by hand: Poterie Not Frères, near the village of Mas-Saintes-Puelles.

The Not family has been manufacturing *cassoles* in this spot for decades. "We still use clay from around Issel," says Aimé Not. The brothers make the *cassole* in the traditional way, glazed in the interior and along the rim but unglazed on the outside. Aimé's brother Robert adds that in the old days this was done in order to save money, but it has the additional convenience of making the *cassole* much easier to hold when taken out of the oven.

Robert says that the *cassole* predates the invention of cassoulet and was used for cooking meat in salted water. But when used to make cassoulet, the *cassole* allowed more beans to be exposed to the oven's heat, thus forming the brown crust.

SWEET & SOUR GLAZED PORK CHOPS
Maiale in Agrodolce
SERVES 4

Honey and balsamic vinegar are the sweet-and-sour agents in this quintessentially Roman grilled recipe.

4   10-oz. bone-in pork chops, frenched
3   tbsp. extra-virgin olive oil
    Kosher salt and freshly ground black pepper, to taste
⅓   cup balsamic vinegar
2   tbsp. honey
4   tbsp. unsalted butter
1   sprig fresh rosemary, torn into 1" pieces

1 Put chops on a plate, drizzle with oil, season generously with salt and pepper, and let sit for 30 minutes.

2 Meanwhile, build a medium-hot fire in a charcoal grill or heat a gas grill to medium-high. (Alternatively, arrange an oven rack 4″ below the broiler and heat broiler.) Combine vinegar and honey in a 1-qt. saucepan and cook over medium heat until reduced to ¼ cup. Stir in butter and rosemary and set aside.

3 Put pork chops on grill (or foil-lined baking sheet) and cook, occasionally turning and basting with balsamic mixture, until browned and cooked through, 12–14 minutes. Transfer to a platter and let sit for 5 minutes before serving.

SPIEDIES

SERVES 2–4 (SEE PHOTO, PAGE 227)

These tangy pork kebabs are rubbed with garlic and dry herbs and basted with a vinegar wash. A regional favorite of New York State's Southern Tier, their name derives from the Italian *spiedino* or *spiedo* ("skewer" and "spit").

1½	lb. trimmed pork loin, cut into 1¼″ cubes
¾	cup olive oil
¼	cup white wine vinegar
5	tbsp. finely chopped fresh mint
5	tbsp. finely chopped fresh flat-leaf parsley
2	tbsp. finely chopped fresh oregano
1	tsp. fresh lemon juice
1	bay leaf, finely crushed
	Kosher salt and freshly ground black pepper, to taste
1½	tsp. crushed red chile flakes
6	8″ bamboo skewers, soaked in water for 30 minutes
2	10″-long Italian hoagie rolls, split, toasted, and halved
	Lemon wedges, for serving

1 In a large bowl, toss together pork, ¼ cup oil, vinegar, 2 tbsp. mint, 2 tbsp. parsley, the oregano, lemon juice, bay leaf, and salt and pepper; cover with plastic wrap and chill for at least 3 hours or up to overnight. In a small bowl, whisk together remaining oil, mint, and parsley with chile flakes, then season with salt and pepper. Set sauce aside.

2 Meanwhile, build a medium-hot fire in a charcoal grill or heat a gas grill to medium-high. (Alternatively, arrange an oven rack 4″ below the broiler and heat broiler.) Thread 4 or 5 pork cubes onto each skewer. Transfer to grill (or foil-lined baking sheet) and cook, turning once, until charred and cooked through, about 10 minutes. Place skewers on rolls, drizzle with sauce, and serve with lemon wedges.

BACON-WRAPPED STUFFED PORK LOIN

SERVES 6–8 (SEE PHOTO, PAGE 425)

Wrapping a lean cut of meat such as pork loin in bacon helps keep it moist when grilling. Stuffed with spinach and feta and with a hint of heat from chile flakes, this makes an irresistible main course.

2	lb. boneless pork loin
	Kosher salt and freshly ground black pepper, to taste
¼	cup olive oil
1	tsp. crushed red chile flakes
6	cloves garlic, finely chopped
1	shallot, finely chopped
8	cups baby spinach
3	oz. feta, crumbled
¾	lb. sliced bacon

1 Slice pork loin lengthwise three-quarters of the way through the middle. Lay open and season with salt and pepper. Heat oil in a 12″ skillet over medium-high heat. Add chile flakes, garlic, and shallots and cook until golden, 3–4 minutes. Add spinach and cook, stirring occasionally, until wilted, 2–3 minutes. Let cool, squeeze excess water from spinach, and finely chop; transfer to a bowl. Stir in feta, salt, and pepper. Spread mixture over pork; fold closed and wrap bacon around pork. Using kitchen twine, tie pork securely at 1″ intervals.

2 Build a hot fire in a charcoal grill or heat a gas grill to high; bank coals or turn burner off on one side for indirect grilling (page 191). Cook pork, turning as needed, until bacon is crisp and pork is cooked through, 45 minutes to 1 hour. If outside starts to burn before pork is fully cooked, move pork to cooler section of the grill until done. Rest pork for 15 minutes before slicing.

MEMPHIS-STYLE DRY RIBS

SERVES 4–6

Charles Vergos, the late proprietor of the beloved Memphis restaurant Rendezvous, invented this style of ribs served "dry," with a tangy spice mixture but no sauce.

2 racks St. Louis–cut pork spareribs (about 3 lb. each)

⅔ cup Memphis-Style Dry Rub (page 588)

¾ cup apple cider

4 tbsp. kosher salt

1 Rub pork all over with all but 2 tbsp. of the spice mixture. Let sit at room temperature for 1 hour or chill overnight. Whisk together remaining spice mixture with apple cider, salt, and ¾ cup water in a bowl; set basting sauce aside.

2 Prepare for barbecuing using the kettle grill, bullet smoker, or gas grill method (see Barbecue Fuel, page 192, and Barbecue Flavor, page 193), using applewood chunks or chips. Place ribs, top side down, on grate. Maintaining a grill temperature of 225° to 275° (if using a kettle grill or bullet smoker, replenish fire with unlit coals, as needed, to maintain temperature), cook, turning once and basting with apple cider mixture every 20 minutes, until the tip of a small knife slips easily in and out of meat, 2–4 hours.

RIB TIPS

Here are six simple tips for barbecuing ribs, straight from Kansas City's "Baron of Barbecue," Paul Kirk. (See his dry rub recipe on page 193.)

STEP 1 The most common pork ribs are baby backs and spareribs, which can be cut into St. Louis ribs and a 2″ slab of rib tips.

STEP 2 To remove membrane from baby backs (if butcher hasn't done so), use your fingers and start from center. For spares, use a clean screwdriver and begin at one end.

STEP 3 Dry rubs should be sprinkled onto, not massaged into, meat.

STEP 4 Laying ribs flat in a cooker is okay, but Kirk prefers to hang them so dripping fat acts as a baste.

STEP 5 If you're cooking for a crowd, try this tip for fitting several slabs of spareribs onto a standard-size grill: Trim breastbone from each slab, then pull around into a circle, secure with string, and cook for 4–5 hours, until bones can be pulled apart. If you opt to baste, untie ribs, return to grill, and baste with sauce until heated through. A final tip: The tied ribs may be wrapped and frozen.

STEP 6 Ribs are just fine without sauce.

VIETNAMESE PORK CHOPS

Sườn Nướng

SERVES 4–6

Thin pork chops—you can cut three of them from one hefty American-style pork chop—are flavored with a caramel-lemongrass marinade in this essential Vietnamese dish.

½ cup plus 2 tbsp. sugar

⅓ cup thinly sliced shallots

¼ cup thinly sliced lemongrass

2 tbsp. peanut oil

2 tbsp. soy sauce

1½ tbsp. nuoc mam (Vietnamese fish sauce)

1 tbsp. freshly ground black pepper

8 cloves garlic, finely chopped

1 lb. ¼″-thick pork blade chops, pounded thin
Cooked white rice and Nuoc Cham (page 594), for serving

1 Heat ½ cup of sugar in a 1-qt. heavy bottomed saucepan over medium-high heat, swirling pan often, until sugar dissolves and turns to liquid caramel. Remove from heat; add ¼ cup boiling water. Return pan to heat and cook, swirling pan gently, until caramel dissolves in water. Remove from heat and let cool. Transfer to a food processor along with remaining 2 tbsp. sugar, shallots, lemongrass, oil, soy sauce, fish sauce, pepper, and garlic; purée until smooth. Place pork chops in a 9″×13″ baking dish and pour purée over top. Cover and chill for at least 1 hour or overnight.

2 Heat a 12″ cast-iron grill pan over high heat. Working in batches, add chops and cook, turning once, until charred in spots and cooked through, about 2 minutes. Serve immediately with rice and chile-garlic sauce.

BAMONTE'S PORK CHOPS WITH PICKLED PEPPERS

SERVES 2

These juicy pork chops topped with halved cherry peppers have been a menu staple at Bamonte's Italian restaurant in Williamsburg, Brooklyn, since the 1950s.

2 1″-thick bone-in pork chops
Salt and freshly ground black pepper, to taste

3 tbsp. olive oil

5 cloves garlic, thinly sliced

12 pickled cherry peppers, halved

¼ cup dry white wine

¼ cup chicken stock

> "Grilling, broiling, barbecuing—whatever you want to call it—
> is an art, not just a matter of building a pyre and throwing on a piece
> of meat as a sacrifice to the gods of the stomach."
>
> **JAMES BEARD**

1 Heat oven to 425°. Season chops with salt and pepper.

2 Heat 2 tbsp. olive oil in an ovenproof 12″ skillet over medium-high heat. Fry chops, flipping once, until browned, 5–8 minutes. Transfer pan to oven; roast until pork is cooked through, 18–20 minutes. Transfer chops to a plate.

3 Return pan to medium heat, add remaining 1 tbsp. oil, garlic, and peppers and cook until garlic is golden, 3–4 minutes. Raise heat to high, add wine and stock, and cook until reduced by half, 3–4 minutes. Spoon sauce over chops.

HAWAIIAN PANFRIED PORK CHOPS
SERVES 4

This dish is an adaptation of the panfried island pork chops (also known as "pork chop bones") served at Honolulu's Side Street Inn. The late chef Colin Nishida used locally raised pork and treated his customers to a colossal portion of four chops each. We've scaled back the quantity a bit.

- 1 cup flour
- ½ cup cornstarch
- 1–2 cups cottonseed oil
- 4 1″-thick pork loin chops (2½–3 lb. total)
- 4 1″-thick pork rib chops (2½–3 lb. total)
- 2 tbsp. garlic salt
- 1 tbsp. freshly ground black pepper
- ½ head cabbage, cored and thinly sliced
- 1 cup ketchup, for dipping

1 Put flour and cornstarch into a wide, shallow dish and whisk to combine. Set aside.

2 Heat 1 cup oil in a large skillet over medium-high heat until a deep-fry thermometer reads 375°. Season pork chops generously with garlic salt and pepper. Working in batches, dredge chops in flour mixture, gently shake off any excess, and fry, turning once, until well browned and cooked through, 5–6 minutes per side. Transfer pork chops to a baking sheet fitted with a rack. (If oil becomes too dark, carefully discard it, wipe out skillet with paper towels, and continue with 1 cup clean oil.)

3 Transfer pork chops to a cutting board and cut meat away from bones (don't discard bones). Slice meat into 1″-thick pieces. Divide cabbage among 4 plates and top with meat and bones. Serve with ketchup on the side for dipping.

POT-ROASTED PORK WITH THYME
Roti de Porc au Thym
SERVES 6–8

This French approach to pot-roasted pork is remarkably versatile. We prefer a rib roast for the cut, but it works equally well with a loin, shoulder, or blade.

- 1 4½-lb. pork rib roast, boned
  Kosher salt and freshly ground
  black pepper, to taste
- 1 tbsp. butter
- 1 tbsp. peanut oil
- ⅔ cup Dijon mustard
- 1 tbsp. Herbes de Provence (page 587)
- 2 branches fresh thyme

1 Heat oven to 425°. Generously season pork all over with salt and pepper and set aside.

2 Heat butter and oil together in a large heavy-bottomed pot with a tight-fitting lid over medium-high heat. Add meat and cook until well browned on all sides, 3–4 minutes per side.

3 Turn meat fat side up, spread mustard in an even layer on top, then sprinkle with herbes de Provence, crushing the herbs between your fingers as you season the meat. Lay thyme branches on top of meat, then add 1 cup water to pot and cover with lid.

4 Put pot into oven and roast meat, basting with rendered juices every 15 minutes or so, until meat is tender and an instant-read thermometer inserted into center reads 135°, about 45 minutes. Remove pot from oven, set lid ajar to partially uncover pot, and allow meat to rest for 15–20 minutes. Remove and discard thyme branches, then transfer meat to a carving board and thinly slice. Serve with pan juices spooned over top.

ADOBO
SERVES 4

Adobo is the national dish of the Philippines, where variations on the classic recipe abound. In this textbook version from Amy Besa—co-owner of the Brooklyn restaurant Purple Yam—pork is braised in seasoned palm vinegar and soy sauce.

2½	lb. boneless pork shoulder, cut into 2″ pieces
½	cup palm vinegar
3	tbsp. soy sauce
1	tsp. black peppercorns, crushed
12	cloves garlic, crushed
1	bay leaf
2	tbsp. lard or canola oil
	Cooked white rice, for serving
	Patis (Filipino fish sauce), for serving (optional)

1 Place pork, vinegar, soy sauce, peppercorns, garlic, and bay leaf in a large bowl and toss to combine. Cover and refrigerate for at least 8 hours or up to overnight.

2 Heat pork mixture and 2 cups water in a 6-qt. Dutch oven over medium-high heat; bring to a boil. Skim the foam that rises to the surface, and then reduce the heat to medium-low; cover and cook until tender, about 1½ hours.

3 Pour pork into a colander set over a medium bowl; discard bay leaf, and set pork and garlic aside. Return broth to pot and cook over medium heat until reduced to 1½ cups, about 25 minutes. Transfer broth to a bowl and set aside.

4 Melt lard in same pot over medium-high heat. Set garlic aside, then, working in batches, add pork and cook, turning, until browned all over, about 10 minutes. Add garlic and cook, stirring occasionally, until garlic is lightly browned, about 2 minutes. Stir broth back into pot, reduce heat to medium-low, and cook to meld flavors, about 5 minutes.

5 Divide rice among 4 bowls; top with pork and broth. Season with fish sauce, if you like.

DR PEPPER PULLED PORK
SERVES 6–8

It's not uncommon in the American South for soft drinks to factor into cooking: Their high sugar content and relative acidity contribute to many a terrifically tender roast and braise. Here, tender pork shoulder braises in a Dr Pepper barbecue sauce, which we like for its tart fruity flavor, though you could easily substitute cola or root beer. Whatever your poison, try to use a soda sweetened with cane sugar rather than corn syrup; it will reduce down to a deeper, more complex flavor.

FOR THE SAUCE

4	tbsp. unsalted butter
4	cloves garlic, minced
1	large onion, minced
1	cup ketchup
½	cup cider vinegar
½	cup packed light brown sugar
⅓	cup Worcestershire sauce
3	tbsp. tomato paste
2	tsp. ancho chile powder
1	tsp. kosher salt
1	tsp. ground white pepper
1	12-oz. can Dr Pepper soda

FOR THE PORK

3	tbsp. olive oil
3	lb. boneless pork shoulder
	Kosher salt and freshly ground black pepper
¼	cup dark brown sugar
1½	tbsp. cayenne pepper
1	large onion, sliced ¼″ thick
3	12-oz. cans Dr Pepper soda
	Hamburger buns, lightly toasted, for serving
	Sliced bread-and-butter pickles, for serving (optional)

1 Make the sauce: Melt butter in a 4-qt. saucepan over medium-high heat. Add garlic and onion and cook until soft, 4–6 minutes. Add ketchup, vinegar, sugar, Worcestershire, tomato paste, chile, salt, pepper, and soda and bring to a simmer. Cook until thickened, about 30 minutes; set aside.

2 Make the pork: Heat oven to 325°. Heat oil in a 6-qt. Dutch oven over medium-high heat. Season pork with salt and pepper; cook, turning as needed, until browned, 10–12 minutes. Transfer pork to a plate and rub with brown sugar and cayenne. Pile onion slices in center of pan and arrange pork over top; pour Dr Pepper around pork. Bake, covered, until pork is tender and an instant-read thermometer inserted into pork reads 190°, about 2½ hours. Uncover and cook until browned on top and meat is very tender, 30–45 minutes more. Let cool slightly, then transfer to a work surface. Using 2 forks or your hands, shred pork; transfer to a bowl with half the sauce and toss to combine. Serve on buns with remaining sauce on the side and, if you like, pickles.

COOK'S NOTE Only one Dr Pepper bottling plant—in Dublin, Texas—still used cane sugar as recently as 2012. You can still find bottles of Dublin Dr Pepper from online sellers, but they're increasingly rare.

ST. LOUIS COUNTRY-STYLE RIBS

SERVES 6

Our riff on pork steaks simmered in a St. Louis–style sauce calls for braising tender country-style ribs—thick cut and meaty, dissimilar to slab ribs—in the oven until they're meltingly tender.

- 4 slices bacon, finely chopped
- 1 tbsp. ancho chile powder
- 4 cloves garlic, finely chopped
- ¼ medium onion, chopped
- 2 cups canned whole, peeled tomatoes, puréed
- ½ cup packed dark brown sugar
- ½ cup cider vinegar
- ¼ cup whole-grain mustard
- 1 tbsp. Worcestershire sauce
- 1 tbsp. kosher salt, plus more to taste
  Freshly ground black pepper, to taste
- 6 country-style pork ribs (about 3¼ lb.)
- 3 tbsp. canola oil

1 Heat oven to 350°. Heat bacon in a 4-qt. saucepan over medium heat and cook, stirring, until fat renders, about 6 minutes. Add chile powder, garlic, and onion and cook, stirring, until soft, about 5 minutes. Add tomatoes, sugar, vinegar, mustard, Worcestershire, salt, and pepper, bring to a boil, and cook for 5 minutes. Remove from heat and set aside.

2 Season ribs with salt and pepper. Heat oil in a 12″ skillet over medium-high heat. Working in batches, add ribs and cook, turning once, until browned on both sides, about 8 minutes. Transfer ribs to a 9″×13″ baking dish and pour sauce over to cover. Bake ribs until the tip of a small knife slips easily in and out of meat, about 1 hour.

PORK LOIN BRAISED IN MILK & CREAM

Brasato di Maiale al Latte

SERVES 4–6

This dish is based on a classic from the Bologna region of Italy, where milk-braised meat is a culinary art form.

- 1 5-lb. pork rib roast, ribs and roast separated by butcher
  Kosher salt and freshly ground black pepper, to taste
- 1 tbsp. olive oil
- 3 tbsp. butter
  Leaves from 1 bunch fresh sage
- 2 cups whole milk
- 2 cups heavy cream
  Zest of 1 lemon, in wide strips

1 Tie roast with kitchen twine, then generously season with salt and pepper. Heat oil and 1 tbsp. butter in a medium heavy-bottomed pot over medium-high heat until butter melts. Add roast, fat side down, and ribs and cook until browned on all sides, 2–3 minutes per side.

2 Pour off fat from pot, reduce heat to medium, and add remaining 2 tbsp. butter. When butter melts, add half the sage leaves and fry for a few seconds. Slowly add milk and cream; then add lemon zest, season with salt, and bring to a simmer. Reduce heat to medium-low, partially cover pot, and gently simmer for 1 hour, turning pork after 30 minutes.

3 Coarsely chop remaining sage leaves and add to pot. Continue simmering, partially covered, for 1 hour more, turning meat after 30 minutes. Uncover casserole and continue simmering, turning every 30 minutes, until meat is very tender and milk mixture is pale golden and thick, about 1½ hours more.

4 Transfer meat to a warm serving platter and remove twine, then slice meat. Discard ribs and spoon sauce over meat.

RED-BRAISED PORK BELLY

Hong Shao Rou

SERVES 4

Two types of soy sauce and a touch of sugar give this dish—beloved throughout China—its signature glossiness and a deep red-brown tint. Serve the tender pork belly morsels and boiled eggs with a light vegetable, like bok choy.

6 eggs
1 spring onion, white part only
¾ oz. ginger (about a 2″ piece)
1¾ lb. pork belly, skin on if desired
1 tbsp. canola or vegetable oil
1 star anise pods
1 cinnamon stick
3 tbsp. Shaoxing wine
3 cups hot water or stock
2 tbsp. light soy sauce
1 tbsp. plus 1 tsp. dark soy sauce
3 tbsp. superfine sugar or 1½ oz. rock sugar
   Cooked white rice, for serving

1 Combine eggs and enough water to cover by 1″ in a small saucepan; bring to a rapid boil and let cook for 2 minutes. Remove and let eggs rest in water for 10 minutes. Let cool, then shell. In each egg, make 6–8 shallow slashes lengthwise to allow the flavors of the stew to enter.

2 Smack spring onion and ginger gently with the flat side of a cleaver or a rolling pin to loosen their fibers.

3 Combine pork and enough water to cover in a medium saucepan; bring to a boil, then let boil for 5 minutes. Drain and rinse pork with cold water. When cool enough to handle, cut into 1″ cubes.

4 Heat oil in a seasoned wok over high heat. Add ginger, onion, star anise, and cinnamon and stir-fry until aromatic, about 2 minutes. Add pork and cook until meat is faintly golden and some of the fat is rendering, 1–2 minutes. Splash the Shaoxing wine around the edges of the pan. Add eggs, hot water, light soy sauce, 2 tsp. dark soy sauce, and sugar. Bring to a boil, then reduce to a simmer; cover and let cook for 45 minutes, stirring occasionally.

5 Pour into a bowl, let cool, then chill until the fat congeals (a few hours or overnight). Remove and skim away any fat that has settled on the surface. Pour meat and liquid back into a wok, then boil, stirring constantly, to reduce the sauce by half, 10–15 minutes. Discard ginger, spring onion, and whole spices. Stir in remaining 2 tsp. dark soy sauce.

6 Shortly before serving, bring back to a boil over high heat and reduce sauce to about 1″ of dark, glossy gravy. Transfer to a rimmed serving dish. Serve with rice.

PORK VINDALOO

SERVES 4–6

This tangy, spice-infused curry from Goa, India, has roots in *carne de vinh d'alho,* a stew brought to the region by Portuguese colonists. Now an Anglo-Indian restaurant staple, it comes in countless variations—some fiery, some mild—from the subcontinent to the British Isles.

1 tbsp. black peppercorns
1 tbsp. black mustard seeds
2 tsp. cumin seeds
2 tsp. coriander seeds
1 tsp. fenugreek seeds
5 whole cloves
1 1″ stick cinnamon
¼ cup Hungarian paprika
¼ cup palm vinegar
1 tsp. ground turmeric
1 tsp. light brown sugar
16 cloves garlic, minced
1 2″ piece fresh ginger, peeled and minced
2 lb. boneless pork shoulder, cut into 1–2″ pieces
3 tbsp. canola oil
2 large yellow onions, finely chopped
10 thin green bird's eye chiles, stemmed, seeded, and minced
1 lb. small new potatoes, cut in half (quarters if large)
   Kosher salt, to taste
   Cooked white rice, for serving

1 Heat peppercorns, mustard, cumin, coriander, fenugreek, cloves, and cinnamon in a 12″ skillet over medium-high heat and cook, swirling pan occasionally, until lightly toasted, about 2 minutes. Transfer to a bowl and let cool. Working in batches, transfer spices to a spice grinder and process until finely ground. Transfer to a small food processor along with paprika, vinegar, turmeric, sugar, one-quarter of garlic, and half the ginger; purée until smooth. Transfer to a large bowl and add pork; rub pork with spice mixture. Cover and refrigerate for at least 4 hours or up to overnight.

2 Heat oil in a 6-qt. saucepan over medium-high heat. Add onions and cook, stirring, until caramelized, about 25 minutes. Add remaining garlic and ginger along with chiles and cook, stirring, until soft, about 5 minutes. Add pork along with any paste in bowl, potatoes, and 2 cups water and bring to a boil. Reduce heat to medium-low and cook, covered and stirring occasionally, until pork is cooked through, about 25 minutes. Remove from heat and season with salt. Serve with rice.

MEATBALLS WITH ONION GRAVY

SERVES 4-6

The Cwmcerrig Farm Shop in Wales serves these hearty liver-enriched pork meatballs doused in a buttery onion gravy.

FOR THE ONION GRAVY

- 4 tbsp. unsalted butter
- 1 large yellow onion, thinly sliced
- 1 tbsp. flour
- 2 cups beef stock
- ⅓ cup madeira wine
- ½ tsp. Worcestershire sauce
  Kosher salt and freshly ground black pepper

FOR THE MEATBALLS

- 10 slices bacon, finely chopped
- 1 tbsp. finely chopped fresh sage
- 1½ tsp. finely chopped fresh thyme
- 1 small yellow onion, finely chopped
  Kosher salt and freshly ground black pepper, to taste
- 1 lb. ground pork
- ¼ lb. pig's liver, finely chopped
- 1½ cups dried bread crumbs
- ½ cup milk
- ¼ tsp. freshly grated nutmeg
- ½ cup dry white wine

1 Make the onion gravy: Melt butter in a 4-qt. saucepan over medium-low heat. Add onion and cook, stirring occasionally, until golden brown, about 40 minutes. Stir in flour and cook 2 minutes. Add stock, madeira, Worcestershire, salt, and pepper and bring to a boil. Cook until slightly thick, about 5 minutes; set gravy aside and keep warm.

2 Make the meatballs: Heat oven to 350°. Heat bacon in a 12″ skillet over medium-high heat; cook until fat is rendered and bacon is slightly crisp, 4–6 minutes. Add sage, thyme, onion, salt, and pepper and cook, stirring occasionally, until golden, 7–9 minutes. Transfer to a bowl; let cool.

3 Add pork, liver, bread crumbs, milk, nutmeg, salt, and pepper to bacon mixture; mix gently to combine. Form mixture into eight 4-oz. balls. Place in a 9″×13″ baking dish and add wine; bake, basting occasionally with pan juices, until cooked through, about 25 minutes. Serve with onion gravy.

PINEAPPLE-CHIPOTLE GLAZED HAM

SERVES 14-20

The New York City–based cookbook author Zarela Martinez gave us the recipe for this smoky, Coca-Cola–glazed ham, a picture-perfect centerpiece for a festive meal.

- 1 12–15-lb. whole semiboneless ham
- 8 fresh or canned pineapple slices
- 64 whole cloves
- 2 12-oz. cans Coca-Cola
- 2 chipotle peppers in adobo, drained and finely chopped
- ⅓ cup honey

1 Put ham into a 16-qt. pot; cover with water. Bring to a boil, reduce heat to medium-low, and simmer for 1 hour.

2 Heat oven to 350°. Transfer ham to a rack in a roasting pan. Using toothpicks, secure pineapple to ham; stud with cloves. Pour 2 cups Coca-Cola over ham; pour 1 cup water into pan. Cover loosely with foil; bake for 1 hour.

3 Meanwhile, combine the remaining ¾ cup Coca-Cola, chipotles, and honey in a 2-qt. saucepan and bring to a boil. Reduce the heat to medium; cook, stirring the glaze, until syrupy, 12–15 minutes. Uncover the ham; brush with some of the glaze. Increase oven to 500°. Bake the ham, brushing occasionally with glaze, until browned and glossy, 15–20 minutes. Let cool for 20 minutes before carving.

COOK'S NOTE To cut slices of fresh pineapple into perfect circles, use a 3″ round cookie cutter to trim the outer edges of the slices and a 1″ round one to cut out the center.

HAM STEAKS WITH HAZELNUT SAUCE

SERVES 2-4

The sauce in this German dish is filling and creamy, enriched with ground hazelnuts and brightened by brandy.

- 3 tbsp. unsalted butter
- 2 white onions, thinly sliced
- 1 tbsp. canola oil
- 2 ¼″-thick cooked ham steaks, smoked or unsmoked
- ¼ cup apple brandy
- 1 cup heavy cream
- 3 tbsp. Dijon mustard

½ cup hazelnuts, toasted and finely ground
Kosher salt and freshly ground black pepper, to taste
6 tbsp. dried bread crumbs
4 sprigs fresh rosemary
1 tbsp. finely chopped fresh chives, for garnish

1 Heat oven to 400°. Grease an 11″ × 14½″ baking pan with 1 tbsp. butter. Arrange onions on bottom; bake until soft, about 15 minutes. Set aside.

2 Heat oil in a 12″ skillet over medium-high heat. Working in 2 batches, sear ham steaks, about 3 minutes per side. Transfer to a plate. Add brandy to skillet and return to high heat. Cook, scraping up any browned bits, until brandy has almost evaporated, about 1 minute. Add cream and mustard and cook for 2 minutes. Add hazelnuts and season with salt and pepper; pour sauce over reserved onions. Place steaks on top of onions. Melt remaining 2 tbsp. butter and combine with bread crumbs; coat tops of steaks with crumbs and arrange rosemary on top. Bake until hot, about 15 minutes. Garnish with chives.

HAM SAUPIQUET
SERVES 2–4

In the Morvan and neighboring portions of Burgundy, France, a *saupiquet* is usually either sliced ham or wild game (hare is classic) cooked in a piquant sauce of vinegar or red wine. Starting with cooked ham slices makes this an exceptionally quick supper to come together.

2 tbsp. butter
10 oz. cooked ham, sliced
6 shallots, finely sliced
2 cloves garlic, finely sliced
3½ tbsp. red wine
2 tbsp. red wine vinegar
1 tbsp. juniper berries
⅔ cup heavy cream
Sprig of thyme
Kosher salt and freshly ground black pepper, to taste

1 Heat oven to 400°. Melt butter in a skillet over medium heat, add ham, and sauté until lightly browned. Transfer to a gratin dish. Add shallots and garlic to skillet and cook gently until golden, about 1 minute.

2 Meanwhile, put wine and vinegar into a small saucepan with the juniper berries and reduce to 2 tbsp. Add to the shallots, together with the cream, thyme, and salt and pepper. Simmer gently until thickened, then spoon over ham in gratin dish. Put the dish in the oven and bake until top is golden, 10–15 minutes.

TOAD IN THE HOLE
SERVES 6

Onion gravy is a delicious match for this comforting, classic British dish of sausages baked in a Yorkshire pudding batter.

4 tbsp. unsalted butter
2 large yellow onions, sliced
1½ cups plus 1 tbsp. flour
2 cups beef stock
⅓ cup madeira wine
½ tsp. Worcestershire sauce
Kosher salt and freshly ground black pepper, to taste
2 tsp. dry mustard
1¼ cups milk
3 eggs, lightly beaten
8 tbsp. rendered bacon fat
6 slices prosciutto
6 large pork sausages

1 To make onion gravy, melt butter in a 4-qt. saucepan over medium-low heat. Add onions and cook until golden brown, about 40 minutes. Stir in 1 tbsp. flour; add stock, madeira, and Worcestershire, and bring to a boil. Cook for 5 minutes. Season with salt and pepper. Set aside.

2 Heat oven to 425°. Whisk remaining 1½ cups flour, mustard, and pepper in a bowl. Whisk in milk and eggs; let rest for 15 minutes. Pour 6 tbsp. bacon fat into a 9″ × 11″ baking dish; heat in oven for 10 minutes. Heat remaining 2 tbsp. bacon fat in a 12″ skillet over medium heat. Wrap 1 slice prosciutto around each sausage; place in skillet and cook until browned all over, about 8 minutes. Pour batter into hot baking dish. Arrange sausages in dish and bake until golden, 25–30 minutes. Serve with gravy.

Lamb & Goat

LEG OF LAMB WITH HERB–GARLIC CRUST
SERVES 8

This recipe from the late, great R. W. Apple conjures up the era when people knew their butcher by name. If you are lucky enough to have that kind of relationship today, ask him or her to french the shank bone, so you can use it as a sort of handle when you're carving the meat.

- 1   7–8 lb. leg of lamb, at room temperature
- 4   cloves garlic, peeled
- ¼   cup chopped fresh flat-leaf parsley
- ¼   cup chopped fresh rosemary
- 1   cup fresh bread crumbs
     Kosher salt and freshly ground black pepper, to taste
- 2   tbsp. olive oil
- 2   tbsp. Dijon mustard

1 Heat oven to 350°. If your butcher has not already done so, remove all excess fat from the lamb, leaving a very thin layer to protect the meat while cooking. Use the tip of a paring knife to make small incisions all over lamb. Cut 3 of the garlic cloves into small pieces and slip them into the incisions.

2 Mince remaining garlic clove and combine with parsley, rosemary, bread crumbs, and salt and pepper to taste. Mix well. Rub lamb with olive oil, then brush with mustard. Sprinkle bread-crumb mixture over lamb and pat down with your hands to form a thick, even coating.

3 Place lamb, fat side up, in a roasting pan. Roast until an instant-read thermometer inserted into center of meat reads 130°, 1¼–1½ hours. Remove lamb from oven and allow to rest for 20 minutes before carving.

INDIAN-STYLE LAMB POT ROAST
SERVES 8

Belonging to the family of slow, steam-cooked Moghul dishes called *dum pukht,* this lamb is coated in a spice paste made with saffron, coconut, almonds, and yogurt. It's typically prepared in a South Asian clay pot called a *handi,* but any deep-sided, flat-bottomed clay or enamel roaster or Dutch oven will do.

- 8   cloves garlic
- 1   small onion, quartered
- 1   3″ piece fresh ginger, peeled and roughly chopped
- 1½   cups golden raisins
- ½   cup unsweetened flaked dried coconut
- ⅓   cup blanched almonds
- 2   tbsp. plus 1 tsp. garam masala
- 2   tbsp. light brown sugar
- 3   tsp. saffron threads
- 4   serrano chiles, stemmed
- 1½   cups yogurt
- 1   6–7-lb. leg of lamb, boned
     Kosher salt, to taste
     Juice of 1 lime
- 1   large onion, thinly sliced
- 2   tbsp. chopped fresh cilantro leaves

1 In a food processor, pulse garlic, onion, ginger, raisins, coconut, almonds, 2 tbsp. garam masala, sugar, 2 tsp. saffron, and 3 chiles to a paste. Add ½ cup yogurt and pulse to combine. With a sharp knife, make ¼″-deep cuts all over lamb. Season inside of lamb with salt; rub with half the yogurt mixture, working it into the cuts. Roll lamb into a cylinder; tie at 1″ intervals with kitchen twine. Season outside of lamb with salt; rub with remaining yogurt mixture. Cover and let marinate for 1 hour at room temperature.

2 Finely chop remaining chile; combine with lime juice and remaining garam masala, saffron, and yogurt in a small bowl. Refrigerate sauce.

3 Put sliced onion into bottom of roasting pot; top with lamb. Cover, place in a cold oven, and turn heat to 325°. Bake until lamb is tender, about 3 hours. Uncover and cook, basting occasionally with juices, until browned, about 30 minutes more. Transfer lamb to a cutting board. Pour juices and onions into a 2-qt. saucepan; boil over high heat until reduced to 2 cups, about 15 minutes. Transfer onions to a platter with a slotted spoon. Slice lamb and lay over onions; drizzle with reduced juices and garnish with cilantro. Serve with the yogurt sauce.

LAMB MARINADES

Lamb goes well with all sorts of distinctively flavored rubs and marinades. The quantities shown below are for cuts large enough to feed four; scale quantities up or down as necessary so that you have enough rub or marinade to cover the meat. Once marinated, the cuts mentioned in the following recipes can be grilled, broiled, or roasted.

CHILE RUB This recipe is based on one given to us by chef Rick Bayless. Stem and seed 12 dried guajillo chiles (or 8 ancho chiles) and put them into a bowl; cover with boiling water to soften for 30 minutes. Drain and transfer to a blender along with 5 cloves garlic, 3 tbsp. water, 3 tbsp. cider vinegar, 2 tsp. sugar, 1 tsp. kosher salt, ¾ tsp. black pepper, ¼ tsp. ground cumin, and ¼ tsp. ground cinnamon. Purée until smooth. Rub mixture over a 3-lb. piece of shoulder or leg. Refrigerate for at least 2 hours before cooking.

LEMON-DILL MARINADE Fresh herbs marry beautifully with lamb. In a small bowl, whisk together 1 cup dry red wine, ¾ cup olive oil, 1 cup roughly chopped fresh dill, ½ cup fresh lemon juice, 3 tbsp. fresh oregano leaves, 1 tbsp. kosher salt, and 1 tbsp. dry mustard. Rub marinade onto two 1-lb. sirloin chops and marinate for up to 4 hours in the refrigerator before cooking.

SOY-HONEY MARINADE This delicious marinade brings out lamb's natural sweetness. In a bowl, whisk together ½ cup soy sauce, ⅓ cup honey, ¼ cup fresh lime juice, 3 tbsp. sesame oil, 3 tbsp. minced fresh ginger, 6 star anise pods, 2 stemmed and chopped chiles de árbol, and 2 minced garlic cloves. Rub marinade onto two 1-lb. arm or blade chops and marinate for 1 hour at room temperature or overnight in the refrigerator before cooking.

SAFFRON-ROASTED LAMB
SERVES 4–6

We were introduced to this flavorful lamb dish by Middle Eastern food expert Charles Perry. The saffron steeps in tangy onion juice, which kicks its floral pungence to a higher level.

1 large yellow onion, peeled
    Large pinch of saffron threads
1 2–2½-lb. boneless leg of lamb
1 tsp. ground sumac
    Coarsely chopped fresh mint, for garnish
    Coarsely chopped fresh cilantro, for garnish
    Thinly sliced scallions, for garnish

1 Grate onion or purée in a food processor. Put onions into a fine sieve and press onions with the back of a wooden spoon to strain the onion juice into a large nonreactive dish. Discard solids and set juice aside.

2 Toast saffron in a small skillet over high heat for 1 minute. Crumble toasted saffron into onion juice in dish and stir until juice turns golden. Put lamb into dish and turn to coat well. Cover tightly with plastic wrap and marinate in the refrigerator for at least 8 hours, turning and basting several times.

3 Heat oven to 350°. Roll up and firmly tie lamb with kitchen twine and put on a rack in a roasting pan. Roast until an instant-read thermometer inserted into center of meat reads 120° for rare or 130° for medium, 30–45 minutes. Remove from the oven and allow lamb to rest for 15 minutes.

4 Sprinkle lamb with sumac, then slice, discarding twine. Serve garnished with mint, cilantro, and scallions.

RACK OF LAMB WITH ROSEMARY & THYME
SERVES 2–4

The classic presentation for a roasted rack of lamb calls for frenching the meat—removing the layer of muscle and fat that extends to the end of the rib bones. Ask the butcher to do this if it's not already done.

1 1¾-lb. rack of lamb, frenched
    Kosher salt and freshly ground black pepper, to taste
2 tbsp. extra-virgin olive oil
2 tbsp. roughly chopped fresh rosemary
1 tbsp. chopped fresh thyme, plus 4 sprigs
10 cloves garlic, smashed

1 Heat oven to 450°. Season lamb with salt and pepper. Heat oil in a 12″ cast-iron skillet over medium-high heat. Add lamb, fat side down, and cook, using tongs to flip and sear bottom and sides of rack, until browned, about 10 minutes. Turn lamb fat side up in the skillet and scatter herbs over the top.

2 Add garlic to skillet and transfer to oven. Roast until an instant-read thermometer inserted into center of meat reads 130° for medium rare, about 10 minutes. Let cool for 5 minutes before slicing into chops and serving.

RACK OF LAMB WITH POMEGRANATE GLAZE

SERVES 4

Pomegranates and their juice have been an essential part of Mediterranean and Middle Eastern cuisines for millennia. Their sweet-tart flavor is perfect for this Armenian-inspired variation on a classic roasted rack of lamb.

- 3 cups pomegranate juice
- ½ cup sugar
  Leaves from 2–3 sprigs fresh oregano
- 2 cloves garlic, minced
- 1 2½-lb. rack of lamb, trimmed
  Kosher salt and freshly ground black pepper, to taste

1 Cook pomegranate juice and sugar in a medium saucepan over medium-high heat, stirring constantly, until a thick syrup forms, 20–30 minutes. Remove saucepan from heat and place in a larger pan of hot water to keep syrup warm and liquid.

2 Heat oven to 500°. Chop oregano leaves into minced garlic as finely as possible to make a paste, then smear it over all surfaces of lamb. Season with salt and pepper and place, bone side down, on a rack in a roasting pan. Brush lightly with pomegranate syrup and place in upper third of oven for 5 minutes. Lower oven to 375° and roast for 15 minutes per pound for medium rare (center registers 125° on an instant-read thermometer). After first 20 minutes, add some water to bottom of pan and brush roast with more pomegranate syrup.

3 Allow meat to rest for 10 minutes before cutting into chops. Mix pan juices into remaining syrup, pour over chops, and serve.

LAMB & ONION CURRY

Gosht Dopiaza

SERVES 6–8

Caramelized onions infused with cardamom, fennel, and cumin form the basis for this elemental Indian curry, made with lamb and small, flat cipolline onions and topped with crispy fried onions. ("Dopiaza" means "two onions.")

- 1 tbsp. paprika
- 1 tbsp. garam masala
- 4 tsp. ground turmeric
- 2 tsp. dried mint
- 2 tsp. kosher salt
- 12 cloves garlic, finely chopped
- 1 4" piece fresh ginger, peeled and finely chopped
- 1 jalapeño, stemmed, seeded, and finely chopped
- 2 lb. lamb shoulder, cut into 1½" cubes
- ¼ cup Greek yogurt
- 12 tbsp. unsalted butter
- 1 tbsp. coriander seeds
- 2 tsp. cumin seeds
- 1 tsp. fennel seeds
- 6 green cardamom pods, crushed
- 1 stick cinnamon
- 2 large yellow onions, thinly sliced lengthwise
- 1 16-oz. can whole, peeled tomatoes in juice, crushed by hand
- 12 cipolline or large pearl onions, peeled
  Fried onions, for garnish
  Cooked white rice, for serving

1 Make the spice paste: Combine paprika, garam masala, 2 tsp. turmeric, mint, salt, garlic, ginger, jalapeño, and ¼ cup water in a small food processor and purée until smooth. Transfer half the spice paste to a bowl and add lamb and yogurt; toss until evenly coated. Cover bowl with plastic wrap and marinate in the refrigerator for 4 hours.

2 Heat 8 tbsp. butter in an 8-qt. Dutch oven over medium-high heat. Add coriander, cumin, fennel, cardamom, and cinnamon and cook, stirring, until cinnamon stick unfurls and spices are fragrant and lightly toasted, about 5 minutes. Add yellow onions and and cook, stirring often, until deeply caramelized, about 25 minutes (add up to 4 tbsp. water, if necessary, to keep onions from sticking to bottom of pot). Add remaining spice paste and continue cooking until no longer raw, about 2 minutes. Add lamb along with any marinade and cook, stirring, until marinade is no longer raw, about 2 minutes. Add tomatoes and 3 cups water and bring to a boil. Reduce heat to medium-low and cook, stirring occasionally, until lamb is tender, about 1 hour.

3 Meanwhile, bring a 2-qt. saucepan of water to a boil over high heat. Add cipolline onions and cook until just tender, about 5 minutes; drain. Heat remaining turmeric and 4 tbsp. butter in a 10″ skillet over medium-high heat. Add onions and cook, stirring, until caramelized all over, about 10 minutes. Remove curry from heat and stir in caramelized onions. Sprinkle with fried onions and serve with rice.

LAMB STEWED WITH PARSNIP, BACON, FENNEL & RED WINE
SERVES 4–6

Chef Dano Hutnik, of Dano's Heuriger on Seneca, in New York's Finger Lakes region, gave us the recipe for this lamb stew; the rich meat and earthy parsnips and fennel are a natural match for the spicy, fragrant wine produced in the area.

- ½ lb. bacon, cut into ½″ pieces
- 2 tbsp. olive oil
- 1 lb. boneless lamb shoulder, trimmed and cut into 2″ cubes
  Kosher salt and freshly ground black pepper, to taste
- ½ cup flour
- 1 tbsp. fennel seeds
- 2 cloves garlic, roughly chopped
- 1 medium yellow onion, roughly chopped
- 1 bay leaf
- 2 cups dry red wine
- 1 cup chicken stock
- 2 parsnips, peeled and cut into 1″ pieces
- 1 medium fennel bulb, trimmed and cut into 1″ wedges
  Crusty bread, for serving

1 Heat bacon and oil in a 6-qt. saucepan over medium-high heat and cook until fat renders and bacon is crisp, about 8 minutes. Using a slotted spoon, transfer bacon to paper towels to drain; set aside.

2 Season lamb with salt and pepper, and toss with flour in a bowl, shaking off excess flour. Add lamb to pan and cook, turning as needed, until browned all over, about 10 minutes.

3 Add fennel seeds, garlic, onion, and bay leaf, season with salt and pepper, and cook, stirring, until onion is soft and golden, about 6 minutes. Add wine and cook, stirring

to scrape bottom of pan, until wine is reduced by half, about 15 minutes. Add stock and bring to a boil; reduce heat to medium and cook, covered, until meat is tender, about 1 hour.

4 Stir in reserved bacon, parsnips, and fennel and cook until vegetables are tender, about 30 minutes. Season with salt and pepper before serving with bread.

SHEPHERD'S PIE
SERVES 6

Shepherd's pie gets its name from the romantic notion that it was eaten by shepherds in the north of England long ago. Keeping the spirit of the idea, it's traditionally made with lamb; when made with beef, this casserole is called cottage pie.

- 14 tbsp. butter
- 2 lb. lamb shoulder, trimmed and cut into ½″ cubes
- 2 leeks, white part only, finely chopped
- 2 medium carrots, peeled and chopped
- 2 tbsp. flour
- 1½ cups beef stock
- 1 tbsp. Worcestershire sauce
- 1 tbsp. finely chopped fresh rosemary
- 1 tbsp. finely chopped fresh thyme leaves
- ⅛ tsp. freshly grated nutmeg
  Kosher salt and freshly ground black pepper, to taste
- 1½ cups fresh or thawed frozen peas
- 3 large russet potatoes (about 2 lb.), peeled and quartered
- ½ cup half-and-half

1 Melt 2 tbsp. of butter in a large pot over high heat. Add one-third of the lamb and brown on all sides, 4–5 minutes. Using a slotted spoon, transfer lamb to a plate, leaving fat in pot. Repeat process 2 more times, using 2 tbsp. of the butter and one-third of the lamb for each batch. Add leeks and carrots to pot, reduce heat to medium, and cook until softened, scraping up any browned bits, 3–4 minutes. Return lamb and its juices to pot along with flour and cook, stirring frequently, for 1 minute. Whisk in stock, Worcestershire, rosemary, thyme, nutmeg, and salt and pepper. Increase heat to medium-high and bring to a boil. Reduce heat to medium-low and simmer, covered, until lamb is tender, about 40 minutes. Uncover pot and simmer, stirring often, until thickened, 35–40 minutes more. Remove from heat, stir in peas, and set aside.

2 Meanwhile, put potatoes into a large pot and cover with salted water; bring to a boil. Reduce heat to medium-low and simmer until tender, 20–25 minutes. Drain and transfer potatoes to a bowl. Add 6 tbsp. butter, half-and-half, and salt and pepper; mash smooth with a potato masher.

3 Heat oven to 375°. Transfer lamb mixture to a 2-qt. casserole dish. Top evenly with mashed potatoes, making swirls and whorls with the back of a spoon. Cut remaining 2 tbsp. butter into small cubes; scatter over potatoes. Bake until golden brown and bubbling, about 30 minutes.

MOUSSAKA
SERVES 12–16

A good *moussaka*—a baked casserole of eggplant and lamb or beef under a lush layer of béchamel sauce—is one of the most famous of all Greek recipes, but compared to other Greek classics, it has a short history. Though a similar casserole had existed previously, the added layer of Frenchified béchamel was popularized by chef Nicholas Tselementes in the late 1920s.

- 2 cups plus 3 tbsp. extra-virgin olive oil
- 6 bay leaves
- 2 sticks cinnamon
- 1 large yellow onion, finely chopped
- 2 lb. ground beef
- ¼ cup tomato paste
- 1½ tsp. ground cinnamon, plus more for dusting
- ½ tsp. freshly grated nutmeg
- ¼ tsp. ground cloves
- 1 tbsp. red wine vinegar
- 1 tsp. sugar
- 1 28-oz. can whole, peeled tomatoes in juice, crushed by hand
- 1½ tsp. kosher salt, plus more to taste
  Freshly ground black pepper, to taste
- 8 tbsp. unsalted butter
- 1 cup flour
- 4 cups milk
- 4 eggs, beaten
- 3 large eggplants, cut into ¼"-thick slices
- 5 medium russet potatoes, peeled and thinly sliced crosswise
- 1 cup coarsely grated graviera or Gruyère cheese

1 Heat 3 tbsp. oil in a 6-qt. saucepan over medium-high heat. Add bay leaves, cinnamon sticks, and onion and cook until soft, about 5 minutes. Add beef and cook until all liquid evaporates and meat is browned, about 30 minutes. Add tomato paste, 1¼ tsp. ground cinnamon, ¼ tsp. nutmeg, and cloves; cook until lightly caramelized, about 2 minutes. Add vinegar, sugar, tomatoes, and 2 cups water and bring to a boil. Reduce heat to medium-low and cook, covered partially, until almost all liquid is evaporated, about 1½ hours. Remove from heat; discard cinnamon and bay leaves. Season with salt and pepper; set meat sauce aside. Melt butter in a 2-qt. saucepan over medium-high heat. Add flour and cook until smooth, about 2 minutes. Add 1½ tsp. salt, remaining cinnamon and nutmeg, and milk and cook until thickened, about 10 minutes. Remove from heat; pour into a blender with eggs. Blend until smooth; set béchamel aside.

2 Heat oven to 350°. Heat remaining 2 cups oil in a 12″ skillet over medium-high heat. Dust eggplant with cinnamon; working in batches, fry in oil until golden brown, about 10 minutes. Transfer to paper towels to drain; set aside. Bring a large pot of salted water to a boil. Add potatoes and cook until barely tender, about 10 minutes. Drain and transfer to a bowl of ice water to stop cooking. Drain; set aside.

3 Spread 1 cup béchamel on bottom of a 10″×14″ baking dish; sprinkle with ⅓ cup cheese. Spread potatoes over cheese; top with eggplant. Pour meat sauce over eggplant; spread remaining béchamel over meat sauce. Sprinkle with remaining cheese and bake until golden brown, about 1 hour.

SPICED LAMB KEBABS
SERVES 4

Variations on these bullet-shaped ground lamb kebabs are found in virtually every Mediterranean country; with its cumin, Aleppo pepper, and mint, this is a particularly Middle Eastern variation.

- 1½ lb. ground lamb
- 6 tbsp. grated onion
- 2 tbsp. extra-virgin olive oil
- 4 tbsp. ground dried Aleppo pepper or paprika
- 1 tbsp. kosher salt
- 2 tsp. ground cumin
- 2 tsp. dried oregano
- 2 tsp. dried mint, crumbled with your fingers
- 1 tsp. freshly ground black pepper

1 Combine lamb and onion in a large bowl; set aside. Heat oil in a 10″ skillet over medium-high heat. Add Aleppo pepper, salt, cumin, oregano, mint, and pepper and cook, stirring constantly, until fragrant, about 45 seconds. Pour spice mixture over reserved lamb mixture and mix thoroughly with your hands.

2 Divide lamb mixture into 4 portions and roll each into a thin cylinder about 10″ long and 1″ thick. Slide a flat metal skewer into each cylinder and press the meat around the skewer. Transfer skewers to a parchment-lined baking sheet and refrigerate for 30 minutes to firm up.

3 Meanwhile, build a medium-hot fire in a charcoal grill or heat a gas grill to medium-high. (Alternatively, position an oven rack 7″ from broiler and heat broiler.) Grill or broil kebabs, turning once, until browned and nicely charred on the outside and medium on the inside, about 4 minutes per side.

COOK'S NOTE Wide, flat metal skewers are ideal for grilling this style of ground-meat kebab, but the spiced meat mixture can also be formed into patties if you don't have skewers.

LAMB RISSOLES

MAKES 12

Use leftover roast leg of lamb and gravy to make these bread crumb–crusted meat patties. The term *rissoles* comes from the French *rissoler*, "to brown."

- 4 cups diced roast leg of lamb
- 2 cups pan drippings or lamb or beef stock
- ¼ bunch fresh flat-leaf parsley, leaves chopped
- 5 cups fresh bread crumbs
  Kosher salt and freshly ground black pepper, to taste
- 3 eggs
- ¼ cup vegetable oil

1 Working in 2 batches, put lamb into a food processor and process until texture resembles that of ground beef, about 30 seconds per batch, or finely chop with a large sharp knife or cleaver, then transfer to a large bowl. Add drippings, parsley, and 2 cups of the bread crumbs, season with salt and pepper, and stir until well combined. Shape meat mixture into twelve 3″ patties and set aside.

2 Put remaining 3 cups bread crumbs into a medium dish and set aside. Lightly beat eggs in another medium dish and set aside. Heat oil in a large nonstick skillet over medium heat. Meanwhile, lightly dredge 1 lamb patty at a time in the bread crumbs, dip into eggs, then dredge again in the bread crumbs, coating entire surface.

3 Fry patties in batches, until golden brown on both sides, 3–5 minutes per side. Serve hot or at room temperature.

MUGHAL GOAT CURRY

Bhuna Gosht

SERVES 4–6

This recipe employs an Indian technique called *gosht,* in which the meat, spices, and wet ingredients are stewed together until the mixture reduces and the main ingredient browns.

- 9 cloves garlic, chopped
- 3 lb. bone-in goat shoulder, trimmed and cut into 4″ pieces
- 4 cups plain yogurt
- 2 tbsp. amchoor (sour mango powder)
- 1 tbsp. cardamom pods
- 1 tbsp. ground coriander
- 1 tbsp. black peppercorns
- 2 tsp. cumin seeds
- 2 tsp. Kashmiri red chile powder or paprika
- 1 tsp. whole cloves
- 3 cups canola oil
- 1 3″ piece fresh ginger, peeled and julienned
  Salt, to taste
- 6 shallots, thinly sliced
  Basmati rice, for serving

1 Purée garlic and ⅓ cup water in a blender. Put garlic paste, goat, yogurt, amchoor, cardamom, coriander, peppercorns, cumin, chile powder, cloves, ⅔ cup oil, ginger, and salt into a pot and stir well. Bring to a boil, reduce heat to medium, and boil gently, stirring up browned bits from bottom of pot, until meat is almost tender, about 2 hours.

2 Heat remaining 2⅓ cups oil in a pot over medium heat until oil reads 325° on a deep-fry thermometer. Add shallots and cook, stirring constantly, until brown, 3–5 minutes. Using a slotted spoon, transfer shallots to a paper towel–lined plate. When cool, pulse shallots to a coarse paste in a spice grinder. Add shallots and 2 cups water to pot and cook, stirring, until goat is tender and beginning to brown and sauce is thickened, about 45 minutes more. Season with salt. Serve with basmati rice.

SOURCING NOTE You can find sour mango powder online, or substitute with dried sumac or dried lemon zest (page 588).

Offal

NIÇOISE-STYLE TRIPE STEW

Tripes à la Niçoise

SERVES 4

A favorite among the locals in Nice, France, this fragrant stew must be cooked very slowly to tenderize the tripe properly. If you skimp on the cooking time, it will be chewy and bland.

- 2 lb. beef tripe, cut into 2″ × ½″ strips
- ¼ cup white vinegar
- ¼ cup extra-virgin olive oil
- 2 cups dry white wine
- 4 tomatoes, peeled, seeded, and roughly chopped
- 4 cloves garlic, finely chopped
- 2 onions, sliced
- 1 Bouquet Garni (page 86)
- 1 small dried red chile (optional)
  Kosher salt and freshly ground black pepper, to taste
  Grated Parmigiano-Reggiano, for serving

1 Rinse tripe very well in several changes of cold water. Bring a large pot of water to a boil over high heat and add vinegar. Blanch tripe for 20 seconds in boiling water; drain.

2 Heat oil in a medium pot over medium heat and add tripe. Cook for about 2 minutes, stirring frequently. Stir in wine, tomatoes, garlic, onions, bouquet garni, chile (if using), and salt and pepper to taste.

3 Cover, reduce heat to low, and simmer for at least 8 hours. Season with salt and pepper and serve with grated cheese.

VENETIAN CALF'S LIVER & ONIONS

Fegato alla Veneziana

SERVES 6

When we visited Venice, we asked the locals where to find the definitive calf's liver and onions. Everyone said Harry's Bar, and, after trying it there, we had to agree. This is Harry's recipe.

- 2 lb. calf's liver, trimmed and membrane removed
- 6 tbsp. extra-virgin olive oil
- 6 small onions, halved and very thinly sliced

Kosher salt and freshly ground black pepper
- 3 tbsp. butter
- ½ bunch fresh flat-leaf parsley, chopped
  Grilled Polenta (page 401), for serving

1 Cut liver lengthwise into 4 long pieces, then, using a very sharp knife and pressing the palm of your hand firmly against the meat, slice each piece crosswise into pieces as thin as possible.

2 Heat 4 tbsp. oil in a large skillet over medium heat. Add onions and cook, stirring frequently, until soft and deep golden brown, about 20 minutes. Transfer onions with a slotted spoon to a bowl and set aside.

3 Increase heat to medium-high and add remaining 2 tbsp. oil. When oil is sizzling hot, add liver, in batches to avoid crowding the skillet, and cook, stirring constantly with a wooden spoon, until brown and crispy on the edges, 3–5 minutes. Season liberally with salt and pepper, then add reserved onions and accumulated juices. Cook for 2 minutes, stirring and turning liver and onions constantly while shaking skillet over heat. Transfer to a warm serving platter.

4 Add butter to skillet and scrape up any browned bits stuck to bottom of skillet as butter melts. Remove skillet from heat and stir in parsley. Spoon butter and parsley over liver and onions. Serve with grilled polenta.

SWEETBREADS WITH BLACK MUSHROOMS

SERVES 4

Jock Livingston, owner of Ports, an erstwhile L.A. hangout for the famous and infamous, loved sweetbreads and was adept at cooking Chinese food. He invented this dish.

- 8 Chinese dried black mushrooms
- 1 lb. veal sweetbreads, cleaned
- 2 slices lemon
- ½ cup chicken stock
- ¼ cup oyster sauce
- 3 tbsp. dry sherry or sake

1 tbsp. soy sauce
1 tsp. sugar
3 tbsp. extra-virgin olive oil
1 medium onion, minced
1 clove garlic, minced
1 1"-piece ginger, peeled and minced
2 scallions, finely chopped, for garnish

1 Soak mushrooms in a medium bowl of hot water until soft, about 1 hour. Meanwhile, bring a medium pot of water to a boil over high heat. Add sweetbreads and lemon slices, reduce heat to medium, and simmer for 10 minutes. Drain, discarding lemon slices. Arrange sweetbreads in a single layer on a plastic wrap–lined baking sheet. Cover sweetbreads loosely with plastic wrap, then set another baking sheet directly on top and weight it down with several heavy, unopened cans. Refrigerate for 30 minutes. Slice sweetbreads on the diagonal into ½"-thick pieces; set aside.

2 Remove mushrooms from soaking liquid, trim off stems, then chop caps and set aside. Discard soaking liquid and stems. Whisk together stock, oyster sauce, sherry, soy sauce, and sugar in a small bowl and set sauce aside.

3 Heat oil in a large skillet over medium-high heat. Add onion, garlic, and ginger and cook, stirring, until onions are soft, 3–4 minutes. Add sweetbreads and mushrooms, reduce heat to medium, and cook, gently shaking skillet, until sweetbreads are heated through, about 1 minute. Add sauce and simmer, stirring and spooning sauce and mushrooms over sweetbreads, until thickened, 1–2 minutes. Transfer to a serving platter and garnish with scallions.

OXTAIL TATIN WITH TOMATO JAM

Tatin de Cua de Bou

SERVES 8

We tried this elegant dish of braised oxtail on top of puff pastry topped with a spoonful of tomato jam at the Hotel Empordà on Spain's Costa Brava. There, the chef adds *mistela negra*—new red wine dosed with brandy—to the braising liquid for the oxtail. It's rarely available in the United States, but tawny port is a fine substitute.

6   lb. oxtails
6   cups red wine
2¼   cups tawny port
¾   cup cognac
2   ribs celery, cut into batons
2   medium carrots, cut into batons
1   large onion, halved and thickly sliced
2   cloves garlic, crushed
2   tsp. juniper berries
2   bay leaves
3   large sprigs fresh thyme
     Kosher salt and freshly ground black pepper
6   tbsp. peanut oil
⅓   cup flour
2   tbsp. olive oil
4   medium tomatoes, peeled, seeded, and coarsely chopped
1   tsp. sugar
1   tsp. brewed strong coffee
8   baked 4" puff pastry circles, warm

1 Put oxtails, wine, port, cognac, celery, carrots, onion, garlic, juniper berries, bay leaves, and 2 sprigs thyme in a bowl. Cover and let marinate in the refrigerator for 3 days.

2 Heat oven to 300°. Strain marinade into a bowl and reserve. Set vegetables and aromatics aside in another bowl. Transfer oxtail to a clean surface, pat dry, then season with salt and pepper. Heat peanut oil in a large, heavy ovenproof pot with a tight-fitting lid over medium-high heat. Working in batches, brown oxtails all over, 7–10 minutes. Return oxtails to pot and roast in oven, uncovered, for 1½ hours.

3 Reduce oven temperature to 250°. Transfer pot to medium heat on top of stove. Add reserved vegetables and aromatics and cook, stirring occasionally, until browned, 10–12 minutes. Stir in flour. Pour in reserved marinade, increase heat to high, and bring to a boil, skimming any foam that rises. Cover pot, transfer to oven, and braise, stirring occasionally, until meat is very tender, about 4 hours.

4 To make the tomato jam, heat olive oil in a small pot over medium heat. Add tomatoes, sugar, coffee, and remaining 1 sprig thyme. Simmer, stirring occasionally and reducing heat, if necessary, to prevent jam from boiling, until thick, about 1 hour. Season with salt and pepper. Discard thyme. Keep jam warm over low heat.

5 Strain sauce from braised meat into a medium pot, skim off fat, and boil over medium-high heat, skimming occasionally, until reduced to 2¼ cups, 15–20 minutes. Meanwhile, pick meat off bones and return to large pot, discarding fat, sinew, bones, vegetables, and aromatics. Strain sauce through a sieve into pot with meat. Season with salt and pepper. Keep warm over lowest heat.

6 Put a puff pastry circle on each plate and spoon some meat and sauce on top, then garnish each with a spoonful of jam.

Game

RABBIT IN MUSTARD SAUCE

SERVES 8

This French-inspired recipe, with soft herbal notes and a pointed mustard flavor, came to us from the chef and writer David Tanis.

- 2   2½-lb. rabbits, each cut into 6 pieces
       Kosher salt and freshly ground black pepper, to taste
- ½   lb. pancetta or unsmoked bacon, cut into ¼"-thick strips
- 1½   cups crème fraîche
- ¾   cup Dijon mustard
- 2   tbsp. roughly chopped fresh thyme
- 2   tbsp. roughly chopped fresh sage
- 2   tsp. black or yellow mustard seeds, crushed
- 8   cloves garlic, thinly sliced
- 4   bay leaves

1 Season rabbit generously with salt and pepper and place in a large bowl along with remaining ingredients. Mix together with your hands until rabbit pieces are coated. Cover bowl with plastic wrap and let marinate at room temperature for at least 1 hour or up to overnight in the refrigerator.

2 If rabbit has been chilled, allow it to come to room temperature. Heat oven to 400°. Divide rabbit in a single layer between 2 shallow roasting pans and top with any of the remaining marinade. Roast the rabbit, turning once and basting with pan juices occasionally, until the juices have reduced and rabbit is cooked through, about 55 minutes. Heat broiler and cook until golden brown, about 5 minutes more. Serve rabbit with pan juices.

MALTESE RABBIT IN RED WINE

SERVES 4

In Malta, rabbit (called *fenek*) is almost a national dish—so much so, the Maltese coined a new word for those dining on rabbit: *fenkata*. This red-wine preparation results in a crispy outside and moist interior, thanks to a stove-top browning followed by a slow finish in the oven.

- 1   2-lb. rabbit, cut into 6 pieces
- 5   tbsp. extra-virgin olive oil
- 6–8 cloves garlic, minced
- 4   scallions, white part only, finely chopped
       Leaves from 3 sprigs each fresh mint, thyme, marjoram, and flat-leaf parsley, chopped
- 1   cup red wine

1 Heat oven to 350°. Heat 4 tbsp. oil in a large ovenproof skillet over medium-high heat. Add rabbit pieces and brown, turning frequently. Remove rabbit from pan and reserve. Pour off fat from pan and lower heat to medium.

2 Add remaining 1 tbsp. oil to pan and add garlic, scallions, and all but a bit of the herbs; cook for about 3 minutes. Deglaze skillet with wine and return rabbit to it. Place skillet in oven and cook uncovered until meat is firm, about 25 minutes. Serve garnished with remaining herbs.

BRAISED RABBIT WITH MUSHROOMS & CELERY ROOT

SERVES 4–6

Wild rabbit, a favorite among hunters in Kansas, is braised in beer and chicken stock to make this autumnal dish. It's often served with corn on the cob on the side.

- 3   slices bacon, roughly chopped
- 1   3-lb. rabbit, cut into 6 pieces
       Kosher salt and freshly ground black pepper, to taste
- ½   cup flour
- 3   tbsp. olive oil
- 7   oz. oyster mushrooms, trimmed
- 4   cloves garlic, roughly chopped
- 2   small yellow onions, quartered
- 2   ribs celery, cut into 1" pieces
- 1   medium carrot, peeled and cut into 1" pieces
- 1   bay leaf
- 3½   tbsp. tomato paste
- 1   cup chicken stock
- 1   cup lager-style beer
- ½   medium celery root, peeled and cut into 1" pieces
- 2   tbsp. chopped fresh flat-leaf parsley, for garnish

1 Heat bacon in a 6-qt. Dutch oven over medium-high heat; cook until fat is rendered and bacon is crisp, about 10 minutes. Using a slotted spoon, transfer bacon to a bowl. Season rabbit with salt and pepper, and dredge in flour, shaking off excess. Working in batches, cook rabbit, flipping once, until browned, about 10 minutes; transfer to a plate.

2 Add oil and mushrooms to pan and cook until browned, 4–5 minutes; transfer to the plate with rabbit. Add garlic, onion, celery, and carrot to pan and cook, stirring occasionally, until garlic is browned, 3–4 minutes. Add bay leaf and tomato paste and cook, stirring, until slightly caramelized, about 3 minutes. Add stock and beer and bring to a boil. Reduce heat to medium-low and return rabbit and mushrooms to the pan. Stir in celery root, partially cover, and braise until rabbit is cooked through, 35–40 minutes. Garnish with parsley and reserved bacon.

RABBIT & ONION STEW
Kouneli Stifado
SERVES 4

Sweetened with prunes and studded with pearl onions, this country-style rabbit stew is a home-cooked specialty on the Greek island of Crete.

- 1 3-lb. rabbit, cut into 6 pieces
  Kosher salt and freshly ground black pepper, to taste
- ½ cup olive oil
- 2 lb. pearl onions, peeled
- 1 lb. medium tomatoes, roughly chopped
- ½ cup chicken stock
- 1 tbsp. tomato paste
- 12 prunes
- 6 whole cloves
- 5 cloves garlic, smashed
- 3 bay leaves
- 2 small sprigs fresh rosemary
- 1 2″ stick cinnamon
  Fresh flat-leaf parsley, for garnish

1 Season rabbit with salt and pepper. Heat oil in a 5-qt. Dutch oven over medium-high heat. Working in 3 batches, add rabbit and cook, turning once, until browned, about 8 minutes. Transfer rabbit to a plate; set aside. Add onions and cook, stirring occasionally, until golden brown, about 5 minutes. Add tomatoes, stock, tomato paste, prunes, cloves, garlic, bay leaves, rosemary, and cinnamon. Nestle

rabbit in the pot, cover, and bring to a boil. Reduce heat to low and cook until rabbit is very tender, about 45 minutes.

2 Transfer rabbit to a large platter. Set a medium strainer over a 1-qt. saucepan. Strain the cooking liquid, discarding bay leaves and rosemary. Transfer the onions and prunes to the platter. Simmer the strained sauce over medium-high heat until slightly thickened, about 8 minutes. Skim excess fat from surface, season sauce with salt and pepper, and spoon over rabbit. Serve garnished with parsley.

VENISON SAUSAGE BRAISED IN BEER
SERVES 6

Butter-sautéed apples and carrots highlight venison sausage's nuanced nature; a braise in beer enhances its earthy, dusky flavor.

- 4 tbsp. butter
- 1 tbsp. extra-virgin olive oil
- 12 venison sausages
- 4 medium carrots, peeled and cut into large pieces
- 2 leeks, white part only, cut into 1″ pieces
- 2 Granny Smith apples, peeled, cored, and cut into wedges
  Kosher salt and freshly ground black pepper, to taste
- 1 12-oz. bottle lager beer
- ¼ cup Demi-Glace (page 571, or store-bought; optional)
- 1 small savoy cabbage, cored and cut into large pieces

1 Melt 2 tbsp. butter with oil in a large, heavy skillet over medium heat. Working in batches, add sausages and brown on all sides, about 10 minutes total. Transfer sausages to a plate, cover with aluminum foil to keep warm, and set aside.

2 Melt remaining 2 tbsp. butter in the same skillet, then add carrots, leeks, and apples, stirring to coat vegetables and apples with butter. Season with salt and pepper and cook until everything in the pan is glazed and slightly browned, about 10 minutes. Pick apple wedges out of skillet and set aside. Add beer and demi-glace (if using), and, with a wooden spoon, loosen any browned bits stuck to the bottom of the skillet. Reduce heat to medium-low, then cover and cook for 20 minutes. Return sausages and apples to the skillet, then add cabbage. Cover and cook until vegetables are tender, about 20 minutes. Serve sausages arranged on top of vegetables, apples, and cabbage.

RACK OF VENISON WITH SOUR CHERRY–PORT SAUCE

SERVES 4–8

When venison is surrounded by a garlicky bread-crumb mixture and paired with a tart cherry sauce, its gamy sweetness shines.

FOR THE VENISON

1	cup fresh bread crumbs
1	clove garlic, minced
2	tbsp. minced fresh thyme
3	juniper berries, crushed and ground
2	tbsp. extra-virgin olive oil
	Kosher salt and freshly ground black pepper
1	8-chop rack venison, cut into two 4-chop racks

FOR THE SAUCE

1	cup port
¼	cup Demi-Glace (page 571), or 1 cup beef or veal stock reduced to ¼ cup
1	cup preserved sour cherries, with a little of their juice
	Kosher salt and freshly ground black pepper, to taste

1 Make the venison: heat oven to 375°. Mix together bread crumbs, garlic, thyme, juniper berries, and oil in a large bowl. Season with salt and pepper. Pat bread-crumb mixture on meat of both racks, then place in a small, heavy roasting pan, interlocking bones to hold chops upright. Roast until an instant-read temperature inserted into center (away from bone) reads 150° for medium rare, about 45 minutes. Remove venison from oven, transfer meat to a serving platter, and set roasting pan aside. Cover venison loosely with foil and let rest for 15 minutes before carving.

2 Make the sauce: Place roasting pan on top of stove over medium heat. Add port, deglazing pan by stirring to scrape up any browned bits stuck to the bottom of the pan, and cook until port is reduced by half, about 10 minutes. Add demi-glace, juices from the resting venison, and cherries with their juice. Season with salt and pepper and serve with venison.

ALSATIAN VENISON STEW

SERVES 6

This Alsatian dish is a rich game stew traditionally thickened with the blood of the animal; our recipe uses flour for a lighter interpretation. Serve with slices of toasted country bread.

3	lb. boneless venison shoulder, cut into large pieces
1	medium carrot, diced
1	medium yellow onion, diced
3	cloves garlic, peeled
12	sprigs fresh flat-leaf parsley
2	sprigs fresh thyme
2	bay leaves
15	black peppercorns
1	750-ml bottle dry red wine
¼	lb. slab bacon, sliced and julienned
	Kosher salt and freshly ground black pepper
2	tbsp. canola oil
2	tbsp. flour
1	lb. pearl onions, peeled
1	tsp. sugar
4	tbsp. butter
½	lb. white mushrooms, sliced
2	tbsp. cognac

1 Combine venison, carrot, yellow onion, garlic, 2 sprigs parsley, thyme, bay leaves, peppercorns, and wine in a large bowl. Cover and refrigerate for 24 hours to tenderize venison.

2 Cook bacon in a heavy pot or Dutch oven over medium heat until crisp, 8–10 minutes. Remove with a slotted spoon; drain on paper towels.

3 Remove venison, then strain marinade into a bowl, discarding herbs and vegetables. Season meat with salt and pepper. Add oil to bacon fat in pot, increase heat to medium-high, add meat, and brown, turning occasionally, 7–10 minutes. Sprinkle flour over meat and return bacon to pot. Cook, stirring, until flour turns a nut-brown color, about 1 minute. Add marinade, bring to a simmer, then reduce heat to medium-low, cover, and cook until venison is tender, 2–2½ hours.

4 Bring a medium pot of salted water to a boil. Add pearl onions and sugar and simmer over medium heat until tender, 25–30 minutes. Drain. Heat 2 tbsp. butter in a medium skillet over medium-high heat. Add mushrooms and cook, stirring, until golden, about 3 minutes.

5 Remove venison from pot to finish sauce. Increase heat to medium-high, add cognac, and cook for 5 minutes. Remove pot from heat and whisk in remaining 2 tbsp. butter. Return venison to sauce, add onions and mushrooms, and mix thoroughly. Chop remaining parsley and sprinkle on top.

Seafood

SEAFOOD

SUCCULENT FRIED CLAM BELLIES from a Maine seafood shack; a delightfully messy stone-crab dinner served up at a Florida shanty; a fragrant, saffron-infused fish stew enjoyed in a Mediterranean port—the pleasure to be found in eating seafood is as deep and as wide as the ocean itself.

Of course, the delights of seafood are not limited to sun-soaked days by the shore. We've been plumbing lakes, rivers, and seas for protein-rich sustenance since the beginning of human memory, and today, fish markets around the world—Tokyo's Tuskiji Market, Barcelona's Boqueria, the Feskekörka in Götenberg, Sweden—hawk a wide variety of choices: purple curls of squid, slippery lengths of eel, ruddy crabs, snowy cod filets, coin-shaped pearly scallops. And the ways cooks prepare these fresh- and saltwater harvests are almost as myriad: roasting, smoking, salt baking, poaching, stewing, frying, and searing.

But not all preparations rely on fire. Among the most wonderful ways to enjoy fish and shellfish are those in which their delicate, briny flavor speaks for itself in raw and cured preparations, such as Japanese sushi and sashimi, Peruvian ceviche, Italian *crudo,* Scandinavian gravlax and pickled herring, and the raw bivalves slurped happily by the dozen in European and American oyster bars.

Seafood can also serve as both a foil and a showcase for the flavors emblematic of a region: the diverse fish curries of South and Southeast Asia, the rich Creole favorites of New Orleans like gumbo and crawfish étouffée, and Kenya's fiery ginger and coconut crab. And while casual seafood plates like Britain's fish and chips or Maryland's cracker meal–bound crab cakes are no anomaly, seafood's haute reputation stretches back to Greek antiquity, when fish was considered an upper-class preserve.

That tradition is reflected in wonderfully dignified classics like pike quenelles and creamy *homard à l'armoricaine.* Its special station is also held up in religious repasts such as southern Italy's Christmastime Feast of the Seven Fishes, or Portugal's ubiquitous *bacalao* (salt cod) dishes, which take on special status during meatless Catholic holidays. And across different faiths, cultures, and seasons, the arrival of a whole fish brings a celebratory moment to any table or meal.

Whole Fish

MOROCCAN FISH WITH CUMIN SEEDS

SERVES 6

A Marrakesh home cook presented us with this cumin-infused roasted fish at a supper in Morocco. The fish bakes on a bed of vegetables, which absorbs its aromatic juices.

- 3 tbsp. cumin seeds, toasted
- 12 cloves garlic, crushed
- 1 bunch fresh flat-leaf parsley, chopped
- 1 tbsp. kosher salt
  Juice of 3 lemons, plus 1 lemon, sliced
- 2 3-lb. whole red snappers, cleaned
- 3 carrots, peeled and sliced
- 12 new potatoes, sliced
- 4 tomatoes, sliced
- 1 green bell pepper, seeded and sliced
- 5 whole mild green chiles
- ½ cup extra-virgin olive oil

1 Using a spice grinder or a mortar and pestle, grind together cumin, garlic, parsley, and salt. Transfer to a small bowl and mix in the lemon juice.

2 Place the fish in a large, shallow baking pan and rub marinade all over them. Cover with plastic wrap and marinate in refrigerator for 30 minutes.

3 Heat oven to 500°. Remove fish from refrigerator and scatter carrots, potatoes, tomatoes, pepper, lemon slices, and chiles around fish. Pour oil and ½ cup water over fish and vegetables. Bake, basting often, until fish is cooked through, about 30 minutes. Serve fish on a bed of the roasted vegetables.

SALT-ROASTED SEA BASS WITH CELERY SALSA VERDE

SERVES 2 (SEE PHOTO, PAGE 222)

The technique of baking a whole fish inside a crust of salt bound with egg whites essentially creates an oven within the oven, a clever method that keeps the fish moist as it roasts. Chef Jody Adams of the Boston restaurant Rialto adds fresh herbs to her salt crust, which infuses the fish with a subtle flavor that's enhanced by a tart celery salsa verde.

FOR THE SALSA VERDE

- 1¼ cups roughly chopped fresh flat-leaf parsley leaves
- ⅓ cup roughly chopped celery leaves
- ⅓ cup rinsed and chopped capers
- 1½ tbsp. roughly chopped fresh tarragon leaves
- 3 oil-packed anchovy filets, rinsed and minced
  Grated zest of ½ lemon
- ¾ cup extra-virgin olive oil
- ½ tbsp. fresh lemon juice
- 1 clove garlic, minced
- 1 rib celery, minced
  Kosher salt and freshly ground black pepper, to taste

FOR THE FISH

- 1 cup kosher salt
  Freshly ground black pepper, to taste
- ½ cup roughly chopped fresh thyme leaves
- ¼ cup lightly toasted coriander seeds
- ¼ cup lightly toasted fennel seeds
- 3 cups coarse sea salt
- 4 egg whites
- 1 1½-lb. whole black sea bass, branzino, or porgy, cleaned, scales left on
- 2 thin slices lemon
- 6 sprigs fresh flat-leaf parsley

1 Make the salsa verde: Combine parsley leaves, celery leaves, capers, tarragon, anchovies, and lemon zest in a food processor. Add ½ cup oil and pulse into a coarse paste. Transfer to a bowl along with lemon juice, garlic, and celery. Season lightly with salt and pepper and stir in remaining ¼ cup oil; cover and set sauce aside.

2 Make the fish: Heat oven to 400°. Combine salt, pepper, thyme, coriander, and fennel in a food processor. Process until herbs are minced and salt takes on a green tint. Add sea salt and pulse to combine. In a large bowl, whip egg whites until foamy. Stir in salt mixture. Arrange 1 cup egg-salt mixture in a thin layer on a baking sheet. Lay fish over top and stuff cavity with lemon slices and parsley sprigs. Top fish with remaining egg-salt mixture and pat with your hands to form a smooth, sealed mound (keep fish mouth and tail uncovered, if you like). Bake fish until an instant-read thermometer inserted into thickest part of fish reads 140°, 20–25 minutes. Transfer baking sheet to a rack and let fish rest for 5 minutes.

3 To serve, crack open salt shell by tapping it with the back of a spoon. Peel away and remove top layer of salt. Peel off skin and transfer top filet of fish to a warm serving plate. Remove bones and transfer remaining filet to another warm serving plate, leaving skin and bottom layer of salt behind. Spoon reserved salsa verde over fish.

BROILED RED SNAPPER WITH FENNEL & TOMATOES

Vivaneau Rouge Rôti avec Fenouil & Tomates

SERVES 4

Garlic, coriander, and thyme season this robustly flavored baked fish, inspired by a similar dish served at the restaurant Le Brûlot in Antibes, in the south of France. Serve it with crusty bread for soaking up the juices.

3 plum tomatoes, cored and halved lengthwise
1 medium bulb fennel, trimmed, cut into 12 wedges
1 medium onion, cut crosswise into 12 slices
4 cloves garlic
  Kosher salt, to taste
½ cup fresh lemon juice
⅓ cup extra-virgin olive oil
1 tsp. lightly crushed coriander seeds
1 tsp. lightly crushed black peppercorns
1 tsp. dried thyme
2 bay leaves
2 1-lb. whole red snappers, cleaned
  Freshly ground black pepper, to taste
1 tbsp. finely chopped fresh flat-leaf parsley
  Baguette slices, for serving

1 Heat oven to 400°. Spread tomatoes, fennel, and onion evenly in a large oval baking dish. Mince garlic on a cutting board and sprinkle heavily with salt; using a knife, scrape garlic and salt together to form a smooth paste. Transfer to a bowl and whisk in lemon juice, oil, coriander, peppercorns, thyme, and bay leaves; pour half of this dressing over the vegetables. Bake vegetables until tender, about 35 minutes.

2 Heat broiler. Season inside and outside of fish with salt and ground pepper and place over vegetables in dish; pour remaining dressing evenly over fish. Place under broiler and cook, turning fish once, until fish are cooked through, about 18 minutes. Sprinkle with parsley before serving with bread.

HOW TO BUTTERFLY RED SNAPPER

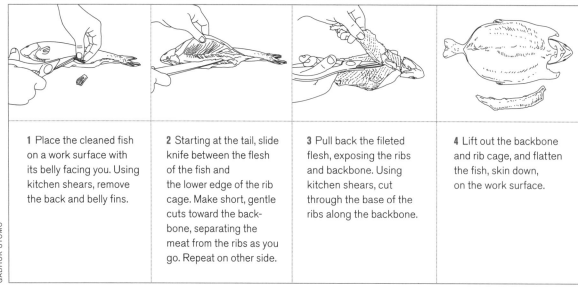

1 Place the cleaned fish on a work surface with its belly facing you. Using kitchen shears, remove the back and belly fins.

2 Starting at the tail, slide knife between the flesh of the fish and the lower edge of the rib cage. Make short, gentle cuts toward the backbone, separating the meat from the ribs as you go. Repeat on other side.

3 Pull back the fileted flesh, exposing the ribs and backbone. Using kitchen shears, cut through the base of the ribs along the backbone.

4 Lift out the backbone and rib cage, and flatten the fish, skin down, on the work surface.

GABHOR UTOMO

HOW TO FILET SARDINES

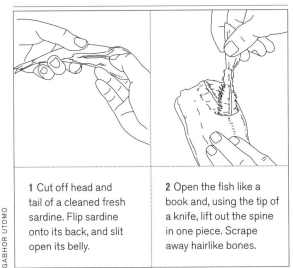

1 Cut off head and tail of a cleaned fresh sardine. Flip sardine onto its back, and slit open its belly.

2 Open the fish like a book and, using the tip of a knife, lift out the spine in one piece. Scrape away hairlike bones.

GABHOR UTOMO

FISH STUFFED WITH PICO DE GALLO

Pescado Encarcelado

SERVES 4

Baking butterflied fish in foil packets preserves their natural juices. In this dish, red snappers are stuffed with savory tomato salsa, a popular preparation along Mexico's Pacific coast.

- 2 tbsp. minced jalapeños
- 4 tsp. Worcestershire sauce
- 2 plum tomatoes, finely chopped
- 1 medium white onion, minced
  Kosher salt and freshly ground black pepper, to taste
- 2 1-lb. whole red snappers, cleaned and butterflied (see How to Butterfly Red Snapper, left)
- 1 lime, cut into wedges, for serving

1 Combine jalapeños, Worcestershire, tomatoes, and onion in a bowl; season with salt and pepper and set pico de gallo aside. Heat broiler.

2 Place each fish, backbone side down, on a 12″ square of foil, and crimp foil around bottom of fish to form a canoe shape. Season fish with salt and pepper, and divide pico de gallo between fish cavities. Transfer fish packets to a baking sheet, and broil until fish is cooked through and charred at the edges, about 15 minutes. Serve fish with lime wedges.

GRILLED WHOLE FISH WITH TAMARIND

Samaki Wa Kupaka

SERVES 2–4

This Swahili recipe calls for ingredients that have been staples along the Kenyan coast since seafarers from the Arabian Peninsula and India landed in Mombasa centuries ago: chiles, turmeric, cloves, and tamarind paste.

- 1 2–3-lb. whole fish, such as red snapper, porgy, or striped bass, cleaned
  Kosher salt and freshly ground black pepper, to taste
- 6 cloves garlic, minced
- 2 pili pili or red bird's eye chiles, stemmed, seeded, and minced
- 1 2″ piece fresh ginger, peeled and minced
  Juice of 2 limes
- 1 cup canned coconut milk
- ¼ cup tamarind extract
- ½ tsp. curry powder
- ½ tsp. ground coriander
- ¼ tsp. cayenne pepper
  Canola oil, for brushing

1 Put fish into a 9″×13″ baking dish and cut 3 evenly spaced ¼″-deep crosswise slits into each side of fish. Season fish cavity and skin with salt and pepper. Combine garlic, chiles, ginger, and lime juice in a small bowl and rub cavity and skin of fish with garlic mixture. Cover dish with plastic wrap and refrigerate for 1 hour.

2 Meanwhile, heat coconut milk, tamarind extract, curry powder, coriander, and cayenne in a 2-qt. saucepan over low heat and cook, stirring often, until tamarind is dissolved, about 15 minutes. Remove pan from heat and set aside. Build a medium-hot fire in a charcoal grill or heat a gas grill to medium-high. (Alternatively, arrange a rack 4″ from broiler element and heat broiler.) Brush the inside of a grilling basket with oil. Uncover fish, transfer it to grilling basket, and brush with some of the tamarind sauce. Cook fish, flipping every few minutes and basting often with tamarind sauce, until cooked through, about 15 minutes. Transfer fish to a serving platter; serve hot or at room temperature.

COOK'S NOTE This recipe works best with a grilling basket, a narrow steel cage with a long handle that allows you to turn over flaky fish without damaging it.

SWEET & SOUR SARDINES

Sarde in Saor

SERVES 6

This sumptuous *cicchetto*—Venetian small plate—is traditionally made with sardines that are fried, but the dish is just as delicious when the fish are broiled.

- ½ cup white wine
- ¼ cup raisins
- 2 lb. sardines, cleaned
  Kosher salt and freshly ground black pepper, to taste
- ¾ cup olive oil
- 1 large white onion, thinly sliced
- ⅓ cup white wine vinegar
- ¼ cup pine nuts

1 Combine wine and raisins in a bowl. Soak for 30 minutes; drain, and set aside. Meanwhile, heat broiler. Season sardines with salt and pepper on a baking sheet. Broil, until cooked, about 2 minutes; let cool.

2 Heat oil in a 4-qt. pan over medium-high heat. Add onion and cook until browned, 10–12 minutes. Add vinegar, reduce heat to medium-low, and cook until soft, 6–8 minutes. Stir in raisins, nuts, salt, and pepper; let cool. Place half the sardines on bottom of an 8″×8″ dish and cover with half the onion mixture. Place remaining sardines on top and cover with remaining onion mixture. Marinate in refrigerator for 4 hours before serving.

CREOLE-STYLE FRIED FISH

SERVES 4

This Louisiana recipe was given to us by the writer Lonnée Hamilton, who recommends spooning some bacon grease into the frying oil to give the fish a smokier flavor.

- 4 cups vegetable shortening or oil
- 3 tbsp. bacon grease (optional)
- 1 cup flour
- 1 cup yellow cornmeal
  Lawry's seasoned salt and ground black pepper, to taste
- 1 cup milk
- 8 6–8-oz. whole head-on bluegill, perch, or other small freshwater fish, cleaned
  Tartar Sauce (page 591), for serving

1 Heat shortening and bacon grease in a 12″ skillet over medium-high heat until a deep-fry thermometer reads 350°.

2 Whisk together flour, cornmeal, Lawry's, and pepper in a bowl. Transfer half the cornmeal mixture into another bowl. Pour milk into a medium bowl. Working in batches, roll fish in cornmeal mixture, transfer to milk, shake off excess, and dredge in second bowl of cornmeal mixture.

3 Using tongs, fry 4 fish, turning occasionally, until golden brown and cooked through, about 5 minutes. Repeat with remaining fish. Serve with tartar sauce.

BREAKFAST TROUT WITH BACON

SERVES 4

In the American South, eating a sweet, fresh-caught trout fried in rendered bacon fat is one of the best parts of getting up early to cast a line. This dish is traditionally eaten for breakfast, but we also like it for dinner.

- 4 thick slices bacon
- 4 8–10-oz. whole trout, cleaned
  Kosher salt and ground black pepper, to taste
- 1 cup yellow cornmeal
- ⅓ cup vegetable oil

1 Fry bacon in a large, heavy skillet until brown and crisp, about 15 minutes. Drain on paper towels and set aside. Reserve bacon fat in pan.

2 Rinse fish, season with salt and pepper, and dredge in cornmeal. Add vegetable oil to bacon fat. Heat pan over high heat until smoking, then fry fish for about 5 minutes. Carefully turn fish and fry the other sides. Shake the pan frequently to ensure the fish don't stick. Trout should be golden and crisp on the outside, moist and tender inside. (If your pan is too small, cook fish in batches and keep warm in a low oven.) Serve 1 trout per person, garnished with bacon.

CHINESE STEAMED FISH WITH SCALLIONS

SERVES 2

Chunyi Zhou, a cooking-school instructor in Beijing, shared this recipe with us. While we love the sweetness of black sea bass, any whole firm-fleshed white fish that fits in a stackable bamboo steamer will do.

2 12–14-oz. whole branzino or black sea bass, cleaned
1 1″ piece fresh ginger, peeled and julienned
3 scallions, white parts discarded, green parts cut into 1″ pieces and thinly julienned
3 tbsp. sesame oil
4 tbsp. light soy sauce

1 Rinse fish under cold running water and pat dry with a paper towel. Transfer each fish to a 10″ plate. Using kitchen shears, trim the tail and fins of each fish. With a knife, score both sides of fish with 4 diagonal slices. Place strips of ginger in the cavity of each fish and strew the remaining ginger on top.

2 In a shallow pot large enough to hold an 11″-wide bamboo steamer, add 1″ of water; bring to a boil over high heat. Place the first tray of bamboo steamer in the pot. Transfer 1 plate of fish to the steamer; repeat with the second steamer tray and second plate of fish. Cover and steam over boiling water until fish is cooked through (a chopstick inserted into the thickest part of the fish enters with ease), about 6 minutes. Using tongs in one hand and a dry kitchen towel in the other, carefully remove hot plates of fish from steamer and sprinkle with scallions; set aside.

3 Meanwhile, heat sesame oil in a small saucepan over high heat for about 1 minute. Spoon oil and soy sauce over scallions and fish.

COOK'S NOTE Make sure your steamer is approximately ½″ wider in diameter than the plate of fish; this helps the fish cook properly and ensures easy removal of the plate when the process is finished.

HAITIAN POACHED SNAPPER

Poisson Rouge

SERVES 2–4

This flavorful poached snapper, an essential recipe in Haitian cuisine, is topped with a colorful salad of fresh, boiled vegetables whose sweetness balances the piquant broth.

2 1-lb. whole red snappers, cleaned
1 cup thinly sliced shallots
½ cup fresh lime juice
1 tbsp. finely chopped scallion
½ tsp. dry mustard
1 sprig fresh thyme
1 Scotch bonnet chile, split

Kosher salt and freshly ground black pepper, to taste
¼ cup canola oil
6 cloves garlic, chopped
1 tbsp. tomato paste
1 tbsp. sugar
Boiled sliced carrots and beets, for serving
Sliced tomatoes, for serving

1 Score sides of fish with 4 diagonal slices and place in a shallow dish. Whisk together half the shallots, the lime juice, scallion, mustard, thyme, chile, salt, and pepper in a bowl and pour over fish; marinate for 30 minutes.

2 Heat oil in a 12″ skillet over medium-high heat. Add garlic and cook, stirring, until fragrant, about 1 minute. Add tomato paste and cook until it begins to caramelize, about 2 minutes. Add 1 cup water and bring to a boil; cook, stirring, until almost evaporated, 8–10 minutes. Remove fish from marinade and set aside; add marinade and sugar to skillet and cook, stirring, until shallots are soft, 4–5 minutes. Add fish and ¾ cup water, cover skillet, and cook, turning once, until fish is cooked through, 8–12 minutes. Transfer fish to a large serving platter. Season cooking liquid with salt and pepper and pour through a fine-mesh sieve over fish. Garnish with remaining shallots and the carrots, beets, and tomatoes.

FRUIT & FIRE

When a recipe calls for Scotch bonnet chiles (like Haitian Poached Snapper, this page), you can substitute another kind, but it's worth seeking out the real thing. A variety of the species *Capsicum chinense*, Scotch bonnets are typically red, orange, or yellow when ripe. They're short, round, and ruffled at the top; some say the chile got its name because of its resemblance to a Scottish tam-o'-shanter hat. This chile is one of the hottest peppers around—as much as 60 times as hot as a jalapeño—but it's got flavor as well as heat. Widely used in both Haiti and Jamaica, the Scotch bonnet has a distinctive floral, fruity character that is perfectly suited to the spicy-sweet curries and citrus marinades of the Caribbean.

Fileted Fish

CEDAR-ROASTED SALMON

SERVES 6

You don't need a smoker to lend a hint of the outdoors to fresh salmon. Simply soak pieces of untreated aromatic cedar (sold by the bundle at lumberyards and hardware stores) and roast them with your salmon. Be sure not to cut the salmon all the way through into separate steaks: You want to create pockets in which to nestle the cedar.

- 1 untreated cedar slat, about 6″ × 12″
- 5 untreated cedar slats, about 3″ × 6″
- 3 lb. center-cut salmon, in 1 piece, cut almost all the way through into 6 steaks
  Kosher salt and freshly ground black pepper, to taste
- 1 lemon, thinly sliced
- 15 sprigs fresh dill
- 6 tbsp. unsalted butter, melted

1 Soak cedar slats in a pan of water overnight, then drain. Alternatively, place them in a large pot of water and bring to a boil over medium-high heat, then drain.

2 Heat oven to 450°. Place large cedar slat on a foil-lined baking sheet. Season salmon with salt and pepper, then place on cedar and slip 1 of the smaller cedar pieces, 1 or 2 lemon slices, and 2 dill sprigs into each of the cuts between salmon steaks, reserving additional dill sprigs and a few lemon slices for garnish. Brush all over with melted butter.

3 Roast salmon until pink, 20–25 minutes, then remove from oven. Remove smaller slats of cedar from salmon and scatter them on top of fish, then wrap foil around baking sheet, sealing salmon tightly. Set aside for 15 minutes. (For more well-done fish, return wrapped salmon to oven and roast for 5 minutes more at 450°.)

4 Unwrap salmon and, when it's cool enough to handle, finish slicing through steaks. Serve fish garnished with reserved lemon slices and dill.

RUSSIAN BAKED SALMON WITH MAYONNAISE

Keta Zapechenaya pod Mayonezom

SERVES 4

Mayonnaise made its way into Russia's everyday culinary vernacular in the 19th century, when it was first known as *sauce provençale*. In this dish, it enrobes salmon seasoned with soy sauce and transforms into a golden crust as it bakes. This luxurious dish goes well with roast potatoes, sautéed vegetables, or a cold beet salad.

- 1 tsp. canola oil
- 8 2″ × 3″ skin-on salmon filets (about 2 lb.)
- 1 tbsp. plus 2 tsp. soy sauce
- ¾ cup mayonnaise

1 Grease 8″× 8″ baking dish with oil. Rub salmon filets with 1 tbsp. soy sauce, then arrange them snugly, skin side up, in prepared dish. Rub the salmon skin with remaining soy sauce; cover dish with plastic wrap and refrigerate for 30 minutes.

2 Heat oven to 425°. Remove baking dish from refrigerator and set aside for 15 minutes to come to room temperature. Brush mayonnaise evenly over the salmon, spreading it out to the edges of the baking dish. Bake, rotating back to front once, until skin is golden brown and salmon is cooked through, 20–25 minutes. Remove from oven and set aside to rest for 5 minutes before serving.

SEARED COD WITH MUSHROOMS AGRODOLCE

SERVES 2

A cast-iron skillet is the perfect pan to use for searing, then oven-roasting fish; firm-fleshed, creamy-flavored cod takes particularly well to the technique. Sautéed mushrooms and onions, finished with vinegar, make for a tart counterpart to the rich filet.

- 5 tbsp. extra-virgin olive oil
- 4–6 cipolline onions, peeled
- 4–6 white mushrooms, stems trimmed flush

Kosher salt and freshly ground
black pepper, to taste
½ cup sherry vinegar
1½ lb. center-cut cod filet
6 sprigs fresh thyme

1 Heat oven to 400°. Heat 3 tbsp. oil in a medium cast-iron skillet over medium-high heat. Add onions and mushrooms, season with salt and pepper, and sauté, shaking skillet over heat occasionally, until well browned, about 5 minutes. Reduce heat to medium and continue cooking until onions soften, about 5 minutes more. Add vinegar to skillet and cook for 1 minute, using a wooden spoon to scrape any browned bits stuck to bottom of skillet. Transfer onions, mushrooms, and pan juices to a bowl and set aside.

2 Wipe skillet clean with paper towels and return to high heat. Rub cod with remaining 2 tbsp. oil, then season generously with salt and pepper. When skillet is very hot, add cod, skin side up, and sear until a good brown crust develops, 2–3 minutes. Turn cod skin side down, arrange reserved onions, mushrooms, and pan juices around fish, then scatter with thyme. Place skillet in oven and roast until fish is cooked through, 12–15 minutes.

HALIBUT WITH BRAISED FENNEL
SERVES 4

In this recipe inspired by a dish served by English chef Michael Caines, fennel and fish are cooked in an intensely aromatic oil infused with lemongrass, ginger, and orange peel.

FOR THE INFUSED OIL
Peel of 1 orange, cut into large strips
3 stalks lemongrass, trimmed and chopped
1 3″ piece fresh ginger, peeled and thinly sliced
½ fennel bulb, cored and thinly sliced
1 cup extra-virgin olive oil

FOR THE FISH
2 lb. small fennel bulbs, trimmed and thickly sliced lengthwise
4 6-oz. skin-on halibut filets
Kosher salt and freshly ground black pepper, to taste
1 tbsp. chopped fresh basil, for garnish
1 tbsp. chopped fresh thyme, for garnish
1 medium tomato, seeded and finely diced, for garnish

1 Make the infused oil: Combine orange peel, lemongrass, ginger, fennel, and oil in a small pan; bring to a near boil over medium-high heat. Remove from heat, cover, and let steep overnight. Strain and reserve oil.

2 Make the fish: Cook fennel in 2 tbsp. infused oil in a 12″ skillet over medium heat until golden, about 5 minutes. Lower heat, add ½ cup water, cover, and simmer until very tender, about 30 minutes. Transfer to a bowl and set aside.

3 Season fish with salt and pepper. Add 3 tbsp. infused oil to skillet and heat over high heat. Cook fish, flipping once, until just cooked, 4–6 minutes. Lower heat to medium, cover, and cook until cooked through, about 7 minutes. Serve fish over fennel, drizzled with remaining infused oil and garnished with basil, thyme, and tomato.

LOUISIANA BLACKENED REDFISH
SERVES 6

This lip-smacking recipe is based on one served by the late chef Paul Prudhomme, one of the key figures in elevating Cajun and Creole cuisine to the national stage. To get the proper char on the fish, make sure your cast-iron skillet is very, very hot.

1 tbsp. sweet paprika
2½ tsp. salt
1 tsp. onion powder
1 tsp. garlic powder
1 tsp. cayenne pepper
¾ tsp. freshly ground black pepper
¾ tsp. freshly ground white pepper
½ tsp. dried thyme
½ tsp. dried oregano
¾ lb. unsalted butter, melted
6 ½″-thick 8-oz. skinless red drum, black drum, or red snapper filets

1 Combine paprika, salt, onion and garlic powders, cayenne, black and white pepper, thyme, and oregano in a small bowl and set aside. Put 2 tbsp. butter into each of 6 small ramekins; set aside and keep warm. Put remaining butter into a wide, shallow dish. Dip each filet in butter and place on a parchment paper–lined baking sheet. Dust each filet generously on both sides with spice mixture, pressing spices and herbs into fish with your hands. Pour remaining butter from dish into a small bowl.

2 Heat oven to 200°. Turn on ventilation system and open windows, if possible. Heat a large cast-iron skillet over high heat until white and ashy, 8–10 minutes. Carefully place 2–3 filets in pan. Stand back to avoid smoke and pour 1 tsp. butter over each filet. Cook until bottom of each filet appears charred, about 2 minutes. Turn filets over and pour 1 tsp. butter over each. Continue cooking until fish is cooked through (time will vary according to heat of pan). Transfer to a rack on a baking sheet and keep warm in oven. Repeat cooking process with remaining fish and butter. Serve with reserved ramekins of warm melted butter.

SEARED SALMON WITH SALSA VERDE
SERVES 4

Chef Johnny Schmitt, whose family ran the French Laundry before Thomas Keller bought it in 1994, makes a flavorful green sauce by picking handfuls of fresh herbs from the bountiful gardens behind northern California's Boonville Hotel. Rather than using a food processor or blender, he crushes them with a mortar and pestle, a method he says better preserves their color and flavor.

FOR THE SALSA VERDE
- ½ cup chopped fresh chives
- ½ cup chopped fresh basil
- ½ cup chopped fresh flat-leaf parsley
- 1 clove garlic, chopped
  Grated zest of 1 orange
- ½ cup extra-virgin olive oil
  Kosher salt and freshly ground black pepper, to taste

FOR THE SALMON
- 2 tbsp. white wine
- 5 tbsp. extra-virgin olive oil, plus more for tossing
- ½ cup coarse cornmeal
- 2 tbsp. chopped fresh thyme
  Kosher salt and freshly ground black pepper
- 4 ¼-lb. salmon filets
- 1 tbsp. Clarified Butter (page 595)
- 2 tbsp. balsamic vinegar
- 2 cups cherry tomatoes, stemmed
- 4 cups mizuna or arugula, for serving

1 Make the salsa verde: Crush chives, basil, parsley, garlic, and orange zest into a coarse paste with a mortar and pestle. Drizzle oil into the paste while stirring with the pestle. Season with salt and pepper and set aside.

2 Make the salmon: Mix together wine and 2 tbsp. oil on a plate and set aside. Mix together cornmeal, thyme, salt, and pepper on another plate and set aside. Moisten salmon filets in the wine mixture, then dredge in the cornmeal mixture. Heat 1 tbsp. oil with the clarified butter in a large skillet over medium-high heat. Add salmon filets and sear, turning once, until fish is golden on both sides and just cooked through, about 3 minutes total. Transfer filets to a plate.

3 Wipe skillet clean with paper towel and return to medium heat. Add remaining 2 tbsp. oil and the vinegar, then add tomatoes, salt, and pepper and cook, shaking pan often, until tomatoes are heated through, about 2 minutes. Remove from heat.

4 Toss mizuna with a little oil in a medium bowl. Divide mizuna among 4 plates. Lay salmon over greens, spoon warm tomatoes and sauce over salmon, and serve with salsa verde.

RED SNAPPER WITH CHERRY TOMATOES
SERVES 4 (SEE PHOTO, PAGE 224)

This recipe from economist Nicola Ceteorelli is included in food writer John Donohue's anthology of essays by men who cook at home, *Man with a Pan*. A snap to make for an easy weeknight meal, the recipe is also elegant enough to serve on special occasions.

- 2 tbsp. extra-virgin olive oil
- 4 ¼-lb. skin-on red snapper filets
  Kosher salt and freshly ground black pepper, to taste
- 1 medium yellow onion, thinly sliced lengthwise
- 1½ lb. cherry tomatoes
- 2 tbsp. finely chopped fresh flat-leaf parsley

Heat oil in a 12″ nonstick skillet over medium-high heat. Season fish with salt and pepper and add to skillet, skin side down. Cook until skin is browned and crisp, about 4 minutes. Remove from skillet; set aside. Add onion to pan and season with salt and pepper. Cook, stirring, until soft, about 4 minutes. Add tomatoes, cover, and cook until soft and releasing their juices, about 8 minutes. Add fish, skin side up, and cook until fish is cooked through, 3–4 minutes. Sprinkle with parsley before serving.

BURNT-SCALLION FISH

SERVES 2

We like sea bass for this dish, which showcases the sweetness of charred green onions, but any firm white fish, such as cod, halibut, or snapper, can be substituted.

- 8 tbsp. butter
- 2 8-oz. firm white fish filets, such as sea bass
- 2 bunches scallions, minced

1 Melt butter in a 12″ skillet over high. Sear fish, flipping once, until golden, 2–3 minutes. Add half of the scallions and cook until charred, 3–4 minutes.

2 Reduce heat to medium-low, add remaining scallions, and cook until fish is cooked through, 6–8 minutes.

SOLE À LA GRENOBLOISE

SERVES 2

In the realm of classic French cuisine, any preparation bearing the designation *à la grenobloise*—literally, "of Grenoble," a city in southeastern France—is served with a sauce of browned butter, capers, parsley, and pieces of lemon.

- 2 whole skinless sole filets (about ¼ lb. each), halved lengthwise down center line
   Kosher salt and freshly ground black pepper
- ¼ cup milk
- 1 lemon, peeled
- ½ cup flour
- 2 tbsp. Clarified Butter (page 595)
- 2 tbsp. unsalted European-style butter
- 2 tsp. capers, drained
- 2 tsp. coarsely chopped fresh flat-leaf parsley

1 Season filets with salt and pepper and place in a shallow dish. Cover with milk and set aside.

2 Using a knife, cut white pith away from lemon and remove segments by slicing between membranes. Cut half the segments into ½″ pieces; set aside. (Reserve the other half for another use.) Place flour on a plate and season with salt and pepper; set aside.

3 Heat clarified butter in a large skillet over medium-high heat. Remove filets from milk and fold the thin, tapered ends under to create an even thickness. Dredge both sides in flour, shake off excess, and add to skillet. Cook, turning once, until golden brown, about 2 minutes per side. Transfer to plates; cover with foil to keep warm.

4 Add whole butter to skillet and cook, stirring, until it turns a deep brown and smells nutty, about 3 minutes. Remove from heat and stir in lemon pieces, capers, and parsley, swirling skillet to combine. Spoon sauce over sole and serve immediately.

SWORDFISH WITH CUBAN ESCABECHE

Pescao en Escabeche Cubano

SERVES 6

The oil-and-vinegar marinade used for *escabeche* starts with a *sofrito*, the iconic Spanish and Latin American flavor base subject to infinite permutations. So it's not surprising to see that *escabeches*, too, vary tremendously. This version, with a *sofrito* of bay leaves, peppers, and onion, came to us from Cuban-born chef Maricel Presilla.

- 6 ½-lb. swordfish steaks, about ½″ thick
- 12 cloves garlic, minced
   Kosher salt and freshly ground black pepper, to taste
- 2 cups flour
- 1 cup extra-virgin olive oil
- 4 bay leaves
- 2 large green bell peppers, seeded and cut into ¼″-thick rings
- 1 large onion, cut into ¼″-thick rings
- 2 cups distilled white vinegar

1 Rub fish with half the garlic and season with salt and pepper on both sides; let sit for 20 minutes. Place flour in a shallow plate, and dredge each fish steak in flour to coat, shaking to remove excess.

2 Heat oil in a 12″ skillet over medium-high heat. Working in batches, add fish steaks, and cook, turning once, until browned on both sides and cooked through, about 5 minutes. Using a slotted spoon, transfer fish steaks to a serving bowl or platter; set aside. Add remaining garlic to oil and cook, stirring, until golden brown, about 1 minute. Add bay leaves, peppers, and onion and cook, stirring, until softened, about 4 minutes. Add vinegar and bring to a boil; cook for 2 minutes. Pour over fish steaks and let sit at room temperature for 1 hour before serving.

SWORDFISH PUTTANESCA

SERVES 6

Italy's puttanesca sauce—briny with anchovies, olives, and capers—pairs beautifully not only with pasta, but with swordfish or any other meaty fish.

- 6 tbsp. extra-virgin olive oil
- 6 swordfish steaks, about 6 oz. each and ½" thick, skin removed
  Kosher salt and freshly ground black pepper, to taste
- 3 cloves garlic, finely chopped
- 2 oil-packed anchovy filets, finely chopped
- 3 cups canned whole, peeled tomatoes in juice, crushed by hand
- ¾ cup large green olives, pitted and roughly chopped
- ¼ cup capers, rinsed and drained
- ½ tsp. crushed red chile flakes
- 3 tbsp. roughly chopped fresh flat-leaf parsley
- 4 tsp. fresh lemon juice

1 Heat oil in a 12" skillet over high heat. Working in batches, season swordfish with salt and pepper, and add to skillet; cook, flipping once, until brown outside and medium-rare inside, about 3 minutes. Transfer fish to a plate and set aside.

2 Return skillet to medium heat. Add garlic and anchovies and cook until soft, about 2 minutes. Add tomatoes, olives, capers, and chile flakes and cook until almost all the liquid evaporates, about 10 minutes. Return swordfish to skillet and add parsley and lemon juice; cook until fish is cooked through, about 2 minutes. Divide swordfish among 6 serving plates and top with sauce.

SAUERKRAUT WITH TROUT IN CREAM SAUCE

Choucroute au Poisson

SERVES 2

Traditionally, *choucroute au poisson* was a dish made only in Alsatian riverside villages. Today, restaurants throughout Alsace serve a version in which filets of flaky, white-fleshed fish are panfried or poached and served on a bed of seasoned sauerkraut and topped with a creamy riesling sauce.

- 3 tbsp. extra-virgin olive oil
- ¼ lb. smoked bacon, cut into ½" cubes
- 4 shallots, finely chopped
- 1 tsp. finely chopped fresh thyme
- ½ tsp. cumin seeds
- 2 star anise pods
- 1 bay leaf
- ½ lb. sauerkraut, drained and rinsed
- 1¼ cups white wine, preferably dry riesling
  Kosher salt and freshly ground black pepper, to taste
- 2 6–8-oz. skin-on trout filets
- ¼ cup flour, sifted
- 4 tbsp. unsalted butter
- ½ cup heavy cream
  Fresh chervil leaves, for garnish (optional)

1 Heat 1 tbsp. oil in a 10" skillet over medium-high heat. Add bacon and cook, stirring occasionally, until browned and crisp, about 8 minutes. Pour off all but 1 tbsp. fat. Reduce heat to medium and add half the shallots along with the thyme, cumin, star anise, and bay leaf and cook, stirring occasionally, until shallots are soft, about 4 minutes. Stir in sauerkraut, ½ cup wine, and ⅓ cup water and season with salt and pepper. Bring to a boil, cover skillet, reduce heat to low, and cook, stirring occasionally, until sauerkraut softens and flavors meld, about 25 minutes. Remove skillet from heat and set aside; discard bay leaf and star anise. Keep warm.

2 Season trout filets with salt and pepper. Put flour on a plate and dredge trout in flour, shaking off excess. Heat remaining oil in a 12" nonstick skillet over medium-high heat until almost smoking. Add trout, skin side down, and cook, flipping once, until golden brown and cooked through, 4–6 minutes. Transfer trout to a plate and loosely cover with foil. Return skillet to medium-high heat and add 2 tbsp. butter and remaining shallots. Cook until shallots are soft, about 4 minutes. Remove skillet from heat, pour in remaining ¾ cup wine, and cook until wine is almost evaporated, about 4 minutes. Add cream and cook, stirring occasionally, until sauce thickens, about 3 minutes. Season with salt and pepper, remove from heat, and stir in remaining 2 tbsp. butter. To serve, divide sauerkraut between 2 plates and top each with trout. Spoon sauce around fish and garnish with chervil.

SMOKED TROUT HASH

SERVES 2

A twist on a breakfast classic, this hash is buttery and luxurious with layers of flavor from caramelized onions, bright fresh dill, and a creamy horseradish sauce.

> ## "Fish, to taste right, must swim three times—
> ## in water, in butter, and in wine."
> POLISH PROVERB

4 tbsp. unsalted butter

1 lb. russet potatoes, boiled, cooled, and cut into ½" cubes

1 small yellow onion, finely chopped

¼ lb. smoked trout filets, flaked into ½" chunks

¼ cup heavy cream

1 tbsp. finely chopped fresh dill

¼ tsp. cayenne pepper

1 clove garlic, finely chopped

Kosher salt and freshly ground black pepper, to taste

3 tbsp. crème fraîche

2 tsp. prepared horseradish

Finely chopped fresh chives, for garnish

Lemon wedge, for garnish

1 Heat 3 tbsp. butter in a 10″ skillet over medium-high heat. Add potatoes and cook, stirring, until lightly browned, 8–10 minutes.

2 Add remaining 1 tbsp. butter and onion. Cook, stirring occasionally, until onion softens, about 10 minutes. Add trout, cream, dill, cayenne pepper, garlic, salt, and pepper. Stir to combine.

3 Turn hash every 2 minutes, loosening any browned bits, until potatoes are golden brown, about 12 minutes.

4 Divide hash between 2 plates. Combine crème fraîche with horseradish. Garnish hash with sauce, chives, and a squeeze of lemon.

YANKEE FISH CAKES
SERVES 4–6

These lemony fish cakes are a favorite weeknight supper in the fishing towns of northeastern Massachusetts.

9 tbsp. unsalted butter

1 medium onion, roughly chopped

1 rib celery, roughly chopped

1 lb. skinless haddock or cod filets, cut into 4 large pieces

⅓ cup heavy cream

1½ cups bread crumbs

3 tbsp. mayonnaise

2 tbsp. minced fresh dill

1 tbsp. Dijon mustard

1 tbsp. fresh lemon juice

1 tbsp. dill pickle relish

1 tsp. lemon zest

½ tsp. Tabasco sauce

1 egg

Kosher salt and freshly ground black pepper, to taste

½ cup yellow cornmeal

1 Heat 3 tbsp. butter in a 12″ skillet over medium heat. Add onion and celery and cook, stirring, until soft, 5–6 minutes. Add fish and cream and bring to a boil over medium-high heat. Cook, covered, until fish is cooked through, 6–8 minutes. Let mixture cool for 15 minutes. Flake fish in the skillet with a fork, then transfer mixture to a large bowl. Add bread crumbs, mayonnaise, dill, mustard, lemon juice, pickle relish, lemon zest, Tabasco, egg, salt, and pepper. Toss mixture together until well combined. Shape fish mixture into twelve ½″-thick patties. Dredge each patty in cornmeal; refrigerate on parchment paper–lined baking sheet for 30 minutes.

2 Heat 3 tbsp. butter in a 12″ skillet over medium heat; add 6 patties to the skillet and cook, turning once, until golden, 8–10 minutes. Wipe out skillet; repeat with remaining butter and fish cakes. Serve immediately.

MISSISSIPPI FRIED CATFISH
SERVES 2

The cooks at Carmack Fish House in Vaiden, Mississippi, serve this dish with tartar sauce and a side of hush puppies.

Canola or peanut oil, for frying

2 cups yellow cornmeal

1⅓ cups flour

¼ cup Lawry's seasoned salt

2 tbsp. baking powder

1 tbsp. freshly ground black pepper

4 3–5-oz. skinless catfish filets

½ lemon, cut into wedges
Tartar Sauce (page 591), for serving

1 Pour oil to a depth of 3″ into an 8-qt. pot and heat over medium-high heat until a deep-fry thermometer reads 350°.

2 Meanwhile, combine cornmeal, flour, Lawry's, baking powder, and pepper in a large bowl. Add catfish and toss to coat. Gently shake off the excess cornmeal mixture and transfer catfish to a rack.

3 Working in 2 batches, fry catfish in the hot oil until golden brown and cooked through, about 6 minutes. Using tongs, transfer catfish to a wire rack set on a baking sheet to drain. Transfer fish to 2 plates and serve with a lemon wedge and tartar sauce.

REDFISH ON THE HALF SHELL
SERVES 4–6

The "half shell" in this classic Texas dish isn't an actual shell; it's actually the scales-on skin of the fileted fish.

6 tbsp. unsalted butter, softened

1 tbsp. finely chopped shallots

1 tbsp. finely chopped fresh cilantro

1 tsp. finely chopped fresh thyme

½ tsp. chile powder

½ tsp. paprika

4 10–12-oz. skinless redfish, snapper, or sea bass filets, scales left on

1 tbsp. canola oil
Kosher salt and freshly ground black pepper, to taste

12 thin lemon rounds

1 Build a medium fire in a charcoal grill or heat a gas grill to medium. (Alternatively, heat a cast-iron grill pan over medium-high heat). Put butter, shallots, cilantro, thyme, chile powder, and paprika into a bowl. Using a hand mixer, whip mixture until fluffy. Brush scales of fish with oil. Flip filets; season flesh with salt and pepper and smear each with 1 tbsp. butter mixture. Top each filet with 3 lemon rounds.

2 Place fish, scale side down, on grill and cover. Cook, basting occasionally with remaining butter mixture, until scales are blackened and fish is cooked through, 12–15 minutes, or cooked to taste. Serve immediately.

GRILLED FISH TACOS WITH CREAMY CHIPOTLE SAUCE
SERVES 8–10

These delectable fish tacos are a dinnertime staple in the home of the Bunker family, sixth-generation Nevadans whose forebears, some of the state's early Mormon pioneers, arrived by covered wagon in 1877.

FOR THE CHIPOTLE SAUCE

½ cup mayonnaise

⅓ cup Greek yogurt

½ tsp. dried oregano

¼ tsp. ground cumin

¼ tsp. dried dill

1 canned chipotle chile in adobo sauce, plus 1 tsp. sauce
Kosher salt, to taste

FOR THE FISH

1 tsp. garlic powder

1 tsp. paprika

½ tsp. cayenne pepper

½ tsp. ground cumin

½ tsp. dried oregano

2½ lb. skinless tilapia filets, sliced in half lengthwise
Kosher salt, to taste
Canola oil, for grilling

FOR SERVING

8 corn or flour tortillas, warmed

¼ small head green cabbage, very thinly shredded

1 small white onion, minced

1 medium tomato, cored and finely chopped

2 limes, cut into wedges

1 Make the sauce: Combine all sauce ingredients in a blender or food processor and purée until smooth. Refrigerate until ready to use.

2 Make the fish: Build a medium-hot fire in a charcoal grill or heat a gas grill to high. (Alternatively, heat a cast-iron grill pan over medium-high heat). In a small bowl, mix garlic powder, paprika, cayenne, cumin, and oregano. Pat the fish dry, season with salt, and sprinkle with mixed spices; refrigerate for 15 minutes. Brush the grill with oil. Working in batches if necessary, grill fish, flipping once, until cooked through, about 5 minutes.

3 Serve grilled fish on warm tortillas with cabbage, onion, tomato, and a drizzle of chipotle sauce as desired with a squeeze of lime.

ED KOCH'S BROILED SWORDFISH WITH OLIVES

SERVES 1

Former New York City mayor Ed Koch famously cooked for himself at least two nights a week. This was one of his favorite main courses, which he enjoyed with a glass of chilled grape juice.

- 1 lb. swordfish steak, about 1″ thick
- 2 tsp. extra-virgin olive oil
  Kosher salt and freshly ground black pepper, to taste
- 8 large green olives, such as Cerignola, pitted

Arrange an oven rack 4″ from broiler and heat broiler. Place swordfish in a small oval baking dish. Rub swordfish all over with oil and season both sides with salt and pepper. Arrange olives around the swordfish. Place dish under broiler and broil until the swordfish is lightly browned and just cooked through and the olives have become a burnished brown, 8–10 minutes. Using a spatula, transfer the swordfish and olives to a plate. Serve at once.

RED SNAPPER BAKED IN PACKETS

Poisson en Papillote

SERVES 4

This simple preparation of red snapper, inspired by one served at the restaurant Le Brûlot in Antibes in the south of France, calls for cooking the fish with white wine, lemon, and fresh herbs in a parchment packet, which traps the juices of the fish, keeping it moist.

- 4 ¼-lb. red snapper filets
  Kosher salt and freshly ground black pepper, to taste
- 16 sprigs fresh thyme
- 8 sprigs fresh rosemary
- 4 bay leaves
- 4 tbsp. unsalted butter
- 4 tbsp. extra-virgin olive oil
- ½ cup white wine
- ¼ cup finely chopped fresh herbs, such as parsley, chives, tarragon, or chervil, for serving
- 1 lemon, cut into 4 wedges, for serving

1 Heat oven to 450°. Cut out four 16″ × 10″ heart-shaped pieces of parchment paper and fold each in half lengthwise to form a crease down the middle. Place a filet in the center of one-half of a heart, placing it next to the crease; season with salt and pepper, and place 4 sprigs thyme, 2 sprigs rosemary, 1 bay leaf, 1 tbsp. butter, and 1 tbsp. oil on top. Fold other half of heart over filet and, starting at the narrow end, begin folding up open edges; move ½″ down the fold and create another fold. Repeat folding until packet is almost closed at the wide end; pour 2 tbsp. wine in opening, and then fold to close it tightly. Transfer packet to a baking sheet, and repeat with remaining parchment paper hearts, filets, herbs, butter, oil, and wine.

2 Bake packets until fish is cooked through, about 8 minutes. To serve, open packets and discard whole herbs; transfer filets to serving plates, sprinkle with finely chopped herbs, and serve with lemon wedges.

SALMON & SCALLOPS À LA NAGE

SERVES 4

The aroma of a California bay leaf lends subtle sharpness to this French dish. If you can't find California bay leaves, available from specialty food purveyors, a couple of regular ones will do.

- 1½ cups dry white wine
- 1 large fresh California bay leaf, or 2 dried regular bay leaves
  Kosher salt and freshly ground black pepper, to taste
- 2 ribs celery, cut into matchsticks
- 1 medium carrot, peeled and cut into matchsticks
- 1 small onion, thinly sliced
- 1 lb. skinless salmon filets, cut into 4 pieces
- 8 sea scallops
- ¼ cup heavy cream
- 6 tbsp. cold unsalted butter, cubed
  Juice of 1 lemon

1 Bring wine, bay leaf, salt, and 1½ cups water to a simmer in a 12″ skillet over medium-high heat. Add celery, carrot, and onion and cook until tender, 8–10 minutes. Using a slotted spoon, transfer vegetables to a bowl and keep warm.

2 Season salmon and scallops with salt and pepper. Add to pan and cook, covered, until cooked through, 6–8 minutes. Divide fish among plates; garnish with vegetables. Add cream, butter, lemon juice, and salt and pepper to skillet.

Cook, stirring occasionally, until sauce is slightly reduced, about 3 minutes. Spoon sauce over fish.

COD WITH BRAISED KALE & POTATOES
SERVES 4

Earthy kale is a great counterpoint to meaty, hearty cod. With the addition of potatoes, you have an essential cold-weather one-dish meal.

- 1 lb. leeks
- 4 tbsp. extra-virgin olive oil
- 2 cloves garlic, minced
- 1 lb. new potatoes, halved
- 3 packed cups stemmed and roughly chopped kale leaves
- 1 cup fish stock or dry white wine
- 1 lb. skinless thick cod or halibut filets, cut into large pieces
   Kosher salt and freshly ground black pepper, to taste

1 Trim off and discard green tops of leeks. Roughly chop white part, place in a colander, and wash thoroughly in running water to remove all sand. Drain and dry on paper towels. Heat 3 tbsp. oil in a large sauté pan over low heat. Add leeks and garlic and cook slowly until leeks are tender, about 20 minutes.

2 Dry potatoes well and add to pan. Raise heat to medium-high and sauté until lightly browned, 3–5 minutes. Add kale and stock, cover, lower heat, and simmer until potatoes are tender and kale has cooked down, about 15 minutes.

3 Meanwhile, sear fish in a lightly oiled nonstick pan over medium-high heat until golden, about 1 minute per side. Add fish to kale mixture and continue to simmer until fish is opaque, about another 5 minutes. Season to taste with salt and pepper and serve.

TUNISIAN FISH STEW
Chreime
SERVES 4–6

This Tunisian-Jewish Sabbath specialty, given to us by Israeli chef and spice merchant Lior Lev Sercarz, features tender fish braised in a thick chile-spiced tomato sauce.

- 6 skin-on fish filets (about ¼ lb. each), such as sea bass or grouper
- 3 tbsp. fresh lemon juice

   Kosher salt and freshly ground black pepper, to taste
- ¼ cup olive oil
- 10 cloves garlic, roughly chopped
- 3 small red bird's eye chiles, stemmed and roughly chopped
- ¾ cup tomato paste
- 2 cups minced fresh cilantro

1 Combine fish, lemon juice, salt, and pepper in a bowl.

2 Heat oil in a 12″ skillet over medium-high heat. Add garlic and chiles and cook, stirring, until soft, 1–2 minutes. Add paste and cook, stirring, until slightly caramelized, about 2 minutes. Add cilantro and 1¼ cups water and bring to a boil. Reduce heat to medium; cook until sauce is slightly reduced, about 6 minutes. Add fish, skin side up, with accumulated juices and cover; cook until fish is cooked through, 18–20 minutes.

INDONESIAN SPICE-BRAISED TUNA
Ikan Bumbu Rujak
SERVES 4

This classic dish from Indonesia's Maluku Islands has an appealing sweet-spicy taste. Swordfish can be substituted for tuna.

- 2 thick stalks lemongrass, trimmed
- 1 tbsp. tamarind extract
- 3 cloves garlic, chopped
- 3–5 long red chiles, such as Holland or cayenne, stemmed and chopped
- 2 shallots, chopped
- 1 2″ piece fresh ginger, peeled and thinly sliced crosswise
- 1 2″ piece fresh galangal, peeled and thinly sliced crosswise (optional)
- 5 tbsp. peanut oil
- 3 cassia or cinnamon sticks
- 2 whole nutmegs, cracked open with a nutcracker
- 1 tsp. whole cloves
- 1½ lb. skinless tuna filets, cut into 2″ chunks
- ¼ cup kecap manis (Indonesian sweet soy sauce)
   Kosher salt, to taste

1 Remove and discard outer leaves of lemongrass and, using a blunt object like the smooth side of a meat mallet, bruise stalks until they are slightly shredded and flexible, then tie each in a knot; set aside.

2 Put tamarind extract, garlic, chiles, shallots, ginger, galangal, and 1 tbsp. water into a food processor and purée, scraping down sides of bowl often, to form a fairly smooth paste, about 2 minutes. Transfer paste to a small bowl; set aside.

3 Heat oil in a medium pot over medium heat. Add paste and cook until oil begins to separate and paste no longer smells raw, about 6 minutes. Add cassia, nutmeg, cloves, and lemongrass and cook, stirring, until aromatic, about 2 minutes. Add tuna and cook, stirring often, until outside of tuna is cooked and opaque, 3–5 minutes. Add sweet soy sauce and ¼ cup water and stir to combine. Reduce heat to medium-low and simmer gently until tuna is just cooked and still faintly pink in middle, 6–8 minutes. Season with salt and transfer tuna and its sauce to a serving bowl. Let rest for at least 10 minutes before serving to allow the flavors to intensify.

VIETNAMESE CATFISH SIMMERED IN CARAMEL SAUCE

Cá Kho Tộ

SERVES 4

This sweet-and-savory Vietnamese fish dish is traditionally prepared in a clay pot, but if you don't have one in your kitchen, we've found that braising in a skillet is equally effective.

- ¼ cup granulated sugar
- 1½ tsp. light brown sugar
- 3 tbsp. nuoc mam (Vietnamese fish sauce)
- ½ tsp. kosher salt
- ¼ tsp. freshly ground black pepper
- 2 cloves garlic, chopped
- 4 1"-thick catfish steaks (about ½ lb. each)
- 1 tbsp. canola oil
- 1 cup coconut water
- 5 bird's eye chiles, stemmed and halved crosswise
- 4 scallions, cut into 1" lengths
  Cooked white rice, for serving

1 Combine granulated sugar and ¼ cup water in a 1-qt. saucepan over medium-low heat and cook, without stirring, until sugar dissolves and sauce becomes dark brown, about 25 minutes. Remove pan from heat and let cool slightly. Vigorously stir in brown sugar, fish sauce, salt, pepper, and garlic to make a marinade. Put fish steaks into a shallow baking dish and pour marinade over, flipping to coat; set aside to marinate for 15 minutes.

2 Heat oil in a 12" skillet over medium-high heat. Add fish and marinade and cook, flipping fish once, until marinade thickens, about 5 minutes. Add coconut water and bring to a boil. Reduce heat to medium-low and simmer, flipping fish once and basting with cooking liquid, until liquid thickens slightly and fish is cooked through, about 15 minutes. Using a spatula, transfer fish to 4 serving plates. Raise heat to medium-high, add chiles and scallions, and cook until scallions soften, 2–3 minutes. Spoon sauce over fish and serve with rice.

FISH & COCONUT STEW WITH MASHED PLANTAINS

Hudutu

SERVES 4–6

Cooks on Honduras' Garifuna coast serve a basil- and culantro-laced fish stew with a starchy plantain mash akin to African *fufu*.

- 2 lb. skin-on kingfish or swordfish filets
  Kosher salt and freshly ground black pepper, to taste
- ¼ cup fresh lime juice
- 2 tsp. ground cumin
- 5 cloves garlic, minced
- 6 green plantains, plus 2 ripe plantains, peeled and cut into 2" pieces
- 7 cups canned coconut milk
- ½ tsp. ground annatto (achiote)
- 6 sprigs fresh culantro or cilantro, chopped
- 4 large fresh basil leaves, chopped
- ½ small onion, minced

1 Season fish with salt and pepper and place in a large resealable plastic bag; add lime juice, 1 tsp. cumin, and garlic, and toss to combine. Seal bag and let marinate in the refrigerator for at least 1 hour.

2 Place all plantains in a 6-qt. saucepan of salted water and bring to a boil over high heat. Reduce heat to medium-low and cook until tender, about 12 minutes. Drain; transfer to a food processor. Season with salt and pepper and purée until smooth, about 5 minutes. Transfer to a bowl and keep warm.

3 Bring coconut milk and 1 cup water to a boil in a 6-qt. saucepan over high heat. Reduce heat to medium, add remaining 1 tsp. cumin, the annatto, culantro, basil, and onion and cook until onions are soft, about 10 minutes.

> ## "Fish is meant to tempt as well as nourish, and everything that lives in water is seductive."
>
> ### JEAN-PAUL ARON

Add fish along with marinade and cook until fish is tender, about 8 minutes. Ladle soup into bowls and serve alongside plantain mixture.

SOY-MARINATED TUNA OVER RICE

Maguro no zuke Donburi

SERVES 4

This Japanese rice bowl preparation showcases the rich flavor of fresh, high-quality tuna, a fish traded in abundance at Tsukiji wholesale seafood market in Tokyo.

- 4   3-oz. pieces sashimi-grade yellowfin or bluefin tuna
- ¼   cup soy sauce
- 2   tbsp. sake
- 2   tsp. mirin
- 4   cups cooked sushi rice
    Thinly sliced pickled ginger, for garnish
    Finely chopped nori (seaweed), for garnish
    Thinly sliced shiso leaves, for garnish
    Wasabi paste, for serving

1 Bring a 4-qt. saucepan of water to a boil. Working with 1 piece of tuna at a time, submerge tuna in water for 5 seconds. Using a slotted spoon, immediately transfer tuna to a bowl of ice water and chill for 10 seconds. Remove and pat dry. Repeat with remaining tuna. Place tuna in a resealable plastic bag; add soy sauce, sake, and mirin. Seal bag and marinate tuna, turning once, at room temperature for 30 minutes.

2 To serve, remove tuna from the bag, reserving marinade, and cut each piece into 6 slices. Divide rice among 4 serving bowls; top each serving with 6 slices of tuna. Garnish with ginger, nori, and shiso. Drizzle with reserved marinade; serve with wasabi.

PARMESAN-CRUSTED HALIBUT WITH PARSLEY SAUCE

SERVES 4

At Pacific Way Bakery and Café in Astoria, Oregon, flaky cheese-crusted halibut filets are topped with a bright parsley sauce. The restaurant pairs the fish with slow-cooked broccoli rabe (page 304) and creamy mashed potatoes (page 409), a perfectly balanced combination.

FOR THE PARSLEY SAUCE
- 1   cup roughly chopped fresh flat-leaf parsley
- ¼   cup olive oil
    Kosher salt and freshly ground black pepper, to taste

FOR THE HALIBUT
- ¾   cup flour
- 2   eggs, beaten
- 1   cup panko bread crumbs
- ½   cup grated Parmigiano-Reggiano
- ¾   cup olive oil
- 4   6-oz. skinless halibut filets
    Kosher salt and freshly ground black pepper, to taste

1 Make the parsley sauce: Purée parsley, ¼ cup oil, salt, and pepper in a food processor until smooth; set aside.

2 Make the halibut: Place flour and eggs in 2 separate shallow dishes; mix panko and Parmigiano in another shallow dish. Heat oil in a 12″ nonstick skillet over medium-high heat. Season halibut with salt and pepper; dredge in flour, dip in eggs, and coat in panko mixture. Fry, flipping once, until golden brown and cooked through, 3–4 minutes. Serve halibut with parsley sauce spooned on top.

Shrimp

SPICED SALT-ROASTED SHRIMP

SERVES 4

We use the largest head-on shrimp we can find for this dish. The recipe came to us from Vitaly Paley, the chef and co-owner of Paley's Place in Portland, Oregon.

- 4 lb. Himalayan pink salt or coarse rock salt
- ⅓ cup star anise pods
- ¼ cup green cardamom pods
- 1 tbsp. whole cloves
- 8 bay leaves
- 4 sticks cinnamon, preferably Vietnamese
- 2 lb. head-on large shrimp, unpeeled
  Melted butter, for serving

1 Heat oven to 500°. Combine salt, star anise, cardamom, cloves, bay leaves, and cinnamon in a 9″ × 13″ baking dish. Bake until fragrant, about 8 minutes.

2 Remove dish from oven and, using a large spoon, transfer half the salt mixture to a heatproof bowl. Place shrimp over salt in baking dish; cover with salt from bowl. Return to oven and bake until shrimp are cooked through, about 8 minutes. Discard salt and serve shrimp with melted butter for dipping.

PIRI PIRI SHRIMP

SERVES 4

Piri piri, or the Swahili variation *pili pili,* refers both to a chile cultivar originally introduced to Africa by Portuguese traders and a variety of sauces made with them. These grilled shrimp came to us from a fisherman of the Lamu Archipelago in Kenya.

- 2 lb. head-on large shrimp, unpeeled
- ¼ cup peanut oil
- 3 tbsp. fresh lemon juice
- 3 tbsp. fresh lime juice
- 1 tbsp. minced fresh cilantro
- 6 cloves garlic, minced
- 5 piri piri or red bird's eye chiles, stemmed, seeded, and minced
  Kosher salt and freshly ground black pepper
  Lime Pickle (page 578) or lime wedges, for serving

1 Working with 1 shrimp at a time, lay shrimp on its side. Make a ¼″-deep cut along length of shrimp on its outer side. Pull out the vein with the tip of a knife and transfer shrimp to a large bowl. Repeat with remaining shrimp. Add oil, lemon and lime juices, cilantro, garlic, and chiles; toss to coat. Cover with plastic wrap and refrigerate for at least 1 hour or up to 4 hours.

2 Build a medium-hot fire in a charcoal grill or heat a gas grill to medium-high. (Alternatively, arrange an oven rack 4″ from broiler and heat broiler.) Transfer shrimp to a baking sheet and season with salt and pepper. Grill shrimp, turning once, until browned and cooked through, about 5 minutes. Serve with lime pickle or lime wedges.

THAI-STYLE BROILED SHRIMP

SERVES 4

Kung (goong) mae nam, the huge freshwater shrimp common in Thailand, are typically grilled. This recipe, served with a lemongrass and coconut sauce, is an elaboration on the traditional preparation.

- 5 dried bird's eye chiles, stemmed
- 5 cloves garlic, peeled
- 1 bunch fresh cilantro, stems chopped, leaves reserved for garnish
- ½ tsp. ground turmeric
- 1 2″ piece fresh galangal, peeled and coarsely chopped
- 1 4″ piece fresh ginger, peeled and coarsely chopped
- 2 stalks lemongrass, trimmed and coarsely chopped
- 2 tsp. shrimp paste
- ½ cup canned coconut milk
- 2 tbsp. nam pla (Thai fish sauce)
- 2 tbsp. sugar
- 1 tbsp. vegetable oil
- 1½ lb. head-on large freshwater shrimp, unpeeled
- 2 limes, quartered

1 Rinse chiles, then place in a medium bowl. Cover with hot water and set aside until soft, about 15 minutes. Drain chiles and remove and discard veins and seeds.

(It is best to wear rubber gloves when handling chiles because oils can irritate skin.) Place chiles in a blender with garlic, cilantro stems, turmeric, galangal, and ginger. Add lemongrass, shrimp paste, coconut milk, fish sauce, sugar, and ¼ cup water and purée until smooth.

2 Heat broiler. Heat oil in a small saucepan over medium-high heat. Carefully add chile mixture (it may spatter) and cook, stirring, until sauce thickens and turns brick red, 5–10 minutes. Set aside to cool.

3 Butterfly shrimp by slicing each one lengthwise through underside, leaving shell intact along back. Pull out and discard dark vein that runs along back. Place shrimp, shell side down, on an oiled baking sheet, flatten, and then brush chile sauce over meat. Broil until shrimp are pink and firm, about 7 minutes, then transfer to a platter. Serve garnished with lime wedges and reserved cilantro leaves.

STIR-FRIED SHRIMP WITH SNOW PEAS
SERVES 4

This Cantonese-style recipe from Chinese cooking expert Eddie Schoenfeld involves coating and marinating the shrimp in a mixture of sherry, egg white, salt, cornstarch, and oil, which gives them a luscious consistency. Before cooking the shrimp, Schoenfeld tosses them in ice water and salt to firm them up. He also prefers to thicken the sauce with potato starch, which produces a lighter result than cornstarch—it's a trick he learned from professional Chinese chefs.

¾	lb. medium shrimp, peeled, deveined, and halved lengthwise (see Out with the Vein, this page)
1½	tbsp. salt
2½	tbsp. dry sherry
¼	tsp. freshly ground white pepper
1	egg white
1½	tbsp. cornstarch
1	tbsp. plus 3 cups peanut oil
¼	cup chicken stock
2	tsp. potato starch, mixed with 1 tbsp. water
½	tsp. sugar
¼	tsp. white vinegar
4	canned water chestnuts, rinsed and halved
¼	lb. snow peas, strings removed
3	scallions, white and light green parts only, cut crosswise into ⅓" pieces
1	clove garlic, finely chopped
1	1" piece fresh ginger, peeled and thinly sliced against the grain
½	tsp. sesame oil

1 Put shrimp, 1 tbsp. salt, and 2 cups ice-cold water into a large bowl and toss well; drain. Pour 1 cup ice-cold water over shrimp and toss well again; drain. Pat shrimp and bowl dry; return shrimp to dry bowl. Add ¼ tsp. salt, 1 tbsp. sherry, ⅛ tsp. pepper, and egg white to shrimp; mix with your hands until evenly coated and egg white is dispersed. Add cornstarch and 2 tsp. peanut oil and toss well. Transfer shrimp to another bowl, discarding any marinade that clings to original bowl. Cover and refrigerate for 1 hour.

2 Mix remaining 1½ tbsp. sherry, remaining 1¼ tsp. salt, remaining ⅛ tsp. pepper, stock, potato starch mixture, sugar, and vinegar together in a bowl. Set sauce mixture aside.

3 Heat 3 cups peanut oil in a wok over medium-high heat until a deep-fry thermometer reads 300°. Carefully add shrimp and gently stir until shrimp turn white, about 30 seconds. Using a slotted spoon, transfer shrimp to a sieve set over a medium pot. Let oil in wok reach 350°, then add water chestnuts and cook, stirring constantly, for 20 seconds. Add snow peas and cook for 2–3 seconds, then quickly and carefully pour entire contents of wok (vegetables and oil together) into the sieve with the shrimp, and allow oil to drain into the pot below; discard oil when cool.

4 Wipe out wok and heat remaining 1 tsp. peanut oil over high heat. Add scallions, garlic, and ginger and cook, stirring, for 10 seconds. Add reserved sauce mixture and stir constantly until it comes to a boil and thickens, 20–30 seconds. Return shrimp and vegetables to wok and toss quickly. Drizzle with sesame oil and serve immediately.

OUT WITH THE VEIN

Here's a foolproof (but little-known) way to devein a raw shrimp without removing its shell or cutting into it. Insert a toothpick between the two middle shell segments. Slide the tip of the toothpick just underneath the vein (which is actually the shrimp's digestive tract) and lift slowly. Unless it's broken, the entire vein will emerge in a single piece.

SPANISH-STYLE SHRIMP IN GARLIC BREAD SAUCE

SERVES 4

Plenty of garlic and a generous pinch of cayenne make themselves known in this bold dish, but it's the luxurious texture of the sauce—thickened with bread and almonds, rather than cream—that makes this Valencian dish truly wonderful.

½ cup extra-virgin olive oil
8 cloves garlic; 4 crushed, 4 minced
1 slice country-style bread or baguette, about 3" in diameter, ¾" thick, with crust removed, plus more for serving
1 sprig fresh flat-leaf parsley, minced
1 cup sliced blanched almonds, toasted
2 cups fish stock
1 bay leaf
½ tsp. cayenne pepper
Kosher salt and freshly ground black pepper, to taste
2 lb. large shrimp, unpeeled

1 Heat oil in a large skillet over medium-low heat. Add crushed garlic and cook for 10 minutes. Remove garlic with a slotted spoon and discard.

2 Increase heat to medium, add bread, and fry, turning once, until browned, about 2 minutes per side. Remove from heat, reserving oil in skillet, and drain bread on paper towels.

3 Crumble bread into a food processor. Add minced garlic, parsley, almonds, and 3 tbsp. stock, then purée to make a fine paste.

4 Carefully pour remaining stock into skillet (it will spatter if oil is too hot). Add bay leaf and cayenne and season with salt and pepper. Simmer over medium heat for 10 minutes.

5 Stir in bread paste, mix well, adjust seasoning, then add shrimp and simmer until pink and firm to the touch, about 5 minutes. Discard bay leaf and serve in shallow bowls.

SHRIMP WITH TOMATOES & FETA

Garides Saganaki

SERVES 2 (SEE PHOTO, PAGE 224)

This bubbling concoction of shrimp, tomatoes, onions, peppers, and feta spiked with a shot of ouzo and flambéed tableside exploded in popularity in the 1950s, with restaurants in seaport towns like Thessaloníki serving hundreds of plates a night. It's now a standard on Greek menus, but it's also quick and satisfying to make at home.

2 tbsp. extra-virgin olive oil
½ small yellow onion, finely chopped
½ medium hot green chile, stemmed and finely chopped
1¼ cups canned whole, peeled tomatoes in juice, crushed by hand
Kosher salt and freshly ground black pepper, to taste
¾ lb. large shrimp, peeled and deveined with head and tail shell intact
¼ lb. feta, coarsely crumbled
2 tbsp. ouzo
1 tbsp. finely chopped fresh flat-leaf parsley

1 Heat broiler. Heat oil in an 8" round metal gratin dish or a heavy ovenproof skillet over medium heat. Add onion and chile and cook, stirring often, until soft, about 5 minutes. Stir in tomatoes and season with salt and pepper; cook until slightly thickened, about 4 minutes.

2 Arrange shrimp in dish, spoon some sauce on top, and continue to simmer until shrimp are pink and just cooked through, about 2 minutes per side. Scatter feta around shrimp, then transfer dish to broiler and broil until feta begins to melt, about 2 minutes. Remove dish from broiler. Warm ouzo in an 8" stainless-steel skillet over low heat, then ignite it with a kitchen match and pour over shrimp and feta. When flames die out, garnish dish with parsley and serve.

SHRIMP UGGIE

SERVES 4

Anthony Uglesich, founder of Uglesich's Restaurant and Bar in New Orleans, named this dish after his son, John, who was nicknamed Uggie by the kids at school. If you can't find super-spicy Melinda's brand hot sauce, Tabasco or Crystal brands can be substituted.

1½ cups vegetable oil
½ cup ketchup
2–3 tbsp. Melinda's brand hot sauce
1 tbsp. fresh lemon juice
1 tbsp. kosher salt, plus more to taste
2 tsp. crushed red chile flakes
1 tsp. sweet paprika
1 green bell pepper, seeded and cut into 1" pieces

1 tsp. chopped fresh flat-leaf parsley
1 small red onion, peeled and chopped
2 lb. medium shrimp, peeled and deveined,
   with tail shell intact
3 medium red-skinned potatoes, cut into
   2″ pieces and boiled
4 fresh chives, chopped

1 Put oil, ketchup, hot sauce, lemon juice, 1 tbsp. salt, chile flakes, paprika, bell peppers, parsley, and onion into a medium bowl and mix well. Cover with plastic wrap and refrigerate for at least 2 days or up to 1 week. Allow marinade to come to room temperature before using.

2 Spoon off and discard most of the top layer of oil from marinade. Put marinade into a large skillet, add shrimp, and cook over medium heat until shrimp turn opaque, 3–5 minutes. Turn shrimp, add potatoes, and cook until potatoes are heated through, 2–3 minutes more. Season to taste with salt.

3 Divide shrimp and sauce among 4 plates and garnish with chives.

SHRIMP & GRITS

SERVES 4

This quintessentially Southern combination of sweet shrimp and soft, creamy grits gets a boost of flavor from bacon and white wine.

4 slices bacon, cut crosswise into 1″ pieces
1 lb. medium shrimp, peeled and deveined
1 small clove garlic, chopped
¼ cup white wine or dry sherry
½ cup heavy cream
2 tbsp. minced fresh parsley
4 cups prepared grits (page 401)

1 Fry bacon in a medium skillet over medium heat until browned and crisp, then transfer with a slotted spoon to paper towels to drain. Discard all but a thin film of bacon drippings from skillet.

2 Increase heat to medium-high and add shrimp, garlic, and three-quarters of the bacon to same skillet; sauté, stirring often, until shrimp are just pink, about 3 minutes. Add wine, scrape any browned bits stuck to bottom of skillet with a wooden spoon, and cook until alcohol has evaporated and reduced slightly, about 2 minutes.

Add cream and cook, stirring constantly, until sauce has thickened, about 2 minutes more; stir in parsley. Divide grits among 4 bowls, then spoon shrimp and sauce over grits.

SHRIMP & RICE PILAF

Machbuss Rubian

SERVES 6–8

This classic seafood pilaf, flavored with dried limes and *bzar* (an Emirati spice blend) came to us from author Annisa Helou.

2   cups basmati rice
5   tsp. kosher salt, plus more to taste
½   cup canola oil
15 fresh or dried curry leaves
3   whole cloves
2   medium yellow onions, thinly sliced lengthwise
2   tsp. Bzar (page 587)
1   tsp. ground turmeric
3   cloves garlic, minced
1   2″ piece fresh ginger, peeled and minced
3   dried black limes, pricked with a knife (optional)
2   plum tomatoes, finely chopped
2⅔ cups vegetable stock
2   lb. head-on jumbo shrimp, unpeeled, deveined
3   tbsp. finely chopped fresh flat-leaf parsley
3   tbsp. finely chopped fresh cilantro

1 Place rice, 3 tsp. salt, and 3 cups water in a medium bowl; let soak for 1 hour.

2 Heat oven to 375°. Heat oil in a 6-qt. Dutch oven over medium-high heat. Add curry leaves and cloves and cook, stirring constantly, until fragrant, about 1 minute. Add onions and cook, stirring occasionally, until lightly caramelized, about 20 minutes. Add bzar, turmeric, garlic, and ginger and cook, stirring often, until fragrant, about 1 minute. Add limes, if using, and tomatoes and cook, stirring, until tomatoes begin to soften, about 5 minutes. Drain rice and add to pot along with remaining 2 tsp. salt and stock; bring to a boil and then arrange shrimp on top of ingredients in pot. Cover and transfer to oven; bake until rice is tender and shrimp are cooked through, about 25 minutes.

3 Transfer shrimp to a plate and set aside; stir 2 tbsp. each parsley and cilantro into rice. Transfer rice to a large serving platter and arrange shrimp on top; sprinkle with remaining parsley and cilantro.

SHRIMP WITH SPICY GARLIC & TOMATO SAUCE

Gamberoni con Salsa Vigliacca

SERVES 6

Vigliacca can mean "scoundrel," which in the case of an Italian sauce means that it's spiced with chiles. This concoction has been served at Trattoria Garga in Florence since its 1979 opening. The owners like it atop everything from pasta to meat loaf; we're particularly taken by it when paired with shrimp.

8	tbsp. extra-virgin olive oil
2	cloves garlic, minced
3	medium tomatoes, cored and quartered
3–4	Italian whole dried red chiles, crushed, or ¼–½ tsp. crushed red chile flakes
	Salt
1½	lb. medium shrimp, peeled and deveined with head and tail shell intact
2	tbsp. cognac
½	tbsp. chopped fresh flat-leaf parsley

1 Heat 4 tbsp. oil in a large skillet over medium heat. Add garlic and cook, stirring with a wooden spoon, until golden, about 30 seconds. Add tomatoes and chiles, season to taste with salt, and cook, crushing pieces of tomato with the back of the spoon and stirring occasionally, until sauce thickens, 8–10 minutes. Set sauce aside.

2 Heat 2 tbsp. oil in another large skillet over high heat. Add half the shrimp in a single layer and cook, turning once, until cooked halfway through, about 2 minutes per side. Transfer shrimp to a plate and set aside. Repeat process with the remaining 2 tbsp. oil and shrimp.

3 Return same skillet to medium-high heat. Carefully add cognac and cook, gently shaking skillet over heat, until alcohol evaporates, about 30 seconds. Add reserved tomato sauce and shrimp and cook, stirring occasionally, until shrimp are cooked through, 3–4 minutes.

4 Divide shrimp and sauce among 6 medium plates, spooning sauce over and around shrimp, then garnish each plate with parsley.

SWEET & SOUR SHRIMP

Gan Shao Xia

SERVES 4

Home cook Eatty Du makes these Shanghainese shrimp bathed in a sweet and tangy sauce.

¼	cup ketchup
2	tbsp. Shaoxing wine
1	tbsp. soy sauce
1	tbsp. mirin
1	tbsp. sugar
2	tbsp. canola oil
1	tbsp. minced fresh ginger
3	scallions, cut into 2″ pieces
1	lb. large shrimp, peeled and deveined with head intact
	Kosher salt and freshly ground black pepper, to taste
	Cooked white rice, for serving

1 Whisk together ketchup, wine, soy sauce, mirin, sugar, and 1 tbsp. water in a bowl; set sauce aside.

2 Heat oil in a 14″ flat-bottomed wok or skillet over high heat. Add ginger and scallions and cook, stirring, until fragrant, about 1 minute. Add shrimp and cook, stirring, until beginning to turn pink, about 2 minutes. Add sauce and cook, stirring, until thick, about 1 minute. Remove from heat; season with salt and pepper. Serve with rice.

SHRIMP MOZAMBIQUE

SERVES 4

This spicy shrimp dish, a Portuguese classic named for Portugal's former African colony, is served at the Liberal Club in Fall River, Massachusetts, over white rice with French fries (page 407) on the side.

4	tbsp. unsalted butter
2	lb. jumbo shrimp, peeled and deveined, with tail shell intact
	Kosher salt and freshly ground black pepper, to taste
1	medium onion, finely chopped
4	cloves garlic, finely chopped
1	tsp. ground annatto
1	tsp. ground coriander
1	tsp. ground cumin
1	tsp. dried oregano
1	12-oz. bottle lager-style beer
8	tbsp. hot sauce
	Chopped fresh flat-leaf parsley, for garnish
	Cooked white rice, for serving
	Lemon wedges, for serving

1 Melt 2 tbsp. butter in a 12″ skillet over medium-high heat. Season shrimp with salt and pepper. Working in 2 batches, add shrimp and cook, turning once, until just pink, about 2 minutes; transfer to a bowl and set aside.

2 Heat remaining 2 tbsp. butter in skillet. Add onion and garlic and cook, stirring occasionally, until soft, about 6 minutes. Stir in annatto, coriander, cumin, and oregano and cook until fragrant, about 1 minute. Add beer and bring to a boil; cook until reduced by half, 8–10 minutes. Stir in hot sauce and cook until sauce has thickened slightly, about 4 minutes.

3 Add reserved shrimp and cook until warmed through, 2–3 minutes more. Season with salt and pepper; garnish with parsley and serve over rice with lemon wedges.

LERUTH'S RED SHRIMP RÉMOULADE

SERVES 2–4

Spicy paprika and whole-grain mustard sauce coats plump shrimp in this signature New Orleans red rémoulade from the late Warren LeRuth, chef-owner of LeRuth's, one of southern Louisiana's most celebrated restaurants in the late 1960s and 1970s.

- ¾ cup Creole mustard
- 2 tbsp. paprika
- 1 tsp. sugar
  Kosher salt, to taste
- 1 cup cottonseed, corn, or canola oil
- 2 lb. medium cooked shrimp, peeled and deveined
- 2 tbsp. minced fresh flat-leaf parsley, plus more for garnish
- 2 inner ribs celery, minced
- ½ small yellow onion, minced
  Tabasco sauce, to taste
- ½ head red leaf lettuce, leaves torn

Whisk mustard, paprika, sugar, and salt in a bowl. Slowly drizzle in oil until sauce is emulsified; stir in shrimp, parsley, celery, onion, and Tabasco. Serve immediately or chill overnight, if you like. Divide lettuce among plates; top with shrimp and garnish with parsley.

SPECIAL SAUCE

As is true of many New Orleans dishes, the origins of shrimp rémoulade are French. The tartar sauce–like white version that appears in the 1938 *Larousse Gastronomique* is made by "adding mustard, gherkins, capers, and chopped herbs to mayonnaise," sometimes with anchovies mixed in at the end. In France it was, and still is, used as a dressing for julienned celery root.

But all this is a far cry from Louisiana's brick-red shrimp rémoulade. The turning point from white French to red New Orleans sauce came in 1920, when the famed Arnaud's restaurant opened. The chefs there, fueled by the spirit of innovation and eager to appeal to customers who adored sweet shrimp, riffed on a rémoulade base to create a dish they called shrimp Arnaud. With the addition of celery, paprika, horseradish, and grainy Creole mustard—a move that reflected the distinctive local love of piquancy—the preparation was indistinguishable from today's Creole rémoulade.

Scallops

BEA CONNER'S BAKED BAY SCALLOPS

SERVES 4

On Nantucket, bay scallops have been a culinary staple as far back as anyone can remember, and for many islanders, including Bea Conner, the scalloper's wife who gave us this recipe, they are the ultimate convenience food. Conner sometimes adds a few tablespoons of heavy cream to the sauce, to make it even richer.

- 2 cloves garlic, minced
- 4 tbsp. unsalted butter
- 4 dozen bay scallops
- 4 tbsp. dry white wine
- 16 Ritz crackers
- 4 tbsp. grated Parmigiano-Reggiano

1 Set oven rack in upper third of oven and heat oven to 400°. Divide garlic among 4 small gratin dishes, add 1 tbsp. butter to each, and place in oven until butter melts.

2 Remove dishes from oven and add 1 dozen bay scallops and 1 tbsp. wine to each dish; spoon sauce over scallops until evenly coated.

3 Crumble 4 crackers over scallops in each dish; then sprinkle each with 1 tbsp. Parmigiano. Bake scallops until they are hot and have turned opaque, about 10 minutes. Turn heat to broil and cook until cracker crumbs and cheese are lightly browned.

GRILLED SCALLOPS WITH YUZU KOSHO VINAIGRETTE

SERVES 4

Yuzu kosho, a paste made from salt, chiles, and the rind of the lemon-like Asian citrus fruit yuzu, pairs beautifully with simple grilled foods. The spicier green version goes with rich beef and chicken, and the mellower red version is at its best with seafood, like these grilled scallops.

- 3 tbsp. extra-virgin olive oil
- 2 tbsp. yuzu juice
- 1 tbsp. minced scallions, white part only
- 1 tbsp. red yuzu kosho
- 2 tsp. soy sauce
- 16 sea scallops
- 1 tbsp. minced fresh flat-leaf parsley
  Kosher salt, to taste

1 Combine oil, yuzu juice, scallions, yuzu kosho, and soy sauce in a bowl and mix well. Put scallops in a small bowl and pour one-third of yuzu mixture over scallops; toss to combine.

2 Build a medium fire in a charcoal grill or heat a gas grill to medium-high. (Alternatively, heat a cast-iron skillet over medium-high heat.) Grill scallops, turning once, until golden brown and just cooked through, about 4 minutes.

3 Transfer scallops to 4 warm serving plates and drizzle remaining yuzu vinaigrette over scallops. Garnish with parsley, season lightly with salt, and serve hot.

SEA SCALLOPS WITH BELGIAN ENDIVE & CHERRY TOMATOES

SERVES 2

Chef Jonathan Waxman, of the New York City restaurant Barbuto, pairs sweet scallops with bitter endive and tart cherry tomatoes in this colorful dish. When they are in season, diver scallops are ideal.

- 5 tbsp. extra-virgin olive oil
- 2 heads Belgian endive, trimmed and quartered lengthwise
- 1 small sweet onion, thickly sliced
  Salt and freshly ground black pepper
- ½ pint cherry tomatoes, halved crosswise
- 1 tbsp. fresh lemon juice
- 1 tsp. fresh lime juice
  Leaves from 1 sprig fresh tarragon
- 12 sea scallops, halved crosswise

1 Heat oven to 400°. Put 4 tbsp. oil into a large enameled cast-iron or other heavy-bottomed pot. Add endive, onion,

> ## "In the hands of an able cook, fish can become an inexhaustible source of perpetual delight."
>
> ### JEAN-ANTHELME BRILLAT-SAVARIN

¼ cup water, salt, and pepper and gently toss until well coated. Cover pot, transfer to oven, and roast until vegetables begin to caramelize, 25–30 minutes.

2 Add tomatoes to pot, gently toss until well coated, then return pot to oven, uncovered, and roast until tomatoes release their juices and soften, about 15 minutes. Remove pot from oven. Add lemon and lime juices and tarragon and adjust seasonings. Set aside to cool.

3 Heat remaining 1 tbsp. oil in a large, heavy-bottomed skillet over medium-high heat. Generously season scallops with salt and pepper. Working in batches, sear scallops on both sides until golden, about 1 minute per side.

4 Transfer vegetables and juices to a serving dish; arrange scallops on top.

COQUILLES ST-JACQUES
SERVES 6

Although *coquilles St-Jacques* simply means "scallops" in French, in the idiom of American cooks, the term is synonymous with the old-time French dish of scallops poached in white wine, placed atop a purée of mushrooms in a scallop shell, covered with a sauce made of the scallop poaching liquid, and gratinéed under a broiler.

- ½ lb. button mushrooms, minced
- 6 tbsp. unsalted butter
- 3 small shallots, minced
- 2 tbsp. minced fresh flat-leaf parsley
- 1 tbsp. minced fresh tarragon, plus 6 leaves, for garnish
  Kosher salt and freshly ground black pepper, to taste
- ¾ cup dry vermouth
- 1 bay leaf
- 6 large sea scallops
- 2 tbsp. flour
- ½ cup heavy cream
- ⅔ cup grated Gruyère cheese
- ½ tsp. fresh lemon juice

1 Heat mushrooms, 4 tbsp. butter, and two-thirds of shallots in a 4-qt. saucepan over medium heat and cook until mixture forms a loose paste, about 25 minutes. Stir parsley and minced tarragon into mushroom mixture; season with salt and pepper. Divide mixture among 6 cleaned scallop shells or shallow gratin dishes.

2 Bring remaining shallots, vermouth, bay leaf, salt, and ¾ cup water to a boil in a 4-qt. saucepan over medium heat. Add scallops and cook until barely tender, about 2 minutes. Remove scallops and place them over mushrooms in shells. Continue boiling cooking liquid until reduced to ½ cup, about 10 minutes; strain.

3 Heat broiler. Heat remaining 2 tbsp. butter in a 2-qt. saucepan over medium heat. Add flour and cook, stirring, until smooth, about 2 minutes. Add reduced cooking liquid and cream and cook until thickened, about 8 minutes. Add cheese, lemon juice, salt, and pepper; spoon sauce evenly over scallops. Broil until browned on top, about 3 minutes. Garnish each with a tarragon leaf.

Lobster, Crayfish & Crab

MAINE-STYLE LOBSTER BOILED IN SALT WATER

SERVES 4

Sweet-fleshed lobster stands up to complex, richly spiced preparations, but its subtle meat lends itself just as well to simplicity: We love a fresh lobster boiled in salt water. Kippy Young, the Maine seaman who shared his method with us, uses seawater, but plenty of kosher salt replicates the flavor. Once the lobster's cooked, it needs little more than a dunk in clarified butter (page 595) or a vibrant sauce like one of the three that follow.

> Kosher salt
> 4 1½–2½ lb. live Maine lobsters

Bring a large pot of well-salted water to a rolling boil. Plunge in lobsters; cook for 5 minutes per pound. Drain, and allow to cool a bit before serving.

COOK'S NOTE Maine lobster (the variety with large claws, also identified as American lobster) is best purchased live; look for the most active, mobile specimen available. If you've brought home a particularly aggressive lobster, let it spend 15 minutes in the freezer immediately prior to cooking. This makes things easier on both you and the lobster.

Brandy Mayonnaise

MAKES ABOUT 1¾ CUPS

This tangy dip, which makes a perfect sauce for simply cooked shellfish (like the basic boiled lobster, above, or steamed crab or shrimp), gets a sweet-and-sour kick from ketchup, brandy, and sour cream.

> 1 cup mayonnaise
> 3 tbsp. brandy
> 3 tbsp. ketchup
> 2 tbsp. sour cream
> 2 tsp. Dijon mustard
> Grated zest and juice of 1 lemon
> Kosher salt and freshly ground black pepper, to taste

Combine mayonnaise, brandy, ketchup, sour cream, mustard, lemon zest and juice in a bowl. Stir until smooth and season with salt and pepper.

Chive Emulsion

MAKES ABOUT 1 CUP

Fresh chives infuse a blend of canola and olive oils for the base of this vibrant sauce, which we like to serve as a dip for lobster or crab.

> 2 cups thinly sliced fresh chives
> 1 cup canola oil
> ¼ cup extra-virgin olive oil
> 1½ tbsp. fresh lemon juice
> 1 tbsp. Dijon mustard
> 2 egg yolks
> Kosher salt and freshly ground black pepper, to taste

Combine chives, canola oil, and olive oil in a blender; purée until very smooth. Pour through a cheesecloth-lined sieve set over a measuring cup; set aside. Whisk lemon juice, mustard, egg yolks, salt, and pepper in a bowl until smooth. While whisking constantly, slowly drizzle in chive oil until sauce is emulsified.

Diablo Sauce

MAKES ABOUT 2 CUPS

This complex tomato-based dipping sauce, which makes a lovely accompaniment to lobster or crab, presumably gets its name from its fiery hue and its mix of serrano chile and spicy chile powder.

> 2 tbsp. olive oil
> 2 tbsp. unsalted butter
> 6 cloves garlic, roughly chopped
> 1 serrano chile, stemmed, seeded, and roughly chopped
> ½ small yellow onion, roughly chopped
> 1 tbsp. dark red chile powder
> 2 tsp. packed brown sugar
> 1 tsp. smoked paprika

1 16-oz. can crushed tomatoes
   Kosher salt and freshly ground black pepper,
   to taste
1 tbsp. fresh lemon juice

Heat oil and butter in a 2-qt. saucepan over medium-high heat. Add garlic, chile, and onion and cook, stirring occasionally, until golden, about 5 minutes. Stir in chile powder, sugar, paprika, tomatoes, salt, and pepper and bring to a boil. Reduce heat to medium-low and cook, stirring occasionally, until sauce is slightly reduced, 6–8 minutes. Let cool slightly, then transfer to a blender. Add lemon juice and purée until smooth.

BOURBON-ROASTED LOBSTER

SERVES 1–2 (SEE PHOTO, PAGE 224)

Loads of herbs and butter makes for a lavish lobster pan roast, and a flambé with bourbon lends as much flavor as it does drama.

1 1½-lb. live lobster
3 tbsp. canola oil
3 shallots, minced
1 clove garlic, minced
½ cup bourbon
¼ cup dry white wine
6 tbsp. unsalted butter, cubed
3 tbsp. minced fresh herbs, such as flat-leaf
   parsley, chives, and chervil
   Kosher salt and freshly ground black pepper,
   to taste

1 Heat oven to 500°. Using a cleaver, split lobster in half lengthwise through its head and tail. Scoop out and discard the yellow-green tomalley. Remove claws and tails from the body of the lobster so it is divided into 6 pieces; crack claws.

2 Heat 1 tbsp. oil in a 12″ skillet over high heat. Cook lobster pieces, shell side up and turning as needed, until shells are bright red, about 15 minutes. Add remaining oil, the shallots, and garlic; cook until shallots and garlic are soft, 1–2 minutes. Add bourbon and, using a match, carefully ignite; cook until the flames subside, about 1 minute.

3 Add wine and place pan in oven; cook until lobster is tender, 3–5 minutes. Transfer lobster to a serving platter. Add butter, herbs, salt, and pepper to skillet and stir until butter is melted, then pour sauce over lobster.

GRILLED LOBSTER WITH GARLIC-PARSLEY BUTTER

SERVES 1–2

In this recipe, shared with us by Australian chef and avid griller Curtis Stone, lobster is flash-grilled, then poached in its own shell in a pool of melted garlic-parsley butter.

8   tbsp. unsalted butter, softened
2   tbsp. finely chopped fresh flat-leaf parsley
1½ tsp. crushed red chile flakes
4   cloves garlic, finely chopped
    Grated zest of 1 lemon
    Kosher salt and freshly ground black pepper,
    to taste
1   1–1½ lb. live lobster
¼   cup extra-virgin olive oil

1 Combine butter, parsley, chile flakes, garlic, lemon zest, salt, and pepper in a bowl; set aside. Using a cleaver, split lobster in half lengthwise through its head and tail. Scoop out and discard the yellow-green tomalley and break off claws. Transfer lobster halves, shell side down, to a baking sheet; crack claws and place them on the baking sheet. Drizzle halves and claws with oil, and season with salt and pepper.

2 Build a hot fire in a charcoal grill or heat a gas grill to high; bank coals or turn off burner on one side for indirect grilling (page 191). Place lobster halves, flesh side down, and claws on hottest part of grill; cook until slightly charred, 2–3 minutes. Flip lobster over, and using a spoon, spread lobster with the garlic-parsley butter; continue grilling until lobster meat is tender, 3–5 minutes more.

BALLYMALOE'S HOT BUTTERED LOBSTER

SERVES 4

This recipe is based on one used at Ballymaloe, the famed Irish restaurant founded by Myrtle Allen, who shared with us her belief that the most humane way to dispatch live lobsters is to lull them to sleep in slowly warming water.

2   2-lb. live lobsters
2½ cups dry white wine
1   carrot, peeled, sliced
1   medium yellow onion, sliced
3   sprigs fresh flat-leaf parsley
3   sprigs fresh thyme

3 black peppercorns
1 bay leaf
8 tbsp. unsalted butter

1 Put lobsters into a large pot, cover with lukewarm water, and bring to a simmer over medium heat. This should take about 40 minutes in all. Meanwhile, put 2½ cups water, wine, carrot, onion, parsley, thyme, peppercorns, and bay leaf into a large nonreactive pot and bring to a boil over medium-high heat. When water in lobster pot comes to a simmer and lobsters begin to turn red, transfer lobsters to vegetable pot, cover, reduce heat to medium, and steam until lobsters turn bright red, about 20 minutes. Transfer lobsters to a baking sheet and let cool slightly, discarding cooking liquids.

2 Heat oven to 350°. Once lobsters are cool enough to handle, remove their claws. Halve lobsters lengthwise. Extract meat from bodies and claws in pieces as large as possible and transfer to a warm medium bowl. Scrape out the yellow-green tomalley from near the head area of the shells into the bowl. Cut meat into 1″–2″ pieces. Place the empty lobster shells on a baking sheet and heat in the oven, about 5 minutes.

3 Melt butter in a large skillet over medium-high heat until just foaming, 1–2 minutes. Add meat and tomalley and toss until heated through, about 1 minute. Fill shells with meat and serve with melted butter and juices from the skillet.

HOMARD À L'ARMORICAINE

Lobster with Shallots, Tomatoes & Cayenne

SERVES 4

Armorique is the old name for the western French region of Brittany, and this creamy lobster preparation is the most famous Breton seafood dish. Its aromatic, vegetable-laden sauce brings out the lobster's inherent sweetness.

2 3-lb. live lobsters
¼ cup extra-virgin olive oil
1 medium onion, finely chopped
3 medium shallots, minced
1 clove garlic, minced
2 carrots, peeled and finely diced
2 tomatoes, chopped
2 tbsp. tomato paste
2 cups white wine
3 tbsp. unsalted butter, softened
½ tsp. cayenne pepper

2 tbsp. crème fraîche
   Cooked white rice, for serving
   Minced fresh flat-leaf parsley, for garnish

1 Cook lobsters in a large pot of boiling water for about 10 minutes. When cool, split open, remove meat, and cut into pieces. Reserve tomalley, coral, and shells.

2 Heat oil in a large skillet over medium-low heat. Add onions, shallots, and garlic and cook for 15 minutes. Add carrots, tomatoes, tomato paste, wine, and 1 cup water. Reduce heat to low and simmer for 8 minutes.

3 Wrap shells in a dish towel and crush with a rolling pin. Add to sauce and cook until sauce is reduced by half, 6–8 minutes. Strain through a fine sieve and return to heat. Make a paste with tomalley, coral, and butter and stir into sauce. Add lobster, season with cayenne pepper, and cook for 2–4 minutes. Stir in crème fraîche. Serve over rice; garnish with parsley.

CAJUN SEAFOOD BOIL

SERVES 6–8

This spicy boil of crawfish, shrimp, potatoes, and corn is inspired by one served at Charlie's Seafood in Harahan, Louisiana.

1¼ cups kosher salt
5 lb. whole live crawfish or frozen seasoned, boiled crawfish, thawed
6 ribs celery, cut into 3″ pieces
2 onions, quartered
1 head garlic, halved crosswise
1 lemon, halved, plus wedges
½ cup Creole seasoning
½ cup Old Bay seasoning
¼ cup Worcestershire sauce
3 tbsp. cayenne pepper
2 lb. medium waxy potatoes
3 lb. head-on jumbo shrimp, unpeeled
3 ears corn, shucked and halved
   Cocktail sauce, for serving
   Hot sauce, preferably Original Louisiana, for serving

1 Whisk 1 cup salt in a large stockpot filled with 2 gallons cold water until dissolved. Add crawfish and let sit for 20 minutes; drain, rinse, and chill.

2 Add remaining ¼ cup salt, celery, onions, garlic, halved lemon, Creole seasoning, Old Bay, Worcestershire,

> **"Always remember that the guest has to wait for the soufflé,
> but the soufflé can't wait for the guest."**
>
> MICHEL BOURDIN

cayenne, potatoes, and 2 gallons water to stockpot; bring to a boil. Reduce heat to medium and cook until potatoes are just tender, 10–12 minutes.

3 Add crawfish, shrimp, and corn and cook, covered, until seafood is cooked through, 5–7 minutes more. Drain contents of pot, discarding the liquid; transfer crawfish, shrimp, potatoes, corn, celery, and onions to a large platter. Serve with lemon wedges and cocktail and hot sauces.

LOBSTER SOUFFLÉ WITH SAUCE NANTUA

SERVES 4

Sauce Nantua is an opulent, classical French concoction of butter and cream studded with chunks of lobster. Cooked into a delicate cheese soufflé, it's even more luxurious. We got this recipe from chef Michel Bourdin, formerly of London's famed Connaught restaurant.

FOR THE SAUCE NANTUA

- 3 tbsp. butter
- 3 tbsp. flour
- 2 cups milk, heated
- 1 cup heavy cream
- ¼ cup Crustacean Butter (this page)
    Meat from one boiled 1–1¼-lb. Maine lobster, cut into 1″ pieces
    Salt and freshly ground white pepper

FOR THE SOUFFLÉ

- 7 tbsp. butter
- ½ cup freshly grated Parmigiano-Reggiano
- 8 eggs
    Kosher salt
- ⅓ cup flour
- 1 cup milk, heated
- ½ cup grated Gruyère cheese
    Cayenne pepper
    Freshly ground white pepper

1 Make the sauce: Melt butter in a large saucepan over medium-low heat. Add flour and cook, stirring,

for 2 minutes. Slowly whisk in hot milk, increase heat to medium, and cook, stirring constantly, until thickened, about 7 minutes. Add ½ cup of cream and simmer, stirring, until reduced by one-quarter, about 6 minutes. Add remaining ½ cup cream and crustacean butter, stirring until melted. Add lobster meat and season to taste with salt and pepper. Cover surface with plastic wrap to prevent a skin from forming, and keep warm over very low heat.

2 Make the soufflé: Heat oven to 475°. Butter four 8-oz. soufflé dishes with 1 tbsp. butter, evenly coat insides with 1 tbsp. grated Parmigiano, and refrigerate. Poach 4 eggs in a medium skillet of simmering salted water over medium heat for 3 minutes. Transfer eggs with a slotted spoon to paper towels to drain, then set aside.

3 Melt remaining 6 tbsp. butter in a large saucepan over medium-low heat. Add flour and cook, stirring, for 2 minutes. Gradually add hot milk, whisking until smooth and thick, 2–3 minutes. Remove pot from heat. Separate remaining 4 eggs, setting whites aside in a large mixing bowl. Whisk yolks into hot flour-milk mixture 1 at a time. Add Gruyère, stirring until melted. Season to taste with cayenne, salt, and pepper. Transfer soufflé base to a large bowl. Working quickly, whisk reserved whites until they hold stiff peaks, then gently fold into soufflé base along with remaining Parmigiano.

4 Spoon ⅓ cup of soufflé mixture into each dish. Add poached egg and 2 tbsp. of sauce Nantua with lobster to each. Spoon remaining soufflé mixture on top. Bake for 5 minutes, reduce heat to 400°, and bake until puffed and browned, about 10 minutes. Serve with remaining sauce.

Crustacean Butter

MAKES ABOUT ¼ CUP

Sauce Nantua is traditionally flavored with crayfish shells—but lobster shells, which you'll have anyway if you're making Lobster Soufflé with Sauce Nantua (this page), work just as well.

1 lb. live crayfish or shells from one
    boiled 1½-lb. whole lobster
1 tbsp. unsalted butter

1 If using crayfish, bring a large pot of water to a boil over high heat. Add crayfish and cook for 5–8 minutes, then drain. Remove tail meat from shells and reserve for another use. If using lobster shells, crack shells into small pieces with a heavy cleaver.

2 Put shells and butter into the bowl of a stand mixer fitted with the paddle attachment and beat on low speed until butter and shells begin to come together, about 5 minutes. Increase speed to medium and beat until butter turns a rich orange color and is almost smooth, about 30 minutes more.

3 Heat oven to 250°. Transfer butter to a medium ovenproof saucepan and heat over medium-low heat, stirring often, until melted, about 5 minutes. Transfer pan to oven and cook for 45 minutes. Remove pan from oven, stir in 2 cups water, and set aside to cool. Transfer to a medium bowl and refrigerate until butter is solid, about 8 hours.

4 Lift solid butter from liquid and shells at bottom of bowl and transfer to a small saucepan. Discard liquid and shells. Melt butter over medium-low heat, then pour through a fine-mesh sieve into a small bowl to remove remaining shell particles. Cover tightly and store in the refrigerator for up to 1 week.

CRAYFISH PIE

SERVES 6–8

Firm and sweet, crayfish meat goes well just about anywhere you'd use lobster. Here, it's combined with peppers, celery, tomatoes, and cayenne pepper and baked in a flaky pastry dough for a spicy twist on pot pie.

FOR THE CRUST
3 cups flour
14 tbsp. unsalted butter, cubed and chilled
2 tsp. kosher salt
½ cup ice cold water

FOR THE FILLING
4 tbsp. unsalted butter
1 medium green bell pepper, seeded and minced
1 medium yellow onion, minced
1 rib celery, minced
½ tsp. cayenne

1 16-oz. can whole, peeled canned tomatoes,
    crushed by hand
1 lb. cooked, peeled crayfish tails
2 tbsp. cornstarch, dissolved in ½ cup water
1 tbsp. minced fresh flat-leaf parsley
2 scallions, minced
    Kosher salt and freshly ground
    black pepper, to taste
1 egg yolk beaten with 1 tbsp. water

1 Make the crust: Pulse flour, butter, and salt in a food processor into pea-size crumbles. Add water and pulse until dough forms. Divide dough in half and flatten into disks. Wrap in plastic wrap; chill for 1 hour.

2 Make the filling: Melt butter in a 12″ skillet over medium heat. Add bell pepper, onion, and celery and cook until golden, 10–12 minutes. Add cayenne and tomatoes and cook about 5 minutes. Add crayfish and cornstarch mixture and cook, stirring constantly, until thickened, about 5 minutes. Stir in parsley, scallions, salt, and pepper; set aside.

3 Heat oven to 450°. On a lightly floured surface, roll 1 disk of dough into a 12″ round. Fit into a 9″ pie plate, trimming edges and leaving 1″ dough overhang. Fill with crayfish mixture. Roll remaining disk into a 12″ round and place over top of pie. Pinch top and bottom edges together and fold under; crimp edges. Brush with egg mixture and cut three 1″-long slits in top of pie. Bake until crust is golden brown and filling is bubbling, 45 minutes to 1 hour. Let cool slightly before serving.

MARYLAND CRAB CAKES

SERVES 4–6

When it comes to crab cakes, we believe the simpler the better. This exceptional version is served at Nick's Inner Harbor Seafood in Baltimore. Saltines are our preferred base for the cracker meal (just crush them to a fine powder), but any plain cracker will do.

2 eggs
2 tbsp. mayonnaise
1 tsp. Dijon mustard
1 tbsp. Worcestershire sauce
¼ cup fresh flat-leaf parsley leaves, minced
2 lb. jumbo lump crabmeat, picked of shells
6 tbsp. cracker meal
    Vegetable oil, for frying

1 Mix together eggs, mayonnaise, mustard, Worcestershire, and parsley in a bowl. Add crab, taking care not to break up crabmeat. Add cracker meal, then shape mixture into 6 large cakes. Cover with plastic wrap and refrigerate for 1 hour.

2 Pour vegetable oil into a large skillet to a depth of ¼″ and heat over medium-high heat. Fry the cakes until golden brown, turning once, about 5 minutes per side.

PAN-FRIED SOFTSHELL CRABS WITH GARLIC-HERB BUTTER

SERVES 4

Softshell crabs are just regular old blue crabs. What makes them special is that they're harvested just after molting, so the entire crab—minus its gills, abdominal plate, and face—is edible. Flash-freezing means softshell crabs are available year-round, but Manhattan's Grand Central Oyster Bar serves this delectable, herbaceous dish only in the spring, during fresh softshell season.

8	tbsp. salted butter, softened
2	small cloves garlic, minced
1	small shallot, minced
1½	tsp. white wine
½	tsp. minced fresh dill
½	tsp. minced fresh thyme
½	tsp. minced fresh chives
½	tsp. minced fresh cilantro
½	tsp. minced fresh parsley
½	tsp. minced fresh tarragon
½	tsp. minced fresh basil
½	cup flour
	Kosher salt and freshly ground black pepper
½	cup olive oil
8	jumbo softshell crabs, cleaned
2	lemons, 1 juiced and 1 cut into quarters
4	sprigs fresh curly parsley

1 Combine butter, garlic, shallot, wine, dill, thyme, chives, cilantro, minced parsley, tarragon, and basil in a bowl and set aside.

2 Combine flour, salt, and pepper in a wide dish. Heat half the oil in a large skillet over medium-high heat. Dredge half the crabs in the flour, then sauté crabs, turning once, until golden brown, 2–2½ minutes per side. Drain on paper towels. Repeat process with remaining oil and crabs.

3 Remove skillet from heat, add garlic-herb butter and lemon juice, and swirl until melted. Divide crabs among

4 plates; spoon butter over crabs. Garnish with lemon wedges and parsley sprigs.

CRAWFISH ÉTOUFFÉE

SERVES 8

A dark brown roux is the flavor base for this Cajun classic. The dish is a cousin of gumbo (page 99), but instead of a mixture of meats, sausages, and seafood, it's made with just one star ingredient—traditionally crawfish, though shrimp will do in a pinch.

2	tsp. kosher salt
1	tsp. cayenne pepper
1	tsp. freshly ground white pepper
1	tsp. freshly ground black pepper
1	tsp. dried basil
½	tsp. dried thyme
¾	cup canola oil
¾	cup flour, sifted
¼	cup finely chopped onion
¼	cup finely chopped celery
¼	cup finely chopped green bell pepper
3	cups chicken stock
12	tbsp. unsalted butter, cubed
2	lb. peeled crawfish tails or peeled medium shrimp
1	cup finely chopped scallions
	Cooked white rice, for serving

1 In a small bowl, combine salt, cayenne, white pepper, black pepper, basil, and thyme; set spice mixture aside. In a 4-qt. heavy-bottomed pot, heat oil over high heat until it just begins to smoke. Sprinkle in flour, whisking constantly, and cook for 30 seconds. Reduce heat to medium-low and cook, whisking constantly, until roux is the color of dark chocolate, about 30 minutes. Add onion and cook, stirring constantly with a wooden spoon, until onion softens, about 5 more minutes. Remove pot from heat and stir in 1 tbsp. reserved spice mixture, along with celery and bell pepper. Continue stirring until roux has cooled and darkened slightly, about 5 minutes; set aside.

2 In a 2-qt. saucepan over medium-high heat, bring 2 cups stock to a boil. Gradually add roux and whisk until incorporated. Reduce heat to low and cook for 2 minutes more. Remove pan from heat; set stock mixture aside.

3 In a 4-qt. saucepan, melt 8 tbsp. butter over medium-high heat. Stir in crawfish tails and scallions and cook for about 1 minute. Add remaining spice mixture and reserved stock mixture, along with remaining 1 cup stock and 4 tbsp.

YOU CALL THAT A ROUX?

Don't rely on *Larousse Gastronomique* or Escoffier to get you through a New Orleans menu. Although Creole sauces almost always go by French names, they seldom resemble their classical French counterparts. Most New Orleans restaurants, for example, make shrimp rémoulade (page 280) with a spicy red vinaigrette, not a briny mayonnaise. Here's a guide to Gallic-Creole culinary dissonances:

SAUCE BÉARNAISE

French: Shallots, chervil, tarragon, thyme, and vinegar cooked together, then thickened with egg yolks and butter.

Creole: Tarragon and vinegar added to a classic *sauce hollandaise* of lemon juice, egg yolks, and butter.

SAUCE BORDELAISE

French: Sauce espagnole (French brown veal sauce) enhanced with red wine. Traditionally served with grilled meats.

Creole: Clarified butter or oil flavored with garlic and scallion. Used on grilled meats or, nowadays, pasta.

MEUNIÈRE

French: A preparation of fish that is floured, fried in butter, and sprinkled with lemon juice, brown butter, and parsley.

Creole: Fish prepared the same way as the French version, but often with roux and veal stock added to the pan to form a sauce.

RAVIGOTE

French: From *ravigoter*, meaning to "perk up," vinaigrette or a velouté (white sauce) seasoned with herbs, shallots, and sometimes capers.

Creole: Mayonnaise with lemon, parsley, scallions, and capers or olives—similar to the French *mayonnaise à la ravigote.*

RÉMOULADE

French: A mayonnaise flavored with mustard, gherkins, capers, herbs, and anchovies. Similar to a Creole *ravigote.*

Creole: Not mayonnaise at all, but a vinaigrette spiced and colored with paprika, cayenne pepper, and Creole mustard.

ROUX

French: A thickener made by cooking together equal amounts of butter and flour. Usually white, but sometimes brown.

Creole: Flour combined with lard or oil instead of butter and usually cooked to a very dark brown resembling chocolate.

---

butter, and stir until combined and glossy. Remove pan from heat and serve étouffée with rice.

PICKLED DUNGENESS CRAB

SERVES 2–4

In North Beach, San Francisco, an "old stove" is a traditional home cook. Old stove Rose Pistola gave us her recipe for pickled crab, a piquant main course.

- 1   cooked 2-lb. Dungeness crab
- ½   cup extra-virgin olive oil
- ¼   cup white wine vinegar
- ½   cup finely diced celery hearts and leaves
- 1   medium carrot, peeled and diced
- 1   shallot, diced
- 2   tbsp. finely chopped fresh chives
- 1   clove garlic, crushed
      Kosher salt and freshly ground black pepper
- 1   lemon, thinly sliced, for garnish

1 Pull top shell off crab and remove gray gills. Scoop out and discard any soft fat. Crack legs with a nutcracker to expose flesh. Split crab in half down middle, then cut into pieces between each of the legs. Place crab pieces in a shallow glass dish.

2 Whisk together oil, vinegar, celery, carrot, shallot, chives, and garlic. Season with salt and pepper. Pour dressing over crab pieces and toss to coat well. Cover and refrigerate for 24 hours.

3 Transfer crab pieces to a platter, drizzle with marinade, and garnish with lemon slices.

HOW TO EAT BLUE CRAB

STEP 1 Turn the crab over so that its belly faces you. Using your fingers, lift up its heart-shaped apron, or tail, and pull it back to snap it off of the body.

STEP 2 Where you've pried off the apron, wedge a table knife between the top and bottom shells and remove the top shell, twisting and prying it off.

STEP 3 Remove the gills, often called "dead man's fingers," which are attached to either side of the crab. (The yellowish "mustard" and orange roe are edible.) Crack the body down the center.

STEP 4 Press lightly on the body where the back legs, or "swimmers," are attached and pop out the backfin meat in the rear of the crab. Extract the rest of the body meat with your fingers. Remove the claws.

STEP 5 Using a cracker or a small wooden mallet, gently crack open the claws. Scrape the meat out of the claws with your fingers or a table knife.

MARYLAND STEAMED BLUE CRABS
SERVES 6

On summer weekends in the Mid-Atlantic states, it often feels like everyone is up to their elbows in steamed blue crab, cracking the sharp shells and slurping the Old Bay–spiced juices.

- ⅓ cup Old Bay seasoning
- 3 tbsp. kosher salt
- 2 tsp. freshly ground black pepper
- 2 tsp. ground ginger
- 2 tsp. garlic powder
- 1 tsp. onion powder
- 1 tsp. dried thyme
- 1 tsp. cayenne pepper
- 1 tsp. dry mustard
- 1 tsp. yellow mustard seeds
- 4⅓ cups lager-style beer
- 2⅔ cups cider vinegar
- 30 live blue crabs

1 To make the seasoning mix, combine Old Bay, salt, pepper, ginger, garlic and onion powders, thyme, cayenne, and dry mustard and mustard seeds in a small bowl.

2 Combine beer and vinegar in an 8-qt. saucepan fitted with a steamer insert and bring to a boil over high heat. Using tongs, layer crabs in steamer, sprinkling some seasoning mix between layers and on top of final layer. Cover pan and cook until crabs are cooked through, about 10 minutes. Remove from heat and let cool for 10 minutes before serving. (See How to Eat Blue Crab, this page, for instructions on eating this dish.)

SINGAPOREAN BLACK PEPPER CRAB
SERVES 2–4

An abundant amount of freshly ground coarse black pepper mixed with fragrant garlic, turmeric, and ginger spices up sweet crab legs in this popular Singaporean recipe.

- 6 tbsp. black peppercorns
- 8 cloves garlic, roughly chopped
- 1 7½″ piece fresh turmeric, peeled and thinly sliced, or 2 tbsp. ground turmeric
- 1 3″ piece fresh ginger, peeled and thinly sliced
  Kosher salt, to taste
- 3 tbsp. peanut oil
- 3 lb. cooked king or snow crab legs, thawed if frozen

1 Pulse peppercorns in a spice grinder until coarsely ground; set aside. Combine garlic, turmeric, ginger, salt, and 2 tbsp. water in a food processor. Purée into a smooth paste and transfer to a bowl; stir in reserved pepper.

2 Heat oil in a 14″ wok or skillet over medium-low heat. Add paste and cook, stirring occasionally, until mixture is fragrant and paste begins to separate, about 10 minutes. Increase heat to medium-high and add crab and ¾ cup water; bring to a boil. Cook, stirring constantly, until crab shells are bright red and meat is heated through, 5–7 minutes.

CHINESE-STYLE BLACK PEPPER CRAB
SERVES 2–4

Meaty Dungeness crabs, a large-bodied Pacific species, are stir-fried with a sweet-spicy sauce in this toothsome Chinese recipe.

- 3 tbsp. vegetable oil
- 2 1½-lb. cooked and cleaned Dungeness crabs, bodies cut in half, legs and claws cracked
- 3 cloves garlic, finely chopped
- 1 tbsp. finely chopped fresh ginger

4 Thai or green serrano chiles, stemmed, seeded, and finely chopped
2 tbsp. oyster sauce
2 tbsp. dark soy sauce
2 tbsp. soy sauce
1 tbsp. sugar
2 tbsp. coarsely ground black pepper
Fresh cilantro leaves, for garnish

1 Heat oil in a wok or a large skillet over high heat. Sauté crab pieces for 2 minutes. Remove from pan and reserve.

2 Turn down heat to medium, add garlic, ginger, and chiles and cook for 3 minutes, stirring frequently. Add oyster sauce, dark soy sauce, soy sauce, and sugar. Reduce heat to low and simmer for 30 seconds.

3 Add pepper and return crab to wok; stir until coated with sauce. Serve garnished with cilantro.

SWAHILI GINGER CRAB

Mkamba Wa Tangawizi

SERVES 2–4

The cuisine of Africa's Swahili coast is characterized by bold flavors—chiles, ginger, and spices—often tempered by cooling coconut. In this Kenyan recipe, the crab cooks in an aromatic broth that's worth slurping up on its own once the crab is finished.

2 lb. cooked whole Dungeness or king crab or frozen and thawed snow crab legs and claws
2 tbsp. canola oil
4 green bird's eye chiles, stemmed and minced
3 cloves garlic, minced
2 shallots, minced
1 2″ piece fresh ginger, peeled and minced
1 large tomato, chopped
2 cups canned coconut milk
3 fresh or frozen makrut lime leaves
¼ cup fresh lime juice, preferably from makrut or Key limes
Kosher salt and freshly ground black pepper
2 cups cooked rice, for serving

1 Bring 2 cups water to a boil in a 6-qt. pot over high heat. Add crab and cook, covered, for about 4 minutes. Remove crab from pot and set aside to let cool slightly. Strain and reserve cooking liquid. If using whole crab, twist off the claws, crack the claw shells, and transfer to a bowl. Pry off

and discard top shell of the crab's body, remove and discard the innards and fingerlike gills, and rinse out any sand that may be left inside. Roughly chop crab body into 3″–4″ pieces and transfer to bowl with claws; set aside. (If using just legs and claws, chop them into 3″ pieces and set aside.)

2 Wipe out pot, add oil, and heat over medium heat. Add chiles, garlic, shallots, ginger, and tomato and cook, stirring often, until soft, about 5 minutes. Add reserved crab along with the coconut milk, makrut lime leaves, and 2 cups water. Bring to a simmer and cook, stirring occasionally, until crab is warmed through. Stir in lime juice and season with salt and pepper. To serve, spoon crab pieces into bowls and ladle the cooking liquid over the top. Serve with rice.

VIETNAMESE BEER-STEAMED CRABS

Cua Hap Bia

SERVES 2–4

In this dish, ubiquitous throughout Vietnam, fresh blue crabs are steamed in a flavorful mixture of chile, garlic, lime, and beer.

FOR THE DIPPING SAUCE
4 tbsp. nuoc mam (Vietnamese fish sauce)
2 small red or green bird's eye chiles, stemmed and sliced into thin rings
Juice of 2 limes

FOR THE CRABS
12 live blue crabs (about 4 lb.)
4 12-oz. bottles lager-style beer
2 tsp. kosher salt
10 cloves garlic, smashed
3 bird's eye chiles, stemmed and split
1 bunch fresh cilantro
2 limes, halved

1 Make the sauce: Whisk together fish sauce, chiles, and lime juice. Set aside.

2 Rinse crabs under running water. Pour beer into a 6-qt. pot; bring to a boil over high heat. Add salt, garlic, chiles, and cilantro. Squeeze in juice from halved limes; add limes.

3 Add crabs to pot; cook, covered, until they turn a vibrant reddish orange, about 8 minutes. Using tongs, transfer crabs to a platter. Serve with sauce. (See How to Eat Blue Crab, facing page, for instructions on eating this dish.)

Oysters, Clams & Mussels

JOHN DORY'S OYSTER PAN ROAST

SERVES 2–4

You'll be fighting for more toast to sop up this dish's velvety, cream-based sauce touched with a hint of vermouth, garlic, and tarragon. Served at the John Dory Oyster Bar in New York, it's the perfect broth for delicate sautéed oysters.

- 4 slices soft French or Italian bread
- 2 cloves garlic, 1 halved, 1 minced
- 1 tbsp. olive oil
- ½ small yellow onion, minced
- ¼ cup dry vermouth
- ¾ cup fish stock
- 12 oysters, shucked, juices reserved
- 1 cup heavy cream
- 4 tbsp. unsalted butter
- 1½ tsp. fresh lemon juice
- 1 tsp. minced fresh tarragon
  Kosher salt and freshly ground black pepper, to taste
- ¼ tsp. cayenne pepper

1 Heat broiler. Place bread on a baking sheet and broil, flipping once, until lightly toasted, 1–2 minutes. Remove from oven and rub with halved garlic; set aside.

2 Heat oil in a 4-qt. saucepan over medium-high heat. Cook minced garlic and onion until soft, 3–4 minutes. Add vermouth and cook until reduced by half, about 2 minutes. Add stock and oyster juices and simmer until slightly reduced, 3–4 minutes. Add cream and cook until sauce is slightly thick, about 5 minutes more. Remove from heat and stir in oysters, butter, lemon juice, tarragon, salt, and pepper. Spoon into bowls and sprinkle with cayenne; serve with toast on the side.

CLAMS IN SHERRY SAUCE

Almejas à la Gaditana

SERVES 4–6

This classic dish from Spain's Andalusia region is traditionally served with lots of crusty bread, to soak up the spicy, briny, sherry-spiked broth.

- 3 tbsp. olive oil
- 5 cloves garlic, finely chopped
- 3 lb. small clams, such as littlenecks, scrubbed
- 1 cup dry white wine
- ½ cup dry sherry
- ¼ cup finely chopped fresh flat-leaf parsley
- 2 small red bird's eye chiles, stemmed and finely chopped
  Kosher salt and freshly ground black pepper, to taste
  Country bread, for serving

Heat oil in a 6-qt. saucepan over medium-high. Add garlic and cook, stirring, until golden brown, about 2 minutes. Add clams, wine, sherry, parsley, and chiles and season with salt and pepper. Bring to a boil and cook, covered, until the clams open, about 12 minutes. Uncover the pan and remove and discard any clams that don't open. Divide clams and broth among individual bowls. Serve with bread on the side.

CLAM CAKES

MAKES 1 DOZEN

These delectable fritters are a great accompaniment for chowder (page 116). The recipe is adapted from *The New England Yankee Cook Book*, published in 1939.

  Canola oil, for frying
- 1 cup flour
- 4 tsp. baking powder
- 1 tsp. kosher salt, plus more to taste
- ⅛ tsp. freshly ground black pepper
- 2 cups (about ¾ lb.) chopped clams (preferably quahogs)
- ½ cup milk
- 2 tbsp. melted butter
- 1 egg, lightly beaten

1 Pour oil to a depth of 2″ into a large pot and heat over medium-high heat until a deep-fry thermometer reads 350°.

2 Meanwhile, sift flour, baking powder, salt, and pepper into a bowl.

> ## "He was a bold man that first ate an oyster."
> JONATHAN SWIFT

3 In a bowl, stir together clams, milk, butter, and egg. Add flour mixture to clam mixture and stir to combine. Working in batches, carefully drop spoonfuls of batter (about 3 tbsp. each) into oil. Fry, turning once, until golden brown and just cooked through, 3–4 minutes. Transfer fritters to a paper towel–lined plate and sprinkle with salt.

PINE-GRILLED MUSSELS
Terrée de Moules
SERVES 4

Pine needles impart a delicious, smoky tang to briny mussels in a classic *terrée de moules,* or "mussel bake," which in the south of France is traditionally done on the beach. The same results (and dramatic spectacle) can be achieved by means of a standard kettle grill. If you have access to dried, pesticide-free longleaf pine needles (from a species like leppo or umbrella), you can collect your own—just make sure they're completely brown.

1½ lb. mussels, scrubbed and debearded
3–4 qt. dry, brown, pesticide-free pine needles

Place mussels, rounded side up, about 1"–2" apart, between the slats of a grill grate. Pile lightly packed dried pine needles atop mussels to a height of about 12". Light needles with a match; stand back. Allow needles to burn to ash, 4–5 minutes. Dust away excess ash. Eat the mussels straight from the grill. (Discard any that don't open.)

MOULES À LA GUEUZE
Mussels Steamed in Gueuze
SERVES 2–4

Beer-steamed mussels are a Belgian classic—*gueuze,* a blended lambic ale with a dry, pleasingly sour flavor, is an ideal choice. Of course, you should serve these mussels with fries (page 407).

1 tbsp. lard or butter
1 rib celery, julienned
1 small onion, halved and thinly sliced
1 sprig fresh thyme

1 bay leaf
3 lb. mussels, scrubbed and debearded
  Pinch of ground nutmeg
  Pinch of kosher salt
  Freshly ground black pepper, to taste
1 cup gueuze or other unsweetened lambic beer
  Leaves from 6 sprigs fresh flat-leaf parsley, chopped

1 Melt lard in a large pot over medium-high heat. Add celery, onion, thyme, and bay leaf and cook until soft, 5–8 minutes. Add 1 cup water and cook for 5 minutes. Add mussels, nutmeg, salt, and pepper, cover, and steam until mussel shells just begin to open, about 4 minutes. Add beer, cover, and continue steaming until shells completely open, about 4 minutes more. (Discard any that don't open).

2 Spoon into large bowls, discarding bay leaf and thyme, and garnish with parsley.

VALENCIAN-STYLE MUSSELS
Clochinas Valencianas
SERVES 2–4

In Spain, it is common for a bar to be known for a single variety of tapas; we found this paprika-spiced take on mussels at Valencia's Bar Pilar. Almost everyone at the bar has a dish of these in front of them.

1 tbsp. fresh lemon juice
1 tbsp. extra-virgin olive oil
2 bay leaves
1½ tsp. sweet Spanish paprika
¼ tsp. cayenne pepper
1½–2 lb. mussels, scrubbed and debearded

1 Put 2 cups cold water, lemon juice, oil, bay leaves, paprika, and cayenne into a large pot with a tight-fitting lid and bring to a boil over high heat.

2 Add mussels, cover, and give pot a few shakes to mix mussels and liquid together. Steam mussels over high heat, shaking pot once or twice, until shells open, 2–3 minutes.

3 Discard bay leaves and any mussels that do not open. Spoon mussels and broth among warm serving bowls.

> **"Fish is held out to be one of the greatest luxuries of the table and not only necessary, but even indispensable at all dinners where there is any pretense of excellence or fashion."**
>
> MRS. BEETON

MOULES FRITES

SERVES 2

Mussels and fries are both Belgian staples; they've long been paired together at the country's famous fry shops, known as *friteries* in French, or *freetkoken* in Dutch, the language of Flemish Belgium. Most menus offer a long list of variations, from tomato sauced to curried. The classic, though, is a simple mixture of wine, butter, and aromatics.

FOR THE MAYONNAISE

1	tsp. Dijon mustard
1	egg yolk
1	cup canola oil
2	tsp. white wine vinegar
2	tsp. fresh lemon juice
½	tsp. kosher salt, plus more to taste
	Freshly ground black pepper, to taste

FOR THE MUSSELS

2½	lb. mussels, scrubbed and debearded
⅔	cup dry white wine
2	tbsp. unsalted butter, cubed
3	ribs celery, finely chopped
1½	leeks, light green and white parts, cut into ¼"-thick slices
½	large yellow onion, finely chopped
	Kosher salt and freshly ground black pepper, to taste
	French fries (page 407)

1 Make the mayonnaise: In a large bowl, whisk mustard and egg yolk. Whisking constantly, slowly add oil, drop by drop at first until it begins to emulsify and then in a thin stream. Whisk in vinegar, lemon juice, salt, and pepper. Set aside.

2 Make the mussels: Heat a high-sided 12″ skillet over high heat. Add mussels, wine, butter, celery, leeks, and onion, season with salt and pepper, and cover skillet. Cook, occasionally shaking skillet, until mussels have opened, about 5 minutes. Divide mussels between 2 large bowls, discarding any that did not open. Serve with fries and mayonnaise.

Squid

SQUID ON THE GRIDDLE

SERVES 4

In her book *Lidia's Italian Table*, chef Lidia Bastianich reminisces about catching squid with her uncle, using a light and strips of white cloth to attract them: "Soon the first calamari appeared, waving their tentacles and looking like puffs of pink smoke floating in the water. My uncle quickly threw the snag in like a lasso, and then with a splash, the calamari were landed in the boat."

2	lb. squid, cleaned, with skin and tentacles left on
½	cup extra-virgin olive oil
8	cloves garlic, sliced
	Leaves from 1 sprig thyme
1	tsp. crushed red chile flakes
1	tsp. fine sea salt
	Fresh flat-leaf parsley sprigs, for garnish (optional)
	Lemon wedges, for garnish (optional)

1 Combine squid, oil, garlic, thyme, chile flakes, and salt in a medium bowl and marinate for 30 minutes.

2 Heat a large cast-iron skillet over medium-high heat. Transfer squid and marinade to hot skillet and immediately place the clean bottom of a medium cast-iron skillet directly on top of squid to flatten them as they cook. Be sure pans don't trap steam, or squid won't be crisp. Cook, turning squid once, until browned and crispy and juices have caramelized, about 8 minutes per side.

3 Transfer squid and juices to a large platter and serve garnished with parsley sprigs and lemon wedges, if you like.

CALAMARI WITH CHORIZO & ARTICHOKES

SERVES 2–4

At the restaurant Le Grain de Sel in Marseille, squid and artichokes are sautéed in the paprika-laced drippings of chorizo, taking on the spice's rich, dusky flavor.

5	tbsp. olive oil
¼	lb. cured chorizo, peeled and thinly sliced
4	cloves garlic, thinly sliced
4	whole calamari, cleaned, tentacles reserved
	Kosher salt and freshly ground black pepper, to taste
2	cups artichoke hearts (whole canned, drained and halved, or defrosted frozen quarters)
1	orange, zested, then supremed and cut into ¼" pieces

1 Heat 3 tbsp. oil in a 12″ skillet over medium-high heat. Add chorizo and garlic and cook until golden, 3–4 minutes. Spoon onto plates; keep warm.

2 Add remaining 2 tbsp. oil to pan and return to medium-high heat. Pat calamari and tentacles dry with paper towels. Season with salt and pepper and cook, flipping once, until browned and slightly curled, 4–6 minutes; spoon onto plates. Add artichokes, salt, and pepper to pan and cook until browned, 3–4 minutes, then add to plates. Garnish with orange zest and chopped orange.

Vegetables

VEGETABLES

A S COOKS, WE DEFINE the change of seasons by the bounty of the harvest. Whether it's at a farmers' market, a roadside produce stand, or a supermarket, the year is marked by what's on display. The spring's first peas announce the end of winter and are a green reminder of summer's soon-to-arrive tomatoes, while root vegetables and members of the big Brassicaceae family—broccoli, cabbage, kale—sustain us through the colder months.

When the new season's vegetables appear, our menus shift to incorporate the change, moving from the brightly colored abundance of spring and summer to cool-weather standbys like roots, tubers, and hearty greens. But no matter the time of year, vegetables infuse our meals with flavor, texture, and color.

Select cooking methods for vegetables that will intensify their flavors. For example, grilling infuses corn with smoky sweetness, oil-braising asparagus concentrates its grassy taste, and roasting cauliflower imparts nuttiness. Likewise, the right preparation will transform a vegetable's texture: A slow braise turns kale into a luscious heap of greens, and a quick fry renders long beans blistered yet tender.

Although vegetables are often relegated to the realm of sides, they can easily stand on their own. A squash gratin or an Irish-inspired casserole of cabbage, potatoes, and ham is robust enough to serve as a main dish; *saag paneer* and flatbread make for a simple, satisfying meal; and an assortment of seasonal sides makes a colorful supper.

Of course, the success of any vegetable dish depends on the quality and freshness of the vegetable itself. Today, vegetables from all over the globe are available year-round at the neighborhood grocery store. We can find tomatillos from Central America and lotus root from Asia, artichokes in winter and sweet potatoes in summer. Although this bounty opens up our kitchens to a world of different cuisines, we should never forget about the bonanza of produce that is available in our own backyard. Nothing can compare to buying local, in-season vegetables from a nearby farmers' market or farm: freshly harvested, handled with care to preserve their taste, and available in a wide array of heirloom varieties seldom found anywhere else. These are the vegetables that shine in any meal, simple or complex, and that keep us coming back for more.

Artichokes

SAUTÉED ARTICHOKES BAKED WITH MOZZARELLA

Carciofi Saltati e Fusi al Forno con la Mozzarella

SERVES 4–6

Among English cooking terms, there is no direct equivalent for *insapiore,* the verb Italians derive from their word for taste, *sapore.* A literal, if awkward definition is "to make something tasty"—the process of drawing out and developing the flavor of your ingredients. Marcella Hazan gave us this recipe for artichokes seared until very dark and rich and then draped in creamy cheese; she cites it as a prime example of *insapiore* in action.

- 1 tbsp. fresh lemon juice
- 2 lb. baby artichokes (about 20), or 8 full-size artichokes
- 2 tbsp. extra-virgin olive oil
- 4 cloves garlic, peeled
  Kosher salt and freshly ground black pepper, to taste
- 2 tbsp. butter
- ⅓ cup grated Parmigiano-Reggiano
- ½ lb. mozzarella, sliced ¼" thick
  Crusty bread, for serving

1 Fill a large bowl halfway with water and the lemon juice. Trim artichokes, stripping them of all the tough inedible portions of their leaves. If you are working with baby artichokes, cut them in half lengthwise. If you are using full-size ones, cut them into quarters. As you trim each piece, drop it into the bowl of water. (You can prepare the artichokes up tho this point several hours in advance.) When ready to proceed with the cooking, drain the artichokes and rinse them in cold water to wash off the lemon from their soak.

2 Heat olive oil and garlic over medium-high heat in a skillet wide enough to contain the artichokes in a single uncrowded layer. Cook garlic to a golden brown, stirring from time to time, about 3 minutes. Remove garlic from the pan, discard it, and arrange artichokes in the pan in a single layer, cut side down.

3 Cook artichokes, turning frequently, until completely tender and brown all over, 25 minutes or more. If they stick to the pan, as is likely and even desirable, add 2–3 tbsp. water and loosen them from the bottom using a wooden spoon or spatula. When done, add salt and pepper, turn them over once or twice more, and remove from heat.

4 Heat oven to 400°. Grease the bottom of a 7"×11" baking dish with 1 tbsp. butter. Spread artichokes in the dish along with any juices from the skillet. Sprinkle half the Parmigiano over them. Cover with mozzarella. Top with remaining Parmigiano and dot with remaining 1 tbsp. butter, cut into small pieces.

5 Bake artichokes just until mozzarella melts and becomes partly colored light brown, about 5 minutes. Serve at once with crusty bread to sop up the juices.

STUFFED ARTICHOKES

SERVES 4

Stuffed with bread crumbs and pecorino, these hearty artichokes are a satisfying side dish.

- 4 large, full-size artichokes
- 1 lemon, halved
- 1¾ cups dried bread crumbs
- 1 cup grated pecorino romano
- ⅓ cup chopped fresh flat-leaf parsley
- 2 tsp. kosher salt
- 1 tsp. freshly ground black pepper
- 8 cloves garlic, finely chopped
- 5 tbsp. extra-virgin olive oil

1 Using a serrated knife, cut off artichoke stems to create a flat bottom. Cut top third off each artichoke, pull off tough outermost leaves, and trim tips of leaves with kitchen shears. Rub cut parts with lemon halves. Open artichoke leaves with your thumbs to make room for stuffing; set artichokes aside.

2 Heat oven to 425°. In a large bowl, combine bread crumbs, ¾ cup pecorino romano, parsley, salt, pepper, and garlic. Working over a bowl with 1 artichoke at a time, sprinkle one-quarter of bread crumb mixture over artichoke and work it in between leaves. Transfer stuffed artichoke to a shallow baking dish. Drizzle each artichoke with 1 tbsp. oil. Pour in boiling water to a depth of 1". Rub remaining 1 tbsp. oil on a sheet of aluminum foil, cover artichokes with foil (oiled side down), and secure foil tightly around dish with kitchen twine. Bake until a knife easily slides into the base of an artichoke, about 45 minutes. Remove foil, sprinkle tops with remaining ¼ cup cheese, and turn oven to broil. Broil until tops of artichokes are golden brown, about 3 minutes.

ARTICHOKES IN CILANTRO & POMEGRANATE SAUCE

Ardî Shawkî bil-Hâmid

SERVES 4

For thousands of years, the northern Syrian city of Aleppo has been one of the culinary capitals of the Middle East. The cuisine makes great use of strong flavors, like cilantro and pomegranate—both on vibrant display in this dish, a favorite among Aleppan home cooks.

2–3	medium tomatoes, halved
3	tbsp. extra-virgin olive oil
1	medium onion, finely chopped
8	cloves garlic, minced
¾	cup finely chopped fresh cilantro
	Kosher salt, to taste
8	fresh or thawed frozen artichoke hearts, halved if large
2	tbsp. pomegranate molasses

1 Place tomatoes in a medium-mesh sieve set over a small bowl. Use a spoon to press juice through. Reserve juice; discard seeds and skin.

2 Heat oil in a skillet over medium-high heat. Add onion and cook for 2 minutes. Stir in garlic and cilantro, season with salt, and cook until fragrant, about 1 minute.

3 Reduce heat to medium, add reserved tomato juice, artichokes, and 1 cup water, and simmer until liquid is reduced by half, about 15 minutes. Using a slotted spoon, transfer artichokes to a serving platter. Increase heat to medium-high, add pomegranate molasses, and cook, stirring constantly, until sauce thickens, 1–2 minutes. Spoon pomegranate sauce over artichokes and serve.

BRAISED ARTICHOKE HEARTS WITH MINT

Carciofi alla Romana

SERVES 6

This classic Roman *contorno*, or side dish, is a showpiece for fresh mint, which—like its cousin, basil—is a popular herb in Italian kitchens.

6	large artichoke hearts, trimmed with stems intact
2	cups white wine
1	cup extra-virgin olive oil
3	tbsp. minced fresh flat-leaf parsley
3	tbsp. minced fresh mint leaves
2	tbsp. fresh lemon juice
4	cloves garlic, minced
	Kosher salt and freshly ground black pepper, to taste

1 Place artichokes in a 3-qt. saucepan along with wine, oil, parsley, mint, lemon juice, garlic, and 2 cups water. Season with salt and pepper and bring to a boil. Reduce heat to medium-low and simmer artichokes, turning occasionally, until tender, 15–20 minutes.

2 To serve, transfer artichokes, stem side up, to a platter and drizzle with some of the cooking liquid.

Asparagus

MOTHER'S ASPARAGUS LUNCHEON DISH

SERVES 4–6

Cream, butter, bread crumbs, and cheese make this asparagus casserole a deliciously decadent side dish. This recipe was given to us by Margaret Barstow, organizer of the annual asparagus supper at the First Congregational Church in Hadley, Massachusetts, a town famous for its asparagus farms. She in turn got it from a friend's 89-year-old grandmother.

	Kosher salt, to taste
2	lb. asparagus
6	tbsp. butter
4	tbsp. flour
1	cup heavy cream
1	tsp. paprika
4	hard-cooked eggs, thinly sliced
1	loaf country-style white bread, cut into 1″ cubes (about 2 cups)
1	cup coarsely crumbled Cabaret or Ritz crackers
½	cup grated Parmigiano-Reggiano

1 Heat oven to 350°. Bring a large pot of salted water to a boil over high heat. Prepare asparagus by holding bottom half of each spear with both hands and gently bending it until it snaps where it naturally breaks, separating tough fibrous end from tender part. Discard ends. Cut asparagus into 2″ pieces, add to pot, and cook until soft, 4–6 minutes. Reserve 1 cup cooking water, then drain asparagus.

2 Melt 4 tbsp. butter in a saucepan over medium-low heat. Add flour and cook, stirring, for 2 minutes.

Whisk in reserved cooking water, then cream, stirring until smooth and thick, 8–10 minutes. Add paprika, then season to taste with salt. Layer asparagus, eggs, and sauce alternately in a medium baking dish, ending with sauce. Sprinkle with bread cubes, cracker crumbs, and Parmigiano. Dot with remaining 2 tbsp. butter. Bake until bubbling and golden, 25–30 minutes.

OIL-BRAISED ASPARAGUS
SERVES 1–2

The long, slow cooking of asparagus in oil caramelizes the vegetable, intensifying its sweet, grassy flavor.

- 1 lb. asparagus
- 2 tbsp. vegetable oil
  Kosher salt and freshly ground black pepper, to taste

PREPPING ASPARAGUS

Techniques for preparing asparagus vary according to its size, origin, and freshness, but in general, you'll want to go through these three steps.

CLEANING Commercially grown asparagus, which is washed before shipping, needs only a quick rinse in cold water prior to cooking. Spears that come from your garden, however, require extra care. Soak in cold water for about 15 minutes, gently agitating every so often to loosen any sandy soil trapped in tips or "fins," then lift asparagus from the water, leaving grit behind.

TRIMMING For thin spears, hold stalk with one hand at the base, the other hand about 2" away; then bend the spear. If it doesn't break, move hands up a little and try again. For thick spears, which tend to break anywhere, use a knife to cut where you see a slight color change.

PEELING Thin or very fresh spears are tender enough to eat unpeeled. Thick asparagus is peeled both for presentation and so that stalks and tips cook more evenly. Peel asparagus two-thirds of the way up using downward strokes with an old-style metal swivel peeler. (These fine-bladed peelers remove only skin, leaving flesh behind.)

1 Prepare asparagus by holding bottom half of each spear with both hands and gently bending it until it snaps where it naturally breaks, separating tough fibrous end from tender part. Discard ends. Cut asparagus into 2" pieces.

2 Heat oil in a large skillet over medium-low heat. Add asparagus, season with salt and pepper, and cook, stirring often, until browned, 15–30 minutes.

WHITE ASPARAGUS RAGOUT WITH CHERRY TOMATOES
SERVES 4

White asparagus is the same plant as its green counterpart, it's just been kept from sunlight so chlorophyll isn't given the chance to develop—a practice that dates back to 17th-century France. But it's particularly beloved in Germany, where its arrival is celebrated every spring. Hans Röckenwagner, a German-born, Los Angeles–based chef and restaurateur, serves this as an appetizer or as a side dish.

	Kosher salt and freshly ground white pepper, to taste
5	tbsp. fresh lemon juice
15	tbsp. butter
2	lb. fresh white asparagus
1	cup dry white wine
1	shallot, thinly sliced
½	cup heavy cream
¼	tsp. Tabasco sauce
3–4	tbsp. fresh chervil leaves
16–20	small red cherry tomatoes

1 Bring 16 cups water to a boil in a medium pot over high heat. Add 2 generous pinches of salt, 4 tbsp. lemon juice, and 3 tbsp. butter. Meanwhile, trim about ½" from ends of asparagus. Lay spears on a work surface, then peel thin skin from each with a sharp swivel-blade vegetable peeler, starting 1½" from the top and running the length of the spear. Gather spears into 4 bundles, tie loosely with kitchen twine, and lower into simmering water. Simmer, increasing heat to medium-high if necessary, until spears are tender when pierced with the tip of a knife, 8–30 minutes, depending on thickness. Lift bundles from simmering water and drain on paper towels.

2 Boil wine and shallots in a medium heavy pan over medium-high heat until reduced by three-quarters, 10–15 minutes. Add cream and reduce again by half,

> "Training is everything. The peach was once a bitter almond;
> cauliflower is nothing but cabbage with a college education."
>
> MARK TWAIN

5–7 minutes; reduce heat to low. Cut remaining 12 tbsp. butter into pieces, then whisk into pan, a few pieces at a time, until smooth. Whisk in salt and pepper to taste, Tabasco, and remaining 1 tbsp. lemon juice. Cover and keep warm.

3 Chop half the chervil and set aside. Untie twine from asparagus, then cut spears into 1½" lengths and add to warm beurre blanc. Cook for 1 minute, stirring gently until well coated. Add tomatoes and chopped chervil and stir gently, then spoon into a warm serving dish. Garnish with remaining chervil. Serve warm.

ASPARAGUS SHANDONG STYLE
Liang Ban Lu-Sun
SERVES 2–4

A specialty of China's Shandong province, this dish was traditionally reserved for banquets because, at one time, asparagus was very expensive there. These days, both in China and the United States, the vegetable is more widely available, so there's no reason not to take advantage of this flavorful dish more often.

1½	lb. asparagus, trimmed and cut crosswise on the diagonal into 2" pieces
1	tbsp. soy sauce
1	tsp. sesame oil
2	drops red chile oil
½	tsp. sesame seeds, toasted, for garnish

1 Bring a medium pot of water to a boil over high heat. Add asparagus to pot and cook until tender-crisp and bright green, 1½–2 minutes. Do not overcook. Drain, then immediately plunge into a large bowl of ice water; set aside to cool, 2–3 minutes. Drain again, then transfer to paper towels, pat dry, and set aside.

2 Whisk together soy sauce, sesame oil, and chile oil in a medium bowl. Add asparagus and toss. Transfer to a serving bowl and garnish with sesame seeds.

Broccoli & Broccoli Rabe

CLASSIC BROCCOLI-CHEESE CASSEROLE
SERVES 8–10

Broccoli and cheddar are a classic pair; their mellow flavors marry in this creamy casserole, a weeknight staple from SAVEUR associate food editor Kellie Evans' mother, Patricia.

MASSACHUSETTS GRASS

The asparagus harvest is a rite of spring in Hadley and a handful of other towns, including Hatfield, Sunderland, and Whately, along the Connecticut River in western Massachusetts. From the 1930s through the 1970s, this area, blessed with a deep layer of sandy loam—the sediment of a glacial lake that once covered the valley—was one of America's premier asparagus-growing regions. In this fertile soil, the vegetable—and especially the standard Mary Washington variety—thrived as it did nowhere else, sending down strong roots and often producing for 30 years or more.

Hadley "grass"—as the crop is still called in these parts (it's short for "sparrow grass," a corruption of asparagus popular in the 17th and 18th centuries)—was once a mainstay of the local economy and an important source of community spirit. But in the mid-1970s, a soil-borne fungus known as fusarium attacked and destroyed the asparagus crop. Nowadays, total production is barely a tenth of what it used to be, and what little asparagus is still grown is sold almost exclusively in the area, at farm stands and small markets.

Kosher salt, to taste

4 heads broccoli, cut into small florets

2 tbsp. olive oil

8 tbsp. unsalted butter

½ lb. white mushrooms, thinly sliced

1½ cups panko bread crumbs

2 tsp. dried sage

Freshly ground black pepper, to taste

3 cloves garlic, finely chopped

1 small onion, finely chopped

3 tbsp. flour

2 cups milk

2 tsp. dry mustard

¼ tsp. freshly grated nutmeg

3 oz. cream cheese, softened

2 cups shredded cheddar cheese

½ cup mayonnaise

2 eggs, lightly beaten

1 Bring a large pot of salted water to a boil over high heat. Add broccoli and cook until just tender, about 2 minutes. Drain and transfer to a 9″×13″ baking dish and set aside. Heat oil and 2 tbsp. butter in a 10″ skillet over medium-high heat. Add mushrooms and cook, stirring, until browned, about 5 minutes; transfer to a bowl and set aside. Add 3 tbsp. butter to skillet and melt. Remove from heat and add bread crumbs and sage; season with salt and pepper and set aside.

2 Heat remaining 5 tbsp. butter in a 2-qt. saucepan over medium-high heat. Add garlic and onion and cook until soft, about 4 minutes. Add flour and cook, stirring, for 2 minutes. Add milk, mustard, and nutmeg and bring to a boil. Reduce heat to medium and cook, stirring often, until sauce is slightly thickened, about 3 minutes. Remove from heat and stir in cream cheese, 1 cup cheddar, mayonnaise, and eggs until smooth; season with salt and pepper and set sauce aside.

3 Heat broiler. Pour sauce evenly over the top of broccoli and sprinkle with mushrooms, bread crumbs, and remaining 1 cup cheddar. Broil until cheese is melted and lightly browned, about 2 minutes.

BROCCOLI STRASCINATI

Broccoli with Garlic & Hot Pepper

SERVES 2–4

This Roman dish, which pairs beautifully with pork chops, can be made with regular broccoli, broccoli rabe, cauliflower, or romanesco.

¼ cup extra-virgin olive oil

1 head broccoli, cut into florets

3 cloves garlic, smashed

½ tsp. crushed red chile flakes

Kosher salt, to taste

Heat oil in a 12″ skillet over medium-high heat. Add broccoli and cook, turning occasionally, until lightly browned, 6–8 minutes. Sprinkle in 2 tbsp. water, add garlic, and cook until golden, 2–3 minutes. Add chile and cook until toasted, about 2 minutes. Season with salt.

BROCCOLI WITH SICILIAN SAUCE

SERVES 8

"For me, Thanksgiving isn't a holiday unless there is some piece of Italy on the table," says radio host Lynne Rossetto Kasper, who gave us this recipe. "No region does tomato sauces like Sicily, and this sauce, which straddles the line between a pasta sauce and vegetable dressing, is intensely delicious, with its mass of sautéed onions, its reduction of wine, vinegar, garlic, and tomato, and its near-to-Arabic finish of olives, raisins, and pine nuts." It's perfect over broccoli.

2 heads broccoli, cut into florets

Kosher salt and freshly ground black pepper, to taste

3 tbsp. extra-virgin olive oil

4 sprigs fresh flat-leaf parsley, finely chopped

3 medium red onions, thinly sliced

½ cup dry red wine

2 tbsp. red wine vinegar

1 heaping tbsp. tomato paste

½ tsp. dried oregano

⅛ tsp. crushed red chile flakes

3 cloves garlic, thinly sliced

1 28-oz. can whole, peeled tomatoes in juice, crushed by hand

⅓ cup pitted black Sicilian olives

⅓ cup seedless raisins

⅓ cup pine nuts, toasted (optional)

1 Set a collapsible steamer in the bottom of a tall pot. Add water to just below the steamer. Cover and bring to a boil over high heat. Lay broccoli in a crosshatch pattern in steamer and steam, covered, until tender, 6–8 minutes. Transfer broccoli to a serving dish and season with salt. Set aside at room temperature.

2 Heat oil in a large skillet over medium-high heat. Add the parsley and onions, season with salt and pepper, and cook, stirring often, until onions are softened and browned, 10–15 minutes. Add wine, vinegar, tomato paste, oregano, chile flakes, and garlic and cook, stirring occasionally, until mixture is reduced to a glaze, 4–5 minutes. Stir in tomatoes with their liquid and bring sauce to a boil. Lower heat to medium-low and simmer uncovered, stirring occasionally, until somewhat thick, 8–10 minutes. Add olives and simmer until sauce thickens further, about 10 minutes more. Stir in raisins. Spoon the tomato sauce over room-temperature broccoli and sprinkle with pine nuts, if you like.

SLOW-COOKED BROCCOLI RABE

Cime di Rapa Fritte

SERVES 4–6

Notoriously bitter and tough, broccoli rabe becomes mellow and supple when cooked slowly in a bath of water and olive oil. Simply seasoned with garlic and chile flakes, this Italian home-cooking classic is true comfort food.

1¼	cups olive oil
1½	tsp. crushed red chile flakes
12	cloves garlic, thinly sliced
2¼	lb. broccoli rabe, thick stems removed, cut into 2″ pieces
	Kosher salt and freshly ground black pepper, to taste

1 Heat ¾ cup oil, chile flakes, and half the garlic in a 12″ skillet over medium-high heat and cook, stirring occasionally, until garlic is lightly browned, about 2 minutes. Add broccoli rabe and ½ cup water, reduce heat to medium-low, and cover skillet. Cook, stirring occasionally, until very soft, about 1¼ hours.

2 Meanwhile, place remaining ½ cup oil and garlic in a 1-qt. saucepan over medium-high heat. Cook, stirring occasionally, until garlic is crisp and golden, about 5 minutes. Drain and set garlic chips aside.

3 To serve, season broccoli rabe with salt and pepper and top with reserved garlic chips.

Brussels Sprouts

BRUSSELS SPROUTS GRATIN

SERVES 4

This recipe blends sweet roasted Brussels sprouts with roasted garlic and a silky mornay sauce. A panko topping with lemon zest adds crunch and zing.

½	cup panko bread crumbs
2	tsp. unsalted butter, melted
2	tsp. minced fresh flat-leaf parsley
2	tsp. grated lemon zest
1½	oz. Gruyère cheese, grated
1½	tsp. kosher salt, plus more to taste
½	tsp. freshly ground black pepper, plus more to taste
4	cloves garlic, unpeeled
3	tbsp. olive oil
1	lb. Brussels sprouts, trimmed and halved lengthwise
6	shallots, thinly sliced
3	slices bacon, chopped
1	tbsp. fresh lemon juice
1	tbsp. unsalted butter
2	tsp. flour
1	cup heavy cream
2	sprigs fresh thyme
1	oz. Parmigiano-Reggiano, grated

1 Make the gratin topping: In a small bowl, combine panko, butter, parsley, 1 tsp. lemon zest, 1 oz. Gruyère, and salt and pepper to taste. Toss lightly and set aside.

2 Heat oven to 400°. Make a pouch with a sheet of aluminum foil that has been folded in half. Place garlic and 2 tbsp. olive oil into the pouch and fold the sides over to seal. Roast in oven for 15 minutes. Remove and let cool. Press the garlic from the peels and set confit aside.

3 Heat oven to 400°. In a medium bowl, toss sprouts with remaining 1 tbsp. oil, 1 tsp. salt, and ¼ tsp. pepper. Place sprouts on a baking sheet that can hold them in a single layer. Roast until browned and can be pierced by a fork with a little resistance, about 10 minutes. Set aside.

4 Heat a sauté pan over medium heat. Add shallots and bacon, stirring frequently until fat is rendered and shallots begin to caramelize, about 4 minutes. Add reserved garlic confit and remaining lemon zest. Deglaze the pan with lemon juice. Stir and remove from heat. Toss with Brussels sprouts.

5 Make the mornay sauce: In a 4-qt. saucepan, melt the butter. Add flour to make a roux and cook until it smells toasted and is light brown, about 30 seconds. Add cream and thyme, stirring vigorously to avoid lumps. Heat to a simmer, stirring continuously, about 2 minutes. Remove from heat and pour sauce through a sieve, removing thyme. Return sauce to the saucepan and add remaining ½ oz. Gruyère and the Parmigiano. Stir until cheeses melt. Season with ½ tsp. salt and ¼ tsp. pepper.

6 Pile sprouts into a 10″ oval gratin dish. Pour mornay sauce over sprouts and sprinkle bread crumb mixture over the top. Cover loosely with foil and bake until bubbling, about 15 minutes. Remove foil and cook until top is nicely browned, about 5 minutes. Remove from oven and let rest for 10 minutes. Serve warm.

BRUSSELS SPROUTS WITH BACON

SERVES 6–8

Brussels sprouts caramelized in rich bacon fat makes for an absolutely divine sweet-salty combination.

¾	lb. slab bacon, cut into ½″ matchsticks
1	tbsp. olive oil
2	tbsp. unsalted butter
2	lb. Brussels sprouts, trimmed and halved lengthwise Kosher salt and freshly ground black pepper, to taste

1 Heat slab bacon and oil in a heavy skillet over medium-high heat. Cook, stirring occasionally, until bacon is crisp and fat is rendered, about 15 minutes. Using a slotted spoon, transfer bacon to paper towels to drain, then pour off all but 2 tbsp. bacon drippings.

2 Return skillet to heat and add butter. Add Brussels sprouts and cook, stirring occasionally, until golden brown and caramelized, about 15 minutes. Season with salt and pepper and serve garnished with reserved bacon.

Cabbage

GUJARATI-STYLE CABBAGE

Sambharo

SERVES 6–8

In this dish from the western Indian state of Gujarat, simple shredded cabbage is transformed into a fragrant side dish with the addition of cilantro, lime, and an array of spices including turmeric and cumin. It's crucial to salt the cabbage to extract some of its moisture.

1	green cabbage, cored and shredded Kosher salt, to taste
2	tbsp. peanut oil
2	tsp. black mustard seeds
2	tsp. asafoetida
2	tsp. cumin seeds
10	fresh curry leaves
2	tsp. ground turmeric
3	plum tomatoes, chopped
3	cubanelle peppers, seeded and thinly sliced crosswise
1	serrano chile, thinly sliced
5	tbsp. roughly chopped fresh cilantro
¼	cup fresh lime juice
2	tbsp. sugar

1 Toss cabbage and salt in a bowl. Let wilt for 1 hour. Squeeze excess liquid from cabbage; set cabbage aside and discard liquid.

2 Heat oil in a 12″ skillet over medium-high heat. Add mustard seeds, asafoetida, cumin, and curry leaves and cook, stirring, until fragrant, about 2 minutes. Add reserved cabbage, turmeric, tomatoes, peppers, and serrano and cook, stirring, until cabbage is crisp-tender, 6–7 minutes. Stir in cilantro, lime juice, and sugar. Season with salt and cook until flavors meld, 3–5 minutes.

BRAISED GREEN CABBAGE WITH SLAB BACON

SERVES 6–8

Smoky bacon and plenty of garlic and onion boost the flavor of the cabbage in this winter side dish, a staple on the Christmas dinner table of chef and writer Mike Colameco.

½	lb. slab bacon, cut into ½″ matchsticks
6	cloves garlic, thinly sliced
1	large onion, thinly sliced
1	large head green cabbage, cored and sliced ½″ thick Kosher salt and freshly ground black pepper, to taste

Heat bacon in an 8-qt. saucepan over medium-high heat and cook, stirring occasionally, until fat is rendered and bacon is crisp, 7–9 minutes. Add garlic and onion and cook, stirring occasionally, until golden, 5–7 minutes. Add cabbage, salt, and pepper and cook until slightly wilted, about 6 minutes. Reduce heat to medium and cook, covered and stirring occasionally, until cabbage is tender, 45 minutes to 1 hour. Season with more salt and pepper.

GERMAN BRAISED RED CABBAGE

Blaukraut

SERVES 6–8

The secret to this dish, a classic German accompaniment to a meat course, is keeping the pot covered, which helps preserve the cabbage's deep purple hue.

- 6 slices bacon, roughly chopped
- 1 tbsp. sugar
- 1 large onion, finely chopped
  Kosher salt and freshly ground black pepper, to taste
- 1 large Granny Smith apple, peeled, cored, and coarsely chopped
- ⅓ cup port wine
- ¼ cup red wine vinegar
- 1 large head red cabbage, cored and finely shredded
- 2 cups chicken stock
- ¼ cup red currant jelly

1 Cook bacon in a large, wide pot over medium-high heat until just crisp, about 5 minutes. Add sugar and cook, stirring constantly, for 30 seconds more. Add onions and salt and pepper and cook, stirring occasionally, until onions are golden and soft, about 10 minutes. Stir in apples, reduce heat to medium-low, cover, and cook until tender, 6–8 minutes.

2 Add port, vinegar, and cabbage to the onion-apple mixture; stir to combine. Cover pot and cook until cabbage is bright purple and slightly wilted, 5–7 minutes. Add stock, salt, and pepper. Increase heat to medium-high and bring to a boil. Reduce heat to medium-low, cover, and cook until cabbage is tender but still red, about 1¼ hours. Stir in red currant jelly, season with more salt and pepper, and cook briefly, 4–5 minutes more. Serve warm.

CABBAGE & BACON PIE

SERVES 6–8

In Ireland, the term "bacon" is used loosely; the meat in this hearty cabbage-and-potato casserole is actually ham.

- 6 russet potatoes, peeled and quartered
- 14 tbsp. butter
- 6 tbsp. flour
- 5 cups milk
- ⅔ cup chopped fresh flat-leaf parsley
  Kosher salt and freshly ground black pepper, to taste
- 1 head Savoy cabbage, chopped
- 1 cup heavy cream
- 2 scallions, finely chopped
- 1½ lb. baked ham, diced

1 Heat oven to 400°. Put potatoes into a medium pot, cover with cold water, and bring to a boil over medium-high heat until soft, 30–35 minutes.

2 Meanwhile, melt 6 tbsp. butter in a medium saucepan over medium heat. Add flour and cook, stirring, for 2 minutes. Add milk and cook, stirring often, until sauce thickens, 8–10 minutes. Add parsley, salt, and pepper and set aside.

3 Boil cabbage in a medium pot of boiling salted water over high heat until soft, about 5 minutes. Drain and set aside.

4 Drain potatoes, return them to pot, and mash until smooth. Stir in cream, the remaining 8 tbsp. butter, scallions, salt, and pepper and set aside.

5 Scatter ham in bottom of a large baking dish, cover with cabbage, then sauce, then mashed potatoes, piping potatoes through a pastry bag fitted with a ½" star tip, if you like. Bake until bubbling hot and golden on top, 30–35 minutes.

Carrots

MAPLE-GLAZED CARROTS

SERVES 8

Braising carrots slowly in butter, rather than steaming or boiling them, brings out their natural sugars. Maple syrup adds a delicate glaze and a rich flavor.

- 12 large carrots, peeled
- 8 tbsp. butter
- ¼ cup maple syrup
- ½ tsp. fresh lemon juice
  Kosher salt and freshly ground black pepper, to taste
- 1 tbsp. fresh thyme leaves

1 Cut carrots into 2″ lengths, then halve or quarter pieces lengthwise so that all carrots are equal-size strips.

2 Melt butter in a large heavy sauté pan over medium-low heat. Add carrots, cover, and braise, stirring occasionally, until carrots are fork-tender, 20–30 minutes.

3 Increase heat to medium and stir in syrup and lemon juice. Cook for 2 minutes, then season with salt and pepper. Add thyme and mix well.

INDIAN-STYLE CARROTS WITH MUSTARD SEEDS

Gadjar Kari

SERVES 4–6

These carrots are stewed long enough to concentrate their sweetness. Mustard seeds, curry leaves, and chiles provide warm and earthy notes.

- 2 tbsp. canola oil
- 1 tsp. brown mustard seeds
- 2 tsp. yellow split peas, lightly crushed
- 1 tsp. ground turmeric
- ½ tsp. paprika
- 24 fresh or dried curry leaves
- 2 dried chiles de árbol, stemmed and torn into small pieces
- 1¼ lb. small to medium carrots, thinly sliced crosswise
    Kosher salt and freshly ground black pepper, to taste
    Cooked white rice, for serving

1 Heat oil in a 12″ skillet over medium-high heat. Add mustard seeds, cover skillet with lid, and cook, shaking pan occasionally, until seeds stop popping, about 30 seconds.

2 Remove lid and stir in peas, turmeric, paprika, curry leaves, and chiles. Cook, stirring often, until fragrant, about 2 minutes. Add carrots along with 1 cup water and bring to a boil. Reduce heat to medium-low and cook, covered and stirring occasionally, until carrots are very soft, about 20 minutes.

3 Uncover pan, raise heat to high, and cook, stirring occasionally, until excess liquid evaporates, about 5 minutes. Season with salt and pepper. Serve hot or at room temperature with rice.

Cauliflower

ROASTED CAULIFLOWER WITH TAHINI SAUCE

SERVES 4–6

In this addictive Lebanese side dish, roasting cauliflower in a very hot oven gives it an appealing crisp-tender texture and toasty flavor that pairs perfectly with a tart tahini dipping sauce.

- ¼ cup extra-virgin olive oil
- 4 tsp. ground cumin
- 2 medium heads cauliflower, cored and cut into 1½″ florets
    Kosher salt and freshly ground black pepper, to taste
- ½ cup tahini
- 3 cloves garlic, smashed and minced into a paste
- 2 tbsp. fresh lemon juice

1 Heat oven to 500°. Toss together oil, cumin, cauliflower, salt, and pepper in a large bowl. Transfer to 2 baking sheets; spread out evenly. Bake, rotating pans from top to bottom and front to back, until cauliflower is browned and tender, 25–30 minutes.

2 Meanwhile, combine tahini, garlic, lemon juice, and ½ cup water in a small bowl and season with salt. Serve cauliflower hot or at room temperature with tahini sauce.

LEMONY FRIED CAULIFLOWER

Culupidia Frita con Limón

SERVES 4–6

In this take on this traditional Sephardic Jewish dish, cauliflower florets are coated in a flour-and-egg batter, fried, and then bathed in lemon juice. As a side or a snack, this dish is crunchy and tender, brimming with fresh, tangy flavor.

- 1 large head cauliflower, cored and cut into 1″ florets
    Canola oil, for frying
- 1½ cups flour
- 1 tbsp. grated lemon zest, plus lemon wedges for serving
- 1 tsp. ground turmeric
- 1 tsp. cayenne pepper
    Kosher salt and freshly ground black pepper, to taste

5   eggs
     Roughly chopped fresh flat-leaf parsley,
     for garnish

1 Bring a large pot of salted water to a boil; add cauliflower and cook until just tender, about 5 minutes. Using a slotted spoon, transfer to an ice bath until chilled; drain and dry completely with paper towels.

2 Heat 2″ oil in a 6-qt. saucepan until a deep-fry thermometer reads 350°. Mix together flour, lemon zest, turmeric, cayenne, salt, and pepper into a shallow baking dish. Whisk eggs in a bowl. Working in batches, dip cauliflower in flour, shaking off excess, then in egg, and once again in flour. Fry, flipping as needed, until golden and crisp, about 45 seconds. Using a slotted spoon, transfer to paper towels to drain; season with salt and pepper. Garnish with parsley and serve with lemon wedges.

CAULIFLOWER MANCHURIAN
SERVES 4

India's Chinese population has given rise to a rich Indo-Chinese culinary tradition; notably, this iconic dish of fried cauliflower in a sweet-sour-spicy sauce, which draws inspiration from the techniques and pantries of both cuisines.

 12   cloves garlic
  4   2″ pieces fresh ginger, peeled; 3 cut into
       thin coins, 1 julienned
  1   head cauliflower, cored and cut into large florets
  ½   tsp. kosher salt, plus more to taste
  ⅔   cup cornstarch
  ⅔   cup flour
  1   tsp. cayenne pepper
       Freshly ground white pepper
  2   tsp. plus 3 tbsp. soy sauce
       Peanut oil, for frying
  2   small onions, chopped
8–10   bird's eye chiles, stemmed and thinly sliced
  ½   cup ketchup
 1½   tbsp. sesame oil
  2   scallions, thinly sliced, for garnish
       Fresh cilantro leaves, for garnish
       Cooked white rice, for serving (optional)

1 Purée garlic, ginger coins, and ⅓ cup water in a blender; set aside. Boil cauliflower in a pot of salted water until tender, 6–7 minutes; drain.

2 Whisk together cornstarch, flour, cayenne pepper, ½ tsp. salt, and ¼ tsp. white pepper in a bowl. Stir in half the garlic-ginger paste, 2 tsp. soy sauce, and ¾ cup water to make a batter. Pour oil into a large, deep skillet to a depth of 1″ and heat over medium-high heat until a deep-fry thermometer reads 350°. Working in batches, dip cauliflower in batter and fry, flipping as needed, until golden, 5–6 minutes. Using a slotted spoon, transfer to a paper towel–lined plate.

3 Drain all but about 6 tbsp. of the oil from the skillet. Add onions and cook for 3–4 minutes. Add chiles and remaining garlic-ginger paste; cook until paste is lightly browned, 3–4 minutes. Add ketchup, remaining 3 tbsp. soy sauce, sesame oil, and ⅓ cup water. Bring to a boil, lower heat to medium-low, and simmer until thick, 1–2 minutes. Season with salt and pepper, then toss cauliflower in sauce. Garnish with remaining julienned ginger, scallions, and cilantro. Serve with white rice, if you like.

OLIVE OIL–BRAISED CAULIFLOWER & BROCCOLI
SERVES 4–6

Based on a recipe from Traci Des Jardins, chef and co-owner of Jardinière in San Francisco, this flavorful mix of broccoli, cauliflower, zucchini, and potatoes is utterly transformed by a slow braise in aromatic olive oil.

  1   cup extra-virgin olive oil
  1   tbsp. anchovy paste
  ½   tsp. crushed red chile flakes
  6   sun-dried tomatoes, thinly sliced lengthwise
  6   cloves garlic, smashed
  6   sprigs fresh rosemary
  1   lemon, ends trimmed, thinly sliced crosswise,
       and seeds removed
  1   large zucchini, cut on diagonal into 1½″-long pieces
  1   lb. baby Yukon gold or new potatoes
  1   medium head broccoli, cored and cut into florets,
       stalk cut into large pieces
  ½   medium head cauliflower, cored and cut into
       florets, stalk cut into large pieces
  2   tbsp. finely chopped fresh flat-leaf parsley
       Leaves from 2 sprigs fresh marjoram
       Kosher salt and freshly ground black pepper,
       to taste

1 Put oil, anchovy paste, chile flakes, tomatoes, garlic, rosemary, and lemon slices into a 6-qt. Dutch oven. Place over medium-high heat and cook, stirring occasionally, until fragrant and garlic and lemon slices are lightly browned, about 5 minutes.

2 Add zucchini in a single layer and cook, without stirring, until lightly browned, about 5 minutes. Flip the zucchini and cook for 5 minutes more.

3 Add potatoes, broccoli, and cauliflower to the pot and stir once or twice to coat in oil. Cook, covered, without stirring, until vegetables begin to brown and soften, about 30 minutes.

4 Stir vegetables gently, replace the lid, and reduce the heat to medium-low. Cook until vegetables are very soft and tender, about 1 hour more.

5 Remove vegetables from heat and stir in parsley and marjoram. Season with salt and pepper. Serve immediately.

ALOO GOBI

Curried Cauliflower & Potatoes

SERVES 6–8

This Indian classic derives its great depth of flavor from a base of caramelized onions and an abundance of spices.

- ½ cup canola oil
- 2 medium russet potatoes, halved lengthwise and cut crosswise into 1½″ pieces
- 1 large head cauliflower, cored and cut into medium florets
- 3 medium onions, finely chopped
- 1 2″ piece fresh ginger, peeled and cut into 1″ matchsticks
- 2 canned whole, peeled tomatoes, crushed by hand
- 1½ tsp. ground coriander
- ½ tsp. cayenne pepper
- ½ tsp. ground turmeric
  Kosher salt and freshly ground black pepper, to taste
- ½ cup fresh or thawed frozen green peas
- ½ tsp. ground cumin
- ½ tsp. garam masala

1 Heat oil in a 12″ skillet over medium-high heat. Add potatoes and cook, turning as needed, until browned all over and barely cooked through, about 12 minutes. Using a slotted spoon, transfer potatoes to paper towels to drain; set aside. Add cauliflower to oil and cook, turning as needed, until browned all over and barely cooked through, about 10 minutes. Transfer to paper towels to drain and set aside.

2 Return skillet to medium-high heat, add onions, and cook, stirring, until lightly browned, about 12 minutes. Add ginger and cook, stirring, until onions are slightly darker, about 2 minutes. Add tomatoes and cook, stirring, until caramelized, 4–6 minutes. Add coriander, cayenne, turmeric, and salt and pepper and cook until fragrant, about 1 minute. Add potatoes, cauliflower, peas, and 1 tbsp. water, stir to combine, and cover skillet. Cook until potatoes and cauliflower are cooked through, about 5 minutes. Remove from heat and stir in cumin and garam masala. Serve hot.

Corn

ELOTE

Grilled Corn on the Cob with Mayonnaise, Cheese & Chile

SERVES 6

Smoky, chewy corn slathered with an array of savory toppings is a ubiquitous Mexican street-food snack.

- 6 ears corn, in husks
- 3 tbsp. butter, melted
- ½ cup mayonnaise
- ⅓ cup finely crumbled queso añejo (aged cows' milk cheese), or grated pecorino romano or Parmigiano-Reggiano
- 1 tbsp. ground dried chile de árbol or cayenne

1 Put corn in a large, deep bowl, cover with cold water, and weight with a plate to submerge. Soak corn for 30 minutes, then drain. Meanwhile, build a medium-high fire in a charcoal grill or heat a gas grill to medium-high, and adjust grill rack to 5″ above heat.

2 Grill corn, turning frequently, until husks are blackened, 10–15 minutes. Remove from heat, let cool, then peel off husks and remove silk.

3 Brush corn with butter, return to grill, and cook, turning frequently, until browned all over, about 5 minutes. Spread each ear with some mayonnaise, roll in cheese, and sprinkle with chile.

MAQUE CHOUX

SERVES 4

This Cajun dish of corn, peppers, and okra is Native American in both its composition (it's similar to succotash, this page, another New World dish adapted by European settlers), and its name, most likely a French-Creole transliteration. It's often served as a side dish, but it pairs well with rice and seafood or chicken to make a main course. This version, a classic rendition, comes from Commander's Palace in New Orleans.

- 2 slices bacon, chopped
- 2 tbsp. unsalted butter
- 3 cloves garlic, finely chopped
- 1 shallot, finely chopped
- 1 red bell pepper, seeded and finely chopped
- 1 jalapeño, stemmed, seeded, and finely chopped
- 5 small okra, stemmed and thinly sliced crosswise
- 4 ears corn, shucked, kernels sliced off (or one 10-oz. package frozen corn, about 2 cups)
- 4 scallions, thinly sliced
   Kosher salt and freshly ground black pepper, to taste

In a 12″ skillet over medium-high heat, cook bacon, stirring occasionally, until crisp, about 7 minutes. Using a slotted spoon, transfer bacon to a paper towel–lined plate; set aside. Melt 1 tbsp. butter in hot bacon fat. Add garlic, shallots, peppers, and jalapeños and cook over medium-high heat, stirring occasionally, until lightly browned, about 5 minutes. Increase heat to high, add okra and corn, and cook, stirring occasionally, until crisp-tender, about 6 minutes. Stir in scallions and remaining butter and season with salt and pepper. Garnish with reserved bacon.

SUMMER CORN SUCCOTASH
SERVES 6–8

This version of the American summer mainstay, elevated with grilled sweet corn plus fresh edamame in place of the traditional limas, came to us from home cook Neal Ballard of Lawrence, Kansas.

- 8 ears corn, in husks
- 1 large Vidalia onion, cut crosswise ½″ thick
- 2 cups frozen shelled edamame
   Kosher salt and freshly ground black pepper, to taste
- 1 cup olive oil
- ¼ cup white wine vinegar
- ¼ cup roughly chopped fresh tarragon
- 2 pints cherry or grape tomatoes, halved

1 Pull husks back from corn but don't remove; discard silk and replace husks. Soak in cold water for 30 minutes; drain.

Build a medium-hot fire in a charcoal grill or heat a gas grill to medium-high. Grill corn, turning as needed, until husks are slightly charred and kernels are tender, 15–20 minutes; let cool, discard husks, and slice kernels off cobs into a large bowl. Grill the onion, flipping once, until slightly charred and tender, 3–5 minutes. Roughly chop; add to the bowl with corn.

2 Boil edamame in a 2-qt. saucepan of salted water until tender, 2–3 minutes. Transfer edamame to a bowl of ice water until chilled. Drain and add corn and onion along with oil, vinegar, tarragon, tomatoes, salt, and pepper. Toss to combine and serve.

MRS. APPLE'S CREAMED CORN
SERVES 6

The late author and food and wine expert R. W. Apple Jr. shared this old family recipe with us. It is based on dried sweet corn, a Pennsylvania Dutch staple ingredient that's rarely found outside the area (except, of course, online!). The dried corn lends this dish a firmer texture and a nutty taste.

- 4 cups (1 lb.) dried corn
- 4 cups milk
- 3 cups heavy cream
- 1 tbsp. sugar
- 1 tbsp. salt, plus more to taste
- 4 tbsp. butter
   Freshly ground black pepper

1 Place dried corn in a large bowl and cover with milk and cream. Cover with plastic wrap and refrigerate overnight.

2 Transfer corn mixture to a large saucepan. Add sugar, 1 tbsp. salt, and butter. Bring to a boil over medium-high heat, stirring frequently. Reduce heat to low and simmer, stirring occasionally, for about 30 minutes. Adjust seasoning with salt and pepper and serve.

EAST HAMPTON CORN PUDDING
SERVES 8

This corn pudding recipe is adapted from the *Neighborhood House Cookbook*, compiled by East Hampton's Women's Service Club, a "small group of ladies still carrying on the tradition of old-fashioned, home-cooked covered dish suppers."

5 ears corn, shucked, kernels sliced off
(about 2½ cups)
2 tsp. sugar
3 eggs
2 cups half-and-half
2 tbsp. melted butter
¼ tsp. freshly grated nutmeg
Salt and freshly ground black pepper

1 Heat oven to 350°. Put half the corn in a blender or food processor; set aside remaining corn.

2 Add sugar, eggs, half-and-half, butter, nutmeg, and salt and pepper to blender. Process for 1–2 minutes, then pour into a greased 9″× 5″ loaf pan. Gently mix in the remaining corn. Bake until golden and a toothpick inserted in the middle of the pudding comes out clean, about 1 hour.

CORN SOUFFLÉ

SERVES 1–2

Take advantage of fresh summer corn—white corn, if available—for this garlicky, gingery soufflé.

5 tbsp. butter
¾ cup grated Gruyère cheese
2 cloves garlic, minced
2 ears corn, shucked, kernels sliced off
(about 1 cup)
½ tsp. minced fresh ginger
Kosher salt and freshly ground white pepper
2½ tbsp. flour
¾ cup milk, warm
3 eggs, separated, at room temperature

1 Heat oven to 450°. Grease a small soufflé dish (6½″ diameter, 2½″ deep) with 1 tbsp. butter. Sprinkle with ¼ cup Gruyère.

2 Melt 2 tbsp. butter in a small skillet over medium heat. Add garlic and cook until fragrant, about 1 minute. Add corn and ginger and cook, stirring occasionally, until corn begins to soften, 2–4 minutes. Remove from heat, season with salt and pepper, and set aside to cool.

3 Melt 2 tbsp. butter in a heavy-bottomed small saucepan over medium heat. Add flour and cook, stirring constantly with a wooden spoon, for 2 minutes (do not brown). Remove from heat and, when bubbling subsides, whisk in half of milk. Return to heat and stir in remaining milk. Cook, stirring, until very thick, about 2 minutes.

Season with salt and pepper, transfer to a large bowl, and whisk in egg yolks, one at a time.

4 Beat egg whites in a nonreactive bowl until stiff peaks form. Add one third of egg whites to egg yolk mixture and gently fold together. While folding in remaining egg whites, sprinkle in corn mixture and remaining ½ cup Gruyère. Do not overmix.

5 Spoon into soufflé dish. Make sure oven rack is low enough to allow soufflé room to rise about 2″ above rim of dish. Bake until soufflé is browned, 18–22 minutes. Serve immediately.

Cucumber

JULIA CHILD'S BUTTER-BAKED CUCUMBERS

SERVES 4–6

This artful technique—in which cucumber batons are slowly roasted with butter and fresh herbs, inspired by a recipe in Julia Child's *Mastering the Art of French Cooking*—transforms a famously crispy vegetable into something meltingly sweet and tender.

3 large cucumbers, peeled, quartered lengthwise, and seeded
1 tbsp. kosher salt
1 tbsp. sugar
1 tbsp. white wine vinegar
3 tbsp. roughly chopped mixed fresh herbs, such as dill and parsley
2 tbsp. unsalted butter, melted
Freshly ground black pepper, to taste

1 Cut cucumbers into ½″ triangles and place in a colander set over a bowl. Toss with salt, sugar, and vinegar; let sit for 30 minutes to drain, then pat dry using paper towels.

2 Heat oven to 375°. Toss reserved cucumbers with herbs, butter, and pepper in a 9″× 13″ baking dish; spread into an even layer. Bake, stirring once halfway through, until cucumbers are crisp-tender, 15–20 minutes.

FRIED CUCUMBERS

SERVES 8–12

This appetizer plays with cucumber's crunchy appeal by coating slices with a spiced cornmeal crust and frying them up until piping hot. A cool green goddess dip squelches the heat.

> Canola oil, for frying
> 2 cups cornmeal
> 1½ cups flour
> 2 tbsp. baking powder
> 1 tbsp. celery salt
> 1½ tsp. sweet paprika
> 1½ tsp. kosher salt, plus more for sprinkling
> 1½ tsp. freshly ground black pepper
> 1½ tsp. garlic powder
> 1½ tsp. onion powder
> 1 tsp. cayenne pepper
> 1½ lb. cucumbers, halved lengthwise, seeded, and cut into 3″ × ½″ sticks
> Green Goddess Sauce (page 592), for dipping

Pour oil to a depth of 2″ into a 6-qt. Dutch oven and heat over medium-high heat until a deep-fry thermometer reads 375°. Whisk together cornmeal, flour, baking powder, celery salt, paprika, kosher salt, pepper, garlic powder, onion powder, and cayenne in a large bowl. Working in batches, add cucumber slices to cornmeal mixture and toss evenly to coat; transfer to oil and fry until golden brown and crisp, about 2 minutes. Using a slotted spoon, transfer slices to a wire rack set over a baking sheet to drain. Serve hot, with dipping sauce.

INDIAN-STYLE CUCUMBER WITH BLACK-EYED PEAS
Olan

SERVES 6

This simple Keralan curry is traditionally made with ash gourd, but author Maya Kaimal's Aunty Kamala prepared her version using fresh and watery cucumbers.

> 1 cucumber, peeled, seeded, quartered lengthwise, and cut crosswise into ⅛″ slices
> ½ cup canned coconut milk
> 2 fresh hot green chiles (serrano or bird's eye), slit lengthwise down one side
> 15 fresh or dried curry leaves
> ½ tsp. salt
> ⅔ cup canned black-eyed peas
> 2 tsp. coconut oil

1 Put cucumbers, ¼ cup coconut milk, ½ cup water, chiles, curry leaves, and salt in a medium saucepan and bring to a boil over medium-high heat. Reduce heat to medium-low,

add black-eyed peas, and simmer until cucumbers are soft and translucent, about 5 minutes.

2 Add remaining ¼ cup coconut milk to the cucumber and peas and bring just to a simmer, then remove from heat. Stir in coconut oil and add salt to taste. Serve warm.

STUFFED CUCUMBER KIMCHI
Oi Sobagi
MAKES ABOUT 20 PIECES (SEE PHOTO, PAGE 427)

Cucumber rounds stuffed with a spicy vegetable filling are a well-loved snack in Korea, especially during the hot summer months. The filling varies depending on what a home cook might have on hand, but the version in this recipe—a tangy, savory combination of garlic, carrot, ginger, and Asian pear—is one of the most popular.

> 1¼ lb. Japanese or Kirby cucumbers
> 1 tbsp. kosher salt
> 3 tbsp. gochugaru chile powder
> 1½ tbsp. finely chopped saeu jeot salted shrimp
> 1 tbsp. finely chopped carrot
> 1 tbsp. aek jeot (Korean anchovy sauce) or fish sauce
> 2 tsp. sesame seeds
> 2 tsp. sugar
> 30 fresh garlic chives, cut into 1″ pieces
> 4 cloves garlic, finely chopped and mashed into a paste
> 3 scallions, white and light green parts only, thinly sliced on the diagonal
> 1 1″ piece fresh ginger, peeled, finely chopped, and mashed
> ¼ Asian pear, peeled, cored, and finely chopped
> 1 tbsp. pine nuts

1 Trim the round ends off of cucumbers, then slice them crosswise into 1½″ lengths. Working with 1 cucumber piece at a time, stand piece on its end and make 1 deep vertical cut roughly three-quarters of the way to the bottom; make another, identical cut perpendicular to the first one to form a cross-shaped opening. Transfer cucumber pieces cut side up to a large bowl. Sprinkle salt over cucumbers, gently working some of the salt into the openings; let sit for 30 minutes. Rinse cucumbers and pat dry; set aside.

2 In a medium bowl, stir together the chile powder, salted shrimp, carrot, anchovy sauce, sesame seeds, sugar, garlic chives, garlic, scallions, ginger, and Asian pear. Working with 1 cucumber piece at a time, stuff about 2 tsp. of filling into the opening. Press 3 or 4 pine nuts into the stuffing of each cucumber. Transfer to a platter and serve immediately.

COOK'S NOTE *Oi sobagi* are also delicious when allowed to ferment: Nestle cucumber pieces, stuffed side up, in a plastic container; cover and let sit for 1 day at room temperature, then refrigerate until chilled. Cucumbers will continue to soften and will keep in the refrigerator for up to 1 week.

Eggplant

EGGPLANT IN CHARMOULA

SERVES 4

Charmoula, a Moroccan relish, is best known as a tart marinade for fish. Here, its fresh taste is a perfect complement to the warm creaminess of eggplant. This dish should be prepared at least an hour ahead, to give the eggplant time to absorb the charmoula.

2	medium eggplants (about 1½ lb. total)
	Coarse salt
1	clove garlic, minced
1	tsp. sweet paprika
	Pinch hot paprika
¾	tsp. ground cumin
3	tbsp. finely chopped fresh cilantro
3	tbsp. finely chopped fresh flat-leaf parsley
3	tbsp. fresh lemon juice
½	cup extra-virgin olive oil

1 Slice eggplant into ¾" rounds and sprinkle lightly on both sides with salt. Place in a colander, cover with a cloth, and weight down the slices with a heavy pot or cans for 30 minutes, until the eggplant exudes its bitter juices.

2 Heat oven to 350°. Whisk together garlic, paprikas, cumin, half of cilantro and parsley, lemon juice, 2 tbsp. oil, and salt to taste in a small bowl; set aside.

3 Pat eggplant slices dry with paper towels and lightly brush each slice with oil. Spread them in a single layer on a baking sheet and bake until tender and golden, 25–30 minutes. This will prevent eggplant from absorbing too much oil during frying. Remove eggplant from oven and set aside to cool completely.

4 Heat remaining oil in a medium skillet over high heat. Add slices, one at a time, to hot oil and fry until crisp and brown on both sides, about 1 minute per side. Drain on paper towels and transfer to a shallow dish.

5 Whisk sauce once more and drizzle over eggplant. Sprinkle remaining cilantro and parsley on top. Let stand for 1 hour, then serve at room temperature.

CHARRED EGGPLANT WITH CHILE SAUCE & TAHINI

SERVES 2–4

To make Israeli chef Erez Komarovsky's delectable charred eggplant, choose young eggplants, which are more delicate and less bitter than their older counterparts. If you have a gas burner, try cooking each eggplant over the open flame for a few minutes to impart a smoky flavor.

2	small Italian eggplants (about 1 lb. total)
2	cups fresh cilantro leaves, chopped
1	cup fresh mint leaves, chopped
1	cup olive oil
¼	cup honey
6	cloves garlic, peeled
1	serrano chile, stemmed and seeded
	Zest and juice of 1 lemon
	Kosher salt and freshly ground black pepper, to taste
½	cup tahini, for serving
6	soft-boiled eggs, halved

1 Heat broiler. Place eggplant on a foil-lined baking sheet. Broil, turning as needed, until tender and charred, 8–10 minutes.

2 Purée cilantro, mint, oil, honey, garlic, chile, lemon zest and lemon juice, salt, and pepper in a food processor to make a smooth sauce. To serve, slice eggplant in half lengthwise, leaving stem attached. Season with salt and pepper. Spoon chile sauce and tahini over eggplant and arrange egg halves around eggplant on serving platter.

EGGPLANT WITH BALSAMIC VINEGAR, BASIL & CAPERS

SERVES 4

Sweet, mild eggplant pairs with briny capers, floral basil, and a drizzle of balsamic reduction in this recipe inspired by a dish served at Marseille's Le Bistrot d'Edouard.

½	cup balsamic vinegar
1	cup olive oil

2 small eggplants (about 1 lb. total), trimmed and sliced crosswise ⅓" thick
Kosher salt and freshly ground black pepper, to taste
2 tbsp. capers, drained
4 fresh basil leaves, thinly sliced

1 Simmer vinegar over medium heat in a 1-qt. saucepan until reduced to a thick syrup, about 15 minutes.

2 Heat half the oil in a 12" skillet over medium-high heat. Working in batches and adding more oil as needed, fry eggplant, flipping once, until golden brown, 5–7 minutes; transfer to paper towels to drain and season with salt and pepper. Arrange on a platter; drizzle with balsamic and garnish with capers and basil.

FRIED EGGPLANT WITH WALNUT SAUCE

Badridzhani Nigvsit

SERVES 6–8

Tender Japanese eggplant work best in this Georgian side dish of fried eggplant slices sandwiching a pesto-like walnut sauce.

1 cup walnuts, toasted
⅓ cup packed fresh cilantro leaves
¼ cup packed fresh basil leaves
¼ cup packed fresh flat-leaf parsley leaves
1 tsp. ground fenugreek
½ tsp. hot paprika
¼ tsp. ground turmeric
1 tbsp. red wine vinegar
1 clove garlic, minced
½ small yellow onion, roughly chopped
Kosher salt and freshly ground black pepper, to taste
1½ cups canola oil
4 small Japanese eggplants, trimmed and sliced lengthwise ½" thick
½ small red onion, thinly sliced crosswise into rings

1 Place walnuts, half each of the cilantro, basil, and parsley, plus fenugreek, paprika, turmeric, vinegar, garlic, yellow onion, salt, pepper, and ⅓ cup water in a food processor; purée until very smooth, about 2 minutes. Set sauce aside.

2 Heat oil in a 12" skillet over medium-high heat. Working in batches, fry eggplant, flipping once, until golden and cooked through, about 5 minutes. Transfer to paper towels to drain and cool; season with salt and pepper.

3 Spread each slice of eggplant with about 2 tbsp. walnut sauce and fold in half; transfer to a serving platter and garnish with remaining cilantro, basil, and parsley leaves and the red onions.

Escarole

ESCAROLE WITH PROSCIUTTO

SERVES 4

Fried slices of prosciutto provide a crisp contrast to sautéed escarole in this earthy Italian side dish.

Kosher salt, to taste
2 large heads escarole or chicory, tough outer leaves discarded, inner leaves roughly chopped
5 tbsp. extra-virgin olive oil
4 thin slices prosciutto, torn into strips
2 oz. cooked ham, finely chopped
6 cloves garlic, thinly sliced
½ tsp. crushed red chile flakes
Freshly ground black pepper, to taste
2 tbsp. fresh lemon juice

1 Bring a large pot of salted water to a boil. Add escarole and cook until tender, about 3 minutes. Drain escarole, reserving ¼ cup cooking liquid; transfer to a bowl. Heat 1 tbsp. oil in a 12" skillet over high heat. Add prosciutto strips and cook, flipping once, until crisp, about 1 minute. Use a slotted spoon to transfer prosciutto to paper towels; set aside. Add cooked ham to skillet and cook, stirring, until browned, about 5 minutes. Add reserved cooking liquid and scrape up any browned bits. Pour liquid into a bowl; set aside.

2 Return skillet to medium-high heat, add remaining 4 tbsp. oil, along with the garlic and chiles, and cook for 30 seconds. Add escarole, reserved ham, and cooking liquid and cook until hot, 2–3 minutes. Season with salt and pepper. Stir in the lemon juice. Garnish with prosciutto.

Fennel

FENNEL BAKED IN CREAM

Finocchio al Forno

SERVES 6–8

Chef Gabrielle Hamilton of Prune restaurant in New York City turned us on to this simple, classic Italian preparation, which calls for baking fennel in the oven with cream and Parmigiano to create a luxurious gratin.

- 2 large fennel bulbs, trimmed, halved lengthwise, and cut into ½″ wedges
- 2 cups heavy cream
- 1½ cups grated Parmigiano-Reggiano
  Kosher salt and freshly ground black pepper, to taste
- 4 tbsp. unsalted butter, cubed

1 Heat oven to 425°. In a bowl, toss together fennel, cream, and 1 cup Parmigiano; season with salt and pepper. Transfer to a 3-qt. baking dish and dot with butter. Cover dish with foil and bake for 1 hour.

2 Uncover dish and sprinkle with remaining ½ cup Parmigiano. Bake until fennel is tender, about 30 minutes.

FRIED FENNEL

Finocchio Fritto

SERVES 6–8

Fennel's bright licorice flavor stands up well to a crispy batter in this popular Italian appetizer or snack.

- 1¾ cups flour
- ¼ tsp. kosher salt, plus more for serving
- 1 egg, separated
- 1 tbsp. extra-virgin olive oil
- 2 tbsp. white wine
- 4 medium fennel bulbs, trimmed and cut into wedges
- 2 cups canola oil

1 Mix together ¾ cup flour and salt in a medium bowl and make a well in the center of the flour. Lightly beat egg yolk, olive oil, and wine in a small bowl, then pour into well. Gradually incorporate flour into liquid, stirring with a wooden spoon. Slowly add ¾ cup cold water, stirring constantly, until batter is smooth but still thick. Cover and refrigerate for at least 2 hours and up to 12 hours.

2 Bring a medium pot of salted water to a boil over high heat. Add fennel and cook until tender when pierced with a fork, 5–10 minutes. Use a slotted spoon to transfer fennel to paper towels to drain. Set fennel aside to cool.

3 Whisk egg white in a medium bowl until stiff (but not dry) peaks form, then fold into chilled batter with a rubber spatula. Heat canola oil in a large skillet over medium-high heat until a deep-fry thermometer reads 350°. Put remaining 1 cup flour in a medium bowl, dredge fennel wedges, and shake off excess flour. Dip fennel in batter to coat completely, then carefully put in hot oil and fry, turning once or twice, until crispy and golden, 1–2 minutes per side. Use a slotted spoon to transfer fennel to paper towels to drain. Sprinkle liberally with salt and serve hot.

Green Beans

GREEN BEANS ALMONDINE

SERVES 8

This iconic recipe—a Thanksgiving staple in many homes—is best with young green beans, as tender as you can find them.

- 2 lb. green beans, trimmed
- 2 tbsp. butter
- 1 cup slivered almonds
- 3 shallots, chopped
  Kosher salt and freshly ground black pepper, to taste

1 Cook green beans in a large pot of boiling salted water for 3–8 minutes, depending on tenderness desired. Drain and transfer to a large bowl of ice water to cool. Drain again, pat dry, and set aside.

2 Melt 2 tbsp. butter in a medium pot over medium heat. Add almonds and cook, stirring frequently with a wooden spoon, until golden, 2–3 minutes. Add shallots and cook, stirring often, until translucent, about 1 minute.

3 Add green beans, tossing to coat, and cook until heated through, about 5 minutes. Season to taste with salt and pepper.

HARICOTS VERTS & SNOW PEAS SAUTÉED IN BUTTER

SERVES 4

This simple, sweet dish is a showpiece for good produce. It's best made with young, fresh vegetables.

- ½ lb. haricots verts, trimmed
- ½ lb. snow peas, trimmed

2 tbsp. unsalted butter
1 tsp. extra-virgin olive oil

1 Bring a pot of salted water to a boil, add haricots verts, and cook for 2 minutes. Add snow peas and continue cooking until just tender, about 2 minutes more. Drain vegetables, rinse in cold water, then drain again.

2 Melt butter with olive oil in a skillet over medium heat, add cooked beans and peas, and sauté for about 3 minutes. Serve hot.

CHINESE DRY-FRIED LONG BEANS

Gan Bian Si Ji Dou

SERVES 2–4

The long beans in this dish are shallow-fried, a method that blisters them on the outside and renders them tender on the inside, with a whisper of a chew. Just enough pork for flavor cinches this dish, though the addition of preserved Sichuan mustard greens, with their salty, *xian-wei* flavor, makes it truly transcendent. If you can't find long beans, green beans may be substituted.

¼ cup canola oil
10 oz. long beans or green beans, cut into 2″ pieces
2 oz. ground pork
3 tbsp. finely chopped Pickled Mustard Greens (page 577)
1 tbsp. Shaoxing wine
1 tbsp. soy sauce
1 tsp. sesame oil
  Kosher salt and freshly ground black pepper, to taste

Heat 2 tbsp. oil in a 14″ flat-bottomed wok or 12″ skillet over medium-high heat. Add beans and cook, stirring often, until tender, about 5 minutes. Transfer to a bowl and set aside. Return wok to high heat. Add remaining oil and then pork. Cook, stirring constantly, until browned, about 2 minutes. Return beans to wok along with mustard greens, wine, and soy sauce and cook, stirring, until heated through, about 3 minutes. Remove from heat, stir in sesame oil, and season with salt and pepper.

GREEN BEANS & TOMATOES

SERVES 8

In so many green bean casseroles, the beans are cooked well past the point of mushy. SAVEUR editor-in-chief James Oseland lets his beans retain some snap in this recipe: the richness here comes from luscious, cooked-down tomatoes.

¼ cup olive oil
10 cloves garlic, roughly chopped
4 whole tomatoes, fresh or canned, peeled and crushed
2 lb. green beans, trimmed
  Kosher salt and freshly ground black pepper, to taste

Heat oil in a 12″ skillet over medium-high heat. Add garlic and cook, stirring often, until soft, about 2 minutes. Add tomatoes and cook, stirring, until broken down and soft. Add green beans and ½ cup water; cover pan with lid and cook, stirring occasionally, until beans are tender, about 8 minutes. Remove from heat, and season with salt and pepper.

GREEN BEANS WITH PANCETTA, MINT & HAZELNUTS

SERVES 6

This green bean dish is mildly creamy, thanks to a quick blanching in milk, which also sweetens the beans slightly. A garnish of toasted chopped hazelnuts adds a lovely nutty crunch.

4 cups milk
2 tbsp. kosher salt, plus more for seasoning
2 tbsp. sugar
2 lb. green beans, trimmed
⅓ lb. pancetta, diced
3 tbsp. unsalted butter
4 tbsp. chopped fresh mint
4 tbsp. chopped fresh flat-leaf parsley
  Freshly ground black pepper, to taste
¼ cup toasted chopped hazelnuts

1 Bring milk, 4 cups water, 2 tbsp. salt, and sugar to a boil in a 6-qt. saucepan.

2 Add green beans to saucepan and cook until crisp-tender, 5–6 minutes. Drain, reserving ⅓ cup cooking liquid. Chill beans in ice water. Drain; set aside.

3 Meanwhile, combine pancetta and 1½ cups water in a 12″ skillet; cook over medium heat until water evaporates and pancetta crisps, about 25 minutes. Using a slotted spoon, transfer pancetta to a plate, leaving 1 tbsp. fat in skillet. Place skillet over high heat, add beans and reserved cooking liquid, and cook until liquid evaporates, about 5 minutes.

4 Add butter and 2 tbsp. each mint and parsley. Cook until butter melts. Season with salt and pepper. Transfer to a platter and sprinkle with pancetta, hazelnuts, and remaining mint and parsley.

LEBANESE-STYLE GREEN BEANS WITH CHICKPEAS

Loubieh Wa Hommus Bi-Ziet

SERVES 4–6 (SEE PHOTO, PAGE 429)

Slow-cooked vegetable dishes like this one, a cumin-and-paprika-spiced stew of beans and tomatoes, are a standby in Lebanon. Here, tomatoes and green beans release some of their essence into the cooking liquid, creating a flavorful broth.

- ¼ cup olive oil
- 2 tsp. cumin seeds
- 4 cloves garlic, finely chopped
- 1 medium onion, thinly sliced
  Kosher salt and freshly ground black pepper, to taste
- 2 tbsp. tomato paste
- 1 tbsp. paprika
- 1½ lb. green beans, trimmed
- 1 28-oz. can whole, peeled tomatoes with juice, crushed by hand
- 1 15-oz. can chickpeas, drained and rinsed

1 Heat oil in an 8-qt. saucepan over medium-high heat. Add cumin seeds and cook, stirring often, until fragrant, about 1 minute.

2 Add garlic and onion, season with salt and pepper, and cook, stirring often, until soft and lightly browned, about 12 minutes.

3 Add tomato paste and paprika and cook, stirring occasionally, until tomato paste is lightly caramelized, about 2 minutes. Add the green beans, tomatoes, chickpeas, and 3 cups water and bring to a boil. Reduce heat to medium-low, and cook, partially covered and stirring occasionally, until very tender, about 1 hour. Let sit for at least 15 minutes before serving to allow the flavors to meld.

Greens

ETHIOPIAN COLLARD GREENS

Ye'abesha Gomen

SERVES 4

These fragrant collards are cooked with an Ethiopian-style spiced butter flavored with cardamom, fenugreek, and nigella seeds.

- 4 tbsp. unsalted butter
- ⅛ tsp. black cardamom seeds
- ⅛ tsp. ground fenugreek
- ⅛ tsp. nigella seeds
- ¼ cup extra-virgin olive oil
- 1 large onion, minced
- 3 cloves garlic, minced
- 2 bird's eye chiles, stemmed, seeded, and minced
- 1 1″ piece fresh ginger, peeled and minced
- 1½ lb. collard greens, stemmed and cut crosswise into ¼″-wide strips
  Kosher salt and freshly ground black pepper, to taste
  White wine vinegar, to taste

Melt butter in a 6-qt. pot over medium heat. Add cardamom, fenugreek, and nigella and cook, stirring often, until fragrant, 1–2 minutes. Increase heat to medium-high and add oil; add onion and cook, stirring often, until browned, 10 minutes. Add garlic, chiles, and ginger and cook, stirring often, until soft and fragrant, 3 minutes. Add collards, 1⅓ cups water, and salt and pepper, cover, and bring to a boil. Reduce heat to low and cook, stirring occasionally, until collards are tender, 50–55 minutes. Stir in vinegar and serve collards hot.

LONNÉE'S COLLARDS

SERVES 4

Writer Lonnée Hamilton simmers her collards in a chicken stock fortified with onions and garlic until they're tender and silky.

- 2 tbsp. extra-virgin olive oil
- 2 tbsp. unsalted butter
- 3 cloves garlic, roughly chopped
- 2 small yellow onions, minced
- 5 cups chicken stock
- 1½ lb. collard greens, stemmed and roughly chopped
  Kosher salt, freshly ground black pepper, and crushed red chile flakes, to taste

Heat oil and butter in a 6-qt. pot over medium heat. Add garlic and onions and cook, stirring often, until soft, 6–8 minutes. Pour in chicken stock and bring to a simmer. Add collard greens, cover, and cook, stirring occasionally, until very tender, about 1 hour. Season with salt, pepper, and chile flakes and serve immediately.

CHOY SUM WITH GARLIC SAUCE

SERVES 4 (SEE PHOTO, PAGE 426)

A lightning-quick, deceptively simple dressing of oil, garlic, and soy sauce elevates a dark leafy green like choy sum (Chinese flowering cabbage), bok choy, or broccoli rabe, bringing out its sweetness while masking some of its bitter notes.

> Kosher salt, to taste
> 1½ lb. choy sum, bok choy, or broccoli rabe
> 1 tbsp. peanut oil
> 2 tbsp. coarsely chopped garlic
> 2 tbsp. soy sauce

1 Bring a pot of lightly salted water to a boil. Meanwhile, trim ends from choy sum. Blanch greens in the water until just tender, about 1 minute. Drain greens and set aside on a plate.

2 Heat oil in a wok or a skillet over medium-high heat. Add garlic and cook until lightly browned, 1–2 minutes. Add soy sauce and 1 tbsp. water and cook for 1 minute. Pour garlic sauce over greens and serve immediately.

Kale

BRAISED TUSCAN KALE

SERVES 4–6

The leaves of Tuscan kale (also known as *cavolo nero*, lacinato kale, or dinosaur kale) cook slowly into a luscious heap when braised whole.

> ¼ cup extra-virgin olive oil
> 1 tbsp. fennel seeds
> 1 tsp. crushed red chile flakes
> 12 cloves garlic, thinly sliced
> 2 oil-packed anchovy filets, finely chopped
> 4 cups chicken stock
> 4 lb. Tuscan kale, stemmed
> Kosher salt and freshly ground black pepper, to taste

1 Heat oil in a wide pot over medium-high heat. Add fennel seeds, chile flakes, garlic, and anchovies and cook until fragrant, 1–2 minutes.

2 Add stock and bring to a boil. Add kale and salt and pepper to taste. Cover and cook, stirring occasionally, until leaves are somewhat wilted, 4–5 minutes. Reduce heat to medium-low and simmer, covered, until very tender, 40–45 minutes more.

KALE TARTS WITH FENNEL & OLIVES

MAKES 18 TARTS

Kale and fennel lend a unique sweetness to these briny puff pastry tarts. They're perfect as appetizers, savory breakfasts, or as an accompaniment to a bowl of warm, wintry soup.

> 2 tbsp. olive oil, plus more for drizzling
> 1 medium onion, diced
> 1 medium fennel bulb, quartered lengthwise, cored, and thinly sliced
> 3 cloves garlic, finely chopped
> 1 medium bunch Tuscan kale, stemmed and finely chopped
> ⅓ cup crumbled feta, plus more for topping
> ¼ cup Kalamata olives, pitted and finely chopped
> 2 tbsp. chopped fresh flat-leaf parsley
> Freshly ground black pepper, to taste
> 1 17-oz. package (2 sheets) puff pastry, thawed
> 3 tbsp. unsalted butter, melted

1 Heat oil in a large pan over medium heat. Add onion and cook, stirring occasionally, until softened and lightly browned, 5–7 minutes. Add fennel and garlic and cook, stirring occasionally, until softened, about 5 minutes. Lower heat, add kale, cover, and cook until kale is soft and wilted, adding 1 tsp. water if necessary, about 5 minutes. Remove pan from heat and fold in feta, olives, and parsley. Season with pepper.

2 Heat oven to 375° and line 2 baking sheets with parchment paper. Unroll both puff pastry sheets onto a floured work surface. Cut each sheet into 9 squares. Cut L-shaped slits on opposite corners of each square (creating a frame-like shape). Take hold of both corners and fold them toward the opposite sides, passing one corner under the other and pressing them in place, to create a diamond-shaped pocket to hold the filling.

3 Mound 1–2 tbsp. filling into each pocket; top with a little

> **"No vegetable exists which is not better slightly undercooked."**
>
> JAMES BEARD

more feta and a drizzle of oil. Place pockets on the prepared baking sheets and brush the outer edges with melted butter. Bake until golden brown and puffed, 30–35 minutes. Serve warm, topped with more feta.

KALE & SWEET POTATO GRATIN

SERVES 6–8

Don't limit traditional pie spices like cinnamon and nutmeg to the dessert table. In this cheesy, rich gratin, the spices sing alongside kale, sweet potatoes, and sharp white cheddar.

- 5 tbsp. butter
- 3 cloves garlic, peeled
  Kosher salt and freshly ground black pepper, to taste
- 1 bunch Tuscan kale, stemmed and roughly chopped
- 3 large sweet potatoes (about 2½ lb.), peeled and sliced ⅛" thick
- 2 cups half-and-half
- 2 tsp. ground cinnamon
  Whole nutmeg
- 1 cup grated white cheddar cheese

1 Heat oven to 400°. Grease an 8"×8" baking dish with 1 tbsp. butter. Smash garlic with side of a knife and sprinkle generously with salt. Chop and scrape garlic into a paste.

2 Combine garlic paste, kale, potatoes, half-and-half, cinnamon, and remaining 4 tbsp. butter (cut into ½" pieces) in a pot. Stir, then season with salt and pepper and taste the creamy liquid—it should be seasoned generously. Grate in a hint of nutmeg. Bring to a boil over medium-high heat while stirring the mixture with a wooden spoon. After 8–10 minutes the potatoes will be a little tender, and their starch will have thickened the liquid considerably.

3 Transfer the mixture to the prepared dish; smooth the top as much as possible. Cover the gratin with cheddar and bake until deeply golden brown, 20–30 minutes. Let gratin cool and set for 15 minutes before serving.

Kohlrabi

BUTTER-BRAISED KOHLRABI

SERVES 4

With its turnip-like flavor, this member of the cabbage family takes well to a slow simmer on the stove with chicken stock, butter, and thyme. Serve this dish with roast chicken or grilled pork chops.

- 2 lb. kohlrabi, trimmed but unpeeled and cut into 1" cubes
- 1 cup chicken stock
- 4 tbsp. unsalted butter, cubed
- 1½ tsp. fresh thyme leaves
  Kosher salt and freshly ground black pepper

Put kohlrabi, chicken stock, 2 tbsp. butter, and thyme into a 12" skillet over medium-high heat. Season with salt and pepper and cover with a parchment-paper circle cut to fit inside rim of skillet. Cook, stirring occasionally, until kohlrabi is tender, about 15 minutes. Uncover, remove pan from heat, and add remaining 2 tbsp. butter, swirling skillet until butter melts. Serve warm.

Leeks

GRILLED LEEKS & STEWED GARLIC ON TOAST

SERVES 6

Garlic and leeks are a natural pair: Both are members of the allium family, biting when raw and sweetly mellow when cooked. Chef and writer Alice Waters introduced us to this idea of putting them on toast.

- Kosher salt, to taste
- 6 small leeks, white and pale green parts only
- 7–9 tbsp. extra-virgin olive oil
- 20–25 cloves garlic, peeled
- 6 slices crusty country bread
- 4–5 oil-packed anchovy filets, cut into strips (optional)
  Freshly ground black pepper, to taste

1 Bring a medium pot of salted water to a boil. Cut leeks almost in half lengthwise, starting about 2″ above base, and wash thoroughly. Add leeks to pot and cook over medium heat until soft, 6–8 minutes. Drain well, transfer to a plate, and let cool. Toss leeks with 2 tbsp. oil and set aside.

2 Build a medium-hot fire in a charcoal grill or heat a gas grill to medium-high. Meanwhile, put garlic in a small pot, cover with cold water, bring to a simmer over medium heat, and simmer for 5 minutes. Drain and repeat process with fresh water. Drain again and repeat process once more, cooking garlic until very soft but not falling apart, 5–8 minutes. Drain well. Crush garlic with the side of a heavy knife, pressing and scraping to form a coarse paste. Stir in 1 tbsp. oil and set aside. Grill leeks, turning once, until lightly charred in places, 2–3 minutes. Brush bread with 2–3 tbsp. oil and grill, turning once, until golden, about 2 minutes. Cut bread crosswise into thirds.

3 Spread toasts with garlic paste. Split leeks into thirds lengthwise and top each toast with leeks. Garnish with anchovies, if using, then drizzle each toast with a little more oil. Season to taste with salt and pepper.

LEEKS VINAIGRETTE

Poireaux Vinaigrette

SERVES 4 (SEE PHOTO, PAGE 426)

The origins of leeks vinaigrette—poached leeks in a mustardy dressing—are unknown, but it's easy to imagine someone pulling these hearty aromatics out of the stockpot once they had worked their magic, and then making a stand-alone dish of them.

- 8 medium leeks, white and pale green parts only
  Kosher salt, to taste
- 5 tbsp. red wine vinegar
- 2 tsp. Dijon mustard
  Freshly ground white pepper, to taste
- 7 tbsp. canola oil
  Leaves from 4 sprigs fresh flat-leaf parsley, chopped
- 1 hard-cooked egg, chopped

1 Cut leeks almost in half lengthwise, starting about 2″ above base, and wash thoroughly. Bring a 12″ deep-sided skillet of salted water to a boil, add leeks, and cook over medium heat until soft but not mushy, about 6 minutes. Transfer leeks to a large bowl of ice water to stop them from cooking further. Carefully split leeks completely

in half lengthwise and transfer to a rack, cut side down, to drain thoroughly.

2 Whisk vinegar, mustard, salt, and pepper together in a small bowl. Gradually add oil, whisking constantly, until vinaigrette is smooth and creamy. Adjust seasonings and set aside.

3 Divide leek halves equally among 4 warm salad plates. Drizzle vinaigrette over leeks and sprinkle with chopped parsley and egg.

Mushrooms

CHANTERELLE SALAD

SERVES 4

Fresh, fruity chanterelle mushrooms—delicious in simple preparations, like this one—grow wild in many areas in the United States; their season depends on the climate of the region. Look for them in specialty gourmet shops and farmers' markets.

- ¼ cup walnut halves
- 5 tbsp. walnut oil
- 2 large cloves garlic, minced
- ½ lb. chanterelle mushrooms, trimmed
  Kosher salt and freshly ground black pepper, to taste
- 1 medium tomato, seeded and diced
- 2 oz. thinly sliced smoked ham, diced
- 1 tbsp. finely chopped fresh flat-leaf parsley
- ¼ lb. mixed baby lettuces

1 Place walnuts in a single layer in a large skillet. Toast over medium heat for 10 minutes, turning once. Coarsely chop and set aside.

2 Heat 3 tbsp. oil in a large skillet over medium heat. Add garlic and cook, stirring, until fragrant, about 2 minutes. Increase heat to medium-high, add mushrooms, season with salt and pepper, and cook, stirring, until mushrooms soften, about 5 minutes.

3 Reduce heat to low, add tomatoes, ham, and parsley and cook, stirring, for 1 minute. Remove from heat and set aside.

4 Place lettuce in a small bowl and dress with remaining 2 tbsp. oil. Season with salt and pepper, then divide among

4 small plates. Arrange mushroom mixture over lettuce, garnish with walnuts, and serve.

CRÊPES WITH MUSHROOMS, GRUYÈRE & SPINACH
SERVES 8

Savory beer-batter crêpes get stuffed with mushrooms, eggs, Gruyère, and spinach in this dish from the Perierra Crêperie cart in Portland, Oregon.

- 2 cups flour
- 1 cup milk
- ¾ cup cold lager beer
- 2 eggs
  Kosher salt and freshly ground black pepper, to taste
- 2 cups sautéed sliced mushrooms
- 1 cup grated Gruyère cheese
- 4 cups baby spinach
- 8 fried eggs

1 To make the crêpes, combine flour, milk, beer, eggs, salt and pepper, and ¾ cup cold water in a blender and blend until smooth; cover and refrigerate for at least 2 hours.

2 Heat a 12″ nonstick skillet over medium-high heat. Pour about ⅓ cup batter into skillet, tilting skillet to let batter cover bottom completely; sprinkle ¼ cup mushrooms, 2 tbsp. Gruyère, and ½ cup spinach over batter and season with salt and pepper. Cook until crêpe is lightly browned on the bottom, about 4 minutes; fold crêpe in half over fillings, place a fried egg on one side of the folded crêpe, and then fold again to sandwich the egg in the crêpe. Serve immediately; repeat with remaining batter, mushrooms, Gruyère, spinach, and fried eggs to make 8 crêpe sandwiches total.

IOWA FRIED MORELS
SERVES 4

The morels for this indulgent dish, whose name recalls Minneapolis-based chef Mitch Omer's Midwestern American youth, must be plump and fresh to hold up to the breading.

- 1 cup flour
  Salt and freshly ground black pepper
- 2 eggs, beaten
- 25 medium morels
- 6 tbsp. unsalted butter
  Lemon wedges, for serving

1 Season flour with a pinch of salt and a pinch of pepper, then divide between 2 small bowls. Combine eggs with ¼ cup water in a third small bowl.

2 Clean and trim morels. Melt butter in a large straight-sided skillet over medium heat.

3 Prepare morels for frying by dipping them into first bowl of flour, then into egg, then into second bowl of flour. Shake off excess flour, then cook, in 2 batches, turning once, until crisp, about 8 minutes. Drain on paper towels, sprinkle with salt, and serve with lemon wedges.

MORELS IN CREAM SAUCE
SERVES 4

Fresh morels are best in this rich, savory dish, but dried, rehydrated morels may be used if it's not morel season.

- 35–40 small morels
- 2 tbsp. butter
- 2 tsp. finely chopped shallots
- 1 tbsp. madeira wine
- 1 cup heavy cream
- 4 slices white Pullman loaf sandwich bread
- 1 tsp. arrowroot, or 1 tbsp. flour
  Kosher salt and freshly ground black pepper, to taste
  Finely chopped fresh flat-leaf parsley

1 Clean and trim morels. Melt butter in a large skillet over medium heat. Add morels and shallots and cook, stirring, until morels begin to soften, about 3 minutes.

2 Increase heat to high, add madeira and cream, and bring to a boil. Reduce heat to medium and simmer, stirring frequently, for 8 minutes.

3 Meanwhile, remove and discard crusts from bread. Toast bread, cut on diagonal, and arrange on 4 small plates.

4 Dissolve arrowroot in 1 tbsp. water in a small bowl. Stir mixture into mushroom sauce, season with salt and pepper, and simmer until sauce thickens, 1–2 minutes. Spoon over toast. Garnish with parsley and serve.

YUNNANESE MUSHROOMS TOSSED WITH CHILES
SERVES 4

Mushrooms, boiled until firm and succulent, are tossed with a dressing of chiles and sesame oil for this salad from the southwest Chinese province of Yunnan.

14 dried chiles de árbol, stemmed
2 tbsp. minced scallions
2 tbsp. sesame oil
2 tbsp. rice vinegar
2 tbsp. soy sauce
Kosher salt
12 large button mushrooms,
stemmed and thinly sliced

1 Working in batches, place chiles in a spice grinder and process until finely ground. Transfer to a medium bowl and stir in scallions, oil, vinegar, and soy sauce to form a thick sauce; set sauce aside.

2 Bring a 4-qt. saucepan of salted water to a boil over high heat. Add mushrooms and cook until lightly chewy, about 5 minutes. Drain mushrooms and transfer to a kitchen towel; squeeze out as much liquid as possible. Transfer mushrooms to bowl with sauce and toss until evenly coated. Let sit for 10 minutes before serving.

WILD MUSHROOM RAGOUT

SERVES 4–6

This delicate "stew" can be made when fresh wild mushrooms are plentiful, then frozen to enjoy later. Serve with toasted country bread, over pasta or polenta, or as an accompaniment to roast meat.

1 lb. mixed wild mushrooms, such as black trumpets, fairy rings, and porcini
1 tbsp. unsalted butter
2 shallots, finely chopped
1 clove garlic, minced
¾ cup Brown Chicken Stock (page 568)
¼ cup heavy cream
2 sprigs fresh thyme
1 tbsp. chopped fresh chives
Kosher salt and freshly ground black pepper, to taste

1 Trim mushrooms, reserving stems for another use. Slice large caps into fairly even pieces; leave smaller caps whole.

2 Melt butter in a large skillet over medium heat. Add shallots and garlic and cook, stirring occasionally, until tender, about 15 minutes. Add mushrooms and cook until they release their liquid. Add stock and cook for about 5 more minutes. Stir in cream and cook for another 5 minutes. Add thyme and chives, then season to taste with salt and pepper.

Okra

FRIED OKRA

SERVES 4–6

Tabasco sauce adds tang and spice to fried okra, an essential Southern side dish, while cornmeal gives it a pleasant crunchiness.

¼ cup buttermilk
¼ tsp. Tabasco sauce, plus more for serving
1 lb. okra, stems trimmed
1 cup flour
¾ cup stone-ground yellow cornmeal
1 tbsp. kosher salt
½ tsp. cayenne pepper
½ tsp. freshly ground black pepper
Canola oil, for frying

1 In a large bowl, stir together the buttermilk and Tabasco. Add okra to the buttermilk mixture, and set aside to rest for 10 minutes.

2 In a large bowl, combine flour, cornmeal, salt, cayenne pepper, and black pepper. Drain the okra in a colander. Working in batches, dredge the okra in the flour mixture, coating evenly. Shake off excess flour and transfer okra to a parchment-lined baking sheet.

3 Heat 1″ of oil in a 12″ cast-iron skillet over medium heat until a deep-fry thermometer reads 350°. Working in batches, fry the okra (do not crowd the pan), turning the pods occasionally, until golden brown, about 4 minutes. Using a slotted spoon, transfer fried okra to a paper towel-lined plate. Serve with more Tabasco, if you like.

OKRA WITH TOMATOES & CHICKPEAS

Bamiya

SERVES 6–8

Okra stews are popular throughout the Middle East and North Africa, where they often include lamb. This vegetarian version from Egypt is brightened with tomatoes and lemon juice.

2 cups chickpeas, soaked overnight and drained
Kosher salt and freshly ground black pepper, to taste
¼ cup extra-virgin olive oil
3 cloves garlic, minced

1¼ lb. small okra
1 28-oz. can whole, peeled tomatoes, drained
  and coarsely chopped
1 tbsp. ground cumin
1 cup chicken stock
2 tbsp. fresh lemon juice
½ cup coarsely chopped fresh flat-leaf parsley

1 In a medium saucepan, cover chickpeas with water and bring to a boil over medium-high heat. Reduce heat to medium-low and gently simmer until chickpeas are tender, 20–30 minutes. Remove from heat and season with salt and pepper. Let beans cool in cooking liquid. Transfer beans and liquid to a large bowl and store, covered, in the refrigerator until ready to use.

2 Heat oil in a large, deep skillet over medium heat. Add garlic and cook, stirring occasionally, until fragrant, about 2 minutes. Add okra and cook, stirring once or twice, until it turns bright green, about 3 minutes.

3 Stir in tomatoes and cumin and cook for 1–2 minutes. Add stock and lemon juice and season with salt and pepper. Cover, reduce heat to medium-low, and cook until okra is soft, about 35 minutes.

4 Drain chickpeas. Add to okra mixture, cover, and cook just until chickpeas are heated through, 5–10 minutes. (Chickpeas should still hold their shape.) Add parsley, adjust seasoning with salt and pepper, and serve warm.

Onions

ROASTED VIDALIA ONIONS WITH HERBED BREAD CRUMBS

SERVES 4–6 (SEE PHOTO, PAGE 430)

Sweet Vidalia onions, grown in and around their namesake Georgia city, turn even sweeter when roasted with a savory herbed bread crumb topping.

2 large Vidalia onions, cut crosswise
  into ½"-thick slices
4 tbsp. extra-virgin olive oil
  Kosher salt and freshly ground black pepper,
  to taste
6 tbsp. dried bread crumbs
2 tbsp. unsalted butter, melted

1 tbsp. finely chopped fresh flat-leaf parsley
1 tsp. finely chopped fresh oregano
1 tsp. finely chopped fresh thyme
2 cloves garlic, minced

1 Heat oven to 450°. On a foil-lined baking sheet, coat onion slices in oil, keeping rings as intact as possible; season with salt and pepper. Bake, turning once, until soft and lightly caramelized, about 15 minutes.

2 Meanwhile, stir together bread crumbs, butter, parsley, oregano, thyme, garlic, and salt and pepper in a small bowl; sprinkle evenly over onion slices. Continue baking until topping is golden brown, about 15 minutes more.

ONIONS BAKED WITH ROSEMARY & CREAM

SERVES 6

Baking onions brings out their gentle sweetness; adding cream at the last minute softens the rosemary's pungency.

6 large onions, unpeeled
2 cups chicken stock
3–4 tbsp. extra-virgin olive oil
  Kosher salt and freshly ground black pepper,
  to taste
  Leaves from 3–4 sprigs fresh rosemary, chopped
½ cup heavy cream

1 Heat oven to 425°. Slice about ¼" off the bottoms and tops of the onions so that they will sit upright, then slice in half crosswise. Arrange onions, cut side up, in a baking dish.

2 Pour stock over and around the onions in baking dish. Drizzle oil over onions, then liberally season with salt and pepper. Scatter rosemary over onions and into the stock in the baking dish.

3 Transfer baking dish to oven and bake the onions, basting them often with the stock, until they are soft when pierced with the tip of a paring knife and stock has been reduced by about three-quarters, 1–1¼ hours.

4 Remove baking dish from oven and pour cream over onions. Return dish to oven and bake until pan juices have thickened slightly and tops of onions have browned, 20–30 minutes more.

IRAQI STUFFED ONIONS

Dolma Mahshi

SERVES 6–8

Pomegranate molasses, coriander, and curry powder perfume the filling for these tender stuffed onion rolls once served at Aladdin's Castle Café, a now-defunct Iraqi food cart in Portland, Oregon.

- 2 cups jasmine rice
- 1 cup finely chopped flat-leaf parsley
- ½ cup extra-virgin olive oil
- ⅓ cup finely chopped fresh cilantro
- ¼ cup pomegranate molasses
- ¼ cup tomato paste
- 2 tsp. ground cumin
- 2 tsp. ground coriander
- 2 tsp. curry powder
  Salt and freshly ground black pepper, to taste
- 4 large white onions, peeled
- 1 cup chicken stock
- 1 14-oz. can whole, peeled tomatoes in juice, puréed
- 2 tsp. ground sumac, plus more for garnish
  Greek yogurt, for serving

1 Make the stuffing: Combine rice, parsley, oil, cilantro, pomegranate molasses, tomato paste, cumin, coriander, curry powder, salt and pepper, and 1½ cups water in a bowl; let sit until the rice begins to soak up some of the liquid, about 30 minutes.

2 Meanwhile, trim the tops and bottoms from onions and peel off outer layer; place in a 6-qt. saucepan and cover with water. Bring to a boil over medium-high heat, and cook until onions are tender to the core, about 30 minutes; drain and let cool.

3 Cut each onion halfway around the side and peel off each whole layer to get about 4–5 large layers each. Stuff each layer with 2 tbsp. stuffing and roll up into a football-shaped roll; place rolls in a single layer in a 9″×13″ baking dish. Pour stock and tomatoes over rolls and sprinkle with sumac; season with salt and pepper.

4 Heat oven to 375°. Bake until filling is cooked through and sauce is reduced around rolls, about 1 hour. Divide rolls among serving plates and sprinkle with more sumac; serve with yogurt.

SWEET & SOUR ONIONS

Cipolline in Agrodolce

SERVES 4–6

This piquant yet delicate dish is beloved in Rome, where it is often paired with roasted meats.

- ½ cup raisins
- 3 tbsp. extra-virgin olive oil
- 1½ lb. cipolline or pearl onions, peeled
- ¼ cup balsamic vinegar
- 1½ tbsp. sugar
  Kosher salt, to taste

1 Put raisins into a small bowl, cover with hot water, and let soften for 30 minutes.

2 Heat oil in a 12″ skillet over medium-high heat. Add onions and cook until golden brown, 8–10 minutes; pour off oil. Drain raisins. Add raisins, vinegar, and sugar and season with salt. Cook, stirring, until sauce thickens, 2–3 minutes.

BEER-BATTERED ONION RINGS

SERVES 6–8 (SEE PHOTO, PAGE 219)

Batter-fried onions have been a staple of American county fairs, fast-food restaurants, and backyard barbecues for nearly a century. Some onions are simply dredged in flour, others get a cornmeal crust, but our favorite variation is an airy, flavorful batter infused with honey, paprika, and lager beer.

- 1¾ cups flour
- ½ cup cornstarch
- 1½ tbsp. hot paprika
- 1 tbsp. dry mustard
- 1 tbsp. baking powder
- 1 tbsp. kosher salt, plus more to taste
- 2 tsp. honey
- 12 oz. lager-style beer
  Canola oil, for frying
- 2 large yellow onions, cut crosswise into ½″-thick slices and separated into rings

1 In a large bowl, whisk together flour, cornstarch, paprika, mustard, baking powder, and salt. Add honey and beer and whisk until smooth; let sit for 10 minutes.

2 Pour oil to a depth of 2″ into a 6-qt. Dutch oven and heat over medium-high heat until a deep-fry thermometer reads 375°. Working in batches, dip onion rings into batter, shaking off excess, and lower into oil; fry, flipping once, until golden brown, about 3 minutes. Transfer to paper towels to drain briefly and season with more salt; serve immediately.

CURRIED CREAMED ONIONS

SERVES 4–6

Luscious pearl onions are rendered even more delicious with a kick of curry powder and Tabasco. This is a classic Thanksgiving side dish in the American South.

Kosher salt, to taste
2 lb. white pearl onions, unpeeled
2 tbsp. unsalted butter
3 tbsp. flour
1 tsp. curry powder
1 cup half-and-half
2 tsp. Dijon mustard
⅛ tsp. Tabasco sauce
Freshly ground black pepper, to taste

1 Bring a 6-qt. pot of salted water to a boil. Add onions and cook until just tender, about 15 minutes. Using a slotted spoon, transfer onions to bowl. Reserve ¾ cup cooking liquid. Using a paring knife, peel onions and set aside.

2 Meanwhile, melt butter in a 2-qt. saucepan over medium heat. Add flour and curry powder and cook, stirring frequently, until golden and thick, about 1 minute. Slowly whisk in half-and-half, the reserved cooking liquid, and mustard and bring to a simmer. Reduce heat to medium-low and cook, stirring occasionally, until sauce has thickened, about 5 minutes. Add onions and season with Tabasco and salt and pepper. Cook, stirring occasionally, until onions soften a little and the flavors meld, about 10 more minutes. Transfer onions to a platter or a bowl with a slotted spoon and pour some of the cream sauce over them.

Peas

PEAS IN LETTUCE CUPS

SERVES 4

Leaves of baby lettuce become nests for barely cooked fresh green peas, in this delicate side dish.

2 lb. green peas in the pod, shelled
  to yield 2 cups
4 heads baby Bibb lettuce

½ tbsp. butter
Kosher salt and freshly ground black pepper, to taste

1 Bring 3 cups salted water to a boil in a medium saucepan over medium-high heat. Add peas to boiling water, reduce heat to medium-low, and simmer until tender, about 5 minutes.

2 Meanwhile, remove outer leaves of the lettuce heads and pull out the inner cores so that you have only the tender middle leaves.

3 Drain peas in a colander and run briefly under cold water to stop the cooking. Toss peas with butter while they are still warm and season to taste with salt and pepper. To serve, spoon hot peas into lettuce "cups." (Peas will slightly cook lettuce.)

PEAS BRAISED WITH DILL & ONIONS

Arakás me Ánitho & Kremythákia

SERVES 4

Dishes such as this one belong to the category of Greek cookery known as *latherá,* which, loosely translated, means "oil-based stews." The liberal use of olive oil produces a surprisingly light and sweet side dish.

4 tbsp. extra-virgin olive oil
2 medium onions, finely chopped
4–6 scallions, white part only, thinly sliced
1 clove garlic, minced
4 cups fresh or frozen peas
½ cup finely chopped fresh dill
Kosher salt and freshly ground black pepper, to taste

1 Heat oil in a large, deep skillet over low heat. Add onions, scallions, and garlic, cover, and cook until soft, 15 minutes.

2 Stir in peas. Add water just to cover, replace lid, and cook, stirring occasionally, for 30 minutes. Add dill, season with salt and pepper, and cook, covered, for 20 minutes.

3 Uncover, raise heat to medium-low, and cook until most of the liquid has evaporated, about 10 minutes. Season with salt and pepper and serve warm or at room temperature.

PEA SHOOTS WITH FERMENTED BEAN CURD
Dòu Miáu

SERVES 4

Dòu miáu—the phrase means "bean grass" in Mandarin, and they're often called "pea shoots" or "snow pea shoots" in English—are the soft leaves and tendrils of the pea plant. Their sweet flavor needs little help, just a bit of savory intensity from a sauce of garlic and fermented bean curd.

1½	lb. pea shoots
2–3	tbsp. vegetable oil
2	cloves garlic, thinly sliced
2	cubes fermented bean curd

1 Remove leaves, including those with tendrils, from pea shoots and discard stems. Rinse leaves in cold water. Place a wok over high heat for 2 minutes. Add leaves and toss until wilted, about 1 minute. Transfer to a sieve and allow leaves to drain.

2 Pour oil into the hot wok. Add garlic and sauté just until golden. Add bean curd and stir vigorously, breaking up the curd to make a smooth, thick sauce. Add leaves and toss in sauce for 1 minute over medium heat. Serve at once.

Peppers

ROASTED PEPPERS & ANCHOVIES

SERVES 6–8

At Mamma 'Zu's restaurant in Richmond, Virginia, this simple, satisfying Italian small dish is served with crusty bread. It pairs nicely with other small vegetable plates, like Fried Eggplant with Walnut Sauce (page 314), as part of an appetizer spread.

12	oil-packed anchovy filets
6	roasted red bell peppers, skins, stems, and seeds removed, cut into large strips
¼	cup roughly chopped fresh flat-leaf parsley
2	cloves garlic
3	tbsp. extra-virgin olive oil
	Kosher salt and freshly ground black pepper, to taste

Alternately lay anchovy filets and strips of pepper on a serving platter in one layer. Combine parsley and garlic on a cutting board and finely chop together; sprinkle parsley-garlic mixture evenly over anchovies and peppers. Drizzle with oil and season with salt and pepper. Let sit for 10 minutes before serving to allow flavors to marry.

PADRÓN PEPPERS WITH SERRANO HAM

SERVES 4

The thumb-size *pimiento de padrón* pepper is a specialty of Galicia, Spain. In chef Maricel Presilla's interpretation of a classic Spanish preparation, the peppers are stir-fried with garlic and serrano ham to give them an extra-savory flavor.

¼	cup extra-virgin olive oil
40	pimientos de padrón or shishito peppers
2	oz. thinly sliced serrano ham or prosciutto, torn into 2" pieces
2	cloves garlic, roughly chopped
	Flaky sea salt, to taste
	Lemon wedges, for serving

1 Heat a 12" cast-iron skillet over high heat. Add oil and heat until it ripples and smokes lightly. Add peppers and ham and cook, flipping peppers occasionally with a spoon, until peppers have blistered and softened, about 2 minutes. Add garlic and cook, stirring occasionally, until golden, about 1 more minute.

2 Transfer peppers to a platter, sprinkle generously with salt, and serve with lemon wedges.

PEPERONATA
Stewed Sweet Peppers

MAKES 2 CUPS

This sweet, simple pepper stew is an ideal use for summer's bounty of sweet peppers. It makes a great antipasto atop bruschetta.

⅓	cup extra-virgin olive oil
4	assorted red, yellow, and orange bell peppers, cored, seeded, and cut into ¼" strips
4	cloves garlic, thinly sliced crosswise
½	medium white onion, thinly sliced
	Kosher salt and freshly ground black pepper, to taste
3	tbsp. red wine vinegar

Heat oil in a 4-qt. saucepan over medium-high heat. Add peppers, garlic, onion, and ½ cup water and season with salt and pepper. Cook, partially covered and stirring occasionally, until peppers are soft, about 1 hour. Stir in vinegar and transfer to a serving bowl.

Plantains

MASHED PLANTAINS WITH TOMATO SAUCE

Mofongo con Salsa de Tomate

SERVES 6

Mashed with bacon and garlic and served with a quick tomato sauce, this is a Puerto Rican take on a ubiquitous Caribbean plantain dish.

	Canola oil, for frying
5	yellow ripe plantains, peeled, cut into 1″ chunks, soaked in hot water
¾	cup chicken stock
½	lb. bacon, cut into ¼″ cubes
7	cloves garlic, minced
8	tbsp. olive oil
	Kosher salt and freshly ground black pepper, to taste
1	small yellow onion, minced
1	28-oz. can whole, peeled tomatoes, drained and crushed by hand
	Shredded iceberg lettuce and tomato wedges, for garnish

1 Pour canola oil to a depth of 2″ into a 6-qt. Dutch oven and heat over medium-high heat until a deep-fry thermometer reads 325°. Drain and dry plantains, then fry until tender, about 6 minutes. Finely chop plantains in a food processor with stock; set aside. Cook bacon in a 10″ skillet over medium heat until browned, about 15 minutes. Stir bacon and fat into plantains with half the garlic and 5 tbsp. olive oil. Season with salt and pepper and set mofongo aside.

2 Heat remaining 3 tbsp. oil in skillet over medium heat. Add remaining garlic and onion and cook until soft, about 15 minutes. Add tomatoes and cook until broken down, about 10 minutes. Serve mofongo on a platter, garnish with lettuce and tomato, and top with sauce.

TWICE-FRIED GREEN PLANTAINS WITH GARLIC DIPPING SAUCE

Tostones con Mojo Verde

SERVES 6

These smashed, fried plantains—a Cuban specialty—are crisp outside and soft inside. With an herbaceous, garlicky *mojo* sauce, they're an addictive snack, or a wonderful accompaniment to roast chicken.

FOR THE MOJO

3–4	cloves garlic, crushed
	Kosher salt
3–6	fresh cilantro sprigs, leaves chopped
2–3	fresh culantro leaves, trimmed and chopped (optional, or substitute more cilantro)
½	cup extra-virgin olive oil

FOR THE TOSTONES

3	green unripe plantains
	Vegetable oil, for frying
	Kosher salt

1 Make the mojo: Put garlic and a pinch of salt in a mortar. Crush to a rough paste, then add cilantro and culantro (if using) and crush until bruised. Add oil while grinding in a circular motion. Adjust seasoning. Set aside.

2 Make the tostones: To remove tough green skin from plantains, trim off both ends with a sharp knife, then make a few slits through skin the length of each plantain. Push your thumb between skin and flesh; pry skin away from flesh. It will come off in pieces, like bark from a tree. Trim off any woody fiber stuck to plantains. Cut plantains into 1″-thick rounds.

3 Pour oil to a depth of 1″ into a large heavy skillet and heat until a deep-fry thermometer reads 325°. Fry plantains, in 2 batches, until lightly golden and hollow-sounding when tapped, about 3 minutes. Transfer plantains with a slotted spatula to paper towels to drain. Working quickly, press warm tostones with the clean bottom of a small pan or a flat pot lid, flattening them to about half their original thickness.

4 Return flattened tostones to oil in batches and fry until crisp around edges and deeply golden, about 2 minutes more. Transfer tostones to paper towels to drain and season to taste with salt while still hot. Serve tostones hot with mojo as a dipping sauce.

Radishes

ROASTED RADISHES

SERVES 2–4

Roasted in a hot oven, radishes lose their bite and take on a creamy sweetness that has been known to convert even the most ardent radish foe. This recipe, taught to students at the Viking Cooking School in Greenwood, Mississippi, is a testament to the transformative power of a little bit of heat.

- 3 bunches assorted radishes, trimmed
- 3 tbsp. extra-virgin olive oil
- 6 sprigs fresh thyme
  Kosher salt and freshly ground black pepper, to taste

1 Heat oven to 425°. Wash radishes, pat dry, and transfer to a large bowl with oil and thyme. Toss to combine; season with salt and pepper.

2 Put radishes into a shallow baking dish and cook, turning occasionally, until golden brown and a small knife slides easily into radishes, 40–50 minutes.

DAIKON RADISH WITH WHITE MISO SAUCE

Furofuki Daikon

SERVES 8

This salty, savory Japanese dish calls for daikon, a mild (and very large) type of radish, but other root vegetables, such as turnips, rutabagas, or parsnips, may be used.

- 1 2″ square piece kombu (dried kelp)
  Pinch salt
- 1 9″ piece daikon, peeled, trimmed, and cut crosswise into eight 1″-thick rounds
- ⅔ cup white miso
- 3 tbsp. sake
- 2 tbsp. mirin
- 1 tbsp. sugar
- 1 egg yolk
- 3 tbsp. dashi
- 1 1″ piece fresh ginger, peeled and grated

1 Cut out a circle of parchment paper just large enough to fit inside a wide medium pot, then cut a ½″ vent hole in center and set paper aside. Put kombu, 8 cups water, and salt into the wide medium pot and bring to a simmer over medium heat. Add daikon and return to a simmer. Lay parchment paper circle on surface of liquid in pot, reduce heat to medium-low, and gently simmer until daikon is soft when pierced with the tip of a small sharp knife, 50–60 minutes.

2 Put miso into a medium pan set over another medium pan of simmering water over medium heat and cook, stirring constantly with a wooden spoon, until paste loosens, about 1 minute. Gradually add sake, then mirin, stirring until smooth. Add sugar and egg yolk and cook, stirring constantly, until sauce is thick and creamy, 1–2 minutes. Stir in dashi and ginger.

3 Using a slotted spoon, divide daikon, cut sides up, among 8 small bowls and discard cooking liquid. Spoon some of the miso sauce on top of each piece of daikon, spreading it out with the back of the spoon to cover top of daikon completely.

Scallions

GRILLED SCALLIONS WITH ROMESCO SAUCE

Calçots amb Romesco

SERVES 4–6

Traditionally, this Barcelonan springtime recipe calls for *calçots* (young green onions) and *ñora* peppers. Scallions and ancho chiles are good substitutes.

- 1 dried ancho chile, stemmed, halved, and seeded
- ¾ cup extra-virgin olive oil
- ½ cup whole blanched almonds
- 1 slice crustless white bread, roughly chopped
- 3 cloves garlic, smashed
- 1 medium onion, thinly sliced
- 4 tsp. smoked paprika
- 1½ cups roughly chopped roasted red peppers
- 2½ tbsp. sherry vinegar
  Kosher salt and freshly ground black pepper, to taste
- 3–4 bunches scallions

1 Put chile and 2 cups boiling water into a bowl; let soften for 5 minutes. Drain chile and roughly chop. Heat ½ cup oil in a 10″ skillet over medium-high heat. Add almonds and bread and cook until golden, 3–4 minutes. Transfer almond mixture to a bowl with a slotted spoon. Return skillet to medium heat. Add chile, garlic, and onion and cook until golden, 3–4 minutes. Add paprika and cook for 1 minute. Put chile mixture, almond mixture, peppers, and vinegar into a food processor and purée. Season romesco sauce with salt and pepper; set aside.

2 Build a medium-hot fire in a charcoal grill or heat a gas grill to medium-high. Drizzle scallions with remaining oil and season with salt and pepper. Grill until charred and tender, 5–6 minutes. Serve with romesco sauce.

Spinach

SPINACH WITH PINE NUTS & RAISINS
SERVES 4

Federal Hill, the Italian-American section of Providence, Rhode Island, is home to some amazing dishes, including this one. Earthy spinach showcases its sweet side thanks to plump raisins and soft-cooked garlic and onion, with a sprinkling of pine nuts for good measure.

- 2 tbsp. raisins
- 3 tbsp. extra-virgin olive oil
- ½ small onion, chopped
- 2 cloves garlic, thinly sliced
- 2 bunches spinach, trimmed
- 3 tbsp. pine nuts, toasted
- 1 tbsp. fresh lemon juice
- 8 thin strips lemon zest
  Salt and freshly ground black pepper
  Lemon wedges, for serving (optional)

1 Soak raisins in a bowl of cold water for 10 minutes; drain and set aside.

2 Heat olive oil in a large skillet over medium heat. Add onion and garlic and cook until soft, 4–5 minutes.

3 Add spinach and cook, stirring, for 1 minute. Cover and cook, stirring, until wilted, 2–3 minutes. Add pine nuts, lemon juice, lemon zest, and raisins. Season to taste with salt and pepper. Serve with lemon wedges, if you like.

SPINACH MADELEINE
SERVES 6

A sauce of unabashedly rich ingredients—including evaporated milk and, yes, Velveeta cheese—makes for a spectacularly luxurious take on creamed spinach. We adapted this recipe from one found in the *River Road Cookbook,* one of Louisiana's best-known Junior League cookbooks.

- 8 tbsp. unsalted butter
- 3 lb. spinach
  Kosher salt and freshly ground black pepper, to taste
- 2 tbsp. flour
- 2 tbsp. chopped onion
- ½ cup chicken stock
- ½ cup evaporated milk
- 6 oz. Velveeta cheese, chopped
- 2 jalapeños, stemmed and finely chopped
- 2 tsp. Worcestershire sauce
- ¾ tsp. celery salt
- ¾ tsp. garlic salt

1 Melt 4 tbsp. butter in an 8-qt. saucepan over medium heat. Add spinach and cook in batches until wilted, about 10 minutes. Season with salt and pepper; set aside.

2 Melt remaining 4 tbsp. butter in a 4-qt. saucepan over medium heat. Add flour and stir until blended and smooth but not brown. Add onion and cook until soft, about 2 minutes. Slowly add stock and evaporated milk, stirring constantly to avoid lumps. Cook until smooth and thick, about 3 minutes. Add Velveeta, jalapeños, Worcestershire, celery and garlic salts, salt, and pepper and stir until cheese is melted. Combine with cooked spinach and serve.

SAAG PANEER
Spinach with Fresh Indian Cheese
SERVES 4

It's not hard to love northern Indian *saag paneer*—meltingly soft greens strewn with chunks of mild *paneer,* or fresh cheese—especially when it's scooped up with hot flatbread.

- 4 cloves garlic, chopped
- 1 1″ piece fresh ginger, peeled and chopped
- 1 serrano chile, stemmed and chopped

SILKY GREENS

No one knows exactly how *saag paneer* originated, but it is indisputably a specialty of northern India, specifically the Punjab region, where dairy products are common. The dish came to the U.S. courtesy of immigrant Punjabis, who established most of the Indian restaurants here. But it's beloved throughout India, too, partly because it's a traditional staple of roadside snack stops in the Punjab and has been spread all over the country by travelers who've encountered it. Also, it's a protein-rich vegetarian food ideal for meat-eschewing Hindus, a large portion of India's population. *Saag* just means "greens" in Hindi, and although spinach is what's most often used in the U.S., in India the dish is made with not only spinach but also mustard, collard, fenugreek, or beet greens and even amaranth or purslane. *Paneer,* though, always means fresh cheese, made by separating cow's milk into curds and whey and then pressing the curds. *Saag paneer* is easy to make and tastes best when fresh—convincing arguments for cooking this restaurant dish at home.

6   tbsp. Ghee (page 595)
6   cups finely chopped spinach
    or other tender greens
    Kosher salt, to taste
6   tbsp. heavy cream
½   tsp. garam masala
¼   tsp. cayenne pepper
7   oz. paneer
    Naan (page 459, or store-bought)
    or cooked white rice, for serving

1 Place garlic, ginger, chiles, and ¼ cup water in a blender and purée into a smooth paste. Heat ghee in a skillet over medium-high heat. Add ginger-garlic paste and cook, stirring, until fragrant, about 30 seconds. Add spinach and salt and cook, stirring often, until spinach wilts, about 1 minute. Reduce heat to medium-low, cover, and cook, stirring often, until spinach is very soft, about 15 minutes. Stir in cream, garam masala, and cayenne.

2 Add paneer to skillet, cover, and continue cooking until liquid thickens and spinach is soft, about 15 minutes. Serve with flatbread or rice.

Squash

ROASTED KABOCHA SQUASH WITH SAGE BREAD CRUMBS
SERVES 6–8

Sage, a member of the mint family, livens up any dish, including this classic autumn squash roast. But remember, too much sage will make food taste bitter or medicinal.

1   large kabocha squash (3–5-lb.)
6   tbsp. butter
    Sea salt and freshly ground black pepper, to taste
2   cups fresh bread crumbs
2   tbsp. chopped fresh sage, plus sprigs for garnish

1 Heat oven to 400°. Halve the kabocha squash crosswise and scoop out and discard seeds. Rub each half with 1 tbsp. softened butter, season with salt and pepper, and put cut side up on a baking sheet. Cover with foil and bake until tender, about 1 hour.

2 Meanwhile, combine bread crumbs, 4 tbsp. melted butter, sage, and salt and pepper in a bowl.

3 Uncover squash, divide mixture between halves, and roast until golden, 15–20 minutes more. Garnish with fresh sage sprigs.

TAIWANESE-STYLE SQUASH WITH GINGER
Chao Nan Gua
SERVES 4

This fragrant side dish, a favorite in Taipei, can be made with several different kinds of squash; we've found that kabocha and butternut work best.

1   tbsp. canola oil
1   1½" piece fresh ginger, peeled and cut crosswise into ⅛"-thick coins
2   tsp. sugar
½   tsp. kosher salt
1   small kabocha or butternut squash (about 2½ lb.), peeled, seeded, and cut into 1½" pieces

1 Heat oil in a 10" skillet or wok over high heat. Add ginger and cook until fragrant, about 2 minutes.

2 Add sugar, salt, squash, and ½ cup water. Bring to a boil, reduce heat to medium, cover, and cook, stirring occasionally, until squash is tender, 8–12 minutes. Transfer to a serving bowl and serve hot.

SQUASH GRATIN
Gratin de Courge
SERVES 8–10

The Provençal original of this gratin calls for a French pumpkin called *potiron* that can be hard to find outside of Europe. A combination of acorn and butternut squash makes a good substitute.

- 2 large butternut squash (5–6 lb.), peeled, seeded, and cut into 1½″ chunks
- 1 large acorn squash (about 2 lb.), peeled, seeded, and cut into 1½″ chunks
- 3 medium Yukon gold potatoes (about 1¾ lb.), peeled, halved lengthwise, and thickly sliced
- 8 cloves garlic, chopped
  Kosher salt and freshly ground black pepper, to taste
- 2 cups milk
- 4 cups grated Gruyère cheese

1 Heat oven to 400°. Put both squash into a large pot, cover with salted water, and bring to a boil. Reduce heat to medium-low and simmer, partially covered, until tender, about 20 minutes. Drain, pressing out any excess water. Meanwhile, put potatoes in a pot, cover with salted water, and bring to a boil. Reduce heat to medium-low and simmer until just tender, about 10 minutes. Drain.

2 Put squash into a large bowl and mash coarsely with a potato masher. Add potatoes, garlic, and salt and pepper to taste and gently fold together. Transfer squash mixture to a deep 9″×14″ roasting pan or baking dish. Pour milk evenly over top and sprinkle with Gruyère. Bake until golden brown and bubbly, about 30 minutes. Let cool slightly before serving.

SQUASH-BLOSSOM BEIGNETS
SERVES 6

Light and delicate, these fried squash blossom fritters are an irresistible summer treat.

- 1½ cups flour
- 1 tsp. salt
- 1 tbsp. extra-virgin olive oil
- 1 egg, lightly beaten
- 18 large or 36 small squash blossoms
  Vegetable oil, for frying
- 1 clove garlic, finely chopped
- 2 tbsp. finely chopped fresh flat-leaf parsley

1 Sift flour and salt into a medium bowl. Whisk in 2 cups water, olive oil, and egg.

2 Remove stems and stamens from squash blossoms; wash blossoms and pat dry.

3 Heat 1″ vegetable oil in a large, heavy saucepan over high heat. Just before frying, add garlic and parsley to batter, stirring well. Dip flowers in batter, coating them inside and out. Fry for 1–3 minutes, turning frequently. Drain and sprinkle with salt.

STUFFED SQUASH BLOSSOMS
Fiori di Zucca Ripieni
SERVES 6–8

You'll find fried zucchini and other squash blossoms all over Italy—stuffed, as they are here, or unstuffed. This recipe, with its savory filling of cheese and anchovy, comes from the restaurant Antico Ristoranti Pagnanelli in the town of Castel Gandolfo, near Rome.

- 24 squash blossoms
- ¾ lb. fresh mozzarella
- 12 oil-packed anchovy filets
- 4 eggs
- 1 cup flour
  Freshly ground black pepper, to taste
  Vegetable oil, for frying
  Salt

1 Remove stems and stamens from squash blossoms; wash blossoms and pat dry.

2 Cut mozzarella into small dice, coarsely chop anchovy filets, and combine in a bowl. Stuff each blossom with mixture and twist petals to retain stuffing.

3 Beat eggs in a small bowl. Mix flour with pepper in a second shallow pan. Heat 2½″ vegetable oil in a skillet over high heat until very hot.

4 Working in small batches, dredge each stuffed blossom in flour, dip into eggs, turning to coat well, and then dredge in seasoned flour. Fry blossoms, turning frequently, until crisp, 3–5 minutes. Drain on paper towels, sprinkle with salt, and serve immediately.

SOY-BRAISED KABOCHA SQUASH

SERVES 6

Braising is one of our favorite ways to bring out the texture and flavor of winter squash. With ginger, garlic, soy, and mirin, the flavors in this braise make for a versatile accompaniment to almost any main dish.

- 2 tbsp. canola oil
- 1 1½" piece fresh ginger, minced
- 2 cloves garlic, minced
- 3 scallions, minced, plus more for garnish
- ¼ cup chicken or vegetable stock
- 3 tbsp. soy sauce
- 1 tbsp. mirin
- 1 tbsp. sugar
- ½ medium kabocha squash, peeled, seeded and cut into 1" × 4" wedges

1 Heat oil in a 12" skillet over medium-high heat. Add ginger, garlic, and scallions and cook until fragrant, 1–2 minutes.

2 Add stock, soy sauce, mirin, and sugar and bring to a simmer. Add squash and cook, turning once, until softened, about 8 minutes.

3 Reduce heat to low, cover, and cook until tender, turning once to glaze evenly, about 15 minutes more.

STEWED PATTYPAN SQUASH WITH TOMATOES

SERVES 4

When served with chicken fried steak, fried okra, and pecan pie, a side of stewed squash and tomatoes completes Oklahoma's official state meal. Use tiny yellow and green pattypan squash and fresh tomatoes for the best results.

- ¼ cup extra-virgin olive oil
- 1 large onion, roughly chopped
- 1 lb. small green and yellow pattypan squash, cut into 1" wedges
- 1½ tsp. kosher salt
- 3 medium tomatoes, cored and cut into eighths
- 2 cloves garlic, finely chopped
- 2 tbsp. butter
- 8 fresh basil leaves, thinly sliced
  Freshly ground black pepper, to taste

1 Heat olive oil in a 12" skillet over medium-high heat. Add onion and cook, stirring occasionally, until soft, about 10 minutes. Add squash and salt and cook, stirring occasionally, until squash begins to soften and brown, about 15 minutes.

2 Add 1 cup water, tomatoes, and garlic to skillet and stir to combine. Cook until liquid has reduced by half and the squash is cooked through, about 5 more minutes. Stir in butter and basil and season with pepper to taste.

Sweet Potato

SWEET POTATO CASSEROLE WITH PECAN CRUMBLE

SERVES 6–8 (SEE PHOTO, PAGE 434)

In 1917, the marketers of Angelus Marshmallows published a booklet designed to encourage home cooks to embrace the candy as an everyday ingredient. It featured plenty of instant classics, including the first documented appearance of mashed sweet potatoes baked with a marshmallow topping. In this version, a pecan crumble adds an additional layer of decadence to the Thanksgiving classic.

FOR THE FILLING

- 3 lb. sweet potatoes
- ⅓ cup packed dark brown sugar
- 6 tbsp. unsalted butter, melted
- ¼ cup heavy cream
- 1 tsp. vanilla extract
- 1 tsp. ground cinnamon
- ½ tsp. freshly grated nutmeg
- ½ tsp. kosher salt
- 2 eggs, lightly beaten
- 1 1" piece fresh ginger, peeled and finely grated
  Freshly ground black pepper, to taste

FOR THE CRUMBLE TOPPING

- ½ cup flour
- ½ cup rolled oats
- ½ cup packed dark brown sugar
- ¼ cup finely chopped pecans
- ½ tsp. kosher salt
- 5 tbsp. cold unsalted butter, cubed
- ¼ cup mini marshmallows

1 Make the filling: Heat oven to 425°. Place sweet potatoes on a parchment paper–lined baking sheet and bake until soft, about 1½ hours; let cool for 30 minutes, then remove skins. Pass potatoes through a food mill into a large bowl; stir in sugar, butter, cream, vanilla, cinnamon, nutmeg, salt, eggs, ginger, and pepper. Pour mixture into a 1½-qt. baking dish and smooth top; set aside.

2 Make the topping: Reduce oven temperature to 350°. Stir together flour, oats, sugar, pecans, and salt in a bowl; add butter and, using your fingers, rub butter into flour mixture until large crumbles form. Mound crumble mixture over filling, dot with marshmallows, and bake until filling is hot and topping is browned, about 30 minutes. Let cool for 15 minutes before serving.

SWEET POTATO FRIES
SERVES 4

Fries made from pale yellow sweet potatoes (not to mention the moister, orange-fleshed American "yam," which is actually a variety of potato) are an exuberant alternative to conventional French fries. Add a dusting of black pepper as well as salt—its floral warmth dovetails beautifully with the sweet potato's subtle honey flavor.

3	lb. sweet potatoes or yams
	Vegetable oil, for frying
	Kosher salt, to taste
	Freshly ground black pepper, to taste (optional)

1 Peel sweet potatoes, if you like, then trim ends. Cut each sweet potato into 8–10 thin wedges about 4″ long. Set aside.

2 Heat oven to lowest setting. Heat 2″ oil in a deep, heavy-bottomed skillet over medium-high heat. When oil is hot (about 325° on a deep-fry thermometer), fry sweet potatoes in small batches, turning frequently, for 3 minutes per batch or until golden and crisp. Remove from oil with tongs or a slotted spoon. Drain on paper towels and keep warm in oven while you fry remaining sweet potatoes. Serve hot, sprinkled with salt and, if desired, pepper.

TZIMMES
Root Vegetable Stew
SERVES 6–8

Flavored with honey and warm spices, this autumnal stew is a staple at Jewish holiday tables. Some versions are heavier on the carrot, while ours relies more on sweet potatoes; all include dried fruit for a hearty sweetness.

3	tbsp. olive oil
2	lb. beef chuck, cut into 1½″ cubes
	Kosher salt and freshly ground black pepper, to taste
1½	tsp. ground cinnamon
½	tsp. ground ginger
¼	tsp. freshly grated nutmeg
2	large yellow onions, minced
4	cups beef stock
2	lb. sweet potatoes, peeled and cut into 1½″ cubes
½	lb. pitted prunes, halved
2	carrots, cut into 1½″ lengths
1	tbsp. honey
1	tbsp. finely chopped fresh flat-leaf parsley

1 Heat oil in a 6-qt. Dutch oven over medium-high heat; season beef with salt and pepper. Working in batches, add beef to pot and cook, turning, until browned all over, about 8 minutes; transfer to a plate and set aside. Add cinnamon, ginger, nutmeg, and onions, season with salt and pepper, and cook, stirring, until soft, about 5 minutes. Return beef to pot along with stock and bring to a boil; reduce heat to medium-low and cook, covered partially, until beef is barely tender, about 1 hour.

2 Add potatoes, prunes, and carrots and cook, uncovered, until tender, about 1 hour. Remove from heat, stir in honey, and sprinkle with parsley.

Tomato

ROASTED TOMATOES
SERVES 6 (SEE PHOTO, PAGE 426)

The recipe for these aromatic roasted tomatoes easily scales to match your backyard bounty—or a summer farmers' market haul. Serve the tomatoes with slices of crusty baguette, or as a side dish with grilled fish or chicken.

6	medium tomatoes
6	cloves garlic, unpeeled and lightly crushed
5	sprigs fresh thyme
½	cup extra-virgin olive oil
	Kosher salt and freshly ground black pepper, to taste

Heat oven to 425°. Place tomatoes, garlic, and thyme on a baking sheet and drizzle with oil; season with salt and pepper. Bake, brushing tomatoes occasionally with the oil, until tomatoes soften and their skins split, about 25 minutes. Transfer tomatoes, along with juices, to a serving dish and serve warm.

SCALLOPED TOMATOES

SERVES 6

Ripe and juicy tomato slices baked with herbs, butter, and toasty bread crumbs make a wonderful summer side.

- 4 cups fresh bread crumbs
- 4 tbsp. butter, melted, or extra-virgin olive oil
- 2 tbsp. chopped fresh chives
- 2 tbsp. chopped fresh flat-leaf parsley
- 1 tbsp. fresh thyme leaves
  Kosher salt and freshly ground black pepper, to taste
- 6 tomatoes, thickly sliced

1 Heat oven to 375°. Combine bread crumbs, butter (or oil), chives, parsley, thyme leaves, and salt and pepper.

2 Press half the bread crumb mixture into a large baking dish to form a "crust." Bake until lightly golden, about 10 minutes.

3 Remove dish from oven, arrange a layer of tomatoes over bread crumbs, and sprinkle with more bread crumbs. Repeat process until tomatoes are used up, ending with a layer of bread crumbs. Bake until crumbs are golden and tomatoes are warm, about 10 minutes.

FRIED GREEN TOMATOES

SERVES 2–4

A fresh green tomato has a more vegetal flavor than a fully ripe fruit has, with just a hint of sweetness that lends itself to a spiced, crisp breading. Northerners tend to eat green tomatoes in late summer or fall, just before the peak of harvest, but in the South, where tomatoes can be red and juicy as early as May and June, fresh green tomatoes are enjoyed throughout the warm months.

- 1 lb. firm green tomatoes, sliced ⅓" thick
  Kosher salt, to taste
- 1½ cups canola oil
- 2 cups fine yellow cornmeal
- 1½ tsp. paprika
- 1 tsp. cayenne pepper
- 1 cup buttermilk

1 Toss tomatoes generously with salt in a colander set over a bowl; let sit for 30 minutes to drain, then pat completely dry using paper towels.

2 Heat oil in a 12" skillet over medium-high heat. Whisk together cornmeal, paprika, cayenne, and salt in a shallow bowl. Working in batches, dip tomatoes in buttermilk and dredge in cornmeal mixture; fry, flipping once, until golden and crisp, 1–2 minutes. Transfer to paper towels to drain; season with salt.

SOY-MARINATED GRILLED TOMATOES

SERVES 6–8

Ripe tomatoes develop umami-rich flavor when grilled with a soy sauce marinade. Mitsuba, a Japanese relative of parsley, contributes a mild cilantro-like freshness.

- ¼ cup olive oil
- 5 cloves garlic, finely chopped
- 3 tbsp. soy sauce
- 1 tbsp. red yuzu kosho (see Cook's Note)
- 1 tsp. sansho or Sichuan peppercorns
- 1 tsp. kosher salt
- 4 medium tomatoes, cored and halved crosswise
- 1 cup roughly chopped fresh mitsuba, flat-leaf parsley, or cilantro leaves and stems

1 Whisk together oil, garlic, soy sauce, yuzu kosho, sansho, and salt in a 9"×13" baking dish. Add tomatoes, toss to coat, then lay cut side down in dish. Let tomatoes marinate at room temperature for 15 minutes.

2 Build a hot fire in a charcoal grill or set a gas grill to high; bank coals or turn off burner on one side for indirect grilling (page 191). Reserve marinade and grill tomatoes, cut side down, on hottest part of grill until slightly charred, 2–4 minutes. Flip tomatoes, move to cooler part of grill, and spoon reserved marinade over tops; continue to grill without flipping until tomatoes are slightly caramelized, 6–8 minutes. Garnish with mitsuba.

COOK'S NOTE *Yuzu kosho*, a tart-hot relish of citrus, chiles, and salt, can be found online or at Japanese markets. It has a green variant, which is hotter than the red version.

TOMATOES STUFFED WITH LIMA BEANS

SERVES 4–6

Tomatoes stuffed with a mixture of lima beans, rice, and herbs make a beautiful vegetarian dish. If the tomatoes still have their stems, take care to leave them intact for the presentation.

6 large tomatoes
Kosher salt and freshly ground black pepper, to taste
2 cups cooked baby lima beans
1 cup cooked white rice
1 cup shredded arugula
¼ cup chopped fresh flat-leaf parsley
¼ cup chopped fresh chives
6 tbsp. extra-virgin olive oil
2 tbsp. fresh lemon juice

1 Blanch tomatoes in a large pot of boiling water for 30 seconds. Slip off skins and cut off the top quarter of each tomato on the stem end, saving tops. Carefully scoop out and reserve seeds and flesh. Lightly salt tomatoes inside and out. Turn upside down and allow to drain.

2 Combine reserved tomato seeds and flesh, lima beans, rice, arugula, parsley, and chives in a medium bowl. Drizzle 4 tbsp. of the olive oil and 2 tbsp. of the lemon juice into the vegetables, add a few grinds of pepper, and mix lightly. Taste and add more lemon juice, salt, or pepper as needed.

3 Fill tomato shells with lima bean mixture. Place tomatoes on a platter, replace tops, and scatter leftover beans around them. Drizzle with remaining 2 tbsp. olive oil.

TOMATO PUDDING

SERVES 8–10

This satisfying mush of homemade croutons, tomatoes, and pecorino cheese is based on a recipe from chef Mary Sue Milliken of the Border Grill in Los Angeles. It's a staple on her Thanksgiving table.

1 1-lb. loaf country bread, cut into 1″ pieces
¾ cup olive oil
Kosher salt and freshly ground black pepper, to taste
8 tbsp. unsalted butter
1 medium onion, thinly sliced
½ cup chicken stock
½ cup grated pecorino romano or aged Manchego
2 tbsp. dark brown sugar
2 tbsp. fresh lemon juice
2 tbsp. roughly chopped fresh thyme
1 28-oz. can whole, peeled tomatoes in juice, crushed by hand
1 16-oz. can tomato purée

1 Heat oven to 375°. Toss bread with ½ cup oil, salt, and pepper on a baking sheet; spread into an even layer. Bake, stirring occasionally, until slightly crisp, 10–15 minutes. Transfer to a large bowl and set aside.

2 Melt butter in a 6-qt. saucepan over medium-high heat. Add onion and cook until golden, 5–7 minutes. Stir in stock, half the pecorino, sugar, lemon juice, thyme, tomatoes, and tomato purée and cook until slightly reduced, about 20 minutes.

3 Remove sauce from heat and pour over bread; let sit until slightly cooled, then, using hands, lightly mash and stir together. Transfer to a 9″×13″ baking dish. Sprinkle remaining pecorino over top and drizzle with remaining oil. Bake until golden brown and bubbling, 25–30 minutes.

TOMATO-ZUCCHINI TIAN

SERVES 6

This striking dish epitomizes summer, especially when using vegetables just plucked from the garden. Fresh herbs enhance its appeal.

1 medium eggplant, peeled
Kosher salt and freshly ground black pepper, to taste
2 medium onions, peeled and chopped
3 cloves garlic, minced
8 tbsp. extra-virgin olive oil
2 medium zucchini, sliced on diagonal
6 ripe medium tomatoes, sliced
3–4 sprigs fresh herbs, such as thyme, rosemary, basil, or oregano
½ cup grated Parmigiano-Reggiano

1 Cut eggplant in 1″ cubes, sprinkle with salt, and place in a colander. Drain for 30 minutes, then pat dry.

2 Cook onions and garlic in 3 tbsp. oil in a medium skillet over medium heat until slightly browned, about 10 minutes. Transfer to a medium baking dish. In the same skillet, cook eggplant in 2–3 tbsp. oil until tender and slightly browned, about 10 minutes. Season with salt and pepper and stir into onion mixture.

3 Heat oven to 400°. Arrange zucchini and tomatoes in layers over eggplant. Top with herbs, drizzle with remaining 2–3 tbsp. oil, season to taste with salt and pepper, and bake for 30–40 minutes. Sprinkle with Parmigiano cheese and serve.

TOMATO ASPIC

SERVES 8

Savory tomato aspic is a midcentury luncheon classic. This version comes from the now-closed Woman's Industrial Exchange restaurant in Baltimore.

4	cups tomato juice
1	small onion, chopped
2	ribs celery, chopped
6	sprigs fresh flat-leaf parsley
1	tbsp. fresh lemon juice
1	tbsp. sugar
1	bay leaf
3	whole cloves
	Pinch of kosher salt
4	black peppercorns
2	tbsp. unflavored powdered gelatin
	Mayonnaise, for serving (optional)

1 Mix together tomato juice, onion, celery, parsley, lemon juice, sugar, bay leaf, cloves, salt, and peppercorns in a pot and bring to a boil. Reduce heat to low and simmer 30–40 minutes.

2 Soften gelatin in ½ cup water. Strain tomato juice mixture, discarding solids. Return to pot and stir in gelatin until dissolved. Pour into a lightly oiled 8″×8″ pan or ring mold, cover with plastic wrap, and chill until firm, about 4 hours. Serve with mayonnaise, if you like.

Turnips

TURNIP GALETTE

SERVES 4–6

This variation on a classic potato galette (page 407) takes on a bit of an edge from the turnips' sharp flavor.

	Butter, for greasing
15	medium turnips, peeled
	Kosher salt and freshly ground black pepper, to taste

1 Heat oven to 375°. Generously butter a 9″ glass pie dish. Thinly slice turnips and layer slices in dish, slightly overlapping. Season with salt and pepper.

2 Weight turnips with another 9″ glass pie dish. Bake until golden, 1–1½ hours. Uncover and invert onto a large plate.

TURNIP SOUFFLÉ

SERVES 4–6

If you don't boil it into oblivion, the humble, dependable turnip may surprise you with its sweet warmth. This soufflé comes by way of Clementine Paddleford, the pioneering early-20th-century food writer.

4	tbsp. butter
4	tbsp. flour, plus more for dusting
4	small, young turnips, peeled and diced
⅓	cup heavy cream
2	tbsp. yellow onion, minced
	Sea salt and freshly ground white pepper, to taste
4	eggs, separated

1 Heat oven to 350°. Grease a 6-cup soufflé dish with 1 tsp. butter, dust with flour (tap out excess), and set aside.

2 Boil turnips in a pot of salted water over high heat until soft, 8–10 minutes; drain well and mash until smooth. Melt remaining butter in a medium pan over medium heat. Add flour and cook, stirring, for 2 minutes. Stir in cream and turnips and cook, stirring, until thick, about 5 minutes.

3 Add onions and salt and pepper to taste. Remove pot from heat and gradually stir in egg yolks. Transfer mixture to a large bowl and set aside.

4 Whisk egg whites in a large bowl until stiff peaks form, then gently fold into turnip mixture. Spoon into prepared dish. Bake until puffed and golden, 35–40 minutes.

Yucca

YUCCA WITH PARSLEY-GARLIC SAUCE

Yuca con Mojo

SERVES 4

We discovered this distinctly Cuban side dish at La Fontana, a *paladar*—a privately run home-restaurant—in Havana.

2	lb. yucca, halved crosswise, peeled, and cut into thick wedges
	Kosher salt, to taste
¼	cup olive oil
¼	cup vegetable oil
3	scallions, minced
3	cloves garlic, minced

1   tbsp. chopped fresh flat-leaf parsley
Juice of 1 lime

1 Put yucca in a medium pot, cover with cold water by 2″, and add a pinch of salt. Simmer over medium-high heat until very soft and slightly translucent, 30–40 minutes. Drain, then arrange on a platter.

2 Meanwhile, heat olive and vegetable oils in a medium skillet over medium heat. Add scallions and garlic, season with salt, and cook, stirring often, until soft, about 5 minutes. Remove skillet from heat and stir in parsley and lime juice. Serve yucca drizzled with the warm garlic sauce.

Zucchini

ZUCCHINI STUFFED WITH RICOTTA

Zucchine Ripiene con Ricotta

SERVES 6

In this Italian dish, zucchini are stuffed with the twin stars of Calabrian cheese making: ricotta and pecorino. Flecked with tomato and mint, they are equally good eaten hot or at room temperature.

6	medium zucchini (about 2 lb.), halved lengthwise
7	tbsp. extra-virgin olive oil
3	cloves garlic, finely chopped
1	medium onion, finely chopped
2	medium tomatoes, seeded and chopped
2	cups ricotta
¾	cup grated pecorino
¾	cup fresh bread crumbs
3	tbsp. finely chopped fresh flat-leaf parsley
2	tsp. dried mint, crumbled
2	tsp. chopped fresh oregano
2	egg yolks, beaten
	Kosher salt and freshly ground black pepper, to taste

1 Scoop out and discard pulp from each zucchini half, leaving a ¼″ rim around the edges. Heat 3 tbsp. oil in a 10″ skillet over medium heat. Add garlic and onion and cook, stirring occasionally, until translucent, about 6 minutes. Add tomatoes and cook, stirring occasionally, until soft, 4 minutes more. Remove from heat and set aside.

2 In a medium bowl, stir together ricotta, ¼ cup pecorino, ¼ cup bread crumbs, parsley, mint, oregano, and egg yolks. Fold in onion mixture and season with salt and pepper. Set filling aside.

3 Arrange an oven rack 7″ from broiler and heat broiler. Rub the insides of zucchini halves with 2 tbsp. oil and season lightly with salt. Place zucchini, cut side up, on a foil-lined baking sheet and broil for 5 minutes. Remove from oven and fill each zucchini half with enough of the ricotta mixture that it mounds slightly but doesn't spill over the edges of the zucchini. Sprinkle stuffed zucchini with remaining ½ cup pecorino and bread crumbs and drizzle with remaining 2 tbsp. oil. Broil until zucchini are soft and tops are lightly browned, 10–15 minutes.

ZUCCHINI FRITTERS

Kolokitho Keftedes

SERVES 4

This fresh-flavored, crisp Cretan mezze dish can be served hot or at room temperature.

1	lb. zucchini, coarsely grated
2	tsp. kosher salt
½	cup minced fresh flat-leaf parsley
½	cup grated pecorino romano
½	cup dried bread crumbs
1	medium onion, grated
1	egg, beaten
	Freshly ground black pepper, to taste
	Pinch of cayenne pepper, to taste
	Olive oil or canola oil, for frying

1 Mix zucchini and salt in a sieve; set a weighted plate on top and let drain for 30 minutes. Transfer zucchini to a tea towel and squeeze out liquid. Mix zucchini, parsley, pecorino, bread crumbs, onion, and egg in a bowl. Season with pepper and cayenne; divide mixture into 12 balls. Press balls into ¾″-thick patties.

2 Pour oil to a depth of 2″ into a 4-qt. pot and heat over medium-high heat until a deep-fry thermometer reads 315°. Working in 2 batches, fry patties until browned and crisp, 5–6 minutes. Using a slotted spoon, transfer fritters to paper towels.

Pastas, Noodles & Dumplings

PASTAS, NOODLES & DUMPLINGS

ELICATE AND HEARTY, tender and chewy, and formed into myriad intriguing shapes, pasta satisfies like nothing else. It serves as the perfect canvas for all sorts of preparations, from Italy's herbaceous pestos, luscious cream sauces, and meat-enriched gravies to Asia's fragrant broths and fiery oils to America's cheese-laden casseroles.

As it turns out, humankind has been happily slurping noodles for millennia. In 2005, archaeologists in western China unearthed a 4,000-year-old bowl of noodles. Made of millet flour, those ancient strands were virtually identical to contemporary pasta, which everywhere is made according to the same formula: Flour of some sort is combined with water into a pasty dough (the word *pasta* is Italian for "paste"), which is then shaped, cooked, and dressed.

This fundamental process has given rise to infinite permutations that are the cornerstones of global cooking: Pasta is cut into strips, stretched into ropey strands, extruded to form tubes, and shaped into fanciful forms named for the objects they resemble: spiral *cavatappi,* meaning "corkscrew"; cupped *conchiglie,* or "shells." It might be left in broad sheets for layering in a crowd-pleasing lasagna, and its pliability allows it to wrap ingredients for dumplings filled with everything from lamb, onion, and garlic to a brothy mix of pork and scallion that must be slurped like soup.

The composition of pasta can vary almost as broadly. Practically every type of grain is used, and ingredients are sometimes added to enhance the final texture and flavor. In Italy's Emilia-Romagna region, cooks work eggs into the dough for tagliatelle, delicate, flat, golden noodles whose rough, broad surface clings to a thick Bolognese sauce. In much of Asia, rice flour is transformed into chewy, slippery rice noodles that are perfect for searing in the wok for a smoky pad thai or for fishing from a bowl of Vietnamese *pho.*

Dried pastas, which require only a short stint in boiling water, became widespread with the rise of industrialization, greatly increasing the food's popularity. But pastas have traditionally taken time and artistry. In Japanese noodle restaurants, chefs cut buckwheat-flour soba precisely by hand, exhibiting skill that takes years to master, and in North Africa, couscous makers painstakingly roll dough into tiny pearls for steaming to create the fluffy grains that cradle grilled or braised meats and spiced vegetables.

Pastas & Noodles

CAPPELLINI WITH WHITE CLAM SAUCE

SERVES 4

The secret to this simple and satisfying pasta dish is boiling the cappellini until it's barely al dente, so that it will absorb plenty of the briny, winey sauce when the two are cooked together—along with tender chopped clams—just before serving.

- ⅓ cup extra-virgin olive oil
- 3 cloves garlic, thinly sliced
- 2¼ lb. littleneck clams in their shells, cleaned
- ⅓ cup dry white wine
- ½ tsp. crushed red chile flakes
- 1 lb. dried cappellini
- 2 tbsp. finely chopped fresh flat-leaf parsley
  Kosher salt and freshly ground black pepper, to taste
- 3 tbsp. unsalted butter

1 Heat oil in a 12″ skillet over medium heat. Add garlic and cook, stirring, until fragrant, about 1 minute. Add clams, wine, and chile flakes, cover, and cook, shaking pan occasionally, until clams open, 8–10 minutes (discard any that don't open).

2 Meanwhile, bring a large pot of salted water to a boil and add cappellini; cook until barely al dente. Reserve ½ cup of the cooking water, then drain.

3 Transfer clams to a cutting board, letting them drain back into the skillet as you remove them, and remove meat from shells; roughly chop meat and return to skillet. Add pasta, reserved pasta water, parsley, salt, and pepper and toss until pasta is heated through, about 2 minutes. Add butter and toss until melted. Serve immediately.

STIR-FRIED RICE NOODLES WITH BLACK PEPPER & GARLIC CHIVES

Mee Teow

SERVES 4

Bangkok, and to a lesser extent Thailand's southern coastal provinces, are home to a minority population of Thai Chinese, originally of Teochew, Han, and Hainanese descent, and their vibrant foods, like this garlic chive-and-pepper-spiked noodle dish, are similar to recipes found in neighboring Malaysia and Singapore.

- 5 oz. sen mee or other thin rice noodles
- 4 tsp. peanut oil
- 2 cloves garlic, roughly chopped
- 30 garlic chives or scallions, trimmed and cut into ½″ pieces (about 2 cups)
- 2 cups mung bean sprouts
- 1 tbsp. soy sauce
- 2 tsp. freshly ground black pepper
  Kosher salt, to taste

1 Bring a medium pot of water to a boil. Add noodles and press down to submerge them. Immediately cover pot and turn off heat; let rest for 3 minutes. Drain noodles, rinse well in cold water, and drain again. Cut noodles in half and spread them out on a paper towel–lined baking sheet. Set aside to let dry slightly, 2–3 minutes.

2 Meanwhile, heat oil in a large nonstick skillet over medium-high heat. Add garlic and cook until golden, about 30 seconds. Add garlic chives and cook until just softened, about 30 seconds. Reduce heat to medium-low, add bean sprouts, soy sauce, pepper, salt, and reserved noodles, and toss together. Cook until chives are wilted, about 1 minute more. Serve immediately.

BETTY'S SPAGHETTI

SERVES 4

This recipe, from chef Thomas Keller, is an exuberantly updated version of a simple, creamy pasta dish often prepared by his mother, Elizabeth Marie "Betty" Keller, during his childhood.

- ¼ cup flour
- 1 cup plus 2 tbsp. canola oil
- 2 large shallots, 1 cut into ⅛″ rings, 1 finely chopped
- ½ cup unsalted butter
- ½ tsp. white wine vinegar
  Kosher salt and freshly ground black pepper
  Stems from 2 sprigs fresh parsley, cut into ½″ pieces, plus 1 tsp. finely minced, for garnish
- ½ lb. dried spaghetti
- ⅔ cup ricotta cheese
- 1 tbsp. extra-virgin olive oil

1 Put flour into a wide shallow dish. Heat 1 cup canola oil in a small pot over medium heat until it reaches 325° on a deep-fry thermometer. Working in 2 batches, toss shallot rings in flour to coat and shake off any excess. Fry shallots, stirring gently, until golden brown, about 90 seconds. Using a slotted spoon, transfer fried shallots to a paper towel–lined plate to drain. Set shallot rings aside.

2 Heat remaining 2 tbsp. canola oil in a large skillet over medium heat. Add chopped shallots and cook just until beginning to caramelize, 3–4 minutes. Add butter, vinegar, and 1 cup water and cook until reduced by about one-third, 18–20 minutes.

3 Meanwhile, bring a large pot of salted water to a boil. Add parsley stems and cook for 10 seconds. Transfer stems to a colander and rinse under cold water. Add spaghetti to boiling water and cook until al dente, 8–10 minutes. Drain spaghetti and add to skillet with shallot reduction; toss to combine. Add cooked parsley stems, ricotta, olive oil, salt, and pepper and toss to combine. Divide spaghetti among 4 warm bowls. Top with minced parsley and fried shallot rings. Serve immediately.

SPAGHETTI COLLINS

SERVES 6

This lovely, aromatic pasta recipe is a showpiece for scallions' sweet flavor. It's adapted from a dish served at the restaurant Pascal's Manale in New Orleans.

- Kosher salt and freshly ground black pepper, to taste
- 1 lb. dried spaghetti
- ⅓ cup olive oil
- 2 cloves garlic, minced
- 6 bunches scallions, chopped
- ⅓ cup white wine
- ½ cup beef or chicken stock
- 4 tbsp. butter
- ½ cup grated Parmigiano-Reggiano, for serving

1 Bring a large pot of salted water to a boil. Add spaghetti to boiling water and cook until al dente, 8–10 minutes.

2 Meanwhile, heat oil in a skillet over medium heat. Add garlic, scallions, and white wine and cook until soft, 2–3 minutes. Add stock and butter, season with salt and pepper, and cook until creamy, 1–2 minutes.

3 Drain pasta, add to skillet, and toss. Sprinkle with Parmigiano just before serving.

FOUR PERFECT PASTA TIPS

Everyone boasts that they can make great pasta—it's as simple as boiling water, right? But what makes humble foods like Spaghetti Carbonara (facing page) or Cacio e Pepe (page 346) so special is the way they are prepared: with subtle and time-honored techniques that make the whole considerably greater than the sum of the parts.

1. TOAST YOUR BLACK PEPPER Merely sprinkling preground pepper over the finished pasta won't come close to achieving the desired flavor in a classic sauce. Instead, crush whole black peppercorns in a mortar and pestle or grind them on the coarsest setting in a spice grinder. Then "toast" the cracked pepper by frying it in the olive oil you'll be using for the pasta sauce, heating it until it smells very fragrant.

2. FINISH YOUR PASTA IN THE SAUCE Here's a case where undercooking is the right thing to do. Boil your pasta until it's just short of al dente, then finish cooking it in the hot pan or skillet containing your sauce, tossing the pasta and the sauce together vigorously. This technique will cause the sauce to coat the pasta more thoroughly; it's the key to dishes like Bucatini all'Amatriciana (page 349).

3. RESERVE SOME OF YOUR PASTA WATER Adding a few ladlefuls of salty, starchy pasta water to the pasta and the sauce as you toss them together will moisten your sauce and add an additional layer of flavor and body to the final dish. In the case of the Cacio e Pepe, it will also help the cheese to melt evenly, ensuring a creamy, emulsified sauce.

4. SERVE IT RIGHT AWAY Pastas that are gilded with silky sauces don't do well resting on the counter, waiting to be served. Don't wait to eat them; serve them as soon as you pull them off the stove.

ANTS CLIMBING A TREE

Ma Yi Shang Shu

SERVES 4

The name for this Sichuanese dish means "ants climbing a tree," a reference to the way the ground pork clings to the strands of glass noodles.

- ¼ lb. dried bean thread (glass) noodles
- 2 tsp. toasted sesame oil
- 3 tbsp. canola oil
- ¼ lb. ground pork
- 4 cloves garlic, minced
- 1 3″ piece fresh ginger, peeled and minced
- 3 tbsp. red chile bean paste
- 2 tbsp. light soy sauce
- 1 tbsp. Shaoxing wine
- 1½ cups chicken stock
- 2 tbsp. dark soy sauce
- 3 garlic chives or scallions, thinly sliced

1 Place noodles and 4 cups boiling water in a bowl; let sit until soft, about 4 minutes. Drain and toss noodles with sesame oil; set aside.

2 Heat canola oil in a 14″ flat-bottomed wok over medium-high heat. Add pork and cook, breaking up meat, until browned, 5–7 minutes. Add garlic and ginger and cook, stirring, until fragrant, about 1 minute. Add bean paste, light soy, wine, and stock and bring to a boil. Add noodles and cook, stirring occasionally, until liquid is reduced by half, 8–10 minutes more. Stir in dark soy sauce and chives.

SPAGHETTI CARBONARA

SERVES 4

Real Roman spaghetti carbonara gets its richness from whole eggs, pancetta or *guanciale* (cured pork jowl), and Parmigiano-Reggiano and pecorino romano cheeses—never cream. Cooking the pancetta in the wine adds a hint of sweetness.

- 3 tbsp. extra-virgin olive oil
- 4 cloves garlic, crushed
- 10 oz. pancetta, cut into ½″-long by ¼″-square matchsticks
- ⅔ cup white wine
- 1 lb. dried spaghetti
- ⅔ cup grated Parmigiano-Reggiano
- ¼ cup grated pecorino romano

- 2 tbsp. finely chopped fresh flat-leaf parsley
- 2 eggs
  Kosher salt and freshly ground black pepper

1 Heat oil in a 12″ skillet over medium-high heat. Add garlic and cook until golden, about 1 minute. Remove and discard garlic. Add pancetta and cook until edges are crisp, about 6 minutes. Add wine and cook until thickened, about 3 minutes. Remove from heat.

2 Bring a large pot of salted water to a boil. Add spaghetti, and cook until al dente, about 7 minutes. Drain, reserving ¼ cup pasta water. In a large bowl, whisk together Parmigiano, pecorino, parsley, and eggs. While whisking constantly, slowly drizzle in reserved pasta water until smooth. Add spaghetti along with reserved pancetta mixture. Season with salt and a generous amount of pepper. Toss to combine and serve immediately.

DI PALO'S SPAGHETTI & MEATBALLS

SERVES 8

Lou Di Palo shared his grandmother's recipe for the meatballs that he sells at his family's store, Di Palo's Fine Foods in New York City. Serve them on top of spaghetti—food doesn't get more classic than that.

- ¼ cup olive oil
- 5 cloves garlic, finely chopped
- 1 tbsp. dried parsley
- 1 tbsp. dried basil
- 2 28-oz. cans whole, peeled tomatoes in juice, crushed by hand
  Kosher salt and freshly ground black pepper, to taste
- ¼ cup sugar
- 10 oz. ground pork
- 5 oz. ground beef chuck
- 5 oz. ground veal
- ⅓ cup shredded provolone
- ⅓ cup whole-milk ricotta
- ¼ cup grated Parmigiano-Reggiano
- ¼ cup grated pecorino romano, plus more for serving
- ¾ cup dried bread crumbs
- 3 eggs, lightly beaten
- 1 lb. dried spaghetti, cooked
- 2 tbsp. finely chopped fresh flat-leaf parsley, for serving

1 Heat 2 tbsp. oil and 3 cloves garlic in a 6-qt. saucepan over medium heat and cook until lightly browned, about 3 minutes. Add dried parsley, basil, tomatoes, salt, and pepper and cook for 1 hour. Add sugar and cook until reduced and thick, about 20 minutes.

2 Mix remaining garlic, pork, chuck, veal, provolone, ricotta, Parmigiano, pecorino, bread crumbs, eggs, salt, and pepper in a bowl. Form into eight 2½″ meatballs, about 6 oz. each.

3 Heat remaining oil in a 12″ skillet over medium-high heat. Working in batches, add meatballs and cook, turning, until browned, about 10 minutes. Transfer to sauce and simmer until cooked through, about 30 minutes. Serve meatballs and sauce over spaghetti. Sprinkle with fresh parsley.

BARBECUE SPAGHETTI

SERVES 6–8

This Memphis-style dish, a cockeyed cousin of traditional spaghetti with tomato sauce, is a great way to use leftover pulled pork (page 240).

- 3 cups tomato sauce
- ½ cup cane syrup
- 1½ tbsp. cider vinegar
- ¾ tsp. ground allspice
- ½ tsp. ground cinnamon
- ½ tsp. cayenne pepper
  Pinch of ground cloves
  Kosher salt and freshly ground black pepper, to taste
- 1 cup chopped pulled pork (page 240)
- 1 lb. dried spaghetti

1 In a 4-qt. saucepan, bring tomato sauce, syrup, vinegar, allspice, cinnamon, cayenne, cloves, salt, and pepper to a boil over medium-high heat. Cook, stirring, until thickened, about 10 minutes. Add pulled pork and cook until heated through.

2 Meanwhile, bring a large pot of salted water to a boil, add spaghetti, and cook until al dente, 8–10 minutes. Drain and toss with the sauce.

JAPCHAE

Korean Noodles with Beef and Vegetables

SERVES 4

This Korean noodle dish is a festive combination of slippery, transparent sweet potato–starch noodles (turned golden from the cooking juices) mixed with soy sauce, crunchy vegetables, and tender, juicy beef.

- 3 tbsp. canola oil
- 2 cups julienned carrots
  Kosher salt and freshly ground white pepper, to taste
- 2 cups thinly sliced onions
- 1 cup julienned red bell pepper
- 1 cup julienned button mushrooms
- 1 cup julienned filet mignon
- 1 clove garlic, minced
- ½ cup soy sauce
- ½ cup sugar
- 1 lb. dried dangmyeon (Korean sweet potato–starch noodles), soaked in very hot water until al dente
- 2 tbsp. sesame oil
- 2 tbsp. thinly sliced scallions, for garnish
- 1 tbsp. toasted sesame seeds, for garnish

1 Heat 1 tbsp. oil in a 12″ skillet over medium-high heat. Add carrots, season with salt and pepper, and cook, stirring, until half-tender, about 3 minutes. Transfer to a large bowl. Repeat with 1 tbsp. oil, onions, peppers, and mushrooms and add to bowl.

2 Wipe skillet clean; heat remaining oil. Add steak and garlic and cook until browned, about 4 minutes. Add soy sauce and sugar and cook until sugar dissolves. Pour over vegetables in bowl, add noodles and sesame oil, and toss. Garnish with scallions and sesame seeds.

WHOLE WHEAT SPAGHETTI WITH ANCHOVY SAUCE

Bigoli in Salsa

SERVES 4

We got the recipe for this traditional Venetian pasta dish—nutty from the whole wheat pasta, salty and savory from the anchovy—from Venice's Da Fiore restaurant, purveyor of some of the best food in that city.

8 oz. salt-packed whole anchovies (about 32)
1½ cups dry white wine
½ cup extra-virgin olive oil
1 large yellow onion, halved and thinly sliced
Kosher salt
¾ lb. dried whole wheat spaghetti
2 tbsp. finely chopped fresh flat-leaf parsley, for garnish

1 Soak anchovies in ½ cup of the white wine and 2 cups water in a large bowl for 30 minutes. Gently pull anchovies apart into lengthwise halves from the head end and remove and discard spines and all tiny bones. Wash anchovies in the soaking liquid, discard the soaking liquid, set aside 6 anchovy halves for garnish, then chop remaining halves into small pieces and set aside.

2 Heat oil in a large skillet over medium heat. Stir in onion and chopped anchovies, breaking up anchovies with the back of a wooden spoon, until onions are very soft and anchovies have "melted," about 10 minutes. Add remaining 1 cup wine and stir, scraping up any brown bits stuck to bottom of skillet. Reduce heat to low, cover, and cook for about 30 minutes, stirring occasionally.

3 Meanwhile, bring a large pot of lightly salted water to a boil. Add spaghetti and cook until pasta is just tender, about 8 minutes. Drain, add pasta to sauce, mix well, and serve garnished with reserved anchovies and parsley.

SPAGHETTI WITH GRILLED ARTICHOKES
SERVES 4

Baby artichokes, minimally dressed with olive oil and garlic and slightly charred from a few minutes on the grill, take center stage in this springtime dish.

1 lb. baby artichokes with stems, trimmed and halved lengthwise, tough outer leaves discarded
Zest and juice of 1 lemon
6 tbsp. extra-virgin olive oil
Kosher salt and freshly ground black pepper, to taste
½ lb. dried spaghetti
4 tbsp. unsalted butter
¼ tsp. crushed red chile flakes
4 cloves garlic, minced
⅔ cup finely grated Parmigiano-Reggiano
2 tbsp. minced fresh flat-leaf parsley, for garnish

1 Put artichokes, 2 tbsp. lemon juice, and 6 cups water in a 4-qt. saucepan. Bring to a boil, reduce heat, and simmer until crisp-tender, about 5 minutes. Drain artichokes; transfer to a medium bowl and toss with 4 tbsp. oil and salt and pepper. Heat a 12″ grill pan over high. Place artichokes cut side down on grill pan and cook until tender, 6 minutes per side. Return grilled artichokes to the bowl and cover with plastic wrap; set aside.

2 Bring a large pot of salted water to a boil and add pasta; cook, stirring occasionally, until al dente, 6–7 minutes. Drain pasta, reserving 1 cup pasta water; set aside. Heat remaining oil and 3 tbsp. butter in a 12″ skillet over medium heat. Add chile flakes and garlic and cook, stirring, until garlic is soft, 4–5 minutes. Add remaining lemon juice along with zest, cooked pasta, and ½ cup Parmigiano and toss together, adding reserved pasta water as needed to create a smooth sauce. Stir in remaining butter and parsley and season with salt and pepper. To serve, divide pasta evenly among 4 bowls and top with artichokes; garnish with remaining Parmigiano and parsley.

LO MEIN
Egg Noodles with Beef and Chinese Broccoli
SERVES 4

Lo mein, literally "tossed noodles," is a generic Cantonese term for any combination of fresh egg noodles, stir-fried vegetables, and (occasionally) meat. Beef and Chinese broccoli are a common—and delicious—version.

3 tbsp. light soy sauce
3 tbsp. oyster sauce
1 tsp. sugar
½ lb. top sirloin steak, halved lengthwise and thinly sliced
3 tbsp. vegetable oil
½ lb. gai lan, trimmed, leaves and stems thinly sliced on the diagonal
1 cup unsalted chicken stock
1 tbsp. dark soy sauce
1 lb. fresh or frozen Chinese thick egg noodles
½ tsp. toasted sesame oil
Freshly ground black pepper, to taste

1 Combine 1 tbsp. light soy sauce, 1 tbsp. oyster sauce, and sugar in a bowl. Add beef and marinate for 20 minutes.

2 Heat vegetable oil in a wok over high heat. Add beef and stir-fry until it begins to brown. Add broccoli and stir-fry until tender, about 3 minutes. Transfer to a plate and set aside.

3 Bring stock, remaining 2 tbsp. light soy sauce, remaining 2 tbsp. oyster sauce, and dark soy sauce to a boil in wok over high heat. Add noodles, stir, and cook until most of liquid has been absorbed, 5–10 minutes. Stir in sesame oil, beef, and broccoli. Season with pepper and serve.

SPAGHETTI ALLA PRIMAVERA

SERVES 4–6 (SEE PHOTO, PAGE 432)

This cream-laced pasta dish, tossed with vibrant vegetables and toasted pine nuts, was made famous by Sirio Maccioni of New York City's famed Le Cirque.

1	lb. dried spaghetti
7	tbsp. olive oil
3	cloves garlic, minced
6	oz. button mushrooms, quartered
1	cup asparagus tips, blanched
1	cup small broccoli florets, blanched
½	cup frozen peas, blanched
1	small zucchini, quartered lengthwise, cut into 1″ lengths and blanched
1	cup heavy cream
⅔	cup grated Parmigiano-Reggiano
2	tbsp. unsalted butter
	Kosher salt and freshly ground black pepper, to taste
1	cup grape tomatoes, halved
2	tbsp. thinly shredded fresh basil
½	cup pine nuts, lightly toasted, for garnish

1 Bring a large pot of salted water to a boil. Add spaghetti and cook until al dente, about 8 minutes. Drain, toss with 1 tbsp. oil, and reserve pasta.

2 Heat 5 tbsp. oil in a 12″ skillet over medium heat. Add two-thirds of the garlic and cook until golden, about 2 minutes. Add mushrooms and cook until golden, about 3 minutes. Add asparagus, broccoli, peas, and zucchini and cook for 3 minutes. Add pasta, cream, Parmigiano, and butter, season with salt and pepper, and toss to combine; transfer to a platter.

3 Bring remaining 1 tbsp. oil and garlic, tomatoes, and basil to a simmer and pour over pasta, then garnish with nuts.

OUT OF THE KITCHEN

"I believe it started in 1975, when I visited Prince Edward Island with a number of colleagues, including Craig Claiborne of the *New York Times*. To eat, we had only lobster and wild boar. After a week of this, everyone said, "Can we have some pasta?" I set out to make two dishes, one with vegetables, one Alfredo style. But in the end I mixed it all together, vegetables with spaghetti and cream. After Claiborne wrote about it in the *Times*, everybody started to come to Le Cirque and ask for *spaghetti alla primavera*. But my French chef said, "You want to do spaghetti? I don't want spaghetti in my kitchen!" I didn't want a crisis. So I decided to prepare it in the dining room on a cart, tableside. It looked nice, and it tasted nice. We've never put it on the menu, but people still ask for it."

SIRIO MACCIONI
co-owner of Le Cirque restaurant in New York City

SPAGHETTI CACIO E PEPE

Cheese & Pepper Pasta

SERVES 4

Less is more in this elemental Roman pasta dish, which gets its spiciness from black pepper toasted in oil.

1	lb. dried spaghetti
4	tbsp. extra-virgin olive oil
2	tsp. freshly cracked black pepper, plus more to taste
1¾	cups finely grated pecorino romano

1 Bring a large pot of salted water to a boil. Add pasta and cook until al dente, 8–10 minutes. Reserve 1 cup pasta water and drain pasta.

2 Meanwhile, heat oil in a 12″ skillet over medium heat until shimmering. Add pepper and cook until fragrant, 1–2 minutes. Ladle ¾ cup pasta water into skillet and bring to a boil. Using tongs, transfer pasta to skillet and spread it out evenly. Sprinkle ¾ cup pecorino over pasta and toss to combine until sauce is creamy and clings to the pasta without clumping, about 2 minutes, adding a little pasta water if necessary. Transfer to 4 plates and sprinkle with remaining pecorino and more pepper.

PASTA SHAPES

There are hundreds of Italian pasta shapes, each with its own regional and familial variations. Here's a rundown of our favorites.

CASARECCI

Thick, rolled *casarecci* were traditionally homemade across southern Italy; now commercial versions are available.

FARFALLE

Farfalle, "butterflies," are a perennial favorite throughout Italy; an egg version, called stricchetti, is popular in Bologna.

PENNE RIGATE

In Italian the name means "ridged quills"; this pasta allows sauces to adhere to its ribbed exterior and cylindrical cavity.

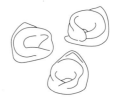

TORTELLINI

The distinctively shaped stuffed pasta called tortellini often goes by the name *ombelichi di Venere*, "Venus' navels," in Bologna.

SPAGHETTI

Spaghetti remains quasi-sacred in Rome, especially when it's used in the luscious cheese-and-pepper-sauce pasta dish known as *cacio e pepe* (facing page).

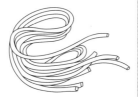

TONNARELLI

Tonnarelli are square noodles often made with eggs. Many Roman cooks prefer tonnarelli for tomato-based sauces and simple cheese-and-oil preparations.

PAPPARDELLE

The ultrawide ribbons of egg pasta known as pappardelle (*pappare* means "to gobble up") are usually consumed fresh, though good dried versions are increasingly available.

BUCATINI

This long, hollow noodle is made from durum wheat and water and is among the most classically Roman pasta shapes. In the dish known as *bucatini all'amatriciana* (page 349), it is paired with tangy tomato sauce.

ORECCHIETTE

Orecchiette ("little ears") are small, circular noodles with ridges—thumbprints left while hand-shaping the pasta that are ideal for chunky sauces.

GARGANELLI

Egg-based *garganelli* are a specialty of Bologna. The grooved edges of the pasta are perfect for gripping the meaty sauces celebrated in this region.

LASAGNETTE

Lasagnette, which are popular in southern Italy, look like the ruffly lasagne sheet common in that area, but are thinner and longer.

RADIATORI

The name literally translates to "radiators," but this pasta's deep-corrugated pieces make wonderful vessels for thick sauces.

COLD SESAME NOODLES

SERVES 4

Peanut butter, sesame paste, and chile-garlic paste combine to make a silky, savory sauce for these noodles—a Chinese-American restaurant staple. Chopped peanuts and a flurry of slivered cucumber and carrot add crunch.

- 1 lb. fresh or frozen Chinese egg noodles
- 4 tbsp. sesame oil
- 3½ tbsp. soy sauce
- 2 tbsp. rice vinegar
- 2 tbsp. sesame paste
- 2 tbsp. smooth peanut butter
- 1 tbsp. sugar
- 2½ tsp. jarred chile-garlic paste, such as sambal oelek
- 2 tsp. toasted sesame seeds
- 2 cloves garlic, finely chopped
- 2 scallions, thinly sliced
- 1 1½" piece fresh ginger, peeled and finely chopped
- 1 small cucumber, peeled, seeded, and julienned
- 1 carrot, peeled and julienned
  Chopped roasted peanuts, for garnish

1 Bring a large pot of water to a boil. Add noodles and cook until barely tender, about 5 minutes. Drain in a colander, rinse with cold water, and drain again. Transfer to a bowl, add 3 tbsp. sesame oil, and toss until evenly coated and set aside.

2 In another bowl, whisk together remaining sesame oil, soy sauce, vinegar, sesame paste, peanut butter, sugar, chile-garlic paste, sesame seeds, garlic, scallions, and ginger. Pour over noodles, add cucumber and carrot, and toss until evenly combined. Transfer to a serving bowl and garnish with peanuts.

PASTA ALLA NORMA

Pasta with Tomato Sauce & Eggplant

SERVES 4–6

Chef Sara Jenkins of New York City's Porchetta gave us her recipe for this spicy, comforting dish, one of the essential Sicilian pasta recipes. Allegedly, it's named for the heroine (and title character) of the Bellini opera *Norma*.

- 2 medium eggplants, cut into ¾" cubes
- 7 tbsp. extra-virgin olive oil
  Kosher salt and freshly ground black pepper, to taste
- 1 small yellow onion, minced
- 1 tsp. crushed red chile flakes
- 5 cloves garlic, minced
- 1 28-oz. can whole, peeled tomatoes in juice, crushed by hand
- 16 fresh basil leaves, torn
- 1 lb. dried bucatini
- ¼ lb. ricotta salata, grated

1 Heat oven to 500°. Put eggplant into a bowl and drizzle with 4 tbsp. oil. Toss to combine and season with salt and pepper. Transfer eggplant to 2 baking sheets and bake, turning occasionally, until soft and caramelized, about 20 minutes. Transfer to a rack; set aside.

2 Heat remaining 3 tbsp. oil in a 5-qt. pot over medium heat. Add onions and cook, stirring, until soft, about 10 minutes. Add chile flakes and garlic and cook, stirring, until garlic softens, about 3 minutes. Add tomatoes and half the basil, season with salt, and cook until heated through, about 5 minutes.

3 Meanwhile, bring a large pot of salted water to a boil. Add pasta and cook, stirring occasionally, until just al dente, about 8 minutes. Drain pasta and transfer to tomato sauce. Stir in reserved eggplant and toss to combine. Stir in remaining basil and season with salt. To serve, transfer pasta to a platter and garnish with ricotta salata.

LOBSTER FRA DIAVOLO

SERVES 6–8

This spicy seafood pasta, an Italian-American restaurant classic, gets an extra boost of flavor from the lobster shells that are used when making the zesty tomato sauce.

- ½ cup extra-virgin olive oil
- 2 1¼-lb. live lobsters, cleaned, tails cut into 6 pieces, claws cracked open, bodies reserved
- ½ cup flour
- 2 tsp. crushed red chile flakes
- 1 tsp. dried oregano
- 5 cloves garlic, finely chopped
- 2 tbsp. tomato paste
- ½ cup cognac or brandy
- 1 cup seafood or fish stock
- 1 28-oz. can whole, peeled tomatoes in juice, crushed by hand
- 1 bay leaf
  Kosher salt and freshly ground black pepper
- 1 lb. dried bucatini or spaghetti
- 1 tbsp. chopped fresh flat-leaf parsley

1 Heat oil in an 8-qt. Dutch oven over medium-high heat. Toss lobster pieces (including reserved bodies) in flour, shake off excess, and add to pot; cook until shells turn red, about 6 minutes. Transfer lobster pieces to a plate; set aside.

2 Add chile flakes, oregano, and garlic to pot and cook until lightly toasted, about 3 minutes. Add tomato paste and cook until lightly caramelized, about 2 minutes. Add cognac and cook until almost evaporated, about 2 minutes. Add stock, tomatoes, and bay leaf and bring to a boil. Reduce heat to medium-low and cook, partially covered, until thickened, about 30 minutes. Meanwhile, bring a large pot of salted water to a boil, add bucatini, and cook until al dente, about 8 minutes. Drain and reserve.

3 Return lobster to pot and sauté until cooked through, about 10 minutes. Season with salt and pepper. Add pasta and toss with sauce. Transfer to a large serving platter and garnish with parsley.

BUCATINI ALL'AMATRICIANA

SERVES 6–8

Chef Rachael Grossman of Portland, Oregon, provided this exceptional version of the Italian pasta classic, named for the central Italian town of Amatrice. In it, she uses bacon in place of the traditional *guanciale* (cured pork jowl). It's perfect served with Carbone's Garlic Bread (this page).

¾	lb. thick-cut bacon, cut crosswise into ¼″ strips
2	tbsp. unsalted butter
2	medium carrots, peeled and finely chopped
1	large yellow onion, finely chopped
	Kosher salt, to taste
4	cloves garlic, finely chopped
1	sprig rosemary
1	sprig sage
2	tbsp. red wine
1	28-oz. can whole, peeled tomatoes in juice, crushed by hand
2	tbsp. extra-virgin olive oil
2	tsp. freshly ground black pepper, plus more to taste
1	tsp. crushed red chile flakes
1	lb. dried bucatini
	Grated pecorino romano, for garnish
	Finely chopped fresh flat-leaf parsley, for garnish

1 Heat bacon in a 6-qt. saucepan over medium heat and cook until fat renders and bacon is crisp, about 15 minutes. Using a slotted spoon, transfer bacon to paper towels to drain; set aside.

2 Add butter to pan with drippings and then add carrots and onion and season with salt. Cook, stirring, until soft, about 6 minutes. Add half the garlic and the rosemary and sage and cook, stirring, until fragrant, about 2 minutes. Add wine and cook, stirring, until evaporated, about 5 minutes. Add tomatoes and bring to a boil; reduce heat to medium-low and cook, partially covered and stirring occasionally, until reduced and thickened, about 2 hours. Remove and discard rosemary and sage and transfer sauce to a blender; purée and then return to pan. Stir in three-quarters of the reserved bacon, along with remaining garlic and oil, pepper, and chile flakes; keep warm.

3 Meanwhile, bring a large pot of salted water to a boil, and add bucatini. Cook, stirring occasionally, until al dente, about 8 minutes. Drain pasta and add to pan with sauce; toss to coat. Divide pasta and sauce among serving bowls and garnish each bowl with remaining reserved bacon, pecorino, and parsley.

Carbone's Garlic Bread

SERVES 4–6

The recipe for this cheesy, herb-flecked exemplar of garlic breads comes from Manhattan's Carbone restaurant.

1	large baguette, halved lengthwise
6	tbsp. unsalted butter, softened
1	tbsp. olive oil
1	tsp. crushed red chile flakes
1	tsp. dried oregano
4	cloves garlic, smashed into a paste
	Kosher salt and freshly ground black pepper, to taste
⅓	cup grated Parmigiano-Reggiano
1	tbsp. finely chopped fresh chives
1	tbsp. finely chopped fresh flat-leaf parsley

Heat broiler. Place baguette cut side up on a foil-lined baking sheet. Stir butter, oil, chile flakes, oregano, garlic, salt, and pepper in a bowl; spread evenly over cut sides of baguette and sprinkle with Parmigiano. Bake until golden and slightly crisp, 2–3 minutes. Sprinkle with chives and parsley; cut into 2″ pieces.

PASTA WITH TOMATO-BEER PUTTANESCA SAUCE

SERVES 4

In this dish, based on one served at Birrificio Italiano, a brewery and restaurant in Italy's Lombardy region, the piquant puttanesca-style pasta sauce is enriched with Bibock, the brewery's malty, bock-style beer.

- 3 tbsp. extra-virgin olive oil
- ¼ cup salt-packed capers, rinsed
- 8 oil-packed sun-dried tomatoes, chopped
- 8 cloves garlic, smashed
- 6 oil-packed anchovy filets, chopped
- 4 red Fresno chiles, seeded and chopped
- 4 gherkins, chopped
- 2 red onions, chopped
- 1 28-oz. can whole, peeled tomatoes in juice, crushed by hand
- 1 12-oz. bottle bock or other malty, dark beer
- ¾ cup Kalamata olives, pitted and halved
  Kosher salt and freshly ground black pepper, to taste
- 1 lb. dried pasta, such as scialatielli or linguine
- 8 caper berries, for garnish
- 2 tbsp. finely chopped fresh flat-leaf parsley, for garnish

1 Heat oil in a 4-qt. saucepan over medium-high heat. Add capers, sun-dried tomatoes, garlic, anchovies, chiles, gherkins, and onions and cook, stirring occasionally, until browned, about 20 minutes. Add canned tomatoes and beer and bring to a boil. Reduce heat to medium-low and simmer until sauce thickens, about 1½ hours. Purée sauce in a blender, then return to low heat. Stir in olives and season with salt and pepper.

2 Bring a large pot of salted water to a boil. Add pasta and cook until al dente. Drain pasta and transfer pasta to sauce; toss to combine. Stir in a little pasta water to loosen the sauce, if you like. Serve garnished with caper berries and parsley.

PAD THAI WITH PORK & SHRIMP

SERVES 2

Variations on this popular noodle dish abound. This recipe, adapted from chef Andy Ricker's version, captures the vibrance of the sweet-sour-salty-spicy balance emblematic of pad thai—which was reportedly created in the 1930s by a Thai politician promoting national identity.

- 1 cup Thai Tamarind Water (page 351)
- ¾ cup Palm Sugar Syrup (page 351)
- ½ cup Thai fish sauce, plus more for serving
- 4 oz. wide sen lek (semi-dried, flat rice noodles)
- 1 tbsp. plus 1 tsp. medium dried shrimp
- 2 tbsp. lard or canola oil
- 4 medium fresh shrimp (2 oz.), peeled and deveined
- 3 tbsp. (1½ oz.) ground pork
- 1 large egg, at room temperature
- ¼ cup unflavored pressed (extra-firm) tofu (1¼ oz.), sliced ¼" thick
- 2 tbsp. shredded Thai salted radish, soaked in cold water for 10 minutes, rinsed, and drained well
- 1 cup lightly packed soybean sprouts
- ¼ cup fresh garlic chives, sliced into 1½" lengths, plus more for topping
- 1 tbsp. chopped unsalted roasted peanuts, plus more for topping
  Lime wedges, thinly sliced banana blossoms, and raw cane sugar, for serving
  Phrik Pon Khua (Toasted Thai Chile Powder; page 589), for serving

1 Combine tamarind water, palm sugar syrup, and fish sauce in a small bowl and stir well to combine.

2 Using kitchen shears, snip noodles into 8" pieces. Combine cut noodles and enough lukewarm water to cover by 1" in a medium bowl. Set aside to soak until very pliable, about 30 minutes. Drain and set noodles by stove.

3 Combine dried shrimp and enough cold water to cover them by 1" in a small bowl. Let soak for 10 minutes, then drain, briefly rinse, and pat dry.

4 In a flat-bottomed wok or small, dry skillet over medium heat, add rehydrated dried shrimp and cook, stirring frequently, until they are slightly crispy, about 10 minutes. Transfer to a bowl, and let cool.

5 Return the wok to high heat, add lard or oil, and swirl to coat inner surface and sides. Once smoking, add fresh shrimp and pork and cook, using a wok spatula or large wooden spoon to continuously stir and break up pork for about 15 seconds. Push shrimp and pork to one side of wok, then crack egg into empty side. Lower heat to medium, and cook until the edges of the whites are lightly golden and crispy, about 30 seconds. Add tofu, radish, and toasted dried shrimp to an empty area of wok. Use wok spatula to flip egg (it's okay if yolk breaks) and cook, without stirring, for 1 minute. Use spatula to break egg into several rough pieces, then stir everything together vigorously and continuously for 1 minute more. Add noodles on top of ingredients in wok and cook, without stirring, for 45 seconds. (Moisture clinging to noodles will steam up dramatically.) Vigorously stir everything together, then add ¼ cup plus 2 tablespoons of prepared sauce, and stir again. Add bean sprouts and cook, stirring occasionally, until noodles are fully tender and have absorbed sauce, and bean sprouts are tender but still crunchy, 1–1½ minutes. Add ¼ cup garlic chives and 1 tablespoon peanuts, and stir fry briefly.

6. Transfer pad thai to a serving platter. Sprinkle with additional garlic chives and peanuts, and serve. On the side, arrange whole banana blossoms, if using, and offer small dishes of toasted chile powder, fish sauce, and raw cane sugar for guests to customize their plates.

Thai Tamarind Water

MAKES 1¼ CUPS

The sticky pulp of the tamarind fruit is popular in sweet and savory dishes, and beverages in tropical regions.

- 1 3″ square (2 oz.) Thai or Vietnamese tamarind pulp

1 Combine tamarind pulp and 1¾ cups water in a small pot. Bring to a boil over high heat, using a spoon to break up tamarind as it softens. Immediately turn off heat, cover pot, and set aside until tamarind is very soft and hydrated, about 30 minutes.

2 Use a whisk or spoon to mash and stir tamarind mixture, breaking up any remaining large clumps.

3 Set a medium mesh strainer over a heatproof bowl. Pour mixture into strainer, pressing solids to extract as much liquid as possible. (There might be pulp clinging to outside of strainer; add that to the bowl too.) Discard remaining solids. Use or refrigerate in an airtight container for up to 1 week, or freeze for up to 3 months. Stir well before using.

Palm Sugar Simple Syrup

MAKES 2 CUPS

Dissolving palm sugar makes it easier to incorporate into a sauce. Look for the soft and scoopable version, sold in small tubs at Asian markets.

- 1½ cups (10 oz.) coconut palm sugar (preferably Thai)

Combine palm sugar and 1¼ cups water in a small pot. Bring to a boil over high heat, then immediately turn off heat and whisk until sugar has completely dissolved. Let cool to room temperature. Use immediately, or refrigerate in an airtight container for up to 3 months.

THE ORIGINAL FETTUCCINE ALFREDO

SERVES 4–6

A Roman named Alfredo di Lelio is credited with the invention of this decadent dish, just after the turn of the 20th century. As the story goes, after di Lelio's wife gave birth to their son, she lost her appetite. Di Lelio, determined to get her to eat, transformed his *fettuccine al burro*—a homely preparation of pasta tossed with butter and parmesan—by significantly increasing the amount of butter he used. The result was a more lavish dish, which neither his wife nor his customers could resist. Mixing the ingredients on a warmed platter helps them melt quickly to make a satiny sauce.

- 1 lb. dried fettuccine
- 1 cup (2 sticks) unsalted butter
- ½ lb. Parmigiano-Reggiano, grated (about 3¼ cups)

1 Bring a large pot of salted water to a boil. Add fettuccine and cook, stirring occasionally, until pasta is al dente, about 8 minutes.

2 Meanwhile, cut butter into ¼″ pats and transfer to a large, warmed platter. Drain pasta, reserving ¾ cup pasta water, and place pasta over butter on platter.

3 Sprinkle Parmigiano over pasta and drizzle with ¼ cup of the reserved pasta water.

4 Using a large spoon and fork, gently toss the pasta with the butter and cheese, lifting and swirling the noodles and adding more pasta water as necessary. (The pasta water will help create a smooth sauce.) Work in any melted butter and cheese that pools around the edges of the platter. Continue to mix the pasta until the cheese and butter have fully melted and the noodles are coated, about 3 minutes. Serve the fettuccine immediately on warmed plates.

COOK'S NOTE For the best results, use dried pasta, which doesn't break as easily during tossing as fresh egg pasta does.

FOOLPROOF FETTUCCINE

Making pasta at home takes time and effort, but store-bought fresh pasta cannot compare with the flavor and lightness of homemade.

STEP 1 Stir together 1 cup all-purpose flour and ½ cup semolina flour in a large bowl and form a well in the center; pour 2 beaten eggs into well and stir with a fork until dough forms. Transfer dough to a work surface and knead until smooth, about 10 minutes. Cover with plastic wrap and let sit for 30 minutes.

STEP 2 Cut homemade pasta dough into manageable pieces. Using a hand-crank pasta-rolling machine, pass the dough through the rollers repeatedly, decreasing the thickness each time, until the sheets of pasta are about 1/16″ thick and smooth.

STEP 3 Drape the sheets of pasta over a pasta drying rack (you can use a tie rack, dish-drying rack, or sweater-drying rack) for about 5 minutes to allow the moisture to evaporate from the surface of the pasta. This keeps the sheets from sticking to one another and makes them easier to cut.

STEP 4 Sprinkle some cornmeal across your work surface, then stack the sheets of pasta one on top of another, sprinkling more cornmeal between each layer. Beginning at one end of the stack, roll the sheets into a tight cylinder and position the cylinder seam side down.

STEP 5 Using a chef's knife, slice the cylinder crosswise into ¼″-wide ribbons of pasta. Unravel the ribbons by tossing them with a small amount of cornmeal and separating the ribbons with your fingers. Let the pasta sit uncovered for 10 minutes to dry before cooking or transfer to a storage container to use later.

FRESH FETTUCCINE WITH HEIRLOOM TOMATOES

SERVES 6–8

Homemade pasta doesn't need a lot of embellishment, as this simple summer recipe from the Portland food cart Artigiano proves.

6   cups roughly chopped heirloom tomatoes
1   cup halved heirloom cherry tomatoes
¼   cup extra-virgin olive oil
15   fresh basil leaves, thinly sliced
2   cloves garlic, finely chopped
    Kosher salt and freshly ground black pepper, to taste
    Foolproof Fettuccine (this page)
    Thinly shaved Parmigiano-Reggiano, for serving

1 Combine tomatoes, oil, basil, garlic, salt, and pepper in a bowl; cover and let sit at room temperature for 30 minutes to meld flavors.

2 Bring a large pot of salted water to a boil over high heat. Add pasta and cook, stirring, until al dente, about 3 minutes. Drain pasta and add to bowl of sauce; toss to combine. Divide among serving bowls and garnish with Parmigiano.

BROWN BUTTER PASTA WITH SUNNY-SIDE-UP EGGS

SERVES 4

Chef Gabrielle Hamilton of New York City's Prune restaurant gave us her recipe for this delicious pasta, which is tossed in brown butter and pine nuts, then topped with butter-basted sunny-side-up eggs.

½   lb. fresh fettuccine or tagliatelle
1   cup (2 sticks) unsalted butter
¾   cup pine nuts
4   eggs
    Kosher salt and freshly ground black pepper, to taste
    Freshly grated Parmigiano-Reggiano, to taste
    Freshly grated nutmeg, to taste

1 Bring a large pot of salted water to a boil. Add pasta and cook, stirring occasionally, until al dente, about 4 minutes. Drain pasta, reserving ½ cup of pasta water. Set aside separately.

2 Melt butter in a 12″ skillet over medium heat. Add pine nuts and cook, stirring often, until golden brown, about 10 minutes. Using a slotted spoon, transfer pine nuts to a bowl. Working in two batches, crack eggs into butter and cook, spooning butter over yolks, until whites are set but yolks are still runny, about 3 minutes. Transfer eggs to a plate and keep warm.

> ## "Spaghetti can be eaten most successfully if you inhale it like a vacuum cleaner."
>
> #### SOFIA LOREN

3 Add pasta and half the pine nuts to skillet and toss until hot. Stir in reserved pasta water to create a sauce, and season with salt and pepper. To serve, divide pasta among 4 serving plates and top each serving with a fried egg. Sprinkle with remaining pine nuts, Parmigiano, and nutmeg.

STIR-FRIED RICE NOODLES

Char Kuey Teow

SERVES 2

Shrimp, lap cheong sausage, chiles, and chives bring intense flavor to these wok-fried noodles, a popular street food in Singapore and Malaysia.

- 1 tbsp. dried shrimp paste
- 3 dried chiles de árbol, stemmed, torn into pieces, and soaked in very hot water for 5 minutes, drained
- 3 tbsp. peanut oil
- 2 cloves garlic, chopped
- 12 medium shrimp, peeled, deveined, and tails removed
- 1 6″ dried lap cheong sausage, peeled and thinly sliced
- 10 oz. fresh broad hé fěn rice noodles, rinsed and drained
- 1 tbsp. dark soy sauce
- 1 tsp. sugar
- 1 egg
- ¼ lb. mung bean sprouts
- 6 garlic chives or scallions, cut into 2″ lengths

1 Place shrimp paste on a small piece of foil and wrap foil around paste to form a packet; heat broiler and broil packet until fragrant, about 8 minutes. Let paste cool slightly, then transfer to a cutting board and add chiles; using a chef's knife, cut and mash shrimp paste and chiles together until a smooth paste forms; set paste aside.

2 Heat oil in a 12″ wok or nonstick skillet over high heat. Add chile-shrimp paste and cook, stirring, until fragrant, about 1 minute. Add garlic and cook, stirring, until just

golden, about 30 seconds. Add shrimp and sausage and cook, flipping shrimp once, until barely pink, about 1 minute. Break noodles apart with your fingers and add to wok along with soy sauce and sugar; cook, stirring often, until noodles are evenly coated and heated through, about 1 minute.

3 Make a well in the center of the noodles and add egg. Cook, without stirring, until white is half-set, about 45 seconds. Add sprouts and chives and stir noodles and egg until evenly incorporated and sprouts and chives begin to wilt, about 1 minute. Serve immediately.

TAGLIARINI DEL MAGNIFICO

Tagliarini with Citrus Zest

SERVES 4

Trattoria Garga in Florence named this dish for the 16th-century Florentine statesman Lorenzo de' Medici, known as "Il Magnifico" (The Magnificent). It is inspired by the yeast cakes made with lemon and orange zest that are eaten locally during Carnival.

- 1 large lemon
- 1 orange
- 1 cup heavy cream
- 1 cup half-and-half
- 2 tbsp. cognac
  Leaves from 4 sprigs mint
  Kosher salt, to taste
- 10 oz. fresh tagliarini or linguine
- 1 cup freshly grated Parmigiano-Reggiano

1 Bring a large pot of salted water to a boil. Meanwhile, gently scrub lemon and orange under warm running water to remove any waxy residue, then pat dry with paper towels. Finely grate zest from lemon and orange and set aside.

2 Put cream, half-and-half, and lemon and orange zests into a large skillet and boil over medium heat, stirring often with a wooden spoon, until reduced by one-quarter, about 10 minutes. Add cognac and mint and cook until alcohol evaporates, about 2 minutes. Season to taste with salt.

3 Add 2 generous pinches salt to boiling water, then add pasta and cook, stirring often, until just tender, 1½–2 minutes. Using a pair of kitchen tongs, transfer pasta to skillet with sauce. Add Parmigiano to skillet and cook over medium heat, stirring pasta constantly, until sauce thickens, about 1 minute more. Serve immediately.

PENNE ALLA VODKA

SERVES 4–6

Whether or not this dish of penne pasta lavished with a peppery, vodka-laced cream-and-tomato sauce was created in Italy is a matter of heated debate in some quarters. Whatever the case, it has become firmly entrenched as an Italian-American classic.

    1   lb. dried penne
    ¼   cup olive oil
    1   tsp. crushed red chile flakes
    12 cloves garlic, thinly sliced lengthwise
    1   32-oz. can whole, peeled tomatoes in juice,
        crushed by hand
    ¼   cup vodka
    ¾   cup heavy cream
    1   cup finely grated Parmigiano-Reggiano
        Kosher salt and freshly ground
        black pepper, to taste
        Finely chopped fresh flat-leaf parsley, for garnish

1 Bring a large pot of salted water to a boil. Add penne and cook, stirring occasionally, until al dente, about 8 minutes.

2 Meanwhile, heat oil in a 6-qt. saucepan over medium heat. Add chile flakes and garlic, and cook, stirring, until soft and lightly browned, about 3 minutes. Add tomatoes and vodka and cook, stirring, until slightly reduced, about 5 minutes. Stir in cream and Parmigiano, season with salt and pepper, and stir until smooth. Drain pasta and transfer to pan with sauce; toss pasta with sauce until evenly coated. Transfer to a serving platter and sprinkle with parsley.

KALE & SAUSAGE PENNE WITH LEMON CREAM SAUCE

SERVES 6–8

This is a hearty dish of strong flavors: dark, earthy kale offset by bright lemon cream and a warm, aromatic heat from crushed red chiles and garlic. It's the creation of SAVEUR associate food editor Kellie Evans, who served it regularly when she was an on-set caterer for film and television. It's our kind of new classic.

    ¼   cup olive oil
    4   cloves garlic, finely chopped
    1   small onion, finely chopped
    1   tsp. crushed red chile flakes
    1   pound sweet Italian sausage,
        casing removed
    1   bunch kale, stemmed and roughly chopped
        Kosher salt and freshly ground
        black pepper, to taste
    2½ cups half-and-half
    ⅓   cup grated Parmigiano-Reggiano
        Juice and zest of 1 lemon
        Freshly grated nutmeg, to taste
    1   lb. dried penne
    3   tbsp. finely chopped fresh flat-leaf parsley,
        for garnish

1 Heat oil in a 6-qt. saucepan over medium-high heat. Add garlic, onion, and chile flakes and cook, stirring occasionally, until golden brown, about 10 minutes. Add sausage and cook, using a wooden spoon to break it up into small pieces, until browned, 16–18 minutes. Add kale, season with salt and pepper, and cook until wilted, about 3 minutes. Add half-and-half and bring to a simmer. Cook, stirring occasionally, until reduced by one third, 7–8 minutes. Stir in Parmigiano, lemon juice and zest, nutmeg, and season with salt and pepper; set aside and keep warm.

2 Bring a large pot of salted water to a boil. Add penne and cook, stirring occasionally, until al dente, about 8 minutes. Drain, reserving ¼ cup cooking water; add both pasta and water to reserved sauce and cook for about 5 minutes more. Serve garnished with parsley.

GARGANELLI WITH PEAS & PROSCIUTTO

Garganelli al Prosciutto & Piselli

SERVES 4–6

This creamy, fresh dish calls for the quill-shaped pasta *garganelli,* a specialty of the Romagna region of Italy, where they're also known for their salty, funky prosciutto. Sweet peas and a hint of cream provide perfect balance.

    1   lb. dried garganelli
    2   cups heavy cream
    1½ cups fresh or frozen peas
    ½   cup grated Parmigiano-Reggiano
        Kosher salt and freshly ground
        black pepper, to taste

¼ lb. thinly sliced prosciutto, torn into strips
1 cup fresh mint leaves, torn

1 Bring a large pot of salted water to a boil. Add pasta and cook until al dente, about 8 minutes. Drain pasta, reserving ¼ cup pasta water.

2 Meanwhile, boil the cream in a 12″ skillet over high heat until reduced by half, about 8 minutes. Add the pasta with the peas and cook, tossing occasionally, until the sauce begins to cling to the pasta, about 2 minutes. Add the Parmigiano and season with salt and pepper. Add the reserved pasta water as needed to loosen the sauce. Fold in the prosciutto and mint and serve immediately.

ORECCHIETTE WITH BROCCOLI RABE
SERVES 6

The small, disk-shaped pasta known as *orecchiette* ("little ears") are typical of the Southern Italian region of Puglia. They are classically served with bitter greens, like broccoli rabe.

2 lb. broccoli rabe, stems removed
1 lb. dried orecchiette
¾ cup extra-virgin olive oil
7 cloves garlic, minced
   Kosher salt and freshly ground
   black pepper, to taste
   Freshly grated pecorino romano, for serving

1 Place broccoli rabe in a deep saucepan and cover with cold salted water. Bring to a simmer over high heat. When bubbles appear, remove broccoli rabe from heat, drain, and plunge into ice water. Drain again, pat dry, and set aside.

2 Bring a large pot of salted water to a boil. Add orecchiette and cook until al dente, 12 minutes. Meanwhile, heat oil in a large sauté pan over medium heat and sauté garlic until fragrant and just golden, about 3 minutes. Add broccoli rabe, season with salt and pepper, and cook until warmed through, about 5 minutes. Reduce heat to low and keep warm until pasta is ready.

3 Drain pasta, add to broccoli rabe, and toss to mix well. Remove from heat, transfer to a platter, and serve with pecorino.

KASHA VARNISHKES
Bow-Tie Pasta with Buckwheat Groats
SERVES 8

This classic Russian-Jewish dish of sautéed onions tossed with pasta and buckwheat groats is earthy, savory, and sweet all at once.

1¼ cups kasha (roasted buckwheat groats)
1   egg, lightly beaten
3   cups chicken stock
    Kosher salt, to taste
1   lb. dried bow-tie pasta
1   cup rendered chicken fat or canola oil
2   large yellow onions, roughly chopped
4   cloves garlic, minced
    Freshly ground black pepper, to taste
    Thinly sliced fresh flat-leaf parsley,
    for garnish

1 Toss kasha and egg in a bowl until well coated. Heat a 12″ skillet over medium-high heat. Add kasha and cook until egg is dry and kasha is lightly toasted, about 2 minutes. Add stock and salt and bring to a boil. Reduce heat to medium-low and cook, covered, until tender, about 14 minutes. Remove from heat and set aside. Bring a large pot of salted water to a boil. Add pasta and cook until al dente, about 10 minutes. Drain and set aside.

2 Heat fat in a 6-qt. saucepan over medium heat. Add onions and cook until deeply caramelized, about 40 minutes. Add garlic and cook until soft, about 1 minute. Add kasha and pasta and cook, tossing, until heated through and coated in chicken fat, about 3 minutes. Season with salt and pepper, transfer to a serving platter and garnish with parsley.

Sauces & Ragùs

PESTO GENOVESE

Classic Basil Pesto

MAKES ABOUT 1½ CUPS

Pesto genovese has been a culinary touchstone in the Liguria region of Italy for centuries; its rise in popularity in the 1980s coincided with the period when Americans started exploring regional Italian cooking and embracing all things Mediterranean. With its harmonious combination of fresh basil, extra-virgin olive oil, aged cheese, sharp garlic, and sweet pine nuts, pesto was—and remains—an essential addition to our arsenal of condiments and sauces.

- 4 cups packed fresh basil leaves
- ½ cup extra-virgin olive oil
- ½ cup finely grated Parmigiano-Reggiano
- ¼ cup pine nuts
- 3 tbsp. finely grated pecorino romano
- 2 cloves garlic, finely chopped
  Kosher salt, to taste

Process basil, oil, Parmigiano, pine nuts, pecorino, and garlic in a food processor until smooth; season with salt.

OREGANO-HAZELNUT PESTO

MAKES ABOUT 1 CUP (SEE PHOTO, PAGE 433)

Spicy, fresh oregano is the star in this unexpected take on pesto, with sweet hazelnuts adding an earthy, sweet note. It's a great match for Butternut Squash Ravioli (page 370).

- 1½ cups packed fresh oregano leaves
- 1 cup extra-virgin olive oil
- ½ cup packed fresh basil leaves
- ½ cup finely grated Parmigiano-Reggiano
- ¼ cup hazelnuts, toasted
- 2 cloves garlic, finely chopped
  Kosher salt and freshly ground black pepper, to taste

Process oregano, oil, basil, Parmigiano, hazelnuts, and garlic in a food processor until finely ground; season with salt and pepper.

PESTO ROSSO

Red Pesto

MAKES ABOUT 1½ CUPS

This flavorful pesto from Sicily is traditionally served with homemade *busiate,* a spiral-shaped pasta. Dried fusilli is a fine substitute.

- 1 pint cherry tomatoes
- ¾ cup sliced almonds, toasted
- ½ cup packed fresh basil leaves
- ½ cup finely grated Parmigiano-Reggiano, plus more for serving
- 5 tbsp. extra-virgin olive oil
- 2 tbsp. golden raisins
- 2 tbsp. capers, drained
- ¼ tsp. crushed red chile flakes
- 3 anchovy filets in oil, drained
- 2 cloves garlic, chopped
- 1 peperoncino, stemmed, seeded, and roughly chopped
  Kosher salt and freshly ground black pepper, to taste

Put tomatoes in a food processor and process until finely chopped; pour into a fine-mesh sieve and drain off excess juices. Return tomatoes to food processor along with almonds, basil, Parmigiano, olive oil, raisins, capers, chile flakes, anchovies, garlic, and peperoncino and process until finely ground. Season with salt and pepper.

ANGELO'S MARINARA SAUCE

MAKES ABOUT 3 CUPS

This tomato sauce, based on one served at Angelo's Fairmount Tavern in Atlantic City, New Jersey, tastes just as good tossed with spaghetti as it does in baked pasta dishes or *secondi* like veal parmesan.

- 1 28-oz. can whole, peeled tomatoes in juice
- 3 tbsp. extra-virgin olive oil
- 1 clove garlic, finely chopped
- 1 dried bay leaf
- ½ small onion, finely chopped

½ tsp. dried oregano
¼ tsp. dried thyme
1 tbsp. finely chopped fresh flat-leaf parsley
Kosher salt and freshly ground black pepper, to taste

1 Put tomatoes and their liquid into the bowl of a food processor and pulse until coarsely chopped. Set aside.

2 Heat oil in a 4-qt. saucepan over medium heat. Add the garlic, bay leaf, and onions and cook, stirring occasionally, until the onions are translucent, about 10 minutes. Add the tomatoes along with the oregano and thyme. Cook, stirring occasionally, until the sauce thickens slightly and its flavors come together, about 20 minutes. Stir in parsley and season with salt and pepper. Remove bay leaf before serving.

TOMATO SAUCE WITH ONION & BUTTER
MAKES 3 CUPS

This simple yet transcendent tomato sauce recipe, one of Italian culinary icon Marcella Hazan's greatest legacies, is as delicious as it is easy to prepare.

½ cup unsalted butter, cubed
¼ tsp. sugar
1 28-oz. can whole, peeled tomatoes in juice, crushed by hand
1 medium yellow onion, quartered lengthwise
Kosher salt and freshly ground black pepper, to taste

Bring butter, sugar, tomatoes, and onion to a boil in a 4-qt. saucepan over medium-high heat. Reduce heat to medium-low and cook, stirring occasionally, until flavors meld and sauce is slightly reduced, about 45 minutes. Discard onion, and season sauce with salt and pepper before serving.

HEARTY VEGETABLE TOMATO SAUCE
MAKES 5 CUPS

This savory vegetarian tomato sauce is enriched with chopped squash and mushrooms.

⅓ cup extra-virgin olive oil
6 cloves garlic, finely chopped
1 large onion, finely chopped
1 carrot, peeled and finely chopped
1 tbsp. ground fennel seeds
1 tsp. crushed red chile flakes

2 bay leaves
¼ cup tomato paste
½ lb. white button mushrooms, finely chopped
1 medium zucchini, finely chopped
1 medium yellow squash, finely chopped
2 28-oz. cans whole, peeled tomatoes in juice, crushed by hand
Kosher salt and freshly ground black pepper, to taste

1 Heat oil in a 6-qt. saucepan over medium-high heat. Add garlic, onion, and carrot and cook, stirring, until golden, about 6 minutes. Add fennel, chile flakes, and bay leaves and cook for 1 minute. Add tomato paste and cook, stirring, until caramelized, about 3 minutes. Add mushrooms, zucchini, and squash and cook until soft, about 10 minutes. Add tomatoes and 1½ cups water and bring to a boil.

2 Reduce heat to medium and cook, partially covered, stirring occasionally, until thick and slightly reduced, about 2 hours. Season with salt and pepper.

RAW TOMATO–CAPER SAUCE
MAKES 3–4 CUPS

Salty, deeply savory capers and anchovies are a perfect complement to the bright taste of chopped fresh tomatoes. Serve this flavorful sauce on hot pasta, toasted Italian bread, grilled fish, or roasted vegetables.

½ cup salt-packed large capers
3 large tomatoes, coarsely chopped
2 cloves garlic, crushed
3 oil-packed anchovy filets, minced
½ cup extra-virgin olive oil
Freshly ground black pepper, to taste
Fresh flat-leaf parsley or basil, roughly chopped (optional)

Soak capers in water for 15 minutes, changing water once or twice. Rinse well, chop roughly, and place in a bowl. Add tomatoes, garlic, anchovies, and oil. Mix together and season with pepper. Let stand for at least 1 hour to allow flavors to develop. Discard garlic. If desired, add parsley.

COOK'S NOTE The sauce becomes saltier if left to sit overnight.

> "Once the pasta is sauced, serve it promptly, inviting your guests and family to put off talking and start eating."
>
> MARCELLA HAZAN

RAGÙ ALLA BOLOGNESE

MAKES 8 CUPS

In Bologna, you'll find home cooks making versions of this sauce that take all day to come together. This variation spends far less time on the stove, but rich lard and a splash of wine give it a complexity that belies its mere two-hour cooking time.

½ cup lard
3 small yellow onions, finely chopped
2 medium carrots, peeled and finely chopped
2 ribs celery, finely chopped
2 lb. ground beef chuck
½ cup dry red wine
2¾ cups canned tomato purée
Kosher salt and freshly ground black pepper, to taste

1 Heat lard in a heavy-bottomed pot over medium heat. Add onions, carrots, and celery and cook, stirring frequently, until vegetables are somewhat softened, about 8 minutes.

2 Raise heat to medium-high, add beef, and cook, stirring constantly, until meat is broken up and just cooked through, 6–8 minutes. Add the wine and cook, stirring occasionally, until evaporated, about 4 minutes. Stir in tomato purée and 1½ cups water and bring to a boil over high heat.

3 Reduce the heat to low and simmer, partially covered, stirring occasionally, until the sauce is thick, about 2 hours. Season with salt and pepper.

RAGÙ ALLA NAPOLETANA

SERVES 6

Tender rolls of beef stuffed with a garlicky mixture of pine nuts and raisins anchor this savory pasta sauce, based on a recipe that Sandro Manzo, an Italian art dealer who lives in New York, learned from his mother during his youth in southern Italy.

½ cup pine nuts, chopped
½ cup raisins, chopped
4 cloves garlic, finely chopped

2 lb. beef chuck, sliced to ⅛" thickness
Kosher salt and freshly ground black pepper, to taste
5 tbsp. extra-virgin olive oil
1 onion, sliced
½ cup red wine
1–2 35-oz. cans diced tomatoes
1 12-oz. can tomato paste
1 lb. dried penne or ziti, cooked, for serving
Grated Parmigiano-Reggiano, for serving

1 In a small bowl, combine pine nuts, raisins, and garlic. Lay meat slices on a work surface and season them lightly on both sides with salt and pepper. Sprinkle pine nut and raisin mixture on one side of the slices. Roll slices up and secure them with a toothpick or kitchen twine.

2 Place rolls in a large, deep sauté pan and add oil, onion, and 4 cups water. Place over medium heat and simmer, uncovered, until water has evaporated, about 1 hour. Continue cooking, turning rolls with tongs, until they are lightly browned on all sides. Add wine to pan and cook until evaporated. Add tomatoes and tomato paste and bring to a simmer. Cook until sauce is very thick, about 2 hours.

3 Remove meat from pan with tongs; remove toothpicks or cut twine. Season sauce with salt and pepper. Spoon sauce over a cooked tubular pasta, such as penne or ziti, top with meat, and serve with grated Parmigiano on the side.

SUNDAY GRAVY

SERVES 6

This gravy—the Italian-American term for red sauce—is enriched with a variety of meats: links of hot Italian sausage, slender baby back ribs, hearty pork neck bones, and thin-cut lamb shoulder chops. Before adding the meat to the sauce, be sure to roast it all until it's completely caramelized; the sauce will taste richer.

1 lb. pork baby back ribs, cut into individual ribs
1 lb. pork neck bones
¾ lb. hot Italian sausage links, cut into 2"–3" pieces
2 thin-cut lamb shoulder chops (about 1 lb.)

2 28-oz. cans whole, peeled tomatoes
in juice
1 tbsp. extra-virgin olive oil
1 clove garlic
2 6-oz. cans tomato paste
Kosher salt and freshly ground black pepper,
to taste
¼ cup white wine
1 tbsp. roughly chopped fresh basil leaves
1 tbsp. roughly chopped fresh flat-leaf
parsley leaves
½ tsp. dried oregano
⅛ tsp. crushed red chile flakes
⅓ cup finely grated pecorino romano cheese

1 Heat oven to 400°. Line a large baking sheet with aluminum foil and arrange ribs, neck bones, sausage, and lamb chops in a single layer on top. Roast meat, turning with tongs occasionally, until deep golden brown and cooked through, about 40 minutes for sausage and 1 hour for ribs, bones, and lamb. Set roasted meat aside.

2 Meanwhile, run the tomatoes and their juice through a food mill twice; discard any remaining seeds or skin. Set puréed tomatoes aside.

3 Heat oil in a large pot over medium-high heat. Add garlic and cook, stirring frequently, until golden brown, about 2 minutes. Add tomato paste and fry, stirring constantly, for 1 minute. Add 3 cups water and salt and pepper and stir well. Reduce heat to medium-low and simmer, stirring occasionally, for 15 minutes. Add wine, basil, parsley, oregano, and reserved tomato purée. Stir well and cook for 10 minutes more. Partially cover pot and cook until slightly thickened, about 30 minutes.

4 Transfer roasted meat to the pot with tomato sauce. Add red chile flakes and salt and pepper and simmer, partially covered, until thickened, about 30 minutes more. (The sauce will appear glossy.) Stir in the pecorino and cook briefly, partially covered, until flavors have melded.

VEAL PASTA SAUCE WITH RED, GREEN, & YELLOW PEPPERS

SERVES 6

The recipe for this sweet, meaty ragù was given to us by cookbook author Marcella Hazan. Her trick to achieving the ideal texture is simple but makes all the difference: The veal is cooked separately and combined later with the peppers to preserve its juiciness.

¼ cup extra-virgin olive oil
7 whole cloves garlic, peeled
2 large red bell peppers, stemmed, seeded,
peeled, and cut into strips
2 large yellow bell peppers, stemmed, seeded,
peeled, and cut into strips
2 large green bell peppers, stemmed, seeded,
peeled, and cut into strips
½ tsp. kosher salt, plus more to taste
4 very firm plum tomatoes
2 tbsp. canola oil
2 tbsp. butter
½ cup finely chopped onion
½ lb. ground veal
¼ tsp. freshly ground black pepper, plus
more to taste
1 lb. fresh fettuccine or pappardelle,
or 10 oz. dried, cooked just al dente, for serving
¼ cup freshly grated Parmigiano-Reggiano,
for serving

1 Add the olive oil to a 12″ skillet. Add garlic, heat over medium-high heat, and cook, turning from time to time, until the garlic turns medium brown, about 4 minutes. Remove garlic from pan and discard.

2 Add peppers and ¼ tsp. salt and lower heat to medium. Cook the peppers, turning them from time to time, until they are quite tender and considerably diminished in bulk, about 45 minutes.

3 Meanwhile, peel the tomatoes using a swivel-blade vegetable peeler (don't peel them by scalding them in hot water, because you want them to remain very firm), and coarsely chop.

4 Add the canola oil to a 10″ skillet and add the butter and onion. Turn the heat to medium-high and cook, stirring from time to time, until the onion has softened and turned a pale gold color, 5–7 minutes.

5 Add the ground veal, ¼ tsp. salt, and ¼ tsp. black pepper and reduce heat to medium. Cook the meat, turning it once or twice, until it has completely lost its raw color. Add the tomatoes with any of their accumulated juices, reduce heat to medium-low, and simmer gently for about 20 minutes.

6 Transfer the contents of the skillet with the veal to the pan with the peppers, gently tossing all the ingredients to combine them thoroughly. Simmer, stirring from time to time, for about 15 minutes. Add salt and pepper to taste. Serve immediately over pasta, and garnish with Parmigiano.

Baked Pastas

MACARONI & FOUR CHEESES

SERVES 6–8

The secret to this rich, ultra-creamy macaroni and cheese is mixing in a little Velveeta—yes, Velveeta; no other ingredient will quite do—with the cheddar, Gruyère, and blue cheese.

- 3 slices white bread, crust removed
- 6 tbsp. unsalted butter
- ½ tsp. paprika
- 3 sprigs fresh thyme
- 2 shallots, minced
- 1 bay leaf
- ¼ cup flour
- ⅛ tsp. cayenne pepper
- 3 cups milk
- 10 oz. sharp white cheddar, grated (about 4 cups)
- 10 oz. Gruyère cheese, grated (about 4 cups)
- 6 oz. Velveeta, cut into ½" cubes (about 1¼ cups)
- 1 oz. blue cheese, crumbled (about ¼ cup)
- ½ lb. dry hollow pasta, preferably elbow macaroni or shells, cooked and drained
  Freshly ground black pepper, to taste

1 Heat oven to 375°. Tear bread into small pieces and transfer to the bowl of a food processor. Process until finely ground; set aside. Melt 3 tbsp. butter in a sauté pan over medium heat; add bread crumbs and stir to combine. Transfer bread crumb mixture to a plate and set aside.

2 Wipe out pan and set over medium heat. Melt the remaining butter and add the paprika, thyme, shallots, and bay leaf. Cook, stirring often, until shallots are soft, about 5 minutes. Add flour and cayenne and stir until mixture thickens, about 1 minute. Whisk in milk and cook, continuing to whisk often, until sauce has thickened and coats the back of a spoon, about 10 minutes. Discard thyme and bay leaf and remove pan from heat.

3 Stir in cheddar, half the Gruyère, the Velveeta, and the blue cheese; continue stirring until smooth. Stir in pasta

and season sauce with salt and pepper. Transfer mixture to an 8″×8″ baking dish. Sprinkle remaining Gruyère over top of pasta and then top with bread crumbs.

4 Transfer baking dish to a foil-lined baking sheet and bake until macaroni and cheese is golden brown and bubbly, about 30 minutes. Let cool for 10 minutes before serving.

GREEK MAC & CHEESE

SERVES 8–10

Studded with spinach, topped with salty feta, and infused with a hint of sweet cinnamon, this savory casserole is based on a recipe from New York City chef Michael Psilakis. If you can't find a semifirm Greek cheese like Graviera or Kefalotyri, Gruyère is an acceptable substitute.

- 3 slices crustless white bread, torn into small pieces
- 9 tbsp. unsalted butter, melted
  Kosher salt, to taste
- ½ lb. hollow pasta, preferably elbow macaroni
- ¼ cup flour
- 3 cups milk
- 4 cups grated Graviera, Kefalotyri, or Gruyère cheese (about ¾ lb.)
- ¾ tsp. ground cinnamon
- ⅛ tsp. freshly grated nutmeg
  Freshly ground black pepper, to taste
- 2 tbsp. extra-virgin olive oil
- 8 large shallots, finely chopped
- 1 lb. baby spinach, roughly chopped
- 8 scallions cut into ¼"-thick rounds
- ⅓ cup roughly chopped fresh dill
- 1¾ cups crumbled feta (about ½ lb.)

1 Put bread into the bowl of a food processor and pulse until finely ground. Put bread crumbs and 3 tbsp. butter into a small bowl and combine; set aside. Bring a 6-qt. pot of salted water to a boil. Add pasta and cook until cooked halfway through, about 3 minutes. Drain pasta, rinse with cold water, and set aside.

2 Heat remaining butter in a 4-qt. saucepan over medium heat. Add flour and cook, whisking constantly, for 1 minute. Still whisking constantly, slowly drizzle in milk and cook until sauce has thickened and coats the back of a spoon, 10–15 minutes. Remove pan from heat. Stir in Graviera, cinnamon, and nutmeg and season with salt and pepper; set béchamel sauce aside.

3 Heat oven to 350°. Heat oil in a 5-qt. pot over medium heat. Add shallots and cook, stirring often, until soft, 3–4 minutes. Add spinach and scallions and cook, covered, stirring occasionally, until wilted, about 3 minutes. Stir in the béchamel sauce, dill, and pasta and transfer mixture to a 9″×13″ baking dish. Sprinkle evenly with reserved bread crumbs and the feta. Bake until golden brown and bubbly, about 30 minutes. Let cool for 10 minutes before serving.

THE MELTDOWN

There are a couple of factors that contribute to the creamy texture of a good macaroni and cheese, and the cheese itself is the most important. Firm cheeses like cheddar, Comté, Fontina, and Gruyère are perfect melters; in small amounts, hard cheeses like parmesan and pecorino romano work well, too. Fresh mozzarella and goat cheese do not: the former becomes stringy, and the latter will hardly melt at all, ending up instead as sticky clumps. Why? The proteins in those cheeses break down less readily when heated, and so they'll stick together rather than disperse in the sauce. Whichever kinds of cheese you're using, let them come to room temperature before you begin cooking, and grate them as finely as possible; doing so increases the surface area that's exposed to the heat, making for more uniform melting. Also, heat the cheese gently with the sauce; a blast of high heat can cause proteins to break away from the fats, resulting in a grainy texture.

MACARONI & CHEESE WITH COUNTRY HAM

SERVES 6–8

This creamy recipe puts leftover country ham and biscuits to good use. You can use coarse, day-old bread crumbs if you don't have biscuits on hand.

- 3 cups elbow macaroni
  Kosher salt, to taste
- 8 tbsp. unsalted butter
- 2 day-old breakfast biscuits, split, toasted, and crumbled
- 6 tbsp. flour
- 3 cups milk, scalded
  Freshly ground black pepper, to taste
- 10 oz. mild cheddar, grated
- ¼ tsp. cayenne pepper
- ¾ cup diced country ham

1 Heat oven to 375°. Meanwhile, cook macaroni in a large pot of salted boiling water until tender, 5–8 minutes. Drain, rinse under cold water, and set aside.

2 Melt 2 tbsp. butter in a small pan. Grease a 2-qt. baking dish with half the melted butter. Toss biscuit crumbs in remaining melted butter. Toast flour in a small cast-iron skillet over medium heat, stirring frequently, until golden, 10 minutes. Transfer to a bowl.

3 Melt remaining 6 tbsp. butter in a large saucepan over medium-high heat. Add flour and cook for 1 minute. Gradually whisk in milk and bring to a boil. Reduce heat to medium-low, add black pepper, and stir until thick, 10 minutes. Remove pan from heat. Gradually add 1½ cups cheddar, whisking until melted. Stir in cayenne, then pasta and ham. Transfer to prepared dish and sprinkle with remaining cheddar and buttered crumbs. Bake until crust is golden and sauce is bubbling, about 30 minutes.

LOBSTER MACARONI & CHEESE

SERVES 8–10

The standard mac 'n' cheese is transformed into an indulgent entrée with the addition of lobster and a splash of brandy.

- Kosher salt, to taste
- ¾ lb. elbow macaroni or other hollow pasta

4   tbsp. unsalted butter
¼   cup flour
4   cups milk
11 oz. Fontina, grated (about 4 cups)
½   lb. mascarpone (about 1 cup)
3   tbsp. lobster or fish stock
3   tbsp. brandy or cognac
1   tsp. Tabasco sauce
¼   tsp. freshly grated nutmeg
    Freshly ground black pepper, to taste
½   lb. cooked lobster meat, cut into
    1″ chunks
⅓   cup minced fresh chives
2   scallions, thinly sliced crosswise
2   oz. sharp aged white cheddar, grated
    (about 1 cup)

1 Heat oven to 375°. Bring a 4-qt. saucepan of salted water to a boil. Add pasta and cook, stirring occasionally, until cooked halfway through, about 3 minutes. Drain pasta, transfer to a bowl, and set aside.

2 Melt butter in a 4-qt. saucepan over medium heat. Add flour and cook, whisking constantly, until smooth, about 1 minute. Whisk in milk and cook, continuing to whisk often, until sauce has thickened and coats the back of a spoon, about 10 minutes. Remove pan from heat and stir in 2 cups Fontina, along with the mascarpone, broth, brandy, Tabasco, and nutmeg; season with salt and pepper. Add reserved pasta to cheese sauce. Stir in half each of the lobster, chives, and scallions.

3 Transfer mixture to a 9″×13″ baking dish and sprinkle with remaining Fontina and the cheddar. Bake until golden brown and bubbly, about 30 minutes. Let cool for 10 minutes. Garnish with remaining lobster, scallions, and chives.

MEXICAN NOODLE CASSEROLE
Sopa Seca
SERVES 4

This comforting casserole—the name means "dry soup"—is dense with thin *fideo* noodles bathed in a chile sauce. Serve it with a salad or pickled chiles on the side.

¼   cup canola oil, plus more for greasing
½   lb. fideos or vermicelli noodles,
    broken into 1″ pieces
4   canned chipotle chiles in adobo, minced
4   cloves garlic, minced

1   15-oz. can whole, peeled tomatoes
    in juice, crushed by hand
½   small white onion, roughly chopped
½   cup chicken stock
    Kosher salt and freshly ground black
    pepper, to taste
1   cup crumbled Cotija cheese
¾   cup crema or sour cream
2   tbsp. minced fresh cilantro

1 Heat oven to 350°. Grease an 8″×8″ baking dish with oil; set aside. Heat oil in a 12″ skillet over medium-high heat. Working in two batches, add pasta and cook, stirring, until lightly browned and toasted, about 4 minutes. Using a slotted spoon, transfer to paper towels to drain; set aside.

2 Purée chipotles, garlic, tomatoes, and onion in a blender until very smooth, at least 2 minutes. Return skillet to heat, add tomato purée, and cook, stirring constantly, until almost all liquid is evaporated, about 18 minutes. Add stock and cook, stirring, for 1 minute. Add noodles, stir to combine, and season with salt and pepper. Transfer to prepared baking dish and cover with foil. Bake until pasta is tender and sauce is absorbed, about 10 minutes. Divide among serving plates, sprinkle with Cotija, and drizzle with crema. Sprinkle with cilantro before serving.

SAVORY NOODLE KUGEL
Lokshen Kugel
SERVES 8–10

Jewish-style noodle casserole comes in sweet or savory versions. This savory rendition is flavored with garlic and onions.

1½ cups sour cream
1¼ cups cottage cheese
½   cup unsalted butter, melted
4   eggs, lightly beaten
    Kosher salt, to taste
½   lb. wide egg noodles
    Freshly ground black pepper, to taste
4   cloves garlic, minced
1   large yellow onion, minced

1 Heat oven to 350°. Whisk sour cream, cottage cheese, 6 tbsp. butter, and eggs in a bowl; set aside. Meanwhile, bring a 4-qt. pot of salted water to a boil. Add noodles and cook until al dente. Drain; stir into cheese mixture. Season with salt and pepper.

2 Heat remaining 2 tbsp. butter in a 12″ cast-iron skillet over medium-high heat. Add garlic and onions and cook, stirring, until lightly caramelized, about 8 minutes. Stir in noodles and bake until browned, 35–40 minutes.

JOHNNY MARZETTI

SERVES 6

It's a home-cooking classic now, but this cheesy, beefy noodle casserole began life in a restaurant: The bygone restaurant Marzetti's in Columbus, Ohio, is credited with its invention.

10	tbsp. olive oil
3	cloves garlic, chopped
2	medium yellow onions, roughly chopped
½	lb. white button mushrooms, thinly sliced
1½	lb. ground beef
1	tsp. dried oregano
1	28-oz. can whole, peeled tomatoes in juice, crushed by hand
	Kosher salt and freshly ground black pepper, to taste
2	tbsp. finely chopped fresh parsley
10	oz. wide egg noodles
2	tbsp. unsalted butter
½	lb. cheddar, shredded
3	oz. mozzarella, shredded
3	tbsp. bread crumbs

1 Heat 3 tbsp. oil in a 12″ skillet over medium-high heat. Add garlic and onions and cook until soft, about 8 minutes. Transfer to a bowl and set aside. Return skillet to heat with 3 tbsp. oil, add mushrooms, and cook until browned, about 5 minutes. Add to bowl with onions; return skillet to heat with 2 tbsp. oil. Add beef and cook until browned, about 8 minutes. Return onions and mushrooms to skillet along with oregano and tomatoes and bring to a boil. Reduce heat to medium-low and cook until thickened, about 15 minutes. Remove from heat, season with salt and pepper, and stir in parsley; let sauce cool.

2 Heat oven to 325°. Bring a large pot of salted water to a boil over high heat. Add noodles and cook until al dente, about 7 minutes. Drain and toss with butter in a bowl; set aside.

3 Spread 2 cups sauce on bottom of a 9″×13″ baking dish; cover with noodles. Spread two-thirds of the cheddar over the noodles; top with remaining sauce. Sprinkle remaining cheddar, mozzarella, and bread crumbs over sauce; drizzle with remaining 2 tbsp. oil. Bake until browned on top, about 25 minutes.

TURKEY TETRAZZINI

SERVES 8

The original turkey tetrazzini, attributed to Auguste Escoffier, was a rich mixture of sherry-spiked cream, turkey, and cheese, named in honor of Luisa Tetrazzini, a celebrated early-20th-century opera singer. Our home-style version, slightly less opulent, is a great use for leftover roast turkey (page 177).

2	tbsp. unsalted butter
7	cups chicken stock
1	green bell pepper, seeded and finely chopped
1	large yellow onion, finely chopped
1	clove garlic, finely chopped
	Kosher salt and freshly ground black pepper, to taste
1	lb. dried spaghetti
1	lb. skinless boneless roasted turkey, torn into large chunks (about 3 cups)
2	cups fresh or thawed frozen peas
1	cup ketchup
7	oz. white button mushrooms, sliced
¼	cup finely chopped drained pimientos
3	cups grated cheddar (about ½ lb.)

1 Heat oven to 350°. Butter an 11″×13″ casserole dish with 1 tbsp. butter. Combine stock, peppers, onions, garlic, salt, and pepper in a large pot and bring to a boil. Add spaghetti in broken pieces, reduce heat to medium, and boil gently, stirring often, until spaghetti is al dente, 12–14 minutes. Remove from heat, add remaining 1 tbsp. butter, turkey, peas, ketchup, mushrooms, pimientos, and salt and pepper to taste, and fold together.

2 Transfer spaghetti mixture to buttered dish and cover with grated cheese. Bake until golden and bubbly, about 30 minutes. Let cool slightly to set, then serve.

LASAGNE BOLOGNESE

SERVES 8–12

This rich, complex version of lasagne is typical of the Italian region of Emilia-Romagna, and especially of its capital, Bologna.

2 tbsp. unsalted butter
Kosher salt, to taste
1 lb. no-boil lasagne noodles
5 cups Ragù alla Bolognese (page 358)
1 cup freshly grated Parmigiano-Reggiano
2 cups Besciamella (this page)

1 Set oven rack in top third of oven, then heat oven to 450°. Grease a 9″×12″ baking dish with butter and set aside.

2 Line bottom of prepared baking dish with a layer of noodles, breaking sheets so that they fit in 1 even layer (patch if necessary). Spread evenly with about 1 cup meat sauce, then sprinkle lightly with some Parmigiano. Add another layer of noodles, evenly spread 1 cup of the béchamel sauce on pasta, then sprinkle lightly with Parmigiano. Repeat layers (you will have 3 layers of meat sauce and 2 of béchamel), ending with meat sauce and Parmigiano. Reserve any extra meat sauce for another use.

3 Bake lasagne for 10 minutes. Increase oven temperature to 500° and cook until lasagne is bubbling around the edges and browned on top, 5–7 minutes more. Do not overcook. Let lasagne rest for 8–10 minutes before serving.

....

Besciamella

Italian-Style Béchamel Sauce

MAKES 2 CUPS

Although widely recognized by its French name, béchamel, this sauce has been known in Italy as besciamella *(or balsamella or bechimella) for centuries. The sauce functions as a binding element in many pasta and vegetable dishes.*

3 tbsp. unsalted butter
¼ cup sifted flour
2 cups scalded milk
Kosher salt and freshly ground black pepper, to taste

1 Melt butter in a heavy medium saucepan over medium-low heat. Add flour and whisk for 1½ minutes (do not allow to brown).

2 Gradually add hot milk, whisking constantly. Season with salt and pepper and stir constantly with a wooden spoon until sauce is the consistency of thick cream, about 15 minutes.

....

VEGETARIAN LASAGNE

SERVES 6–8

This vegetarian take on the classic, creamy lasagne Bolognese calls on a shallot-infused béchamel and uses earthy shiitake mushrooms instead of meat.

FOR THE BÉCHAMEL
½ cup unsalted butter
1 shallot, chopped
1 carrot, peeled and chopped
½ cup flour
5 cups milk
1 tsp. freshly grated nutmeg
Kosher salt and freshly ground black pepper, to taste

FOR THE TOMATO SAUCE
12 dry-packed sun-dried tomatoes
Kosher salt and freshly ground black pepper, to taste
3 tbsp. extra-virgin olive oil
3 tbsp. unsalted butter
2 lb. shiitake mushrooms, stemmed and quartered
½ lb. spinach, chopped
6 cloves garlic, chopped
3 tbsp. chopped fresh flat-leaf parsley
2 tbsp. chopped fresh oregano
1 tbsp. chopped fresh thyme
1 tbsp. chopped fresh rosemary
1 tbsp. tomato paste
5 cups canned whole, peeled tomatoes, crushed by hand
1 tbsp. unsalted butter

1 lb. no-boil lasagne noodles
2½ cups grated grana padano or Parmigiano-Reggiano
2½ cups grated Fontina

1 Make the béchamel: Melt butter in a 4-qt. saucepan over medium heat. Add shallots and carrots and cook for 5 minutes. Add flour and cook for 2 minutes. Whisk in milk and bring to a boil. Reduce to medium-low; simmer, whisking, until thick, 20–25 minutes. Add nutmeg; season with salt and pepper.

2 Make the tomato sauce: Cover dried tomatoes with 1 cup boiling water; soak for 20 minutes. Drain and chop. Heat oil and butter in a 6-qt. pot over medium-high heat. Add mushrooms and cook for 10 minutes. Add dried tomatoes,

> ## "Life is a combination of magic and pasta."
> ### FEDERICO FELLINI

spinach, garlic, parsley, oregano, thyme, rosemary, and tomato paste and cook for 3 minutes. Add canned tomatoes and cook, stirring occasionally, for 8–10 minutes. Season with salt and pepper. Set sauce aside.

3 Heat oven to 375°. Grease a 9″×13″ baking pan with 1 tbsp. butter. Spread 2 cups tomato sauce in baking dish. Cover with a layer of noodles. Spread 1 cup béchamel over top; sprinkle with ½ cup of each cheese and 2 cups tomato sauce. Repeat layering 2 more times. Top with remaining noodles, tomato sauce, béchamel, and cheeses. Cover with foil and bake on a baking sheet for 1 hour. Remove foil; raise oven to 500°. Bake until bubbling and golden, about 15 minutes. Let rest for 8–10 minutes before serving.

PASTITSIO
Greek Lasagne
SERVES 10–12

This rich casserole of ground beef, macaroni, and béchamel is enjoyed throughout Greece.

FOR THE MEAT SAUCE
- ⅓ cup extra-virgin olive oil
- 2 green bell peppers, seeded and minced
- 2 medium yellow onions, minced
- 1 lb. ground beef, veal, or pork
- 3 oz. cured chorizo, minced
- 2 cups canned crushed tomatoes
- ⅓ cup red wine
- ¼ tsp. crushed red chile flakes
- 2 fresh or dried bay leaves
- 1 2″ cinnamon stick
  Kosher salt and freshly ground black pepper, to taste
  Freshly grated nutmeg, to taste

FOR THE BÉCHAMEL
- ½ cup unsalted butter
- 1 cup flour
- 4 cups milk
- 1 cup grated Parmigiano-Reggiano

- 3 eggs, separated
  Kosher salt and freshly ground black pepper, to taste
  Freshly grated nutmeg, to taste

- 1 lb. no. 2 Greek macaroni or elbow macaroni
- 2 tbsp. extra-virgin olive oil

1 Make the meat sauce: Heat oil in a 12″ skillet over medium-high heat. Add peppers and onions and cook, stirring often, until soft, 8–10 minutes. Using a slotted spoon, transfer onion mixture to a plate and set aside. Add ground meat and chorizo to skillet and cook, breaking meat into tiny pieces, until browned, 6–8 minutes. Add reserved onion mixture, along with tomatoes, wine, chile flakes, bay leaves, and cinnamon and bring to a boil. Reduce heat to medium and cook, stirring often, until sauce thickens, about 15 minutes. Remove sauce from heat, discard bay leaves and cinnamon, and season with salt, pepper, and nutmeg; let cool.

2 Make the béchamel: Melt butter in a 4-qt. saucepan over medium-high heat. Add flour and cook, whisking constantly, until smooth and slightly toasted, 1–2 minutes. Add milk and cook, whisking often, until sauce coats the back of a spoon, 8–10 minutes. Remove from heat, add ¾ cup Parmigiano and egg yolks, and season with salt, pepper, and nutmeg. Stir until smooth; set aside.

3 Heat oven to 350°. Bring a large pot of salted water to a boil; add pasta and cook halfway through, about 5 minutes. Meanwhile, whisk egg whites in a large bowl until frothy. Stir in remaining Parmigiano. Drain pasta in a colander and then toss with egg white–cheese mixture to coat evenly. Set aside.

4 Grease a deep 9″×13″ baking dish with olive oil. Place half the pasta mixture on bottom of dish and cover evenly with meat sauce. Top with remaining pasta mixture. Pour béchamel over pasta, spreading it evenly with a rubber spatula. Bake until the top is golden brown, about 1 hour. Transfer to wire rack; cool for 20 minutes before serving.

BRAZILIAN PASTA & SHRIMP CASSEROLE

Camusquim de Camarão

SERVES 8

This zesty north Brazilian casserole is like a punched-up version of macaroni and cheese. It combines shrimp, melted cheese, and béchamel, along with a generous dose of fresh and pickled vegetables and herbs.

1½	lb. medium shrimp, peeled, deveined, and roughly chopped
2	tbsp. fresh lime juice
3	tbsp. olive oil
1	small yellow onion, minced
2	tbsp. minced Brazilian Pickled Chiles (page 578) or pickled jalapeños
1	tbsp. minced garlic
½	cubanelle pepper, seeded and minced
2	tomatoes, cored and minced
1	tsp. ground annatto seed
½	cup minced fresh basil
⅓	cup minced fresh cilantro
	Kosher salt and freshly ground black pepper, to taste
3½	cups dried elbow macaroni
3	tbsp. unsalted butter
¾	cup flour
4	cups milk
3	cups grated Parmigiano-Reggiano
10	oz. fresh mozzarella, grated

1 Toss together shrimp and lime juice in a bowl; let marinate for 10 minutes. Meanwhile, heat 2 tbsp. oil in a 12″ skillet over medium-high heat. Add onion and cook until soft, about 4 minutes. Add chiles, garlic, and pepper and cook until soft, about 3 minutes. Add tomatoes and cook until lightly caramelized, about 10 minutes. Add shrimp and annatto and cook until shrimp are just cooked through, about 3 minutes. Remove from heat and stir in basil, cilantro, and salt and pepper; set mixture aside.

2 Bring a large pot of salted water to a boil. Add pasta and cook until al dente, about 9 minutes. Meanwhile, heat remaining oil and butter in a 4-qt. saucepan over medium-high heat. Add flour and cook until smooth, about 2 minutes. Add milk, whisk until smooth, and bring to a boil. Reduce heat to medium-low and cook until sauce thickens, about 5 minutes. Season with salt and pepper and add drained pasta; stir to combine.

3 Heat oven to 425°. Spread half the pasta over bottom of a 9″×13″ baking dish; top with half each of the shrimp mixture, Parmigiano, and mozzarella. Repeat layering. Bake until browned, about 30 minutes. Let casserole rest for 10 minutes to set before serving.

TUNA-NOODLE CASSEROLE

SERVES 6

This stalwart of American cooking is often topped with a crunchy layer of crushed potato chips and traditionally made with a can or two of cream of mushroom soup. Our "from scratch" version is respectfully updated (though we do on occasion revert to the potato-chip option).

10	tbsp. butter
4½	cups (about 10 oz.) flat egg noodles
5	scallions, chopped
3	tbsp. flour
1½	tsp. dry mustard
3⅓	cups milk
	Kosher salt and freshly ground black pepper, to taste
1	12-oz. can tuna packed in oil, drained and broken into small chunks
1½	cups homemade fresh white bread crumbs

1 Preheat oven to 375°. Rub the inside of a 2½-qt. casserole dish with 1 tbsp. butter. Bring a large pot of salted water to a boil over high heat. Add noodles and cook until al dente, 5–7 minutes. Drain and transfer noodles to a large bowl.

2 Melt 4 tbsp. butter in a medium saucepan over medium-high heat. Add half the scallions and cook until softened, 1–2 minutes. Add flour and mustard and cook, stirring frequently, for 1 minute. Gradually pour in milk, whisking constantly, and bring to a boil. Cook sauce, stirring frequently, until smooth and thickened, 16–18 minutes. Season with salt and pepper. Transfer sauce to the bowl with the noodles. Add tuna and stir gently to combine. Transfer tuna-noodle mixture to prepared dish.

3 Melt remaining 5 tbsp. butter and toss with remaining scallions, bread crumbs, and salt and pepper to taste in a bowl. Scatter seasoned bread crumbs over tuna-noodle mixture and bake until golden brown and bubbling, 20–25 minutes. Let casserole cool slightly before serving.

Couscous

PALESTINIAN COUSCOUS WITH CHICKEN & CHICKPEAS

Maftoul

SERVES 4

This hearty couscous preparation, perfumed with cumin, cardamom, and other spices, is layered with chickpeas, bathed in a garlic and lemon broth, and served with crisp-skinned chicken.

- 1 3½–4-lb. chicken, quartered
- 8 whole allspice, plus ⅛ tsp. ground
- 2 cloves garlic, crushed
- 1½ lemons, thinly sliced
- 2 medium yellow onions, 1 halved, 1 minced
- 1 stick cinnamon, plus ⅛ tsp. ground
   Kosher salt, to taste
- ¾ cup olive oil
- 2½ tsp. ground cumin
- 1½ tsp. ground cardamom
- 1 cup maftoul (Palestinian large-grain bulgur couscous) or Israeli couscous
   Freshly ground black pepper, to taste
- 1 15-oz. can chickpeas, drained and rinsed
   Roughly chopped fresh flat-leaf parsley, for garnish
   Greek yogurt, for serving

1 Bring chicken, whole allspice, half each of the garlic and lemon, halved onion, cinnamon stick, salt, and 8 cups water to a boil in a 6-qt. saucepan. Reduce heat to medium-low and cook, covered partially, until chicken is cooked, 15–20 minutes. Using tongs, transfer chicken to a bowl. Add ¼ cup oil, half the cumin, and the cardamom to the chicken and toss to coat; set aside. Increase heat to medium and simmer until stock is reduced to 4 cups, 20–25 minutes. Strain into a bowl, discarding solids.

2 Heat ¼ cup oil in a 4-qt. saucepan over medium-high heat. Add remaining garlic and lemons and the minced onion and cook, stirring occasionally, until golden, 6–8 minutes. Add ground allspice and cinnamon, the remaining cumin, and the maftoul; season with salt and pepper and cook, stirring, until couscous is lightly toasted, about 4 minutes. Add

1½ cups reserved stock and bring to a boil. Reduce heat to low and cook, covered, until couscous is tender and all the liquid is absorbed, 16–18 minutes. Uncover, fluff with a fork, and transfer to a serving platter; keep warm.

3 Heat remaining ¼ cup oil in a 12″ skillet over medium-high heat. Add chicken, skin side down, and cook, flipping once, until browned, 5–7 minutes. Transfer to platter with couscous. Add chickpeas to skillet with remaining stock; boil. Cook until liquid is reduced to about ½ cup, 8–10 minutes. Spoon chickpeas over chicken; garnish with parsley and serve with yogurt.

SEVEN-VEGETABLE COUSCOUS

SERVES 4–8

Moroccans consider it lucky to combine seven vegetables in one dish; substitutions are acceptable so long as the total number remains the same.

- 6 tbsp. unsalted butter
- 1 lb. boneless veal shank, cut into several pieces
- 1 onion, minced
   Pinch of saffron threads
- 1 small green cabbage, quartered
- 2 medium tomatoes
- 2 small chiles, stemmed and seeded
   Salt and freshly ground black pepper
- 2 cups fine-grain couscous
- 1 waxy potato, peeled and quartered
- 1 small eggplant, quartered
- 3–4 medium carrots, peeled and quartered
- 1 red bell pepper, seeded and quartered
- 1 white turnip, peeled and quartered
- 1 small butternut squash, peeled, seeded, and cut into 4 large chunks
- 2 small zucchini, quartered
- 1 cup rinsed canned chickpeas
- 1 cup chopped fresh cilantro

1 Melt 4 tbsp. butter in a large pot over medium-high heat. Add veal, onion, saffron, cabbage, tomatoes, chiles, 2 tsp. salt, and 1 tsp. pepper and cook, stirring often, for about

367

5 minutes. Add enough water (about 4 cups) to just cover meat and vegetables. Bring to a boil, then reduce heat to low, cover, and simmer for 1 hour.

2 Meanwhile, place couscous in a bowl, add 6 cups cold water, and soak for 10 minutes. Drain and transfer to a large platter. Allow to rest until all moisture has been absorbed, about 10 minutes. Use your fingers to separate couscous grains, breaking up any lumps, then transfer to large fine-mesh sieve or colander that can be suspended in the pot over veal mixture. Set couscous aside.

3 After veal mixture has simmered, add potatoes, eggplant, carrots, red peppers, turnips, and butternut squash. Suspend sieve with couscous in pot. So that all steam is forced up through couscous, tightly seal space between sieve and pot with aluminum foil. Allow couscous to steam, uncovered, for 20 minutes. Using a large spoon, transfer couscous to same large platter. Break up any more lumps with your fingers, using a small amount of cold water if necessary. Return couscous to sieve and steam for 20 minutes more.

4 Transfer couscous to platter again, break up lumps, then use a fork to mix in ½ cup veal cooking liquid and remaining 2 tbsp. butter. Remove sieve from pot; add zucchini, chickpeas, and cilantro to veal mixture. Return couscous to sieve and place on top of pot, then reseal with aluminum foil and steam for a final 20 minutes.

5 Remove pot from heat. Transfer couscous to a serving platter and fluff with a fork. Mound couscous into a cone shape. Using a slotted spoon, remove veal and vegetables from cooking liquid and put veal at peak of cone and some of vegetables around sides, alternating different colors. Then place more vegetables around top, covering meat. Serve hot, with veal cooking liquid on the side.

COUSCOUS ROYALE
Couscous with Grilled Meats

SERVES 8

A plate of fluffy couscous is lavished with meatballs, lamb chops, chicken skewers, *merguez* sausage, and a saffron-scented chickpea stew in this celebratory dish, a centerpiece at Paris' *maghrébin* (North African) restaurants.

FOR THE GRILLED MEAT

- 1 lb. ground lamb
- 3 tbsp. paprika
- 3 tbsp. ground cumin
- 6 cloves garlic, minced
- 1 small onion, grated
- 1 bunch fresh cilantro, minced
- 1 egg
  Kosher salt and freshly ground black pepper, to taste
- 8 8″ bamboo skewers, soaked in water for 30 minutes
- 1 lb. boneless, skinless chicken thighs, cut into 1″ × 2″ pieces
- 8 baby lamb chops
- 8 merguez sausages

FOR THE STEW

- ⅓ cup olive oil
- ¾ lb. boneless lamb shoulder, trimmed and cut into 1″ pieces
  Kosher salt and freshly ground black pepper, to taste
- ½ cup flour
- 4 cloves garlic, finely chopped
- 2 medium carrots, peeled and cut into ¼″-thick slices
- 2 ribs celery, roughly chopped
- 2 small serrano chiles, stemmed, seeded, and chopped
- 1 medium yellow onion, roughly chopped
- 1 medium white turnip, peeled and cut into 1″ pieces
- 1 medium zucchini, cut into 1″ pieces
- ½ cup golden raisins
- 2 tbsp. tomato paste
- 1 tsp. paprika
- ½ tsp. ground ginger
- ¼ tsp. crushed saffron threads
- 2 sticks cinnamon
- 2 bay leaves
- 4 cups chicken stock
- 1 cup dried chickpeas, soaked overnight, drained
- 1 15-oz. can whole, peeled tomatoes in juice, crushed by hand
- 1 small head cabbage, cored and roughly chopped
- 1 bunch fresh flat-leaf parsley, finely chopped
  Juice of 1 lemon

FOR THE COUSCOUS
- 4 tbsp. unsalted butter
- 3 tbsp. olive oil
- 3 cups fine-grain couscous
  - Harissa (page 592), for serving

1 Season the meat: Place ground lamb, 1½ tbsp. paprika, 1½ tbsp. cumin, half the garlic, onion, three-quarters of the cilantro, egg, and salt and pepper in a bowl and mix until evenly combined. Divide mixture into 12 oval balls, about 1 oz. each, and place 3 balls on each of 4 skewers; place skewers on a plate and refrigerate until ready to grill. Place remaining paprika, cumin, garlic, and cilantro in a bowl, add chicken and lamb chops, and season with salt and pepper; toss to combine. Cover and marinate in the refrigerator for at least 1 hour. Reserve merguez.

2 Make the stew: Heat oil in an 8-qt. saucepan over medium-high heat. Working in batches, season lamb with salt and pepper, dredge in flour, and cook, turning as needed, until browned all over, about 6 minutes. Using a slotted spoon, transfer meat to a bowl; set aside. Add garlic, carrots, celery, chiles, onion, turnip, and zucchini to saucepan and cook, stirring, until golden brown, about 12 minutes. Add raisins, tomato paste, paprika, ginger, saffron, cinnamon, and bay leaves and cook, stirring, until lightly caramelized, about 3 minutes.

3 Return lamb to pan along with stock, chickpeas, tomatoes, and cabbage and bring to a boil. Reduce heat to medium, and cook, covered, stirring occasionally, until meat and chickpeas are very tender, about 2½ hours. Season with salt and pepper and stir in parsley and juice; keep warm.

4 Make the couscous: Bring butter, oil, and 6 cups water to a boil over high heat. Stir in couscous, season with salt and pepper, and cover. Remove from the heat and let sit until water is absorbed, about 10 minutes. Fluff couscous with a fork; set aside in a warm place.

5 Build a medium-hot fire in a charcoal grill or heat a gas grill to medium-high. (Alternatively, heat a cast-iron grill pan over medium-high heat.) Remove chicken from marinade, divide and thread among 4 more skewers, and working in batches, add to grill. Cook, turning once,

until charred in spots and cooked through, about 10 minutes. Transfer to a serving platter and repeat with lamb skewers, lamb chops, and sausages, about 16 minutes for lamb skewers, about 7 minutes for lamb chops, and about 18 minutes for sausages. Serve stew, couscous, and grilled meats together on the table with harissa on the side.

PARIS ROYALE

" Expats from the Maghreb—the name means "place of the sunset" or "west" in Arabic, and denotes the western edge of the Arab world—constitute the largest immigrant group in France. Those immigrants have been arriving in waves since the 1920s, when they began settling on the edges of Paris as the French colonial era came to a close. Even as second- and third-generation North Africans identify as French, new immigrants from the region continue to pour in, populating sections of the city that are as fragrant with spices and teeming with hijab-clad women as the Marrakech Kasbah.

Morocco—as in vogue today among Europeans as it was in the '60s, when Yves Saint-Laurent unveiled his Moroccan-inspired couture—has a long history of hospitality that also took root firmly and enduringly in Paris.

Though Morocco's cuisine is the Maghreb's most regal, with the most complex spice blends and elaborate dishes, you're not likely to find any food in that country dubbed *royale*. These fancy presentations were Parisian innovations, intended to seduce the French palate; in Morocco, couscous is traditionally served with only one meat, and just one day a week, usually after Friday prayers. "

JAY CHESHES

Filled Pastas & Dumplings

SPINACH & RICOTTA RAVIOLI

SERVES 10–12

Delicate ravioli filled with spinach and cheese are easily available at any store, but our homemade version is fresher, lighter, and undeniably more flavorful. We love them paired with Hearty Vegetable Tomato Sauce (page 357).

- ¼ lb. mozzarella, shredded
- 2 cups ricotta cheese
- 2 tbsp. thinly sliced fresh basil leaves
- ¼ tsp. freshly grated nutmeg
- 1 10-oz. package frozen spinach, thawed, squeezed completely dry, and finely chopped
  Kosher salt and freshly ground black pepper, to taste
- 20 sheets fresh pasta (about 6½″ × 5½″, or 2 12-oz. packages)

1 Combine mozzarella, ricotta, basil, nutmeg, spinach, and salt and pepper in a bowl; refrigerate filling until ready to use.

2 Lay 1 pasta sheet on a work surface and lightly brush with water. Place 2 tsp. of the filling in the upper left-hand corner of the sheet, and repeat with 3 more portions, forming a grid of 4, each portion about 1″ from the edge of the sheet and spaced about 2″ apart from each other. Lay another sheet of pasta on top of the filling portions, and press down around the filling to press out any air and push the 2 pasta sheets together. Using a crimped pasta cutter or knife, trim the border of dough, and then cut a cross in between the 4 mounds of filling to create 4 ravioli. Repeat with remaining pasta sheets and filling to make 40 ravioli. (At this point, ravioli can be refrigerated for up to 1 week, or frozen for up to 2 months.)

3 To cook ravioli: Bring a large pot of salted water to a boil over high heat. Add ravioli and cook until al dente and filling is heated through, about 4 minutes. Using a slotted spoon, transfer ravioli to serving bowls and spoon the sauce of your choice on top.

BUTTERNUT SQUASH RAVIOLI

SERVES 6–8 (SEE PHOTO, PAGE 433)

The delicate filling of these ravioli—roasted garlic, butternut squash, and browned butter—is shown off when the usual heavy pasta is swapped for store-bought wonton wrappers, ethereal and delicate. It's a perfect match for Oregano-Hazelnut Pesto (page 356).

- 4 cloves garlic, unpeeled
- 1 small butternut squash, halved lengthwise and seeds removed
- 2 tbsp. olive oil
- 1 cup finely grated Parmigiano-Reggiano, plus more for serving
- 4 tbsp. unsalted butter, browned
- 1 tbsp. freshly grated nutmeg
- 2 tsp. minced fresh sage, plus ½ cup packed whole leaves
- 2 tsp. minced fresh oregano
  Kosher salt and freshly ground black pepper, to taste
- 1 cup canola oil
- 80 square wonton wrappers
- 1 egg, lightly beaten

1 Heat oven to 450°. Rub garlic and squash with olive oil. Place squash, cut sides down, on a baking sheet. Bake until tender, about 30 minutes. Let cool briefly, then scoop out the squash flesh and garlic cloves from their skins and pass both through a potato ricer or food mill into a large bowl. Mix in Parmigiano, browned butter, nutmeg, minced sage, oregano, and salt and pepper. Set filling aside.

2 Heat canola oil in a 10″ skillet over medium-high heat. Add whole sage leaves and fry until crisp, about 20 seconds. Transfer to paper towels to drain and set aside.

3 Place 1 wonton wrapper on a work surface and place 1 tbsp. filling in center; brush edge of wrapper with egg and top with another wrapper. Press edges to seal. Repeat with remaining wrappers and filling.

4 Bring a large pot of salted water to a boil. Working in batches, add ravioli and cook until tender, about 2 minutes. Transfer to a large bowl and toss with the sauce of your choice.

RAVIOLI CACIO E PERE

Pear & Cheese Ravioli

SERVES 4–6

At the Manhattan restaurant Felidia, chef-owner Lidia Bastianich mixes tender, sweet Bartlett pears with sharp pecorino romano and creamy mascarpone to make the filling for this rich ravioli.

FOR THE DOUGH
- 2⅔ cups flour, plus more for dusting
- ½ tsp. kosher salt, plus more to taste
- 1 tsp. olive oil, plus more
- 4 eggs
- ¾ cup unsalted butter
  Freshly ground black pepper, to taste

FOR THE FILLING
- 1 lb. pecorino romano, grated, plus more for serving
- ¾ cup mascarpone
- 6 Bartlett pears, peeled, cored, and grated

1 Make the dough: Mix flour and salt in a food processor. With the motor running, add oil, eggs, and 1–2 tbsp. water and process until dough forms. Transfer dough to a lightly floured surface and knead until dough is elastic, 8–10 minutes. Transfer to a greased bowl and cover with plastic wrap; let rest 1 hour at room temperature.

2 Make the filling: Stir pecorino, mascarpone, and pears together in a bowl; chill until ready to use.

3 On a lightly floured surface, divide dough into 3 balls. Working with 1 ball at a time, and keeping the remaining dough covered with a damp cloth, roll ball into an 11″×30″ rectangle. With a long side facing you, place 1½ tbsp. mounds of filling in 2 rows of 10 on the top half of the dough, leaving a 1½″ border at the edges and spacing the mounds about 2½″ apart. Brush dough with water. Fold bottom half of dough up and over filling. Press dough to seal, squeezing out air pockets around filling. Using a pastry cutter or knife, cut out ravioli; transfer to a parchment paper–lined baking sheet.

4 Bring a large pot of salted water to a boil. Cook ravioli until al dente, 3–4 minutes. Meanwhile, melt butter in a 12″ skillet over medium-high heat. Using a slotted spoon, transfer ravioli to skillet, along with 1 cup cooking water, salt, and pepper; toss to combine. Transfer ravioli to a serving platter; garnish with more pecorino and pepper.

VEAL & ESCAROLE AGNOLOTTI

SERVES 10

Tender veal and bittersweet escarole fill these small, rectangular ravioli. They're traditionally served in a shallow bowl of hot chicken stock.

- 3 cups flour, plus more for dusting
- 1½ tsp. kosher salt, plus more to taste
- 5 eggs
- ½ head escarole, cored and chopped
- 3 tbsp. unsalted butter
- ¼ lb. ground veal
- ¼ cup grated Parmigiano-Reggiano
- ¼ tsp. freshly grated nutmeg
- 1 egg white
  Freshly ground black pepper, to taste

1 In a large bowl, whisk together flour and salt. Make a well in center and add 4 eggs and 5–6 tbsp. water to well. Mix with a fork until a dough forms. Transfer to a lightly floured work surface and knead until smooth, about 8 minutes. Wrap dough in plastic wrap and chill for 1 hour.

2 Meanwhile, make the filling: Bring a large pot of salted water to a boil and add escarole. Cook until just tender, about 1 minute. Drain escarole and transfer to a kitchen towel. Gather up ends of towel and squeeze out liquid; set aside. Melt butter in a 10″ skillet over medium-high heat. Add escarole and cook for 4 minutes. Transfer escarole to a food processor along with remaining egg, veal, Parmigiano, nutmeg, egg white, and salt and pepper; pulse until just smooth. Transfer filling to a bowl, cover with plastic wrap, and chill.

3 Divide dough into 16 pieces. Working with 1 piece of dough at a time (cover remaining dough with a tea towel), flatten it into a rectangle, sprinkle with flour, and pass through a hand-cranked pasta machine set at its widest setting. Fold dough into thirds like a letter, creating another rectangle, and feed short edge through pasta roller at its widest setting; repeat folding process twice more. Decrease one setting and roll dough again; repeat, decreasing one setting each time until you've reached the second to last setting, creating a $\frac{1}{16}''$-thick sheet of pasta.

4 Cut sheet in half crosswise; set one half aside. Using a teaspoon-size measuring spoon, place balls of filling, spaced about ½″ apart, on dough. Top with reserved pasta, using your fingers to press around each ball to push out any trapped air. Using a knife, divide individual ravioli, trimming edges. Transfer ravioli to a lightly floured baking sheet; repeat with remaining dough and filling.

5 To cook: Bring a large pot of salted water to a boil. Working in 4 batches, add the ravioli and cook, stirring occasionally, until the pasta is al dente, 3–4 minutes.

SPINACH GNOCCHI WITH BROWN BUTTER & SAGE
SERVES 4–6

A regional dish from the Italian province of Parma, these plump spinach gnocchi are excellent sprinkled with the local cheese—Parmigiano-Reggiano.

1	lb. russet potatoes, unpeeled
	Kosher salt, to taste
¼	lb. spinach
1¼	cups semolina flour, sifted, plus more for dusting
2	eggs, beaten
18	tbsp. unsalted butter
16	leaves fresh sage, minced
¼	tsp. freshly grated nutmeg
	Freshly ground black pepper, to taste
4	tbsp. olive oil
3	tbsp. finely grated Parmigiano-Reggiano, for serving

1 Put potatoes into a 4-qt. pot of salted water and bring to a boil. Reduce heat to medium-low and simmer until tender, 25 minutes. Drain; let cool. Peel potatoes and pass through medium plate of a food mill into a bowl.

2 Meanwhile, heat a 12″ skillet over medium-high heat. Add spinach and 1 tbsp. water and cook until wilted. Press on spinach in a sieve to extract liquid. Finely chop spinach; stir together with potatoes and semolina and form a well in center. Add eggs and salt and, using a fork, beat eggs into potato mixture. Transfer dough to a work surface dusted with semolina; knead to combine. Divide dough into 6 portions. Roll each portion into a ½″-thick rope. Cut ropes into ½″-wide pieces; transfer to a semolina-dusted baking sheet.

3 Melt 10 tbsp. butter in a 10″ skillet over medium heat; cook, swirling, until butter browns, about 6 minutes. Add sage and nutmeg and season with salt and pepper. Remove from heat; set aside.

4 Working in 4 batches, add 2 tbsp. butter and 1 tbsp. oil to a 12″ skillet over medium-high heat. Add dough pieces and cook, flipping once, until golden brown, 3–4 minutes. Transfer to a baking sheet. Wipe out skillet and repeat with remaining butter, oil, and dough pieces in 3 batches. Toss dumplings and brown butter sauce in the skillet until hot. Serve sprinkled with Parmigiano.

HALUŠKY
Boiled Potato Dumplings
SERVES 8–10

These earthy potato dumplings, a staple of families of Eastern European descent in Pennsylvania's Pocono Mountains, are delicious tossed with sweet caramelized onions and bacon and topped with sour cream.

1	tbsp. unsalted butter
3	slices bacon, cut into ½″ pieces
2	small yellow onions, 1 thinly sliced, 1 finely grated
	Kosher salt, to taste
1¾	lb. russet potatoes, peeled and finely grated (soak in water until needed, then drain)
2	cups flour
¾	tsp. baking soda
2	eggs, lightly beaten
	Freshly ground black pepper, to taste
	Sour cream, for serving

1 Heat butter and bacon in a 10″ skillet over medium-high heat and cook, stirring occasionally, until bacon is crisp and its fat has rendered, about 6 minutes. Using a slotted spoon, transfer bacon to paper towels to drain and set aside. Add sliced onion to skillet and cook, stirring occasionally, until soft and lightly caramelized, about 6 minutes. Transfer to a small bowl and set aside.

2 Bring a 6-qt. saucepan of salted water to a boil over high heat. Meanwhile, stir together grated onion, potatoes, flour, baking soda, eggs, and salt and pepper in a bowl with a fork until a thick dough forms. Working in batches, drop teaspoon-size balls of dough into the water and cook until the dumplings float to the surface and are cooked through, about 3 minutes. Drain dumplings, then divide among serving plates. Top each portion with bacon, caramelized onions, and sour cream before serving.

SPÄTZLE SHORTCUT

Spätzle, literally "little sparrows" in German, are tiny egg dumplings. Despite their apparent simplicity, making them can be tricky. Veteran cooks cut the batter into tiny ribbons or push it through a colander or even just pinch off bits of dough. We discovered a foolproof alternative: a tool called the Viennese Spätzle Maker, available at cookware stores and online. Place it over a pot of boiling water, spoon batter into the hopper, then push and pull it across the perforated screen. The small dollops of dough that emerge cook into perfect spätzle.

GABHOR UTOMO

SPÄTZLE
Garlic Dumplings with Emmentaler
SERVES 4

Spätzle are a ubiquitous comfort food in southwestern Germany. They're even more comforting served under a generous blanket of broiled cheese.

- 2 heads garlic
- 2 tbsp. extra-virgin olive oil
- 6 tbsp. unsalted butter
- ½ cup milk
- ¼ cup finely chopped fresh flat-leaf parsley
- ¼ cup finely chopped fresh basil
- ¼ tsp. kosher salt
- 3 eggs, beaten
- 2 cups flour
- 1 cup grated Emmentaler cheese

1 Heat oven to 450°. Halve both heads of garlic crosswise with a knife and brush with oil; wrap with foil. Roast until soft, 1 hour. Let cool and squeeze roasted garlic cloves from their skins into a bowl; mash with a fork to a paste.

2 Melt 2 tbsp. butter and add to paste. Then add milk, parsley, basil, salt, and eggs; stir until smooth. Put flour into a large bowl and form a well in center. Slowly pour in the garlic-milk mixture, stirring with a fork to form a smooth batter.

3 Bring a 5-qt. saucepan of salted water to a boil over high heat. Set a perforated spätzle-making disk over the pot. Working in batches, scrape batter through holes into water. Cook until dumplings rise to surface, about 1 minute. Using a slotted spoon, transfer dumplings to a baking sheet.

4 Heat remaining 4 tbsp. of butter in a 12″ ovenproof skillet over high heat. Add dumplings and cook, stirring, until lightly browned, 6–8 minutes. Meanwhile, arrange an oven rack 5″ from broiler and heat broiler. Sprinkle dumplings with cheese and broil until melted, about 2 minutes.

TURKISH LAMB DUMPLINGS
Manti
SERVES 6

These dense lamb-filled dumplings are traditionally served with both a thick yogurt sauce and a spicy brown-butter sauce, textural counterpoints that harmonize beautifully. Pay special attention to the size of your *manti*: According to Turkish tradition, the smaller the dumpling, the more respect you have for your guests.

- 1 cup flour, plus more for dusting
- ½ tsp. kosher salt, plus more to taste
- 1 egg
- 7 oz. ground lamb
- 1 clove garlic, minced
- ½ small yellow onion, minced
   Freshly ground black pepper, to taste
- ½ cup unsalted butter
- 2 tsp. dried mint
- 2 tsp. paprika
- 1 tsp. crushed red chile flakes
- 1 cup Greek yogurt
   Thinly sliced fresh mint, for garnish

> "The greatest delight the fields and woods minister is the suggestion of an occult relation between man and the vegetable. I am not alone and unacknowledged. They nod to me and I to them."
>
> RALPH WALDO EMERSON

1 Combine flour, salt, and egg in a food processor. With the motor running, slowly add ¼ cup water until a soft dough forms. Transfer dough to a lightly floured surface and knead until smooth and elastic, 2–3 minutes. Transfer to a bowl and cover with plastic wrap; chill for 30 minutes.

2 Mix lamb, garlic, onion, salt, and pepper in a bowl; chill for 20 minutes.

3 Divide dough into 2 balls. Working with 1 ball of dough at a time (keep remaining ball of dough covered with a damp cloth), roll out on a lightly floured surface into a 10″ square about ⅛″ thick. Cut dough into twenty-five 2″ squares. Place ½ tsp. of the lamb mixture onto each square. Working with 1 square at a time, brush corners of dough with water, then lift up and over filling so they join in the middle and pinch closed. Transfer dumplings to a parchment paper–lined baking sheet; cover with a damp cloth until ready to cook. Bring an 8-qt. saucepan of salted water to a boil. Working in batches, cook the dumplings until they rise to the surface, 4–5 minutes. Drain dumplings and transfer to a serving bowl; keep warm.

4 Melt butter in a 12″ skillet over medium heat; cook until butter is dark golden brown with dark brown flecks and it gives off a nutty aroma, 20–25 minutes. Stir in dried mint, paprika, and chile flakes. Whisk yogurt until smooth. Drizzle over dumplings, then drizzle brown butter sauce over dumplings and garnish with fresh mint.

GEORGIAN DUMPLINGS
Khinkali

MAKES 25 DUMPLINGS

A specialty of dumpling houses in Tbilisi, Republic of Georgia, these large, juicy pork-and-beef-filled pockets are flavored with chiles, cilantro, and fenugreek.

- 4 cups flour, plus more for dusting
- 1¼ tsp. kosher salt, plus more to taste
- ½ lb. ground beef
- ½ lb. ground pork

- 2 tbsp. finely chopped fresh cilantro
- 1 tsp. dried fenugreek leaves
- ½ tsp. crushed red chile flakes
- 3 small yellow onions, minced
  Freshly ground black pepper, to taste

1 Stir together flour, salt, and 1¼ cups warm water in a bowl until a dough forms. Transfer to a work surface and knead until smooth, about 6 minutes. Wrap dough in plastic wrap and refrigerate for 40 minutes. Meanwhile, combine beef, pork, cilantro, fenugreek, chile flakes, and onions in a bowl until evenly mixed. Season generously with salt and pepper and set filling aside.

2 Divide dough into 25 equal pieces and shape each piece into a ball. Using a rolling pin, roll a ball into a 6″ round. Place about 2 tbsp. filling in center of round and fold edges of dough over filling, creating pleats in dough as you go, until filling is covered. Holding dumpling in the palm of one hand, grasp top of dumpling where pleats meet and twist to seal pleats and form a knot at top of dumpling. Repeat with remaining dough rounds and filling.

3 Bring a large pot of salted water to a boil. Working in batches, boil dumplings until they float and dough is tender, about 8 minutes. Drain and serve hot. Season with black pepper.

POTATO PIEROGI

MAKES 4–5 DOZEN DUMPLINGS

This is the basic pierogi recipe used by the Pierogi Ladies of St. Josaphat's Ukrainian Catholic Cathedral in Parma, Ohio, where they sell thousands of dumplings each week in order to support their church.

FOR THE DOUGH

- 1 egg
- 3 tbsp. unsalted butter, melted and cooled
- 2 tsp. kosher salt
- 5½ cups flour

FOR THE FILLING

- 3 medium boiling potatoes, peeled and quartered
  Kosher salt, to taste
- 5 tbsp. unsalted butter, melted
- 1 tbsp. vegetable oil

1 Make the dough: Put egg, butter, salt, and 2 cups warm water in the bowl of a standing mixer fitted with a paddle and beat on low speed until combined. Gradually add flour, continuing to beat. Increase speed to medium and beat until a soft, elastic dough forms. Transfer dough to a floured surface and knead several times to form a smooth ball. Cover dough with a damp cloth and set aside for 30 minutes.

2 Make the filling: Put potatoes in a medium pot of cold salted water, bring to a boil over high heat, and cook until tender, 20–30 minutes. Drain, then return potatoes to pot. Add butter and mash potatoes with a potato masher or fork until smooth. Season to taste with salt.

3 Divide dough into 2 balls. Roll out 1 dough ball about ⅛" thick on a floured surface, then cut out 3" circles. Spoon 1 heaping tsp. of filling into the center of each circle, then fold in half to form a semicircle. Pinch edges together to seal. Repeat with remaining dough and filling. (Freeze pierogi, if you like, and cook later without thawing.)

4 Bring a large pot of salted water to a boil, then add oil. Cook pierogi, in batches, until dough is tender, about 5 minutes. Lift pierogi from boiling water with a slotted spoon and drain well. Serve hot with melted butter or sour cream, if you like.

COOK'S NOTE To make the Pierogi Ladies' cheese pierogi, add a few tablespoons of Cheez Whiz to the filling in step 2.

SHANGHAI SOUP DUMPLINGS

Xiao Long Bao

MAKES 16 DUMPLINGS

These shots of savory broth encased in steamed dough are made using a collagen-rich pork stock that gels as it cools. The soup reliquefies as the dumplings steam, ready to be slurped out upon serving.

- ¼ lb. pork skin, rinsed and finely diced
- 2 scallions, trimmed and chopped
- 1 3" piece fresh ginger, peeled, cut into matchsticks
- 8 large napa cabbage leaves, trimmed and blanched
- 4 tbsp. black vinegar
- 5 oz. pork belly, cubed
- 1 tsp. sugar
- 1 tsp. soybean paste
- 1 tsp. dark soy sauce
- 1 tsp. sesame oil
- 1 tsp. kosher salt
- ¼ tsp. freshly ground white pepper
- ½ cup flour

1 Place pork skin, half the scallions, one-third the ginger, and 1½ cups cold water in a 4-qt. pot. Bring to a simmer over medium-low heat and continue to simmer until most of the gelatin from the pork skin has leached out and broth has reduced to ½ cup, about 1 hour. Strain broth through a sieve into a shallow bowl, discarding solids, and refrigerate until firmly gelled, 1–1½ hours. Line bottoms of 2 medium (about 9" in diameter) bamboo steamer baskets with 3 of the cabbage leaves each and set aside. Divide remaining ginger between 2 small dipping bowls. Add 2 tbsp. of the vinegar to each bowl and set sauce aside.

2 Place pork belly and remaining scallions in a bowl; mix well. Pass pork mixture through a meat grinder fitted with the fine-hole disk into a medium bowl. Add sugar, bean paste, soy sauce, sesame oil, and salt and pepper, and mix well. Finely dice pork jelly and stir into ground pork mixture. Cover and set filling aside in the freezer to set.

3 Put flour into a medium bowl, add 5 tbsp. warm water, and stir until a dough begins to form. Press dough together into a rough ball, transfer to a lightly floured surface, and knead until smooth, 8–10 minutes. Shape dough into a ball, cover with plastic wrap, and set aside to let rest for 30 minutes. Roll dough into a 6"-long rope on a lightly floured surface with your hands, cut into 16 equal pieces, roll into balls, and cover with plastic wrap to keep from drying out.

4 To form the dumplings, lightly dust 1 of the dough balls with flour, then flatten into a disk. Roll out until disk is about 3" in diameter. Put 1 tbsp. of the filling on the thick center of dough. Pleat dough at ¼" intervals to encase filling. Hold dumpling in one hand, put tip of index finger of your other hand in center of pleated dough, then gently twist pleats shut, removing index finger as you twist, to completely encase filling. Repeat rolling, filling, pleating, and twisting with remaining dough to make 16 dumplings in all. Put 8 dumplings into each steamer basket, adding them as they are formed; cover dumplings with remaining cabbage leaves to keep them from drying out as you work.

5 Remove and discard cabbage leaves from tops of dumplings (not the leaves lining the baskets), stack baskets, and put lid on top basket. Steam dumplings over a wok of boiling water over high heat until pork is cooked through and jelly has melted into soup, 8–10 minutes. Serve dumplings immediately, with dipping sauce on the side.

COOK'S NOTE To eat soup dumplings, take a small bite from the top of the doughy top, making a hole out of which you can slurp the broth. Then dip the deflated—but still delicious!—dumpling in the dipping sauce and eat.

SICHUAN PORK WONTONS

Chao Shou

MAKES ABOUT 40 WONTONS

The recipe for these tasty pork wontons drowned in fiery chile oil is from Chengdu, China, noodle shop owner Ma Yingjun.

- 1½ lb. ground pork
- 3 tbsp. cornstarch
- 2 tbsp. dry sherry
- 2 tbsp. light soy sauce
- 1 tbsp. Shaoxing wine
- 4 cloves garlic, minced
- 1 4″ piece fresh ginger, peeled and minced
- 40 3½″-square wonton wrappers
- 1 egg, beaten
   Kosher salt, to taste
- ½ cup Sichuan Red Chile Oil (this page, or store-bought), plus more for serving
- 2 tbsp. black vinegar, plus more for serving

1 Mix pork, cornstarch, sherry, soy, wine, garlic, and ginger in a bowl. Working with 1 wrapper at a time, place ½ tbsp. filling in center, brush edges with egg, and fold in half, forming a triangle; overlap opposite corners, brushing with egg to seal together. Repeat with remaining wrappers and pork mixture; set aside.

2 Bring a large pot of salted water to boil over high heat; working in batches, cook wontons until firm and cooked through, 5–7 minutes. Using a slotted spoon, transfer to paper towels to drain briefly, then place in a bowl; season with salt and toss with red chile oil and vinegar. Serve additional red chile oil and vinegar on the side, if you like.

Sichuan Red Chile Oil

Hong You

MAKES ABOUT 2 CUPS

This versatile, ruby red chile-and-spice-infused oil is a key ingredient in all kinds of Sichuan dishes.

- 2 cups canola oil
- 4 star anise pods
- 3 cloves garlic, smashed
- 3 black cardamom pods (cao guo)
- 3 whole cloves
- 2 bay leaves
- 1 stick cinnamon, broken in half
- 1 3″ piece fresh ginger, smashed
- 1 cup (about 32) chiles de árbol, stemmed and chopped
- 3 tbsp. Sichuan peppercorns
- 1 tbsp. light soy sauce
- ½ tsp. kosher salt

Combine oil, star anise, garlic, cardamom, cloves, bay, cinnamon, and ginger in a 2-qt. saucepan over medium heat. Cook, stirring occasionally, until garlic is golden, 15–20 minutes. Transfer to a 1-qt. glass jar and add chiles, peppercorns, soy, and salt; let cool to room temperature. Using a slotted spoon, remove and discard garlic and ginger; seal jar and let sit for at least 24 hours. To use, strain oil, discarding solids. Store refrigerated for up to 3 months.

HAR GAO

Shrimp Dumplings

MAKES ABOUT 40 DUMPLINGS

These traditional shrimp dumplings are encased in *har gao* dough, glutinous dumpling skins that are opaque when raw and become luminously translucent once cooked. The pea "eyes" are purely decorative; Buddakan co-executive chef Yang Huang likes them because they make the dumplings look like little goldfish.

FOR THE FILLING

- 1 lb. shrimp, peeled, deveined, and diced
- 1 cup bamboo shoots, diced
- 1 cup water chestnuts, diced
- 1 cup pea shoots, coarsely chopped
- 1 clove garlic, finely minced
- 2 tsp. salt
- 1 tsp. sugar
- 1 tsp. white pepper

2 tsp. vegetable oil

1 tsp. toasted sesame oil

¼ cup green peas

FOR THE DOUGH & SERVING

1⅓ cups wheat starch

⅔ cup tapioca flour

¼ tsp. salt

Vegetable oil

½ cup soy sauce

¼ cup rice vinegar

1 scallion, green parts only, sliced very thin

1 Make the filling: In a large nonreactive bowl, combine all filling ingredients except peas. Work mixture aggressively with hands until thoroughly combined. Cover and refrigerate.

2 Make the dough: Mix together wheat starch, tapioca flour, and salt in a medium bowl. Gradually stir in 1 cup plus 3 tbsp. boiling water a little at a time, then add 2 tbsp. oil. Mix until dough forms a ball. Knead dough on a lightly oiled surface until silky, about 1 minute. Quarter dough, roll into 10″ ropes, cut each rope into 10 pieces, roll pieces into balls, then flatten balls with palm of your hand. Flatten skins further using the flat side of an oiled Chinese cleaver until very thin. Keep dough and skins covered with plastic to prevent them from drying out.

3 Spoon about 2 tsp. filling in center of each skin, folding dough over and pleating edges together until halfway closed; place two peas on the edge of the dumpling skin and fold dough around them to form "eyes."

4 Fit a bamboo steamer basket over boiling water and steam dumplings over high heat for about 5 minutes, or until translucent. Serve accompanied with combined soy sauce, rice vinegar, and scallion.

CHAR SIU BAO

Roast Pork Buns

MAKES 16 BUNS

Char siu bao is a Cantonese specialty consisting of sweet-savory marinated pork encased in a spongy dough that is then steamed or baked. It's a popular—and hearty—breakfast or snack.

FOR THE DOUGH

1 tsp. active dry yeast

½ cup lukewarm water (115°)

3½ cups cake flour

1 tbsp. sugar

1 tsp. baking powder

2 tbsp. diced lard or vegetable shortening

FOR THE FILLING

1 tbsp. canola oil

3 scallions, white part only, finely chopped

1½ cups diced roast pork

3 tbsp. soy sauce

3 tbsp. oyster sauce

1 tbsp. sugar

1 tsp. cornstarch

1 Make the dough: Combine yeast and water in a bowl; let sit until foamy, about 10 minutes. Combine flour, sugar, and baking powder in the bowl of a stand mixer fitted with a paddle attachment. Add yeast mixture and mix on low speed until combined. Add lard 1 piece at a time, then increase speed to medium, and continue mixing until dough comes together in a ball, about 5 minutes. Remove bowl from mixer, cover with plastic wrap, and let sit in a warm place until doubled in size, about 2 hours. Knead dough until smooth and elastic, about 5 minutes. Shape into 16 equal-size balls.

2 Make the filling: Heat oil in a 10″ nonstick skillet over medium-high heat. Add scallions and cook for 1 minute. Add roast pork, soy and oyster sauces, and sugar and cook until scallions have softened and pork is heated through, about 3 minutes. Dissolve cornstarch in 2 tbsp. water in a small cup, add to pork mixture, and cook until sauce thickens, about 1 minute more. Remove from heat and let cool.

3 Place a dough ball in the palm of one hand and, with the thumb of your other hand, make a well in the center. Fill well with about 1½ tbsp. pork filling, then seal by pinching dough closed toward the center. Place a 2″-square piece of parchment paper over pinched area. Turn bun over and use scissors to make a ½″ crisscross incision in the center of the bun. Repeat process, filling remaining buns and placing on parchment squares. Keep filled buns covered with a damp towel.

4 Place 8 buns, paper side down, in an 11″ bamboo steamer; close tightly with lid. Meanwhile, bring 2 cups water to a boil in a 14″ flat-bottomed wok over high heat. Fit bamboo steamer into wok, and steam until buns are puffed, about 12 minutes. Repeat with remaining buns.

Rolls

POPIAH

Malaysian-Style Fresh Spring Rolls

MAKES 6

Fresh, crunchy shrimp- and tofu-filled spring rolls are a popular street snack in Ipoh, Malaysia's capital city. Writer Jayanthi Daniel learned to make this version from a young man working at her aunt's favorite *pasar malam*, or night market.

- 2¼ cups canola oil
- 2 cloves garlic, finely chopped
- 10 oz. jicama, julienned
- 1½ tbsp. sugar
- ½ tsp. ground white pepper
  Kosher salt, to taste
- 2 eggs, lightly beaten
- 5 oz. dried spiced bean curd, julienned
- ½ small yellow onion, very thinly sliced
- ½ cup small dried shrimp, soaked in boiling water for 20 minutes and drained
- 6 8"-square wheat spring roll wrappers
- 1½ tsp. *each* Sriracha chile sauce and hoisin sauce, plus more to taste
- 1 small head green leaf lettuce

1 Heat 2 tbsp. oil in a small pot over medium-high heat. Add garlic and cook, stirring, for 1 minute. Add jicama, sugar, pepper, and salt, and cook, stirring, for 2 minutes. Add 1 cup water and bring to a boil; cook, stirring, until crisp-tender, 7 minutes. Remove from heat and let cool.

2 Heat 2 tbsp. oil in a medium nonstick skillet over medium-high heat. Add eggs; cook, flipping once, until a firm omelette forms, about 4 minutes. Transfer to a cutting board, roll up like a cigar, and slice very thinly crosswise; set aside. Add another 1 tbsp. oil to skillet and, when hot, add bean curd; cook, stirring, until golden brown, about 8 minutes. Set aside.

3 Heat remaining oil in a small pot over medium-high until a deep-fry thermometer reads 350°. Add onion and fry until crisp, about 4 minutes. Using a slotted spoon, transfer onion to paper towels to drain. Add shrimp to oil, and fry until crisp and browned, about 2 minutes; transfer to paper towels to drain, and set onion and shrimp aside. Remove oil from heat.

4 To assemble, arrange 1 spring roll wrapper on a work surface like a diamond (so a corner faces you). Brush bottom third of wrapper with ¼ tsp. each chile and hoisin sauces; place 1 leaf of lettuce on top, followed by ¼ cup jicama, 1½ tbsp. sliced omelette, and 1 tbsp. each bean curd, fried onions, and fried shrimp. Lift corner nearest to you over filling, then pull top corner of wrapper back down against filling to tighten. Fold in sides, and roll up and away from you to form a tight cylinder. Repeat with remaining wrappers and fillings to make 5 more rolls. Transfer to a serving platter, and cut each roll crosswise into 4 pieces. Drizzle with more chile sauce and hoisin, if you like, and serve.

LUMPIA

Deep-Fried Pork Spring Rolls

MAKES ABOUT 2 DOZEN

Lumpia are often deep-fried, but not always; some come wrapped in fresh egg crêpes, while others are wrapper-less. The freshly fried version is a marvel, the wrapper crisp, the filling's texture delicate and yielding. Instead of the common sweet-sour dipping sauce, chef Dale Talde opts for the condiment he enjoyed growing up—a mixture of vinegar and soy sauce spiked with raw garlic and fiery chiles—which he calls the salt and pepper of Filipino food.

FOR THE ROLLS

- 1 lb. ground pork
- ½ cup finely chopped yellow onion
- ½ cup finely chopped carrot
- 3 cloves garlic, finely chopped
- 1½ tsp. kosher salt, plus more
- ¼ tsp. freshly ground black pepper
- 1 14-oz. package 6" square spring roll wrappers
- 1 large egg, lightly beaten, for egg wash
  Vegetable oil for frying

FOR THE DIPPING SAUCE

- 1 cup white vinegar
- ¼ cup soy sauce
- 2 tbsp. sugar
- ¾ tsp. black peppercorns
- 2 cloves garlic, minced
- 2 red bird's eye chiles, stemmed and thinly sliced

1 Make the rolls: Combine pork with onion, carrot, garlic, salt, and pepper in a medium bowl, and mix with your hands until evenly combined. Position 1 spring roll wrapper in front of you so that a corner points to you, and place 1 tbsp. filling on the wrapper's bottom half. Lift corner nearest you up over filling. Fold left and right corners in toward the center, then brush top corner of wrapper lightly with some of the beaten egg and continue rolling up and away from you to form a tight cylinder. Transfer to a parchment paper–lined baking sheet, and repeat to use up remaining wrappers and filling.

2 Make the dipping sauce: In a small jar, combine vinegar, soy sauce, sugar, peppercorns, garlic, and chiles. Shake to mix.

3 Pour oil to a depth of 2″ in a medium Dutch oven. Heat over medium-high until a deep-fry thermometer reads 350°. Working in batches, add spring rolls to oil and fry until outsides are golden and filling is cooked, 8 minutes. Using a slotted spoon, transfer rolls to paper towels to drain. Season with salt and serve hot with dipping sauce.

KIMBAP
SERVES 4

Korean kimbap (also written "gimbap") is similar to Japanese sushi, except the ingredients in it are typically all cooked or pickled, even the veggies. It's a popular street food. Here's a recipe for making it at home with a sushi mat. It's the perfect light meal (or snack).

- 3   cups short-grain rice
- 1   tbsp. plus 1 tsp. sesame oil
- 2   tsp. kosher salt
- 2½   tbsp. soy sauce
- 1   tsp. plus 1 tbsp. sugar
- 1   clove garlic, minced
- 1   scallion, finely chopped
- 6   oz. beef sirloin, thinly sliced across the grain
- 2   tbsp. vegetable oil
- 1   tsp. rice wine
- 4   burdock roots (about 4 oz.), peeled and quartered
- 1   cucumber, julienned lengthwise
- 1   carrot, peeled and julienned lengthwise
- 2   eggs, lightly beaten
- 1   pickled daikon radish (about 3 oz.), cut into ¼″ julienne
- 4   sheets laver (dried nori seaweed)
- 2   tbsp. soy sauce
- 1   tbsp. chile sauce

1 Combine rice and 3¾ cups water in a medium pot and bring to a boil; reduce heat to maintain a simmer and cook, covered, for 12 minutes. Remove from heat and stir in 1 tbsp. sesame oil and 1 tsp. salt.

2 Meanwhile, combine 1 tbsp. soy sauce, 1 tsp. sugar, the garlic, and scallion in a bowl. Add beef, toss to coat, and marinate for 15 minutes.

3 Heat 1 tsp. vegetable oil in a large skillet over high heat. Add beef and cook, stirring, until browned, about 3 minutes. Transfer beef to a bowl, wipe skillet clean, and return to high heat.

4 Combine remaining soy sauce and sugar, plus rice wine and 1 tbsp. water in a bowl; add to skillet along with burdock root and cook, stirring, until soft, about 12 minutes. Transfer burdock root to a bowl, wipe skillet clean, and return to high heat.

5 Meanwhile, toss cucumber with remaining salt and let stand for 10 minutes; rinse cucumber and squeeze dry.

6 Add remaining vegetable oil to skillet and heat over medium-high heat. Add carrot and cucumber and cook for 30 seconds. Transfer vegetables to a bowl, wipe skillet clean, and return to medium heat.

7 Pour eggs into skillet and cook, undisturbed, until almost set, 2–3 minutes. Flip omelette in skillet and cook until completely set, about 1 minute more. Transfer omelette to a cutting board and let cool. Roll omelette up like a cigar and cut crosswise into ½″ thick strips.

8 Working with one sheet of seaweed at a time, place laver on a bamboo sushi rolling mat, shiny side down. Using wet fingers, press one-fourth of the rice onto the seaweed in an even layer, leaving a ½″ border on the side furthest from you. Working from the side closest to you, arrange one-quarter each of the beef, burdock root, cucumber, carrot, pickled daikon, and egg side-by-side over the rice.

9 Using the mat as a guide, lift the edge of the mat closest to you to roll seaweed up and over ingredients, forming a tight cylinder (take care to pull back the edge of the mat so as to not roll it into the kimbap). Transfer the kimbap to a cutting board and repeat with the remaining laver, rice, beef, burdock root, cucumber, carrot, pickled daikon, and egg. Slice crosswise into 10 equal pieces.

10 Mix soy sauce and chile sauce together in a bowl and serve with kimbap.

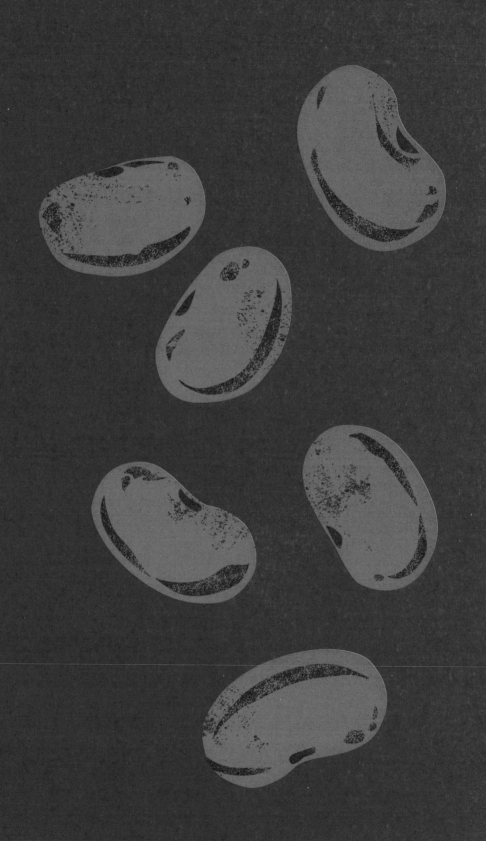

Beans, Grains & Potatoes

BEANS, GRAINS & POTATOES

A DRIED BEAN, A GRAIN OF RICE, a single potato—these are small things, unassuming. They are pantry staples, often afterthoughts. But within them lie universes of culinary pleasure: As long as we have beans, grains, or potatoes on hand, we know we will have something delicious to eat.

Very little is needed to transform dried beans and other legumes into satisfying, hearty dishes. Slow cooking imbues them with a meaty flavor and a silky texture, bringing nourishing heartiness to everything from dal, a richly spiced Indian lentil dish, to New England–style baked beans simmered in a sauce flavored with maple syrup, molasses, bacon, and mustard. Beans also shine in fried preparations: dried favas are soaked then ground, shaped into balls, and fried until crisp for falafel, and thin, crisp fritters made from just chickpeas ground into flour and mixed with water are addictive street snacks in Sicily.

Grains are the classic accompaniment to beans, and the two together make up celebratory and everyday dishes around the world, including Creole beans and rice, the coconut-rich *resanbinsi* of Honduras, and Hoppin' John, the Southern black-eyed pea stew whose luck-conferring properties are legendary. But rice without beans gets plenty of mileage, too. It's the world's most popular grain, eaten daily by more than half of the global population.

Fluffy, filling, and versatile, rice serves as the perfect canvas for all kinds of ingredients, soaking up flavors that can transform it from a side dish into a full-fledged meal: Enriched with parmesan cheese and tinted with saffron, it yields a toothsome *risotto alla Milanese;* tossed in a wok with pork, eggs, scallions, ginger, and peas, it becomes Chinese pork fried rice; sweetened with sugar and scented with orange zest and rose water, it is *shirin polow,* a sweet-savory Iranian pilaf. Although rice is undoubtedly the king of grains, many other grains are equally versatile. New World cornmeal yields smoky grilled polenta and butter-bolstered grits, and nutritious ancient grains, such as quinoa, bulgur, and farro, bring a nutty flavor and heft to the table.

But it's the potato that transforms like no other. Native to South America, the starchy, sweet, mild tubers feature in our most beloved dishes. Potatoes star in the creamy gratins and crisp *pommes frites* of France, the chile-spiked *patatas rajas* of Mexico, and Switzerland's crisp potato pancakes. They also make appearances in Indonesian gado-gado salad, Indian vegetable curries, Irish stews, and American potato salad. To borrow a phrase from Will Rogers, we never met a potato we didn't like.

Beans & Other Legumes

SOUPY BEANS

MAKES ABOUT 4 CUPS

A ham hock adds depth and richness to this simple preparation, a staple technique throughout the American Southeast. We like to use white beans, though they can easily be swapped out for black-eyed peas, red beans, or pinto beans.

- 2 cups dried white beans, such as great northern, navy, or cannellini, picked over and rinsed
- 1 ham hock, split, or about ½ lb. smoked pork necks, ham bone, or ham
- 1 medium onion, halved
  Kosher salt and freshly ground black pepper, to taste

1 Put beans in a 6-qt. saucepan and cover with 10 cups water. Let soak overnight. (Or, as a shortcut, simply cover beans with cold water and bring just to the boiling point over high heat. Remove from heat, cover, and allow to sit for 1 hour.)

2 Drain beans and return to pan. Cover with 2″ cold water. Add ham hock and onion halves and bring to a boil over high heat. Reduce heat, cover, and simmer until beans are very tender. (Some of the beans will fall apart and form a thick sauce.) This will take anywhere from 1½–3 hours, depending on the age of the beans. (If desired, remove ham hock from beans. Pull off meat, cut it into bits, and return meat to beans. Discard bone and gristle.)

3 Taste beans and adjust seasoning with salt and plenty of pepper. The beans will keep—and even improve—for several days in the refrigerator.

STEWED WHITE BEANS WITH TOMATO & LAMB

SERVES 6–8

Simmering beans with a lamb shoulder chop, a flavorful cut of meat, gives this saucy, spicy Middle Eastern dish a silky texture and deeply savory flavor.

- 2 cups dried white beans, such as cannellini, picked over and rinsed
- 2–3 chiles de árbol
- 2 medium yellow onions, 1 halved, 1 finely chopped
- ¼ cup extra-virgin olive oil
- 1 6-oz. lamb blade chop
- 3 cloves garlic, finely chopped
- 1 large banana pepper or cubanelle pepper, stemmed, seeded, and chopped
- 1½ cups tomato sauce
- 1 tsp. ground Aleppo pepper or paprika
- ½ tsp. dried oregano
- 2 medium tomatoes, halved and grated, skins discarded
- 1¾ cups chicken stock
  Kosher salt, to taste
- 1 lemon, cut into wedges

1 Put beans in a 6-qt. saucepan and cover with 10 cups water. Let soak overnight. (Or, as a shortcut, simply cover beans with cold water and bring just to the boiling point over high heat. Remove from heat, cover, and allow to sit for 1 hour.)

2 Drain beans, then put into a medium pot and cover with 10 cups cold water. Add chiles de árbol and halved onion to the pot and bring to a boil. Reduce heat to medium-low and simmer until beans are tender, about 1 hour. Discard onion and drain beans and chiles; set aside.

3 Heat oil in a 4-qt. saucepan over high heat. Add lamb and cook, turning once, until browned, 8 minutes. Add remaining onions, garlic, and banana pepper and cook, stirring occasionally, until softened, about 8 minutes. Add tomato sauce, Aleppo pepper, oregano, and grated tomatoes and cook, stirring occasionally, until the mixture is very thick, about 10 minutes. Add stock and the reserved beans and bring to a boil. Reduce heat to medium-low and simmer, stirring occasionally, until the flavors have melded, about 15 minutes more.

4 Transfer lamb to a plate and chop it into small pieces; discard bone. Return lamb to saucepan. Season beans with salt; ladle beans into bowls and squeeze lemon wedges over the top.

TUSCAN-STYLE WHITE BEANS

Fagioli Lessi

SERVES 6–8

Tuscany is known as the home of the *mangiafagioli,* or "bean eaters," thanks to the Italian region's culinary dedication to beans. The most common preparation is this one: a humble simmer with garlic and sage.

- 2 cups dried cannellini beans, picked over and rinsed
- 4 tbsp. extra-virgin olive oil
- 2 cloves garlic, crushed
- 4–5 fresh sage leaves
- 3–4 black peppercorns
  Kosher salt and freshly ground black pepper, to taste

1 Put beans in a 6-qt. saucepan and cover with 10 cups water. Let soak overnight. (Or, as a shortcut, simply cover beans with cold water and bring just to the boiling point over high heat. Remove from heat, cover, and allow to sit for 1 hour.)

2 Drain beans, then combine in a large flameproof earthenware casserole with 12 cups cold water, 2 tbsp. oil, garlic, sage, and peppercorns. Cover casserole, and bring to a simmer over medium heat, about 1 hour. Season with salt, reduce heat to medium-low, and gently simmer, stirring occasionally with a wooden spoon, until bean skins are tender and interiors are soft, 1–2 hours more.

3 Remove from heat, set aside, and allow beans to cool in the cooking liquid. To serve, reheat beans in the liquid over medium-low heat, drain them, and season with salt and pepper. Drizzle beans with remaining 2 tbsp. oil.

GIANT BEANS IN TOMATO-DILL SAUCE

SERVES 4–6

This Mediterranean preparation of beans in a spiced tomato-dill sauce is a favorite at the deli counter at Kalustyan's specialty store in Manhattan.

- 2 cups dried giant beans, picked over and rinsed
- 1 cup olive oil
- 1 small yellow onion, chopped
- 2 cloves garlic, chopped
- 1 28-oz. can diced tomatoes
- ½ tsp. sweet paprika
  Pinch ground allspice
  Kosher salt and freshly ground black pepper, to taste
- 1 tbsp. chopped fresh basil
- 1 tbsp. chopped fresh dill

1 Put beans in a 6-qt. saucepan and cover with 10 cups water. Let soak overnight. (Or, as a shortcut, simply cover beans with cold water and bring just to the boiling point over high heat. Remove from heat, cover, and allow to sit for 1 hour.)

2 Drain beans, then put in a medium pot and cover with cold water by 2″. Bring to a boil over high heat, reduce heat to medium-low, and simmer until soft, 1–1½ hours.

3 Meanwhile, heat ½ cup of the oil in a medium pot over medium heat. Add onion and garlic and cook, stirring often, until soft, about 10 minutes. Add tomatoes, paprika, and allspice and cook until sauce thickens slightly and oil rises to the top, about 20 minutes. Transfer to a blender and purée until smooth. Return sauce to pot and season with salt and pepper. Keep sauce warm over low heat.

4 Drain beans and add to sauce. Stir in basil, dill, and the remaining ½ cup oil. Increase heat to medium and simmer, stirring occasionally, 15–20 minutes. Adjust seasonings and serve warm or at room temperature.

NEW ENGLAND–STYLE BAKED BEANS

SERVES 6–8

Flavored with molasses, maple syrup, and rum, this substantive bean dish is easy to prepare; all it takes is time: Six hours of cooking yields thick, rich results. Serve it with hearty brown bread (page 416) to mop up the flavorful sauce.

- 2 cups dried navy beans, picked over and rinsed
- 1 medium yellow onion, ends trimmed, peeled, and left whole
- 4 whole cloves
- ½ lb. slab bacon or salt pork, trimmed and cut into 2″ × 14″ pieces
- ¼ cup plus 2 tbsp. maple syrup
- ¼ cup unsulfured molasses
- 2 tsp. dry mustard
- ½ cup ketchup
- 1 tbsp. cider vinegar

1 tbsp. dark rum
   Kosher salt and freshly ground black
   pepper, to taste

1 Put beans in a 4-qt. saucepan and cover with 10 cups cold water. Let soak overnight. (Or, as a shortcut, simply bring beans just to the boiling point over high heat. Remove from heat, cover, and allow to sit for 1½ hours.) Drain beans in a colander and discard cooking liquid.

2 Heat oven to 250°. Stud onion with the cloves and place in a 4-qt. Dutch oven along with the beans, bacon, maple syrup, molasses, mustard, and 3 cups boiling water; stir to combine. Cover pot with a lid, place in the oven, and cook, lifting the lid and stirring occasionally, for 3 hours. Stir in ketchup and vinegar. Cover again, return to the oven, and cook, stirring occasionally, until beans are tender and the liquid has reduced to a thick glaze, about 3 hours more. Just before serving, stir in rum and season with salt and pepper.

FULL OF BEANS

Baked beans, rich and sweet, are one of the original Colonial American foods. English settlers brought pea seeds with them to North America so they could make pease pottage, a nourishing stew flavored with salted meat, but the plants weren't hardy enough for New England's harsh climate. Beans, however, were indigenous to North America and grew well, so the settlers used them in the dish instead.

The tradition of a Saturday bean supper, which still thrives in parts of New England, emerged from two aspects of Colonial life: routine and religion. Saturday was a baking day, and once the bread was done, beans slowly simmered in the oven's residual heat. Along with other early American foods, brown bread (page 416) was typically eaten with the beans. Together, the beans and bread formed a protein-rich meal. In observance of the Puritan Sabbath, cooking was forbidden from sundown on Saturday until sundown on Sunday. The beans cooked all day Saturday, were ready for supper that night, and were eaten again the following day.

BARBECUED BAKED BEANS
SERVES 6–8

These sweet-spicy baked beans are an irresistible way to use up the leftover meat and sauce from a barbecue feast.

10 slices bacon, chopped
 1 medium yellow onion, chopped
 2 cups barbecue sauce
1¼ cups dark brown sugar
 1 cup beef stock
 1 cup leftover chopped beef brisket (page 604) or pulled pork (page 240)
¼ cup molasses
 1 tbsp. dry mustard
 2 tsp. kosher salt
⅛ tsp. ground cloves
 4 15-oz. cans navy beans, drained and rinsed
 1 16-oz. can whole, peeled tomatoes, crushed by hand
    Freshly ground black pepper, to taste

Heat oven to 325°. Heat bacon in an 8-qt. Dutch oven over medium-high heat and cook, stirring, until fat renders, about 8 minutes. Add onion and cook, stirring, until soft, about 5 minutes. Add sauce, sugar, stock, meat, molasses, mustard, salt, cloves, beans, tomatoes, and pepper and bring to a boil. Cover pot and place in oven; bake until thick and fragrant, about 2 hours. Let cool for 10 minutes.

NEW ORLEANS RED BEANS & RICE
SERVES 6–8

In New Orleans, this Creole classic was traditionally served on laundry day, so a cook could leave her beans and rice simmering for hours on the stove while she went about her washing. Ham hocks cooked along with the beans give the dish a smoky depth.

 2 cups dried kidney beans, picked over and rinsed
¼ cup canola oil
 8 cloves garlic, finely chopped
 6 ribs celery, finely chopped
 2 large yellow onions, finely chopped
 2 green bell peppers, seeded and finely chopped
    Kosher salt, to taste
 1 tbsp. ground white pepper
 1 tbsp. dried thyme
 2 tsp. dried oregano
1½ tsp. cayenne pepper
 1 tsp. freshly ground black pepper

4   bay leaves
2   smoked ham hocks
1   tbsp. Tabasco sauce
    Cooked white rice, for serving
    Thinly sliced scallions, for garnish

1 Put beans in a 6-qt. saucepan and cover with 10 cups water. Let soak overnight. (Or, as a shortcut, simply cover beans with cold water and bring just to the boiling point over high heat. Remove from heat, cover, and allow to sit for 1 hour.) Drain beans.

2 Heat oil in an 8-qt. Dutch oven over medium-high heat. Add garlic, celery, onions, and peppers, season with salt, and cook, stirring, until soft, about 12 minutes. Add white pepper, thyme, oregano, cayenne, and black pepper and stir until fragrant, about 2 minutes. Add beans, bay leaves, ham hocks, and 6 cups water and bring to a boil.

3 Reduce heat to medium-low and cook, covered, until beans and ham hocks are tender, about 2 hours. Remove hocks from pot, remove and discard bones and skin, and finely chop meat; return to pot along with hot sauce and stir until combined. Serve over rice in bowls and sprinkle with scallions.

RESANBINSI
Garifuna Rice & Beans with Coconut Milk
SERVES 8–10

Coconut milk is an essential ingredient in many dishes from Honduras' Garifuna coast, including this creamy take on rice and beans.

¼   cup canola oil
5   cloves garlic, minced
1   small onion, minced
1   rib celery, minced
½   small red bell pepper, seeded and minced
2½ cups long-grain white rice
1½ tsp. ground cumin
1   tsp. freshly ground black pepper
1   tsp. sugar
3½ cups canned coconut milk
2   cups chicken stock
2   15-oz. cans small dark red kidney beans, rinsed and drained
2   sprigs fresh culantro or cilantro, chopped
    Kosher salt, to taste

Heat oil in a 6-qt. saucepan over medium-high heat. Add garlic, onion, celery, and bell pepper and cook until soft,

about 10 minutes. Add rice, cumin, black pepper, and sugar and cook for 1 minute. Add coconut milk and stock and bring to a boil. Reduce heat to medium-low, add beans and cilantro, and season with salt. Cover and cook, stirring occasionally, until rice is tender, about 30 minutes.

CUBAN-STYLE BLACK BEANS
Frijoles Negros Cubanos
SERVES 4–6

The secret of good black beans—and of many other Cuban dishes—is a slow-cooked *sofrito* of onions or scallions, garlic, and green peppers.

1½ lb. dried black beans, picked over and rinsed
1   bay leaf
1   sprig fresh oregano
4   tbsp. olive oil
1   tbsp. ground cumin
12 scallions, finely chopped
8   cloves garlic, finely chopped
1   small green bell pepper, seeded and finely chopped
    Kosher salt and freshly ground black pepper, to taste

1 Put beans, bay leaf, oregano, and 1 tbsp. oil into a large pot, then cover with cold water by 3". Bring to a boil over high heat, reduce heat to medium-low, and simmer, adding more water as needed to keep beans covered, until beans are tender, about 2 hours.

2 Heat remaining 3 tbsp. oil in a small skillet over medium heat. Add cumin, scallions, garlic, and green peppers and sauté, stirring often, until peppers are soft and scallions are golden, about 10 minutes. Season with salt and pepper, then add to beans. Continue cooking beans, stirring occasionally, for 10–15 minutes. Adjust seasonings. Remove bay leaf before serving.

FRIJOLES DE OLLA
Stewed Pot Beans
SERVES 6

These stewed pinto beans can be eaten with tortillas for a light meal, or served as a side dish with grilled or roasted meats.

2   cups dried pinto beans, picked over and rinsed
½   small white onion, thinly sliced
2   tbsp. lard or canola oil

1 Kosher salt, to taste
Mexican crema or sour cream
1 cup shredded queso Oaxaca or mozzarella cheese

1 Bring beans, onion, lard, and 10 cups warm water to a boil in a 4-qt. saucepan over medium-high heat. Reduce heat to medium-low and cook, covered and stirring occasionally, until beans are just tender and begin to split open, about 2 hours. Add salt and continue cooking, mashing some of the beans in the pot as they cook, until beans are completely soft, about 30 minutes more.

2 To serve, ladle beans into serving bowls and top with a spoonful of crema and some of the cheese.

HOPPIN' JOHN

SERVES 8–10

This humble Southern dish of black-eyed peas and rice makes good use of leftover ham scraps. Considered a good-luck dish, it's frequently eaten on New Year's Day.

1 lb. dried black-eyed peas
1 smoked ham bone or 2 ham hocks
¼ cup canola oil
½ cup finely chopped cooked ham
¼ tsp. crushed red chile flakes
2 cloves garlic, finely chopped
1 jalapeño, stemmed, seeded, and finely chopped
1 large carrot, finely chopped
1 large onion, finely chopped
1 rib celery, finely chopped
1 bay leaf
1 lb. collard greens, ribs removed, leaves roughly chopped
2 tbsp. cider vinegar
Kosher salt and freshly ground black pepper, to taste
Cooked rice, for serving
Chopped tomatoes and scallions, for garnish

1 Bring peas, ham bone, and 8 cups water to a boil in a 6-qt. Dutch oven. Reduce heat to medium-low and cook, skimming foam occasionally, until peas are tender, about 45 minutes. Drain peas, reserving 1 cup cooking liquid along with ham bone; set aside.

2 Heat oil in a 12-qt. pot over medium-high heat. Add chopped ham, chile flakes, garlic, jalapeños, carrot, onion, celery, and bay leaf and cook, stirring occasionally, until soft, about 8 minutes. Add reserved black-eyed peas, ham bone, and reserved cooking liquid, along with collards and 12 cups water. Bring to a boil, reduce heat to medium-low, and simmer until collards are tender, about 1 hour. Stir in vinegar and season with salt and pepper. Serve soup over rice with garnishes.

SPICED BLACK-EYED PEAS WITH CURRY LEAVES

SERVES 4–6

In this earthy legume stew from the state of Gujarat, in northwest India, chickpea flour is used to both thicken the dish and add a nutty undertone.

2 tbsp. peanut oil
1 tsp. cumin seeds
10 fresh curry leaves
¼ cup chickpea flour
2 tsp. ground turmeric
1–2 tsp. hot paprika
⅛ tsp. asafoetida
1½ tbsp. tamarind extract
1 tbsp. finely chopped jaggery or packed brown sugar
2 15-oz. cans black-eyed peas, drained
Kosher salt, to taste
2 tbsp. finely chopped fresh cilantro

1 Heat oil in a 4-qt. saucepan over medium-high heat. Add cumin and curry leaves; cook, stirring, until fragrant, about 2 minutes. Stir in flour, turmeric, paprika, and asafoetida and cook, stirring, until fragrant, 1–2 minutes. Stir in 2¾ cups water and bring to a boil. Stir in tamarind and jaggery and stir to dissolve.

2 Add black-eyed peas, season with salt, and bring to a boil. Reduce heat to medium-low and simmer until thickened, 3–5 minutes. Stir in cilantro before serving.

FUL MEDAMES

Egyptian Stewed Fava Beans

SERVES 2–4

Egypt's unofficial national dish, *ful medames,* is a hearty stew of warmed fava beans topped with olive oil, lemon juice, and garlic. It's usually eaten for breakfast, with warm pita.

2 15-oz. cans fava beans, drained and rinsed
¼ cup fresh lemon juice

> **"The discovery of a new dish does more for the happiness of the human race than the discovery of a star."**
>
> JEAN ANTHELME BRILLAT-SAVARIN

- ¼ cup extra-virgin olive oil, plus more for drizzling
- 2 tsp. ground cumin
- ¼ tsp. cayenne pepper
- 4 cloves garlic, mashed
  Kosher salt and freshly ground black pepper, to taste
- 2 hard-cooked eggs, each cut into 6 wedges
- 2 tbsp. finely chopped fresh flat-leaf parsley

1 Place beans in a 2-qt. saucepan and cover with water by 1″. Place over medium heat, bring to a boil, and cook until beans are beginning to fall apart, about 8 minutes.

2 Drain beans and transfer to a bowl; add lemon juice, oil, cumin, cayenne, garlic, salt, and pepper. Stir until beans are lightly broken up. Transfer to a serving platter and surround with egg wedges. Drizzle with more oil and sprinkle with parsley before serving.

GRILLED FAVA BEANS IN THEIR PODS
SERVES 4

Young, tender fava beans work best for this preparation; you can pop them right out of the grilled pods and eat them without having to peel them first.

- 2 lb. fava beans in the pod
- 3 tbsp. extra-virgin olive oil, plus more for drizzling
  Sea salt and freshly ground black pepper, to taste
- 1 lemon, halved
- 2 oz. Parmigiano-Reggiano

1 Build a medium-hot fire in a charcoal grill or heat a gas grill to medium-high. Put favas into a large bowl, drizzle with 3 tbsp. oil, and season with salt and pepper.

2 Grill favas, turning occasionally, until charred and soft, about 6 minutes.

3 Transfer favas to a serving platter. Drizzle with oil and squeeze lemon juice over the top. Season with salt and, using a vegetable peeler, peel thin strips of Parmigiano over favas. Let cool for 5 minutes before serving.

FAVA FALAFEL
MAKES ABOUT 30

Falafel, a Middle Eastern street-food favorite, takes on a lighter, greener flavor when made with favas. Like their chickpea counterpart, they're often served as part of a pita sandwich with Israeli Chopped Salad (page 59), but are delicious on their own as well, dressed with tahini.

- ½ lb. dried peeled split fava beans, soaked overnight
- 2 cloves garlic, minced
- 1¾ cups chopped fresh flat-leaf parsley
- 1 bunch scallions, green parts only, coarsely chopped
- 1½ tsp. ground cumin
- ½ tsp. baking powder
- 1¼ tsp. salt
- 2 tbsp. coarsely chopped fresh cilantro
  Vegetable oil, for frying

1 Drain beans and place in a food processor. Add garlic and purée until ground. Add parsley, scallions, cumin, baking powder, salt, and cilantro and pulse until beans are thoroughly ground and mixture holds together.

2 Wet hands (mixture will be sticky) and form mixture into 30 balls. Flatten each slightly, to ensure even cooking, and place on waxed paper. Cover and refrigerate until ready to cook.

3 Meanwhile, heat 2″ oil in a medium saucepan over medium heat. Drop fava falafel balls in hot oil a few at a time and fry until golden, 5–10 minutes; repeat with remaining balls. Drain on paper towels and serve.

CHANA MASALA
Spiced Chickpeas
MAKES ABOUT 6 CUPS

Chana masala is a simple chickpea stew with many variations, eaten all across India. This version is aromatic with ginger and cardamom, and has a bit of heat as well.

2 tbsp. finely chopped fresh ginger
3 tsp. garam masala
2 tsp. ground turmeric
8 cloves garlic, chopped
¼ cup canola oil
2 tsp. coriander seeds
1 tsp. cumin seeds
3 green cardamom pods
2 chiles de árbol, stemmed
1 stick cinnamon
2 large yellow onions, chopped
1 15-oz. can whole, peeled tomatoes, crushed by hand
2 tbsp. tamarind extract
3 15-oz. cans chickpeas, drained and rinsed
2 tbsp. fresh lemon juice
¼ tsp. amchoor (green mango powder, optional)
Kosher salt, to taste
Fresh cilantro leaves, for garnish
Cooked rice, for serving

1 Purée ginger, 1 tsp. garam masala, turmeric, garlic, and 3 tbsp. water in a small food processor; set paste aside.

2 Heat oil in a 6-qt. saucepan over medium-high heat. Add coriander, cumin, cardamom, chiles, and cinnamon and cook until fragrant, about 1 minute. Add onions and cook until lightly browned, about 8 minutes. Add reserved paste and cook for 3 minutes. Add tomatoes and cook until slightly reduced, about 4 minutes. Add tamarind and chickpeas and bring to a boil. Reduce heat to medium-low and cook until liquid is reduced by one-fourth, about 45 minutes.

3 Add remaining garam masala, juice, amchoor, and salt. Garnish with cilantro. Serve with rice.

PANELLE
Chickpea Fritters
MAKES 48 FRITTERS

These addictive triangular fritters are a traditional Sicilian street food.

2⅓ cups chickpea flour
Kosher salt and freshly ground black pepper
Canola oil, for frying

1 In a 4-qt. saucepan, whisk together chickpea flour, salt, pepper, and 3 cups water until smooth. Cook over medium-high heat, stirring constantly with a wooden spoon, until mixture becomes a thick paste, about 6 minutes. Reduce heat to low and continue stirring until mixture pulls away from side of pan, about 2 minutes more. Working quickly in batches, with a rubber spatula, spread ½ cup of the mixture into circles 9″ in diameter and ¼″ thick on parchment paper or aluminum foil. (Keep saucepan warm so that dough remains spreadable.) Let dough disks sit until cool, 15–20 minutes.

2 When dough disks are cool, peel off paper and stack disks together like pancakes; cut stack into 8 wedges. Pour oil into a 6-qt. Dutch oven to a depth of 2″ and heat over medium-high heat until a deep-fry thermometer reads 375°. Working in batches, add wedges and fry, turning occasionally, until golden and crisp, about 3 minutes. Using a slotted spoon, transfer wedges to a paper towel–lined plate and sprinkle with salt. Serve hot.

ETHIOPIAN LENTIL STEW
Misr Wot
SERVES 4–6

Ethiopian cook Alemtshaye Yigezu made this rich lentil dish for us when we visited her home. Its complex flavor is thanks to *nit'r qibe*, Ethiopia's ubiquitous clarified butter, generously spiced with cardamom and fenugreek.

4 tbsp. Nit'r Qibe (page 595) or unsalted butter
1 small yellow onion, finely chopped
4 cloves garlic, finely chopped
1 cup red lentils, rinsed
2 tbsp. Berbere (page 586)
1 small tomato, cored and chopped
Kosher salt, to taste

Melt butter in a medium saucepan over medium heat. Add onion and cook, stirring occasionally, until golden brown, about 10 minutes. Add garlic and cook, stirring constantly, until fragrant, about 30 seconds. Add reserved lentils, 1 tbsp. berbere, tomato, and 4 cups water to the saucepan. Reduce heat to medium-low and simmer, stirring occasionally, until thick and lentils are tender, 45–50 minutes. Stir in remaining 1 tbsp. berbere and season generously with salt. Serve immediately.

CREAMY SPICED INDIAN LENTILS

Dal Makhani

SERVES 6–8

This intensely creamy dish takes its name from *makkhan*, the Hindi word for butter.

- 1½ cups kali sabut urad dal (whole black lentils)
- ½ cup channa dal (split yellow lentils)
- ½ cup rajma dal (small red kidney beans)
- 1 tbsp. mustard or canola oil
- 6 cloves garlic, coarsely chopped
- 2 green bird's eye chiles, stemmed and coarsely chopped
- 1 2″ piece fresh ginger, peeled and coarsely chopped
- 6 tbsp. Ghee (page 595)
- 1 tsp. cumin seeds
- 1 medium red onion, chopped
- 1 tsp. ground coriander
- 1 tsp. ground turmeric
- 1 cup canned peeled, whole tomatoes, puréed
- 2 tbsp. garam masala
- 1 tbsp. dried fenugreek leaves (optional)
- 1 tsp. Kashmiri red chile powder
  Salt to taste
- 1½ cups milk
- ½ cup butter, cut into pieces
- ½ cup heavy cream

1 Combine dals and wash under running water until it runs clear. Toss with oil in a bowl; set aside. Purée garlic, chiles, ginger, and ¼ cup water in a blender; set paste aside.

2 Heat ghee in a large pot over medium-high heat. Add cumin; cook for 1 minute. Add onion and cook until browned, 8–10 minutes. Add paste, coriander, and turmeric; cook for 3 minutes. Add tomatoes and cook, stirring and scraping until thickened, 6–7 minutes. Add dals and 8 cups water; bring to a boil. Reduce heat to medium-low; simmer, covered, until tender, about 2 hours. Add garam masala, fenugreek (if using), chile powder, and salt; simmer for 5 minutes. Stir in milk and butter; simmer for 5 minutes. Drizzle cream on top and serve.

FRENCH LENTIL SALAD

Salade de Lentilles

SERVES 6–8

This hearty lentil salad, lightened with fresh parsley, thyme, and shallots, is an essential part of the French culinary canon. It's a versatile side dish or, over lettuce, a delicious main course.

ALL ABOUT DAL

The Hindi word *dal* means pulses (peas and beans as well as lentils), both raw and cooked. But in India and Pakistan, you might be invited to come over for *dal* and rice or *dal* and bread, whether or not legumes are on the menu: The word has come to be synonymous with dinner. *Dal* is eaten by those of all castes, classes, and religions, and in every region. Northerners like to cook *chana dal* (split lentils) or *urad dal* (split gram beans) into thick stews, while southerners make *toovar dal* (pigeon peas) and *masoor dal* (split red lentils) into soupy purées. The *tarka* (fried spice mixture) with which most *dals* are finished not only adds flavor but is believed to aid digestion.

FOR THE LENTILS

- 1 lb. lentilles du Puy, picked over and rinsed
- 1 medium yellow onion, halved
- 6 sprigs fresh flat-leaf parsley
- 1 sprig fresh thyme
- 1 bay leaf

FOR THE DRESSING

- ¼ cup Dijon mustard
- ¼ cup red wine vinegar
- 5 tbsp. extra-virgin olive oil
  Kosher salt and freshly ground black pepper, to taste
- 3 shallots, thickly sliced

1 Make the lentils: Put lentils into a large pot, cover with cold water by 1½″, and add onion halves, parsley, thyme, and bay leaf. Bring to a boil over high heat, reduce heat to medium-low, and simmer until lentils are tender, about 15 minutes.

2 Make the dressing: Put mustard, vinegar, and oil into a large bowl. Season with salt and pepper and stir with a wooden spoon until just combined but not emulsified. Set dressing aside.

3 Drain lentils, then remove and discard bay leaf, thyme, parsley, and onions. Transfer warm lentils to the bowl with dressing, add shallots, and toss with a wooden spoon until lentils are evenly coated. Adjust seasonings. Serve at room temperature.

> **"If you really want to make a friend, go to someone's house and eat with him ... the people who give you their food give you their heart."**
>
> CESAR CHAVEZ

YUBA STIR-FRY WITH EDAMAME

SERVES 2

Stir-frying yuba—noodle-like tofu skins popular in Japanese and Chinese cookery—crisps its edges, intensifying its nutty flavor and chewy texture.

- 6 tbsp. sesame oil
- 4 tsp. minced garlic
- 4 tsp. minced fresh ginger
- 6 scallions, thinly sliced
- ½ lb. fresh, frozen, or dried yuba sheets (thawed, if frozen; reconstituted in cold water, if dried), cut lengthwise into ½"-wide strips
- 1 cup shelled edamame, frozen or fresh
- 2 tsp. chile bean paste or sauce
- 2 tbsp. soy sauce

Heat oil in a 12" skillet over high heat. Add garlic, ginger, and half the scallions and cook until fragrant, about 30 seconds. Add yuba, edamame, and chile bean paste and cook until hot, about 1 minute. Add soy sauce and ¼ cup water and cook, tossing, until almost evaporated, about 30 seconds more. Divide between 2 serving bowls, and garnish with remaining scallions.

DRY-COOKED CABBAGE WITH TOFU & PEAS

SERVES 4

This aromatic recipe is based on a dish served by Satya, the head cook at Radha Govinda Mandir, an International Society for Krishna Consciousness temple in Brooklyn, New York.

- 1 cup flour
- 1 12-oz. package firm tofu, cut into ½" cubes and patted dry
- 10 tbsp. Ghee (page 595)
- 2 tsp. mustard seeds
- 2 tbsp. peeled grated fresh ginger
- 3 tsp. ground coriander
- 1 tsp. ground turmeric
- ½ tsp. asafoetida
- 1 serrano chile, stemmed and finely chopped
- ½ small head cabbage, cored and thinly sliced
  Kosher salt, to taste
- 1 cup frozen peas, thawed

1 Put flour in a large, wide dish. Add half of the tofu and toss gently to coat; shake off excess flour. Heat 4 tbsp. of the ghee in a large skillet over medium-high heat. Add floured tofu and fry, turning occasionally, until light golden brown all over, about 5 minutes total. Using a slotted spoon, transfer to a large, paper towel–lined plate. Carefully clean out skillet, then repeat process with 4 more tbsp. ghee and remaining tofu.

2 Heat remaining 2 tbsp. ghee in a medium pot over medium heat. Add mustard seeds and cook, stirring, until they begin to pop, about 30 seconds. Carefully stir in ginger, 2 tsp. of the coriander, turmeric, asafoetida, and chile and cook, stirring and scraping the ginger mixture, until fragrant and ginger is no longer raw, 1–2 minutes. Add cabbage and salt and cook, covered, stirring frequently, until tender, about 15 minutes. Add remaining coriander, reserved tofu, peas, and salt and cook until heated through, 1–2 minutes more. Serve immediately.

HUNANESE HOME-STYLE TOFU

Jia Chang Dou Fu

SERVES 4

This stir-fry flavors smooth, earthy-tasting fried tofu with pork, garlic, and chile paste.

- 4 dried shiitake mushrooms
- ¼ lb. pork loin, cut into 2"-long slices about ⅛" thick
- 1 tsp. Shaoxing wine
- ¾ cup peanut oil
- 1 14-oz. package firm tofu, drained, patted very dry, sliced into 2" squares about ½" thick, and halved diagonally

2 tbsp. dou ban jiang (Sichuan chile paste)
1 tbsp. chopped garlic
¾ cup chicken stock
1 tsp. dark soy sauce
¾ tsp. cornstarch mixed with 1 tbsp. cold water
3 garlic chives or scallions, green parts only,
   cut into 1″ pieces
1 tsp. sesame oil

1 Put mushrooms into a bowl and cover with hot water; let soak for 30 minutes. Drain, then trim and discard stems. Cut caps into 2″-long pieces about ⅛″ wide; set aside. Toss pork and wine together in a small bowl and set aside.

2 Heat oil in a wok over high heat. Working in 3 batches, fry tofu, turning once, until light golden brown, about 4 minutes. Transfer tofu to a plate with a slotted spoon.

3 Discard all but 3 tbsp. of oil from wok. Reduce heat to medium-high, add pork with wine, and stir-fry until pieces separate, about 30 seconds. Add chile paste and stir-fry until fragrant, about 30 seconds. Add mushrooms and garlic and cook until fragrant, about 30 seconds more. Add tofu, stock, and soy sauce and bring to a boil. Reduce heat to medium-low and simmer for 3 minutes. Add cornstarch mixture, stir well, and cook until just thickened, about 30 seconds. Add chives and toss to combine. Stir in sesame oil and transfer to a serving plate.

MAPO TOFU

Sichuan Tofu & Ground Meat in Red Chile Sauce
SERVES 4

Sichuan's most famous dish, this spicy braise of tofu and ground meat is famous for mouth-numbing Sichuan peppercorns.

1 14-oz. package firm tofu, drained
   and cut into 1″ cubes
   Kosher salt, to taste
½ cup Sichuan Red Chile Oil (page 376)
6 cloves garlic, minced
1 6″ piece fresh ginger, peeled and minced
6 oz. ground beef or pork
4 garlic chives, blossoms discarded,
   or scallions, thinly sliced, plus more
   for garnish
1 red bird's eye chile, stemmed and minced
2½ tbsp. red chile bean paste
1 tbsp. fermented black soybeans
1¼ cups chicken stock
1 tbsp. sugar
1 tbsp. light soy sauce
¼ cup cornstarch mixed with 6 tbsp. water
¼ tsp. ground Sichuan peppercorn, for garnish
   Cooked rice, for serving

1 Place tofu in a bowl with 3 cups boiling salted water; let sit 15 minutes. Drain and spread on paper towels to dry; set aside.

2 Heat oil in a 14″ flat-bottomed wok over medium-high heat. Add garlic and ginger and cook until fragrant, about 1 minute. Add beef and cook, stirring and breaking up meat, until browned, 4–6 minutes. Add chives, chile, paste, and beans and cook, stirring, until chives are wilted, about 2 minutes. Add stock and tofu and bring to a boil, stirring gently, so as not to break up the tofu. Add sugar and soy and cook, stirring, until sugar is dissolved, about 1 minute. While stirring, slowly add cornstarch mixture, then cook until sauce has thickened, about 2 minutes more. Transfer to a dish and garnish with chives and Sichuan pepper. Serve with rice.

Rice & Grains

PERFECT WHITE RICE

SERVES 4

Rice plays a key role in the majority of meals eaten worldwide, from Brazil to Senegal to Indonesia. It's important, therefore, to make it correctly; you want grains that are fluffy, moist, and distinct, not sticky. For perfect long-grain white rice, follow these steps.

- 1 cup long-grain white rice, such as jasmine

1 Place rice in a 2-qt. saucepan and fill pot halfway with cold water. If any rice hulls float to the surface, scoop them aside with your hand and discard them. Gently swirl your fingers through the rice until the water becomes cloudy from the surface starch on the rice grains, about 20 seconds. Allow rice to settle for a few seconds. Tilt the pot over a sink and drain out all the water, cupping the rice with your hand to prevent it from spilling out of the pot. Repeat this process with 3 more changes of water. Leave the rinsed rice in the pot.

2 Add 1¼ cups water to the rinsed rice. Gently shift the pot back and forth a few times, letting the rice settle in a flat, even layer at the bottom.

3 Place the pot over high heat and bring the water to a rolling, noisy boil. Allow rice to boil vigorously for 15 seconds. Immediately reduce the heat to the lowest possible setting and cover the pot tightly with the lid. Continue cooking for 15 minutes. Don't be tempted to lift or remove the lid during this time. You'll lose essential cooking steam if you do.

4 Remove from the heat and allow rice to continue to steam, covered, away from the heat for an additional 10 minutes. This period ensures the rice will be fully tender and makes it less prone to sticking to the bottom of the pot. Open the pot and fluff rice gently with a fork, being careful to break as few grains as possible.

5 Transfer rice to a deep serving bowl and fluff it again well with a fork, lifting it into a peaked mound before serving.

PERFECT BROWN RICE

SERVES 4

Cooking brown rice well can be tricky. The goal is to soften each grain's fibrous bran coating without causing the grains inside to become mushy. We've learned through trial and error that brown rice looks and tastes the best when it has been boiled and drained like pasta, and then steamed in the small amount of moisture that remains in the pot.

- 1 cup short-, medium-, or long-grain brown rice
  Kosher salt, to taste

1 Rinse rice in a sieve under cold running water for 30 seconds. Bring 12 cups water to a boil in a large pot with a tight-fitting lid over high heat. Add rice, stir it once, and boil, uncovered, for 30 minutes. Pour rice into a colander in the sink.

2 Let the rice drain for 10 seconds, then return it to the pot, off the heat. Cover the pot and set it aside to allow rice to steam for 10 minutes. Uncover rice, fluff with a fork, and season with salt.

PERFECT WILD RICE

SERVES 6

Why is some wild rice beautiful and firm when cooked, while some turns into a mushy mess? The secret is to buy the highest grade of genuine (and genuinely wild) wild rice and to cook it gently. Using stock instead of water helps complement the rice's nutty flavor.

- 1½ cups long-grain wild rice
- 4 cups chicken stock, vegetable stock, or water

1 Rinse rice, soak in 3 cups cold water for 1 hour, and then drain.

> ## "Rice is great if you're hungry and want 2,000 of something."
> ### MITCH HEDBERG

2 Bring stock to a boil in a medium saucepan. Add rice, cover, and allow to return to a boil. Lower heat and simmer until tender but firm, about 45 minutes or longer.

3 Drain off any excess stock, then fluff with a fork and serve immediately.

COCONUT RICE
Nasi Lemak
SERVES 8–10

This coconut rice dish, perfumed with makrut lime and lemongrass, is a breakfast staple in Malaysia.

- 2   cups jasmine rice
- 1   cup canned coconut milk
- 1½ tsp. ground turmeric
- 1   tsp. kosher salt
- 3   fresh or frozen makrut lime leaves
- 1   6″ piece lemongrass, bruised with a mallet until pliable and tied into a knot
- 1   1″ piece ginger, peeled and bruised until flattened

Stir together rice, coconut milk, turmeric, salt, lime leaves, lemongrass, ginger, and 1½ cups water in a 2-qt. saucepan, and bring to a boil over high heat. Cover tightly with lid and reduce heat to low; cook, without stirring, until all liquid is absorbed and rice is tender, about 20 minutes. Discard lime leaves, lemongrass, and ginger before serving.

JOOK
Chinese Rice Porridge
SERVES 4

This comforting rice dish, also known as congee, is eaten for breakfast throughout China and other parts of Asia.

- ½ cup long-grain white rice
- 1 tsp. kosher salt

  Chile oil, for garnish
  Thinly sliced scallions and small red chiles, for garnish
  Fried shallots, for garnish

In a sieve, rinse rice under cold water and let drain. Put rice, 8 cups water, and salt into a 4-qt. saucepan. Bring to a boil over high heat, reduce heat to medium-low, and cook, partially covered and stirring occasionally, until rice takes on the consistency of porridge, about 1½ hours. Divide porridge among 4 bowls and garnish each with chile oil, scallions, chiles, and shallots.

MEXICAN RICE
Arroz a la Mexicana
SERVES 6–8

This vibrant, red-hued rice is an essential component of a traditional Mexican meal.

- 2   cups chicken stock
- 2   ripe tomatoes, cored and chopped
- 2   cloves garlic, smashed
- ½   small yellow onion, chopped
- 2   tbsp. canola oil
- 1   cup long-grain white rice
     Kosher salt and freshly ground black pepper, to taste

1 Place stock, tomatoes, 1 clove garlic, and onion in a blender and purée until smooth; set tomato mixture aside.

2 Heat oil in a 4-qt. saucepan over medium-high heat. Add remaining garlic and rice and cook, stirring occasionally, until golden brown, about 6 minutes. Stir in tomato mixture, season with salt and pepper, and reduce heat to low. Cook, covered, until rice is tender and has absorbed all liquid, 25–30 minutes. Remove from heat and let sit, covered, for 10 minutes. Gently fluff rice with a fork before serving.

NIGERIAN RED RICE
Jollof Rice
SERVES 4–6

Author Yewande Komolafe, originally from Lagos, Nigeria, gave us her family's recipe for this unifying West African rice dish, smothered in a tomato-pepper sauce called *obe ata*. Serve it with fried plantains (page 327), stewed greens (page 317), and meat or fish.

- 4 plum tomatoes, cored
- 4 cloves garlic, plus 1 clove minced
- 2 medium red onions, plus ½ red onion sliced into rings
- 1 red bell pepper, stemmed and seeded
- 1 red habanero chile, stemmed and seeded
- ¼ cup canola oil
- 1 1″ piece fresh ginger, peeled and minced
- 1½ tbsp. Madras curry powder
- 1 tbsp. minced fresh thyme leaves
- ½ cup tomato paste
- 2 cups long-grain white rice
- 2¼ cups chicken stock or water
  Kosher salt and freshly ground black pepper, to taste

1 Roughly chop tomatoes, 4 cloves garlic, 2 onions, bell pepper, and habanero and transfer to the bowl of a food processor with 1 cup water; purée and set tomato mixture aside.

2 Heat oil in a 4-qt. saucepan over medium-high heat. Add the remaining onions and garlic, the ginger, curry powder, and thyme and cook, stirring occasionally, until the onions begin to brown, about 5 minutes. Add tomato paste, stir vigorously, and stir in reserved tomato mixture. Cook, stirring occasionally, until the flavors meld, about 5 minutes. Add rice and stir to coat the grains. Add stock and season with salt and pepper. Bring to a boil, reduce heat to low, and cook, covered, until rice is tender, about 20 minutes. Remove pot from heat and let sit, covered, for 10 minutes. Uncover, fluff rice with a fork, and serve hot.

IRANIAN RICE PILAF
Shirin Polō
SERVES 8–10

This rice pilaf is prized for its *tahdig* crust—the crisp, browned crust of rice that forms at the bottom of the pot, considered the best part of the dish—as well as its crown of sweet garnishes.

- ½ cup sugar
- ¾ tsp. crushed saffron threads
- ¾ cup thinly sliced orange peel
- 1 tbsp. rose water
- 4 cups long-grain white rice
- 2 tbsp. kosher salt
- ½ cup milk
- ½ cup canola oil
- 2 tbsp. unsalted butter, melted
- ¾ cup finely shredded carrots, for garnish
- ½ cup slivered almonds, for garnish
- ½ cup chopped pistachios, for garnish

1 Bring sugar, ½ tsp. saffron, and ½ cup water to a boil in a saucepan over high heat. Add ½ cup orange peel and cook until tender, 8–10 minutes. Let cool, and stir in rose water; set aside.

2 Make the rice: Rinse rice in a sieve under water until water runs clear. Place rice in a 6-qt. pan. Add salt and 4 cups water, cover, and soak for 2 hours. Place pan over high heat and bring to a boil. Cook until rice begins to rise to the surface, about 12 minutes; drain. Return pan to medium-high heat and add remaining ¼ tsp. saffron, milk, and oil. Return rice to pan, forming it into a mound. Using handle of a wooden spoon, poke 5 holes in the mound (to let steam escape), then cover and cook for 15 minutes.

3 Pour butter and 1 cup boiling water over rice, re-cover, then reduce heat to medium-low and cook until a golden crust forms on bottom, 30–35 minutes. Transfer rice to a platter, separating the grains as you go; break up crust from bottom of pot and stir into rice. Garnish rice with remaining orange peel, carrots, almonds, and pistachios.

SPICED RICE WITH TOASTED ALMONDS
SERVES 8–10

White rice is enlivened with an aromatic mix of warm spices and a garnish of fried almonds in this appealing dish, a common preparation throughout the Middle East.

- 1 tbsp. black peppercorns
- 2 tsp. whole allspice
- 2 tsp. whole cloves
- 1 stick cinnamon, broken in half
- ¾ cup olive oil
- 1 cup whole blanched almonds
  Kosher salt, to taste
- 2 cups long-grain white rice
- ¾ cup roughly chopped fresh flat-leaf parsley, for garnish

1 Heat peppercorns, allspice, cloves, and cinnamon in a 6-qt. saucepan over medium heat until fragrant, 1–2 minutes. Let cool slightly, then transfer to a spice grinder; grind into a powder and set aside.

2 Add ¼ cup oil to pan and place over medium-high heat. Add almonds and cook until golden, 3–5 minutes. Transfer to a bowl and season with salt.

3 Add remaining oil to pan and return to medium-high heat. Add rice and cook, stirring occasionally, until lightly toasted, 5–7 minutes. Add spice mixture and 3½ cups water and bring to a boil. Reduce heat to low and cook, covered, until rice is tender, about 30 minutes.

4 Remove pan from heat and let sit for 10 minutes. Uncover and fluff rice with a fork. Transfer to a platter, garnish with almonds and parsley, and serve.

BUTCHER'S CHOICE RISOTTO
SERVES 4

Cesare Benelli of Ristorante Al Covo in Venice, who shared this recipe with us, makes his risotto with a richly marbled cut of beef. We've found that a meaty short rib also works well.

5	tbsp. extra-virgin olive oil
1	1-lb. short rib, bone in
3	cups beef stock
3	cups chicken stock
	Kosher salt and freshly ground black pepper, to taste
1	clove garlic, minced
4	small shallots, minced
1	rounded cup Carnaroli or Arborio rice
½	cup cold dry white wine
2	tbsp. finely chopped fresh flat-leaf parsley
¼	cup grated Parmigiano-Reggiano
1	tbsp. brandy

1 Heat oven to 350°. Meanwhile, heat 1 tbsp. oil in a small ovenproof skillet over high heat. Add short rib and brown evenly, about 2 minutes per side. Remove skillet from heat, place in oven, and roast until meat is crispy on the outside and tender on the inside, about 1½ hours. Remove from oven and set aside to cool. When rib is cool enough to handle, remove meat, discard bone, and shred meat. Set aside.

2 Bring beef stock and chicken stock to a simmer in a medium saucepan over low heat. Season with salt and pepper. Keep warm over lowest heat.

3 Heat 2 tbsp. oil in a wide, heavy saucepan over medium heat. Add garlic and shallots and sauté until golden, about 2 minutes. Add rice and cook, stirring constantly, until rice is coated and lightly toasted, about 3 minutes.

4 Stir in wine and cook until wine evaporates, about 1 minute. Reduce heat to medium, add shredded meat and enough stock to cover rice, then stir once and cook until almost all stock is absorbed, about 4 minutes. Add remaining stock, about ½ cup at a time, stirring once each time and adding more stock as liquid is absorbed. (Make sure rice never dries out and is always just covered by stock.) This process should take about 25 minutes.

5 Just before serving, add parsley, Parmigiano, brandy, and remaining oil, then lift and shake pan to swirl ingredients together. Let rest for 5 minutes, then serve.

RISOTTO ALLA MILANESE
SERVES 4

Chef Marc Vetri gave us his luxurious recipe for *risotto alla milanese*, the creamy rice dish that gets its vivid color and flavor from saffron. Allegedly, we have the master glazier of Milan's cathedral to thank for the dish: In 1574, the master hired a disciple nicknamed Zafferano because he used saffron to stain the glass gold. The master teased, "You'll be putting saffron in your risotto next!" At the master's daughter's wedding celebration, a table held four steaming pots of risotto. The guests were amazed to see it was tinted gold—the wedding gift of all wedding gifts.

6	cups chicken stock
1	tbsp. saffron threads
3	tbsp. unsalted butter
2	small yellow onions, minced
2	cups Carnaroli or Arborio rice
1	cup dry white wine
2	oz. raw bone marrow (optional)
½	cup grated Parmigiano-Reggiano Kosher salt and freshly ground black pepper, to taste

1 Bring stock and saffron to a simmer in a medium saucepan over low heat. Keep warm.

2 Melt butter in a 4-qt. saucepan over medium-high heat. Add onions and cook until soft, about 4 minutes. Add rice and cook until lightly toasted, about 4 minutes. Add wine and cook until evaporated, about 2 minutes. Add ½ cup warm stock and cook, stirring, until absorbed, about 2 minutes. Continue adding stock, ½ cup at a time and cooking until absorbed before adding more, until rice is tender and creamy, about 16 minutes total.

3 Stir in marrow, if using, and Parmigiano; season with salt and pepper.

RISOTTO WITH SHRIMP & RADICCHIO
Risotto con Scampi & Radicchio
SERVES 4

For an authentic Venetian iteration of this rich dish, bitter with radicchio and sweet with seafood and good white wine, you'll need true *scampi*—Adriatic crayfish—but they can be difficult to find in the United States. Small shrimp are a perfect substitute.

5	cups fish stock
3	tbsp. extra-virgin olive oil
1	small white onion, minced
2	cloves garlic, minced
1¼	lb. small shrimp, peeled and deveined
1⅔	cups Carnaroli or Arborio rice
1	cup tocai friulano or other dry white wine
1	medium head Treviso radicchio, trimmed and chopped
1	tbsp. unsalted butter
¼	cup grated Parmigiano-Reggiano Kosher salt, to taste

1 Bring fish stock to a simmer in a medium saucepan over low heat. Keep warm over lowest heat.

2 Heat oil in a medium heavy pot over medium-low heat. Add onion and garlic and cook, stirring often with a wooden spoon, until soft, about 10 minutes. Increase heat to medium-high, add shrimp, and cook for 1 minute.

3 Add rice, stir to coat well, then add wine and cook until alcohol evaporates, about 3 minutes. Add ¾ cup warm stock at a time and cook, stirring constantly, until stock has been absorbed before adding more. After 15 minutes, add radicchio. Continue cooking until rice is tender but firm, about 5 minutes more. Remove from heat, stir in butter and Parmigiano, and season with salt.

RISOTTO BY EAR

When we went looking for the best way to cook risotto, we discovered a most surprising technique from Cesare Benelli, the handsome, mustachioed chef-owner of the celebrated Ristorante Al Covo in Venice, Italy, and originator of our Butcher's Choice Risotto recipe (facing page). "You cook risotto by ear," Benelli told us; one need only to pay attention to the symphony of sounds signaling different stages in the cooking process to guarantee success.

He started by making a risotto base, sautéing aromatics in olive oil. Once the sizzling subsided, he added all the rice at once. Flavor, he noted, is coaxed out of the rice by toasting, not browning—which seals the grain, impeding its ability to soak up liquid in later steps. "The rice will whistle when it's time to scrape whatever is stuck on the bottom of the pan," he said. "This is the moment to deglaze, to shock the rice with cold wine—it must be cold. Let it evaporate completely." There was a crackling sound as the rice started to open and to release its starch. At this point, he began to pour in the warm broth slowly, in increments—always just enough to cover the rice.

"Don't let the rice get dry," he said. "Keep it 'loose' during the simmering so that it opens up slowly, releasing its starches as it absorbs the broth." Periodically Benelli gripped the skillet firmly and shook it back and forth—we heard swishing—so that the starches from the rice could bind with the reduced flavors from the broth. Stirring, he warned, will smash the grains of rice. "The rice is ready when it has a creamy consistency." He added oil and cheese, let it sit for a couple of minutes, and then plated a perfectly wavy risotto.

VENETIAN RICE FRITTERS
Arancini Veneziani
SERVES 6–8

These cheesy rice fritters are often made with leftover risotto. But they're an addictive enough snack to merit being made from scratch, as in this recipe.

6	cups chicken stock
4	tbsp. unsalted butter

3 cloves garlic, minced
1 small yellow onion, minced
1⅓ cups Arborio rice
⅓ cup white wine
¼ lb. prosciutto, minced
¼ lb. fresh mozzarella, minced
1 cup grated Parmigiano-Reggiano
½ cup finely chopped fresh flat-leaf parsley
¼ tsp. freshly grated nutmeg
Kosher salt and freshly ground black pepper, to taste
Canola oil, for frying
½ cup flour
4 eggs, lightly beaten
1½ cups plain bread crumbs

1 Heat stock in a 2-qt. saucepan over medium heat; keep warm. Melt butter in a 4-qt. saucepan over medium heat. Add garlic and onion and cook until soft, about 8 minutes. Add rice and cook, stirring, until lightly toasted, about 2 minutes. Add wine and cook until evaporated, about 1 minute. Add ½ cup stock and cook, stirring often, until liquid is absorbed. Repeat until all stock is used and rice is tender, about 40 minutes. Transfer to a bowl and stir in prosciutto, mozzarella, Parmigiano, parsley, nutmeg, salt, and pepper. Using wet hands, shape rice mixture into about fifty 1½″ logs; transfer to a parchment paper–lined baking sheet and chill.

2 Pour oil to a depth of 2″ into a 6-qt. Dutch oven and heat over medium-high until a deep-fry thermometer reads 350°. Place flour, eggs, and bread crumbs in 3 separate shallow bowls. Dredge logs in flour, coat in eggs, and coat in bread crumbs. Working in batches, fry until golden brown, about 5 minutes. Drain on paper towels.

CHINESE PORK FRIED RICE

SERVES 4

Stir-frying day-old cooked rice with ground pork, eggs, scallions, ginger, and peas brings the grains back to life.

2 tbsp. peanut oil
½ lb. ground pork
1 carrot, cut into ¼″ pieces
1 2″ piece fresh ginger, peeled and minced
3 cups cold cooked white rice
½ cup frozen peas, thawed
2 tbsp. soy sauce
1 egg, lightly beaten
1 tsp. sesame oil

3 scallions, thinly sliced
Kosher salt, to taste

Heat a wok over high heat. Add half the peanut oil, pork, carrot, and ginger and stir-fry until pork is browned and carrot is soft, 2–3 minutes. Stir in remaining peanut oil, rice, and peas and stir-fry until rice is heated through, about 1 minute. Stir in soy sauce. Make a well in center of rice and add egg; cook until the egg is lightly set, about 1 minute, then mix it into the rice. Stir in sesame oil, half the scallions, and salt. Garnish with remaining scallions.

INDONESIAN FRIED RICE

Nasi Goreng

SERVES 4–6

For *nasi goreng,* a common Indonesian breakfast, last night's rice is stir-fried with a seasoning paste made from chiles, shrimp paste, and sugar and topped with a fried egg. It's made in a variety of ways throughout the country; this is the classic iteration.

1 tsp. dried shrimp paste
1 tbsp. dark brown sugar
2 shallots, roughly chopped
2 cloves garlic, minced
2 red Holland or serrano chiles, stemmed, seeded, and roughly chopped
¼ cup peanut oil
4 eggs
Kosher salt, to taste
5 cups cold cooked white rice
4½ tsp. kecap manis (Indonesian sweet soy sauce)
2 Kirby cucumbers, halved lengthwise, and sliced crosswise on diagonal, for serving

1 Place shrimp paste on a small piece of foil and wrap foil around paste to form a packet; Turn a gas or electric burner on to medium-high heat; using tongs, hold packet on burner and cook, turning once, until toasted and fragrant, about 2 minutes; cool. Unwrap and transfer to a mini food processor with sugar, shallots, garlic, chiles, and 2 tbsp. water; purée until smooth. Set flavoring paste aside.

2 Heat oil in a 12″ skillet over medium-high heat. Add eggs, season with salt, and cook until yolks are just cooked through and whites are crisp at the edges, about 4 minutes. Transfer to a plate and set aside. Return skillet to medium heat, add flavoring paste, and cook, stirring, until fragrant, about 3 minutes. Increase heat to high, add rice, breaking up clumps, and cook, stirring, until heated through,

6–8 minutes. Add soy sauce and cook, stirring, until evenly combined, about 30 seconds more. Season with salt and divide among serving plates; place an egg on top of each serving. Serve cucumbers on the side.

HAWAIIAN FRIED RICE

SERVES 4

Chinese char siu (barbecued pork), Japanese dashi (soup base), and Portuguese linguiça sausage, which reflect three of Hawaii's most influential cultures and cuisines, come together in Honolulu restaurant Side Street Inn's version of this classic.

1¼	cups medium-grain white rice
3	slices bacon, chopped
½	link (about 3 oz.) hot linguiça, chopped
3	tbsp. oyster sauce
1	tbsp. instant dashi granules
½	cup (2½ oz.) chopped char siu (page 377)
½	cup mixed frozen peas and carrots, thawed
3	scallions, thinly sliced

1 Put rice into a medium bowl, cover with cold water, and swish around with your hand until water clouds. Drain. Repeat process until water remains clear, 4–5 more times. Put rice and 2 cups water into a medium pot and bring to a boil over medium-high heat. Cover pot, reduce heat to medium-low, and simmer until water is absorbed, about 15 minutes. Remove pot from heat and let sit, covered, for 10 minutes. Spread rice out in a single layer on a baking sheet and let cool, uncovered, in refrigerator for 6 hours or overnight.

2 Put bacon and sausage into a wok or large skillet and cook over medium heat until bacon is crisp, about 6 minutes. Increase heat to medium-high, add rice, and stir-fry vigorously to prevent sticking until hot, about 2 minutes. Add oyster sauce and dashi and mix well. Add char siu, peas and carrots, and two-thirds of the scallions. Continue to stir-fry until all ingredients are hot, about 2 minutes more. Transfer rice to a serving dish and garnish with remaining scallions.

JAPANESE-STYLE FRIED BROWN RICE

SERVES 2

This flavorful side dish is based on one served by Yumiko Kanou, the chef and owner of Nakaiseki Sen, a vegetarian restaurant in Tokyo.

2	tbsp. sesame oil
7	scallions, thinly sliced on the diagonal
2	tbsp. pine nuts
2	cups cold cooked short-grain brown rice
1	tbsp. light soy sauce
2	dried chiles de árbol, cut into thin rings

1 Heat sesame oil in a 10″ nonstick skillet over high heat. Add scallions and pine nuts and cook, stirring frequently, until the scallions wilt slightly and pine nuts take on a light golden color, about 2 minutes.

2 Add rice and soy sauce and cook, stirring to break up the clumps, until rice is hot and all ingredients are fully combined, about 3 minutes. Top with chiles.

JAMBALAYA

SERVES 6–8

Jambalaya is traditionally made in one pot using meats and vegetables. It is different from other South Louisiana dishes like gumbo or etouf because the rice is not cooked separately, but is added raw to the broth to absorb the flavors of the dish as it cooks.

3	lb. chicken, cut into serving pieces
1	tsp. salt
½	tsp. cayenne pepper
4	large cloves garlic, peeled, 2 whole and 2 minced
4–5	tbsp. vegetable oil
1	cup finely chopped onion
½	cup finely chopped green bell pepper
2	bay leaves
1½	cups long-grain white rice
1	lb. Cajun andouille sausage, sliced ¼″ thick
3	cups chicken stock or water, heated
¼	cup finely chopped scallions
¼	cup finely chopped fresh flat-leaf parsley

1 Season chicken with salt and cayenne. Smash whole garlic cloves with the flat side of a knife. Rub smashed garlic on chicken and discard garlic. Brown chicken in vegetable oil in a large, heavy pot over medium heat. Cook in batches to ensure even browning, adding more oil as needed. Remove chicken from pot as it browns and set aside.

2 In the same pot, combine onions, peppers, minced garlic, and bay leaves. Cook over medium heat, stirring occasionally, until onions are golden brown, about 20 minutes. Add rice and andouille and cook, stirring frequently, until lightly browned, 15–20 minutes. Add chicken and stock and bring to a simmer. Reduce heat to low, cover, and cook until stock is absorbed, about 30 minutes.

3 Fluff rice with a fork and adjust seasoning. Just before serving, stir in scallions and parsley.

BIBIMBAP

SERVES 4 (SEE PHOTO, PAGE 220)

This classic Korean dish, with its array of cooked and raw vegetables atop white rice, is beautiful to behold. It can be made with meat or seafood and served hot, but we love this fresh-tasting cold, vegetarian version, served with a sweet-hot sauce.

FOR THE SAUCE

¾ cup gochujang (Korean spicy soybean paste)
6 tbsp. lemon-lime soda, such as Sprite
3 tbsp. doenjang (Korean soybean paste) or miso
2 tbsp. light corn syrup
2 tbsp. sesame oil
2 tbsp. minced garlic
2 tbsp. minced fresh ginger
1 tbsp. brown rice vinegar
1½ tsp. sesame seeds

FOR THE BIBIMBAP

¼ lb. mung bean sprouts
½ lb. baby spinach
12 dried shiitake mushrooms
6 tbsp. canola oil
3 tsp. sesame oil
2 tbsp. plus 2 tsp. minced garlic
2½ tsp. minced fresh ginger
Kosher salt and freshly ground black pepper, to taste
6 oz. gosari (bracken fern), cut into 3″ pieces (optional)
2 small zucchini, halved and cut crosswise into ¼″-thick slices
2 medium carrots, peeled and julienned
¼ small daikon radish, peeled and julienned
¾ tsp. sesame seeds
½ lb. firm tofu, cut into ½″-thick slices
4 cups cooked white sushi rice
4 eggs, fried
2 leaves chicory, thinly sliced
2 leaves green-leaf lettuce, thinly sliced
1 scallion, thinly sliced, for garnish

1 Make the sauce: In a bowl, whisk together all ingredients until smooth; set aside.

2 Make the bibimbap: Bring a 4-qt. saucepan of water to a boil and add sprouts; cook until crisp-tender, about 30 seconds. Transfer to a bowl of ice water, drain, and dry with paper towels; set aside. Repeat procedure with spinach (squeeze out as much liquid as possible when draining). When finished, pour boiling water into a bowl and add mushrooms; let soften for 30 minutes. Drain, remove stems, and slice ¼″ thick.

3 Heat 1 tbsp. canola oil and ½ tsp. sesame oil in a 10″ nonstick skillet over medium heat. Add 1 tsp. garlic, ½ tsp. ginger, and mushrooms, season with salt and pepper, and cook until hot, about 2 minutes. Transfer to a bowl. Repeat procedure, using same amounts of canola oil, sesame oil, garlic, and ginger, with the gosari (if using), zucchini, carrot, and radish; season each with salt and pepper. Set aside in separate bowls and add ¼ tsp. sesame seeds to radishes. Add 1½ tsp. garlic, ¼ tsp. sesame oil, salt, and pepper each to sprouts and spinach; stir. Heat remaining canola oil in skillet, add tofu, and cook, turning once, until browned, 4–6 minutes. Transfer to a plate; cut each in half.

4 To serve, place 1 cup rice in center of each of 4 bowls, and top each with a fried egg. Mound one-fourth of mushrooms on rice in each bowl. Working clockwise, arrange one-fourth each of zucchini, carrot, radish, spinach, sprouts, gosari (if using), chicory, and lettuce around mushrooms. Place tofu on lettuces and sprinkle with remaining sesame seeds and the scallions. Serve sauce on the side.

BASIC POLENTA

SERVES 4–6

Cornmeal, water, and butter are alchemical together, producing savory, versatile polenta. Always add the cornmeal to cold water to ensure lump-free results.

1⅔ cups polenta or coarse-grained yellow cornmeal
4 tbsp. unsalted butter
Kosher salt and freshly ground black pepper, to taste

Combine polenta with 7 cups cold salted water in a large pot. Bring to a boil over medium-high heat. Reduce heat to low and cook, stirring constantly with a wooden spoon, until polenta pulls away from the sides of the pot, 30–40 minutes. Add butter and stir until melted. Season with salt and pepper.

Grilled Polenta

SERVES 6

In Venice, polenta is often served grilled as a side dish.

> 1 recipe Basic Polenta (facing page), just prepared (about 5 cups)

Pour just-cooked polenta into a wet ceramic or glass mold, let cool, turn out, and cut into pieces with a wet knife. Grill on a very hot, dry grill or sear in a nonstick skillet until golden brown.

CHESTNUT FLOUR POLENTA

SERVES 6–12

This dense, filling polenta variation from Corsica is made with nutty chestnut flour rather than cornmeal. It's traditionally allowed to set, then sliced, and served in small wedges.

> 1 tsp. salt
> 6 cups chestnut flour

1 Bring 6¼ cups water to a boil in a heavy nonreactive pot over medium-high heat. Sift together salt and chestnut flour, then add to boiling water. Stir constantly with a wooden spoon until polenta pulls away from sides of pot, about 20 minutes.

2 Spoon polenta into center of a clean kitchen towel liberally dusted with chestnut flour. Wrap towel around polenta and pat with your hands into a 1½"-thick round. Set aside for 10 minutes, then unwrap, quarter, and slice into small wedges.

OLD-FASHIONED CREAMY GRITS

SERVES 4–6

This is a basic recipe for this Southern staple, typically served with savory accompaniments like shrimp, sausage, or redeye gravy (page 479) for breakfast. But the great doyenne of Southern cooking, Edna Lewis, took a dim view of adding fancy ingredients to grits. "People should really leave grits alone," said Lewis.

> 2 cups milk, plus more if necessary
> 1 cup stone-ground or regular grits
> Kosher salt, to taste
> ¼ cup heavy cream
> 2 tbsp. unsalted butter

1 Heat 2 cups water and the milk in a heavy-bottomed saucepan until just simmering.

2 While the mixture is heating, put stone-ground grits into a large bowl and cover with cool water. Stir the grits assertively so that the chaff floats to the top. Skim the surface carefully, removing the chaff. Drain grits in a fine-mesh sieve. If using regular grits, skip this step. Stir grits into simmering water and milk. Cook, stirring often, until grits are tender to the bite and have thickened to the consistency of thick oatmeal. As grits thicken, stir them more often to keep them from sticking and scorching. Regular grits are done in about 20 minutes, but stone-ground require an hour or a little more to cook, and you will have to add additional milk and water as needed.

3 Season grits generously with salt and stir in cream and butter. Remove from heat and let rest, covered, until serving. Serve hot.

POLENTA VS. GRITS

What's the difference between grits and that other popular cornmeal mush, polenta? It turns out that the best answer is based on particle size: grits are of a coarser grind. Glenn Roberts, maker of artisanal grits and polenta (he even ground the latter for Marcella Hazan), pegs the particle size of grits at ⅛ inch to 1/20 inch, and of polenta at 1/12 inch to 1/80 inch.

To complicate matters further, Roberts explains, both grits and polenta come in white and yellow varieties, depending on the type of corn used to make them. In general, he says, white grits are preferred by those who live near coastal port cities (such as Charleston, South Carolina), while yellow grits are traditional for inlanders. As for polenta, yellow is ubiquitous, but Roberts also makes white, which is preferred in Italy's Veneto region. Either way, Roberts assures us, grits and polenta may be used interchangeably in recipes, even though their respective genealogies and heritages are quite different (and cooking times vary).

FARRO RISOTTO WITH BUTTERNUT SQUASH & MUSHROOMS

SERVES 4–6

In this wintry risotto, the farro remains perfectly springy and al dente, creating a nice contrast to the softer textures of butternut squash and mushrooms.

2½	cups cubed butternut squash, in ½-inch cubes
3	tbsp. olive oil
	Kosher salt and freshly ground black pepper, to taste
1	tbsp. plus 1 tsp. fresh sage, chopped
1	cup farro (pearled or semipearled)
2	cups chopped shiitake mushrooms
3	tbsp. unsalted butter
4	shallots, minced
2	cloves garlic, minced
1	sprig fresh thyme
½	cup white wine
1	cup chicken or vegetable stock
1½	cups shredded Parmigiano-Reggiano
1	tbsp. crème fraîche

1 Heat oven to 400°. Toss squash with 2 tbsp. oil and season with salt and pepper. Place on parchment-lined baking sheet and roast until edges are browned and crisp, 25–30 minutes. Remove from oven and sprinkle 1 tbsp. sage over still-hot squash.

2 Meanwhile, bring 4 cups water to a boil over medium heat. Stir in farro and cook for 15 minutes. Drain, reserving 1 cup of cooking liquid, and set aside.

3 In a 4-qt. saucepan, heat remaining 1 tbsp. oil over medium heat. Add shiitakes and sauté until tender, about 3 minutes. Remove from pan and set aside.

4 Melt butter in the same pan over medium heat. Add shallots, garlic, and thyme and let cook until shallots are slightly caramelized, about 3 minutes. Add farro and stir, coating each kernel with butter. Pour in wine and simmer until evaporated.

5 Turn heat to low and begin alternately adding stock and farro cooking liquid a ¼ cup at a time, stirring continuously with each addition. Do not add more liquid until the previous ¼ cup has been completely absorbed. This process should take 25–30 minutes. After last addition, stir until about two-thirds of the liquid has been absorbed, then stir in reserved mushrooms and squash and heat through.

6 Fold in Parmigiano and stir just until melted. Fold in crème fraîche and season with salt and pepper. Garnish with remaining 1 tsp. sage.

BULGUR WHEAT & WALNUT SALAD

SERVES 6

Fine-grain bulgur wheat is essential to give this Middle Eastern dish, flavored with tamarind and lemon juice, the proper airy texture. Serve with wedges of toasted pita bread or alongside a skewer of beef or chicken.

1½	cups fine-grain bulgur wheat
3	tbsp. extra-virgin olive oil
1	tbsp. tamarind extract
½	cup finely chopped walnuts
¼	cup pine nuts
¼	cup finely chopped fresh flat-leaf parsley
2	scallions, green parts only, finely chopped
1	tbsp. tomato paste
	Pinch cayenne pepper
2	tbsp. fresh lemon juice
	Kosher salt and freshly ground black pepper, to taste

1 Combine bulgur with 2 cups water and 1 tbsp. oil. Set aside until water is absorbed, about 20 minutes. Meanwhile, combine tamarind and ⅓ cup warm water in a medium bowl.

2 Add walnuts, pine nuts, parsley, and scallions to bulgur and mix well. Add remaining 2 tbsp. olive oil, tomato paste, cayenne pepper, and lemon juice to tamarind mixture, season with salt and pepper, and pour over bulgur. Cover and set aside for 2 hours before serving.

EASY SQUEEZING

A cold lime or lemon doesn't yield juice as readily as a room-temperature one, because cold makes the fruit's cell membranes more rigid. Don't break a sweat trying to juice brick-hard citrus for a lemony recipe like tabbouleh (facing page). Pop it in the microwave for 10 or 12 seconds, and the fruit will willingly yield its juice.

TABBOULEH

SERVES 6–8

Tabbouleh, a staple in any Middle Eastern spread, is a salad made primarily from bulgur wheat and parsley. Combinations of spices and vegetables vary subtly from country to country: Egyptians add finely diced cucumbers; Armenians include paprika and cumin; in Turkey, the addition of tomato and red pepper pastes results in a dish called *kisir*. This Lebanese version is bright with scallions and lemon; it's often served with large lettuce leaves for scooping.

- 1 cup fine-grain bulgur wheat
- 1⅓ cups fresh lemon juice
- 3 bunches scallions, finely chopped
- 3 cups chopped fresh flat-leaf parsley leaves
- 3 large ripe tomatoes, cored and chopped
- ⅓ cup extra-virgin olive oil
  Kosher salt, to taste

1 Put bulgur into a large glass or ceramic bowl, then stir in 1 cup lemon juice and 2 cups water. Cover bowl and set aside at room temperature until most of the liquid has been absorbed and bulgur is tender, about 2 hours.

2 Drain bulgur in a sieve, gently pressing to remove excess liquid. Transfer to a large clean glass or ceramic bowl and add scallions, parsley, tomatoes, olive oil, and the remaining ⅓ cup lemon juice. Season to taste with salt and toss well.

MUESLI

MAKES 6 CUPS

Credit for inventing the mixture of nuts, grains, and fruit known as muesli goes to the Swiss, but it's now a ubiquitous breakfast throughout Europe. When mixing up this homemade muesli, which makes a hearty breakfast with the addition of fresh fruit and yogurt, work with what you have available: pear juice instead of apple juice, or dried blueberries, figs, or fresh dates instead of apricots, for example.

- 3 cups rolled oats
- 1 cup sunflower seeds
- ¾ cup almonds
- ½ cup pumpkin seeds
- ½ cup unsweetened shredded dried coconut
- ½ cup apple cider
- ¼ cup sesame seeds

- 2 tbsp. vegetable oil
- 1 cup thinly sliced dried apricots
  Yogurt, for serving (optional)
  Fresh fruit, for serving (optional)

1 Heat oven to 325°. Combine oats, sunflower seeds, almonds, pumpkin seeds, coconut, apple cider, sesame seeds, and oil in a large bowl and stir to blend.

2 Spread mixture out evenly on a baking sheet and bake, stirring occasionally, until lightly browned, about 30 minutes. Remove from oven and set aside to cool.

3 Sprinkle apricots over cooled muesli and toss to combine. Store in an airtight container at room temperature for up to 2 weeks. Serve with yogurt and fresh fruit on the side, if you like.

SAVORY PROVENÇAL GRANOLA

MAKES 3½ CUPS

Chef Daniel Humm of Eleven Madison Park in New York City uses savory granolas like this to add a spicy, herbal crunch to roasted beets or tomato salad. Use it as a substitute for croutons in green salad, too.

- ½ cup canola oil
- 1 cup fresh basil leaves
- 2 cups puffed rice
- 1 cup pine nuts
- ¼ cup finely grated Parmigiano-Reggiano
- 2 tbsp. basil seeds
- 2 tsp. piment d'Espelette
  Kosher salt, to taste
- 1 tbsp. minced garlic
- ¼ cup honey

1 Heat oil in a 10″ skillet over medium-high heat. Working in batches, add basil leaves and fry until crisp, about 10 seconds. Transfer basil to paper towels; let cool. Transfer to a bowl along with puffed rice, pine nuts, Parmigiano, basil seeds, piment d'Espelette, salt, and garlic; set aside.

2 Heat oven to 250°. Heat honey in a small saucepan over medium heat until loose; pour over puffed rice mixture and toss to coat evenly. Transfer to a baking sheet and spread out evenly. Bake, tossing occasionally, until toasted and golden brown, about 40 minutes. Transfer to a wire rack and let cool. To serve, sprinkle over vegetables or salad, or eat on its own with yogurt as a savory cereal. Granola will keep, covered, for up to 2 weeks.

Potatoes

POTATOES ROASTED WITH SAFFRON

SERVES 4

The pleasantly bitter and floral taste of saffron is often reserved for luxurious risottos and silky stews, but we love pairing it with otherwise basic roasted potatoes.

- Large pinch saffron threads
- 2 cups chicken stock
- 16 small potatoes
- 3 tbsp. butter, softened
  Kosher salt and freshly ground black pepper, to taste
  Chopped fresh flat-leaf parsley, for garnish

1 Heat oven to 400°. Toast saffron threads in a small skillet over high heat for 1 minute. Crumble saffron into stock in a saucepan and bring to a simmer over medium heat.

2 Rub potatoes with softened butter. Sprinkle with salt and pepper. Arrange potatoes in a single layer in a baking pan and pour hot stock over potatoes. Roast until tender, 30–45 minutes. Serve garnished with parsley.

TWICE-BAKED POTATOES

SERVES 8

The buttery, creamy indulgence of mashed potatoes meets the visceral joy of digging into a baked potato in this iconic steakhouse side dish. For the full experience, use a pastry bag to artfully pipe the potato-cheese mixture into the scooped-out skins.

- 4 russet potatoes (about 2½ lb.)
- 1 cup grated aged cheddar cheese
- 1 cup grated Gruyère cheese
- ½ cup sour cream
- 4 tbsp. unsalted butter, softened
- 2 tbsp. finely chopped fresh chives
- 1 tbsp. finely chopped fresh flat-leaf parsley
- ¼ tsp. Tabasco sauce
- ¼ tsp. Worcestershire sauce
- 8 slices bacon, cooked and cut into ¼″ strips
  Kosher salt and freshly ground black pepper, to taste
- ¼ tsp. paprika

1 Heat oven to 450°. Put potatoes on a baking sheet and bake, turning occasionally, until tender, about 1 hour. Transfer to a rack and let cool slightly.

2 Halve potatoes lengthwise and scoop out insides with a spoon into a medium bowl, leaving ¼″ of the outer layer of flesh and skin behind; transfer empty potato halves to a baking sheet. Combine scooped potato insides, ½ cup each cheddar and Gruyère, and sour cream, butter, chives, parsley, Tabasco, Worcestershire, and bacon and season with salt and pepper. Spoon mixture into potato halves and sprinkle with remaining cheese and the paprika.

3 Bake until cheese is browned and bubbly, about 10 minutes.

OLD-FASHIONED SCALLOPED POTATOES

SERVES 8

Thinly sliced potatoes and onions are baked in a rich, thyme-scented cream sauce in this classic American crowd-pleaser.

- 4 tbsp. unsalted butter, plus more for greasing
- 3 cloves garlic, finely chopped
- 1 medium yellow onion, thinly sliced
- ¼ cup flour
- 1½ cups heavy cream
- ½ cup milk
- 3 tbsp. finely chopped fresh thyme
  Kosher salt and freshly ground black pepper, to taste
- 2½ lb. Yukon gold potatoes, peeled and very thinly sliced
- ¼ tsp. paprika

Heat oven to 350°. Grease an 8″ square baking dish with butter; set aside. Melt butter in a 6-qt. saucepan over medium-high heat. Add garlic and onion and cook, stirring occasionally, until golden, 8–10 minutes. Add flour and cook, stirring, until smooth, about 2 minutes. Add cream, milk, thyme, salt, and pepper and bring to a boil. Add potatoes and cook, stirring occasionally, until just tender, 8–10 minutes. Transfer mixture to prepared baking dish.

Using a spoon, press mixture down; sprinkle with paprika. Bake until golden brown and a knife inserted into center slides in easily, about 40 minutes.

JANSSEN'S TEMPTATION

SERVES 6–8

This traditional Swedish side—popular on the Christmas *julbord* table—combines spiced anchovies with potatoes, onions, and cream. The origins of its name are disputed, but most Swedes associate it with the 19th-century opera singer Pelle Janssen, who sang weekly in the Stockholm opera house and who was as famous for his ravenous appetite as he was for his voice.

4	tbsp. unsalted butter, plus more for greasing
1	3½ oz. can anchovy filets
2	medium onions, thinly sliced
1	leek, white part only, thinly sliced
6–8	medium potatoes, peeled and thinly sliced
1	cup heavy cream
½	cup fine bread crumbs

1 Heat oven to 350° and butter a square baking dish. Drain anchovies and cut into bite-size pieces.

2 Sauté onions and leek in butter in a skillet over medium heat until soft. In a bowl, mix together the onion mixture, potatoes, and anchovies and transfer to the baking dish. Pour cream over top and cover the dish with aluminum foil. Bake until the potatoes are tender and most of the liquid is absorbed, about 50 minutes. Remove foil, sprinkle with bread crumbs, and return dish to oven until the top is golden brown.

RÖSTI

Swiss Potato Pancake

SERVES 4 (SEE PHOTO, PAGE 435)

Good potatoes coarsely grated, pressed, and fried are one of life's great pleasures. In their native Switzerland, recipes include bacon, rosemary, caraway seeds, eggs, pasta, cheese, even coffee. These variations can be delicious, but we found the definitive version in Bern, at Restaurant Della Casa: golden, impeccable, ideal.

2¼	lb. russet potatoes
2	tbsp. lard or unsalted butter
2	tbsp. canola oil
1	tbsp. kosher salt, plus more to taste

1 Place potatoes in a large saucepan, cover with cold water, and bring to a boil over medium-high heat. Cook until tender, about 30 minutes. Drain potatoes, and set aside to cool for about 10 minutes. Peel potatoes, then refrigerate until chilled, at least 1 hour. Grate potatoes using the large holes on a cheese grater.

2 Heat lard and oil in an 8″ nonstick skillet over medium-low heat. When lard has melted, add potatoes, sprinkle with salt, and mix well, coating potatoes with fat. Using a metal spatula, gently press potatoes, molding them to fit the skillet. Cook, shaking skillet occasionally, until edges are golden brown, about 20 minutes.

3 Cover skillet with a large inverted plate, invert the rösti onto the plate, then slide it back into the skillet, cooked side up. Cook until golden brown on the bottom, about 20 minutes. Transfer to a cutting board, sprinkle with salt, and cut into wedges to serve.

BUBBLE & SQUEAK

SERVES 6–8

This hearty fried vegetable hash, a British pub classic and a perfect use for leftovers, includes roasted Brussels sprouts, carrots, and parsnips. The name is a reference to the sounds the vegetable mixture makes while cooking.

½	lb. Brussels sprouts, halved
6	medium carrots, chopped
3	medium parsnips, chopped
6	tbsp. olive oil
	Kosher salt and freshly ground black pepper, to taste
2	lb. russet potatoes, cubed
6	tbsp. unsalted butter
1	small yellow onion, minced
¼	cup heavy cream
3	tbsp. finely chopped fresh chives

1 Heat oven to 400°. Place Brussels sprouts, carrots, and parsnips on a foil-lined baking sheet and toss with 4 tbsp. oil and salt and pepper. Roast until tender, about 25 minutes; let cool.

2 Put potatoes in a 4-qt. saucepan; cover with salted water, and bring to a boil. Cook until tender, about 20 minutes. Drain and set aside. Return pan to heat with 2 tbsp. butter. Add onion and cook until soft, 8–10 minutes. Remove from heat, add potatoes, cream, chives, salt, and pepper, and mash until smooth. Stir in roasted vegetables.

3 Heat remaining oil and butter in a 12″ skillet over medium-high heat. Add vegetable mixture and cook, flipping once, until browned, 18–20 minutes.

SAUTÉED POTATOES & CHILES

Papas con Rajas

SERVES 4

Smoky roasted poblano chiles add deep flavor to starchy potatoes in this side dish typical of central Mexico.

- ¾ lb. small waxy potatoes, cut into ¼″-thick disks
- 3 tbsp. canola oil
- 1 medium white onion, thinly sliced
- 3 cloves garlic, finely chopped
- 3 poblano chiles, roasted, peeled, stemmed, seeded, and thinly sliced
- 4 sprigs fresh epazote or cilantro, roughly chopped
   Kosher salt, to taste

HOT CHILE HOW-TO

The principal heat-giving compound in chiles, capsaicin, is not concentrated in the fruit's seeds, as is often thought, but rather in the pithy, seed-studded flesh, or placenta, that is located near the stem and extends along the inner ribs. Many cooks wear rubber gloves when handling very hot chiles; others halve the chile lengthwise and scrape away seeds with a small spoon. Whatever your method, take care when handling the chile's hottest parts: Keep from touching your face, and wash your hands when you've finished.

When shopping, choose chiles with the greenest stems (brown patches indicate that the pepper is less than fresh). Most fresh chiles can be left out for a couple of days, though some—especially those sold unripe, like green bells, or thin-skinned varieties like the habanero—will lose moisture more quickly and should be refrigerated after a day. Store the chiles in a tightly sealed plastic bag on the top shelf of the fridge (chiles store the best at between 45° and 55°). You can also freeze almost any kind of chile for as long as a year; just seal them snugly in plastic bags.

1 Place potatoes in a 4-qt. saucepan, cover with water by 1″, and bring to a boil over high heat. Cook until just tender, about 20 minutes. Drain and set aside.

2 Heat oil in a 12″ skillet over medium-high heat. Add onion and cook, stirring, until slightly caramelized, about 12 minutes. Add garlic and chile, and cook, stirring, until heated through, about 2 minutes. Add potatoes and cook, stirring, until potatoes are very tender, about 10 minutes. Remove from heat, stir in epazote, and season with salt.

POTATOES WITH MUSTARD SEEDS & ONIONS

SERVES 6

This is an essential Tamil dish from South India, demonstrating the vibrant palate of Tamilian food—curry leaves, turmeric, hot pepper, and mustard seeds.

- 2–3 tbsp. vegetable oil
- 1 tsp. brown mustard seeds
- 2 tbsp. urad dal (black gram beans)
- 1–3 dried hot red chiles, halved lengthwise
- 20 fresh curry leaves
- 2 medium onions, quartered and thinly sliced
- 1 tsp. salt
- ½ tsp. ground turmeric
- ½ tsp. cayenne pepper
- 1 lb. potatoes, peeled and cut into ½″ dice
- 1 tomato, chopped
- ¼ tsp. asafoetida

1 Heat oil in a well-seasoned wok or a large nonstick frying pan over medium heat. Add mustard seeds, urad dal, and chiles and stir until the seeds start to pop and the dal begins to turn red, a few seconds.

2 Stir in curry leaves. Add onions and fry until the edges begin to brown. Add salt, turmeric, and cayenne and stir for 5 seconds. Add potatoes, then stir and fry for 2 minutes.

3 Add tomato and asafoetida and stir for 1 minute. Add 1 cup plus 2 tbsp. water and bring to a boil. Cover, reduce heat slightly, and cook vigorously until the potatoes are just tender and the water is absorbed. Remove lid, stir, and fry, turning potatoes over often, until they are reddish yellow, 5–8 minutes. Serve hot.

POTATO GALETTE

Galette de Pomme de Terre

SERVES 2–4

This decadent, crusty potato cake has a savory depth thanks to generous amounts of both duck fat and butter. This recipe is inspired by the one served at the restaurant L'Ami Louis in Paris.

- 2 lb. Yukon gold potatoes, peeled and cut into ½″ × ¼″ pieces
- 2 tbsp. duck fat
- 2 tbsp. unsalted butter
  Kosher salt and freshly ground black pepper, to taste
- 1 tbsp. minced fresh flat-leaf parsley
- 1 tsp. minced garlic

1 Put potatoes into a 4-qt. pot, add salted water to cover by 1″, and bring to a boil. Reduce heat to medium-low and simmer until potatoes are tender, 20–30 minutes. Drain potatoes, transfer to a baking sheet, and chill.

2 Heat oven to 400°. Melt fat and butter in a 6″ cast-iron skillet or ovenproof nonstick skillet over medium heat. Put chilled potatoes into a bowl. Pour fat and butter over potatoes (reserving skillet) and season with salt and pepper; toss to coat. Transfer potatoes to reserved skillet and cover with a piece of parchment paper cut to fit inside rim of skillet. Cook, smashing potatoes into skillet with a metal spatula, until edges begin to crisp and brown, about 30 minutes. Transfer skillet to oven and bake until potato cake is golden brown, 10–15 minutes (to check, use a fork to lift up one edge of the potato cake). Invert a small serving plate over skillet. Using two tea towels, hold plate and skillet together firmly and invert skillet. Remove skillet and garnish potato cake with parsley and garlic. Serve hot.

POMMES DUCHESSE

SERVES 4

These rosettes of piped mashed potatoes were the epitome of elegance in the 1960s and 1970s, though the recipe dates to the early 19th century. They're brushed with an egg wash before baking for color and crunch.

- 2½ lb. russet potatoes
- 4 tbsp. unsalted butter, softened
- 2 egg yolks, plus 1 egg mixed with 1 tsp. heavy cream, lightly beaten
- ⅛ tsp. freshly grated nutmeg
  Kosher salt and freshly ground black pepper, to taste

1 Heat oven to 400°. Using a fork, prick potatoes all over; place on a baking sheet. Bake until tender, 1½ hours. Let cool, then peel and pass through a food mill or ricer.

2 Mix potatoes, butter, yolks, nutmeg, salt, and pepper in a bowl; transfer to a piping bag fitted with a ¾″ star tip. On a parchment paper–lined baking sheet, and working in a tight circular motion, pipe twelve 2½″ cones about 2″ high. Brush with egg mixture, then bake until golden brown, 40–45 minutes.

BISTRO FRENCH FRIES

SERVES 4

The secret to these spectacular bistro fries is duck fat, a superior frying medium that gives the potatoes a meaty flavor.

- 7 cups duck fat
- 3 cups canola oil
- 4 large russet potatoes, cut lengthwise into ¼″-thick batons
  Kosher salt, to taste

1 Heat duck fat and oil in a 6-qt. Dutch oven over medium-high heat until a deep-fry thermometer reads 325°. Working in small batches, add potatoes and cook, turning occasionally and maintaining a temperature of 300° (the temperature will drop when you add the potatoes), until pale and tender, 5–6 minutes. Using a slotted spoon, transfer fries to a wire rack set over a baking sheet. Remove pot from heat and refrigerate fries for 1 hour.

2 Return oil to medium-high heat until a deep-fry thermometer reads 400°. Working in small batches, add chilled fries to oil and cook, turning occasionally and maintaining a temperature of 375°, until golden brown and crisp, 1–2 minutes. Using a slotted spoon, transfer fries to a rack set over a baking sheet; season with salt. Serve hot.

SHOESTRING FRIES

SERVES 2

These thin, crisp, quick-frying potatoes straddle the line between French fries and potato chips.

> ## "I have made a lot of mistakes falling in love, and regretted most of them, but never the potatoes that went with them."
>
> ### NORA EPHRON

Canola or peanut oil, for frying
2 large russet potatoes, peeled
Kosher salt, to taste

1 Pour oil to a depth of 2″ into a 6-qt. Dutch oven and heat over medium-high heat until a deep-fry thermometer reads 375°.

2 Meanwhile, julienne potatoes lengthwise using the narrowest setting of a mandoline with a julienne attachment or by hand with a sharp knife. Transfer potatoes to a colander and rinse them briefly under cold water for 1 minute so that they won't stick together as they fry in the oil. Drain potatoes, transfer to kitchen towels, and pat dry.

3 Working in 4 batches, fry potatoes, stirring constantly with a slotted spoon and maintaining an oil temperature of at least 350° (adding the potatoes will cause the temperature to drop), until potatoes are light golden brown and crisp, about 2 minutes. Using a slotted spoon, transfer fried potatoes to a wire rack set over a baking sheet; season potatoes with salt. Serve hot.

POUTINE

French Fries with Gravy & Cheese Curds

SERVES 4–6

The province's gastronomic achievements may reach dizzying heights, but Quebec may forever be known as the place where *poutine* began. An unabashedly savory collage of French-fried potatoes, beef gravy, and squeaky-fresh cheese curds, it's perhaps the ultimate late-night snack.

4 lb. russet potatoes, washed and dried
4 tbsp. unsalted butter
¼ cup flour
1 shallot, minced
1 clove garlic, minced
4 cups beef stock
2 tbsp. ketchup
1 tbsp. cider vinegar
1 tbsp. green peppercorns
½ tsp. Worcestershire sauce
Kosher salt and freshly ground black pepper
Canola oil, for frying
2 cups cheddar cheese curds

1 Cut potatoes into lengths of about ¼″×¼″×4″. Place in a large bowl, cover with cold water, and refrigerate for about 2 hours.

2 Meanwhile, heat butter in a 2-qt. saucepan over medium-high heat. Add flour and cook, stirring, until smooth, about 2 minutes. Add shallot and garlic and cook until soft, about 2 minutes. Add stock, ketchup, vinegar, peppercorns, Worcestershire, and salt and pepper and bring to a boil. Cook, stirring, until thickened, about 6 minutes. Remove from heat and keep gravy warm.

3 Pour oil to a depth of 3″ into a 6-qt. Dutch oven and heat over medium heat until a deep-fry thermometer reads 325°. Drain potatoes, then dry thoroughly with paper towels. Working in small batches, add potatoes and fry, tossing occasionally, until tender and slightly crisp, about 4 minutes. Drain on paper towels and let cool for 20 minutes.

4 Increase temperature to medium-high and heat oil until thermometer reads 375°. Working in small batches, return potatoes to oil and fry, tossing occasionally, until crisp and golden brown, about 2 minutes. Transfer fries to paper towels to drain briefly and then divide among serving bowls. Pour gravy over each serving of fries and top with cheese curds; serve immediately.

JOËL ROBUCHON'S WHIPPED POTATOES

SERVES 6–8

When Joël Robuchon first prepared this dish at his restaurant Jamin in Paris in the early 1980s, he stunned a world that was familiar only with basic mashed spuds. Since then, this incredibly rich potato purée has become so popular that customers demand it at every one of his restaurants. The key to the dish is to keep the potatoes hot as you mix in so much chilled butter—a pound for every two pounds of potatoes. It takes vigorous and constant stirring to keep them smooth and silky.

- 2 lb. yellow-fleshed potatoes, such as Yukon gold
  Kosher salt, to taste
- ¼ cup milk
- 1 lb. unsalted butter, cubed and chilled

1 Place potatoes in an 8-qt. pot, cover with salted water, and bring to a boil. Cook until tender, about 25 minutes. Drain and let cool slightly. Meanwhile, bring milk to a boil in a saucepan; remove from heat, cover, and set aside.

2 Peel potatoes and pass them through a food mill or ricer into a 4-qt. saucepan set over medium-low heat. Using a rubber spatula, turn potatoes frequently until they take on a drier, fluffier consistency, 2–3 minutes. Reduce heat to low. Working in batches, vigorously stir in the butter until mixture is creamy. Whisk in warmed milk, season with salt, and transfer to a warmed serving bowl.

SISTER MILDRED'S CREAMED POTATOES

SERVES 4–6

This satisfying dish, named after a late member of the Sabbathday Lake community of Shakers in New Gloucester, Maine, may also be made with leftover boiled potatoes.

- 3 large russet potatoes, peeled and cut into ½" cubes
- ½ cup butter

- 1 cup half-and-half
  Kosher salt, to taste
  Chopped fresh chives, for garnish (optional)

1 Place potatoes in a medium pot, cover with cold water, and bring to a boil over high heat. Reduce heat to medium and simmer until potatoes are just soft when pierced with a fork, about 3 minutes. Drain and set aside.

2 Melt butter in same pot over medium heat. Add half-and-half and bring to a gentle simmer. Add potatoes, reduce heat to low, and simmer, stirring very gently from time to time, until nearly all the cream mixture has been absorbed by the potatoes, about 30 minutes. Season with salt and garnish with chives, if you like.

NEEPS 'N' TATTIES

Mashed Rutabagas & Potatoes

SERVES 8

This classic Scottish side dish of buttered, salted neeps (rutabagas) and tatties (potatoes) is traditionally served with haggis.

- 2 lb. russet potatoes, peeled and diced
- 2 lb. medium rutabagas, peeled and diced
- 8 tbsp. unsalted butter
  Kosher salt and freshly ground black pepper, to taste

1 Put potatoes and rutabagas into 2 separate medium pots of cold water and bring them to a boil over high heat. Reduce heat to medium and gently boil each until potatoes and rutabagas are very soft, 15–20 minutes each. Drain separately and return them to their pots.

2 Coarsely mash potatoes with 5 tbsp. butter and season with salt and pepper; cover and set aside. Coarsely mash rutabagas with remaining 3 tbsp. butter and season with salt and pepper. Serve mashed rutabaga and mashed potatoes side by side on the same platter.

Breads

BREADS & ROLLS

"GOOD BREAD IS THE MOST FUNDAMENTALLY SATISFYING OF ALL FOODS," said the great James Beard, and we couldn't agree more. The sight and scent of a freshly baked loaf symbolizes all that is good and nourishing in the world. And perhaps there is no pleasure more immediate than ripping off a hunk of fresh, warm, homemade bread, slathering it with sweet butter or dunking it into fruity olive oil, and promptly eating it.

Bread has been a part of our culinary DNA since man first discovered the magical alchemy of mixing crushed grains with water and applying heat. The original artisanal food, it has been baked, grilled, steamed, fried, and fashioned into a multitude of shapes and varieties. We've added herbs and oils, fruits and nuts, spices and seeds, but its essence is always the same: flour, water, and usually leavening, ably prepared with just a modicum of attentiveness. Bread baking is also very democratic. For those of us with the inclination and time, yeasted breads, with their highly anticipatory aura, cannot be beat for delivering a sense of accomplishment. For the ingénue baker, slicing into a loaf of quickly assembled Irish soda bread to reveal its dense, currant-studded crumb is equally satisfying.

More than just a countertop staple, our daily bread displays great cultural significance in how it is eaten around the globe. Americans have a long tra-

dition of quick breads, like buttermilk biscuits and cornbread, thanks to our pioneering past. Ethiopians quite literally eat the plate their food is served on, making the delicately spongy *injera* highly practical. For Swedes, Christmas is not complete without yeasted sweet rolls infused with saffron, while every self-respecting German beer hall serves tangy giant pretzels.

Universally, we love to use bread as a vehicle to hold other things. Try delicate crêpes filled with mushrooms, Gruyère, and spinach, or the Turkish favorite *lahmacun,* a crisp flatbread topped with a spiced lamb and tomato sauce. For an impromptu party, pair an olive-studded Provençal *fougasse* with a crisp, dry rosé.

The art of making bread keeps us honest and grounded. Indeed, there is a natural soulfulness that comes with mixing together such simple components to create something so immediately gratifying.

Yeast Breads

ITALIAN BREAD

MAKES 2 LOAVES

A crusty loaf of Italian bread with a pillowy center is the star in sandwiches such as Muffuletta (page 125) or a worthy base for garlic bread (page 349). It's also just great to eat out of hand.

- 2 tbsp. sugar
- 2 tsp. active dry yeast
- 2 cups water, heated to 120°
- 2 tbsp. olive oil
- 6 cups bread flour
- 1 tbsp. kosher salt

1 Place 1 tbsp. sugar, yeast, and water in the bowl of a stand mixer fitted with a hook; let sit until foamy, about 10 minutes. Add remaining 1 tbsp. sugar and the oil, and then add flour and salt. Mix on low speed until dough forms; increase speed to medium-high and knead dough until smooth, 8–10 minutes. Remove bowl from mixer and cover with plastic wrap; let sit until doubled in size, 1½–2 hours.

2 On a lightly floured work surface, knead dough briefly and form into a ball. Divide dough in half. Using your hands, roll each half into a 16″-long rope. Place each rope on a parchment paper–lined baking sheet and cover loosely with plastic wrap. Let sit until doubled in size, 1–1½ hours.

3 Heat oven to 375°. Using a sharp knife, slash a long line down the middle of each loaf, about ½″ deep. Bake loaves until lightly golden and an instant-read thermometer inserted into the center of each loaf reads 208°–212°, 18–20 minutes. Let cool for 15 minutes before serving.

FILONE

MAKES 2 LOAVES

This recipe, from Daniel Leader of the Bread Alone bakeries in upstate New York, produces an airy loaf with a nice crust similar to a ciabatta. It's made with a lightly fermented traditional Italian starter called a *biga*.

- 1⅔ cups water, heated to 115°
- 1½ tsp. active dry yeast
- 3¼ cups plus ⅔ cup flour, plus more for dusting
- ⅓ cup olive oil, plus more for greasing bowl
- 2¼ tsp. kosher salt
- ½ cup ice cubes

1 In a medium bowl, whisk together ⅓ cup water and ½ tsp. yeast; let sit until foamy, about 10 minutes. Add ⅔ cup flour, and mix until a smooth dough forms. Transfer to a lightly floured surface and knead until fairly smooth, about 2 minutes. Transfer ball of dough to a greased bowl and cover with plastic wrap. Place bowl in a cold oven and let sit for 1 hour. Transfer bowl to refrigerator and let sit for at least 8 hours or up to 24 hours to ferment. This ball of dough is the biga, a quick and simple starter that imparts large bubbles and a lightly fermented flavor to the dough.

2 Remove biga from refrigerator, and let sit to come to room temperature, about 30 minutes. Transfer biga to a large bowl and add remaining 1⅓ cups water and 1 tsp. yeast; stir until biga breaks up and is partly dissolved in water. Add remaining 3¼ cups flour, along with oil and salt, and stir until dough forms. Let the dough sit to allow flour to hydrate, about 20 minutes.

3 Knead dough, which will be very wet and sticky, in the bowl until it begins to tighten and becomes smooth, about 4 minutes. (The dough for this bread must be very wet to achieve its light and airy texture.) Transfer the dough to a lightly floured work surface and continue kneading, using a bench scraper to help if necessary, until smooth and elastic, about 6 minutes more. At this point, the dough will be sticky to the touch but will release from your hands fairly easily. It will also have formed a tight skin on the outside that can hold its shape when stretched lightly.

4 Transfer dough ball to a lightly greased bowl and cover it with plastic wrap. Place the bowl in a cold oven, and let dough rest until it doubles in size, about 2 hours. (When you press your finger into the dough, the fingerprint should spring back slowly.) Lightly dust a sheet of parchment paper with flour and set it on a rimless baking sheet.

5 Lightly dust a work surface with flour, and transfer dough to work surface. Using a bench scraper or a chef's knife, cut dough into 2 equal-size pieces and flatten slightly. Fold the top and bottom edges of 1 piece toward the middle, and flatten dough at the seam with the palm of your hand; turn dough over, seam side down, and shape into a 12″ log. Transfer log to the prepared, floured parchment paper and repeat this folding and shaping procedure with remaining dough piece. Lift the parchment paper between the loaves slightly. Loosely cover dough logs on baking sheet with plastic wrap, and transfer to a cold oven. Let sit until dough logs double in size, about 1½ hours.

6 Remove proofed loaves on baking sheet from oven, and place a cast-iron skillet on bottom rack of oven; position another rack above skillet and place a baking stone on top of it. Heat oven to 425°.

7 Uncover dough logs and sprinkle with flour (this looks aesthetically pleasing and adds another dimension of flavor from the toasted flour). Using the corner of the parchment paper as a guide, slide the loaves, still on the paper, onto the baking stone and position evenly on the stone. Place ice cubes in skillet (this produces steam that allows the loaves to rise fully before a crust forms on the exterior). Bake loaves until dark golden brown and crisp, about 50 minutes; let cool before serving.

COOK'S NOTE Given the temperature in kitchens can vary widely, thus speeding up or slowing down a dough's rise, placing the dough in a cold oven maintains the temperature.

FOUR-HOUR BAGUETTE
MAKES 3 LOAVES

Traditional French baguettes are 24 to 30 inches long and are baked in ovens that produce steam, which delays crust formation so the loaves can fully rise. Our version creates shorter loaves that can easily fit in home ovens, and calls for adding ice cubes to a hot cast-iron skillet to simulate a steam oven.

- 1½ cups water, heated to 115°
- 1 tsp. active dry yeast
- 3¼ cups flour
- 1½ tsp. kosher salt
  Canola oil, for greasing bowl
- ½ cup ice cubes

1 In a large bowl, whisk together water and yeast; let sit until foamy, about 10 minutes. Add flour and stir with a fork until dough forms and all flour is absorbed; let dough sit to allow flour to hydrate, about 20 minutes. Add salt; transfer dough to a lightly floured work surface and knead until smooth and elastic, about 10 minutes. Transfer dough ball to a lightly greased bowl, cover bowl with plastic wrap, and place bowl in a cold oven. Let dough rest until doubled in size, about 45 minutes.

2 Transfer dough to a floured surface and shape into an 8″×6″ rectangle. Fold the 8″ sides toward the middle, then fold the shorter sides toward the center. Return dough, seam side down, to bowl. Cover with plastic again and return to oven; let sit until doubled in size, about 1 hour.

3 Remove bowl with dough from oven, and place a cast-iron skillet on the bottom rack of oven; position another rack above skillet, and place a baking stone on it.

4 Heat oven to 475°. Transfer dough to a floured surface and cut into 3 equal pieces; shape each piece into a 14″ rope. Flour a sheet of parchment paper on a rimless baking sheet; place ropes, evenly spaced, on paper. Lift paper between ropes to form pleats; place 2 tightly rolled kitchen towels under long edges of paper, creating supports for the loaves. Cover loosely with plastic wrap; let sit until double in size, about 50 minutes.

5 Uncover; remove towels and flatten paper to space out loaves. Using a sharp razor or paring knife, slash the top of each baguette at a 30-degree angle in 4 spots; each slash should be about 4″ long. Using the corner of the parchment paper as a guide, slide loaves, still on the parchment paper, onto the baking stone. Place ice cubes in skillet (this produces steam that lets the loaves rise fully before a crust forms). Bake until darkly browned and crisp, about 30 minutes; let cool before serving.

APPLE CIDER LEVAIN LOAF
MAKES 1 LOAF

Tart, tangy, and sweet from the addition of apple cider and dried cranberries, this flavorful white bread can also be made without those ingredients; simply substitute the same amount of water for the apple cider and omit the cranberries. Be sure to begin the starter 10 days before baking.

- 6½ cups plus ⅓ cup water, heated to 115°
- 4¾ cups plus ⅔ cup and 2 tbsp. all-purpose flour
- ¼ tsp. active dry yeast
- 4 cups bread flour

1 cup apple cider, at room temperature
½ cup dried cranberries
2 tsp. kosher salt
   Canola oil, for greasing
½ cup ice cubes

1 In a large bowl, stir together ⅔ cup water, ¼ cup plus 2 tbsp. all-purpose flour, and yeast until a smooth paste forms; cover with plastic wrap and let sit for 24 hours. Repeat this process for the next 8 days, adding ⅓ cup each water and flour the second and third days and ¾ cup the remaining days, to make the starter (which you can keep alive, in the fridge, by adding the same amounts once weekly).

2 On the 10th day, place ¼ cup starter in a bowl and stir in ⅓ cup water, ¾ cup bread flour, and ¼ cup apple cider to create sourdough culture; let sit for 12–24 hours, until ready to bake.

3 Uncover culture and add remaining ⅔ cup water, 3¼ cups bread flour, and ¾ cup cider, along with cranberries and salt. Stir until dough forms; let dough sit to let flour hydrate, about 20 minutes. Transfer dough to a floured surface and knead, using a bench scraper to help remove dough from surface, until smooth and elastic, about 10 minutes. Transfer to a greased bowl; cover with plastic wrap and place in a cold oven. Let rest until slightly inflated, about 1 hour. Transfer dough to a floured surface and flatten slightly. Fold top and bottom edges toward middle. Return dough, seam side down, to bowl; cover. Let sit until doubled in size, about 3 hours.

4 Repeat folding procedure, then place dough, seam side down, into a greased 8″×4″×2½″ loaf pan. Cover with plastic again and return to oven. Let sit until dough reaches top of loaf pan, about 3 hours. One hour before baking, place a cast-iron skillet on bottom rack of oven; position another rack above skillet and place a baking stone on top of it. Heat oven to 475°.

5 Using a razor, slash top of loaf at an angle in 4 spots. Place loaf on baking stone; place ice cubes in skillet. Bake until brown, about 50 minutes; let cool before serving.

SEEDED RYE LOAF

MAKES 1 LOAF

Dark and deeply flavored from a rye sourdough starter that's made 10 days in advance, this earthy loaf can be easily customized with whatever seeds and grains you have on hand.

6 cups rye flour
3¼ cups plus ⅓ cup water, heated to 115°
¼ tsp. active dry yeast
2¼ cups bread flour
1½ tsp. kosher salt
¼ cup each sunflower, pumpkin, or sesame seeds, or cracked wheat or rye (any combination), mixed together in a bowl
   Canola oil, for greasing
½ cup ice cubes

1 In a bowl, stir together ½ cup rye flour, ¼ cup water, and yeast until a smooth paste forms. Cover with plastic wrap and let sit for 24 hours. Repeat this process for the next 8 days, adding the same amounts of rye flour and water, to make the starter (which you can keep alive for longer in the fridge by adding the same amounts once weekly).

2 On the 10th day, place ¼ cup starter in a bowl. Stir in ½ cup rye flour and ⅓ cup water until smooth to create sourdough culture for this loaf. Let sit for 8–24 hours.

3 Uncover culture and add remaining 1 cup rye flour and ½ cup water, along with bread flour, salt, and half the seed mix. Stir until dough forms; let dough sit to let flour hydrate, about 20 minutes. Transfer to a floured surface; knead until smooth and elastic, about 10 minutes. Transfer to a greased bowl; cover with plastic wrap and place in a cold oven. Let sit until slightly inflated, about 1 hour.

4 Transfer to a floured surface and flatten. Fold top and bottom edges toward middle. Return dough to bowl, seam side down; cover and return to oven. Let sit until doubled in size, about 3 hours.

5 Transfer dough to a floured surface. Positioning your hands on outside edge of dough, rotate dough over surface to form a taut dome, pinching edges underneath. Transfer, seam side up, to a floured kitchen towel in a colander. Cover loosely with plastic wrap; let sit until doubled in size, about 3 hours. One hour before baking, place a cast-iron skillet on bottom rack of oven; position another rack above skillet and place a baking stone on top of it. Heat oven to 400°.

6 Invert dough onto a parchment paper sheet on a rimless baking sheet. Spray with water and cover with remaining seed mix. Using a razor, slash a hashtag pattern in top of dough. Using paper, slide loaf onto stone. Place ice in skillet. Bake until loaf is dark brown, about 1 hour; let cool before serving.

DORIS GRANT'S BROWN BREAD

MAKES 2 LOAVES

Myrtle Allen, founder of the famed Irish restaurant Ballymaloe, adapted this recipe from the simple no-knead, one-rise bread developed by English cookbook writer Doris Grant at the request of the British government during World War II.

- 1 tbsp. unsalted butter
- 2 tsp. active dry yeast
- 2 tbsp. molasses
- ½ cup water, heated to 115°
- 10 cups stone-ground whole wheat flour
- 1½ tbsp. fine sea salt

1 Heat oven to 200°. Grease two 8×4×2½″ loaf pans with butter and set them aside in a warm spot. Put yeast into a small glass bowl, add molasses and water, and stir to dissolve. Set aside and let sit until foamy, about 10 minutes.

2 Put flour and salt into a large ovenproof bowl and stir well to combine. Place bowl in oven and let rest until flour mixture is warmed through, about 10 minutes. Remove bowl from oven, add yeast mixture and 3½ cups lukewarm water, and mix together with your hands until a sticky dough forms.

3 Increase heat to 400°. Divide dough evenly between the 2 prepared loaf pans, cover with a clean kitchen towel, and let rise in a warm spot until bread has grown by one-third, 15–20 minutes. Bake bread until loaves are browned on top, about 45 minutes. Loosely cover loaves with foil, then continue to bake for 25–30 minutes more.

4 Let bread cool in pans for 10 minutes, then gently run a table knife around inside edge of each pan to loosen. Turn loaves out onto a wire rack to cool completely before serving, about 2 hours.

GLUTEN-FREE SANDWICH BREAD

MAKES 1 LOAF

Silvana Nardone of the blog Silvana's Kitchen developed this gluten-free recipe for us when we asked her to make a perfect wheat-free sandwich bread. It uses a mix of sorghum flour, brown rice flour, whey powder, and tapioca starch to achieve a light crumb.

- 1¼ cups brown rice flour, plus 1 tbsp. for dusting
- 1 cup sorghum flour
- 1 cup tapioca starch
- ⅔ cup plus 1 tbsp. whey powder
- 2 tbsp. granulated sugar
- 1½ tbsp. xanthan gum (see Cook's Note)
- 1½ tsp. salt
- 1 tsp. active dry yeast
- 2 large eggs, at room temperature
- ¼ cup canola oil, plus more for greasing
- 1¼–1½ cups seltzer, at room temperature
- 1 tsp. rice bran, plus more for coating

1 In a large bowl, whisk together both flours, tapioca starch, whey powder, sugar, xanthan gum, salt, and yeast. Meanwhile, in a small bowl, whisk together eggs and oil.

2 Place flour mixture in the bowl of a stand mixer fitted with the paddle attachment. Add egg mixture and with the motor on low speed, slowly stream in seltzer until a sticky, stretchy, batter-like dough forms. Increase speed to medium-high and mix for 4 minutes.

3 Meanwhile, grease an 8×4×2½″ loaf pan with oil and coat with rice bran. In one motion, scoop dough into pan and very gently smooth out top with greased fingers (to avoid deflating). Cover loosely with plastic wrap and let proof at room temperature until the dough peeks over top of pan, about 1½ hours.

4 Place a pizza stone on the middle rack of the oven and heat to 350°. In a small bowl, stir together rice bran and 1 tbsp. rice flour. Lightly dust loaf with the rice bran mixture. Using a serrated knife, diagonally score loaf three times, ¼″ deep. Bake until golden brown, about 1 hour. Remove the loaf from the pan and place directly on pizza stone. Bake on the pizza stone until the loaf sounds hollow when thumped on the bottom, about 15 minutes. Place loaf on its side on a wire rack to cool completely before slicing, about 1 hour.

COOK'S NOTE Depending on the brand of flours and starches used, as well as the humidity level on any given day, water absorption can vary when mixing the batter. Typically, it can range by about ¼ cup, so add seltzer slowly until you get the right texture. Xanthan gum is a natural emulsifier and thickener derived from seaweed that's often added to gluten-free baked goods to mimic the viscosity and texture that's lost thanks to the absence of wheat flour. It's available at most health food stores and specialty groceries.

FOUGASSE

Provençal Bread with Olives & Herbs

MAKES 5 LOAVES

Cookbook author Patricia Wells gave us the recipe for this herb-and-olive-topped Provençal loaf. Its distinctive flat shape (see Shaping Fougasse, this page) is a common sight in markets throughout the south of France.

- 1 tsp. active dry yeast
- 1 tsp. sugar
- 1⅓ cups water, heated to 115°
- 4½ cups flour, plus more for dusting
- 2 tbsp. extra-virgin olive oil, plus more for brushing loaves
- 1 tsp. kosher salt
  Cornmeal, for dusting
- ½ cup minced Kalamata olives
- ¼ cup minced green olives
- 2 tbsp. minced fresh flat-leaf parsley
- 2 tbsp. minced fresh thyme
- 1 tbsp. minced fresh rosemary
  Sea salt and freshly ground black pepper, to taste

1 In a large bowl, stir together yeast, sugar, and water; let sit until foamy, about 10 minutes. Stir in flour, oil, and salt and mix until a dough forms. Transfer dough to a floured surface. Knead for 6 minutes. Cover with a damp kitchen towel; let sit until doubled in size, about 1½ hours.

2 Heat oven to 500°. Divide dough into 5 equal pieces. Working with 1 dough piece at a time on a floured work surface, roll into a rough 8″×5″ triangle about ¼″ thick. Transfer triangle to a cornmeal-dusted, parchment paper–lined baking sheet. Using a sharp knife, cut 3 lengthwise parallel slashes in the middle of the dough and 1 small slash below and parallel to the middle large slash. Spread slashes apart with your fingers. Cover with a damp kitchen towel; let rest until puffed, about 30 minutes.

3 Combine olives and herbs in a bowl. Lightly brush each dough piece with oil, sprinkle with olive mixture, and season with salt and pepper. Bake, one at a time, until golden brown, about 15 minutes each.

SHAPING FOUGASSE

The Provençal flatbread known as *fougasse* (this page) is a crust lover's dream: The dough is flattened and scored, maximizing surface area exposed to direct heat, which means plenty of crunch and lots of room for toppings. Here's how to shape the dough:

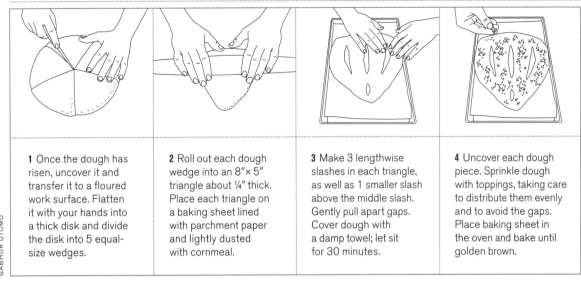

1 Once the dough has risen, uncover it and transfer it to a floured work surface. Flatten it with your hands into a thick disk and divide the disk into 5 equal-size wedges.

2 Roll out each dough wedge into an 8″× 5″ triangle about ¼″ thick. Place each triangle on a baking sheet lined with parchment paper and lightly dusted with cornmeal.

3 Make 3 lengthwise slashes in each triangle, as well as 1 smaller slash above the middle slash. Gently pull apart gaps. Cover dough with a damp towel; let sit for 30 minutes.

4 Uncover each dough piece. Sprinkle dough with toppings, taking care to distribute them evenly and to avoid the gaps. Place baking sheet in the oven and bake until golden brown.

GABHOR UTOMO

ROSEMARY-LEMON FOCACCIA

MAKES 1 LOAF

With a pleasantly crisp crust and a chewy interior, this rosemary-flecked focaccia decorated with lemon slices was inspired by a similar version shared with us by the celebrated cookbook author Marcella Hazan.

- 1 tsp. active dry yeast
- ½ cup water, heated to 115°
- 5 tbsp. extra-virgin olive oil, plus more for greasing
- 4 cups flour
- 1 tbsp. kosher salt
- 8 sprigs fresh rosemary
   Cornmeal, for dusting
- 2 lemons, thinly sliced into rounds
   Coarse sea salt, to taste

1 Dissolve yeast in water in a small bowl and let stand for 10 minutes, then add 2 tbsp. oil. Combine flour and salt in a large bowl. Strip and chop leaves from 5 rosemary sprigs and stir into flour. Add yeast mixture and 1¼ cups water and stir until dough becomes too stiff to stir. Turn out dough onto a floured surface and knead until smooth. Shape dough into a ball, transfer to a large oiled bowl, and cover with a damp cloth. Allow dough to rise in a warm spot for 2 hours.

2 Transfer dough to a floured surface. Using your fingertips, press dough out to form a 12″ circle, then transfer to a baker's peel or inverted baking sheet dusted with cornmeal. Cover with a damp cloth and set aside for 1 hour.

3 Put a pizza stone in the oven and heat oven to 400°. Whisk together remaining 3 tbsp. oil and 1 tbsp. water in small bowl. Remove cloth from dough and dimple dough with your fingertips, then brush with oil-and-water emulsion. Arrange lemon slices and small sprigs of rosemary from remaining 3 branches over dough and sprinkle with salt. Slide dough onto pizza stone and bake until golden, about 30 minutes.

VARIATION Omit the lemons and rosemary and spread the shaped but uncooked focaccia with pesto and scatter with halved cherry tomatoes, thinly sliced red onion, and grated Parmigiano. Bake as directed. Just before serving, scatter with fresh basil leaves.

BRIOCHE À TÊTE

MAKES 12 ROLLS

The French name for this type of brioche means "brioche with a head" and refers to the confection's shape: a large sphere topped with a smaller one. Golden on the outside, with a feathery, rich-tasting interior, it's a perfect showcase for high-quality butter.

- ⅓ cup milk, heated to 105°–115°
- ¼ cup sugar
- 1 tsp. active dry yeast
- 5 eggs, at room temperature
- 4 cups flour
- 1 tsp. fine salt
- 1 cup unsalted butter, plus more
   for greasing, softened

1 Pour milk into a large bowl. Add a pinch of the sugar and the yeast. Let stand until foamy, about 10 minutes.

2 Whisk 4 eggs into the milk-yeast mixture and set aside. In the bowl of a stand mixer fitted with a paddle attachment, combine remaining sugar, flour, and salt. With mixer on low speed, add egg mixture and butter and mix until combined. Increase mixer speed to medium and beat, stopping to scrape the bowl down occasionally with a rubber spatula, until dough is satiny smooth and clings to the paddle, about 8 minutes.

3 Knead dough several times to bring it together, then transfer to a large buttered bowl, turning to coat. Cover bowl with plastic wrap and set in a warm place to let rise until doubled in size, 1½–2 hours. Punch dough down, cover, and let rise for another hour.

4 Generously butter 12 fluted 3″ brioche molds and put them on a baking sheet. Punch dough down again, transfer it to a floured surface, and divide into 12 portions. Firmly roll each portion of dough on the table in a circular motion with the palm of your hand to form a smooth ball.

5 Using the edge of your hand (holding it as you would if performing a karate chop), gently roll dough ball into a shape resembling that of a squat bowling pin, creating a small ball (the "head" of the brioche) that's roughly a third the size of the larger mass (the "body"). Lift the brioche by the head and place it body first into a buttered brioche mold. Press your fingers into the dough around the small ball to form an indentation, then gently push the small ball down into the center of the brioche. Repeat with remaining dough balls, cover with a towel, and let rise in a warm place for 1 hour.

6 Heat oven to 375°. Whisk the remaining egg in a small bowl. Brush the top of each brioche with egg and bake until deep golden brown, 25–30 minutes. Let cool in the molds for 10 minutes before serving. Brioches are best when eaten straight from the oven but, once cooled, may be stored in an airtight container or plastic bag at room temperature for up to 3 days.

CHALLAH

MAKES 1 LOAF

This slightly sweet, brioche-like braided egg bread is traditionally served at Shabbat meals and Jewish festival holidays. Leftovers make excellent French toast (page 480).

- ¾ cup plus 2 tbsp. milk, heated to 115°
- ¼ cup plus 1 tsp. sugar
- 2 tsp. active dry yeast
- 4 tbsp. unsalted butter, melted, plus more for greasing
- 2 eggs, lightly beaten
- 4 cups flour
- 1½ tsp. kosher salt
- 1 egg yolk
  Sesame seeds, for garnish

1 Stir together milk, 1 tsp. sugar, and yeast in a large bowl; let sit until foamy, about 10 minutes. Meanwhile, in a small bowl, whisk together butter and eggs. Add to yeast mixture and stir to combine. Add flour, remaining ¼ cup sugar, and salt and stir with a wooden spoon until a dough forms.

2 Transfer dough to a floured surface and knead until smooth, 6–8 minutes. Transfer to a lightly greased large bowl and cover with plastic wrap; let sit until doubled in size, about 1 hour. Punch dough down, cover, and let sit until slightly puffed, about 30 minutes.

3 Transfer dough to a floured surface, divide into 4 equal portions, and roll each into a 16"-long rope. Align dough ropes side by side, perpendicular to you, and pinch together ends farthest from you to form one end of loaf. Braid ropes and pinch ends together to seal (see How to Braid Challah & Pulla Breads, page 420). Transfer braided loaf to a parchment paper–lined baking sheet and cover loosely with plastic wrap; let rise for 1 hour.

4 Heat oven to 375°. Stir together egg yolk and 1 tbsp. water in a small bowl and brush all over surface of loaf; sprinkle evenly with sesame seeds. Bake until loaf is dark golden brown, 30–35 minutes. Transfer to a wire rack; let cool for 30 minutes before serving.

PULLA

Braided Cardamom Bread

MAKES 2 LOAVES

This Finnish cardamom-spiced sweet bread is usually served as a snack with coffee or tea.

- 1⅓ cups milk, heated to 115°
- ⅔ cup sugar
- 4 tsp. ground cardamom
- 1 tsp. active dry yeast
- 3 eggs, lightly beaten
- 6½ cups flour
- 1 tsp. kosher salt
- 5 tbsp. unsalted butter, cut into ½" cubes, softened, plus more for greasing
- 1 tbsp. heavy cream
- 1 egg yolk
  Crushed lump sugar, for garnish
  Sliced almonds, for garnish

1 In the bowl of a stand mixer fitted with a paddle attachment, stir together milk, sugar, 3 tsp. cardamom, and yeast; let sit until foamy, about 10 minutes. Add eggs and mix to combine. Add flour and salt; mix until a dough forms. Replace paddle with hook attachment and knead dough on medium speed for 2 minutes. While kneading, slowly add butter in batches, mixing until incorporated before adding next batch, 3–4 minutes; continue kneading for 4 minutes more after last of butter is added. Transfer dough to a greased bowl and cover with plastic wrap; let sit until doubled in size, about 1 hour. Punch dough down, cover, and let sit until fully risen, about 30 minutes.

2 Heat oven to 375°. Transfer dough to a floured surface and divide into 2 equal pieces. Set 1 piece aside and divide other piece into 3 equal portions. Roll each portion between your palms and work surface to create a 16" rope. Braid ropes together to form a loaf and pinch ends together to seal (see How to Braid Challah & Pulla Breads, page 420). Transfer loaf to a parchment paper–lined baking sheet. Repeat with second dough piece. Cover loaves with plastic wrap and let sit until slightly puffed up, about 20 minutes.

3 Whisk together remaining 1 tsp. cardamom, cream, and egg yolk in a small bowl; brush over loaves. Sprinkle with lump sugar and almonds; bake, 1 loaf at a time, until golden brown, 20–25 minutes. Transfer to a rack; let cool for 10 minutes before serving.

HOW TO BRAID CHALLAH & PULLA BREADS

Certain breads have doughs elastic enough to stand up to elaborate shaping and braiding, like the traditional Jewish egg bread Challah (page 419), or cardamom-scented Finnish Pulla (page 419). The three ropes of dough combine in the oven, but the surface of the loaf retains the beautiful visual rhythm of the braid.

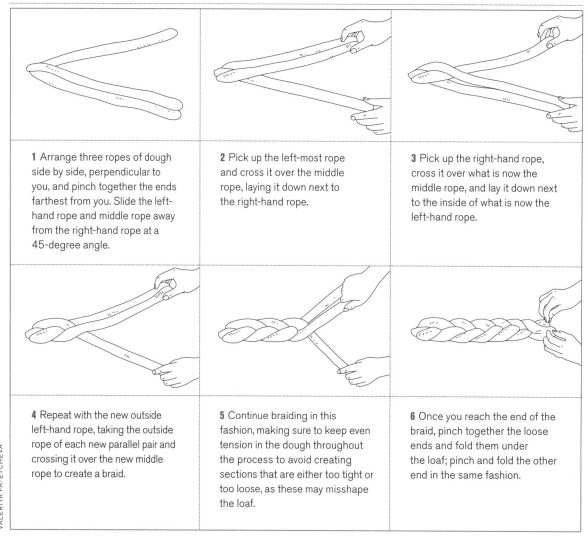

1 Arrange three ropes of dough side by side, perpendicular to you, and pinch together the ends farthest from you. Slide the left-hand rope and middle rope away from the right-hand rope at a 45-degree angle.

2 Pick up the left-most rope and cross it over the middle rope, laying it down next to the right-hand rope.

3 Pick up the right-hand rope, cross it over what is now the middle rope, and lay it down next to the inside of what is now the left-hand rope.

4 Repeat with the new outside left-hand rope, taking the outside rope of each new parallel pair and crossing it over the new middle rope to create a braid.

5 Continue braiding in this fashion, making sure to keep even tension in the dough throughout the process to avoid creating sections that are either too tight or too loose, as these may misshape the loaf.

6 Once you reach the end of the braid, pinch together the loose ends and fold them under the loaf; pinch and fold the other end in the same fashion.

VALERIYA FATEYCHEVA

CROATIAN WALNUT SWIRL BREAD

Povitica

SERVES 8–10

Sweet walnut paste is rolled into yeasted dough in this *babka*-like loaf that—with its uncountable layers—puts conventional cinnamon breads to shame. In Croatian, the name means "swaddled," referring to the rolled layers of buttery cinnamon. This recipe is adapted from Toni's Country Kitchen in Laurium, Michigan, a one-room diner famed for its fresh pastries and breads.

FOR THE DOUGH

- 1 tsp. active dry yeast
- 4 tbsp sugar
- ¾ cup milk, heated to 115°
- ½ tbsp. kosher salt
- 4 tbsp. unsalted butter, melted, plus more for greasing
- 1 egg
- 2½ cups flour

FOR THE FILLING

- 1 cup walnut halves, toasted
- ½ cup sugar
- 4 tbsp. unsalted butter
- 2 tbsp. milk
- 1 tsp. ground cinnamon
- 2 egg whites

1 Make the dough: Combine yeast, 1 tbsp. sugar, and half the milk in the bowl of a stand mixer fitted with a paddle attachment; let sit until foamy, about 10 minutes. Add remaining 3 tbsp. sugar and milk, plus salt, butter, and egg and stir to mix. With the motor running, slowly add flour; beat until smooth. Cover with plastic wrap; set in a warm place until doubled in size, about 1 hour.

2 Make the filling: Purée walnuts, sugar, butter, milk, and cinnamon in a food processor into a smooth paste. Beat egg whites until stiff peaks form; fold in walnut paste.

3 Grease a 9″×5″×2¾″ loaf pan with butter. On a floured surface, roll dough into a 10″×4″-long oval about 1⁄16″ thick. Spread dough with walnut mixture. Starting from one narrow end, roll dough into a tight cylinder. Trim ends and transfer to pan; set in a warm place until doubled in size, about 1 hour.

4 Heat oven to 350°. Bake until a toothpick inserted into middle comes out clean, about 1 hour. Let cool.

GRUYÈRE, ROSEMARY & HONEY MONKEY BREAD

SERVES 8–10

This indulgent pull-apart bread glazed with honey is the perfect savory-sweet combination. It makes a great addition to a brunch spread.

- 18 tbsp. unsalted butter, plus more for greasing
- 4 cups flour, plus more for dusting
- 1½ cups grated Gruyère cheese
- 1 tbsp. finely chopped fresh rosemary
- 2 tsp. kosher salt
- 1 tsp. freshly ground black pepper
- 1 cup milk
- ¼ cup sugar
- 2 tsp. active dry yeast
- 1 cup honey

1 Grease a 10″ Bundt pan with butter and dust with flour; set aside. Whisk flour, Gruyère, rosemary, salt, and pepper in a bowl; set aside. Heat 2 tbsp. butter with milk and ⅓ cup water in a 1-qt. saucepan over medium-high heat until an instant-read thermometer reads 115°. Transfer to the bowl of a stand mixer fitted with a hook attachment. Stir in sugar and yeast; let sit until foamy, about 10 minutes. With the motor running, slowly add dry ingredients and beat until dough is smooth. Transfer to a lightly greased bowl and cover loosely with plastic wrap; set in a warm place until doubled in size, about 1 hour.

2 Melt remaining 16 tbsp. butter in a 2-qt. saucepan; whisk in honey and set aside.

3 Heat oven to 350°. On a floured surface, pat dough out into an 8″ square about 1″ thick. Cut dough into 1″ pieces and fit snugly into prepared Bundt pan. Pour butter mixture evenly over dough; bake until golden and a toothpick inserted in the middle of the bread comes out clean, about 35 minutes. Let cool slightly before serving.

PÃO DE QUEIJO

Brazilian Cheese Bread

MAKES 16 ROLLS

If you can't find sour tapioca starch to make these classic Brazilian cheese bread bites, sweet tapioca starch will yield equally delicious results.

- 1 cup sour tapioca starch
- 1 cup grated Parmigiano-Reggiano
- ½ cup plus 2 tbsp. flour

> "The smell of good bread baking, like the sound of lightly flowing water, is indescribable in its evocation of innocence and delight."
>
> M. F. K. FISHER

1 tsp. kosher salt
½ tsp. active dry yeast
¾ cup milk
4 tbsp. unsalted butter, cubed
2 eggs

1 Heat oven to 350°. In a large bowl, whisk together tapioca starch, Parmigiano, flour, salt, and yeast. Heat milk and butter in a small saucepan over medium-high heat until butter melts. Pour mixture into dry ingredients along with 1 egg and stir until dough forms; cover and let sit for 30 minutes.

2 Using a tablespoon, portion out dough and roll each into a ball. Place on parchment paper–lined baking sheets, spaced 2″ apart; beat remaining egg in a small bowl and brush balls with egg. Bake until browned, 25–30 minutes.

ONION & POPPY SEED BIALYS

MAKES ABOUT 1½ DOZEN (SEE PHOTO, PAGE 439)

Soft and chewy cousins to the bagel, bialys are a stalwart of Polish bakeries, where their hole-less centers are filled with caramelized onions and poppy seeds.

1 tbsp. barley malt syrup or dark corn syrup
1 tsp. active dry yeast
1½ cups water, heated to 115°
5 cups flour
2 tsp. kosher salt, plus more to taste
2 tbsp. canola oil
4 cloves garlic, finely chopped
2 small yellow onions, finely chopped
1 tbsp. poppy seeds
Freshly ground black pepper, to taste

1 Make the dough: In the bowl of a stand mixer fitted with a dough hook, stir together syrup, yeast, and water; let sit until foamy, about 10 minutes. Add flour and salt and mix on low speed until dough forms; increase speed to medium and knead until smooth, about 8 minutes. Cover bowl with plastic wrap and let sit until doubled in size, about 1½ hours.

2 Meanwhile, make the filling: Heat oil in a 12″ skillet over medium-high heat. Add garlic and onions and cook, stirring occasionally, until deeply caramelized, about 30 minutes. Remove from heat and stir in poppy seeds and salt and pepper; set aside to cool.

3 Uncover and punch dough down; cover and let sit until doubled in size again, about 1 hour. Uncover dough and transfer to a clean work surface; portion and shape into about eighteen 2-oz. balls. Place 6 balls each on 3 parchment paper–lined baking sheets, spaced evenly apart; cover with plastic wrap and let sit until puffed, about 30 minutes. Uncover balls and, using the palm of your hand, gently flatten each into a disk; cover again and let sit until puffed, about 30 minutes.

4 Heat oven to 450°. Uncover balls and, using your fingers, press the center of each to indent; continue pressing and stretching center of each dough ball until you're left with a thin center membrane surrounded by a thick ring of dough on the outer edge. Fill the center of each dough round with about 1 tsp. onion-poppy seed filling. Working with 1 baking sheet at a time, place in oven and spray bialys with water until completely coated. Bake until lightly browned and still soft, about 16 minutes.

HOMEMADE BAGELS

MAKES 8

Briefly boiled before baking to get their characteristic thin, chewy crust, homemade bagels beat those from the grocery store every time.

1½ tsp. active dry yeast
3 tbsp. barley malt syrup or dark corn syrup
1½ cups water, heated to 80°
4 tsp. wheat gluten
4 cups flour, plus more for dusting
1 tbsp. kosher salt
3 tbsp. cornmeal

1 Mix together yeast, 2 tbsp. barley malt, and water in the bowl of a stand mixer fitted with a dough hook. Meanwhile, sift together gluten, flour, and salt into a bowl. Sift twice more, then add flour mixture, 1 cup at a time, to yeast mixture, beating at the lowest speed until all the flour has been added and the dough is rough looking and just barely holding together, about 4 minutes. Increase speed to medium-slow and continue mixing until dough forms a smooth, stiff ball, 8–10 minutes.

2 Put dough on a floured surface and cut into 8 equal pieces (about 4 oz. each), then roll into smooth balls. Cover with plastic wrap and set aside for 5 minutes.

3 Shape each ball into a thick, 11″-long rope. Form into bagels by overlapping the ends of each rope by about 1½″, dampening with a little water to hold the ends together. Then place on a cornmeal-dusted baking sheet, cover tightly with plastic wrap, and refrigerate for about 10 hours.

4 Put a baking stone on the center oven rack and heat oven to 450°. Remove dough rings from refrigerator. Bring a large pot of water to a boil over high heat. Add remaining 1 tbsp. barley malt, then drop rings, 3 or 4 at a time, into boiling water for 30 seconds. Turn over with a large skimmer and cook for another 30 seconds. Remove rings from water and drain, bottom side down, on a wire rack.

SECRETS OF BAGELRY

Getting the loftiness and chew of a bakery-quality bagel at home requires good ingredients and good technique. We found that the real secret to the dough is high-gluten flour. By mixing our own—sifting 1 tsp. wheat gluten, available at any good healthfood store, into each cup of flour—we got a better texture than by using bread flour.

Once the dough is made, be patient: Prepare the dough the night before and bake it in the morning; it's the slow, cold rise in the refrigerator that gives bagels the right texture and color. Don't let the boiling turn you off; it's a 1-minute sealing step that keeps bagels from blowing up.

5 Slide boiled rings onto the baking stone in the oven and bake until deep golden brown and crisp, about 14 minutes. Cool on a wire rack. Serve warm or at room temperature.

GERMAN PRETZELS

Laugenbrezel

MAKES 2 LARGE PRETZELS

These giant pretzels from the Hofbräuhaus beer hall in Munich have a similar chew to bagels, but a tangier outer crust, thanks to the inclusion of baking soda in the water with which they are brushed. Instead of the more common mustard, they're served with soft butter.

- 1½ tbsp. barley malt syrup or dark corn syrup
- 1 tsp. active dry yeast
- 1½ cups water, heated to 115°
- 3 tbsp. unsalted butter, softened, plus more for serving
- 4 cups flour
- ¼ tsp. kosher salt
- 2 tbsp. baking soda
  Coarse salt, for sprinkling
  Butter, for serving

1 Put a baking stone on the center oven rack and heat oven to 500°. Stir together syrup, yeast, and water in a large bowl; let sit until foamy, about 10 minutes. Add butter, flour, and salt, and stir until dough forms.

2 Transfer to a floured surface and knead until smooth and elastic, about 8 minutes. Halve dough and, working with one piece at a time, roll dough into a 4′ rope about 1″ thick. Transfer rope to the bottom edge of a sheet of parchment paper and, keeping the center of the rope on the paper, pick up both ends, cross one end over the other, about 2″ from the ends, and twist; attach each end to the sides of the pretzel. Repeat with remaining dough and set aside to rest for 20 minutes.

3 Bring baking soda and 1 cup water to a simmer in a 2-qt. saucepan over medium-high heat, stirring constantly until baking soda dissolves. Brush each pretzel generously with the baking soda solution and sprinkle with coarse salt. Using a sharp paring knife, make a 6″ slash about ¼″ deep across the bottom edge of the pretzel. Slide 1 pretzel on parchment paper onto the stone and bake until dark brown, about 15 minutes. Repeat with remaining pretzel. Let cool for about 10 minutes, then serve warm with butter.

Quick Breads

POPOVERS

MAKES 8

Don't open the door to check on these light, airy popovers until about 5 minutes before they're finished baking, or they will deflate.

- 1 cup flour
- ½ tsp. kosher salt
- 2 eggs
- 1¼ cups milk
- 1 tbsp. unsalted butter, melted, plus more for greasing

1 Heat oven to 425°. Sift together flour and salt into a bowl. Whisk together eggs, milk, and butter in a separate bowl. Add to flour, stirring with a wooden spoon until combined (some lumps may remain).

2 Butter an 8-mold popover tin or 8 standard muffin-pan wells. Pour batter into prepared molds, filling two-thirds to three-fourths full. Bake for 15 minutes, reduce heat to 350°, then continue baking until puffed and browned, about 20 minutes more.

3 Unmold, pierce sides of popovers with a toothpick to allow steam to escape, and serve immediately.

PINT-GLASS BREAD

MAKES ONE 7½″ ROUND LOAF

Peter Ward, founder of the Country Choice grocery in County Tipperary, Ireland, devised this simple recipe—all of the ingredients of which can be measured out with a pint glass—for his son Jeff, who was off at college. If you use the same means to measure the ingredients, note that the vessel in question is a 20-ounce imperial pint glass.

- 1 pint glass (2½ cups) all-purpose flour
- 1 pint glass (2½ cups) stone-ground whole wheat flour
  Enough baking soda to coat the bottom of a pint glass (¾ tsp.)
  Enough salt to coat the bottom of a pint glass (¾ tsp.)
  Enough butter to coat the bottom of a pint glass (1 tbsp.)
- ¾ pint glass (1¾ cups) buttermilk

1 Heat oven to 375°. Sprinkle 1 tsp. of the all-purpose flour over the center of a baking sheet and set aside. Put 2 tsp. of the all-purpose flour into a small bowl and set aside. Meanwhile, put remaining all-purpose flour, whole wheat flour, baking soda, and salt into a large bowl and mix well with your hands. Add butter, breaking it up into small pieces with your fingers, and mix until combined. Make a well in the center of the flour mixture and add buttermilk. Slowly incorporate buttermilk into flour mixture with your hands until a rough ball forms, then turn out onto a floured surface and form into a neat ball (without kneading).

2 Transfer dough to center of baking sheet and press gently to form a 7½″-wide round. Using a sharp knife, slash a cross ½″ deep across the entire top of the loaf and dust top of loaf with the reserved flour. Bake until bread is light golden and sounds hollow when tapped on the bottom, about 70 minutes. Wrap bread in a clean kitchen towel, prop against a windowsill, and allow to cool for about 2 hours.

A LESSON IN PRACTICAL BAKING

When Jeff Ward went off to study commerce at University College in Dublin, he missed something about home right away: good bread. "I can't eat the parbaked rolls they serve here," he told his parents, Peter and Mary Ward, who run Country Choice, a market and café in the Tipperary town of Nenagh, Ireland. "I'll starve." Peter suggested that he bake his own bread. But Jeff had no experience and few utensils in his student-housing kitchen. "I knew that every Irish student has a pint glass that he's brought home from a pub," says Peter, "so I invented a recipe for the simplest bread in the world, one whose ingredients he could measure out with a pint glass. And I told him he could mix it in the wash basin if he didn't have a bowl. He didn't starve after all."

Preceding page: Bacon-Wrapped Stuffed Pork Loin (page 237); this page, clockwise from top left: Choy Sum with Garlic Sauce (page 318); Peppers Stuffed with Feta (page 35); Leeks Vinaigrette (page 320); Roasted Tomatoes (page 323); facing page: Stuffed Cucumber Kimchi (page 312).

Facing page: Rhode Island Clam Chowder (page 117); this page: Lebanese-Style Green Beans with Chickpeas (page 317); following spread: Roasted Vidalia Onions with Herbed Bread Crumbs (page 323).

Facing page: Spaghetti alla Primavera (page 346); this page: Butternut Squash Ravioli (page 370) with Oregano-Hazelnut Pesto (page 356); following page: Sweet Potato Casserole with Pecan Crumble (page 332).

Preceding page: Rösti (page 405); this page: Ham, Cheese, Egg & Lemon Sandwich (page 123); facing page: Eggs Hussarde (page 171).

Facing page: Churros (page 486); this page; clockwise from top left: Rolls with Cracklings & Prune Jam (page 482); Onion & Poppy Seed Bialys (page 422); Hot Cross Buns (page 482); Chapati (page 459).

Facing page: Painkiller Cocktail (page 545); this page: Nutmeg Ice Cream (page 526); following page: Rhubarb Upside-Down Cake (page 494).

Preceding page: Pineapple Upside-Down Cake (page 493); facing page: Dark Chocolate Matzo Brittle (page 509); this page: Flourless Chocolate Soufflé (page 533); following page: Baked Ricotta with Orange Blossom Cherry Sauce (page 530).

Preceding page: Blueberry Slump (page 522); this page, clockwise from top left: Hungarian Sour Cherry Cake (page 498); Very Moist Chocolate Layer Cake (page 497); Brennan's Bananas Foster (page 525), Chocolate Mousse (page 530).

THE RISE OF SODA BREAD

Although ancestors of the Irish had likely been baking unleavened breads as early as 4000 B.C., the first record of risen breads dates from the seventh century. Back then, barm (yeast from fermenting malt) and sourdough were common leaveners, but Ireland's wheat, with its unpredictable gluten content, didn't always respond fully to them. It wasn't until 1790, when French chemist Nicolas Leblanc discovered an easy, inexpensive way to make sodium carbonate—essential in the production of baking soda—that people were given a more reliable option. When combined with an acidic liquid (like buttermilk), baking soda—which was convenient, cheap, and easy to store—created gases that caused dough to rise. Not only that; it also reacted well with Ireland's wheat. The Irish soon began using baking soda in their doughs—and from then on, any bread made with baking soda and sour milk or buttermilk became known as soda bread.

By the mid-1800s, soda bread had become an Irish staple. The dough was typically scored with an X—some said it symbolized the cross; others insisted it was "to let the devil out"—then baked in the hearth, either on a griddle or in a pot oven, a covered iron pot topped with smoldering turf. Slices of the resulting loaf were fried and served with soft-boiled eggs for breakfast, used to sop up gravy at midday dinner, and slathered with butter and jam for evening tea.

While store-bought soda bread is popular in Ireland today, many families still have a favorite recipe. Some use currants, raisins, or caraway seeds; others prefer whole wheat to white flour; some say "Never knead"; others claim quick kneading is the secret to their loaf's success.

IRISH SODA BREAD

MAKES 1 LOAF

It seems every Irish family has its own recipe for soda bread, a dense loaf that became popular in the 1800s and remains ubiquitous today. Some versions incorporate little more than flour, baking soda, and buttermilk, while others add various fruits and spices—ours is lightly sweetened and studded with raisins.

- 4 cups flour, plus more for dusting
- 2 tbsp. sugar
- 1 tsp. kosher salt
- 1 tsp. baking soda
- 4 tbsp. unsalted butter, plus more for greasing
- 1 cup raisins
- 1 egg, lightly beaten
- 2 cups buttermilk

1 Heat oven to 425°. Sift together flour, sugar, salt, and baking soda into a large mixing bowl. Using a pastry cutter or 2 knives, work butter into flour mixture until it resembles coarse meal, then stir in raisins.

2 Make a well in the center of the flour mixture. Add egg and buttermilk to well and mix in with a wooden spoon until dough is too stiff to stir. Dust hands with a little flour, then gently knead dough in the bowl just long enough to form a rough ball. Transfer dough to a floured surface and shape into a round loaf.

3 Transfer dough to a large, lightly greased cast-iron skillet or a baking sheet. Using a serrated knife, score top of dough about ½" deep in an X shape. Transfer to oven and bake until bread is golden and bottom sounds hollow when tapped with a knife, about 40 minutes. Transfer bread to a rack to let cool briefly. Serve bread warm, at room temperature, or sliced and toasted.

STRAWBERRY BREAD

MAKES 2 LOAVES

SAVEUR test kitchen director Farideh Sadeghin grew up making this fruit-filled quick bread with her mother, Teresa. While the recipe calls for strawberries, just about any seasonal fruit works.

-   Unsalted butter, for greasing
- 3 cups flour, plus more for dusting
- 1 tsp. baking powder
- 1 tsp. ground cinnamon
- ½ tsp. kosher salt
- 2 cups sugar
- 1¼ cups canola oil
- 4 eggs
- 4 cups roughly chopped fresh strawberries

1 Heat oven to 350°. Grease two 9″×5″×2¾″ loaf pans with butter and dust with flour; set aside. Whisk together flour, baking powder, cinnamon, and salt in a large bowl; set aside.

2 In a separate bowl, whisk together sugar, oil, and eggs. Pour wet ingredients over dry ingredients and whisk until just combined. Stir in strawberries and pour batter into prepared pans. Bake until loaf is golden brown and a toothpick inserted in the middle of the loaves comes out clean, about 1 hour. Let cool for 30 minutes before unmolding, slicing, and serving.

MANGO BREAD
MAKES 1 LOAF

Mango's tanginess pairs well with warm spices and rich coconut in this dense, sweet loaf, a recipe from writer Victoria Pesce Elliott's mother. Substitute dates for mango when they aren't available.

- ⅓ cup vegetable oil, plus more for greasing
- 1½ cups flour, plus more for dusting
- ¾ tsp. baking soda
- 1 tsp. cinnamon
- ½ tsp. freshly grated nutmeg
- ½ tsp. kosher salt
- 1 cup sugar
- 2 eggs plus 1 yolk
- ½ cup mango purée
- ½ tsp. vanilla extract
- 1 large very ripe mango, peeled, pitted, and cut into ¼″ dice (about 2 cups)
- ½ cup chopped walnuts
- ½ cup shredded unsweetened coconut

1 Heat oven to 350°. Grease a 9″×5″×2¾″ loaf pan with oil and dust with flour; set aside.

2 Whisk together flour, baking soda, cinnamon, nutmeg, and salt in a bowl, then make a well in center. Whisk together oil, sugar, eggs and yolk, mango purée, and vanilla in a bowl; add to well and stir. Fold in diced mango, nuts, and coconut, then pour into prepared pan. Bake until a toothpick inserted into middle of bread comes out clean, about 1 hour and 20 minutes.

SOUTHERN CORNBREAD
SERVES 8–10

In some parts of the South, cooks prefer cornbread that's slightly sweet, like this recipe, to counterbalance the salty, smoky flavors of vegetables stewed with pork.

- ⅓ cup butter, melted, plus more for greasing
- 1 cup flour, plus more for dusting
- 1 cup yellow cornmeal
- ¼ cup sugar
- 4 tsp. baking powder
- 1 tsp. kosher salt
- 1 cup buttermilk
- 1 egg, lightly beaten

1 Heat oven to 425°. Grease and flour an 8″ square baking pan; set aside.

2 Whisk together flour, cornmeal, sugar, baking powder, and salt in a large bowl. Add butter, buttermilk, and egg and whisk until smooth. Pour into prepared pan and smooth top. Bake until golden brown and a toothpick inserted into middle of bread comes out clean, about 25 minutes.

JALAPEÑO CORNBREAD
SERVES 10

This skillet-cooked cornbread has a toothsome bite thanks to the addition of whole corn kernels and sliced pickled jalapeños.

- 2 cups yellow cornmeal
- 2 cups flour
- 1½ tbsp. sugar
- 1 tbsp. plus 1 tsp. baking powder
- 2½ tsp. salt
- 2 cups milk
- ½ cup corn oil
- 2 eggs, beaten
- ¾ cup fresh or frozen corn kernels
- ¾ cup sliced pickled jalapeños
- 2 tbsp. unsalted butter

1 Heat oven to 425°. Whisk together cornmeal, flour, sugar, baking powder, and salt in a large bowl. Whisk in milk, oil, and eggs. Using a rubber spatula, fold in corn and jalapeños; set batter aside.

2 Heat a 12″ cast-iron skillet over medium-high; grease with butter. Pour in batter; transfer skillet to oven and bake until bread is golden brown and a toothpick inserted into middle of bread comes out clean, about 35 minutes.

Biscuits, Scones, Rolls & Buns

LOLA MAE'S BUTTERMILK BISCUITS

MAKES 12 BISCUITS

Lola Mae Autry, a cook from Whippoorwill Valley in Hickory Flat, Mississippi, recommends rolling out these simple buttermilk biscuits a little thinner than is typical, for a better ratio of crusty exterior to pillowy interior. For the softest biscuits, don't overwork the dough.

- 3 cups unsifted self-rising flour
- 6 tbsp. vegetable shortening
- 1½ cups buttermilk

1 Heat oven to 425°. Put flour in a large bowl. Use a pastry cutter to work shortening into flour until mixture resembles coarse meal. Add buttermilk and stir with a wooden spoon until mixture just holds together.

2 Gather dough into a rough ball, then turn out onto a floured surface. Dust hands with flour and gently knead dough 4–5 times. Roll dough out into a 12″–13″ circle about ½″ thick, dusting rolling pin and dough with just enough flour to keep dough from sticking. Cut out 12 biscuits with a cookie cutter or the rim of a juice glass and place in a well-seasoned 12″ cast-iron skillet. Biscuits will fit snugly.

3 Bake until biscuits are just beginning to color, about 15 minutes, then turn heat to broil and bake until tops are lightly browned, 1–2 minutes longer.

BAKING-POWDER BISCUITS

MAKES ABOUT 6 BISCUITS

One of the pillars of the Southern table, buttery biscuits raised to lofty heights with baking powder are served at virtually every meal. At breakfast, we like them best smothered in a sausage-studded white Sawmill Gravy (page 196), with a dash or two of hot sauce.

- 2½ cups flour
- 3½ tsp. baking powder
- 1½ tsp. kosher salt
- ½ cup unsalted butter, cubed and chilled, plus 2 tbsp. melted
- 1½ cups buttermilk

1 Heat oven to 425°. Combine flour, baking powder, and salt in a large bowl and whisk to blend. Add butter and, using your fingers, rub mixture together until pea-size crumbles form. Add buttermilk and stir with a fork until just combined.

2 Transfer to a floured surface and gently pat dough into a 6″×4″ rectangle about 1″ thick. Dip a 3″ round cutter into a bowl of flour and cut out rounds of dough. Press scraps together and repeat with remaining dough until you have about 6 rounds.

3 Brush a 9″ round cake pan with melted butter, arrange biscuits in pan, and brush the tops with butter. Bake until golden brown, about 25 minutes.

EDNA LEWIS' HOMEMADE BAKING POWDER

Edna Lewis, the great pillar of traditional Southern cooking, started making her homemade baking powder after becoming bothered by the chemical additives and tinny aftertaste of store-bought. The difference was subtle but important—a cleaner flavor and a slightly better rise. Here is her formula:

To make ½ cup baking powder, sift ¼ cup cream of tartar, 2 tbsp. baking soda, and 1 tbsp. cornstarch together 3 times. Transfer to a clean, tight-sealing jar. Store at room temperature, away from sunlight, for up to 6 weeks.

> ## "Blues is to jazz what yeast is to bread—without it, it's flat."
>
> CARMEN McRAE

HONEY & HERB BISCUITS

MAKES ABOUT 2 DOZEN BISCUITS

These fluffy biscuits, fragrant with rosemary and thyme, are an elevated alternative to plain dinner rolls.

7½	cups flour
¼	cup finely chopped fresh rosemary
3	tbsp. baking powder
2	tsp. finely chopped fresh thyme
2	tsp. kosher salt
1	tsp. baking soda
1	tsp. freshly ground black pepper
¾	cup unsalted butter, cut into ½" cubes and chilled
2	cups buttermilk
¾	cup half-and-half
¼	cup honey

1 Heat oven to 375°. Whisk together flour, rosemary, baking powder, thyme, salt, baking soda, and pepper in a large bowl. Add butter and, using your fingers, rub butter into flour mixture until pea-size crumbles form.

2 In a medium bowl, whisk together buttermilk, half-and-half, and honey; add to dry ingredients and stir together with a fork until just combined. Transfer dough to a well-floured surface, and pat into a 1"-thick disk. Using a 3" round cutter, cut out biscuits and transfer to a parchment paper–lined baking sheet, arranging them so their edges touch. Reroll scraps and cut out more biscuits until all dough is used. Bake until golden brown, about 35 minutes.

SULTANA SCONES

MAKES 20 SCONES

The main difference between scones and biscuits is the inclusion of an egg in the dough—plus, of course, the matter of provenance. Biscuits are a decidedly American bread, while scones are the anchor of British tea, served with butter or clotted cream and often incorporating sweet or savory ingredients—like the sultanas (golden raisins) here.

6¼	cups flour
½	cup sugar
2	tsp. baking powder
1	cup (2 sticks) unsalted butter, cut into pieces, plus more for serving
¾	cup golden raisins
1¾	cups milk
1	egg
	Marmalade or jam, for serving

1 Heat oven to 400°. Line 2 baking sheets with parchment paper and set aside. Whisk together flour, sugar, and baking powder in a large bowl. Using a pastry cutter or 2 table knives, cut butter into flour mixture until it resembles coarse meal flecked with pea-size pieces of butter. Stir in sultanas. Add milk and stir until dough just comes together.

2 Turn dough out onto a floured surface. Dust hands with flour and gently knead with the heels of your hands several times until dough forms a rough ball. (Do not over-knead dough, or scones will be tough.)

3 Divide dough into 20 equal pieces, gently shape each into a round, and arrange on prepared baking sheets 1"–2" apart. Beat egg and 1 tsp. water together in a small bowl. Using a pastry brush, brush tops of dough rounds with egg wash.

4 Bake scones until golden brown, 30–35 minutes. Set aside to cool on wire racks for 5–10 minutes. Serve warm with butter and marmalade or jam.

CRUMPETS

MAKES 1 DOZEN CRUMPETS

The addition of baking soda helps to create the classic "nooks and crannies" in these light and fluffy English muffins, which are fried in a shallow ring on a griddle.

3¼	cups flour
1	tsp. kosher salt
½	tsp. baking soda
2	cups milk (1 cup heated to 115°, 1 cup room temperature)

2 tbsp. sugar
1 tsp. active dry yeast
  Unsalted butter, for greasing and serving
  Jam, for serving

1 Whisk together flour, salt, and baking soda in a bowl. Combine heated milk, sugar, and yeast in the bowl of a stand mixer fitted with a paddle attachment; let sit until foamy, about 10 minutes. With the motor running, slowly add dry ingredients, then remaining milk until a smooth dough forms. Cover dough loosely with plastic wrap and set in a warm place until doubled in size, about 1 hour.

2 Heat a 12″ cast-iron skillet over medium heat; place a greased 4″ ring mold on pan. Fill ring with ⅓ cup batter. Cook until bubbles appear on the surface, about 6 minutes. Carefully remove the ring and flip crumpet over; cook until crumpet is golden and cooked through, about 5 minutes. Repeat with remaining batter, greasing ring mold each time. Serve with butter and jam.

HUSH PUPPIES
MAKES ABOUT 30 FRITTERS

These crisp-fried, cayenne-spiced cornmeal balls are traditionally served alongside fried fish and tartar sauce throughout the South.

1½ cups flour
1½ cups cornmeal
2 tbsp. baking powder
2 tbsp. sugar
1 tbsp. baking soda
2 tsp. kosher salt
½ tsp. cayenne pepper
1¼ cups buttermilk
2 eggs
1 large yellow onion, grated
  Canola oil, for frying
  Tartar Sauce (page 591, or store-bought), for serving

1 Whisk together flour, cornmeal, baking powder, sugar, baking soda, salt, and cayenne in a large bowl. Stir together buttermilk, eggs, and grated onion with its juice in a medium bowl. Pour over dry ingredients and stir together until just combined. Set aside to rest for 1 hour.

2 Pour oil to a depth of 2″ into a 6-qt. Dutch oven and heat over medium-high until a deep-fry thermometer reads 350°.

Using a tablespoon, drop small rounds of batter into the oil, making sure to not crowd the pan. Cook, stirring occasionally and flipping halfway through, until golden on the outside and crisp, 3–4 minutes. Remove hush puppies from oil and drain on paper towels. Serve with tartar sauce on the side for dipping.

THREE TYPES OF TEA

British teatime, our favorite setting for eating scones and crumpets, can take many forms. Here are the three principal types of tea.

AFTERNOON TEA Not until the 1840s, when the seventh duchess of Bedford complained that a "sinking feeling" would strike her between lunch and dinner, was the custom of taking afternoon tea established. At first, the meal consisted simply of tea and light cakes, but soon bread and butter were added. Today, afternoon tea may also include dainty sandwiches, scones with jam and clotted cream, and petits fours. Afternoon tea is the fanciest and most elaborate of them all, the one you dress up for and enjoy at Fortnum & Mason or at a posh London hotel like the Ritz.

CREAM TEA Also known as Devonshire tea, this mid- to late-afternoon fortifier, comprising scones, clotted cream, and preserves, is the specialty of the southwest of England, notably Devon and Cornwall, where the high butterfat content of the milk of Channel Islands cows (Guernseys and Jerseys) enables the cream to clot. Cream tea was once served in the fields and on the farms to tide the laborers over until the evening meal, but nowadays it is eaten at home or in village tearooms.

HIGH TEA Contrary to what its name may imply, high tea is neither exalted nor, strictly speaking, a tea; it's a working-class supper, eaten at around five or six in the evening, that could as likely be accompanied by mugs of tea made with strong tea in bags as by the more ceremonial service. The term *high* is thought to refer to the fact that this tea was originally taken at the "high" dining table rather than at a lower table in the parlor, where one would take afternoon tea.

> "Bread is the king of the table, and all else is merely the court that surrounds the king. The countries are the soup, the meat, the vegetables, the salad ... but bread is king."
>
> LOUIS BROMFIELD

GEORGENE'S FLUFFY ROLLS

MAKES ABOUT 2½ DOZEN ROLLS

These light and buttery rolls are named for Georgene Hall, a cook near Memphis, Tennessee, who perfected them in the early 1950s.

1¼	cups milk
¼	cup vegetable shortening
¾	cup sugar
1	tsp. kosher salt
1	tsp. active dry yeast
¼	cup tap water, heated to 115°
2	eggs, lightly beaten
4	cups flour
¾	cup butter, melted

1 Combine milk, shortening, sugar, and salt in a saucepan over medium heat and cook, stirring, until sugar dissolves. Remove from heat; set aside to cool. Meanwhile, dissolve yeast in water in a large bowl; set aside until foamy, about 10 minutes.

2 Pour milk mixture into yeast. Stir in eggs and gradually add flour. Stir with a wooden spoon until dough gets stiff, then use your hands (dough will be sticky, so grease your hands with a little butter). Brush a small amount of butter on the inside of a large bowl and on one side of a sheet of wax paper. Place dough in bowl, cover with buttered wax paper, and lay a damp cloth on top. Set aside to rise until doubled in size, at least 3 hours.

3 Turn out dough onto a floured surface. Knead until elastic, then roll out to ½" thickness. Cut dough with a 3" biscuit cutter, dip each round into melted butter, and fold in half. Line up, round edges up and sides touching, on a baking sheet. Cover as in step 2 and set aside to rise, at least 2½ hours.

4 Heat oven to 350°. Bake until rolls are golden, about 15 minutes. Serve warm.

TOM COLICCHIO'S PARKER HOUSE ROLLS

MAKES 14 ROLLS

Chef Tom Colicchio's fluffy, buttery dinner rolls, served at his New York City restaurant Colicchio & Sons, may be the best we've ever eaten. The secret? Barley malt syrup, a molasses-thick liquid sweetener that adds a hint of malty flavor.

¾	cup milk, heated to 115°
1	tsp. active dry yeast
1	tsp. barley malt syrup or dark corn syrup
2	cups flour
1½	tsp. kosher salt
2½	tbsp. unsalted butter, cut into ½" cubes, softened
¼	cup Clarified Butter (page 595), for greasing and brushing
	Fleur de sel or other flaky sea salt, for garnish

1 Stir together milk, yeast, and syrup in a large bowl; let sit until foamy, 10 minutes. In a medium bowl, whisk together flour and salt; add to milk mixture along with butter and stir with a wooden spoon until a dough forms. Transfer to a floured surface and knead until smooth, 5–6 minutes. Transfer dough to a lightly greased bowl and cover with plastic wrap; let sit until nearly doubled in size, about 1 hour. Punch dough down, cover, and let sit until puffed, about 45 minutes.

2 Heat oven to 325°. Portion dough into fourteen 1½"-diameter balls and transfer to a greased 8" cast-iron skillet or 8"×8" baking pan, nestling them side by side; cover loosely with plastic wrap and let sit until doubled in size, about 2 hours. Brush with clarified butter and bake until puffed and pale golden brown, 20–22 minutes. Transfer to a rack and brush with more clarified butter; sprinkle each roll with a small pinch of fleur de sel and serve warm.

PAN DE SAL

Sweet Filipino-Style Bread Rolls

MAKES 20 ROLLS

The dough for these classic Filipino rolls—which, despite their name (*pan de sal* means "salt bread" in Spanish), are sweet rather than salty—is rolled to achieve a pillow-soft texture and then dusted with bread crumbs prior to baking.

- 6 cups bread flour
- 1 cup, plus 1 tbsp. sugar
- 1½ tsp. kosher salt
- 2½ cups milk, heated to 115°
- 1 tbsp. active dry yeast
- 4 tbsp. unsalted butter, melted, plus more for greasing
- 1 egg
- 1 cup dried bread crumbs

1 Whisk flour, 1 cup sugar, and salt in a bowl. Stir together 1 tbsp. sugar, 1 cup milk, and yeast in another bowl; let sit until foamy, about 10 minutes. Add remaining milk, plus melted butter and egg; whisk until smooth. Slowly stir in dry ingredients until dough comes together. Turn out dough onto a floured surface and knead until smooth, about 3 minutes. Transfer to a lightly greased bowl and cover loosely with plastic wrap; set in a warm place until doubled in size, about 1 hour.

2 Place bread crumbs on a plate. On a floured surface, divide dough into 4 equal pieces. Working with 1 piece at a time, pat dough into a 4″×9″ rectangle about ½″ thick.

SHAPING PAN DE SAL

To achieve the airy structure of Pan de Sal (this page), a sweet Filipino-style bread, the key is not to overwork the dough. Once the dough comes together, gently flatten it with your fingers on a lightly floured surface and then roll it to create a series of layers that expand in the oven, yielding a wonderfully light crumb.

1 On a lightly floured surface, divide dough into 4 equal pieces. Working with 1 piece at a time, pat dough into a 4″x 9″ rectangle about ½″ thick.

2 Working from one long end, roll up the dough evenly to form a tight, uniform cylinder.

3 Use a sharp knife to cut the cylinder of dough crosswise into 5 rolls about 1½″ wide.

4 Handling the dough with care, coat the sticky, cut sides of each roll with bread crumbs. Place rolls cut side up on a parchment-lined baking sheet about 2″ apart, and proof in a warm place until doubled in size, about 1 hour.

VALERIYA FATEYCHEVA

Working from one long end, roll dough into a tight cylinder. Cut dough crosswise into five 1½″ rolls. Gently coat cut sides of rolls in bread crumbs; place cut side up on parchment paper–lined baking sheets, spaced about 2″ apart. Cover loosely with plastic wrap; set in a warm place until doubled in size, about 1 hour.

3 Heat oven to 350°. Bake rolls until golden, 15–20 minutes.

DONEGAL OATCAKES
SERVES 4

These hearty and filling Irish cakes are a great alternative to biscuits. They're best slathered with butter or jam.

- 1½ cups stone-ground oatmeal, preferably Macroom's
- ¾ cup boiling water
- 2 tbsp. unsalted butter or lard
- ½ tsp. kosher salt
  Flour, for dusting
  Unsalted butter and jam, for serving (optional)

1 Place oatmeal in a mixing bowl; set aside. Stir water, butter, and salt in another bowl until butter is dissolved; pour over oatmeal and stir until dough forms. If necessary, add more boiling water. Gently knead until dough is pliable. Transfer dough to a lightly floured surface. Press a sheet of parchment paper over dough and, using a rolling pin, roll dough into a ½″-thick rectangle; let sit 1 hour to dry slightly.

2 Heat oven to 250°F. Using a 3″ round cutter, cut out cakes; gather and reuse scraps. Transfer cakes to a baking sheet; bake, flipping once, until golden and slightly crisp, 2–2½ hours. The more slowly the oatcakes cook, the better the flavor will be. Let cool slightly; serve with butter and jam, if you like. Store in an airtight container at room temperature for up to 1 week.

CHEDDAR CHEESE BISCUITS
MAKES ABOUT 40 BISCUITS

Fourth-generation cheese maker Sid Cook, of "Wisconsin's Carr Valley Cheese," explained to us that the best cheese biscuits are made with extra-sharp cheddar—the older the better, as the flavor intensifies as it ages—so the cheese holds its own against the rich butter and cream.

- 3 cups flour
- 1½ tbsp. baking powder
- 1 tbsp. sugar
- 2¼ tsp. salt
- 2½ cups heavy cream
- 1 cup grated aged extra-sharp cheddar
- 3 tbsp. butter

1 Heat oven to 375°. Whisk together flour, baking powder, sugar, and salt in a large bowl. Add cream and cheddar and stir gently with a wooden spoon, mixing just until dough holds together.

2 Turn out dough onto a floured work surface. Knead once or twice, just enough to incorporate cream and cheddar into flour mixture. (Handle dough as little as possible, or biscuits will not rise.)

3 Roll out dough about 1″ thick on a floured work surface. Cut with a 1¾″ round biscuit cutter or a thin-edged glass (a champagne flute works well). Place biscuits about 2″ apart on ungreased baking sheets, then set aside for 10 minutes for dough to rest. (This produces taller, lighter biscuits.)

4 Melt butter in a small skillet over low heat, then cool slightly. Brush biscuit tops with butter. Bake until golden brown, about 20 minutes.

Flatbreads, Crêpes & Crackers

FLOUR TORTILLAS

MAKES 16 SIX-INCH OR 8 TWELVE-INCH TORTILLAS

When making tortillas at home, remember that they will shrink a bit when cooked.

- 4 cups flour
- 1½ tsp. kosher salt
- 1 tsp. baking powder
- 4 tbsp. lard

1 Put flour, salt, and baking powder into a bowl and mix well. Work lard into flour mixture with your fingers until it resembles coarse meal. Add 1½ cups warm water and stir until a soft dough forms. Turn dough out onto a floured surface and knead 15–20 times. Cover and set aside for 10 minutes.

2 To make 6″ tortillas, divide dough into 16 equal balls and roll out on a floured surface into 7″ circles; to make 12″ tortillas, divide dough into 8 equal balls and roll out into 13″ circles. (Tortillas will shrink when cooked.)

3 Heat a large dry cast-iron skillet over medium heat until hot. Cook tortillas, one at a time, until blistered and charred in spots, 1½–2 minutes per side. Wrap in a clean dish towel to keep warm.

HOW TO MAKE CORN TORTILLAS

Tortillas are one of the most elemental of foods; it's hard to imagine Mexican cuisine without them. Making supple homemade tortillas is easier than you might think— the only special equipment you need is a tortilla press, available at most cooking supply shops or online. The results are incomparable.

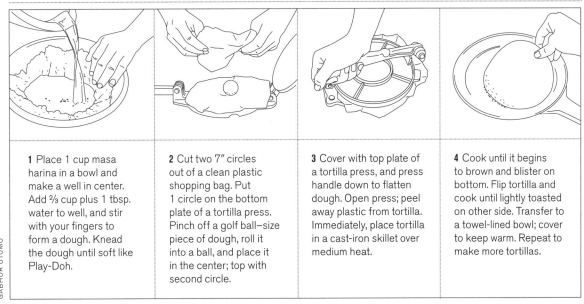

1 Place 1 cup masa harina in a bowl and make a well in center. Add ⅔ cup plus 1 tbsp. water to well, and stir with your fingers to form a dough. Knead the dough until soft like Play-Doh.

2 Cut two 7″ circles out of a clean plastic shopping bag. Put 1 circle on the bottom plate of a tortilla press. Pinch off a golf ball–size piece of dough, roll it into a ball, and place it in the center; top with second circle.

3 Cover with top plate of a tortilla press, and press handle down to flatten dough. Open press; peel away plastic from tortilla. Immediately, place tortilla in a cast-iron skillet over medium heat.

4 Cook until it begins to brown and blister on bottom. Flip tortilla and cook until lightly toasted on other side. Transfer to a towel-lined bowl; cover to keep warm. Repeat to make more tortillas.

GABHOR UTOMO

THE ESSENTIAL TORTILLA

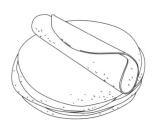

"Tortillas are Mexico's most cherished food. I like to think it was a huge moment when Mesoamericans figured out how to unlock corn's nutrients through nixtamalization, the soaking of the grain in a slaked lime solution that makes the corn more digestible and easier to grind into the substance called masa, the base for corn tortillas. Of course, tortillas are different everywhere. There are wheat-flour tortillas, beloved in the north, and thicker tortillas in the Yucatán that are made, often by hand, from corn washed so thoroughly that the grain becomes as white and soft as wheat flour. In Mexico City, the tortillas are rougher, with bits of corn still visible. When you spend so much time with a foodstuff, you begin to know it intimately; every household develops its own quirky ways with the tortilla. My favorite innovation was my grandmother's *tacos de barriga,* "belly tacos." She and I would go to the *tortillería,* and as the tortillas came out onto the conveyor belt, she'd take a knife and cut off the thin layer that puffs up during cooking, the part that looks like a pudgy belly. She stuffed these tortillas with chicken, rolled them up, and fried them. They were so fine, like puff pastry. From a very young age, I knew that a tortilla could be anything."

ROBERTO SANTIBAÑEZ

GABHOR UTOMO

PITA BREAD

MAKES 6 PITAS

Chef Jim Botsacos showed us his technique for fluffy, fresh pita, perfect for eating with your favorite dip or hummus.

1 tbsp. active dry yeast
1 tbsp. sugar
½ cup water, heated to 115°
2 tbsp. kosher salt
4 cups bread flour, plus more for rolling
¼ cup plus 1 tbsp. olive oil, plus more for greasing

1 In a small bowl, dissolve yeast and sugar in the water. Cover and set aside for 15 minutes.

2 In the bowl of a stand mixer fitted with a dough hook, dissolve salt in 1 cup warm water. Add flour and turn the mixer on. Slowly add the yeast mixture and 1 tbsp. oil. Mix until the dough combines (it will be tacky), about 2 minutes. Turn out dough onto a floured work surface and knead for 10 minutes.

3 Shape dough into a ball and place on a lightly greased baking pan. Coat lightly with oil. Cover with plastic wrap and place in a warm area until it doubles in size, about 1 hour.

4 Punch dough down and knead for 5 minutes. Divide dough into 6 pieces and roll each piece into a ball. Place on a baking sheet lined with parchment paper. Cover balls with plastic wrap, being careful not to let the plastic wrap stick to the balls (you can do this by placing coffee mugs or short glasses on the pan). Let the balls proof for 15 minutes.

5 Lightly dust 1 piece of dough at a time on both sides with flour. Push dough out with your fingers in a circular motion to create a disk that is about 5″ in diameter and ½″ thick. Using a lightly floured rolling pin, roll dough in a clockwise motion to get 7″ in diameter and ⅛″ thick.

6 Heat oven to 350°. Transfer dough to an inverted lightly floured baking sheet. Place in oven and bake for 3 minutes. Flip bread over and bake for another 3 minutes. Remove bread from oven and transfer to a parchment paper–lined baking sheet. Place a second piece of parchment paper on top of bread and cover with a damp kitchen towel. Let bread sit until cooled, about 10 minutes.

7 When ready to serve, lightly brush pitas with remaining ¼ cup oil and grill for 1–1½ minutes on each side. Cut into wedges and serve.

NAAN

Tandoori Flatbread

MAKES 12 FLATBREADS

The ubiquitous Indian flatbread is traditionally made in a tandoor oven, but we replicated the intense ambient heat of clay with the combination of a cast-iron skillet and a baking stone.

- 4 cups flour
- 1 tbsp. plus 1 tsp. baking powder
- 1 tbsp. kosher salt
- 1 tbsp. sugar
- 1¼ cups milk
- ⅓ cup plain yogurt
- 2 tbsp. canola oil
- 1 egg, lightly beaten
  Ghee (page 595, or store-bought), for serving

1 Whisk together flour, baking powder, salt, and sugar in a bowl.

2 In another bowl, whisk together milk, yogurt, oil, and egg. Pour milk mixture into flour mixture; mix into a dough. Knead dough on a floured surface until smooth, 10–12 minutes. Form dough into a ball; cover with a kitchen towel and let rest for 30 minutes.

3 Place a baking stone on the middle oven rack; heat oven to 500° (or 550°, if possible). Divide dough into 12 equal pieces; cover with a kitchen towel. Working with 1 dough piece at a time, stretch it over a medium inverted bowl into a 6"–8" circle. Heat a large cast-iron skillet over high heat until very hot. Peel dough off bowl and lay it in skillet; transfer hot skillet to bottom rack of oven (below baking stone) and bake just until bread is puffed, 2–3 minutes Repeat process with remaining pieces of dough. Brush naan with ghee before serving.

BUSS-UP-SHUT

Trinidadian Griddle-Cooked Flatbread

MAKES 12 FLATBREADS

This Trinidadian flatbread, also known as paratha roti, takes its name from how it looks: like a "busted-up shirt."

- 6¾ cups flour (about 2 lb.), plus more for dusting
- 1 tbsp. baking powder
- 2 tsp. kosher salt
- 1 cup milk
- 6 tbsp. unsalted butter, softened
- ½ cup canola oil

1 Combine flour, baking powder, and salt in a large bowl. Add milk and 2 cups water. Using your hands, work ingredients together until a soft dough forms, 1–2 minutes. Turn dough out onto a floured surface and knead for 3 minutes; shape into a sticky ball. Cover dough with a damp kitchen towel and let rest for 40 minutes, kneading it for 30 seconds every 10 minutes.

2 Heat oven to 200°. Divide dough into 12 equal balls and cover with a damp cloth. Working with 1 ball at a time, press dough out with your fingers into a 7" disk. Spread ½ tbsp. butter on disk. Using a pair of kitchen shears, cut disk from edge to middle. Starting with one end of cut circle, roll dough around circle to form a cone. Press top point of cone down into middle of the base, then cover with damp cloth. Repeat process with remaining dough and butter. Let rest for 30 minutes.

3 Heat a very large (at least 15") cast-iron griddle or skillet over medium heat; brush with oil. Roll 1 piece of dough out to a 12" circle, flouring dough lightly as you go. Transfer dough to griddle, brush with oil, and spread dough out so that none of its edges overlap. Dough will break apart as it's worked. Continue to break dough apart, turning and tossing until both sides are lightly golden, about 4 minutes total. Transfer to a plate and keep warm in oven. Repeat process with remaining dough and oil.

CHAPATI

Indian Flatbread

MAKES 10 FLATBREADS (SEE PHOTO, PAGE 439)

Thinner and chewier than naan, these earthy Indian flatbreads are made with whole durum wheat flour, called *atta* in Hindi.

- 2 cups durum wheat flour
- 1 tbsp. kosher salt
- 1 tbsp. Ghee (page 595, or store-bought) or canola oil, plus more for brushing

1 Stir together flour, salt, ghee, and 1 cup water in a bowl until dough forms. Transfer to a floured surface and knead until smooth, about 4 minutes. Cover with plastic wrap and let sit for 1 hour.

2 Divide dough into 10 equal pieces and shape each piece into a ball. Using a rolling pin, roll each ball into a 5" round. Heat a 12" cast-iron skillet over high heat. Add 1 dough round and cook, turning once, until cooked through and charred in spots, about 2 minutes. Transfer to a plate and brush on both sides with ghee; repeat with remaining rounds. Serve hot.

INJERA

Ethiopian Flatbread

MAKES 18 FLATBREADS

Injera, the spongy, crêpe-like sourdough flatbread served with most Ethiopian meals, is usually made from *tef,* a hardy Ethiopian grain. Our version can be easily made at home with all-purpose flour, yeast, and a nonstick skillet.

1	cup water, heated to 115°
1	tsp. active dry yeast
3	cups flour
½	tsp. kosher salt

1 Pour warm water into a small bowl, sprinkle with yeast, and let stand until foamy, about 10 minutes. Sift flour into a large bowl; add the yeast mixture along with 2 cups water and whisk until a very smooth batter has formed. Cover tightly with plastic wrap and let sit at room temperature for 4 hours.

2 Briskly whisk the bubbling batter until smooth; add salt and whisk to combine.

3 Heat a 6″ nonstick skillet over medium-low heat. Pour in ¼ cup batter, tilting and swirling the skillet to coat it evenly with batter. Cook until just set, about 1 minute. Cover and cook until the edges pull away slightly from the sides, about 1 minute more. Using a heatproof rubber spatula, transfer injera to a paper towel–lined plate, cover with another paper towel, and repeat, stacking the flatbreads as you go. (Whisk the batter while each flatbread cooks.)

4 Let injera cool completely; wrap with plastic wrap until ready to serve. The injera may be stored overnight in the refrigerator; bring to room temperature before serving.

FLATBREAD WITH LAMB & TOMATOES

Lahmacun

SERVES 4–6

Bake these Turkish spiced lamb and tomato flatbreads on a heated pizza stone in the oven so that the crust and topping cook evenly.

1	tsp. sugar
1	tsp. active dry yeast
¾	cup water, heated to 115°
2	cups flour, plus more for dusting

1½	tsp. kosher salt
¼	cup extra-virgin olive oil
3	tbsp. tomato paste
1	tbsp. minced fresh flat-leaf parsley
½	tsp. cayenne pepper
¼	tsp. ground cumin
¼	tsp. sweet paprika
⅛	tsp. ground cinnamon
3	oz. ground lamb
2	cloves garlic, minced
1	plum tomato, grated
1	small onion, grated
½	serrano chile, stemmed, seeded, and minced

1 Combine sugar, yeast, and water in a small bowl; let sit until foamy, about 10 minutes. Combine flour and salt in a bowl and make a well in the center. Add yeast mixture and stir to form a dough. Turn dough out onto a floured surface; knead until smooth, about 6 minutes. Transfer dough to a lightly oiled bowl and cover with plastic wrap; let sit until doubled in size, about 1 hour.

2 Punch dough down, divide into 4 portions, and roll each portion into a ball. Transfer dough balls to a floured baking sheet. Cover with a damp kitchen towel and let rest for 45 minutes.

3 Meanwhile, make the topping: In a large bowl, combine oil, tomato paste, parsley, cayenne, cumin, paprika, and cinnamon and stir vigorously with a fork. Stir in lamb, garlic, tomatoes, onions, and chiles and season with salt; set topping aside.

4 Put a pizza stone in bottom third of oven and heat oven to 475°. Working with 1 dough ball at a time, use a rolling pin to roll dough into a 10″ disk. Brush off excess flour and transfer dough to a piece of parchment paper. Spoon 3–4 tbsp. topping onto dough and, using your fingers, spread topping evenly to edges. Season with salt. Holding parchment paper by its edges, transfer to baking stone. Bake until dough is golden brown and topping is cooked, 6–8 minutes. Repeat with remaining dough and topping; serve warm or at room temperature.

BUCKWHEAT CRÊPES

Crêpes de Blé Noir

SERVES 4–6

These French crêpes, made with nutty buckwheat flour, are a common sight on tables in Brittany, where they take the place of bread or rolls.

1½ cups buckwheat flour
½ tsp. sea salt
1 egg, beaten until foamy
1 cup milk
½ cup salted butter

1 Combine flour and salt in a bowl; form a well in the center. Pour in egg. Using one hand, with fingers spread wide, mix egg into flour while pouring in 1½ cups cool water. Stir batter upward with your right hand, scooping it up from the bottom. Continue with increasing speed and force, lifting and slapping the batter to make a hollow, spanking noise with the impact. Continue this process until batter is smooth and elastic, 3–4 minutes. Transfer batter to a medium bowl and pour 2 tbsp. water evenly over the top (this protects the batter from drying out). Cover surface with plastic wrap, tucking in the edges. Cover and refrigerate overnight.

2 Stir milk and ⅔ cup water into batter. Heat a well-seasoned 10¼″ crêpe pan over medium heat and brush with a bit of butter, wiping off any excess. Pour about ¼ cup batter onto pan, swirling quickly to spread batter out to edges. Cook until light golden and just crisp, about 2 minutes. Using a spatula, flip and cook until light golden on the second side, about 2 minutes more. Repeat with remaining batter. Spread a dab of butter onto each crêpe and serve hot.

CHICKPEA-FLOUR CRÊPES

Socca

SERVES 4–6

This rosemary-scented chickpea-flour crêpe is a mainstay in southern French markets. Serve it as an appetizer, or with a salad for a light meal.

1 cup chickpea flour
½ cup olive oil
1½ tbsp. minced fresh rosemary
¾ tsp. kosher salt
¼ tsp. ground cumin
Freshly ground black pepper, to taste

1 Whisk together flour, 2 tbsp. oil, 1 tbsp. rosemary, salt, and 1 cup water in a medium bowl until smooth; cover and let batter sit at room temperature for 2 hours.

2 Heat broiler and heat a 10″ cake pan under broiler for 10 minutes. Add 3 tbsp. oil to pan, and then pour in half the batter, tilting pan to spread it over bottom of pan. Broil until crisp and browned all over, about 4 minutes. Remove from

oven, and sprinkle with half each the remaining rosemary and salt and with cumin and pepper; repeat with remaining oil, batter, rosemary, salt, cumin, and pepper.

ALGERIAN TOMATO CRÊPES

Mahjouba

SERVES 8

These thick, flaky semolina crêpes stuffed with a jammy tomato-based filling are a typical street snack in Algeria.

6 small yellow onions, roughly chopped
3 serrano chiles, stemmed and seeded
2 medium carrots, peeled and roughly chopped
¼ cup olive oil, plus more for greasing
3 tbsp. tomato paste
1 15-oz. can whole, peeled tomatoes, drained and crushed by hand
2 tbsp. kosher salt, plus more to taste
Freshly ground black pepper, to taste
1 cup packed fresh cilantro leaves, finely chopped
4¼ cups fine semolina flour, plus more for dusting

1 Combine onions, chiles, and carrots in a food processor and process until finely chopped. Heat oil in a 12″ skillet over medium-high heat. Add chopped vegetables and cook, stirring, until soft and caramelized, about 20 minutes. Add tomato paste and cook until lightly caramelized, about 3 minutes. Add tomatoes, season with salt and pepper, and cook, stirring, until mixture is thick and slightly dry, about 45 minutes. Remove from heat and stir in cilantro; let filling cool.

2 Meanwhile, combine 2 tbsp. salt, semolina, and 2 cups water in a bowl and stir until dough forms. Transfer to a floured surface and knead until dough is smooth and no longer sticky, about 8 minutes. Divide dough into 8 equal pieces, shape into balls, and place on a lightly oiled baking sheet; cover loosely with plastic wrap and let rest for 30 minutes.

3 Lightly oil a work surface. Working with 1 ball at a time, flatten dough ball into a disk using the heel of your hands until it is about ⅛″ thick. Gently pull the edges to stretch the dough into a paper-thin rectangle, about 15″ long and 12″ wide. Place a scant ½ cup filling in the center of the dough and spread it out to a 6″×4″ rectangle. Fold the long sides of the rectangle over the filling, and then fold over the short sides, pressing to seal and enclose the filling. Repeat with remaining dough and filling.

4 Heat a 12″ nonstick skillet over medium heat, place 1 packet, seam side down, in skillet and cook, flipping once, until browned in spots, about 12 minutes; repeat with remaining packets.

SWEDISH CRISPBREAD
Knäckebröd
MAKES FOUR 9″ ROUNDS

Knäckebröd, or crispbread, has been part of the Swedish diet since antiquity. It is said that the Vikings ate the nutritious and nearly imperishable nutty rye flour cracker. Traditionally, it is baked with a center hole for drying on a wooden pole, and its grooves, which help it cook evenly, are created by a stud-covered rolling pin. Swedes eat crispbread often, but it's especially popular on Midsummer's Eve paired with pickled herring and a shot of strong drink.

- 1 cup milk, heated to 115°
- 1½ tsp. honey
- 1½ tsp. barley malt syrup or dark corn syrup
- 1 tsp. active dry yeast
- 1½ cups whole wheat graham flour
- ⅔ cup rye flour
- ¼ cup spelt flour
- ¼ cup whole wheat flour
- 1½ tsp. lightly crushed fennel seeds
- ½ tsp. kosher salt
- 1 tsp. flaked sea salt

1 Stir together milk, honey, syrup, and yeast in a large bowl; let sit until foamy, about 10 minutes. Add the 4 flours, fennel seeds, and kosher salt and stir until dough forms; cover with plastic wrap and let sit until slightly puffed, about 1 hour.

2 Heat oven to 450°. Working on a floured surface, divide dough into 4 pieces. Working with 1 piece at a time, use a rolling pin to roll dough into a 9″ circle about ⅛″ thick. Transfer circle to a parchment paper–lined baking sheet and, using a 1½″ round cutter, cut out a hole in the center of the circle. Prick dough all over with a fork and brush circle lightly with water; sprinkle with ¼ tsp. flaked sea salt. Bake until lightly browned and crisp, about 10 minutes. Using tongs, flip bread and continue baking until underside is browned, about 4 minutes more. Repeat with remaining dough pieces and sea salt.

GRISSINI
Italian Breadsticks
MAKES ABOUT 30 BREADSTICKS

According to legend, *grissini*—crunchy, thin Piedmontese breadsticks—were invented in 17th-century Turin as an easy-to-digest foodstuff. Napoleon is said to have had a penchant for their crisp deliciousness. This version will make you a convert, too.

- 4 cups farina "00" (Italian-style flour)
- 3 tbsp. extra-virgin olive oil
- 2 tsp. sugar
- 2 tsp. kosher salt
- 1 tsp. active dry yeast

1 Put flour, oil, sugar, salt, yeast, and 1⅓ cups water into a large bowl and stir well to combine (the mixture should be sticky). Cover bowl with plastic wrap and let rest for 1 hour.

2 Heat oven to 350°. Form dough into thirty 1½″-wide balls. Working with 1 ball of dough at a time (keep others covered with a kitchen towel), roll and stretch dough into a 16″ rope. Transfer to parchment paper–lined baking sheets as done, keeping the ropes about 1″ apart. Bake until light golden brown and crisp, about 25 minutes. Transfer to a rack to cool.

CHEESE CRACKERS
MAKES ABOUT 10 DOZEN CRACKERS

In Charleston, South Carolina, tins of these savory little homemade crackers are a popular hostess gift, usually to be served with cocktails. The better-quality the cheese you use, the better the crackers will be.

- ¾ cup unsalted butter, softened
- 6 oz. sharp white cheddar, grated on small holes of a box grater (about 1½ cups)
- ¼ cup grated Parmigiano-Reggiano
- 1½ cups flour
- 1 tsp. kosher salt
- ¾ tsp. cayenne pepper

1 Put butter into a medium bowl and beat with an electric mixer on high speed until light and fluffy. Add cheeses and beat well. Sift flour, salt, and cayenne together into another bowl. Using your hands, quickly work flour mixture into butter mixture without overworking the dough. If dough remains crumbly, stir in 2 tbsp. ice water. Gather dough into a ball. Quarter dough, shape each piece into a disk, wrap in plastic wrap, and refrigerate for 2–3 hours.

2 Heat oven to 450°. Roll out 1 piece of dough on a floured surface to 1/16″ thickness. Using a 1½″ round cookie cutter, cut out about 30 rounds and transfer to a parchment paper–lined baking sheet about ½″ apart. Repeat process with remaining dough.

3 Bake crackers until puffed and golden, 6–8 minutes. Transfer crackers to a clean paper bag or paper towels to let cool completely. Crackers will keep in an airtight container for up to 1 month.

CHEESE STRAWS
MAKES ABOUT 24 14″ STRAWS

Serve these crisp, savory little crackers—a 1950s entertaining classic—instead of bread at lunchtime or for supper. They go superbly with cocktails, too.

- ¾ cup grated Parmigiano-Reggiano
- 1 package frozen puff pastry, thawed

1 Heat oven to 375°. Dust work surface with ¼ cup Parmigiano. Lay unfolded sheet of puff pastry on top of cheese, then sprinkle with ½ cup more grated cheese. Gently roll dough out with a rolling pin, pressing cheese into dough, to a thickness of about ⅛″. Dust with more cheese as needed.

2 Cut pastry into long ½″-wide strips. Give each strip several twists, then lay ½″ apart on a parchment-lined baking sheet. Bake until golden, about 10 minutes. Allow to cool slightly, then remove from paper and serve.

FLAXSEED CRACKERS
MAKES ABOUT 30 CRACKERS

These crispy crackers studded with nutty flaxseeds epitomize the California health food craze of the 1980s— but they've endured thanks to their salty deliciousness. Try them spread with soft goat cheese alongside a bowl of creamy tomato soup (page 94), or crumbled on a green salad.

- 1½ cups flour, plus more for dusting
- ½ cup flaxseeds
- 1 tsp. garlic salt
- ½ tsp. baking powder
- 2 tbsp. butter, softened
- ½ cup milk
- 2 tbsp. extra-virgin olive oil
- ½ tsp. salt, preferably fleur de sel

1 Heat oven to 375°. Combine flour, flaxseeds, garlic salt, and baking powder in a large bowl. Using your fingers, work butter into flour mixture until mixture resembles coarse cornmeal. Gradually add milk, stirring until a crumbly dough forms (dough will be on the dry side, but should be moist enough to hold together). Shape dough into a ball, wrap in plastic wrap, and transfer to the refrigerator to chill for 10–15 minutes.

2 Divide chilled dough in half. Wrap 1 dough half in plastic wrap to keep it from drying out. Roll other piece of dough out on a floured surface into a rectangle about 10″×12″ and ⅛″-thick . Trim off ragged edges. Brush dough with half the oil and sprinkle with half the salt. Cut dough into fifteen 1½″×5″ rectangles. Using a thin metal spatula, transfer dough rectangles to a parchment paper–lined baking sheet about ½″ apart and set aside. Repeat process with remaining dough, oil, and salt, making 30 crackers in all.

3 Bake crackers until golden brown, about 10 minutes, rotating pans back to front halfway through baking time. Transfer crackers to a wire rack to cool completely before serving.

COOK'S NOTE Flaxseeds, which can be found in health food stores, turn rancid quickly and should be stored in the refrigerator.

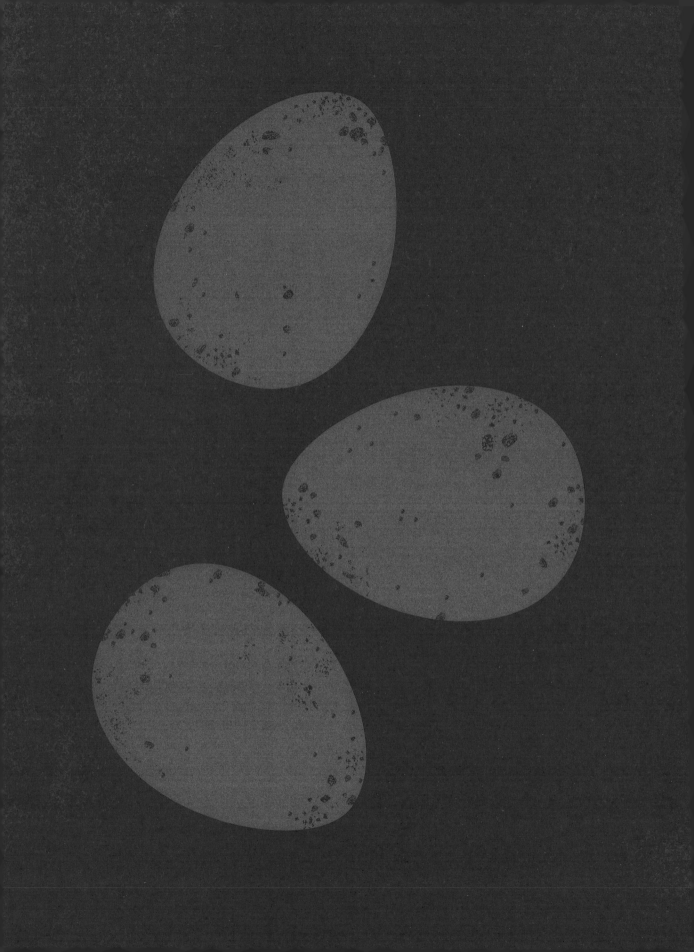

Breakfast & Brunch

BREAKFAST & BRUNCH

W E DON'T NEED THE EXPERTS to tell us that we shouldn't skip breakfast. Perish the thought: We look forward to the first food of the day, that delicious moment when we break our nightlong fast. It might be a towering stack of pancakes or salsa-smothered huevos rancheros, Colombian egg-stuffed *arepas* or just coffee and a sticky bun.

Breakfast defines who we are more than any other meal. For many, it's an on-the-go affair, a quick jolt of caffeine and a few bites to rev the engine: a bagel and cream cheese, cereal and milk, a power bar and an apple. For others, it's a contemplative repast that offers several focused moments in which they nourish their body with healthful foods like oatmeal and fruit and they ready their mind for the day. Still others make breakfast a daily occasion of celebration and indulgence, laying a foundation for the hours ahead with a big spread of eggs, sausage, home fries, and slices of buttered toast.

Even for those folks whose workweek breakfasts are eaten in a rush, the weekend is a time of welcome opportunity. The table transforms as diets and office schedules are forgotten, providing the chance to reconnect with family and friends over a morning meal of greater complexity—of eggs draped in tangy, creamy hollandaise sauce, smoked trout and potato hash under a creamy horseradish dressing, from-scratch yeast-risen waffles, and impossibly decadent brown sugar–coated bacon.

Although many of the elements that anchor our mornings are common to much of the world—sweet breads, for example, or eggs cooked every which way—the methods by which they are prepared reflect regional tastes: the earthy cumin and paprika in the spicy tomato sauce that blankets poached eggs in *shakshouka* locates us squarely in the Middle East; the unimpeachable Frenchness of rich Gruyère and ham in silky quiche Lorraine; the eye-opening power of the coffee-spiked redeye gravy that adorns a slab of salty country ham in the American South. But in whatever way we choose to satisfy our appetite in the early hours of the day, the diversity of the global breakfast foods gathered here is proof of one thing: The first bite of the day has no excuse not to be one of the best.

BAKED EGGS WITH SPINACH & TOMATO

SERVES 2

Baked eggs (sometimes called shirred eggs) are a simple, hearty all-in-one breakfast. The technique can be applied to almost any combination of meats, vegetables, and cheese; here, the flavors of layered spinach, tomato, bacon, and egg meld together beautifully, tied together by Parmigiano and a hint of nutmeg.

- 1 tbsp. unsalted butter
- 4 tbsp. cooked chopped spinach, squeezed to extract excess liquid
- 4 eggs
- ½ tomato, cut into 4 wedges
- 2 tbsp. heavy cream
- 1 slice bacon, cooked and chopped
- 2 tbsp. grated Parmigiano-Reggiano
- ½ tsp. chopped fresh thyme
- ¼ tsp. grated freshly nutmeg
  Kosher salt and freshly ground black pepper, to taste

1 Arrange an oven rack 10″ from broiler and heat broiler. Grease two 8-oz. gratin dishes with butter. To each dish, add 2 tbsp. spinach. Using your fingers, make 2 wells in each pile of spinach and crack 2 eggs into each dish.

2 Nestle 2 wedges of tomato on opposite sides of each dish. Pour 1 tbsp. heavy cream into each dish. Add half of the bacon to each dish.

3 Sprinkle each dish with 1 tbsp. Parmigiano, ¼ tsp. thyme, ⅛ tsp. nutmeg, salt, and pepper. Transfer to oven rack and broil until cheese is golden brown, whites of eggs are set, and yolks are still slightly soft, about 5 minutes.

COOK'S NOTE Serve the hot gratin dishes on top of serving plates lined with paper napkins to prevent the dishes from slipping.

EGG-IN-A-HOLE

SERVES 1

Additional names for this easy breakfast recipe are gashouse eggs, eggs in a pocket, one-eyed jack, and baby-in-the-hole. Whatever you call it, use good bread and good butter. If you prefer your egg over easy rather than sunny-side up, crack it into the hole in the bread right after you put the bread into the skillet.

- 1 slice good white bread, such as Pullman loaf
- 2–3 tbsp. butter
- 1 egg
  Kosher salt and freshly ground black pepper, to taste

1 Use a sturdy glass 2″–3″ in diameter to cut a hole out of the center of the slice of bread. Set bread slice and round cutout aside. Melt butter in a medium skillet over medium heat. Fry bread and cutout on 1 side in skillet until golden, 2–3 minutes.

2 Turn bread and cutout over. Melt a small nugget of butter in the hole in the bread, crack egg into hole, and cook until white of egg is set but yolk is still runny, 2–3 minutes. Season to taste with salt and pepper. Serve with toasted cutout for dipping in the yolk.

HUEVOS RANCHEROS

SERVES 4

This dish of tortillas and fried eggs smothered in a warm, spicy tomato salsa makes for a hearty breakfast, though adding a side of refried beans and Mexican rice (page 394) qualifies it for dinner, too.

- 14 plum tomatoes, cored
- 12 tbsp. canola oil
- 3 cloves garlic, minced
- ½ jalapeño, stemmed and minced
- ½ medium yellow onion, chopped
- 1 tbsp. fresh lime juice
  Kosher salt and freshly ground black pepper, to taste
- 8 corn tortillas
- 8 eggs
  Pickled jalapeño slices (page 578), for garnish

1 Heat a 12″ cast-iron skillet over high heat. Add tomatoes and cook, turning, until skins blacken, 8–10 minutes. Peel tomatoes, purée in blender, strain, and set aside.

2 Heat 4 tbsp. oil in a 4-qt. pan over medium heat. Add garlic, jalapeños, and onion and cook until soft, 6–8 minutes. Add tomatoes and bring to a boil. Stir in lime juice; season with salt and pepper.

3 Working in 4 batches, heat 1 tbsp. oil in a 12″ nonstick skillet over medium-high heat, add 2 tortillas, and cook, flipping once, until warmed, about 20 seconds. Transfer tortillas to 4 plates. Working in 2 batches, heat remaining 4 tbsp. oil in skillet over medium heat and fry eggs to desired doneness. Top each tortilla with a fried egg and tomato sauce. Garnish with pickled jalapeños.

WILD GREENS WITH FRIED EGGS

Horta me Avga Tiganita

SERVES 6

This dish from the Epirus region of Greece marries the silky richness of oil-basted fried eggs with the pleasing, mild bitterness of wild greens. It's versatile enough to be served any time of day, but we particularly like it as a simple, elegant brunch dish.

- 1¼ cups extra-virgin olive oil
- 10 scallions, minced
- 1¾ lb. mixed greens, such as nettles, lamb's-quarter, spinach, Swiss chard, and arugula, washed and minced
- 1 cup chopped fresh flat-leaf parsley
- 1 cup chopped fresh mint
- ½ cup chopped fennel fronds
- 6 cloves garlic, minced
  Kosher salt and freshly ground black pepper, to taste
- 6 eggs

1 Heat ½ cup oil in a 5-qt. pot over medium-high heat. Add scallions and cook for 4 minutes. Add greens, parsley, mint, fennel, garlic, and ½ cup water and season with salt and pepper. Cook, stirring, until greens are tender, 18–20 minutes. Remove from heat.

2 Heat ¾ cup oil in a 12″ skillet over medium-high heat. Working in 2 batches, crack eggs into skillet and cook, constantly spooning oil over yolks, until yolks are just set, about 2 minutes. Using a slotted spoon, transfer eggs to a plate. Divide greens among 6 plates and top each serving with a fried egg.

HOW FRESH ARE YOUR EGGS?

To test eggs' freshness, gently drop them into a bowl of cold water. The freshest ones will immediately sink on their sides, while slightly older ones will tilt or even sit upright at the bottom of the bowl. Just be careful to avoid using eggs that float to the surface, a sure sign that they are past their prime.

PERFECT SCRAMBLED EGGS

SERVES 1

These scrambled eggs employ the slow-and-low approach, for the creamiest possible outcome. They're aided by butter, chives, and a splash of heavy cream added just before the eggs are done.

- 1½ tbsp. unsalted butter
- 3 eggs
- ¼ tsp. kosher salt
- 1 tbsp. heavy cream
- 3 tbsp. finely chopped fresh chives
  Freshly ground black pepper, to taste

1 Grease a 10″ nonstick skillet with 1 tbsp. unsalted butter. Heat skillet over medium-low heat. Crack eggs into a small bowl and whisk with a fork until whites and yolks are just combined, about 10 seconds. Transfer beaten eggs to skillet.

2 Let eggs sit until they just begin to stick to the bottom of the skillet, about 30 seconds. Begin stirring vigorously with a wooden spoon to break up the curds. Cook, stirring constantly, until eggs are almost set but still runny, 3–4 minutes.

3 Add salt, remaining ½ tbsp. butter, cream, and 2 tbsp. chives and stir to combine. Return the skillet to medium-low heat and cook, stirring occasionally, until the eggs cook to desired doneness, 1–2 minutes.

4 Transfer to a plate and season with pepper. Top with remaining 1 tbsp. chives.

BREAKFAST AROUND THE WORLD

AUSTRALIA

Weetabix may look like health food, but Australian children hanker for these flaky whole wheat biscuits, softened in milk and eaten as cereal.

BRAZIL

A simple meal of coffee, bread, and jam is elevated in Brazil by the inclusion of the country's famous fruits: Papaya, guava, or passion fruit often show up at the breakfast table.

DOMINICAN REPUBLIC

The cornerstone of Dominican breakfasts is *mangú,* a creamy mash of boiled plantains, milk, and butter, usually served with eggs and sausage.

COLOMBIA

The small, round cornmeal pancakes called *arepas* (page 476) are so popular that many Colombian kitchens have an appliance that exists solely for cooking them. Called an *arepera,* it's a distant relative of the waffle iron, with circular molds that turn out perfectly shaped disks. In their traditional breakfast incarnation, the cakes are often stuffed with eggs, cream cheese, or butter and honey.

EGYPT

Ful medames (page 387), a stew of dried fava beans simmered with garlic, is Egypt's national dish. With fresh pita, scrambled or hard-cooked eggs, and a salad of chopped tomatoes, it makes for a savory morning meal. Many claim that it's as old as the pyramids, based on the evidence of favas found in pharaonic-era tombs.

ENGLAND

The "full English," as it's called, is a hearty plate of sausages, bacon, beans, fried tomatoes and mushrooms, fried eggs, and buttered toast. For most, a cup of strong tea is essential as well.

ITALY

Gianduja, a paste-like confection of chocolate and hazelnuts native to Italy's Piedmont region, was the inspiration for the breakfast spread Nutella, which was introduced to the world in the 1940s by the Italian pastry maker Pietro Ferrero.

JAPAN

It wouldn't be breakfast in Japan without *natto,* the pungent fermented soybean condiment that's often served with rice and an array of additional garnishes like grated daikon or chopped scallion, raw quail eggs, hot mustard, or soy sauce.

RUSSIA

Kasha, a porridge made from an assortment of grains such as buckwheat, oats, and wheat, is a key player in the traditional Russian breakfast.

SCANDINAVIA

Throughout Scandinavia, mornings are a time for a slice of dense bread topped with something salty and savory: cheese, cold cuts, fish pâté, or eggs.

SOMALIA

A Somali breakfast wouldn't be complete without *laxoox,* a sourdough flatbread, similar to Ethiopian *injera,* that's traditionally eaten with honey, butter, or beans.

SPAIN

Breakfast in Spain is mostly a coffee-and-bread affair, but the country lays claim to at least one decadent morning option: cinnamon-and-sugar-dusted fried dough, which is particularly wonderful dunked in a mug of hot chocolate.

VIETNAM

A steaming bowl of the aromatic noodle soup known as *pho* (page 87) starts the day for much of Vietnam. Indeed, it could be considered the country's national dish.

WORLDWIDE

Just as a French rooster sounds unlike an American one, the onomatopoeic Rice Krispies mascots Snap! Crackle! Pop! have different names in other countries. In Sweden, they're *Piff! Paff! Puff!;* in Finland, *Poks! Riks! Raks!;* in Germany, *Knisper! Knasper! Knusper!;* and in South Africa, *Knap! Knaetter! Knak!*

INTERNATIONAL SCRAMBLE

Worldwide, scrambled eggs are used as a vehicle for everything from seasonal vegetables to savory meats and cheeses. Some of our favorites include:

BRAZIL In Brazil, scrambled eggs are tossed with butter-fried *farofa* (toasted cassava flour) and green onions to make *farofa de ovo e cebolinha*.

CHINA Tomatoes and chives are stir-fried with egg to make *xihongshi chao jidan*, a staple of Chinese home cooking.

FRANCE In France, butter-and-cream-enriched scrambled eggs are augmented with luxurious ingredients such as shaved truffle and morels.

INDIA Ghee-fried raisins and onions bolster *bharuchi akuri*, an egg scramble from Gujarat, in northeast India.

IRAQ Lamb is sautéed in olive oil with tomatoes, seasoned with *bahar asfar* (yellow spice mix), and scrambled with eggs to make *makhlama lahm*, a beloved Iraqi breakfast dish.

JEWISH TRADITION Matzo *brei*, a crushed matzo cracker and egg scramble, is a staple in Jewish households the world over, particularly during the Passover holiday.

PORTUGAL Matchstick-size fried potatoes and shredded salt cod are scrambled with eggs to make Portugal's *bacalhau à Brás*.

SPAIN Tiny, delicate shrimp are sautéed with garlic for *revuelto de gambas*, a seafood and egg scramble from coastal Spain.

SYRIA For breakfast in Syria, garlicky fried artichokes are folded into scrambled eggs to make *ardî shawkî bil-bayd*.

TAIWAN Oysters are scrambled with eggs to make *o-a-tsian*, a popular Taiwanese snack.

SCRAMBLED EGGS WITH BREAD & CHORIZO

Migas con Chorizo

SERVES 4

This classic Spanish-style egg scramble, made with spicy chorizo and chunks of olive oil–crisped bread, is a practical—and delicious—way to use up day-old bread.

> 3½ tbsp. olive oil
> 2 oz. Spanish chorizo, thinly sliced
> 4 oz. crusty bread, such as French, Italian, or a kaiser or Portuguese roll, torn into 1″ pieces
> 8 eggs, lightly beaten
> 1½ tsp. crushed red chile flakes
> Kosher salt and freshly ground black pepper, to taste

1 Heat 1 tbsp. oil and chorizo in a 10″ skillet over medium heat. Cook until just browned, about 1 minute. Using a slotted spoon, transfer chorizo to a plate.

2 Add remaining oil to skillet and add bread. Cook, stirring occasionally, until golden and slightly crisp, 5–7 minutes. Transfer to plate with chorizo.

3 Add eggs, chile flakes, salt, and pepper to skillet and cook, stirring constantly, until eggs are soft-scrambled, 8–10 minutes. Remove from heat and stir in reserved chorizo and bread before serving.

COOK'S NOTE Spanish chorizo is sold in links and is generally fully cooked; it is distinct from Mexican *chorizo fresco*, which resembles ground meat and needs to be cooked before serving.

MEXICAN-STYLE SCRAMBLED EGGS

Huevos a la Mexicana

SERVES 4–6

This quick breakfast dish is made *a la mexicana* with red tomatoes, white onions, and green jalapeños, which mirror the colors of the Mexican flag.

> 3 tbsp. canola oil
> 1 small white onion, finely chopped
> 1 jalapeño, stemmed, seeded, and finely chopped
> 1 plum tomato, cored, seeded, and finely chopped
> Kosher salt and freshly ground black pepper, to taste
> 2 tbsp. thinly sliced fresh cilantro leaves
> 8 eggs, lightly beaten

1 Heat oil in a 12″ skillet over medium-high heat. Add onion, jalapeño, and tomato, season with salt and pepper, and cook, stirring, until soft, about 6 minutes.

2 Add cilantro and eggs, and cook, folding eggs over in large curds occasionally, until cooked through, about 4 minutes. Serve hot.

HANGTOWN FRY
SERVES 4–6

This rich oyster and bacon omelette is based on one from the Tadich Grill in San Francisco, where it's been served for over 160 years, since the dish's invention back in gold rush days. It's generally served with a side of sliced tomatoes.

12 oysters, such as kumamoto, shucked
    Kosher salt and freshly ground
    black pepper, to taste
¼ cup flour
7 eggs
½ cup dried bread crumbs
4 tbsp. unsalted butter
4 slices bacon, cooked and crumbled
2 scallions, thinly sliced
    Hot sauce, for serving
    Sliced tomatoes, for serving

1 Pat oysters dry and season with salt and pepper; set aside. Put flour, 1 beaten egg, and bread crumbs in 3 separate bowls. Dip each oyster in flour, then egg, then crumbs and place on a floured plate.

2 Heat butter in a 12″ nonstick skillet over medium-high heat. Add oysters and fry, flipping once, until golden brown, 6–8 minutes.

3 Whisk remaining eggs in a bowl; season with salt and pepper. Add eggs to pan with half the bacon and scallions. Cook until eggs are just set, about 3 minutes. Smooth over top; cover and cook until top is set, about 5 minutes. Transfer omelette to a plate, and garnish with remaining bacon and scallions. Serve with hot sauce and sliced tomatoes.

PERFECT CHEESE OMELETTE
SERVES 2

This simple French-style omelette relies entirely on its method: Chef André Soltner, the chef-owner of New York's now-closed but iconic restaurant Lutèce, showed us how to roll it up into a clean cylinder. It's proof that practice makes perfect: The technique can be tricky to master, but once you have it down, it's exquisite to behold.

6 eggs
½ cup grated Gruyère cheese
    Kosher salt and freshly ground
    white pepper, to taste
2 tbsp. unsalted butter

1 Heat a medium nonstick skillet over high heat. Meanwhile, beat eggs with a fork until yolks and whites are completely incorporated. Add Gruyère, season with salt and pepper, and mix well.

2 Melt butter in heated skillet. Pour eggs into skillet and, working quickly, stir surface of eggs constantly with a fork to make small, tight curds. When eggs are about halfway set, use the fork to carefully roll the edge of the omelette closest to you about a third of the way toward center of the omelette. Hold skillet in one hand and give handle several quick raps with other hand to gently force the outside edge of the omelette to slide up the edge of the skillet farthest from you and roll over on itself. Quickly and carefully invert omelette onto a large plate, and serve immediately.

DINER-STYLE AMERICAN-CHEESE OMELETTE
SERVES 1

At virtually every diner, breakfast joint, truck stop, and pancake house we've visited, we've encountered variations on this exquisitely simple omelette: a fluffy disk of cream-enriched scrambled eggs folded around a gooey core of molten American cheese. With a side of crisp hash browns and a rasher or two of bacon, it occupies a well-deserved position in the pantheon of all-time great breakfasts.

1½ tbsp. unsalted butter
5 eggs
    Kosher salt and freshly ground
    black pepper, to taste
3 tbsp. heavy cream, whipped into stiff peaks
2 slices American cheese

1 Heat oven to 400°. Melt butter in an ovenproof 10″ nonstick skillet over medium heat. Meanwhile, whisk eggs, salt, and pepper in a bowl until fluffy and fold in whipped cream; add to skillet. Using a rubber spatula, cook, stirring occasionally to form large curds, until eggs are almost set but not browned, 2–3 minutes.

2 Pat eggs into an even layer. Lay cheese slices, overlapping slightly, over one side of eggs. Using the spatula, lift and fold other side of eggs over cheese. Bake until omelette is set and lightly golden and cheese is melted, 1–2 minutes.

FRIED-RICE OMELETTE

SERVES 2

In this dish, a popular order at Teshima's, a restaurant in the Hawaiian town of Kealakekua, a thin omelette is folded around a filling of fried rice and sausage. The cooks at Teshima's use linguiça, a Portuguese-style sausage, for this Hawaiian version of Japanese omurice.

- 5 tbsp. unsalted butter
- ¼ lb. linguiça, chopped into small pieces
- 1 small onion, thinly sliced
- 1 small carrot, cut into matchsticks
- 1½ cups cooked short-grain rice
- 2 tsp. soy sauce
- 2 tsp. oyster sauce
- 4 eggs, beaten

1 Heat 1 tbsp. butter in a 12″ nonstick skillet over medium-high heat. Add sausage; brown for 6 minutes. Add onion and carrot and cook until golden, about 4 minutes. Add rice; cook, stirring, until hot, 3–4 minutes. Stir in soy and oyster sauces; set fried rice aside, covered.

2 Heat 2 tbsp. butter in a skillet over medium-high heat. Beat 2 eggs in a bowl; pour into the skillet and turn to coat bottom. Cook, swirling pan, until omelette sets but top is still slightly wet, about 1 minute. Arrange half the fried rice down center. Using a rubber spatula, slide omelette onto a plate; roll around filling. Repeat with remaining butter, eggs, and fried-rice mixture.

ABBEVILLE CRAWFISH OMELETTE

SERVES 4

Abbeville, Louisiana, has its annual Giant Omelette Celebration every November. The festival features every kind of Cajun specialty, but the main event is the preparation and communal consumption of a giant crawfish omelette. The original recipe feeds the whole town; this adaptation makes a more manageable portion.

- 4 tbsp. unsalted butter
- 1 onion, chopped
- 1 green bell pepper, seeded and chopped
- 1 cup crawfish tails, peeled and cooked
- 10 eggs
- ½ cup milk
  Sea salt and freshly ground black pepper
- 3 scallions, chopped
- 3 sprigs fresh flat-leaf parsley, chopped
  Tabasco sauce, to taste
  Warmed French bread, for serving

1 Heat butter in a nonstick skillet over medium heat. Add onions and peppers and cook until soft, about 10 minutes. Stir in crawfish tails.

2 Beat together eggs and milk in a bowl. Season with salt and pepper. Pour eggs into skillet and cook, stirring occasionally, until soft curds form. Just before eggs are cooked to your liking, add scallions, parsley, and Tabasco. Serve with French bread.

DENVER OMELETTE

SERVES 2

Legend has it that the Denver omelette got its name from the cowboys who ate this hearty scramble sandwich of ham, onion, and pepper while out riding the trail through Colorado.

- 2 tbsp. butter
- ¼ lb. smoked ham, diced
- 1 small yellow onion, coarsely chopped
- ½ small green bell pepper, seeded and coarsely chopped
- 4 eggs, lightly beaten
  Kosher salt and freshly ground black pepper, to taste
- 4 thick slices white bread, toasted and buttered

1 Heat butter in a large nonstick skillet (preferably a cast-iron one) over medium-high heat. Add ham and cook, stirring frequently, until just golden brown, about 4 minutes. Add onion and pepper and cook, stirring frequently, until softened, 3–4 minutes.

2 Pour in eggs, season with salt and pepper, and stir gently. Cook until eggs are light golden brown, then use a spatula to gently cut eggs in half down the middle. Carefully flip over each half and cook until light golden brown on the second side. Sandwich each half between 2 slices toast.

EGGS BENEDICT, ETC.

There are as many variations of eggs Benedict as there are chickens that lay eggs, many of which have become mainstays at brunch palaces all over the country, from the Plaza Hotel in New York City to Brennan's in New Orleans. Here are a few of our favorites.

EGGS FLORENTINE Sautéed spinach provides a bed for the poached eggs, which are coated with hollandaise sauce. This dish is sometimes sprinkled with grated parmesan and then broiled until the cheese is hot and bubbly.

EGGS BENEDICT ARNOLD Recipes vary, but a popular one calls for poached eggs nestled on biscuits and smothered with sausage gravy—a distinctly Southern take on the Yankee original.

EGGS CHESAPEAKE This dish is prepared the same way as eggs Benedict, except that the Canadian bacon is replaced with crab cakes.

EGGS HUSSARDE This New Orleans specialty (page 474) consists of rusks topped with thick slices of tomato and tasso ham, both covered with a veal stock–enriched red wine sauce called *marchand de vin* and crowned with poached eggs, which, in turn, are coated with hollandaise sauce.

EGGS PROVENÇAL Thin slices of fried bread are topped with poached eggs and doused with a garlicky Mediterranean-style tomato sauce.

EGGS SARDOU One of the signature dishes of Antoine's in New Orleans, where it was invented, Eggs Sardou (this page) is made by filling hollowed-out artichoke bottoms with creamed spinach, topping them with poached eggs, and ladling hollandaise sauce over it all.

EGGS BENEDICT

SERVES 2–4

Credit for this opulent brunch classic is generally given to the New York City restaurant Delmonico's, where the story goes that the chef topped a muffin half with ham, a poached egg, and a generous pour of hollandaise in order to appease a Mrs. Benedict, who found nothing on the menu to her liking. Poaching the eggs in salted, vinegared water helps them hold their shape.

Kosher salt
2 tbsp. white vinegar
4 eggs
2 English muffins, split and toasted
3 tbsp. butter
4 slices Canadian bacon
1½ cups Blender Hollandaise (page 591)
Fresh flat-leaf parsley leaves, for garnish

1 Bring a medium skillet of salted water to a simmer over medium heat; add vinegar. Crack eggs into individual small dishes. Slip eggs into simmering water, turn off heat, cover, and cook until whites are just firm, 4 minutes. Transfer eggs with a slotted spoon to a bowl of ice water and set aside.

2 Heat oven to 200°. Spread toasted muffins with some of the butter. Transfer to 2–4 plates; keep warm in oven. Melt remaining butter in a medium skillet over medium heat. Fry bacon in butter until browned, about 5 minutes. Place bacon on muffins; keep warm in oven.

3 Reheat eggs in a skillet of simmering water for 1 minute; transfer with a slotted spoon to paper towels to drain. To serve, carefully place egg on bacon and spoon some hollandaise on top. Garnish with parsley.

EGGS SARDOU

SERVES 4

In any other city you might order eggs Sardou and get poached eggs served over artichoke hearts nestled in a bed of creamed spinach. But the original eggs Sardou, served at the iconic New Orleans restaurant Antoine's since its invention in 1908, has far more pizzazz. Anchovies are tucked in between the egg and artichoke, and a thick hollandaise sauce blankets the entire dish, which is scattered with handfuls of minced black truffle, parsley, and ham and served with fried asparagus spears.

Kosher salt
2 tbsp. white vinegar
8 eggs
8 large frozen artichoke bottoms, thawed
Canola oil, for frying
1 cup flour
2 eggs, lightly beaten
1 cup dried bread crumbs
8 asparagus spears, trimmed
8 oil-packed anchovies, drained
1½ cups Blender Hollandaise (page 591)

2 tbsp. minced cooked ham

2 tbsp. minced black truffles

2 tbsp. minced fresh parsley,
plus sprigs for garnish

1 Bring a large skillet of salted water to a simmer over medium heat; add vinegar. Crack eggs into individual small dishes. Slip eggs into simmering water, turn off heat, cover, and cook until whites are just firm, 4 minutes. Transfer eggs with a slotted spoon to a bowl of ice water and set aside.

2 Bring a large pot of water to a boil, add artichokes, and cook until tender, about 3 minutes. Drain and keep warm. Pour oil to a depth of 2″ into a 6-qt. Dutch oven over medium-high heat and heat until a deep-fry thermometer reads 365°. Place flour, eggs, and bread crumbs in 3 separate shallow dishes. Toss asparagus in flour, dip in eggs, and then dredge in bread crumbs. Working in batches, fry asparagus until golden brown, about 2 minutes. Transfer to paper towels to drain.

3 To serve, place 2 artichoke bottoms in the center of each plate. Fold each anchovy in half and place in an artichoke. Top with a poached egg; pour hollandaise sauce evenly over eggs. Sprinkle with ham, truffles, and parsley. Place 2 fried asparagus on each plate and garnish with parsley sprigs.

EGGS HUSSARDE

SERVES 4 (SEE PHOTO, PAGE 437)

This luxurious dish, served at the New Orleans restaurant Brennan's, incorporates a rich red wine sauce into the standard eggs Benedict construction, and exchanges the more common English muffin base for Holland rusks, a type of packaged round toast available at specialty shops. It's made all the more decadent thanks to its partner on the plate, parmesan-topped broiled tomatoes.

Kosher salt

2 tbsp. white vinegar

8 eggs

3 tbsp. unsalted butter

1 clove garlic, finely chopped

1 scallion, finely chopped

¼ yellow onion, finely chopped

¼ cup finely chopped ham

¼ cup minced mushrooms

1 tbsp. flour

¾ cup beef stock

¼ cup dry red wine

2 tsp. Worcestershire sauce

½ tsp. dried thyme

1 bay leaf

4 tbsp. finely chopped fresh parsley
Kosher salt and freshly ground
black pepper, to taste

1 medium tomato, cut into 4 slices

⅓ cup grated Parmigiano-Reggiano

8 slices Canadian bacon

8 Holland rusks

1½ cups Blender Hollandaise (page 591)

1 Bring a large skillet of salted water to a simmer over medium heat; add vinegar. Crack eggs into individual small dishes. Slip eggs into simmering water, turn off heat, cover, and cook until whites are just firm, 4 minutes. Transfer eggs with a slotted spoon to a bowl of ice water and set aside.

2 Heat 2 tbsp. butter in a 2-qt. saucepan over medium-high heat. Add garlic, scallion, and onion and cook until soft, 2–3 minutes. Add ham and mushrooms and cook for 4 minutes. Add flour and cook, stirring, for 1 minute. Add stock, wine, Worcestershire, thyme, and bay leaf and bring to a boil. Reduce heat to medium and cook briefly until slightly thick. Stir in 2 tbsp. parsley and season with salt and pepper; keep red wine sauce warm.

3 Set oven to broil. Place tomato slices on a baking sheet. Season with salt and pepper, sprinkle with cheese, and broil until cheese is melted and browned, 2–3 minutes; set aside.

4 Heat remaining butter in a 12″ skillet over medium heat. Add bacon and cook until warmed. Divide rusks among 4 plates and put 1 bacon slice on each. Spoon 2 tbsp. red wine sauce over bacon and top with a poached egg. Spoon hollandaise evenly over eggs. Garnish plates with broiled tomatoes and remaining 2 tbsp. parsley.

SHAKSHOUKA

Eggs Poached in Tomato Sauce

SERVES 4–6

This savory, richly spiced Middle Eastern breakfast can be served as a main course for any meal of the day. Be sure to include plenty of warm pita to sop up the delectable sauce.

¼ cup extra-virgin olive oil

5 Anaheim chiles or 3 jalapeños, stemmed, seeded, and finely chopped

1 small yellow onion, chopped

8 cloves garlic, crushed
1 tsp. ground cumin
1 tbsp. paprika
1 28-oz. can whole, peeled tomatoes, undrained
Kosher salt, to taste
8 eggs
½ cup crumbled feta
1 tbsp. chopped fresh flat-leaf parsley
Warm pita, for serving

1 Heat oil in a 12″ skillet over medium-high heat. Add chiles and onion and cook, stirring occasionally, until soft and golden brown, about 6 minutes. Add garlic, cumin, and paprika and cook, stirring frequently, until garlic is soft, about 2 more minutes.

2 Put tomatoes and their liquid into a medium bowl and crush with your hands. Add crushed tomatoes and their liquid to skillet along with ½ cup water, reduce heat to medium, and simmer, stirring occasionally, until thickened slightly, about 20 minutes. Season sauce with salt.

3 Crack eggs over sauce so that eggs are evenly distributed across sauce's surface. Cover skillet and cook until yolks are just set, about 5 minutes. Using a spoon, baste the whites of the eggs with tomato mixture, being careful not to disturb the yolk. Sprinkle shakshouka with feta and parsley and serve with pita.

BACON & EGG PIE
SERVES 12

Flaky pastry, rich egg yolks, and salty bacon make this classic New Zealander pie a dish with mass taste-bud appeal.

½ cup ketchup
¼ cup Worcestershire sauce
2 9″ × 11″ sheets frozen puff pastry, thawed and chilled
20 eggs
1 tbsp. heavy cream
1 lb. sliced bacon, roughly chopped
Kosher salt and freshly ground black pepper, to taste

1 Heat oven to 400°. Whisk together ketchup and Worcestershire in a small bowl; set aside. Using a rolling pin, roll 1 sheet of puff pastry on a floured work surface into an 11″×14″ rectangle; transfer to a 9″×12½″ baking pan and let

excess hang over sides. Separate 1 egg and place the yolk in a small bowl; stir in cream and set egg wash aside. Place egg white on top of pastry. Crack the remaining eggs and drop them in rows across top of pastry, spacing them evenly apart, and sprinkle with bacon; drizzle ketchup mixture over eggs and bacon and season with salt and pepper.

2 Fold dough hanging over the edge of the pan back over eggs and bacon and brush with some of the egg wash. Roll second pastry sheet into a 10″×13″ rectangle and place on top of eggs and bacon, tucking edges into sides of pan. Cut 4 slits in the top of the pastry with a paring knife, and then brush completely with egg wash. Bake until golden brown and eggs and bacon are cooked through, about 1 hour. Cut into squares to serve.

QUICHE LORRAINE
SERVES 6–8

These eggy, creamy, bacon-filled tarts epitomized the quiche craze of the 1980s—and they're still delicious today. The sprinkle of nutmeg adds a subtle depth to the luxuriant combination of ingredients.

2 eggs
¾ cup grated Gruyère cheese
½ cup heavy cream
½ cup milk
¼ tsp. cayenne pepper
¼ tsp. freshly grated nutmeg
Kosher salt and freshly ground black pepper, to taste
3 slices bacon, finely chopped
Perfect Quiche Crust (page 476)
Chopped fresh chives, for garnish

1 Whisk together eggs, Gruyère, cream, milk, cayenne, nutmeg, salt, and pepper in a bowl. Cook bacon in an 8″ skillet over medium heat to render its fat, about 12 minutes. Let cool, then add to egg mixture.

2 Heat oven to 325°. Pour filling into crust, then bake until just set, about 20 minutes. Garnish with chives.

CRAB & SHRIMP QUICHE
SERVES 6–8

Sweet shrimp and crabmeat elevate a cheese-filled quiche in this recipe from Long Island's Modern Snack Bar, which has been around since 1960.

½ lb. small shrimp, peeled
  and deveined
  Perfect Quiche Crust (this page)
4 oz. jumbo lump crabmeat,
  picked of shells
2 oz. shredded cheddar
2 oz. shredded mozzarella
¾ cup mayonnaise
¾ cup sour cream
2 tbsp. finely chopped fresh basil
¼ tsp. Old Bay seasoning
5 eggs
  Kosher salt and freshly ground
  white pepper, to taste

Heat oven to 325°. Arrange shrimp over bottom of crust and sprinkle with crab. Whisk together half each of the cheddar and mozzarella, plus mayonnaise, sour cream, 1 tsp. basil, the Old Bay, eggs, salt, and white pepper in a bowl; pour evenly over shrimp and crab. Sprinkle with remaining cheeses and basil. Bake until filling is set, 45 minutes to 1 hour.

PERFECT QUICHE CRUST

MAKES 1 CRUST

A buttery, flaky crust is an important part of any quiche's appeal. This recipe can be made ahead through step 2 and kept in the refrigerator, covered in plastic wrap or in a large airtight container, for up to 2 days.

1¾ cups flour, plus more for dusting
6 tbsp. unsalted butter, cubed and chilled
1 tsp. kosher salt
3 tbsp. ice-cold water

1 Pulse flour, butter, and salt in a food processor until pea-size crumbles form. Add water and pulse until dough comes together. Flatten dough into a disk and wrap in plastic wrap and chill for 1 hour.

2 On a lightly floured surface, roll dough into a 13″ circle. Transfer to an 11″ tart pan with a removable bottom,

pressing into bottom and sides. Trim excess dough and discard. Chill for 30 minutes.

3 Heat oven to 375°. Using a fork, prick dough all over the bottom. Line dough with parchment paper and fill with pie weights or dried beans. Bake until golden, about 20 minutes. Remove paper and weights and let crust cool before pouring in quiche filling of your choice.

EGG-STUFFED CORN CAKES

Arepas de Huevo

SERVES 8

Twice-fried *arepas* are a classic street food in Colombia. Often they're stuffed with soft-cooked eggs, as they are here, but the corn cakes make for a good vehicle for almost any filling—including breakfast staples like cream cheese or butter and honey.

2 cups masarepa (see Cook's Note)
1½ tsp. kosher salt
1 tbsp. canola oil, plus more for frying
8 eggs
  Hot sauce, for serving

1 Mix corn flour and salt in a bowl. Stir in 2½ cups warm water and 1 tbsp. oil until dough forms; knead until smooth, 2–3 minutes. Divide dough into eight 4-oz. balls. Heat 2″ oil in a 6-qt. saucepan until a deep-fry thermometer reads 325°. Flatten balls into 5″ disks about ¼″ thick. Working in batches, fry, flipping once, until puffed, 3–4 minutes. Transfer to paper towels to drain.

2 Increase oil temperature to 375°. Working with one arepa at a time, slice a 3″ incision horizontally without cutting all the way through to make a pocket. Crack an egg into the pocket and fry until egg is set, 2–3 minutes. Drain on paper towels. Serve with hot sauce.

COOK'S NOTE Masarepa, which is precooked corn flour, is readily available online. Our preferred brand is Harina P.A.N.

Breakfast Meats

BREAKFAST SAUSAGE PATTIES

SERVES 4–6

Making your own breakfast sausage—a simple mixture of ground pork and spices—is easier than you might think. For the best results, ask your butcher to grind together a blend of pork shoulder and fatback for a combination that is 70 percent lean.

1	bay leaf
1	tsp. crushed red chile flakes
1	tbsp. finely chopped fresh sage
1	tsp. dry mustard
¼	tsp. ground nutmeg
1	lb. ground pork
2½	tsp. kosher salt
2	tsp. freshly ground black pepper
1	tbsp. canola oil

1 Using a spice grinder, grind bay leaf and chile flakes to a fine powder. Add sage, mustard, and nutmeg and pulse twice to combine.

2 Combine spice mixture with ground pork in a large bowl along with salt and pepper and mix with your hands until the spices are evenly combined throughout the meat.

3 Form the mixture into 6 patties, each about 3″ wide and ½″ thick. Make a small depression in the center of each patty with your thumb and forefinger. (This will help to keep the patties flat as they cook.) Refrigerate for at least 1 hour or up to overnight so that the flavors can meld. (The raw patties may be covered and refrigerated for up to 4 days or frozen, wrapped well in plastic wrap, for up to 3 months.)

4 Heat oil in a 12″ skillet over medium-high heat. Fry patties, turning once, until well browned, 8–10 minutes.

GOETTA

SERVES 6–8

Steel-cut oats bulk up this hearty sausage loaf, an Ohio breakfast staple of Germanic origin usually served alongside eggs and toast.

1½	lb. boneless beef chuck, cut into 1″ pieces
¾	lb. boneless pork shoulder, cut into 1″ pieces
4	cups beef stock
	Kosher salt, to taste
1	cup steel-cut oats
¼	cup dried onion flakes
1¼	tsp. ground white pepper
¼	cup canola oil

1 Line a 9″×5″ loaf pan with plastic wrap, letting at least 4″ hang over the edges; set aside. Bring beef, pork, stock, salt, and 4 cups water to a boil in a 6-qt. saucepan over high heat. Reduce heat to medium-low and cook until meat is very tender, 1½–2 hours. Drain meat, reserving ⅓ cup cooking liquid. Transfer meat to a food processor and pulse until finely ground.

2 While meat is cooking, bring 3⅓ cups water to a boil in a 4-qt. saucepan over high heat. Stir in oats and salt, reduce heat to medium, and cook, stirring occasionally, until oats are tender, about 15 minutes. Transfer oats to a food processor with meat and reserved cooking liquid, onion flakes, white pepper, and salt. Purée until mixture becomes a thick paste. Press into prepared loaf pan and fold excess plastic wrap over top; refrigerate overnight.

3 To serve, heat oil in a 12″ cast-iron skillet over medium-high heat. Unwrap goetta and slice crosswise into ½″-thick pieces. Working in batches, fry slices, flipping once, until crisp and browned, 4–5 minutes.

BILLIONAIRE'S BACON

SERVES 8–10

Caramelized brown sugar adds an irresistible layer of sweetness to crispy bacon. According to our sources, the late chef and food consultant Gene Hovis gave this recipe to Mortimer's in New York City; it was subsequently adopted by that restaurant's successor, Swifty's, and served at cocktail parties both on premises and off. Be sure to line your sheet pans with parchment paper—the bacon-infused caramel can be a chore to clean up.

1 lb. medium-cut sliced bacon
1½ cups packed light brown sugar

1 Heat oven to 425°. Line 2 baking sheets with parchment paper.

2 Separate bacon slices and blot dry with paper towels. Put sugar in a wide dish. Coat both sides of bacon in sugar, firmly pressing sugar into each slice. Lay bacon out on pans as slices are coated (some sugar will fall off).

3 Bake bacon, turning once, until browned and lacquered, about 15 minutes. Transfer to a lightly oiled baking sheet to cool before serving.

HOW TO COOK BACON

There's more than one way to turn sliced raw bacon into the crisp strips we find so appealing. All methods fundamentally work well; it's just a matter of personal preference. (It might be pointed out, though, that baking is convenient for cooking large amounts of bacon, whereas using a skillet, handy for fewer slices, will leave you with a pan of leftover bacon grease useful for sautéing vegetables or making biscuits.)

FRY Lay slices of bacon in an unheated heavy skillet in a single layer. Fry over medium heat, turning often, for 5–15 minutes, depending on desired crispness. Transfer to paper towels to let drain.

BAKE Heat oven to 325°. Lay bacon slices, slightly overlapping, on an unheated broiler rack set over a pan. Bake until bacon is as crisp as you like, 10–15 minutes.

BROIL Heat broiler. Place slices of bacon in a single layer on an unheated broiler rack set over a broiler pan. Broil bacon, checking on it often to prevent it from burning, until cooked to desired crispness, turning strips once or twice, 6–8 minutes.

MICROWAVE Lay bacon slices, without overlapping, on a microwave-safe rack set over a microwave-safe dish, cover with paper towels, and microwave for approximately 1 minute per slice of bacon. Or lay slices of bacon in a single layer between sheets of paper towels and microwave for about 1 minute per slice.

SCRAPPLE
SERVES 15–20

Eaten throughout the mid-Atlantic, scrapple—known as *panhaas* to the Pennsylvania Dutch—is an old-fashioned blend of pork heart, liver, and rib meat, cooked with cornmeal and spices before being fried into patties crisp on the outside and meltingly tender on the inside.

    Unsalted butter, for greasing
2 lb. pork liver
1 lb. pork ribs
1 ½-lb. pork heart, trimmed, cleaned, and quartered
2 cups fine yellow cornmeal
1½ cups buckwheat flour
2½ tbsp. ground sage
2½ tbsp. kosher salt
1½ tbsp. freshly ground black pepper
½ tsp. ground cloves
2 tbsp. canola oil

1 Grease three 9"×5"×2¾" loaf pans with butter; set aside. Bring liver, ribs, heart, and 12 cups water to a boil in an 8-qt. saucepan over medium-high heat. Reduce heat to medium-low, cover, and cook, skimming occasionally, until the meat is falling off the ribs, 2½–3 hours. Using a slotted spoon, transfer meat to a plate; let cool.

2 Discard bones from ribs and grind all the meat through a meat grinder; return to pan and bring to a simmer. Add cornmeal, buckwheat flour, sage, salt, pepper, and cloves and cook, stirring occasionally, until cornmeal is cooked and mixture is very thick, about 30 minutes. Pour scrapple into prepared pans and let cool. Cover with plastic wrap; chill overnight or up to 1 week or freeze up to 1 month.

3 Turn scrapple out onto a cutting board and slice crosswise 1" thick. Heat oil in a 12" cast-iron skillet over medium-high heat. Working in batches, cook scrapple, flipping once, until browned and crisp, 8–10 minutes.

HAP TOWNES' HAM STEAKS WITH STEWED TOMATOES
SERVES 4–6

Most memorable of the repertoire of vegetable sides at Nashville's now-closed Hap Townes Restaurant were the stewed tomatoes, simmered with bread and sugar to become a fruity compote that is an ideal companion for

"All happiness depends on a leisurely breakfast."

JOHN GUNTHER

ham or pork chops. The kitchen staff said that most of the old-time cooks they knew made their stewed tomatoes with biscuits, but they all agreed that Hap's use of toasted white bread makes a more buoyant dish.

- 8 tbsp. unsalted butter
- 4 cloves garlic, finely chopped
- 1 rib celery, finely chopped
- ½ small onion, finely chopped
- 8 ripe plum tomatoes, peeled and halved
- 2 tbsp. sugar
- 1 bay leaf
- 1 sprig fresh oregano
- 2 slices white bread, lightly toasted and torn into 1″ pieces
- 2 tbsp. fresh lemon juice
  Kosher salt and freshly ground black pepper, to taste
- 1 tbsp. finely chopped fresh parsley
- 1 lb. thin-cut ham steaks, cut into quarters

1 Heat 4 tbsp. butter in a 6-qt. saucepan. Add garlic, celery, and onion and cook until soft, 6–8 minutes. Add tomatoes, sugar, bay leaf, and oregano and bring to a simmer. Cook until tomatoes are very soft, about 45 minutes. Reduce heat to medium-low, add bread and lemon juice, and season with salt and pepper. Cook, stirring, until bread is soft, about 5 minutes more. Stir in 2 tbsp. butter and the parsley. Set aside in a warm place.

2 Heat remaining 2 tbsp. butter in a 12″ skillet over medium-high heat. Working in 2 batches, add ham and cook, flipping once, until browned, about 8 minutes. Serve topped with the stewed tomatoes.

FRIED COUNTRY HAM WITH REDEYE GRAVY

SERVES 1–2

Redeye gravy, a simple but essential component of the full-on Southern ham breakfast, is the alchemical result of ham drippings cut with black coffee: Salty and earthy, bitter and sweet.

- 1 1¼″-thick slice bone-in country ham
- ½ cup boiling coffee

1 Fry ham in a large skillet over medium heat, turning once, until browned on both sides, about 10 minutes. Transfer ham to a warm plate.

2 Add coffee to skillet and stir with a wooden spoon, scraping up any brown bits on bottom of pan. Pour gravy over ham.

THE BITTER TRUTH

" According to Southern-food historian Joseph E. Dabney, the term 'redeye gravy' is attributed to President Andrew Jackson, who thought the hole left by a bone in a slice of ham resembled an eye. Dabney reports a theory that one of Jackson's drunken companions created the original recipe. I can attest to the curative power of pork grease mixed with coffee. The flavor is not, however, universally adored. To enjoy it requires the appreciation for what writer Jim Auchmutey calls 'the exquisite taste of rot.' My father, raised in a house where the smell of redeye gravy penetrated the draperies, agrees. 'Redeye gravy had a stinking taste,' he says. 'But like a dog with an old bone, we liked it that way.' My grandfather used to scrape ham bits from the bottom of the skillet and then pour in black coffee, but every Southern family has its own method. One contingent prefers Coca-Cola to coffee. In my book, that's taking the easy way out. The bitterness is what you must learn to love. "

LOUISE JARVIS

Breakfast Breads

MARION CUNNINGHAM'S YEAST-RAISED WAFFLES

MAKES 20 WAFFLES

An overnight rise and a last-minute addition of baking soda to the batter make these classic waffles—one of the great food writer Marion Cunningham's favorite recipes—especially airy and crisp.

1½	tsp. active dry yeast
½	cup tap water, heated to 115°
2	cups milk
½	cup unsalted butter, melted
1	tsp. kosher salt
1	tsp. sugar
2	cups flour
2	eggs
¼	tsp. baking soda

1 Dissolve yeast in water; set aside until foamy, 8–10 minutes. Add milk, butter, salt, sugar, flour, and eggs and whisk until combined. Cover with plastic wrap and refrigerate overnight.

2 Heat a nonstick waffle iron. Whisk baking soda into batter. Pour ¼ cup batter onto iron and let set for 30 seconds. Lower lid and cook until golden and crisp, 4–5 minutes. Repeat with remaining batter.

BELGIAN WAFFLES

MAKES 8 WAFFLES

Maurice Vermesch first introduced America to Belgian waffles at the 1962 Seattle World's Fair, but only after he sold them at the 1964–65 New York fair did they soar in popularity in this country. Vermersch wouldn't divulge his family's recipe, but we think we've come very close.

1¾	cups self-rising flour
1	tsp. sugar
4	eggs, separated
½	tsp. vanilla extract
1	cup unsalted butter, melted

1 Heat a nonstick Belgian waffle iron. Meanwhile, combine flour and sugar in a large mixing bowl. Add 1¼ cups water, egg yolks, and vanilla and whisk until smooth. Whisk in melted butter. Beat egg whites in a medium mixing bowl with an electric mixer on medium speed until frothy, 1–2 minutes, then increase speed to high and beat until stiff peaks form, about 1 minute. Gently but thoroughly fold egg whites into batter half at time.

2 Pour about 1 cup batter (or enough batter to fill pockets in iron) into hot waffle iron; immediately lower waffle iron lid and cook until waffles are golden brown and crisp, about 5 minutes. Separate sheet of waffles into individual waffles. Repeat with remaining batter.

BRIOCHE FRENCH TOAST WITH APRICOTS & PEARS

SERVES 6

An elegant French toast, this recipe makes an indulgent breakfast. Take it to the next level by topping it with a scoop of vanilla ice cream.

8	dried apricots
12	tbsp. unsalted butter
4	pears, peeled, cored, quartered
1	lemon, zested and halved
¼	cup plus 3 tbsp. sugar
2	eggs
½	cup milk
1	tbsp. orange blossom water
6	thick slices brioche or challah
	Vanilla ice cream, for serving

1 Soften apricots in boiling water. Melt 4 tbsp. butter in a pot over medium-high heat and add apricots, 2 pears, juice of ½ lemon, and 1 tbsp. sugar. Cook, stirring, until fruit is tender and golden around the edges, about 15 minutes. Remove from heat.

2 In a medium pot over medium-high heat, cook the remaining 2 pears, lemon zest, juice of remaining ½ lemon, ¼ cup sugar, and ½ cup water until pears are tender, about 20 minutes. Purée with poaching liquid to make a sauce.

3 Beat eggs with remaining 2 tbsp. sugar, milk, and orange blossom water. Melt remaining 8 tbsp. butter in a large sauté pan over medium-high heat. Dip brioche into egg-milk mixture. Cook, flipping once, until golden brown on both sides, about 5 minutes total.

4 Arrange 1 brioche slice on each plate and add pears and apricots and a spoonful of pear sauce. Serve with ice cream.

SHOPSIN'S PUMPKIN PANCAKES
SERVES 8

Iconoclastic chef Kenny Shopsin serves this popular autumn breakfast dish at his tiny, beloved namesake restaurant in New York City's Essex Street Market.

- 1¾ cups flour
- 3 tbsp. sugar
- 1 tbsp. ground cinnamon
- 2 tsp. baking powder
- 1 tsp. ground cloves
- 1 tsp. ground ginger
- ½ tsp. kosher salt
- ¼ tsp. ground allspice
- 1 cup canned pumpkin purée
- 1 cup heavy cream
- ½ cup milk
- 2 eggs, lightly beaten
- 6 tbsp. canola oil
  Butter, for serving
  Maple syrup, for serving

1 In a bowl, whisk together flour, sugar, cinnamon, baking powder, cloves, ginger, salt, and allspice. Add pumpkin, cream, milk, and eggs and whisk until smooth.

2 Heat 1 tbsp. oil in a 12″ nonstick skillet over medium-high heat. Using a ¼-cup measuring cup, pour batter into skillet to make three 3″ pancakes. Cook until bubbles begin to form on the edges, 1–2 minutes. Flip and cook until done, 1–2 minutes more. Repeat with remaining oil and pancake batter. Serve pancakes hot with butter and syrup.

HELEN'S CORN CAKES
SERVES 4–6

Helen Nixon, an Arkansas native and the owner of the now-called Helen's Restaurant on Chicago's South Side,

learned how to cook these cakes from her mother, who would use a cast-iron skillet to prepare cornbread-like flapjacks when it was too hot to turn on the oven.

- 1½ cups flour
- 1½ cups coarse yellow cornmeal
- 3 tbsp. baking powder
- 2 tbsp. sugar
- 2 tsp. salt
- 1 cup buttermilk
- ½ cup canola oil
- 3 eggs, lightly beaten
- 8 tbsp. butter, plus more for serving

1 Put flour, cornmeal, baking powder, sugar, and salt into a large bowl and whisk to combine. Set flour mixture aside. Put buttermilk, oil, eggs, and ½ cup warm water into a second large bowl and whisk together. Add buttermilk mixture to flour mixture and stir just until combined. (Overmixing can produce tough corn cakes.)

2 Melt 2 tbsp. butter in a large seasoned cast-iron skillet or on a large griddle over medium-high heat. Pour about ¼ cup batter onto the griddle to form two or three 3″-wide circles, keeping them spaced about 2″ apart. Cook, flipping once, until golden brown on both sides and cooked through, about 5 minutes total. Transfer the finished cakes to a plate and cover them with a kitchen towel to keep them warm. Repeat with remaining butter and batter. Serve warm, with plenty of butter.

LEMON POPPY SEED MUFFINS
MAKES 12 MUFFINS

The nutty flavor of poppy seeds is complemented by a generous hit of fresh lemon zest in this quintessential muffin recipe.

- 3 cups flour
- 1 tbsp. baking powder
- ½ tsp. kosher salt
- 1 cup, plus 1 tbsp. sugar
- ¾ cup milk
- ¾ cup unsalted butter, melted and cooled
- 2 tbsp. poppy seeds
- 3 eggs
  Zest of 2 lemons

1 Heat oven to 375°. Line a 12-cup muffin tin with paper liners; set aside. Whisk together flour, baking powder, and salt in a large bowl, and set aside. Whisk together 1 cup sugar, milk, butter, poppy seeds, eggs, and zest in a medium bowl. Pour over dry ingredients, and stir until just combined.

2 Divide batter evenly among muffin cups and sprinkle the tops with remaining sugar. Bake until golden brown, about 22 minutes.

ROLLS WITH CRACKLINGS & PRUNE JAM
Tepertős Pogácsa

MAKES 24 ROLLS (SEE PHOTO, PAGE 439)

A blend of rendered pork fat and cracklings adds a smoky depth to these flaky Hungarian rolls, filled with a thick prune jam called *lekvár*.

3	tbsp. milk, heated to 115°, plus ¾ cup
2	¼-oz. packages active dry yeast
3¼	cups flour, plus more for dusting
1	tbsp. kosher salt
1	tsp. freshly ground black pepper
1½	cups minced pork cracklings
½	cup lard, melted, plus more for greasing
1	tbsp. light rum
4	eggs, lightly beaten, plus 1 yolk
½	cup prune lekvár or prune jam
¼	cup boiling water

1 Combine heated milk and yeast in a bowl; let sit until foamy, about 10 minutes. In a large bowl, whisk together flour, salt, and pepper. Add yeast mixture, remaining ¾ cup milk, cracklings, lard, rum, and beaten eggs and stir until dough comes together. Knead in bowl until smooth, about 2 minutes. Cover loosely with plastic wrap and set in a warm place until doubled in size, about 1 hour.

2 Grease a 9″×13″ baking dish with lard; set aside. Stir prune lekvár and boiling water together in a bowl. On a heavily floured surface, roll dough into a 14″×17″ rectangle about ¼″ thick. Spread evenly with lekvár mixture, leaving a ½″ border; fold dough in half lengthwise. Cut dough into eighteen 2″-square rolls. Transfer to greased dish; cover loosely with plastic wrap and set in a warm place until doubled in size, about 1 hour.

3 Heat oven to 350°. Stir egg yolk and 1 tsp. water together in a bowl. Brush tops of rolls lightly with egg yolk mixture and bake until golden brown and cooked through, about 30 minutes.

SWEDISH SAFFRON BUNS
Lussekatter

MAKES 32 BUNS

The secret to making these mildly sweet pastries—served for breakfast on St. Lucia's day—is to steep the saffron in hot milk before incorporating it into the dough.

3	tsp. active dry yeast
2	cups milk, heated to 115°
2	tsp. saffron threads, lightly crushed
¾	cup plus 1 tsp. sugar
6½	cups flour
¾	tsp. kosher salt
3	eggs
¾	cup unsalted butter, cut into ½″ cubes, softened
	Canola oil, for greasing
64	raisins

1 In the bowl of a stand mixer fitted with a paddle attachment, mix together yeast, milk, saffron, and 1 tsp. sugar; let sit until foamy, about 10 minutes. Stir in remaining ¾ cup sugar, along with the flour, salt, and 2 eggs. Mix on low speed until dough forms and gathers around the paddle. Replace paddle with dough hook and add butter; knead on medium-high speed until dough pulls away from sides of bowl, about 8 minutes. Transfer dough to a large bowl greased with oil and cover with plastic wrap; let rest in a warm place until doubled in size, 1 hour.

2 Divide dough into 32 pieces and roll each piece into an 8″-long rope. Form each rope into an S shape and then roll each end into a tight spiral. Place shaped dough pieces 2″ apart on parchment paper–lined baking sheets; cover with plastic wrap and let rise in a warm place for 30 minutes.

3 Heat oven to 400°. Uncover the dough pieces and place a raisin at the center of each of the spirals. Lightly beat remaining egg with 1 tbsp. water and brush each bun with egg mixture. Bake until buns are golden brown and cooked through, about 16 minutes. Transfer buns to a wire rack and let cool for at least 10 minutes before serving.

HOT CROSS BUNS

MAKES 10 BUNS (SEE PHOTO, PAGE 439)

These sweet, spiced buns are best when fresh out of the oven. Traditionally served on Easter, they're marked with a cross to symbolize Jesus' crucifixion.

FOR THE FRUIT MIXTURE

- 1 cup granulated sugar
- 1 navel orange
- 1 lemon
- ¾ cup currants
  Pinch each ground cinnamon, nutmeg, and allspice

FOR THE DOUGH

- 1½ tsp. active dry yeast
- 1 cup milk, heated to 115°
- 2 cups bread flour
- 2 cups all-purpose flour
- 2 tsp. kosher salt
- ½ cup sugar
- 2 eggs, at room temperature
- 6 tbsp. unsalted butter, at room temperature
  Canola oil, for greasing

FOR THE GLAZE AND CROSS

- ¼ cup orange marmalade
- ¼ cup confectioners' sugar

1 Make the fruit mixture: In a small saucepan, combine sugar and 1 cup of water and bring to a boil, stirring until the sugar dissolves. Keep on a slow simmer. Remove sections of the orange peel in 1″ strips and, using a paring knife, trim off any white pith. Julienne the strips, then repeat the process with the lemon. Add julienned pieces to the simple syrup and let simmer for 8 minutes. Remove from heat and let cool. Once cooled, drain and combine with the currants and spices and set aside. You should have 1 cup total.

2 Make the dough: In the bowl of a stand mixer, dissolve yeast in milk. In a separate bowl, combine flours, salt, and sugar. Lightly beat 1 egg and add to yeast mixture. Add dry ingredients and butter. Using the dough hook, mix dough on low speed. When it comes together, knead on low speed for 8 minutes; remove from bowl and place on a lightly floured surface. Fold in candied citrus and currant mix by hand, working just until evenly distributed.

3 Place dough in a lightly greased bowl, cover with a kitchen towel, and let rise in a warm place until doubled in size, 60–80 minutes. When dough is ready, measure out 4-oz. portions, form each portion into a round, and place on a parchment paper–lined baking sheet. Cover with a kitchen towel and let rise again until doubled in size, 45–60 minutes.

4 Heat oven to 325°. Beat remaining egg with 1 tbsp. water and lightly brush each bun with egg wash. Place in oven and bake until golden brown, about 20 minutes, rotating back to front midway during baking. Fit another baking sheet with a wire rack and set aside.

5 Make the glaze: In a small saucepan over low heat, combine orange marmalade and 1 tbsp. water and stir until marmalade loosens.

6 When buns are done, place them on rack on baking sheet and let them cool for about 15 minutes. Brush each with marmalade glaze and let stand for 10 minutes until glaze sets.

7 Make the cross: Combine the confectioner's sugar and 2 tsp. water. The mixture should be loose enough to pipe but stiff enough not to run off the bun. Pour into a piping bag and pipe a cross on each bun. Serve warm.

PECAN STICKY BUNS

MAKES 12 BUNS

Three types of sugar sweeten these syrupy, caramel-drizzled pecan swirl buns, adapted from the version made at Sweet Auburn Bread Company in Atlanta, Georgia.

- ¼ cup tap water, heated to 115°
- 1½ tsp. active dry yeast
- 1¼ cups, plus 1 tsp. granulated sugar
- 8 tbsp. unsalted butter, melted, plus 20 tbsp., softened, and more for pan
- ½ cup milk, at room temperature
- 2 tbsp. packed light brown sugar
- ¾ tsp. kosher salt
- ½ tsp. vanilla extract
- 1 egg, plus 1 yolk
- 3¼ cups flour, plus more for dusting
- ⅔ cup packed dark brown sugar
- 1 cup finely chopped pecans
- 3 tbsp. ground cinnamon

1 Combine water, yeast, and 1 tsp. granulated sugar in the bowl of a stand mixer fitted with a dough hook; let sit until foamy, about 10 minutes. Stir in ¼ cup granulated sugar, 8 tbsp. melted butter, milk, light brown sugar, salt, vanilla, egg, and yolk. Add flour and mix on low speed until dough forms. Increase speed to medium-high and knead until smooth, about 8 minutes. Cover dough with plastic wrap and set in a warm place until doubled in size, about 1½ hours.

2 Meanwhile, bring 10 tbsp. softened butter and dark brown sugar to a boil in a 2-qt. saucepan and cook, stirring occasionally, until sugar is melted, about 3 minutes. Pour sauce evenly into a greased 9″×13″ baking dish; sprinkle ⅔ cup pecans over the top. Stir together remaining 10 tbsp. butter, 1 cup granulated sugar, and ⅓ cup pecans and the cinnamon in a bowl; set baking dish and filling aside.

3 On a lightly floured surface, roll dough into a 10″×18″ rectangle; spread filling evenly over dough. Working from a long side, roll dough into a log; trim ends, then cut into 12 rounds. Place rounds cut side up over sauce in baking dish. Cover with plastic wrap; chill 6 hours or overnight.

4 Heat oven to 375°. Uncover buns and bring to room temperature. Bake until golden brown, about 30 minutes. Let pan cool for 5 minutes, then invert onto a serving tray. Immediately spoon pecan sauce from dish over buns.

SWEET ORANGE BUNS

SERVES 12

Home cook Linda Worsley gave us her recipe for these luscious buns filled with fragrant orange-flavored butter. As they bake, the kitchen fills with an irresistible citrus perfume.

1¼	cups milk, heated to 115°
1½	tsp. active dry yeast
⅓	cup granulated sugar
2	tbsp. unsalted butter, melted, plus 1 cup, softened
1½	tsp. kosher salt
1	egg, lightly beaten
4	cups flour, plus more for dusting
½	cup packed light brown sugar
⅓	cup orange zest (from about 4 oranges)
3	cups confectioners' sugar
1	tsp. orange extract
1	tsp. vanilla extract
1	tbsp. fresh orange juice
	Canola oil, for greasing

1 Make the dough: Combine milk and yeast in the bowl of a stand mixer fitted with a dough hook; let sit until foamy, about 10 minutes. Stir in granulated sugar, melted butter, 1 tsp. salt, and egg; add flour and mix on low speed until dough forms. Increase speed to medium-high and knead until smooth, about 8 minutes. Cover with plastic wrap; let dough sit in a warm place until doubled in size, about 1½ hours.

2 Meanwhile, combined softened butter, brown sugar, and zest in another bowl and beat on high speed until smooth, about 2 minutes. Add remaining ½ tsp. salt, confectioners' sugar, and extracts; beat until smooth, about 2 minutes. Transfer ¼ cup filling to a bowl; stir in orange juice to make an icing. Set filling and icing aside.

3 Transfer dough to a lightly floured work surface and roll into a 10″×18″ rectangle. Spread filling evenly over dough. Working from a long side, roll dough into a log; trim ends, then cut into 12 rounds. Place rounds cut side up in a greased 9″×13″ baking dish. Cover with plastic wrap; chill 6 hours or overnight.

4 Heat oven to 375°. Uncover buns and bake until golden brown, about 25 minutes. Drizzle icing over rolls before serving.

CRÊPES WITH MAPLE SUGAR & SYRUP

Crêpes au Sucre & au Sirop d'Érable

SERVES 12

This recipe for crêpes comes from Bas-St-Laurent, Quebec's second-largest maple syrup–producing region. Layered and rolled with sweet amber sugar and syrup, they make an indulgent breakfast or dessert.

1½	cups milk
10	tbsp. unsalted butter, melted
1	egg
1	cup flour
3	tbsp. sugar
½	tsp. baking powder
6	tbsp. maple sugar
12	tbsp. maple syrup

1 In a medium bowl, whisk milk, 4 tbsp. butter, and egg. In a large bowl, whisk flour, sugar, and baking powder; add milk mixture and whisk until smooth. Set aside for 10 minutes.

2 Grease a 10″ nonstick skillet or crepe pan with ½ tbsp. butter and heat over medium-high heat. Add ¼ cup batter and swirl pan to spread batter. Cook crêpe, turning once, until browned, 1–2 minutes. Transfer to a warm plate and repeat with remaining butter and batter. To serve, sprinkle ½ tbsp. maple sugar onto each crêpe and drizzle with 1 tbsp. maple syrup. Roll up into a cylinder and serve immediately.

Doughnuts & Fried Doughs

VANILLA-GLAZED YEAST DOUGHNUTS

MAKES ABOUT 1½ DOZEN DOUGHNUTS

The glaze on these airy doughnuts achieves its satiny consistency thanks to a combination of clarified butter and evaporated milk.

- 1 tbsp. active dry yeast
- ½ cup granulated sugar
- 6 tbsp. tap water, heated to 115°
- 1½ cups milk, scalded and cooled
- 1 tsp. kosher salt
- 2 eggs
- 6 tbsp. vegetable shortening, plus more for greasing
- 5 cups flour, sifted, plus more for dusting
  Canola oil, for greasing and frying
- ½ cup plus 2 tbsp. unsalted butter
- ⅓ cup evaporated milk
- 2½ tsp. vanilla extract
- 2½ cups confectioners' sugar

1 Combine yeast, 1 tbsp. granulated sugar, and water in the bowl of a stand mixer fitted with a paddle attachment; let sit until foamy, about 10 minutes. Add remaining 7 tbsp. granulated sugar, milk, salt, eggs, and shortening and mix until combined. With the motor running, slowly add flour; beat until dough is smooth. Transfer to a lightly greased bowl and cover loosely with plastic wrap; set in a warm place until doubled in size, about 1½ hours.

2 Turn dough onto lightly floured surface and roll dough into a 13″ round about ½″ thick. Using floured 3½″ and 1½″ ring cutters, cut out doughnuts and holes; gather and reuse scraps. Place on greased parchment paper–lined baking sheets, at least 3″ apart, and cover loosely with plastic wrap; set in a warm place until doubled in size, about 45 minutes.

3 Heat 2″ of oil in a 6-qt. Dutch oven until a deep-fry thermometer reads 325°. Using scissors, cut the doughnuts out of the parchment paper, leaving about 1″ of paper around the sides of each doughnut (the paper makes it easier to transfer them to frying oil). Working in batches, place doughnuts in oil, paper side up, using tongs to peel off and discard paper. Fry, flipping once, until puffed and

golden, 3–4 minutes. Using a slotted spoon, transfer to a wire rack on a baking sheet; let cool completely.

4 Melt butter in a 1-qt. saucepan over medium-low heat. Using a small ladle, skim and discard white film from surface. Slowly pour liquid from pan into a bowl, leaving sediment behind; let cool for 1 minute. Add evaporated milk, vanilla, ¼ cup water, and confectioners' sugar and whisk until smooth. Dip doughnuts in glaze, coating completely; return to wire rack until glaze is set.

COOK'S NOTE To avoid oily doughnuts, remember: The less shortening you use in your dough, the lighter the doughnut will be after frying. Also, go light on flour when rolling out dough, and use a brush to remove any excess. Loose flour particles attract and absorb oil.

CINNAMON SUGAR–CIDER DOUGHNUTS

MAKES ABOUT 1 DOZEN DOUGHNUTS

These cinnamon-rich doughnuts will leave you licking your fingers thanks to their sugary coating. In New England, they're ubiquitous during cider season—both because cider is used in the batter, and because the doughnuts are excellent with a mug of hot cider alongside.

- 1¾ cups flour, sifted
- ¼ cup whole wheat graham flour
- 3½ tsp. ground cinnamon
- 2 tsp. baking powder
- 1 tsp. baking soda
- ½ tsp. kosher salt
- 2 tbsp. unsalted butter, softened
- 1½ cups sugar
- 2 egg yolks
- 1 tsp. vanilla extract
- ¼ cup apple cider
- ¼ cup buttermilk
  Canola oil, for forming and frying

1 Whisk flours, 2 tsp. cinnamon, baking powder, soda, and salt in a bowl; set aside. In the bowl of a stand mixer fitted with a paddle attachment, beat butter and ½ cup sugar until fluffy. Add yolks, vanilla, cider, and buttermilk and mix until smooth. With the motor running, slowly add dry ingredients and mix until a soft, sticky dough forms.

2 Combine remaining 1½ tsp. cinnamon and 1 cup sugar in a bowl; set aside. Heat 2″ oil in a 6-qt. Dutch oven until a deep-fry thermometer reads 350°. Using lightly oiled hands, roll about ¼ cup batter into a loose, sticky ball; pat gently into a disk. With your thumb, make a 1½″ hole in the center of dough; carefully slide into oil and fry, flipping once, until golden, 3–4 minutes. Using a slotted spoon, transfer to a wire rack on a baking sheet; repeat with remaining dough. Let doughnuts cool completely, then toss in cinnamon-sugar mixture.

VARIATION These doughnuts can also be dipped in a simple glaze made from boiled-down apple cider, butter, and confectioner's sugar.

JELLY DOUGHNUTS

MAKES ABOUT 2 DOZEN DOUGHNUTS

Jelly doughnuts are one of the most satisfying desserts to eat—half the fun is catching the oozing jam with your tongue (that is, if your shirt doesn't get to it first).

> 3 tsp. active dry yeast
> 1½ cups milk, heated to 115°
> 1½ cups sugar
> 4 tbsp. unsalted butter, softened, plus more for greasing
> 1 tbsp. vanilla extract
> 1 tsp. kosher salt
> 1 egg, plus 3 yolks
> 4¾ cups flour, sifted, plus more for dusting
> Canola oil, for frying
> 2 cups seedless strawberry jam, for filling

1 Combine yeast and milk in a bowl; let sit until foamy, about 10 minutes. In a stand mixer fitted with a paddle attachment, beat ½ cup sugar and butter until fluffy. Add yeast mixture, vanilla, salt, egg, and yolks; beat until combined. With the motor running, slowly add flour; beat until dough is smooth. Transfer to a lightly greased bowl and cover loosely with plastic wrap; set in a warm place until doubled in size, about 1½ hours.

2 On a lightly floured surface, roll dough into a 14″ round about ½″ thick. Using a floured 3″ ring cutter, cut dough into 20 rounds; gather and reuse scraps. Transfer rounds to lightly greased parchment paper–lined baking sheets, at least 3″ apart. Cover loosely with plastic wrap and set in a warm place until doubled in size, about 30 minutes.

3 Heat 2″ oil in a 6-qt. Dutch oven until a deep-fry thermometer reads 350°. Using scissors, cut the doughnuts out of the parchment paper, leaving about 1″ of paper around the sides of each doughnut (the paper makes it easier to transfer them to frying oil). Working in batches, place doughnuts in oil, paper side up, using tongs to quickly peel off and discard paper. Fry, flipping once, until puffed and golden, 2–3 minutes. Using a slotted spoon, transfer to a wire rack on a baking sheet; let cool completely.

4 Place remaining sugar in a large bowl; set aside. Fill a pastry bag fitted with a plain ¼″ tip with jam. Working with one doughnut at a time, insert tip about ½″ deep into the side of doughnut, pipe 2–3 tbsp. jam, and toss generously in sugar.

COOK'S NOTE If piping the jelly into the donuts proves challenging, use a paring knife to hollow out the side of the donut, making a cavity for the jelly.

CHURROS

MAKES ABOUT 5 DOZEN DOUGHNUTS

(SEE PHOTO, PAGE 438)

Ruben Ortega, a native of Puebla, Mexico, and the pastry chef at the restaurant Hugo's in Houston, Texas, shared his recipe for these long, fluted fritters, best served with thick hot chocolate for dunking.

> 6 tbsp. unsalted butter
> 1 tsp. kosher salt
> 1 tsp. vanilla extract
> 1 stick cinnamon, preferably canela, plus 1 tbsp. ground cinnamon
> 2¼ cups flour
> 1 egg
> 2 cups sugar
> Canola oil, for frying

1 Bring butter, salt, vanilla, cinnamon, and 2¼ cups water to a boil in a 4-qt. saucepan over medium-high heat. Remove and discard cinnamon, and add flour; cook, stirring constantly with a wooden spoon, until a smooth dough forms, about 5 minutes. Transfer dough to a bowl, add egg, and stir vigorously until dough is smooth. Transfer dough to a piping bag fitted with ⅜″ star tip and set aside.

Meanwhile, combine sugar and ground cinnamon in a large brown paper bag or a 9″×13″ baking dish; set aside.

2 Pour oil to a depth of 2″ into an 8-qt. Dutch oven and heat over medium-high heat until a deep-fry thermometer reads 400°. Working in batches, hold piping bag above oil and pipe about four 6″ lengths of dough. Fry, turning often, until golden brown, about 2 minutes.

3 Transfer to paper towels to drain briefly, and then transfer to bag or dish with cinnamon-sugar mixture and quickly shake or roll until evenly coated. Repeat with remaining dough in piping bag.

SOPAIPILLAS

MAKES 1 DOZEN SOPAIPILLAS

We're not sure what's more attractive about these fried Mexican pillows of dough: their alluring smell while frying or the beautiful golden brown pastry they become when pulled from the fryer.

- 2 cups flour
- 1½ tsp. sugar
- 1½ tsp. canola oil, plus more for frying
- 1 tsp. kosher salt
- 1 tsp. baking powder
- ¼ cup milk
- 1 cup honey, for serving

1 Place flour, sugar, oil, salt, and baking powder in a large bowl and mix with your fingertips to combine. Add milk and ½ cup lukewarm water and stir until a sticky dough forms. Turn dough out onto a lightly floured surface and knead vigorously until soft and no longer sticky, about 1 minute. Cover dough with a damp cloth and let rest for 15 minutes. Divide dough into 3 equal balls, cover again, and let rest for 30 minutes.

2 Pour oil to a depth of 2″ in a 6-qt. Dutch oven and heat over medium heat until a deep-fry thermometer reads 400°. Meanwhile, using a rolling pin, gently roll 1 dough ball out on a lightly floured surface into an 8″ square, keeping other balls covered until ready to use. Cut square into 4 equal squares. Trim and discard any ragged edges. Repeat process with remaining dough.

3 Place 1 square gently in the oil. When dough rises to the top (this will happen almost immediately), turn it over. Continue to turn dough until it puffs up to form a pillow

and turns light golden brown, about 1 minute. (If dough remains on one side for too long, it will not puff up entirely.) Drain on paper towels. Repeat process with remaining dough. Serve immediately, drizzled with honey.

GULAB JAMUN

Cardamom Syrup–Soaked Doughnuts

MAKES 16 DOUGHNUTS

These South Asian confections, soaked in an aromatic syrup of saffron, cardamom, and rose water, are made from *khoya*, a rich curd that is the result of reducing milk for several hours.

- 8 cups milk
- 2½ cups sugar
- ⅛ tsp. saffron threads
- 1 tsp. rose water
- 8 cardamom pods, cracked
- ¼ cup flour, sifted
- ¼ cup semolina flour
- ½ tsp. baking powder
- 3 tbsp. Ghee (page 595) or Clarified Butter (page 595), plus more for frying
- 1 tbsp. plain yogurt
- 1 egg

1 Bring milk to a boil in a 4-qt. nonstick pan. Reduce heat to medium-low and cook, stirring occasionally, until very thick, about 5 hours. You should have 1½ cups thickened milk; let cool to room temperature.

2 Bring sugar, saffron, rose water, cardamom, and 1¾ cups water to a boil in a 1-qt. saucepan. Cook, stirring, until sugar dissolves, 4–6 minutes; let cool.

3 Combine thickened milk, the flours, and baking powder into bowl of a stand mixer fitted with a paddle attachment and mix. Add ghee, yogurt, and egg and continue to beat until dough forms. Cover with plastic wrap and set aside for 10 minutes.

4 Heat 2″ ghee in a 6-qt. Dutch oven until a deep-fry thermometer reads 275°. Using wet hands, divide dough into 16 pieces; roll into balls. Working in batches, fry, stirring to keep balls submerged, until cooked through, 12–15 minutes. Using a slotted spoon, transfer to paper towels to drain briefly; transfer hot doughnuts to syrup and let soak for at least 30 minutes before serving.

Desserts

DESSERTS

THERE ARE FEW THINGS MORE WONDERFUL than finishing a satisfying dinner and realizing the best is yet to come—dessert. Whether it's a refreshing bowl of ripe seasonal fruits, crunchy mixed nuts drizzled with honey, or an elegant, cool, creamy spoonful of crème brûlée, dessert can be the most unforgettable element of any dining experience.

The word dessert comes from the French *desservir,* "to clean the table," and although desserts are traditionally served at the end of a meal after the other plates have been removed, we all know that they are welcome any hour of the day.

No matter where in the world you happen to live, a perfect morning is made all the brighter when it starts with a ricotta-stuffed cannoli or a rustic French *clafoutis* studded with seasonal cherries served alongside a cup of freshly brewed coffee. A cool, tangy mango ice can be the perfect antidote to the hot afternoon sun. And, come dinnertime, you might opt to finish your meal with *kheer,* a creamy Asian rice pudding, or with a fruit-topped Irish custard. Finally, once the dishes are done and the counter is wiped down, there's no shame in enjoying one last indulgence—a chocolate chip cookie dipped in cold milk—before heading to bed.

For some, desserts bring back memories of long-ago gatherings and celebrations. The Boston cream pie your mom had cooling in the fridge when you came home from school one day; the dense chocolate sheet cake topped with buttercream served at a childhood birthday party; the flaky-crusted apple pie Dad baked each year to round out the Thanksgiving dinner menu; or the chocolate *babka* your Eastern European grandmother made better than anyone else.

Desserts are also deeply ingrained in long-standing national traditions. Pavlova, a light, crisp meringue, is ubiquitous at summer barbecues in New Zealand, while moist, braided King Cake (page 611) is typically served at the end of the Christmas season in some countries and in the days leading up to Mardi Gras in New Orleans.

Despite the joys desserts bring, many cooks shy away from them, feeling they are too daunting or difficult to pull off at home. This holds especially true when it comes to baking, which presents its own unique set of scientific challenges, as well. Yet, when you find that perfect recipe—when you bake that first cinnamon-laced coffee cake, or that perfectly executed Indonesian layer cake that fills your kitchen with the aromas of vanilla and clove—it is an achievement worth celebrating.

Cakes

ROSE'S FAMOUS CARAMEL CAKE

MAKES ONE 9" CAKE

Rose Deshazer-White, a home cook on Chicago's South Side, earned local fame for this buttery cake. For the best results, have all ingredients at room temperature.

FOR THE CAKE

- 16 tbsp. unsalted butter, softened, plus more for greasing pans
- 3¼ cups cake flour, plus more for dusting pans
- 1 tbsp. baking powder
- ½ tsp. kosher salt
- 2½ cups sugar
- 2 tsp. vanilla extract
- 4 eggs
- 1¼ cups milk

FOR THE ICING

- 3¾ cups sugar
- 16 tbsp. salted butter
- 2 12-oz. cans evaporated milk

1 Make the cake: Heat oven to 350°. Grease and flour two 9" round cake pans and set aside. Sift flour, baking powder, and salt together; set aside. Beat unsalted butter and 2½ cups sugar in a bowl with an electric mixer on medium-high speed until fluffy. Add vanilla and then eggs one at a time, beating after each addition. On low speed, add flour mixture in 3 batches alternately with milk in 2 batches, beginning and ending with flour and beating until smooth after each addition. Divide batter between pans. Bake until golden, 30–35 minutes. Let cool on a rack for 10 minutes; remove cakes and let cool completely.

2 Make the icing: Cook sugar and butter in a pot over high heat, stirring constantly, until light brown, 7–8 minutes. Carefully stir in evaporated milk; reduce heat to medium-low and cook, stirring constantly, until smooth, 8–10 minutes. Cook, stirring occasionally, until icing registers 240° on a candy thermometer, about 1½ hours. Remove from heat; beat with a wooden spoon until thick, glossy, and spreadable, 20–25 minutes. (A dollop dropped on a plate should ooze only slightly.) Ice bottom layer of cake; top with second layer and ice the top and sides. Chill cake until set before serving.

LADY BALTIMORE CAKE

MAKES ONE 8" CAKE

This cake is the queen of Maryland confections, a real ladies'-circle kind of offering. It's made up of three dreamy layers of white cake with a mixture of chopped pecans, dried fruits, and rose water–infused buttercream sandwiched in between.

FOR THE CAKE

- 16 tbsp. unsalted butter, plus more for greasing pans
- 3½ cups sifted cake flour, plus more for dusting pans
- 4 tsp. baking powder
- ½ tsp. kosher salt
- 2 cups sugar
- 1 cup milk
- ½ tsp. rose water
- 8 egg whites

FOR THE ICING

- 4 cups sugar
- 6 egg whites
- ½ tsp. rose water
- ½ cup chopped raisins
- ½ cup chopped figs
- 2 tbsp. chopped candied orange peel
- 1½ cups chopped pecans

1 Make the cake: Heat oven to 375°. Grease and flour three 8" cake pans and set aside. Mix flour, baking powder, and salt together in a bowl; set aside. Put butter in bowl of a stand mixer fitted with a paddle attachment and beat on medium-high for 2 minutes, then gradually add sugar, beating until light and fluffy. On low speed, add flour mixture in 3 batches alternately with milk in 2 batches, beginning and ending with flour and beating until smooth after each addition. Add rose water and set aside.

2 Beat egg whites in a clean bowl on high speed until stiff but not dry. Gently stir about one-third of the whites into batter to lighten it, then gently fold in remaining whites in 2 batches. Divide batter among cake pans and bake until a toothpick inserted into center of each cake comes out clean, about 25 minutes. Let cool, then invert onto wire racks.

3 Make the icing: Bring 2 cups water to a boil over medium-high heat, add sugar, and stir until dissolved. Continue to boil for 5 minutes more, then remove from heat. Beat egg whites in bowl of a stand mixer on medium speed until stiff but not dry, about 1 minute. Still beating, pour sugar syrup in a thin stream into whites and beat until icing is room temperature, about 10 minutes. Beat in rose water. Reserve 3 cups icing, then mix raisins, figs, orange peel, and ½ cup pecans into remaining icing.

4 Place bottom layer of cake on a plate, spread with one-third of fruit-and-nut icing, and top with second layer. Spread with same icing and top with third layer, icing it, too. With plain icing, ice top (over fruit-and-nut icing) and sides. Press remaining 1 cup pecans onto sides.

COCONUT CAKE

MAKES ONE 9″ CAKE

This flavorful, delicate cake, passed down to us from writer Ben Mims' grandmother Jane Newson, calls for both fresh coconut water and freshly grated coconut.

FOR THE CAKE

- 16 tbsp. unsalted butter, softened, plus more for greasing pans
- 2½ cups cake flour, sifted, plus more for dusting pans
- 1 tsp. baking soda
- 1 tsp. kosher salt
- 1 cup buttermilk
- 1 tbsp. vanilla extract
- 2 cups sugar
- 5 eggs

FOR THE FROSTING

- 4 egg whites
- ½ tsp. cream of tartar
- 2¼ cups sugar
- ¼ cup light corn syrup
- 1 tsp. kosher salt
- 2 tsp. vanilla extract

- ¾ cup fresh coconut water
- 3 cups freshly grated coconut

1 Make the cake: Heat oven to 350°. Grease and flour two 9″ cake pans and set aside. Whisk together flour, baking soda, and salt in a bowl; set aside. Whisk together buttermilk and vanilla in a bowl; set aside. In the bowl of a stand mixer fitted with a paddle attachment, cream butter and sugar on medium-high speed until pale and fluffy, about 3 minutes. Add eggs one at a time, beating well after each addition. On low speed, alternately add dry ingredients in 3 batches and wet ingredients in 2 batches. Increase speed to high and beat until batter is smooth, 5 seconds. Divide batter between prepared pans and smooth top with a rubber spatula; drop pans lightly on a counter to expel large air bubbles. Bake cakes until a toothpick inserted into middle comes out clean, about 35 minutes. Let cakes cool for 20 minutes in pans; invert onto wire racks and let cool. Using a serrated knife, halve each cake horizontally, producing 4 layers.

2 Make the frosting: Place egg whites and cream of tartar in the bowl of the stand mixer fitted with a whisk and beat on medium-high speed until soft peaks form; turn mixer off. Bring sugar, syrup, salt, and ½ cup water to a boil in a 2-qt. saucepan over high heat, stirring to dissolve sugar; attach a candy thermometer to side of pan and cook, without stirring, until thermometer reads 250°, 4–5 minutes. Turn mixer to medium speed and very slowly drizzle hot syrup into egg whites while beating. Add vanilla and increase speed to high; beat until meringue forms stiff peaks and is slightly warm to the touch, 3 minutes.

3 To assemble, place one layer on a cake stand, drizzle with 3 tbsp. coconut water, spread with 1½ cups frosting, and sprinkle with ½ cup grated coconut; top with another layer, drizzle with 3 tbsp. coconut water, spread with 1½ cups frosting, and sprinkle with ½ cup coconut. Place another layer over frosting, drizzle with 3 tbsp. coconut water, spread with 1½ cups frosting, and sprinkle with ½ cup grated coconut; top with remaining layer and drizzle with remaining coconut water. Cover top and sides with remaining frosting, and cover outside of cake with remaining coconut, pressing it lightly to adhere; chill cake to firm frosting. Serve chilled or at room temperature.

GRAPEFRUIT CAKE

MAKES ONE 9″×13″ CAKE

Grapefruit juice and zest brighten a buttery sheet cake—a staple at Texas potluck dinners—with its welcome kick of citrusy zing.

3	pink grapefruits
10½	tbsp. unsalted butter, softened, plus more for greasing pan
3	cups cake flour, plus more for dusting pan
1	tbsp. baking powder
1	tsp. kosher salt
1¾	cups sugar
2	eggs
¾	cup milk
1½	tbsp. vanilla extract
1	lb. cream cheese, softened
2½	cups confectioners' sugar

1 Zest 1 grapefruit to make 2 tsp. zest; set aside. Peel and segment grapefruits; set aside. Squeeze juice from remaining pulp, reserving ½ cup plus 1 tbsp.; set aside.

2 Heat oven to 350°. Grease and flour a 9″×13″ baking dish; set aside. In a bowl, whisk together flour, baking powder, and salt. In a large bowl, beat butter and sugar with a handheld mixer until fluffy. Beat in eggs one at a time. Add ½ cup of the reserved juice, milk, and vanilla and stir. Add flour mixture and stir until combined. Line bottom of prepared pan with half the reserved grapefruit, add batter and smooth top with a spatula. Bake until a toothpick inserted into cake comes out clean, 40–45 minutes; let cool.

3 In a large bowl, beat reserved zest, remaining 1 tbsp. juice, and cream cheese until fluffy. Add confectioners' sugar, ½ cup at a time, and beat until smooth. Spread frosting over cake and top with remaining grapefruit segments. Chill before serving.

THE BEST DAMN MEYER LEMON CAKE

MAKES ONE 8½″ LOAF CAKE

Meyer lemons—a cross between a lemon and either a mandarin or an orange (botanists aren't sure which)—are the perfect citrus fruit: a thinner-rind lemon without the pucker punch. Its bright flavor cuts through this buttery rich lemon cake.

1	tbsp. unsalted butter, for greasing pan, plus 8 tbsp. melted
2	tbsp. fine dried bread crumbs, for dusting pan
½	cup whole blanched almonds
1½	cups cake flour
1	tsp. baking powder
¾	tsp. fine salt
1⅓	cups plus 2 tbsp. sugar
2	eggs
½	cup milk, at room temperature
2	tbsp. lemon extract
	Grated zest and juice of 2 Meyer lemons

1 Heat oven to 350°. Grease a 8½″×4½″×2¾″ loaf pan with butter and dust with bread crumbs. Invert and tap out excess crumbs; set pan aside. In a food processor, grind almonds until very fine, about 1 minute; set aside. In a bowl, sift together flour, baking powder, and salt; set aside.

2 Put the melted butter into a large bowl and add 1 cup sugar. Mix with a handheld mixer on low speed until combined, about 1 minute. Add eggs one at a time, beating just long enough to incorporate, about 30 seconds. Add flour mixture in 3 batches alternately with milk in 2 batches, beginning and ending with the flour. Beat until mixed after each addition, scraping down the sides of the bowl with a rubber spatula, about 3 minutes total. Mix in lemon extract. With the spatula, fold in lemon zest and ground almonds. (The mixture will be thin.) Turn batter into prepared pan and bake until a toothpick inserted into middle of cake comes out clean and dry, about 65 minutes.

3 Transfer the pan to a wire rack. Prepare the glaze: Combine remaining ⅓ cup plus 2 tbsp. sugar and lemon juice in a small saucepan over medium heat and cook, stirring, until sugar is dissolved, about 2 minutes; do not boil. Brush the glaze over the hot cake. (The excess liquid may pool along the sides of the pan; it will absorb completely as it sits.) Once the cake has absorbed all the liquid, turn it out of the pan and let it cool upright on a rack. Once cool, wrap with plastic wrap and let stand at room temperature for 24 hours for flavors to meld before serving.

COOK'S NOTE For the best results, use a light-colored metal loaf pan. A dark-colored loaf pan will cause the cake to overbrown, and glass loaf pans do not conduct heat as well as metal.

PINEAPPLE UPSIDE-DOWN CAKE

MAKES ONE 10″ CAKE (SEE PHOTO, PAGE 443)

When this cake is baked to a golden brown and inverted onto a serving platter, the juices from the pineapple and caramel drizzle down the sides, making it incredibly moist. This recipe comes from the chief of the Arcata Fire Department in Humboldt County, California, and is considered an all-time favorite among the firemen.

1¾	cups cake flour
2	tsp. baking powder
¼	tsp. fine salt
21	tbsp. unsalted butter
1	cup sugar
1	tbsp. white vinegar
3	tsp. vanilla extract
3	eggs
1⅓	cups buttermilk
10	tbsp. dark brown sugar
2	tbsp. brandy
7	rings canned pineapple
1½	cups stemmed maraschino cherries

1 Heat oven to 350°. In a bowl, sift together flour, baking powder, and salt; set aside. Using an electric mixer, cream together 12 tbsp. butter, sugar, vinegar, and 2 tsp. vanilla until fluffy, 3–4 minutes. Add eggs one at a time, beating for 15 seconds after each addition. On low speed, add flour mixture in 3 batches alternately with buttermilk in 2 batches, beating after each addition. Set mixer speed to medium and beat batter until smooth, about 3 minutes. Set aside.

2 Melt remaining 9 tbsp. butter in a 10″ nonstick ovenproof skillet over medium-high heat. Whisk in remaining 1 tsp. vanilla, brown sugar, and brandy until dissolved, 1 minute. Remove skillet from heat; arrange pineapple slices across bottom of skillet. Arrange cherries evenly between the slices. Pour in cake batter. Bake until golden and set, about 35 minutes. Let cool for 30 minutes and invert onto a serving plate.

RHUBARB VARIATION (SEE PHOTO, PAGE 442)
The caramel sweetness of an upside-down cake lends itself to plenty of fruits beyond pineapple. In spring, swap fresh rhubarb for a sweet-tart take: Follow the instructions above, but instead of pineapple rings, combine ¾ lb. rhubarb, trimmed and chopped, with 1 cup sugar, 4 tbsp. butter, 1 tbsp. lemon juice, 2 tsp. vanilla, and ¼ tsp. salt in a 10″ cast-iron skillet over medium heat. Cook, stirring occasionally, until sugar is melted and rhubarb is tender and slightly caramelized, 8–10 minutes. Then pour in cake batter and bake according to instructions above.

CHARLOTTE À LA FRAMBOISE
Raspberry Charlotte
MAKES ONE 9″ CAKE

The Les Halles quarter of Paris may no longer have its famed food market, but its spirit lives on in the classic French bistro dishes it inspired, such as this cool and creamy raspberry mousse sandwiched between two layers of fluffy cake.

FOR THE CAKE

1	tbsp. unsalted butter
4	eggs, separated
½	cup sugar
7	tbsp. cake flour
1¼	tsp. vanilla extract

FOR THE FILLING

9	cups fresh or frozen raspberries
¾	cup sugar
1	package unflavored gelatin
¼	cup eau-de-vie de poire (pear brandy)
2	cups heavy cream

FOR THE SAUCE

3	tbsp. superfine sugar
2	tbsp. fresh lemon juice
2	tbsp. eau-de-vie de poire (pear brandy)

1 Make the cake: Heat oven to 400°. Butter a 9″ springform pan and line bottom with buttered parchment and set aside. Whisk together egg yolks and sugar in a bowl until pale yellow. Gradually beat in flour until mixture is smooth. Add vanilla and set aside. Whisk egg whites in a medium bowl until stiff peaks form, then fold whites into yolk mixture, taking care not to deflate whites. Pour into pan and bake until brown, 25–30 minutes. Set aside to cool.

2 Make the filling: Put raspberries, sugar, and 1 cup water into a medium saucepan. Simmer over medium heat until sugar dissolves and berries break down, about 10 minutes. Press through a sieve set over a bowl to catch purée. Return 2 cups purée to pan and set over low heat. Reserve remaining purée for sauce. Sprinkle gelatin in ¼ cup cold water, let soften for 3–5 minutes, then add to purée in pan, stirring until dissolved, 1–2 minutes. Remove from heat, add eau-de-vie, and set aside to cool. Whip cream in a large bowl until soft peaks form. Gently fold cooled purée into cream.

3 Unmold cake and discard parchment. Slice cake in half horizontally, making 2 layers, then return cake bottom to pan with ring reattached. Pour in filling, then replace cake top, brown side up. Cover with plastic; refrigerate for 24 hours.

BAKING BETTER CAKES

Baking takes patience and precision. A few extra tips never hurt, either.

THE FLOUR For the best results when baking a cake, you need to use cake flour, a finely milled variety of flour made from soft winter wheat. With a lower content of gluten-producing proteins than all-purpose flour, cake flour yields baked goods with a fine, soft texture. In a pinch, substitute ¾ cup all-purpose flour mixed with 2 tbsp. cornstarch for each cup of cake flour called for in the recipe.

THE TEMPERATURE The key to a smooth batter is making sure the milk, butter, and eggs are at room temperature when you mix them into the batter. Ideally, leave the eggs out overnight so that they can come to room temperature naturally. But if you are pressed for time, you can quickly warm up refrigerated eggs by placing them in a bowl of warm tap water. Let the eggs sit in the water for about 5 minutes so that they reach the proper temperature before being added to the batter.

THE BEATING Most home bakers learn not to beat their batter in order to prevent a tougher crumb. While this may be a concern when using all-purpose flour, cake batter is less prone to gluten production. Beating a cake batter for a short period of time actually helps aerate it. Once the batter is just mixed, beat it on high speed for 5 seconds—it immediately transforms into a smooth emulsion.

THE SMOOTHING A random air bubble can wreak havoc on a sliced cake's appearance. This aesthetic imperfection can be avoided easily: Once you pour your batter into the pan, smooth its top with a rubber spatula. Next, drop the pan from a height of about a foot onto a countertop. The impact of the fall forces large air bubbles out, producing a more even shape. Only do this for cakes leavened with baking soda or baking powder; egg foam cakes, like Raspberry Charlotte (facing page), need their air bubbles in order to rise.

4 Make the sauce: Combine reserved berry purée, sugar, lemon juice, and eau-de-vie in a bowl and stir until sugar has dissolved. Serve cake with sauce alongside.

SMITH ISLAND CAKE
MAKES ONE 9″ CAKE

Smith Island, one of two inhabited islands in the Chesapeake Bay, is home to an amazing cake composed of wafer-thin, well-frosted layers. Our recipe for this towering dessert, featuring eight layers of buttery yellow cake with chocolate-fudge icing, was inspired by a decadent version served at Becca's Smith Island Cakes in Tasley, Virginia.

FOR THE CAKE
- 24 tbsp. unsalted butter, melted, plus more for greasing pans
- 3½ cups cake flour, plus more for pans
- 4 tsp. baking powder
- 1½ tsp. kosher salt
- 2¼ cups sugar
- 2 cups milk
- 1 tbsp. vanilla extract
- 6 eggs

FOR THE ICING
- 2 oz. unsweetened chocolate, chopped
- 2 oz. semisweet chocolate, chopped
- 2 cups sugar
- 1 cup evaporated milk
- 6 tbsp. unsalted butter, melted
- 2 tsp. vanilla extract

1 Make the cake: Heat oven to 350°. Butter and flour four 9″ cake pans; set aside. Whisk together flour, baking powder, and salt in a large bowl; set dry ingredients aside. Whisk together butter, sugar, milk, vanilla, and eggs in another bowl. Pour wet ingredients over dry ingredients and, using a whisk, stir together until just combined; let batter rest for 15 minutes. Stir batter again until smooth, and then divide half the batter among prepared pans; tilt cake pans around to let batter cover entire bottom. Bake cakes, rotating pans halfway through cooking, until barely browned, about 15 minutes. Let cakes cool for 20 minutes in pans, and then invert onto wire racks to cool completely. Clean and dry pans, and grease and flour again; divide remaining batter among pans, and repeat baking process.

2 Make the icing and assemble the cake: Bring both chocolates, sugar, milk, and butter to a boil in a 6-qt. saucepan over medium-high heat; cook, stirring often, until sugar dissolves, chocolate melts, and mixture is smooth and shiny, about 8 minutes. Remove from heat and stir in vanilla; let icing sit until thick enough to spread, about 30 minutes. Place 1 cake layer on a cake stand and, using an offset spatula, spread with ¼ cup icing; repeat with remaining cake layers, leaving top layer uniced. Chill cake to set icing between layers, about 30 minutes. Rewarm remaining icing, if necessary, and spread over top and sides of cake; let icing cool before serving.

RED VELVET CAKE

MAKES ONE 8″ CAKE

According to legend, red velvet cake was invented in the 1950s at Oscar's in New York's Waldorf-Astoria Hotel. However, baker Raven Dennis of New York's Cake Man Raven Confectionery (whose triple-layer recipe we've adapted) claims red velvet cake originated during the Civil War, and that Southern ladies made it "to keep their husbands home."

FOR THE CAKE

1	tbsp. unsalted butter
3	cups plus 2 tbsp. cake flour, plus 2 tbsp. for dusting pans
1½	cups sugar
1	tsp. baking soda
1	tsp. unsweetened cocoa powder
1	tsp. kosher salt
2	eggs
1½	cups vegetable oil
1	cup buttermilk
2	tbsp. red food coloring
1	tsp. vanilla extract
1	tsp. white vinegar

FOR THE FROSTING

12	oz. cream cheese, softened
24	tbsp. unsalted butter, softened
1½	tsp. vanilla extract
3	cups confectioners' sugar
1½	cups chopped pecans

1 Make the cake: Heat oven to 350°. Grease three 8″ round cake pans with butter. Dust with 2 tbsp. of the flour and set aside. Sift remaining flour, sugar, baking soda, cocoa, and salt into a bowl. Beat eggs, oil, buttermilk, food coloring, vanilla, and vinegar in a bowl with an electric mixer until combined. Add dry ingredients and beat until smooth, 1–2 minutes. Divide batter evenly among pans. Bake cakes, rotating halfway through, until a toothpick inserted into middle of each cake comes out clean, 25–30 minutes. Let cakes cool for 5 minutes, then invert each onto a plate, then invert again onto a rack. Let cakes cool.

2 Make the frosting: Beat cream cheese, butter, and vanilla in a bowl with an electric mixer until well combined. Add sugar and beat until frosting is light and fluffy, 5–7 minutes.

3 Put 1 cake layer on a cake stand; spread one-quarter of the frosting on top. Set another layer on top and repeat frosting. Set remaining layer on top and frost top and sides with remaining frosting. Press pecans into sides of cake.

ELVIS PRESLEY'S POUND CAKE

MAKES TWO 9″ LOAF CAKES

This southern classic, made by Elvis Presley's good friend Janelle McComb, is a testament to the fact that homemade comfort foods never go out of style—no matter how famous you become.

16	tbsp. unsalted butter, softened, plus more for greasing pans
3	cups cake flour, sifted, plus more for dusting
3	cups sugar
2	tsp. vanilla extract
¾	tsp. kosher salt
7	eggs
1	cup heavy cream

1 Heat oven to 350°. Grease and flour two 9″×5″×3″ loaf pans; set aside. Beat butter, sugar, vanilla, and salt in a bowl on medium-high speed of a hand mixer until pale and fluffy, about 6 minutes. Add eggs one at time, beating well after each until smooth. Add flour in 3 batches alternately with cream in 2 batches, beginning and ending with flour and beating until smooth. Increase speed to high and beat batter until smooth and light, 5 minutes.

2 Divide batter between prepared pans and smooth tops with a rubber spatula. Bake until a toothpick inserted into the middle comes out with a couple crumbs adhering to it,

EATING LIKE ELVIS

"When we wrote our book *Elvis World*, we often dined with fans of the King. As they discussed what they loved about him, it became clear that one of the reasons people felt so close to Elvis was that he never lost his down-home taste. You can see it in the decor at Graceland, a poor Mississippi boy's idea of how a rich person's house should look; and it is apparent in what he ate. He could afford filet mignon but preferred well-done burgers. Instead of champagne, he drank Pepsi. For dessert, he favored Deep South diner classics. One of Elvis' favorite sweets was the pound cake made by his childhood friend Janelle McComb. She gave us her recipe in 1987, on the 10th anniversary of Elvis' death. Every year at Christmas, she'd bake two loaves and bring them to Graceland. Elvis could eat one all by himself. Fans know about McComb and place her in the firmament of those who practice TCE ("Taking Care of Elvis"); to serve her cake is to keep the legend alive. "

JANE AND MICHAEL STERN

about 1¼ hours. Let cool for 30 minutes, then unmold onto a cooling rack; let cool completely before serving.

VERY MOIST CHOCOLATE LAYER CAKE

MAKES ONE 9" CAKE (SEE PHOTO, PAGE 448)

This opulent chocolate cake offers a velvety crumb, a rich chocolate taste, and a creamy icing. It's a foolproof recipe for birthdays, celebrations, or just having on hand for when a craving for cake arises.

FOR THE CAKE

- 1 cup milk
- 4 oz. unsweetened chocolate, finely chopped
- 1 cup vegetable shortening, plus more for greasing pans
- 2 cups flour, plus more for dusting pans
- ½ tsp. kosher salt
- 1 tsp. baking soda
- 1 cup packed dark brown sugar
- 1 cup granulated sugar

- 3 large eggs
- 1 tsp. vanilla extract

FOR THE ICING

- 2 oz. unsweetened chocolate, finely chopped
- 2 cups sugar
- ½ cup milk
- ¼ cup light corn syrup
- 8 tbsp. unsalted butter
- ¼ tsp. kosher salt
- 1 tsp. vanilla extract

1 Make the cake: Bring milk to a boil in a 1-qt. saucepan. Remove from heat, add chocolate, and cover; set aside for 5 minutes. Stir until smooth.

2 Heat oven to 350°. Grease and flour three 9" cake pans; set aside. Whisk together flour and salt in large bowl; set aside. Dissolve baking soda in ⅓ cup hot water; set aside.

3 In the bowl of a stand mixer fitted with a paddle attachment, beat both sugars and shortening until fluffy, about 3 minutes. Add eggs one at a time, beating well after each, until smooth. Add flour mixture in 3 batches alternately with chocolate mixture in 2 batches, beginning and ending with flour mixture and beating until smooth. Beat in soda water and vanilla. Divide batter evenly among pans and smooth tops. Bake until a toothpick inserted into middle of each cake comes out clean, about 30 minutes. Let cool for 10 minutes, then invert cakes onto a wire rack to cool completely.

4 Make the icing: Heat chocolate, sugar, milk, corn syrup, butter, and salt in a saucepan over medium-high heat; attach a candy thermometer to side of pan, and cook until mixture thickens and reaches 220°.

5 Pour icing into a mixing bowl; beat with a hand mixer on medium speed until slightly cooled. Add vanilla, increase speed to high, and beat until consistency of frosting. Working quickly, place 1 cake on a cake stand; spread about ½ cup icing on top. Cover with second cake; spread with another ½ cup icing. Cover with third cake, and spread icing over top and sides of cakes. Let cool to set before serving.

ROOT BEER CAKE

MAKES ONE 9"× 13" SHEET CAKE

Using soda pop for baking was popular during World War II because sugar was rationed and soda syrups were a good substitute. We think root beer gives this sheet cake extra levity and a zippy flavor.

1 lb. unsalted butter, softened, plus more for greasing pan
2½ cups cake flour, plus more for dusting pan
2½ tsp. baking powder
1 tsp. kosher salt
1 cup root beer
5 tsp. root beer extract
1½ cups sugar
4 eggs, at room temperature
4½ cups confectioners' sugar
2 tbsp. heavy cream
Root beer candies, for decoration

1 Heat oven to 350°. Grease and flour a 9″×13″ pan.

2 Sift cake flour, baking powder, and salt into a bowl; set aside. Whisk together root beer and 2 tsp. root beer extract in a bowl; set aside.

3 Beat sugar and 1 cup butter in a large bowl until fluffy. Add eggs one at a time, beating briefly after each addition. Add flour mixture and root beer mixture alternately in 3 batches, waiting for each to be incorporated before adding the next. Mix briefly, then transfer batter to pan; smooth out top. Bake, rotating once, until a toothpick inserted into middle of cake comes out clean, 30 minutes. Let cool.

4 Put confectioners' sugar and remaining 1 cup butter into a bowl; beat with an electric mixer to combine. Add cream and remaining 3 tsp. root beer extract; beat to make a fluffy frosting. Spread frosting on cake, making swirls and whorls. Decorate with root beer candies.

CINNAMON COFFEE CAKE

MAKES ONE 8″ CAKE

Ground cinnamon gives the topping on this classic coffee cake its signature zing; the cake itself gets an extra boost of flavor from cinnamon extract.

16 tbsp. unsalted butter, melted, plus more for greasing pan
3¾ cups cake flour, plus more for dusting pan
1¼ cups plus 2 tsp. granulated sugar
6 tbsp. plus 1½ tsp. packed light brown sugar
2 tbsp. plus ½ tsp. ground cinnamon
1¼ tsp. kosher salt
⅓ cup finely chopped pecans

2½ tsp. baking powder
1 cup milk
6 tbsp. sour cream
2¼ tsp. vanilla extract
1½ tsp. cinnamon extract
2 eggs

1 Heat oven to 325°. Grease and flour an 8″×8″ baking pan; set aside. To make the topping, in a bowl, mix 8 tbsp. melted butter, ¼ cup granulated sugar, 6 tbsp. brown sugar, 2 tbsp. ground cinnamon, and ½ tsp. salt until smooth. Add 1½ cups flour and mix with a fork until crumbly. Refrigerate until chilled, at least 1 hour.

2 Meanwhile, make the filling. In a bowl, mix remaining 1½ tsp. brown sugar, 2 tsp. granulated sugar, ½ tsp. ground cinnamon, and pecans; set aside.

3 To make cake batter, in another bowl, whisk together flour, remaining 1 cup sugar, salt, and baking powder; set aside. In a large measuring cup, whisk together remaining 8 tbsp. butter, milk, sour cream, vanilla, cinnamon extract, and eggs until smooth. Pour wet ingredients over dry ingredients and whisk to combine.

4 Pour half the batter into prepared baking pan. Sprinkle filling over top and pour remaining batter over it. Break up topping with fingers and sprinkle over top. Bake until a toothpick inserted into middle of cake comes out clean, 1¼ hours. Let cool before serving.

HUNGARIAN SOUR CHERRY CAKE

MAKES ONE 9″X13″ CAKE (SEE PHOTO, PAGE 448)

Sour cherries grow abundantly in Hungary and are a staple in the country's markets in summer. This cake is typically served with coffee for breakfast.

2 lb. fresh sour cherries, stemmed and pitted, or thawed frozen and pitted sour cherries
¼ cup cake flour, plus more for dusting pan
16 tbsp. unsalted butter, softened, plus more for greasing pan
1½ cups sugar
3 tbsp. kirsch (cherry brandy) or regular brandy
1 tsp. vanilla extract
1 egg
2¼ cups whole wheat flour
1 tbsp. baking powder
¾ tsp. kosher salt
1 cup milk

1 Heat oven to 400°. Toss cherries with ¼ cup flour in a bowl; set aside.

2 Grease a 13″×18″×1″ baking sheet and dust with flour; set aside. In a large bowl, beat together butter, sugar, kirsch, and vanilla with a hand mixer on medium speed until pale and fluffy. Add egg and beat until incorporated.

3 In a medium bowl, whisk together whole wheat flour, baking powder, and salt. With the mixer on low speed, add flour mixture and milk alternately in 3 batches each, beating until smooth. Spoon batter onto prepared baking sheet and smooth evenly. Sprinkle cherries over the top. Bake until cake is golden brown, 45–50 minutes. Let cake cool for 30 minutes, then cut into 12 squares.

INDONESIAN SPICE CAKE

Spekkuk Bumbu

MAKES ONE 8″ CAKE

This aromatic dessert is a layer cake unlike any other: Rather than baking four cakes separately and layering them, as with most layer cakes, you pour each layer on top of the one before, with a wash of butter between them. The result is rich and moist, with a subtle gradient from one layer to the next.

- 1½ cups plus 3 tbsp. unsalted butter, softened, plus more for greasing
- 2 cups cake flour, sifted, plus more for dusting
- 1 tbsp. ground cinnamon
- 1 tsp. freshly grated nutmeg
- ½ tsp. baking powder
- ½ tsp. ground cloves
  Pinch kosher salt
- 1⅔ cups sugar
- 4 eggs
- 3 egg yolks, lightly beaten
- 2 tsp. vanilla extract

1 Heat oven to 325°. Grease and flour an 8″×8″×2″ cake pan and set aside. Sift flour, cinnamon, nutmeg, baking powder, cloves, and salt together into a medium bowl. Repeat and set aside.

2 Beat 1½ cups butter in a large bowl, using a wooden spoon, until it is soft and very pliant, about 4 minutes. Add sugar and beat together until pale and fluffy, 5–6 minutes. Add whole eggs one at a time, beating until mixture is light and fluffy, about 4 minutes. Add flour mixture in 3 equal batches, stirring with a wooden spoon after each addition,

to make a smooth batter. Add egg yolks and vanilla and mix until well combined, about 30 seconds more.

3 Pour one-quarter of the batter into prepared pan, spreading it evenly over bottom, and bake until golden brown and a toothpick inserted into middle of cake comes out clean, 20 minutes. Remove cake from oven, brush cake with one-third of remaining butter, and carefully top with another one-quarter of the batter; repeat the baking process. Repeat the process 2 more times to use up all the batter and remaining butter. The cake will have 4 layers.

4 When its final layer is golden brown and a toothpick inserted into it comes out clean, remove cake from oven and set aside to cool for 10 minutes. Run a knife carefully around edges of pan to loosen cake, then invert it onto a large plate. Invert again and let cool completely.

COOK'S NOTE This cake is also great baked as one whole square, without the layers (just eliminate the extra 3 tbsp. butter).

LINDY'S CHEESECAKE

MAKES ONE 9″ CHEESECAKE

New York deli man Arnold Reuben (owner of the now-closed Reuben's Restaurant and Delicatessen, and alleged inventor of the eponymous sandwich) claimed he was the first to serve New York–style cheesecake. But it was his competitor, Leo Lindemann, who hired away Reuben's pastry chef to re-create the dessert at his place, Lindy's, and made it an icon. Lindy's is gone now, but the cheesecake recipe remains.

FOR THE CRUST
- 1 cup flour
- 8 tbsp. cold unsalted butter, cubed
- ¼ cup sugar
- 1 tsp. grated lemon zest
- ¼ tsp. kosher salt
- 1 egg yolk
- ½ vanilla bean, seeds scraped and reserved

FOR THE FILLING
- 2½ lb. cream cheese, softened
- 1¼ cups sugar
- 3 tbsp. flour
- 1½ tsp. grated orange zest
- 1½ tsp. grated lemon zest
- ½ tsp. vanilla extract

> ## "If you're afraid of butter, use cream."
> ### JULIA CHILD

5   whole eggs, plus 2 yolks
¼   cup heavy cream

1 Make the crust: Combine flour, butter, sugar, lemon zest, salt, yolk, and vanilla seeds in a bowl; rub with fingers until dough forms. Form dough into 2 rounds and wrap each in plastic wrap. Chill for 1 hour. Press 1 round onto bottom of a 9″ springform pan; pull pieces from remaining round and press around sides of pan. Set aside.

2 Make the filling: Heat oven to 500°. Beat cream cheese, sugar, flour, citrus zests, and vanilla in a large bowl on medium-high speed of a hand mixer until smooth. Add eggs and yolks one at a time, beating after each addition until smooth; stir in cream. Pour filling into pan and bake until top begins to brown, about 15 minutes. Reduce heat to 200° and bake until just set, 1 hour more. Let cool completely on a rack. Cover and refrigerate for at least 8 hours or overnight. Remove cake from pan and cut into slices to serve.

CORSICAN-STYLE CHEESECAKE
MAKES ONE 8″ CHEESECAKE

Corsicans use *brocciu,* a tangy local cheese made from sheep's or goat's milk, for their cheesecake, but it's nearly impossible to find in the States. Swap in ricotta—sheep's milk ricotta, if you can find it—to lend a similar rich, savory character to this sweet, minimal dessert.

    Unsalted butter, for greasing pan
8   eggs
2½ cups sugar
4½ cups whole-milk ricotta, drained in cheesecloth
    or fine-mesh sieve for 1 hour
    Grated zest of 2 large lemons

Heat oven to 350°. Butter an 8″×8″ baking pan. Line bottom of pan with parchment paper and grease parchment. Whisk together eggs, sugar, ricotta, and lemon zest in a medium bowl. Pour into prepared pan. Bake until dark brown on top and a toothpick inserted into center comes out clean, 1¼ hours. Allow to cool for 20 minutes then run a knife around sides of pan, turn out onto large plate, peel off paper, then turn cake face up.

PERSIMMON PUDDING
SERVES 8–10

While their Asian counterparts may be better known, persimmons are also indigenous to North America. In the Midwest, the fruit is traditionally used in a spiced, cakelike pudding. Eva Powell, a former elementary-school librarian in Mitchell, Indiana, has won the town's pudding contest numerous times with this recipe.

2   cups persimmon pulp
     (from about 5 ripe persimmons)
2   cups sugar
2   eggs, beaten
1½   cups buttermilk
1   tsp. baking soda
1½   cups flour
1   tsp. baking powder
½   tsp. ground cinnamon
     Pinch kosher salt
¼   cup heavy cream
4   tbsp. unsalted butter, melted
     Whipped cream, for serving

1 Heat oven to 350°. Put pulp and sugar into a large mixing bowl. Mix well. Beat in eggs. Put buttermilk and baking soda into a small bowl and stir. Add to pulp and mix well.

2 Sift together flour, baking powder, cinnamon, and salt into a medium bowl. Gradually add to pulp, stirring until well combined. Add heavy cream and mix well.

3 Grease a 9″×13″ baking dish with some of the butter. Stir remaining butter into batter. Pour batter into dish. Bake until dark brown and toothpick inserted into center comes out clean, about 1 hour. Set aside to cool. Serve with whipped cream.

PLUM PUDDING
MAKES 8 INDIVIDUAL PUDDINGS

This English classic's name is a bit misleading; traditional English plum pudding studded with fruit and nuts hasn't had real plums in it for generations. After tasting it doused with a brandy syrup and a rum-spiked hard sauce, no one will mind the discrepancy.

FOR THE PUDDING

- 4 tbsp. unsalted butter, softened
- 2 eggs
- ¼ cup brandy
- 1 Granny Smith apple, peeled, cored, and diced
- ½ cup dried currants
- ¼ cup raisins
- ¼ cup pecans, chopped
- ⅓ cup packed dark brown sugar
- 1 cup fresh bread crumbs
- ½ tsp. ground cinnamon
- ¼ tsp. ground cloves
  Pinch of freshly grated nutmeg

FOR THE BRANDY SYRUP

- ½ cup sugar
- 1¼ cups brandy

FOR THE HARD SAUCE

- 4 tbsp. unsalted butter, softened
- ¾ cup confectioners' sugar
- ½ tsp. vanilla extract
  Pinch freshly grated nutmeg
- 1 tbsp. dark rum

1 Make the pudding: Grease eight 6-oz. ramekins with 1 tbsp. butter and set aside. Grease eight 3″ squares of foil on one side with 1 tbsp. butter and set aside. Melt remaining 2 tbsp. butter in a small saucepan and set aside to cool slightly.

2 Whisk together eggs and brandy in a medium bowl. Add apples, currants, raisins, pecans, brown sugar, bread crumbs, cinnamon, cloves, nutmeg, and melted butter and mix well. Divide batter among prepared ramekins. Tightly cover each with prepared foil, buttered side down, and put on a rack set in the bottom of a wide, deep pot with a tight-fitting lid. Add enough boiling water to reach halfway up sides of ramekins. Cover pot and steam puddings over medium heat until toothpick inserted into center comes out clean, 15–20 minutes.

3 Make the brandy syrup: Combine sugar and brandy in a small pot and simmer over medium heat, stirring often, until sugar dissolves and mixture is syrupy, about 5 minutes. Keep warm over lowest heat.

4 Make the hard sauce: Put butter, sugar, vanilla, and nutmeg into a bowl and whisk until light and fluffy, about 1 minute. Gradually add rum, whisking constantly until completely incorporated.

5 Remove puddings from pot, uncover, and invert each onto a dessert dish to unmold. Spoon some of the brandy syrup over each pudding and put a dollop of the hard sauce on top (or put hard sauce into a piping bag fitted with a star tip and pipe a rosette on top of each).

CROQUEMBOUCHE
SERVES 16

"The fine arts are five in number," wrote the chef Marie-Antoine Carême, "painting, sculpture, poetry, music, and architecture—whereof the principal branch is confectionery." He knew what he was talking about. After all, he created *croquembouche,* a dramatic spire of caramelized cream puffs that—at some traditional French weddings—takes the place of a wedding cake.

FOR THE PÂTE À CHOUX DOUGH

- 12 tbsp. unsalted butter
- ¼ tsp. kosher salt, plus pinch
- 2 cups flour
- 9 eggs

FOR THE FILLING

- 1½ cups milk
- ½ cup sugar
- 3 tbsp. cornstarch
- 4 egg yolks
- 1½ tsp. vanilla extract
- 16 tbsp. unsalted butter, softened

FOR THE CARAMEL

- 4 cups sugar

1 Make the pâte à choux dough: Heat oven to 425°. Bring butter, ¼ tsp. salt, and 1½ cups water to a boil in a 4-qt. saucepan over high heat. Remove pan from heat, add flour all at once, and stir vigorously with a wooden spoon until mixture forms a thick dough and pulls away from sides of pan, about 2 minutes. Return pan to heat and cook, stirring constantly, until dough is lightly dried, about 2 minutes more. Transfer dough to a bowl and let cool for 5 minutes; using a wooden spoon, beat in 8 eggs one at a time, making sure each egg is completely incorporated before adding the next. Dough will come together and be thick, shiny, and smooth.

2 To shape puffs, dip 2 spoons in water, shake off excess, and scoop a walnut-size piece of dough with 1 spoon. With other spoon, scrape dough onto parchment-lined baking sheet, spacing pieces 1″ apart. Lightly beat remaining egg with pinch of salt and brush each piece of dough with mixture. Bake until puffed and light brown, about 10 minutes. Reduce oven to 350° and continue to bake until well browned, about 15 minutes. Remove from oven and let cool.

3 Make the filling: Bring 1 cup milk and sugar to a boil in a 4-qt. saucepan over medium heat. Meanwhile, whisk remaining ½ cup milk, cornstarch, and egg yolks together in a large bowl. Slowly pour half the hot milk into yolk mixture, whisking constantly, then return mixture to saucepan and cook, stirring constantly with a wooden spoon, until it thickens and just returns to a boil. Stir in vanilla and transfer to a bowl; cover with plastic wrap and refrigerate until chilled. In a large bowl, beat butter on medium speed of a hand mixer until pale and fluffy. Add cold filling and beat until smooth and fluffy, about 4 minutes. Spoon filling into a piping bag fitted with a ¼″ plain tip. Gently poke a hole in flat side of each baked, cooled puff with tip and pipe in filling.

4 Make the caramel: Place 2 cups sugar and ½ cup water in a shallow saucepan and stir to combine. Cover and cook over medium heat until sugar turns light amber, 15–20 minutes. Remove from heat.

5 Using tongs, dip top of filled puffs in hot caramel. Place puffs, glazed side up, on a plastic-lined tray. Form base with 12–14 glazed, cooled puffs, sticking them together with more caramel. Add puffs, layer by layer, to form a hollow cone. (Reheat caramel until liquid again if it becomes too thick; repeat making more caramel with remaining sugar and ½ cup water when first batch of caramel becomes too thick to work with.) Allow caramel to cool until it is the consistency of honey. With a spoon, drizzle thin strings of caramel around cone; let cool until brittle and set. Serve croquembouche within 4 hours of making to ensure the filling doesn't soften the puffs.

KOUIGN AMANN

Breton Butter Cake

MAKES ONE 9″ CAKE

The traditional Breton dessert *kouign amann* (pronounced KWEEN ah-man) is an intensely buttery yeasted pastry with folds and rolls reminiscent of a sweet croissant. Served warm, it's a transportive end to a decadent meal—or an indulgent breakfast or afternoon snack.

2	tsp. active dry yeast
⅓	cup water, heated to 115°
1	tsp. kosher salt
2	cups flour, plus more for dusting pan
11	tbsp. unsalted butter (keep 8 tbsp. in refrigerator until ready to use), plus more for greasing bowl and pan
1¼	cups sugar, plus more for work surface and cake top

1 Mix yeast and water in a large bowl; let sit until foamy, about 10 minutes.

2 Add salt and 1 cup flour to yeast mixture, stirring with a wooden spoon. Add ⅓ cup water and when well blended, add remaining 1 cup flour and another ⅔ cup water. Stir until dough forms into a ball, then transfer to a floured surface and knead with the heels of your palms until smooth and elastic, about 10 minutes. Coat the inside of a large bowl with butter, place dough in bowl, and cover with a damp kitchen towel or plastic wrap. Set aside to rise until doubled in size, 1 hour.

3 Heat oven to 450°. Grease a 9″ pie pan with butter and dust with flour; set aside. Roll out dough on a lightly floured work surface into a large rectangle about 12″×18″, with the shorter side nearest you.

4 Cut chilled stick of butter into 10–12 pieces. Dot middle portion of dough with butter pieces and sprinkle with ¾ cup sugar. Working quickly, fold short sides toward the center, over butter and sugar. Edges should slightly overlap. Sprinkle dough with sugar and roll over seams to seal. Turn dough again so shorter side is nearest you, then fold into thirds as you would a letter. Let dough rest for 15 minutes in refrigerator.

5 Sprinkle work surface with sugar. Roll out dough, dusting with ¼ cup sugar as you go, into a large rectangle. Fold into thirds again and let dough rest for 15 minutes in refrigerator.

6 Again sprinkle work surface with sugar. Roll out dough, dusting with remaining ¼ cup sugar as you go, into a square slightly larger than the pie pan. Ease dough into pan. Melt remaining 3 tbsp. butter and drizzle over dough. Sprinkle with sugar and bake until golden, 35–40 minutes. Remove from pan while hot and serve warm.

Bars, Cookies & Pastries

KATHARINE HEPBURN'S BROWNIES

MAKES 9 BARS

This recipe accompanied a 1975 *Ladies' Home Journal* interview with the actress Katharine Hepburn, who was a great lover of chocolate. The result is a brownie that's incredibly rich, mellow, and chewy.

8	tbsp. unsalted butter, plus more for greasing pan
2	oz. unsweetened chocolate
1	cup sugar
2	eggs, beaten
½	tsp. vanilla extract
1	cup roughly chopped walnuts
¼	cup flour
¼	tsp. fine salt

1 Heat oven to 325°. Grease an 8″×8″ baking pan with butter. Line pan with parchment paper, and grease paper. Set pan aside.

2 Melt butter and chocolate together in a 2-qt. saucepan over low heat, stirring constantly. Remove pan from heat and stir in sugar. Add eggs and vanilla and stir to make a smooth batter. Add walnuts, flour, and salt and stir until incorporated. Pour batter into pan and spread evenly. Bake until a toothpick inserted into the center comes out clean, 40–45 minutes. Let cool on a rack. Cut and serve.

BLONDIES

MAKES 12 BARS

Like a brownie in shape and texture, blondies are packed with all the brown sugar and butterscotchy goodness of chocolate chip cookies, but are softer and more substantial.

12	tbsp. unsalted butter, melted, plus more for greasing pan
2	cups flour, plus more for dusting pan
1½	tsp. baking powder
¼	tsp. kosher salt
1¼	cups packed light brown sugar
½	cup granulated sugar
1	tsp. vanilla extract
2	eggs
2	cups roughly chopped white or dark chocolate

1 Heat oven to 350°. Grease and flour a 9″×13″ baking pan and set aside. Whisk together flour, baking powder, and salt and set aside.

2 Whisk together sugars, vanilla, and eggs in a bowl until smooth. Add butter and stir until smooth. Add flour mixture and stir until just combined. Stir in chocolate and spread batter in prepared pan.

3 Bake until a toothpick inserted into the center comes out with a few crumbs attached, about 20 minutes. Cut and serve.

NANAIMO BARS

MAKES 9 BARS

The Nanaimo bar—an intensely sweet 1950s-era refrigerator confection—takes its name from a city on Vancouver Island in Canada (even though the bar was quite possibly created in the nearby town of Ladysmith). The no-bake square consists of a chocolate-, almond-, and coconut-enriched graham crust supporting a dense layer of buttercream, topped with a slick of semisweet chocolate. The tricky part isn't making them; it's eating one cleanly.

20	tbsp. unsalted butter, softened
5	tbsp. Dutch-process unsweetened cocoa powder
¼	cup granulated sugar
1¼	cups graham cracker crumbs
1	cup unsweetened shredded dried coconut
½	cup ground almonds
1	egg
2	cups confectioners' sugar
3	tbsp. heavy cream
2	tbsp. powdered milk
2	tsp. vanilla extract
8	oz. bittersweet chocolate

1 Heat 8 tbsp. butter, cocoa, and sugar in a 2-qt. saucepan over medium heat until melted and smooth; stir in crumbs, coconut, almonds, and egg. Transfer to a parchment paper–lined 8″×8″ baking pan and press evenly into bottom; set aside.

2 Beat 8 tbsp. butter, confectioners' sugar, cream, powdered milk, and vanilla in a bowl on medium speed of a hand mixer until smooth and fluffy; spread over chocolate layer.

3 Melt remaining 4 tbsp. butter and the chocolate in a 2-qt. saucepan over medium-low heat; spread over vanilla layer. Chill until set, at least 4 hours. Cut into squares to serve.

LEMON BARS

MAKES 16 BARS

This simple, superlatively flavorful take on lemon bars from writer Helen Rosner takes on extra brightness from the use of zest as well as juice in the curd, its intensity well-balanced against buttery-rich shortbread.

FOR THE LEMON CURD
- 1 cup granulated sugar
- 3 eggs
  Grated zest of 2 large lemons
- 4 tbsp. fresh lemon juice
- 8 tbsp. unsalted butter, cubed and chilled

FOR THE SHORTBREAD CRUST
- 12 tbsp. unsalted butter, softened
- 2½ tbsp. granulated sugar
- 2½ tbsp. confectioners' sugar, plus more for dusting
- 1⅓ cups flour

1 Make the lemon curd: Whisk together sugar and eggs in a 2-qt. saucepan until smooth and stir in lemon zest and juice. Place over medium heat and cook, stirring often, until thickened to the consistency of loose pudding. Remove from heat and whisk in butter, 2–3 cubes at a time, until smooth. Transfer to a bowl and cover with plastic wrap. Refrigerate until firm, at least 2 hours.

2 Make the shortbread crust: Heat oven to 325°. Combine butter, both sugars, and flour in a bowl and beat on medium speed until smooth and evenly combined. Transfer to a parchment paper–lined 8″×8″ baking pan and press into the bottom. Bake until lightly golden and set, about 30 minutes.

3 Reduce oven temperature to 300°, pour lemon curd over crust, and continue baking until slightly loose in the center, about 10 minutes longer. Let cool completely and then refrigerate until firm. Cut into squares and dust with confectioners' sugar to serve.

BLUEBERRY POPPY SEED SQUARES

Boruvkovy Kolac

MAKES 2 DOZEN SQUARES

The floral character of poppy seeds shines even more when the seeds are ground, as in this ubiquitous Hungarian dessert.

- 20 tbsp. unsalted butter, softened, plus more for greasing pan
- 3 cups flour, plus more for pan
- 1½ cups sugar
- ¾ tsp. kosher salt
- ¼ tsp. vanilla extract
- 4 cups blueberries
- 2 tbsp. fresh lemon juice
- ½ tsp. ground cinnamon
- 1½ cups ground poppy seeds
- ½ cup heavy cream

1 Heat oven to 350°. Butter and flour a 9″×13″ metal baking pan; set aside. Beat 16 tbsp. butter and ½ cup sugar on medium-high speed until pale and fluffy, about 2 minutes. Add 2½ cups flour and ½ tsp. salt and beat until just combined. Press dough into bottom and halfway up sides of prepared pan; chill for 20 minutes. Bake crust until lightly browned, about 12 minutes, then let cool. Meanwhile, stir remaining butter, flour, and salt, ¼ cup sugar, and vanilla in a bowl until coarse crumbles form; set streusel aside.

2 Heat remaining sugar, 3 cups blueberries, lemon juice, and cinnamon in a 2-qt. saucepan over medium-high heat. Cook until berries burst, about 20 minutes. Remove from heat and stir in remaining 1 cup berries; let cool. Stir together poppy seeds and cream in a bowl, then spread evenly over cooled crust. Pour blueberry mixture over poppy seeds and sprinkle with streusel mixture. Bake until filling is bubbly and streusel is lightly browned, about 40 minutes. Let cool, cut into squares, and serve.

CHOCOLATE CHIP COOKIES

MAKES ABOUT 2 DOZEN COOKIES

These chocolate chip cookies have more in common with biscuits than with the traditional drop cookie: Here, the dough is rolled out and then layered with the chocolate chips, with a result that's crisp outside, and richly marbled and moist within.

- 2¼ cups flour
- ¾ tsp. baking soda

- ¾ tsp. kosher salt
- 16 tbsp. unsalted butter, softened
- ¾ cup packed dark brown sugar
- ¾ cup granulated sugar
- 1 tsp. vanilla extract
- 4 egg yolks
- 9 oz. bittersweet chocolate, roughly chopped

1 Heat oven to 375°. Whisk together flour, baking soda, and salt in a bowl; set aside. Combine butter, both sugars, and vanilla in a large bowl and beat on medium-high speed until smooth and fluffy, about 3 minutes. Add yolks two at a time, beating after each addition. Add dry ingredients and beat on low speed until just combined. Transfer dough to a floured work surface and divide into 3 equal pieces. Flatten each into a 4″×6″ rectangle and wrap in plastic wrap. Chill for 30 minutes.

2 Place 1 dough rectangle on floured work surface and sprinkle with half the chocolate. Top with another rectangle, sprinkle with remaining chocolate, and cover with last rectangle. Using a floured rolling pin, flatten rectangles into a 9″×6″×1½″ rectangle. Using a 2″ round cutter, cut out cookies and transfer to parchment paper–lined baking sheets, spacing them 3″ apart. Gather scraps, reroll into a 1½″-thick disk, and cut out more cookies. Bake, rotating baking sheets halfway through cooking, until lightly browned and set, about 15 minutes.

FLOURLESS PEANUT BUTTER COOKIES
MAKES 3–4 DOZEN COOKIES

The absence of flour brings out the pure peanut butter flavor of these cookies. They have a wonderful chewy texture and a great balance between sweetness and saltiness.

- 1¾ oz. creamy peanut butter
- 1 cup granulated sugar
- 1 cup packed light brown sugar
- 2 eggs
- 1 tsp. vanilla extract
- 2 tsp. baking soda
- ½ tsp. salt
- ½ tsp. cinnamon
- 1 cup demerara sugar

1 Heat oven to 350° with racks in the upper and lower thirds. Line 2 baking sheets with parchment paper and set aside. In a medium bowl, cream together peanut butter, granulated sugar, and brown sugar. Beat in

eggs, vanilla, baking soda, salt, and cinnamon until thoroughly combined.

2 Place demerara sugar in a small bowl. Form peanut butter mixture into 2″ balls and roll in demerara sugar, coating completely. Place balls 4″ apart on prepared baking sheets and flatten with the tines of a fork in a perpendicular crosshatch pattern, if desired.

3 Bake until puffed and lightly golden at edges, 10–12 minutes. Allow to cool on pans for 10–15 minutes on trays to set before serving.

POTATO-CHIP SUGAR COOKIES
MAKES ABOUT 2 DOZEN COOKIES

Chef Mary Sue Milliken of the Border Grill restaurants reimagines the classic butter cookie by studding it with crushed potato chips–giving this treat unexpected salt and crunch.

- 16 tbsp. unsalted butter, softened, plus more for brushing
- ½ cup sugar, plus more for topping
- 1½ tsp. vanilla extract
- ¾ tsp. kosher salt
- 2 cups flour
- ½ cup finely chopped pecans
- ½ cup crushed plain potato chips
- 4 oz. semisweet chocolate, melted, for garnish

1 Heat oven to 350°. Using a hand mixer, beat butter and sugar until light and fluffy. Beat in vanilla and salt until smooth. Fold in flour, pecans, and potato chips until just combined.

2 Working in batches, shape dough into 1″ balls and transfer to a parchment paper–lined baking sheet, spacing them about 2″ apart. Brush the bottom of a heavy glass with butter and dip in sugar. Press glass onto each dough ball and flatten into a 3″ circle. Bake until cookies are golden brown at edges, 8–10 minutes. Transfer to a wire rack and let cool completely. Dip tines of a fork into chocolate and drizzle over cookies, then return to rack until set.

BUTTER BALLS
MAKES 4 DOZEN COOKIES

Dredging these melt-in-your-mouth walnut cookies twice—first while still warm and again after they've cooled—ensures a generous covering of powdery sugar. They're a classic American Christmas cookie.

1 cup finely ground walnuts
2¼ cups flour
½ tsp. kosher salt
16 tbsp. unsalted butter, softened
¼ cup confectioners' sugar, plus 1 cup for dredging
1 tsp. vanilla extract

1 Heat oven to 400°. Combine walnuts, flour, and salt in a medium bowl. Mix well and set aside. Beat butter with an electric mixer on medium speed. Gradually add ¼ cup sugar and beat until mixture is fluffy. Beat in vanilla, then reduce speed and add flour mixture, mixing until just combined.

2 Using your hands, shape dough, 1 tbsp. at a time, into small balls, then place about 1″ apart on buttered nonstick baking sheets. Bake until cookies are slightly golden, about 10 minutes. Remove from oven and let cool for 10 minutes.

3 Meanwhile, place remaining 1 cup sugar on a large plate. Roll cookies, while still warm, in sugar, then transfer to a wire rack to cool. Once cookies are completely cool, roll them again in sugar.

LEBKUCHEN

Chocolate-Glazed Almond Spice Cookies

MAKES 8–10 COOKIES

This unique German cookie, a holiday season staple, is actually two cookies in one: Raw batter is heaped on crisp wafer cookies known as *Oblaten*, and then baked. The cookies are finished with a chocolate glaze.

1½ cups sugar
1 tbsp. vanilla extract
3 eggs
10 oz. mixed candied citrus peel, finely chopped
2¼ cups finely ground almonds
1 tbsp. milk
½ cup flour
1 tbsp. ground cinnamon
½ tsp. ground cloves
½ tsp. ground cardamom
½ tsp. freshly grated nutmeg
½ tsp. kosher salt
14 3½″ Oblaten wafers
2 tbsp. light corn syrup
4 oz. semisweet chocolate, finely chopped

1 Whisk together 1 cup sugar, vanilla, and eggs in a bowl, then beat with a hand mixer until thickened. Stir in candied peel, almonds, milk, flour, cinnamon, cloves, cardamom,

nutmeg, and salt. Place a heaping ¼ cup of batter on an Oblaten wafer; spread batter to edges, leaving it mounded in center. Repeat with remaining wafers and transfer to parchment paper–lined baking sheets, spacing them 1″ apart. Let sit until slightly dried, about 1 hour.

2 Heat oven to 275°. Bake cookies until a toothpick inserted into the middle comes out clean, about 25 minutes. Meanwhile, heat remaining ½ cup sugar, corn syrup, and ¼ cup water in a 1-qt. saucepan over high heat, stirring until sugar dissolves. Pour over chocolate, then let sit for 1 minute. Stir until glaze is shiny. Brush cookies with glaze and let cool to set.

ALFAJORES

Dulce de Leche Cookie Sandwiches

MAKES 20 COOKIES

Variations on this elegant, buttery sandwich cookie can be found throughout Latin America, but alfajores are associated above all with the café culture of Buenos Aires. They're served year-round with coffee, but during the holidays home cooks all over Argentina break out their trusted family recipes—each one unique but always with a decadent filling of dulce de leche.

1⅔ cups cornstarch
1¼ cups flour
1 tsp. baking powder
⅔ cup sugar
10 tbsp. unsalted butter, softened
1 tbsp. cognac or brandy
½ tsp. grated lemon zest
4 egg yolks
½ cup dulce de leche, for filling cookies

1 Heat oven to 350°. In a bowl, sift together cornstarch, flour, and baking powder; set aside.

2 In a mixer fitted with a paddle, beat together sugar and butter until fluffy. Beat cognac and lemon zest and then yolks one at a time. Mix in dry ingredients.

3 Transfer dough to a floured surface, knead briefly, and divide into thirds. Working with 1 dough piece at a time, roll out ¼″ thick . Using a 2½″ round cookie cutter, cut out cookies; transfer to parchment paper–lined baking sheets, spacing them 1″ apart. Reroll scraps, then repeat with remaining dough. Bake until golden, 12–15 minutes. Let cool.

4 Flip half the cookies over; top each with about 1 heaping tsp. dulce de leche. Top with remaining cookies.

CANNOLI

MAKES 24 FILLED COOKIES

Sweetened ricotta fills crisp-fried cookie shells in this Italian classic. While the American version generally uses cow's milk ricotta, in Italy the sheep's milk variety is the norm—we prefer its lightness.

FOR THE FILLING

- 3 cups sheep's milk ricotta
- ½ cup sugar
- ½ tsp. vanilla extract
- ½ cup minced candied citron

FOR THE SHELLS

- 2 cups flour, plus more for kneading
- ¼ cup sugar
- ¼ tsp. kosher salt
- 4 tbsp. unsalted butter, cut into small cubes
- 5 tbsp. marsala wine
- 2 eggs, lightly beaten
  Canola oil, for frying

  Chopped pistachios or thinly sliced candied citron, for garnish

1 Make the filling: Put ricotta, sugar, vanilla, and minced citron into a medium bowl and stir to combine. Cover and refrigerate.

2 Make the shells: Put flour, sugar, and salt into a large bowl and stir to combine. Add butter and work with fingers until mixture resembles fine meal. Add marsala and 1 egg and mix until dough can be formed into a ball. Turn out onto a lightly floured surface and knead until elastic and silky, 10 minutes. Wrap dough in wax paper and let rest in a cool place for 2 hours.

3 Divide dough into 8 balls. Run 1 dough ball through a pasta machine on its widest setting, then repeat several times, gradually moving to narrower settings, until it can be run through at the narrowest setting. Transfer to a clean surface and cut out three 4" circles; discard scraps. Cover with a kitchen towel and repeat with remaining dough balls to make 24 circles in all.

4 Pour oil to a depth of 3" into a heavy medium pot and heat over medium heat until a deep-fry thermometer reads

375°. Working in batches, wrap each dough circle around a 1"×4¾"-long cannoli form (see Cook's Note), sealing ends with a brushing of egg, and fry until light golden brown, about 20 seconds. Transfer to a rack and let cool slightly. Slide shells off forms; let cool completely.

5 To assemble, transfer filling to a piping bag; pipe into both ends of each shell to fill. Dip ends of each cannolo in pistachios to garnish. Serve immediately.

COOK'S NOTE To make the cylindrical shells, you'll need a set of cannoli forms, hollow metal tubes around which the dough is wrapped before being plunged into the hot oil. They're available at most cooking supply stores, Italian groceries, or online.

KNAFEH

Syrup-Soaked Cheese Pastry

SERVES 10-20

This dessert, a staple at celebrations throughout the Middle East, sandwiches fresh cheese between layers of *kataif*, a bird's nest–like phyllo dough. The whole thing is then doused in a sweet, rich, amber-hued syrup.

- 1 cup sugar
- 2 tsp. fresh lemon juice
- 1 tsp. red food coloring (optional)
- ½ cup milk
- 3 tbsp. semolina flour
- 1 lb. whole-milk ricotta
- 1 lb. kataif (shredded phyllo dough), crumbled
- 2 cups unsalted butter, melted, plus more for greasing
- ¼ cup chopped pistachios

1 Boil sugar and ½ cup water in a 2-qt. saucepan and cook, stirring until sugar is dissolved, 1–2 minutes. Stir in juice and food coloring; set aside. Boil milk and semolina in a 1-qt. saucepan and cook, whisking, until slightly thickened, 1–2 minutes. Whisk in ricotta and set aside.

2 Heat oven to 350°. Lightly grease a 9"×13" baking dish. Toss kataif and butter in a bowl until butter is absorbed; press half into the bottom of the dish. Spread ricotta mixture evenly over kataif, then top with remaining kataif. Press layers firmly together. Bake until crisp and golden, 1–1½ hours. Let cool to room temperature. Transfer pastry to a serving platter. Spoon syrup over the top and sprinkle with pistachios.

Candies & Confections

BRIGADEIROS

Brazilian Fudge Balls

MAKES ABOUT 2 DOZEN

You can find many versions of *brigadeiros* in Brazil, but chocolate is the traditional flavor for these dense, chewy fudge balls rolled in sprinkles.

- 4 tbsp. unsalted butter
- 2 tbsp. heavy cream
- 2 14-oz. cans sweetened condensed milk
- 3 oz. semisweet chocolate, finely chopped
- 1 tbsp. unsweetened cocoa powder, sifted
- 1 cup chocolate sprinkles

1 Bring butter, cream, and milk to a boil in a 4-qt. saucepan over medium heat. Add chocolate and cocoa powder and reduce heat to low. Cook, stirring constantly, until mixture is the consistency of dense, fudgy batter, about 15 minutes. Transfer to a bowl and chill until set, at least 4 hours.

2 Using a tablespoon, portion out fudge and roll into balls. Roll each ball in chocolate sprinkles until evenly coated. Chill until ready to serve.

PEANUT BUTTER BUCKEYES

MAKES 2½ DOZEN

Silky peanut butter is whipped with butter and sugar, making a creamy confection that is then rolled and dipped into semisweet chocolate. They're called "buckeyes" because the tan dome of peanut butter left atop the chocolate coating makes these treats resemble the nuts of the buckeye tree.

- 2 cups sifted confectioners' sugar
- ¾ cup creamy peanut butter
- 4 tbsp. unsalted butter, melted
- ½ tsp. vanilla extract
- ¼ tsp. kosher salt
- 6 oz. semisweet chocolate chips
- ½ tsp. vegetable shortening

1 Put sugar, peanut butter, butter, vanilla, and salt into a bowl and beat well with a wooden spoon. Roll peanut

butter mixture into 1" balls and transfer to a wax paper–lined baking sheet in a single layer. Freeze until firm, 15–20 minutes.

2 Melt chocolate and shortening in a small heatproof bowl set over a small pot of simmering water, stirring often. Remove pot and bowl together from heat.

3 Working with about 6 peanut butter balls at a time, insert a toothpick into the center of a ball and dip about three-quarters of the ball into the melted chocolate, leaving about a 1" circle of peanut butter visible at the top. Twirl toothpick between your finger and thumb to swirl off excess chocolate, then transfer to another wax paper–lined baking sheet, chocolate side down. Slide out toothpick and repeat dipping process with remaining peanut butter balls and chocolate, reheating chocolate if necessary.

4 Freeze buckeyes until firm. Smooth out toothpick holes left in peanut butter. Buckeyes will keep well sealed in a cool place for up to 1 week and in the refrigerator up to 2 weeks. Serve at room temperature or chilled.

ALMOND HALVAH

SERVES 4–6

This dense confection is popular in the Middle East, where it comes in numerous variations. We fell in love with this rose water–perfumed halvah in Turkey—a denser, flour-based recipe compared to nut-butter varieties.

- ½ cup high-protein all-purpose flour, such as King Arthur
- ½ cup whole wheat flour
- 3 tbsp. blanched almond halves, toasted
- ¼ tsp. kosher salt
- 8 tbsp. unsalted butter
- 1 cup sugar
- 1 tsp. rose water

1 Stir together both flours, 2½ tbsp. almonds, and salt in a medium bowl. Melt butter in a medium pot over medium-high heat. Add flour mixture and stir with a wooden spoon

> ## "Chocolate is a perfect food, as wholesome as it is delicious, a beneficent restorer of exhausted power. It is the best friend of those engaged in literary pursuits."
>
> ### JUSTUS VON LIEBIG

until combined. Reduce heat to low and cook, stirring occasionally, until mixture darkens slightly and looks moist, about 30 minutes.

2 Meanwhile, put sugar and 1⅔ cups water into a small pot; bring to a boil over medium-high heat, stirring to dissolve sugar. Allow syrup to boil for 2 minutes; remove from heat. Add syrup to flour-almond mixture and stir until well combined (the result should look like cookie dough). Cover pot and cook over low heat for 8 minutes. Uncover pot, transfer mixture to a serving plate, and smooth into a 7″–8″ round with the back of a spoon. With a large soup spoon, press indentations around edges of almond halvah to form a decorative pattern, then sprinkle with rose water. Gently press remaining ½ tbsp. almonds into center of halvah in a radiating flower pattern. Serve warm or at room temperature.

PECAN PRALINES

MAKES ABOUT 2 DOZEN

Pralines, named for an 18th-century French soldier whose cook invented the recipe, are sweets made by coating nuts with sugar syrup.

2	tbsp. unsalted butter
2	cups sugar
¾	cup milk
½	tsp. baking soda
1½	tsp. vanilla extract
1½	cups pecan halves or pieces

1 Line 2 large baking sheets with wax paper, butter the paper with 1 tbsp. of the butter, and set aside. Combine sugar, milk, and baking soda in a medium pot and cook over medium heat, stirring constantly, until a candy thermometer reads 240°, 18–20 minutes.

2 Remove pot from heat, add remaining 1 tbsp. butter and the vanilla, and stir quickly until completely incorporated

and creamy, about 20 seconds. Add pecans and stir well to coat.

3 Working quickly—before the mixture sets—drop generous spoonfuls of pecan mixture onto the prepared pans to form disks about 2″ wide. Let them cool and harden completely, about 2 hours. Carefully peel pralines from wax paper. Serve at once, or store in an airtight container at room temperature for 2–3 days.

DARK CHOCOLATE MATZO BRITTLE

MAKES ABOUT 2 POUNDS (SEE PHOTO, PAGE 444)

You can tailor this caramel-topped brittle—a popular snack during Passover, when matzo shows up at virtually every meal—with any toppings you have on hand, such as cranberries, sliced almonds, or flaky sea salt.

5	unsalted matzo crackers
10	tbsp. unsalted butter, plus more for greasing
1	cup granulated sugar
1	cup packed light brown sugar
1	tsp. vanilla extract
1	tbsp. kosher salt
10	oz. semisweet chocolate, finely chopped
⅓	cup roasted pistachios, roughly chopped

1 Heat oven to 350°. Line a 13″×18″ baking sheet with 2 layers of aluminum foil; grease completely with butter. Place matzos in one layer over foil, breaking into pieces and slightly overlapping, if necessary; set aside.

2 Heat sugars in a 4-qt. saucepan over medium-high heat. Cook, swirling pan often, until golden amber and completely liquefied, about 7 minutes. Add butter and cook, stirring, until caramel is liquid again and butter is melted, about 2 minutes. Add vanilla and salt and stir to combine. Pour caramel over matzo and, using a rubber spatula, spread into an even layer. Bake until matzo has absorbed caramel and is slightly crisp, about 8 minutes.

3 Remove from oven. Sprinkle chocolate evenly over caramel and spread in an even layer. Before chocolate is set, sprinkle with pistachios. Refrigerate for at least 30 minutes. Break into pieces to serve. Store between layers of wax paper in an airtight container for up to 1 week.

SEA SALT CARAMELS

MAKES ABOUT 50

These sweet, velvety, vanilla-infused caramels are perfectly balanced with a sprinkling of coarse sea salt.

- 1¾ cups heavy cream
- ¾ cup liquid glucose or light corn syrup
- 1 tsp. fine sea salt
- 1 vanilla bean, halved lengthwise, seeds scraped and reserved
- 1¾ cups sugar
  Fleur de sel or other flaky sea salt, for garnish

1 Heat cream, glucose, salt, and vanilla seeds in a 4-qt. saucepan over medium heat until mixture begins to simmer; remove from heat and let sit for 10 minutes. Line bottom and sides of an 8″×8″ baking pan with parchment paper; set aside.

2 Stir together sugar and ¾ cup water in a 2-qt. saucepan. Heat over medium-high heat, without stirring, until mixture turns a medium-dark amber and a candy thermometer reads 370°. Remove pan from heat and slowly pour cream mixture into caramel. Return saucepan to medium heat and stir until caramel dissolves. Transfer mixture to a 4-qt. saucepan and cook, without stirring, until candy thermometer reads 246°. Pour mixture into prepared pan and smooth top. Let cool completely, then cut into 1″ squares. Sprinkle with fleur de sel and wrap individually in wax paper squares. Store at room temperature.

NIGERIAN COCONUT MILK CARAMELS

Shuku Shuku

MAKES 64 CARAMELS

Coconut-milk caramels are a common Nigerian snack. Street vendors sell them as caramel spheres rolled in toasted coconut, but at home, they just as often go unadorned. Be sure to use full-fat coconut milk for the best texture and richest flavor.

- 2 tbsp. coconut oil, melted, plus more for cutting caramels
- 2 cups canned coconut milk
- ¾ cup light corn syrup
- 1 tsp. coarse sea salt
- 1¾ cups sugar
- ¾ cup water

1 Line the bottom and sides of an 8″×8″ baking dish with parchment paper and brush with coconut oil; set aside.

2 Combine coconut milk, corn syrup, and salt in a 4-qt. saucepan. Heat over medium-low heat, stirring constantly, until mixture is just warm and any coconut milk clumps are dissolved, 2–3 minutes. Remove from heat and set aside.

3 In an 8-qt. saucepan, combine sugar and water and stir until sugar is wet. Place over medium-high heat and let cook, without stirring, until sugar turns a light amber and a candy thermometer reads 310°. Immediately remove from heat and pour melted sugar into coconut milk mixture. Be careful, as the mixture will bubble and splash. Return saucepan to medium-low heat, stirring continuously until all the caramel is dissolved. Raise heat to medium-high and cook, stirring continuously, until caramel becomes quite thick and a candy thermometer reads 240°F. Immediately remove from heat and pour into prepared pan. Let cool completely and cut into 1″ squares. (Brush your knife with melted coconut oil before each cut to avoid sticking.) Wrap individually in wax paper squares. Store at room temperature.

CANDIED ORANGE PEELS
MAKES 40–50 STRIPS

Turning leftover citrus rinds into a chewy, sweet confection takes two simple ingredients: oranges and sugar. They're a lovely garnish for cakes and cocktails, irresistible dipped in dark chocolate, or simply perfect eaten on their own.

- 3 navel oranges
- 1 cup sugar, plus more for dredging
  Melted dark chocolate, for dipping (optional)

1 Trim ½″ off ends of navel oranges, then make a slit in rinds and scoop out flesh, reserving for another use. Slice peels into ⅛″-wide strips, put in a bowl, cover with water, and refrigerate overnight.

2 Drain strips, transfer to a medium pot, cover with water, and bring to a boil over medium heat. Drain strips and set aside. In same pot, bring sugar and ½ cup water to a boil until sugar dissolves. Add strips and simmer until soft and glazed, about 30 minutes.

3 Dry strips on a rack until tacky. Dredge in sugar and dip ends in melted chocolate, if you like.

BLACK LICORICE TWISTS
MAKES ABOUT 3 DOZEN

Why buy licorice in the store when you can make the freshest, most aromatic version you've ever tasted at home? Made with herbaceous, slightly bitter licorice extract (available at health food stores or online), it's unlike anything you're likely to find in the candy aisle.

- 8 tbsp. unsalted butter, plus more for greasing pan
- 1 cup sugar
- ½ cup dark corn syrup
- ½ cup sweetened condensed milk
- ¼ cup blackstrap molasses
- ⅛ tsp. kosher salt
- ¾ cup whole wheat flour
- 1½ tbsp. licorice extract or anise extract
- 1½ tsp. black food coloring

1 Line a glass 8″×8″ baking dish with parchment; grease. Combine butter, sugar, corn syrup, milk, molasses, and salt in a 2-qt. saucepan fitted with a candy thermometer, bring to a boil over high heat, and boil until temperature reads 265°. Remove from heat and stir in flour, licorice extract, and food coloring; pour into pan. Chill until firm, 30–45 minutes.

2 Invert onto a cutting board, peel off paper, and cut into ¼″-thick ropes; twist each rope to shape. Place on baking sheets; chill for 20–30 minutes until set.

COOK'S NOTE Licorice twists can be stored in the refrigerator for up to 2 weeks, though they will harden considerably as they rest. To serve, just microwave them briefly to soften.

Tarts & Pies

CHOCOLATE CARAMEL TART

SERVES 8

We swooned over this oozing caramel tart, topped with a solid layer of chocolate ganache and sprinkled with sea salt, at Brooklyn's Marlow & Sons restaurant. On their ever-changing menu, it's one of the few things available every night. One bite and you'll understand why.

FOR THE TART SHELL

1½	cups flour
¼	cup plus 1 tbsp. Dutch-process unsweetened cocoa powder
¼	tsp. kosher salt
10	tbsp. unsalted butter, cubed and softened
½	cup plus 2 tbsp. confectioners' sugar
2	egg yolks, at room temperature
½	tsp. vanilla extract

FOR THE CARAMEL

1½	cups granulated sugar
3	tbsp. light corn syrup
¼	tsp. kosher salt
6	tbsp. unsalted butter
6	tbsp. heavy cream
1	tbsp. crème fraîche

FOR THE GANACHE

½	cup heavy cream
4	oz. bittersweet chocolate, finely chopped

Sea salt, for garnish

1 Make the tart shell: Heat oven to 350°. Combine flour, cocoa powder, and salt in a medium bowl and set aside. Using a handheld mixer, cream butter and sugar in a large bowl until mixture is pale and fluffy; mix in yolks and vanilla. Mix in dry ingredients. Transfer dough to a 9″ fluted tart pan with a removable bottom and press dough evenly into bottom and sides of pan. Refrigerate for 30 minutes. Prick the tart shell all over with a fork and bake until cooked through, about 20 minutes. Transfer to a rack and let cool.

2 Make the caramel: In a 1-qt. saucepan, whisk together sugar, corn syrup, salt, and 6 tbsp. water and bring to a boil. Cook, without stirring, until a candy thermometer inserted into syrup reads 340°. Remove pan from heat and whisk in butter, cream, and crème fraîche (the mixture will bubble up) until smooth. Pour caramel into cooled tart shell and let cool slightly; refrigerate until firm, 4–5 hours.

3 Make the ganache: Bring cream to a boil in a 1-qt. saucepan over medium heat. Put chocolate into a medium bowl and pour in hot cream; let sit for 1 minute, then stir slowly with a rubber spatula until smooth. Pour ganache evenly over tart and refrigerate until set, 4–5 hours. Sprinkle tart with sea salt, slice, and serve chilled.

FRENCH APPLE TART

SERVES 8

New York City chef and writer Sara Moulton taught us how to make this beautiful tart in which the apples are arranged to resemble a blooming rose.

FOR THE TART SHELL

1¼	cups flour, plus more for dusting
8	tbsp. unsalted butter, cubed and chilled
¼	tsp. kosher salt

FOR THE FILLING

7	Golden Delicious apples, peeled, halved, and cored
¼	cup sugar
4	tbsp. unsalted butter, cut into small pieces
½	cup apricot jam

Whipped cream, for serving

1 Make the tart shell: Combine flour, butter, and salt in a food processor and pulse until pea-size crumbles form, about 10 pulses. Drizzle in 3 tbsp. ice-cold water and pulse until dough is moistened, 3–4 pulses. Transfer dough to a work surface and form into a flat disk; wrap in plastic wrap and refrigerate for 1 hour. Unwrap dough and transfer to a floured surface. Using a rolling pin, flatten dough into a 13″ circle, transfer to an 11″ tart pan with a removable bottom, and trim edges. Chill for 1 hour.

2 Heat oven to 375°. Make the filling: Working with 1 apple half at a time, thinly slice into ⅛″ wedges. Arrange apple slices in an overlapping pattern, working from outer edge of tart dough. Repeat with remaining apple halves until dough is completely covered and any gaps are filled in. Sprinkle with sugar and dot with butter. Bake until golden brown, 60–70 minutes.

3 Meanwhile, heat apricot jam in a small saucepan until warmed and loose; pour through a fine sieve into a small bowl and set aside. Transfer tart to a wire rack. Using a pastry brush, brush top of tart with jam. Let cool completely before slicing. Serve with whipped cream.

PEAR TARTE TATIN

Tarte Tatin aux Poires

SERVES 6

Firm-fleshed pears transform into tender, juicy slices after steaming under a homemade crust and bathing in a caramel sauce in this variation on the classic French upside-down tart, traditionally made with apple.

FOR THE PASTRY
- 1 cup flour
- 1 tsp. kosher salt
- 6 tbsp. cold unsalted butter, cut into small pieces
- 2 tbsp. cold shortening

FOR THE FILLING
- 2 lb. firm pears, peeled, cored, and halved lengthwise
- 2 tbsp. fresh lemon juice
- 1¼ cups sugar
- 6 tbsp. unsalted butter

1 Make the pastry: In a large bowl, combine flour and salt, then rub in butter and shortening with your fingers until mixture resembles coarse crumbs. Sprinkle 3 tbsp. ice water, 1 tbsp. at a time, into flour mixture and knead until dough just holds together. Wrap in plastic wrap and refrigerate.

2 Heat oven to 425°. To fan pears for filling, place core side down on a cutting board. Starting just below stem, cut each one into 4 lengthwise slices, leaving stem end attached.

Place in a bowl, gently toss with lemon juice and ¼ cup sugar, and set aside for 20 minutes.

3 Meanwhile, melt butter in a 9″ ovenproof skillet over medium heat. Add remaining 1 cup sugar and cook, stirring constantly, until golden brown and caramelized, 3–5 minutes. Remove skillet from heat. Stir to cool, as the sugar will continue to darken even off the heat.

4 Drain pears and place in skillet on caramelized sugar, round side down, stems facing center. Gently fan slices out.

5 Roll out dough on a floured work surface into a 10″ round about ¼″ thick. Place dough on top of pears, covering edge of skillet. Press edges down between pears and inside of skillet and cut four ¼″ steam holes in center. Bake until pastry is golden brown, about 25 minutes.

6 Remove skillet from oven and tilt it carefully, using a baster to draw off excess juices. Transfer juices to a small saucepan and reduce over high heat until thick. Place a large, flat serving platter on top of skillet and invert quickly and carefully. Spoon reduced caramelized juices over the pears. Serve warm or at room temperature.

BUTTERSCOTCH PIE SUPREME

SERVES 8

Dense custard is mixed with warm butterscotch to make the filling for home cook Louise Piper's cream pie recipe, which won Best of Fair at Iowa's State Fair in 1997. It's one of the best versions of this diner classic we've ever tried.

- ½ recipe Flaky Butter Pie Dough (page 521)
- 1 cup packed dark brown sugar
- ¼ cup unsalted butter
- 1 tbsp. corn syrup
- 3 tbsp. flour
- 3 tbsp. cornstarch
- 1¾ cups milk
- 3 egg yolks
- ½ cup sugar
- ¾ tsp. kosher salt
- 1 tsp. vanilla extract
  Whipped cream, for serving
  Chopped walnuts, for garnish

1 On a lightly floured surface, roll out dough into a 12″ round. Fit into a 9″ pie plate. Trim and crimp edges; chill for 30 minutes.

> "If you wish to make an apple pie from scratch,
> you must first invent the universe."
>
> CARL SAGAN

2 Heat oven to 400°. Bake crust (using pie weights, if desired) until lightly set and beginning to color at edges, 10–12 minutes. (If weights were used, remove now.) Reduce oven to 350° and continue to bake until crust is golden brown, about 15 minutes. Let cool completely.

3 Mix together brown sugar, butter, corn syrup, and ¼ cup water in a heavy-bottomed medium saucepan. Cook, stirring constantly, over medium heat until a candy thermometer reads 250°, about 15 minutes. Immediately lower heat to keep temperature at 250°, keeping butterscotch warm over low heat.

4 Mix together flour and cornstarch in a medium bowl. Add ½ cup milk, whisking until smooth. Whisk in egg yolks, then set aside. Combine sugar, salt, and remaining 1¼ cups milk in a heavy saucepan and bring just to a boil over medium heat, about 10 minutes. Whisk ½ cup hot milk mixture into yolk mixture, then whisk yolk mixture into remaining hot milk. Cook over low heat, whisking constantly, until thick and boiling, about 1 minute. Boil for 1 minute more, remove from heat, and stir in vanilla.

5 Immediately mix together warm butterscotch and custard mixture. Pour into baked crust. Let cool to room temperature, then refrigerate until set, about 2 hours. Just before serving, top pie with whipped cream, leaving butterscotch exposed in center. Sprinkle with nuts.

BLUE-RIBBON PECAN PIE
SERVES 8

Sweet, gooey pecan pie is a holiday essential—and, in the American South, a year-round staple. This version's toffee-like interior and beautiful bronze top layer of halved pecans won baker Rubyanne Surritte first place in the 2012 pie contest at Oklahoma's Drummond Ranch.

FOR THE CRUST
- 1½ cups flour
- 1 tsp. kosher salt

- 7 tbsp. unsalted butter, cubed and chilled
- ¼ cup ice-cold water

FOR THE FILLING
- 1 cup light corn syrup
- ¾ cup granulated sugar
- ¼ cup packed light brown sugar
- 2 tbsp. unsalted butter, melted and cooled
- 2 tsp. vanilla extract
- ½ tsp. kosher salt
- 3 eggs, lightly beaten
- 1¼ cups roughly chopped pecans, plus ½ cup halves

1 Make the crust: Pulse flour, salt, and butter in a food processor into pea-size crumbles. Add water and pulse until dough comes together. Flatten dough into a disk. Wrap disk in plastic wrap and chill for 1 hour. On a lightly floured surface, roll disk into a 12″ round. Fit into a 9″ pie plate. Trim edges and crimp; chill for 30 minutes. Heat oven to 350°.

2 Make the filling: Whisk corn syrup, sugars, butter, vanilla, salt, and eggs in a bowl, then fold in chopped pecans. Distribute filling evenly over dough, then arrange pecan halves decoratively around the inside edge of crust. Bake until crust is golden brown and filling is set, about 1 hour. Let cool completely before serving.

SALTED CARAMEL APPLE PIE
SERVES 8

Adapted from a recipe from Brooklyn's Four & Twenty Blackbirds pie shop, this deep-dish delight is packed with apples and a thick salted caramel sauce. Choose both sweet and tart apples to balance the caramel's richness.

- 1 recipe Flaky Butter Pie Dough (page 521)
- 3 tbsp. flour, plus more for dusting
- 7 baking apples, such as Golden Delicious, Granny Smith, or Honeycrisp (about 3 lb.), peeled, halved, cored, and thinly sliced

3 tbsp. plus 1 cup granulated sugar
Juice of 2 lemons
8 tbsp. unsalted butter, cubed
½ cup heavy cream
8 tbsp. demerara sugar
½ tsp. Angostura bitters
¼ tsp. freshly grated nutmeg
¼ tsp. ground allspice
¼ tsp. ground cinnamon
¼ tsp. kosher salt
⅛ tsp. freshly ground black pepper
½ tsp. flaky sea salt
1 egg, lightly beaten with 1 tsp. water

1 On a lightly floured surface, roll out 1 dough disk into a 12″ round. Fit into a 9″ deep-dish pie plate. Trim edges with a knife, leaving 1″ dough overhanging edge of plate; chill for 30 minutes. On a lightly floured piece of parchment paper, roll out remaining dough disk into a 12″ round; trim, discarding edges, into a 9″ square. Slice into six 1½″-wide strips; chill for 30 minutes.

2 Toss apples with 2 tbsp. granulated sugar and the lemon juice; cover with plastic wrap and set aside for 1 hour. Whisk 1 cup sugar and ¼ cup water in a 2-qt. saucepan over medium heat and cook, without stirring, until the sugar dissolves, 2–3 minutes. Add butter and bring to a boil. Continue cooking until the mixture turns a deep red-brown and a candy thermometer inserted in sauce reads 325°, about 25 minutes. Remove from heat. Carefully add cream, stirring until sauce is smooth.

3 Heat oven to 375°. Stir 5 tbsp. demerara sugar, 2 tbsp. flour, bitters, nutmeg, allspice, cinnamon, kosher salt, and pepper together in a large bowl. Drain apples, discarding juices, add to bowl, and toss to coat in spice mixture. Sprinkle remaining 1 tbsp. flour and sugar over crust and tightly arrange apples over dough, mounding them slightly higher in the center. Pour caramel sauce evenly over apples. Sprinkle with half the sea salt.

4 Make a lattice top: Lay 3 dough strips vertically across top of pie about 1½″ apart. Fold first and third strips in half upward. Lay 1 horizontal strip at pie's center. Unfold first and third vertical strips over it. Fold second vertical strip upward. Lay another horizontal strip below the first. Unfold second vertical strip over bottom horizontal strip, then fold it again downward. Lay a third horizontal strip just above the pie's center and unfold second vertical strip. Pinch bottom crust and lattice edges together, roll toward center of pie to hide lattice edges, and crimp edges. Brush egg over crust, then sprinkle lattice with remaining 3 tbsp. demerara sugar and ¼ tsp. sea salt. Bake until crust is golden and filling is bubbly, about 1 hour. Let cool completely before serving.

MOCK APPLE PIE

SERVES 8

Mock apple pie consists of little more than crackers and lemony syrup baked in a pie crust (see Putting on the Ritz, this page), but once baked, it will trick your taste buds into thinking you're eating an apple pie.

FOR THE CRUST
1¾ cups flour
1 tbsp. sugar
1 tsp. fine salt
12 tbsp. unsalted butter, cubed and chilled, plus 2 tbsp. to top filling

FOR THE FILLING
2 cups sugar
2 tsp. cream of tartar
2 tbsp. fresh lemon juice
1 tbsp. grated lemon zest
½ tsp. ground cinnamon
2 cups coarsely broken Ritz, saltine, or soda crackers (about 36)

1 egg, beaten

PUTTING ON THE RITZ

We assumed mock apple pie's persuasive texture and flavor were the invention of Nabisco's test kitchen: The company first issued a back-of-the-box recipe for it in 1935, a year after the introduction of the Ritz cracker. But as it happened, thrifty cooks had long since discovered that crackers, when combined with cream of tartar, lemon juice, cinnamon, and sugar, bore an uncanny resemblance to apple filling. Civil War soldiers used their hardtack rations to simulate homemade apple pies, and even at that time the recipe was on its way west. As the food historian Barbara Haber told us, "We may never know who was the first person to substitute crackers for apples, but my money is on some lady in a poke bonnet in a covered wagon."

1 Make the crust: Combine flour, sugar, and salt in a food processor and pulse to combine. Add 12 tbsp. butter and pulse until pea-size pieces form. Drizzle in 3–4 tbsp. ice water and pulse until dough just comes together. Turn dough out onto a floured surface and knead briefly into a ball. Divide dough in half, form into 2 disks, and wrap tightly in plastic wrap. Chill for at least 1 hour or up to overnight.

2 Make the filling: Put sugar, cream of tartar, and 1¾ cups water into a medium saucepan and bring to a boil. Reduce heat to medium-low and simmer for 15 minutes. Remove from heat and add lemon juice and zest, and cinnamon. Let cool to room temperature.

3 Heat oven to 400°. On a floured surface, roll out 1 dough disk into a 12″ circle, transfer to a 9″ pie pan, fill with crackers, and pour syrup over top. Dot mixture with remaining 2 tbsp. butter. Roll out remaining dough into an 11″ circle and place on top of pie; trim dough, leaving a ½″ overhang. Fold edges up over rim, press to seal, and crimp with the tines of a fork. Cut 6 slits in top of pie, brush with the egg, and bake until crust is golden brown, about 35 minutes. Let cool completely before slicing.

RHUBARB-STRAWBERRY PIE

SERVES 8

Radiant stalks of rhubarb, sharp and tart, show up at the markets right around the same early-summer moment as the season's first sweet strawberries; it's no wonder they so often find themselves sharing a pie crust. In this version, which won home baker Louise Piper a blue ribbon at the Iowa State Fair, thin-sliced rhubarb makes a jammy backdrop to big, juicy chunks of strawberry.

FOR THE CRUST

2⅔	cups flour
1	tsp. kosher salt
⅔	cup vegetable oil
6	tbsp. cold milk

FOR THE FILLING

1¼	cups plus 2 tsp. sugar
⅓	cup flour
¼	tsp. ground nutmeg
¼	tsp. ground cinnamon
2	cups thinly sliced rhubarb
3	cups hulled and halved strawberries
2	tbsp. unsalted butter, cut into small pieces
2	tsp. milk

1 Make the crust: Heat oven to 400°. Sift together flour and salt into a bowl. Measure oil into a measuring cup, then add milk, but don't stir together. Pour oil and milk into flour mixture. Stir until dough just holds together. Divide dough in half, shape into 2 balls, and flatten slightly. Roll out each ball between 2 sheets of wax paper into 12″ rounds. Transfer 1 pastry round (discarding wax paper) into a 9″ pie plate and set other pastry round aside.

2 Make the filling: Mix together 1¼ cups of the sugar, flour, nutmeg, and cinnamon in a large bowl, then add rhubarb and strawberries, tossing well to coat evenly.

3 Fill bottom crust with rhubarb-strawberry mixture and scatter butter on top. Cover with remaining pastry round (discarding wax paper) and crimp edges together to seal. Score top to allow steam to escape, brush with milk, and sprinkle with remaining 2 tsp. sugar. Place pie on a baking sheet and bake until crust is golden and filling is bubbling, about 50 minutes. If edge of crust browns too quickly, cover edge with a strip of aluminum foil to prevent burning. Let pie cool for 1 hour before serving.

LATTICE-TOP RED RASPBERRY PIE

MAKES ONE 9″ PIE

Strawberries may get all the summer berry-pie glory, but we're partial to raspberries—especially under a classic lattice crust, so the top of the filling caramelizes and browns.

FOR THE CRUST

2	cups flour
1	tsp. kosher salt
⅔	cup plus 2 tbsp. vegetable shortening, chilled
1	tbsp. milk
1	tbsp. sugar

FOR THE FILLING

1	cup sugar
3–4	tbsp. flour
	Pinch kosher salt
5	cups fresh or thawed frozen raspberries
2	tbsp. unsalted butter, cut into small pieces

1 Make the crust: Whisk together flour and salt in a large bowl. Using a pastry cutter or 2 table knives, cut shortening into flour mixture until it resembles coarse meal flecked

> **"There is something eternal about the freshness a lemon imparts.... They make you pucker and gnash, but you can't stay mad at lemons for long."**
> MOLLY O'NEILL

with pea-size pieces of shortening. Sprinkle in 6–8 tbsp. ice water, stirring dough with a fork until it begins to hold together. Press dough into a rough ball, then transfer to a lightly floured surface. Give dough several quick kneads until it becomes smooth. Divide dough into 2 balls, one slightly larger than the other, and flatten each slightly to make a disk. Wrap disks individually in plastic wrap and refrigerate for 1 hour.

2 Make the filling: Combine sugar, flour, and salt in a large bowl. Add raspberries and gently toss until well coated. Set filling aside.

3 Heat oven to 375°. Roll larger dough disk out on a lightly floured surface into an 11″ round, then fit it into a 9″ glass pie plate. Transfer filling to pastry bottom and scatter butter over fruit. Roll the remaining dough disk out on the lightly floured surface into a 10″ round, then cut it into eight 1″-wide strips. Weave dough strips on top of filling to make a lattice-top crust (see Salted Caramel Apple Pie, Step 4, page 515), fold edges of dough under, and crimp edges. Brush lattice crust with milk and sprinkle with sugar. Bake until pastry is deep golden (cover edges of crust with foil if browning too quickly), 60–70 minutes. Let pie cool for several hours before serving.

KEY LIME PIE
SERVES 8

Although this pie can be made with bottled Key lime juice, we prefer the flavor of fresh Key limes, which add that signature zip to this tangy crowd-pleaser. Key limes are available by mail order year-round and at supermarkets in the late summer and early winter months.

FOR THE CRUST

    7   tbsp. unsalted butter, melted
    1½ cups graham cracker crumbs (about 10 crackers)
    3   tbsp. sugar

FOR THE FILLING

    4   pasteurized egg yolks
    1   14-oz. can sweetened condensed milk
    ½   cup fresh Key lime juice (8–10 Key limes)
    1½ cups heavy cream
    2   tbsp. sugar

1 Make the crust: Heat oven to 375°. Butter a 9″ glass pie plate with some of the melted butter and set aside. Combine graham cracker crumbs, sugar, and remaining melted butter in a medium mixing bowl, then transfer to prepared pie plate. Spread crumbs evenly on bottom and up sides of pie plate, then, using your fingertips, firmly press down on crumbs to form a crust. Bake crust until lightly browned, 8 minutes. Remove crust from oven and let cool to room temperature on a wire rack.

2 Make the filling: Briefly whisk egg yolks in a large bowl; then gradually add condensed milk, whisking until smooth. Add lime juice and mix until just combined.

3 Pour filling into prepared crust (filling will thicken as it sits). Cover pie with plastic wrap, being careful not to let it touch the surface of the filling, and refrigerate until well chilled, at least 6 hours or overnight.

4 Just before serving, put cream and sugar into a large, well-chilled bowl. Beat with a whisk or an electric beater on high speed until cream just forms soft peaks (do not overbeat). Decorate pie with large dollops of whipped cream.

SHAKER LEMON PIE
MAKES ONE 9″ PIE

This pie, with its marmalade-like filling, is said to have been a specialty of the Ohio branch of the Shaker community—descendants of an ascetic 18th-century English-born religious group.

FOR THE FILLING

2	large lemons
2	cups sugar
¼	tsp. kosher salt
4	eggs
4	tbsp. unsalted butter, melted
3	tbsp. flour

FOR THE CRUST

1¾	cups flour
1	tsp. kosher salt
10	tbsp. unsalted butter, chilled and cut into pieces
2	tbsp. vegetable shortening

1 Start the filling: Thoroughly wash lemons, then dry with paper towel. Finely grate lemon zest into a bowl. Using a mandoline or a sharp knife, slice lemons very thin and remove seeds. Add slices to zest and toss with sugar and salt. Cover and set aside at room temperature for 24 hours.

2 Make the crust: Sift flour and salt together into a large bowl. Use a pastry cutter or 2 table knives to work butter and shortening into flour until it resembles coarse meal. Sprinkle in up to 5 tbsp. ice water, stirring dough with a fork until it just begins to hold together. Press dough firmly into a rough ball, then transfer to a lightly floured surface. Give the dough several kneads with the heel of your hand to form it into a smooth ball. Divide dough into 2 balls, wrap in plastic wrap, and refrigerate for 1 hour.

3 Heat oven to 425°. Finish the filling: Whisk eggs in bowl until frothy. Add butter and flour, whisking until smooth. Stir into lemon mixture.

4 Roll out dough on a lightly floured surface into two 12″ rounds. Fit 1 round into a 9″ pie plate and pour in filling. Cover pie with remaining pastry round. Fold edges of dough under, then crimp edges. Cut steam vents in top crust. Bake until edges begin to brown, about 30 minutes. Reduce heat to 350° and bake until crust is golden brown, 25–30 minutes more. Remove from oven and let cool for at least 30 minutes before slicing.

CONCORD GRAPE PIE

MAKES ONE 9″ PIE

This recipe comes from Irene Bouchard, the undisputed Grape Pie Queen of Naples, New York, who started baking these sweet pies in the early 1970s.

FOR THE CRUST

2½	cups flour
1	tsp. kosher salt
18	tbsp. unsalted butter, chilled and cut into small pieces

FOR THE FILLING

2	lb. Concord grapes, stemmed
¾–1	cup sugar
2	tbsp. quick-cooking tapioca
1	tbsp. unsalted butter, cut into small pieces

1 Make the crust: Whisk flour and salt together in a large bowl. Using a pastry cutter or 2 table knives, work butter into flour until mixture resembles coarse meal. Sprinkle in up to 10 tbsp. ice water, stirring dough with a fork until it just holds together. Press dough into a rough ball, then transfer to a lightly floured surface. Give dough several quick kneads until smooth. Divide dough into 2 balls, one slightly larger than the other, wrap each in plastic wrap, and refrigerate for 2 hours.

2 Make the filling: Slip pulp of each grape out of its skin into a medium saucepan, put skins into a large bowl, and set aside. Cook pulp over medium heat, stirring often, until soft, 8–10 minutes, then strain into bowl with skins, pressing on solids with the back of a spoon. Discard seeds. Set aside to cool completely. Stir sugar and tapioca into grapes and set aside.

3 Heat oven to 400°. Roll the larger dough ball out on a lightly floured surface into a 12″ round, then fit into a 9″ pie plate. Transfer grape filling to pastry bottom and scatter butter on top. Roll the remaining dough ball out on the lightly floured surface into a 10″ round, cut a 1″ hole in center of dough to let steam escape, then cover filling with pastry round. Fold edges of dough under and crimp edges. Bake pie for 20 minutes, reduce oven temperature to 350°, and continue baking until pastry is golden brown, 45–50 minutes more. Let pie cool completely before serving, 3–5 hours.

DEEP-DISH PEACH PIE

SERVES 8–10

This rectangular pie was born out of Nicodemus, Kansas, a now-withering town that was once a fruitful farmland for more than 20,000 free African-Americans in the late 1870s; today it has fewer than 100 residents. Elizabeth

Williams—a once-renowned baker in the community—made this pie with her daughters in the 1930s, using peaches from the orchard behind their house.

FOR THE CRUST

4	cups flour
½	tsp. kosher salt
16	tbsp. unsalted butter, chilled and cut into small pieces
1	cup vegetable shortening, chilled and cut into small pieces

FOR THE FILLING

10	cups sliced fresh peaches
1	cup sugar
	Juice of 1 lemon
¼	cup flour
1	tsp. ground cinnamon
¼	tsp. ground nutmeg

1 Make the crust: Sift flour and salt together into a large bowl. Using a pastry cutter or 2 knives, work butter and shortening into flour until mixture resembles coarse meal. Sprinkle in up to 8 tbsp. ice water, stirring the dough with a fork until it just holds together. Using your hands, press dough firmly into a rough ball. Give dough several quick kneads with the heel of your hand to form a smooth dough, then shape into a ball. Divide ball in half, dust each half with flour, and wrap in plastic wrap. Refrigerate for at least 1 hour.

2 Make the filling: Gently mix peaches, sugar, lemon juice, flour, cinnamon, and nutmeg together in a large bowl and set aside.

3 Heat oven to 375°. Roll out 1 dough ball between 2 sheets of wax paper into a 12″×15″ rectangle. Remove paper and ease pastry into a 9″×12″ baking pan, then fill pastry with peaches and any accumulated juices.

4 Roll out second chilled dough ball between 2 new sheets of wax paper into a 10″×13″ rectangle, then remove paper and carefully place dough on top of peaches. Fold edge under, then crimp with a fork. Make several slits with a sharp knife down the center of the top crust to allow steam to escape during baking. Bake until pie is golden brown and bubbling, 1 hour and 25 minutes. Let cool for at least 1 hour before serving.

BOSTON CREAM PIE
SERVES 10

The French pastry chef who invented the Boston cream pie at the city's Parker House Hotel probably didn't anticipate that the dessert would still be around well over a century later, sold in supermarkets, interpreted as cupcakes, and ice cream, and even finding prominence as a doughnut flavor. But there's an unwavering appeal to those two layers of golden sponge cake sandwiching thick custard, all topped with a glossy chocolate glaze.

FOR THE CAKE

12	tbsp. unsalted butter, softened, plus more for greasing pan
1½	cups flour, plus more for dusting pan
2	tsp. baking powder
½	tsp. kosher salt
1	cup sugar
2	tsp. vanilla extract
3	eggs
⅔	cup buttermilk

FOR THE FILLING & GLAZE

1	cup sugar
¼	cup cornstarch
½	tsp. kosher salt
½	vanilla bean, halved lengthwise, seeds scraped and reserved
6	egg yolks
1½	cups milk
4	tbsp. unsalted butter, cubed and chilled
1	tsp. vanilla extract
4	oz. bittersweet chocolate (60 percent cacao), finely chopped
½	cup heavy cream

1 Make the cake: Heat oven to 350°. Grease and flour a 9″ round cake pan; set aside. Whisk together flour, baking powder, and salt in a bowl; set aside. In another bowl, beat butter, sugar, and vanilla on medium-high speed of a hand mixer until pale and fluffy, about 3 minutes. Add eggs one at a time, beating well after each until smooth. Add dry ingredients in 3 batches alternately with buttermilk in 2 batches, beginning and ending with dry ingredients; beat until just combined. Pour into pan and smooth top with a rubber spatula. Bake until a toothpick inserted into the middle comes out clean, about 35 minutes. Let cool for 15 minutes, then invert onto a wire rack; let cool completely.

"Promises and pie crusts are made to be broken."

JONATHAN SWIFT

2 Make the filling: Whisk together sugar, cornstarch, salt, and vanilla seeds in a 4-qt. saucepan; add yolks and whisk until smooth. Stir in milk and place pan over medium heat; cook, stirring constantly, until thickened, about 10 minutes. Remove from heat and add butter one cube at a time, whisking until smooth. Stir in vanilla extract. Transfer pudding to a bowl, cover with plastic wrap, and chill until firm, at least 2 hours.

3 Make the glaze and assemble cake: Place chocolate in a bowl. Bring cream to a boil in a 1-qt. saucepan over high heat; pour over chocolate and let sit for 1 minute. Slowly stir chocolate and cream until smooth and shiny; set aside to cool for 10 minutes. Using a serrated knife, split cake horizontally into 2 layers so that the top layer is slightly thicker than the bottom. Spread chilled pudding over cut side of bottom layer and cover with top layer; pour chocolate glaze evenly over cake, letting it drip down the sides of the cake. Refrigerate cake until glaze is set, at least 30 minutes. Serve chilled or at room temperature.

BANOFFEE PIE

SERVES 8

Banana slices, sticky toffee, and whipped cream are arranged in layers over a cookie-like crust in this dense, cool treat. (The name is a portmanteau of the two dominant flavors, banana and toffee.) A traditional British dessert, banoffee pie has its share of fanatics on this side of the pond, too.

FOR THE CRUST

- 1 10-oz. package digestive biscuits, such as McVities brand
- 8 tbsp. unsalted butter, melted

FOR THE FILLING

- 8 tbsp. unsalted butter
- ½ cup packed dark brown sugar
- 1 14-oz. can condensed milk
- 4 ripe bananas
- 2 cups heavy cream
  Grated chocolate, for garnish

1 Make the crust: Crush the digestive biscuits in a food processor until you get a fine crumb texture. Transfer to a bowl and stir in melted butter. Press onto bottom of 9″ tart pan with a removable bottom. Press the mixture up the sides of the tart pan with the back of a spoon. Chill the crust in refrigerator for at least 1 hour.

2 Make the filling: Melt butter in a small saucepan. Stir in the brown sugar and melt over low heat. Add condensed milk and bring mixture to a boil for a few minutes, stirring continuously. The toffee should darken slightly. Pour filling into crust. Cool and chill again until the caramel is firm, at least 1 hour.

3 To serve, remove the tart from pan and carefully transfer to a serving plate. Peel and slice bananas and place in a single layer on top of the caramel. Whip the cream and spoon it over the toffee and bananas, sealing the filling in. Sprinkle the top with chocolate.

CARDAMOM-BUTTERMILK PIE

MAKES ONE 10″ PIE

Buttermilk pie, an American classic, is a forerunner of cheesecake and pairs beautifully with dusky, floral cardamom. Real, old-fashioned buttermilk—which, unless you have access to a dairy farm, can be hard to find—is the liquid left over from the churning of ripened cream for butter; it has a tangier, more complex flavor than the version found in stores today. In this recipe, sour cream helps replicate the taste of true buttermilk. A slightly unconventional vinegar-based pie crust lends an extra-flaky, extra-buttery note.

FOR THE CRUST

- 1½ cups flour
- 1 tbsp. sugar
- ¼ tsp. fine salt
- 10 tbsp. cold butter
- 2 tsp. white vinegar

FOR THE FILLING

- 3 tbsp. flour
- ¼ tsp. fine salt

4 tbsp. butter, melted and cooled slightly
1 tsp. ground cardamom
3 egg yolks
1 cup sour cream
1 cup sugar
2 cups buttermilk
   Grated zest of 1 lemon
1 tbsp. fresh lemon juice

1 Make the crust: Combine flour, sugar, salt, and butter in a sealable plastic bag and freeze completely. (This may be done up to 3 months in advance.) When ready to make the crust, mix vinegar and ½ cup ice water in a bowl. Turn the freezer bag's contents out into a food processor; pulse until chunks of the butter have been reduced to the size of large peas. Add vinegar mixture to flour mixture and pulse briefly just to incorporate. Form dough into a disk, wrap in plastic wrap, and refrigerate for at least 1 hour or overnight.

2 On a well-floured surface, roll dough out to a 13″ circle about ⅛″ thick. Fit into a 10″ pie pan; cut away excess dough, leaving a 1½″ border. Tuck the overhanging dough underneath itself to form a thick edge; using your fingers, pinch the edge to create a wavy pattern. Cover and chill for 1 hour.

3 Heat oven to 400°. Prick bottom of dough with a fork; line with foil and fill with pie weights or dried beans. Bake for 10 minutes. Remove weights and foil and bake until light brown, about 10 minutes. Let cool on a rack.

4 Make the filling: Whisk together flour, salt, butter, cardamom, egg yolks, and sour cream; beat in sugar, buttermilk, and lemon zest and juice. Pour into cooled pie shell, place in oven, and reduce heat to 325°. Bake until set on the edges but slightly wobbly in center, about 1 hour. Let pie cool completely on a rack and refrigerate until ready to serve. Allow pie to warm slightly before serving.

FLAKY BUTTER PIE DOUGH
MAKES ENOUGH FOR 2 CRUSTS

This lightly sweetened buttery pie dough makes an incomparably flaky crust for all types of fruit, nut, and custard pies.

2¼ cups flour
1 tbsp. sugar
1 tsp. kosher salt
12 tbsp. unsalted butter, cubed
   and chilled
6 tbsp. ice-cold water

Whisk flour, sugar, and salt in a bowl. Using a pastry cutter, 2 forks, or your fingers, cut butter into flour mixture, forming pea-size crumbles. Add water and work dough until smooth but with visible flecks of butter. (Alternatively, pulse ingredients in a food processor.) Divide dough in half and flatten into disks. Wrap disks in plastic wrap; chill for 1 hour before using.

GLUTEN-FREE PIE CRUST
MAKES 1 CRUST

This subtly sweet, shortbread-like crust is wheat- and gluten-free, and perfect with any filling of your choice.

1 cup white rice flour
¼ cup cornstarch
2 tbsp. confectioners' sugar
½ tsp. baking powder
½ tsp. baking soda
¼ tsp. cream of tartar
¼ tsp. kosher salt
7 tbsp. vegetable shortening or
   unsalted butter, cubed and chilled
1 egg, lightly beaten

1 Pulse flour, cornstarch, sugar, baking powder, baking soda, cream of tartar, salt, and butter in a food processor into pea-size crumbles. Add egg and pulse until dough comes together. Form dough into a ball, flatten slightly, and press evenly into pie plate with fingers; crimp edges. Chill for 30 minutes.

2 To prebake the crust: Heat oven to 400°. Bake crust (using pie weights, if desired) until lightly set and beginning to color at edges, 10–12 minutes. (Remove weights, if used.) Reduce oven to 350°. Remove crust from oven, add filling, and bake as directed in pie recipe. Or continue to bake the unfilled crust until golden brown, about 15 minutes more, then let cool completely and fill as desired.

Fruit Desserts

APPLE CRUMBLE WITH HOT CUSTARD

SERVES 8

To be considered a true crumble, a dessert must comprise a layer of fruit covered in crunchy, buttery crumbs. This version, which we were served on a visit to a sheep farm in New Zealand, ups the ante by smothering the crumble with a scoop of piping-hot custard.

FOR THE CRUMBLE
- 12 Granny Smith apples, peeled, quartered, cored, and thickly sliced
- ½ cup sugar
- 2 cups flour
- 1½ cups packed brown sugar
- 1 tsp. ground cinnamon
- ¼ tsp. ground cloves
- 8 tbsp. unsalted butter, cut into pieces

FOR THE CUSTARD
- 2⅓ cups milk
- ¼ cup sugar
- 4 tbsp. unsalted butter, melted
- ¼ cup flour
- 1 egg
- 1 tsp. vanilla extract

1 Make the crumble: Heat oven to 350°. Put apples and 1 cup water into a large, deep skillet and cook over medium heat, stirring occasionally, until some of the apples are very soft, 20–30 minutes. Stir in sugar and transfer to a large baking dish. Combine flour, brown sugar, cinnamon, and cloves in a large bowl. Work butter into flour mixture until it resembles coarse meal, then spread over apples. Bake until golden, 40–45 minutes.

2 Make the custard: Warm milk in a medium pan over medium heat. Meanwhile, whisk sugar, butter, flour, and egg together in a large bowl. Whisk 1 cup of the milk into the sugar–flour mixture. Gradually add mixture back into the milk in the pan and cook, stirring constantly, until thick, 5–8 minutes. Remove from heat. Add vanilla. Serve crumble with hot custard spooned on top.

BLUEBERRY SLUMP

SERVES 8 (SEE PHOTO, PAGE 447)

Rounds of sticky biscuit dough are dropped onto a skillet full of sweet blueberries in this classic New England dessert, which is variously called a "slump," "grunt," or "cobbler," depending on who you're asking. Scoops of cool vanilla ice cream add a creamy flourish.

- 2 cups flour
- 1¾ cups sugar, plus more for sprinkling
- 4½ tsp. baking powder
- 1 tsp. kosher salt
- 4 tbsp. unsalted butter, cubed and chilled
- 1¼ cups milk
- 1½ lb. blueberries
- 1 cup fresh orange juice
- ¼ cup fresh lemon juice
- Vanilla ice cream, for serving

1 Whisk together flour, ¼ cup sugar, baking powder, and ½ tsp. salt in a large bowl. Add butter and, using your fingers, rub butter into flour until pea-size crumbles form. Add milk and stir just until a moist dough forms; cover and refrigerate dough for 30 minutes, or until ready to use.

2 Heat oven to 400°. Bring remaining 1½ cups sugar and ½ tsp. salt along with blueberries and citrus juices to a boil in a 12″ ovenproof skillet over high heat, stirring to dissolve sugar. Remove pan from heat, and, using 2 tablespoons, portion and form chilled dough into 2–3″ oval dumplings and drop them evenly on top of the blueberry mixture. Sprinkle dough dumplings with sugar and transfer skillet to oven. Bake until biscuits are cooked through and blueberry mixture is reduced, about 25 minutes. Serve hot with vanilla ice cream.

CHERRY CLAFOUTIS

SERVES 8

This classic dessert from rural southern France resembles a slightly thick crêpe that's brimming with ripe, juicy cherries. The recipe is simple, but the

"Life is uncertain. Eat dessert first."

ERNESTINE ULMER

presentation is impressive: Once pulled from the oven, this dessert puffs like a soufflé into a golden brown pillow studded with ruby cherries.

1	tbsp. unsalted butter, softened
1¼	cups milk
6	tbsp. granulated sugar
2	tbsp. kirsch (cherry brandy)
1	tbsp. vanilla extract
6	eggs
	Kosher salt, to taste
¾	cup flour
3	cups cherries, pitted or unpitted
	Confectioners' sugar, for dusting

1 Heat oven to 425°. Grease a 9″ cast-iron skillet or baking dish with butter; set aside. Combine milk, granulated sugar, kirsch, vanilla, eggs, and salt in a blender. Blend for a few seconds to mix ingredients, then add flour and blend until smooth, about 1 minute.

2 Pour batter into buttered skillet, then distribute cherries evenly over top. Bake until a skewer inserted into the center comes out clean and a golden brown crust has formed on top and bottom of clafoutis, about 30 minutes. Dust with confectioners' sugar before serving.

PEACH MELBA

SERVES 4

Auguste Escoffier invented this classically simple dessert of poached peaches, raspberry sauce, and vanilla ice cream in the late 1800s; it's famously named for Australian opera singer Dame Nellie Melba.

4	ripe peaches
1	vanilla bean
1	cup plus 4 tsp. sugar
1	pint vanilla ice cream, softened
1	cup raspberries
½	tsp. fresh lemon juice

1 Bring a large pot of water to a simmer over high heat. Lower peaches into simmering water and blanch just long enough to loosen their skins, about 1 minute. Transfer peaches with a slotted spoon to a bowl of ice water to cool, then peel, halve lengthwise, and discard pits. Put peach halves and vanilla bean into a wide dish and sprinkle with 1 cup sugar. Cover with plastic wrap and set aside until peach juices run and most of the sugar dissolves, about 1 hour.

2 Bring 3 cups water to a boil in a medium pot over high heat. Add peaches and their sugary juices and vanilla bean, reduce heat to medium, and poach, gently stirring occasionally, until peaches are just soft when pierced, 8–12 minutes. Remove pot from heat, partially cover, and set aside until peaches are cool, 1–2 hours. Transfer pot to the refrigerator until peaches are thoroughly chilled, 2–3 hours.

3 Meanwhile, divide ice cream among 4 wide dessert dishes, making a smooth, even layer in bottom of each dish; transfer to freezer until ice cream is solid. Purée raspberries in a blender, then strain through a sieve into a bowl, pressing purée through with a rubber spatula; discard seeds. Add the remaining 4 tsp. sugar and lemon juice to purée, stirring until sugar dissolves.

4 To serve, arrange 2 peach halves, pit side down, in each dish of ice cream (save poaching liquid for another use). Spoon some of the raspberry sauce over peaches. Allow ice cream to soften slightly before serving.

PLUM STRUDEL

SERVES 8–12

This satisfying Eastern European pastry layers plum preserves and walnuts for a gooey, crumbly cake.

2	cups flour
½	cup sugar
4	tbsp. unsalted butter, chilled and cut into ½″ pieces

> "I know the look of an apple that is roasting and sizzling on the hearth on a winter's evening, and I know the comfort that comes of eating it hot, along with some sugar and a drench of cream . . . . I know how the nuts taken in conjunction with winter apples, cider, and doughnuts, make old people's tales and old jokes sound fresh and crisp and enchanting."
>
> MARK TWAIN

1½ tsp. baking powder
½   tsp. kosher salt
3   eggs, lightly beaten
1   cup walnuts
1   12-oz. jar plum preserves

1 Process flour, ¼ cup sugar, butter, baking powder, and salt in a food processor until pea-size crumbles form. Add 2 eggs and ¼ cup ice-cold water and pulse until dough forms. Form into a disk, wrap in plastic wrap, and chill for 1 hour. Finely chop remaining ¼ cup sugar and nuts in food processor; set aside. Purée preserves in processor.

2 Heat oven to 375°. Cut dough into thirds; roll each into an 11″×7″ rectangle. Line an 11″×7″ baking dish with a rectangle. Spread with half the preserves and sprinkle with one-third of the walnuts. Top with second rectangle and spread with remaining preserves and sprinkle with half of the remaining nuts. Top with last rectangle and prick with tines of a fork. Brush with remaining egg and sprinkle with remaining walnuts. Bake until golden, 25–30 minutes.

CRÊPES SUZETTE
SERVES 6

The legend behind crêpes Suzette is almost as rich as the dish itself: Authorship of the recipe is claimed by French restaurateur Henri Charpentier, who writes in his memoirs that in 1894, at age 14, while an assistant waiter, he accidentally set a sauce aflame when serving dessert to the Prince of Wales. Once the fire subsided, the sauce was so delicious that the prince asked that the dish be named for a young girl in his entourage, Suzette.

FOR THE CRÊPES
6   tbsp. flour
6   eggs
6   tbsp. milk
3   tbsp. heavy cream
    Unsalted butter, for greasing

FOR THE SAUCE
3   oranges
16 tbsp. unsalted butter, softened
½   cup plus 2 tbsp. sugar
7   tbsp. Cointreau
1   tbsp. kirsch (cherry brandy)
1   tsp. orange flower water
5   tbsp. cognac

1 Make the crêpes: Whisk together flour and eggs in a medium bowl. Add milk and cream and whisk until smooth. Pour through a fine sieve into a bowl, cover, and refrigerate for 2 hours or up to overnight.

2 Make the sauce: Use a vegetable peeler to remove zest from 2 of the oranges; mince zest and set aside. Juice all 3 oranges and set juice aside. In a medium bowl, beat butter and ½ cup sugar on high speed of a hand mixer until light and fluffy, 2 minutes. Add zest to butter and beat for 1 minute. Gradually drizzle in juice, 2 tbsp. Cointreau, kirsch, and orange flower water, beating constantly until very light and fluffy, about 2 minutes.

3 Heat a seasoned crêpe pan or small nonstick skillet over medium-high heat until hot. Grease pan with a little butter, then pour in ¼ cup batter. Working quickly, swirl batter to just coat pan and cook until edges brown, about 1 minute. Turn with a spatula and brown other side for 30 seconds. Transfer to a plate and repeat with remaining batter, greasing pan only as needed.

4 Melt orange butter sauce in a 12″ skillet over medium heat until bubbling. Dip both sides of 1 crêpe in sauce, then, with best side facing down, fold in half, then in half again. Repeat process with remaining crêpes, arranging and overlapping them around the perimeter of the pan. Sprinkle with remaining sugar. Remove pan from heat, pour remaining 5 tbsp. Cointreau and the cognac over crêpes, and carefully ignite with a match. Spoon sauce over crêpes until flame dies out and then serve immediately.

BRENNAN'S BANANAS FOSTER

SERVES 4–6 (SEE PHOTO, PAGE 448)

Banana liqueur heightens the flavor of the bananas in this flambéed dessert, a signature at the New Orleans restaurant Brennan's.

- 8 tbsp. unsalted butter
- 1 cup packed brown sugar
- ½ tsp. ground cinnamon
- ¼ cup banana liqueur
- 4 bananas, peeled and quartered
- ¼ cup white rum
    Vanilla ice cream, for serving

1 Melt butter, sugar, and cinnamon in a 12″ skillet over medium-high heat. Cook, stirring, until sugar is dissolved, about 4 minutes.

2 Add liqueur and bananas and cook until bananas are soft and slightly caramelized, 4–6 minutes. Add rum and, using a match or lighter, ignite to flambé. Cook until flame dies out. Spoon bananas and sauce over ice cream.

THAI FRIED BANANAS

Kluai Khaek

SERVES 8

Many varieties of banana are grown in Thailand, and the Thai often grill, broil, or fry them. Here, bananas are fried in a delicate batter that's flavored with sweet shredded coconut.

- ½ cup flour
- ½ cup rice flour
- 2 tsp. baking powder
- 1 tsp. ground turmeric
- ¼ cup sugar
- ½ cup sweetened shredded dried coconut
    Vegetable oil, for frying
- 16 firm, ripe baby bananas, peeled and sliced lengthwise

1 To make batter, sift together both flours with baking powder, turmeric, and sugar into a medium bowl. Stir in coconut and ½ cup water and mix well. (Batter should be the consistency of heavy cream; if it is too thick, add a little more water.)

2 Pour oil to a depth of 3″ in a wok and heat over medium-high heat. Working in batches, dip bananas in batter, shake off excess, and fry until crisp and golden brown, 1–2 minutes. Drain on paper towels and serve warm.

COOK'S NOTE For this simple dish, small, firm bananas are preferred. Large supermarket bananas don't work well because they tend to fall apart when heated.

UTAH'S FAMOUS GREEN JELL-O SALAD

SERVES 12

Jell-O mixed with fruit and cream has been a potluck and Mormon church supper staple for decades. (The people of Utah, incidentally, have traditionally been among the nation's top consumers of the product.)

- ½ cup sugar
- 1 6-oz. package lime Jell-O
- 2 tbsp. fresh lemon juice
- 1 8-oz. can crushed pineapple with its juice
- 2 cups heavy cream

1 Put sugar, Jell-O, and 1 cup boiling water into a medium heatproof bowl and stir until Jell-O is dissolved, 2–3 minutes. Add lemon juice and pineapple with its juice, and stir well. Refrigerate until the mixture has a syrupy consistency, 45–50 minutes.

2 Whip cream until stiff peaks form, then gently fold cream into Jell-O mixture. Transfer mixture to a 9″×13″ pan, smooth the top with a spatula, and refrigerate until firm. Serve chilled.

Ice Creams, Sorbets & Granitas

NUTMEG ICE CREAM

MAKES 1 QUART (SEE PHOTO, PAGE 441)

Nutmeg does a delightful thing to this ice cream—it gives it a surprisingly warm sensation, just like cinnamon does to apple pie. Serve this spiced ice cream on its own or scooped on top of warm fruit crisps, cobblers, or pies.

- 2 tsp. freshly grated nutmeg
- 2 cups half-and-half
- 1 whole nutmeg, cracked
- ¾ cup sugar
- 6 egg yolks
- 1 cup heavy cream

1 Toast grated nutmeg in a skillet over medium heat, 1–2 minutes. Remove pan from heat and set aside.

2 Heat half-and-half and cracked nutmeg in a 4-qt. saucepan until it just begins to simmer. Remove from heat and let steep for 10 minutes.

3 In a bowl, whisk together sugar and yolks. While whisking, slowly pour in half-and-half mixture. Return mixture to pan and cook, stirring, until mixture thickens, 8–10 minutes. Pour through a fine sieve into a large bowl.

4 Whisk in toasted nutmeg and cream, cover custard, and chill. Pour custard into an ice cream maker and process according to manufacturer's instructions until churned and thick. Transfer to an airtight container and freeze until set before serving, at least 4 hours.

PISTACHIO KULFI

Indian Ice Cream

SERVES 10

What makes *kulfi,* or Indian-style ice cream, so thick and luscious, and what makes it slower to melt than most styles of ice cream, is that it isn't churned to incorporate air; instead, milk is very slowly simmered until it reduces to become as thick as heavy cream, then cooled, and promptly frozen.

- 8 cups milk
- ⅛ tsp. saffron threads
- ½ cup sugar
  Cardamom seeds from 2 pods, crushed
- 4 tbsp. finely chopped pistachios

1 Heat milk in a 6-qt. Dutch oven over medium-high heat, stirring constantly, until it just reaches a boil. Stir in saffron, reduce heat to low, and gently simmer milk, stirring occasionally, until reduced to 3 cups, about 4 hours. Remove pan from heat and whisk in sugar and cardamom seeds, then let cool to room temperature.

2 Stir in pistachios. Pour mixture into 10 paper cups or kulfi molds. Freeze until set, about 6 hours. To serve, tap cups or pinch molds to release kulfi onto plates.

RUM RAISIN ICE CREAM

MAKES ABOUT 1½ QUARTS

How rum raisin ice cream originated is anyone's guess, but it may have reached its apotheosis in the 1980s, when it became Häagen-Dazs' ultimate cult flavor. When applied to a vanilla custard base, the flavors truly shine: a concentrated burst of dried fruit cut by the boozy kick of rum, all cushioned by creamy dairy. It's kid-friendly sweetness and grown-up complexity, all in one spoonful.

- 1 cup raisins
- 1 cup dark rum
- ¾ cup sugar
- 6 egg yolks
- 2 cups milk
- 2 cups heavy cream
- 1 tbsp. vanilla extract

1 Place raisins and rum in a small bowl, cover with plastic wrap, and let sit until raisins soften and absorb some rum, at least 8 hours or up to overnight. Drain, reserving 2 tbsp. rum, and set raisins and rum aside.

2 Place sugar and yolks in a 4-qt. saucepan and whisk until pale yellow and lightened slightly, about 2 minutes.

> "I don't cry over spilt milk, but a fallen scoop of ice cream
> is enough to ruin my whole day."
>
> TERRI GUILLEMETS

Add milk and stir until smooth. Place over medium heat and cook, stirring often, until mixture thickens and coats the back of a spoon, about 10 minutes. Pour through a fine sieve into a large bowl. Whisk in drained raisins along with reserved rum, cream, and vanilla; cover custard with plastic wrap, pressing it against the surface of the custard, and refrigerate until chilled.

3 Pour custard into an ice cream maker and process according to manufacturer's instructions until churned and thick. Transfer to an airtight container and freeze until set before serving, at least 4 hours.

AZUKI BEAN ICE CREAM

MAKES 1 QUART

A common ingredient in Asian cuisines—particularly in Japan, where they are often used for confections and sweets—red azuki beans are wonderful in both sweet and savory dishes. Here, they provide a perfect ripple of flavor in vanilla ice cream.

FOR THE AZUKI PASTE

- 1 cup washed azuki beans
- ¾ cup sugar
  Pinch of kosher salt

FOR THE ICE CREAM

- 2 vanilla beans
- 1 cup sugar
- 3 egg yolks
- 1½ cups milk
- 1½ cups heavy cream

1 Make the azuki paste: Put beans in a saucepan full of water, bring to a boil, then drain in a colander. Return beans to pan, add 3–4 cups water, cover, and simmer until beans are very soft and have absorbed all the water, 30–40 minutes. Stir in sugar and cook over low heat until sugar has dissolved and beans form a soft, chunky paste. Add salt and allow paste to cool.

2 Make the ice cream: Slice vanilla beans lengthwise down the center with a sharp paring knife. With your fingers, spread beans open, then scrape out and reserve black seeds, reserving pods for another use. Put seeds in a small bowl, add ¼ cup sugar, and mix well.

3 In a medium bowl, blend remaining ¾ cup sugar, vanilla-sugar combination, and egg yolks and beat until mixture becomes creamy and turns a pale yellow. Add milk and cream and mix well into a custard-like consistency. Refrigerate until ready to use, preferably overnight.

4 Pour custard into an ice cream maker and process according to manufacturer's instructions until churned and thick. About 10 minutes before ice cream is ready, feed ½ cup of the azuki paste into ice cream maker. (Reserve the rest for another batch of ice cream.) Serve immediately, or freeze in an airtight container until ready to use.

TART RED CHERRY SORBET

MAKES ABOUT 3½ CUPS

Traditionally, granita has a pleasingly granular texture, obtained by stirring the base mixture frequently with a fork as it freezes. Although that method works with this sour cherry recipe, you can also use an ice cream maker, which will yield a smoother, sorbet-like dessert.

- 1 cup dry white wine
- ¾ cup sugar
- 1 lb. sour cherries, stemmed and pitted
- 6 oz. sweet red cherries, stemmed and pitted
- 3 tbsp. kirsch (cherry brandy)
- 1 tsp. fresh lemon juice

1 Put wine and sugar into a large, heavy-bottomed saucepan and boil over high heat, stirring occasionally, until sugar dissolves, about 5 minutes. Add sour and sweet cherries and return to a boil. Reduce heat to medium and simmer, stirring occasionally, until cherries are soft, about 15 minutes.

2 Remove saucepan from heat and stir in kirsch and lemon juice. Transfer cherry mixture to a large bowl and set aside to cool to room temperature, then cover and refrigerate until thoroughly chilled.

3 Working in batches, purée cherry mixture in a blender until mixture is flecked with bits of cherries. Strain through a sieve into a medium bowl, pressing on solids with the back of a wooden spoon. Discard solids.

4 Process cherry mixture in an ice cream maker according to manufacturer's directions. Serve immediately, or freeze in an airtight container until ready to use.

MANGO ICE
Raspado de Mango
SERVES 6–8

This refreshing and tangy frozen treat is a Mexican version of granita. A touch of salt helps to heighten the sweet-tart flavor.

- 4 cups fresh or bottled mango juice or nectar
- 1 cup sugar
- ½ tsp. kosher salt
- 2 tbsp. fresh lime juice

1 Heat 2 cups mango juice, sugar, and salt in a 2-qt. saucepan over medium-high heat and cook, stirring, until sugar dissolves. Remove from heat and stir in remaining 2 cups mango juice and lime juice; let cool.

2 Pour into an 8″×8″ baking dish and place in freezer. Freeze, scraping and stirring mixture with a fork thoroughly every hour as ice crystals form to prevent it from freezing into a solid mass, until mixture is the consistency of shaved ice, about 4 hours. Spoon into chilled bowls to serve.

MILK GELATO
MAKES ABOUT 1 QUART

Jon Snyder of Il Laboratorio del Gelato, an innovative gelato parlor in New York City, gave us his simple recipe for a silky, perfect milk gelato.

- 1 cup heavy cream
- 3 cups milk
- 1 cup sugar
- 7 tsp. cornstarch
- 1 tbsp. apricot preserves

1 Bring cream and 2 cups milk to a simmer in a medium saucepan over medium heat. Meanwhile, dissolve sugar and cornstarch in remaining 1 cup milk in a bowl.

2 Remove pan from heat and stir in milk-cornstarch mixture. Return pan to medium heat and cook, stirring constantly, until mixture comes to a boil and thickens slightly, 10 minutes. Stir in preserves, strain into a bowl, and set aside to cool. Cover and refrigerate until well chilled, 2–3 hours.

3 Process mixture in an ice cream maker according to manufacturer's directions. Serve immediately, or freeze in an airtight container until ready to use.

OLIVE OIL GELATO
MAKES 1½ QUARTS

Smooth, grassy, and faintly savory, this rich gelato makes an elegant dessert, especially when topped with sea salt.

- 1 cup sugar
- 6 egg yolks
- ⅔ cup extra-virgin olive oil
- 3 cups milk
- 1 cup heavy cream
- 2 tsp. vanilla extract
- 1 tsp. kosher salt
  Fleur de sel or other flaky sea salt, for serving

1 With a hand mixer, beat sugar and egg yolks in a large bowl until pale yellow, about 5 minutes. Add oil in a steady stream and continue beating until smooth and airy, about 3 minutes. Add milk, cream, vanilla, and salt and beat until combined.

2 Pour into an ice cream maker and freeze according to manufacturer's instructions. Serve immediately, or freeze in an airtight container until ready to use. Serve with a sprinkling of fleur de sel.

HOT FUDGE SAUCE
MAKES 2 CUPS

A hot fudge sundae is arguably the quintessential American dessert, and arguably the best part of it is the glorious juxtaposition of freezing cold ice cream and a warm river of hot fudge. In our experience, the commercial stuff never actually tastes as good as the lush, dark liquid chocolate we love at the ice cream parlor; this rich recipe solves that problem.

8   oz. unsweetened chocolate,
    chopped
1   cup sugar
1   cup light corn syrup
8   tbsp. unsalted butter
1   tbsp. vanilla extract
¼   tsp. kosher salt
1⅓ cups water

1 In a 2-qt. saucepan, combine all ingredients. Place over medium-high heat and bring to a boil. Cook, stirring constantly, until sauce thickens and becomes smooth and shiny, about 10 minutes.

2 Let cool slightly before serving, or transfer to a glass jar with a lid and store in the refrigerator for up to 1 week. Before serving, reheat sauce in a saucepan over low heat or in a bowl in the microwave for 30 seconds, as it will thicken when refrigerated.

MARSHMALLOW SAUCE

MAKES 2 CUPS

Step aside, jarred marshmallow fluff. This homemade version—from Itgen's Ice Cream Parlour in Valley Stream, New York—is a wholesome rendition of liquefied marshmallows that begs to be drizzled over chocolate ice cream.

1   tsp. unflavored powdered gelatin
½   cup cold water
1½ cups sugar
1   cup light corn syrup
    Pinch kosher salt
1   tsp. vanilla extract

1 Stir together gelatin and cold water in the bowl of a stand mixer fitted with a whisk.

2 Meanwhile, bring sugar, light corn syrup, kosher salt, and ½ cup water to a boil in a 2-qt. saucepan over medium heat, and cook, without stirring, until a candy thermometer reads 240°. Pour syrup over gelatin mixture and add vanilla extract; beat on low speed for 2 minutes. Increase speed to high and beat until syrup becomes thick, shiny, and white.

3 Serve, or transfer to a glass jar with a lid and store in the refrigerator for up to 1 month. Before serving, reheat sauce in a saucepan over low heat or in a bowl in the microwave for 30 seconds, as it will thicken when refrigerated.

CARAMEL SAUCE

MAKES ABOUT 1 CUP

A veil of luscious caramel sauce is the perfect cloak for a creamy gelato or a dense bread pudding.

8   tbsp. unsalted butter
2   tbsp. light corn syrup
¾   cup packed light brown sugar
¼   cup granulated sugar
⅓   cup heavy cream
1   tbsp. dark rum
½   tsp. fresh lemon juice
½   tsp. kosher salt

1 Heat butter, corn syrup, and ¼ cup water in a 2-qt. saucepan over medium-low heat. Cook, stirring constantly, until butter is melted, about 3 minutes.

2 Stir in both sugars and scrape down sides of pan with a rubber spatula. Bring mixture to a boil and cook, without stirring, until it is golden brown and a candy thermometer inserted in sauce reads 245°, 8–10 minutes.

3 Remove from heat. Carefully add cream, rum, lemon juice, and salt and stir until sauce is smooth. Let caramel sauce cool to room temperature. Store in the refrigerator in a lidded container for up to 1 month.

DATE SHAKE

MAKES 2 SHAKES

Supposedly invented in the 1930s by a California date farmer, date shakes are a popular drink at roadside stands in the Coachella Valley. This recipe is from Oasis Date Gardens, which serves up to 300 shakes a day.

1   cup dates, such as Deglet Noor or (for a more intense date flavor) Medjool, pitted and chopped
1   cup milk
2   cups quality vanilla ice cream

Put dates and milk into jar of a blender and purée until smooth. Add ice cream and purée again. Divide shake between 2 tall cups or glasses.

Mousses, Puddings, Custards & Creams

CHOCOLATE MOUSSE

SERVES 6 (SEE PHOTO, PAGE 448)

This classic French dessert has been a hit with home cooks in America for decades (it took off in popularity in 1955, when the *New York Times* published a recipe for the airy, creamy confection). This version is inspired by Julia Child's take on the classic.

6 oz. semisweet chocolate, cut into small chunks
¼ cup dark rum or orange liqueur
4 eggs, separated
¾ cup sugar
¼ cup strong coffee
8 tbsp. unsalted butter, softened and cut into chunks
¼ tsp. cream of tartar
Pinch kosher salt
½ cup heavy cream

1 Combine chocolate and rum in a small pot; nestle it inside a larger pot filled partway with boiling water. Cover smaller pot and set aside to let chocolate melt.

2 Beat yolks in another small pot until pale and frothy. Combine sugar and coffee in another pot; cook over medium heat until dissolved, 5–6 minutes. Pour into yolks in a stream, while whisking; set aside. Pour water to a depth of 2″ into a large pot and heat over medium-low heat until hot but not simmering. Nestle pot containing yolk mixture over pot and cook, whisking vigorously, until thick and creamy, 8–9 minutes. Transfer yolk mixture to a clean bowl; beat with an electric mixer until cool, about 5 minutes. Uncover chocolate mixture and stir; add butter and whisk until smooth. Fold chocolate-butter mixture into yolk mixture; set aside.

3 Beat egg whites in a bowl until just frothy. Add cream of tartar and salt and beat to stiff peaks. Stir one-quarter of the egg whites into chocolate-yolk mixture; gently fold in the rest. Spoon mousse into 6 serving cups or dishes; cover and chill until set. Beat cream to stiff peaks; transfer to a piping bag with a star tip. Pipe a rosette of cream onto each mousse.

RICOTTA & COFFEE MOUSSE

Spuma di Ricotta al Caffè

SERVES 6

A decadent and elegant dessert, this *spuma* combines ricotta with heavy cream and infuses it with espresso. The recipe is based on one prepared at Ristorante Dattilo in Calabria, Italy.

2 cups whole-milk ricotta
1 cup heavy cream
⅓ cup sugar
2 tbsp. instant espresso powder
1 tbsp. unflavored powdered gelatin
Shaved bittersweet chocolate, for garnish

1 Purée ricotta in a blender until smooth. Transfer to a large bowl; set aside.

2 Whip together cream and sugar in a large bowl until soft peaks form. Set aside.

3 Bring ¼ cup water to a boil in a small saucepan; remove from heat. Whisk 2 tbsp. of the water with espresso in a small bowl. Whisk remaining water with gelatin in another small bowl until dissolved.

4 Stir espresso mixture into ricotta, then stir in gelatin mixture. Fold in cream in 3 batches. Chill mixture for 1 hour, then transfer to a piping bag fitted with a star tip. Pipe mixture into 6 sundae glasses; refrigerate until set, about 1 hour. Garnish with shaved chocolate.

BAKED RICOTTA WITH ORANGE BLOSSOM CHERRY SAUCE

SERVES 4–6 (SEE PHOTO, PAGE 446)

Whipped with an egg and lightened with lemon zest, ricotta transforms into a simple, custard-like dessert once baked. Topped with a cherry sauce perfumed with orange and orange blossom water, it's a beautifully rustic summer dessert.

FOR THE RICOTTA

Unsalted butter, for greasing
1½ cups whole-milk ricotta cheese,
     drained overnight
3 tbsp. honey
1 tsp. grated lemon zest
1 egg

FOR THE CHERRIES

1 cup fresh or frozen pitted cherries, halved
3 tbsp. sugar
2 tbsp. freshly squeezed orange juice
1 tsp. orange blossom water

1 Make the ricotta: Heat oven to 400°. Lightly grease four 4-oz. ramekins with butter and place on a baking sheet. Whisk ricotta, honey, lemon zest, and egg in a bowl until smooth. Divide ricotta mixture among ramekins and smooth the tops with a spatula. Bake until lightly puffed and golden brown on top, 30–35 minutes. Remove from oven and let cool slightly.

2 Make the cherries: Bring cherries, sugar, and orange juice to a boil in a 1-qt. saucepan over medium-high heat. Reduce heat to medium-low and cook, stirring occasionally, until cherries soften and liquid reduces to a syrup, 20–25 minutes. Remove from heat and stir in orange blossom water; let cool slightly. Transfer ramekins to serving plates; spoon cherries and syrup over top.

BUTTERSCOTCH BUDINO

SERVES 8

In 2007, chef Nancy Silverton put an Italian spin on butterscotch pudding, calling it a "budino" and topping it with caramel sauce and fleur de sel. The sweet-salty revelation inspired all sorts of tributes, including this one from chef Jeff Mahin of Stella Rosa Pizza Bar in Santa Monica, who sets the pudding with gelatin instead of eggs for a lighter feel. Call it what you will, it is still, at its core, everything we've always loved about butterscotch pudding.

FOR THE PUDDING

2 tbsp. milk
1 tbsp. unflavored powdered gelatin
10 oz. high-quality butterscotch chips
2 tbsp. bourbon
4 cups heavy cream
3 tbsp. light brown sugar

1 tbsp. granulated sugar
1 tsp. kosher salt
½ vanilla bean, halved lengthwise,
     seeds scraped and reserved

FOR THE CARAMEL SAUCE

⅔ cup granulated sugar
6 tbsp. unsalted butter, cubed
3 tbsp. light corn syrup
2½ cups heavy cream
1 tsp. kosher salt
     Flaky sea salt, for serving

1 Make the pudding: Combine milk, gelatin, and 1 tbsp. water in a bowl; let sit to soften gelatin, about 5 minutes. Place butterscotch and bourbon in a blender; set aside. Combine cream, both sugars, salt, and vanilla seeds in a 2-qt. saucepan, bring to a boil over medium-high heat, and boil until sugar dissolves. Remove from heat, add gelatin mixture, and stir until gelatin dissolves. Pour into blender, let sit for 5 minutes, and then purée until smooth. Divide among eight 6-oz. serving glasses. Chill until set, about 4 hours.

2 Make the caramel sauce: Heat sugar, butter, and corn syrup in a 4-qt. saucepan over medium-high heat; cook, without stirring, until mixture turns dark amber. Meanwhile, boil cream and kosher salt in a 2-qt. saucepan. Pour into caramel and cook, stirring, until smooth. Let cool; divide sauce among set pudding cups. Sprinkle lightly with sea salt before serving.

DANISH RED BERRY PUDDING WITH CREAM

Rødgrød med Fløde

SERVES 4

Fresh strawberries, raspberries, and currants are cooked down into a syrup and then transformed into a thick, silky pudding in this Danish dish, which can be served warm or cold with whipped cream.

1½ lb. mixed red berries, such as strawberries,
     raspberries, and red currants
1 cup sugar
¼ cup cornstarch
     Whipped cream, for serving

1 Combine berries, sugar, and 3 cups water in a 4-qt. saucepan over medium heat and cook until berries begin to break down, about 25 minutes.

2 Strain syrup through a cheesecloth-lined sieve; discard berries or save for another use. Return syrup to pan; bring to a boil.

3 Whisk cornstarch and ½ cup water in a bowl until combined, then whisk into syrup. Cook, whisking constantly, until a thick pudding forms, 8–10 minutes. Transfer pudding to a bowl, cover with plastic wrap, pressing it directly on the surface of the pudding, and chill for 1 hour. Divide among serving dishes and garnish with whipped cream.

BANANA & CHEESE PUDDING

Sombremesa de Banana com Queijo

SERVES 6–8

Fresh bananas layered with cinnamon-perfumed sweetened condensed milk and cream cheese constitute this sumptuous Brazilian dessert.

- 1   14-oz. can sweetened condensed milk
- 1   12-oz. can evaporated milk
- 1   stick cinnamon
- 4   ripe bananas, peeled and cut crosswise into 2″ pieces, then lengthwise into ¼″-thick slices
- 12 oz. cream cheese, cubed
- ¼   tsp. ground cinnamon

1 Heat oven to 350°. Boil milks and cinnamon stick in a 12″ nonstick skillet over medium heat until reduced by half, about 30 minutes; discard cinnamon.

2 Spread one-third of reduced milk over bottom of an 8″×8″ baking dish; top with half the bananas and half the cream cheese. Repeat layering, ending with reduced milk, then sprinkle with ground cinnamon. Bake until bubbly, about 30 minutes.

COCONUT STICKY RICE WITH MANGOES

Kao Niow Mamuang

SERVES 6

In Chiang Mai, the second-largest province in Thailand, locals steep sticky rice (*kao niow*; also known as glutinous or sweet rice) in fresh coconut cream rather than milk, for a rich, sweet flavor. Topped with slices of ripe mango (*mamuang*), it's a fresh dessert to cap off a spicy meal.

- 1   cup sweet rice
- 1   cup coconut cream, or 13.5–oz. can coconut milk
- ½   cup sugar
- 1   tsp. kosher salt
- 2   mangoes, peeled and sliced

1 Place rice in a large bowl, add water to cover by 3″, and soak for 3 hours, then drain.

2 Fill a wok with water and bring to a boil over high heat. Fit with a bamboo steamer, add rice to steamer, reduce heat to medium-low, and steam until rice is tender, 20–25 minutes. Transfer rice to a bowl and set aside.

3 Place coconut cream in a medium saucepan (if using canned coconut milk, spoon cream off the top). Add sugar and salt. Bring to a boil over medium-high heat and cook, stirring, until sugar dissolves, about 1 minute. Pour over rice, mix well, then set aside until liquid has been absorbed, about 30 minutes. To serve, spoon rice onto 6 plates and garnish with mangoes.

INDIAN RICE PUDDING

Kheer

SERVES 4–6

This traditional cardamom-scented Indian rice pudding owes its particular richness to the inclusion of whole milk, which has been reduced by half during the cooking process to produce a thick, creamy base.

- 6   tbsp. jasmine rice
- 2   tbsp. unsalted butter
- ½   tsp. lightly crushed saffron threads
- ½   tsp. ground cardamom
- 6   cups milk
- 3   oz. jaggery, or 6 tbsp. light brown sugar
- ¼   cup slivered almonds, toasted
- ¼   cup thinly sliced pistachios

1 Place rice in a fine sieve, and rinse under running water until water runs clear; drain thoroughly.

2 Melt butter in a 10″ skillet over medium heat. Add rice, saffron, and cardamom and cook, stirring, until lightly toasted, about 2 minutes. Add milk and cook, stirring occasionally, until milk is reduced by half and rice is tender, 1 hour and 20 minutes.

3 Add jaggery, almonds, and half the pistachios and cook, stirring, until sugar dissolves, about 2 minutes. Transfer to a serving bowl and garnish with remaining pistachios before serving.

"Look, there's no metaphysics on earth like chocolates."

FERNANDO PESSOA

CORTLANDT'S WHISKEY BREAD PUDDING

SERVES 12

This recipe was named after Cortlandt Inge, chef and owner of the now-closed 14 South Restaurant in Fairhope, Alabama. Inge's whiskey sauce is what gives this bread pudding its deep, rich color.

FOR THE WHISKEY SAUCE

16	tbsp. unsalted butter
1⅓	cups light brown sugar
1	cup heavy cream
¼	cup whiskey
1	cup unsalted, roasted whole cashews
½	cup coarsely chopped pecans
1	tbsp. vanilla extract

FOR THE PUDDING

1	tbsp. unsalted butter, for greasing
1½	cups milk
5	tbsp. light brown sugar
2	eggs
2	tsp. vanilla extract
1	tsp. ground cinnamon
	Pinch kosher salt
1	loaf Italian bread, cut into 1"-thick slices

FOR THE WHIPPED CREAM

2	cups heavy cream, cold
6	tbsp. brown sugar
4	tsp. whiskey
1	tsp. vanilla extract

1 Make the whiskey sauce: Put butter and sugar in a medium, heavy-bottomed saucepan over medium heat. Stir mixture with a wooden spoon until butter melts, then stop stirring and continue cooking until syrup reaches 280° on a candy thermometer, about 10 minutes. Remove pan from heat, stir in cream, whiskey, cashews, pecans, and vanilla, then set aside.

2 Make the pudding: Heat oven to 350°. Butter a medium baking dish and set aside. Beat together milk, sugar, eggs, vanilla, cinnamon, and salt in a bowl. Soak bread slices in milk mixture, then fit snugly in a single layer in prepared dish. Pour any remaining milk mixture over bread. Spoon two-thirds of the whiskey sauce over bread and bake until crusty and brown, 45–50 minutes.

3 Make the whipped cream: Beat together heavy cream, sugar, whiskey, and vanilla in a bowl until soft peaks form. Serve bread pudding with reserved whiskey sauce and whipped cream.

FLOURLESS CHOCOLATE SOUFFLÉ

SERVES 3–4 (SEE PHOTO, PAGE 445)

We prefer this delicate but intensely chocolate flourless soufflé to the more traditional flour-stabilized version.

3	tbsp. milk
5½	tbsp. granulated sugar, plus more for dusting
4	oz. semisweet chocolate, coarsely chopped
2	egg yolks
3	egg whites
	Confectioners' sugar, for garnish

1 Heat oven to 375°. Place milk and 4 tbsp. granulated sugar in a small saucepan and stir over medium-low heat until sugar dissolves, about 45 seconds. Stir in chocolate and cook until melted, 1–2 minutes. Transfer to a nonreactive bowl, cool for 5 minutes, then beat in egg yolks.

2 Beat egg whites in a bowl until foamy, then sprinkle in remaining 1½ tbsp. sugar, beating until stiff peaks form.

3 Butter a small soufflé dish (2½" deep, 6" diameter; soufflé will not rise in a larger dish), then lightly dust with granulated sugar. Gently mix one-third of the egg whites into chocolate mixture, then fold in remaining whites, one-third at a time. Do not overmix. Spoon batter into dish.

4 Make sure oven rack is low enough to allow soufflé room to rise as much as 2″ above the dish. Bake until puffed, about 25 minutes. Dust with confectioners' sugar and serve immediately. (Soufflé will begin to deflate after about 2 minutes.)

FLAN

SERVES 8

Many cultures have devised desserts around the simple formula of cooking eggs, sugar, and milk until thick and velvety, but it's the Spanish who had the brilliant idea to add a layer of caramel to the top of the molded custard. The result is flan, quite possibly the most beloved dessert throughout Latin America.

FOR THE CARAMEL

- 1   cup sugar
- 2   tbsp. fresh lemon juice

FOR THE CUSTARD

- ¾   cup sugar
- 3¼   cups milk
- 2   tsp. vanilla extract
- 1   2″ strip lemon zest
- 6   eggs

1 Make the caramel: Heat oven to 350°. Set a kettle of water on to boil. Combine sugar and lemon juice in a small saucepan. Bring to a boil over medium-high heat, stirring with a fork, just until sugar dissolves, about 3 minutes. Stop stirring and let the sugar gradually caramelize until deep golden brown, about 4 minutes. Remove from heat and carefully divide caramel among eight 3¼″-wide flan molds or ramekins to form a layer in the bottom of each. Set the molds aside.

2 Make the custard: Put 6 tbsp. sugar, milk, vanilla, and lemon zest into a small pot. Bring just to a boil over medium-high heat, then remove from the heat. Discard the lemon zest. Whisk together the remaining 6 tbsp. sugar and eggs in a large bowl. Slowly pour the milk mixture into the egg mixture, whisking constantly until well combined.

3 Arrange the molds in a deep baking dish and pour the milk-egg mixture into them, dividing evenly. Put the baking dish into the oven and pour in hot water from the kettle to reach halfway up the sides of the molds. Bake until flans are set around the edges but still slightly wiggly in the center when the sides are tapped with a spoon, about 30 minutes.

Let flans rest in water bath for 5 minutes, then remove and transfer to the refrigerator to chill completely.

4 To serve, carefully run a sharp knife around edges of each mold. Dip the bottom of each mold briefly into a bowl of hot water to warm slightly. Invert flans onto small plates, knock on bottoms for good luck, and lift the molds off to reveal flans.

IRISH CUSTARD WITH STRAWBERRIES

SERVES 6

The Irish love their puddings—especially a thick, creamy egg custard like this one, scented with vanilla bean and topped with jewel-like fresh summer strawberries.

- 1   vanilla bean
- 3   cups milk
- 7   large egg yolks
- ¾   cup sugar
- 4   cups strawberries, hulled

1 Halve vanilla bean lengthwise and add to milk in a heavy saucepan. Bring just to a boil over medium heat. Remove from heat and set aside to cool.

2 Place egg yolks in a medium bowl and slowly whisk in ½ cup sugar until sugar has almost dissolved and mixture thickens.

3 Remove vanilla bean from milk and save for another use. Pour milk into egg-sugar mixture in a thin stream, stirring constantly. Return custard mixture to saucepan and place over medium-low heat. Stir constantly until custard is the consistency of pancake batter (a little thicker than heavy cream), 15–20 minutes. Do not boil.

4 Strain custard through a sieve and pour into 6 individual dishes or a large serving bowl. Allow the custard to cool at room temperature, then chill.

5 Sprinkle strawberries with remaining ¼ cup sugar, mix gently, and let macerate for 1 hour at room temperature. Spoon berries over custard.

PAVLOVA

SERVES 6–8

For decades, Australians and New Zealanders have argued over who gets to claim responsibility for originating this colorful, fruit-filled meringue dessert.

"It seems to me that our three basic needs, for food and security and love, are so mixed and mingled and entwined that we cannot straightly think of one without the others. So it happens that when I write of hunger, I am really writing about love and the hunger for it, and warmth and the love of it and the hunger for it; and then the warmth and richness and fine reality of hunger satisfied; and it is all one."

M. F. K. FISHER

Early variations on the dish are found in archival documents from both countries, but one thing everyone can agree on: The name is in honor of the early 20th century ballet dancer Anna Pavlova, who visited Wellington, New Zealand, while on a world tour in 1926. Our version of the recipe borrows the best elements of versions by Robyn Hedges and Pop Hoar, two New Zealand bakers.

3	cups sugar
1	egg
	Grated zest and juice of 1 lemon
2	tbsp. unsalted butter, cubed and chilled
¼	cup cornstarch
1	tbsp. white vinegar
1	tbsp. vanilla extract
8	egg whites at room temperature
1	cup heavy cream, chilled
½	cup plain yogurt, chilled
	Strawberries, hulled and halved, for garnish
	Kiwifruit, peeled and sliced, for garnish

1 Make lemon curd: In a small saucepan over medium heat, whisk together ½ cup sugar, 1 egg, and lemon zest and juice. Cook, whisking constantly, until thickened, 8–10 minutes. Remove pan from heat and whisk in unsalted butter, letting each cube incorporate before adding the next. Strain curd through a fine sieve set over a small bowl; press plastic wrap against the surface of the curd and refrigerate until well chilled.

2 Make meringue: Heat oven to 350°. In a small bowl, stir together cornstarch, vinegar, and vanilla extract; set aside. In the bowl of a stand mixer fitted with a whisk, beat remaining 2½ cups sugar and egg whites on low speed until combined. Increase speed to medium-high and beat until soft peaks form. Add cornstarch mixture to egg whites, and continue beating until very stiff and glossy peaks form, about 5 minutes more.

3 Place a 9″ round cake pan in the center of a 13″×18″ sheet of parchment paper and use a pencil to trace a circle around the outside of the pan. Flip the sheet of parchment paper marked side down and transfer it to a 13″×18″ baking sheet. Transfer meringue to center of the parchment paper.

4 Using a rubber spatula, shape meringue into a 9″ disk by making the meringue conform to the traced circle; smooth top and sides with spatula. Transfer meringue to the oven; reduce oven temperature to 215° and bake for 1¼ hours. Turn off oven and let meringue sit in oven until cooled, 3–4 hours. Gently peel parchment paper from meringue and, using 2 metal spatulas, transfer meringue to a cake stand.

5 In the bowl of a stand mixer fitted with a whisk, beat cream and yogurt on medium-high speed until stiff peaks form. Pour the whipped cream mixture onto the cooled meringue and, using the rubber spatula, spread evenly over the top.

6 Decorate the top of the Pavlova with strawberries and kiwifruit. Remove the reserved lemon curd from the refrigerator and stir vigorously; drizzle the curd over the Pavlova, reserving a few tbsp. for individual servings. Cut Pavlova into slices and serve immediately with lemon curd.

Drinks

DRINKS

IT MAY JUST BE A COINCIDENCE of language that the phrase "good spirits" refers to both a happy mood and a delicious drink, but we're inclined to read a little something into it. There's a profound pleasure to be found in the thoughtful combination of liquids. That means that what winds up in our glasses deserves the same amount of care in its making—and appreciation in its consumption—as the food on our plates receives.

The first drink ever to be called a "cocktail" was likely made and consumed in the early part of the 19th century, but the precise details—as is so often the case when cocktails are involved—are murky. That particular story may be lost to us, but much of the history of drink has been well documented, with origin stories and invention credit as much of a cocktail's identity as its name. We know—or at least, so the stories go—that the sugar-spiked Old Fashioned likely came about in Tennessee as a bartender's solution for a Civil War veteran who disliked the taste of bourbon; that the rummy Singapore Sling is generally attributed to a bartender working a century ago at Singapore's Raffles hotel; and that the first sip ever taken of the peach-flavored Bellini occurred at Harry's Bar in Venice at some point during World War II.

Cocktails as we know them today may have their origins in the early 1800s, but we've been mixing up drinkable concoctions for far longer: Adding a splash of fruit juice or soda water or a good dose of sugar was an easy way to mask the unpleasant flavors of harsh barreled spirits and rough homemade hooch or—as in the case of a lemonade shandy or a wine-and-soda spritzer—to lighten the alcohol content of something meant to be sipped all day.

Of course, not all libations are intoxicating—at least not by virtue of their alcoholic content. Ritual and history are found in softer drinks, as well: Lime juice, sugar, and salt are an alchemical combination in India's ubiquitous fresh lime soda. In North Africa and the Middle East, almost any visit to someone's home begins with small cups of bracingly sweet hot tea perfumed with fresh mint.

But the one thing that all of these glasses have in common—regardless of whether they hold a tee-totaler's lime rickey or a potent poolside slush—is that we can raise them up in a toast to one another, enjoying the company of our friends and family as much as we enjoy the drink itself.

Cocktails

BRANDY OLD FASHIONED

MAKES 1 COCKTAIL

For Wisconsinites of a certain age, the brandy old-fashioned is the only cocktail worth sipping. This recipe comes from Milwaukee bartender Ellen Diehl, who uses her mother's formula for the old-fashioned mix.

FOR THE OLD-FASHIONED MIX
- 1 cup sugar
- 5 tbsp. Angostura bitters

FOR THE COCKTAIL
- 2 oz. brandy
- 2 dashes Angostura bitters
- ½ cup lemon-lime soda
- 2 maraschino cherries, for garnish
  Small orange slice, for garnish

1 Make the old-fashioned mix: Combine sugar and 1 cup water in a 2-qt. saucepan over medium heat. Cook, stirring occasionally, until sugar has dissolved, 3–4 minutes. Let cool, then stir in bitters. Transfer to an airtight jar and set aside. Mix will keep for up to 2 weeks in the refrigerator.

2 Make the cocktail: Fill a 10-oz. rocks glass with ice. Add brandy, bitters, and 1 oz. of the old-fashioned mix and stir. Top with soda and garnish with cherries and an orange slice.

THE EARTHQUAKE

Tremblement de Terre

MAKES 1 COCKTAIL

This intense potion is adapted from one served at parties by the 19th-century French artist Henri de Toulouse-Lautrec.

- 2½ oz. cognac
- ¼ oz. absinthe
  Strip lemon peel, for garnish

Stir cognac and absinthe in a cocktail shaker filled with ice. Strain into a chilled cocktail glass. Twist strip of peel over the top and drop it in.

BRANDY CRUSTA

MAKES 1 COCKTAIL

Invented in antebellum New Orleans, this citrus-kissed cognac cocktail was a precursor to the sidecar.

- 2 oz. cognac
- 1 tsp. fresh lemon juice
- 1 tsp. orange liqueur, such as Grand Marnier
- 1 tsp. Simple Syrup (this page)
- 2 dashes Angostura bitters
  Strip lemon peel, for garnish

Combine cognac, lemon juice, orange liqueur, simple syrup, and bitters in a cocktail shaker filled with ice. Shake vigorously and strain into a chilled cordial glass. Garnish with lemon peel.

Simple Syrup

MAKES ABOUT 1 CUP

An essential ingredient in many drinks, from cocktails to iced tea to juices, this sweet syrup is a good thing to keep on hand. It can be stored indefinitely in the refrigerator.

- 1 cup sugar

Combine sugar with 1 cup water in a small pot. Cook over low heat, stirring until sugar dissolves. Remove from heat and let cool; store in an airtight container.

CAIPIRINHA

MAKES 1 COCKTAIL

Brazil's national spirit is *cachaça*, a brandy made from sugarcane that takes well to a simple combination of sugar and lime. Substitute vodka in this classic drink and the result is called a *caipiroska*.

- 2–3 tbsp. sugar
- 2 limes, each cut into 6 wedges, plus 1 slice for garnish
- 1½–2 oz. cachaça

Combine sugar and lime wedges in a cocktail shaker and muddle. Add cachaça to taste, pour into a rocks glass filled with ice, and garnish with lime slice.

FRENCH 75

MAKES 1 COCKTAIL

This elegant libation was created in 1915 at Paris' New York Bar. It's named for a type of 75mm gun—powerful and to the point, much like this drink.

- 1¼ oz. cognac
- ¼ oz. fresh lemon juice
- ¼ oz. Simple Syrup (page 539)
  Champagne, chilled
  Strip lemon peel, for garnish

Combine cognac, lemon juice, and simple syrup in a cocktail shaker filled with ice; shake and pour into a champagne flute. Top with champagne and garnish with lemon peel.

NEGRONI

MAKES 1 COCKTAIL

There's no room for variation in the Negroni, which calls for equal parts Campari, gin, and sweet vermouth. But you don't need variation here: It's clean, potent, and flawless. Swap whiskey for the gin and you have what's known as a *boulevardier*.

- 1 oz. Campari
- 1 oz. gin
- 1 oz. sweet vermouth
  Strip orange peel, for garnish

1 Fill a rocks glass with ice. Combine Campari, gin, and vermouth in a cocktail shaker filled with ice; stir and strain into glass.

2 Holding a lit match in one hand and the twisted peel in the other, squeeze peel over both the match and glass, so the oils from the peel briefly flare up. Set match aside and drop the twist in the drink.

AMERICANO

MAKES 1 COCKTAIL

Bright red and bittersweet, the Americano, a cousin of the Negroni, was born as the Milano-Torino at Caffè Camparino in the 1860s (the Campari came from Milan,

the sweet vermouth from Turin). The cocktail eventually became known as the Americano due to its popularity with American expats during Prohibition.

- 1½ oz. Campari
- 1½ oz. sweet vermouth
  Soda water
  Orange slice or strip of orange peel, for garnish

Fill a highball glass with ice. Add Campari and vermouth and top generously with soda. Garnish with an orange slice or peel.

PERFECT MARTINI

MAKES 1 COCKTAIL

A London dry gin can stand up to a lot more vermouth than you might suspect. The original 1910s-era formula for this iconic drink demonstrates that fact elegantly. ("Perfect" refers not to its quality—though it is that—but to the equal portions of vermouth and gin.)

- 2 oz. dry vermouth
- 2 oz. London dry gin
- 2 dashes orange bitters
  Strip orange peel, for garnish

Fill a martini glass with crushed ice to chill. Combine vermouth, gin, and bitters in a cocktail shaker filled with ice. Stir for 15 seconds. Empty ice from glass and strain cocktail into chilled glass. Twist strip of peel over the top and drop it in.

GIBSON MARTINI

MAKES 1 COCKTAIL

Order a Gibson from a knowledgeable barkeep and you'll get this: A dry martini garnished not with an olive but with a tiny, piquant pickled onion.

- 3 oz. gin
- 1 oz. dry vermouth
- 1 Vermouth-Spiked Cocktail Onion (facing page), plus a little of its pickling liquid

Fill a martini glass with crushed ice to chill. Combine gin and vermouth in a cocktail shaker filled with ice; stir for 10 seconds. Empty ice from glass and strain cocktail into chilled glass. Add cocktail onion plus a drop or two of its pickling liquid.

Vermouth-Spiked Cocktail Onions

MAKES ABOUT 2½ CUPS

Vermouth adds sweet depth to these bar essentials, the key to a classic Gibson martini.

- 1 tsp. black peppercorns
- ⅛ tsp. freshly grated nutmeg
- 3 sprigs fresh thyme
- 2 cups dry vermouth
- 1 cup white wine vinegar
- ½ cup sugar
- 1 tbsp. kosher salt
- 10 oz. white pearl onions, peeled

Combine peppercorns, nutmeg, and thyme in a 1-qt. sterilized glass jar; set aside. Bring vermouth, vinegar, sugar, salt, and ½ cup water to a boil in a 2-qt. saucepan over high heat, stirring until sugar and salt dissolve; add onions and cook for 1 minute. Transfer onions and brine to jar and seal with lid; let cool to room temperature. Refrigerate at least 4 hours before using.

MARTINEZ

MAKES 1 COCKTAIL

In the 1880s, Old Tom gin, made with quite a bit more sweetness than London dry, was just beginning to gain popularity in America. This drink—a dark, sultry red libation—put it over the top.

- 2 oz. Old Tom gin
- 1 oz. red vermouth
- ½ tsp. maraschino liqueur
- 2 dashes bitters
  Strip lemon peel, for garnish

Combine gin, vermouth, maraschino liqueur, and bitters in a cocktail shaker filled with ice; stir for 15 seconds and strain into a chilled cocktail glass. Twist strip of peel over the top and drop it in.

SINGAPORE SLING

MAKES 1 COCKTAIL

The Singapore sling was ostensibly created in the early 1900s in the Long Bar at Singapore's legendary Raffles Hotel by bartender Ngiam Tong Boon. The original recipe was never recorded, but the hotel's modern-day version—based on bartenders' remembrances and

THE MARTINI VARIATIONS

The martini, the gin cocktail par excellence, has, like gin itself, undergone a remarkable evolution over the years. American bartenders have been mixing gin with vermouth since the latter decades of the 19th century, though initially the gin would have been a rich, sweet genever and the vermouth a sweet one, too. The martinez (this page), an 1880s cocktail widely cited as the martini's starting point, was actually more like a Manhattan than a dry martini. It featured the Old Tom style of gin, still sweet but lighter than genever, that was just then catching on in the U.S., coinciding with a trend toward lighter cocktails. Whether "martini" is a riff on "martinez" or has another root—some credit Gilded Age bon vivant Randolph B. Martine as the drink's inventor; others point to the Martini brand of vermouth—remains open to debate. But there's no question that the turn to light, crisp drinks continued, opening the floodgates not only to the new London dry style of gin but also to dry vermouth from France and Italy. By the early 20th century, the two had converged in the dry martini, though the version coming across bars circa 1910, with its high proportion of dry vermouth and double dash of orange bitters (see Perfect Martini, facing page), was still a step removed from the minimalist take—nothing more than ice-cold gin and the merest hint of vermouth—that's reigned since the 1940s. Still, even the mutable martini has its limits. There are ingredients—vodka or acid-green apple schnapps—that never a true martini make, no matter what kind of glass they're served in.

some written notes—remains popular: The bar serves thousands of slings every day.

- 4 oz. pineapple juice
- 1 oz. gin
- ½ oz. cherry brandy
- ½ oz. lime juice
- ⅓ oz. grenadine
- ¼ oz. Cointreau
- ¼ oz. Bénédictine
  Dash Angostura bitters
  Maraschino cherry, for garnish
  Slice pineapple, for garnish

Combine pineapple juice, gin, cherry brandy, lime juice, grenadine, Cointreau, Bénédictine, and bitters in a cocktail shaker filled with ice; shake vigorously, then strain into a highball glass. Garnish with cherry and pineapple slice.

MONKEY GLAND

MAKES 1 COCKTAIL

Credited to Harry McElhone, the famed proprietor of the New York Bar in Paris, the Monkey Gland is a 1920s cocktail that balances gin and fresh orange juice with a splash of absinthe and a little grenadine. As for the name, it's a reference to a controversial medical practice designed to boost vitality. We prefer to stick with the cocktail.

3 oz. gin
1½ oz. fresh orange juice
¼ oz. grenadine
Dash absinthe
Strip orange peel, for garnish

Combine gin, orange juice, grenadine, and absinthe in a cocktail shaker filled with ice; shake vigorously and strain into a coupe glass. Twist strip of peel over the top and drop it in.

WHITE LADY

MAKES 1 COCKTAIL

This citrusy sour was—like the Monkey Gland (above)—invented by Harry McElhone. The egg white gives the drink a ghostly opacity, hence its name.

FOR THE SOUR MIX
1 cup fresh lemon juice
1 tbsp. superfine sugar
1 egg white

FOR THE COCKTAIL
1½ oz. gin
¾ oz. Cointreau
¼ tsp. granulated sugar

1 Make the sour mix: Combine lemon juice, superfine sugar, and egg white; set aside. Mixture will keep in the refrigerator for 2 weeks.

2 Make the cocktail: Fill a cocktail shaker with ice. Add 1½ oz. sour mix, gin, Cointreau, and granulated sugar. Shake vigorously, then pour into a chilled cocktail glass.

PIMM'S CUP

MAKES 1 COCKTAIL

The classic Pimm's Cup is the essential summer cocktail in Britain.

2 oz. Pimm's No. 1
½ oz. fresh lemon juice
Ginger ale
2 cucumber slices, for garnish

Combine Pimm's and lemon juice in an ice-filled highball glass; top with ginger ale. Garnish with cucumber slices.

STRAWBERRY PIMM'S CUP

MAKES 1 COCKTAIL

A twist on the classic, this summer cooler takes on spicy, herbal notes from makrut lime, while strawberries lend sweet balance to the pleasingly bitter liqueur.

3 strawberries, hulled and thinly sliced
1 makrut lime leaf
¼ cup ginger ale
¼ cup Pimm's No. 1
½ tbsp. balsamic vinegar

Muddle half of sliced strawberries and the makrut lime leaf in the bottom of a tall glass. Fill glass with ice and stir in ginger ale, Pimm's, balsamic vinegar, and remaining strawberry slices.

CORPSE REVIVER #2

MAKES 1 COCKTAIL

Popularized by the 1930 *The Savoy Cocktail Book* by Harry Craddock, this cocktail is part of a succession of "corpse revivers" originally devised as hangover cures. An ice-cold nip of this elixir is refreshing, astringent, and strong enough to perk up the senses—reviving, indeed.

1 oz. Cocchi Americano or Lillet Blanc
1 oz. Cointreau
1 oz. fresh lemon juice
1 oz. gin
Dash absinthe
Strip orange peel, for garnish

Combine Cocchi Americano, Cointreau, lemon juice, gin, and absinthe in a cocktail shaker filled with ice; shake vigorously and strain into a chilled martini glass. Garnish with orange peel.

AVIATION

MAKES 1 COCKTAIL

This Prohibition-era cocktail enjoyed a renaissance with the craft-cocktail boom of the early 2000s. Slightly bitter maraschino liqueur tempers the floral flavors of the crème de violette.

2 oz. gin
½ oz. maraschino liqueur
½ oz. fresh lemon juice
¼ oz. crème de violette
Strip lemon peel, for garnish

Combine gin, maraschino liqueur, and lemon juice in a cocktail shaker filled with ice; shake well and strain into a coupe glass. Gently pour in the crème de violette, then twist strip of peel over the top and drop it in.

THE ULTIMATE GIN & TONIC

MAKES 1 COCKTAIL

The addition of aromatics like juniper berries and lemon verbena brings out the floral, herbal notes of both gin and tonic water. Use a high-end tonic water made with cane sugar to help the flavors shine.

1½ oz. gin
1 lime slice
1 lemon slice
2 juniper berries
1 fresh lemon verbena leaf
1 edible flower, such as nasturtium
Tonic water

Combine gin, lime and lemon slices, juniper berries, lemon verbena leaf, and flower in an ice-filled rocks glass. Top with tonic water to taste.

RAMOS GIN FIZZ

MAKES 1 COCKTAIL

A mix of orange flower water and gin gives this New Orleans cocktail—invented by Henry C. Ramos in 1888—a floral character and a hint of juniper. Traditionally the egg white is shaken with ice for 12 minutes to fully aerate it, which makes the shaker so cold that it needs to be wrapped in a towel for comfort. If you don't quite have it in you, a minute of shaking will do.

1 tbsp. superfine sugar
2 tsp. fresh lime juice
1 tsp. fresh lemon juice
1½ oz. gin
1 oz. heavy cream
¼ tsp. orange flower water
1 egg white
1 oz. soda water

Combine sugar, lime juice, and lemon juice in a cocktail shaker and stir to dissolve. Add gin, cream, orange flower water, and egg white. Cover and shake vigorously for 15 seconds; add crushed ice, cover, and shake vigorously for about 45 seconds more. Strain into a chilled rocks or highball glass and top with soda water.

FOUR STYLES OF GIN

Gin's roots reach back to 16th-century Holland, and the various types that have emerged since then are as different as the eras that produced them. From clear and bone-dry to honey colored, sweet, and fruity, these gins are hardly interchangeable when it comes to mixing drinks. Here's a guide to the most popular styles, and the cocktails best suited to each one.

GENEVER This style—the original—uses a malt-spirit base, making it not unlike a flavored whiskey. Less botanical than the English styles, we like it best for sipping, straight and chilled.

LONDON DRY Very dry, light bodied, and pungent, this is what most of us think of when we think of gin. Good for gin and tonics and dry martinis.

PLYMOUTH Though originally as rich as a Dutch genever, today this regional gin, made only in Plymouth, England, is as clean and bracing as a London dry, and is good for most any drink in which you might use one.

OLD TOM London dry's sweeter, fuller-bodied parent has only recently come back on the market after decades in suspended animation. It's perfect for a Tom Collins (page 544) or Martinez (page 541).

TOM COLLINS

MAKES 1 COCKTAIL

This gin sour has spawned a thousand variations, but the classic still stands above all of them.

- 2 oz. gin
- 2 oz. fresh lemon juice
- 1 oz. Simple Syrup (page 539) or 2 tbsp. superfine sugar
  Soda water
  Maraschino cherry, for garnish

Put the gin, lemon juice, and simple syrup in a cocktail shaker half full of ice; shake well and strain into a highball glass filled with ice. Top with soda water and garnish with maraschino cherry.

POINSETTIA PUNCH

MAKES 1 COCKTAIL

This brightly spiced punch recipe, imagined by Frank Cisneros, mixologist at Gin Palace in New York's East Village, is perfect for holiday gatherings.

- 2 oz. floral gin
- ¾ oz. fresh lemon juice
- ½ oz. grenadine
- ¼ oz. allspice liqueur
- ¼ oz. Cinnamon Syrup (page 547, or store-bought)
- 2 dashes Angostura bitters
  Slice lemon, for garnish

Combine gin, lemon juice, grenadine, allspice liqueur, syrup, and bitters in a cocktail shaker filled with ice; shake vigorously and strain into a chilled rocks glass filled with cracked ice. Garnish with lemon slice.

THE LAST WORD

MAKES 1 COCKTAIL

Equal parts gin, Chartreuse, maraschino liqueur, and fresh lime juice, this is an old-fashioned cocktail that feels awfully modern. Its equally portioned ingredients make for easy scaling: Mix up a triple or quadruple batch to serve several drinkers at once.

- ¾ oz. gin
- ¾ oz. green Chartreuse
- ¾ oz. maraschino liqueur, such as Luxardo
- ¾ oz. fresh lime juice
  Strip lime peel, for garnish

Combine gin, Chartreuse, maraschino liqueur, and lime juice in a cocktail shaker filled with ice; shake vigorously and strain into a martini glass or coupe. Twist strip of peel over glass and drop it in.

ICE CREAM GRASSHOPPER

MAKES 1 COCKTAIL

At the Greenwood Supper Club in Fish Creek, Wisconsin, the minty grasshopper gets a soda-shop twist with vanilla ice cream—instead of the more traditional heavy cream—and whipped cream on top.

- 2 cups vanilla ice cream
- 1 oz. green Crème de Menthe (below)
- 1 oz. white crème de cacao
  Whipped cream, for garnish

Purée ice cream, ½ oz. crème de menthe, and the crème de cacao in a blender; pour into a cocktail glass. Top with dollop of whipped cream, then drizzle remaining ½ oz crème de menthe over the top. Serve immediately.

CRÈME DE MENTHE

MAKES 1 QUART

An essential ingredient in a grasshopper, this bright potion is given the distinction of being a crème liqueur not because it has cream or any dairy product added to it, but because of the thick, luscious texture resulting from the amount of sugar in the recipe.

- 2 cups vodka
- 3 cups packed fresh mint leaves
- 1 cup sugar
- 5–6 drops green food coloring (optional)

1 Put vodka and half the mint in a sterilized 1-qt. glass jar. Cover with a lid and set aside in a cool, dark place for 1 week.

2 Bring sugar and 2 cups water to a boil. Cook, stirring, until sugar is dissolved, about 2 minutes. Remove from heat and add remaining mint; let syrup cool.

3 Strain vodka and syrup through a fine-mesh sieve lined with cheesecloth into a sterilized 1-qt. glass bottle, discarding mint. Add food coloring, if using; cover bottle and shake gently to combine. Refrigerate for up to 3 months.

IRISH CREAM

MAKES 3 CUPS

Cream, whiskey, vanilla, and coffee combine with sweetened condensed milk for a silky-smooth alternative to store-bought Irish cream. We love it added to coffee, used to sweeten cake frosting, or just on its own, enjoyed over a little ice.

- 1 cup heavy cream
- 1 tsp. instant coffee powder
- ½ tsp. cocoa powder
- ¾ cup Irish whiskey
- 1 tsp. vanilla extract
- 1 14-oz. can sweetened condensed milk

Combine 1 tbsp. cream and the coffee and cocoa powders to make a smooth paste. Slowly add remaining cream, whisking until smooth. Add whiskey, vanilla extract, and sweetened condensed milk and stir to combine. Pour into a 24-oz. jar and keep refrigerated until ready to serve, up to 2 weeks. To serve, pour into a tumbler filled with ice.

PORTO FLIP

SERVES 1

In the classic canon, flips contain egg yolk or whole egg, simple syrup, heavy cream, and a spirit. This light and fruity version adapted from Jerry Thomas' 1887 *Bartender's Guide: How to Mix Drinks, or the Bon Vivant's Companion*, forgoes the cream, getting its richness from a jammy fortified wine.

- 1 whole large egg
- 1½ oz. ruby port
- 1 oz. brandy
- ¼ oz. simple syrup
- Freshly grated nutmeg, for garnish

1 In a cocktail shaker, combine egg, port, brandy, and simple syrup. Shake vigorously for 10 seconds to emulsify, then fill shaker with ice and continue shaking until the outside of the shaker feels frosty, 10–15 seconds more.

2 Strain into a coupe glass, garnish lightly with freshly grated nutmeg, and serve immediately.

PAINKILLER COCKTAIL

MAKES 1 COCKTAIL (SEE PHOTO, PAGE 440)

Very boozy and very well-shaken, this British Virgin Islands classic gets a creamy, frothy head similar to a flip or fizz from the addition of sweetened cream of coconut. While Pusser's Rum trademarked the name in the 1990s, it was the iconic Soggy Dollar bar on Jost Van Dyke that invented the Painkiller in 1970. Pusser's rum is a non-negotiable in the drink today; for the best results, look for their "Gunpowder Proof" (black label) bottle.

- 4 oz. fresh pineapple juice
- 3 oz. Pusser's dark rum
- 1 oz. cream of coconut, such as Coco Lopez
- 1 oz. fresh orange juice
- Lemon wedge
- Lime wedge
- Freshly grated nutmeg, for garnish

In a cocktail shaker filled with ice, combine pineapple juice, rum, cream of coconut, and orange juice. Squeeze lemon and lime wedges into the shaker, then add them too. Shake until chilled and frothy, 20–30 seconds. Pour into a chilled highball or rocks glass, garnish with freshly grated nutmeg, and serve immediately.

MAI TAI

MAKES 1 COCKTAIL

"Trader Vic" Bergeron came up with this floral drink to showcase a 17-year-old gold Jamaican rum. Once all his bottles were gone, he re-created the drink's complex flavor by layering two very different rums in the same drink.

- 1 oz. dark Jamaican rum
- 1 oz. rhum agricole vieux (aged rum)
- 1 oz. fresh lime juice, plus 1 lime wedge, for garnish
- ½ oz. orange curaçao
- ¼ oz. orgeat or almond syrup
- ¼ oz. Simple Syrup (page 539)
- Sprig fresh mint, for garnish

Combine rum, rhum agricole, lime juice, curaçao, and syrups in a cocktail shaker and fill with ice; shake vigorously and pour into a rocks glass. Garnish with reserved lime wedge and mint.

CLASSIC DAIQUIRI

MAKES 1 COCKTAIL

A far cry from the sweet frozen concoctions that most often bear the name, a true daiquiri—said to have been invented in Cuba in 1896—is a showpiece for good gold rum, with lime and sugar rounding things out.

1   oz. fresh lime juice
1   tsp. superfine sugar
2   oz. gold rum

Put all ingredients in a cocktail shaker filled with ice; shake well. Strain into a martini glass.

BANANA DAIQUIRI

MAKES 2 COCKTAILS

The banana daiquiri, an indulgent smoothie of a cocktail, was allegedly first mixed some 50 years ago at St. Thomas' Mountaintop bar in the U.S. Virgin Islands.

6   oz. dark rum
2   tbsp. sugar
½   oz. fresh lime juice
2   oz. banana liqueur
2   very ripe bananas, peeled

Put rum, sugar, lime juice, banana liqueur, 2 oz. water, bananas, and 2 cups ice into a blender; purée until smooth and thick. Pour into 2 tall chilled glasses.

PIÑA COLADA

MAKES 2 COCKTAILS

A poolside classic, this blended coconut cooler is heightened with a splash of aromatic bitters.

3   oz. pineapple juice
2   oz. cream of coconut, such as Coco López
½   oz. light rum
½   oz. dark rum
3   tbsp. crushed canned pineapple
2   tbsp. half-and-half
2   dashes Angostura bitters
2   maraschino cherries, for garnish
2   wedges pineapple, for garnish

Combine pineapple juice, cream of coconut, rums, crushed pineapple, half-and-half, and bitters in a blender filled with ice and blend until smooth. Pour into 2 chilled cocktail glasses. Garnish with a cherry and pineapple wedge.

THE BLACK & STORMY

MAKES 1 COCKTAIL

This recipe for a modified dark and stormy, the trademarked combination of spiced rum and sweet ginger beer, comes to us from the Cliff Restaurant in Barbados. The addition of fresh ginger juice to the drink provides a kick of clean heat for an especially invigorating cocktail.

2   oz. dark rum
1   oz. fresh lime juice
1   oz. Simple Syrup (page 539)
1   oz. Fresh Ginger Juice (below, or store-bought)
     Ginger beer

Combine rum, lime juice, simple syrup, and ginger juice in a mixing glass; stir well. Fill a highball glass with ice and add rum and syrup mixture. Top off with ginger beer and stir before serving.

Fresh Ginger Juice

MAKES ABOUT ¼ CUP

Nothing compares to the fire and sweetness of just-made ginger juice.

¼   lb. fresh ginger, peeled and coarsely chopped

Combine ginger and ½ cup water in a blender; process until fully liquefied. Strain through cheesecloth into a glass jar. Refrigerate for up to 3 days.

MOJITO

MAKES 1 COCKTAIL

Sugarcane and rum are lifelines of Cuba's economy, and their marriage in the mojito is a delicious expression of the island's identity. At celebrated Havana bars, mojitos are an essential part of the nightly proceedings.

1   tsp. sugar
1   tbsp. fresh lime juice
½   bunch fresh mint
1   oz. dry white rum
2   oz. club soda

Mix sugar with lime juice in a tall glass. Add 3–4 ice cubes and several sprigs of mint, then pour in rum and club soda. Stir well, garnish with a bit more mint, and serve.

CUBA LIBRE

MAKES 1 COCKTAIL

This simple drink lives or dies by the freshness of the lime juice.

- 3 oz. light rum
- 1½ oz. fresh lime juice
  Coca-Cola

Combine rum and lime juice in a highball glass filled with ice. Top with cola and stir gently.

FLAMINGO

MAKES 1 COCKTAIL

Bartender Jim Meehan of PDT in New York City created this alternative to rum and Coke, utilizing lighter, brighter grapefruit soda, which lets the bold character of a pot-distilled English-style rum shine through.

- 2 oz. English-style white rum
- ¾ oz. fresh lime juice
- 3 oz. pink grapefruit soda
  Lime slice, for garnish

Combine rum and lime juice in a cocktail shaker filled with ice; shake vigorously and strain into a rocks glass with ice. Top with soda and garnish with lime slice.

PETIT PUNCH VIEUX

MAKES 1 COCKTAIL

Ben Jones of Clément rum distillery shared with us his version of Martinique's national drink, the cool and bracing ti' punch.

- 2 lime wedges
- 2 oz. rhum agricole vieux
- ½ oz. cane syrup or Simple Syrup (page 539)

Squeeze juice from lime wedges into a rocks glass and add one spent wedge to glass; rub rim of glass with second spent wedge and then discard. Add rhum agricole, syrup, and ice to fill; stir until chilled.

ZOMBIE

MAKES 1 COCKTAIL

The famous bartender Don the Beachcomber set a limit of two per customer for this potent drink, made with three kinds of rum, citrus, and spice.

- 2 oz. Spanish-style ron añejo
- 1½ oz. Jamaican gold rum
- 1 oz. 151-proof Demerara rum
- ¾ oz. fresh lime juice
- ½ oz. falernum
- 2 tsp. fresh white grapefruit juice
- 1 tsp. Cinnamon Syrup (below, or store bought)
- 1 tsp. grenadine
- ⅛ tsp. Pernod or other anise liqueur
  Dash Angostura bitters
- 1 sprig fresh mint, for garnish

Combine rums, lime juice, falernum, grapefruit juice, cinnamon syrup, grenadine, Pernod, and bitters in a blender filled with ice; blend on high for 5 seconds to crush ice. Pour into a chimney glass or highball glass, add more ice to fill, and garnish with mint.

Cinnamon Syrup

MAKES ABOUT 1 CUP

Great in cocktails, this flavored simple syrup is also wonderful stirred into coffee or drizzled over pancakes.

- 1 cup sugar
- 4 sticks cinnamon, broken in half
- ½ vanilla bean, split, seeds scraped

Bring sugar, cinnamon, vanilla bean and seeds, and 1 cup water to a boil in a small saucepan. Cook briefly to dissolve sugar. Cool; strain. Refrigerate for up to 3 months.

MARGARITA

MAKES 2 COCKTAILS

Where the margarita was invented and by whom is a matter of much debate. Among the many who have claimed the honor: a Texan hostess named Margarita Sames; the Kentucky Club in Ciudad Juárez; and the Tail o' the Cock in Los Angeles. What *is* certain is that fresh lime juice and good tequila are essential to a real margarita, and that no sweet-and-sour mix should be anywhere near it.

- 2 limes, halved and juiced, rinds reserved, plus slices for garnish
  Kosher salt
- 4 oz. Cointreau or triple sec
- 4 oz. tequila

Fill 2 stemmed cocktail glasses with crushed ice and let chill. Empty ice from glasses, rub rims with pulp side of the lime rinds, then dip moistened rims into a saucer of salt. Combine lime juice, Cointreau, and tequila in a cocktail shaker filled with ice; shake vigorously and strain into prepared glasses. Garnish with lime slice.

PALOMA
MAKES 1 COCKTAIL

One of Mexico's most popular cocktails, the Paloma is a perfectly refreshing combination of sweet and tart with grapefruit, lime, and a pinch of salt.

- 2 oz. blanco tequila
  Juice of ½ lime
  Pinch salt
- 3 oz. grapefruit juice
- 3 oz. soda water
  Lime wedge, for garnish

Combine tequila, lime juice, and pinch salt in a highball glass. Add ice and top with grapefruit juice and soda water. Stir gently and garnish with lime wedge.

VAMPIRO
MAKES 1 COCKTAIL

The name of this popular Mexican cocktail literally translates to "vampire," but its blend of fresh juices—tomato, orange, and a hint of lime—is anything but ghoulish.

- 1 ripe tomato, finely chopped, juices reserved
  Juice of 2 oranges
- 1 tbsp. fresh lime juice
- 1 tbsp. sugar
- 2 oz. tequila
- ⅛ tsp. cayenne pepper
  Dash celery salt
  Seltzer water
  Rib celery, for garnish

1 Combine tomato and its juices, orange juice, lime juice, and sugar; strain into a shaker; add tequila and ice; shake until cold.

2 Mix together the cayenne pepper and celery salt; wet the rim of a glass and dip into pepper mixture; strain in cocktail and top with seltzer. Garnish with celery.

RAISING THE BAR

As far as we're concerned, the ability to make an elegant, well-balanced cocktail is an essential component of the home cook's repertoire. Here are four time-honored bartender's techniques that will serve the home mixologist well.

THE STIR Clear drinks like martinis should be stirred, not shaken (which causes bubbles and froth to form). The key is to stir long enough for the ice to chill the ingredients thoroughly without watering it down.

THE CRUSH Cracking ice cubes into jagged pieces increases their surface area, allowing them to melt faster and mellow the alcohol's bite while also making the drink easier to stir. Place ice in a canvas (or plastic) bag, and smash with a mallet.

THE SHAKE As a general rule, cocktails that contain heavy ingredients like eggs, dairy products, fruit juices, or cream liqueurs should be shaken so that you get a substantive froth.

THE FLAME Applying fire to citrus oils enhances their flavor. Cut a thick, 1″ circle of rind from a fresh orange. Light a match and hold it above the glass; grip the piece of rind by the edges, hold it skin side down above and to the side of the match, and sharply pinch the peel. This will send a spray of oil through the flame and onto the surface of the drink.

TEQUILA SUNRISE
MAKES 1 COCKTAIL

The recipe for this colorful cocktail originally appeared in *Bottoms Up! Y Como!*, a brochure published by the Agua Caliente resort in Tijuana, Mexico, in 1934.

- 2 oz. blanco tequila
- 2 tsp. crème de cassis
- 1 tsp. grenadine
  Juice of ½ lime, spent lime half reserved
- 2 oz. soda water

Combine tequila, crème de cassis, grenadine, and lime juice and lime half in a highball glass filled with crushed ice; stir to combine and top with soda water.

CLASSIC BLOODY MARY

MAKES 1 COCKTAIL

Probably invented in the early 20th century (one account, likely apocryphal, features a Palm Beach socialite named Mary Warburton who spilled a tomato-and-vodka drink down her white dress and thus inspired the name), this now ubiquitous brunch cocktail has lent itself to countless interpretations, most of them revolving around the basic theme of a peppery kick complemented by tangy, vodka-spiked tomato juice.

- 4 oz. tomato juice
- 2 oz. vodka
- 1 tbsp. fresh lemon juice
- ¼ tsp. Worcestershire sauce
- 1 tsp. prepared horseradish
  Freshly ground black pepper, to taste
  Lemon wedge, for garnish

Combine tomato juice, vodka, lemon juice, Worcestershire, horseradish, and black pepper in a mixing glass. Pour the mixture into a second mixing glass and then back and forth again several times to combine. (This is a mixing technique called "rolling," which blends the ingredients without aerating or diluting them.) Pour into a highball glass full of cracked ice and garnish with lemon wedge.

TOMATILLO BLOODY MARY

MAKES 2 COCKTAILS

Tomatillos give this Bloody Mary—based on one served at Whist at the Viceroy Hotel in Santa Monica, California—its green hue.

- 3 tomatillos, husked, rinsed, and cored
- 2 medium green tomatoes
- 2 cloves garlic
- 1 small cucumber
- 1 sprig each fresh cilantro and flat-leaf parsley, plus more sprigs for garnish
- ½ serrano chile, seeded
  Kosher salt, to taste
- 3 oz. vodka
- 2 whole scallions, for garnish
- 2 lime wedges, for garnish

Combine tomatillos, tomatoes, garlic, cucumber, cilantro, parsley, and chile in a blender; purée until smooth. Season with salt. Fill 2 glasses with ice and pour in tomatillo mixture and vodka. Add herb sprigs and scallions to glasses and garnish rims with lime wedges.

BLOODY CAESAR

MAKES 1 COCKTAIL

This briny, light take on a Bloody Mary uses Clamato, a brand of tomato juice blended with clam liquor. The Caesar is Canada's unofficial national drink—it's estimated that this is the country's most-consumed cocktail.

- 1 tsp. celery salt
- ½ tsp. freshly ground black pepper
- 1 oz. vodka
- ½ tsp. Worcestershire sauce
- ½ tsp. Tabasco sauce
  Clamato juice (or a mixture of 2 parts clam juice to 1 part tomato juice)
- ½ lime, in 2 wedges
  Leafy rib celery, for garnish

Combine celery salt and pepper in a shallow dish. Wet the edge of a pint glass and dip the rim in the celery salt–pepper mixture. Fill the rimmed glass with ice. Pour in vodka, Worcestershire, and Tabasco; top with Clamato. Gently squeeze the lime wedges into the glass, and drop in the juiced pieces. Garnish with leafy celery rib.

SALTY DOG

MAKES 1 COCKTAIL

Vodka is the traditional spirit for this bright cooler. If you leave off the salt rim, what you have is a Greyhound.

- 1 tbsp. kosher salt
- 1 tsp. grated grapefruit zest
- 1 2"-wide strip grapefruit peel
- 2 oz. fresh grapefruit juice
- 2 oz. vodka

Combine salt and zest on a small plate. Rub grapefruit peel around rim of a glass and dip rim into salt mixture. Combine grapefruit juice and vodka in a cocktail shaker filled with ice. Shake and pour into rimmed glass. Twist strip of peel over glass and drop it in.

DALMATIAN
MAKES 1 COCKTAIL

Another variation on a Greyhound, this pink drink looks demure, but it packs serious heat with a slow, lingering burn from the vodka and the black pepper syrup, which lends the drink its name.

- 3 oz. fresh grapefruit juice
- 1½ oz. vodka
- 1½ oz. Black Pepper Simple Syrup (below)

Combine grapefruit juice, vodka, and syrup in a cocktail shaker filled with ice; shake vigorously and strain into an ice-filled rocks glass.

Black Pepper Simple Syrup
MAKES 1 CUP

This peppercorn-infused simple syrup has a warm, floral heat.

- 1 cup sugar
- ¼ cup crushed black peppercorns

Put sugar, peppercorns, and 1 cup water in a small saucepan and bring to a boil, stirring occasionally. Once sugar is dissolved, take off heat and let cool. Leave the peppercorns in the syrup to lend it a stronger flavor; strain them out when it is spiced to taste. Syrup will keep, covered, for up to 1 week in the refrigerator.

MANHATTAN
MAKES 1 COCKTAIL

In the early 1800s, "cocktail" connoted a drink mixed with bitters. The recipe for this one comes from Keen's Steakhouse in Manhattan, which has been open about as long as this classic drink has been around.

- 3 oz. rye whiskey
- 1 oz. sweet vermouth
- 3 dashes Angostura bitters
  Maraschino cherry, for garnish

Combine whiskey, vermouth, and bitters in a shaker with ice and stir. Strain into a martini glass or a rocks glass filled with ice and garnish with cherry.

OLD FASHIONED
MAKES 1 COCKTAIL

A bartender at the Pendennis Club in Louisville, Kentucky, invented this drink, ostensibly to mask the taste of bourbon for a Civil War veteran and club member who didn't cotton to its flavor.

- 2 orange slices
- 2 maraschino cherries, stems removed
- 2 dashes Angostura bitters
- ½ tsp. superfine sugar
- 2½ oz. bourbon

Put 1 orange slice, 1 cherry, bitters, 1 tsp. water, and sugar into a rocks glass. Using a pestle or the back of a teaspoon, muddle the fruit and sugar until the fruit is a little mashed and the sugar has dissolved. Add several ice cubes to the glass and add the bourbon. Stir gently and garnish with remaining orange and cherry.

BLOOD & SAND
MAKES 1 COCKTAIL

This smoky-sweet cocktail, created in London in the 1920s, was named for the 1922 film starring Rudolph Valentino.

- 1 oz. peated scotch
- ¾ oz. Cherry Heering liqueur
- ¾ oz. fresh orange juice
- ¾ oz. sweet vermouth
  Maraschino cherry, for garnish

Combine scotch, Cherry Heering, orange juice, and vermouth in a cocktail shaker filled with ice; shake vigorously and strain into a chilled coupe glass. Garnish with cherry.

BROWN DERBY
MAKES 1 COCKTAIL

Named in honor of the famous hat-shaped restaurant, this was the signature drink at Los Angeles' 1930s Vendome Club.

- 1 oz. bourbon
- 1 oz. fresh grapefruit juice
- 1½ tsp. honey mixed with 1½ tsp. warm water

Mix bourbon, juice, and honey mixture in a cocktail shaker filled with ice; shake vigorously and strain into coupe glass.

THE THOUSAND-DOLLAR MINT JULEP
MAKES 1 COCKTAIL

This version of the classic three-ingredient cocktail—which combines three parts bourbon to one part simple syrup bracingly infused with fresh spearmint—is sanctioned by the Kentucky Derby itself as the official mint julep recipe.

FOR THE MINT SIMPLE SYRUP
- 1 cup sugar
- 1 cup roughly chopped fresh mint

FOR THE COCKTAIL
- 3 oz. bourbon
- Fresh mint sprig, for garnish

1 Make the mint simple syrup: Combine sugar and 1 cup water in a small saucepan. Bring to a boil and stir until sugar is fully dissolved. Put the mint into a heatproof container and pour in hot syrup. Cover and refrigerate for 8 hours or overnight; strain and discard mint. Syrup will keep for up to 3 weeks in the refrigerator.

2 Make the cocktail: Fill a glass or julep cup with crushed ice. Add bourbon and 2 tbsp. of mint simple syrup; stir gently until the glass is thoroughly chilled. Garnish with mint sprig.

SEELBACH
MAKES 1 COCKTAIL

This classic recipe was named after the Louisville, Kentucky, hotel where it was first created in 1917.

- 1½ oz. bourbon
- ½ oz. Cointreau
- 3 dashes Angostura bitters
- 3 dashes Peychaud's bitters
- Champagne, chilled
- Strip orange peel, for garnish

Combine bourbon, Cointreau, and bitters in a cocktail shaker filled with ice; shake vigorously and strain into a champagne coupe. Top with champagne and garnish with orange twist.

LA LA LOLA
MAKES 1 COCKTAIL

Jill Schulster of New York restaurant Joe and Misses Doe created this boozy riff on a cherry cola—the name refers to the Kinks song "Lola," which references the fruity soft drink.

- 1 cup cola
- 2 oz. rye whiskey
- ¾ lb. cherries, pitted
- 1 tsp. fresh lemon juice
- 4–5 cola ice cubes (allow cola to flatten, then freeze)

Combine cola, 1 oz. rye, and cherries in a bowl; cover and chill for 1–2 hours. Place 5 cherries plus 1 tsp. of the cherry marinade in a rocks glass and muddle cherries. Combine remaining whiskey and cherry marinade in a cocktail shaker filled with ice, shake vigorously, and strain into glass with cherries. Add cola ice cubes to fill.

WHISKEY SOUR
MAKES 1 COCKTAIL

This timeless recipe is often undone by syrupy premade sour mix. Here, we elevate it back to its original glory with fresh lemon juice and frothy egg white.

- 1½ oz. bourbon
- 1 oz. Simple Syrup (page 539)
- ¾ oz. fresh lemon juice
- ¼ oz. egg white
- Maraschino cherry
- Orange slice, for garnish

Mix bourbon, syrup, lemon juice, and egg white in a shaker with ice; shake vigorously. Strain into a rocks glass filled with ice and garnish with cherry and orange slice.

SAZERAC
MAKES 1 COCKTAIL

The Sazerac, potent and celebratory, is the official cocktail of New Orleans.

- ½ oz. absinthe
- 2 oz. rye
- ¼ oz. Simple Syrup (page 539)
- 3 dashes Peychaud's bitters
- Dash Angostura bitters
- Strip lemon peel, for garnish

JAZZY STANDARD

Like New Orleans, the Sazerac has its own mythology. Invented, it is said, as a cognac-based cocktail in the 1830s by Antoine Peychaud, whose family's bitters are essential to the drink, it was eventually adopted by the Sazerac Coffee House in the French Quarter, named for a then-popular brand of cognac called Sazerac de Forge et Fils. Peychaud's supposed invention soon took on the Sazerac moniker. In 1870, a gentleman named Thomas Handy became the proprietor of the coffeehouse; he amended the drink further, replacing the cognac with rye whiskey. By 1876, another ingredient had been added: absinthe, the bitter green liqueur flavored with wormwood much favored by artists in 19th-century Paris (and New Orleans) and subsequently banned almost everywhere for its supposed inducing of madness (Herbsaint, an anise-flavored liqueur, was substituted). In 1949, the Crescent City's Roosevelt Hotel bought the rights to the joint, recipe and all—relocating it first to a spot next door to the hotel and eventually to its present location, inside the hotel lobby.

Pour absinthe into a rocks glass, swirl to coat, and discard liqueur. Fill glass with ice to chill. Combine rye, simple syrup, and bitters in a cocktail shaker filled with ice; shake vigorously. Discard ice in glass and strain cocktail into glass. Rub the rim with lemon peel, twist the strip over the glass, and drop it in.

VIEUX CARRÉ

MAKES 1 COCKTAIL

The recipe for this powerful drink, named for the French Quarter, or Vieux Carré ("old square" in French), comes from the Hotel Monteleone's famous rotating Carousel Bar.

½ oz. Bénédictine
½ oz. cognac
½ oz. rye whiskey
½ oz. sweet vermouth
  Dash Peychaud's bitters
  Dash Angostura bitters
  Strip lemon peel, for garnish

Combine Bénédictine, cognac, rye, vermouth, and bitters, in a rocks glass filled with ice and stir. Twist strip of peel and drop it in.

BOURBON CIDER

MAKES 1 COCKTAIL

Perfect for fall, this apple-and-bourbon recipe comes from Jennifer Pittman of Proof on Main in Louisville, Kentucky.

FOR THE GINGER SYRUP

1 cup sugar
2 tbsp. whole cloves, crushed
1 3″ piece fresh ginger, peeled and thinly sliced
1 cinnamon stick

FOR THE COCKTAIL

3 oz. apple cider
1½ oz. bourbon
1 tsp. fresh lemon juice
  Dried apple slice, for garnish

1 Make the ginger syrup: Bring 1 cup water to boil in a small saucepan. Remove from heat, stir in sugar, cloves, ginger, and cinnamon, and let sit for 1 hour. Strain and chill syrup; it will keep for up to 1 month in the refrigerator.

2 Make the cocktail: Mix ¾ oz. ginger syrup with cider, bourbon, and lemon juice in a cocktail shaker filled with ice; shake vigorously and strain into a martini glass. Garnish with apple slice.

Beer, Wine & Champagne Cocktails

MICHELADA

MAKES 1 COCKTAIL

Mexican lager is refreshing on a hot beach day. Mixed with the ingredients usually associated with the Bloody Mary, it's even more restorative.

- 1 tsp. kosher salt
- 1 tsp. chile powder
- 1 lime wedge
- 2 oz. tomato juice
- 1 oz. fresh lime juice
- 1 tsp. Worcestershire sauce
- ¼ tsp. hot sauce
- 2 dashes Maggi seasoning or 1 dash soy sauce and 1 dash Worcestershire sauce
- 1 12-oz. bottle Mexican lager, chilled
- 1 pickled jalapeño, for garnish

Combine salt and chile powder in a small dish. Run lime wedge around the rim of a tall beer glass and dip rim into salt mixture. Add tomato juice, lime juice, Worcestershire, hot sauce, Maggi seasoning, and beer to the glass and stir gently to combine. Garnish with pickled jalapeño.

SHANDY

MAKES 1 COCKTAIL

Ale mixed with lemonade is a classic pairing that dates back to 19th-century England, when beer—an all-day drink—was often diluted to reduce its alcoholic effects. For variation, try a spicy ginger ale instead of the lemonade.

FOR THE LEMONADE
- 3 oz. Simple Syrup (page 539)
- 3 oz. fresh lemon juice

FOR THE COCKTAIL
- Chilled ale, to top
- Lemon slice, for garnish

1 Make the lemonade: In a small pitcher or large glass, combine simple syrup, lemon juice, and 1 cup water. Lemonade will keep for up to 1 week in the refrigerator.

2 Make the cocktail: Pour ¼ cup lemonade into a pint glass; top with ale. Add more lemonade to taste, if desired. Garnish with lemon slice.

KALIMOTXO

MAKES 1 COCKTAIL

A popular refresher on Spain's Basque coast, this drink—the best-known version of wine mixed with cola—is found in parts of Eastern Europe and in South America under different names. Some say the best approach is using the cheapest plonk you can get. We prefer a slightly better dry, tannic red.

- 3 oz. cola
- 3 oz. dry red wine
- 1 oz. fresh lemon juice
  Lemon wedge, for garnish

Combine cola, wine, and lemon juice in a glass filled with ice. Garnish with lemon wedge.

TINTO DE VERANO

MAKES 1 COCKTAIL

Tinto de verano, which translates to "red wine of summer," is a combination of red wine and lemon-lime soda. This cool Spanish spritzer is a perfect refreshment for hot summer days.

- 1 cup lemon-lime soda
- 1 cup red wine, such as rioja
  Soda water, to top
  Lemon wedge, for garnish

Combine lemon-lime soda and wine in a glass filled with ice and add soda water to taste. Garnish with lemon wedge.

SHERRY COBBLER

MAKES 1 COCKTAIL

Fruit-and-wine cobblers were popular in the United States in the mid-1800s. Cocktail historian David Wondrich considers this one to be "as simple and tasty a drink as has ever been concocted by the hands of mankind." In it, a touch of citrus offsets the sherry's nutty character.

- 4 oz. dry amontillado or oloroso sherry
- ¼ oz. Simple Syrup (page 539)
- 2 orange slices

Combine sherry, simple syrup, and 1 orange slice in a cocktail shaker filled with ice; shake vigorously and strain into a highball glass filled with crushed ice. Garnish with remaining orange slice.

A TOAST TO TOASTS

The term *toasting*, dating from 1600s England, was inspired by an older practice of immersing toast or spiced bread in bitter wine to improve its flavor. Here are some of the world's favorite toasts—with attendant lore.

KANPAI ("EMPTY YOUR GLASS"; JAPAN) Each drinker's glass is filled by one of his companions and must be kept full throughout the entire evening.

HERE'S MUD IN YOUR EYE (U.S., ENGLAND) Perhaps a way of wishing American pioneers land so fertile and soft that it would splash in their faces when plowed. But the English say it originated in the muddy trenches of World War I.

SLÀINTE ("GOOD HEALTH TO YOU"; IRELAND) Pronounced "slahn-cha," this toast is properly declared while one fully extends the right arm, glass in hand. In days of yore, this was a sign of friendship and peaceful intentions, as the drinker couldn't draw his sword while toasting.

SKÅL ("CHEERS"; SWEDEN) This toast sprang from a practice, said to be common until the 11th century, of drinking mead or ale from the skulls of fallen enemies (*skål* once meant "skull"). The toast is found, spelled variously, throughout Scandinavia.

NA ZDOROVIE ("BE HEALTHY"; RUSSIA) An ironic wish in a society where a bottle of alcohol is often finished *do dna*, or "to the bottom!" After the toast—pronounced "naz-dorovyeh"—is made, glasses are promptly emptied.

CHAMPAGNE COCKTAIL
MAKES 1 COCKTAIL

The straightforwardly named champagne cocktail is, in fact, quite complex in flavor: A bitters-soaked sugar cube calls attention to the sparkling wine's woodsy notes and brings its own robust floral finish.

- 1 sugar cube
  Angostura bitters
  Champagne

Put the sugar cube in a champagne flute; add 2 drops of bitters and allow to soak in. Top with champagne. (Pour slowly; the sugar encourages lots of frothing.)

KIR ROYAL
MAKES 1 COCKTAIL

Unlike a Kir, which is made with white wine and is far less exciting, a Kir royal is a splash of blackcurrant liqueur topped with sparkling wine.

- ½ oz. crème de cassis
- 6 oz. champagne, to top
  Blackberries, for garnish

Pour crème de cassis into a champagne flute and top with champagne. Garnish with blackberries.

MOONWALK
MAKES 1 COCKTAIL

Joe Gilmore, head barman at the Savoy Hotel's American Bar, invented this cocktail in 1969 to commemorate the first moon landing. The drink—a combination of grapefruit, orange liqueur, and a hint of rose water, topped with champagne—was the first thing Neil Armstrong and Buzz Aldrin sipped upon returning to earth.

- 1 oz. fresh grapefruit juice
- 1 oz. orange liqueur, such as Grand Marnier
- 2–3 drops rose water
  Champagne

Combine grapefruit juice, Grand Marnier, and rose water in a cocktail shaker filled with ice. Shake vigorously and strain into a champagne flute; top with champagne.

"Come quickly, I am tasting the stars!"

DOM PERIGNON, UPON DISCOVERING CHAMPAGNE

MIMOSA

MAKES 1 COCKTAIL

This simple method of imbibing at breakfast, popularized in Paris and London in the 1920s, is named for the mimosa flower, which has a similarly lovely yellow-orange color.

- 1 oz. fresh orange juice
  Champagne

Pour orange juice into a champagne flute. Top with champagne and stir to combine.

HEMINGWAY'S DEATH IN THE AFTERNOON

MAKES 1 COCKTAIL

Named after Ernest Hemingway's 1932 novel about the rituals of bullfighting, this champagne cocktail takes its greenish hue from a splash of absinthe.

- 1 oz. absinthe
  Champagne

Pour absinthe into a champagne flute. Top with champagne and stir to combine.

SGROPPINO

MAKES 1 COCKTAIL

Sgroppino, a slushy combination of lemon sorbet, vodka, and prosecco, is commonly served in Italy as a palate cleanser, dessert, or predinner drink. Whisking the ingredients together instead of shaking or blending creates a magnificently frothy libation.

- ⅓ cup lemon sorbet
- 3 oz. prosecco
- 1 oz. vodka

In a stainless steel bowl or cocktail shaker, whisk together sorbet and a splash of prosecco until fully incorporated. While whisking, slowly pour in vodka and then the remainder of prosecco. Serve in a martini glass or coupe.

CHAMPAGNE VARIATIONS

As the mimosa and its brethren prove, an ounce or so of fruit juice topped with sparkling wine has enduring appeal. Try any of these variations—or experiment and invent your own.

BELLINI Famously invented at Harry's Bar in Venice, the Bellini calls for an ounce and a half of fresh white peach purée combined with an equal amount of high-quality peach brandy, topped with prosecco.

ROSSINI An ounce of fresh strawberry purée (or, out of season, no-sugar-added strawberry jam) turns a pour of sparkling wine a brilliant pink; garnish with a thin slice of strawberry.

BIANCHINI A half ounce of coconut milk makes creamy champagne even creamier; lighten it with a quarter ounce of fresh lime juice and garnish with a lime twist.

ELDERFLOWER COCKTAIL A splash of elderflower syrup—found at Scandinavian specialty stores—poured over brut champagne brings out the wine's floral notes. Garnish with fresh elderflowers, if available.

CHAMPAGNE FRANGIPANE Take a cue from the classic French pear-almond tart and combine an ounce of pear purée with a quarter ounce of amaretto; top with champagne.

BELLINI TROPICALE Instead of peach, use fresh mango purée—and a squeeze of lime juice—for an equatorial riff on the Venetian classic.

BLUEBERRY THRILL Muddle a handful of blueberries and basil in a glass, then add bubbly, for a refreshing summertime sip.

POMPAGNE Brighten your holiday party by adding a splash of pomegranate liqueur to your flute of champagne; garnish with mint.

Punches & Pitchers

SANGRIA

SERVES 4–6

This version of a Spanish sangria is ripe with summer fruit; its light, refreshing flavors are made effervescent by the addition of blood-orange soda.

- ⅓ cup honey
- 1 stick cinnamon
- ½ vanilla bean
- 1½ cups sparkling blood-orange soda
- 4 cups rosé wine
- ½ cup brandy
- 3 cups roughly chopped stone fruit, such as plums and nectarines
- 1 cup halved grapes
- ½ cup blueberries
- 3 sprigs fresh mint

Bring honey, cinnamon, vanilla bean, and blood-orange soda to a boil in a 4-qt. saucepan; let cool. Stir in wine and brandy. In a pitcher, layer chopped fruit, grapes, blueberries, and mint. Strain wine mixture over fruit; chill for at least 4 hours or up to overnight before serving.

REFAJO

SERVES 4–6

Crisp and bittersweet, this Colombian lager-based pitcher cocktail is the perfect accompaniment to an afternoon around the grill.

- 1 liter Colombiana soda
- ¾ cup aguardiente or Pastis
- 3 12-oz. bottles pale lager
  Lime wedges, for garnish
  Orange wedges, for garnish

Pour soda, aguardiente, and lager into a chilled pitcher; do not stir. Serve over ice and garnish with lime and orange wedges.

GREEN MONSTER

SERVES 4–6

Floral, tropical passion fruit juice pairs with white rum and cool mint in this vibrant drink based on a Costa Rican cocktail.

- ¼ cup sugar
- 4 cups passion fruit juice
- 1½ cups white rum
- ⅓ cup fresh lime juice
- 1½ cup fresh mint leaves
  Thin lime slices, for garnish

Boil sugar with ¼ cup water in a 1-qt. saucepan until sugar is dissolved; let simple syrup cool and transfer to a blender. Add passion fruit juice, rum, lime juice, and mint leaves; purée until smooth. Strain into a pitcher and garnish with lime wheels. Serve chilled.

WATERMELON COOLER

SERVES 4–6

Sweet watermelon balances the heat of a Scotch bonnet chile in this summery, tequila-based drink.

- 1 8-lb. watermelon, flesh cut into 1″ cubes
- ¼ cup sugar
- 1 Scotch bonnet chile, halved
- ½ cup fresh lime juice
- 2 cups silver tequila

Freeze one-fourth of the watermelon cubes. Purée the remaining watermelon and strain; you should have about 8 cups juice. Boil sugar and ¼ cup water in a 1-qt. saucepan until sugar is dissolved. Add chile and let syrup cool; strain into a pitcher. Stir in watermelon juice and frozen cubes, lime juice, and tequila.

CHILLED CIDER PUNCH

SERVES 15–20

Effervescent with ginger beer and dry hard cider and spiked with a generous dose of whiskey, this concoction combines the fall flavors of a mulled cider with the celebratory feel of a sparkling punch.

8 cups apple cider
1 750-ml. bottle dry hard cider
3 12-oz. bottles ginger beer
1½ cups whiskey
2 oz. fresh lemon juice
Several dashes orange bitters
1 orange, sliced into rounds, for garnish
Cinnamon sticks, for garnish

Combine the ciders, ginger beer, whiskey, lemon juice, and bitters in a large punch bowl or pitcher. Stir to combine. Top with orange slices and cinnamon sticks. Ladle into punch glasses filled with ice.

FLAMING PUNCH
Punschglühbowle
SERVES 12

The name of this flaming red wine punch translates from the German as "punch glow bowl." This recipe is based on one in the 1905 collection *Coolers and Punches* from the German army's *Maneuvers and Field Deployment* manual.

3 bottles light-bodied red wine
1 750-ml bottle arrack liquor or cachaça
½ cup sugar
1 Seville orange (also called bitter or sour orange) thinly sliced, seeds removed
1 lemon, thinly sliced, seeds removed

1 In a 6-qt. pot, bring red wine and arrack liquor to a boil over medium-high heat. Reduce heat to medium-low and stir in sugar and orange and lemon slices. Simmer, stirring occasionally, for 5 minutes. Transfer the punch to a heavy heatproof bowl.

2 Ignite the punch. Dip a small metal ladle into the hot punch; touch a lit match to the surface of the punch in the ladle to ignite it. Pour the flaming punch back into the bowl. Serve immediately so that punch remains aflame in the glass.

TOM & JERRY
SERVES 12

This traditional Christmas punch gets its body from briskly beaten eggs and its flavor from a riot of baking spices.

2 eggs, separated
⅛ tsp. cream of tartar
1½ cups plus 2 tsp. dark rum
⅔ cup superfine sugar
¼ tsp. ground cinnamon
⅛ tsp. ground allspice
⅛ tsp. ground cloves
4½ cups milk
1½ cups VSOP cognac
Freshly grated nutmeg

1 In a large bowl, whisk egg whites and cream of tartar to stiff peaks. In another bowl, whisk yolks, 2 tsp. rum, sugar, cinnamon, allspice, and cloves until thick. Working in 2 batches, fold egg whites into yolk mixture. Cover bowl with plastic wrap; chill batter.

2 To serve, heat milk in a 2-qt. saucepan over medium-low heat; keep warm. Put 1 heaping tbsp. batter into a mug; stir in 1–2 tbsp. each cognac and rum. Fill mug with 6 tbsp. milk; stir until frothy and garnish with nutmeg. Repeat.

ULTIMATE EGGNOG
SERVES 6

Chef Mary Sue Milliken showed us how to craft this decadent eggnog, which incorporates whipped cream, egg whites, and spices into a pudding-like zabaglione base.

1 cup light rum, plus more for serving (optional)
½ cup plus 2 tbsp. sugar
6 eggs, separated
¾ cup heavy cream
½ tsp. ground cinnamon, plus more for garnish
⅛ tsp. freshly grated nutmeg, plus more for garnish
⅛ tsp. ground allspice
⅛ tsp. ground anise
1 cup milk

1 Whisk rum, ½ cup sugar, and egg yolks in a heatproof bowl set over a saucepan of simmering water until very thick, 2–3 minutes; chill. Whip cream in a bowl until soft peaks form, then chill.

2 In a large bowl, whip egg whites, 2 tbsp. sugar, cinnamon, nutmeg, allspice, and anise until soft peaks form. Fold whipped cream and cooled egg yolk mixture into whites; stir in milk. To serve, ladle eggnog into mugs and garnish with cinnamon and nutmeg. Serve additional rum on the side, if you like.

Hot Drinks

HOT TODDY

MAKES 1 COCKTAIL

This time-honored concoction of whiskey, lemon, and honey soothes colds (the illness) and cold (the temperature) with equal force.

- 2 oz. whiskey
- 1 oz. honey
- ½ oz. fresh lemon juice
- Ground cinnamon, for garnish

Combine whiskey, honey, and lemon juice in a sturdy mug. Top with hot water and stir until honey is dissolved. Sprinkle a bit of cinnamon on top.

HOT CHAI TODDY

MAKES 1 COCKTAIL

Spiced black chai adds a warming, deeply spiced, pleasantly tannic twist to the classic hot toddy.

- 1 bag black tea with chai spices
- 1 tbsp. honey
- 1 tbsp. fresh lemon juice
- 2 oz. bourbon
- Lemon wedge, for garnish

Pour 1 cup hot water over tea bag in a heatproof glass or mug. Add honey and stir until completely dissolved. Allow to steep for 3–4 minutes, then discard tea bag. Add lemon juice and bourbon and stir until combined. Garnish with lemon wedge.

CALVADOS TODDY

MAKES 1 COCKTAIL

Bartender Jose Torrella of the Barclay Bar in New York City combines calvados (French apple brandy) with hot cider for a variation on a toddy that's autumn in a glass.

- ¼ cup sugar
- 1 tsp. cinnamon, plus more for garnish

- ¾ cup apple cider, plus more for rimming glass
- ½ cup heavy cream
- 1½ oz. calvados
- 1 cinnamon stick, for garnish

Mix sugar and cinnamon together in a bowl wide enough to fit the rim of a heat-proof glass. Pour apple cider into a bowl of similar size to about a depth of ¼". Dip the rim of the glass in apple cider and then cinnamon-sugar mixture. Whip cream and ½ oz. calvados until stiff peaks form. Refrigerate until ready to use. Heat apple cider in a small saucepan. Remove from heat and add 1 oz. calvados. Pour into sugared glass and top with whipped cream. Garnish with ground cinnamon and cinnamon stick.

HOT COCONUT MILK PUNCH

MAKES 1 COCKTAIL

Coconut milk adds richness to this bourbon drink, adapted from a recipe by mixologist and writer Toby Cecchini.

- ¾ cup milk
- ¼ cup canned coconut milk
- 1 tbsp. light brown sugar
- 1½ tsp. vanilla extract
- 2 oz. bourbon
- Freshly grated nutmeg, for garnish

Heat milks, sugar, and vanilla in a small saucepan over high heat and cook, whisking, until frothy and steaming. Stir in bourbon, then pour into a coffee mug and garnish with nutmeg.

GLÖGG

Mulled Wine

SERVES 8–10

This version of the Scandinavian classic is served at Aquavit in New York City as part of the restaurant's traditional *Julbord* Christmas spread.

2 oranges
2 750-ml bottles dry red wine
1½ cups port
1 cup vodka
¼ lb. dried figs, sliced
¼ lb. raisins
1 cup packed light brown sugar
2 star anise
4 Indonesian long peppers
5 cloves
7 cardamom pods
3 cinnamon sticks
Blanched almonds, for serving
Raisins, for serving
Pepparkakor or gingersnaps,
for serving

Peel the zest from oranges in ribbons, then juice the oranges. Combine zest, juice, wines, vodka, fruits, sugar, and spices in a large pot and bring mixture to a simmer, stirring from time to time. Remove from heat and allow glögg to macerate for 2 hours. When ready to use, strain, reheat, and serve with blanched almonds and raisins in the cup, and pepparkakor on the side for dipping.

BITTERSWEET HOT CHOCOLATE WITH RED WINE
SERVES 2

We love nibbling dark chocolate alongside a glass of red wine; the two flavors combined in a mug of hot chocolate is an unexpected treat. Use a fruity merlot, shiraz, or beaujolais.

6 oz. bittersweet chocolate,
finely chopped
⅓ cup fruity red wine
1 cup milk
Pinch kosher salt
Sugar, for serving

Combine chocolate and wine in a 1-qt. saucepan over low heat; bring wine to a simmer and cook, whisking, until chocolate is melted, about 3 minutes. Add ⅔ cup water, milk, and salt, bring to a boil, and cook, whisking, for 3 minutes more. Pour into 2 mugs and serve with sugar on the side to sweeten to taste.

ARNAUD'S CAFÉ BRÛLOT DIABOLIQUE
SERVES 4–6

Our simplified version of the flaming coffee cocktail—served, with great fiery spectacle, at Arnaud's in New Orleans—uses strong black coffee spiced with whole cloves.

⅓ cup orange curaçao
¼ cup brandy
10 whole cloves
3 cinnamon sticks
1 orange, quartered
Peel of 1 lemon
3 cups strong black coffee
3–5 tbsp. sugar

Simmer orange curaçao, brandy, cloves, cinnamon sticks, orange, and lemon peel in a 4-qt. saucepan over medium-high heat. Using a match or lighter, carefully ignite and cook, swirling pan until flames die out. Stir in coffee and sugar; cook, stirring, until sugar is dissolved. Strain coffee into brûlot or demitasse cups.

HOT BUTTERED RUM
SERVES 16

Hot buttered rum is part of an American colonial tradition in which strongly flavored ingredients were added to soften the harsh rum available at the time.

1½ cups unsalted butter, softened
1 cup packed dark brown sugar
¼ tsp. freshly grated nutmeg
¼ tsp. ground cinnamon
¼ tsp. ground cloves
Kosher salt, to taste
24 oz. rhum agricole vieux (aged rum)

1 Beat butter and sugar in a bowl with an electric mixer until fluffy. Add nutmeg, cinnamon, cloves, and pinch of salt and beat again to combine. Chill buttered rum base until ready to use, for up to 2 weeks.

2 To make each hot buttered rum, put 2 heaping tbsp. buttered rum base and 1½ oz. rum into an 8-oz. mug and fill with boiling water. Stir to melt and mix; serve at once.

Cordials & Liqueurs

RASPBERRY CORDIAL

MAKES 2 CUPS

This liqueur is delightfully sweet, with just a little kick, and makes good use of a summer bounty of raspberries.

- 4 pt. fresh raspberries, plus a few berries
- ¾ cup sugar
- ¾ cup vodka

1 Put raspberries into a large heatproof bowl set over a large pot of water simmering over low heat. Cook undisturbed until berries begin to collapse into their juices, 3–4 hours.

2 Using a rubber spatula, gently stir berries. Continue cooking berries undisturbed until most of their juices have been released, about 2 hours more.

3 Pour berries and juice into a clean jelly bag suspended over a bowl and drain overnight. (Don't squeeze bag, or cordial will be cloudy.)

4 Meanwhile, heat sugar and ½ cup water together in a small pot over medium-low heat, stirring until sugar dissolves, 3–5 minutes. Cover and simmer for 2 minutes more. Remove from heat, uncover, and set aside to cool.

5 Combine juice (you should have about 1 cup), syrup, and vodka in a pitcher, then pour into a 16-oz. bottle. Add a few raspberries. Refrigerate for up to 3 months.

LIMONCELLO

MAKES TWO 750-ML BOTTLES

True limoncello is produced in Sorrento, Italy, and served well chilled in the summer months as an after-dinner drink. It's easy to make but requires patience—it takes several weeks before the final product is ready to drink.

- 8–12 lemons
- 4 cups Everclear or other neutral high-proof spirit
- 2½ cups sugar

1 Peel zest from lemons with a vegetable peeler, being careful to avoid removing the white pith. (Reserve lemons for another use.) Put zest into a large glass jar with a tight-fitting lid and add spirits (there should be enough to cover the zest; if there isn't, add more). Set aside in a cool, dark place for 3–4 days. (The higher the proof of the alcohol, the faster the essence of the lemon will be extracted.) When peels turn pale and liquid is a deep yellow, strain through a sieve and store in another glass container. Discard peels.

2 Combine sugar and 6 cups water in a medium saucepan over medium heat; do not boil. Stir until the sugar dissolves and the syrup is clear, about 10 minutes, then set aside to cool.

3 Pour syrup into lemon-infused alcohol (mixture will turn cloudy). Adjust flavor to your palate by either diluting with water or adding more alcohol in small amounts. Then pour liqueur into 2 clean, dry 750-ml bottles, using a funnel. Close tightly with corks or screw tops. Set aside for a few weeks to allow liqueur to mellow.

PEANUT BUTTER–INFUSED BOURBON

MAKES ONE 750-ML BOTTLE

"Effleurage" is an age-old perfumers' technique used to extract botanicals from flowers by pressing the fresh petals into a layer of vegetable fat. To similar effect, you can spread a high-quality, unsweetened peanut butter across a baking pan to maximize surface area, and then float some bourbon on top to pull out the flavors.

- 16 oz. creamy, all-natural peanut butter
- 1 750-ml bottle of bourbon

1 Drain the oil away from a jar of creamy, all-natural peanut butter, then spread the peanut butter in an even layer over the bottom of a 9″×13″ baking dish.

2 Pour the bottle of bourbon over the peanut butter (reserving the bottle) and cover tightly with plastic wrap. Set aside at room temperature for 24 hours.

3 Line a fine strainer with cheesecloth or a coffee filter and set over a bowl.

4 Strain the bourbon, then use a funnel to return it to the bottle.

CLEMENTINE-RUM LIQUEUR

Creole Shrubb

MAKES ONE 750-ML BOTTLE

In the French Caribbean territory of Guadeloupe, this slightly sweet liqueur is prepared with the abundant citrus fruits that appear around the holidays. Known as a "shrubb" (not to be confused with the vinegar-based shrub), it's prepared with rhum agricole, a local rum distilled from fresh sugarcane juice instead of molasses. Culinary historian Jessica B. Harris prepares this, her version, every year.

- 1 750-ml bottle dark rhum agricole, such as Clément brand
- ¼ cup sugar, or more to taste
  Peels from 8 clementines, satsumas, kumquats, or other citrus of choice, white pith removed
- 1 vanilla bean, scraped
- 1 cinnamon stick

1 In a large lidded jar, combine rhum and sugar and stir until fully dissolved. Add citrus peels, vanilla bean pod and seeds, and cinnamon stick. Taste and add more sugar if desired. Cover and let macerate in a sunny spot for 2 weeks.

2 Strain twice through a few layers of cheesecloth. Serve, or store covered in a cool place.

CRAB APPLE LIQUEUR WITH CINNAMON

MAKES ABOUT 5 CUPS

Goldschläger's far subtler (but still gold-flecked) relative, this after-dinner sipper has sweetness, a cinnamon aroma, and an apple finish. Crab apples, which can be dropped in whole to steep, are ideal due to their low water content. "If you're from somewhere warmer and your crab apples are not as tart," says Red Morin of Quebecois restaurant Joe Beef, "add a splash of good cider vinegar at the end."

- 2 lb. hard, fragrant crab apples, scrubbed clean
- 1 cinnamon stick
- 4 cups Everclear or high-proof vodka or rye whiskey
- ⅓ cup maple syrup
- ⅓ cup sugar
  Gold flake, crumbled (optional)

1 In a 4-qt. jar or other tight-sealing container, combine apples and cinnamon. Cover with alcohol, and seal.

2 Store in a cool dark place for at least 1 month and up to 2 months. Then strain and reserve liquid, discarding apples.

3 Combine maple syrup, sugar, and ⅓ cup water in a small pot over medium heat. Bring to a boil, stirring to dissolve sugar. Remove and let cool completely. Add syrup to infused spirit, stirring to incorporate. Stir in some gold flake, if desired.

4 Using a funnel, transfer liqueur to a clean glass bottle. Shake to distribute gold flake before serving. Serve chilled or at room temperature.

HOW TO MAKE YOUR OWN AMARO

SPIRIT Start with any over-proof clear spirit that strikes your fancy (think vodka, rum, or Everclear), but keep it neutral so the flavors you choose can develop fully and shine through. Choosing 150 proof or higher is ideal; don't go below 100 proof, or the alcohol won't absorb the flavors as well.

BITTER Arguably the most important component, the bitter taste provides the backbone of the finished product. Choose one or two bittering agents to add to the infusion—like cherry tree bark, cinchona bark, wormwood, licorice root, angelica root, or gentian root—and use about a tablespoon per 750 ml of spirit.

DRIED The dried ingredients lend depth and complexity to an amaro, and allow for a more diverse flavor experience than you can get with fresh ingredients alone (unless, of course, you happen to live on an alpine hillside). Use about a teaspoon each of 5 to 10 nontoxic dried components that appeal to you, such as lemongrass, anise seeds, cardamom, dried cranberries, hyssop, hops, or elderflower.

FRESH The liveliness of fresh herbs or citrus peel adds top notes of brightness to amaro, but use them sparingly, as ingredients like these can easily become overpowering. Use a handful of fresh mint, sage, or rosemary, and a few strips of orange, grapefruit, or lemon zest.

SWEET Once everything gets muddled together and infuses for several weeks, the inedible alcohol infusion needs to be diluted and sweetened to taste. Simple syrup made with cane sugar is a classic, but for more depth of flavor, you can make a demerara syrup, or dilute honey or maple syrup with fresh water before stirring into your filtered amaro.

—Alexander Testere.

Nonalcoholic Drinks

LIME RICKEY

MAKES 1 COCKTAIL

A refreshing warm-weather drink, the lime rickey offers up a bit of sweet cold citrus heaven, well worth the labor of making it.

- ½ lime, quartered, plus 2 tbsp. fresh lime juice
- 2½ tbsp. sugar
- 1 cup club soda

Place lime wedges and sugar in a pint glass and, using a muddler or wooden spoon, crush and stir until sugar dissolves. Fill glass with ice, add lime juice and club soda, and stir to combine.

SALTY LIME SODA

MAKES 1 DRINK

Ubiquitous throughout India, this soda is bright, bracing, and not too sweet thanks to a generous pinch of salt, which embellishes the lime's flavor.

- 2 tbsp. superfine sugar
- 1½ tbsp. fresh lime juice
- ¼ tsp. kosher salt
- Club soda
- Lime slice, for garnish

Fill a glass with ice cubes, then add sugar, lime juice, and salt. Add soda water and stir well until sugar and salt are mostly dissolved. Garnish with lime slice.

FINNISH LEMON SODA

Sima

MAKES ABOUT 1 QUART

Bright and fruity with a caramelized depth of flavor thanks to brown sugar and a four-day ferment, this homemade lemon soda is enjoyed during the May Day celebration in Finland.

- ⅛ tsp. fresh yeast
- 3 cups filtered water
- ½ cup packed dark brown sugar
- 3 tbsp. fresh lemon juice
- 1 tsp. granulated sugar
- 5 golden raisins

1 Mix yeast and ¼ cup filtered water heated to 115°; let sit until foamy, about 10 minutes. Put brown sugar in a heatproof bowl. Bring 1¼ cups water to a boil; pour over sugar and stir until sugar is dissolved. Stir in remaining 1½ cups water, lemon juice, and granulated sugar; let cool. Stir in yeast mixture and drape a kitchen towel over bowl; let sit at room temperature (70°–75°) for 24 hours.

2 Using a funnel, pour soda into a sterilized 1-quart plastic soda bottle, filling to within 1″ of the top or lower. Add raisins and close bottle tightly with top. Let sit at room temperature for 24 hours (the bottle should become rock-hard with the pressure that builds up within). Refrigerate soda for 2 days before carefully opening and serving. Drink soda within 1 week of opening and store in the refrigerator.

AGUA DE SANDÍA

Watermelon Punch

MAKES 1 GALLON

Simple to make, this cooling Mexican beverage is a marvelously summery refresher.

- 1 8–10-lb. watermelon
- 3–5 limes, quartered
- ¼–½ cup sugar

Seed the watermelon, then purée the pulp in a blender or food processor. Strain into a large widemouthed jar to catch stray seeds. Squeeze 3 limes into jar, adding the rinds. Add ¼ cup sugar and 6–8 cups water and mix well. Adjust flavor with more sugar or limes, if you like. Add plenty of ice, then ladle into tall glasses.

AGUA DE JAMAICA

Sweet Hibiscus Drink

SERVES 4

This sweet-tart, magenta-hued drink is a popular street-side cooler in Mexico.

1½ cups sugar

2 cups (about 2 oz.) dried hibiscus flowers

3 whole allspice

1 stick canela (Mexican cinnamon) or cinnamon

Bring 5 cups water to a boil in a 4-qt. saucepan over high heat. Add sugar and cook, stirring, until sugar dissolves, about 1 minute. Remove from heat, stir in hibiscus flowers, allspice, and canela; let sit, covered, at room temperature for 1 hour. Pour through a fine sieve into a pitcher and discard solids; chill for 2 hours. Pour over ice to serve.

FRUIT PUNCH

MAKES 2 GALLONS

"This recipe dates to before the Civil War," claims Alabama native Betty Wright of her citrusy punch. "It looks like lemonade until you drink it. The flavor blossoms after it sits in the refrigerator for a few days, and it freezes well. I just pull it out of the freezer and add water whenever the grandkids come over."

3 oranges, halved

3 lemons, halved

¼ cup citric acid

2 tbsp. plus 1 tsp. cream of tartar

4 cups sugar

1 Juice oranges and lemons, discarding seeds and reserving rinds. Set juices aside.

2 Put reserved orange and lemon rinds into a large heatproof bowl, sprinkle with citric acid and cream of tartar, and toss to combine. Pour 2 cups boiling water over rinds and set aside to steep for 15 minutes. Strain fruit-infused liquid, discarding rinds, and set aside.

3 Put sugar and 2 cups water into a medium pot and cook over medium heat until sugar is dissolved. Place sugar syrup aside to cool.

4 To make concentrate, combine reserved fruit juices, fruit-infused liquid, and sugar syrup in a 2-qt. glass jar with a tight-fitting lid. Stir well with a wooden spoon. Cover and refrigerate for at least 2 days and up to 2 weeks before using, to let the flavors come together. When ready to use, mix 1 part fruit punch concentrate with 3 parts water. Serve over crushed ice. Refrigerate leftover concentrate for up to 2 weeks.

CHOCOLATE EGG CREAM

MAKES 1 DRINK

This soda-jerk classic famously contains neither egg nor cream. What it does have is an effervescent sweetness and plenty of nostalgic appeal.

½ cup cold milk

1¼ cups cold seltzer

2 tbsp. chocolate syrup

Pour milk into a 16-oz. drinking glass and then slowly pour in seltzer, using a long-handled spoon to stir constantly until foamy. Add syrup and stir from the bottom until just blended, leaving the foamy head at the top white.

ROOT BEER

MAKES 22 TWELVE-OUNCE BOTTLES

It's crucial to sanitize all your gear before tackling this project. The bottles and capper, as well as your kitchen tools (mesh sieve, funnel, long-handled spoon, and stockpot) are easiest to sanitize by running through a dishwasher on its "sanitize" setting. To ready the caps, place them in a pot of cold water over high heat; once the water comes to a boil, let cook for 5 minutes.

½ oz. dried birch bark (see Cook's Note)

½ oz. dried sarsaparilla root

½ oz. dried sassafras root bark

¼ oz. dried licorice root

SODA-JERK SPEAK

Drugstores in the South in the late 1930s had their own language. Soda jerks used fountainese for the fixtures of drugstore life and for calling out orders. Here are some examples:

FINAGLING The art of manipulating a soda fountain pinball machine without tilting it (and thereby losing your nickel).

FLATWICH A sandwich flattened in a double-sided grill. Messy sometimes.

PICCOLO Jukebox

SHOOT ONE, WALKING Coke in a cup, to go

SHOOT ONE, BLOODY Cherry coke

FIZZ A VAN A vanilla ice cream soda

1 2" piece of fresh ginger, thinly sliced

2 vanilla beans, split lengthwise, seeds scraped and reserved

4 cups molasses (not blackstrap)

¼ tsp. active dry yeast

1 Combine birch bark, sarsaparilla root, sassafras root bark, licorice root, ginger, vanilla bean and seeds, and 4 quarts cold water in a large pot. Bring to a boil over medium heat, then remove from heat, cover, and let steep for 2 hours.

2 Place a fine-mesh sieve over a large (at least 21/2-gallon) stockpot. Strain liquid and discard solids. Stir in molasses and 4 quarts of cold, filtered water, then let cool to 75°F. Sprinkle in yeast and stir to combine; cover and let ferment for 15 minutes.

3 Stir mixture once more, then funnel into sanitized bottles, filling to within 2 inches of the top, but no higher. Cap using a bottle capper (follow manufacturer's instructions). Leave bottles to ferment in a cool place (65–75°) for 12 hours, then refrigerate for 5 days to let flavor develop before enjoying or gifting.

COOK'S NOTE: Because this recipe calls for steeping and straining the botanicals, coarsely chopped varieties are preferred. Measurements are listed by weight, which is more accurate than volume when dealing with chunky ingredients.

CARDAMOM LASSI

SERVES 2

India's lassis—yogurt-based drinks—are a cooling treat and come in a dizzying array of flavors. Cardamom, with its dusty, floral notes, is a popular version.

2 cups plain whole-milk yogurt

3 tbsp. sugar

1 tsp. ground cardamom

Put yogurt, sugar, and cardamom into a blender and purée until well combined. Divide lassi between 2 glasses and chill until cold, about 30 minutes, or serve at once.

MANGO LASSI

MAKES 4 DRINKS

To make this yogurt-enriched Indian fruit shake, use the ripest, sweetest mango you can find.

3 cups plain whole-milk yogurt

¼ cup sugar

½ tsp. kosher salt

1 large ripe mango, peeled, pitted, and roughly chopped

Combine all ingredients in a blender, and purée until smooth. Refrigerate until chilled, at least 1 hour. Pour into glasses and serve with straws.

SOUTHERN SWEET TEA

MAKES 1 GALLON

Southerners take "sweet tea"—as genuine iced tea is known in the South—very seriously.

4 qt.-size tea bags, preferably black tea

2 cups sugar

1 Bring 8 cups water to a boil in a pot over high heat. Add tea bags, remove pot from heat, and let steep for 4 minutes.

2 Meanwhile, combine 8 cups cold water with sugar in a one-gal. jug. Remove tea bags from pot, pour hot tea into jug, and stir well. (Adding the hot tea to the cold sugared water, rather than the other way around, helps keep the tea clear and preserves its flavor.) Fill the biggest glasses you can find with ice and pour tea into them. Refrigerate leftover tea: It tastes even better the next day.

MASALA CHAI

Spiced Indian Tea

SERVES 4

Throughout India, sweet, milky black tea is suffused with ginger, clove, and cardamom, with vibrant results.

1 tsp. fennel seeds

8 green cardamom pods

8 whole cloves

1 stick cinnamon, halved

1 1" piece ginger, peeled and crushed

2 cups whole milk

¾ cup jaggery or sugar

6 Assam tea bags

1 sprig mint

Heat an empty 4-qt. saucepan over medium-high. Cook fennel seeds, cardamom, cloves, and cinnamon until lightly toasted and fragrant, 1–2 minutes. Let spices cool slightly and transfer to a spice grinder; grind into a powder and return to pan. Add ginger and 4 cups water and bring to a boil. Stir in milk, sugar, tea bags, and mint; remove from heat and let steep 6 minutes. Strain into glasses and serve hot.

NORTH AFRICAN MINT TEA
SERVES 4–6

Mint tea is served throughout North Africa and the Middle East. It's not possible for it to be too minty or too sweet.

- **2** tbsp. Chinese gunpowder tea or green tea
- **16** lumps sugar or ⅓ cup granulated sugar
- **1** bunch fresh mint, stems discarded (about 25 sprigs)

Combine tea, sugar, mint, and 4 cups boiling water in a teapot and stir until sugar dissolves; let sit for 10 minutes. To serve, strain tea into serving glasses.

HORCHATA
SERVES 4

The New York–based Mexican chef Fany Gerson gave us the recipe for this clean, refreshing toasted-rice horchata, served all over Mexico.

- **1** 1″ piece canela (Mexican cinnamon), plus freshly ground cinnamon for garnish
- **⅓** cup medium- or long-grain rice
- **¼** cup sugar
- **½** tsp. vanilla extract

Toast cinnamon piece and rice in a heavy skillet over medium-low heat until fragrant. Remove from heat and process in a blender to a fine powder. Add 2 cups water, sugar, and vanilla and blend well. Strain through wet cheesecloth into a large pitcher and stir in 2 more cups water. Chill, then serve over ice topped with ground cinnamon.

YUENG YUENG
Hong Kong–Style Coffee with Sweetened Tea
SERVES 2–4

Soothing milk tea blends beautifully with the assertive flavors of coffee in this distinctive Hong Kong drink popularized in *cha chaan tengs* (tea cafés).

- **4** small black tea bags, paper and strings removed
- **1** 14-oz. can sweetened condensed milk
- **2** cups strong brewed coffee

Simmer tea and 1 cup water in a 2-qt. saucepan over medium heat for 3 minutes. Squeeze out and discard tea bags. Stir in milk, bring to a boil, and cook, stirring, for 3 minutes. Stir in coffee, heat through, and pour into glasses.

THAI-STYLE ICED COFFEE
SERVES 2

Traditionally, coffee in Thailand is made using a cloth filter that resembles a wind sock. Known as *kafae thung* or *kafae boran*, literally "bag coffee" or "old-fashioned coffee" in Thai, this method of brewing, coupled with dark-roasted robusta beans, leads to coffee with a distinctly burnt flavor and aroma, lots of caffeine, and not much body. When it comes to iced coffee—pretty much the standard in Thailand's heat—this intensity is mellowed with a splash of evaporated milk. Sweetened condensed milk and or sugar can be added if, like most Thais, you prefer your coffee sweet.

- **¼** cup plus 2 tbsp. coarsely ground very dark roasted robusta coffee
- Sugar or sweetened condensed milk (optional)
- **1** can evaporated milk

1 In a small pot, bring a few cups of water to a boil. Moisten filter, then add coffee grounds to it. Pour 1½ cups boiling water into a heatproof glass measuring cup. Submerge filter in water, alternatively steeping and agitating grounds, for 1 minute.

2 While grounds are steeping, fill 2 tall glasses with chipped ice.

3 Lift filter from hot liquid and position it over a second glass measuring cup. Pour brewed coffee through filter, lowering the bag into the measuring cup to steep briefly once more. Lift filter, position it over one of the glasses, and pour half of the coffee through the grounds once more. Add sugar or condensed milk to taste (if desired), stirring to combine. Top with evaporated milk to taste. Repeat with the second glass and serve immediately.

KOPI JAHE
Indonesian Coffee with Ginger
SERVES 6

This bittersweet Indonesian coffee gets a jolt from smashed fresh ginger.

- **6** tbsp. coarsely ground coffee
- **1** 3″ piece fresh ginger, smashed
- **3½** oz. palm sugar, coarsely chopped

Bring coffee, ginger, sugar, and 6 cups water to a boil in a 2-qt. saucepan. Reduce heat to medium and cook, stirring, until sugar is dissolved. Serve immediately.

The Pantry

Stocks

CHICKEN STOCK

MAKES ABOUT 8 CUPS

We learned this recipe from a Roman restaurateur, Jane Mariani, who advised us to use an old hen—the older the bird, she said, the better the flavor. Your basic chicken, however, makes a fine stock for many diverse dishes.

- 1   3-lb. chicken, or 3 lb. chicken parts
- 2   carrots, roughly chopped
- 2   ribs celery
- 1   medium onion, peeled
- 6   black peppercorns

1 Combine all ingredients with 12 cups water in a large stockpot. Bring to a boil over medium-high heat.

2 Reduce heat to low and simmer uncovered, skimming occasionally, for 3 hours. (After 1 hour of cooking, you may remove chicken, pick meat from the bones to reserve for another use, and return carcass to the pot.) Remove from heat and strain through a fine-mesh sieve. Skim off fat before using. Use immediately or refrigerate or freeze.

PRESSURE-COOKER CHICKEN STOCK

MAKES ABOUT 8 CUPS

Making a rich, flavorful homemade stock generally calls for simmering the ingredients for hours on the stove top. Here, a pressure cooker speeds up the process to just about an hour.

- 3   lb. chicken parts
- ¼   tsp. black peppercorns
- 2   carrots, roughly chopped
- 1   head garlic, halved
- 1   leek, roughly chopped
- 1   onion, quartered

1 Combine all ingredients with 8 cups water in a pressure cooker. Cover pressure cooker with lid and seal according to manufacturer's directions. Heat on high for 5 minutes, then reduce heat to low and cook for 30–40 minutes. (If pressure builds too much and steam escapes rapidly from release valve, remove pot from heat for a few minutes to prevent overpressurizing. Return to low heat when pressure stabilizes.)

2 Remove pot from heat; allow pressure cooker to depressurize, but do not take off lid. Let cool for 20 minutes. The cooling process will decrease pressure naturally. This depressurizing also allows the extraction process to continue gently. Once pot has fully depressurized, remove lid.

3 Pour stock through a fine-mesh sieve set over a bowl. Skim off fat before using. Use immediately or refrigerate or freeze.

BROWN CHICKEN STOCK

MAKES ABOUT 12 CUPS

French stocks fall into two categories, white and brown. Brown stocks, the basis for many classic sauces and stews, are made by roasting bones and vegetables until dark brown, then simmering them on the stovetop with wine, water, and aromatics.

- 5   lb. chicken bones
- 3   carrots, chopped
- 3   onions, chopped
- 3   ribs celery, chopped
- 2   tbsp. tomato paste
- 2   cups white wine
- 2   medium tomatoes, chopped
- 2   cloves garlic, peeled
- 2   bay leaves
- 10   black peppercorns
- 3   sprigs fresh flat-leaf parsley

1 Heat oven to 400°. Place chicken bones in a large roasting pan. Roast until they begin to brown, 1–1½ hours, then add carrots, onions, celery, and tomato paste. Mix well and continue roasting until vegetables and bones are well browned, about 40 minutes.

2 Place roasting pan over 2 burners on stovetop and transfer bones and vegetables to a large stockpot. Heat roasting pan over medium-high heat, add white wine, then scrape up browned bits on bottom of pan. Simmer for about 1 minute, then add deglazing liquid to stockpot.

3 Add tomatoes, garlic, bay leaves, peppercorns, parsley, and 16 cups water. Simmer uncovered over medium heat, skimming occasionally, for 3 hours. Remove from heat and strain through fine-mesh sieve. Skim off fat before using. Use immediately or refrigerate or freeze.

ICHIBAN-DASHI
Japanese Seafood Stock
MAKES ABOUT 2½ CUPS

Dashi, the stock at the heart of Japanese cooking, should taste of the sea. With only three ingredients, it's incredibly simple to make.

- 1   oz. wide-cut kombu (dried kelp)
- 4   cups katsuobushi (dried smoked bonito flakes)

1 Place kombu in a medium saucepan with 4 cups water. Heat over medium-high heat until water just begins to simmer. Reduce heat to medium-low and cook—without allowing stock to come to a full simmer—until kombu is soft, about 2 minutes.

2 Remove kombu and discard. Increase heat to medium-high and bring stock to a full boil. Add ¼ cup cold water to lower temperature of stock, then add bonito flakes. Do not stir. Return to a boil, then immediately remove pan from heat. (If bonito flakes boil for more than a few seconds, flavor will be too strong.) Allow bonito flakes to settle, skim foam, then carefully pour stock through a sieve lined with cheesecloth, discarding bonito flakes. Use immediately.

RICH BEEF STOCK
MAKES ABOUT 12 CUPS

Enriched with smoked ham hock and beef marrow bones, this stock is an ideal base for hearty, Eastern European–style soups and stews, like German Barley Soup (page 86).

- 2   lb. beef chuck
- 1   lb. beef marrowbones
- 1   smoked ham hock
- 2   medium parsnips, peeled
- 2   medium carrots, peeled
- 2   ribs celery
- 1   yellow onion, peeled
- 3   sprigs fresh dill
- 3   sprigs fresh flat-leaf parsley
- 4   bay leaves
- 10   black peppercorns
- 2   large dashes kosher salt

1 Put beef, marrowbones, ham hock, and 14 cups water into a large pot and bring to a boil over high heat, skimming any foam that rises to the surface.

2 Add parsnips, carrots, celery, onion, dill, parsley, bay leaves, peppercorns, and salt and return to a boil. Reduce heat to medium-low, cover partially, and simmer until beef is very tender, 1–1½ hours. Strain through a colander into a large bowl. Reserve beef and ham hock for another use or discard. Use immediately or refrigerate or freeze. Skim off fat before using.

FISH STOCK
MAKES ABOUT 10 CUPS

When your recipe calls for a good fish stock (like Bouillabaisse, page 111), look no further than this savory preparation.

- 3   tbsp. extra-virgin olive oil
- 3   small leeks, white part only, diced and rinsed
- 1   rib celery, diced
- 1   fennel bulb, diced
- 2   medium carrots, peeled and diced
     Grated zest of ½ orange
- 3   cloves garlic, crushed
- 3   tomatoes, coarsely chopped
- 4   sprigs fresh flat-leaf parsley
- 1   sprig fresh thyme
- 1   bay leaf
- 5   black peppercorns
- 6   lb. fish bones and carcasses (with heads), chopped into large pieces
- 1   750-ml bottle dry white wine

1 Heat oil in a large stockpot over medium-low heat. Add leeks, celery, fennel, carrots, and orange zest and cook, stirring occasionally, until vegetables are soft, about 15 minutes.

2 Add garlic, tomatoes, parsley, thyme, bay leaf, and peppercorns and cook for 1–2 minutes more. Add fish pieces to vegetables along with wine and 16 cups water. Increase heat to medium-high, bring stock to a boil, then reduce heat to medium and simmer uncovered, skimming occasionally, for 1 hour.

3 Allow stock to cool slightly, then strain through a fine-mesh sieve, return to pot, and reduce by about half over medium-high heat, about 30 minutes. Use immediately or refrigerate or freeze.

LOBSTER STOCK

MAKES ABOUT 16 CUPS

A great way to use up otherwise discarded lobster shells, this subtly sweet stock makes an excellent addition to seafood gumbos, chowder, risotto, and more.

- 3 tbsp. unsalted butter or vegetable oil
- 3 yellow onions, chopped
- 1 rib celery, chopped
- 2 leeks, white part only, chopped
  Broken shells from 7 lb. raw, boiled, or steamed lobsters (about 5 lb. shells)
- 2 cups dry white wine

1 Melt butter in a large stockpot over medium heat. Add onions, celery, and leeks and cook until vegetables begin to soften, about 10 minutes.

2 Add lobster shells and cook, crushing shells with a heavy wooden spoon, for 5 minutes, then add wine and 18 cups water. Bring stock to a boil, reduce heat to medium, and simmer, skimming occasionally, until reduced by one-quarter, about 1 hour.

3 Strain through a fine-mesh sieve lined with cheesecloth. Use immediately or refrigerate or freeze.

COOK'S TIP Shrimp shells can be substituted for some or all of the lobster shells.

SIMPLE VEGETABLE STOCK

MAKES 8 CUPS

This versatile recipe is a great use for any vegetables in your pantry that may be slightly past their prime.

- 3 tbsp. extra-virgin olive oil
- 1 carrot, roughly chopped
- 2 ribs celery, roughly chopped
- 2 medium onions, roughly chopped
- 6 cloves garlic, roughly chopped
- 1 large leek, roughly chopped
- 1 bulb fennel, roughly chopped
- 1 small tomato, roughly chopped
- 1 cup dry white wine

- 5 sprigs fresh flat-leaf parsley
- 6 black peppercorns
- 1 bay leaf

Heat oil in a large pot over medium heat, add vegetables, and cook for 15 minutes. Add wine, 7 cups water, parsley, peppercorns, and bay leaf. Bring stock to a boil, skimming off foam. Lower heat, cover, and simmer for 45 minutes. Strain through a fine-mesh sieve. Use immediately or refrigerate or freeze.

SKIMMING 101

One of the keys to making a good stock is the careful and continuous skimming away of the fat and impurities that rise to the top of the pot as your stock simmers. There are several different methods for skimming, but all of them have the same goal: To remove as much of the unwanted foam as possible without removing the stock along with it. Here are four tried-and-true techniques we've come to rely on in the SAVEUR test kitchen:

THE COLD-SPOON METHOD Dip a large metal spoon in ice water and run the bottom of the spoon along the surface of the stock. The cold metal will cause fats in the foam to coagulate and stick to the bottom of the spoon.

THE SPIN METHOD Dip the bottom of a long-handled ladle into the stock and begin swirling it in a circular motion, working from the center outward, until the foam accumulates around the edge of the pot, at which point it can be easily spooned away.

THE CONVECTION METHOD Move the stockpot partially off the burner (using an overturned plate or a pie dish to prop up the overhanging section of the pot) so that only one side of the stock continues to simmer actively. The foam will accumulate toward the calm side of the pot, becoming easier to remove.

THE BIG-SKIMMER METHOD Students at the École Supérieure de Cuisine Française in Paris use a wide, shallow perforated skimming tool, which, when wielded deftly, captures the fatty foam while allowing the pure stock to drain back into the pot.

DEMI-GLACE

MAKES 2 CUPS

Rich and concentrated, demi-glace—a classic French sauce used in a variety of preparations—is well worth the time it takes to make. You can buy it ready-made, but if you make your own, you can refrigerate it for up to 2 weeks or freeze it for up to 6 months. Browning veal bones—which have more collagen than beef bones, yielding a thicker, richer stock—and vegetables in a roasting pan in the oven before simmering them in a pot with water gives this reduced stock a pronounced flavor and deeper color. Traditionally, the stock for demi-glace was thickened with a roux, but modern chefs have shunned thickeners in favor of reducing stock to a pure, more syrupy consistency.

10	lb. veal bones
3	carrots, roughly chopped
2	onions, roughly chopped
1	leek, white part only, roughly chopped (optional)
1	Bouquet Garni (page 86)
1	6-oz. can tomato paste

1 Heat oven to 500°. Put bones into a roasting pan large enough to hold them in a single layer and roast until lightly browned, 1–1½ hours. Add carrots, onions, and leeks and spread them evenly around the bones. Roast the bones and vegetables until deeply browned, about 45 minutes more.

2 Transfer bones and vegetables to a 15-qt. stockpot. Pour off and discard any fat in the roasting pan and place pan over 2 burners on stove top over medium heat. Add 3 cups water to pan; begin scraping up any browned bits from bottom of pan with a wooden spoon. (These caramelized morsels of concentrated juice, called the fond—literally, "the foundation"—will enrich the stock.) Simmer for 3 minutes; transfer liquid to pot of bones. Add bouquet garni and tomato paste. Cover bones with 6–8 qt. cold water and set pot over medium-high heat. (Starting with cold water encourages the proteins and fats contained in bones to rise to the surface in large pieces, where they can be skimmed and discarded.)

3 When the first bubbles begin to appear on the surface of the liquid, reduce heat to medium-low and maintain a very gentle simmer; a bubble should rise to the surface about once per second. Simmering slowly prevents the fat and impurities from being churned back into the stock and clouding it. The strength and concentration of your demi-glace will be determined by the length of time the stock simmers. For the minimum amount of extraction, it should simmer for at least 6–8 hours, but we recommend 12–24 hours for a richer, more gelatinous sauce. Check every few hours and add more cold water if necessary so bones are always covered.

4 Skim fatty froth from surface of stock with a ladle every 5–10 minutes during first hour of cooking to prevent it from clouding stock. After first hour, skim stock every 30 minutes or so.

5 When stock is ready, set a chinois (a fine-mesh conical sieve) or a fine metal sieve over a clean 8-qt. pot. Strain stock through sieve into pot. Tap edge of sieve with a wooden spoon to loosen any solids that impede the straining, but do not force liquid through. Discard bones, vegetables, and bouquet garni. The stock should yield 4–5 qt. If storing stock for another use, you can cool it quickly by placing the pot in a sink half filled with ice water. Once it's cooled, skim the surface again to remove any fat. Transfer stock you don't plan to use right away to storage containers and refrigerate. Stock will keep refrigerated for up to 1 week or frozen for up to 6 months. To transform the stock into demi-glace, proceed to the next step.

6 Simmer stock over medium-high heat, skimming occasionally, for 4–5 hours until reduced to 2 cups. Use immediately or store as directed in headnote.

ENRICHED DUCK STOCK

MAKES ABOUT 8 CUPS

An enriched stock refers to a stock at double strength. It can be made by making a classic standard recipe but using an already-made stock in lieu of water, or—as here—by stirring in satiny, concentrated demi-glace. It can be made with any stock, but we particularly like it with duck: Using the carcass from a roast duck (page 180) allows the bird's rich flavor to live on well past its initial starring turn at the dinner table.

- 1   duck carcass, chopped into about 16 pieces
- 1   medium onion, quartered
- 8   black peppercorns
- 1   bay leaf
- 2   tsp. salt
- 2   cups duck demi-glace (see Sourcing Note)

1 Heat oven to 500°. Put duck pieces in a heavy roasting pan with onion, peppercorns, and bay leaf. Season with salt and roast until deeply browned, about 45 minutes.

2 Remove duck from oven and add 12 cups water to roasting pan. Using a wooden spoon, scrape any browned bits stuck to bottom of pan, then return pan to oven and roast until stock has reduced by half, about 30 minutes. Strain stock, discarding solids, and stir in demi-glace until fully incorporated. Use immediately or refrigerate or freeze. Skim off fat before using.

SOURCING NOTE You can buy duck demi-glace from specialty purveyors suck as D'Artagnan; alternately, make your own using the recipe for Demi-Glace (page 571) and substituting an equivalent quantity of duck bones for the veal bones called for in the recipe.

CLOUDS & CLARITY

When a stock is allowed to boil (rather than simmer), it runs the risk of becoming cloudy, the result of particles of fat from the meat, fish, or fowl becoming emulsified with the water. There's nothing wrong with a cloudy stock, taste-wise, but it can occasionally have a heavier texture, and, when used as the base of a broth-based soup, can make the final product look less beautiful than it otherwise might.

Fortunately when it comes to stock making, what's been done can often be undone. If you have time, the simplest method to clarify stock is just to put it in the refrigerator. As it cools, the fat will rise to the surface and solidify and can be scooped or sliced right off the top and discarded. If you're using your stock right away and need to clarify it immediately, make an egg raft: Beat 1 egg white per 4 cups stock and stir the beaten whites into the simmering stock. Stop stirring and the egg whites will rise to the surface, forming a raft; as the soup simmers, the raft will attract stray particles. Continue simmering on low heat for 30 minutes, then scoop out and discard the cooked egg whites—along with anything clinging to them.

Pickles & Preserves

RUSSIAN-STYLE CUCUMBER PICKLES

Solionye Ogurtsky

MAKES 2 QUARTS

Pickling is occasionally referred to as Russia's national pastime. These spiced cucumber pickles are a staple of Russian pantries.

½	cup kosher salt
16–20	small Kirby cucumbers, tips trimmed
1	tbsp. sugar
2	cups cider vinegar
12	black peppercorns
8	cloves garlic, peeled
1	bay leaf
1	bunch fresh dill with seed heads
1–2	horseradish, oak, or grape leaves (optional)

1 Dissolve ¼ cup salt in 10 cups water in a large bowl. Add cucumbers and set aside for 12 hours. Drain and rinse.

2 Combine remaining ¼ cup salt, sugar, vinegar, and 2 cups water in a saucepan. Bring to a boil over high heat. Add peppercorns, garlic, and bay leaf and boil for 2 minutes. Fit cucumbers upright in 2 hot, sterilized quart-size canning jars. Tuck in dill. Pour hot vinegar mixture over cucumbers to cover. Add leaves, if using. Put lids on jars, screw on bands, and process in a boiling water bath for 15 minutes. Remove jars from pot and cool. Store in a cool, dark place for at least 3 weeks before using. They will keep for up to 1 year.

MINNESOTA BREAD-AND-BUTTER PICKLES

MAKES 2 QUARTS

These sweet-sour refrigerator pickles, flavored with onion, mustard seeds, and cider vinegar and colored with turmeric, are based on a recipe we tried at the Minnesota State Fair.

8	medium cucumbers, cut into ¼"-thick slices
1	medium yellow onion, thinly sliced
1	clove garlic, thinly sliced
½	red bell pepper, seeded and thinly sliced
½	green bell pepper, seeded and thinly sliced
2	tbsp. kosher salt
1⅔	cups sugar
1	cup cider vinegar
1½	tsp. brown mustard seeds
½	tsp. celery seeds
½	tsp. ground turmeric

1 Combine cucumbers, onion, garlic, and peppers in a large bowl and sprinkle with salt; add 2 cups cracked ice and toss together. Let sit for 3 hours. Transfer vegetables to a colander and rinse lightly with cold water. Divide vegetables between two 1-qt. glass jars with resealable lids and set aside.

2 Bring sugar, vinegar, mustard and celery seeds, and turmeric to a boil in a 1-qt. saucepan; divide mixture evenly between jars and seal jars with lids. Let cool to room temperature and then store in refrigerator for up to 2 weeks.

JAVANESE CUCUMBER & CARROT PICKLE

Acar Timun

MAKES ABOUT 2½ CUPS

This relish is a variation of the ubiquitous Indonesian quick-pickle, and makes a cool, crisp counterpoint to grilled satay.

1½	tbsp. kosher salt
3	shallots, thinly sliced
1½	cucumbers, cut into 2"-long by ¼"-wide sticks
1	large carrot, cut into 2"-long by ¼"-wide sticks
2½	tbsp. sugar
2	tbsp. rice vinegar
2	green bird's eye chiles, stemmed and sliced into ⅛" rings

Stir together salt, shallots, cucumbers, carrot, and 2 cups boiling water in a bowl. Let sit for 15 minutes; drain.

Squeeze out liquid and transfer to a bowl. Stir in sugar, vinegar, and chiles. Let sit for 15 minutes before serving.

VIETNAMESE CARROT & DAIKON PICKLE
Do Chua

MAKES ABOUT 3 CUPS

Eat this crunchy pickle as a stand-alone snack, or add it to Asian dipping sauces, *bánh mì* (page 126), and salads.

- ½ lb. carrots, peeled and cut into matchsticks
- 1½ lb. small daikon, peeled and cut into matchsticks
- 2 tsp. kosher salt
- 1 tsp. plus ¼ cup sugar
- ½ cup plus 2 tbsp. white vinegar

1 In a bowl, combine carrots, daikon, salt, and 1 tsp. sugar. Let sit until the vegetables have wilted slightly and liquid pools at the bottom of the bowl, about 30 minutes. Drain vegetables; rinse and pat dry with paper towels. Transfer vegetables to a medium bowl.

2 Whisk together the remaining ¼ cup sugar, vinegar, and ½ cup warm water, pour mixture over vegetables. Stir to combine. Set aside to marinate for at least 1 hour before serving. Cover and refrigerate for up to 4 weeks.

SMASHED CUCUMBERS WITH GINGER
SERVES 4

This quick pickle calls on ingredients from the Asian pantry and indeed variations on the dish are popular throughout east and southeast Asia. Its cooling flavor makes it the ideal accompaniment to grilled meats and rich braises.

- 4 Kirby cucumbers
-    Kosher salt
- 1 1″ piece fresh ginger, peeled
- 1 tbsp. sugar
- 1½ tbsp. rice vinegar
- 1 tsp. sesame oil
- 2 cloves garlic, roughly chopped

1 Cut cucumbers into irregular chunks about 2″ long and ¼″ thick. Transfer cucumber slices to a medium bowl, sprinkle with 2 tsp. salt, mix, and set aside at room temperature to extract excess liquid and soften, about 1 hour.

2 Meanwhile, julienne ginger, transfer to a medium bowl, and set aside.

3 Drain and gently squeeze cucumbers to extract more liquid, then pat dry with a kitchen towel. Add cucumbers to the bowl of ginger along with sugar, vinegar, sesame oil, and garlic. Toss to combine and season with salt to taste.

4 Let rest at room temperature for at least 15 minutes before serving to allow the flavors to come together.

CHINESE HOT & SOUR CABBAGE PICKLE
Suan Cai

SERVES 6

Try this gently pickled cabbage as an accompaniment to Jook (page 394), a savory rice porridge. The heat is variable; use more chiles and chile oil for a hotter pickle.

- 1 large napa cabbage (3–4 lb.)
- 2 tbsp. kosher salt
- 4 tbsp. sugar
- 8–12 dried red chiles
- ½–1 tsp. Red Chile Oil (page 376, or store-bought)
- 1 cup white vinegar

1 Peel away green leaves from napa cabbage until you reach pale yellow–tipped inside leaves. (Discard green leaves or save for another use.) Quarter cabbage lengthwise, core, then slice lengthwise into 1½″-wide strips.

2 Transfer to a bowl, sprinkle with salt, cover, and set aside to release water and until leaves are pliable and translucent, 3–4 hours.

3 Drain, then squeeze to release more water. Arrange half the cabbage in a bowl and sprinkle with 2 tbsp. sugar and 4–6 dried red chiles. Repeat with remaining cabbage, 2 tbsp. sugar, and 4–6 dried red chiles. Add red chile oil and white vinegar. Cover and refrigerate for 24 hours. Serve cold.

CHOWCHOW
MAKES ABOUT 3 CUPS

This tart-sweet Southern relish, which makes use of a bumper crop of late-summer produce, is the perfect condiment for crab cakes (page 287), cold roast meats, or as a sandwich topping.

- 1½ lb. green tomatoes, finely chopped
- 1 medium onion, finely chopped
- 1 rib celery, finely chopped
- ½ green bell pepper, seeded and finely chopped
- ½ red bell pepper, seeded and finely chopped

2 tbsp. kosher salt
½ cup sugar
⅓ cup white vinegar
1½ tsp. dry mustard
1½ tsp. yellow mustard seeds
1 tsp. celery seeds
1 tsp. crushed red chile flakes
¼ tsp. ground coriander

1 Toss tomatoes, onion, celery, and peppers in a large bowl with salt; cover with plastic wrap and let sit at room temperature for 4 hours or overnight. Transfer vegetables to a sieve and press to extract excess juices; discard juices.

2 Transfer vegetables to a 6-qt. saucepan and add remaining ingredients. Cover, bring mixture to a boil, reduce heat to medium-low, and simmer, stirring occasionally, until vegetables are very soft, about 2½ hours. Transfer relish to a glass jar and let cool. Cover and refrigerate for up to 2 weeks.

APPLE-CRANBERRY RELISH
MAKES ABOUT 4 CUPS

This sweet-tart relish gets its body from the natural pectin in the poached, puréed cranberries. A twist on Thanksgiving's traditional cranberry sauce, the recipe was given to us by Michael Sandoval, culinary developer at Bouchon Bistro in Yountville, California. His staff prepares it as part of the restaurant's annual Thanksgiving meal for veterans and their families.

¼ cup olive oil
12 cloves garlic, minced
1 medium yellow onion, thinly sliced
4 cups fresh or thawed frozen cranberries
2 sweet apples, such as Red Delicious, cored, peeled, and roughly chopped
2½ cups unsweetened apple juice
   Kosher salt and freshly ground black pepper, to taste

1 Heat oil in a medium pot over medium heat. Cook garlic and onion until soft, 6–8 minutes. Add cranberries and apples and cook until cranberries burst and apples are tender, about 15 minutes. Add apple juice and salt and pepper to taste and bring to a boil. Reduce heat to medium and cook, stirring occasionally, until mixture is slightly dry, about 45 minutes.

2 Let mixture cool slightly and transfer to a food processor. Pulse until coarsely ground. Serve cold or at room temperature.

YELLOW HOT RELISH
MAKES 2½ CUPS

Rosaura Guerrero, co-founder of the Rosarita brand, typically used up a whole batch of this lively condiment at one family meal, but her granddaughter Susan likes to refrigerate some for later use. The Guerrero family recommends serving it alongside pork chops or steak.

1½ lb. small medium-hot or hot fresh yellow chiles, such as Caribes
½ medium white onion, chopped
8 cloves garlic, chopped
1 tsp. crushed dried oregano (preferably Mexican)
½ tsp. kosher salt
1¼ cups white vinegar, or as needed

1 Stem, seed, and chop chiles, then put into a medium bowl. (Wear rubber gloves, or wash hands thoroughly with soap and hot water after handling chiles.) Add onion, garlic, oregano, and salt to bowl and mix well.

2 Put relish into a clean 24-oz. ceramic or glass jar. Add enough vinegar to cover relish by about ¼". Cover jar and refrigerate for at least 2 weeks before serving. Relish keeps, refrigerated, for up to 6 weeks.

CORN RELISH
MAKES ABOUT 2 QUARTS

This bright-tasting relish is one of our favorite uses for summer corn.

4 cups fresh corn kernels
2 cloves garlic, minced
1 small red onion, minced
1 jalapeño, stemmed, seeded, and minced
½ green bell pepper, cored, seeded, and minced
½ red bell pepper, cored, seeded, and minced
2 cups apple cider vinegar
3 tbsp. dark brown sugar
1 tbsp. kosher salt
½ tsp. dried mustard powder
½ tsp. ground turmeric
   Juice of 1 lime

1 Combine corn, garlic, onion, jalapeño, and peppers in a bowl. Divide corn mixture evenly between two clean 1-qt. glass jars with tight-fitting lids.

2 Combine vinegar, sugar, salt, mustard, turmeric, and 1 cup water in a 4-qt. saucepan. Bring to a boil over high heat; stir until sugar and salt dissolve. Remove pan from heat and stir in lime juice.

3 Pour vinegar mixture over corn and seal jars. Let cool. Refrigerate for up to 2 weeks.

PICKLED CAULIFLOWER

MAKES 6 PT.

We added coriander, turmeric, cumin, chiles, and black mustard seeds to brighten and add verve to this otherwise everyday cauliflower and carrot pickle, giving the resulting dish a South Asian accent.

3	tsp. coriander seeds
1½	tsp. turmeric
1½	tsp. cumin seeds
1½	tsp. black mustard seeds
6	bay leaves
6	dried chiles de árbol, split
2	lb. cauliflower
1	large carrot
1	small red onion
3	cups white wine vinegar
6	tbsp. sugar
6	tbsp. kosher salt

1 Bring a 6-qt. pot of water to a boil. Place six 1-pt. canning jars along with their bands and lids in the boiling water. After about 30 seconds, remove the lids from the water with tongs and transfer to a kitchen towel on the counter. After about 10 minutes, use tongs to transfer jars and bands to the kitchen towel and let air-dry.

2 When jars are dry, add ½ tsp. coriander seeds, ¼ tsp. turmeric, ¼ tsp. cumin seeds, ¼ tsp. black mustard seeds, 1 bay leaf, and 1 split chile to each jar.

3 Bring a 4-qt. saucepan of salted water to a boil. Cut cauliflower into 1″ florets. Peel and slice carrot into ⅛″-thick coins. Halve and thinly slice the onion.

4 Boil cauliflower and carrots for 3 minutes; drain and transfer to a large bowl. Add the onion and stir to combine. Divide vegetables among the jars, leaving about ¾″ headspace at top of each jar.

5 In a 4-qt. saucepan, bring vinegar, 4 cups water, sugar, and salt to a boil over high heat, whisking occasionally to dissolve it, about 5 minutes.

6 Pour vinegar solution into jars, to within ½″ of rim. Wipe jar rims with a hot damp towel. Cover and seal each jar with a lid and screw the bands on tightly.

7 Place jars in a large pot fitted with a rack; pour in enough water to cover the jars by at least 3″. Bring to a boil over high heat and boil for 15 minutes.

8 Using tongs or a rubber-handled jar lifter, transfer jars, not touching, to a kitchen towel on the counter; let cool for 6 hours. Store cauliflower in a cool, dark place for up to 1 year. Refrigerate after opening.

PICKLED EGGPLANT

MAKES 4–6

With their delicate flavor, tender skin, and paucity of seeds, Japanese eggplants are delicious preserved in a simple, rustic brine of puréed walnuts, cayenne, salt, and olive oil.

4–6	small Japanese eggplants
2	tsp. kosher salt
1	tbsp. ground walnuts
½	tsp. cayenne pepper
	Olive oil, to cover

1 Poach eggplants in gently boiling water until slightly soft, 5–10 minutes. Slit each eggplant from blossom end almost to stem end twice, so that eggplant splays into 4 "fingers" attached to stem end.

2 Process salt, walnuts, and cayenne in a food processor into a smooth paste. Rub paste on exposed eggplant flesh, reassemble the eggplants, and place in a tall glass jar, stem ends upward, for 12 hours.

3 Discard brine at bottom of jar. Fill jar with oil, covering eggplants completely. A ball of foil on top of eggplants will keep them submerged. Close jars and pickle for 10–14 days. They will keep refrigerated for up to 2 weeks.

PERSIAN EGGPLANT & HERB PICKLE

Torshi Liteh

MAKES 1½ CUPS

Serve this tart, herbaceous eggplant pickle with Persian stews or rice dishes, like Shirin Polō (page 395).

"Salt is born of the purest of parents: the sun and the sea."
PYTHAGORAS

1¼ lb. Japanese eggplants, peeled
    and halved lengthwise
    Kosher salt, to taste
¾ cup cider vinegar
½ tsp. ground turmeric
½ tsp. ground coriander
½ tsp. caraway seeds
2 cloves garlic, minced
1 tbsp. chopped fresh tarragon
1 tbsp. finely chopped fresh flat-leaf
    parsley
1 tbsp. finely chopped fresh cilantro
1½ tsp. dried mint

1 Sprinkle eggplants heavily with salt and place on a wire rack set over paper towels; let drain for 20 minutes. Roughly chop eggplants and place in a 4-qt. saucepan along with ½ cup vinegar, turmeric, coriander, caraway, garlic, and ½ cup plus 2 tbsp. water. Bring to a simmer over medium heat and cook until tender, about 20 minutes.

2 Combine remaining ¼ cup vinegar, tarragon, parsley, cilantro, and mint in a bowl. Stir herb mixture into eggplant mixture, then transfer to a bowl. Chill and serve.

PICKLED MUSTARD GREENS
MAKES 1 QUART

Japanese, Chinese, and Korean cooks are masters of the art of pickling. Pickled greens like these are often served in all these countries as an accompaniment to meat dishes.

2 tbsp. sugar
1 tbsp. kosher salt
¼ cup white vinegar
½ lb. gai choy or other mustard greens
3 red or green serrano chiles,
    split lengthwise

1 In a small saucepan, combine 2 cups water, sugar, salt, and vinegar. Bring to a boil over high heat, then remove from heat. Let cool slightly.

2 Using a paring knife, trim stems of mustard greens from leaves. Cut stems into 2″ pieces and place in a 1-qt. measuring cup. Coarsely chop enough greens to fill measuring cup when added to stems and packed down gently.

3 Pack stems, leaves, and chiles into a clean 1-qt. glass jar. Pour hot liquid onto greens, making sure stems are completely submerged. Cover and refrigerate for at least 3 days before serving.

OKRA PICKLES
MAKES 1 QUART

Spicy okra refrigerator pickles are a Southern classic and make a great snack or accompaniment to any meal. We particularly love them on the Thanksgiving table, where their tart crunch cuts through the richness of turkey, potatoes, and gravy.

1 lb. okra
4 cloves garlic, peeled
3 sprigs fresh dill
1 habanero or Scotch bonnet chile,
    stemmed and halved
2 cups white wine vinegar
2 tbsp. kosher salt
1½ tbsp. yellow mustard seeds
½ tbsp. fennel seeds
8 black peppercorns

Combine okra, garlic, dill, and chile in a sterilized 2-qt. glass jar; set aside. Bring vinegar, salt, seeds, peppercorns, and 1¾ cups water to a boil in a 4-qt. saucepan over high heat, stirring to dissolve salt. Pour into jar, seal, and let cool to room temperature; refrigerate for at least 24 hours before serving. They will keep refrigerated for up to 1 month.

YUCATECAN PICKLED RED ONIONS
Escabeche de Cebolla
MAKES ABOUT 1¾ CUPS

Red onions soak up the flavors of oregano and cumin in this vibrant pickle relish. It's served with fresh seafood in Yucatán, Mexico, but we have yet to find a sandwich, taco, or salad these onions don't feel right at home on.

- 1 tbsp. kosher salt
- 1 large red onion, thinly sliced lengthwise
- 1 tsp. black peppercorns
- 1 tsp. dried oregano
- 1 tsp. cumin seeds
- 3 cloves garlic, halved lengthwise
- 1½ cups red wine vinegar

In a bowl, toss salt and onion together; let sit until onion releases some of its liquid, about 15 minutes. Transfer to glass jar along with peppercorns, oregano, cumin, and garlic, then pour in vinegar; seal with lid. Refrigerate for at least 4 hours before using.

MEXICAN-STYLE PICKLED JALAPEÑOS
Jalapeños Escabeche

MAKES ABOUT 1 QUART

These vinegary pickled jalapeños are an essential condiment for all kinds of street foods throughout Mexico.

- 2 tbsp. extra-virgin olive oil
- 1 small white onion, thinly sliced
- 1 medium carrot, peeled and thinly sliced crosswise
- 1 clove garlic, minced
- 10 red or green jalapeños, pricked with a paring knife
- 1 cup white vinegar
- 1½ tsp. kosher salt
- 1 tsp. dried oregano
- 1 bay leaf

1 Heat oil in a 4-qt. saucepan over medium heat. Add onion, carrot, and garlic and cook, stirring, until barely tender, about 3 minutes.

2 Add jalapeños, and cook, stirring, for 4 minutes. Add vinegar, salt, oregano, bay leaf, and 2 cups water and bring to a boil; remove from heat and let cool to room temperature. Transfer to a storage container and refrigerate for at least 1 week and up to 2 weeks before using.

BRAZILIAN PICKLED CHILES
Conserva de Pimenta

MAKES 2 QUARTS

Fiery Brazilian pickled chiles are a tabletop condiment served alongside rice and beans, roast pork, or fish.

- 1 lb. mixed hot fresh chiles, such as Scotch bonnet, habanero, jalapeño, and serrano
- ½ cup red wine vinegar
- ½ tsp. fennel seeds
- 3 bay leaves
- 2 whole cloves
- 2 star anise pods
- 2 juniper berries
- 2 sticks cinnamon
- ¾ cup canola oil
- ¾ cup white wine vinegar
- 1 tbsp. sugar
- 1 tsp. kosher salt

1 Bring a 6-qt. saucepan of water to a boil, add chiles, and cook for 1 minute. Drain and transfer to a bowl of ice water; let sit for 1 minute. Drain and dry chiles; set aside. Mix red wine vinegar, fennel, bay leaves, cloves, star anise, juniper, and cinnamon in a bowl and let sit for 15 minutes. Drain, reserving spices, and save vinegar for another use.

2 Place spices in a sterilized 2-qt. glass jar and add chiles. Whisk oil, white wine vinegar, sugar, and salt in a bowl until sugar dissolves; pour over chiles and spices. Cover jar with lid and let sit at room temperature for 1 week before using.

COOK'S NOTE For less intense heat, remove the seeds from the chiles before pickling.

LIME PICKLE
Nimbu ka Achaar

MAKES ABOUT 2 CUPS

Tangy, tender lime pickles are a staple of Indian cuisine, a condiment that adds sour, spicy punch to meals. The classic recipe calls for fermenting the citrus with salt in the sun before blending it with a spice paste and lime juice.

- 25 small limes
- ¼ cup kosher or sea salt
- ⅓ cup canola oil
- 1½ tsp. brown mustard seeds
- ½ tsp. fenugreek seeds
- 20 fresh or frozen curry leaves
- 2 tsp. cayenne pepper
- 1 tsp. ground turmeric
- ½ tsp. asafoetida
- 1 cup fresh lime juice

1 Using a paring knife, quarter limes lengthwise, leaving them attached by ½" at the stem ends. Using your fingers, rub the limes inside and out with salt in a bowl. Transfer limes and salt to a sterilized 1-pt. glass jar, packing them in tightly to fit. Cover jar with lid and place jar near a window or any other spot indoors where it will receive a lot of sunlight and warmth; let the jar sit in this environment for 1 week, shaking the jar once a day to disperse brine evenly.

2 After limes have sat for 1 week, heat oil in a 10″ skillet over medium-high; add mustard seeds, fenugreek seeds, and curry leaves and cook, stirring, until lightly toasted, about 2 minutes. Transfer to a spice grinder or small food processor and process into a smooth paste. Stir in cayenne, turmeric, and asafoetida. Mix spice mixture with lime juice, and then pour mixture into jar with limes; seal with lid. Shake jar to evenly disperse ingredients and store in the refrigerator for at least 1 week to infuse flavors. They will keep refrigerated for up to 1 year.

PICKLED PEACHES
MAKES 2 QUARTS

These spiced peaches are a pleasure to eat alongside grilled or roasted meats year-round—but make them only in summer peach season, with fruit that's fully ripe but not too soft.

3½	cups sugar
1½	cups white vinegar
14–16	ripe medium peaches, peeled
8	whole cloves
2	sticks cinnamon
1	1″ piece ginger, peeled and thinly sliced

1 Bring a 6-qt. pot of water to a boil. Place two 1-qt. canning jars and their lids and ring bands in boiling water. After about 30 seconds, remove the lids from the water with tongs and transfer to a kitchen towel on the counter. After about 10 minutes, use tongs to transfer jars and bands to the kitchen towel and let air-dry.

2 Combine sugar, vinegar, and 1½ cups water in a heavy, medium pot and bring to a boil over medium-high heat, stirring until sugar dissolves. Working in batches, slide peaches into pickling liquid and cook, turning once or twice, until peaches soften but before they turn fuzzy, 4–5 minutes per batch. Transfer peaches to a bowl as done.

3 Divide cloves, cinnamon, and ginger between the 2 jars. Cut any peaches with brown spots into halves or quarters, discarding pits, and trim away the brown spots. Spoon peaches into the jars, filling the gaps with the halves and quarters and packing the jars as tightly as possible.

4 Return pickling liquid to a boil, then pour boiling liquid into each jar, covering peaches and filling to within ¼″ of rims. Let liquid settle in jars, then add more boiling liquid as necessary. Discard any remaining liquid. Wipe jar rims with a hot damp towel. Cover and seal each jar with a lid and screw the bands on tightly.

5 Place jars in a large pot fitted with a rack; pour in enough water to cover the jars by at least 3″. Bring to a boil over high heat and boil for 10 minutes. Carefully lift jars from water with jar tongs and place on a kitchen towel at least 1″ apart. Let cool undisturbed for 24 hours. To test that jars have properly sealed, press on center of each lid, then remove your finger. If lid stays down, it's sealed. Refrigerate any jars of pickled peaches that aren't sealed and use within 4 weeks. Store properly sealed jars in a cool, dark place for up to 1 year. Refrigerate after opening.

RUSSIAN PICKLED TOMATOES
MAKES ABOUT 2 QUARTS

Whole pickled tomatoes flavored with dill and garlic are a tart, unexpected way to preserve summer's bounty. The prepared pickles, finely chopped, make a delicious sandwich relish.

1	tsp. black peppercorns
6–8	small tomatoes
8	small peperoncini
4	small fresh bay leaves
4	sprigs fresh dill, stemmed
2	cloves garlic, thinly sliced
1	cup red wine vinegar
2½	tbsp. kosher salt
1	tbsp. sugar

Combine peppercorns, tomatoes, peperoncini, bay leaves, dill, and garlic in a sterilized 2-qt. glass jar with a tight-fitting lid. Bring vinegar, salt, sugar, and 1¼ cups water to a boil in a saucepan; stir until salt and sugar dissolve. Pour vinegar mixture over tomatoes. Seal jar; let cool. Refrigerate for up to 2 weeks.

PICKLED BLUEBERRIES
MAKES 3½ CUPS

Chef Tyler Kord of No. 7 Sub Shop in New York City created these sweet-tart pickled blueberries as a condiment for a sandwich of Brie, pistachios, and chervil. We also love them with grilled or roasted chicken or on a cheese board.

1 cup white vinegar
¼ cup sugar
1¾ tbsp. kosher salt
1¼ lb. blueberries
1 small red onion, thinly sliced

Whisk vinegar, sugar, salt, and ¼ cup water in a medium bowl until sugar and salt dissolve. Add blueberries and onion and cover with plastic wrap. Refrigerate overnight before using.

RUSSIAN PICKLED WATERMELON
SERVES 6

Russian-style watermelon pickles—which, unlike its American counterparts (this page), use the whole watermelon, not just the rind—make a bright, pretty snack or hors d'oeuvre for a summer gathering.

¼ cup kosher salt
¼ cup sugar
1 tbsp. pickling spices
¾ tsp. cayenne pepper
½ tsp. white vinegar
8 cloves peeled garlic, smashed
5 ribs celery, coarsely chopped
½ bunch fresh dill
1 2-lb. piece watermelon, rind left on, cut into 1"-thick wedges

In a large, nonreactive bowl or pot, stir together salt, sugar, pickling spices, cayenne, vinegar, garlic, celery, dill, and 8 cups water until salt and sugar dissolve. Submerge the watermelon wedges. Cover with plastic wrap and refrigerate for at least 1 week and up to 2 weeks before serving.

WATERMELON RIND PICKLES
MAKES 6 CUPS

Crunchy, sweet watermelon rind pickles are a staple at any Southern barbecue; they offer a vibrant contrast to smoked meats.

1¾ lb. peeled watermelon rind, cut into 1" pieces
4 cups sugar
2 cups cider vinegar
3 whole cloves
1 cinnamon stick

Bring a large pot of water to a boil, add rind, and cook until just tender, about 15 minutes. Divide rinds between

2 sterilized 1½-pt. glass jars. Bring sugar, vinegar, cloves, and cinnamon to a boil in a 4-qt. saucepan over high heat, stirring until sugar dissolves. Pour over rinds. Seal jars with lids and let cool. Refrigerate for 1 day before serving.

PICKLED BEETS WITH ORANGE & GINGER
MAKES ABOUT 1 QUART

This lacto-fermented recipe is inspired by *rosl,* a Jewish specialty from the Ukraine that calls for pickling beets in brine. The sweet, spiced beets make for a delicious accompaniment to roast meats or fish.

4 medium beets, peeled and sliced into ⅛"-thick rounds
1 tsp. brown mustard seeds
1 tsp. whole allspice
1 tsp. black peppercorns
1 tsp. whole cloves
2 sticks cinnamon
1" piece ginger, peeled and cut into matchsticks
Zest of 1 orange, cut into wide strips
2 tbsp. whey
2 tbsp. honey
3 cups filtered water, warmed
Kosher salt, to taste

1 Bring a 4-qt. saucepan of salted water to a boil and add beets; cook until just tender, about 3 minutes. Drain, transfer to a bowl of ice water, and let sit for 2 minutes to chill. Drain and place beets in a sterilized 1-qt. glass jar along with mustard seeds, allspice, peppercorns, cloves, cinnamon, ginger, and orange. In a medium bowl, stir together whey, honey, and filtered water; pour over beets until covered. Pour any remaining brine or water into a resealable plastic bag, and place bag on top of beets to keep them submerged.

2 Drape a large kitchen towel over the jar and let sit at room temperature until beets have cured, about 1 week. Once beets are cured, season them with salt to taste, cover jar with lid, and refrigerate for up to 1 week before serving.

PRESERVED LEMONS
MAKES ABOUT 1 QUART

As lemons cure in a mixture of salt and spices, their flesh softens and sweetens; after a month, they're ready to be finely chopped and added to everything from Moroccan tagines (page 173) to vinaigrettes.

6 medium lemons
¼ cup kosher salt
2 cups fresh lemon juice
1 tsp. black peppercorns
1 tsp. cumin seeds
½ tsp. coriander seeds
½ tsp. nigella seeds
¼ tsp. fenugreek seeds
8 whole allspice
1 stick cinnamon
1 bay leaf

1 Quarter each lemon lengthwise so that it stays attached by about ½" at the stem end. Place lemons in a bowl and stuff with salt.

2 Transfer lemons to a sterilized 1-qt. glass jar and add the lemon juice, peppercorns, cumin, coriander, nigella, and fenugreek seeds, allspice, cinnamon, and bay leaf; seal with a tight-fitting lid and set aside in a dark place, shaking jar every other day or so, until lemons are soft, about 1 month. Refrigerate after opening and use within 2 weeks.

PEAR & CURRANT CHUTNEY

MAKES 2½–3 CUPS

This chutney, which we serve with everything from poultry to rich roasts, is ready right away, but improves with age; it's best when left to ripen in the refrigerator before using.

1 cup dried currants
6 tbsp. pear brandy
4 Bosc pears, cored and cut into ½" pieces
2 ribs celery, cut into ¼" pieces
½ cup sugar
⅓–½ cup fresh lemon juice
1 3"–3½" piece ginger, peeled and grated
Pinch of cayenne pepper

1 Put currants and brandy into a medium saucepan and simmer over medium heat until currants are plump and have absorbed most of the liquor, about 7 minutes. Add pears, celery, sugar, lemon juice, ginger, and cayenne and stir well. Return to a simmer, reduce heat to medium-low, and simmer until pears are very soft and translucent and juices are thick and syrupy, about 1 hour.

2 Put chutney into a clean jar with a tight-fitting lid; set aside to let cool. Cover and refrigerate for up to 2 weeks. Serve at room temperature.

APRICOT CHUTNEY

MAKES 2 CUPS

This savory-sweet English curried chutney goes well with lamb roasts (page 245 or 603) or braised lamb shanks.

3 tbsp. canola oil
1 tsp. curry powder
1 small onion, minced
1 clove garlic, minced
1 1" piece ginger, peeled and minced
¾ cup chopped dried apricots
⅓ cup raisins
2 tbsp. fresh lime juice
2 tbsp. sugar

1 Heat oil and curry powder in a 2-qt. saucepan over medium heat. Cook, stirring frequently, until curry powder is fragrant, about 2 minutes. Add onion, garlic, and ginger and cook, stirring occasionally, until soft, about 10 minutes.

2 Add apricots and raisins along with 1 cup water, lime juice, and sugar. Cook, stirring occasionally, until thickened, about 20 minutes. Serve immediately or refrigerate for up to 2 weeks.

CRANBERRY-GINGER CHUTNEY

MAKES ABOUT 3 CUPS

This sophisticated take on Thanksgiving cranberry sauce, laced with spices and plenty of fresh ginger, gets an extra boost from chopped celery and tart apples.

1 tbsp. unsalted butter
2 ribs celery, finely chopped
1 small yellow onion, finely chopped
1 lb. fresh or frozen cranberries (about 4 cups)
½ cup packed light brown sugar
¼ cup honey
2 tbsp. granulated sugar
2 tsp. ground cinnamon
1½ tsp. finely grated fresh ginger
¼ tsp. ground allspice
1 Granny Smith apple, cored and finely chopped

1 Melt butter in a 4-qt. saucepan over medium heat, add celery and onion, and cook, stirring, until soft, about 12 minutes.

2 Add cranberries, brown sugar, honey, granulated sugar, cinnamon, ginger, allspice, apple, and 1 cup water and bring to a boil. Cook, stirring until cranberries burst and release their juices, about 15 minutes. Reduce heat to medium-low and cook, stirring often, until berries are tender and chutney is the consistency of thick jam, about 1 hour. Transfer chutney to sterilized glass jars and refrigerate for up to 2 weeks.

MAJOR GREY'S CHUTNEY
MAKES 5 CUPS

Order a curry in many Anglo-Indian restaurants, and Major Grey's—a spiced mango chutney—comes alongside it; in a pub, a dollop might complement cheddar cheese.

- 2¼ lb. mangoes, peeled, pitted, and finely chopped
- 1 cup granulated sugar
- 1 cup packed light brown sugar
- 1 cup cider vinegar
- 1 cup raisins
- ½ cup finely chopped ginger
- 3 tbsp. fresh lemon juice
- 2 tsp. chile powder
- 1 tsp. freshly grated nutmeg
- 1 tsp. kosher salt
- ½ tsp. ground cloves
- ½ tsp. finely ground black pepper
- 2 cloves garlic, minced
- 1 large yellow onion, finely chopped
- 1 stick cinnamon

Combine all ingredients in a 4-qt. saucepan and bring to a boil over medium-high heat. Reduce heat to medium-low and cook, stirring, until reduced and thick, about 2 hours. Transfer chutney to sterilized glass jars and refrigerate for up to 2 weeks.

MOSTARDA DI FRUTTA
Spicy Mustard & Fruit Preserves
MAKES ABOUT 5½ CUPS

A salty-sweet, pleasantly spicy fruit relish, Italian *mostarda* is traditionally served with boiled meat, or as an accompaniment to soft cheeses that can take its sharpness.

- ½ lb. dried apricots, quartered
- ¼ lb. dried cherries, halved
- 1½ cups sugar
- 3 tbsp. Dijon mustard
- 2 tbsp. brown mustard seeds
- 2 tbsp. canola oil
- ¼ tsp. cayenne pepper
- 4 green apples, such as Granny Smith, peeled, cored, and cut into ½" cubes

- 3 bay leaves
  Kosher salt, to taste

Bring all ingredients and 3 cups water to a boil in a 4-qt. saucepan over medium-high heat; cook, stirring occasionally, until apricots and cherries are plumped, apples are tender, and liquid is reduced, about 40 minutes. Let cool. Serve immediately or transfer to an airtight container and refrigerate for up to 2 weeks.

TOMATO-VANILLA PRESERVES
MAKES 2 CUPS

Vanilla bean brings out the musky qualities of cherry tomatoes in this jammy compote, perfect paired with goat cheese, or alongside firm white-fleshed fish, like cod or halibut.

- ⅔ cup sugar
- 1 tsp. powdered pectin
- 1 pint red cherry tomatoes, halved crosswise
- ½ vanilla bean
- 1 tbsp. fresh lemon juice

1 Combine 1 tbsp. sugar with pectin. Set aside.

2 In a nonreactive bowl, combine remaining sugar with cherry tomatoes. Slice vanilla bean lengthwise and scrape out seeds. Add to tomatoes and sugar along with the bean itself. Toss until tomatoes are evenly coated with sugar and vanilla. Cover and let macerate until most of the sugar is dissolved and tomatoes have released their juices, about 30 minutes. Pour mixture into a nonreactive pot and place over medium-high heat. Bring to a boil, reduce heat to a simmer, and cook, stirring occasionally and skimming any foam off the top, until mixture is reduced to three-quarters of its original volume, about 12 minutes.

3 Stir in lemon juice. Whisk in pectin mixture, mixing well to eliminate clumps. Simmer for 5 minutes more to cook the pectin.

4 Divide between 2 sterilized ½-pt. glass jars. Refrigerate and use within 2 weeks, or process according to instructions in Step 5 of Pickled Peaches (page 579), then store in a cool, dark place for up to 1 year.

BEET EINGEMACHTES

Beet Jam

MAKES 5–6 PINTS

This recipe for beet *Eingemacht*—the word means "gravy" in German, but here it's more of a jam—comes to us straight from an Eastern European grandma, who serves it on Passover with matzo.

7	lb. beets, peeled
4½	lb. sugar (10¾ cups)
6	lemons
1	heaping tbsp. ground ginger
1	cup whole blanched almonds

1 Bring a large pot of water to a boil over medium-high heat. Boil beets until you can just get a fork through them, about 1 hour. Drain and set aside to cool. Cut beets into wedges, then into small, even, triangular shapes. Place in a large saucepan with sugar and ½ cup water. Heat gently, stirring frequently. Once liquid starts to come out of the beets, turn up the heat so it bubbles gently.

2 Bring a large pot of water to a boil over medium-high heat. Boil lemons for 1 minute and drain. Peel off skin and pith and discard; cut lemons into ½" slices, then into quarter triangles. Discard seeds.

3 After beets have been cooking for 1 hour, add lemons and continue simmering. After another 30 minutes, add ginger. Cook until thick and jam-like (it will thicken even more as it cools), about 1½ hours. To determine if jam is ready to fill, drop a teaspoonful on a chilled plate. Let it sit briefly, then push gently with a fingertip; if the surface of the jam wrinkles, it is ready. (Take pan off heat while you are testing.)

4 Add almonds and mix well. Pour into warm, sterilized jars. Cool before covering. Store in refrigerator for up to 1 month.

RHUBARB-GINGER JAM

MAKES 4 PINTS

Lip-puckering rhubarb isn't just for pies—pair it with spicy-sweet ginger and you've got a lovely jam.

1½	lb. rhubarb stalks, cut into 2" pieces
2	cups sugar
1	2" piece ginger, peeled

1 Place rhubarb in a large saucepan with sugar, ginger, and 1 cup water. Simmer over medium-low heat, stirring occasionally and skimming foam as it rises, until rhubarb is soft and syrup begins to thicken, about 15 minutes. Remove rhubarb with a slotted spoon and set aside.

2 Continue simmering syrup until very thick, another 7–10 minutes. Remove from heat. Discard ginger, return rhubarb to pan, stir, and cool for 5–10 minutes.

3 Sterilize four 1-pt. jars, lids, and ring bands according to instructions in Step 1 of Pickled Peaches (page 579). Ladle jam into jars, seal, and let stand at room temperature to set. Store in refrigerator for up to 1 month.

RASPBERRY FREEZER JAM

MAKES 6 HALF PINTS

This easy method for freezer-set raspberry jam delivers a brighter fresh-fruit flavor than the cooked version.

2	pints fresh raspberries
4	cups superfine sugar
6	tbsp. liquid fruit pectin
3	tbsp. fresh lemon juice

1 Crush raspberries in a large bowl. Add sugar and stir frequently until sugar dissolves, about 20 minutes.

2 Stir together pectin and lemon juice in a small bowl. Add pectin mixture to berries and stir for 3 minutes. Pour raspberry mixture into 6 sterilized ½-pt. jars, cover, and set aside at room temperature for 24 hours. Store jam in freezer. Thaw before serving; store opened jam up to 4 weeks in refrigerator.

Living Larder

HOMEMADE YOGURT

MAKES 1 QUART

You'll find no shortage of yogurt brands on supermarket shelves these days. Still, as far as we're concerned, nothing beats homemade; doing it yourself allows you to make creamy, fresh-tasting yogurt that's exactly as tart as you like. Electric makers are easy to use, but the process is simple even without one. You'll need a bit of yogurt with live active cultures (bacteria that kick off fermentation) to use as your starter and a warm oven to provide the right conditions for bacteria activation.

    4   cups milk
    1   tbsp. plain full-fat yogurt

1 Bring milk to a boil in a small pot, then transfer to a 1-qt. heatproof glass bowl or plastic container. Allow to sit until an instant-read thermometer inserted into the milk registers 90°, which could take up to an hour depending on the ambient temperature in your kitchen.

2 Preheat oven to 200°. Stir yogurt into milk and cover tightly with plastic wrap or a lid. Wrap in a large, thick dish towel and fasten with rubber bands or string; transfer to oven and immediately turn off the heat. Let sit until slightly thickened, 12–24 hours. (The longer the yogurt sits, the thicker and more sour it will become.) Remove towel and chill yogurt for 1 hour before serving.

FERMENTED SAUERKRAUT

MAKES 8 CUPS

When making sauerkraut—essential for Bigos (page 105), the Polish stew, and a vibrant topping for hot dogs and sandwiches—use firm, dense heads of cabbage with tightly packed leaves. A Japanese-style mandoline works well for shredding the cabbage.

    5   lb. white cabbage, cored and shredded
    3½   tbsp. kosher salt

1 Combine shredded cabbage and salt in a large bowl. Using a potato masher or a wooden spoon, pound cabbage for 10 minutes to bruise it and extract juices. Working in batches, transfer cabbage and juices to a 1-gal. glass jar, pressing each layer down with the masher before adding the next batch. Press a small plate into the jar onto the surface of the cabbage to weight it down. Cover jar with 4 layers of cheesecloth secured with kitchen twine.

2 Let cabbage sit and ferment at room temperature, skimming any white froth from surface of liquid every other day and discarding portions of the cabbage that turn brown, for up to 3 weeks before transferring it to two 1-qt. glass jars and refrigerating. The flavor of the sauerkraut will deepen as it sits. Use it after about 10 days for a brighter new-sauerkraut flavor or after a couple of months for a stronger classic sauerkraut flavor. Sauerkraut will keep in the refrigerator for up to 6 months.

CABBAGE KIMCHI

MAKES ABOUT 4½ QT.

In Korea, kimchi—a spicy, pungent, earthy-tasting dish of fermented vegetables—is on the table for breakfast, lunch, dinner, and everything in between. In this version, cabbage is rubbed with a handful of ingredients including chile powder and garlic before fermenting at room temperature.

    1½   cups plus 1 tsp. sea salt
    3   medium-size napa cabbages, quartered
         lengthwise with core left intact, outer
         leaves discarded
    1½   lb. daikon radishes, peeled and julienned
    1   cup plus 2 tbsp. gochugaru chile powder
    3   tbsp. aek jeot (Korean anchovy sauce)
         or fish sauce
    2½   tbsp. finely chopped saeu jeot salted shrimp
    2   tbsp. sesame seeds
    30   garlic chives, cut into 1″ pieces
    14   cloves garlic, finely chopped and mashed
         into a paste

10   scallions, white and light green parts only, thinly sliced on diagonal

10   sprigs minari or watercress, trimmed and roughly chopped

2   2″ pieces ginger, peeled, finely chopped, and mashed into a paste

1   large carrot, peeled and julienned

1   Asian pear, cored and julienned

1 In a large bowl, combine 1¼ cups salt and 8 qt. cold water and stir until salt dissolves. Add cabbages and massage the salt water into the leaves. Drain cabbages, transfer to a baking sheet, and work remaining ¼ cup salt in between the leaves down to the root. Put cabbages into a large bowl and let sit, turning occasionally, until softened, about 4 hours. Rinse cabbages and squeeze to extract excess water; set aside.

2 In a large bowl, vigorously stir together the remaining ingredients to make the kimchi seasoning paste. Working with one-quarter of cabbage at a time over the bowl of seasoning, use your fingers to work some of the paste between the leaves, starting with the innermost leaves and working outward. Repeat with remaining cabbages, reserving a handful of filling. Transfer seasoned cabbages to a clean 6-qt. glass jar, adding some of the remaining seasoning paste and ¼ tsp. salt between each layer and pressing down to compact the cabbages. Rub any remaining paste over top of packed cabbages and cover jar with 2 layers of plastic wrap. Let kimchi ferment at room temperature for 4 days.

3 Uncover the jar to release any carbon dioxide. Re-cover and refrigerate for at least 4 more days to let flavors meld further. The kimchi will keep, refrigerated, for at least 6 months (its flavor will sharpen over time). To serve, remove desired amount of cabbage and snip leaves into 1″–2″ pieces.

FERMENTED CARROT, CHILE & TOMATO SAUCE

MAKES 2 CUPS

Left to ferment, this sauce takes on a tangy, spicy-sweet flavor. Oregon pizzaiola Sarah Mininick likes to use fresh cayenne peppers to make this zippy condiment at her Portland pizzeria, Lovely's Fifty-Fifty, but any hot red chile will do.

1   cup peeled, shredded carrots (5 oz.)

1   cup puréed hot red chiles, from about 14 oz. fresh chiles such as cayenne or Fresno

1   tbsp. kosher salt

2   cups drained crushed tomatoes (14 oz.)

1   tbsp. fresh lemon juice

1 Combine carrots and chiles. Season with salt and transfer to an airtight pint jar. Store at room temperature until fermented and fizzy (about 1 week). Transfer to the refrigerator, and use within 3 months.

2 When ready to serve, combine tomatoes, lemon juice, and 2–3 tbsp. of fermented chile mixture in a bowl. (Save the extra chile mixture for more batches of sauce.)

SPROUT KRAUT

MAKES ABOUT 3 CUPS

For a twist on traditional sauerkraut, cookbook author Karen Solomon likes to soak Brussels sprouts in a briny mixture of peppercorn, dill, garlic, and chiles.

1   lb. Brussels sprouts (about 35), trimmed and halved

¼   cup packed dill fronds

2   tbsp. whole black peppercorns

4   cloves garlic, crushed

3   dried chiles de árbol

¼   cup kosher salt

1 Place sprouts, dill, peppercorns, garlic, and chiles in a clean 2-qt. glass jar and set aside.

2 Whisk salt and 4½ cups water in a bowl until salt is almost dissolved, making a brine. Pour 3 cups brine over sprouts; pour remaining brine into a resealable plastic sandwich bag, and place bag on top of sprouts to keep them submerged. Drape a large kitchen towel over jar and let sit at room temperature (ideally 70–75°) until sprouts have cured to your taste, about 3–4 weeks. Once kraut is soured, cover jar with a lid and refrigerate for up to 2 months.

Spices, Rubs & Blends

BERBERE

Ethiopian Spice Blend

MAKES ABOUT ¾ CUP

Berbere, whose name means "pepper" in Amharic, is a blend of chiles and spices that's essential to many Ethiopian dishes, including Doro Wot (page 173).

- 2   tsp. coriander seeds
- 1   tsp. fenugreek seeds
- ½   tsp. black peppercorns
- ¼   tsp. whole allspice
- 6   green cardamom pods
- 4   whole cloves
- ½   cup dried onion flakes
- 5   dried chiles de árbol, stemmed, seeded, and broken into small pieces
- 3   tbsp. paprika
- 2   tsp. kosher salt
- ½   tsp. freshly grated nutmeg
- ½   tsp. ground ginger
- ½   tsp. ground cinnamon

1 In a small skillet, combine coriander seeds, fenugreek seeds, black peppercorns, allspice, cardamom pods, and cloves. Toast spices over medium heat, swirling skillet constantly, until fragrant, about 4 minutes.

2 Let cool slightly; transfer to a spice grinder along with onion flakes and grind until fine. Add chiles and grind with the other spices until fine. Transfer mixture to a bowl and stir in paprika, salt, nutmeg, ginger, and cinnamon. Store away from direct sunlight in an airtight container for up to 6 months.

CALIFORNIA HERB SALT SEASONING BLEND

MAKES ABOUT ¼ CUP

Pioneering California restaurant the Ranch House was defined by their generous and often innovative use of herbs. We adapted this fresh herb-salt blend from chef-owner Alan Hooker's original recipe.

- 1   tbsp. coarse salt
- 1   tbsp. chopped onion
- 1   clove garlic, peeled
- 2   tbsp. fresh flat-leaf parsley leaves
- 2   tsp. fresh basil leaves
- 1   tsp. fresh thyme leaves

In a small food processor, combine salt, onion, garlic, parsley, basil, and thyme. Pulse ingredients until smooth. Mixture may be used immediately or stored in an airtight container in the refrigerator for up to 1 week.

BAHARAT

Middle Eastern Spice Blend

MAKES ABOUT ¼ CUP

Basic to many cuisines of the Middle East, this ground spice mixture is formulated a little differently by every cook who makes it. The aromatic blend, which can also include paprika, sumac, coriander, cumin, and cardamom, flavors stews and ground meat mixtures.

- 2   tbsp. black peppercorns
- 2   tbsp. whole allspice
- 1   tsp. ground cinnamon
- ½   tsp. freshly grated nutmeg

Grind peppercorns and allspice in a spice grinder or with a mortar and pestle, then transfer mixture to a small bowl. Add cinnamon and nutmeg and mix thoroughly. Store away from direct sunlight in an airtight container for up to 6 months.

BAHARAT KARISIMI

Turkish Herb & Spice Blend

MAKES ABOUT 2 TBSP.

Seasoning mixtures of this kind are common in kitchens throughout Turkey. We particularly like this blend on grilled lamb.

- 1½   tsp. dried winter savory
- 1   tbsp. pickling spice

½ tsp. ground cinnamon

½ tsp. freshly grated nutmeg

½ tsp. dried mint leaves, crumbled

½ tsp. ground cumin

1 tsp. freshly ground black pepper

In a spice grinder, grind together winter savory, pickling spice, cinnamon, nutmeg, mint, cumin, and pepper until fine. Store away from direct sunlight in an airtight container for up to 3 months.

HERBES DE PROVENCE
MAKES ABOUT ½ CUP

This classic herb blend from the south of France works best with dried herbs—they're easier to crush, so the flavors intermingle more harmoniously.

3 tbsp. dried tarragon leaves

1½ tbsp. dried savory leaves

1 tbsp. dried sage leaves

1 tbsp. dried thyme leaves

1 tbsp. dried lavender buds

1 tbsp. dried marjoram leaves

Combine tarragon, savory, sage, thyme, lavender, and marjoram, rubbing any whole leaves between fingers to crush them. Store away from direct sunlight in an airtight container for up to 6 months.

BZAR
Emirati Spice Mix
MAKES ABOUT 1¼ CUPS

This spice blend is a common Emirati flavoring; it's often combined with clarified butter or sprinkled directly into soups, stews, and other dishes.

¼ cup black peppercorns

¼ cup cumin seeds

¼ cup coriander seeds

1 tbsp. whole cloves

1 tbsp. green cardamom pods

3 dried chiles de árbol, stemmed

2 cinnamon sticks, broken in half

1 whole nutmeg, broken into pieces

1½ tbsp. ground ginger

1 tbsp. ground turmeric

Working with 1 spice at a time, grind peppercorns, cumin, coriander, cloves, cardamom, chiles, cinnamon, and nutmeg in a spice grinder until finely ground. Transfer to a bowl and stir in ginger and turmeric. Store away from direct sunlight in an airtight container for up to 6 months.

MOROCCAN SEVEN-SPICE MIXTURE
MAKES ABOUT 5 TBSP.

Many different traditional spice blends exist in Moroccan cooking, each used for a different purpose. We love the brilliant flavor in this one, which is typically added to stews and braised dishes.

4 tsp. sweet paprika

½ tsp. hot paprika

4 tsp. ground cumin

4 tsp. freshly ground black pepper

1 tsp. ground ginger

½ tsp. ground turmeric

1 tsp. ground cinnamon

Combine sweet paprika, hot paprika, cumin, pepper, ginger, turmeric, and cinnamon in a jar, cover tightly, and shake well. Store away from direct sunlight for up to 6 months.

TEXAS-STYLE BARBECUE RUB
MAKES ABOUT ¾ CUP

Spice rubs like this one are essential to the sweet-smoky flavor of slow-cooked brisket.

1½ tbsp. kosher salt

1½ tbsp. dark brown sugar

1 tbsp. sweet paprika

2 tsp. garlic powder

2 tsp. dry mustard powder

1½ tsp. finely ground black pepper

½ tsp. ground coriander

½ tsp. ground cumin

½ tsp. dried thyme

Combine salt, sugar, paprika, garlic powder, mustard, pepper, coriander, cumin, and thyme in a jar, cover tightly, and shake well. Store away from direct sunlight for up to 6 months.

"Pepper is small in quantity and great in virtue."

PLATO

MEMPHIS-STYLE DRY RUB

MAKES ABOUT ¾ CUP

In Memphis, Tennessee, pork ribs are often served "dry"—no barbecue sauce, just a dry marinade in a flavorful spice mixture like this one.

- 2 tbsp. kosher salt
- 2 tbsp. dark brown sugar
- 2 tbsp. paprika
- 1 tbsp. dried oregano
- 1 tbsp. ground black pepper
- 2 tsp. garlic powder
- 1 tsp. onion powder
- 1 tsp. dried thyme
- 1 tsp. dried marjoram
- 1 tsp. dried parsley
- 1 tsp. ground cumin
- 1 tsp. dry mustard
- 1 tsp. celery seeds
- ½ tsp. cayenne pepper
- ½ tsp. ground fennel seeds
- ½ tsp. ground white pepper

Combine salt, sugar, paprika, oregano, black pepper, garlic powder, onion powder, thyme, marjoram, parsley, cumin, mustard, celery seeds, cayenne pepper, fennel seeds, and white pepper in a jar, cap tightly, and shake well. Store away from direct sunlight for up to 6 months.

DRIED LEMON ZEST

MAKES ABOUT 6 TBSP.

A sprinkling of this dried zest brightens the flavor of roasted beets or squash, salads, sauces, and soups.

- 10 unwaxed lemons, scrubbed

1 Use a Microplane or the smallest holes on a box grater to zest lemons. Spread zest on a sheet of wax paper; let dry at room temperature for at least 24 hours.

2 Fold paper and press to smash the zest into a powder. Store in an airtight container in the refrigerator for up to 2 weeks.

HOMEMADE FRESH POULTRY SEASONING

MAKES ABOUT ½ CUP

Our fresh poultry seasoning blend puts the jarred stuff to shame. This pungent, lively mix leaves out salt, so you can add it directly to turkey, stuffing, or chicken without fear of overseasoning.

- 3 tbsp. finely chopped fresh thyme
- 3 tbsp. finely chopped fresh rosemary
- 3 tbsp. finely chopped fresh sage
- 1 tbsp. finely chopped fresh marjoram
- ½ tbsp. freshly ground black pepper
- 1 tsp. celery seeds
- 1 tsp. freshly grated nutmeg
- 1 tsp. ground ginger
- 1 tsp. smoked paprika

Combine thyme, rosemary, sage, marjoram, pepper, celery seeds, nutmeg, ginger, and paprika in a bowl or jar and mix well. Store in an airtight container in the refrigerator for up to 3 days.

CAIN'S BARBECUE SPICE BLEND

MAKES ABOUT ½ CUP

The famous Hickory House in Dallas used this spice blend, no longer made, as its dry rub. This recipe is chef Rick Bayless' interpretation of that now-unobtainable product.

- 2 large cloves garlic, finely chopped
- ¼ cup ground chile powder, such as ancho, New Mexico, or guajillo, or paprika
- 4 tsp. kosher salt
- 2 tsp. freshly ground black pepper
- 2 tsp. sugar
- 2 tsp. dried oregano, preferably Mexican
- 1 tsp. dried thyme

Combine garlic, chile powder, salt, pepper, sugar, oregano, and thyme in a bowl and mix well. Store in a small, tightly capped jar in the refrigerator for up to 1 month.

TOASTED THAI CHILE POWDER

Phrik Pon Khua

MAKES ⅔ CUP

Phrik pon khua is a common spice in Thailand, where it is often a part of the seasonings served at the table with pad thai. It has a tame heat and a roasted, dark-fruit flavor. Be sure to toast your chiles in a very well-ventilated area or, even better, outdoors on a small charcoal grill.

- 2 oz. dried puya chiles (about 30 medium chiles), stems removed

1 Moisten a paper towel and set it by stove. Heat a large, dry skillet or flat-bottomed wok over high heat, then lower heat to low. Add chiles and cook, stirring and flipping constantly, until they are brittle and browned all over, 10–15 minutes. As loose seeds fall into pan, use a wet paper towel to quickly remove them to prevent burning and smoking.

2 Remove individual chiles from pan as soon as they are toasted. Let cool to room temperature, then, working in batches, use a heavy mortar and pestle or a spice grinder to pulverize them into a flaky powder. Use immediately, or transfer to an airtight container and store in a cool, dry place for up to 1 month.

HOMEMADE VANILLA EXTRACT

MAKES ONE 750-ML BOTTLE

Vanilla extract is beautifully easy to make at home. Order a pound of Grade B vanilla beans from an online seller and half your work is done. Split the beans, plunge them into booze, and time does the rest.

- 1 750-ml bottle vodka, with bottle
- 24 grade B vanilla beans, split lengthwise, seeds scraped and reserved
- 1 cup dark rum

1 Remove about 1½ cups vodka from vodka bottle and reserve it for another use.

2 Using a narrow funnel, push vanilla seeds into the bottle of vodka. Cap and shake to distribute. Remove cap and put the scraped beans into the bottle. Top off the bottle with rum and cap once more.

3 Store bottle in a cool, dark place for 4–6 months. Extract is ready when the liquid is dark, nearly syrupy, and fragrant with the scent of vanilla.

HOMEMADE TOMATO PASTE

MAKES ABOUT 1 CUP

Tomato paste lends depth and flavor to many dishes; making it from scratch is a great way to preserve and concentrate the flavor of ripe summer tomatoes.

- ¼ cup plus 2 tbsp. extra-virgin olive oil
- 5 lb. plum tomatoes, roughly chopped
  Kosher salt, to taste

1 Heat oven to 300°. Heat ¼ cup oil in a 12″ skillet over high heat. Add tomatoes and season lightly with salt; bring to a boil. Cook, stirring, until very soft, about 8 minutes.

2 Pass tomatoes through the finest plate of a food mill, pushing as much of the pulp through the sieve as possible.

3 Rub a 13″×18″ baking sheet with remaining 2 tbsp. oil and spread tomato purée evenly over sheet. Bake, using a spatula to turn the purée over on itself occasionally, until most of the water evaporates and the surface darkens, about 3 hours. Reduce heat to 250° and cook until thick and brick colored, 20–25 minutes. Store in an airtight container in the refrigerator for up to 1 month, or freeze, wrapped in plastic wrap, for up to 6 months.

SOFRITO

MAKES ABOUT 2 CUPS

Sofrito is essential to building flavor for a host of Latin-American dishes. Many Puerto Rican and Cuban cooks make it in large batches and store it in ice-cube trays in the freezer, popping out cubes to use as needed.

- ¼ lb. aji dulce chiles or cubanelle peppers, seeded, and roughly chopped
- 8 sprigs fresh cilantro
- 6 fresh flat-leaf parsley leaves
- 1 medium yellow onion, roughly chopped
- 1 medium green bell pepper, seeded and chopped
- 1 clove garlic
- 1 tbsp. vegetable oil

Combine chiles, cilantro, parsley, onion, bell pepper, garlic, and oil in a food processor and purée, stopping occasionally to scrape down the sides of the bowl with a rubber spatula, until a semicoarse paste forms, about 1 minute. Store in an airtight container in the refrigerator for up to 1 month or freeze for up to 3 months.

Sauces & Condiments

HOMEMADE KETCHUP

MAKES 3 CUPS

Our favorite homemade version of this ubiquitous condiment combines tomato purée, jalapeño, garlic, cider vinegar, and a host of spices, including ground cloves, allspice, and cinnamon.

- 1   28-oz. can tomato purée
- 1   medium yellow onion, quartered
- 1   clove garlic, crushed
- ½   fresh jalapeño, stemmed and seeded
- 2   tbsp. dark brown sugar
- ½   cup cider vinegar
- Pinch cayenne pepper
- Pinch celery salt
- Pinch dry mustard
- Pinch ground allspice
- Pinch ground cloves
- Pinch ground ginger
- Pinch ground cinnamon
- Kosher salt and freshly ground black pepper, to taste

1 Put tomato purée, onion, garlic, jalapeño, and sugar into a blender or food processor and pulse until blended. Add vinegar and 1 cup water and purée until smooth.

2 Transfer to a medium saucepan; add cayenne, celery salt, mustard, allspice, cloves, ginger, and cinnamon. Cook over low heat, stirring occasionally, for 45 minutes. Season to taste with salt and pepper. Store in sealed jars in refrigerator for up to 1 month.

TERIYAKI SAUCE

MAKES 1⅓ CUPS

This authentic formula is not as sweet as the sugary bottled version available in most American supermarkets.

- 7   tbsp. sake
- 7   tbsp. mirin
- 7   tbsp. dark soy sauce
- 1   tbsp. sugar

Bring sake, mirin, soy sauce, and sugar to a boil in a small saucepan over medium heat and cook until sugar dissolves, stirring constantly. Use at once, or cool, bottle, and store in the refrigerator for up to 2 weeks.

HOMEMADE STEAK SAUCE

MAKES ABOUT 1 CUP

Steak sauce as we know it—dark, sweet, and tangy with aromatic spices—is a British invention. In fact, A.1. Steak Sauce, the bottled condiment of choice for many American steak lovers, was invented by Henderson William Brand, the cook to King George IV in the 1820s. This recipe has similarly rich, acidic, savory notes but with a brighter, cleaner flavor.

- ½   cup vodka
- 2   tsp. crushed whole allspice
- 2   tsp. broken cinnamon stick
- 10 whole cloves, crushed
- ½   cup plus 6 tbsp. red wine vinegar
- ½   cup soy sauce
- 2   tsp. hot sauce
- 4   cloves garlic, crushed
- 4   medium tomatoes, cored and grated, skins discarded
- ¼   cup sugar
- ¼   cup tamarind extract or pomegranate molasses

1 Put vodka, allspice, cinnamon, and cloves into a small bowl. Cover with plastic wrap and let sit at room temperature for 8 hours. Strain vodka mixture; set aside.

2 Put ½ cup vinegar, soy sauce, hot sauce, and garlic into a bowl; set aside. Scrape grated tomatoes through a sieve to make 1 cup tomato pulp; set aside.

3 Cook sugar and 6 tbsp. vinegar in a skillet over medium heat, stirring constantly, to make a deep brown caramel, 6–7 minutes. Carefully stir in tomato pulp. Reduce heat to medium-low and cook until thick, 4–5 minutes. Remove and discard garlic from soy sauce mixture, then add mixture to skillet. Bring to a boil, add tamarind paste along with vodka mixture, and cook until thickened, 10–12 minutes. Store in sealed jars in refrigerator for up to 2 months.

KANSAS CITY BARBECUE SAUCE

MAKES ABOUT 2 CUPS

We got the recipe for this tangy sauce from Remus Powers, who founded the Diddy-Wa-Diddy National Barbecue Sauce Contest, now part of the American Royal BBQ Contest, the world's biggest competitive BBQ cookoff. It's perfect over ribs, chicken, or any barbecued meat.

¼	tsp. ground allspice
¼	tsp. ground cinnamon
¼	tsp. ground mace
¼	tsp. freshly ground black pepper
½	tsp. curry powder
½	tsp. chili powder
½	tsp. paprika
¼	cup white vinegar
½	tsp. hot sauce
1	cup ketchup
⅓	cup dark molasses

1 Mix together allspice, cinnamon, mace, pepper, curry powder, chili powder, and paprika in a bowl. Stir in vinegar, then add hot sauce, ketchup, and molasses and mix until very well blended.

2 Serve warm or at room temperature. Store in sealed jars in refrigerator for 2–3 weeks or in freezer for up to 6 months.

SPICY GUINNESS MUSTARD

MAKES 3½ CUPS

This piquant recipe uses brown mustard seeds and Guinness beer, which lends a malty character and hints of sweetness.

1	12-oz. bottle Guinness Extra Stout
1½	cups brown mustard seeds
1	cup red wine vinegar
1	tbsp. kosher salt
1	tsp. freshly ground black pepper
¼	tsp. ground cinnamon
¼	tsp. ground cloves
¼	tsp. ground nutmeg
¼	tsp. ground allspice

1 Combine ingredients in a nonreactive mixing bowl. Cover with plastic wrap and let sit at room temperature for 1–2 days so that the mustard seeds soften and the flavors meld.

2 Transfer mixture to a food processor and process, stopping occasionally to scrape down the sides of the bowl with a rubber spatula, until seeds are coarsely ground and mixture thickens, about 3 minutes. Transfer to a jar and cover.

3 Refrigerate overnight before using. Store in sealed jars in refrigerator for up to 6 months. The flavor of the mustard will mellow as the condiment ages.

TARTAR SAUCE

MAKES ABOUT 1 CUP

Traditional recipes for tartar sauce use homemade mayonnaise, but high-quality store-bought mayo yields good results, too.

3	cornichons or gherkins, finely chopped
2–3	tsp. nonpareil capers, drained and chopped
1	cup mayonnaise
1	tbsp. fresh lemon juice
1	tsp. pickling brine from jar of cornichons
1	tsp. pickling brine from jar of capers
	Kosher salt and freshly ground black pepper, to taste

Put cornichons and capers in medium mixing bowl. Add mayonnaise, lemon juice, and both pickling brines and mix with a wooden spoon until well blended. Season to taste with salt and pepper. Adjust seasonings with a little more mayonnaise, lemon juice, or pickling brine, if you like.

BLENDER HOLLANDAISE

MAKES ABOUT 1 CUP

When you're making hollandaise the traditional stovetop way, there's always the chance it will curdle. We've found Julia Child's blender method, which she says is "within the capabilities of an 8-year-old child," to be nearly fail-proof and it gives the resulting sauce a welcome lightness.

16	tbsp. unsalted butter
6	egg yolks
4–6	tbsp. fresh lemon juice
½	tsp. kosher salt
¼	tsp. freshly ground white pepper

"Woe to the cook whose sauce has no sting."
CHAUCER

1 Melt butter in a medium saucepan over medium-low heat until it begins to foam, 15–20 minutes.

2 Meanwhile, put egg yolks, 4 tbsp. lemon juice, salt, and pepper in a blender. Cover and blend on high speed for 2 seconds; then, with the motor running, gradually add butter in a slow, steady stream, leaving milky solids behind. Adjust seasonings with more lemon juice, salt, and pepper.

ROASTED GARLIC CHIPOTLE MAYONNAISE
MAKES ½ CUP

This smoky, gently spicy staple sauce is terrific with everything from French fries (page 592) to roast beef.

- 5 cloves garlic, peeled
- ¾ cup mayonnaise
- 1½ tbsp. fresh lemon juice
- 2 chipotle peppers in adobo
  Kosher salt and freshly ground black pepper, to taste

Cook garlic in a dry skillet over medium-high heat until cloves are golden with some black spots, about 9 minutes. Transfer to a food processor along with mayonnaise, lemon juice, and peppers and process until combined. Season with salt and pepper.

GREEN GODDESS SAUCE
MAKES ⅓ CUP

This classic sauce combines fresh herbs with a creamy base. It's great with crudités, salmon, or slathered atop turkey sandwiches.

- 2 tbsp. chopped fresh flat-leaf parsley
- 2 tbsp. chopped fresh tarragon
- 2 tbsp. chopped scallions
- 2 tbsp. chopped fresh chives
- ½ cup mayonnaise
- 2 tbsp. crème fraîche
- 2 tbsp. white wine vinegar
  Kosher salt and freshly ground black pepper, to taste

Combine herbs in a small food processor and blend until a smooth paste forms. In a bowl, combine mayonnaise with crème fraîche and vinegar. Add paste to mayonnaise mixture and stir to combine; season with salt and pepper.

HARISSA
North African Pepper Paste
MAKES 1 CUP

Salty and spicy, this vibrant red condiment enlivens grilled meats or fish, sandwiches, stews, and more. If traditional Tunisian Baklouti chiles are unavailable, substitute an equal portion of dried guajillo and dried red New Mexico chiles.

- 16 dried Baklouti chiles, stemmed and seeded
- ½ tsp. caraway seeds
- ¼ tsp. coriander seeds
- ¼ tsp. cumin seeds
- 1 tsp. dried mint leaves
- 3 tbsp. extra-virgin olive oil, plus more for topping
- 1½ tsp. kosher salt
- 5 cloves garlic, peeled
- 2 tbsp. fresh lemon juice

1 Put chiles into a medium bowl, cover with boiling water, and let sit until softened, about 20 minutes. Heat caraway, coriander, and cumin in an 8″ skillet over medium heat. Toast spices, swirling skillet constantly, until very fragrant, about 4 minutes. Transfer spices to a spice grinder with the mint and grind to a fine powder. Set aside.

2 Drain chiles and transfer to a food processor with the ground spices, olive oil, salt, garlic, and lemon juice. Purée, stopping occasionally to scrape down the sides of the bowl, until the paste is very smooth, about 2 minutes. Transfer to a sterilized 1-pt. glass jar and fill with oil until ingredients are submerged by ½″. Refrigerate, topping off with more oil after each use. Harissa paste will keep for up to 6 weeks.

TEQUILA HOT SAUCE

MAKES 1 PINT

Chef Elizabeth Karmel of Hill Country Barbecue in New York City serves this infused tequila drizzled over dishes ranging from grilled fish to grilled peaches.

- ¼ tsp. whole allspice
- ¼ tsp. black peppercorns
- ¼ tsp. cumin seeds
- 1 1-pt. bottle tequila blanco
- 3–5 fresh or dried red bird's eye chiles, smashed with side of a knife
- 1 black cardamom pod

1 Heat allspice, peppercorns, and cumin in an 8″ skillet over medium heat and cook, swirling skillet, until toasted and fragrant, about 3 minutes. Remove pan from heat; set aside.

2 Pour off 1″ of tequila from bottle (reserve for another use), then add toasted spices, chiles, and black cardamom to bottle, cover, and shake to mix. Add a pour spout or original cap to bottle; let sit for 1 week before using.

DILL MOUSSELINE SAUCE

MAKES 2 CUPS

Mousselines are French sauces similar to hollandaise, but with the addition of cream alongside the egg, lemon, and butter. This recipe came to us from David Lesh of the Gustavus Inn in Glacier Bay, Alaska, about 50 miles west of Juneau. It's exquisite served with poached salmon.

- ½ cup heavy cream
- 3 egg yolks
- 2 tbsp. fresh lemon juice
- 1 cup unsalted butter, kept hot
- 1 tbsp. chopped fresh dill
  Kosher salt and freshly ground white pepper, to taste

1 Whip cream in a small bowl until soft peaks form. Set aside.

2 Combine egg yolks and lemon juice in a blender or food processor; process until well mixed, then, while blending, slowly pour in butter and continue blending until thick.

3 Transfer to a saucepan and fold in whipped cream. Stir in dill and season with salt and pepper. Keep warm over simmering water or very low heat until ready to serve.

SCANDINAVIAN MUSTARD-DILL SAUCE

Gravlaxsas

MAKES ½ CUP

This tangy sauce is a classic pairing for gravlax (page 43) or roasted salmon (page 593); its acidic brightness cuts through the fatty richness of the fish.

- ¼ cup Dijon mustard
- 1 tsp. dry mustard
- 1 tbsp. sugar
- ½ tsp. kosher salt
- 1 tbsp. fresh lemon juice
- ¼ cup extra-virgin olive oil
- 2 tbsp. minced fresh dill

Mix together mustards in a bowl. Whisk in sugar, salt, and lemon juice. While whisking, drizzle in oil to make an emulsion. Add dill. The sauce will keep, covered, in the refrigerator for up to 2 weeks.

MINT SAUCE

MAKES 1¼ CUPS

In England, roast lamb is generally served with mint sauce, a combination of fresh mint, sugar, and vinegar.

- 2¼ cups fresh mint leaves, finely chopped
- 1 tbsp. sugar
- ½ tsp. kosher salt
- 1 cup white vinegar

Combine mint, sugar, salt, and ¼ cup boiling water and stir until sugar dissolves. Add vinegar, cover, and let sit for 1 hour to allow the flavors to meld.

WORCESTERSHIRE SAUCE

MAKES ABOUT 2 CUPS

Tart, vinegary, and deeply savory, the bottled condiment known as Worcestershire sauce likely has its origins in *garum,* a fermented fish sauce from the Roman era. The name's reference to the British county of Worcestershire is likely a bit of 19th-century marketing on the part of Lea & Perrin's, the brand that popularized the sauce.

- 2 cups white vinegar
- ½ cup dark molasses
- ½ cup soy sauce
- ¼ cup tamarind extract or pomegranate molasses
- 3 tbsp. yellow mustard seeds

3 tbsp. kosher salt
1 tsp. black peppercorns
1 tsp. whole cloves
½ tsp. curry powder
5 green cardamom pods, smashed
4 chiles de árbol, chopped
2 cloves garlic, smashed
1 1″ stick cinnamon
1 oil-packed anchovy filet, chopped
1 onion, chopped
1 1½″ piece ginger, peeled and crushed
½ cup sugar

1 Combine all ingredients except sugar in a 2-qt. saucepan and bring to a boil. Reduce heat and simmer for 10 minutes.

2 Meanwhile, cook sugar in a skillet over medium-high heat until dark amber and syrupy, about 5 minutes. Add caramelized sugar to vinegar mixture, whisk to combine, and cook sauce for 5 minutes.

3 Transfer sauce to a sterilized glass jar with a tight-fitting lid and refrigerate, covered, for 3 weeks. Strain out solids and return to jar. Use at once or refrigerate for up to 8 months.

SOY-CHILE DIPPING SAUCE
MAKES ¾ CUP

This dipping sauce is the perfect balance between spicy, sweet, salty, and acidic; serve it with steamed dumplings or fried chicken wings.

½ cup soy sauce
2 tbsp. seasoned rice vinegar
1 tbsp. chile paste, such as sambal oelek
1 tbsp. honey
1 tsp. freshly grated ginger
1 tsp. sesame seeds, toasted

In a small bowl, stir together all ingredients. Stir to blend. Store in an airtight container in the refrigerator for up to 4 weeks.

NUOC CHAM
Vietnamese Chile-Garlic Sauce
MAKES 1½ CUPS

This classic sweet-sour condiment is an ideal dipping sauce for spring rolls.

4 tbsp. sugar
2 cloves garlic, peeled
2 bird's eye chiles, stemmed
¼ cup fish sauce
2 tbsp. fresh lime juice
2 tbsp. finely shredded carrots

1 Place 1 tbsp. sugar, garlic, and 1 chile on a cutting board and roughly chop everything together. Using the side of the knife, scrape the garlic–chile mixture into a rough paste.

2 Transfer paste to a bowl and whisk in remaining 3 tbsp. sugar and 1 cup warm water, then whisk until sugar dissolves, about 30 seconds. Whisk in fish sauce and lime juice. Thinly slice remaining chile crosswise and add to sauce along with carrots. Let sauce sit until the flavors meld, at least 30 minutes. Stir well before serving.

GEORGIAN CILANTRO SAUCE
Kindzis Satsebela
MAKES 2 CUPS

Sweet-savory sauces made with a variety of vegetables, fruits, herbs, and nuts are essential to Georgian cuisine. Serve with crudités or grilled meats.

2 tbsp. apricot preserves
4 cloves garlic, crushed
2 scallions, chopped
1½ cups fresh cilantro
½ cup fresh basil leaves
½ cup fresh dill leaves
½ cup fresh flat-leaf parsley leaves
½ cup fresh tarragon leaves
½ cup walnuts
¼ cup fresh lemon juice
1 cup walnut oil
Dash cayenne pepper
Kosher salt and freshly ground black pepper, to taste

1 Place apricot preserves, garlic, scallions, cilantro, basil, dill, parsley, tarragon, walnuts, and lemon juice in a blender. Pulse until smooth. With motor running, gradually add walnut oil, processing until sauce is thick.

2 Transfer sauce to a bowl, season with cayenne, salt, and pepper, and set aside for about 2 hours to allow flavors to develop. Sauce will keep in an airtight container in refrigerator for up to 1 week.

PEANUT SAUCE

MAKES 1 CUP

The piquancy of this sauce is balanced by the peanuts. It's the classic accompaniment to satay.

- 2 tsp. Thai hot red curry paste
- 1½ cups canned Thai coconut milk
- ½ cup finely ground peanuts
- 1 tsp. tamarind extract
- ¼ cup finely chopped fresh cilantro leaves

Heat curry paste and coconut milk in a heavy saucepan over medium-low heat, stirring for 1 minute. Add peanuts and tamarind extract, lower heat, and simmer for 10 minutes, stirring constantly. Remove from heat and add cilantro.

NIT'R QIBE

Ethiopian Spiced Butter

MAKES ABOUT ¾ CUP

This seasoned, clarified butter is a key component of many Ethiopian dishes, including Doro Wot (page 173). It's also delicious stirred into coffee.

- 16 tbsp. unsalted butter
- ¼ tsp. ground black cardamom seeds
- ¼ tsp. ground fenugreek powder
- ¼ tsp. ground nigella seeds

1 Melt butter in a small saucepan over medium-low heat, skimming the foam off the surface. Once butter has begun to simmer gently, continue removing foam until butter is completely clear, about 30 minutes. Strain butter through a fine-mesh sieve set over a bowl, leaving behind the milk solids at the bottom of the pan.

2 Stir cardamom, fenugreek, and nigella into butter and mix well to combine. Let cool and transfer to an airtight container; store in the refrigerator for up to 3 months.

CLARIFIED BUTTER

MAKES ABOUT 1 CUP

Clarifying butter removes the milk solids, enabling this fat to stand up to higher heat. Try it for griddling pancakes for a crispy edge and pure butter flavor.

- 16 tbsp. unsalted butter, cubed

Melt butter in a medium pan over medium heat and cook until cloudy milk solids form in the bottom of the pan, about 3 minutes. Skim and discard foam from surface. Pour clarified butter off, leaving milky sediment behind. Use at once or store in an airtight container in the refrigerator for up to 3 months.

GHEE

Indian Clarified Butter

MAKES 2½ CUPS

Ghee, the basis for almost all Indian cooking, is clarified butter that's been browned to intensify and deepen its rich, nutty flavor. Ready-made *usli* ("pure") ghee is available in Indian grocery stores, but making your own is easy and guarantees freshness.

- 1½ lb. unsalted butter, cubed

1 Melt butter in a large skillet over medium-low heat. Let it sputter and bubble until a fine foam covers the surface, about 20 minutes. Continue cooking, gently pushing foam cover aside with a spoon occasionally to check the color of the milk solids at the bottom of the skillet.

2 Once milk solids turn golden brown and butter just begins to smell nutty, 10–15 minutes more, pour butter through a cheesecloth-lined sieve into a medium bowl. Transfer ghee to a clean jar and let cool. Ghee will keep, tightly covered in the refrigerator, for up to 6 months.

Holiday Entertaining

HOLIDAY ENTERTAINING

WHICHEVER HOLIDAYS YOU HAPPEN TO OBSERVE, there's no more joyful place to mark a festive occasion than around the dinner table. The pleasure in sharing a celebratory meal crafted with care is an experience treasured across borders and generations, and one that encapsulates our deeply held belief that food is a gesture of belonging.

Starters take on a heightened significance when entertaining around the holidays, when that first course must walk the line between elegant edible prequel and family-friendly comfort food. Dainty hors d'oeuvres topped with soft-ripened cheese and glistening pomegranate arils, painstakingly pleated pork dumplings, and crispy salt cod cakes allow you to go big on flavor and presentation, while still doing a bit of prep ahead. Or consider kicking off a marathon of feasting with offbeat-yet-elegant charcuterie. An Icelandic winter terrine—made from either seasonally apropos reindeer meat or the more readily available venison—makes for a tasty conversation piece on the holiday table, while foie gras, perfumed with a whiff of truffle, lends heady luxury to any special occasion.

Likewise, holiday entertaining is also a welcome opportunity to splurge on some of the more lavish ingredients—like caviar. Flip to page 602 for a brief overview of the most prized varieties of sturgeon roe. How you choose to serve those briny pearls—atop Shanghainese tea-smoked eggs, alongside classic Russian blini, or irreverently scooped up with potato chips—is entirely up to you.

The expected whole holiday birds (like Christmas Goose with Stuffing, page 181, or Tamarind & Honey–Glazed Roast Turkey, page 178) are the cornerstone of some classic holiday tables, but experienced entertainers looking for an impressive alternative around which to build their feast will find in this section epic centerpieces like a fruity glazed rib roast, retro bone-in lamb leg, and garlicky, tomato-braised brisket.

Pastry, too, has a place of honor on the holiday table, where restraint is wont to fly out the window in the presence of the year's most majestic sweets. Savory mincemeat pie and sculpted moon cakes are rich both in ingredients and in tradition, while sweet breads like kugelhopf, king cake, and Latvian klingeris make particularly lovely holiday desserts, with leftovers segueing seamlessly—as they should—into a leisurely festive brunch.

Festive Appetizers

ROBIOLA-STUFFED FIGS WITH POMEGRANATE

MAKES 15

Oozy and mild robiola cheese may be substituted with Brie, ricotta, or any other soft cheese in this simple no-cook appetizer.

- 15 fresh figs, stemmed
- 8 oz. robiola cheese, rind removed, at room temperature
- 2 tbsp. honey
  Kosher salt and freshly ground black pepper, to taste
- 2 tbsp. pomegranate seeds
  Fresh dill, for garnish

Working from the stem end of each fig and using a paring knife, cut an X toward the base about halfway through each fruit; set aside. Mix robiola, honey, salt, and pepper in a bowl. Spoon filling into a piping bag fitted with a plain ½″ tip and pipe about 1 tsp. into each fig. Garnish with pomegranate seeds and fresh dill.

MARINATED SARDINE CROSTINI WITH SALSA VERDE & FENNEL

SERVES 8

Chef Tony Mantuano combines the tangy flavors of tarragon and chive salsa verde with a zesty lemon and fennel salad in this marinated sardine crostini.

FOR THE SALSA VERDE
- ½ cup finely chopped fresh tarragon
- ½ cup finely chopped fresh chives
- ⅓ cup finely chopped fresh flat-leaf parsley
- 1 hard-boiled egg (page 31), peeled and chopped
- ½ tsp. Dijon mustard
- ⅓ cup extra-virgin olive oil
- 1½ tbsp. capers, rinsed, drained, and chopped

FOR THE SARDINES & SERVING
- Sea salt and freshly ground pepper, to taste
- 4 fresh sardines, deboned and fileted

- ½ cup extra-virgin olive oil
- 1 cup fresh orange juice
- ½ cup white wine vinegar
- 1 bulb fennel, trimmed
  Juice of ¼ lemon
- 8 1″ thick slices ciabatta bread, halved

1 Prepare the salsa verde: In a medium bowl, combine tarragon, chives, parsley, egg, mustard, olive oil, and capers. Stir to mix thoroughly and let stand for at least 1 hour to allow flavors to blend. The sauce can be made ahead and refrigerated for up to a week.

2 Prepare the sardines: Lightly salt sardines and let stand for 10 minutes. In a bowl, whisk together olive oil, orange juice, and vinegar. Put sardines in a shallow dish and pour marinade over. Marinate for 30 minutes. Remove sardines from marinade and lightly pat dry. Set aside until ready to use.

3 Prepare the fennel salad: Using a mandolin, thinly shave fennel into a medium bowl. Dress with lemon juice and season to taste with salt and freshly ground pepper.

4 Prepare the crostini: Arrange an oven rack 4″ from broiler and heat broiler. Lay out the slices of ciabatta on a baking sheet. Toast under broiler until brown, about 1 minute. Flip slices over and repeat. Remove from oven. (Alternatively, you can grill bread over an open flame.)

To assemble, spread a teaspoon of salsa verde onto each piece of toast. Top with a sardine filet and some shaved fennel salad. Serve immediately.

POTTED FOIE GRAS WITH BLACK TRUFFLES

Foie Gras Souvarov

SERVES 6–8

The term "Souvarov" (or "Souvaroff") implies the presence of foie gras and truffles. This over-the-top preparation was served to us by winemaker Gérard Chave at his Rhône winery in 2004. Whole lobes of foie gras may be ordered online.

2   1½-lb. lobes fresh duck foie gras
    Salt, preferably fleur de sel, and freshly ground
    black pepper
4   tbsp. Armagnac
1   cup demi-glace
½   cup flour
2   oz. fresh or thawed frozen black winter truffles,
    thinly sliced
1   baguette, sliced

1 Put foie gras lobes into a dish just large enough to hold them snugly, generously season all over with salt and pepper, then drizzle with Armagnac. Cover with plastic wrap and transfer to the refrigerator to let marinate for 12–24 hours. Remove foie gras from refrigerator and set aside to come to room temperature, 3–4 hours.

2 Preheat oven to 450°. Put demi-glace into a 12-cup ovenproof earthenware pot or terrine (with lid) large enough to fit lobes snugly side by side, and set aside. Mix flour and ½ cup water together in a medium bowl, transfer to a lightly floured surface, and knead until smooth, about 5 minutes. Roll dough into a rope long enough to wrap around rim of pot or terrine (about 24″ long) and set aside.

3 Heat a large skillet over medium-high heat, then carefully sear foie gras until lightly browned on each side, about 1 minute per side. Transfer to pot and add truffles. Cover with lid and wrap dough around rim, pressing dough into crevices to seal. Transfer to oven and bake for 25–30 minutes. Remove from oven, break dough seal around pot with a fork, and pry off lid.

4 To serve, bring pot to the table. Transfer foie gras to a platter and thickly slice. Serve 2–3 slices of foie gras to each guest, spooning some of the truffles and sauce on top. Pass baguette slices around for guests to eat with the foie gras and truffles.

CLASSIC PORK & CHIVE DUMPLINGS
MAKES 24 DUMPLINGS

The go-to Chinese filling: juicy pork mixed with the fresh oniony flavor of garlic chives. Try to find a fatty blend of ground pork; it will improve the filling's flavor and juiciness. Chopped garlic chives, which have a peppery raw-garlic flavor, and fresh ginger cut through the rich meat. Make sure the dumplings are completely sealed and devoid of air bubbles to prevent any leaks during boiling. This recipe is adapted from Helen You and Max

Falkowitz's acclaimed *The Dumpling Galaxy Cookbook*, published by Clarkson Potter in 2017.

FOR THE DOUGH
2   cups flour, plus more for dusting
⅛   tsp. kosher salt
1   large egg white

FOR THE FILLING
1   lb. ground pork
2   tbsp. dry sherry or rice wine
1   tbsp. freshly grated ginger
2   tsp. soy sauce
½   tsp. kosher salt
½   cup minced garlic chives or scallions

1 Make the dough: In a large bowl, combine flour and salt. Add ¾ cup lukewarm water and the egg white and mix with fingers. (Dough should be shaggy with dry pockets of flour, like biscuit dough.)

2 Knead dough on a well-floured work surface using floured hands, dusting with more flour as needed to prevent sticking, until smooth, about 4 minutes. Transfer to a lightly floured bowl and cover with plastic wrap. Let rest for at least 30 minutes or up to 1 hour.

3 Make the filling: In a medium bowl, combine pork, sherry, ginger, soy sauce, and salt and mix with hands. Fold in chives.

4 On a floured surface, knead dough briefly until satin-smooth. Cut into 4 equal pieces. Roll each piece into a ¾″ thick log and cut with a cleaver or a sharp knife into 6 equal pieces about the size of an egg yolk. On a rimmed baking sheet, toss balls generously with flour and drape with a damp paper towel.

5 Flatten each ball slightly with the palm of your hand. Using a wooden dowel, flatten dough a bit more. Roll from the edge of each dough disk to its center, rotating disk between rolls. Repeat until you have a wrapper 3″ in diameter with edges half as thick as the center. Transfer back to well-floured surface and tent with a damp paper towel.

6 Holding a wrapper in your palm, fill center with a tablespoon of filling. Pinch edges shut to form a half-moon, stretching the dough slightly as needed and squeezing out any air bubbles. Transfer back to tented work surface and repeat with remaining wrappers.

7 Add 6 dumplings at a time to a medium pot of boiling water. Boil for 2 minutes over high heat, then reduce heat to medium-high and cook for 2 minutes more. Reduce heat to medium and cook until dumpling wrappers are puffy, a final 2 minutes.

8 Using a slotted spoon, transfer dumplings to a plate. Serve immediately.

VENISON TERRINE

Dádýrakæfa

SERVES 6–8

Venison is a great substitute for the traditional reindeer meat in this rustic cranberry-and-pistachio-studded terrine from Icelandic cookbook author Nanna Rögnvaldardóttir.

- 3 tbsp. olive oil
- 1 clove garlic, chopped
- 1 small white onion, chopped
- 1 tsp. dried thyme
- ½ tsp. ground ginger
- ⅛ tsp. ground cloves
- 1 lb. boneless venison, chopped
- 8 oz. pork fatback, chopped
- 8 oz. venison or chicken liver
- 3 tbsp. tawny port
- 2 tbsp. potato starch
- 1 tbsp. kosher salt
- 1 tsp. freshly ground black pepper
- 3 eggs
- ½ cup pistachios, roughly chopped
- ½ cup dried cranberries
     Fresh red currants and parsley sprigs, for garnish (optional)

1 Heat oven to 200°. Grease a 1½-qt. terrine mold with 1 tbsp. oil.

2 Heat remaining 2 tbsp. oil in a medium skillet over medium-high heat and cook garlic and onion until soft, 5–7 minutes. Add thyme, ginger, and cloves; cook for 1 minute, then transfer to a food processor.

3 Add venison, fatback, liver, port, potato starch, salt, pepper, and eggs to blender jar. Purée until smooth. Transfer mixture to a bowl and fold in pistachios and cranberries. Spread mixture into prepared mold. Cover with aluminum foil and place in a 9″×13″ baking pan; pour boiling water into outer pan to come halfway up the sides of the terrine. Bake until an instant-read thermometer inserted into the center reads 160°, about 2 hours. Let cool, and garnish with currants and parsley sprigs, if you like, before serving.

TEA-SMOKED EGGS WITH CAVIAR

SERVES 4

These smoky, creamy-in-the-center Shanghainese eggs are topped with spoonfuls of caviar—a luxurious combination of flavors and textures.

- 4 duck eggs
- 1 tsp. salt
- ¼ cup black tea leaves
- 1 tbsp. long-grain rice
- 2 tbsp. flour
- 1 tbsp. sugar
     Pinch of five-spice powder
- 9 shiso leaves, 1 julienned
- 4 tsp. caviar, such as sevruga or osetra

1 Put eggs into a small pot, cover with water, and bring to a boil over high heat. Add salt, reduce heat to low, and simmer, covered, for 1 minute. Remove pot from heat and let sit, covered, to gently cook eggs for 2 minutes. Immediately transfer eggs to a large bowl of ice water and let chill for 10 minutes. Drain. Gently crack and peel eggs. Pat eggs dry.

2 Put tea, rice, and ¼ cup water into a small bowl and let soak for 3 minutes. Drain tea mixture through a fine sieve, shaking out any excess water. Line a large flat-bottomed wok and its lid with heavy-duty aluminum foil, pressing the foil against the bottom. Spread tea mixture in the bottom of the wok, sprinkle flour, sugar, and five-spice powder over the top, and place a small metal heatproof rack over the mixture. Place eggs on rack spaced 2″ apart.

3 Open your windows and turn on the exhaust fan. Heat wok over high heat until tea mixture begins to smoke, 2½–3 minutes. Cover tightly with the lid and continue to smoke until eggs are tinged golden yellow, 5–6 minutes. Remove from heat and transfer eggs to a clean work surface. (Cool and discard tea mixture.) Slice eggs in half lengthwise and place each half atop a whole shiso leaf on a platter. Garnish the yolk of each egg with a dollop of caviar and a little of the julienned shiso leaf. Serve promptly.

CAVIAR WITH BLINI

MAKES 40

The original blini (the word literally means "pancakes") were made with buckwheat flour. Today, as in this recipe, white flour is often added to yield a lighter crumb.

- 1¼ tsp. active dry yeast
- 1 cup lukewarm milk (115°)
- ½ cup buckwheat flour
- ½ tsp. sugar
- ¼ tsp. kosher salt
- ⅔ cup all-purpose flour
- 2 tbsp. sour cream
- ¼ cup heavy cream
- 2 large eggs, lightly beaten
- 1 tbsp. unsalted butter, melted
  Vegetable oil
  Crème fraîche (below), for serving
  Caviar, for serving

1 Combine yeast and milk in a large bowl. Mix well, then add buckwheat flour, sugar, and salt. Mix thoroughly, cover with plastic wrap or a clean dish towel, and set aside to rise until bubbles appear on surface, about 1 hour. Add all-purpose flour, sour cream, heavy cream, eggs, and butter. Mix well, cover, and set aside to rise for 2 hours more.

2 Heat 1 tbsp. oil in a large nonstick skillet over medium heat. Cook blini a few at a time (adding oil as necessary). Spoon batter a tablespoon at a time into the hot pan and smooth with the back of a spoon (blini will flatten as they cook). Cook until edges brown and bubbles appear on surface, about 1 minute. Flip blini; cook for 30 seconds more. Transfer finished blini to a plate and cover with a clean dish towel while finishing cooking. Serve blini warm, brushed with melted butter if desired, and topped with crème fraîche and caviar.

Homemade Crème Fraîche

MAKES 2 CUPS

- 2 cups heavy cream (not "ultra-pasteurized")
- 3 tbsp. buttermilk

In a clean glass pint jar, stir the cream with the buttermilk until evenly combined. Cover the jar with a cheesecloth and secure it in place with a rubber band. Let the cream stand at room temperature for 24 hours or until thickened to your liking (the longer it stands, the thicker the crème fraîche becomes). Once it's thickened, refrigerate the crème fraîche until ready to use.

A SHORT COURSE ON CAVIAR

Caviar was traditionally made from the roe of the Caspian sturgeon. However, these days, certain types of that fish—particularly the massive Beluga—are critically endangered. Overfishing has threatened the continued health of the species, and so the term "caviar" is now being more broadly applied to salted and preserved eggs from related species farmed elsewhere around the world.

The finest quality caviar is said to come from fish caught or raised in the coldest of waters, from late fall to early spring, but purveyor Alexandre Petrossian—who sources the roe for his family's eponymous shop from China, Bulgaria, Israel, Uruguay, Madagascar, and the United States—believes that there's much to be gained from a global approach. "Every territory has brought something new to our understanding of caviar," he explains. The following "big three" sturgeon varieties are the traditional Caspian types, which sustainable caviar producers strive to replicate.

SEVRUGA The smallest and most plentiful of the species, sevruga sturgeons weigh between 50 and 75 pounds, are about three feet long, and mature in seven years, producing small, gray, subtly flavored, creamy eggs.

OSETRA The second largest sturgeons, osetras weigh in at 150 to 300 pounds, grow four to six feet long, mature in 12 to 15 years, and produce medium-size, gray-brown to nearly golden, peppery eggs. One fish in 100 will deliver large, dark gold eggs—the pricey imperial osetra.

BELUGA The largest and rarest of the species, beluga can weigh up to 3,000 pounds, grow to 12 feet in length, and live for up to 50 years. Beluga eggs are unavailable in the United States, though some farms have created hybrid strains in order to approximate the breed's coveted large, gray eggs, with their delicate skin and clear flavor.

Centerpiece Roasts

PEAR-MARINATED ROAST LEG OF LAMB
SERVES 12–15

The enzymes found in pears tenderize this roast lamb, while garlic and herbs add flavor. The dish, from Corey Lee, chef-owner at San Francisco restaurant Benu, goes well with a side dish of roasted pears and shallots. Its simplicity helps it slot nicely into any winter holiday menu.

1	bone-in leg of lamb, 10–12-lb., shank bone exposed
	Kosher salt and freshly ground black pepper, to taste
⅓	cup extra-virgin olive oil
⅓	cup roughly chopped rosemary
2	tbsp. roughly chopped thyme
6	cloves garlic, unpeeled and crushed
	Zest of 1 lemon, removed with a vegetable peeler
1	Asian pear, peeled and coarsely grated
¼	cup canola oil
8	tbsp. cold unsalted butter, cubed

1 Season lamb with salt and pepper. Heat olive oil to a simmer in a 1-qt. saucepan over medium heat. Add rosemary, thyme, garlic, and lemon zest; remove from heat and let cool. Stir in grated pear and rub mixture all over lamb. Place in the fridge to marinate overnight.

2 The next day, preheat oven to 325°. Wipe marinade from lamb and pat dry using paper towels.

3 Heat canola oil in a roasting pan over medium-high heat. Season lamb with salt and pepper; cook, turning as needed, until browned, 15–20 minutes. Add butter and transfer to oven; roast, basting occasionally with pan juices, until an instant-read thermometer inserted into the thickest part of lamb reads 130°, 1 1/2–2 hours for medium-rare. Let rest for 10 minutes before carving.

COFFEE-CRUSTED BEEF TENDERLOIN
SERVES 8

One Christmas morning in the mid-1990s, chef Robert Del Grande spilled coffee grounds all over the cutting board he was about to use to prep the day's roasts—and he decided to just go with it. "He thought back on a conversation he'd once had with a friend about the meaty quality of coffee," wrote Margo True in a 2006 story about Del Grande's Cafe Annie in Houston. "In a second, he was rolling the filets in the coffee. The ground beans formed a rich, unctuous crust." Today the place is called the Annie Cafe & Bar, but Del Grande remains its executive chef, and coffee-crusted beef is still on the menu.

4	guajillo chiles, stemmed and seeded
2	ancho chiles, stemmed and seeded
4	medium garlic cloves, peeled
2	canned chipotle chiles in adobo
½	small white onion, finely chopped (about ¼ cup)
¼	cup extra-virgin olive oil
2	tbsp. light brown sugar
2	tbsp. red-wine vinegar
	Kosher salt and freshly ground black pepper, to taste
1	2-lb. beef tenderloin roast, tied with butcher's twine at ½" intervals
3	tbsp. very finely ground coffee
1	tbsp. cocoa powder
⅛	tsp. ground cinnamon

1 In a large, dry skillet over medium heat, toast guajillo and ancho chiles, turning occasionally, until fragrant, 4–5 minutes. Transfer to a medium bowl, cover with warm water, and soak until softened, 20–25 minutes.

2 In a blender, purée softened chiles, 1 cup of their soaking liquid, and the garlic, chipotles, and onion until smooth.

3 To make a chile sauce, in a small pot over medium-high heat, heat 2 tbsp. olive oil until it shimmers, then add the chile mixture, reduce heat to low, and cook, stirring frequently, until thickened but still pourable, about 30 minutes. Add brown sugar and vinegar, and continue cooking, stirring frequently, until further thickened to a loose paste, 12–14 minutes more. Season to taste with salt and pepper, remove from heat, and let cool to room temperature.

4 Meanwhile, position a rack in the center of the oven and preheat to 400°. Rub roast with remaining 2 tbsp. olive oil, season generously with salt and pepper, then brush all over with 2 tbsp. of the chile sauce (save any remainder for another use).

5 In a large bowl, stir together coffee, cocoa powder, and cinnamon, then roll roast in this mixture to coat. Transfer to a large, rimmed baking sheet fitted with a wire rack and let marinate for 30 minutes.

6 Roast meat for 15 minutes, then lower temperature to 225°. Continue roasting until a thermometer reads 120° for rare, 12–14 minutes. (For medium-rare, cook to 125°–130°.) Let rest at room temperature for 15 minutes, then cut away and discard the twine, and slice against the grain before serving.

STANDING RIB ROAST
SERVES 6–8

This meaty, crowd-pleasing centerpiece dates from former test-kitchen director Kellie Evans' days working as a film and television caterer—a job that required feeding a lot of hungry people. "Imagine making four full 16-pound roasts at a time in a mobile kitchen!" said Evans, who still makes this dramatic dish for her family at Christmas.

- 1   8-lb. bone-in beef rib roast
- 8   medium cloves garlic, peeled and halved
       Kosher salt and coarsely ground black pepper, to taste
- 4   tbsp. unsalted butter
- 1   large shallot, minced (about ½ cup)
- 2   cups ruby port
- 1   cup black currant preserves
- 2   tbsp. red wine vinegar
- 3   tbsp. canola oil

1 Position a rack in the center of the oven and preheat to 350°. Using a paring knife, make 16 incisions, about ½" deep, all over roast; insert garlic halves. Season meat generously with salt and pepper.

2 To make a glaze, melt butter in a small pot over medium-high; when foam begins to subside, add shallot and cook, stirring frequently, until translucent and soft, 4–6 minutes. Add port, bring to a boil, then lower heat to medium-low and cook, stirring occasionally, until liquid is reduced by

a third, 6–8 minutes. Stir in preserves and vinegar, season to taste with salt and pepper, and cook until smooth and syrupy, about 3–5 minutes more. Remove from heat.

3 In a large cast-iron skillet over high heat, heat oil until it shimmers, then add the roast and sear, using tongs or two large forks to turn the meat occasionally, until browned all over, 10–12 minutes. Position roast bone-side down in skillet and transfer to oven. Cook, basting every 15–20 minutes with glaze, until an instant-read thermometer inserted into the thickest part of the meat reaches 120° (for rare), 1 hour and 15 minutes. Carve and serve with remaining glaze on the side.

CLASSIC BRAISED BRISKET
SERVES 6–8

This iconic brisket originated with the grandmother of former SAVEUR staffer Kelly Alexander. "The whole staff loved it and chowed down.... Every year on Jewish holidays I still get emails from SAVEUR readers about how it's become a family staple for them too," says Alexander, now a food anthropologist at Duke University. "When people make this recipe, they pay my mema the best kind of respect."

- 2   tsp. dried oregano
- 1   tbsp. sweet paprika
- 1   tbsp. freshly ground black pepper, plus more to taste
- 1   tbsp. kosher salt, plus more to taste
- 1   5-lb. beef brisket, preferably a flat cut, trimmed of any large pieces of fat
- 3   tbsp. vegetable oil
- 3½ cups low-sodium chicken stock
- 1   14½-oz. can diced tomatoes
- 2   bay leaves
- 3   medium yellow onions, thinly sliced (about 3 cups)
- 3   medium garlic cloves, minced (about 1 tbsp.)

1 Preheat oven to 350°. Meanwhile, in a small bowl, stir together oregano, paprika, pepper, and salt, then rub all over brisket.

2 Heat oil in a large Dutch oven over medium-high heat until it shimmers, then add brisket and sear until browned on both sides, about 10 minutes per side. Remove from pot and set aside.

3 Pour off and discard rendered fat from pot, then return pot to medium-high heat and add the stock, tomatoes, and bay leaves. Bring to a simmer and deglaze pot, using a wooden spoon to scrape up any browned bits stuck to the bottom. Add brisket and its accumulated juices, and scatter onions and garlic atop meat. Cover pot, transfer to oven, and cook for 1 hour. Remove lid and continue cooking until onions begin to melt, about 1 hour more. Push some of the onions and garlic into braising liquid surrounding brisket. Cover pot again, and continue cooking until meat is very tender when pierced with the tip of a sharp knife, about 2 hours more.

4 Transfer meat to a cutting board and loosely tent with foil. The onions and garlic that remain in the pot should be very soft, and braising juices rich and saucy. If juices are watery, return pot to the stove top and simmer over medium heat until juices thicken, about 5 minutes. Season to taste with additional salt and pepper.

5 To serve, slice brisket against the grain, transfer to a serving platter, and spoon vegetables and sauce on top.

ROAST BEEF WITH YORKSHIRE PUDDINGS

SERVES 8

A roast served with the savory pastry known as Yorkshire pudding—a frequent main course at the University of Cambridge's Formal Hall—could be called the quintessential British dinner, quite appropriate for any festive gathering.

1	3- to 4-lb. beef top sirloin roast, tied with kitchen twine
	Kosher salt and freshly ground black pepper, to taste
¼	cup olive oil
2	tbsp. finely chopped fresh thyme
2	tbsp. finely chopped fresh rosemary
4	cloves garlic, finely chopped
1¼	cups milk
1	cup plus 2 tbsp. flour
3	large eggs
1	large shallot, finely chopped
½	cup red wine
1	cup beef stock
	Chopped fresh flat-leaf parsley, for garnish (optional)

1 Season beef generously with salt and pepper. In a small bowl, mix together oil, thyme, rosemary, and garlic. Rub beef with herb mixture. Place beef in a small roasting pan, cover loosely with plastic wrap, and refrigerate for at least 8 hours or overnight.

2 Remove beef from the fridge 2 hours before you are ready to roast to allow it to come to room temperature. Meanwhile, make Yorkshire pudding batter: Whisk together milk, 1 cup flour, 1 tsp. salt, and eggs in a bowl (ideally with a spout) or large pitcher. Cover and let batter sit at room temperature for at least 1 hour.

3 Preheat oven to 500°. Remove plastic wrap and roast the beef until browned, 18–20 minutes. Reduce temperature to 250°. Roast until a thermometer inserted into center of beef reads 125° (for medium rare), about 25 minutes. Remove from oven, transfer to a cutting board, and let rest, tented with foil, while you make the Yorkshire puddings and gravy. Pour pan drippings into a small pitcher, leaving about 3 tbsp. in pan. Set roasting pan aside.

4 Raise oven temperature to 450°. Spoon ½ tsp. reserved drippings from pitcher into each cup of a nonstick popover or muffin pan. Heat in oven for 15 minutes. Uncover batter and whisk in 1 tbsp. drippings from pitcher. Remove pan from oven and pour batter evenly among cups; bake until risen and brown, about 20 minutes. Reduce oven temperature to 350° and bake for 10 minutes more to set puddings. Remove pan from oven and set aside.

5 To make gravy, heat reserved roasting pan over medium heat. Add shallots and cook until soft, 4–6 minutes. Add wine and cook, scraping up browned bits from pan bottom, until reduced by half, 4–6 minutes. Whisk in remaining flour, followed by stock. Cook, whisking, until thick, about 5 minutes. Slice beef and serve with puddings and gravy. Garnish with chopped parsley, if you like.

Celebration Desserts

BAKED ALASKA FLAMBÉ

SERVES 12–14

With three colorful layers of ice cream domed atop a fudgy, flourless chocolate cake, our version of this retro dessert is a project perfect for celebrations. You can vary the assembly as you like—layering the ice cream in any pattern or thickness, or flambéing the meringue topping or not. But whatever you choose, give yourself a day or two in advance to prepare.

FOR THE ICE CREAM AND CAKE

	Nonstick cooking spray or butter, for greasing
1½	cups (13 oz.) nutty ice cream, such as pistachio
11	oz. finely chopped bittersweet chocolate
3	cups (24 oz.) fruity ice cream (not sorbet), such as strawberry
2	cups (20 oz.) vanilla ice cream
4	oz. (1 stick) unsalted butter, plus more for greasing
6	large egg yolks (plus half of a reserved egg shell, gently washed and dried)
¾	cup plus 1 tbsp. (3 oz.) pistachio or almond flour
½	cup (3 oz.) rice flour
6	large egg whites
¾	cup plus 2 tbsp. (7 oz.) superfine sugar

FOR THE MERINGUE TOPPING

4	large egg whites, at room temperature
¾	cup plus 2 tbsp. (7 oz.) superfine sugar
	Pinch of cream of tartar
	Seeds scraped from 1 vanilla bean
⅓	cup overproof spiced rum (optional)

1 At least 1 day and up to 1 week before serving, assemble ice cream dome: Transfer all the ice cream to the refrigerator for 15 minutes to soften. Meanwhile, lightly spray a medium freezer-safe bowl with cooking spray, then line with 2 long sheets of plastic wrap, placed perpendicularly to fully line bowl with a few inches overhang on each side; press to smooth.

2 Remove nutty ice cream and scoop it into prepared bowl; using a rubber spatula or small offset metal spatula, press ice cream into bottom of bowl, smoothing surface into an even, smooth layer. Sprinkle with 3 tbsp. chopped chocolate, pressing lightly to adhere, then transfer bowl to the freezer for 10 minutes to firm up slightly. Remove bowl and fruity ice cream flavor from the refrigerator; spread into an even, smooth layer. Sprinkle 5 tbsp. chopped chocolate evenly over ice cream layer and press lightly to adhere. Transfer bowl back to freezer for another 10 minutes. Finally, remove bowl from freezer and add vanilla ice cream. Smooth it over chopped chocolate into an even, smooth layer. Gently fold plastic edges over ice cream to cover. Freeze until completely solid, about 10 hours.

3 Meanwhile, make the cake layer base: Preheat oven to 350°. Grease a 9″ cake pan with butter, and line with a circle of parchment paper cut to fit the bottom of the pan.

4 In a double boiler (or microwave), combine butter and remaining 8 oz. chocolate and cook, stirring occasionally, until just melted. Remove and set aside.

5 Combine yolks, pistachio flour, and rice flour in the bowl of a food processor, and pulse to combine. With the motor running, slowly drizzle in the warm chocolate mixture. Use a rubber spatula to scrape down the sides of the bowl and the blade and pulse a few times more to combine completely. Transfer mixture to a large bowl, then set aside.

6 In the bowl of an electric mixer fitted with a whisk, beat 6 egg whites on high speed until medium-stiff peaks begin to form, 2–3 minutes. Add sugar in 4 batches, whipping well after each addition to make a glossy, soft-peaked meringue.

7 Using a large rubber spatula and working in two batches, fold meringue into chocolate mixture, mixing well after each addition. Pour batter into prepared cake pan and bake until just set but still quite soft, 35–40 minutes. Remove and let cool completely in pan before inverting onto a rack and removing the parchment lining. Immediately re-invert cake onto a heat-resistant serving plate or cake stand so that the flattest part of the cake is back on the bottom. Cover with plastic wrap and set in the refrigerator to firm up for at least a few hours or ideally overnight.

8 A few hours before you are ready to serve, remove bowl of ice cream from freezer and cake from refrigerator. Unwrap cake and uncover the top of the ice cream. Using the plastic wrap around the sides, lift dome of ice cream from bowl. (If it sticks, dunk bottom of the bowl in large bowl of hot water for a few seconds to help release.) Place ice cream dome, centered and flat-side down, atop cake. Remove plastic wrap from dome and transfer Baked Alaska back to the freezer.

9 Make the meringue topping: Put 4 egg whites in the bowl of a stand mixer fitted with a whisk. Beat on medium speed until whites begin to turn foamy, 30–60 seconds. Add 2 tbsp. sugar, the cream of tartar, and the vanilla seeds and continue beating until silky, soft peaks begin to form, 2–3 minutes. Reduce to medium-low speed and gradually add remaining sugar, 2 tbsp. at a time, until sugar is completely incorporated and meringue holds glossy, stiff peaks.

10 Immediately remove Baked Alaska from freezer. Using a rubber spatula, scoop meringue evenly over ice cream in decorative swoops and swirls. If flambéing, gently nestle half egg shell into the top of the meringue dome. Transfer to freezer.

11 Half an hour before you are ready to serve, transfer Baked Alaska to the refrigerator to soften slightly. To serve, use a crème brûlée torch to evenly brown the meringue. (If it starts to catch fire, gently blow out flame and continue toasting.)

12 To flambé the meringue, in a small pot over low heat, warm rum for 1–2 minutes (do not boil). Place Baked Alaska on table to serve and, using a small metal ladle, carefully pour 2 tbsp. rum into eggshell. Use a long match or grill starter to light the rum in the eggshell, then, slowly and carefully, ladle more rum into the shell, allowing it to flow down meringue like a volcano. Once alcohol has burned off and your guests have been adequately impressed, use a warm knife to slice the Baked Alaska into wedges and serve immediately.

TRADITIONAL MINCEMEAT PIE
MAKES ONE 9″ PIE

This recipe for old-fashioned mincemeat pie, a version of one featured in the classic 1861 volume *Mrs Beeton's Book of Household Management*, was updated in Jane Grigson's *English Food* (Macmillan, 1974). The mincemeat filling should be prepared at least two days (and preferably two weeks) prior to the making of the pies so that the fruit can soften and the flavors can meld.

FOR THE FILLING
2	cups finely chopped beef suet
¾	cup dried currants
¾	cup finely chopped rump steak (about 3 oz.)
½	cup raisins
½	cup packed dark brown sugar
2	tbsp. brandy
1½	tsp. chopped candied citron peel
1½	tsp. chopped candied lemon peel
1½	tsp. chopped candied orange peel
1	tsp. fresh lemon juice, plus grated zest of ½ lemon
¼	tsp. grated nutmeg
1½	Granny Smith apples, cored and finely chopped

FOR THE CRUST
2¼	cups flour, plus more for dusting
1	tbsp. granulated sugar
1	tsp. kosher salt
12	tbsp. (1½ sticks) cold unsalted butter, cubed
6	tbsp. ice-cold water
1	large egg, lightly beaten

1 Make the filling: In a medium bowl, combine beef suet, currants, rump steak, raisins, brown sugar, brandy, candied citrus peels, lemon juice and zest, nutmeg, and apples. Mix well. Transfer the mixture to a 1-qt. jar. Cover and refrigerate for at least 2 days and up to 2 weeks.

2 Make the crust: In a bowl, whisk together flour, granulated sugar, and salt. Using a dough blender, two forks, or your fingers, cut or rub butter into flour mixture, forming pea-size crumbles. Add water; work dough until smooth but with visible flecks of butter. (Alternatively, pulse the ingredients in a food processor.) Divide dough in half and flatten into disks. Wrap disks in plastic; refrigerate for at least 1 hour before using.

3 When ready to bake, remove one of the disks of dough to a lightly floured work surface, and let rest at room temperature for about 5 minutes, or until still chilled but pliable. Using a lightly floured rolling pin, roll out the disk into a ⅛″ thick round, rotating often and flouring the surface more as needed to prevent sticking. Carefully transfer dough to a 9″ pie plate, pressing gently against sides and bottom to fit. Roll out remaining disk of dough into a ⅛″ thick round using the same method. Transfer filling to pie shell, brush edges with water, and cover pie with top crust. Trim excess, leaving a 1″ overhang. Fold top edge over bottom crust to seal, and crimp as desired. Cut a few steam vents in top crust, then refrigerate pie for 1 hour.

4 Meanwhile, preheat oven to 350°. Brush pie with egg wash, then bake until golden, about 1 hour. Transfer to a wire rack and let cool completely.

KUGELHOPF
MAKES 8–10 SERVINGS

If you don't have the cupboard space or the budget to buy a mold specifically for kugelhopf, a standard fluted cake pan works, too. Make sure not to rush the mixing and fermentation periods for this dough; the flavor and open-crumb structure of the delicate cake are at their best when allowed to develop slowly.

- ½ cup raisins
- 2 tbsp. kirsch (cherry brandy)
- 1 cup whole milk
- 1 tbsp. plus 1 tsp. fresh cake yeast (see Cook's Note)
- ⅔ cup plus 2¾ cups bread flour (1 lb. total)
- 2 tbsp. superfine sugar
- 2 tsp. kosher salt
- 1 large egg, lightly beaten
- 13 tbsp. unsalted butter, softened, plus more for greasing
- ¼ cup whole almonds
    Confectioners' sugar, for dusting

1 In a small bowl, soak raisins in kirsch and 2 tbsp. hot water for 30 minutes, then strain, discarding liquid.

2 Mix milk, yeast, and ⅔ cup flour in the bowl of a stand mixer fitted with a hook and stir on low speed just to combine, about 1 minute. Let stand for 15 minutes, then add remaining flour, the sugar, and the salt, and mix on low speed until evenly combined, 1–2 minutes. Add egg and continue mixing on low speed until incorporated, 3–4 minutes. Increase speed by 1 level and continue mixing until dough is smooth and elastic (but still a bit sticky), 3–4 minutes more. Revert to lowest speed, add butter, and continue mixing, using a silicone spatula to occasionally scrape bottom and sides of bowl, until butter is incorporated and dough is very smooth and glossy, 12–15 minutes more. Add raisins and continue mixing on low speed to distribute them throughout dough, about 2 minutes more. Lightly grease a medium bowl with butter, then add dough, cover loosely with plastic wrap, and let rest at room temperature until nearly doubled in volume, 1–1¼ hours.

3 Gently press dough down to deflate, fold in thirds, then cover bowl again. Set aside until dough has nearly doubled in volume again, 30–40 minutes more.

4 Meanwhile, soak almonds in hot water for 5 minutes, then drain. Grease a kugelhopf pan (or fluted cake pan, if using) lightly with butter, then distribute soaked almonds among the grooves of the pan. Using your fist, punch a hole in center of the dough, then gently lift and position it in the prepared pan. Cover loosely with plastic wrap and let rise until nearly doubled, 30–40 minutes.

5 Meanwhile, position a rack in the center of the oven and preheat to 400°F. Transfer kugelhopf to oven, then immediately lower temperature to 350°. Bake until deep golden brown, 40–50 minutes. Immediately, and gently, invert and unmold the cake onto a wire rack, and let cool completely.

COOK'S NOTE Fresh cake yeast, which dissolves well in cool liquid, is the ideal leavening for heavily enriched, high-hydration doughs like this one. Look for it in the fridge or freezer section of well-stocked grocery stores. Can't find it? Substitute one-third the quantity by weight of instant dry yeast; in this case, 1⅔ teaspoons.

LATVIAN BRAIDED BIRTHDAY CAKE
Klingeris
SERVES 18–20

Every family seems to have its own recipe for this traditional yeasted birthday cake. Ruta Gailīte's uses dough similar to brioche dough, but relies on cream instead of butter for its richness. With the addition of plump dried fruit and ground cardamom and cinnamon, it makes a perfect breakfast cake too.

- 2 cups light cream, at room temperature
- 6 tbsp. plus ¾ cup granulated sugar
- 2¼ tsp. instant (not active dry) yeast
- 5 large eggs
- 7⅓ cups flour, plus more for dusting
- 1 tbsp. kosher salt
- 1½ lb. assorted dried fruit (prunes, tart cherries, and/ or raisins)
- 1¾ oz. candied ginger, finely chopped (⅓ cup)
    Butter or lard, for greasing
- 1½ tsp. ground cinnamon
- 1 tsp. ground cardamom
- 1⅓ cups sweetened condensed milk
    Confectioners' sugar, for dusting

1 In a very large bowl, whisk the cream, ¾ cup lukewarm water, 6 tbsp. granulated sugar, and the yeast. Add 4 eggs and whisk until smooth. Add half the flour and all of the salt and whisk until mixture is smooth, shiny, and stringy, about 2 minutes. Swap whisk for a wooden spoon and add remaining flour, stirring until fully incorporated into a very soft dough. Scrape the dough from the sides of the bowl, and cover bowl with a heavy towel. Set aside at room temperature until dough rises a few inches (it won't double), about 1 hour. (When poked, dough will be soft but shouldn't stick to your finger.)

2 Meanwhile, prepare the fruit filling: If the fruit is very hard and dry, cover it in boiling water and soak until tender, about 1 hour. Drain, discard soaking liquid, and coarsely chop. Transfer chopped fruit to a medium bowl, add candied ginger, and stir to combine. Set aside.

3 In a small bowl, combine remaining ¾ cup granulated sugar with cinnamon and cardamom and set aside. In another small bowl, whisk remaining egg with 1 tsp. of cold water and set aside to use as an egg wash.

4 Grease a large, rimmed baking sheet or rectangular cake pan with butter or lard, and line with parchment paper.

5 Generously dust a work surface and rolling pin with flour. Turn dough out onto surface and dust generously with more flour. Use your hands to pat dough into an even rectangle, then roll it out into a ⅛″ thick sheet, about 20″ × 25″. Brush dough with condensed milk, then sprinkle spice mixture over it, followed by dried fruit, spreading fillings evenly over dough all the way to the edges. Divide dough into 5 long strips, and roll each lengthwise into a fat snake, about 1½″ wide, pinching the seams shut. Press one end of all 5 strands together, with opposite ends fanning out toward you, 3 strands to the right and 2 strands to the left. Bring the strand farthest to the right over the center 3 strands so it falls between the 2 strands on the left. (You will now have 2 strands on the left and 2 on the right.) Next, bring the strand farthest to the left over the other 2 strands on the left so it lands in the center of the other 4 strands. Stretching the dough as little as possible, continue braiding strands in this manner until you have a fat, braided loaf. Press ends together, then wrap loaf into a wreath shape, pressing the 2 ends of the braid together. Carefully lift braid into pan (you might need a second set of hands for this) and gently adjust the dough so it keeps its wreath shape, stretching as needed to even out braid and

tucking in ends. Cover cake with a dry towel and let rise at room temperature until dough is slightly puffed, about 45 minutes.

6 Preheat oven to 425°. When the cake has risen, carefully brush it all over with egg wash. Transfer to oven and bake until dark amber-brown, 25–30 minutes. Lower oven to 325°, and continue baking until internal temperature registers 190–195° on an instant-read thermometer, 20–25 minutes more.

7 Remove cake from oven and let cool slightly. Dust with confectioners' sugar, and serve warm or at room temperature.

CHOCOLATE CHIP MOON CAKES WITH ALMONDS & SPICED FRUIT
MAKES ABOUT 28 CAKES

Pastry chef Pichet Ong's whimsical spin on the moon cake—traditionally enjoyed at mid-autumn Moon Festivals across Asia—takes inspiration from American chocolate chip cookies. He folds chocolate chips and candied fruits into a bean- and almond-paste filling and then wraps it in brown sugar–like cookie dough.

FOR THE DOUGH

5	cups cake flour, plus more for rolling
3	tbsp. custard powder, such as Bird's brand
1⅔	cups honey or golden syrup, such as Lyle's brand
¼	cup plus 1 tbsp. unsulfured molasses (not blackstrap)
1	tsp. kosher salt
¼	cup water
1½	tsp. baking soda
¾	cup plus 1 tbsp. peanut oil

FOR THE FILLING

3	lb. lotus seed paste, such as Wu Chung brand
1	lb. almond paste
3	tbsp. vegetable oil
2	tsp. kosher salt
	Finely grated zest of 4 oranges
⅔	cup finely diced dried apricot
½	cup dried cherries or cranberries
½	cup finely diced candied ginger
1	cup finely chopped toasted almonds
½	cup finely chopped toasted pecans
5	oz. high-quality dark chocolate, roughly chopped
5	oz. high-quality milk chocolate, roughly chopped
1	large egg, beaten with 1 tbsp. water, for egg wash

1 In the bowl of a stand mixer fitted with a paddle, combine flour with custard powder. In a medium, high-sided pot, bring honey, molasses, and salt to a boil. Meanwhile, in a small bowl, stir baking soda with ¼ cup water.

2 Add baking soda solution to boiling syrup and cook, stirring, for 3 seconds (the syrup will bubble up). Remove syrup from heat and pour into flour along with the peanut oil. Turn mixer on medium speed and mix dough until smooth, about 90 seconds. Form into a ball and wrap in plastic wrap. Let dough rest at room temperature for at least 2 hours.

3 Divide dough into 2-oz. balls and place on a parchment paper–lined baking sheet. Wrap baking sheet in plastic and let stand at room temperature until ready to use. See Cook's Note: If making the dough more in advance, refrigerate the dough, and allow it to return to room temperature before proceeding.

4 Preheat oven to 375°. In the bowl of a stand mixer fitted with a paddle, beat lotus seed paste with almond paste, oil, salt, and zest on medium-high speed until smooth. Reduce mixer speed to low and add apricots, cherries, and ginger, followed by almonds and pecans. Add chocolates and beat until just combined. Divide filling into about twenty-eight 3½-oz. pieces, and roll each piece into a ball.

5 Using a rolling pin, flatten each ball of dough into a 5″ circle, about ¼″ thick. Place a ball of filling in the middle of each dough circle and wrap dough around filling, sealing it in completely and smoothing out the surface. Place each dough-wrapped ball into the lightly floured cavity of a moon cake paddle (see Cook's Note) and press to fill the mold. Bang moon cake paddle on each side against a work surface to loosen moon cake, and then turn paddle so the cavity is facing down and bang paddle to release moon cake, allowing it to fall onto work surface. Arrange molded moon cakes on parchment paper–lined baking sheets, spaced 2″apart, and spray lightly with water.

6 Bake moon cakes for 10 minutes and then remove from oven and lightly brush each with egg wash. Reduce oven temperature to 350° and bake until golden brown

and warmed in center, 5 minutes more. Remove moon cakes from oven and transfer to a rack to cool completely. Ideally, allow moon cakes to sit at room temperature, sealed in an airtight container, for 2 days to allow to soften before eating.

COOK'S NOTE You can purchase a specialized paddle for molding round or square moon cakes online, and any less-familiar ingredients may be purchased online as well. For best results, start a day or two ahead of time to give dough time to rest and develop taste and texture.

MACANESE COCONUT COOKIES
Beijinhos de Coco
MAKES 24 COOKIES

Though writer and chef Rosa de Carvalho Ross was born and raised in Hong Kong, her family has roots in Macao almost as old as the region itself. As a child, she returned there often, and recalls eating these cookies, which are traditionally packaged in lacy paper wrappers called *cortadinhas* at weddings and other celebrations.

> 2 cups unsweetened finely shredded coconut
> ½ cup sugar
> 1 tbsp. flour
> 4 tbsp. unsalted butter, melted
> 2 large egg yolks
> 1 large egg

1 Preheat the oven to 350°.

2 Meanwhile, in a medium bowl, stir all ingredients together. Using a ½-oz. scoop or a packed tablespoon, divide dough into 24 pieces. Moisten your hands and roll pieces into smooth balls. Space the balls 2″ apart on parchment paper–lined baking sheets and bake until golden, 15–18 minutes, rotating sheets halfway through baking time. Let cookies cool completely on the baking sheets. Stored in an airtight container, cookies will keep for up to 5 days.

MARDI GRAS KING CAKE

SERVES 10–12

In New Orleans, king cake season officially begins on January 6th, the Epiphany, and is kicked off with a Twelfth Night Party. These gatherings always feature the signature ring-shaped, sugar-coated (and sometimes filled) yeast bread—and they continue through Mardi Gras, which marks the last day of excess before Lent. Tradition dictates that you hide a small plastic baby, representing the baby Jesus, in the cake after it's baked and before slathering on the icing. The partygoer who gets the lucky slice is then crowned royalty for the occasion—and must provide the king cake for the next party. Look for miniature plastic babies in your local craft store (the baby shower aisle is usually a good bet), or order a plastic king cake baby online.

FOR THE DOUGH

- 1   ¼-oz. package active dry yeast
- ¼   cup granulated sugar
- ¼   cup lukewarm water (115°)
- ½   cup whole milk
- 2   tbsp. light brown sugar
- ½   tsp. vanilla extract
- 1   egg
- 1   egg yolk
- 2¾ cups flour
- ¾   tsp. kosher salt
- 8   tbsp. unsalted butter, softened

FOR THE FILLING & GARNISH

- 2   8-oz. packages cream cheese, softened
- ½   cup packed dark brown sugar
- ½   cup chopped pecans
- 2   tbsp. cane syrup or maple syrup
- 2   tsp. ground cinnamon
- ½   tsp. kosher salt
- ½   lemon, zested

FOR THE BUTTERMILK GLAZE

- 2   cups confectioners' sugar
- ¼   cup buttermilk

FOR DECORATING

  Green, purple, and yellow sanding sugars

1 Make the dough: In the bowl of a standing mixer fitted with a hook, combine yeast, ½ tsp. of the sugar, and lukewarm water. Stir to combine and let sit until foamy, about 10 minutes. Add remaining granulated sugar, milk, light brown sugar, vanilla, egg, and egg yolk. Beat on low speed until thoroughly combined, 1 minute. Turn mixer off and add flour and salt. Mix on medium speed until the dough just comes together. Turn mixer speed to high and knead dough for 4 minutes. Add the butter and continue kneading until dough is smooth and pulls away from sides of bowl, about 6 minutes. Remove bowl from mixer, cover with plastic wrap, and let sit until doubled in size, 1½–2 hours.

2 Meanwhile, make the filling: Combine cream cheese, brown sugar, pecans, maple syrup, cinnamon, salt, and zest in a large bowl and beat with a hand mixer on medium speed until combined; set aside.

3 Punch down dough and turn it out onto a heavily floured surface. Using a floured rolling pin, roll the dough into a large round, about ¼"-thick. Cut a hole in the center of the round and pull with your fingers to widen. Place dollops of filling evenly around round halfway between outer edge and inner hole. Drape outside edges over filling and continue rolling outside inward until filling is covered, widening inner hole as needed, until dough covers the seam. Transfer rolled dough round to a parchment paper–lined baking sheet; cover with plastic wrap and let sit for 1 hour. Heat oven to 350°. Uncover cake and bake until golden brown, 34–40 minutes. Let cool completely.

4 Meanwhile, make the buttermilk glaze: Whisk together the sugar and buttermilk in a small bowl until smooth.

5 Transfer king cake to a cutting board or serving platter; spread buttermilk glaze evenly over top of cake and sprinkle evenly with sanding sugars.

Recipes by Ingredient

NOTE: Page references in italics indicate photographs.

Recipes by Origin

Related Topics

TABLE OF EQUIVALENTS

The exact equivalents in the following tables have been rounded for convenience.

Liquid and Dry Measurements

U.S.	METRIC
¼ teaspoon	1.25 milliliters
½ teaspoon	2.5 milliliters
1 teaspoon	5 milliliters
1 tablespoon (3 teaspoons)	15 milliliters
1 fluid ounce	30 milliliters
¼ cup	65 milliliters
⅓ cup	80 milliliters
1 cup	235 milliliters
1 pint (2 cups)	480 milliliters
1 quart (4 cups, 32 fluid ounces)	950 milliliters
1 gallon (4 quarts)	3.8 liters
1 ounce (by weight)	28 grams
1 pound	454 grams
2.2 pounds	1 kilogram

Length Measures

U.S.	METRIC
⅛ inch	3 millimeters
¼ inch	6 millimeters
½ inch	12 millimeters
1 inch	2.5 centimeters

Oven Temperatures

FAHRENHEIT	CELSIUS	GAS
250°	120°	½
275°	140°	1
300°	150°	2
325°	160°	3
350°	180°	4
375°	190°	5
400°	200°	6
425°	220°	7
450°	230°	8
475°	240°	9
500°	260°	10

ACKNOWLEDGMENTS

It's no accident that this book is being published on the twentieth anniversary of SAVEUR. In its pages, two decades' worth of writers, editors, cooks, researchers, and photographers will find their handiwork. To every last one of them goes my heartfelt thanks. But more immediately, this book could not have happened without a few specific people. Chief among those is Helen Rosner, who is the book's true steward; her intelligence, thoroughness, and wit are at the heart of every sentence, every recipe step. I'd also like to thank Helen's deputy, Sara Cann, who spent uncountable hundreds of hours making lists and spreadsheets, chasing down headnotes, and generally keeping things humming. Another key player was managing editor Camille Rankin, who remained a beacon of calm in even the most chaotic moments, and made everything in these pages better thanks to her editorial expertise.

As it happens, the SAVEUR masthead handily doubles as a reference list for the bulk of these acknowledgments, which is as much a testament to the skill and passion of this group of editors as it is proof of how much a book of this scope took over the lives of even people who weren't necessarily supposed to be so deeply involved in its production. In particular, senior editors Karen Shimizu and Cory Baldwin uncomplainingly faced down many late nights and early mornings in service of these pages. Gratitude is due also to executive editor Betsy Andrews; senior editors Keith Pandolfi and Mari Uyehara; associate editor Felicia Campbell; associate food editors Kellie Evans and Judy Haubert; associate test kitchen director Farideh Sadeghin; assistant editors Laura Loesch-Quintin, Laura Sant, and Zoe Schaeffer; and intern extraordinaire Laura Grahame. All of these individuals wrote, read, edited, and above all accepted with incredible grace the towering piles of chapter manuscripts that threatened to fully take over Helen's cubicle and, in the end, the entire office.

A book this beautiful doesn't just wake up looking like this: Thanks are due to former photography director Chelsea Pomales and former art director Dave Weaver, who lined up the visuals in this book so that a formidable Weldon Owen crew—led by Kelly Booth and her multi-talented colleague Marisa Kwek—could take over. And something far beyond thanks to everyone at Weldon Owen for their faith in this behemoth of a title—including Terry Newell, Amy Kaneko, Roger Shaw, and, of course, Amy Marr, who has been this book's midwife, cheerleader, taskmaster, compass, and engine since the very beginning—in short, its boss. Slices of Lady Baltimore cake (page 000) for everyone!

JAMES OSELAND
SAVEUR EDITOR-IN-CHIEF

weldon**owen**

A WELDON OWEN PRODUCTION

PO Box 3088
San Rafael, CA 94912
www.weldonowen.com

Conceived and produced with SAVEUR
by Weldon Owen International

ISBN-13: 978-1-68188-757-9
ISBN-10: 1-68188-757-6

Printed in China

Library of Congress Cataloging-in-Publication
data is available.

10 9 8 7 6 5 4 3 2 1

SAVEUR NEW CLASSICS COOKBOOK

Editorial Director **Kat Craddock**
Consulting Editor **Shane Mitchell**
Photography Editor **Thomas Payne**

First Edition Edited & Produced By

Editor-in-Chief **James Oseland**
Executive Editor **Helen Rosner**
Managing Editor **Camille Rankin**

Associate Publisher **Amy Marr**
Creative Director **Kelly Booth**
Art Director **Marisa Kwek**

Weldon Owen International

CEO **Raoul Goff**
Publisher **Roger Shaw**
Managing Editor **Katie Killebrew**
Editorial Assistant **Jourdan Plautz**
VP of Creative **Chrissy Kwasnik**
Designer **Megan Sinead Harris**

Cover design and chapter illustrations
by Marisa Kwek.

ACKNOWLEDGMENTS

Weldon Owen wishes to thank Sarah Putman Clegg,
Eve Lynch, Rachel Lopez Metzger, Elizabeth Parson,
Emma Rudolph, Howie Severson, and Sharon Silva
for their help producing this book.